Shooter's Bible

111TH EDITION

D1294199

SKYHORSE PUBLISHING

Skyhorse Publishing books may be purchased in bulk at special discounts for sales promotion, corporate gifts, fund-raising, or educational purposes. Special editions can also be created to specifications. For details, contact the Special Sales Department, Skyhorse Publishing, 307 West 36th Street, 11th Floor, New York, NY 10018 or info@skyhorsepublishing.com.

Visit our website at www.skyhorsepublishing.com.

10 9 8 7 6 5 4 3 2 1

Library of Congress Cataloging-in-Publication Data is available on file.

Cover design by Brian Peterson
Cover photos courtesy of Pointer, Ruger, and Savage Arms

Print ISBN: 978-1-5107-4812-5
Ebook ISBN: 978-1-5107-4814-9
ISSN: 0080 9365

Printed in the United States of America

Note: Every effort has been made to record specifications and descriptions of guns, ammunition, and accessories accurately, but the Publisher can take no responsibility for errors or omissions. The prices shown for guns, ammunition, and accessories are manufacturers' suggested retail prices (unless otherwise noted) and are furnished for information only. These were in effect at press time and are subject to change without notice.

CONTENTS

INTRODUCTION

The 111th edition of the *Shooter's Bible* is the most recent version of the ultimate firearms reference book. It's the perfect go-to source for millions of people who want information on new guns, ammunition, optics, and accessories, as well as up-to-date prices and specs for thousands of in-production firearms. Since 1925, when it was first published, more than seven million copies of the *Shooter's Bible* have been sold. The *Shooter's Bible* is the most trusted source for complete, up-to-date information for nearly every firearm on the market today.

As an overview, last year proved to be an uneventful year for firearms sales in the US. According to a spokesman for the National Shooting Sports Foundation, "Sales of firearms have leveled off over the past few years and continue to be driven in part by self-defense and personal protection-minded consumers. There are also millions of non-gun owners who have a strong interest in purchasing their first firearm, and they are in need of information and an invitation. Knowing this, the NSSF has developed consumer-facing websites—LetsGoShooting.org and LetsGoHunting.org—and mentoring initiatives including the +ONE Movement and National Shooting Sports Month that are aimed to increase sales and participation."

To meet current and anticipated future demand, firearms manufacturers continue to come out with a host of new products, as well as adding innovative features to guns already on the market.

As you'll read in Robert Sadowski's full new product report, "Guns and Optics 2020," beginning on page 7, long-range target and hunting rifles are continuing to grow in popularity, with new models now available from the likes of Browning (the X-Bolt Max Long Range), FN (the SCAR 20S, based on the Sniper

Editorial director of the *Shooter's Bible* Jay Cassell (left) and hunting buddy Bruce Connor after a day of grouse hunting in the Berkshire Mountains of Massachusetts. Cassell is holding his Browning 20-gauge side-by-side, a perfect shotgun for busting through the thick brushes of grouse country. As frequently happens in grouse hunting, the birds won on this particular fall day.

Shooter's Bible researcher Lindsey Breuer-Barnes trying out a 28-gauge Remington 1100 on a clays course in New York.

Support Rifle), Mossberg (MVP Long Range also in multiple long-range calibers), and Savage (the Rascal Target XP, a new micro tactical .22 LR rimfire). Rifles chambered in .224 Valkyrie and .450 Bushmaster are also hot this year, with a number of companies now offering new models. In shotguns, more compact versions are all the rage, with many manufacturers offering a slightly shorter length of pull on many of their popular models. These models are designed for small-statured users like kids and some women. New affordable target shotguns from Legacy Sports can get you in the game for less. And check out the Stevens

single-shot turkey gun chambered in .410. In an already challenging sport, this new model will help test your skills in both shooting and calling.

The popularity of handguns continues to grow, with new single-stack 9mm pistols for concealed carry available from Glock, Kimber, Ruger, Springfield Armory, and SIG. Even Mossberg, known for shotguns and rifles, has entered the field with its new MC1sc, a 9mm subcompact pistol.

In optics, many scope makers are following the long-range trend and coming out with models specifically designed for the long-range crowd. Reflex

Breuer-Barnes at target practice with a Browning Buck Mark UDX with a Trijicon RMR sight in Ohio.

sights for handguns and new models for MSR/AR15-style guns fill out the optics field . . . almost. Not to be outdone, SIG has come out with the BDX series of riflescopes and rangefinders. The Ballistic Data Xchange projects relevant information in the field of view in real time. You can connect your scope to your smartphone to calculate the ballistic curve based on the rifle you're using and the type of ammo you have loaded. The scope and rangefinder combo is definitely cutting edge.

If you own or are looking to buy currently produced firearms, then you'll want to check out the existing products section starting on page 113. Here is where you'll find every firearm currently in production, with up-to-date prices and specs. If you have a gun that isn't in this section, it is probably out of production, in which case you need to pick up a copy of another Skyhorse publication, the *Gun Trader's Guide*. The forty-first edition came off the presses at the same time this edition of the *Shooter's Bible* did.

The Skyhorse staff is proud of this newest edition of the *Shooter's Bible*, a book that has been continually updated and fact-checked for the past twelve months. Now that this 111th edition is off the presses, we're already starting to work on the 112th edition. It's an ongoing process, one we have to stay on top of and pay close attention to, given all the changes going on in the world of firearms.

For a full listing of *Shooter's Bible* and *Gun Trader's Guide* guidebooks (including the brand-new *Shooter's Bible Guide to Deer Hunting*), please go to www.sky-horsepublishing.com.

—Jay Cassell
Editorial Director
Shooter's Bible

GUNS AND OPTICS 2020
By Robert A. Sadowski

Long-range hunting rifles are popular this year and are available from Browning, Legacy Sports, Mossberg, and Remington. Also rifles chambered in .450 Bushmaster are hot to take advantage of hunting laws that allow straight-wall cartridges. This is the year of compact shotguns, with many brands offering a slightly shorter LOP on many of their popular models. New affordable target shotguns from Legacy Arms can get you in the game for less—and speaking of less, Stevens has a single-shot turkey gun chambered in .410. Single-stack 9mm pistols for concealed carry are the trend this year, with Glock, Mossberg (yes, you read correctly the shotgun manufacture), Kimber, Ruger, Springfield Armory, and SIG, producing new models for concealed carry.

Optic manufacturers are providing scopes for long-range shooting, reflex sights for handguns, and plenty of choices for MSR/AR-15 style guns.

Ammunition continues to be fine-tuned for specific scenarios, be it Hornady's .300 BLK Subsonic or Federal Premium's 3rd Degree turkey hunting loads. Here are the details.

Rifles

Auto-Ordnance (auto-ordnance.com)

The "Airborne" M1 Carbine (MSRP: $1518) has an 18-inch barrel and an engraved walnut folding stock and wood handguard. The Tanker Thompson (MSRP: $1749) is chambered in .45 ACP and features a walnut fixed stock with U.S. logo and horizontal foregrip.

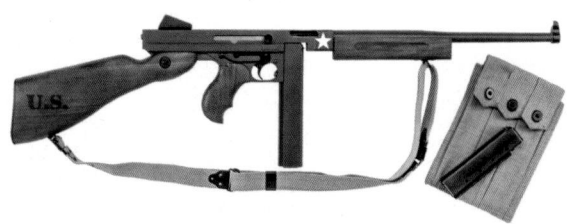

AUTO-ORDNANCE THOMPSON TANKER

Bergara (bergarausa.com)

The Ridgeback (MSRP: $2000) features an adjustable fiberglass stock, medium Palma barrel, and detachable magazine in six calibers, including 6.5 PRC. The Highlander (MSRP: $1850) is a lightweight rifle designed for hard hunting. It boasts the Bergara Premier line of features and comes in nine calibers, including .280 Ackley Improved.

Brownells (brownells.com)

The BRN-PROTO 5.56 (MSRP: $1499) is the latest addition to Brownell's Retro series of AR-10 and AR-15 rifles. This is a reproduction of the first AR-15 prototype.

BROWNELLS BRN-PROTO

Browning (browning.com)

New to the X-Bolt series is the X-Bolt Max Long Range (MSRP: $1270) with a composite MAX stock that is fully adjustable, the X-Bolt Target McMillan A3-5 Ambush (MSRP: $3070) with a composite McMillan A3-5 stock with adjustable comb, fluted bull barrel, and threaded-on muzzle brake, and the X-Bolt Pro Tungsten (MSRP: $2070) with a carbon fiber-wrap stock and tungsten Cerakote finish. All are available in eleven different calibers. The BAR Mark III series now includes a Hell's Canyon Speed (MSRP: $1600) with a Burnt Bronze Cerakote finish and A-TACS AU camo stock and forend. The BAR MK 3 DBM Wood (MSRP: $1530) is a multi-purpose rifle chambered in .308 Win. with an 18-inch barrel and detachable ten-round magazine. The iconic Semi-Auto 22 series now has a Grade II Octagon (MSRP: $1000) is equipped with satin nickel finish receiver with scroll engraving, octagon barrel, and gloss-finish walnut with cut checkering.

Bushmaster (bushmaster.com)

The ACR series of semiautomatic rifle is now chambered in .450 Bushmaster or 6.8 SPC (MSRP: $2250) with either a 16- or 18.5-inch barrel.

CMMG (cmmging.com)

The new Resolute AR-15 platform rifle comes in three variants: Resolute 100, Mk 4 (MSRP: $950), Resolute 200, Mk 4 (MSRP: $1125), and Resolute 300, Mk 4 (MSRP: $1450). All are chambered in .350 Legend and have 16.1-inch barrels.

CMMG RESOLUTE 300 SEREIS

CVA (cva.com)

The Cascade (MSRP: $567) is CVA's first ever bolt-action centerfire rifle equipped with a 22-inch barrel, synthetic stock, matte blue finish, and threaded muzzle. The bolt design incorporates a 70-degree throw.

CZ-USA (cz-usa.com)

The CZ 457 series of rimfire rifles has eight new models. The American (MSRP: $496) has a 24.8-inch barrel, no sights, and walnut stock with a flat comb and a classic checkering pattern. The Lux (MSRP: $522) has a hogback stock fashioned from Turkish walnut, along with iron sights. The Training Rifle (MSRP: $449) has a tangent rear sight and beechwood stock with Schnabel forend. The Scout (MSRP: $365) is designed for young shooters with a 12-inch LOP and iron sights.

Varmints should be scared. The ProVarmint Suppressor-Ready (MSRP: $588) is equated with a heavy 16.5-inch threaded barrel and laminate stock. The Varmint (MSRP: $522) is a heavy-barreled version of the 457. The Varmint AT-ONE (MSRP: $660) uses Boyd's AT-ONE stock that adjusts for LOP and comb height. The Varmint MTR (MSRP: $752) gets a bit more attention than the average 457 Varmint with its match chamber cut to the tightest specification for maximum accuracy. The Varmint Precision Trainer Camo (MSRP: $1144) was designed to provide the same look and feel as a full-size tactical rifle while allowing for more economical training.

The centerfire-chambered CZ 527 line gets two new varmint rifles. The Varmint MTR (MSRP: $879) combined match target accuracy with a walnut stock designed for better ergonomics, and the Varmint Suppressor-Ready (MSRP: $779) features an American-style walnut stock with a 24-inch barrel that's threaded for a suppressor. It chambers 6.5 Grendel.

CZ-USA 457 VARMINT AT-ONE

Daniel Defense (danieldefense.com)

DD has gotten into the bolt-action game with the Delta 5 (MSRP: $2199). This rifle is fully modular with an interchangeable cold hammer forged barrel and a user-configurable stock. Think long-range shooting. Available in three popular calibers.

DPMS (dpmsinc.com)

The M-LOK TAC2 (MSRP: $1249) features a Magpul ACS stock and MOE grip, Midwest Industry M-LOK handguard, and is chambered in 5.56 NATO. The M-LOK RECON (MSRP: $1169) features a Magpul MOE stock and grip,

DPMS M-LOK TAC2

Midwest Industry M-LOK handguard, and is chambered in 5.56 NATO.

FN (fnamerica.com)

The SCAR 20S precision rifle (MSRP: $4499) is based on the FN MK20 SSR or Sniper Support Rifle currently fielded within USSOCOM. Chambered in 7.62x51mm, this rifle is purpose-built to achieve superior long-range accuracy with 1-MOA accuracy to 100 yards with match-grade ammunition out of the box.

Marlin (marlin.com)

Marlin has gone stealth with the Model 1894 CST (MSRP: $1154). This rifle features stainless steel metal and a barrel that accepts a suppressor. The Model 1894 SBL (MSRP: $1145) is now available in .44 Rem. Mag. The iconic Model 336 (MSRP: $899) is gussied up with curly maple stock and forearm with a striking checkered pattern. It's back: The Model 444 Marlin (MSRP: $769) has been reintroduced, which should makes hunters happy in states that allow the use of straight-wall cartridges for deer hunting.

MARLIN FIREARMS MODEL 336C CURLY MAPLE

Mossberg (mossberg.com)

The MVP series (MSRP: $700–$910) of bolt-action rifles is now available in .224 Valkyrie. The semiautomatic rimfire 702 Plinkster line (starting at MSRP: $139) has been revamped with more ergonomic stocks in black or pink. The rimfire bolt-action 802 Plinkster series (starting at MSRP: $191) also gets a new stock treatment. The centerfire Patriot series now has a Predator model (MSRP: $441) with a 16.25-inch barrel, synthetic FDE finish stock, and chambered in .450 Bushmaster. A Cerakote Patriot Brown finish is also available on the Patriot Predator line (MSRP: $524).

Remington (remington.com)

The Model 783 Varmint Laminate (MSRP: $625) is a sharp-looking, no-nonsense varmint rifle with a 26-inch heavy-profile barrel chambered in five varmint-stopping calibers. I've always liked the Model Seven series, and the new Stainless H-S (MSRP: $1149) features a 20-inch

REMINGTON MODEL 783 VARMINT LAMINATE

light-contour barrel and H-S Precision stock with aluminum bedding.

Ruger (ruger.com)

The 10/22 Compact (MSRP: $309) features a 12.5-inch LOP for small-statured shooters. The 10/22 Target Lite (MSRP: $649) feature a radical laminated thumbhole stock in red/black or black finish. The AR-556 series now has the MPR (MSRP: $1099) chambered in .450 Bushmaster and built for hunting. There is an AR-556 Optics Ready (MSRP: $789) that comes sans sights and ready for an optic. The scaled-down Precision Rimfire now comes in .17 HMR and .22 WMR (MSRP: $529). The Scout Rifle is now available in .450 Bushmaster (MSRP: $1199). Col. Cooper would be happy.

Savage (savagearms.com)

New Model 100 series rifles include the 110 Brush Hunter (MSRP: $784) with oversized bolt handle and 20-inch barrel in two dangerous-game calibers; 110 Hog Hunter (MSRP: $594) with 20-inch barrel, AccuStock, and AccuTrigger; 110 Lightweight Storm (MSRP: $749) with stainless barrel/action at under six pounds; 110 Storm (MSRP: $849) with AccuStock, stainless barreled action, and eleven calibers, including 6.5 PRC and .280 Ackley Improved, and a TrueTimber Strata finish; and 110 Tactical (MSRP: $784) with a 20-inch barrel, ten-round detachable magazine, AccuStock, and AccuTrigger. The Axis XP series features a new ergonomic stock and comes factory-mounted with a Weaver 3–9x40mm scope (MSRP: $495.00–$515.00) in nine calibers and a variety of finishes. Need a new micro tactical .22 LR rimfire? The Rascal Target XP (MSRP: $399) features a bi-pod, factory-mounted scope, and threaded muzzle. The single-shot Rascal FV-SR (MSRP: $219) features a black or pink stock. The semiautomatic rimfire 64 Takedown (MSRP: $249) quickly disassembles. The MSR AR-15/10 platform rifle series now includes the MSR 15 Competition (MSRP: $2875) in either .223 Rem. or .224 Valkrie, and MSR 10 Competition (MSRP: $3449) in .308 Win.; both feature a PROOF Research barrel, tunable gas port, and Magpul CTR stock.

SAVAGE ARMS 110 STORM LEFT-HAND

SIG Sauer (sigsauer.com)

The 9mm MPX (MSRP: $2016) semiauto uses a closed bolt piston system for smooth shooting and has the control AR-15 shooters expect. Features include a 16-inch threaded barrel and five-position folding stock. The SIGM400 Tread (MSRP: $951) is a premium entry-level AR-15 rifle with a free-floated 16-inch barrel, M-LOK handguard, and Magpul SL-K stock.

Thompson/Center Arms (tcarms.com)

New finishes have been added to the new T/CR22 series in Realtree EDGE and Mossy Oak Break-Up camouflage (MSRP: $419).

WEATHERBY MARK V WYOMING GOLD EDITION

WEATHERBY MARK V WYOMING SILVER EDITION

Weatherby (weatherby.com)

To commemorate Weatherby's move to Sheridan, Wyoming, Silver Edition (MSRP: $6500) and Gold Edition (MSRP: $10000) Mark V variants have been created and are top of the line in the opulent performance you would expect from Weatherby. The Subalpine series are MK V rifles wrapped in Gore Optifade Subalpine camo. Models include the Subalpine (MSRP: $2700), Subalpine RC (MSRP: $3200), and Camilla Subalpine (MSRP: $2700). At 7.25 pounds, the First Lite (MSRP: $2600) features a sub-MOA accuracy guarantee, fluted barrel, and First Lite camo finish.

Winchester Repeating Arms (winchesterguns.com)

The new Wildcat 22 LR (MSRP: $249) autoloader offers ambidextrous controls, speed-load magazine, striker-fired action, integral picatinny rails, and more. The XPR Hunter series of centerfire bolt-actions now comes in True Timber

Strata (MSRP: $599) and Kryptek Highlander (MSRP: $599). The Model 1892 Large Loop Carbine (MSRP: $1260) features the iconic large loop lever-action seen in cowboy movies.

Shotguns

Benelli (benelliusa.com)

High performance meets lightweight luxury with the Montefeltro Silver (MSRP: $1999) with engraved nickel receiver in either 12- or 20-gauge. Benelli's Performance Shop tweaks the 828U Upland (MSRP: $3499) for fast handling with a shorter LOP and 24-inch barrels.

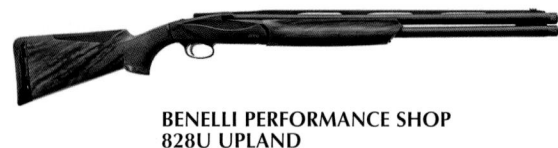

**BENELLI PERFORMANCE SHOP
828U UPLAND**

Browning (browning.com)

The Citori 725 Feather Superlight (MSRP: $2670) will keep you in the field longer. The 12-gauge weighs a mere 6 pounds 2 ounces and the 20-gauge is 5 pounds 7 ounces. Both feature an engraved silver nitride finish, mechanical trigger system, and straight-grip stock with Schnabel forearm. The Citori CXS Micro (MSRP: $2140) is a crossover design chambered in 12- or 20-gauge with lightweight profile barrels and compact 13-inch lengths of pull. The Citori CX (MSRP: $2140) is another crossover designed to be adaptable to all the clay target games, as well as be adept in the game field without being too heavy or cumbersome. The third new CX model is the CX with Adjustable Comb (MSRP: $2540).

Lightning strikes three times this year with the Citori White Lightning (MSRP: $2670), Citori Gran Lightning (MSRP: $3330), and Citori Feather Lightning (MSRP: $2870). The White and Feather models feature a silver engraved receiver while the Gran has a high polished blue receiver. All feature oil finish grade III/IV walnut. Last but not the least in the Citori line is the High Grade Side Plate Four Gauge Combo gun (MSRP: $11330) a four-barrel set in 12-, 20-, 28-gauge and .410-bore, with full-coverage engraved sideplates and gloss oil-finished Grade VI/VIII walnut. The target BT-99 series now has a Max High Grade model (MSRP: $5340)

with a fully adjustable stock, gloss oil-finished wood, hull ejector, Midas Grade choke tubes, and universal BT Trap fitted case.

CZ USA (cz-usa.com)

The 1012 series is CZ's latest evolution in its semiautomatic shotgun line and uses a gasless inertia operating system. The 1012 (MSRP: $659) features a traditional walnut checkered stock and blued finish. The 1012 Synthetic (MSRP: $659–$749) features a polymer stock and black or camo finish. Both are chambered in 12-gauge. All you need to do is add a pointer to the Bobwhite G2 (MSRP: $655–$702). These traditionally styled side-by-sides feature double triggers, an English-style straight-grip, and are chambered in either 12-, 20- or 28-gauge.

Mossberg (mossberg.com)

Mossberg has gone retro with wood stocks and a parkerized finish on the Retrograde models, which include the 590A1 (MSRP: $902), 500 (MSRP: $504), and 590 Nightstick (MSRP: $539). The Shockwave series has a Shock 'n' Saw model (MSRP: $560) with a chainsaw-style forend. Two new 835 Ulti-Mag pumps are the Combo Field/Deer (MSRP: $493) and Tactical Turkey (MSRP: $652) with adjustable stock and Mossy Oak Obsession camo finish.

MOSSBERG 590 SHOCKWAVE SHOCK 'N' SAW

Remington (remington.com)

The V3 series of semiautomatic scatterguns now includes four new models. The V3 Field Sport Waterfowl Pro (MSRP: $1195) features a bronze Cerakote receiver and barrel, and Mossy Oak Shadow Grass camo stock and forearm. The V3 Field Sport Turkey Pro (MSRP: $1195) is decked out for gobbler-busting with a full Cerakote camo finish. Both models have oversize controls to run with gloved hands. The V3 Field Sport Compact (MSRP: $915) has a 13-inch LOP for small-statured shooters and black oxide finish. Defend your

BROWNING CITORI GRAN LIGHTNING

REMINGTON MODEL 870 EXPRESS TACTICAL SIDE FOLDER

turf with a new defensive shotgun. The Model 870 Express Tactical Side Folder (MSRP: $569) with black synthetic stock and six-round magazine tube.

Stevens (savagearms.com)

The 301 Turkey Mossy Oak Bottomlands (MSRP: $199) single-shot, break-action .410-bore shotgun features a 26-inch barrel optimized for Federal Premium TSS shells. *Gobble, gobble*. Sixteen-gauge shooters rejoice. The 555 series of over-and-under shotguns now includes two 16-gauge models: the 555 Enhanced (MSRP: $879) and the 555 Field (MSRP: $705).

Stoeger (stoegerindustries.com)

Play some duck, duck, goose with the semiautomatic Model 3500 Waterfowl Special (MSRP: $849) that uses Stoeger's Inertia-Driven system and is equipped with a 3.5-inch chamber, 28-inch ventrib barrel, Cerakote bronze finish, oversized controls, and paracord sling.

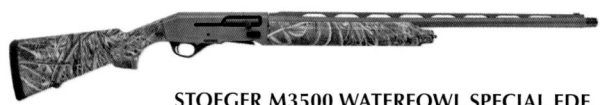

STOEGER M3500 WATERFOWL SPECIAL FDE

Winchester (winchesterguns.com)

The semiauto SX4 series now has an SX4 Compact (MSRP: $799) with a shorter LOP in both 12- or 20-gauge. The SX4 Upland Field (MSRP: $1110) has a satin-finshed walnut stock, matte nickel-finished alloy receiver, and Truglo front sight. The SX4 Waterfowl Hunter Compact - Mossy Oak Shadow Grass Blades (MSRP: $939 to $1070 depend on gauge) gets new camo and a 13-inch LOP in 12- or 20-gauge. The SXP Youth (MSRP: $399) has a 12-inch LOP and satin-finished stock.

Handguns

Beretta (beretta.com)

Ernest Langdon gave his opinion on how a Beretta should be equipped and collaborated on the Px4 Storm Carry (MSRP: N/A). It gets a full-size frame and slide with increased magazine capacity. He also inspired the Elite LTT (MSRP:

$1100), which is equipped with a Vertec/M9A3 slide with front cocking serrations, dovetail fiber optic front sight, and stainless steel barrel. Additions to the striker-fire APX line includes the Compact (MSRP: $575) and Centurion (MSRP: $575). The Compact has a 13+1 capacity in 9mm or 10+1 in .40 S&W with a flush-fit magazine for concealed carry. The Centurion is a mid-size pistol that features a 15+1 capacity in 9mm or 13+1 in .40 S&W with flush-fit magazines. Both pistols have a 3.7-inch barrel. The M9A3 (MSRP: $1099) is now available in a black finish.

BERETTA USA PX4 COMPACT GRAY

Browning (browning.com)

The Buck Mark series addition is the Buck Mark Medallion Rosewood (MSRP: $509) with a blacked stainless steel slab-side 5.5-inch barrel and fiber optic front sight.

CMMG Inc. (cmmginc.com)

The Banshee 100 Series (MSRP: $1249) features an 8-inch barrel, ProMag twenty-round magazine, and CMMG RML7 M-Lok handguard. The Banshee 200 Series (MSRP: $1449) comes equipped with a Magpul MOE pistol grip and CMMG Ripbrace arm brace. The Banshee 300 Series (MSRP: $1599) has a 5-inch barrel, Magpul MOE pistol grip, CMMG Ripbrace arm brace, ambidextrous controls, and more. All are chambered in FN 5.7x28mm caliber.

CZ-USA (cz-usa.com)

The Bren pistol evolves into the Bren 2 Ms (NSRP: $1799) available in multiple barrel lengths and chambered in either 7.62x39mm or 5.56x45mm NATO.

CZ-USA BREN 2 MS

Dan Wesson (danwessonfirearms.com)

Need a Commander-sized 1911 in .45 ACP? The TCP (MSRP: $1725) combines a match-grade bull barrel and railed alloy frame, and is designed for concealability with angled slide cuts and a taper-profiled grip.

Ed Brown (edbrown.com)

Optimized for the 9mm, the KC9 (MSRP: $1895) is smaller, thinner, and lighter than the typical 1911 yet retains 1911 controls and handling characteristics. It also uses standard 1911 magazines and standard 1911 grips with the Ed Brown Bobtail cut.

FN (fnamerica.com)

The 9mm striker-fire FN 509 line expands with the FN 509 Midsize (MSRP: $649) built for concealed carry with

FN AMERICA FN 509 TACTICAL

a 4-inch barrel and 15+1 capacity. The FN 509 Tactical (MSRP: $1049) has a 4.5-inch threaded barrel and 17+1 or 24+1 capacity.

GLOCK (us.glock.com/en)

New to the Slimline series are the G43X (MSRP: $459) and the G48 (MSRP: $459). Both are single-stack 9mm guns with a 10+1 capacity, available in a two-tone finish with a silver slide and matte black frame.

Kel-Tec (keltecweapons.com)

The CP33 (MSRP: $475) holds a total of thirty-three rounds of .22 Long Rifle ammo in a quad-stack magazine. Yes, you read correctly—a quad-stack. It features a 5.5-inch barrel and is optic- and suppressor-ready.

Kimber (kimberamerica.com)

The EVO SP (Striker Pistol) series is a subcompact 9mm striker-fire pistol built with a metal frame. It is designed for concealed carry. The EVO SP TLE (MSRP: $925) features G10 grip panels and a backstrap with an aggressive slant-checkering. The EVO Two-Tone (MSRP: $856) has a matte silver frame and matte black slide. The EVO CDP (MSRP: $949) also features a two-tone finish and checkered G10 grips. The EVO Custom Shop model (MSRP: $1047) features a contoured slide with Stiplex-inspired slide serrations. The KHX Custom/RL (MSRP: $1967) has a milled slide to install

KIMBER KHX CUSTOM/RL (OI)

an optic, a Picatinny accessory rail, and Stiplex-style front grip strap stippling for extra gripability.

Magnum Research (magnumresearch.com)

The iconic semiautomatic Desert Eagle Mark XIX Pistol (MSRP: $2143) is now chambered in .429DE, which is based off the .50 AE cartridge case.

Mossberg (mossberg.com)

Mossberg released the MC1sc (MSRP: $425), a 9mm concealed carry subcompact handgun, to celebrate the company's one hundredth anniversary. The MC1sc weighs 19 ounces empty and is equipped with a 3.4-inch barrel and flush six-round and seven-round extended magazines.

Remington (remington.com)

The Model 700 CP (MSRP: $1020) is engineered for big game and varmint hunting as well as steel silhouettes. Think 300, 500, and 700 yards. Chambered in .300 BLK, .308 Win., or .223 Rem. The RM380 line now includes the RM380 Micro Light Blue (MSRP: $415), which features a "Tiffany"-blue Cerakote frame and matte stainless slide.

Ruger (ruger.com)

The LCP II line now has an extended magazine model (MSRP: $399) with a 7+1 capacity. The inexpensive Security-9 (MSRP: $439) now comes from the factory with a Hogue Beavertail HandALL grip sleeve. The rimfire Mark IV 22/45 line has three new variants ($559–$599): light blue finish and wood laminate target grips; gold and black two-tone finish with checkered 1911-style grips; and a matte black finish. All feature a receiver made of aerospace-grade aluminum that is ventilated, making the pistol extremely light. All feature adjustable rear sights and a threaded barrel.

SIG Sauer (sigsauer.com)

The P320 M17 (MSRP: $768) is similar to the US Army model and now available to civilians. Like the Government model, this one also has a manual thumb safety. The Legion Series now includes two new pistols: a P238 (MSRP: $850), and P938 (MSRP: $904). Both feature the Legion Gray finish, flat trigger, G10 grips, and night sights. The P320 striker-fire series now includes the Compact Lima (MSRP: $884) equipped with an integrated red or green laser. The P320 XCompact (MSRP: $804) uses a compact grip module, night sights, a slide cut for optics, and a 3.4-inch barrel. The P365 line has two new additions. The Nitron Mirco-Compact (MSRP: $599) features a Nitron stainless steel slide, and the P365 Manual Safety model (MSRP: $599) has an ambidextrous manual thumb safety. SIG's 1911, P238, and P938 lines now have a Spartan II variant with MOLON LABE engraved on the slide. The 1911 Spartan II (MSRP: $1359) is a full-size pistol, chambered in .45 ACP, with fixed combat sights and ambidextrous thumb safety. The P938 Spartan II (MSRP: $815) and P238 Spartan II (MSRP: $630) feature custom Spartan grips. All three Spartan II pistols feature a distressed coyote tan finish on the slide and frame. The MPX Copperhead (MSRP: $1835) uses the MPX platform but is

**REMINGTON RM380
MICRO LIGHT BLUE**

SIG SAUER P938 SPARTAN II

compact with a 3.5-inch barrel and comes equipped with the SIG Pivoting Contour Brace.

Smith & Wesson (smith-wesson.com)

Coming out of the Performance Center are Ported M&P Shield M2.0 pistols ($499–$629) in 9mm, .40 S&W, and .45 Auto variants. These feature a ported barrel and slide for reduced muzzle flip, enhanced trigger for a crisp light trigger pull, and HI-VIZ Fiber Optic Sights or tritium night sights. The M&P380 Shield EZ pistol (MSRP: $399) is now available with a Crimson Trace Green Laserguard laser.

Springfield Armory (springfield-armory.com)

The subcompact 9mm 911 pistol ($429–$849) has controls similar to a 1911 and is equipped with 6+1 flush and 7+1 extended magazines. The 911 Alpha series (MSRP: $429) is chambered in .380 and comes with a 6+1 flush-fit magazine. In 10mm are the XD(M) 4.5-inch (MSRP: $652) and 5.25-inch (MSRP: $779). These two XD(M)s take the series to a whole other level of power. Also new to the XD(M) series are the XD(M) OSP with threaded barrel (MSRP:$710) and the XD(M) OSP with threaded barrel and Vortex Venom optic (MSRP: $958). Chambered in 9mm, these pistols have a 19+1 capacity, tall sights, and a 5.3-inch threaded barrel and 4.5-inch non-threaded barrel. The hammer-fired XD-E pistol (MSRP: $542) is now available with longer 3.8- and 4.5-inch barrels. New finishes are available on the XD-S Mod.2 3.3-inch single-stack 9mm pistols (MSRP: $499) including desert FDE, desert FDE/black, and tactical gray/black.

Steyr Arms (steyr-arms.com)

The A2 MF (MSRP: $675) features a redesigned frame with interchangeable grip panels and backstraps.

STEYR A2 MF

Stoeger (stoegerindustries.com)

The economical STR-9 pistol (MSRP: $329–$449) is striker-fired and chambered in 9mm with a 15+1 capacity.

Taurus (taurususa.com)

The full-size TX22 (MSRP: $349) is chambered in .22 Long Rifle and features a polymer frame and adjustable rear sights.

Walther Arms (waltherarms.com)

The Q5 Match Steel Frame Competition pistol (MSRP: $1499) is a match-ready pistol in 9mm with fiber optic front sight and adjustable rear.

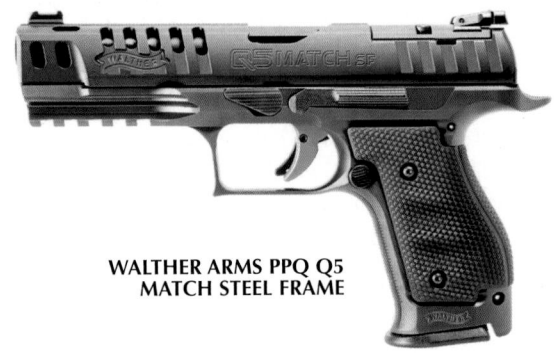

WALTHER ARMS PPQ Q5 MATCH STEEL FRAME

Black Powder

CVA (cva.com)

The new Paramount (MSRP: $1063) is a long-range muzzle-loader chambered in .45-caliber. It is designed for ranges up to 300 yards.

Thompson/Center Arms (tcarms.com)

The new entry-level .50-caliber IMPACT!SB muzzleloader (MSRP: $263) feature a break-open action, hand-removable triple lead thread breech plug, and a Power Rod aluminum ramrod for easy loading. Available in black, Realtree, or Mossy Oak camouflage finishes.

Optics

Bushnell (bushnell.com)

Prime is a features-packed budget line that includes the high-end EXO barrier coating. The same coating is on all its premium lines up to and including Elite Tactical. Prime riflescope models include a 1–4x32mm (MSRP: $156), 3.5–10x36mm (MSRP: $180), 3–9x40mm (MSRP: $216), 4–12x40mm (MSRP: $276), and 6–18x50mm (MSRP: $360). These are all second focal plane scopes. Hunters and precision shooters alike will find the Nitro line of optics offer a higher level of performance. These second focal

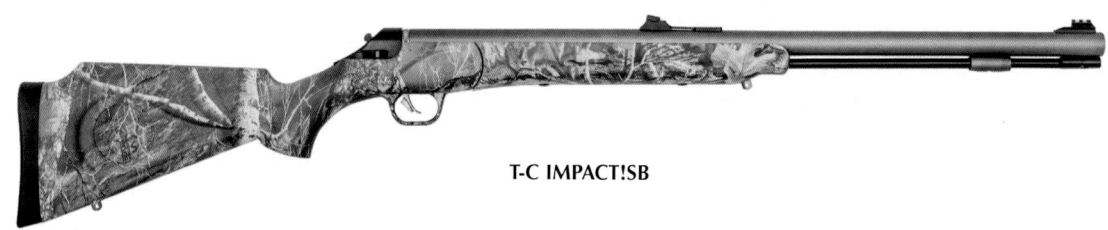

T-C IMPACT!SB

plane riflescopes come in thirty-five configurations and feature EXO Barrier lens coating, side parallax adjustment, flip-up Butler Creek scope covers, sun shade, and multiple ballistic reticle options. Models range from 2.15–10x44mm (MSRP: $420) up to 6–24x50mm (MSRP: $840) and come in either a matte black or matte gray finish. The Forge line of riflescopes offer many of the features and technologies ported over from the high-end Elite Tactical line. Three riflescope models include a 2.5–15x50mm (MSRP: $900–$1020 depending on reticle), 3–18x50mm (MSRP: $960–$1080 depending on reticle), and a 4.5–27x50mm (MSRP: $1080–$1140 depending on reticle). All are second focal plane scopes, with side parallax adjustment, exposed zero stop turrets, and in matte black or matte bronze finish.

BUSHNELL NITRO

Hawke Optics (us.hawkeoptics.com)

The flagship Frontier line of riflescopes (MSRP: $729–$899, depending on reticle style) has been updated with new features like an exposed tactical turret with zero-stop, index-matched lenses, and either a first focal plane (FFP) or second focal plane (SFP) reticle. SFP models include 2.5–15x50mm and 5–30x50mm. FFP variants include a 3–15x50mm and 5–25x56mm models.

Konus (konuspro.com)

Konus uses LCD technology to generate ten different reticle patterns in the Konus EL-30 4–16x44mm riflescope (MSRP: $470). Reticle patterns can be changed at the click of a button to suit a host of varied hunting applications, as well as target shooting, long-range precision, and tactical use.

Nightforce Optics (nightforceoptics.com)

New to the attractively priced SHV line of riflescopes is the SHV 3–10x42mm (MSRP: $985), which is available with illuminated MOAR or Forceplex reticles, ideal for use in low-light situations. New to the ATACR series of premium scopes is the ATACR 4–16x50mm F1 (MSRP: $2500), which features a 50mm objective lens, Nightforce's patented ZeroStop elevation with adjustment of 100 MOA or 30 mils of elevation travel, ED glass, MOAR or Mil-C reticles, and an integrated Power Throw Lever (PTL) that allows fast magnification changes in any conditions.

NIGHTFORCE OPTICS ATACR 4–6X50 F1

SHIELD SIGHTS RMSW

Shield Sights (shieldsightsusa.com)

The new RMSw (MSRP: $499) is a reflex red dot handgun sight designed to resist damage from water or other harsh environmental conditions. A gasket creates a watertight fit between the pistol's slide and the battery compartment without the need of a special mounting plate. It will remain watertight at depths of up to 20 meters for thirty minutes. Features include aerospace-grade aluminum construction, fast automatic brightness adjustment, a low profile to Co-Witness standard iron sights, and an average two- to three-year battery life with standard CR2032 battery.

SIG Sauer (sigsauer.com)

SIERRA3BDX riflescopes ($600–$960) are available in 3.5–10x42mm, 4.5–14x44mm, 4.5–14x50mm, and 6.5–20x52mm. They feature HD glass, 30mm main tubes, side-focus parallax adjustments, and the LevelPlex digital anti-cant system. The new ROMEO8H 1x38mm red-dot sight ($600) is designed for law enforcement, military, and civilian sport shooting. This sight is built for severe conditions and rapid target acquisition in any environment; it features a ballistic reticle for shooting at distance and a quad ballistic circle-dot reticle with ballistic holds.

SIG SAUER SIERRA3BDX

NEW PRODUCTS 2019–2020

NEW Products: **Rifles**

ACCURACY INTERNATIONAL ASR LIMITED EDITION, AXSR

ANDERSON MANUFACTURING AM-15 M-LOK .450 BUSHMASTER

ARSENAL, INC. SAM7SFK WITH GAMBIT DEVICE

ARSENAL, INC. SAS M-7 CLASSIC

AUTO-ORDNANCE AIRBONE M1 CARBINE

AUTO-ORDNANCE TANKER THOMPSON

ACCURACY INTERNATIONAL OF NORTH AMERICA, INC. ASR LIMITED EDITION, AXSR

Action: Bolt
Stock: Synthetic
Barrel: N/A
Sights: None
Weight: 15 lb. 4 oz.
Caliber: .338 Lapua, .338 Norma, .300 Norma, .300 Win. Mag., .308 Win.
Magazine: 10 rounds
Features: A total long-distance package with all the big .300s plus .308 represented; barrels are match grade with cut rifling; front locking action with six lugs; M-LOK on ASR; folding adjustable stock; 20 MOA Stanag rail; Limited Edition rifle system is the same package recently submitted to the US Special Operations Command ASR Trials and ships with three barrels and numerous accessories; AXSR is a stand-alone rifle that swaps out the M-LOK handguard for a key-lok RRS-compatible unit and adds a competition trigger
ASR:. **$19544.00**
AXSR: **$8975.00**

ANDERSON MANUFACTURING AM-15 M-LOK .450 BUSHMASTER

Action: Semiautomatic
Stock: Synthetic
Barrel: 18 in.
Sights: None
Weight: N/A
Caliber: .450 Bushmaster
Magazine: 5 rounds
Features: Special Operations Command (USSOCOM) ASR trials and features QuickLoc barrel change capability, shipping with three barrels and a number of accessories; AXSR is virtually identical to the ASR, but as a standalone rifle with a key-slot RRS-compatible handguard and competition trigger
MSRP. **$909.99**

ARSENAL, INC. SAM7SFK WITH GAMBIT DEVICE

Action: Semiautomatic
Stock: Synthetic
Barrel: 16.2 in.
Sights: A-4-type front, 500m peep rear
Weight: 8 lb.
Caliber: 7.62X39mm
Magazine: 30 rounds
Features: Krinkov configuration rifle with right-side folding tubular stock; hammer-forged chrome-lined barrel; "Krink" handguard with or without quad rail; 500m peep sight; Gambit barrel with four pairs of side-cut baffles; short gas system
MSRP. **$2499.99**
Quad-rail: **$2649.99**

ARSENAL, INC. SAS M-7 CLASSIC

Action: Semiautomatic
Stock: Metal
Barrel: 16.25 in.
Sights: A-4-type front, 800m adjustable rear
Weight: 7 lb. 8 oz.
Caliber: 7.62X39mm

Magazine: 30 rounds
Features: Built in Nevada, a classic AK-47 design with under-folding stock; chrome-lined heavy barrel; left-hand threaded muzzle
MSRP. **$1999.00**

AUTO-ORDNANCE AIRBONE M1 CARBINE

Action: Semiautomatic
Stock: Walnut
Barrel: 18 in.
Sights: Blade front, flip-up rear
Weight: N/A
Caliber: .30 Carbine
Magazine: 15 rounds
Features: Another AO commemorative, this one dedicated to paratroopers; battle-worn flag, St. Michael and "St. Michael Pray for Us" on the forearm; paratrooper, parachutes, and C-47 transport aircraft details; folding stock
MSRP. **$1518.00**

AUTO-ORDNANCE TANKER THOMPSON

Action: Semiautomatic
Stock: Walnut
Barrel: 16.5 in.
Sights: Blade front, fixed battle rear
Weight: 11 lb. 8 oz.
Caliber: .45 ACP
Magazine: 20, 30 rounds
Features: Commemorative firearm dedicated to soldiers who fought in M4 Sherman tanks; Cerakoted in Army O.D. green; Sherman tank white star engraved in front of the mag well; U.S. logo on buttstock; stick magazines
MSRP. **$1749.00**

AUTO-ORDNANCE VENGEANCE M1 CARBINE

BERGARA PREMIER HIGHLANDER

BERGARA PREMIER RIDGEBACK

BIG HORN ARMORY SCOUT

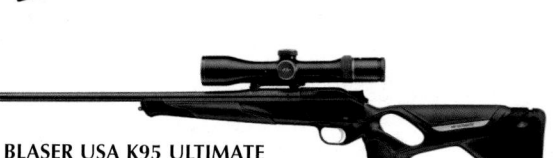

BLASER USA K95 ULTIMATE CARBON

BLASER USA R8 ULTIMATE CARBON

AUTO-ORDNANCE VENGEANCE M1 CARBINE

Action: Semiautomatic
Stock: Walnut
Barrel: 18 in.
Sights: Blade front, flip-up rear
Weight: N/A
Caliber: .30 Carbine
Magazine: 15 rounds
Features: Commemorative recognizing the attack on Pearl Harbor, with imagery from that day engraved on the stock, as well as the B-29 Superfortress Enola Gay
MSRP. **$1391.00**

BERGARA PREMIER HIGHLANDER

Action: Bolt
Stock: Fiberglass
Barrel: 20 in., 24 in.
Sights: None
Weight: 7 lb. 3 oz.–7 lb. 11 oz.
Caliber: 6.5 Creedmoor, 6.5 PRC, .270 Win., 7mm-08 Rem., .28–0 Ackley Improved, .308 Win., .30–06 Spfd., 7mm Rem. Mag., .300 Win. Mag., .300 PRC
Magazine: 3, 4 rounds
Features: For the hunter looking for reach, a rifle featuring Graphite Black Cerakote-finished metalwork; No. 5.5 tapered barrel with threads; TriggerTech Friction Release Technology trigger
MSRP. **$1850.00**

BERGARA PREMIER RIDGEBACK

Action: Bolt
Stock: Fiberglass
Barrel: 20 in., 24 in., 26 in.
Sights: None
Weight: 10 lb.–10 lb. 9 oz.
Caliber: 6mm Creedmoor, 6.5 Creedmoor, 6.5 PRC, .308 Win., .300 Win. Mag., .300 PRC
Magazine: 5, 7 rounds
Features: Dedicated long-range games rifle in all the latest cartridges. Features include: Cerakote black metalwork; medium Palma barrel profile; adjustable cheekpiece with M-LOK compatibility; AICS-type detachable magazine; TriggerTech Frictionless Release Technology trigger
MSRP. **$2000.00**

BIG HORN ARMORY SCOUT

Action: Lever
Stock: Laminate
Barrel: 18 in.
Sights: Blade front, aperture rear
Weight: 7 lb. 10 oz.
Caliber: .500 S&W
Magazine: 7 rounds
Features: A fast-handling lever in the powerhouse .500 S&W cartridge with sling swivels; Hunter Black stainless steel metalwork; black laminate stock with a satin finish; 1:24 twist barrel with a recessed crown
MSRP. **$2799.00**

BLASER USA K95 ULTIMATE CARBON

Action: Break-action
Stock: Carbon fiber
Barrel: 19.5 in., 23.6 in., 25.5 in., 27.5 in.
Sights: None
Weight: N/A
Caliber: More than 25 cartridges ranging from .22 Hornet to .338 Blaser Mag., plus 10.3X60R
Magazine: 1 round
Features: Featuring a unique, two-piece thumbhole stock with an adjustable comb option; special recoil absorption system or optional adjustable recoil pad; Blaser's cocking slide automatically illuminates the dot in Blaser illuminated riflescopes
MSRP. **N/A**

BLASER USA R8 ULTIMATE CARBON

Action: Bolt
Stock: Carbon fiber
Barrel: 19.5 in., 22 in., 25.5 in., 23.6 in., 27.5 in.
Sights: None
Weight: N/A
Caliber: More than 40 cartridges ranging from .204 Ruger to .500 Jeffery, plus 10.3X60R
Magazine: 2, 3, 4 rounds
Features: Similar to the K95 break-action Ultimate Carbon, but in the renowned switch-barrel, box magazine R8 configuration; optional leather or elastomer stock inserts
MSRP. **N/A**

BROWNELLS BRN-605

BROWNELLS BRN-PROTO

BROWNING BAR MARK III HELL'S CANYON SPEED

BROWNING BAR MK 3 DBM, WOOD

BROWNING SEMI-AUTO GRADE II OCTAGON

BROWNING X-BOLT MAX LONG RANGE

BROWNELLS BRN-605

Action: Semiautomatic
Stock: Synthetic
Barrel: 15.5 in.
Sights: Fixed front, adjustable rear
Weight: 6 lb. 11 oz.
Caliber: 5.56 NATO
Magazine: 20 rounds
Features: A copy of Colt's prototype 605 carbine, a firearm that never saw issue, featuring a pinned and welded three-prong flash hider; XM16E1 lower with partial magazine fence; XM16E1 upper; chrome bolt carrier group; forward assist; matte gray anodized metal; black stock
MSRP **$1299.99**

BROWNELLS BRN-PROTO

Action: Semiautomatic
Stock: Synthetic
Barrel: 20 in.
Sights: Fixed front, adjustable rear
Weight: 6 llb. 11 oz.
Caliber: 5.56 NATO
Magazine: 25 rounds
Features: Faithful reproduction of Stoner's original AR prototype, featuring a three-prong duckbill flash hider; brown stock; matt gray anodized finish; rifle-length gas tube; trigger-type charging handle located on top of the receiver; 1:12 twist; slab-side lower
MSRP **$1499.99**

BROWNING BAR MARK III HELL'S CANYON SPEED

Action: Semiautomatic
Stock: Composite
Barrel: 22 in., 23 in., 24 in.
Sights: None
Weight: 6 lb. 10 oz.–7 lb. 8 oz.
Caliber: .243 Win., 7mm-08 Rem., .308 Win., .270 WSM, .300 WSM, .270 Win., .30–06 Spfd., 7mm Rem. Mag., .300 Win. Mag.
Magazine: 4 rounds
Features: Eye-catching gun for the big-game hunter with: Burnt Bronze Cerakote-finish metal; composite stock with grip overmolds in A-TACS AU camo; shim-adjustable stock; Inflex recoil pad; detachable box magazine with hinged floor plate; hammer-forged barrel
MSRP **$1599.99**

BROWNING BAR MK 3 DBM, WOOD

Action: Semiautomatic
Stock: Wood
Barrel: 18 in.
Sights: None
Weight: 6 lb. 10 oz.
Caliber: .308 Win.
Magazine: 10 rounds
Features: With a hybrid military/ European hunting look, this lightweight and fast-handling .308 has detachable box magazine; two top-side scope mount rails; sling swivel studs; matte-finish metal; composite trigger guard; multi-lug rotary bolt; gas-piston functionality
MSRP **$1529.99**

BROWNING SEMI-AUTO GRADE II OCTAGON

Action: Semiautomatic
Stock: Grade II/III black walnut
Barrel: 19.4 in.
Sights: Blade front, notch rear
Weight: 5 lb. 3 oz.
Caliber: .22 LR
Magazine: 10 rounds
Features: A John Browning original gets a gloss-finish black walnut stock; takedown design; octagon barrel; metal buttplate; satin nickel receiver with scroll engraving; steel trigger guard; drilled and tapped for optic mounting
MSRP **$999.99**

BROWNING X-BOLT MAX LONG RANGE

Action: Bolt
Stock: Composite
Barrel: 26 in.
Sights: None
Weight: 8 lb. 3 oz.–8 lb. 7 oz.
Caliber: 6mm Creedmoor, 6.5 Creedmoor, .308 Win., .300 WSM, .26 Nosler, 7mm Rem. Mag., .28 Nosler, .300 Win. Mag., .300 RUM
Magazine: 3, 4 rounds
Features: Viable entry for those looking to get into the long-range game, featuring Composite Max stock with adjustable comb and a black-and-gray textured finish; fluted, stainless steel, heavy contour barrel; TPI threaded muzzle brake and thread protector; length of pull spacers; three swivel studs
MSRP **$1269.99**

BROWNING X-BOLT PRO TUNGSTEN

BUSHMASTER ACR 6.8MM REMINGTON SPC II

CARACAL VERSUS COMPETITION

BROWNING X-BOLT TARGET MCMILLAN A3-5 AMBUSH

BUSHMASTER ACR .450 BUSHMASTER

CENTURY ARMS VSKA

BROWNING X-BOLT PRO TUNGSTEN

Action: Bolt
Stock: Carbon fiber
Barrel: 22 in., 26 in.
Sights: None
Weight: 6 lb. 1 oz.–6 lb. 10 oz.
Caliber: 6.5 Creedmoor, .308 Win., .300 WSM, .26 Nosler, .270 Win., .30–06 Spfd., 7mm Rem. Mag., .28 Nosler, .300 Win. Mag.
Magazine: 3, 4 rounds
Features: Hunter or target master, this sleek rifle features a Tungsten Cerakote finish on the metalwork; full carbon-fiber-wrapped stock; spiral-fluted bolt; threaded on muzzle brake; oversized bolt knob; fluted barrel in lightweight sporter contour
MSRP . . . . **$2069.99–$2129.99**

BROWNING X-BOLT TARGET MCMILLAN A3-5 AMBUSH

Action: Bolt
Stock: Composite
Barrel: 26 in.
Sights: None
Weight: 10 lb.–10 lb. 4 oz.
Caliber: 6.5 Creedmoor, .308 Win., .26 Nosler, 7mm Rem. Mag., .28 Nosler, .300 Win. Mag.
Magazine: 3, 4 rounds
Features: A serious long-range contender in enough calibers to satisfy most and featuring: McMillan's A3-5 adjustable comb composite stock in Urban Carbon Ambush camo; Pachmyr Decelerator recoil pad; TPI suppressor-threaded muzzle brake; over-length bolt handle; 20 MOA Picatinny rail; fluted bull barrel; swivel studs; bipod rail
MSRP . . . . **$3069.99–$3139.99**

BUSHMASTER FIREARMS ACR 6.8MM REMINGTON SPC II

Action: Semiautomatic
Stock: Synthetic
Barrel: 16.5 in.
Sights: None
Weight: 8 lb. 3 oz.
Caliber: 6.8 Rem. SPC II
Magazine: 25 rounds
Features: A new cartridge in an AR carbine platform featuring an BLK square drop modular handguard; seven-position adjustable and folding stock; full ambidextrous controls; Advanced Armament BLK flash hider
MSRP $2249.00

BUSHMASTER FIREARMS ACR .450 BUSHMASTER

Action: Semiautomatic
Stock: Synthetic
Barrel: 16.5 in., 18.5 in.
Sights: None
Weight: 8 lb.–8 lb. 3 oz.
Caliber: .450 Bushmaster
Magazine: 5 rounds
Features: The big .450 Bushmaster at home in an AR platform featuring a folding adjustable stock; ambidextrous controls; .450 muzzle brake
MSRP $2249.00

CARACAL VERSUS COMPETITION

Action: Semiautomatic
Stock: Synthetic
Barrel: 18 in.
Sights: None
Weight: 6 lb. 3 oz.
Caliber: .223 Wylde
Magazine: 10, 30 rounds
Features: A lightweight nimble gun for the 3-Gun crowd in an outside-the-box caliber. Features include carbon fiber-wrapped 416R stainless barrel; two-port, self-timing muzzle brake; 15-inch Caracal free-floating handguard with MLOK and QD attachment points; Caracal grip; direct impingement gas system
MSRP $1799.00

CENTURY ARMS VSKA

Action: Semiautomatic
Stock: American maple
Barrel: 16.3 in.
Sights: A2-style front, ladder-type adjustable rear
Weight: N/A
Caliber: 7.62X39
Magazine: 30 rounds
Features: An upscale, heavy-duty AK-47-style rifle with American maple stock; heat-treated S7 tool steel bolt carrier, front trunnion, and feed ramp; chrome moly 4150 barrel; RAK-1 Enhanced Trigger Group; manganese-phosphate finish
MSRP $735.95

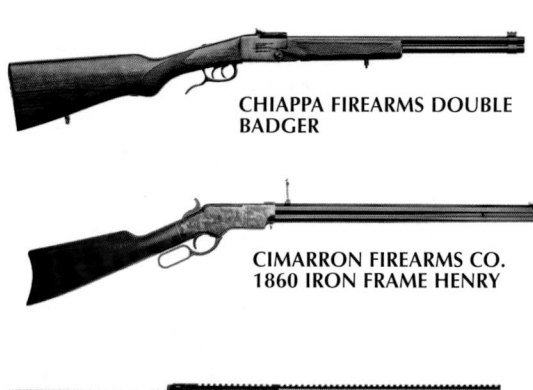

CHIAPPA FIREARMS DOUBLE BADGER

CIMARRON FIREARMS CO. 1860 IRON FRAME HENRY

CMMG INC. ENDEAVOR 200 SERIES

CHIAPPA FIREARMS RAK-9

CHRISTENSEN ARMS TRAVERSE

CMMG INC. ENDEAVOR 100 SERIES

CHIAPPA FIREARMS DOUBLE BADGER

Action: Break-open
Stock: Beech
Barrel: 19 in., 20 in.
Sights: Fixed red fiber optic front, Williams green fiber optic rear
Weight: 5 lb. 13 oz.
Caliber: .22 LR/.410-bore, .243 Win./.410-bore, .22 LR/20-gauge, .22 WMR/.410-bore
Magazine: 2 rounds
Features: A folding combo gun with double triggers; firearm folds by lowering the trigger guard; all shotgun bores are 3-inch chambers; blued finish metalwork; beech stocks
MSRP . . . . $429.00–$619.00

CHIAPPA FIREARMS RAK-9

Action: Semiautomatic
Stock: Synthetic
Barrel: 17.25 in.
Sights: Adjustable military-style
Weight: 6 lb. 10 oz.
Caliber: 9mm
Magazine: 10 rounds
Features: A pistol-caliber take on the AK-47 with a skeletonized synthetic stock; steel frame; adjustable sights
MSRP $719.00

CHRISTENSEN ARMS TRAVERSE

Action: Bolt
Stock: Carbon fiber composite
Barrel: 24 in., 26 in.

Sights: None
Weight: 7 lb. 5 oz.–7 lb. 11 oz.
Caliber: .22–250 Rem., .243 Win., 6.5 Creedmoor, 6.5 PRC, 6.5–284, .26 Nosler, .270 Win., .270 WSM, 7mm-08 Rem., .308 Win., .30–06 Spfd., .30 Nosler, .300 WSM, .300 Win. Mag., .300 RUM
Magazine: 3 rounds
Features: Classically styled and thoroughly modern backcountry rifle with a carbon fiber composite stock with Monte Carlo profile; full palm swell; light target contour, hand-lapped, carbon fiber-wrapped, free-floating threaded barrel with match chamber and 4-inch bottom rail; skeletonized bolt with fluted bolt knob; 0 MOA top rail; Invar pillars; spot bedding; Limbsaver recoil pad; black/gray or green/black spiderweb finish on stock
MSRP $2395.00

CIMARRON FIREARMS CO. 1860 IRON FRAME HENRY

Action: Lever
Stock: Walnut
Barrel: 24 in.
Sights: Ivory front blade, adjustable rear
Weight: 9 lb. 3 oz.
Caliber: .44 WCF, .45 LC
Magazine: 12 rounds
Features: An authentic reproduction any collector would be proud of, featuring case hardened frame; walnut stock; octagon barrel
MSRP $1565.69

CMMG INC. ENDEAVOR 100 SERIES

Action: Semiautomatic
Stock: Synthetic
Barrel: 18 in., 20 in.
Sights: None
Weight: 6 lb. 15 oz.–8 lb. 15 oz.
Caliber: 5.56X45mm, .22 Nosler, .224 Valkyrie, 6.5 Creedmoor, .308 Win.
Magazine: 10, 20, 30 rounds
Features: A full-length direct impingement MSR platform with the long-range game in mind. Features include Type III hard coat anodizing; A2 pistol grip and compensator; A1 buttstock; free-floating CMMG M-LOK handguard
MSRP . . . . $1049.95–$1749.95

CMMG INC. ENDEAVOR 200 SERIES

Action: Semiautomatic
Stock: Synthetic
Barrel: 18 in., 20 in.
Sights: None
Weight: 7 lb. 2 oz.–9 lb. 2 oz.
Caliber: 5.56X45mm, .22 Nosler, .224 Valkyrie, 6.5 Creedmoor, .308 Win.
Magazine: 10, 20, 30 rounds
Features: The 100 Series with added features such as CMMG SV muzzle brake; Magpul MOE stock and pistol grip
MSRP . . . . $1149.95–$1849.95

CMMG INC. ENDEAVOR 300 SERIES

CMMG INC. RESOLUTE 100 SERIES

CMMG INC. RESOLUTE 200 SERIES

CMMG INC. RESOLUTE 300 SERIES

CVA CASCADE

CZ-USA 457 LUX

CZ-USA 457 AMERICAN

CMMG INC. ENDEAVOR 300 SERIES

Action: Semiautomatic
Stock: Synthetic
Barrel: 22 in., 24 in.
Sights: None
Weight: 8 lb. 10 oz.–11 lb. 5 oz.
Caliber: 5.56X45mm, .22 Nosler, .224 Valkyrie, 6.5 Creedmoor, .308 Win.
Magazine: 10, 20, 30 rounds
Features: The top end of the Endeavor Series with upgraded features such as: Geissele two-stage trigger; Magpul MOE pistol grip, PRS stock; CMMG ambidextrous safety selector and charging handle; 10 Premier Cerakote color options
MSRP . . . . $1749.95–$2349.95

CMMG INC. RESOLUTE 100 SERIES

Action: Semiautomatic
Stock: Synthetic
Barrel: 16.1 in., 17 in.
Sights: None
Weight: 6 lb. 1 oz.–7 lb. 2 oz.
Caliber: .22 LR, 5.7X28mm, 9mm, .45 ACP, 5.56X45mm, 6.5 Grendel, .300 BLK, 7.62X39, .308 Win., .458 SOCOM
Magazine: 10, 20, 30 rounds
Features: Carbine-length rifle with an interesting selection of calibers. Features include M4-type buttstock; M-Lok free-float handguards; Type III hard coat anodize; A2 pistol grip and compensator
MSRP . . . . $949.95–$1899.95

CMMG INC. RESOLUTE 200 SERIES

Action: Semiautomatic

Stock: Synthetic
Barrel: 16.1 in.
Sights: None
Weight: 6 lb. 6 oz.–7 lb. 4 oz.
Caliber: .22 LR, 5.7X28mm, 9mm, .45 ACP, 5.56X45mm, 6.5 Grendel, .300 BLK, 7.62X39, .308 Win., .458 SOCOM
Magazine: 10, 20, 30 rounds
Features: A set-up from the 100 series with the addition of CMMG Ripstock and SV muzzle brake
MSRP . . . . $1124.95–$2024.95

CMMG INC. RESOLUTE 300 SERIES

Action: Semiautomatic
Stock: Synthetic
Barrel: 16.1 in.
Sights: None
Weight: 6 lb. 2 oz.–8 lb. 4 oz.
Caliber: .22 LR, 5.7X28mm, 9mm, .45 ACP, 5.56X45mm, 6.5 Grendel, .300 BLK, 7.62X39, .308 Win., .458 SOCOM
Magazine: 10, 20, 30 rounds
Features: The fanciest of the Resolute series, with: 10 Premier Cerakote color options; Geissele two-stage trigger; Magpul MOE pistol grip; "Resolute" engraved on lower receiver
MSRP . . . . $1449.95–$2349.95

CONNECTICUT VALLEY ARMS (CVA) CASCADE

Action: Bolt
Stock: Synthetic
Barrel: 22 in.
Sights: None
Weight: N/A
Caliber: 6.5 Creedmoor, 7mm-08 Rem., .308 Win.

Magazine: 3 rounds
Features: CVA's first centerfire bolt-action featuring: fiberglass-reinforced CVA stock in charcoal gray; 70-degree bolt throw; 4140 carbon steel barrel; flush-fit detachable box magazine; spacers for adjustable length of pull; dual front swivel studs
MSRP $566.95

CZ-USA 457 AMERICAN

Action: Bolt
Stock: Turkish walnut
Barrel: 24.8 in.
Sights: None
Weight: 6 lb. 3 oz.
Caliber: .22 LR, .17 HMR, .22 WMR
Magazine: 5 rounds
Features: Classically styled, walnut-stocked rimfire with a cold hammer-forged barrel; integral 11mm dovetail scope mount cutouts; detachable magazine
MSRP $496.00

CZ-USA 457 LUX

Action: Bolt
Stock: Turkish walnut
Barrel: 24.8 in.
Sights: Hooded front, tangent adjustable rear
Weight: 6 lb. 3 oz.
Caliber: .22 LR, .17 HMR, .22 WMR
Magazine: 5 rounds
Features: A rimfire with a European flair; detachable box magazine; fully adjustable trigger; 60-degree bolt rotation for easier scope use; swappable barrel system
MSRP $522.00

CZ-USA 457 PROVARMINT SUPPRESSOR-READY

CZ-USA 457 SCOUT

CZ-USA 457 TRAINING RIFLE

CZ-USA 457 VARMINT

CZ-USA 457 VARMINT AT-ONE

CZ-USA 457 VARMINT MTR

CZ-USA 457 PROVARMINT SUPPRESSOR-READY

Action: Bolt
Stock: Laminate
Barrel: 16.5 in.
Sights: None
Weight: 7 lb. 4 oz.
Caliber: .22 LR
Magazine: 5 rounds
Features: A short-barreled, suppressor-ready rifle for small varmints: detachable box magazine; laminate stock with black paint; fully adjustable trigger; barrel threaded ½X28
MSRP **$588.00**

CZ-USA 457 SCOUT

Action: Bolt
Stock: Beechwood
Barrel: 16.5 in.
Sights: Skeletonized hooded blade front, leaf rear
Weight: 5 lb.
Caliber: .22 LR
Magazine: 1 round
Features: A youth rifle with a 12-inch length of pull; ½X28 threaded muzzle for suppressor use; modular 457 platform; single-shot adaptor, but accepts all 457/455 magazines; American style beechwood stock; adjustable trigger
MSRP **$365.00**

CZ-USA 457 TRAINING RIFLE

Action: Bolt
Stock: Beechwood
Barrel: 24.8 in.
Sights: Hooded front, tangent adjustable rear
Weight: 6 lb. 3 oz.
Caliber: .22 LR
Magazine: 5 rounds
Features: A serious practice and small-game rifle with: fully adjustable trigger; distance adjustable tangent rear sight, hooded front; slab-sided
MSRP **$449.00**

CZ-USA 457 VARMINT

Action: Bolt
Stock: Turkish walnut
Barrel: 20.5 in.
Sights: None
Weight: 7 lb. 1 oz.
Caliber: .22 LR, .17 HMR, .22 WMR
Magazine: 5 rounds
Features: A maneuverable varmint rifle with: heavy barrel profile; detachable box magazine; swappable barrel system; 60-degree bolt rotation for easier use with optics; laser-cut stippling
MSRP **$522.00**

CZ-USA 457 VARMINT AT-ONE

Action: Bolt
Stock: Laminate
Barrel: 16.5 in., 24 in.
Sights: None
Weight: 7 lb. 12 oz.
Caliber: .22 LR
Magazine: 5 rounds
Features: A varmint-getter made to fit with a Boyd's AT-ONE laminate stock adjustable at cheekpiece and for length of pull; swappable barrel system; fully adjustable trigger
MSRP **$660.00**

CZ-USA 457 VARMINT MTR

Action: Bolt
Stock: Turkish walnut
Barrel: 20.5 in.
Sights: None
Weight: 7 lb. 1 oz.
Caliber: .22 LR
Magazine: 5 rounds
Features: A rock-steady small-varmint or paper-puncher gun- (MTR = Match Target Rifle) with a handsome target-style stock of Turkish walnut; fully adjustable trigger; detachable box magazine; match chamber; heavy barrel profile; flat fore-end; dual QD studs front, single rear
MSRP **$752.00**

CZ-USA 457 VARMINT PRECISION TRAINER CAMO

CZ-USA 527 VARMINT MTR

DAMKO MARTINI RIFLE STANDARD

CZ-USA 527 VARMINT SUPPRESSOR-READY

DAMKO MARTINI RIFLE SCOPE VERSION

DAMKO MARTINI RIFLE PEEP SIGHT

CZ-USA 457 VARMINT PRECISION TRAINER CAMO

Action: Bolt
Stock: Composite
Barrel: 16.5, 20.5 in., 24 in.
Sights: None
Weight: 7 lb. 2 oz.–7 lb. 9 oz.
Caliber: .22 LR
Magazine: 5 rounda
Features: A dedicated rimfire training rifle or small-game getter with a Manners carbon-fiber/fiberglass composite stock in a three-color camo; ½X28 threaded barrel; swappable barrel system
MSRP **$1144.00**

CZ-USA 527 VARMINT MTR

Action: Bolt
Stock: Turkish walnut
Barrel: 25.6 in.
Sights: None
Weight: 8 lb. 11 oz.
Caliber: .223 Rem., 6.5 Grendel
Magazine: 5 rounds
Features: Nicely priced varmint or paper-punching rifle (MTR = Match Target Rifle) with choice of an American pattern heavy target stock; flat fore-end; longer barrel; fully adjustable trigger; .866-inch heavy profile barrel
MSRP **$879.00**

CZ-USA 527 VARMINT SUPPRESSOR-READY

Action: Bolt
Stock: Turkish walnut
Barrel: 24 in.
Sights: None
Weight: 7 lb. 13 oz.
Caliber: 6.5 Grendel
Magazine: 5 rounds
Features: Chambered only for the 6.5 Grendel, this varmint rifle features: single set trigger; controlled round feed; claw extractor; 5/8X24 muzzle threads
MSRP **$779.00**

DAMKO (D. K. PRECISION OUTDOOR, LLC) MARTINI RIFLE STANDARD

Action: Single-shot Martini falling block
Stock: Walnut
Barrel: 20 in., 24 in.
Sights: Hooded bead front, tangent-adjustable flat-top rear
Weight: N/A
Caliber: .25–35 Win., .30–30 Win., .30–40 Krag, .44 Rem. Mag.
Magazine: 1 round
Features: An updated take on a classic Martini falling block action in four popular calibers; .44 Rem. Mag with 20-inch barrel, all others 24 inches; steel butt plate; Chromoly Pac-Nor barrel
MSRP **$1799.00**

DAMKO (D. K. PRECISION OUTDOOR, LLC) MARTINI RIFLE PEEP SIGHT

Action: Single-shot Martini falling block
Stock: Walnut
Barrel: 20 in., 24 in.
Sights: Hooded bead front, threaded rear peep
Weight: N/A
Caliber: .25–35 Win., .30–30 Win., .30–40 Krag, .44 Rem. Mag.
Magazine: 1 round
Features: All the features of the standard Martini, with the addition of DAMKO's own peep sight with a 12–40 thread
MSRP **$1899.00**

DAMKO (D. K. PRECISION OUTDOOR, LLC) MARTINI RIFLE SCOPE VERSION

Action: Single-shot Martini falling block
Stock: Walnut
Barrel: 20 in., 26 in.
Sights: None
Weight: N/A
Caliber: .25–35 Win., .30–30 Win., .30–40 Krag, .44 Rem. Mag.
Magazine: 1 round
Features: An original take on the Martini rifle with a flat-top PAC-NOR barrel mounted with DAMKO's own cantilever scope mount base
MSRP **$1999.00**

DANIEL DEFENSE DDM4
V7 LW RATTLECAN

DANIEL DEFENSE DELTA 5

DEVIL DOG
ARMS DDA
KRP-15

DARK STORM INDUSTRIES DS-15
HURRICANE

DEVIL DOG ARMS
DDA MRP 10

DEVIL DOG ARMS DDA
RIS-15

DANIEL DEFENSE DDM4 V7 LW RATTLECAN

Action: Semiautomatic
Stock: Synthetic
Barrel: 16 in.
Sights: None
Weight: 6 lb. 1 oz.
Caliber: 5.56 NATO
Magazine: 20 rounds
Features: The popular DDM4 platform gets an fresh look with the company's proprietary Rattlecan hybrid paint scheme, a combination of DD's Tornado and mil-spec Cerakote finishes. Other features include mid-length gas system; ½X28 threaded muzzle; H buffer; pinned low-profile gas block; DD's glass-filled polymer stock with soft-touch overmolds
MSRP **$1902.00**

DANIEL DEFENSE DELTA 5

Action: Bolt
Stock: Synthetic
Barrel: 20 in., 24 in.
Sights: None
Weight: 8 lb. 15 oz.–9 lb. 8 oz.
Caliber: .308 Win., 6.5 Creedmoor, 7mm-08 Rem.
Magazine: 5 rounds
Features: DD's first bolt-action featuring a user-interchangeable stainless steel barrel; bedded stainless steel action with integral recoil lug; removeable bolt knob; carbon fiber-reinforced stock adjustable for length of pull and height; 11 M-LOK points on the fore-end, one on the buttstock, and three M-LOK sling points; AICS single-feed mag compatible; adjustable Timney Elite Hunter trigger, single-stage with two-position safety
MSRP **$2199.00**

DARK STORM INDUSTRIES DS-15 HURRICANE

Action: Semiautomatic
Stock: Synthetic
Barrel: 20 in.
Sights: None
Weight: N/A
Caliber: .224 Valyrie
Magazine: N/A
Features: A fixed-magazine semiauto featuring a 3-pound billet drop-in trigger; 15-inch M-LOK forearm; nickel-boron bolt carrier group; stainless steel competition compensator; Hogue overmolded pistol grip; ambidextrous charging handle and safety selector; rifle-length gas system with micro gas block; PMAG removeable magazine option available
MSRP **$1595.00**

DEVIL DOG ARMS DDA KRP-15

Action: Semiautomatic
Stock: Synthetic
Barrel: 16 in.
Sights: None
Weight: 7 lb.
Caliber: .223 Rem./5.56 NATO
Magazine: N/A
Features: KRP is Keymod Rifle Package, an AR platform with miles of rail on its 15-inch free-floating Keymod handguard; billet machined upper and lower; gas impingement system; Type III hard coat anodized receiver finish; nitride finish 1:7 twist barrel; Devil Dog Arms tactical muzzle brake; Magpul six-position MOE buttstock and MOE+ grip
MSRP **$1199.00**

DEVIL DOG ARMS DDA MRP 10

Action: Semiautomatic
Stock: Synthetic
Barrel: 18 in.
Sights: None
Weight: 9 lb. 8 oz.
Caliber: .308 Win./7.62X51 NATO
Magazine: N/A
Features: MRP is MOE Rifle Package featuring 3D billet machined 7075-T6 lower and flattop upper; Devil Dog Arms 15-inch hexagonal free-floating handguard; LM profile barrel with 1:11 twist and DDA tactical flash hider; ALG QMS trigger; Magpul MOE buttstock and MOE+ grip
MSRP **$1499.00**

DEVIL DOG ARMS DDA RIS-15

Action: Semiautomatic
Stock: Synthetic
Barrel: 16 in.
Sights: DDA RIS front, Magpul MBUS rear
Weight: 7 lb.
Caliber: .223 Rem./5.56 NATO
Magazine: N/A
Features: RIS is Rail Integrated Sight; with a 13-inch RIS handguard; Devil Dog Arms front Rail Integrated Sight and Magpul MBUS rear; 7075-T6 lower and flat-top upper; DDA tactical flash hider; magnetic particle inspected NiB-X-coated bolt; ALG QMS trigger
MSRP **$1199.00**

DEVIL DOG ARMS HOG

DOUBLESTAR CORP. ZERO CARBINE RIFLE

DPMS PANTHER ARMS M-LOK RECON

DPMS PANTHER ARMS LCAR

DPMS PANTHER ARMS M-LOK TAC2

DPMS PANTHER ARMS M-LOK TPR

DPMS PANTHER ARMS PRAIRIE PANTHER KUIU VERDE

DEVIL DOG ARMS HOG

Action: Bolt
Stock: Carbon fiber
Barrel: N/A
Sights: None
Weight: 13 lb. 6 oz.–14 lb.
Caliber: 6.5 Creedmoor, .308 Win., .338 Lapua
Magazine: N/A
Features: This is a premium rifle for the long-range crowd, featuring a Kelby Model KTS stock, hand laid with three-way buttplate and adjustable cheekpiece; black nitride action; Calvin Elite two-stage trigger; match-grade M24 Krieger barrel; hand-polished chamber; 5/8X24 threaded muzzle; detachable box magazine
6.5 Creedmoor, .308 Win.: . . . **$4495.00**
.338 Lapua: **$5995.00**

DOUBLESTAR CORP. ZERO CARBINE RIFLE

Action: Semiautomatic
Stock: Synthetic
Barrel: 16 in.
Sights: None
Weight: N/A
Caliber: 5.56 NATO
Magazine: 30 rounds
Features: A premium accuracy rifle with a 1:8 twist Wilson Air Gauge heavy barrel; low-profile gas block; Cloak 15 ½-inch M-LOK handguard; Alpha AR Comp compensator; flattop receiver; billet winter triggerguard and backbone charging handle; forward assist; ACE SOCOM stock; Ergo Ambi Sure Grip; direct gas impingement action
MSRP **$1479.99**

DPMS PANTHER ARMS LCAR

Action: Semiautomatic
Stock: Synthetic
Barrel: 16 in.
Sights: F-marked carbine-height front,Magpul flip-up rear
Weight: 8 lb. 8 oz.
Caliber: 5.56 NATO
Magazine: 20 rounds
Features: Mil-spec carbine with an adjustable M4 stock; Magpul flip-up back-up rear sight; FNC-treated barrel
MSRP **$749.00**

DPMS PANTHER ARMS M-LOK RECON

Action: Semiautomatic
Stock: Synthetic
Barrel: 16 in.
Sights: Magpul flip-up front and rear
Weight: 7 lb. 11 oz.
Caliber: 5.56 NATO
Magazine: 20 rounds
Features: With a Midwest Industries M-LOK handguard; Magpul MOE stock, grip, ad trigger guard; BLK flash hider; bead-blasted stainless steel barrel
MSRP **$1169.00**

DPMS PANTHER ARMS M-LOK TAC2

Action: Semiautomatic
Stock: Synthetic
Barrel: 16 in.
Sights: A2 front, Magpul flip-up rear
Weight: 8 lb. 8 oz.
Caliber: 5.56 NATO
Magazine: 20 rounds

Features: Feature-rich AR with a forged 7075 T6 upper and lower; Magpul adjustable ACS stock; M-LOK handguard with a runway of top rail; Magpul MOE pistol grip; Panther flash hider
MSRP **$1249.00**

DPMS PANTHER ARMS M-LOK TPR

Action: Semiautomatic
Stock: Synthetic
Barrel: 20 in.
Sights: None
Weight: 7 lb. 12 oz.
Caliber: 5.56 NATO
Magazine: 20 rounds
Features: TPR is for Tactical Precision Rifle, with a 20-inch HBAR barrel in bead-blasted stainless; Magpul MOE grip; DMPS M11 modular M-LOK handguard
MSRP **$1349.00**

DPMS PANTHER ARMS PRAIRIE PANTHER KUIU VERDE

Action: Semiautomatic
Stock: Synthetic
Barrel: 20 in.
Sights: None
Weight: 7 lb. 3 oz.
Caliber: 5.56 NATO
Magazine: 20 rounds
Features: A hunting AR platform dressed in Kuiu Verde camo; carbon fiber free-floating handguard; A2 pistol grip; optics rail
MSRP **$1248.00**

NEW Products: **Rifles**

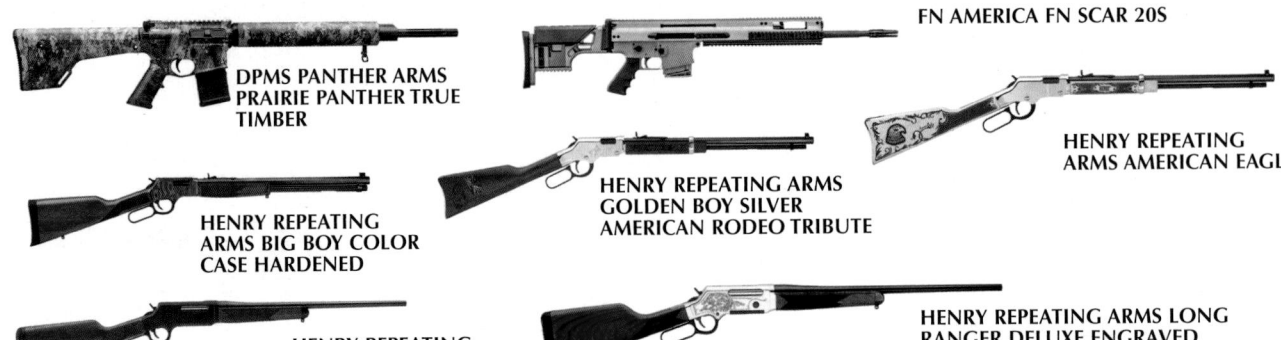

DPMS PANTHER ARMS
PRAIRIE PANTHER TRUE
TIMBER

FN AMERICA FN SCAR 20S

HENRY REPEATING
ARMS AMERICAN EAGLE

HENRY REPEATING ARMS
GOLDEN BOY SILVER
AMERICAN RODEO TRIBUTE

HENRY REPEATING
ARMS BIG BOY COLOR
CASE HARDENED

HENRY REPEATING ARMS LONG
RANGER DELUXE ENGRAVED

HENRY REPEATING
ARMS LONG RANGER

DPMS PANTHER ARMS PRAIRIE PANTHER TRUE TIMBER

Action: Semiautomatic
Stock: Synthetic
Barrel: 20 in.
Sights: None
Weight: 7 lb. 3 oz.
Caliber: 5.56 NATO
Magazine: 20 rounds
Features: A hunting AR platform dressed in True Timber Strata camo; carbon fiber free-floating handguard; A2 pistol grip; optics rail
MSRP $1248.00

FN AMERICA FN SCAR 20S

Action: Semiautomatic
Stock: Synthetic
Barrel: 20 in.
Sights: None
Weight: 11 lb. 3 oz.
Caliber: 7.62X39mm
Magazine: 10 rounds
Features: Slick, short-stroke gas piston semiauto with miles of rail; two-stage match Geissele "Super SCAR" trigger; stock adjustable for length of pull and comb height; Hogue finger-groove pistol grip; monolithic aluminum receiver; left- or right-hand charging handle mounting; polymer trigger module; adjustable cheekpiece
MSRP $4499.00

HENRY REPEATING ARMS AMERICAN EAGLE

Action: Lever
Stock: Walnut
Barrel: 20 in.
Sights: Brass bead front, adjustable buckhorn rear with diamond insert
Weight: 6 lb. 12 oz.
Caliber: .22 LR
Magazine: 16 rounds
Features: A unique salute to America with a ivory-washed walnut stock engraved with border patterns, an American eagle head, and aggressive, distinctive checkering; blued octagon barrel
MSRP $950.00

HENRY REPEATING ARMS BIG BOY COLOR CASE HARDENED

Action: Lever
Stock: Walnut
Barrel: 20 in.
Sights: Brass bead front, adjustable buckhorn rear with diamond insert
Weight: 7 lb. 13 oz.
Caliber: .357 Mag., .44 Mag., .45 LC
Magazine: 7, 10 rounds
Features: Classic handgun cartridges at home in a walnut stocked lever action featuring color case hardened receivers; blued octagon barrels; choice of standard or large loop levers
MSRP $1045.00

HENRY REPEATING ARMS GOLDEN BOY SILVER AMERICAN RODEO TRIBUTE

Action: Lever
Stock: Walnut
Barrel: 20 in.
Sights: Brass bead front, adjustable rear
Weight: 6 lb. 12 oz.
Caliber: .22 LR
Magazine: 16 rounds
Features: A tribute to the sport and cowboys of American rodeo, featuring a blued octagon barrel; engraved stock with 24K gold highlights; bucking bull rider engraved in color on stock
MSRP $1190.00

HENRY REPEATING ARMS LONG RANGER

Action: Lever
Stock: Walnut
Barrel: 20 in., 22 in.
Sights: None; ramp front with ivory bead, adjustable rear
Weight: 7 lb.
Caliber: .243 Win., .308 Win., .223 Rem., 6.5 Creedmoor
Magazine: 4, 5 rounds
Features: A lever for cartridges more commonly found in a bolt-action, featuring; round barrels; flush-fit detachable magazines; sighted and unsighted options
MSRP $1066.00

HENRY REPEATING ARMS LONG RANGER DELUXE ENGRAVED

Action: Lever
Stock: Walnut
Barrel: 20 in.
Sights: Folding fully adjustable rear, ramp front with ivory bead
Weight: 7 lb.
Caliber: .223 Rem./5.56 NATO, .243 Win., .308 Win.
Magazine: 5, 4 rounds
Features: Freshly updated versions of Henry's popular hunting rifle. All have checkered American walnut straight-wrist stocks; solid rubber recoil pads; sling swivels; detachable steel magazines; high-polished nickel receivers with gold-inlay enhanced scroll engraving
MSRP $1850.00

HENRY REPEATING ARMS LONG RANGER WILDLIFE EDITION

HENRY REPEATING ARMS SINGLE SHOT YOUTH RIFLE

HORIZON FIREARMS RIVAL HZ

HOWA AMERICAN FLAG CHASSIS

HOWA MINI EXCL LITE CHASSIS

HOWA ORYX

HOWA ORYX MINI-ACTION

HENRY REPEATING ARMS LONG RANGER WILDLIFE EDITION

Action: Lever
Stock: Walnut
Barrel: 20 in.
Sights: Folding fully adjustable rear, ramp front with ivory bead
Weight: 7 lb.
Caliber: .223 Rem./5.56 NATO, .243 Win., .308 Win.
Magazine: 5, 4 rounds
Features: Similar to the Long Ranger Deluxe Engraved, but each caliber is dedicated to a specific game animal with appropriate portrait engravings highlighted in 24K gold: the Coyote in .223/5.56 NATO; the Antelope in .243; and the Elk in .308
MSRP **$1850.00**

HENRY REPEATING ARMS SINGLE SHOT YOUTH RIFLE

Action: Break-open
Stock: Walnut
Barrel: 22 in.
Sights: Folding fully adjustable leaf rear, brass bead front
Weight: 6 lb. 15 oz.
Caliber: .243 Win.
Magazine: 1 round
Features: The first time Henry's single-shot youth rifle offered in a caliber other than .22. Features include solid rubber recoil pad; blued steel receiver; round blued steel barrel with 1:10 twist
MSRP **$448.00**

HORIZON FIREARMS RIVAL HZ

Action: Bolt
Stock: Synthetic

Barrel: 24 in., 25 in.
Sights: None
Weight: N/A
Caliber: 6.5 Creedmoor, 6.5 PRC, .308 Win.
Magazine: N/A
Features: Semi-custom long-range rifle featuring Horizon Series Stiller action; Benchmark barrel with three-flute spiral; spiral-fluted bolt with Small Tac knob; threaded muzzle; iota KLUTCH stock with adjustable cheekpiece; TriggerTech trigger
MSRP **$4899.00**

HOWA BY LEGACY SPORTS AMERICAN FLAG CHASSIS

Action: Bolt
Stock: Aluminum
Barrel: 20 in., 24 in., 26 in.
Sights: Nikko Sterling Diamond 4–16X50 Long Range scope
Weight: 12 lb.–12 lb. 8 oz.
Caliber: .223 Rem., .22–250 Rem., .243 Win., 6mm Creedmoor, 6.5 Creedmoor, .308 Win.
Magazine: 10 rounds
Features: Chassis rifle Cerakoted in red-white-and-blue or a gray-scale American flag graphics; Nikko Sterling Diamond 4–16X50 Long Range scope; heavy barrel with muzzle three-chamber Midwest Industries muzzle brake (semi-heavy barrel option does not include brake); Hogue finger groove pistol grip; adjustable bipod
MSRP . . . . starting at **$1499.00**

HOWA BY LEGACY SPORTS MINI EXCL LITE CHASSIS

Action: Bolt
Stock: Synthetic

Barrel: 16.25 in., 20 in.
Sights: None
Weight: N/A
Caliber: .223 Rem., .300 BLK. 7.62X39, 6.5 Grendel
Magazine: 5, 10 rounds
Features: An ultra-compact lightweight chassis rifle with threaded barrel; detachable box magazine; adjustable length of pull from 12.75 to 15.75 in.
MSRP . . . . starting at **$699.00**

HOWA BY LEGACY SPORTS ORYX

Action: Bolt
Stock: Aluminum
Barrel: 20 in., 24 in., 26 in.
Sights: None
Weight: 10 lb. 13 oz.–11 lb. 4 oz
Caliber: 6mm Creedmoor, 6.5 Creedmoor, .308 Win.
Magazine: N/A
Features: A full monolithic aluminum chassis with a back end adjustable for length of pull and comb height; heavy barrel; available in grey, green, or flat dark earth; barrel threaded 5/8X24
MSRP . . . . starting at **$1099.00**

HOWA BY LEGACY SPORTS ORYX MINI-ACTION

Action: Bolt
Stock: Aluminum
Barrel: 16 in..25 in., 20 in.
Sights: None
Weight: 8 lb. 3 oz.–8 lb. 23 oz.
Caliber: .300 BLK., .223 Rem., 7.62X39, 6.5 Grendel
Magazine: N/A
Features: The compact chassis footprint of the full-size Oryx and with a different set of caliber offerings
MSRP . . . . starting at **$1059.00**

IRON HORSE FIREARMS
TOR

KIMBER MOUNTAIN
ASCENT (SUBALPINE)

MARLIN FIREARMS
MODEL 1894 CST

MARLIN FIREARMS
MODEL 1894 SBL

MARLIN FIREARMS
MODEL 336C CURLY
MAPLE

MARLIN FIREARMS
MODEL 444 MARLIN

MASTERPIECE ARMS MPA
BA HYBRID HUNTER

IRON HORSE FIREARMS TOR

Action: Semiautomatic
Stock: Synthetic
Barrel: 16 in.
Sights: None
Weight: N/A
Caliber: 5.56 NATO
Magazine: 20 rounds
Features: TOR is for "thumb-operated receiver" and makes for an AR with a unique and original trigger system that improves control by putting the force necessary to activate it in line with the shooter's center of aim; trigger "guard" completely encases the trigger with is within the top rear of the pistol grip; AERO Precision upper, lower, and M-LOK handguard; carbine-length gas system; front handguard and receiver top rails
MSRP $1350.00

KIMBER MOUNTAIN ASCENT (SUBALPINE)

Action: Bolt
Stock: Carbon fiber
Barrel: 22 in., 24 in.
Sights: None
Weight: 5 lb. 6 oz.
Caliber: .308 Win., .280 Ackley Improved, .30–06 Spfd., .300 WSM, .300 Win. Mag.
Magazine: 4 rounds
Features: A very lightweight offering for back-country wilderness hunters featuring reinforced carbon fiber stock wrapped in Gore Optifade SubAlpine camo; four-groove, fluted, sporter-contour barrel; muzzle brake and thread protector; stainless steel 84M action; Mauser claw extractor; spiral-fluted bolt
MSRP $2040.00

MARLIN FIREARMS MODEL 336C CURLY MAPLE

Action: Lever
Stock: Maple
Barrel: 20 in.
Sights: Hooded front post, adjustable semibuckhorn rear
Weight: N/A
Caliber: .30–30 Win.
Magazine: 7 rounds
Features: Curly maple is a hallmark of collectible rifles in many lines, appearing here with fleur-de-lis accents on the checkering; polished blue hardware; micro-groove rifling
MSRP $899.00

MARLIN FIREARMS MODEL 444 MARLIN

Action: Lever
Stock: Walnut
Barrel: 22 in.
Sights: Hooded front post, adjustable semibuckhorn rear
Weight: N/A
Caliber: .444 Marlin
Magazine: 4 rounds
Features: A favorite returns to the Marlin big-bore lineup with a Ballard rifled 22-inch barrel; polished blue hardware
MSRP $769.00

MARLIN FIREARMS MODEL 1894 CST

Action: Lever
Stock: Synthetic
Barrel: 16.5 in.
Sights: XS ghost ring sights
Weight: 6 lb. 8 oz.
Caliber: .357 Mag.

Magazine: 8 rounds
Features: Suppressor-ready comes to this Marlin leaver with a threaded barrel in a satin stainless finish; large loop
MSRP $1154.00

MARLIN FIREARMS MODEL 1894 SBL

Action: Lever
Stock: Laminate
Barrel: 16.5 in.
Sights: XS ghost ring sights
Weight: 6 lb. 8 oz.
Caliber: .44 Mag.
Magazine: 8 rounds
Features: Dressed up lever-action workhorse with all stainless hardware; gray/black laminate stock; XS Sights ghost ring sights; large loop; topside rail
MSRP $1145.89

MASTERPIECE ARMS MPA BA HYBRID HUNTER

Action: Bolt
Stock: Aluminum/Synthetic
Barrel: customer determined
Sights: None
Weight: 9 lb. 6 oz.
Caliber: 6.5 Creedmoor, 6.5 PRC, .300 PRC, .28 Nosler
Magazine: 5 rounds
Features: A chassis rifle for the long-distance hunter with a side-folding, adjustable stock; built-in inclinometer; vertical grip; hand-lapped, pull-button rifled carbon fiber barrel threaded 5/8X24 and with Sendero profile; spiral-fluted one-piece bolt; Cerakote finish; Curtis Axiom action; TriggerTech trigger
MSRP . . . . $3725.00–$4175.00

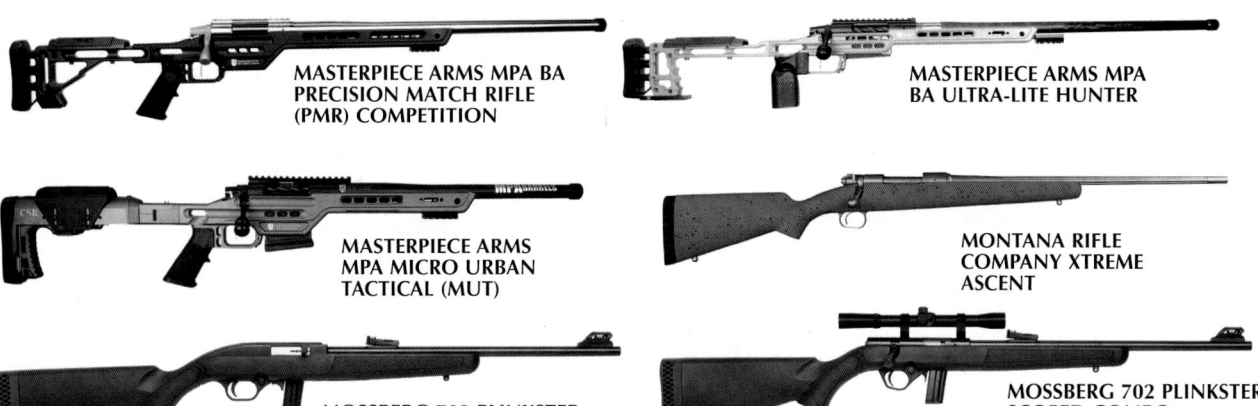

MASTERPIECE ARMS MPA BA PRECISION MATCH RIFLE (PMR) COMPETITION

MASTERPIECE ARMS MPA BA ULTRA-LITE HUNTER

MASTERPIECE ARMS MPA MICRO URBAN TACTICAL (MUT)

MONTANA RIFLE COMPANY XTREME ASCENT

MOSSBERG 702 PLINKSTER

MOSSBERG 702 PLINKSTER SCOPED COMBO

MASTERPIECE ARMS MPA BA PRECISION MATCH RIFLE (PMR) COMPETITION

Action: Bolt
Stock: Aluminum
Barrel: 26 in.
Sights: None
Weight: 11 lb. 8 oz.
Caliber: 6mm Creedmoor, 6.5 Creedmor, .308 Win.
Magazine: 10 rounds
Features: Developed specifically for the Production Class in formal Precision Rifle Series competition, this rifle sport's MPA's BA Hybrid Chassis in Cerakote with v-bedding, built-in inclinometer, thumb notch, and lower rail; MPA/Curtis short action; X-Caliber hand-lapped barrel with a #7 profile threaded 5/8X24; TriggerTech Special trigger; Magpul AICS-type magazine
MSRP **$1999.99**

MASTERPIECE ARMS MPA BA ULTRA-LITE HUNTER

Action: Bolt
Stock: Aluminum
Barrel: customer determined
Sights: None
Weight: 7 lb. 8 oz.
Caliber: 6.5 Creedmoor, 6.5 PRC, .300 PRC, .28 Nosler
Magazine: 3 rounds
Features: Nearly 2 pounds lighter than the Hybrid Hunter, this chassis rifle features a Proof carbon fiber barrel in a Sendero light contour and threaded 5/8X25; Curtis Axiom action; MPA's Ultra-Light Chassis with

V-bedding system; vertical grip; built-in inclinometer; TriggerTech trigger; Cerakote finish
MSRP . . . . **$3499.00–$3950.00**

MASTERPIECE ARMS MPA MICRO URBAN TACTICAL (MUT)

Action: Bolt
Stock: Aluminum
Barrel: 12.75 in., 16 in.
Sights: None
Weight: 8 lb. 9 oz.
Caliber: .308 Win.
Magazine: 5 rounds
Features: Ultra-compact chassis rifle featuring Remington 700-type bolt/action; built-in inclinometer; Curtis Axiom action; throat custom cut for Federal Gold Medal 175-grain; TriggerTech trigger; CSR buttstock; AICS magazines
MSRP **$3025.00**

MONTANA RIFLE COMPANY XTREME ASCENT

Action: Bolt
Stock: Synthetic
Barrel: 22 in., 24 in.
Sights: None
Weight: 5 lb. 10 oz.–5 lb. 14 oz.
Caliber: .243 Win., 6.5 Creedmoor, .270 Win., 7mm-08 Rem., .308 Win.
Magazine: 3, 4 rounds
Features: A very lightweight rifle for back-country treks, featuring a pre-64 Winchester Model 70-style, fully adjustable trigger; Montana's M1999 action; aluminum pillar and glass bedding; hand-lapped control round-

feed bolt; Mauser-style extractor; fluted, featherweight contour, button rifled, hand-lapped barrel; left- or right-hand
MSRP **$1975.00**

MOSSBERG 702 PLINKSTER

Action: Semiautomatic
Stock: Synthetic
Barrel: 18 in.
Sights: Hooded fiber optic front, adjustable rear
Weight: 4 lb.
Caliber: .22 LR
Magazine: 10, 25 rounds
Features: A handy, economical youth rimfire; black or pink marble synthetic stock; rounded fore-end; vented rubber recoil pad
MSRP . . . . **$139.00–$234.00**

MOSSBERG 702 PLINKSTER SCOPED COMBO

Action: Semiautomatic
Stock: Synthetic
Barrel: 18 in.
Sights: Hooded fiber optic front, adjustable rear/4X scope
Weight: 4 lb. 8 oz.
Caliber: .22 LR
Magazine: 10 rounds
Features: Black synthetic stock; adjustable rifle sights with a fiber optic front; factory mounted 4X scope; rounded fore-end; vented rubber recoil pad
MSRP **$202.00**

MOSSBERG 702 YOUTH BANTAM PLINKSTER

MOSSBERG 802 PLINKSTER

MOSSBERG 817 17 HMR

MOSSBERG 802 PLINKSTER SCOPED COMBO

MOSSBERG MVP LR

MOSSBERG MVP LR THUNDER RANCH

MOSSBERG MVP PREDATOR

MOSSBERG 702 YOUTH BANTAM PLINKSTER

Action: Semiautomatic
Stock: Synthetic
Barrel: 18 in.
Sights: Hooded fiber optic front, adjustable rear
Weight: 4 lb.
Caliber: .22 LR
Magazine: 10 rounds
Features: Black synthetic stock; adjustable rifle sights with a fiber optic front; rounded fore-end; Bantam is two inches shorter overall than standard Plinkster
MSRP $190.00

MOSSBERG 802 PLINKSTER

Action: Bolt
Stock: Synthetic
Barrel: 18 in.
Sights: Hooded fiber optic front, adjustable rear
Weight: 4 lb.
Caliber: .22 LR
Magazine: 10 rounds
Features: Black synthetic stock; adjustable rifle sights with a fiber optic front; rounded fore-end; vented rubber recoil pad
MSRP $191.00

MOSSBERG 802 PLINKSTER SCOPED COMBO

Action: Bolt
Stock: Synthetic
Barrel: 18 in.
Sights: Hooded fiber optic front, adjustable rear/4X scope
Weight: 4 lb. 8 oz.
Caliber: .22 LR
Magazine: 10 rounds
Features: Black synthetic stock; adjustable rifle sights with a fiber optic front; factory mounted 4X scope; rounded fore-end; vented rubber recoil pad
MSRP $202.00

MOSSBERG 817 17 HMR

Action: Bolt
Stock: Synthetic
Barrel: 21 in.
Sights: None
Weight: 5 lb.
Caliber: .17 HMR
Magazine: 5 rounds
Features: Nimble rifle for the zippy .17 HMR round; Weaver scope bases included; detachable magazine; rounded fore-end; vented rubber recoil pad
MSRP $275.00

MOSSBERG MVP LR

Action: Bolt
Stock: Synthetic
Barrel: 20 in.
Sights: None
Weight: 8 lb.
Caliber: .224 Valkyrie
Magazine: 10 rounds
Features: Features include a textured OD green stock with adjustable cheekpiece; detachable box magazine; fluted and threaded barrel; topside optics rail; dual swivels front, single rear
MSRP $910.00

MOSSBERG MVP LR THUNDER RANCH

Action: Bolt
Stock: Synthetic
Barrel: 20 in.
Sights: None
Weight: 8 lb.
Caliber: 5.56mm NATO/.223 Rem., 7.62X51 NATO/.308 Win.
Magazine: 10 rounds
Features: Features a medium bull barrel threaded and fluted; matte blued metalwork; stock in Kuiu camo with adjustable comb; topside optics rail; detachable box magazine
MSRP $974.00

MOSSBERG MVP PREDATOR

Action: Bolt
Stock: Laminate
Barrel: 20 in.
Sights: None
Weight: 7 lb. 8 oz.
Caliber: .224 Valkyrie
Magazine: 10 rounds
Features: Medium bull barrel threaded; attractive gray/brown laminate stock; Weaver-type bases; detachable box magazine; single swivel fore and aft; vented rubber recoil pad
MSRP $700.00

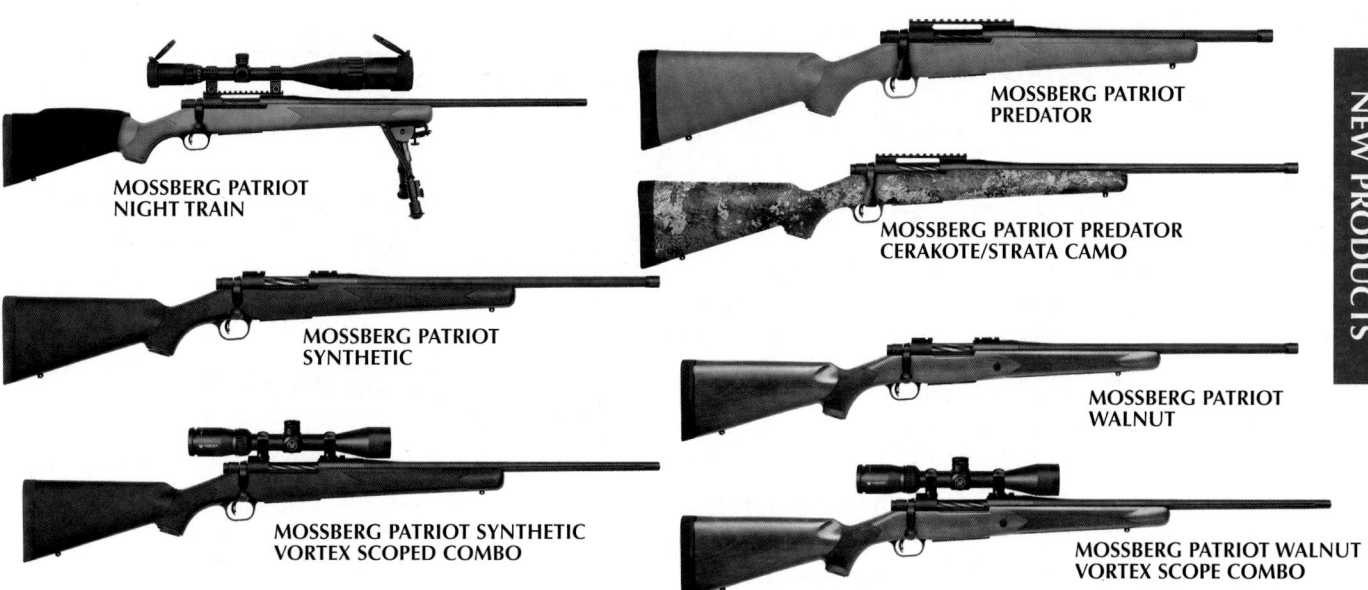

MOSSBERG PATRIOT
NIGHT TRAIN

MOSSBERG PATRIOT
PREDATOR

MOSSBERG PATRIOT PREDATOR
CERAKOTE/STRATA CAMO

MOSSBERG PATRIOT
SYNTHETIC

MOSSBERG PATRIOT
WALNUT

MOSSBERG PATRIOT SYNTHETIC
VORTEX SCOPED COMBO

MOSSBERG PATRIOT WALNUT
VORTEX SCOPE COMBO

MOSSBERG PATRIOT NIGHT TRAIN

Action: Bolt
Stock: Synthetic
Barrel: 24 in.
Sights: 6–24X50mm scope
Weight: N/A
Caliber: 6.5 Creedmoor
Magazine: 5 rounds
Features: A long-range rifle, complete with factory-mounted scope, that won't break the bank; Flat Dark Earth stock; matte finished fluted barrel
MSRP **$794.00**

MOSSBERG PATRIOT PREDATOR

Action: Bolt
Stock: Synthetic
Barrel: 16.25 in.
Sights: None
Weight: 6 lb. 4 oz.
Caliber: .450 Bushmaster
Magazine: 5 rounds
Features: A short-barreled offering in the straight-wall .450 Bushmaster cartridge; Flat Dark Earth stock; threaded barrel; Picatinny optics rail
MSRP **$441.00**

MOSSBERG PATRIOT PREDATOR CERAKOTE/ STRATA CAMO

Action: Bolt
Stock: Synthetic
Barrel: 22 in.
Sights: None

Weight: 6 lb. 8 oz.
Caliber: .243 Win., .308 Win., 6.5 Creedmoor, .22–250 Rem.
Magazine: 5 rounds
Features: Synthetic stock in Strata camo; metalwork in Cerakote Patriot Brown; fluted threaded barrel
MSRP **$524.00**

MOSSBERG PATRIOT SYNTHETIC

Action: Bolt
Stock: Synthetic
Barrel: 20 in.
Sights: None
Weight: 6 lb. 8 oz.
Caliber: .450 Bushmaster
Magazine: 5 rounds
Features: Utilitarian hunting rifle in the straight-wall .450 Bushmaster round; threaded barrel; Weaver-type bases
MSRP **$410.00**

MOSSBERG PATRIOT SYNTHETIC VORTEX SCOPED COMBO

Action: Bolt
Stock: Synthetic
Barrel: 22 in.
Sights: Vortex Crossfire II 3–9X40mm scope
Weight: 7 lb. 8 oz.
Caliber: .22–250 Rem., 7mm-08 Rem., .25–06 Rem., 7mm Rem. Mag., .338 Win. Mag.
Magazine: 3, 5 rounds

Features: Utilitarian hunting rifle featuring a fluted barrel; Vortex scope; matte blue metalwork
MSRP **$536.00**

MOSSBERG PATRIOT WALNUT

Action: Bolt
Stock: Walnut
Barrel: 20 in.
Sights: None
Weight: 7 lb.
Caliber: .450 Bushmaster
Magazine: 4 rounds
Features: A traditionally styled rifle for the straight-wall .450 Bushmaster with walnut stock; matte blue metalwork; vented rubber recoil pad; threaded barrel; Weaver-style bases
MSRP **$542.00**

MOSSBERG PATRIOT WALNUT VORTEX SCOPE COMBO

Action: Bolt
Stock: Walnut
Barrel: 22 in.
Sights: Vortex Crossfire II 3–9X40mm scope
Weight: 8 lb.
Caliber: .22–250 Rem., .25–06 Rem., 7mm Rem. Mag., .338 Win. Mag.
Magazine: 3, 5 rounds
Features: The walnut-stocked Patriot in a variety of common calibers; factory-mounted Vortex scope; fluted barrel; vented recoil pad
MSRP **$686.00**

NEW Products: **Rifles**

MOSSBERG PATRIOT YOUTH
SUPER BANTAM SCOPED
COMBO

PATRIOT ORDNANCE
FACTORY WONDER

REMINGTON MODEL
783 VARMINT LAMINATE

NOSLER M48
MOUNTAIN CARBON

REMINGTON MODEL
700 MAGPUL
ENHANCED

REMINGTON MODEL
SEVEN SS HS PRECISION

MOSSBERG PATRIOT YOUTH SUPER BANTAM SCOPED COMBO

Action: Bolt
Stock: Synthetic
Barrel: 20 in.
Sights: 3–9X40mm scope
Weight: 7 lb. 8 oz.
Caliber: 6.5 Creedmoor, 7mm-08 Rem., .308 Win., .243 Win.
Magazine: 5 rounds
Features: The rifle to take your youth hunter from the rimfire range to the deer stand; stocks available in Strata or Muddy Girl Serenity camo; fluted, matte blue barrel; stock adjustable for length of pull
MSRP $473.00

NOSLER M48 MOUNTAIN CARBON

Action: Bolt
Stock: Carbon fiber
Barrel: 24 in.
Sights: None
Weight: 6 lb.
Caliber: 6mm Creedmoor, 6.5 Creedmoor, .26 Nosler, .28 Nosler, .300 Win. Mag., .30 Nosler, .33 Nosler
Magazine: 3, 4 rounds
Features: Super-light hunter with a carbon-wrapped, Tungsten Grey Cerakote, free-floating barrel with Sendero profile; textured carbon fiber Aramid-reinforced, pillar-bedded Mountain Hunter stock; aluminum floorplate
MSRP $3140.00

PATRIOT ORDNANCE FACTORY WONDER

Action: Semiautomatic
Stock: Synthetic
Barrel: 16.5 in.
Sights: None
Weight: 6 lb. 3 oz.
Caliber: 5.56 NATO
Magazine: 30 rounds
Features: A lightened up and eye-catching AR platform featuring an eye-catching titanium blue Cerakote receiver and 14.5-inch M-LOK Renegade handguard; match-grade Puritan barrel heat-treated and threaded ½X28; single-port Micro-B muzzle brake; carbine length low-profile gas block; direct impingement system
MSRP $1599.99

REMINGTON ARMS COMPANY MODEL 700 MAGPUL ENHANCED

Action: Bolt
Stock: Synthetic
Barrel: 20 in., 24 in.
Sights: None
Weight: 8 lb. 8 oz.
Caliber: .308 Win., 6.5 Creedmoor, 6mm Creedmoor, .300 Win. Mag.
Magazine: 5, 10 rounds
Features: An upgraded version of the standard 700 Magpul Enhanced, featuring a heavy profile fluted barrel threaded for suppressor use; bipod; black Cerakote finish on metalwork; adjustable Magpul Hunter stock in Flat Dark Earth; topside rail; adjustable XMARK Pro trigger; oversized bolt handle; .300 Win. Mag. gets 24-inch barrel and five-

round mag, all others have 20-inch barrels and 10-round mags
MSRP $1249.00

REMINGTON ARMS COMPANY MODEL 783 VARMINT LAMINATE

Action: Bolt
Stock: Laminate
Barrel: 26 in.
Sights: None
Weight: 7 lb. 8 oz.
Caliber: .308 Win., .223 Rem., .22–250 Rem., .243 Win., 6.5 Creedmoor
Magazine: 4, 5 rounds
Features: A mid-weight setup with a durable laminate stock; topside rail; free-floated, button rifled, heavy barrel; adjustable Crossfire trigger; beavertail fore-end; oversized bolt handle
MSRP $625.00

REMINGTON ARMS COMPANY MODEL SEVEN SS HS PRECISION

Action: Bolt
Stock: Synthetic
Barrel: 20 in., 24 in.
Sights: None
Weight: 6 lb. 8 oz.
Caliber: .308 Win., 6.5 Creedmoor; 7mm-08 Rem., .243 Win.
Magazine: 4 rounds
Features: A lightweight, compact hunting rifle with an upgraded black and spruce green aluminum bedding block stock by H-S Precision; adjustable XMark Pro trigger; light contour barrel
MSRP $1149.00

ROCK RIVER ARMS
LAR-15 RRAGE 3G

ROCK RIVER
ARMS LAR-15
RRAGE ALPINE
CARBINE

ROCK RIVER
ARMS LAR-15
RRAGE CARBINE

ROCK RIVER ARMS
LAR-15 RRAGE
PATRIOTIC CARBINE

ROCK RIVER ARMS
LAR-15 RRAGE TAC-
BLACK CARBINE

ROCK RIVER ARMS
LAR-22 MID A4

ROCK RIVER ARMS LAR-
15M .450 BUSHMASTER

ROCK RIVER ARMS LAR-15 RRAGE 3G

Action: Semiautomatic
Stock: Synthetic
Barrel: 16 in.
Sights: None
Weight: 6 lb. 3 oz.
Caliber: 5.56mm NATO/.223 Rem.
Magazine: 30 rounds
Features: For the 3-Gun crowd, a carbine featuring a low-profile carbine-length gas block; single-stage trigger; forged lower; 15-inch RRA 3G handguard; A2 grip; adjustable stock; no forward assist
MSRP $820.00

ROCK RIVER ARMS LAR-15 RRAGE ALPINE CARBINE

Action: Semiautomatic
Stock: Synthetic
Barrel: 16 in.
Sights: None
Weight: 5 lb. 11 oz.
Caliber: 5.56mm NATO/.223 Rem.
Magazine: 30 rounds
Features: Lots of features on this carbine, such as A1 flash hider; free-floating M-LOK handguard; single-stage trigger; no forward assist; full coverage Veil Alpine camo finish
MSRP $925.00

ROCK RIVER ARMS LAR-15 RRAGE CARBINE

Action: Semiautomatic
Stock: Synthetic
Barrel: 16 in.
Sights: None

Weight: 5 lb. 11 oz.
Caliber: 5.56mm NATO/.223 Rem.
Magazine: 30 rounds
Features: Feature-rich AR carbine with an extruded aluminum A4 upper with port door; A2 flash hider; single-stage trigger; six-position tactical CAR stock; CAR-length free-floating aluminum handguard with M1913 top rail and M-LOK compatible;
MSRP $760.00

ROCK RIVER ARMS LAR-15 RRAGE PATRIOTIC CARBINE

Action: Semiautomatic
Stock: Synthetic
Barrel: 16 in.
Sights: None
Weight: 5 lb. 11 oz.
Caliber: 5.56mm NATO/.223 Rem.
Magazine: 30 rounds
Features: The original RRAGE Carbine in an all-over American flag motif; forward assist
MSRP $925.00

ROCK RIVER ARMS LAR-15 RRAGE TAC-BLACK CARBINE

Action: Semiautomatic
Stock: Synthetic
Barrel: 16 in.
Sights: None
Weight: 5 lb. 11 oz.
Caliber: 5.56mm NATO/.223 Rem.
Magazine: 30 rounds
Features: The original RRAGE Carbine dressed up in the mottled Veil Tac-

Black finish on stock, upper, lower, grip, mag, and handguard
MSRP $925.00

ROCK RIVER ARMS LAR-15M .450 BUSHMASTER

Action: Semiautomatic
Stock: Synthetic
Barrel: 16 in.
Sights: None
Weight: 6 lb. 13 oz.
Caliber: .450 Bushmaster
Magazine: N/A
Features: One for the new straight-wall cartridge, featuring cryo-treated 1:14 twist barrel; RRA's Operator muzzle brake with 5/8X24 threads; mid-length gas system; 13-inch free-floating M-LOK rail; two-stage trigger; winter trigger guard
MSRP $1175.00

ROCK RIVER ARMS LAR-22 MID A4

Action: Semiautomatic
Stock: Synthetic
Barrel: 16 in.
Sights: None
Weight: 5 lb. 6 oz.
Caliber: .22 LR
Magazine: N/A
Features: A classic look in a .22 LR featuring single-stage trigger; six-position tactical CAR stock; mid-length handguard with heat shield; choice of poly or forged aluminum A4 upper
Aluminum: $530.00
Poly: $440.00

NEW Products: **Rifles**

ROCK RIVER ARMS
LAR-22 NM 20-INCH
CMP TRAINER

ROCK RIVER ARMS
LAR-22 TACTICAL
CARBINE

RUGER 10/22 CARBINE
COLLECTOR'S SERIES THIRD
EDITION

RUGER 10/22 COMPACT
WITH MODULAR STOCK
SYSTEM

RUGER 10/22 TARGET LITE WITH
RED-AND-BLACK LAMINATE
THUMBHOLE STOCK

RUGER 77/17

ROCK RIVER ARMS LAR-22 NM 20-INCH CMP TRAINER

Action: Semiautomatic
Stock: Synthetic
Barrel: 20 in.
Sights: None
Weight: 8 lb. 13 oz.
Caliber: .22 LR
Magazine: N/A
Features: One for serious small-bore competition with added weight; two-stage chrome match trigger group; stainless steel HBAR barrel with 1:16 twist; NM CMP TRO free-floating rifle-length handguard with rail and swivel; A2 pistol grip; forged aluminum upper and lower
MSRP **$885.00**

ROCK RIVER ARMS LAR-22 TACTICAL CARBINE

Action: Semiautomatic
Stock: Synthetic
Barrel: 16 in.
Sights: None
Weight: N/A
Caliber: .22 LR
Magazine: N/A
Features: AR plinking fun or serious rimfire competition thanks to features such as a two-stage trigger; winter trigger guard; six-position stock; A2 flash hider; Hogue rubber grip; 11-inch free-floating M-LOK handguard; choice of aluminum or poly receiver construction
Aluminum: **$630.00**
Poly: **$550.00**

RUGER 10/22 CARBINE COLLECTOR'S SERIES THIRD EDITION

Action: Semiautomatic
Stock: Synthetic
Barrel: 18.5 in.
Sights: Adjustable ghost ring rear, blade front
Weight: 5 lb.
Caliber: .22 LR
Magazine: 10 rounds
Features: A handy rifle for plinking, ranch work, Rimfire Challenge competition and more, featuring OD Green synthetic Ruger Modular Stock System; satin black finish on metal; factory-installed one-piece scope mount rail; extended magazine release
MSRP **$399.00**

RUGER 10/22 COMPACT WITH MODULAR STOCK SYSTEM

Action: Semiautomatic
Stock: Synthetic
Barrel: 16.12 in.
Sights: Adjustable fiber optic rear, fiber optic front
Weight: 4 lb. 9 oz.
Caliber: .22 LR
Magazine: 10 rounds
Features: The rugged, reliable 10/22 now with a Modular Stock System; low comb and short length of pull; other stock options available for purchase
MSRP **$309.00**

RUGER 10/22 TARGET LITE WITH RED-AND-BLACK LAMINATE THUMBHOLE STOCK

Action: Semiautomatic
Stock: Laminate
Barrel: 16.13 in.
Sights: None
Weight: 5 lb.
Caliber: .22 LR
Magazine: 10 rounds
Features: An eye-catching and maneuverable rifle for the .22 competition crowd; adjustable length of pull; BX-Trigger; cold hammer forged barrel with aluminum alloy sleeve; threaded muzzle; Weaver-style/tip-off combo scope mount; extended magazine release
MSRP **$649.00**

RUGER 77/17

Action: Bolt
Stock: Walnut
Barrel: 20 in.
Sights: None
Weight: 5 lb. 11 oz.
Caliber: .17 WSM
Magazine: 6 rounds
Features: Traditionally styled small-bore for varmint or target work with: detachable rotary magazine; sling swivel studs; integral scope mounts; three-position safety
MSRP **$999.00**

RUGER 77/17 WITH GREEN MOUNTAIN STOCK

RUGER AR-556 MPR

RUGER AR-556 OPTICS CARBINE

RUGER AMERICAN RIFLE PREDATOR LEFT-HAND

RUGER CUSTOM SHOP 10/22 COMPETITION

RUGER HAWKEYE LONG-RANGE TARGET

RUGER 77/17 WITH GREEN MOUNTAIN STOCK

Action: Bolt
Stock: Laminate
Barrel: 18.5 in.
Sights: None
Weight: 7 lb.
Caliber: .17 WSM
Magazine: 6 rounds
Features: Lithe little rifle for small game hunting or predator control, with a laminate stock by Green Mountain; integral scope mounts; cold hammer forged barrel; stainless steel hardware
MSRP. $1069.00

RUGER AMERICAN RIFLE PREDATOR LEFT-HAND

Action: Bolt
Stock: Synthetic
Barrel: 22 in.
Sights: None
Weight: 6 lb. 9 oz.
Caliber: .243 Win., 7mm-08 Rem., .308 Win.
Magazine: 4 rounds
Features: The popular Predator introduced in 2018 now available as a dedicated left-hand model with a Moss Green synthetic stock; factory-installed scope rail; flush-fit magazine; matte blue finish; Ruger Marksman Adjustable Trigger; 70-degree throw, three-lug bolt with dual cocking cams; sling swivel studs
MSRP. $569.00

RUGER AR-556 MPR

Action: Semiautomatic
Stock: Synthetic
Barrel: 18.63 in.
Sights: None
Weight: 7 lb. 6 oz.
Caliber: .450 Bushmaster
Magazine: 5 rounds
Features: Go big or go home with Ruger's AR in .450 Bushmaster loaded with features like its: free-floating MLOK handguard; Type III hardcoat anodized finish; Magpul MOE grip and MOE SL collapsible buttstock; flattop upper with enlarged ejection window; Magpul MLOK accessory attachment points at 3, 6, and 9 o'clock; carbine-length gas system; Ruger muzzle brake
MSRP. $1099.00

RUGER AR-556 OPTICS CARBINE

Action: Semiautomatic
Stock: Synthetic
Barrel: 16.1 in.
Sights: None
Weight: 6 lb. 11 oz.
Caliber: 5.56mm NATO
Magazine: 30 rounds
Features: All you need is a scope. Features include six-position telescoping stock with mil-spec buffer tube; milled gas block with an integral rail mounted at the carbine-length position; flat-top upper with rail; glass-filled nylon handguard; pistol grip angled for extended trigger reach; staked gas key; reduced glare matte black oxide finish; Magpul PMAG magazine
MSRP. $789.00

RUGER CUSTOM SHOP 10/22 COMPETITION

Action: Semiautomatic

Stock: Laminate
Barrel: 16.12 in.
Sights: None
Weight: 6 lb.
Caliber: .22 LR
Magazine: 10 rounds
Features: A next-level .22 for the serious rimfire competitor with features that include: heat-treated and stress-relieved aluminum receiver; 30mm Picatinny rail for optics mounting; adjustable cheekpiece; free-floating barrel with rear cleaning port; extended ambidextrous magazine release; match-grade bolt release; BX Trigger
MSRP. $899.00

RUGER HAWKEYE LONG-RANGE TARGET

Action: Bolt
Stock: Laminate
Barrel: 26 in.
Sights: None
Weight: 11 lb.
Caliber: .300 Win. Mag., 6.5 Creedmoor, 6.5 PRC
Magazine: 5, 10, 30 rounds
Features: Ruger jumps on the long-range trends with a rifle made for the PRS crowd. Features include comb adjustable for height and stock adjustable for length of pull; Mauser-type controlled round feed; Picatinny rail four-screw mounted over integral scope ring bases; lower MLOK rail; two-stage adjustable trigger; free-floated cold hammer forged 4140 chrome-moly steel barrel with 5R rifling; .300 Win. Mag. has 1:9 twist, both 6.5s are 1:8
MSRP. $1279.00

NEW Products: **Rifles**

RUGER PRECISION
RIMFIRE MAGNUM

RUGER SCOUT .450
BUSHMASTER

SAVAGE ARMS 110 APEX
HUNTER XP

SAVAGE ARMS 110 APEX
PREDATOR XP

SAVAGE ARMS 110
APEX STORM XP

SAVAGE ARMS 110 BRUSH
HUNTER WITH ADJUSTABLE
LENGTH OF PULL

RUGER PRECISION RIMFIRE MAGNUM

Action: Bolt
Stock: Synthetic
Barrel: 18 in.
Sights: None
Weight: 6 lb. 13 oz.
Caliber: .17 HMR, .22 WMR
Magazine: 15 rounds
Features: Two new additions to Ruger's highly accurate chassis rimfire platform, now in .17 HMR and .22 WMR. Features include Ruger Marksman Adjustable trigger; one-piece chassis platform; adjustable buttstock; top-side optics rail; Ruger AR pistol grip; reversible safety; oversized bolt knob; free-floating handguard with Magpul M-LOK slots; threaded barrel; includes one new BX-15 Magnum magazine but accepts other Ruger magnum rimfire mags
MSRP **$529.00**

RUGER SCOUT .450 BUSHMASTER

Action: Bolt
Stock: Synthetic
Barrel: 16.1 in.
Sights: Adjustable rear, protected blade front
Weight: 6 lb. 3 oz.
Caliber: .450 Bushmaster
Magazine: 4 rounds
Features: The .450 Bushmaster finds a home in this fast-handling, lightweight rifle featuring: adjustable ghost ring aperture rear sight; Ruger Precision Rifle Hybrid Muzzle Brake; forward-mounted Picatinny rail; integral scope mounts; detachable box magazine; free-floating barrel; one-piece stainless steel bolt
MSRP **$1199.00**

SAVAGE ARMS 110 APEX HUNTER XP

Action: Bolt
Stock: Synthetic
Barrel: 20 in., 22 in., 24 in.
Sights: Vortex Crossfire II 3–9X40mm scope
Weight: 7 lb. 11 oz.–8 lb. 2 oz.
Caliber: .223 Rem., .204 Ruger, .22–250 Rem., .243 Win., 6.5 Creedmoor, .260 Rem., .308 Win., .270 WSM, .300 WSM, .25–06 Rem., 6.5X284 Norma, .270 Win., .30–06 Spfd., 7mm Rem. Mag., .300 Win. Mag., .338 Win. Mag., 7mm-08 Rem.
Magazine: 3, 4 rounds
Features: With a caliber for every hunting pursuit except the most dangerous, the Apex Storm XP comes with a factory-mounted and bore-sighted scope; adjustable AccuTrigger; detachable box magazine; matte black metalwork; sporter barrel profile
MSRP **$684.00**

SAVAGE ARMS 110 APEX PREDATOR XP

Action: Bolt
Stock: Synthetic
Barrel: 20 in., 24 in.
Sights: Vortex Crossfire II 4–12X44mm scope
Weight: 8 lb. 7 oz.
Caliber: .223 Rem., .22–250 Rem., .204 Ruger, .243 Win., 6.5 Creedmoor, .308 Win.
Magazine: 3, 4 rounds
Features: A package rifle with a factory-mounted and bore-sighted Vortex scope; AccuTrigger; button-rifled heavy barrel; adjustable length of pull; matte blue metalwork; Mossy Oak camo coverage on stock; detachable box magazine
MSRP **$739.00**

SAVAGE ARMS 110 APEX STORM XP

Action: Bolt
Stock: Synthetic
Barrel: 20 in., 22 in., 24 in.
Sights: Vortex Crossfire II 3–9X40mm scope
Weight: 7 lb. 11 oz.–8 lb. 2 oz.
Caliber: .270 Win., .223 Rem., .204 Ruger, .22–250 Rem., .243 Win., 6.5 Creedmoor, 7mm-08 Rem., .260 Rem., .308 Win., .270 WSM, .300 WSM, .25–06 Rem., .30–06 Spfd., 7mm Rem. Mag., .300 Win. Mag., .338 Win. Mag.
Magazine: 3, 4 rounds
Features: Similar to the 110 Apex Hunter XP, but with matte stainless metalwork
MSRP **$739.00**

SAVAGE ARMS 110 BRUSH HUNTER WITH ADJUSTABLE LENGTH OF PULL

Action: Bolt
Stock: Synthetic
Barrel: 20 in.
Sights: Adjustable iron
Weight: 7 lb. 6 oz.
Caliber: .338 Win. Mag., .375 Ruger
Magazine: 3 rounds
Features: A smart choice for bear country with a choice of two heavy-hitting calibers. Features include adjustable iron sights; detachable box magazine; matte stainless metalwork; heavy magnum predator barrel contour; adjustable length of pull; AccuTrigger
MSRP **$784.00**

SAVAGE ARMS 110 HIGH COUNTRY

SAVAGE ARMS 110 HOG HUNTER WITH ADJUSTABLE LENGTH OF PULL

SAVAGE ARMS 110 LIGHTWEIGHT STORM WITH ADJUSTABLE LENGTH OF PULL

SAVAGE ARMS 110 PRAIRIE HUNTER

SAVAGE ARMS 110 STORM LEFT-HAND

SAVAGE ARMS 110 TACTICAL LEFT-HAND

SAVAGE ARMS 110 HIGH COUNTRY

Action: Bolt
Stock: Synthetic
Barrel: 22 in., 24 in.
Sights: None
Weight: 8 lb. 1 oz.
Caliber: .243 Win., 6.5 Creedmoor, 6.5 PRC, .270 Win., .280 Ackley Improved, 7mm-08 Rem., 7mm Rem. Mag., .308 Win., .30–06 Spfd., .300 Win. Mag., .300 WSM
Magazine: 3, 4, 5 rounds
Features: One for the backcountry hunters featuring Accufit stock with overmold gripping surfaces and full-coverage TrueTimber Strata camo; PVD-coated stainless action; spiral0fluted bolt and barrel in bronze; threaded barrel (magnum barrels include taplock-interface muzzle brake); detachable box magazine; AccuTrigger; Accufit adjustable stock
MSRP $1129.00

SAVAGE ARMS 110 HOG HUNTER WITH ADJUSTABLE LENGTH OF PULL

Action: Bolt
Stock: Synthetic
Barrel: 20 in.
Sights: Adjustable iron
Weight: 7 lb. 4 oz.
Caliber: .223 Rem., .338 Federal, .308 Win.
Magazine: 4 rounds
Features: A responsive gun for today's growing legions of wild boar hunters with a medium contour, threaded, carbon steel barrel; oversize bolt handle; olive drab stock; detachable box magazine; adjustable length of pull; AccuTrigger
MSRP $594.00

SAVAGE ARMS 110 LIGHTWEIGHT STORM WITH ADJUSTABLE LENGTH OF PULL

Action: Bolt
Stock: Synthetic
Barrel: 20 in.
Sights: None
Weight: 5 lb. 9 oz.–5 lb. 13 oz.
Caliber: .270 Win., .223 Win., 7mm-08 Rem., .308 Win., .243 Win., 6.5 Creedmoor
Magazine: 4 rounds
Features: Savage takes its popular Storm model and shaves off more than a pound with a light-contour barrel that gets spiral fluting. Other features include: detachable box magazine; AccuTrigger; adjustable length of pull; skeletonized receiver
MSRP $749.00

SAVAGE ARMS 110 PRAIRIE HUNTER

Action: Bolt
Stock: Synthetic
Barrel: 22 in.
Sights: None
Weight: 8 lb. 12 oz.
Caliber: .224 Valkyrie
Magazine: 4 rounds
Features: A slightly heavier rifle built around the .224 Valkyrie; carbon steel barrel threaded for suppressor; AccuFit stock in gray; beavertail fore-end; three QD studs; topside 20 MOA rail
MSRP $759.00

SAVAGE ARMS 110 STORM LEFT-HAND

Action: Bolt
Stock: Synthetic
Barrel: 22 in., 24 in.
Sights: None
Weight: 7 lb. 4 oz.
Caliber: .223 Rem., .243 Win., .22–250 Rem., 7mm-08 Rem., .308 Win., .30–06 Spfd., .270 Win., .300 Win. Mag., 7mm Rem. Mag.
Magazine: 4 rounds
Features: Savage continues to provide for Southpaw hunters with a solid range of big-game cartridge choices; gray synthetic stock with AccuFit system; matte stainless metalwork; soft overmolds on grip and fore-end; detachable box magazine
MSRP $849.00

SAVAGE ARMS 110 TACTICAL LEFT-HAND

Action: Bolt
Stock: Synthetic
Barrel: 24 in.
Sights: None
Weight: 8 lb. 14 oz.
Caliber: .308 Win.
Magazine: 10 rounds
Features: Built for stability, this should find favor with law enforcement and competitors with its threaded heavy barrel; oversized bolt handle; AccuStock rail system; adjustable AccuTrigger; AccuFit adjustable stock system; carbon steel receiver; straight barrel fluting pattern
MSRP $784.00

NEW Products: **Rifles**

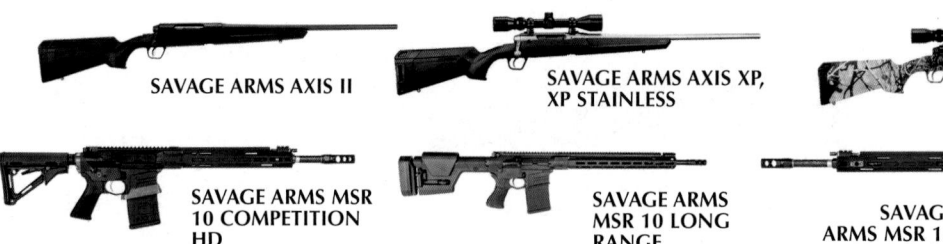

SAVAGE ARMS AXIS II

SAVAGE ARMS AXIS XP, XP STAINLESS

SAVAGE ARMS AXIS XP CAMO

SAVAGE ARMS MSR 10 COMPETITION HD

SAVAGE ARMS MSR 10 LONG RANGE

SAVAGE ARMS MSR 15 COMPETITION HD

SAVAGE ARMS MODEL 64 TAKEDOWN

SAVAGE ARMS AXIS II

Action: Bolt
Stock: Synthetic
Barrel: 22 in.
Sights: None
Weight: 6 lb. 4 oz.
Caliber: .223 Rem., .22–250 Rem., .243 Win., .25–06 Rem., 6.5 Creedmoor, .270 Win., 7mm-08 Rem., .280 Ackley Improved, .308 Win., .30–06 Spfd.
Magazine: 5 rounds
Features: Improved ergonomics with a redesigned stock; adjustable AccuTrigger; four-round detachable box magazine; thread-in headspacing button-rifled sporter barrel
MSRP $429.00

SAVAGE ARMS AXIS XP, XP STAINLESS

Action: Bolt
Stock: Synthetic
Barrel: 22 in.
Sights: Weaver 3–9X40mm scope
Weight: 7 lb. 5 oz.
Caliber: .223 Rem., .22–250 Rem., .243 Win., .25–06 Rem., 6.5 Creedmoor, .270 Win., 7mm-08 Rem., .308 Win., .30–06 Spfd.
Magazine: 5 rounds
Features: A package rifles with a factory-mounted and boresighted Weaver scope; detachable box magazine; sporter-contour barrel
MSRP $515.00

SAVAGE ARMS AXIS XP CAMO

Action: Bolt
Stock: Synthetic
Barrel: 22 in.
Sights: Weaver 3–9X40mm scope
Weight: 7 lb. 5 oz.
Caliber: .223 Rem., .22–250 Rem., .243 Win., .25–06 Rem., 6.5 Creedmoor, .270 Win., 7mm-08 Rem., .308 Win., .30–06 Spfd.
Magazine: 5 rounds
Features: The popular, no-frills, scope-packaged rifle available in Muddy Girl or Mossy Oak Break-Up Country full-coverage stocks; sporter barrel contour; carbon steel barreled action
MSRP $495.00

SAVAGE ARMS MODEL 64 TAKEDOWN

Action: Semiautomatic
Stock: Synthetic
Barrel: 16.5 in.
Sights: Front post, ladder-type leaf rear
Weight: 5 lb.
Caliber: .22 LR
Magazine: 10 rounds
Features: A portable, tear-apart rimfire that comes with an Uncle Mike's Bug-Out Bag; detachable box magazine; available left or right hand; drilled and tapped for scope mount; sling swivel studs
MSRP $249.00

SAVAGE ARMS MSR 10 COMPETITION HD

Action: Semiautomatic
Stock: Synthetic
Barrel: 18 in.
Sights: None
Weight: 9 lb.
Caliber: .308 Win.
Magazine: 20 rounds
Features: For the 3-Gunner shooting outside the .223 class, a souped up rig in .308 with features that include two-stage trigger; non-glare, free-floating rigid hand guard MLOK-ready; ambidextrous selector and mag release; tunable Savage muzzle brake; Hogue pistol grip; Magpul CTR buttstock; aluminum receiver with matte finish; custom-forged upper and lower; custom-length gas system; PROOF Research/Savage carbon-fiber wrapped stainless barrel
MSRP $3449.00

SAVAGE ARMS MSR 10 LONG RANGE

Action: Semiautomatic
Stock: Synthetic
Barrel: 20 in., 22.5 in.
Sights: None
Weight: 9 lb. 12 oz.–10 lb.
Caliber: 6mm Creedmoor, 6.5 Creedmoor, .308 Win.
Magazine: 10 rounds
Features: A serious contender in the long-range game with a direct-impingement system; two-stage trigger; Magpul Gen 3 PRS stock; compact AR10 design via a custom upper and lower; BLACKHAWK! KNOXX pistol grip; fluted heavy barrel with Melonite QPQ finish
MSRP $2284.00

SAVAGE ARMS MSR 15 COMPETITION HD

Action: Semiautomatic
Stock: Synthetic
Barrel: 18 in.
Sights: None
Weight: 5 lb. 13 oz.–7 lb. 14 oz.
Caliber: .223 Rem., .224 Valkyrie
Magazine: 30 rounds
Features: This should be a top pick for 3-Gunners with features like non-glare, free-floating rigid hand guard MLOK-ready; ambidextrous selector and mag release; tunable Savage muzzle brake; Hogue pistol grip; Magpul CTR buttstock; aluminum receiver with matte finish; custom-forged upper and lower; custom-length gas system; PROOF Research/Savage carbon-fiber wrapped stainless barrel; flashy red highlights
MSRP $2875.00

SAVAGE ARMS MSR 15 LONG RANGE

SAVAGE ARMS RASCAL FLV-SR LEFT-HAND

SAVAGE ARMS RASCAL FV-SR

SAVAGE ARMS RASCAL SYNTHETIC LEFT-HAND

SAVAGE ARMS RASCAL TARGET

SAVAGE ARMS RASCAL TARGET XP, TARGET XP LEFT-HAND

SIG SAUER MCX VIRTUS PATROL

SAVAGE ARMS MSR 15 LONG RANGE

Action: Semiautomatic
Stock: Synthetic
Barrel: 22 in.
Sights: None
Weight: 10 lb. 8 oz.
Caliber: .224 Valkyrie
Magazine: 11 rounds
Features: Savage adds weight and stability for the long range crowd. Features include two-port muzzle brake; Hogue pistol grip; free-floating MLOK-capable handguard; low-profile adjustable gas block; Magpul Gen 3 PRS adjustable stock; custom-forged upper and lower; custom length gas system; non-reciprocating side charging handle
MSRP $1849.00

SAVAGE ARMS RASCAL FLV-SR LEFT-HAND

Action: Bolt
Stock: Synthetic
Barrel: 16.125 in.
Sights: None
Weight: 3 lb. 8 oz.
Caliber: .22 LR
Magazine: 1 round
Features: Youth-sized bolt-action for left-handers with a heavy, suppressor-ready barrel; AccuTrigger; in black or pink
MSRP $219.00

SAVAGE ARMS RASCAL FV-SR

Action: Bolt
Stock: Synthetic

Barrel: 16.125 in.
Sights: None
Weight: 2 lb. 11 oz.
Caliber: .22 LR
Magazine: 1 round
Features: A bolt-cocking single-shot for youths, but one with "big gun" features like a heavy barrel with threaded muzzle and AccuTrigger; pink or black synthetic stock
MSRP $219.00

SAVAGE ARMS RASCAL SYNTHETIC LEFT-HAND

Action: Bolt
Stock: Synthetic
Barrel: 16.125 in.
Sights: Peep sights
Weight: 2 lb. 11 oz.
Caliber: .22 LR
Magazine: 1 round
Features: The popular youth rifle in a lightweight synthetic stock for left-handers; available in black or pink
MSRP $191.00

SAVAGE ARMS RASCAL TARGET

Action: Bolt
Stock: Hardwood
Barrel: 16.125 in.
Sights: None
Weight: 4 lb. 8 oz.
Caliber: .22 LR
Magazine: 1 round
Features: A wood-stocked Rascal for the youth shooter ready to improve on the basics, with a rifle two pounds heavier than its synthetic-stocked cousins; a threaded barrel; and

topside Picatinny rail for optics mounting.
MSRP $314.00

SAVAGE ARMS RASCAL TARGET XP, TARGET XP LEFT-HAND

Action: Bolt
Stock: Hardwood
Barrel: 16.125 in.
Sights: 4X32mm scope
Weight: 5 lb. 14 oz.
Caliber: .22 LR
Magazine: 1 round
Features: For the youth shooter getting serious about improving skills and target acquisition with a single-shot .22 LR that includes a factory-installed and sighted 4X32mm scope; heavy barrel; threaded muzzle; AccuTrigger; bipod; swivel mounts; left-hand available
MSRP $399.00

SIG SAUER MCX VIRTUS PATROL

Action: Semiautomatic
Stock: Synthetic
Barrel: 16 in.
Sights: None
Weight: 7 lb. 15 oz.
Caliber: 5.56 NATO, .300 BLK
Magazine: 30 rounds
Features: An AR platform designed for patrol use and featuring user-changeable barrels; free-floating M-LOK handguard in four lengths; ambidextrous controls; adjustable folding stock; available in Stealth Grey or Flat Dark Earth
MSRP $2233.00

NEW Products: **Rifles**

SIG SAUER MPX PCC

SIG SAUER SIGM400 TREAD 16-INCH

SIG SAUER SIGM400 V-TAC ELITE TI

SILVER SHADOW GILBOA M43 CARBINE

SILVER SHADOW GILBOA DBR SNAKE

SMITH & WESSON PERFORMANCE CENTER T/C LRR

SIG SAUER MPX PCC

Action: Semiautomatic
Stock: Synthetic
Barrel: 16 in.
Sights: None
Weight: 6 lb. 9 oz.
Caliber: 9mm
Magazine: 30 rounds
Features: Jumping into the trendy pistol-caliber carbine game with an AR platform featuring a gas piston operating system; free-floating M-LOK handguard; folding, telescoping stock; three-chamber compensator; MPX magazine; 1:10 twist barrel; Timney single-stage MPX trigger
MSRP **$2016.00**

SIG SAUER SIGM400 TREAD 16-INCH

Action: Semiautomatic
Stock: Synthetic
Barrel: 16 in.
Sights: None
Weight: 7 lb.
Caliber: 5.56 NATO
Magazine: 30 rounds
Features: An AR for on-the-go, featuring: reduced weigh MLOK handguard; direct impingement mid-length gas system functionality; aluminum frame; ambidextrous controls; single-stage trigger; Magpul SL-K6 telescoping buttstock
MSRP **$951.00**

SIG SAUER SIGM400 V-TAC ELITE TI

Action: Semiautomatic
Stock: Synthetic
Barrel: 16 in.
Sights: None
Weight: 6 lb. 8 oz.
Caliber: 5.56 NATO
Magazine: 10 rounds
Features: An AR-type with a Titanium Cerakote finish; accepts standard AR mags; nitride barrel with 1:7 twist; direct impingement; six-position adjustable stock
MSRP . . . . **N/A**

SILVER SHADOW ADVANCED SECURITY SYSTEMS, INC. GILBOA DBR SNAKE

Action: Semiautomatic
Stock: Synthetic
Barrel: 11.5 in.
Sights: Flip-up
Weight: 10 lb. 13 oz.
Caliber: 5.56 NATO
Magazine: 40 rounds
Features: Double the fun with a two-barrel, two-magazine, two-trigger gas impingement semiauto that fires two shots at the same time; made in Israel
MSRP **$2299.00**

SILVER SHADOW ADVANCED SECURITY SYSTEMS, INC. GILBOA M43 CARBINE

Action: Semiautomatic
Stock: Synthetic
Barrel: 16 in.
Sights: Flip-up
Weight: 6 lb. 7 oz.
Caliber: 7.62X39mm NATO
Magazine: 30 rounds
Features: Lightweight, Israeli-made; gas impingement system; hard anodized billet aircraft aluminum alloy upper and lower; ample rail; accepts standard AK-47 magazines; free-floating key-mod handguard; Gilboa compensator
MSRP **$1549.00**

SMITH & WESSON PERFORMANCE CENTER T/C LRR

Action: Bolt
Stock: Synthetic
Barrel: 20 in.
Sights: None
Weight: 11 lb.
Caliber: .308 Win., 6.5 Creedmoor, .243 Win.
Magazine: 10 rounds
Features: LRR is Long Range Rifle, loaded with features such as adjustable stock and cheekpiece; numerous Magpul M-LOK cuts; 20 MOA of rail; adjustable Performance Center trigger; Caldwell bi-pod; threaded barrel; muzzle brake; aluminum chassis; available in black or Flat Dark Earth
MSRP **$1211.00**

**S .W .O .R .D .
INTERNATIONAL MK-18
MOD 1 MJÖLNIR**

**SMITH & WESSON
PERFORMANCE CENTER T/CR
22 ALTAMONT**

**SMITH & WESSON
PERFORMANCE CENTER
T/CR 22 HOGUE OVER-
MOLDED**

**SPRINGFIELD
ARMORY SAINT
SBR**

**SPRINGFIELD
ARMORY SAINT
EDGE SBR**

**SPRINGFIELD
ARMORY SAINT
VICTOR**

SMITH & WESSON PERFORMANCE CENTER T/CR 22 ALTAMONT

Action: Semiautomatic
Stock: Laminate
Barrel: 20 in.
Sights: None
Weight: 7 lb.
Caliber: .22 LR
Magazine: 10 rounds
Features: A sound choice for rimfire game competitors and serious small-game hunters alike, featuring 1:15 twist button rifled fluted barrel in blue; oversized bolt handle; push-button safety; ½X28 threaded muzzle; laminate thumbhole stock with generous cheekpiece; topside rail; detachable magazine; aluminum receiver; 10/22 accessory compatible
MSRP **$616.00**

SMITH & WESSON PERFORMANCE CENTER T/CR 22 HOGUE OVER-MOLDED

Action: Semiautomatic
Stock: Hogue Over-Molded
Barrel: 20 in.
Sights: None
Weight: 7 lb.
Caliber: .22 LR
Magazine: 10 rounds
Features: Identical to the Altamont version but replacing the laminate stock with a Hogue Over-Molded synthetic stock and the fluted barrel in stainless
MSRP **$497.00**

SPRINGFIELD ARMORY SAINT EDGE SBR

Action: Semiautomatic
Stock: Synthetic

Barrel: 11.5 in.
Sights: None
Weight: 5 lb. 10 oz.
Caliber: 5.56 NATO
Magazine: 30 rounds
Features: A loaded SBR with features that include a lightened billet lower; ambidextrous safety; Type III hard coat anodized upper and lower; low-profile, adjustable carbine-length gas block; forward assist; Bravo Company Gunfighter buttstock; Carbine "H" heavy tungsten buffer; Melonite finish on barrel and bolt-carrier group; match-grade, short-reset, single-stage trigger; Magpul PMAG; full-length, free-floating handguard M-LOK compatible
MSRP **$1299.00**

SPRINGFIELD ARMORY SAINT SBR

Action: Semiautomatic
Stock: Synthetic
Barrel: 11.5 in.
Sights: None
Weight: 5 lb. 9 oz.
Caliber: 5.56 NATO
Magazine: 30 rounds
Features: A loaded SBR with features that include a forged lower with Accu-Tite tension system; ambidextrous safety; Type III hard coat anodized upper and lower; low-profile, adjustable carbine-length gas block; forward assist; Bravo Company Gunfighter buttstock; Carbine "H" heavy tungsten buffer; Melonite finish on barrel and bolt-carrier group; nickel-boron coated GI-style trigger; Magpul PMAG; full-length, free-floating handguard M-LOK compatible
MSRP **$1049.00**

SPRINGFIELD ARMORY SAINT VICTOR

Action: Semiautomatic
Stock: Synthetic
Barrel: 16 in.
Sights: Flip-up
Weight: 6 lb. 9 oz.
Caliber: 5.56 NATO
Magazine: 30 rounds
Features: Game-ready AR-platform with direct impingement mid-length gas system; Bravo Company six-position buttstock and Mod.3 grip; carbine H heavy tungsten buffer; forged Type III aluminum upper, Accu-Tite lower, both hard anodized; GI-type charging handle; 15-inch M-LOK handguard; spring-loaded flip-up sights; soft rifle case
MSRP **$1072.00**

S.W.O.R.D. INTERNATIONAL MK-18 MOD 1 MJÖLNIR

Action: Semiautomatic
Stock: Synthetic
Barrel: 20 in., 24 in.
Sights: None
Weight: 12 lb. 4 oz.
Caliber: .338 Lapua, .338 Norma, .300 Norma
Magazine: 10 rounds
Features: It's all long-distance business with the MK-18, featuring a proprietary self-regulating short-stroke gas piston system; mil-spec Type 3 hard anodized coating in Coyote Brown; single-point cut-rifled barrel with nitride coating; free-floating M-LOK rail; ambidextrous mag release; tungsten-filled heavy buffer; tuned compensator to reduce muzzle rise
MSRP **$6995.00**

NEW Products: **Rifles**

TACTICAL SOLUTIONS X-RING VR HOGUE STOCK OPEN SIGHTS

TACTICAL SOLUTIONS X-RING TD VR

TACTICAL SOLUTIONS X-RING VR MAGPUL HUNTER X-22 STOCK

TACTICAL SOLUTIONS X-RING VR VANTAGE RS STOCK

THOMPSON/CENTER ARMS T/CR22

TIKKA T1X MTR

TACTICAL SOLUTIONS X-RING TD VR

Action: Semiautomatic
Stock: Synthetic
Barrel: 16.5 in.
Sights: Adjustable rear, fiber-optic front
Weight: 3 lb. 11 oz.–4 lb. 10 oz.
Caliber: .22 LR
Magazine: 1 round, 10 rounds
Features: With a Ruger 10/22 as its backbone, hikers, ranch workers and survivalists get an ultralightweight, packable, takedown (TD) rifle in two options: Mossy Oak Bottomland; Magpul Backpacker stock in metal/stock choices of matte black/black, Gun Metal Gray/black, Quicksand/black, matte black/gray, matte black/Flat Dark Earth, Quicksand/Flat Dark Earth, and a matte black SBX metal paired with choice of black, gray or Flat Dark Earth stock
MO Bottomland: **$1255.00**
Magpul: **$1155.00**

TACTICAL SOLUTIONS X-RING VR HOGUE STOCK, HOGUE STOCK OPEN SIGHTS

Action: Semiautomatic
Stock: Synthetic
Barrel: 16.5 in.
Sights: None, open
Weight: 4 lb. 5 oz.
Caliber: .22 LR
Magazine: 10 rounds
Features: Features an ambidextrous bolt; 15 MOA rail; fully adjustable green fiber optic sights on Open

Sights model; Ruger BX-Trigger; variety of stock color; threaded barrel options; various metal/stock finish options
MSRP **$985.00**

TACTICAL SOLUTIONS X-RING VR MAGPUL HUNTER X-22 STOCK, MAGPUL HUNTER X-22 STOCK OPEN SIGHTS

Action: Semiautomatic
Stock: Synthetic
Barrel: 16.5 in.
Sights: None, open
Weight: 5 lb. 2 oz.
Caliber: .22 LR
Magazine: 10 rounds
Features: Similar in features to the other VRs, but with Magpul's Hunter X-22 chassis stock designed specifically for Ruger 10/22 actions and with M-LOK slots and adjustable length of pull; variety of stock/metal finishes; open sight option features green, fully adjustable fiber optics
MSRP **$1100.00**

TACTICAL SOLUTIONS X-RING VR VANTAGE RS STOCK

Action: Semiautomatic
Stock: Laminate
Barrel: 16.5 in.
Sights: None
Weight: 5 lb. 2 oz.
Caliber: .22 LR
Magazine: 10 rounds

Features: Similar in features to the other VRs, but with a heavier, laminate, one-piece thumbhole stock/forearm; variety of stock/metal finishes; sling swivel studs
MSRP **$1100.00**

THOMPSON/CENTER ARMS T/CR22

Action: Semiautomatic
Stock: Synthetic
Barrel: 17 in.
Sights: Fiber optic front, adjustable rear
Weight: 4 lb. 6 oz.
Caliber: .22 LR
Magazine: 10 rounds
Features: Handy small-game, varmint, or target rimfire with both sights and a topside rail; detachable magazine; blued metalwork with stock in choice of green, Realtree Edge, or Mossy Oak Break-Up Country
Green: **$399.00**
Camo: **$419.00**

TIKKA T1X MTR

Action: Bolt
Stock: Synthetic
Barrel: 20 in.
Sights: None
Weight: N/A
Caliber: .22 LR,.17 HMR
Magazine: 10 rounds
Features: A rimfire for the shooter beyond the beginner, featuring a barrel with a crossover profile that provides stability while being lightweight; detachable magazine; TX3 accessory-compatible pistol grip
MSRP **$499.00**

TROY INDUSTRIES PUMP ACTION RIFLE WITH A2 STOCK

ULTIMATE ARMS WARMONGER

VIGILENCE RIFLES, INC. M18 WINDRUNNER .50 BMG

VOLQUARTSEN FIREARMS LIGHTWEIGHT .17 WSM

VOLQUARTSEN FIREARMS SUMMIT

WEATHERBY MARK V CAMILLA SUBALPINE

TROY INDUSTRIES PUMP ACTION RIFLE WITH A2 STOCK

Action: Pump
Stock: Synthetic
Barrel: 18 in.
Sights: Flip-up front and rear
Weight: 6 lb. 6 oz.
Caliber: .223 Rem.
Magazine: 10 rounda
Features: An AR platform in a pump-action configuration with a Melonite barrel; Medieval flash suppressor; TRX2-style handguard; Troy's folding BattleSight; flattop forged upper; hardcoat anodized lower; choice of black or full-coverage Mossy Oak Shadow Grass Blades
Black:. $849.00
Mossy Oak: $1099.00

ULTIMATE ARMS WARMONGER

Action: Bolt
Stock: Synthetic
Barrel: 18 in., 24 in., 31 in.
Sights: None
Weight: 13 lb. 11 oz.
Caliber: .50 BMG
Magazine: 5 rounds
Features: A shoulder-fired long-distance .50 BMG with a side-loading magazine; four-port muzzle brake
MSRP. $3995.00

VIGILENCE RIFLES, INC. M18 WINDRUNNER .50 BMG

Action: Bolt
Stock: Synthetic
Barrel: 29 in.
Sights: None
Weight: 29 lb. 8 oz.
Caliber: .50 BMG
Magazine: 10 rounds
Features: Adjustable AR-style stock; fixed, screwed-in barrel; Chromoly upper; Windrunner bolt handle; oversized AR-style chromoly extractor; folding, pivoting bipod; aluminum lower; 1:15 twist chromoly bull barrel; 0 MOA rail
MSRP. $3699.00
10-shot repeater: $4299.00

VOLQUARTSEN FIREARMS LIGHTWEIGHT .17 WSM

Action: Semiautomatic
Stock: Synthetic, laminate
Barrel: N/A
Sights: None
Weight: 7 lb. 12 oz.–8 lb. 3 oz.
Caliber: .17 WSM
Magazine: 8 rounds
Features: Employs a carbon-fiber tension barrel to reduce weight; three-pound trigger pull; threaded barrel; removeable forward-blow compensator; available in black McMillan synthetic stock, brown/gray, brown, or gray laminated full or thumbhole stocks; some options available with stainless steel hardware
MSRP . . . . $2195.00–$2300.00

VOLQUARTSEN FIREARMS SUMMIT

Action: Bolt
Stock: Synthetic
Barrel: N/A
Sights: None
Weight: 5 lb. 13 oz.
Caliber: .22 LR, .17 Mach 2
Magazine: 8, 10 rounds
Features: A straight-pull bolt take on the Ruger 10/22 with 20 MOA topside rail; ½X28 threaded lightweight barrel; Magpul adjustable stock with M-LOK slots; available in black, gray, OD Green, and Flat Dark Earth stocks; optional Hogue stock version in .17 Mach 2 only
Magpul:. $1150.00
Hogue: $1135.00

WEATHERBY MARK V CAMILLA SUBALPINE

Action: Bolt
Stock: Composite
Barrel: 22 in., 24 in.
Sights: None
Weight: 5 lb. 12 oz.
Caliber: .240 Wby. Mag., .270 Win., 6.5 Creedmoor, .308 Win., .30–06 Spfd.
Magazine: 4, 5 rounds
Features: Lightweight rifle designed with stock dimensions for women; Gore Optifade Subalpine camo on hand-laminated composite stock; fluted bolt body with 54-degree bolt life; LXX trigger; six-lug action; cocking indicator; hand-lapped chrome-moly barrel with field crown; Flat Dark Earth Cerakote metalwork
MSRP. $2700.00

NEW Products: **Rifles**

WEATHERBY MARK V CAMILLA ULTRA LIGHTWEIGHT

WEATHERBY MARK V CARBONMARK

WEATHERBY MARK V FIRST LITE, FIRST LITE RC

WEATHERBY MARK V SUBALPINE, SUBALPINE RC

WEATHERBY MARK V WYOMING GOLD EDITION COMMEMORATIVE RIFLE

WEATHERBY MARK V CAMILLA ULTRA LIGHTWEIGHT

Action: Bolt
Stock: Composite
Barrel: 22 in., 24 in.
Sights: None
Weight: 5 lb. 12 oz.
Caliber: .240 Wby. Mag., .270 Win., 6.5 Creedmoor, .308 Win., .30–06 Spfd.
Magazine: 4, 5 rounds
Features: One for the hiker with a stock made to better fit a woman's physique; hand-laid composite stock with full-length aluminum bedding block and wearing a Forest Green/black web gel coating; fluted stainless barrel with #1 contour; fluted bolt body; LXX trigger with grooves
MSRP **$2300.00**

WEATHERBY MARK V CARBONMARK

Action: Bolt
Stock: Composite
Barrel: 26 in.
Sights: None
Weight: 7 lb. 12 oz.
Caliber: .257 Wby. Mag., .300 Wby. Mag.
Magazine: 3 rounds
Features: A collaboration with Proof Research featuring a stock with a reduced grip diameter, right-hand palm swell, aluminum bedding block, and a dark gray/black matte gel finish; Proof Research carbon fiber barrel with a stainless steel core, #4 contour,

cut-rifled, hand-lapped, and threaded 5/8X24; Tactical Grey Cerakote metalwork; magnum 9-lug action; fluted bolt body; LXX trigger
MSRP **$4100.00**

WEATHERBY MARK V FIRST LITE, FIRST LITE RC

Action: Bolt
Stock: Composite
Barrel: 24 in., 26 in.
Sights: None
Weight: 7 lb. 4 oz.–8 lb. 4 oz.
Caliber: .257 Wby. Mag., 6.5 Creedmoor, 6.5–3000 Wby. Mag., .270 Wby. Mag., .300 Wby. Mag.
Magazine: 3, 4 rounds
Features: A hunting rifle in Weatherby's most popular cartridges plus the 6.5 Creedmoor, featuring six- or nine-lug actions depending in caliber; hand-laid composite stock dressed in First Lite Fusion camo; fluted, hand-lapped, #3 contour barrel with recessed crown; metalwork in Flat Dark Earth Cerakote; RC version is Range Certified for sub-MOA three-shot groups at 100 yards
MSRP **$2600.00**
RC: **$2100.00**

WEATHERBY MARK V SUBALPINE, SUBALPINE RC

Action: Bolt
Stock: Composite
Barrel: 24 in., 26 in.
Sights: None

Weight: 5 lb. 12 oz.–6 lb. 12 oz.
Caliber: .257 Wby. Mag., 6.5 Creedmoor, 6.5–300 Wby. Mag., .270 Wby. Mag., .300 Wby. Mag.
Magazine: 3, 4 rounds
Features: A light version of the Mark V with a stock dressed in Gore's Optifade Subalpine camo; barrels in #1 or #2 Mod contour with recessed crowns; metalwork in Flat Dark Earth Cerakote; RC version is Range Certified for sub-MOA three-shot groups at 100 yards
MSRP: **$2700.00**
RC: **$3200.00**

WEATHERBY MARK V WYOMING GOLD EDITION COMMEMORATIVE RIFLE

Action: Bolt
Stock: French walnut
Barrel: 26 in.
Sights: None
Weight: N/A
Caliber: .300 Wby. Mag.
Magazine: 3 rounds
Features: Just 1,000 made, the first to roll off the assembly line n Wyoming; AAA exhibition-grade French walnut stock; gold engraved scrollwork; Mark V action; hand-checkered bolt knob; custom mountain scene checkering; gold and silver accent barrel rings; fluted bolt body; LXX trigger; custom leather case
MSRP **$10000.00**

WEATHERBY MARK V WYOMING SILVER EDITION COMMEMORATIVE RIFLE

WEATHERBY VANGUARD BADLANDS

WEATHERBY VANGUARD FIRST LITE

WINCHESTER REPEATING ARMS MODEL 1892 LARGE LOOP CARBINE

WINCHESTER REPEATING ARMS WILDCAT .22 LR

WEATHERBY MARK V WYOMING SILVER EDITION COMMEMORATIVE RIFLE

Action: Bolt
Stock: French walnut
Barrel: 26 in.
Sights: None
Weight: N/A
Caliber: .300 Wby. Mag.
Magazine: 3 rounds
Features: Commemorates Weatherby's historic relocation to Wyoming with custom checkering in a mountain scene; silver engraved scrollwork; AAA exhibition-grade French walnut; LXX trigger; damascened bolt and follower
MSRP $6500.00

WEATHERBY VANGUARD BADLANDS

Action: Bolt
Stock: Composite
Barrel: 25 in., 28 in.
Sights: None
Weight: 7 lb. 8 oz.
Caliber: .240 Wby. Mag., .257 Wby. Mag., 6.5 Creedmoor, 6.5–300 Wby. Mag., .270 Win., .308 Win., .30–06 Spfd., 7mm-08 Rem., 7mm Rem. Mag., .300 Win. Mag., .300 Wby. Mag.
Magazine: 3, 4, 5 rounds
Features: Standard Vanguard features; #2 contour barrel; metalwork in Burnt

Bronze Cerakote; polymer stock with textured gripping surfaces, all dressed in Badlands Approach camo; adjustable match-grade two-stage trigger; fluted, one-piece machined bolt body with fully enclosed bolt sleeve
MSRP $849.00

WEATHERBY VANGUARD FIRST LITE

Action: Bolt
Stock: Composite
Barrel: 26 in., 28 in.
Sights: None
Weight: 7 lb. 8 oz.
Caliber: .240 Wby. Mag., .257 Wby. Mag., 6.5–300 Wby. Mag., .270 Win., .308 Win., .30–06 Spfd., .300 Win. Mag., .300 Wby. Mag.
Magazine: 3, 5 rounds
Features: Cold hammer forged barrel fluted and in #2 contour; metalwork in Flat Dark Earth Cerakote; adjustable match-grade two-stage trigger; Accubrake; stock wears First Lite Fusion camo
MSRP $1090.00

WINCHESTER REPEATING ARMS MODEL 1892 LARGE LOOP CARBINE

Action: Lever
Stock: Walnut
Barrel: 20 in.

Sights: Marble Arms brass bead front, adjustable rear
Weight: 6 lb.
Caliber: .357 Mag., .44 Rem. Mag., .44–40 Win., .45 Colt
Magazine: 10 rounds
Features: Classic saddle rifle with Grade I walnut; large loop with radiused edges; rebounding hammer, metal carbon buttplate; saddle ring; button rifled barrel with recessed crown
MSRP $1259.99

WINCHESTER REPEATING ARMS WILDCAT .22 LR

Action: Semiautomatic
Stock: Polymer
Barrel: 18 in.
Sights: Ramped post front, adjustable ghost ring rear
Weight: 4 lb.
Caliber: .22 LR
Magazine: 10 rounds
Features: Super-fun plinker is super portable at just 4 pounds and has a number of innovative features such as a lower receiver that drops out at the push of a button; removeable rotary magazine; adjustable rear ghost sight; striker-fired mechanism; slide lock; top-side Picatinny rail and a second rail at fore-end tip; ambidextrous skeletonized stock
MSRP $249.99

WINCHESTER REPEATING ARMS XPR HUNTER KRYPTIC HIGHLANDER

WINCHESTER REPEATING ARMS XPR HUNTER TRUE TIMBER STRATA

WINDHAM WEAPONRY 9MM GMC RIFLE

WINDHAM WEAPONRY .223 SUPERLIGHT

WINDHAM WEAPONRY .224 VALKYRIE

WINDHAM WEAPONRY .450 THUMPER

WINCHESTER REPEATING ARMS XPR HUNTER KRYPTIC HIGHLANDER

Action: Bolt
Stock: Composite
Barrel: 22 in., 24 in., 26 in.
Sights: None
Weight: 6 lb. 12 oz.–7 lb. 4 oz.
Caliber: .243 Win., 6.5 Creedmoor, 7mm-08 Rem., .308 Win., .270 WSM, .300 WSM, .325 WSM, .270 Win., .30–06 Spfd., 7mm Rem. Mag., .300 Win. Mag., .338 Win. Mag.
Magazine: 3 rounds
Features: The popular XPR bolt rifle with a stock dressed in Kryptik Highlander camo; Permacoat Gray metalwork finish; MOA trigger system
MSRP $599.99

WINCHESTER REPEATING ARMS XPR HUNTER TRUE TIMBER STRATA

Action: Bolt
Stock: Composite
Barrel: 22 in., 24 in., 26 in.
Sights: None
Weight: 6 lb. 12 oz.–7 lb. 4 oz.
Caliber: .243 Win., 6.5 Creedmoor, 7mm-08 Rem., .308 Win., .270 WSM, .300 WSM, .325 WSM, .270 Win., .30–06 Spfd., 7mm Rem. Mag., .300 Win. Mag., .338 Win. Mag.
Magazine: 3 rounds
Features: The popular XPR bolt rifle with a stock dressed in True Timber Strata camo; Permacoat Flat Dark Earth metalwork finish; MOA trigger system
MSRP $599.99

WINDHAM WEAPONRY 9MM GMC RIFLE

Action: Semiautomatic
Stock: Synthetic
Barrel: 16 in.
Sights: None
Weight: 6 lb. 11 oz.
Caliber: 9mm
Magazine: 17 rounds
Features: GMC stands for "Glock Magazine Compatible"; semiauto blowback; six-position telescoping stock; A2 grip; flat-top upper; Chromoly vanadium steel barrel with 1:10 right twist
MSRP $1148.00

WINDHAM WEAPONRY .223 SUPERLIGHT

Action: Semiautomatic
Stock: Synthetic
Barrel: 16 in.
Sights: Flip-up front and rear
Weight: 6 lb.
Caliber: .223 Rem.
Magazine: 30 rounds
Features: Ultralight .223 MSR with a superlight barrel profile wearing a Melonite QPQ finish and A2 flash suppressor; Mission First Tactical Minimalist buttstock; mil-spec buffer tube; Mission First Tactical Engage pistol grip; Kriss flip-up sights
MSRP $1073.00

WINDHAM WEAPONRY .224 VALKYRIE

Action: Semiautomatic
Stock: Synthetic
Barrel: 22 in.
Sights: None
Weight: 8 lb. 13 oz.
Caliber: .224 Valkyrie
Magazine: 5 rounds
Features: A gas impingement MSR designed specifically for the .224 Valkyrie round, with a fluted barrel threaded ½X28 and 1:7 right-hand twist; flat-top upper hard coat anodized; Luth-AR adjustable buttstock; 15-inch free-floating fore-end; Hogue overmolded beavertail pistol grip
MSRP $1369.00

WINDHAM WEAPONRY .450 THUMPER

Action: Semiautomatic
Stock: Synthetic
Barrel: 16 in.
Sights: None
Weight: 7 lb. 3 oz.
Caliber: .450 Bushmaster
Magazine: 5 rounds
Features: Designed specifically for the straight-wall .450 Bushmaster, with Luth-AR adjustable buttstock; free-floating handguard with rail; Hogue overmolded beavertail pistol grip; chrome-lined barrel with A2 flash hider
MSRP $1219.00

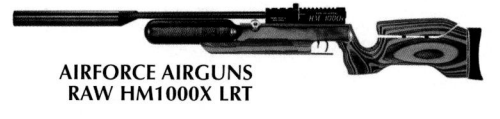

AIRFORCE AIRGUNS
RAW HM1000X LRT

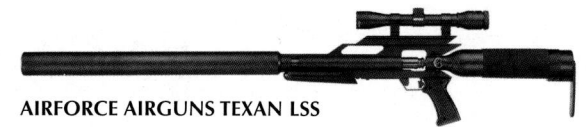

AIRFORCE AIRGUNS TEXAN LSS

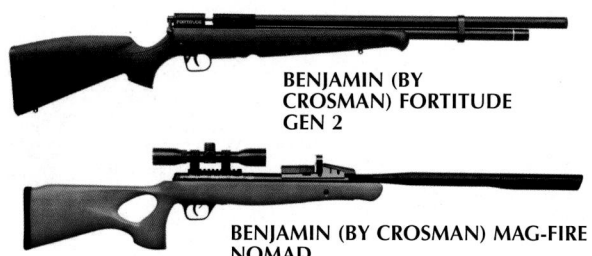

BENJAMIN (BY CROSMAN) FORTITUDE GEN 2

BENJAMIN (BY CROSMAN) MAG-FIRE NOMAD

BENJAMIN (BY CROSMAN) MAG-FIRE MISSION

BENJAMIN (BY CROSMAN) MAG-FIRE ULTRA

AIRFORCE AIRGUNS RAW HM1000X LRT

Action: PCP
Stock: Laminate
Barrel: 24 in.
Sights: None
Weight: 8 lb. 14 oz.
Caliber: .177, .22, .25, .30, .357
Magazine: 12, 9, 7 depending on caliber
Features: A serious competition air rifle, the LRT--Long Range Target--features a 480cc carbon fiber bottle; side-lever action; unique LRT stock with palm swell, steep grip angle, M-LOK slots, adjustable cheekpiece, and adjustable buttstock; rotary magazine; adjustable trigger; choice of red, blue, black, tan, or camo laminate stock
MSRP **$2199.95**

AIRFORCE AIRGUNS TEXAN LSS

Action: PCP
Stock: Synthetic
Barrel: 34 in.
Sights: None
Weight: 8 lb.
Caliber: .257, .308, .357, .457
Magazine: N/A
Features: Capable of taking medium-sized game animals, this suppresses big-bore rifle features adjustable power; pressure relief device; side-cocking lever; two-stage position-adjustable trigger; automatic safety on cocking
MSRP **$1254.95**

BENJAMIN (BY CROSMAN) FORTITUDE GEN 2

Action: PCP
Stock: Synthetic
Barrel: N/A
Sights: None
Weight: N/A
Caliber: .177, .22
Magazine: 10 shots
Features: Cocking force is light; rotary magazine; 3,000 psi regulated pressure gauge; shrouded barrel; suppressor; rifled barrel
MSRP **$399.99**

BENJAMIN (BY CROSMAN) MAG-FIRE MISSION

Action: Break-barrel
Stock: Synthetic
Barrel: N/A
Sights: CenterPoint 4X32 scope
Weight: N/A
Caliber: .177
Magazine: 10 shots
Features: Autoloading magazine; powered by Benjamin's Nitro Piston Elite; SBD suppressor; topside rail; CenterPoint 4X32 scope; adjustable two-stage trigger; synthetic stock with pistol grip
MSRP **$229.99**

BENJAMIN (BY CROSMAN) MAG-FIRE NOMAD

Action: Break-barrel
Stock: Wood
Barrel: N/A
Sights: CenterPoint 4X32 scope
Weight: N/A
Caliber: .177, .22
Magazine: 10 shots
Features: Autoloading magazine; powered by Benjamin's Nitro Piston Elite; SBD suppressor; topside rail; CenterPoint 4X32 scope; adjustable two-stage trigger; wood thumbhole stock
MSRP **$229.99**

BENJAMIN (BY CROSMAN) MAG-FIRE ULTRA

Action: Break-barrel
Stock: Synthetic
Barrel: N/A
Sights: CenterPoint 4X32 scope
Weight: N/A
Caliber: .177, .22
Magazine: 10 Shots
Features: Autoloading magazine; powered by Benjamin's Nitro Piston Elite; SBD suppressor; topside rail; CenterPoint 4X32 scope; adjustable two-stage trigger; traditionally styled synthetic stock
MSRP **$199.99**

NEW Products: Airguns

BENJAMIN MARAUDER
REGULATED WITH LOTHAR
WALTHER BARREL

BUSHMASTER
MPW

CROSMAN 760
PUMPMASTER KIT

CROSMAN CLASSIC
1911 PISTOL KIT

CROSMAN
COWBOY

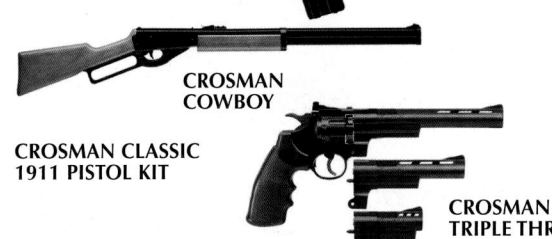

CROSMAN
TRIPLE THREAT

CROSMAN NIGHT
STALKER

BENJAMIN (BY CROSMAN) MARAUDER REGULATED, REGULATED WITH LOTHAR WALTHER BARREL

Action: PCP
Stock: Wood
Barrel: N/A
Sights: None
Weight: N/A
Caliber: .177, .22
Magazine: 10 shots
Features: Fires up to 85 shots per fill with integrated regulator for shot consistency; adjustable cheekpiece; rifled barrel; reversible bolt handle; Picatinny breech; optional Lothar Walther barrel
MSRP **$899.99**

BUSHMASTER (BY CROSMAN) MPW

Action: CO2
Stock: Synthetic
Barrel: N/A
Sights: Red dot
Weight: N/A
Caliber: BB
Magazine: 25 shots
Features: An AR-style CO2 BB gun with adjustable buttstock; quad rail forearm; red dot sight; full-auto and semiauto modes; 25-round drop magazine; can be customized with AR-compatible buffer tubes and grips; speedloader included
MSRP **$239.95**

CROSMAN 760 PUMPMASTER, PUMPMASTER KITS

Action: Pump
Stock: Synthetic

Barrel: N/A
Sights: Ramp blade front, adjustable rear
Weight: N/A
Caliber: BB, .177
Magazine: 18 shots
Features: In 2019, a total revamp of this tried and true airgun, with all new stock, trigger design, 1,000-shot BB reservoir, and easier to access loading port; stocks in turquoise blue, pink and, both available with optional scope; earth brown stock available for Canadian market; kits include 4X scope, supply of Copperhead BBs, Crosman pellets, safety glasses, and targets
MSRP **$44.99**
Kit: **$64.99**

CROSMAN CLASSIC 1911 PISTOL KIT

Action: CO2
Stock: Synthetic
Barrel: 5 in.
Sights: Low-profile blade front, notch rear
Weight: N/A
Caliber: BB
Magazine: N/A
Features: A full-size 1911-type BB pistol with textured grip; skeletonized trigger; under rail; tan frame with black slide and grips; comes with targets and 250 BBs
MSRP **$29.99**

CROSMAN COWBOY

Action: Lever
Stock: Wood
Barrel: N/A
Sights: Ramp blade front, adjustable rear

Weight: N/A
Caliber: BB
Magazine: 1 shot
Features: Have your kid watch a couple John Wayne movies, then buy them this fun lever BB gun with a ratcheted lever that locks to prevent pinched fingers during cocking; all-metal receiver; hardwood stock
MSRP **$49.99**

CROSMAN NIGHT STALKER

Action: CO2
Stock: Synthetic
Barrel: N/A
Sights: Low-profile blade front, notch rear, laser
Weight: N/A
Caliber: BB
Magazine: 18 shots
Features: A Walther lookalike with a built-in red laser; 18-shot BB magazine; blowback action
MSRP **$99.99**

CROSMAN TRIPLE THREAT

Action: CO2
Stock: Polymer
Barrel: 3 in., 6 in., 8 in.
Sights: Ramp front, adjustable rear
Weight: N/A
Caliber: BB, .177
Magazine: 6, 10 shots
Features: A fun CO2 revolver with three barrels, all with vent ribs and rifled; grips remove to replace CO2 cartridge; 10-shot pellet clip; 6-shot BB clip
MSRP **$99.99**

DAISY MODEL 599

GAMO SWARM BONE COLLECTOR

GAMO SWARM FUSION 10X

HATSAN USA AIRMAX BULLPUP

HATSAN USA AIRTRACT

HATSAN USA SPEEDFIRE

HATSAN USA NOVASTAR

DAISY MODEL 599

Action: PCP
Stock: Beechwood
Barrel: N/A
Sights: Hooded front, diopter rear
Weight: N/A
Caliber: .177
Magazine: 1 shot
Features: Competition ready air rifle with integral dovetail scope rail; sling rail; pressure gauge; adjustable stock; position and weight adjustable trigger; cold hammer forged BSA barrel; straight-pull T handle
MSRP **$595.00**

GAMO SWARM BONE COLLECTOR

Action: Break-barrel
Stock: Beechwood
Barrel: N/A
Sights: 4X32mm scope
Weight: N/A
Caliber: .22
Magazine: 10 shots
Features: Gas piston break-barrel action with traditionally styled stock with a raised cheekpiece; Whisper sound dampening; RRR Recoil Reducing Scope Rail; 975 fps; Gamo 10X technology for super-fast 10 repeat shots; 10-round magazine
MSRP **$209.99**

GAMO SWARM FUSION 10X

Action: Break-barrel
Stock: Nylon
Barrel: N/A
Sights: Fiber optic front, adjustable rear, 3–9x40mm scope
Weight: N/A
Caliber: .177, .22

Magazine: 10 shots
Features: Gas piston break-barrel with a glass-filled nylon thumbhole stock; horizontal 10-shot magazine for easy loading; Whisper Fusion noise dampening
MSRP **$269.99**

HATSAN USA AIRMAX BULLPUP

Action: PCP
Stock: Turkish walnut
Barrel: 23 in.
Sights: None
Weight: 10 lb. 14 oz.
Caliber: .177, .22, .25
Magazine: 9, 10 shots
Features: A bullpup design featuring the QuietEnergy fully shrouded barrel; ambidextrous thumbhole stock with adjustable cheekpiece; detachable magazine; Anti-Double Pellet Feed technology; under rail; sling swivels; Quattro adjustable two-stage match trigger
MSRP **$699.99**

HATSAN USA AIRTRACT

Action: Break-barrel
Stock: Synthetic
Barrel: 14.5 in.
Sights: Fiber optic front, adjustable rear, 4X32mm Optima scope
Weight: 5 lb. 11 oz.
Caliber: .177, .22, .25
Magazine: 1 shot
Features: Beginner's single-shot with a slim, skeletonized thumbhole stock; large muzzle break for easy cocking; steel rifled barrel with molded shroud; manual firing safety; automatic cocking safety; adjustable trigger; scope and sights provided
MSRP **$119.99**

HATSAN USA NOVASTAR

Action: PCP
Stock: Turkish walnut
Barrel: 23 in.
Sights: None
Weight: 8 lb. 6 oz.
Caliber: .177, .22, .25
Magazine: 10, 12, 14 shots
Features: Sleek-looking, high-grade precharged-pneumatic air rifle available for use with three pellet sizes; Roto Index magazine system is detachable and caliber specific; heavy, stiffened barrel; thumbhole stock with Monte Carlo cheekpiece; carbon fiber air storage reservoir; Quatto two-stage adjustable trigger
MSRP **$899.99**

HATSAN USA SPEEDFIRE

Action: Break-barrel
Stock: Synthetic
Barrel: 14.5 in.
Sights: Green fiber optic front, red fiber optic rear, Optima 3–9x32mm scope
Weight: 6 lb. 9 oz.
Caliber: .177, .22
Magazine: 10, 12 shots
Features: Modern-looing ergonomically designed stock with raised cheekpiece; removeable Rapid Performance Mag; front sight folds down for use with optics on the topside rail; rifled steel barrel with QuickEnergy synthetic shroud; Quattro two-stage adjustable trigger; manual, automatic cocking, and anti-beartrap safeties; SAS shock absorber system
MSRP **$229.99**

HATSAN USA VECTIS

SIG AIR P320-M17 ASP

STOEGER S4000-E SUPPRESSED, SUPRESSED COMBO

REMINGTON R1100 PUMP RIFLE

UMAREX HAMMER

UMAREX LEGENDS COWBOY RIFLE

HATSAN USA VECTIS

Action: PCP
Stock: Synthetic
Barrel: 17.7 in.
Sights: Flip-up green fiber optic front, red fiber optic rear
Weight: 7 lb. 2 oz.
Caliber: .177, .22, .25
Magazine: 10, 12, 14 shots
Features: A lever-activated thoroughly modern PCP air rifle featuring the QuietEnergy barrel shroud; S/Roto magazines and single-shot tray; Quattro adjustable two-stage trigger; all-weather thumbhole stock with Monte Carlo cheekpiece; removeable fiber optic flip-up sights; acres of rail top and bottom; rifled and choked barrel
MSRP **$399.99**

REMINGTON (BY CROSMAN) R1100 PUMP RIFLE

Action: Pump
Stock: Synthetic
Barrel: N/A
Sights: Blade front, adjustable rear
Weight: N/A
Caliber: BB, .177
Magazine: 1 shot
Features: A variable speed pump-- more pumps equal more velocity--in a shotgun-style stock of youth proportions
MSRP **$59.99**

SIG AIR P320-M17 ASP

Action: CO2
Stock: Polymer
Barrel: N/A
Sights: Fixed
Weight: 34 oz.
Caliber: .177
Magazine: 20 shots
Features: Copy of the U.S. Army's M17 semiautomatic. Features full blowback action for realistic shooting,
MSRP **$119.95**

STOEGER S4000-E SUPPRESSED, SUPRESSED COMBO

Action: Break-barrel
Stock: Synthetic
Barrel: N/A
Sights: Interchangeable fiber optic front, adjustable fiber optic rear; 4X32 scope
Weight: N/A
Caliber: .177, .22
Magazine: 1 shot
Features: Employing the Gas Ram System break-action design; ProAdaptive stock texturing; adjustable two-stage trigger; integral S3 suppressor; MultiGrip system; combo comes with both the fiber optic sights and a 4X32 scope
MSRP **$149.00**
Combo: **$179.00**

UMAREX HAMMER

Action: Stright-pull bolt
Stock: Synthetic
Barrel: 29.5 in.
Sights: None
Weight: 8 lb. 8 oz.
Caliber: .50
Magazine: 5 shots
Features: A big-bore airgun delivering three slugs at full speed of 760 fps and 705 ft-lb of energy, plus two additional lesser-powered shots, achieved by Umarex's Lightspeed valve; straight-pull bolt takes just two pounds of effort to operate; magazine lock-out and trigger block safeties; top-side cantilever optics rail; three M-LOK attachment slots; Magpul AR grip
MSRP **$799.00**

UMAREX LEGENDS COWBOY RIFLE

Action: CO2
Stock: Wood
Barrel: 19.25 in.
Sights: Ramp blade front, adjustable rear
Weight: 5 lb. 15 oz.
Caliber: .177
Magazine: 10 shots
Features: CO2 cartridges hidden in buttstock; realistic lever actioning inserts a "cartridge" with its BB in the chamber and ejects after firing;
MSRP **$249.99**

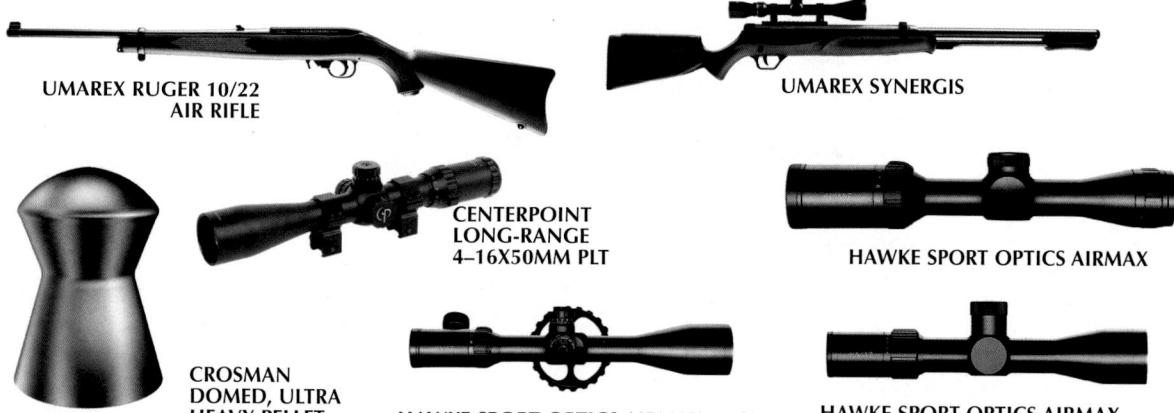

UMAREX RUGER 10/22 AIR RIFLE

UMAREX SYNERGIS

CENTERPOINT LONG-RANGE 4–16X50MM PLT

HAWKE SPORT OPTICS AIRMAX

CROSMAN DOMED, ULTRA HEAVY PELLET

HAWKE SPORT OPTICS AIRMAX 30 SF

HAWKE SPORT OPTICS AIRMAX 30 SF COMPACT

UMAREX RUGER 10/22 AIR RIFLE

Action: CO2
Stock: Synthetic
Barrel: N/A
Sights: Iron
Weight: N/A
Caliber: .177
Magazine: 10 shots
Features: A replica of Ruger's popular 10/22 rimfire; rotary magazine; uses two 12-gram CO2 cartridges; elevation-adjustable rear sight
MSRP. **$129.99**

UMAREX SYNERGIS

Action: Gas piston
Stock: Synthetic
Barrel: N/A
Sights: 3–9x32mm scope
Weight: N/A
Caliber: .177
Magazine: 12 shots
Features: Umarex's first 12-shot repeating gas piston rifle with a fully shrouded fixed barrel; ambidextrous stock; two-stage trigger; Picatinny scope rail and airgun scope; underlever cocking mechanism
MSRP. **$169.00**

Airgun Pellets

CROSMAN DOMED, ULTRA HEAVY PELLET

Available in: .22-cal.
Weight: 19-grain

Features: Crosman says this pellet has 33% more weight than its standard domed pellet
Box of: 200
MSRP. . . . . **N/A**

Airgun Optics

CENTERPOINT LONG-RANGE 4–16X50MM PLT

Available in: 4–16X
Power: 4–16X
Obj. Diameter: 50mm
Main Dia.: 30mm
Features: Nitrogen filled; fast-focus eyepiece; locking turrets with zero reset; fully multi-coated lenses
MSRP. **$164.99**

HAWKE SPORT OPTICS AIRMAX

Available in: 2–7x32mm, 3–9x40mm, 4–12x40mm, 4–12x50mm 16.6 oz.–21.9 oz.
Length: 10.6 in.–13 in.
Power: 2–7X, 3–9X, 4–12X
Obj. Dia.: 32mm, 40mm, 50mm
Main Dia.: 1 in.
Exit pupil: 3.5 in.
Features: Dedicated 1-inch tube air rifle scopes with fully multi-coated optics; integrated adjustable objective; fast-focus eyepiece; ¼-MOA clicks; objective is threaded for accessories; second focal plane AMX reticle, non-illuminated; waterproof and shockproof
MSRP. . . . . **$199.00–$249.00**

HAWKE SPORT OPTICS AIRMAX 30 SF

Available in: 3–12x50mm, 4–15x50mm, 6–24x50mm, 8–32x50mm
Weight: 26.7 oz.–27.5 oz.
Length: 13.6 in.–16.6 in.
Power: 3–12X, 4–16X, 6–24X, 8–32X
Obj. Dia.: 50mm
Main Dia.: 30mm
Exit pupil: 4 in.
Features: Air rifle shooters going long will find favor with this family of 30mm-bodied, 50mm objective lens scopes featuring a red illuminated glass-etch AMX reticle in the second focal plane; ¼-MOA adjustments on exposed, locking, and resettable target turrets; side-focus parallax adjustment; waterproof, shockproof
MSRP. . . . . **$429.00–$499.00**

HAWKE SPORT OPTICS AIRMAX 30 SF COMPACT

Available in: 3–12x40mm, 4–16x44mm, 6–24x50mm
Weight: 20.8 oz.–23.6 oz.
Length: 10.9 in.–13 in.
Power: 3–12X, 4–16X, 6–24X
Obj. Dia.: 40mm, 44mm, 50mm
Main Dia.: 30mm
Exit pupil: 3 in.
Features: Three excellent choices for both precision distance shooters and those hunting game with the large-bore air rifles; red illuminated glass-etched AMX reticle in the second focal plane; resettable target turrets in 1/10-MRAD increments; waterproof and shockproof
MSRP. . . . . **$359.00–$399.00**

NEW PRODUCTS

BENELLI 828U SPORT

BENELLI MONTEFELTRO SILVER FEATHERWEIGHT 12-GAUGE

BENELLI MONTEFELTRO SILVER FEATHERWEIGHT 20-GAUGE

BENELLI NOVA PUMP FIELD MOSSY OAK BOTTOMLAND

BENELLI PERFORMANCE SHOP 828U UPLAND

BENELLI PERFORMANCE SHOP M2 TURKEY EDITION 20-GAUGE

BENELLI PERFORMANCE SHOP M2 WATERFOWL EDITION 20-GAUGE

BENELLI 828U SPORT

Action: Over/under
Stock: Walnut
Barrel: 30 in.
Chokes: Five
Sights: White bead front
Weight: 8 lb.
Bore/Gauge: 12
Capacity: 2 shells
Features: For the sporting clays crowd, the 828U gets an adjustable trigger; automatic ejectors; AA-grade walnut stock; Crio barrel; shim plates for drop and cast adjustments; wide carbon fiber rib with sight channel; balancing weight system; custom hardshell case
MSRP $4399.00

BENELLI MONTEFELTRO SILVER FEATHERWEIGHT 12-GAUGE

Action: Semiautomatic
Stock: Walnut
Barrel: 26 in.
Chokes: Five
Sights: Red bar front
Weight: 6 lb. 3 oz.
Bore/Gauge: 12
Capacity: 3 shells
Features: A lightweight field gun with a 26-inch barrel; AA-grade walnut stock; slim fore-end; low-profile vent rib; engraved nickel-plated alloy receiver; Inertia Driven system; full set of extended Crio chokes
MSRP $1999.00

BENELLI MONTEFELTRO SILVER FEATHERWEIGHT 20-GAUGE

Action: Semiautomatic
Stock: Walnut
Barrel: 24 in.
Chokes: Five
Sights: Red bar front
Weight: 5 lb. 5 oz.
Bore/Gauge: 20
Capacity: 3 shells
Features: A very lightweight and short-barreled 20-gauge with engraved nickel-plated alloy receiver; extended Crio chokes; Inertia Driven system
MSRP $1999.00

BENELLI NOVA PUMP FIELD MOSSY OAK BOTTOMLAND

Action: Pump
Stock: Synthetic
Barrel: 28 in., 26 in.
Chokes: Three
Sights: Red bar front, mid bead
Weight: 8 lb. (12 ga.); 6 lb. 9 oz. (20 ga.)
Bore/Gauge: 12, 20
Capacity: 3 shells
Features: The Nova Pump now available in Mossy Oak Bottomland; 12-gauge chambered for 3 ½-inch and with 28- or 26-inch barrel; 20-gauge chambered for 3-inch, 26-inch barrel only
MSRP $559.00

BENELLI PERFORMANCE SHOP 828U UPLAND

Action: Over/under
Stock: Walnut
Barrel: 24 in.
Chokes: Eight
Sights: Red fiber optic front
Weight: 6 lb. 6 oz.
Bore/Gauge: 12
Capacity: 2 shells
Features: A short-barreled upland gun with upgraded AA walnut stock in a satin finish; five flush-mount chokes plus three Rob Roberts Triple Threat

chokes; carbon fiber stepped rib; drop and cast adjustment shims; no automatic ejectors; lengthened forcing cones; reduced 14.25-inch length of pull; 3-inch chambers; Dark Bronze anodized metalwork
MSRP $3499.00

BENELLI PERFORMANCE SHOP M2 TURKEY EDITION 20-GAUGE

Action: Semiautomatic
Stock: Synthetic
Barrel: 24 in.
Chokes: Six
Sights: Burris Fast-Fire II red dot
Weight: 5 lb. 11 oz.
Bore/Gauge: 20
Capacity: 4 shells
Features: With custom enhancements from patterning expert Rob Roberts; five flush-fit Crio tubes in normal constrictions, plus one extended custom XFT choke; Burris Fast-Fire red dot factory installed; Mossy Oak Bottomland coverage on stock; Burnt Bronze metalwork; ComforTech stock
MSRP $3199.00

BENELLI PERFORMANCE SHOP M2 WATERFOWL EDITION 20-GAUGE

Action: Semiautomatic
Stock: Synthetic
Barrel: 28 in.
Chokes: Three
Sights: Hi-Viz Comp front, metal mid-rib
Weight: 5 lb. 15 oz.
Bore/Gauge: 20
Capacity: 4 shells
Features: Honed and polished action; custom-tuned trigger group; oversized bolt handle; paracord survival sling; three Rob Roberts Triple Threat chokes; chambers 3-inch shells; Gore Optifade Marsh camo on stock; Burnt Bronze metalwork
MSRP $2799.00

BENELLI PERFORMANCE SHOP SUPER BLACK EAGLE 3 TURKEY 12-GAUGE

BENELLI PERFORMANCE SHOP SUPER BLACK EAGLE 3 WATERFOWL 12-GAUGE

BENELLI PERFORMANCE SHOP ULTRA LIGHT UPLAND

BENELLI SUPER BLACK EAGLE 3 RIFLED SLUG

BENELLI SUPER BLACK EAGLE 3 WITH STEADY GRIP

BERETTA A400 XTREME PLUS MAX 5

BENELLI PERFORMANCE SHOP SUPER BLACK EAGLE 3 TURKEY 12-GAUGE

Action: Semiautomatic
Stock: Synthetic
Barrel: 24 in.
Chokes: Six
Sights: Burris Fast-Fire II red dot
Weight: 6 lb. 13 oz.
Bore/Gauge: 12
Capacity: 4 shells
Features: With custom enhancements from patterning expert Rob Roberts; five flush-fit Crio tubes in normal constrictions, plus one extended custom XFT choke; Burris Fast-Fire red dot factory installed; Mossy Oak Bottomland coverage on stock; Burnt Bronze metalwork; ComforTech stock
MSRP $3399.00

BENELLI PERFORMANCE SHOP SUPER BLACK EAGLE 3 WATERFOWL 12-GAUGE

Action: Semiautomatic
Stock: Synthetic
Barrel: 28 in.
Chokes: Three
Sights: Hi-Viz CompSight front
Weight: 7 lb.
Bore/Gauge: 12
Capacity: 4 shells
Features: Honed and polished action; custom-tuned trigger group; lengthened forcing cones oversized bolt handle and release; paracord survival sling; three Rob Roberts Triple Threat chokes; chambers 3 ½-inch

shells; Gore Optifade Marsh camo on stock; Burnt Bronze metalwork
MSRP $3199.00

BENELLI PERFORMANCE SHOP ULTRA LIGHT UPLAND

Action: Semiautomatic
Stock: Walnut
Barrel: 26 in., 24 in.
Chokes: Six
Sights: Hi-Viz Comp front
Weight: 6 lb. 2 oz. (12 ga.); 5 lb. 3 oz. (20 ga.)
Bore/Gauge: 12, 20
Capacity: 3 shells
Features: Satin walnut stock with WeatherCoat treatment; Burnt Bronze Cerakote metalwork; three flush-fit chokes plus three Rob Roberts Triple Threat chokes; shortened magazine tube doesn't need plug; oversized bolt handle and release; alloy receiver; carbon fiber rib
MSRP $2799.00

BENELLI SUPER BLACK EAGLE 3 RIFLED SLUG

Action: Semiautomatic
Stock: Synthetic
Barrel: 24 in.
Chokes: None
Sights: Adjustable rifle sights
Weight: 7 lb. 2 oz.
Bore/Gauge: 12
Capacity: 4 shells
Features: Dedicated rifled bore in an easy to manage 24-inch length; adjustable rifled sights; 3-inch chamber
MSRP $1999.00

BENELLI SUPER BLACK EAGLE 3 WITH STEADY GRIP

Action: Semiautomatic
Stock: Synthetic
Barrel: 24 in.
Chokes: Five
Sights: Red bar front
Weight: 6 lb. 13 oz.
Bore/Gauge: 12
Capacity: 4 shells
Features: The SBE3 now with a Steady Grip and short barrel for turkey hunters; three flush and two extended Crio chokes; stock adjustment shim kit; ComfortTech3 and Combtech pads; Crio barrel; custom fitted hard case; full-coverage Mossy Oak Bottomlands
MSRP $1999.00

BERETTA A400 XTREME PLUS MAX 5

Action: Semiautomatic
Stock: Synthetic
Barrel: 26 in., 28 in.
Chokes: Five
Sights: Red bar front, integral mid bead
Weight: N/A
Bore/Gauge: 12
Capacity: 4 shells
Features: Improved stock features a soft-touch comb; barrels are Steelium Plus and reduce felt recoil; stepped rib with integral mid-rib bead; 3 ½-inch chamber; full-coverage Realtree Max-5; five extended Black Edition choke tubes
MSRP $1900.00

NEW Products: **Shotguns**

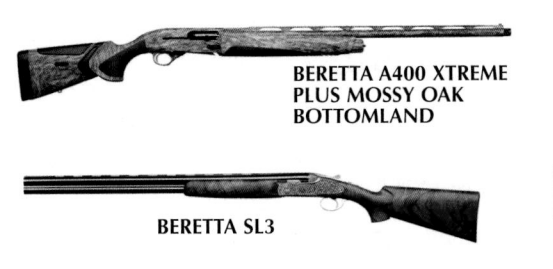

BERETTA A400 XTREME PLUS MOSSY OAK BOTTOMLAND

BERETTA A400 XTREME PLUS SYNTHETIC

BERETTA SL3

BROWNING BT-99 MAX HIGH-GRADE

BROWNING CITORI 725 FEATHER SUPERLIGHT

BROWNING CITORI 725 HIGH GRADE SIDE PLATE FOUR-GAUGE COMBO

BERETTA A400 XTREME PLUS MOSSY OAK BOTTOMLAND

Action: Semiautomatic
Stock: Synthetic
Barrel: 26 in., 28 in.
Chokes: Five
Sights: Red bar front, integral mid bead
Weight: N/A
Bore/Gauge: 12
Capacity: 4 shells
Features: Improved stock features a soft-touch comb; barrels are Steelium Plus and reduce felt recoil; stepped rib with integral mid-rib bead; 3 ½-inch chamber; full-coverage Mossy Oak Bottomland; five extended Black Edition choke tubes
MSRP **$1900.00**

BERETTA A400 XTREME PLUS SYNTHETIC

Action: Semiautomatic
Stock: Synthetic
Barrel: 26 in., 28 in.
Chokes: Five
Sights: Red bar front, integral mid bead
Weight: N/A
Bore/Gauge: 12
Capacity: 4 shells
Features: Kick-Off Mega/Kick-Off3 stock features a soft-touch comb; barrels are Steelium Plus and reduce felt recoil; stepped rib with integral mid-rib bead; 3 ½-inch chamber; black synthetic stock with complementary dark-gray receiver finish; five extended Black Edition choke tubes
MSRP **$1750.00**

BERETTA SL3

Action: Over/under
Stock: Walnut
Barrel: 28 in., 30 in.
Chokes: N/A
Sights: Bead front
Weight: Fixed
Bore/Gauge: 12
Capacity: 2 shells
Features: A handmade boxlock with superior walnut stock; double triggers; Optima Bore HP barrels; rounded body design; light scroll, deep scroll, or game scene engravings, as well as a striking unengraved high-polish receiver option available
MSRP **$19999.00**

BROWNING BT-99 MAX HIGH-GRADE

Action: Break-open
Stock: Grade V/VI walnut
Barrel: 32 in., 34 in.
Chokes: Three extended
Sights: Hi-Viz Pro Comp fiber optic front, mid-rib bead
Weight: 9 lb. 5 oz.
Bore/Gauge: 12
Capacity: 1 shell
Features: Top-of-the-line single-shot trap model with three extended Midas grade choke tubes; Pachmayr Decelerator XLT recoil pad; adjustable Graco buttpad, comb, and recoil reduction system; point of impact adjustable high rib; gloss oil stock finish; fitted Universal BT Trap case
MSRP **$5339.99**

BROWNING CITORI 725 FEATHER SUPERLIGHT

Action: Over/under
Stock: Grade II/III walnut
Barrel: 26 in.
Chokes: Three (F, M, IC)
Sights: Ivory bead front
Weight: 6 lb. 2 oz. (12-ga.); 5 lb. 7 oz. (20-ga.)
Bore/Gauge: 12, 20
Capacity: 2 shells
Features: Super lightweight swinger for the upland hunter who goes all day, featuring: flush-mounted Invector DS chokes; aluminum alloy receiver with silver nitride receiver; gloss-finish straight-grip stock; 2 ¾-inch chrome-plated chambers
MSRP **$2669.99**

BROWNING CITORI 725 HIGH GRADE SIDE PLATE FOUR-GAUGE COMBO

Action: Over/under
Stock: Grade VI/VII walnut
Barrel: 30 in., 32 in.
Chokes: Three (F, M, IC)
Sights: Ivory bead front and mid-rib
Weight: 8 lb. 4 oz.-8 lb. 6 oz.
Bore/Gauge: 12, 20, 28 and .410
Capacity: 2 shells
Features: All the Browning over/unders you ever wanted in one. Features include: top-end black walnut; 3-inch chambers on 12- and 20-gauge and .410-bore, 2 ¾-inch on 28-gauge; Invector Plus flush chokes; Inflex recoil pad; full-coverage engraving with bird and dog accents in gold
MSRP **$11329.99**

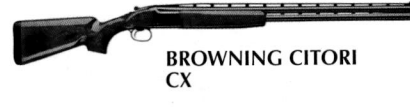

BROWNING CITORI CX

BROWNING CITORI FEATHER LIGHTNING

BROWNING CITORI CX WITH ADJUSTABLE COMB

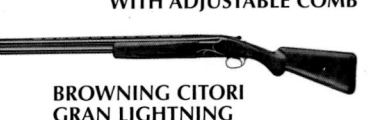

BROWNING CITORI GRAN LIGHTNING

CAESAR GUERINI INVICTUS III SPORTING

BROWNING CITORI CXS MICRO

BROWNING CITORI WHITE LIGHTNING

BROWNING CITORI CX

Action: Over/under
Stock: Grade II American walnut
Barrel: 28 in., 30 in., 32 in.
Chokes: Three extended (F, M, IC)
Sights: Ivory bead front
Weight: 8 lb. 1 oz.–8 lb. 5 oz.
Bore/Gauge: 12
Capacity: 2 shells
Features: Browning calls this a "crossover" gun with a 60/40 point of impact to address targets or game and featuring: high-polished blued finish with CX logo in gold on the receiver; 3-inch chrome chambers; Vector Pro lengthened forcing cones; Inflex recoil pad; gloss-finish stock; Midas-grade extended chokes; ventilated high-post rib and vented barrel joint; Triple Trigger System with one trigger included
MSRP $2139.99

BROWNING CITORI CX WITH ADJUSTABLE COMB

Action: Over/under
Stock: Grade II American walnut
Barrel: 28 in., 30 in., 32 in.
Chokes: Three extended
Sights: Ivory bead front
Weight: 8 lb. 5 oz.–8 lb. 9 oz.
Bore/Gauge: 12
Capacity: 2 shells
Features: Sister to the CX, but with an adjustable comb
MSRP $2539.99

BROWNING CITORI CXS MICRO

Action: Over/under
Stock: Grade II/III American walnut
Barrel: 24 in., 26 in.
Chokes: Three extended (F, M, IC)
Sights: Ivory bead front and mid-rib
Weight: 6 lb. 7 oz.–7 lb. 8 oz.
Bore/Gauge: 12, 20

Capacity: 2 shells
Features: In Browning's "crossover" category of over/unders, this one with shorter barrels for nimble handling on the skeet field or in the grouse woods. Features include: 50/50 point of impact; Inflex recoil pad; shorter 13-inch length of pull; extended Midas-grade chokes; front and mid-rib beads; 3-inch chambers both gauges
MSRP $2139.99

BROWNING CITORI FEATHER LIGHTNING

Action: Over/under
Stock: Grade III/IV walnut
Barrel: 26 in., 28 in.
Chokes: Three extended (F, M, IC)
Sights: Ivory bead front and mid-rib
Weight: 7 lb.–7 lb. 2 oz.
Bore/Gauge: 12
Capacity: 2 shells
Features: A super-lightweight hunter's favorite returns to the Browning family with: three extended Invector Plus chokes; 3-inch chambers; upgraded wood; updated receiver engraving in a pronounced leaf pattern; rounded pistol grip
MSRP $2869.99

BROWNING CITORI GRAN LIGHTNING

Action: Over/under
Stock: Grade V/VI walnut
Barrel: 26 in., 28 in.
Chokes: Three extended (F, M, IC)
Sights: Ivory bead front and mid-rib
Weight: 8 lb.–8 lb. 2 oz.
Bore/Gauge: 12
Capacity: 2 shells
Features: Top-grade wood; rounded pistol grip; all-new leaf-pattern engraving in polished blue with gold

accents; Midas-grade extended chokes tubes; 3-inch chambers
MSRP $3329.99

BROWNING CITORI WHITE LIGHTNING

Action: Over/under
Stock: Grade IIiI/IV walnut
Barrel: 26 in., 28 in.
Chokes: Three extended (F, M, IC)
Sights: Ivory bead front and mid-rib
Weight: 8 lb.–8 lb. 2 oz.
Bore/Gauge: 12
Capacity: 2 shells
Features: Mid-grade wood paired with a silver nitride receiver left naturally "in the white" and polished blue barrels; chrome-plated 3-inch chambers; extended Invector Plus chokes; new engraving in a bold leaf pattern
MSRP $2669.99

CAESAR GUERINI INVICTUS III SPORTING

Action: Over/under
Stock: Walnut
Barrel: 30 in., 32 in.
Chokes: Six
Sights: White Bradley-style front, silver mid-bead
Weight: 8 lb. 1 oz.–8 lb. 3 oz.
Bore/Gauge: 12
Capacity: 2 shells
Features: This one's a head-turner on the sporting clays course, with features like the receiver's hand-polished coin finish gold highlights; ventilated barrel joint; tapered 10mm–8mm top rib; chrome-line barrels; 5-inch DuoCon forcing cones; MAXIS competition chokes; available in left-hand option and with adjustable comb
MSRP . . . . $8445.00–$9005.00

NEW Products: **Shotguns**

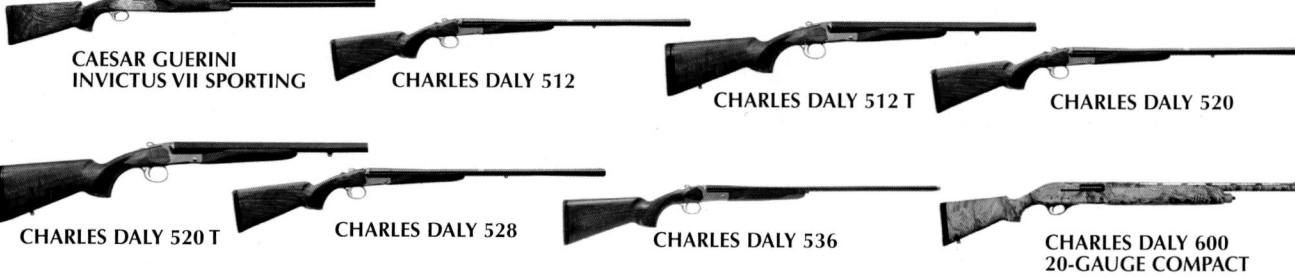

CAESAR GUERINI INVICTUS VII SPORTING | **CHARLES DALY 512** | **CHARLES DALY 512 T** | **CHARLES DALY 520**

CHARLES DALY 520 T | **CHARLES DALY 528** | **CHARLES DALY 536** | **CHARLES DALY 600 20-GAUGE COMPACT**

CAESAR GUERINI INVICTUS VII SPORTING

Action: Over/under
Stock: Walnut
Barrel: 30 in., 32, in.
Chokes: Six
Sights: White Bradley-style front, silver mid-bead
Weight: 8 lb. 1 oz.–8 lb. 3 oz.
Bore/Gauge: 12
Capacity: 2 shells
Features: Similar to the Invictus III Sporting, but with additional gold engravings of five flushing quail on the right side panels, three quail on the rise on the left side, a pheasant and quail on the receiver's underside
MSRP................$9630.00

CHARLES DALY (CHIAPPA FIREARMS) 512

Action: Side-by-side
Stock: Walnut
Barrel: 28 in.
Chokes: Five (F, IM, M, IC, Skeet)
Sights: Bead front
Weight: 5 lb. 10 oz.
Bore/Gauge: 12
Capacity: 2 shells
Features: A lightweight side-by-side with single selective trigger; extractors; Rem Choke threads; gloss blue barrels; receiver left in the white; one sling swivel stud only under barrel joint
MSRP................ $905.00

CHARLES DALY (CHIAPPA FIREARMS) 512 T

Action: Side-by-side
Stock: Walnut
Barrel: 20 in.
Chokes: Five
Sights: Bead front
Weight: 5 lb. 8 oz.

Bore/Gauge: 12
Capacity: 2 shells
Features: The coach gun version of the 512, with matte blue barrels; sling swivel studs under barrel joint and buttstock
MSRP................ $905.00

CHARLES DALY (CHIAPPA FIREARMS) 520

Action: Side-by-side
Stock: Walnut
Barrel: 26 in.
Chokes: Five (F, IM, M, IC, Skeet)
Sights: Bead front
Weight: 5 lb. 10 oz.
Bore/Gauge: 20
Capacity: 2 shells
Features: Single selective trigger; extractors; Rem Choke threads; gloss blue barrels; receiver left in the white; one sling swivel stud only under barrel joint
MSRP................ $905.00

CHARLES DALY (CHIAPPA FIREARMS) 520 T

Action: Side-by-side
Stock: Walnut
Barrel: 20 in.
Chokes: Five
Sights: Bead front
Weight: 5 lb. 4 oz.
Bore/Gauge: 20
Capacity: 2 shells
Features: The coach gun version of the 520, with matte blue barrels; sling swivel studs under barrel joint and buttstock
MSRP................ $905.00

CHARLES DALY (CHIAPPA FIREARMS) 528

Action: Side-by-side
Stock: Walnut

Barrel: 26 in.
Chokes: Five
Sights: Bead front
Weight: 5 lb. 8 oz.
Bore/Gauge: 28
Capacity: 2 shells
Features: Nice little grouse or quail gun with polished blue barrels; single trigger; receiver left in the white; extractors; one sling swivel stud only under barrel joint
MSRP................ $905.00

CHARLES DALY (CHIAPPA FIREARMS) 536

Action: Side-by-side
Stock: Walnut
Barrel: 26 in.
Chokes: Five
Sights: Bead front
Weight: 5 lb. 6 oz.
Bore/Gauge: .410
Capacity: 2 shells
Features: Properly scaled .410 with polished blue barrels with Rem Choke threads; receiver left in the white; single trigger; extractors; extended chokes; no sling swivel studs
MSRP................ $917.00

CHARLES DALY (CHIAPPA FIREARMS) 600 20-GAUGE COMPACT

Action: Semiautomatic
Stock: Synthetic
Barrel: 22 in.
Chokes: Three (IC, M, F)
Sights: Fiber optic front
Weight: 5 lb. 2 oz.
Bore/Gauge: 20
Capacity: 6 shells
Features: A nice semiauto for the youth hunter; 3-inch chamber; chokes with Rem Choke thread; full-coverage Realtree APG camo
MSRP................ $565.00

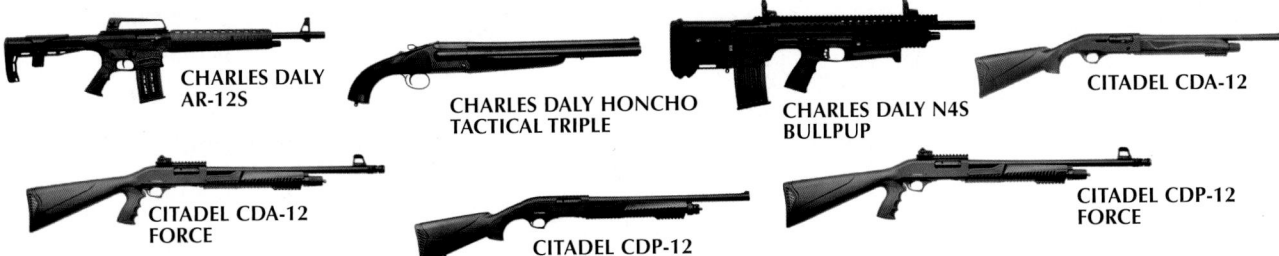

CHARLES DALY
AR-12S

CHARLES DALY HONCHO
TACTICAL TRIPLE

CHARLES DALY N4S
BULLPUP

CITADEL CDA-12

CITADEL CDA-12
FORCE

CITADEL CDP-12

CITADEL CDP-12
FORCE

CITADEL CDP-12 MARINE

CHARLES DALY (CHIAPPA FIREARMS) AR-12S

Action: Semiautomatic
Stock: Synthetic
Barrel: 20 in.
Chokes: One (M)
Sights: A4-style front, adjustable carry handle rear
Weight: 7 lb. 8 oz.
Bore/Gauge: 12
Capacity: 5 shells
Features: Proving the AR really is a do-it-all firearm, this one chambered for the 3-inch 12-gauge and featuring choke with Beretta/Benelli Mobil Choke threads; adjustable buttstock;
MSRP. . . . . **N/A**

CHARLES DALY (CHIAPPA FIREARMS) HONCHO TACTICAL TRIPLE

Action: Over/under
Stock: Rubber-coated walnut
Barrel: 18.5 in.
Chokes: None
Sights: Bead front
Weight: 6 lb.
Bore/Gauge: 12
Capacity: 3 shells
Features: A single over double three-shot self-defense shotgun with rubber-coated walnut fore-end and pistol grip for added weight and improved grip; overall length 27 inches; top-tang safety; single trigger; sling swivels
MSRP. **$1299.00**

CHARLES DALY (CHIAPPA FIREARMS) N4S BULLPUP

Action: Semiautomatic
Stock: Synthetic
Barrel: 20 in.
Chokes: One
Sights: Flip-up
Weight: 9 lb. 5 oz.
Bore/Gauge: 12
Capacity: 5 shells
Features: A bullpup with a little weight for better handling; fixed Modified choke with Beretta/Benelli Mobil Choke thread; adjustable flip-up sights front and rear; detachable magazine
MSRP. **$649.00**

CITADEL BY LEGACY SPORTS CDA-12

Action: Semiautomatic
Stock: Synthetic
Barrel: 20 in.
Chokes: One
Sights: Post front
Weight: 7 lb. 4 oz.
Bore/Gauge: 12
Capacity: 6 shells
Features: Intended for home-defense, an affordable semiauto with a black synthetic stock; oversized bolt handle; prominent front sight; MC-1 Beretta/Benelli Mobil Choke compatibility
MSRP. **$399.00**

CITADEL BY LEGACY SPORTS CDA-12 FORCE

Action: Semiautomatic
Stock: Synthetic
Barrel: 20 in.
Chokes: One
Sights: High post front, adjustable rear
Weight: 6 lb. 13 oz.
Bore/Gauge: 12
Capacity: 6 shells
Features: A home-defense or 3-Gun candidate enhanced with pistol grip; accessory rails on receiver and fore-end; adjustable sights
MSRP. **$439.00**

CITADEL BY LEGACY SPORTS CDP-12

Action: Pump
Stock: Synthetic
Barrel: 20 in.
Chokes: One
Sights: Post front
Weight: 6 lb. 2 oz.
Bore/Gauge: 12
Capacity: 6 shells
Features: The sister pump-action to the semiauto CDA models, with 3-inch chambers; aggressive gripping serrations on fore-end; Marine option is Cerakote finished
MSRP. . . . . **Starting at $249.00**

CITADEL BY LEGACY SPORTS CDP-12 FORCE

Action: Pump
Stock: Synthetic
Barrel: 20 in.
Chokes: One
Sights: High post front, adjustable rear
Weight: 6 lb. 6 oz.
Bore/Gauge: 12
Capacity: 6 shells
Features: A great pump for home-defense or action sports, with an ergonomic fore-end; pistol grip buttstock; topside and under rails; compensated muzzle; 3-inch chamber
MSRP. **$299.00**

CITADEL BY LEGACY SPORTS CDP-12 MARINE

Action: Pump
Stock: Synthetic
Barrel: 20 in.
Chokes: One
Sights: High post front, adjustable rear
Weight: 6 lb. 6 oz.
Bore/Gauge: 12
Capacity: 6 shells
Features: The sister pump-action to the semiauto CDA models, with 3-inch chambers; aggressive gripping serrations on fore-end and pistol grip; muzzle brake; adjustable sights
MSRP. **$299.00**

CITADEL RSS1

CZ-USA CZ 1012

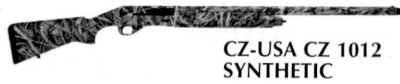

CZ-USA CZ 1012 SYNTHETIC

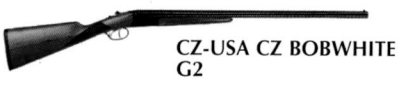

CZ-USA CZ BOBWHITE G2

DICKINSON ARMS ASI

DICKINSON ARMS ECLIPSE

DICKINSON ARMS GREENWING

FABARM L4S DELUXE HUNTER

CITADEL BY LEGACY SPORTS RSS1

Action: Semiautomatic
Stock: Synthetic
Barrel: 28 in.
Chokes: One
Sights: Front post
Weight: 8 lb.
Bore/Gauge: 12
Capacity: 5 shells
Features: A shotgun take on the AK-47 perfect for 3-Gun or home-defense. Features include detachable box magazine; skeletonized stock; 3-inch chamber; Modified choke; optic rail top, accessory rail under fore-end
MSRP. $799.00

CZ-USA CZ 1012

Action: Semiautomatic
Stock: Turkish walnut
Barrel: 28 in.
Chokes: Five (F, MIM, M, IC, C)
Sights: Bead front
Weight: 6 lb. 8 oz.
Bore/Gauge: 12
Capacity: 5 shells
Features: A unique gas-less inertia operating system that features the softest shooting 2 ¾ shells to the hottest 3-inch shells. Features include: 8mm flat vent rib; 14 ½-inch length of pull; choice of Bronze, Grey, or gloss black receiver finishes
MSRP. $659.00

CZ-USA CZ 1012 SYNTHETIC

Action: Semiautomatic
Stock: Synthetic
Barrel: 28 in.
Chokes: Five
Sights: Bead front
Weight: 6 lb. 8 oz.
Bore/Gauge: 12

Capacity: 5 shells
Features: Similar to the standard 1012, but in either a matte black or full-coverage wetlands camo
Matte: $659.00
Aluminum: $749.00

CZ-USA CZ BOBWHITE G2

Action: Side-by-side
Stock: Wood
Barrel: 28 in.
Chokes: Five (F, M, IM, IC, C)
Sights: Bead front
Weight: 5 lb 8 oz.–7 lb. 4 oz.
Bore/Gauge: 12, 20, 28
Capacity: 2 shells
Features: Features a straight, English-style stock; flush-mount choke tubes; double triggers; black chrome finish; gauge-specific frames
MSRP. . . . . $655.00–$702.00

DICKINSON ARMS ASI

Action: Semiautomatic
Stock: Wood, synthetic
Barrel: 26 in., 28 in., 30 in.
Chokes: Five
Sights: Bead front
Weight: 6 lb. 3 oz.–6 lb. 12 oz.
Bore/Gauge: 12
Capacity: 5 shells
Features: A classically styled inertia-operated semiautomatic available wit a stock in either Turkish walnut or in synthetic; synthetic stocks come in black or several camo patterns; cycles a wide variety of loads; recoil spring housed in fore-arm for improved balance and grip
MSRP. N/A

DICKINSON ARMS ECLIPSE

Action: Semiautomatic
Stock: Wood, synthetic
Barrel: 26 in., 28 in., 30 in.
Chokes: Five
Sights: Brass bead front

Weight: 6 lb. 12 oz.–7 lb.
Bore/Gauge: 12
Capacity: 5 shells
Features: A gas-operated semiauto available with either a wood or synthetic stock; squared receiver reminiscent of the more modern iterations of the Browning A5; vent rib; rubber recoil pad
MSRP. . . . . N/A

DICKINSON ARMS GREENWING

Action: Over/under
Stock: Turkish walnut
Barrel: 26 in., 28 in., 30 in.
Chokes: Five
Sights: Bead front
Weight: N/A
Bore/Gauge: 12
Capacity: 2 shells
Features: A budget-priced shotgun with nice features such as automatic ejectors; 22 lines-per-inch checkering; choice of silver or blued receiver with full-coverage scroll engraving
MSRP. . . . . N/A

FABARM L4S DELUXE HUNTER

Action: Semiautomatic
Stock: Turkish walnut
Barrel: 26 in., 28 in.
Chokes: Three
Sights: Fiber optic front
Weight: 6 lb. 5 oz.-6 lb. 13 oz.
Bore/Gauge: 12
Capacity: 4 shells
Features: The highest grade of the three L4S upland models, this one features aluminum alloy frame with a brushed Titanium finish, light diamond and scroll engraving, a gold duck on the right side, and a gold pheasant on the left; deluxe grade Turkish walnut stock with a matte hand-oiled finish; TRIBORE HP barrel; gas-operated with Pulse Piston; 3-inch chamber; INTEGRALE case included
MSRP. $2255.00

FABARM L4S DELUXE SPORTING

FABARM L4S GREY HUNTER

FABARM L4S GREY SPORTING

FABARM L4S INITIAL HUNTER

FABARM L4S SPORTING

HATSAN USA ESCORT DF12

HATSAN USA ESCORT DYNAMAX

FABARM L4S DELUXE SPORTING

Action: Semiautomatic
Stock: Turkish walnut
Barrel: 28 in., 30 in.
Chokes: Five
Sights: White bead front
Weight: 7 lb. 3 oz.
Bore/Gauge: 12
Capacity: 4 shells
Features: The highest grade of the three L4S Sporting models, with highly figured deluxe Turkish walnut stock wearing a matte, hand0oiled finish; Titanium frame finish featuring scroll and diamond pattern engraving, a gold duck on the right side, and a gold pheasant on the left; gas operated with stainless steel piston; five EXIS HP Competition chokes; hard case
MSRP $2765.00

FABARM L4S GREY HUNTER

Action: Semiautomatic
Stock: Turkish walnut
Barrel: 26 in., 28 in.
Chokes: Three
Sights: Fiber optic front
Weight: 6 lb. 5 oz.-6 lb. 13 oz.
Bore/Gauge: 12
Capacity: 4 shells
Features: The middle grade of the three L4S, with a slightly lesser grade of wood than the Deluxe, no gold, but birds engraved in the Titanium finish; INTEGRALE case included
MSRP $1825.00

FABARM L4S GREY SPORTING

Action: Semiautomatic
Stock: Turkish walnut
Barrel: 28 in., 30 in.
Chokes: Five

Sights: White bead front
Weight: 7 Lb. 3 oz.
Bore/Gauge: 12
Capacity: 4 shells
Features: The middle grade of the three L4S Sporting models, similar in features and with nicely figured wood; no gold engravings but flying birds engraved on the receiver; hard case
MSRP $2355.00

FABARM L4S INITIAL HUNTER

Action: Semiautomatic
Stock: Turkish walnut
Barrel: 26 in., 28 in.
Chokes: Three
Sights: Fiber optic front
Weight: 6 lb. 5 oz.-6 lb. 13 oz.
Bore/Gauge: 12
Capacity: 4 shells
Features: The entry level model in the L4S Upland lineup, with basic Turkish walnut stock and black anodized receiver; no case
MSRP $1325.00
Left-handed: $1515.00

FABARM L4S SPORTING

Action: Semiautomatic
Stock: European walnut
Barrel: 28 in., 30 in., 32 in.
Chokes: Five
Sights: White bead front
Weight: 7 lb. 3 oz.
Bore/Gauge: 12
Capacity: 4 shells
Features: Building on the success of the similarly named model in the women's Syren line, the Fabarm L4S Sporting is the base model in this line and features the Tribore HP barrel; five EXIS HP Competition choke tubes; Triwood stock finish; gas operation; 6mm tall rib; oversized controls; shorter action designed

specifically around the 2 ¾-inch 12-gauge load; hard case
MSRP $1950.00
Left-handed: $2140.00

HATSAN USA ESCORT DF12

Action: Semiautomatic
Stock: Synthetic
Barrel: 18 in.
Chokes: Five (F, M, IM, IC, C)
Sights: A4-style front, adjustable rear, flip-up front and rear
Weight: 8 lb. 15 oz.
Bore/Gauge: 12
Capacity: 6 shells
Features: An AR-platform shotgun for the 3-Gun crowd, featuring both A4-style sights with the adjustable rear in the carry handle, plus flip-up sights with a fiber optic front; gas-powered; 3-inch chambers; oxidation-proof chrome-plated barrel; reversible cocking handle; ample rail acreage; elevation-adjustable comb
MSRP $699.99

HATSAN USA ESCORT DYNAMAX

Action: Semiautomatic
Stock: Synthetic
Barrel: 28 in.
Chokes: Five (F, M, IM, IC, C)
Sights: Fiber optic front
Weight: 7 lb.
Bore/Gauge: 12
Capacity: 5 shells
Features: A fast-handling semiauto with three-inch chamber; DaSoft soft-touch stock finish; checkered anti-glare vent rib; Hi-Viz fiber optic front bead; detachable sling swivels; 11mm grooved receiver for optics mounting; steel-shot acceptable chokes; Hybrid Cycling System utilizes both gas and kinetic energy to cycle between shots
MSRP $699.99

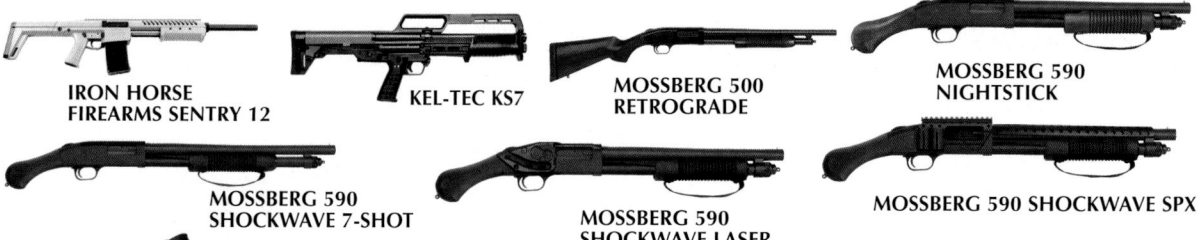

IRON HORSE FIREARMS SENTRY 12

KEL-TEC KS7

MOSSBERG 500 RETROGRADE

MOSSBERG 590 NIGHTSTICK

MOSSBERG 590 SHOCKWAVE 7-SHOT

MOSSBERG 590 SHOCKWAVE LASER SADDLE

MOSSBERG 590 SHOCKWAVE SPX

MOSSBERG 590 SHOCKWAVE SHOCK 'N' SAW

IRON HORSE FIREARMS SENTRY 12

Action: Pump
Stock: Synthetic
Barrel: N/A
Chokes: N/A
Sights: None
Weight: N/A
Bore/Gauge: 12
Capacity: 5 shells
Features: An easy to take apart modular pump shotgun with plenty of rail on top for optics mounting; detachable box magazine; ambidextrous controls
MSRP $899.00

KEL-TEC KS7

Action: Pump
Stock: Synthetic
Barrel: 18.5 in.
Chokes: None
Sights: None
Weight: 5 lb. 15 oz.
Bore/Gauge: 12
Capacity: 8 shells
Features: A shotgun in compact bullpup design with a 13-inch length of pull; carry handle; ambidextrous adjustable stock
MSRP $495.00

MOSSBERG 500 RETROGRADE

Action: Pump
Stock: Walnut
Barrel: 18.5 in.
Chokes: None
Sights: Bead front
Weight: 6 lb. 4 oz.
Bore/Gauge: 12
Capacity: 6 shells
Features: Designed to celebrate Mossberg's 100th anniversary, buyers get a pump shotgun they revere for its technology with the retro look of yesteryear. Features include Cylinder-bore barrel; full-length buttstock; corncob fore-end; single brass bead; blued finish
MSRP $504.00

MOSSBERG 590 NIGHTSTICK

Action: Pump
Stock: Hardwood
Barrel: 14 in.
Chokes: None
Sights: Bead front
Weight: 5 lb. 3 oz.
Bore/Gauge: 12
Capacity: 6 shells
Features: This Talo Distributors exclusive features: five-round magazine; non-NFA (no ATF tax stamp required) fixed Cylinder choke barrel; hardwood bird's-head grip and corncob fore-end; matte blue finish; chambers 3-inch shells
MSRP $539.00

MOSSBERG 590 SHOCKWAVE 7-SHOT

Action: Pump
Stock: Synthetic
Barrel: 18.5 in.
Chokes: None
Sights: Bead front
Weight: N/A
Bore/Gauge: 12
Capacity: 7 shells
Features: The Shockwave with a higher-capacity magazine tube; Raptor grip; sling; corncob fore-end
MSRP $445.00

MOSSBERG 590 SHOCKWAVE LASER SADDLE

Action: Pump
Stock: Synthetic
Barrel: 14 in.
Chokes: None
Sights: Front bead
Weight: N/A
Bore/Gauge: 12
Capacity: 6 shells
Features: The Shockwave with the addition of a Crimson Trace Laser Saddle; Raptor grip, sling; corncob fore-end
MSRP $595.00

MOSSBERG 590 SHOCKWAVE SHOCK 'N' SAW

Action: Pump
Stock: Synthetic
Barrel: 14 in.
Chokes: None
Sights: Bead front
Weight: 6 lb.
Bore/Gauge: 12
Capacity: 6 shells
Features: This non-NFA (no ATF tax stamp required) shotgun features: fixed Cylinder choke barrel; Shockwave's polymer Raptor grip; aluminum MLOK fore-end with Mossberg's own Chainsaw grip; breacher muzzle; matte blue finish; chambers 3-inch shells
MSRP $560.00

MOSSBERG 590 SHOCKWAVE SPX

Action: Pump
Stock: Synthetic
Barrel: 14 in.
Chokes: None
Sights: Bead front
Weight: 5 lb. 12 oz.
Bore/Gauge: 12
Capacity: 6 shells
Features: This non-NFA (no ATF tax stamp required) shotgun features: fixed Cylinder choke barrel; Shockwave's polymer Raptor grip; corncob fore-end with strap; polymer seven-round side-saddle shell holder; heat shield; top-side Picatinny rail; matte blue finish; chambers 3-inch shells
MSRP $560.00

NEW PRODUCTS

MOSSBERG 590 THUNDER RANCH

MOSSBERG 590M SHOCKWAVE

MOSSBERG 835 ULTI-MAG TACTICAL TURKEY

MOSSBERG FLEX 500 SUPER BANTAM ALL-PURPOSE

MOSSBERG 590A1 RETROGRADE

MOSSBERG 835 ULTI-MAG COMBO FIELD/DEER

MOSSBERG 930 THUNDER RANCH

MOSSBERG FLEX 500 YOUTH COMBO FIELD/DEER

MOSSBERG 590 THUNDER RANCH

Action: Pump
Stock: Synthetic
Barrel: 18.5 in.
Chokes: None
Sights: Fiber optic front
Weight: 6 lb. 12 oz.
Bore/Gauge: 12
Capacity: 6 shells
Features: Dressed in Kuiu camo; muzzle sports a door breaching add-on; matte blue metalwork
MSRP $553.00

MOSSBERG 590A1 RETROGRADE

Action: Pump
Stock: Walnut
Barrel: 20 in.
Chokes: None
Sights: Ghost ring
Weight: 7 lb 4 oz.
Bore/Gauge: 12
Capacity: 9 shells
Features: The sister companion to the 500 Persuader Retrograde, features on this MIL-SPEC pump include: Parkerized finish; metal trigger and safety button; heat shield; bayonet lug; full-length stock; corncob fore-end; heavy-wall barrel with Cylinder fixed choke
MSRP $902.00

MOSSBERG 590M SHOCKWAVE

Action: Pump
Stock: Synthetic
Barrel: 15 in.
Chokes: None
Sights: Bead front
Weight: 6 lb. 8 oz.
Bore/Gauge: 12

Capacity: 11 shells
Features: This non-NFA (no ATF tax stamp required) shotgun features: fixed Cylinder choke barrel; Shockwave's polymer Raptor grip; corncob fore-end with strap; increased 11-round overall capacity with a 10-round double-stack removeable magazine; drilled and tapped for optics; chambers 3-inch shells
MSRP $721.00

MOSSBERG 835 ULTI-MAG COMBO FIELD/DEER

Action: Pump
Stock: Walnut
Barrel: 24 in., 28 in.
Chokes: Accu-Mag set
Sights: Dual beads, adjustable rear
Weight: 6 lb. 12 oz.–7 lb.
Bore/Gauge: 12
Capacity: 6 shells
Features: Two for the price of one with a 24-inch fully rifled slug barrel and 28-inch field barrel with interchangeable Accu-Mag chokes; rifled barrel has adjustable rear sight and ramp blade front; wood stock; vented rubber recoil pad; vent rib on field barrel
MSRP $493.00

MOSSBERG 835 ULTI-MAG TACTICAL TURKEY

Action: Pump
Stock: Synthetic
Barrel: 20 in.
Chokes: X-Factor Ported Turkey
Sights: Adjustable fiber optic
Weight: 7 lb.
Bore/Gauge: 12
Capacity: 6 shells
Features: Dedicated turkey gun with fiber optic sights; pistol grip; six-position adjustable stock; vent rib;

ported X-Factor turkey choke tube; full-coverage Mossy Oak Obsession
MSRP $652.00

MOSSBERG 930 THUNDER RANCH

Action: Semiautomatic
Stock: Synthetic
Barrel: 18.5 in.
Chokes: None
Sights: Fiber optic front
Weight: 6 lb. 12 oz.
Bore/Gauge: 12
Capacity: 5 shells
Features: Self-defense gun with a door-breeching muzzle accessory; Kuiu camo stock; matte blue metalwork; Cylinder bore
MSRP $700.00

MOSSBERG FLEX 500 SUPER BANTAM ALL-PURPOSE

Action: Pump
Stock: Synthetic
Barrel: 22 in.
Chokes: Accu-Set
Sights: Front and mid-rib beads
Weight: 6 lb. 8 oz.
Bore/Gauge: 20
Capacity: 6 shells
Features: A gun to grow with thanks to the FLEX stock system; vent rib; chokes; mid-rib and front beads; 12 ½-inch length of pull
MSRP $454.00

MOSSBERG FLEX 500 YOUTH COMBO FIELD/ DEER

Action: Pump
Stock: Synthetic
Barrel: 22 in., 24 in.
Chokes: Accu-Set
Sights: Front and mid-rib beads/ adjustable rifle sights
Weight: 6 lb. 8 oz.–6 lb. 12 oz.
Bore/Gauge: 20
Capacity: 6 shells
Features: A combo youth gun with a 24-inch vent rib barrel with Accu-Set chokes and dual beads; 22-inch fully rifled slug barrel with adjustable sights; FLEX four-position adjustable stock; three-inch chamber
MSRP $531.00

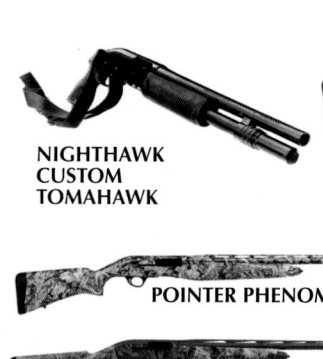

NIGHTHAWK CUSTOM TOMAHAWK

POINTER PHENOMA

POINTER PHENOMA CERAKOTE LASER-ETCHED CAMO

POINTER ARISTA

POINTER PHENOMA CERAKOTE & WOOD

POINTER SCT BASIC BA TRAP

POINTER MXL

NIGHTHAWK CUSTOM TOMAHAWK

Action: Pump
Stock: Hogue
Barrel: 16 in.
Chokes: None
Sights: Bead front
Weight: N/A
Bore/Gauge: 12
Capacity: 6 shells
Features: A non-NFA shotgun featuring a Hogue overmolded pistol grip and fore-end; oversized tactical safety; hand-honed action and rails; rust-resistant black Cerakote finish; 4-round sidesaddle
MSRP $1395.00

POINTER BY LEGACY SPORTS ARISTA, ARISTA YOUTH

Action: Over/under
Stock: Turkish walnut
Barrel: 28 in., 26 in.
Chokes: Five
Sights: Fiber optic front
Weight: 5 lb.–6 lb. 9 oz.
Bore/Gauge: 12, 20, 28, .410
Capacity: 2 shells
Features: Lightweight, fast-swinging upland gun with Turkish walnut stock; 12 ½-inch length of pull and 26-inch barrels in Youth model (14-inch/28-inch standard); vent rib; coin-finished receiver with fine floral engraving
MSRP $589.00

POINTER BY LEGACY SPORTS MXL

Action: Over/under

Stock: Synthetic
Barrel: 28 in.
Chokes: Five
Sights: Fiber optic front
Weight: 6 lb. 6 oz.–6 lb. 9 oz.
Bore/Gauge: 12, 20
Capacity: 2 shells
Features: An budget-friendly over/under made for hard field use three-inch chambers; vent rib; 12- and 20-gauges in all black; 12-gauge available in stock of Mossy Oak Bottomland, Max-5, or Shadow Grass Blades paired with barrels and receiver in Cerakote Burnt Bronze
Black:. $589.00
Camo/Cerakote: $729.00

POINTER BY LEGACY SPORTS PHENOMA

Action: Semiautomatic
Stock: Synthetic
Barrel: 28 in.
Chokes: Five
Sights: Fiber optic front
Weight: 5 lb. 14 oz.–7 lb. 3 oz.
Bore/Gauge: 12, 20, 28, .410
Capacity: 5 shells
Features: A hunter's semiauto featuring: gas-operated system; single-round magazine cutoff; 12-gauge in choice of 3 or 3 ½-inch chambers; all-over matte black or full-coverage camo in Realtree Max-5, Realtree Original; Mossy Oak Bottomland, Mossy Oak Obsession; hard case
MSRP . . . . starting at $529.00

POINTER BY LEGACY SPORTS PHENOMA CERAKOTE LASER-ETCHED CAMO

Action: Semiautomatic

Stock: Synthetic
Barrel: 28 in.
Chokes: Five
Sights: Fiber optic front
Weight: 7 lb. 3 oz.
Bore/Gauge: 12
Capacity: 5 shells
Features: Laser-etched Cerakoting camo designs on the receiver add good looks and resilience in tough hunting conditions. Three combos: Burnt Bronze/Realtree Max-5; Midnight Bronze/Realtree Original; OD Green/Realtree Max-5
MSRP $999.00

POINTER BY LEGACY SPORTS PHENOMA CERAKOTE & WOOD

Action: Semiautomatic
Stock: Turkish walnut
Barrel: 28 in.
Chokes: Five
Sights: Fiber optic front
Weight: 5 lb. 14 oz.–7 lb. 3 oz.
Bore/Gauge: 12, 20, 28, .410
Capacity: 5 shells
Features: A fancier Phenoma for those with more traditional tastes, featuring: Turkish walnut stocks; receivers in choice of Gray or Burnt Bronze Cerakote
MSRP . . . . starting at $669.00

POINTER BY LEGACY SPORTS SCT BASIC BA TRAP, SCT BASIC BA TRAP YOUTH

Action: Break-open
Stock: Turkish walnut
Barrel: 30 in., 28 in.
Chokes: Five
Sights: Fiber optic front
Weight: 7 lb. 15 oz.
Bore/Gauge: 12
Capacity: 1 shell
Features: A dedicated trap gun with adjustable cheekpiece; ported barrel; vent rib; extended choke tubes; Youth model has 12 ½-inch length of pull/28-inch barrel
MSRP $989.00

POINTER SCT BASIC O/U CLAY

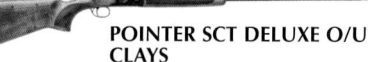

POINTER SCT DELUXE O/U CLAYS

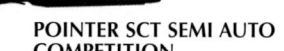

POINTER SCT SEMI AUTO COMPETITION

REMINGTON V3 FIELD SPORT COMPACT

POINTER SCT DELUXE BA TRAP SINGLE BARREL

POINTER BY LEGACY SPORTS SCT SEMI AUTO CLAY

REMINGTON MODEL 870 EXPRESS TACTICAL SIDE FOLDER

POINTER BY LEGACY SPORTS SCT BASIC O/U CLAY, SCT BASIC O/U CLAY YOUTH

Action: Over/under
Stock: Turkish walnut
Barrel: 30 in., 28 in.
Chokes: Five
Sights: Fiber optic front
Weight: 7 lb. 15 oz.
Bore/Gauge: 12
Capacity: 2 shells
Features: A dedicated sporting clays gun with adjustable cheekpiece; high-post vent rib and vented barrel join; ported barrels; extended choke tubes; Youth model has 12 ½-inch length of pull/28-inch barrels
MSRP. **$959.00**

POINTER BY LEGACY SPORTS SCT DELUXE BA TRAP SINGLE BARREL, SCT DELUXE BA SINGLE BARREL YOUTH

Action: Break-open
Stock: Turkish walnut
Barrel: 30 in., 28 in.
Chokes: Five
Sights: Fiber optic front
Weight: 7 lb. 15 oz.
Bore/Gauge: 12
Capacity: 1 shell
Features: Similar to the SCT Basic, but with upgraded wood; high-post rib adjustable for point of impact; stainless-finish choke tubes
MSRP. **$1279.00**

POINTER BY LEGACY SPORTS SCT DELUXE O/U CLAYS, SCT DELUXE O/U CLAYS YOUTH

Action: Over/under
Stock: Turkish walnut
Barrel: 30 in., 28 in.
Chokes: Five
Sights: Fiber optic front
Weight: 7 lb. 15 oz.
Bore/Gauge: 12
Capacity: 2 shells
Features: Similar to the SCT Basic, but with upgraded wood; stainless-finished chokes; ergonomic fore-end
MSRP. **$1199.00**

POINTER BY LEGACY SPORTS SCT SEMI AUTO CLAY

Action: Semiautomatic
Stock: Synthetic
Barrel: 30 in.
Chokes: Yes
Sights: Fiber optic front
Weight: 7 lb. 4 oz.
Bore/Gauge: 12
Capacity: 6 shells
Features: A long-barreled, medium-weight semiauto great for clays games with an ergonomically designed synthetic stock; extended MC-3 Beretta/Benelli Mobil Chokes; length of pull and stock drop spacers; oversized bolt handle; soft-touch stock; 3-inch chambers
MSRP. **$639.00**

POINTER BY LEGACY SPORTS SCT SEMI AUTO COMPETITION

Action: Semiautomatic
Stock: Synthetic
Barrel: 24 in.
Chokes: Yes
Sights: Fiber optic front
Weight: 7 lb.
Bore/Gauge: 12
Capacity: 6 shells
Features: With it's short barrel, we're not sure why this is dubbed a "Competition" model, but it's likely suitable for a turkeys and the tight cover where grouse live; features similar to the SCT Clay semiauto
MSRP. **$639.00**

REMINGTON MODEL 870 EXPRESS TACTICAL SIDE FOLDER

Action: Pump
Stock: Synthetic
Barrel: 18 in.
Chokes: Rem Choke
Sights: Bead front
Weight: 6 lb. 13 oz.
Bore/Gauge: 12, 20
Capacity: 6 shells
Features: Home defense, ranch work or 3-Gun games are good places for this 870 featuring an AK pattern SAW grip by Tapco; M-LOK compatible fore-end; soft-touch cheekpiece; right-side folding; no vent rib but drilled and tapped receiver; QD cup attachment points
MSRP. **$569.00**

REMINGTON V3 FIELD SPORT COMPACT

Action: Semiautomatic
Stock: Synthetic
Barrel: 22 in.
Chokes: Rem Choke
Sights: Bead front
Weight: N/A
Bore/Gauge: 12
Capacity: 4 shells
Features: Three-inch 12-guage wearing a light-contour barrel in a shorter length; drop/cast shim adjustments; length of pull inserts; black oxide finish on metalwork
MSRP. **$915.00**

NEW Products: **Shotguns**

REMINGTON V3 FIELD
SPORT TURKEY PRO

SAVAGE ARMS
212/220 TURKEY

STANDARD
MANUFACTURING
CO. SKO MINI

STEVENS 301 TURKEY

REMINGTON V3 FIELD SPORT
WATERFOWL PRO

STANDARD MANUFACTURING CO.
SKO MINI WORKS PACKAGE

STEVENS 320 FIELD
GRADE

REMINGTON V3 FIELD SPORT TURKEY PRO

Action: Semiautomatic
Stock: Synthetic
Barrel: 22 in.
Chokes: Truglo Headbanger
Sights: Fiber optic front, steel mid-rib bead, Truglo red dot
Weight: 7 lb. 9 oz.
Bore/Gauge: 12
Capacity: 3 shells
Features: A super turkey setup with both fiber optic sights and Truglo's red dot factory mounted and bore-sighted; light contour barrel; full-coverage Realtree Timber; drop and cast adjustment shims; VersaPort gas system; Supercell recoil pad
MSRP $1195.00

REMINGTON V3 FIELD SPORT WATERFOWL PRO

Action: Semiautomatic
Stock: Synthetic
Barrel: 28 in.
Chokes: Three Rem Chokes (I, M, F)
Sights: Fiber optic front, still mid-bead
Weight: 7 lb. 5 oz.
Bore/Gauge: 12
Capacity: 3 shells
Features: Made for the duck blind and goose fields with the VersaPort gas system; sling; shims for drop and cast adjustments; oversized safety, bolt handle and release button. Two finish options: Burnt Bronze Cerakote metalwork with stock in Realtree Max-5 or Mossy Oak Shadow Grass Blades; Patriot Brown Cerakote metalwork with Realtree Timber camo stock
MSRP $1195.00

SAVAGE ARMS 212/220 TURKEY

Action: Bolt
Stock: Synthetic
Barrel: 22 in.
Chokes: Extra-full turkey
Sights: None
Weight: 7 lb.
Bore/Gauge: 12, 20
Capacity: 3 shells
Features: A dedicated turkey gun on a bolt-action platform; Winchester-thread for chokes; adjustable AccuFit stock in Mossy Oak Obsession; matte black metal; topside optics rail; detachable two-round box magazine
12-ga.: $695.00
20-ga.: $779.00

STANDARD MANUFACTURING CO. SKO MINI

Action: Semiautomatic
Stock: Polymer, composite
Barrel: 14.75 in.
Chokes: N/A
Sights: None
Weight: 7 lb. 2 oz.
Bore/Gauge: 12
Capacity: 2, 5, 10 shells
Features: Overall length 27 inches; internal parts salt bath nitride coated; gas-operation; ready for user to add optics, accessories, and chokes, including specialty chokes such as breaking types; accepts most AR-type grips; 3-inch chamber
MSRP $699.00

STANDARD MANUFACTURING CO. SKO MINI WORKS PACKAGE

Action: Semiautomatic

Stock: Polymer, composite
Barrel: 14.75 in.
Chokes: One
Sights: Flip-up AR-style, reflex red dot
Weight: 7 lb. 2 oz.
Bore/Gauge: 12
Capacity: 2, 5, 10 shells
Features: An NFA "other" firearm featuring a 3-inch chamber; gas operation; aluminum receiver; composite fore-end with MOE slots; vertical forward grip; Tru-Choke threading; aluminum tactical grip with built-in red laser and flashlight; flip-up AR-type sights; 45-degree offset sight mount; Door Buster breaching choke; CXHD113 reflex red dot sight; two-point tactical sling
MSRP $1100.00

STEVENS 301 TURKEY

Action: Single-shot
Stock: Synthetic
Barrel: 26 in.
Chokes: Extra-full
Sights: Bead front, rear rail
Weight: 5 lb.
Bore/Gauge: .410
Capacity: 1 shell
Features: Designed to be optimized in barrel length for Federal's HEAVYWEIGHT TSS turkey loads; available in Mossy Oak Bottomland or Obsession; sling swivel studs; removeable front sight can be replaced with TruGlo fiber optics; 3-inch chamber
MSRP $199.00

STEVENS 320 FIELD GRADE, FIELD GRADE COMPACT

Action: Pump
Stock: Synthetic
Barrel: 22 in., 26 in., 28 in.
Chokes: One
Sights: Bead front
Weight: 6 lb. 13 oz.–7 lb. 6 oz.
Bore/Gauge: 12, 20
Capacity: 6 shells
Features: A utilitarian rotary bolt shotgun with dual bars; black synthetic stock; vent rib; matte black metal; one Modified choke provided depending on model; 3-inch chambers across the board; Field Grade in both gauges, Compact in 20-gauge, Security Combo in 12-gauge
Compact: $239.00
Security Combo: $275.00

STEVENS 320 SECURITY

STEVENS 555 16-GAUGE

STEVENS 555 ENHANCED 16-GAUGE

STOEGER M3000 WALNUT/ BURNT BRONZE

STOEGER M3020 WALNUT/BURNT BRONZE

STOEGER M3500 WATERFOWL

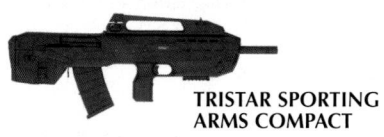

TRISTAR SPORTING ARMS COMPACT

TRISTAR SPORTING ARMS TT-15 FIELD

STEVENS 320 SECURITY

Action: Pump
Stock: Synthetic
Barrel: 18.5 in.
Chokes: None
Sights: Bead front,; ghost ring
Weight: 6 lb. 9 oz.
Bore/Gauge: 12
Capacity: 6 shells
Features: A redesigned buttstock and fore-end make for easier handling than with previous iterations; available with bead front or ghost ring sights; matte finish; 3-inch chamber
Bead: **$239.00**
Ghost ring: **$265.00**

STEVENS 555 16-GAUGE

Action: Over/under
Stock: Turkish walnut
Barrel: 28 in.
Chokes: Five
Sights: Bead front
Weight: 6 lb. 3 oz.
Bore/Gauge: 16
Capacity: 2 shells
Features: The 16-gauge lives again in a Turkish Walnut stock; aluminum receiver; all-over blued finish; manual extractors
MSRP **$705.00**

STEVENS 555 ENHANCED 16-GAUGE

Action: Over/under
Stock: Imperial walnut
Barrel: 28 in.
Chokes: Five
Sights: Bead front
Weight: 6 lb. 7 oz.
Bore/Gauge: 16
Capacity: 2 shells
Features: A fast-handling double for upland field or skeet range with chrome-lined barrels; vent rip and

vent barrel joint; auto ejectors; silver receiver with scroll engraving
MSRP **$879.00**

STOEGER M3000 WALNUT/ BURNT BRONZE

Action: Semiautomatic
Stock: Walnut
Barrel: 28 in.
Chokes: Three
Sights: Red bar front
Weight: 7 lb. 6 oz.
Bore/Gauge: 12
Capacity: 4 shells
Features: Stoeger's Inertia Driven semiauto in a 3-inch 12-gauge, now in a pretty satin-finished walnut stock paired with Burnt Bronze Cerakote metalwork; also available with a Realtree Max-5 stock in place of the walnut; stepped vent rib; drilled and tapped
MSRP **$649.00**

STOEGER M3020 WALNUT/ BURNT BRONZE

Action: Semiautomatic
Stock: Walnut
Barrel: 28 in.
Chokes: Three
Sights: Red bar front
Weight: 5 lb. 12 oz.
Bore/Gauge: 20
Capacity: 4 shells
Features: Who says you have to pay big bucks for today's upgraded finishes? Stoeger adds Burnt Bronze Cerakote metalwork to a satin-finished walnut stock, all within a working man's budget
MSRP **$649.00**

STOEGER M3500 WATERFOWL

Action: Semiautomatic
Stock: Synthetic

Barrel: 28 in.
Chokes: Five
Sights: Red bar front
Weight: 7 lb. 13 oz.
Bore/Gauge: 12
Capacity: 4 shells
Features: Dressed in Realtree Max-5 on the stock and Flat Dark Earth metalwork, this one handles all waterfowl with a 3 ½-inch chamber; extended chokes in Close-Range, Mid-Range, Modified, Improved Cylinder, and XFT; paracord sling; drilled and tapped
MSRP **$849.00**

TRISTAR SPORTING ARMS COMPACT

Action: Semiautomatic
Stock: Synthetic
Barrel: 20 in.
Chokes: One
Sights: Flip-up front, rear
Weight: 8 lb.
Bore/Gauge: 12
Capacity: 5 shells
Features: A gas-operated bullpup design for action shooting games or home defense featuring a detachable magazine; forward grip; carry handle; 30-inch overall length
MSRP **$700.00**

TRISTAR SPORTING ARMS TT-15 FIELD

Action: Over/under
Stock: Walnut
Barrel: 28 in.
Chokes: Five
Sights: Fiber optic front
Weight: 5 lb. 11 oz.–7 lb.
Bore/Gauge: 12, 20, 28, .410
Capacity: 2 shells
Features: Replacing previous TT-15 iterations in TriStars lineup, the Field has a vent rib and ventilated barrel joint; chrome-lined barrel and chamber; ejectors; five Beretta Mobil Choke threaded choke tubes
MSRP . . . . **$840.00–$870.00**

WEATHERBY ELEMENT UPLAND

WEATHERBY ORION SPORTING

WILKINSON TATICAL CR12 MAWS BASIC, MAWS PERFORMANCE

WINCHESTER REPEATING ARMS SX4 COMPACT

WINCHESTER REPEATING ARMS SX4 UPLAND FIELD

WINCHESTER REPEATING ARMS SX4 WATERFOWL HUNTER COMPACT

WINCHESTER REPEATING ARMS SXP YOUTH FIELD

WEATHERBY ELEMENT UPLAND

Action: Semiautomatic
Stock: Walnut
Barrel: 26 in., 28 in.
Chokes: Three (F, M, IM)
Sights: Fiber optic front
Weight: 6 lb. 9 oz.–6 lb. 12 oz.
Bore/Gauge: 12, 20
Capacity: 5 shells
Features: Inertia-operated semiauto made for the grouse woods and pheasant fields, featuring a chrome-line vent rib barrel; both gauges chamber 3-inch shells
MSRP **$699.00**

WEATHERBY ORION SPORTING

Action: Over/under
Stock: Walnut
Barrel: 30 in.
Chokes: Five (F, M, IM, IC, S)
Sights: Fiber optic front
Weight: 7 lb. 8 oz.
Bore/Gauge: 12
Capacity: 2 shells
Features: A dedicated sporting clays gun on the lighter side, featuring an "A"-grade stock with diamond point checkering and an adjustable comb; tapered vent rib; ported barrels; automatic ejectors; chrome-lined bores; 3-inch chamber; knurled extended chokes
MSRP **$1199.00**

WILKINSON TATICAL CR12 MAWS BASIC, MAWS PERFORMANCE

Action: Semiautomatic
Stock: Synthetic
Barrel: 18 in.
Chokes: N/A
Sights: None

Weight: N/A
Bore/Gauge: 12
Capacity: 5, 10, 12 shells
Features: MAWS stands for Modular Advanced Weapons System; .308 AR lower pairs with an upper chambered for 12-ga.; upper can be exchanged for one in .308/7.62X39 NATO or the 6mm and 6.5 Creedmoors in seconds; direct impingement gas operation; smooth barrel threaded for Winchester chokes; FAILZERO EXO nickel boron-plated bolt carrier group; M4-type adjustable stock; black anodized finish; standard buffer on Basic model; Performance model gets Kynshot hydraulic buffer, Carlson breaching muzzle device, PDQ boly catch, and custom color upgrade
MSRP **$2495.00**
Performance: **$2995.00**

WINCHESTER REPEATING ARMS SX4 COMPACT

Action: Semiautomatic
Stock: Composite
Barrel: 24 in., 26 in., 28 in.
Chokes: Three (F, M, IC)
Sights: Fiber optic front
Weight: 6 lb. 8 oz.–6 lb. 12 oz.
Bore/Gauge: 12
Capacity: 5 shells
Features: For youth or shorter-statured shooters with a 13-inch length of pull; all over matte black finish; aluminum alloy receiver; flush Invector-Plus chokes; 3-inch chamber
MSRP **$799.99**

WINCHESTER REPEATING ARMS SX4 UPLAND FIELD

Action: Semiautomatic
Stock: Walnut
Barrel: 26 in., 28 in.
Chokes: Three (F, M, IC)
Sights: Fiber optic front

Weight: 6 lb. 10 oz.
Bore/Gauge: 12
Capacity: 5 shells
Features: A handsome gun featuring Grade II/III walnut stock with a satin finish, 20 lines per inch checkering; aluminum alloy receiver with a matte nickel finish and engraved game bird scenes; Inflex Technology recoil pad; length of pull spacers; 3-inch chamber; flush Invector-Plus chokes
MSRP **$1109.99**

WINCHESTER REPEATING ARMS SX4 WATERFOWL HUNTER COMPACT

Action: Semiautomatic
Stock: Composite
Barrel: 24 in., 26 in., 28 in.
Chokes: Three (F, M, IC)
Sights: Fiber optic front
Weight: 6 lb. 8 oz.–6 lb. 12 oz.
Bore/Gauge: 12
Capacity: 5 shells
Features: For youth or shorter-statured hunters with a 13-inch length of pull; full-coverage Mossy Oak Shadow Grass Blades camo; Inflex-1 recoil pad with hard heel; flush Invector-Plus chokes; vent rib; 3-inch chamber
MSRP **$939.99**

WINCHESTER REPEATING ARMS SXP YOUTH FIELD

Action: Semiautomatic
Stock: Walnut
Barrel: 18 in., 20 in., 22 in., 24 in.
Chokes: Three (F, M, IC)
Sights: Brass bead front
Weight: 5 lb. 14 oz.–6 lb. 6 oz.
Bore/Gauge: 12, 20
Capacity: 5 shells
Features: A youth field shotgun in either 12- or 20-gauge, both with 3-inch chambers; flush Invector-Plus chokes; Grade I walnut stock with satin finish, laser-cut 18 lines per inch checkering; 12-inch length of pull
12-ga.: **$399.99**
20-ga.: **$429.99**

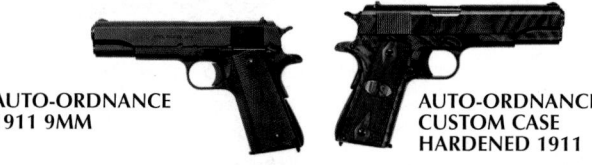

AUTO-ORDNANCE 1911 9MM

AUTO-ORDNANCE CUSTOM CASE HARDENED 1911

AUTO-ORDNANCE "FLY GIRL" 1911

AUTO-ORDNANCE "I STAND" 1911

AUTO-ORDNANCE "SQUADRON" 1911

AUTO-ORDNANCE "VICTORY GIRLS" 1911

BERETTA 92G ELITE LTT

BERETTA APX CENTURION

AUTO-ORDNANCE 1911 9MM

Action: Semiautomatic
Grips: Plastic
Barrel: 5 in.
Sights: Low-profile blade front, notch rear
Weight: 39 oz.
Caliber: 9mm
Capacity: 9 rounds
Features: Faithful GI replica in 9mm; "Model 1911 U.S. Army" on left frame side; brown plastic checkered grips; matte finish
MSRP **$673.00**

AUTO-ORDNANCE CUSTOM CASE HARDENED 1911

Action: Semiautomatic
Grips: Wood
Barrel: 5 in.
Sights: Low-profile blade front, notch rear
Weight: 39 oz.
Caliber: .45 ACP
Capacity: 7 rounds
Features: Gorgeous deep color case hardening on all metalwork; wood grips with raised military "U.S." logo
MSRP **$1327.00**

AUTO-ORDNANCE "FLY GIRL" 1911

Action: Semiautomatic
Grips: Wood
Barrel: 5 in.
Sights: Low-profile blade front, notch rear
Weight: 39 oz.
Caliber: .45 ACP
Capacity: 7 rounds
Features: Honoring WWII's Women Airforce Service Pistols women aviators; right side features Women's Air Corp badge an "Pistol Packin' Mama; left side features "Original Fly Girls" and Walt Disney's Fifinella

character used as a mascot; wood grips with raised military "U.S." logo
MSRP **$1091.00**

AUTO-ORDNANCE "I STAND" 1911

Action: Semiautomatic
Grips: Custom
Barrel: 5 in.
Sights: Low-profile blade front, notch rear
Weight: 39 oz.
Caliber: .45 ACP
Capacity: 7 rounds
Features: Specialty 1911 dedicated to those who've served in the armed forces; "worn" Cerakote finish in gray/black; customer American flag grip on right side, soldier motif with helmet and boots on left; "I Stand" engraved on right side of frame; "Freedom is Not Free" engraved on left side of frame; "All Gave Some, Some Gave All" engraved on dust cover
MSRP **$1313.00**

AUTO-ORDNANCE "SQUADRON" 1911

Action: Semiautomatic
Grips: Wood
Barrel: 5 in.
Sights: Low-profile blade front, notch rear
Weight: 39 oz.
Caliber: .45 ACP
Capacity: 7 rounds
Features: Custom graphics on slide/frame include the "shark mouth" of the P-40 warhawk fighter plane appearing at the muzzle; Army Air Corps insignia; "rivet" pattern; wood grips with raised military "U.S." logo
MSRP **$1106.00**

AUTO-ORDNANCE "VICTORY GIRLS" 1911

Action: Semiautomatic
Grips: Wood
Barrel: 5 in.

Sights: Low-profile blade front, notch rear
Weight: 39 oz.
Caliber: .45 ACP
Capacity: 7 rounds
Features: Honoring all women who supported WWII troops through their industry work at home; "worn" Armor Black and Gunmetal Grey Cerakote finish; "Rosie the Riveter" on left side; classic pin-up girl on right; USAAC rondel on both sides
MSRP **$1240.00**

BERETTA 92G ELITE LTT

Action: Semiautomatic
Grips: G10
Barrel: 4.7 in.
Sights: Red fiber optic front, blacked out notch rear
Weight: 33.3 oz.
Caliber: 9mm
Capacity: 15 rounds
Features: A collaboration with Landon Tactical that features the M9A1 frame; Vertec slide with added front serrations; exclusive radiused trigger guard; beveled mag well; ultra-thin VZ/LTT G10 grips; oversized mag release; no lanyard ring; solid steel guide rod; DA/SA with decocker; ships with three magazines
MSRP **$1100.00**

BERETTA APX CENTURION

Action: Semiautomatic
Grips: Polymer
Barrel: 3.7 in.
Sights: Drift adjustable three-dot front and rear
Weight: 27.7 oz.
Caliber: 9mm, .40 S&W
Capacity: 10, 13, 15 rounds
Features: A mid-size striker-fire suitable for concealed carry; double-stack magazine; ambidextrous slide release, reversible mag release; aggressive slide serrations front and rear; 6-pound trigger with audible reset; under rail
MSRP **$575.00**

NEW Products: Handguns

BERETTA APX COMPACT

BERETTA M9A3 BLACK

BERETTA NANO RE BLUE, SNIPER GREY

BERETTA PX4 COMPACT FDE, GREY

BERETTA PX4 STORM CARRY

BERETTA PICO LAVENDER

BERSA BP9CC WITH THREADED BARREL

BERSA THUNDER 380 WITH THREADED BARREL

BERETTA APX COMPACT

Action: Semiautomatic
Grips: Polymer
Barrel: 3.7 in.
Sights: Drift adjustable three-dot front and rear
Weight: 26.4 oz.–27.2 oz.
Caliber: 9mm, .40 S&W
Capacity: 10, 13 rounds
Features: Short-gripped CCW version of the popular APX with flush-fit magazines; under rail
MSRP $575.00

BERETTA M9A3 BLACK

Action: Semiautomatic
Grips: Polymer
Barrel: 5 in.
Sights: Three-dot night sights
Weight: 33.4 oz.
Caliber: 9mm
Capacity: 10, 17 rounds
Features: An updated classic with night sights; under rail; textured grips; threaded barrel; decocker; lanyard ring; made in Italy
MSRP $1099.00

BERETTA NANO RE BLUE, SNIPER GREY

Action: Semiautomatic
Grips: Polymer
Barrel: 3 in.
Sights: Three-dot white
Weight: 19.8 oz.
Caliber: 9mm
Capacity: 8 rounds
Features: Just a smidge bigger than the tiny Pico in order to take the smidge bigger 9mm, the Nano is now available with a Robin's Egg Blue frame and matte stainless slide or Sniper Gray frame with matte black slide, adding to prior introductions in Ros (bubblegum pink), and Flat Dark Earth
MSRP $450.00

BERETTA PICO FDE, LAVENDER, RE BLUE

Action: Semiautomatic
Grips: Polymer
Barrel: 2.7 in.
Sights: Three-dot white
Weight: 11.5 oz.
Caliber: .380 ACP
Capacity: 6 rounds
Features: The ultra-concealable, ultra-compact Pico .380 gets a fun update with frames in Lavender, Robin's Egg Blue, and Flat Dark Earth, each with contrasting matte stainless slides
MSRP $300.00

BERETTA PX4 COMPACT FDE, GREY

Action: Semiautomatic
Grips: Polymer
Barrel: 3.2 in.
Sights: Drift-adjustable white three dot
Weight: 27.3 oz.
Caliber: 9mm
Capacity: 15 rounds
Features: A super-concealable pistol with a full palm grip thanks to a double-stack magazine; under rail; front and rear slide serrations; DA/SA with decocker; with gray frame and black slide or in all-over Flat Dark Earth
MSRP $650.00

BERETTA PX4 STORM CARRY

Action: Semiautomatic
Grips: Polymer
Barrel: 4 in.
Sights: Illuminated front dot, blacked-out notch rear
Weight: 27.7 oz.
Caliber: 9mm
Capacity: 17, 20 rounds
Features: Featuring the Storm series' rotating barrel and with a heavily

textured grip; dehorned slide profile with front and rear serrations; slimmed grip; under rail; DA/SA with decocker
MSRP . . . . N/A

BERSA (BY EAGLE IMPORTS) BP9CC WITH THREADED BARREL

Action: Semiautomatic
Grips: Polymer
Barrel: 4 in.
Sights: Interchangeable front and rear
Weight: 22 oz.
Caliber: 9mm
Capacity: 8 rounds
Features: An everyday carry gun featuring a threaded barrel; short reset DAO; interchangeable Sig-type front, Glock-type rear sights; matte finish
MSRP $337.00

BERSA (BY EAGLE IMPORTS) THUNDER 380 WITH THREADED BARREL, 22 WITH THREADED BARREL

Action: Semiautomatic
Grips: Polymer
Barrel: 4.3 in.
Sights: blade front, notch/bar rear
Weight: 19.4–20.5 oz.
Caliber: .22 LR, .380 ACP
Capacity: 10, 8 rounds
Features: Reminiscent of Walther's small handguns, features include checkered polymer grips; threaded barrel; magazine disconnect; .380 has a dovetail front sight, while the .22 has a low-profile integral blade
MSRP $317.00

BERSA TPR9C WITH THREADED BARREL

BIG HORN ARMORY AR500 PISTOL

BROWNING BUCK MARK MEDALLION ROSEWOOD

CABOT GUNS CHARLEY

CABOT GUNS GRAN TORINO SS

CARACAL USA CAR816 A2

CENTURY ARMS TP9 ELITE COMBAT

CHARTER ARMS 911 RED, 911 BLUE

BERSA (BY EAGLE IMPORTS) TPR9, TPR9C WITH THREADED BARREL

Action: Semiautomatic
Grips: Polymer
Barrel: 5 in., 4.1 in.
Sights: Interchangeable Sig type front and rear
Weight: 31.2 oz., 23.5 oz.
Caliber: 9mm
Capacity: 17, 13 rounds
Features: Intended as a duty gun and perfectly serviceable as a carry or home-defense pistol, these threaded barrel models feature interchangeable Sig-type sights both front and rear; matte finish; textured grips; alloy frames; steel slides; DA with manual safety; TPR9C is slightly shorter in both barrel and grip length
MSRP **$500.00**

BIG HORN ARMORY AR500 PISTOL

Action: Semiautomatic
Grips: Synthetic
Barrel: 10 in.
Sights: None
Weight: 8 lb. 2 oz.
Caliber: .500 S&W
Capacity: 5 rounds
Features: The big-boy .500 S&W cartridge finds a home in an AR-style pistol with 1:24 threaded barrel with nitride finish; M-LOK-compatible handguard; adjustable gas block
MSRP **$2199.00**

BROWNING BUCK MARK MEDALLION ROSEWOOD

Action: Semiautomatic
Grips: Laminated rosewood
Barrel: 5.5 in.
Sights: TRUGLO/Marble Arms fiber optic front, Pro Target adjustable rear
Weight: 34 oz.
Caliber: .22 LR
Capacity: 11 rounds
Features: A new look for the Buck Mark with blackened, polished-flats

slab-sided barrel; adjustable rear sight and fiber optic front; textured grip panels
MSRP **$509.99**

CABOT GUNS CHARLEY

Action: Semiautomatic
Grips: Ironwood
Barrel: 5 in.
Sights: Reverse dovetail front, ACW fixed rear
Weight: N/A
Caliber: 9mm, .45 ACP
Capacity: 8, 9 rounds
Features: Stylish carry gun featuring a rear sight designed for one-hand manipulation; polished frame and slide flats; aluminum Tristar trigger; satin finished ironwood grip panels; Rhombus checkering on front strap and mainspring housing
MSRP . . . . **starting at $4495.00**

CABOT GUNS GRAN TORINO SS

Action: Semiautomatic
Grips: Carbon fiber
Barrel: 5 in.
Sights: Reverse dovetail front, low-mount fixed rear
Weight: N/A
Caliber: 9mm, .45 ACP
Capacity: 8, 9 rounds
Features: Complete stainless steel construction; chatoyant carbon fiber grips with luminescent silver flakes and inlaid Cabot medallion; Racing Vector rear slide serrations; top slide serrations; hand-fit match grade barrel with custom crown; front of guide rod has engraved star; aluminum Cabot Tristar trigger; machined in place ejector; Rhombus-textured front strap and mainspring housing
MSRP . . . . **starting at $4295.00**

CARACAL USA CAR816 A2

Action: Semiautomatic
Grips: Synthetic

Barrel: 14.5 in.
Sights: None
Weight: 6 lb. 15 oz.
Caliber: 5.56 NATO
Capacity: 10, 30 rounds
Features: Capitalizing on the AR pistol trend and featuring a short-stroke gas operated piston system; modified M4 barrel contour; black nitride finish; EDT Sharp Shooter trigger; SBA3 pistol brace; 9-inch key-lock M-LOK handguard; black or Flat Dark Earth
MSRP . . . . **$1929.00–$1969.00**

CENTURY ARMS TP9 ELITE COMBAT

Action: Semiautomatic
Grips: Polymer
Barrel: 4.73 in.
Sights: Fiber optic front, drift adjustable rear
Weight: 25.8 oz.
Caliber: 9mm
Capacity: 10, 18 rounds
Features: A sleek-looking striker-fired Canik pistol with a fluted, match-grade threaded barrel; aluminum Speed Funnel magwell; flat-faced aluminum trigger; optics-ready slide with adapter plates; extended mag release; retention holster with slide lock release; changeable backstraps; textured grip; all-over Flat Dark Earth; under rail
MSRP **$849.99**

CHARTER ARMS 911 RED, 911 BLUE

Action: Revolver
Grips: N/A
Barrel: 2 in.
Sights: Fixed front and rear
Weight: N/A
Caliber: .38 Spec.
Capacity: 5 rounds
Features: Five-shot snubby with a standard hammer; aluminum frame in black with red or blue stripe
MSRP **$324.00**

NEW Products: **Handguns**

CHARTER ARMS MAG PUG

CHARTER ARMS PITBULL .380

CHARTER ARMS PITBULL .40 S&W

CHARTER ARMS TIGER III

CHIAPPA FIREARMS RHINO NEBULA

CIMARRON FIREARMS 1862 POCKET NAVY CONVERSION

CIMARRON FIREARMS EVIL ROY COMPETITION

CIMARRON FIREARMS MODEL #3 FIRST MODEL AMERICAN

CITADEL M1911 GOVERNMENT AMERICAN FLAG, GRAYSCALE FLAG

CHARTER ARMS MAG PUG

Action: Revolver
Grips: N/A
Barrel: 3 in.
Sights: Fixed front, adjustable rear
Weight: N/A
Caliber: .357 Mag.
Capacity: 5 rounds
Features: A larger-framed .357 Mag. with a high-polished finish; adjustable sights
MSRP $340.00

CHARTER ARMS PITBULL .380

Action: Revolver
Grips: N/A
Barrel: 2.2 in.
Sights: Fixed front and rear
Weight: N/A
Caliber: .380 ACP
Capacity: 6 rounds
Features: A snubby with a large frame holding six rounds of .380 ACP makes a great backup gun; stainless steel finish
MSRP $332.00

CHARTER ARMS PITBULL .40 S&W

Action: Revolver
Grips: N/A
Barrel: 2.2 in.
Sights: Fixed front and rear
Weight: N/A
Caliber: .40 S&W
Capacity: 5 rounds
Features: The power of the .40 S&W in a five-shot larger-frame revolver and a snub profile; adjustable rear sight; stainless steel finish
MSRP $367.00

CHARTER ARMS TIGER III

Action: Revolver
Grips: N/A
Barrel: 4.2 in.
Sights: Fixed front, adjustable rear

Weight: N/A
Caliber: .45 ACP
Capacity: 5 rounds
Features: An XL frame in black with a green stripe houses five rounds of .45 ACP
MSRP $367.00

CHIAPPA FIREARMS RHINO NEBULA

Action: Revolver
Grips: Laminate
Barrel: 6 in.
Sights: Fiber optic front and rear
Weight: 33.6 oz.
Caliber: .357 Mag.
Capacity: 6 rounds
Features: The unique bottom chamber/barre alignment that is the Rhino now in a snazzy, mixed-color PVD metal finish and otherworldly blue laminate grips; top and bottom rails, fiber optics front and back with an adjustable rear; three moon clips provided; DA/SA or SA-only option
MSRP $1509.00

CIMARRON FIREARMS 1862 POCKET NAVY CONVERSION

Action: Revolver
Grips: Walnut
Barrel: 6 in.
Sights: Blade front, integral rear
Weight: N/A
Caliber: .380 ACP
Capacity: 5 rounds
Features: A replica of the original Colt 1862 Pocket Navy, but made to shoot the semiautomatic .380 ACP round--fun!
MSRP $570.00

CIMARRON FIREARMS EVIL ROY COMPETITION

Action: Revolver
Grips: Walnut
Barrel: 4.75 in., 5.5 in.
Sights: Blade front, integral rear

Weight: 38 oz.–40.1 oz.
Caliber: .357 Mag., .44-40, .45 LC
Capacity: 6 rounds
Features: Competition-ready single-action with a tuned action; square notch rear sight paired with a wide front blade; slim walnut grip; some models available with a low, wide hammer
Blued: $778.70
Stainless: $960.70

CIMARRON FIREARMS MODEL #3 FIRST MODEL AMERICAN

Action: Revolver
Grips: N/A
Barrel: 5 in., 8 in.
Sights:
Weight: N/A
Caliber: .45 LC, .44-40, .44 Russian, .44 Special
Capacity: 6 rounds
Features: Wearing military markings in blued or nickel frame with case-colored latch, trigger guard and hammer; two-piece grips
MSRP $1163.00

CITADEL BY LEGACY SPORTS M1911 GOVERNMENT AMERICAN FLAG, GRAYSCALE FLAG

Action: Semiautomatic
Grips: Wood
Barrel: 5 in.
Sights: Blade front, drift-adjustable rear
Weight: 36.8 oz.–38.8 oz.
Caliber: 9mm, .45 ACP
Capacity: 8, 10 rounds
Features: Citadel's 1911 Government wrapped in eye-catching red-white-and-blue or Grayscale American flag graphics; skeletonized trigger and hammer, extended beavertail grip safety; full-length guide rod; ambidextrous safety
MSRP $959.00

CMMG INC . BANSHEE 100 SERIES, 100 SERIES SHORT BARREL RIFLE (NFA)

CMMG INC. BANSHEE 200 SERIES, 200 SERIES SHORT BARREL RIFLE (NFA)

CMMG INC . BANSHEE 300 SERIES, 300 SERIES SHORT BARREL RIFLE (NFA)

CZ-USA BREN 2 MS

ITADEL M1911 OVERNMENT ADAGASCAR CERAKOTE

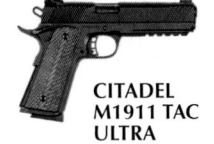

CITADEL M1911 TAC ULTRA

COLT KING COBRA

DAN WESSON TCP

CITADEL BY LEGACY SPORTS M1911 GOVERNMENT MADAGASCAR CERAKOTE

Action: Semiautomatic
Grips: Wood
Barrel: 5 in.
Sights: Blade front, drift-adjustable rear
Weight: 36.8 oz.–38.8 oz.
Caliber: 9mm, .45 ACP
Capacity: 8, 10 rounds
Features: A handsome Government-sized 1911 with laser-etched Cerakote treatment
MSRP $959.00

CITADEL BY LEGACY SPORTS M1911 TAC ULTRA

Action: Semiautomatic
Grips: G10
Barrel: 5 in.
Sights: Fiber optic front, adjustable rear
Weight: 45.12 oz.–48 oz.
Caliber: 9mm, .45 ACP
Capacity: 8, 10 rounds
Features: A competition-ready Government-sized 1911 featuring: skeletonized trigger with over-travel stop; skeletonized hammer; full-length under-barrel accessory rail; full-length guide rod; front and rear slide serrations; dust cover; black parkerized finish; gray G10 grip panels
MSRP $859.00

CMMG INC. BANSHEE 100 SERIES, 100 SERIES SHORT BARREL RIFLE (NFA)

Action: Semiautomatic
Grips: Synthetic
Barrel: 8 in., 8.5 in., 9 in., 10 in., 12.5 in.
Sights: None
Weight: 4 lb. 8 oz.–6 lb. 4 oz.
Caliber: .22 LR, 5.7X28mm, 9mm, .45 ACP, 5.56X45mm, 6.5 Grendel, .300 BLK, 7.62X39mm, .308 Win., .458 SOCOM
Capacity: 10, 13, 20, 25, 30, 32, 33 rounds
Features: An interesting MSR pistol platform in a unique set of caliber offerings. Features include mil-spec trigger, charging handle; free-floating M-LOK handguard; 7075-T6 aluminum receivers; salt bath nitride finish; A2 compensator
MSRP . . . . $849.95–$1799.95

CMMG INC. BANSHEE 200 SERIES, 200 SERIES SHORT BARREL RIFLE (NFA)

Action: Semiautomatic
Grips: Synthetic
Barrel: 8 in., 8.5 in., 9 in., 10 in., 12.5 in.
Sights: None
Weight: 5 lb. 1 oz.–6 lb. 12 oz.
Caliber: .22 LR, 5.7X28mm, 9mm, .45 ACP, 5.56X45mm, 6.5 Grendel, .300 BLK, 7.62X39mm, .308 Win., .458 SOCOM
Capacity: 10, 13, 20, 25, 30, 32, 33 rounds
Features: A step up from the 100 Series with the addition of Magpul MOE pistol grip; CMMG Ripbrace (Ripstock NFA); Type III hard coat anodize; CMMG SV muzzle brake
MSRP . . . . $1049.95–$1949.95

CMMG INC. BANSHEE 300 SERIES, 300 SERIES SHORT BARREL RIFLE (NFA)

Action: Semiautomatic
Grips: Synthetic
Barrel: 8 in., 8.5 in., 9 in., 10 in., 12.5 in.
Sights: None
Weight: 4 lb. 5 oz.–6 lb. 3 oz.
Caliber: .22 LR, 5.7X28mm, 9mm, .45 ACP, .300 BLK, 7.62X39mm
Capacity: 13, 20, 25, 30 rounds
Features: With fewer caliber offerings than the 100 and 200 series but with the addition of Magpul MOE pistol

grip; Premier Cerakote finish in 10 color options; ambidextrous CMMG charging handle and safety; various muzzle brakes depending on caliber; "Banshee" engraved on lower receiver
MSRP . . . . $1199.99–$1799.99

COLT KING COBRA

Action: Revolver
Grips: Hogue
Barrel: 3 in.
Sights: Brass bead front, groove rear
Weight: 28 oz.
Caliber: .357 Mag.
Capacity: 6 rounds
Features: Colt continues reintroductions of long-discontinued classics with the King Cobra .357 Mag.; a brushed stainless finish; Hogue overmolded grips; user-replaceable front sight; Linear Leaf (LL2) trigger; heavy frame; full lug
MSRP $899.00

CZ-USA BREN 2 MS

Action: Semiautomatic
Grips: Synthetic
Barrel: 8 in., 9 in., 11 in., 14 in.
Sights: Folding adjustable
Weight: 5 lb. 6 oz.–5 lb. 14 oz.
Caliber: 5.56X45mm, 7.62X39mm
Capacity: 30 rounds
Features: Totally redesigned Bren replacing the 805 version. Features include trimmed aluminum receiver; carbon fiber-reinforced lower; forward-positioned swappable charging handle; AR-style bolt catch/release system; swappable barrels; designed for add-on buffer tube installation
MSRP $1799.00

DAN WESSON TCP

Action: Semiautomatic
Grips: G10
Barrel: 4 in.
Sights: Brass blade front, notch rear
Weight: 32 oz.
Caliber: 9mm, .45 ACP
Capacity: 8 rounds
Features: TCP is Tactical Commander Pistol. Features aggressive slide serrations; ramped bull barrel with 30-degree crown; tapered grip profile; under barrel accessory rail; flat K-style trigger; top rib for reduced glare; one-piece magwell; square hammer
MSRP . . . . $1700.00–$1725.00

NEW Products: **Handguns**

DARK STORM INDUSTRIES DS-15 TYPHOON PISTOL

DARK STORM INDUSTRIES DS-6TYPHOON PISTOL

DOUBLESTAR CORP. ARP7

EMF COMPANY, INC GREAT WESTERN II DELUXE GRANDE CALIFORNIAN

ED BROWN EVO-KC9, EVO-KC9-G4

ED BROWN/ZEV TECHNOLOGIES EB/ZEV 2019 RMR

FAXON FIREARMS FX-19 HELLFIRE

FAXON FIREARMS FX-19 PATRIOT

DARK STORM INDUSTRIES DS-9 TYPHOON PISTOL

Action: Semiautomatic
Grips: Synthetic
Barrel: 7.5 in.
Sights: None
Weight: N/A
Caliber: 9mm
Capacity: 17 rounds
Features: Similar to the DS-15 Typhoon Pistol but in 9mm and available only with the removeable magazine; choice of black or Flat Dark Earth furniture
MSRP . . . . $1295.00–$1395.00

DARK STORM INDUSTRIES DS-15 TYPHOON PISTOL

Action: Semiautomatic
Grips: Synthetic
Barrel: 7.5 in.
Sights: None
Weight: N/A
Caliber: 5.56 NATO, .300 Blackout
Capacity: 30 rounds
Features: An interesting AR-type pistol in two popular rifle calibers, featuring a billet 7075 aluminum lower; forged upper with forward assist; 6-inch M-LOK forearm with ultra-narrow profile; threaded Nitrite barrel; choice of PMAG or fixed mag configurations; choice of black or Flat Dark Earth furniture; steel micro gas block; pistol gas system
MSRP . . . . $1195.00–$1295.00

DOUBLESTAR CORP. ARP7

Action: Semiautomatic
Grips: Synthetic
Barrel: 7.5 in.
Sights: None
Weight: 5 lb. 6 oz.
Caliber: 5.56 NATO, .300 Blackout, 9mm
Capacity: 30 rounds
Features: An AR-style pistol featuring: free-floating barrel with M4 feed ramp; billet winter trigger guard; billet backbone charging handle; Ergo grip; direct gas impingement;

Doublestar seven-inch Cloak M-LOK handguard
5.56 NATO: $1299.99
.300 Blackout: $1319.99
9mm: $1599.99

ED BROWN EVO-KC9, EVO-KC9-G4

Action: Semiautomatic
Grips: Ed Brown custom
Barrel: 4 in.
Sights: Orange HD XR night sight front, notch rear
Weight: 34 oz.
Caliber: 9mm
Capacity: 9 rounds
Features: EVO is for Evolution, Ed Brown's slimmed and lightened 9mm 1911 featuring Ed's snakeskin treatment to the front strap and his own Bobtail mainspring housing; 7-top custom slide with serrations; bull barrel; flat wire recoil system; two versions, a stainless finish with black textured grips, or a black Gen4 finish with textured brown ombre grips
MSRP $1895.00

ED BROWN/ZEV TECHNOLOGIES EB/ZEV 2019 RMR

Action: Semiautomatic
Grips: G10
Barrel: 4.25 in.
Sights: Tall night sights, Trijicon RMR reflex sight
Weight: 41 oz.
Caliber: 9mm
Capacity: 9 rounds
Features: A collaboration of Ed Brown Products and ZEV Technologies, this unique 9mm 1911 features a stainless steel frame with a black Gen 4 finish; Commander slide on a Government frame; Alien treatment on front strap and mainspring housing; ZEV thread protector and Orion slide cuts; black/gray VZ Alien G10 grips; suppressor-ready barrel with dimple treatment; tall night sights and factory installed Trijicon RMR reflex sight
MSRP $4995.00

EMF COMPANY, INC. GREAT WESTERN II DELUXE GRANDE CALIFORNIAN

Action: Revolver
Grips: Wood
Barrel: 4.75 in.
Sights: Blade front, integral notch rear
Weight: N/A
Caliber: .357 Mag., .45 LC
Capacity: 6 rounds
Features: Gorgeous single-action with a color-case-hardened frame; grips checkered in a pattern reminiscent of fleur-de-lis; Victorian scroll work and sunburst engraving on high-polished blue barrel and cylinder
MSRP $665.00

FAXON FIREARMS FX-19 HELLFIRE

Action: Semiautomatic
Grips: Polymer
Barrel: 4.5 in.
Sights: Suppressor-height night sights
Weight: 18 oz.
Caliber: 9mm
Capacity: 15 rounds
Features: A semi-custom pistol based on the Glock frame--but with a 1911 grip angle--and taking Glock 19 magazines, featuring DLC Diamond-Like-Coating finish; deep slide serrations fore, aft, and top; optics mounting cuts; Overwatch trigger; extended magazine release; suppressor-height night sights; threaded muzzle
MSRP $1499.00

FAXON FIREARMS FX-19 PATRIOT

Action: Semiautomatic
Grips: Polymer
Barrel: 4 in.
Sights: Fiber optic front, blacked-out rear
Weight: 18 oz.
Caliber: 9mm
Capacity: 19 rounds
Features: Similar to the Hellfire, but with a fiber optic front/blacked-out rear sight combo and one standard Glock 19 magazine; unthreaded muzzle
MSRP $1299.00

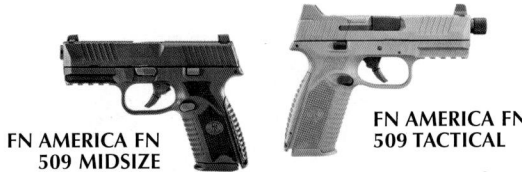

FN AMERICA FN 509 MIDSIZE

FN AMERICA FN 509 TACTICAL

FIME GROUP/AREX D.O.O. REX ALPHA

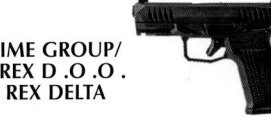

FIME GROUP/ AREX D.O.O. REX DELTA

FULL CONCEAL VIPER

GLOCK G19 GEN5 MOS

GLOCK G17 GEN5 MOS

FIME GROUP/AREX D.O.O. REX ALPHA

Action: Semiautomatic
Grips: Polymer
Barrel: 5 in.
Sights: Fiber optic front, adjustable rear
Weight: 39 oz.
Caliber: 9mm
Capacity: 17 rounds
Features: A hammer-fired competition handgun based on the Zero platform with ambidextrous controls; SA/DA; steel frame; competition-grade trigger; front and rear slide serrations; highly textured grip; under rail; grip panels available in choice of black, white, red, or blue
MSRP $1099.00

FIME GROUP/AREX D.O.O. REX DELTA

Action: Semiautomatic
Grips: Polymer
Barrel: 4 in.
Sights: Steel
Weight: 22.2 oz.
Caliber: 9mm
Capacity: N/A
Features: Arex's first striker-fired pistol featuring a two-stage trigger; angled edges for improved carry; double-stack magazine; front and rear slide serrations
MSRP $449.00

FIME GROUP/AREX D.O.O. REX ZERO 1T

Action: Semiautomatic
Grips: N/A
Barrel: 4.9 in.
Sights: High-profile white three-dot
Weight: 30 oz.
Caliber: 9mm
Capacity: 20 rounds
Features: Adding features to the original Zero 1, including four optics mounting plates; ½X28 threaded barrel; DA/SA; bar stock barrel nitrocarburized; forward slide cocking serrations; ambidextrous mag release and safety; under-rail; decocker; hard

anodized aluminum frame in black, gray, or Flat Dark Earth
MSRP $869.99

FIME GROUP/AREX D.O.O. REX ZERO 1TC

Action: Semiautomatic
Grips: N/A
Barrel: 4.5 in.
Sights: High-profile white three-dot
Weight: 28.7 oz.
Caliber: 9mm
Capacity: 17 rounds
Features: Similar features the full-size Zero 1 Tactical, shaving a bit off barrel and grip length.
MSRP $869.99

FN AMERICA FN 509 MIDSIZE

Action: Semiautomatic
Grips: Polymer
Barrel: 4 in.
Sights: Three-dot luminescent
Weight: 26.5 oz.
Caliber: 9mm
Capacity: 10, 15 rounds
Features: Designed for everyday carry with higher-profile combat-style sights that can make racking in stressed times easier; front and rear slide serrations; striker-fired double-action; loaded chamber indicator; ambidextrous controls; two textured backstraps; under rail
MSRP $649.00

FN AMERICA FN 509 TACTICAL

Action: Semiautomatic
Grips: Polymer
Barrel: 4.5 in.
Sights: Three-dot night sights
Weight: 27.9 oz.
Caliber: 9mm
Capacity: 10, 17, 24 rounds
Features: Duty or competition ready with optics mounting plate; suppressor-height night sights, under rail; threaded barrel; interchangeable backstraps; ambidextrous slide stop and mag release; improved textured

grip; available in black or Flat Dark Earth
MSRP $1049.00

FULL CONCEAL VIPER

Action: Semiautomatic
Grips: Synthetic
Barrel: N/A
Sights: None
Weight: N/A
Caliber: 9mm
Capacity: 21 rounds
Features: A combination of Full Conceal's M3D Glock 19-based pistol and CAA Group's folding-shell Micro-Roni Stabilizer
Gen3: $1249.00
Gen4: $1499.00

GLOCK G17 GEN5 MOS

Action: Semiautomatic
Grips: Polymer
Barrel: 4.49 in
Sights: Drift adjustable rear, post front
Weight: 24.87 oz.
Caliber: 9mm
Capacity: 17, 19, 24, 31, 33 rounds
Features: Fully updated with Gen5 technology, including the Modular Backstrap System, the GLOCK Marksman Barrel, nDLC finish, ambidextrous slide stop, flared mag well and now with the MOS Modular Optics System that allows mounting of multiple electronic red-dot and reflex sights
MSRP $899.00

GLOCK G19 GEN5 MOS

Action: Semiautomatic
Grips: Polymer
Barrel: 4.02 in.
Sights: Drift adjustable rear, post front
Weight: 23.81 in.
Caliber: 9mm
Capacity: 15, 17, 24, 31, 33 rounds
Features: Fully updated with Gen5 technology, including the Modular Backstrap System, the GLOCK Marksman Barrel, nDLC finish, ambidextrous slide stop, flared mag well and now with the MOS Modular Optics System that allows mounting of multiple electronic red-dot and reflex sights
MSRP $899.00

NEW Products: **Handguns**

GLOCK G43X

GLOCK G45

GLOCK G48

IDEAL CONCEAL IC380

KEL-TEC CP33

KIMBER EVO SP (CDP)

KIMBER EVO SP (CS)

KIMBER EVO SP (TLE)

KIMBER EVO SP (TWO-TONE)

GLOCK G43X

Action: Semiautomatic
Grips: Polymer
Barrel: 3.41 in.
Sights: Drift adjustable rear, post front
Weight: 18.7 oz.
Caliber: 9mm
Capacity: 10 rounds
Features: The smaller of two new slimline GLOCK pistols for 2019 intended for CCW practitioners. Features a silver mPVD finish on the slide; forward slide serrations; Gen5 GLOCK Marksman Barrel
MSRP **$459.00**

GLOCK G45

Action: Semiautomatic
Grips: Polymer
Barrel: 4.02 in.
Sights: Drift adjustable rear, post front
Weight: 30.34 oz.
Caliber: 9mm
Capacity: 17, 19, 24, 31, 33 rounds
Features: A second offering in what GLOCK is calling its Crossover pistols. Intended primarily for duty carry, this one combines the slide of the G19 with a full-size G17 frame and adds a non-reflective black hard surface finish
MSRP **$699.00**

GLOCK G48

Action: Semiautomatic
Grips: Polymer
Barrel: 4.17 in.
Sights: Drift adjustable rear, post front
Weight: 20.74 oz.
Caliber: 9mm
Capacity: 10 rounds
Features: The larger of two new slimline GLOCK pistols for 2019 intended for CCW practitioners. Features a silver mPVD finish on the slide; forward slide serrations; Gen5 GLOCK Marksman Barrel
MSRP **$459.00**

IDEAL CONCEAL IC380

Action: Two-shot
Grips: Synthetic
Barrel: N/A
Sights: Ultra-low-profile front blade, raised groove rear
Weight: N/A
Caliber: .380 ACP
Capacity: 2 rounds
Features: A two-shot pistol that folds to look like a cell-phone; one side unfolds to become the grip and provide access to the trigger
MSRP **$575.00**

KEL-TEC CP33

Action: Semiautomatic
Grips: Polymer
Barrel: 5.5 in.
Sights: Adjustable fiber optic
Weight: 24 oz.
Caliber: .22 LR
Capacity: 33 rounds
Features: Loads of target fun with the 33-round double-double-stack magazine; fiber optic adjustable sights; full-length topside rail for optics
MSRP **$475.00**

KIMBER EVO SP (CDP)

Action: Semiautomatic
Grips: G-10
Barrel: 3.16 in.
Sights: Tritium night sights
Weight: 19 oz.
Caliber: 9mm
Capacity: 7 rounds
Features: CDP is Custom Defense Package. Fancier take on the Two-Tone, with the aluminum frame in KimPro Charcoal Gray; FNC Black-finished stainless steel slide; Carry Melt treatment; red/black G10 grips and backstrap with checkering; front strap checkering
MSRP **$949.00**

KIMBER EVO SP (CS)

Action: Semiautomatic
Grips: G-10
Barrel: 3.16 in.
Sights: Tritium night sights
Weight: 18 oz.
Caliber: 9mm
Capacity: 7 rounds
Features: CS is the Custom Shop offering in the EVO line of carry guns, with Stiplex-inspired texturing on the slide, front strap, grips and backstrap; KimPro Charcoal Gray finish on the aluminum frame
MSRP **$1047.00**

KIMBER EVO SP (TLE)

Action: Semiautomatic
Grips: G-10
Barrel: 3.16 in.
Sights: Tritium night sights
Weight: 19 oz.
Caliber: 9mm
Capacity: 7 rounds
Features: The EVO carry gun with KimPro Black finish on the aluminum frame; green/black G10 grips with the unique TLE slant checkering
MSRP **$925.00**

KIMBER EVO SP (TWO-TONE)

Action: Semiautomatic
Grips: Nylon
Barrel: 3.16 in.
Sights: Tritium night sights
Weight: 19 oz.
Caliber: 9mm
Capacity: 7 rounds
Features: Terrific striker-fired CCW pistol featuring an aluminum frame in KimPro Silver finish; stainless steel slide in FNC Black; diamond checkering on grips; bushing-less match-grade barrel; checkered nylon backstrap; front strap checkering
MSRP **$856.00**

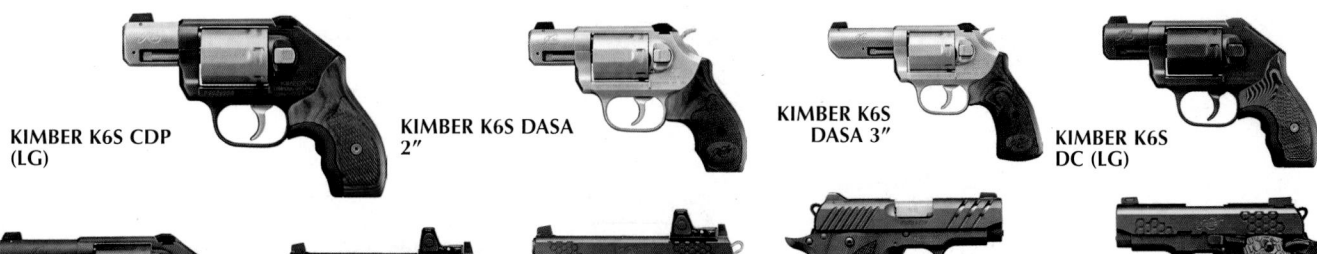

KIMBER K6S CDP (LG)

KIMBER K6S DASA 2"

KIMBER K6S DASA 3"

KIMBER K6S DC (LG)

KIMBER K6S TLE

KIMBER KHX CUSTOM (OI)

KIMBER KHX CUSTOM/RL (OI)

KIMBER MICRO 9 ESV (BLACK)

KIMBER MICRO 9 KHX

KIMBER K6S CDP (LG)

Action: Revolver
Grips: Rosewood
Barrel: 2 in.
Sights: Night sights
Weight: 23 oz.
Caliber: .357 Mag.
Capacity: 6 rounds
Features: CDP is Custom Defense Package, LG is for the Crimson Trace laser grip. Other features include Black DLC over-brush finish on the frame; brushed stainless steel finish on cylinder and barrel; shrouded crane; non-stacking trigger; DAO action
MSRP **$1510.00**

KIMBER K6S DASA 2"

Action: Revolver
Grips: Walnut
Barrel: 2 in.
Sights: White three-dot
Weight: 23 oz.
Caliber: .357 Mag.
Capacity: 6 rounds
Features: Compact powerhouse with Kimber's unique cylinder fluting; boot-style walnut grip; DA/SA exposed hammer; overbrushed stainless finish with minimal engraving; serrated backstrap
MSRP **$949.00**

KIMBER K6S DASA 3"

Action: Revolver
Grips: Walnut
Barrel: 3 in.
Sights: White three-dot
Weight: 25.1 oz.
Caliber: .357 Mag.
Capacity: 6 rounds
Features: The extra inch of barrel also gets you enough grip for a three-finger hold; overbrushed stainless finish with minimal engraving; serrated backstrap
MSRP **$949.00**

KIMBER K6S DC (LG)

Action: Revolver
Grips: G-10
Barrel: 2 in.
Sights: Night sights
Weight: 23 oz.
Caliber: .357 Mag.
Capacity: 6 rounds
Features: A DAO revolver with serrated backstrap; overbrushed black DCL finish; black/gray G-10 Crimson Trace Master Series laser grips
MSRP **$1485.00**

KIMBER K6S TLE (2"), (3")

Action: Revolver
Grips: G-10
Barrel: 2 in.
Sights: Tritium night sights
Weight: 23 oz.
Caliber: .357 Mag.
Capacity: 6 rounds
Features: A DA revolver with an all-over matte black finish; serrated backstrap; green, three-finger G-10 grips with scalloped texturing
MSRP **$999.00**

KIMBER KHX CUSTOM (OI)

Action: Semiautomatic
Grips: G-10
Barrel: 5 in.
Sights: Trijicon RMR red-dot, white-dot co-witness sights
Weight: 38 oz.
Caliber: 9mm, 10mm, .45 ACP
Capacity: 8 rounds
Features: A serious competition or even a home-defense gun, with full-length guide rod; match-grade barrel and bushing; Hogue Magrip G10 panels; aluminum trigger; Trijicon RMR Type 2 red-dot sight with 3.25 MOA dot; co-witness sights; KimPro II Gray finish on frame and slide
MSRP **$1871.00**

KIMBER KHX CUSTOM/RL (OI)

Action: Semiautomatic
Grips: G-10
Barrel: 5 in.
Sights: Trijicon RMR red-dot, white-dot co-witness sights
Weight: 39 oz.
Caliber: 9mm, 10mm, .45 ACP
Capacity: 8 rounds
Features: Similar to the KHX Custom (OI), but with the addition of an under-barrel accessory rail
MSRP **$1967.00**

KIMBER MICRO 9 ESV (BLACK), (GRAY)

Action: Semiautomatic
Grips: G-10
Barrel: 3.15 in.
Sights: Night sights
Weight: 15.35 oz.
Caliber: 9mm
Capacity: 7 rounds
Features: Shaving a couple ounces off the EVO line thanks to slide serrations. Two versions: (Black) has gold Titanium Nitride coating, black Altamont G-10 grips, KimPro II Black slide and frame; (Gray) has Rose Copper coated barrel, black Altamont G-10 grips, KimPro II Gray slide and frame
MSRP **$799.00**

KIMBER MICRO 9 KHX

Action: Semiautomatic
Grips: G-10
Barrel: 3.15 in.
Sights: Red fiber optic front, green fiber optic rear
Weight: 15.6 oz.
Caliber: 9mm
Capacity: 7 rounds
Features: Outstanding features in the CCW pistol include hexagonal dot "serrations" fore and aft on the slide, that pattern repeated in part on the Hogue G-10 grips and backstrap; KimPro II Gray finish on slide and frame
MSRP **$815.00**

NEW Products: Handguns

LES BAER CUSTOM BAER 1911 GUNSITE

MAXIM DEFENSE PDX

LES BAER CUSTOM BAER 1911 KENAI SPECIAL

MOSSBERG MC1SC

LES BAER CUSTOM BAER 1911 PREMIER II HEAVYWEIGHT MONOLITH FRAME

MAGNUM RESEARCH .429 DESERT EAGLE MARK XIX

MAGNUM RESEARCH BFR .500 LINEBAUGH

MOSSBERG MC1SC CENTENNIAL

LES BAER CUSTOM BAER 1911 GUNSITE

Action: Semiautomatic
Grips: Wood
Barrel: 5 in.
Sights: Dovetail tritium front, fixed rear
Weight: N/A
Caliber: .45 ACP
Capacity: 8 rounds
Features: A tribute the legendary Gunsite Academy firearms training center with wood grips bearing the Gunsite logo; serial numbers starting with GAI-; solid match trigger; dehorned; Gunsite logo engraved on slide
MSRP $2255.00

LES BAER CUSTOM BAER 1911 KENAI SPECIAL

Action: Semiautomatic
Grips: Baer Recon
Barrel: 5 in.
Sights: Fiber optic front, low-mount Baer adjustable with hidden leaf rear
Weight: N/A
Caliber: 10mm
Capacity: 9 rounds
Features: Baer jumps into the new-generation 10mm game with all-steel construction; 4-pound speed trigger; beveled mag well; tuned action; checkered high-cut front strap; flat serrated mainspring housing
MSRP $3630.00

LES BAER CUSTOM BAER 1911 PREMIER II HEAVYWEIGHT MONOLITH FRAME

Action: Semiautomatic
Grips: Wood
Barrel: 5 in.
Sights: Dovetail front, low-mount Baer adjustable with hidden leaf rear
Weight: N/A
Caliber: .45 ACP
Capacity: 8 rounds
Features: Unique monolith frame with a flat underside adds 2.8 oz. to normal Government frame weights for

steadier holds, reduced muzzle rise, and improved accuracy; brushed chrome finish; 4-pound Speed trigger; checkered wood Baer logo grips
MSRP $2890.00

LUXURY FIREARMS 7.5 FK FIELD PISTOLS

Action: Semiautomatic
Grips: Aluminum G10
Barrel: 6 in.
Sights: Three-point butterfly
Weight: 44.8 oz.
Caliber: 7.5 FK
Capacity: 16 rounds
Features: Designed for long-distance silhouette and other competitions with the proprietary 7.5 FK cartridge; proprietary recoil attenuating system; streamlined slide, frame, and grip; G10 grips; dark gray nitride finish; SA
MSRP $7500.00

MAGNUM RESEARCH .429 DESERT EAGLE MARK XIX

Action: Semiautomatic
Grips: Soft rubber
Barrel: 6 in.
Sights: Fixed combat type
Weight: 68.3 oz.
Caliber: .429 DE
Capacity: 7 rounds
Features: A new caliber from Magnum Research in a new gun featuring single-action; integral muzzle brake; Picatinny rails topside and under barrel; polygonal rifling with 1:18 twist; stainless finish
MSRP $2143.00

MAGNUM RESEARCH BFR .500 LINEBAUGH

Action: Revolver
Grips: Soft rubber, simulated ivory
Barrel: 5 in., 6.5 in., 7.5 in.
Sights: Fixed ramp front, adjustable rear
Weight: 59 oz.–77.7 oz.
Caliber: .500 Linebaugh
Capacity: 5 rounds
Features: The first production revolver to chamber Linebaugh's famous 500 cartridge, featuring: short cylinder;

unfluted cylinder; brushed stainless finish; optional Bisley grip
MSRP . . . $1399.00 (standard grips);
$1482.00 (Bisley grips)

MAXIM DEFENSE PDX

Action: Semiautomatic
Grips: Aluminum
Barrel: 5.5 in.
Sights: None
Weight: 91 oz.
Caliber: 5.56 NATO, 7.62X29mm NATO
Capacity: N/A
Features: A CQC design featuring Maxim's all-new Heartbrake muzzle "booster"; MD's aluminum SCW stock system with 4-inch length; combo black and Arid tan color finishes; overall length just 18.75 inches
MSRP $2299.00

MOSSBERG MC1SC

Action: Semiautomatic
Grips: Polymer
Barrel: 3.4 in.
Sights: White three-dot
Weight: 19 oz.
Caliber: 9mm
Capacity: 6, 7 rounds
Features: Mossberg's first subcompact striker-fire pistol featuring a button-rifled barrel; front and rear slide serrations; flush-fit six-round magazine; extended seven-round magazine; trigger blade safety; DLC stainless steel slide and barrel finish
MSRP $425.00

MOSSBERG MC1SC CENTENNIAL

Action: Semiautomatic
Grips: Polymer
Barrel: 3.4 in.
Sights: White three-dot
Weight: 19 oz.
Caliber: 9mm
Capacity: 6, 7 rounds
Features: MC1sc with upgraded finishes: slide DLC stainless steel; barrel and guide rod stainless steel and titanium nitride with polished DLC and 24K gold plating; titanium nitride and Cerakote small parts
MSRP $686.00

MOSSBERG MC1SC CROSS-BOLT SAFETY

MOSSBERG MC1SC TRUGLO TRITIUM PRO SIGHTS

MOSSBERG MC1SC VIRIDIAN LASER EQUIPPED

NAROH ARMS N1

NIGHTHAWK CUSTOM AGENT2

NIGHTHAWK CUSTOM CHAIRMAN

NIGHTHAWK CUSTOM FIREHAWK COMPENSATED 1911

NIGHTHAWK CUSTOM HEINIE LADY HAWK 2.0

NIGHTHAWK CUSTOM PRESIDENT

MOSSBERG MC1SC CROSS-BOLT SAFETY

Action: Semiautomatic
Grips: Polymer
Barrel: 3.4 in.
Sights: White three-dot
Weight: 19 oz.
Caliber: 9mm
Capacity: 6, 7 rounds
Features: Same as the base MC1sc but with an additional manual cross-bolt safety
MSRP $425.00

MOSSBERG MC1SC TRUGLO TRITIUM PRO SIGHTS

Action: Semiautomatic
Grips: Polymer
Barrel: 3.4 in.
Sights: TRUGLO Tritium sights
Weight: 19 oz.
Caliber: 9mm
Capacity: 6, 7 rounds
Features: Same as the base MC1sc but with TRUGLO tritium night sights replacing the standard white three-dot sights
MSRP $526.00

MOSSBERG MC1SC VIRIDIAN LASER EQUIPPED

Action: Semiautomatic
Grips: Polymer
Barrel: 3.4 in.
Sights:
Weight: 19 oz.
Caliber: 9mm
Capacity: 6, 7 rounds
Features: Same as the base MC1sc but with the addition of a VIRIDIAN E-Series red laser built into the trigger guard front
MSRP $514.00

NAROH ARMS N1

Action: Semiautomatic
Grips: Polymer
Barrel: 3.13 in.
Sights: Low-profile blade front, low-profile drift adjustable rear
Weight: 16.1 oz.
Caliber: 9mm

Capacity: 8 rounds
Features: A minimalist subcompact DAO striker-fire carry 9mm, the first pistol offered by the company best known for the modernist designs of its hallmark AR accessories
MSRP . . . . N/A

NIGHTHAWK CUSTOM AGENT2

Action: Semiautomatic
Grips: G10
Barrel: 5 in.
Sights: Fiber optic front, Heinie black ledge rear
Weight: 40.1 oz.
Caliber: 9mm, .45 ACP
Capacity: 8, 10 rounds
Features: Match-grade, crowned, flush-cut barrel; Nighthawk/Agency custom trigger; Ultra Hi-Cut front strap; one-piece magwell/mainspring housing; extended and angled magazine release; Agency slide serrations front and aft; Smoke Cerakote finish; Railscales G10 grip
MSRP $4499.00

NIGHTHAWK CUSTOM CHAIRMAN

Action: Semiautomatic
Grips: G10
Barrel: 6 in.
Sights: Gold bead front, adjustable black rear
Weight: 40.9 oz.
Caliber: 9mm, .45 ACP
Capacity: 10 rounds
Features: Long-slide 9mm featuring Nighthawk's aluminum tri-cavity trigger; Ultra Hi-Cut front strap; match-grade crowned barrel; DLC frame/slide finish with cutouts revealing the gold titanium nitride barrel; heavy angle lightning slide cuts; Railscale G10 grips
MSRP $4199.00

NIGHTHAWK CUSTOM FIREHAWK COMPENSATED 1911

Action: Semiautomatic

Grips: Agent 1; G10
Barrel: 5 in.
Sights: Gold bead front, Heinie black slant pro rear
Weight: N/A
Caliber: 9mm, .45 ACP
Capacity: 8, 10 rounds
Features: Government-sized .45 featuring a French border; solid trigger; match-grade barrel; Ultra Hi-Cut front strap; compensator; rear slide serrations only; black finish with Agent 1 grips or stainless with G10 grips
MSRP $4199.00

NIGHTHAWK CUSTOM HEINIE LADY HAWK 2.0

Action: Semiautomatic
Grips: Obsidian; abolone; zinc
Barrel: 4.25 in.
Sights: Tritium front, Heinie straight edge slant pro rear
Weight: 36 oz.
Caliber: 9mm, .45 ACP
Capacity: 8, 10 rounds
Features: Commander frame; match-grade barrel; scalloped front strap and mainspring housing; beveled frame; Nighthawk tri-cavity aluminum trigger; complete dehorning; custom grips in obsidian, abalone, or zinc; DLC frame/slide finish with a rose gold TICN finish on barrel and controls
MSRP $4699.00

NIGHTHAWK CUSTOM PRESIDENT

Action: Semiautomatic
Grips: G10
Barrel: 5 in.
Sights: Gold bead front, Heinie black ledge rear
Weight: 38.2 oz.
Caliber: 9mm
Capacity: 10 rounds
Features: Government frame; Nighthawk tri-cavity trigger; complete dehorning; match-grade crowned barrel; DLC finish with gold titanium nitride barrel; heavy-angle lightning slide cuts; Railscale G10 grips
MSRP $4199.00

NIGHTHAWK CUSTOM THE BULL COMMANDER

NIGHTHAWK CUSTOM TROOPER

NIGHTHAWK CUSTOM VIP BLACK

NORTH AMERICAN ARMS BLACK WIDOW

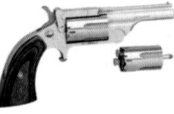

NORTH AMERICAN ARMS RANGER II

NOSLER M48 INDEPENDENCE

PATRIOT ORDNANCE FACTORY RENEGADE, RENEGADE PLUS

REMINGTON MODEL 700 CP

REMINGTON RM380 EXECUTIVE

NIGHTHAWK CUSTOM THE BULL COMMANDER

Action: Semiautomatic
Grips: Carbon fiber
Barrel: 4.25 in., 5 in.
Sights: Tritium front, Heinie Straight Eight tritium ledge rear
Weight: 36.7 oz.
Caliber: .45 ACP
Capacity: 8 rounds
Features: Choice of Government or Commander frames; Nighthawk curved slide stop; coarse rear slide serrations; beveled frame and slide bottom; Nighthawk Bow Tie plug and Bull Nose cut on the front of the slide; French border
MSRP **$3799.00**

NIGHTHAWK CUSTOM TROOPER

Action: Semiautomatic
Grips: G10
Barrel: 5 in.
Sights: Tritium front, Heinie Straight Eight tritium ledge rear
Weight: 37.1 oz.
Caliber: .45 ACP
Capacity: 8 rounds
Features: Government frame; match-grade crowned barrel; Nighthawk tri-cavity trigger; complete dehorning; black nitride finish; Gator Back G10 grips
MSRP **$3199.00**

NIGHTHAWK CUSTOM VIP BLACK

Action: Semiautomatic
Grips: Girrafe bone
Barrel: 5 in.
Sights: Gold bead front, Heinie black slant pro rear
Weight: N/A
Caliber: .45 ACP
Capacity: 8 rounds
Features: Government frame; 14k solid gold front bead sight; giraffe bone grips; hand serrations at rear of slide and at ejection port match the Heinie sight; hand engraving; comes in custom walnut case
MSRP **$7999.00**

NORTH AMERICAN ARMS BLACK WIDOW

Action: Revolver
Grips: Rubber
Barrel: 2 in.
Sights: Marble Arms
Weight: 8.9 oz.
Caliber: .22 Win. Mag.
Capacity: 5 rounds
Features: A short-barreled .22 Win. Mag. with oversized grips to hang onto; SA only; non-fluted cylinder; vent rib
MSRP . . . . **N/A**

NORTH AMERICAN ARMS RANGER II

Action: Revolver
Grips: Rosewood
Barrel: 1.63 in.
Sights: Bead front
Weight: 6.9 oz.
Caliber: .22 Win. Mag.
Capacity: 5 rounds
Features: A bead front helps aim with this new Ranger iteration featuring a rosewood bird's head grip
MSRP . . . . **N/A**

NOSLER M48 INDEPENDENCE

Action: Bolt
Grips: Synthetic
Barrel: 15 in.
Sights: None
Weight: N/A
Caliber: .22 Nosler, .24 Nosler, 6mm Creedmoor, 6.5 Creedmoor, 7mm-08 Rem., .308 Win.
Capacity: 1 round
Features: The bolt handgun comes back to life with a one-piece billet aluminum frame; Nosler's Model 58 short-action; Cerakoted metalwork; bedded action; free-floating barrel
MSRP . . . . **N/A**

PATRIOT ORDNANCE FACTORY RENEGADE, RENEGADE PLUS

Action: Semiautomatic
Grips: Synthetic
Barrel: 10.5 in.
Sights: None
Weight: 5 lb. 13 oz.
Caliber: 5.56 NATO, .300 Blackout
Capacity: 20, 30 rounds
Features: Identical to the company's now discontinued rifle configuration, but in pistol form featuring a nine-inch rail; five-position SB Tactical SBA3 arm brace; M-LOK compatibility; Dictator nine-position gas block; straight gas tube; in black or Burnt Bronze; Plus version gets the additions of the Ultimate Bolt Carrier Group; match-grade trigger; ambidextrous receiver
Black Renegade: **$1499.00**
Burnt Bronze Renegade: . . .**$1599.00**
Black Renegade Plus: **$1899.00**
Burnt Bronze Renegade
    Plus: **$1979.00**

REMINGTON MODEL 700 CP

Action: Bolt
Grips: Synthetic
Barrel: 10.5 in., 12.5 in.
Sights: None
Weight: 5 lb. 15 oz.–6 lb. 3 oz.
Caliber: .300 Blackout, .308 Win., .223 Rem.
Capacity: 10 rounds
Features: CP stands for Chassis Pistol, a new platform for Big Green; short action; top rail; detachable box magazine; rear QD mount; XMARK Pro adjustable trigger; suppressor ready; topside rail; Magpul MIAD pistol grip; M-LOK handguard
MSRP **$1020.00**

REMINGTON RM380 EXECUTIVE

Action: Semiautomatic
Grips: Lamanite Macassar
Barrel: 2.75 in.
Sights: Integral
Weight: 12.2 oz.
Caliber: .380 ACP
Capacity: 6 rounds
Features: A handsome micro-carry with a brushed stainless slide; anodized black frame; low-profile integral sights
MSRP **$405.00**

REMINGTON RM380 MICRO CRIMSON TRACE

REMINGTON RM380 MICRO LIGHT BLUE

REMINGTON RM380 MICRO BLUE/SILVER

REPUBLIC FORGE ULTIMATE COMPETITION 1911

REPUBLIC FORGE ULTIMATE ENGRAVED COMMANDER

ROCK RIVER ARMS LAR-15 7-INCH PISTOL WITH SBA3 ARM BRACE

ROCK RIVER ARMS LAR-22 RRAGE 7-INCH PISTOL WITH SBX-K BRACE

ROCK RIVER ARMS LAR-9 7-INCH PISTOL WITH SBX-K ARM BRACE

REMINGTON RM380 MICRO CRIMSON TRACE

Action: Semiautomatic
Grips: Nylon
Barrel: 2.9 in.
Sights: Integral
Weight: 12.2 oz.
Caliber: .380 ACP
Capacity: 6 rounds
Features: The popular micro carry pistol with a front trigger guard-mounted touch-button Crimson Trace red laser; anodized finish
MSRP **$638.00**

REMINGTON RM380 MICRO LIGHT BLUE

Action: Semiautomatic
Grips: Nylon
Barrel: 2.9 in.
Sights: Integral
Weight: 12.2 oz.
Caliber: .380 ACP
Capacity: 6 rounds
Features: Tiny and slim in a "Tiffany"-type light blue frame; choice of matte blue finish or stainless Cerakote
Blue: **$348.00**
Stainless Cerakote: **$415.00**

REMINGTON RM380 MICRO BLUE/SILVER

Action: Semiautomatic
Grips: Nylon
Barrel: 2.9 in.
Sights: Integral
Weight: 12.2 oz.
Caliber: .380 ACP
Capacity: 6 rounds
Features: Anodized electric blue frame and silver slide
MSRP **$348.00**

REPUBLIC FORGE ULTIMATE COMPETITION 1911

Action: Semiautomatic

Grips: Aluminum; stainless steel
Barrel: 5 in.
Sights: Fiber optic front, adjustable rear
Weight: 40.6 oz.
Caliber: 9mm, .38 Super, .40 S&W, .45 ACP
Capacity: 8, 9 rounds
Features: A ready to win race gun featuring a forged high carbon steel frame; tri-top slide; custom textured grip modules in choice of aluminum or stainless steel; pinned grip safety; Altec competition extractor; Dawson magwell; extended mag release;
MSRP **$4295.00**

REPUBLIC FORGE ULTIMATE ENGRAVED COMMANDER

Action: Semiautomatic
Grips: Mammoth tusk
Barrel: 4.25 in.
Sights: Blade front, drift adjustable rear
Weight: 35.5 oz.
Caliber: 9mm, .38 Super, .40 S&W, .45 ACP
Capacity: 8, 9 rounds
Features: Super high-grade Commander-size 1911 with full-coverage Level D Republic Forge hand engraving; forged high carbon steel frame and slide; case-colored frame; deep blue finished slide; nitrite blue Texas star hammer and other controls; Aftec competition extractor; hand-fitted components; mammoth tusk grips
MSRP **$13250.00**

ROCK RIVER ARMS LAR-9 7-INCH PISTOL WITH SBA3 ARM BRACE

Action: Semiautomatic
Grips: Synthetic
Barrel: 7 in.
Sights: None

Weight: 5 lb. 6 oz.
Caliber: 9mm
Capacity: N/A
Features: Tons of 9mm fun in a rifle featuring an extruded aluminum upper; billet aluminum lower with integral winter trigger guard; flared mag well takes Glock magazines; SBA3 five-position arm brace; two-stage trigger; A2 flash hider with ½X28 threads
MSRP **$1250.00**

ROCK RIVER ARMS LAR-15 RRAGE 7-INCH PISTOL WITH SBX-K BRACE

Action: Semiautomatic
Grips: Synthetic
Barrel: 7 in.
Sights: None
Weight: 4 lb. 13 oz.
Caliber: 5.56mm NATO/.223 Rem.
Capacity: 20 rounds
Features: Featuring a low-profile gas block; A2 pistol grip; A2 flash hider; single-stage trigger; free-floating aluminum M-LOK-compatible handguard; SBX-K stabilizing arm brace; long A2 flash hider
MSRP **$885.00**

ROCK RIVER ARMS LAR-22 7-INCH PISTOL WITH SBX-K ARM BRACE

Action: Semiautomatic
Grips: Synthetic; poly
Barrel: 7 in.
Sights: None
Weight: 3 lb. 13 oz.
Caliber: .22 LR
Capacity: N/A
Features: Super-fun rimfire featuring an A2 flash hider with ½X28 threads; two-stage trigger; chrome-moly barrel; SBX-K arm brace; six-inch free-floating M-LOK handguard; choice of poly or forged aluminum receiver
Poly: **$570.00**
Aluminum: **$660.00**

RUGER CUSTOM SHOP SR1911 COMPETITION

RUGER GP100 MATCH CHAMPION 10MM

RUGER LCP II EXTENDED MAGAZINE

RUGER LCRX 3-INCH .357 MAG.

RUGER MARK IV 22/45 LIT WITH BLACK ANODIZED UPPER AND GOLD THREADED BARREL

RUGER MARK IV 22/45 LITE WITH DIAMOND GRAY ANODIZED FINISH, TARGET LAMINATE GRIPS

RUGER MARK IV 22/45 LITE WITH GOLD ANODIZED UPPER AND BLACK THREADED BARREL

RUGER SECURITY-9 WITH VIRIDIAN E-SERIES LASER

RUGER CUSTOM SHOP SR1911 COMPETITION

Action: Semiautomatic
Grips: Hogue Piranha G10
Barrel: 5 in.
Sights: Adjustable target rear, fiber optic front
Weight: 41 oz.
Caliber: 9mm
Capacity: 11 rounds
Features: Designed in conjunction with champion action shooter Doug Koenig. This pistol's numerous features include hand-fitted slide and frame; match-grade trigger; Koenig Shooting Sports sear and low-mass hammer; ambidextrous mag release; competition barrel with polished ramp target crown and special 1:6 twist; black nitrided stainless frame; front-strap and mainspring housing 25 lpi checkering; undercut trigger guard; and extended mag release; comes with a waterproof case and two 10-round competition mags
MSRP **$2499.00**

RUGER GP100 MATCH CHAMPION 10MM

Action: Revolver
Grips: Hardwood
Barrel: 4.2 in.
Sights: Adjustable rear, fiber optic front
Weight: 37 oz.
Caliber: 10mm
Capacity: 6 rounds
Features: The 10mm truly must be making a comeback if Ruger's housing it in its venerable GP100. Features include stippled hardwood grips by Hogue; half-lug; polished internals with centering boss on trigger and centering shims on hammer trigger; target crown; three half-moon clips included
MSRP **$969.00**

RUGER LCP II EXTENDED MAGAZINE

Action: Semiautomatic
Grips: Glass-filled nylon
Barrel: 2.75 in.
Sights: Integral
Weight: 11 oz.

Caliber: .380 ACP
Capacity: 8 rounds
Features: This handy little CCW .380 keeps you in the game with a seven-round extended magazine that also offers a little extra grip purchase. Comes with a pocket holster. Note: Ruger states that 7-round LCP magazines are not compatible with this LCP II firearm.
MSRP **$399.00**

RUGER LCRX 3-INCH .357 MAG.

Action: Revolver
Grips: Hogue Tamer Monogrip
Barrel: 3 in.
Sights: Pinned front ramp, adjustable blade rear
Weight: 21.3 oz.
Caliber: .357 Mag.
Capacity: 5 rounds
Features: A little extra barrel and the longer Hogue Tamer grip make handling the .357 Mag. in a carry gun more manageable
MSRP **$669.00**

RUGER MARK IV 22/45 LITE WITH BLACK ANODIZED UPPER AND GOLD THREADED BARREL

Action: Semiautomatic
Grips: Checkered 1911-style
Barrel: 4.4 in.
Sights: Adjustable rear, fixed front
Weight: 25 oz.
Caliber: .22 LR
Capacity: 10 rounds
Features: A sleek black finish is complemented by the sight here and there of the gold-finished barrel threaded for suppressor; Picatinny topside rail is standard
MSRP **$559.00**

RUGER MARK IV 22/45 LITE WITH DIAMOND GRAY ANODIZED FINISH, TARGET LAMINATE GRIPS

Action: Semiautomatic
Grips: Laminate

Barrel: 4.4 in.
Sights: Adjustable rear, fixed front
Weight: 27 oz.
Caliber: .22 LR
Capacity: 10 rounds
Features: Updated take on a favorite target pistol with features that include: one-button takedown; polymer frame; laminate grips with target finger grooves; aluminum receiver; ambidextrous safety; drop-free magazine; magazine disconnect; Diamond Gray anodized finish; comes with two magazines
MSRP **$599.00**

RUGER MARK IV 22/45 LITE WITH GOLD ANODIZED UPPER AND BLACK THREADED BARREL

Action: Semiautomatic
Grips: Checkered 1911-style
Barrel: 4.4 in.
Sights: Adjustable rear, fixed front
Weight: 25 oz.
Caliber: .22 LR
Capacity: 10 rounds
Features: A flashy and fun target pistol with a Gold anodized aluminum receiver; polymer frame with black, checkered 1911-style grips; threaded barrel
MSRP **$559.00**

RUGER SECURITY-9 WITH VIRIDIAN E-SERIES LASER

Action: Semiautomatic
Grips: Glass-filled nylon
Barrel: 4 in.
Sights: Dovetailed high-visibility
Weight: 24.3 oz.
Caliber: 9mm
Capacity: 16 rounds
Features: A nice, lightweight carry gun with a built-in red laser from Viridian that adds all of a half-ounce (with battery). Other features include hard-coated aluminum chassis; full-length rails; drift-adjustable rear sight; bladed trigger safety
MSRP **$439.00**

RUGER SP101 WITH BLUED ALLOY STEEL FINISH

RUGER SR1911 OFFICER-STYLE .45 ACP

SIG SAUER 1911 SPARTAN II

SIG SAUER MCX RATTLER CANEBRAKE 5 .5-INCH

SIG SAUER MPX COPPERHEAD

SIG SAUER P238 LEGION MICRO COMPACT

SIG SAUER MPX K TACOPS

SHADOW SYSTEMS MR918 COMBAT

SHADOW SYSTEMS MR918 ELITE

RUGER SP101 WITH BLUED ALLOY STEEL FINISH

Action: Revolver
Grips: Cushioned rubber, engraved wood
Barrel: 2.25 in.
Sights: Integral rear, black ramp front
Weight: 26 oz.
Caliber: .357 Mag.
Capacity: 5 rounds
Features: A lightweight CCW option in the powerful .357 Mag round; prominent feature is the unexposed backstrap, which improves shooter comfort.
MSRP **$719.00**

RUGER SR1911 OFFICER-STYLE .45 ACP

Action: Semiautomatic
Grips: G-10
Barrel: 3.6 in.
Sights: Novak three-dot
Weight: 31 oz.
Caliber: .45 ACP
Capacity: 8 rounds
Features: A sleek carry 1911-style pistol featuring: skeletonized hammer and trigger; round mainspring housing; oversized beavertail grip safety; oversized ejection port; comes with two seven-round magazines; accepts other 1911 magazines, parts and accessories
MSRP **$979.00**

SHADOW SYSTEMS MR918 COMBAT

Action: Semiautomatic
Grips: Polymer
Barrel: 4 in.
Sights: Green tritium outline front, black rear
Weight: N/A
Caliber: 9mm
Capacity: 15 rounds
Features: This company has been making Glock parts and accessories for years, but this is its first production pistol; modeled on the G19 but designed to reduce recoil and muzzle rise; interchangeable grip backstraps; magwell extension for easier reloads;

flat-faced trigger; spiral-fluted barrel in bronze or black; slide is thinned, has front and rear serrations, and can be ordered with an optic cutout
MSRP . . . . **$799.00–$849.00**

SHADOW SYSTEMS MR918 ELITE

Action: Semiautomatic
Grips: Polymer
Barrel: 4 in.
Sights: Green tritium outline front, black rear
Weight: N/A
Caliber: 9mm
Capacity: 15 rounds
Features: Similar to the Combat and with a textured frame of the company's own design; bronze spiral-fluted barrel with conventional rifling; enhanced extractor; optional threaded barrel
MSRP . . . . **$899.00–$959.00**

SIG SAUER 1911 SPARTAN II

Action: Semiautomatic
Grips: SIG Spartan II
Barrel: 4.2 in.
Sights: SIGLITE night sights
Weight: 38.8 oz.
Caliber: .45 ACP
Capacity: 8 rounds
Features: The SA 1911 with updated Spartan cosmetics in a distressed Coyote Tan finish over stainless steel slide and frame; new grip look; MOLON LABE engraved on the slide; under rail; ambi safety
MSRP **$1359.00**

SIG SAUER MCX RATTLER CANEBRAKE 5.5-INCH

Action: Semiautomatic
Grips: PCB
Barrel: 5.5 in.
Sights: None
Weight: 6 lb. 8 oz.
Caliber: .300 Blackout
Capacity: 30 rounds
Features: NFA firearm comes with an inert training device so new owners can head to the range while paperwork clears the feds; suppressor ready; SD handguard; flat, two-stage match trigger; folding PCB brace in

Coyote tan; upper and lower in Cerakote E190
MSRP **$2700.00**

SIG SAUER MPX COPPERHEAD

Action: Semiautomatic
Grips: Synthetic
Barrel: 3.5 in.
Sights: None
Weight: 72 oz.
Caliber: 9mm
Capacity: 30 rounds
Features: A barrel of fun in an uber-small package featuring a monolithic upper; barrel with flared flash hider; two-position Pivoting Contour Brace; completely ambidextrous controls; short-stroke gas piston; fully close bolt firing operation; Elite Series Cerakote finish in an eye-catching FDE
MSRP **$1835.00**

SIG SAUER MPX K TACOPS

Action: Semiautomatic
Grips: Synthetic
Barrel: 4.5 in.
Sights: None
Weight: 96 oz.
Caliber: 9mm
Capacity: 30 rounds
Features: Semiauto take on the submachine gun featuring a dual-side selector switch, magazine release, charging handle, and bolt; full-length Picatinny rail; free-floating eight-inch Keymod handguard; three-position telescoping brace; operation from a fully closed bolt
MSRP **$2298.00**

SIG SAUER P238 LEGION MICRO COMPACT

Action: Semiautomatic
Grips: G-10
Barrel: 2.7 in.
Sights: XRAY3 day/night sights
Weight: 15.2 oz.
Caliber: .380 ACP
Capacity: 7 rounds
Features: A tiny handful of .380 with an upgraded aluminum trigger; black G-10 grips with Legion medallion; ambi safety; Cerakote Elite finish; extended mag well
MSRP **$850.00**

NEW Products: Handguns

SIG SAUER P320 LIMA COMPACT

SIG SAUER P320 M17

SIG SAUER P320 M17 BRAVO

SIG SAUER P320 XCOMPACT

SIG SAUER P365

SIG SAUER P938 LEGION

SIG SAUER P938 SPARTAN II

SMITH & WESSON M&P 45 SHIELD M2.0 WITH CRIMSON TRACE GREEN LASER, RED LASER

SMITH & WESSON M&P 9 M2.0 4-INCH COMPACT WITH CRIMSON TRACE RAIL MASTER UNIVERSAL TACTICAL LIGHT

SIG SAUER P320 LIMA COMPACT

Action: Semiautomatic
Grips: Polymer
Barrel: 3.9 in.
Sights: Contrast; night sights
Weight: 27.8 oz.
Caliber: 9mm
Capacity: 15 rounds
Features: Concealed carry striker-fired pistol featuring the LIMA grip module with a built-in laser; striker and disconnect safety; modular grip; available with contrast or SIGLITE night sights; Nitron finish over stainless steel; M1913 rail
Contrast sights: **$884.00**
SIGLITE night sights: **$952.00**

SIG SAUER P320 M17

Action: Semiautomatic
Grips: Polymer
Barrel: 4.7 in.
Sights: Night sight rear plate, SIGLITE front
Weight: 29.6 oz.
Caliber: 9mm
Capacity: 17 rounds
Features: Recently awarded the MHS--Modular Handgun Contract--from the U.S. Army, this striker-fired mil-spec pistol is now available to the public. Features include optics-ready PVD0-coated slide in Coyote tan; removeable night sight plate; available with or without manual safety; carry-length Coyote grip module
MSRP **$768.00**

SIG SAUER P320 M17 BRAVO

Action: Semiautomatic
Grips: Polymer
Barrel: 4.7 in.
Sights: SIGLITE night sights
Weight: 29.6 oz.
Caliber: 9mm
Capacity: 17 rounds
Features: Similar to the FDE M17, but with in black Nitride and with a black carry-length grip module in three sizes; manual safety; removeable rear sight; optic plate cutout per military Modular Handgun System contract
MSRP **$768.00**

SIG SAUER P320 XCOMPACT

Action: Semiautomatic
Grips: Polymer
Barrel: 3.6 in.
Sights: XRAY3 day/night sights
Weight: 25.3 oz.
Caliber: 9mm
Capacity: 15 rounds
Features: A concealable pistol with stainless steel frame and slide with a black Nitron finish; carbon steel barrel; striker-fired; modular grip panels; compatible with SIG's ROMEO1PRO reflex sight; M1913 rail
MSRP **$804.00**

SIG SAUER P365

Action: Semiautomatic
Grips: Polymer
Barrel: 3.1 in.
Sights: XRAY3 day/night sights
Weight: 17.8 oz.
Caliber: 9mm
Capacity: 10 rounds
Features: This tiny 9mm manages to cram ten rounds into its flush-fit magazine; Nitron-finished stainless steel slide; striker-fired; optional twelve-round mag available
MSRP **$599.99**

SIG SAUER P938 LEGION

Action: Semiautomatic
Grips: Polymer
Barrel: 3 in.
Sights: XRAY3 day/night sights
Weight: 17 oz.
Caliber: 9mm
Capacity: 7 rounds
Features: The smallest of the smallest 9mms in a SAO platform with seven-round magazine; Legion Gray Cerakote finish; front and rear cocking serrations on slide; extended mag well
MSRP **$904.00**

SIG SAUER P938 SPARTAN II

Action: Semiautomatic
Grips: Polymer
Barrel: 3 in.
Sights: XRAY3 day/night sights
Weight: 17 oz.
Caliber: 9mm
Capacity: 7 rounds
Features: As with the other P938s, but with the distressed Coyote Elite Cerakote finish and updated Spartan insignia grips
MSRP **$815.00**

SMITH & WESSON M&P 9 M2.0 4-INCH COMPACT WITH CRIMSON TRACE RAIL MASTER UNIVERSAL TACTICAL LIGHT

Action: Semiautomatic
Grips: Polymer
Barrel: 4 in.
Sights: Steel three dot
Weight: 31 oz.
Caliber: 9mm
Capacity: 15 rounds
Features: Good for games or personal protection, this pistol features an extended stainless steel chassis; four interchangeable grip inserts; aggressive grip texturing; Armonite metalwork finish; built-in under rail-mounted Crimson Trace tactical light
MSRP **$629.00**

SMITH & WESSON M&P 45 SHIELD M2.0 WITH CRIMSON TRACE GREEN LASER, RED LASER

Action: Semiautomatic
Grips: Polymer
Barrel: 3.3 in.
Sights: Steel three dot
Weight: 23.1 oz.
Caliber: .45 ACP
Capacity: 6, 7 rounds
Features: A lightweight carry gun in .45 ACP featuring a built-in Crimson Trace laser in choice of red or green; improved trigger; Armonite finish on metalwork; available with or without manual thumb safety
Red laser: **$549.00**
Green laser: **$499.00**

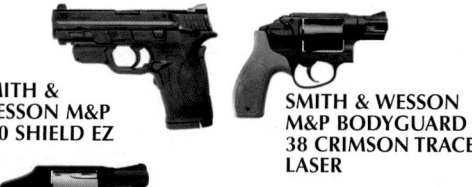

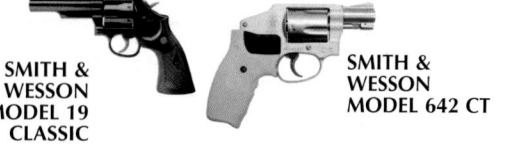

SMITH & WESSON M&P 380 SHIELD EZ

SMITH & WESSON M&P BODYGUARD 38 CRIMSON TRACE LASER

SMITH & WESSON MODEL 19 CLASSIC

SMITH & WESSON MODEL 642 CT

SMITH & WESSON PERFORMANCE CENTER MODEL 19 CARRY COMP

SMITH & WESSON PERFORMANCE CENTER MODEL 442 CRIMSON TRACE LG 105

SMITH & WESSON PERFORMANCE CENTER SW22 VICTORY TARGET MODEL 6-INCH CARBON FIBER BARREL

SMITH & WESSON PERFORMANCE CENTER SW22 VICTORY TARGET MODEL FIBER OPTIC SIGHTS

SMITH & WESSON M&P 380 SHIELD EZ

Action: Semiautomatic
Grips: Polymer
Barrel: 3.675 in.
Sights: Fixed white-dot front, adjustable white-dot rear
Weight: 18.5 o.
Caliber: .380 ACP
Capacity: 8 rounds
Features: An EDC pistol featuring a grip safety; drift adjustable rear sight; under rail; tactile loaded chamber indicator; metalwork including barrel Armonite finished; internal hammer fired; available with or without thumb safety
MSRP **$399.00**

SMITH & WESSON M&P BODYGUARD 38 CRIMSON TRACE LASER

Action: Revolver
Grips: Polymer
Barrel: 1.875 in.
Sights: Black ramp front, groove rear
Weight: 14.4 oz.
Caliber: .38 Spec.
Capacity: 5 rounds
Features: Lightweight snubby carry gun with an aluminum alloy frame; gray polymer grips; top-frame mounted red Crimson Trace laser; PVD coated stainless steel cylinder; ambidextrous cylinder release; DA only
MSRP **$539.00**

SMITH & WESSON MODEL 19 CLASSIC

Action: Revolver
Grips: Wood
Barrel: 4.25 in.
Sights: Red ramp front, adjustable black blade rear
Weight: 37.2 oz.
Caliber: .357 Mag.
Capacity: 6 rounds
Features: A true classic is back in S&W's lineup, featuring a high-polished blue finish; traditional thumbpiece; half-lug; carbon steel frame and cylinder; checkered custom wood grips with S&W silver medallion
MSRP **$826.00**

SMITH & WESSON MODEL 642 CT

Action: Revolver
Grips: Crimson Trace
Barrel: 1.875 in.
Sights: Ramp front, groove rear
Weight: 15.5 oz.
Caliber: .38 Spec.
Capacity: 5 rounds
Features: Part of the Airweight family and +P rated, featuring a Crimson Trace laser grips in Robin's Egg blue; concealed hammer DAO; brushed stainless steel finish
MSRP **$699.00**

SMITH & WESSON PERFORMANCE CENTER MODEL 19 CARRY COMP

Action: Revolver
Grips: Wood/synthetic
Barrel: 3 in.
Sights: Tritium ramp front, adjustable black blade rear
Weight: 34.1 oz.
Caliber: .357 Mag.
Capacity: 6 rounds
Features: The return of the 19K Comp but in a Performance Center iteration featuring a carbon steel frame and cylinder; stainless steel Power Port vented barrel; tritium front sight; PC-tuned action; custom grips of wood and synthetic materials; trigger overtravel stop
MSRP **$1092.00**

SMITH & WESSON PERFORMANCE CENTER MODEL 442 CRIMSON TRACE LG 105

Action: Revolver
Grips: Crimson Trace
Barrel: 1.875 in.
Sights: Ramp front, groove rear, Crimson Trace red laser
Weight: 15 oz.
Caliber: .38 Spec.
Capacity: 5 rounds
Features: Concealed hammer DA only revolver with high-polished parts, including cylinder flutes; carbon steel cylinder in stainless finish; aluminum alloy frame in matte black finish; Crimson Trace LG 105 red laser grips; +P rated; Performance Center tuned action; no internal lock
MSRP **$742.00**

SMITH & WESSON PERFORMANCE CENTER SW22 VICTORY TARGET MODEL 6-INCH CARBON FIBER BARREL

Action: Semiautomatic
Grips: Tandemkross hiveGrip
Barrel: 6 in.
Sights: None
Weight: 33.1 oz.
Caliber: .22 LR
Capacity: 10 rounds
Features: An optics-ready target pistol with carbon fiber barrel; custom muzzle brake; Tandemkross hiveGrip with target thumb rest and texturing; top-side optics rail; flat face trigger; stainless steel frame; extended mag release; adjustable trigger stop
MSRP **$672.00**

SMITH & WESSON PERFORMANCE CENTER SW22 VICTORY TARGET MODEL FIBER OPTIC SIGHTS

Action: Semiautomatic
Grips: Tandemkross hiveGrip
Barrel: 6 in.
Sights: Adjustable fiber optic
Weight: 38.2 oz.
Caliber: .22 LR
Capacity: 10 rounds
Features: One for rimfire match competition, featuring a fluted target barrel; Tandemkross hiveGrip with thumb rest and texturing; flat face trigger; adjustable trigger stop; beveled magazine well; fiber optic sights with adjustable rear; custom muzzle break; Picatinny rail; stainless steel frame and barrel
MSRP **$672.00**

NEW Products: Handguns

SPRINGFIELD ARMORY 1911 RANGE OFFICER ELITE OPERATOR 10MM

SPRINGFIELD ARMORY 1911 TRP 10MM RMR

SPRINGFIELD ARMORY 911 .380 ALPHA

SPRINGFIELD ARMORY 911 9MM

SPRINGFIELD ARMORY PROFESSIONAL MODEL 1911-A1 9M

SPRINGFIELD ARMORY XD-E 3.8-INCH SINGLE STACK

SPRINGFIELD ARMORY XD-E 4.5-INCH SINGLE-STACK

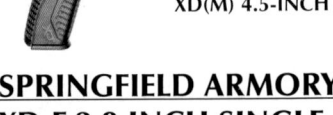

SPRINGFIELD ARMORY XD(M) 4.5-INCH 10MM

SPRINGFIELD ARMORY 911 .380 ALPHA

Action: Semiautomatic
Grips: Polymer
Barrel: 2.7 in.
Sights: Fiber optic front, white-dot rear
Weight: 12.6 oz.
Caliber: .380 ACP
Capacity: 6 rounds
Features: Pocket-worthy, value-priced CCW .380 featuring a hard anodized coated aluminum frame; full-length guide rod; loaded chamber indicator; choice of black nitride finish or stainless steel slide
MSRP $429.00

SPRINGFIELD ARMORY 911 9MM

Action: Semiautomatic
Grips: G10
Barrel: 3 in.
Sights: Pro-Glo tritium front, white outline tritium rear
Weight: 15.3 oz.
Caliber: 9mm
Capacity: 6, 7 rounds
Features: Tiny 9mm CCW pistol with rear slide serrations; tritium night sights; hard coat anodized aluminum frame with Octo-Grip texturing; one flush, one extended magazine; five finish/grip options: black nitride/green G10; stainless/gray G10; black nitride/Hogue wraparound; stainless/Viridian green laser; black nitride/Viridian green laser
Hogue grips: $639.00
G10 grips: $639.00
Viridian laser grips: $849.00

SPRINGFIELD ARMORY 1911 RANGE OFFICER ELITE OPERATOR 10MM

Action: Semiautomatic
Grips: G10
Barrel: 5 in.
Sights: Fiber optic front, white-dot rear
Weight: 41 oz.
Caliber: 10mm
Capacity: 8 rounds
Features: Helping the 10mm resurrection with a GI-style 18.5-pound recoil system; Tactical Rack rear sight; forged steel frame in a black T-finish; ambidextrous safety; under rail; thin-line blue-gray/black G10 grips
MSRP $1145.00

SPRINGFIELD ARMORY 1911 TRP 10MM RMR

Action: Semiautomatic
Grips: G10
Barrel: 5, 6 in.
Sights: Night sights, Trijicon RMR red-dot
Weight: 44 oz., 50 oz.
Caliber: 10mm
Capacity: 8 rounds
Features: A super 10mm competition pistol featuring a forged steel frame 16-pound GI-style recoil spring; match-grade barrel with fully supported ramp; two magazines with slam pads; factory installed Trijicon RMR reflex red-dot sight; 5-inch barrel in all-over black T-finish; 6-inch barrel with a combination black T/OD Green finish
MSRP . . . . $2239.00–$2289.00

SPRINGFIELD ARMORY PROFESSIONAL MODEL 1911-A1 9MM

Action: Semiautomatic
Grips: Cocobolo
Barrel: 6 in.
Sights: Post front; low-mount Novak rear
Weight: N/A
Caliber: 9mm
Capacity: 9 rounds
Features: A competition gun for the minor power factor crowd, featuring a National Match frame, barrel, and bushing; polished feed ramp; fully throated barrel; tuned extractor; lowered ejection port; custom fit one-piece billet mag well; Carry Bevel all-over treatment; black T-finish; checkered cocobolo grips; ambidextrous thumb safety; available with or without rail; six magazines; custom carry case
MSRP $3295.00
Rail: $3395.00

SPRINGFIELD ARMORY XD-E 3.8-INCH SINGLE STACK

Action: Semiautomatic
Grips: Polymer
Barrel: 3.8 in.
Sights: Fiber optic front, white-dot rear
Weight: 24 oz.
Caliber: 9mm
Capacity: 8, 9 rounds
Features: The middle-sized version of the three in this series makes a super carry gun featuring a thumb safety/decocker; dual captive recoil spring; full-length guide rod; forged steel slide with Melonite finish; DA/SA; nine-round mag is extended
MSRP $542.00

SPRINGFIELD ARMORY XD-E 4.5-INCH SINGLE-STACK

Action: Semiautomatic
Grips: Polymer
Barrel: 4.5 in.
Sights: Fiber optic front, white-dot rear
Weight: 25 oz.
Caliber: 9mm
Capacity: 8, 9 rounds
Features: A medium-sized DA/SA pistol with thumb safety/decocker; improved grip texturing; forged steel slide with Melonite finish; one-piece full-length guide rod; nine-round mag is extended
MSRP $542.00

SPRINGFIELD ARMORY XD(M) 4.5-INCH 10MM

Action: Semiautomatic
Grips: Polymer
Barrel: 4.5 in.
Sights: Fiber optic front, low-profile rear; fiber optic front, adjustable rear
Weight: 31.2 oz.
Caliber: 10mm
Capacity: 15 rounds
Features: A full-sized, double-stack breathing life back into the 10mm and featuring interchangeable backstraps; forged steel slide and barrel with Melonite finish; two magazines; full-length guide rod; under rail
MSRP $652.00

SPRINGFIELD ARMORY
XD(M) 5.25-INCH 10MM
(COMPETITION SERIES)

SPRINGFIELD ARMORY
XD(M) OSP WITH
THREADED BARREL

SPRINGFIELD
ARMORY XD-S
MOD.2 9MM

STANDARD
MANUFACTURING
CO. S333
VOLLEYFIRE

STEYR A2 MF

STANDARD
MANUFACTURING
CO. SINGLE ACTION
REVOLVER NICKEL PLATED

STANDARD MANUFACTURING
CO. SINGLE ACTION REVOLVER
NICKEL PLATED C-COVERAGE
ENGRAVING

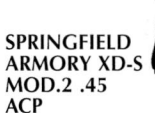

SPRINGFIELD
ARMORY XD-S
MOD.2 .45
ACP

STI
INTERNATIONAL
STACCATO C

SPRINGFIELD ARMORY XD(M) 5.25-INCH 10MM (COMPETITION SERIES)

Action: Semiautomatic
Grips: Polymer
Barrel: 5.25 in.
Sights: Fiber optic front, adjustable target rear
Weight: 32.8 oz.
Caliber: 10mm
Capacity: 15 rounds
Features: Go big or go home with this competition-ready 10mm featuring interchangeable backstrap; under rail; fully adjustable rear sight; three fifteen-round magazines
MSRP **$779.00**

SPRINGFIELD ARMORY XD(M) OSP WITH THREADED BARREL

Action: Semiautomatic
Grips: Polymer
Barrel: 4.5 in., 5.3 in.
Sights: Suppressor height
Weight: 28.8 oz.
Caliber: 9mm
Capacity: 19 rounds
Features: Two times the fun with a 4.5-inch non-threaded barrel and 5.3-inch threaded barrel with thread protector; co-witness suppressor-height sights; in all-over black, Flat Dark Earth, or black with Vortex Venom red-dot sight
MSRP **$710.00**
Vortex Venom sight: **$958.00**

SPRINGFIELD ARMORY XD-S MOD.2 9MM

Action: Semiautomatic
Grips: Polymer
Barrel: 3.3 in.
Sights: Fiber optic front; drift-adjustable steel rear
Weight: 23 oz.
Caliber: 9mm
Capacity: 7, 8 rounds
Features: A CCW gun featuring a dual-spring full-length guide rod; aggressive grip texturing; seven-round flush-fit mag; eight-round mag with Mid-Mag X-Tension
MSRP **$499.00**

SPRINGFIELD ARMORY XD-S MOD.2 .45 ACP

Action: Semiautomatic
Grips: Polymer
Barrel: 3.3 in.
Sights: Fiber optic front; drift-adjustable steel rear
Weight: 21.5 oz.
Caliber: .45 ACP
Capacity: 5 rounds
Features: Similar to the 9mm, but a an ounce and a half lighter; one flush-fit mag supplied
MSRP **$549.00**

STANDARD MANUFACTURING CO. S333 VOLLEYFIRE

Action: Revolver
Grips: Polymer
Barrel: 1.25 in.
Sights: Ramp front, integral raised groove rear
Weight: N/A
Caliber: .22 Win. Mag.
Capacity: 8 rounds
Features: Interesting double-barrel revolver; each pull of the trigger fires two shots simultaneously; DAO
MSRP **$369.00**

STANDARD MANUFACTURING CO. SINGLE ACTION REVOLVER NICKEL PLATED

Action: Revolver
Grips: Walnut
Barrel: 4.75 in., 5.5 in., 7.5 in.
Sights: Blade front, groove rear
Weight: 40 oz.
Caliber: .45 LC
Capacity: 6 rounds
Features: A solid 4140 steel SA revolver with one- or two-piece figured walnut grips; full nickel-plating with fire-blued screws and pins
MSRP **$1995.00**

STANDARD MANUFACTURING CO. SINGLE ACTION REVOLVER NICKEL PLATED C-COVERAGE ENGRAVING

Action: Revolver
Grips: Walnut
Barrel: 4.75 in., 5.5 in., 7.5 in.
Sights: Blade front, groove rear
Weight: 40 oz.
Caliber: .45 LC
Capacity: 6 rounds
Features: Similar to Standard's full nickel-plated SA, but with 75% scroll engraving on frame, barrel, and cylinder; two-piece grip only
MSRP **$3495.00**

STEYR A2 MF

Action: Semiautomatic
Grips: Polymer
Barrel: 4.5 in.
Sights: Trapezoid
Weight: 27 oz.
Caliber: 9mm
Capacity: 10, 17 rounds
Features: MF stands for Modular Frame, which features interchangeable, textured backstraps and grips; trigger, drop, indirect firing pin safeties and manual lock; 5-pound trigger; under rail
MSRP **$675.00**

STI INTERNATIONAL STACCATO C

Action: Semiautomatic
Grips: Aluminum
Barrel: 3.9 in.
Sights: Dawson Precision Perfect Impact sights
Weight: N/A
Caliber: 9mm
Capacity: 8 rounds
Features: A lightweight 9mm carry gun with an all-new 2011 single-stack carry grip; milled aluminum frame; Recoil Master; 3.5-pound trigger; fiber optic front, Stealth Charger rear sight as part of the Dawson Precision Perfect Impact Sights
MSRP **$1495.00**

NEW Products: **Handguns**

STI INTERNATIONAL STACCATO P

STI INTERNATIONAL STACCATO P H.O.S.T.

STOEGER STR-9

TAURUS G2S

TAURUS G2C

TAURUS TX22

UBERTI 1851 NAVY CONVERSION WILD BILL

UBERTI 1873 CATTLEMAN BONNEY

ULTIMATE ARMS MAGNA T5 COMMANDER TAC

ULTIMATE ARMS MAGNA T5 GOVERNMENT

STI INTERNATIONAL STACCATO P

Action: Semiautomatic
Grips: Gen II 2011
Barrel: 4.15 in.
Sights: Dawson Precision Perfect Impact sights
Weight: N/A
Caliber: 9mm, .45 ACP
Capacity: 11, 21 rounds
Features: Billed as a personal protection gun, but certainly suitable for competition with features such as a diamond-like carbon black finish; ambidextrous safety; 4.5-pound trigger; fiber optic front, Stealth Charger rear sight as part of the Dawson Precision Perfect Impact Sights; bull barrel; Recoil Master; Tactical Slim Magwell; 1913 railed frame
MSRP **$1999.00**

STI INTERNATIONAL STACCATO P H.O.S.T.

Action: Semiautomatic
Grips: Gen II 2011
Barrel: 4.15 in.
Sights: Dawson Precision Perfect Impact sights
Weight: N/A
Caliber: 9mm, .45 ACP
Capacity: 11, 21 rounds
Features: Identical to the Staccato P, but with a Gen II reflex optics HOST plate replacing the Dawson Stealth Charger rear sight (no sight included)
MSRP **$2499.00**

STOEGER STR-9

Action: Semiautomatic
Grips: Polymer
Barrel: 4.17 in.
Sights: Three-dot; tritium
Weight: 24 oz.
Caliber: 9mm
Capacity: 15 rounds
Features: Stoeger joins the never-ending striker-fire trend with the STR-9 featuring a double-stack magazine; aggressive slide serrations fore and aft; backstrap and grip texturing; fingergrooves; under rail. Three configurations: 1 magazine/1 backstrap; 3 magazines/3 backstraps; 3 magazines/3 backstraps with tritium sights
MSRP . . . . **$329.00–$449.00**

TAURUS G2C

Action: Semiautomatic
Grips: Polymer
Barrel: 3.2 oz.
Sights: Blade front, adjustable rear
Weight: 22 oz.
Caliber: 9mm, .40 S&W
Capacity: 12, 10 rounds
Features: A double-stack striker-fire good for CCW, target practice, or competition
MSRP **$316.89**

TAURUS G2S

Action: Semiautomatic
Grips: Polymer
Barrel: 3.2 in.
Sights: Blade front, adjustable rear
Weight: 20 oz.
Caliber: 9mm, .40 S&W
Capacity: 7, 6 rounds
Features: A single-stack striker-fire for home-defense and target practice; various frame and slide color options available
MSRP **$332.82**

TAURUS TX22

Action: Semiautomatic
Grips: Polymer
Barrel: 4.1 in.
Sights: Blade front, notch rear
Weight: 17.3 oz.
Caliber: .22 LR
Capacity: 10 rounds
Features: A .22 pistol to fill the hands; striker-fire action; Taurus' Pittman Trigger System
MSRP **$349.00**

UBERTI 1851 NAVY CONVERSION WILD BILL

Action: Revolver
Grips: Simulated ivory
Barrel: 7.5 in.
Sights: Bead front, groove rear
Weight: 43 oz.
Caliber: .38 Special
Capacity: 6 rounds
Features: Based on the 1851 Navy with an unfluted barrel sporting light engraving; classic grip of simulated ivory; front bead; color case hardened frame; cylinder and barre in blue
MSRP **$809.00**

UBERTI 1873 CATTLEMAN BONNEY

Action: Revolver
Grips: Simulated bison horn
Barrel: 5.5 in.
Sights: Blade front, groove rear
Weight: 37 oz.
Caliber: .45 LC
Capacity: 6 rounds
Features: Part of Uberti's 1873 Cattleman Series; SA; bird's head grip of simulated bison; color case hardened frame; blued barrel and cylinder
MSRP **$799.00**

ULTIMATE ARMS MAGNA T5 COMMANDER TAC

Action: Semiautomatic
Grips: Carbon fiber
Barrel: 4.25 in.
Sights: Blade front, drift-adjustable rear
Weight: 23 oz.
Caliber: .45 ACP
Capacity: 8 rounds
Features: Similar to the Government but with a Commander-length slide/barrel; full-size grip
MSRP **$1999.00**
Rail: **$2099.00**

ULTIMATE ARMS MAGNA T5 GOVERNMENT

Action: Semiautomatic
Grips: Carbon fiber
Barrel: 5 in.
Sights: Fiber optic front, adjustable rear
Weight: 28 oz.
Caliber: .45 ACP
Capacity: 8 rounds
Features: A magnesium frame from forged billet makes this a strong and light full-size 1911 featuring a competition trigger; front and rear slide serrations; match-grade barrel; under rail optional
MSRP **$1999.00**
Rail: **$2099.00**

ULTIMATE ARMS MAGNA T5 OFFICERS

VOLQUARTSEN FIREARMS BLACK MAMBA

VOLQUARTSEN FIREARMS SCORPION .22 WMR

VOLQUARTSEN FIREARMS SCORPION 4.5-INCH URBAN CAMO

WALTHER PPQ Q5 MATCH STEEL FRAME

WILSON COMBAT VICKERS ELITE

WINDHAM WEAPONRY 9MM GMC PISTOL

WILSON COMBAT VICKERS ELITE PACKAGE FOR GLOCK

WINDHAM WEAPONRY .450 THUMPER

ULTIMATE ARMS MAGNA T5 OFFICERS

Action: Semiautomatic
Grips: Carbon fiber
Barrel: 3.5 in.
Sights: Blade front, drift-adjustable rear
Weight: 24 oz.
Caliber: .45 ACP
Capacity: 8 rounds
Features: Similar to the Government and Commander, but with the shorter Officer slide; maintains full-size grip and 8-round magazine; rear slide serrations only

MSRP $1999.00
Rail: $2099.00

VOLQUARTSEN FIREARMS BLACK MAMBA

Action: Semiautomatic
Grips: Polymer
Barrel: 4.5 in., 6 in.
Sights: Front ramp blade, adjustable rear
Weight: N/A
Caliber: .22 LR
Capacity: 10 rounds
Features: A combination of Volquartsen's Scorpion target pistol and the takedown functionality of a Ruger 2245 frame; stainless steel threaded barrel with removeable compensator; Tandemkross hiveGrip; Volquartsen accurizing kit, DLC-coated competition bolt, magazine release, and magazine pads; choice of black, OD Green, or Flat Dark Earth upper; top and under rails; Hi-Viz fiber optic front sight available on some versions

MSRP . . . . $1400.00–$1438.00

VOLQUARTSEN FIREARMS SCORPION .22 WMR

Action: Semiautomatic
Grips: G10
Barrel: 6 in.
Sights: Front ramp fiber optic, adjustable tritium rear
Weight: 67 oz.
Caliber: .22 WMR
Capacity: 9 rounds
Features: A dedicated small-game and varmint pistol with compensator; VZ Grips G10 panels in Predator Green; black nitride finish; under rail and topside rail; optional no sight version with black stainless finish; optional target sight version with black VZ Grip panels and black nitride finish

MSRP . . . . $1800.00–$2115.00

VOLQUARTSEN FIREARMS SCORPION 4.5-INCH URBAN CAMO

Action: Semiautomatic
Grips: Hogue
Barrel: 4.5 in.
Sights: Front ramp fiber optic, adjustable target rear
Weight: 32 oz.
Caliber: .22 LR
Capacity: 10 rounds
Features: A 1911-angled frame with Hogue finger-groove grips; competition bolt; compensator; under and top rails; snazzy full-coverage urban camo; anodized aluminum frame and upper

MSRP $1434.50

WALTHER PPQ Q5 MATCH STEEL FRAME

Action: Semiautomatic
Grips: Polymer
Barrel: 5 in.
Sights: Fiber optic front, adjustable rear
Weight: 41.6 oz.
Caliber: 9mm
Capacity: 25, 17 rounds
Features: This is 2018's Q5 Match with a lot of upgrades including a steel frame for added weight; ported and vented slide; Quick Defense trigger at 5.6 pounds; optic read slide cutout; extended frame with under rail; Tenifer coating

MSRP $1493.49

WILSON COMBAT VICKERS ELITE

Action: Semiautomatic
Grips: G10
Barrel: 5 in.
Sights: Battlesight with gold bead front
Weight: 41.6 oz.
Caliber: 9mm, .45 ACP
Capacity: 8, 9 rounds
Features: A full-size competition gun designed with Larry Vickers, featuring a carbon steel frame; high-cut and checkered front strap; Bullet Proof mag well, mag release and thumb safety; carbon steel slide with heavy underside machine chamfering and serrations fore and aft; match-grade barrel with flush cut reverse crown; countersunk slide stop

MSRP . . . . $3850.00–$3960.00

WILSON COMBAT VICKERS ELITE PACKAGE FOR GLOCK

Action: Semiautomatic
Grips: Polymer
Barrel: 4.49 in., 4 in.
Sights: Battlesight with green fiber optic front
Weight: N/A
Caliber: 9mm
Capacity: 15, 17 rounds
Features: Wilson partners with Larry Vickers to take the GLOCK 17 and 19 Gen5 frames and soup them up with Tango Down/Vickers Tactical mag release, grip plug, and magazine base pads; black Armor-Tuff slide finish; stippled frame; front and rear slide cocking serrations; duty action tune

MSRP $1350.00

WINDHAM WEAPONRY .450 THUMPER

Action: Semiautomatic
Grips: Synthetic
Barrel: 9 in.
Sights: Flip-up front and rear
Weight: 93 oz.
Caliber: .450 Bushmaster
Capacity: 5 rounds
Features: Designed specifically for the straight-wall .450 Bushmaster, with SB Tactical pistol arm brace; hardcoat black anodized receiver; mil-spec trigger; Magpul MBUS flip-up sights

MSRP $1081.00

WINDHAM WEAPONRY 9MM GMC PISTOL

Action: Semiautomatic
Grips: Synthetic
Barrel: 9 in.
Sights: None
Weight: 93 oz.
Caliber: 9mm
Capacity: 17 rounds
Features: GMC stands for "Glock Magazine Compatible"; semiauto blowback; five-position SB tactical arm brace; A2 grip; flat-top upper; Chromoly vanadium steel barrel with 1:10 right twist

MSRP $1106.00

NEW Products: **Black Powder**

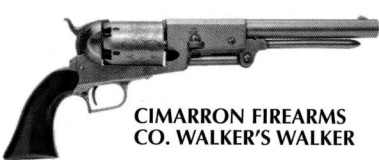

CIMARRON FIREARMS CO. WALKER'S WALKER

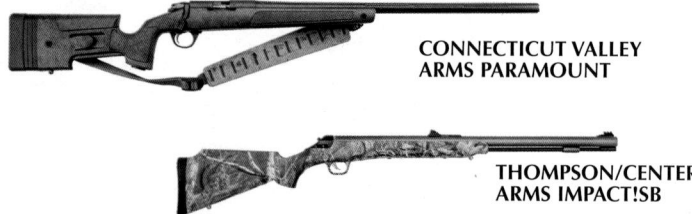

CONNECTICUT VALLEY ARMS PARAMOUNT

THOMPSON/CENTER ARMS IMPACT!SB

CIMARRON FIREARMS CO. WALKER'S WALKER

Action: Revolver
Stock: Walnut
Barrel: 9 in.
Sights: Low blade front
Weight: 72 oz.
Caliber: .44
Features: A beefy revolver with a long barrel in limited edition and featuring a brass trigger guard; steel backstrap; one-piece grips; Cimarron's own original finish with military markings; ships in a glass and walnut presentation case
MSRP **$1127.10**

CONNECTICUT VALLEY ARMS PARAMOUNT

Action: Bolt
Stock: Synthetic
Barrel: 26 in.
Sights: None
Weight: N/A
Caliber: .45
Features: Billed as the world's first long-range muzzleloader capable of killing shots on game 300 yards and beyond. Features include free-floating Bergara barrel; CVA VariFlame breech plus; aluminum chassis; takes new PowerBelt ELR bullets specifically designed for this muzzleloader
MSRP **$1062.95**

THOMPSON/CENTER ARMS IMPACT!SB

Action: Break-open
Stock: Synthetic
Barrel: 26 in.
Sights: Fiber optic front, adjustable rear
Weight: 6 lb. 15 oz.
Caliber: .50
Features: Featuring a hand-removeable triple lead thread breech plug; Power Rod aluminum ramrod; single0shot sliding hood design; adjustable stock with spacers. Five finish/stock options: blued/black; Silver Weather Shield/Realtree Edge; Silver Weather Shield/black; blued/Mossy Oak Bottomland; Silver Weather Shield/Mossy Oak Break-Up Country
MSRP . . . . **$263.00–$324.00**

NEW Products: **Optics**
SCOPES

BARSKA LEVEL HD, LEVEL HD FFP

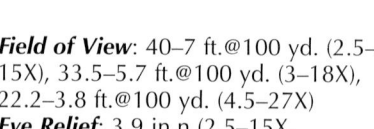

BUSHNELL FORGE

BARSKA LEVEL HD, LEVEL HD FFP

Available in: 1–4x24mm, 1–6x24mm
Weight: 16 oz.
Length: 10 in., 10.5 in.
Power: 1–4X, 1–6X
Obj. Dia.: 24mm
Main Dia.: 30mm
Exit Pupil: 5.88–2.29mm, 8–3.5mm
Field of View: 25–7.6 ft.@100 yd., 18.8 ft.–5.7 ft.@100 yd.
Eye Relief: 4.76–3.94 in., 3.9–3.5 in.
Features: Close and mid-range shooting applications will find favor with the scope featuring an illuminated HRS Quick Shot .223

BDC reticle; fully multi-coated optics; reticle can be red or green and adjusted for brightness; lockable turrets; 1–6X has first focal plane glass-etched reticle
MSRP . . . . **$464.40–$821.50**

BUSHNELL FORGE

Available in: 2.5–15x50mm, 3–18x50mm, 4.5–27x50mm
Weight: 28.9 oz., 29.2 oz.
Length: 14 in., 14.7 in., 14.2 in.
Power: 2.5–15X, 3–18X, 4.5–27X
Obj. Dia.: 50mm
Main Dia.: 30mm

Field of View: 40–7 ft.@100 yd. (2.5–15X), 33.5–5.7 ft.@100 yd. (3–18X), 22.2–3.8 ft.@100 yd. (4.5–27X)
Eye Relief: 3.9 in.n (2.5–15X, 3–18X)., 4 in. (4.5–27X)
Features: Exposed locking turrets; Ultra Wide Band coatings; RevLimiter zero stop; IPX7 waterproof construction; EXO Barrier Protection; second focal plane optics. Available in Black with Deploy MOA, Deploy MOA FFP, or Deploy MIL FFP reticles; Terrain finish available only with Deploy MOA or Deploy MOA FFP reticles
MSRP . . . . **$779.99–$979.99**

BUSHNELL NITRO

BUSHNELL PRIME

GPO PASSION 5X

HAWKE SPORT OPTICS FRONTIER 30

HAWKE SPORT OPTICS FRONTIER 30 SF

HAWKE SPORT OPTICS FRONTIER FFP

BUSHNELL NITRO

Available in: 2.5–10x44mm, 3–12x44mm, 4–16x44mm, 5–20x44mm, 6–24x44mm
Weight: 23.9 oz., 24.2 oz., 23.4 oz., 24.5 oz.
Length: 13.4 in.,13.7 in., 13.9 in.
Power: 2.5–10X, 3–12X, 4–16X, 5–20X, 6–24X
Obj. Dia.: 44mm
Main Dia.: 30mm
Field of View: 37–9 ft.@100 yd. (2.5–10X), 34.8–8.6 ft.@100yd. (3–12X), 23–6 ft.@100 yd. (4–16X, 5–20X), 16–4 ft.@100 yd. (6–24X)
Eye Relief: 3.6 in. (2.5–10X, 4–12X, 5–20X, 6–24X), 3.9 in. (3–18X)
Features: Designed for hunters working at close to middle ranges. Second focal plane copes have a matte gray or black finish; variety of Multi-Plex and Deploy reticles; capped target turrets; Ultra-Wide Band Coating; EXO Barrier Protection; IPX7 waterproofing
MSRP . . . . $369.99–$729.99

BUSHNELL PRIME

Available in: 1–4x32mm, 3–9x40mm, 3.5–10x36, 4-12x40mm, 6–18x50mm
Weight: 13.4 oz., 16.6 oz., 14.8 oz., 18.6 oz., 19 oz.
Length: 10.4 in., 12.8 in., 12.1 in., 12.8 in., 15 in.
Power: 1–4X, 3–9X, 3.5–10X, 4–12X, 6–18X
Obj. Dia.: 32mm, 40mm, 36mm, 50mm
Main Dia.: 1 in.
Field of View: 105–26 ft.@100 yd. (1–4X), 31–11 ft.@100 yd. (3–9X), 38–13 ft.@100 yd. (3.5–10X), 26–9 ft.@100 yd. (4–12X), 18–6 ft.@100 yd. (6–18X)
Eye Relief: 3.9 in. (1–4X), 3.3 in. (3–9X), 3.7 in. (3.5–10X), 3.3 in. (4–12X), 3.5 n. (6–18X)
Features: The most budget-friendly of Bushnell's three new lines offers a lightweight and compact second focal plane package in a power range for every target or hunting application. Features include multi-coated optics; EXO Barrier Protection; IPX7 waterproofing; Ultra Wide Band coatings; Multi-X reticle
MSRP . . . . $139.99–$319.99

GPO PASSION 5X

Available in: 1–5x24imm, 3.5–18x56imm
Weight: 19.4 oz., 26.4 oz.
Length: 10.6 in., 15.4 in.
Power: 1–5X, 3.5–18X
Obj. Dia.: 24mm, 56mm
Main Dia.: 30mm
Exit Pupil: 12.4–5mm (1–5X), 16–3.1mm (3.5–18X)
Field of View: 110–17 ft.@100 yd. (1–5X), 32–6 ft.@100 yd. (3.5–18X)
Eye Relief: 3.5 in.
Features: The somewhat unusual 5X in two units with illuminated reticles; .36-inch/1cm clicks; G4i reticle on 1–5X; mil-base reticle 3.5–18X
MSRP . . . . $699.99–$999.99

HAWKE SPORT OPTICS FRONTIER 30

Available in: 1–6x24mm
Weight: 19.7 oz.
Length: 10.4 in.
Power: 1–6X
Obj. Dia.: 24mm
Main Dia.: 30mm
Exit Pupil: 24–4mm
Field of View: 108–17.6 ft.@100 yd.
Eye Relief: 4 in.
Features: Designed for tactical applications with a wide field of view; generous eye relief; second focal plane; 21 layers fully multi-coated; illuminated etched glass Tactical Dot (6X) Reticle with six brightness levels
MSRP $799.99

HAWKE SPORT OPTICS FRONTIER 30 SF

Available in: 2.5–15x50mm, 5–30x50mm
Weight: 23.4 oz., 24.5 oz.
Length: 13.7 in., 13.9 in.
Power: 5–30X
Obj. Dia.: 50mm
Main Dia.: 30mm
Exit Pupil: 20–3mm (2.5–15X), 10–2mm (5–30X)
Field of View: 42–6.9 ft.@100 yd. (2.5–15X), 22.8–3.9 ft.@100 yd. (5–30X)
Eye Relief: 4 in.
Features: Super tool for hunters especially those shooting magnum calibers, thanks to the 4-inch eye relief; big objective; side focus parallax adjustment; second focal plane; illuminated glass etched LR Dot reticle keeps things simple, or choose the illuminated TMX reticle with mil-dot spacing
MSRP . . . . $799.99–$849.99

HAWKE SPORT OPTICS FRONTIER FFP

Available in: 3–15x50mm, 5–25x56mm
Weight: 26.3 oz., 28.8 oz.
Length: 13.2 in.
Power: 3–15X, 5–25X
Obj. Dia.: 50mm
Main Dia.: 30mm
Exit Pupil: 16.7–3.3mm (3–15X), 11.2–2.3mm (5–25X)
Field of View: 36.7–7.3 ft.@100 yd. (3–15X), 21.7–4.3 ft.@100 yd. (5–25X)
Eye Relief: 4 in.
Features: A mid-size hunter's tool in the underutilized 5X category; 1/10 MRAD locking turrets; first focal plane; illuminated etched glass Mil Ext. reticle with six brightness settings
MSRP . . . . $729.00–$769.00

NEW PRODUCTS

KAHLES K318I

KAHLES K525I

KONUS KONUSPRO EL-30

LEAPERS, INC. UTG 1 BUGBUSTER

LEUPOLD & STEVENS MARK 5 HD

MEOPTA MEOSTAR R2 2.5–15X56MM RD

MEOPTA OPTIKA6

KAHLES K318I

Available in: 3.5–18x50mm
Weight: 33.2 oz.
Length: 12.3 in.
Power: 3.5–18X
Obj. Dia.: 50mm
Main Dia.: 34mm
Field of View: 27.8–5.5 ft.@100 yd.
Eye Relief: 3.6 in.
Features: A solid scope for mid-range work with an illuminated reticle in the first focal plane; TWIST GUARD windage protection; reticle choices of MSR/Ki, SKMR3, and MOAK
MSRP $3199.00

KAHLES K525I

Available in: 5–25x56mm
Weight: 34.2 oz.
Length: 14.8 in.
Power: 5–25X
Obj. Dia.: 56mm
Main Dia.: 34mm
Exit Pupil: 9.5–2.3mm
Field of View: 21.7–4.4 ft.@100 yd.
Eye Relief: 3.74 in.
Features: A big scope for big calibers going big distances featuring an elevation turret with integrated parallax wheel; illuminated first focal plane reticle in reticle choice of SKMR3, SKMR, MOAK, Mil4+, or MSR2/Ki; TWIST GUARD windage system prevents accidental dial movement
MSRP $3299.00

KONUS KONUSPRO EL-30

Available in: 4–16x44mm
Weight: 23.39 oz.
Length: 13.1 in.
Power: 4–16X
Obj. Dia.: 44mm
Main Dia.: 30mm
Exit Pupil: 11–2.7mm
Field of View: 22.6–9.5 ft.@100 yd.
Eye Relief: 3.3–3 in.

Features: Utilizing LCD technology, the EL-30 features 10 interchangeable reticles; 1/10-Mil adjustments; locking tactical turrets; one-piece aluminum tube
MSRP $399.99

LEAPERS, INC. UTG 1 BUGBUSTER

Available in: 3–9x32mm, 3–12x32mm
Weight: 12 oz., 12.7 oz.
Length: 7.8, 8 in.
Power: 3–9X, 3–12X
Obj. Dia.: 32 mm
Main Dia.: 1 in.
Exit Pupil: 10.6–3.6 in., 10.6–2.7mm,
Field of View: 36.6–21.5 ft.@100 yd., 31–10 ft.@100 yd.
Eye Relief: 4.3–3.3 in.
Features: Compact scope with True Strength Platform; mil-dot range-estimating reticle; resettable target turrets; 2-inch sunshade; flip-up lens caps
MSRP . . . . $124.97–$129.97

LEUPOLD & STEVENS MARK 5 HD

Available in: 5–25x56mm
Weight: 30 oz.
Length: 15.67 in.
Power: 5–25X
Obj. Dia.: 56mm
Main Dia.: 35mm
Exit Pupil: 2.2 mm (high)
Field of View: 20.5–4.2 ft.@100 yd.
Eye Relief: 3.58–3.82 in.
Features: European-style fast-focus eye-piece; dual illumination control; 2nd Generation Argon/Krypton waterproofing; side focus parallax adjustment; PR-1MOA reticle
MSRP $2599.99

MEOPTA MEOSTAR R2 2.5–15X56MM RD

Available in: 2.5–15x56mm

Weight: 22.9 oz.
Length: 14 in.
Power: 2.5–15X
Obj. Dia.: 56mm
Main Dia.: 30mm
Exit Pupil: 11.2mm (2.5X), 3.8mm (15X)
Field of View: 45–8 ft.@100 yd.
Eye Relief: 3.8–3.7 in.
Features: A nice choice for big-game and predator hunters, this scope features: Meopta's most advanced lens coating, MeoLux; Schott glass; 98.2% light transmission per lens surface; parallax free to 100 yards. Choice of four illuminated reticles: 4C-RD; 4K-RD; BDC2; BDC3
MSRP $1599.95

MEOPTA OPTIKA6

Available in: 1–6x24mm, 2.5–15x44mm, 3–18x50mm, 3–18x56mm, 4.5–27x56mm, 5–30x56mm
Weight: varies with model
Length: 10.6 in.–15.3 in.
Power: 1–6X, 2.5–15X, 3–18X, 4.5–27X, 5–30X
Obj. Dia.: 24mm, 44mm, 50mm, 56mm
Main Dia.: 30mm
Exit Pupil: varies with model
Field of View: varies with model
Eye Relief: varies with model
Features: Hunting scopes feature a wide variety of second focal plane reticles, including those designed for .223 Rem. and 6.5 Creedmoor rounds; target scopes get first focal plane reticles MIL or MOA adjustments; all reticles are illuminated with a third turret housing the controls; MeoBright TM ion-assisted lens coatings
MSRP . . . . $499.00–$899.00

**NIGHTFORCE OPTICS
ATACR 4–16X50 F1**

**NIGHTFORCE OPTICS
ATACR 7–35X56 F2**

**NIGHTFORCE OPTICS
SHV 3–10X42**

**NIKON BLACK
FORCE 100**

**NIKON
MONARCH M5**

NIKON PROSTAFF P3

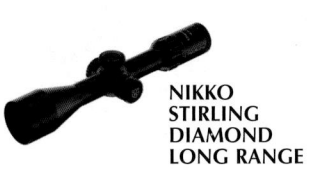

**NIKKO
STIRLING
DIAMOND
LONG RANGE**

NIGHTFORCE OPTICS ATACR 4–16X50 F1

Available in: 4–16x50mm
Weight: 33.3 oz.
Length: 13.1 in.
Power: 4–16X
Obj. Dia.: 50mm
Main Dia.: 34mm
Field of View: 26.9–6.9 ft.@100 yd.
Eye Relief: 3.5 in.
Features: A sound choice for low light and long-range shooting chores with features such as Zero Stop elevation adjustment of 100 MOA/30 mils; MOAR or Mil-C reticles; red and green DigIllum illumination; first focal plane optics
MSRP **$2500.00**

NIGHTFORCE OPTICS ATACR 7–35X56 F2

Available in: 7–35x56mm
Weight: 39.3 oz.
Length: 16 in.
Power: 7–35X
Obj. Dia.: 56mm
Main Dia.: 34mm
Exit Pupil: 6mm (7X), 1.6mm (35X)
Field of View: 97–3.44 ft.@100 yd.
Eye Relief: 3.5 in.
Features: ED glass; 100 MOA total click travel; side parallax adjustment 11 yards to infinity; two-piece locking eyepiece adaptor; power-throw lever; Zero-Stop elevation adjustment; three 30 MOA or 12 MRAD rotation built-in quick-dial options; choice of MOAR-T or MIL-C reticles; second focal plane optics
MSRP **$3100.00**

NIGHTFORCE OPTICS SHV 3–10X42

Available in: 3–10x42mm

Weight: 20.8 oz.
Length: 11.6 in.
Power: 3–10X
Obj. Dia.: 42mm
Main Dia.: 30mm
Exit Pupil: 10.7mm (3X), 4.4mm (10X)
Field of View: 34.9–11 ft.@100 yd.
Eye Relief: 3.5 in.
Features: This popular hunting optic is introduced for the first time with an illuminated reticle. Features include fixed parallax @125m; fast-focus eyepiece; brightness adjustable MOAR Forceplex reticle
MSRP **$985.00**

NIKKO STIRLING DIAMOND LONG RANGE

Available in: 4–16x50mm, 6–24x50mm
Weight: 16.5 oz.
Length: 14.2 in.
Power: 4–16X, 6–24X
Obj. Dia.: 50mm
Main Dia.: 30mm
Field of View: 32–8 ft.@100 yd. (4–16X), 21–5 ft.@100 yd. (6–24X)
Eye Relief: 4.5 in.
Features: Huge eye relief in two long-distance scopes that won't break the bank and featuring illuminated reticles (LR HMD 4–16X; LR Hold Fast 6–24X); multicoated lenses; waterproof, shockproof, and nitrogen filled
MSRP . . . . **$312.00–$328.00**

NIKON BLACK FORCE 100

Available in: 1–6x24mm
Weight: 20.8 oz.
Length: 11.6 in.
Power: 1–6X
Obj. Dia.: 24mm
Main Dia.: 30mm
Exit Pupil: 12.2–4mm

Field of View: 111.2–18.3 ft.@100 yd.
Features: A top choice for 3-Gunners and tactical applications, featuring a quick-focus eyepiece; glass-etched reticle; FORCE MOA reticle; side-mounted illumination controls; capped, low-profile turrets with zero reset
MSRP **$649.95**

NIKON MONARCH M5

Available in: 5–20x50mm
Weight: 22.2 oz.
Length: 15 in.
Power: 5–20X
Obj. Dia.: 50mm
Main Dia.: 30mm
Features: 4X zoom, quick-focus eyepiece; spring-loaded instant zero reset turrets; fully multi-coated lenses; interchangeable turrets; side focus parallax adjustment; MK1-MOA, BDC, or Nikoplex reticles
MSRP **$649.95**

NIKON PROSTAFF P3

Available in: 2–7x32mm, 3–9x40mm, 3–9x50mm, 4–12x40mm, 6–18x40mm
Weight: 14.2 oz.–17.8 oz.
Length: 11.5–14.6 in.
Power: 2–7X, 3–9X, 4–12X, 6–18X
Obj. Dia.: 32mm, 40mm, 50mm
Main Dia.: 1 in.
Field of View: varies with model
Eye Relief: 3.8–3.5 in.
Features: A 3X zoom ratio hunting optic on a new aluminum platform, featuring a nitrogen purged body; spring-loaded instant zero reset turrets that are interchangeable; quick-focus eyepiece; adjustable objective on the largest power model; choice of BDC, mil-dot, or Nikoplex reticles
MSRP . . . .**$149.95–$249.95**

NEW Products: Optics

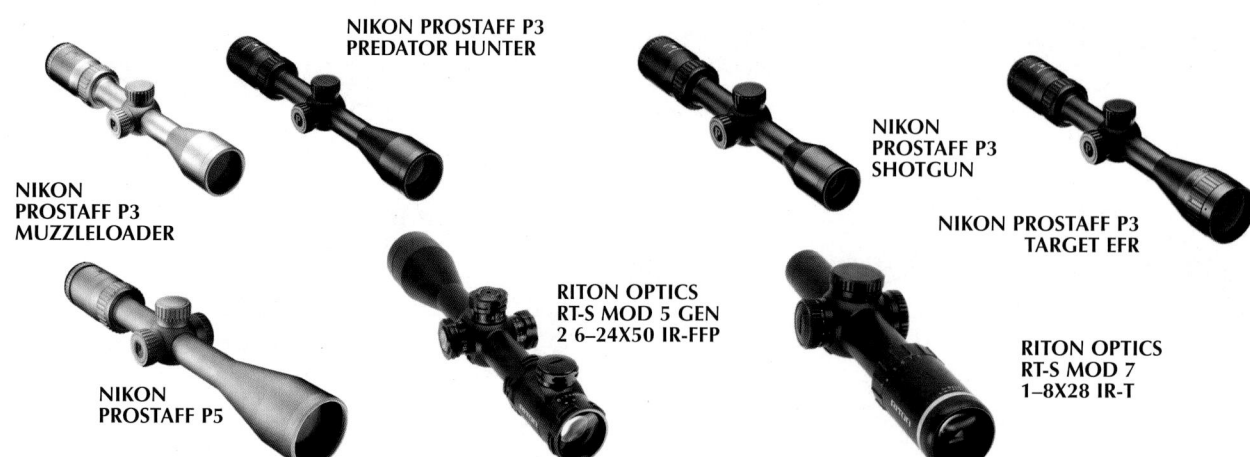

NIKON PROSTAFF P3 PREDATOR HUNTER

NIKON PROSTAFF P3 MUZZLELOADER

NIKON PROSTAFF P5

RITON OPTICS RT-S MOD 5 GEN 2 6–24X50 IR-FFP

NIKON PROSTAFF P3 SHOTGUN

NIKON PROSTAFF P3 TARGET EFR

RITON OPTICS RT-S MOD 7 1–8X28 IR-T

NIKON PROSTAFF P3 MUZZLELOADER

Available in: 3–9x40mm
Weight: 15.2 oz.
Length: 11.4 in.
Power: 3–9X
Obj. Dia.: 40mm
Main Dia.: 1 in.
Field of View: 25.1–8.4 ft.@100 yd.
Eye Relief: 3.6 in.
Features: A muzzleloader-specific scope with generous eye relief and field of view; 3X zoom ratio; in matte black, silver, or TrueTimber KANATI camo; BDC 300 Muzzleloader reticle
MSRP . . . . **$199.95–$219.95**

NIKON PROSTAFF P3 PREDATOR HUNTER

Available in: 3–9x40mm, 4–12x40mm
Weight: 15 oz., 15.5 oz.
Length: 12.4 in., 14.1 in.
Power: 3–9X, 4–12X
Obj. Dia.: 40mm
Main Dia.: 1 in.
Field of View: 33.5–11.5 ft.@100 yd. (3–9X), 23.6–7.9 ft.@100 yd. (4–12X)
Eye Relief: 3.5 in. (3–9X), 3.6 in. (4–12X)
Features: Similar to the other Prostaff 3 series scopes, but with Nikon's proprietary BDC Predator reticle for which aids in shots on moving targets
MSRP . . . . **$249.95–$299.95**

NIKON PROSTAFF P3 SHOTGUN

Available in: 2–7x32mm, 3–9x40mm
Weight: 14.3 oz., 15.2 oz.
Length: 11.5 in., 11.4 in.
Power: 2–7X, 3–9X

Obj. Dia.: 32mm, 40mm
Main Dia.: 1 in.
Field of View: 44.6–12.6 ft.@100 yd. (2–7X), 25.1–8.4 ft.@100 yd. (3–9X)
Eye Relief: 3.8 in.
Features: A 3X zoom ration in a shotgun-specific scope featuring Nikon's BDC 200 Shotgun reticle
MSRP . . . . **$159.95–$199.95**

NIKON PROSTAFF P3 TARGET EFR

Available in: 3–9x40mm
Weight: 16.6 oz.
Length: 12.5 in.
Power: 3–9X
Obj. Dia.: 40mm
Main Dia.: 1 in.
Field of View: 33.5–11.5 ft.@100 yd. (3–9X)
Eye Relief: 3.6 in.
Features: A 3X zoom ratio scope applicable to both air rifles and .22 LR rimfires with Nikon's Precision reticle
MSRP **$189.95**

NIKON PROSTAFF P5

Available in: 2–7x32mm, 2.5–10x42mm, 3–12x42mm, 4–16x50mm, 6–24x50mm
Power: 2–7X, 2.5–10X, 3–12X, 4–16X, 6–24X
Main Dia.: 1 in.
Field of View: varies with model
Eye Relief: 4.0–3.6 in.
Features: A hunting scope with zoom ring in a 4X zoom ratio; focusing eyepiece; knurled controls; all-over aluminum construction; side focus parallax adjustment; fully multi-coated optics
MSRP . . . . **$229.95–$449.95**

RITON OPTICS RT-S MOD 5 GEN 2 6–24X50 IR-FFP

Available in: 6–24x
Weight: 30 oz.
Length: 24 in.
Power: 6–24X
Obj. Dia.: 50mm
Main Dia.: 30mm
Exit Pupil: 8.2–2.1mm
Field of View: 16.8–4.4 ft.@100 yd.
Eye Relief: 3.35 in.
Features: For the long-range game, a budget-friendly first focal plane optic with push-pull locking and zero-reset turrets; ¼-MOA click adjustments; fast-focus eyepiece; Riton HD glass; illuminated ranging reticle
MSRP **$569.99**

RITON OPTICS RT-S MOD 7 1–8X28 IR-T

Available in: 1–8x28mm
Weight: 25 oz.
Length: 10.9 in.
Power: 1–8X
Obj. Dia.: 28mm
Main Dia.: 34mm
Exit Pupil: 14mm
Field of View: 142–17.5 ft.@100 yd.
Eye Relief: 4 in.
Features: A first focal plane optic designed for tactical use with a generous field of view and eye relief that provides fast target acquisition; illuminated reticle with six daylight-bright settings; fixed parallax at 100 yards; ½-MOA clicks; fast-focus eyepiece
MSRP **$1299.99**

RITON OPTICS RT-S MOD 7 4–32X56 IR

SCHMIDT & BENDER 1–8X24 PM II SHORT DOT DUAL CC

SIG SAUER SIERRA3BDX

STEINER H4XI 4–16X56MM

SWAROVSKI OPTIK Z5 2.5–12X50MM

TRACT OPTICS TORIC UHD 30MM

RITON OPTICS RT-S MOD 7 4–32X56 IR

Available in: 4–32x56mm
Weight: 37 oz.
Length: 15 in.
Power: 4–32X
Obj. Dia.: 56mm
Main Dia.: 34mm
Exit Pupil: 14–1.75mm
Field of View: 27–3.4 ft.@100 yd.
Eye Relief: 3.7 in.
Features: First focal plane scope featuring side parallax adjustment; zero stop turrets; illuminated Precision Shooting Reticle; fast-focus eyepiece; fully multi-coated full wideband glass; 30 MRAD adjustment
MSRP **$1469.99**

SCHMIDT & BENDER 1–8X24 PM II SHORT DOT DUAL CC

Available in: 1–8x
Weight: 22 oz.
Length: 11.6 in.
Power: 1–8X
Obj. Dia.: 24mm
Main Dia.: 30mm
Exit Pupil: 9.8–3mm
Field of View: 35.3–4.9m@100m
Eye Relief: 3.54 in.
Features: A true 8X zoom in a compact unit with a first focal plane Mil-dot-based reticle paired with a second focal plane illuminated red-dot; choice of MDR or MDR16 reticles for CQB to mid-range work
MSRP . . . . **N/A**

SIG SAUER SIERRA3BDX

Available in: 3.5–10x42mm, 4.5–14x44mm, 4.5–14x50mm, 6.5–20x52mm
Power: 3.5–10X, 4.5–14X, 6.5–20X
Obj. Dia.: 42mm, 44mm, 50mm, 52mm
Main Dia.: 30mm
Exit Pupil: varies with model
Field of View: varies with model
Features: A rangefinder and scope all in one via SIG's BDX-R1 reticle--BDX stands for Ballistic Data Exchange--which includes an illuminated auto-holdover dot when the scope is paired with Sig's BDX-capable KILO rangefinders; SpectralCoat lenses; anti-cant digital LevelPlex technology; second focal plane
MSRP . . . . **$599.99–$959.99**

STEINER H4XI 4–16X56MM

Available in: 4–16x56mm
Weight: 25 oz.
Length: 14.5 in.
Power: 4–16X
Obj. Dia.: 56mm
Main Dia.: 30mm
Field of View: 13–3 ft.@100 yd.
Eye Relief: 3.8 in.
Features: No worry about scope eye with this one thanks to nearly four inches of eye relief, plus parallax adjustment from 50 yards to infinity with side-focus adjustment; illuminated Plex S1 reticle with 11 settings and rotary control; waterproof to 6.5 meters; ¼-MOA click adjustments with 33 MILs of elevation, 22 MILs windage
MSRP **$1324.99**

SWAROVSKI OPTIK Z5 2.5–12X50MM

Available in: 2.4–12x50mm
Weight: 16.2 oz.
Length: 13.1 in.
Power: 2.4–12X
Obj. Dia.: 50mm
Main Dia.: 1 in.
Exit Pupil: 10–4.1mm
Field of View: 45.9–9 ft.@100 yd.
Features: An ideal scope for American whitetails with light weight, big objective, and ample magnification; second focal plane reticles in Plex or BRX-HEAVY
MSRP **$1277.00**

TRACT OPTICS TORIC UHD 30MM

Available in: 4–20x59mm
Weight: 34 oz.
Length: 13.7 in.
Power: 4–20X
Obj. Dia.: 50mm
Main Dia.: 30mm
Exit Pupil: 12.5–2.5mm
Field of View: 24.5–4.9 ft.@100 yd.
Eye Relief: 3.9 in.
Features: One for the long-range game with first focal plane illuminated glass-etched reticle; quick-focus eyepiece; 11 brightness settings; magnification ring with rear-facing numbers; waterproof, fog-proof with Argon gas; locking turrets with zero stop; side focus parallax adjustment; choice of MRAD or MOA reticles
MSRP **$1294.00**

ACCUFIRE TECHNOLOGY NOCTIS V

BARSKA 1X20 HQ RED DOT

BARSKA 1X30 HQ RED DOT

BARSKA 1X30 ION REFLEX SIGHT

BARSKA 1X40 ION REFLEX SIGHT

BUSHNELL OUTDOOR PRODUCTS NITRO 1 MILE 6X20 LASER RANGEFINDER

BUSHNELL OUTDOOR PRODUCTS PRIME 800 6X24, 1300 5X20 LASER RANGEFINDER

KAHLES HELIA RD

LASERMAX LIGHTNING LASER WITH GRIPSENSE

RED-DOTS, LASERS, RANGEFINDERS

ACCUFIRE TECHNOLOGY NOCTIS V

Type: Nightvision
Power: 1–16X
Features: Compact day/night vision unit with loads of features, including HD-quality night vision; savable presets; ballistic calculations; fifty downloadable reticles; HD video recording in all light levels; built-in Wi-Fi
MSRP **$1499.00**

BARSKA 1X20 HQ RED DOT

Type: Red-dot
Weight: 7 oz.
Length: 2.95 in.
Power: 1X20mm
Obj. Dia.: 20mm
Exit Pupil: 18mm
Field of View: 36 ft.@100 yd.
Eye Relief: Unlimited
Features: Red-dot auto adjusts for external lighting conditions via a light sensor; integrated QD mount; 1 MOA adjustments
MSRP **$178.65**

BARSKA 1X30 HQ RED DOT

Type: Red-dot
Weight: 10.8 oz.
Length: 4.13 in.
Power: 1X30mm
Obj. Dia.: 30mm
Exit Pupil: 26mm
Field of View: 57 ft.@100 yd.
Eye Relief: Unlimited
Features: Similar to the 1X20 version, including auto-adjusting brightness; 1 MOA adjustments
MSRP **$196.50**

BARSKA 1X30 ION REFLEX SIGHT

Type: Reflex sight
Weight: 3.9 oz.
Length: 2.37 in.
Power: 1X30mm
Obj. Dia.: 30mm
Exit Pupil: 26–20mm
Field of View: Unlimited
Eye Relief: Unlimited
Features: A compact, affordable reflex with choice of four reticle patterns; Picatinny rail mount
MSRP **$160.75**

BARSKA 1X40 ION REFLEX SIGHT

Type: Reflex sight
Weight: 6.2 oz.
Length: 3.6 in.
Power: 1X40mm
Obj. Dia.: 40mm
Exit Pupil: 28–44mm
Field of View: Unlimited
Eye Relief: Unlimited
Features: A slightly bigger reflex with choice of four reticles; quick release Picatinny/Weaver-type mount
MSRP **$142.90**

BUSHNELL OUTDOOR PRODUCTS NITRO 1 MILE 6X20 LASER RANGEFINDER

Type: Rangefinder
Weight: 5.5 oz.
Length: 1.5 in.
Power: 6X
Obj. Dia.: 20mm
Features: Ranging capabilities to 1,760 yards (reflective), 1,200 yards (tree), 800 yards (deer); Scan, Bull's-eye, Brush, and Arc modes; EXO Barrier
MSRP **$319.99**

BUSHNELL OUTDOOR PRODUCTS PRIME 800 6X24, 1300 5X20 LASER RANGEFINDER

Type: Rangefinder
Weight: 5.9 oz.
Length: 1.7 in.
Power: 6X, 5X
Obj. Dia.: 24mm, 20mm
Features: 800 Model range capabilities to 800 yards (reflective), 480 yards (tree), 240 yards (deer); 1300 Model range capabilities to 1300 yards (reflective), 550 yards (tree), 350 yards (deer); EXO Barrier protection; Arc and Scan modes; 3-volt CR2 battery included
MSRP . . . . **$159.99–$209.99**

KAHLES HELIA RD

Type: Reflex sight
Weight: 1.4 oz.
Length: 2.16 in.
Power: 1X
Obj. Dia.: 26X22mm
Features: Anti-reflection lens coating for clear view; 2 MOA red-dot with four illumination settings; includes Picatinny rail mount
MSRP **$399.00**

LASERMAX LIGHTNING LASER WITH GRIPSENSE

Type: Laser
Weight: .5 oz.
Features: Dual-activation via the GripSense technology that does not alter grip, or via push-button; steady or pulse beam; ten-minute auto-off; Rail Vise mounting technology; fits Picatinny or Weaver-type rails; choice of red or green beam
MSRP . . . . **$149.99–$199.99**

LEAPERS, INC. UTG REFLEX MICRO DOT

LEICA CAMERA AG RANGEMASTER CRF 2400-R

LEICA CAMERA AG RANGEMASTER CRF 2800 COM

LEICA CAMERA AG TEMPUS ASPH

LEUPOLD & STEVENS RX-950

LEUPOLD & STEVENS VX-FREEDOM RDS

NEWCON OPTIK LRM 3500M

NIGHT OPTICS FIR-I IR ILLUMINATOR

NIGHT OPTICS NIGHT CHASE

LEAPERS, INC. UTG REFLEX MICRO DOT

Type: Reflex sight
Weight: 1.87 oz.
Length: 1.9 in.
Power: 1X
Exit Pupil: Unlimited
Eye Relief: Unlimited
Features: Anodized aluminum body; True Strength Platform; 4 MOA dot; 1 MOA click adjustment; red or green dot options
MSRP **$89.97**

LEICA CAMERA AG RANGEMASTER CRF 2400-R

Type: Rangefinder
Weight: 6.5 oz.
Length: 4.5 in.
Power: 7X
Obj. Dia.: 24mm
Exit Pupil: 3.4mm
Field of View: 347 ft.@1,000 yd.
Eye Relief: 15mm
Features: Updated LED display adjusts to ambient light for better viewing; decimal results to 200 yards; equivalent horizontal range to 1200 yards
MSRP **$499.00**

LEICA CAMERA AG RANGEMASTER CRF 2800 COM

Type: Rangefinder
Weight: 6.7 oz.
Power: 7X
Obj. Dia.: 24mm
Exit Pupil: 3.4mm
Field of View: 115m @1,000 yd.
Eye Relief: 15mm
Features: Leica's ABC ballistic system; measurements to 2800 yards; works in combination with Leica's hunting app to relay information via Bluetooth to calculate holdover and distance corrections for given environmental conditions
MSRP **$1099.00**

LEICA CAMERA AG TEMPUS ASPH

Type: Reflex sight
Weight: 1.41 oz.
Power: 1X
Obj. Dia.: 21X25mm
Features: Utilizes an aspheric lens for a more exacting red-dot image; aluminum housing; choice of 2 or 3.5 MOA dot
MSRP **$599.00**

LEUPOLD & STEVENS RX-950

Type: Rangefinder
Weight: 6.2 oz.
Length: 3.8 in.
Power: 6X
Field of View: 367 ft.@1000 yd.
Features: Line of sight measurements to 950 yards; fully multicoated lens system; waterproof
MSRP **$324.99**

LEUPOLD & STEVENS VX-FREEDOM RDS

Type: Red-dot
Weight: 6.9 oz.
Length: 5.5 in.
Power: 1X
Features: A red-dot that won't break the bank, featuring 1MOA dot reticle; one version has ¼ MOA click adjustments, a second has exposed BDC elevation turrets designed for use with the .223 Rem. 55-grain load; built-in Motion Sensor Technology

saves battery life; scratch resistant lenses; fog-proof and waterproof
MSRP . . . . **N/A**

NEWCON OPTIK LRM 3500M

Type: Rangefinder
Weight: 16 oz.
Length: 4.6 in.
Power: 6.5X
Obj. Dia.: 30mm
Field of View: 7 degrees
Eye Relief: 20mm
Features: A full-featured rangefinder goes the distance to 5 km; etched reticle in mils; last ten readings recall; first/last target logic; declination correction; digital compass; user and target GPS coordinates; bluetooth capability/Android compatible; Kestrel ballistic calculator
MSRP **$5500.00**

NIGHT OPTICS FIR-I IR ILLUMINATOR

Type: IR illuminator
Features: An infrared illuminator that functions to 800 yards; focusable beam; more than one hour of continuous use with a single CR123A battery;
MSRP **$299.99**

NIGHT OPTICS NIGHT CHASE

Type: Laser
Weight: 4 oz.
Length: 4.25 in.
Features: A flip-up backup laser sight for both day and night engagements; laser effective to 500 yards; IR illuminator aids close- and midrange target acquisition
MSRP **$539.99**

NEW Products: Optics

NIGHT OPTICS SENTRY 14 1X 4G

NIKON MONARCH 2000

NIKON PROSTAFF 1000I

SHIELD SIGHTS RMSW

SHIELD SIGHTS SMS2

SIGHTMARK CORE SHOT A-SPEC FMS

SIGHTMARK ULTRA SHOT A-SPEC

SIGHTMARK ULTRA SHOT M-SPEC FMS

SIGHTMARK ULTRA SHOT R-SPEC

NIGHT OPTICS SENTRY 14 1X 4G

Type: Nightvision
Weight: 13.8 oz.
Power: 1X
Obj. Dia.: 26mm
Field of View: 40 degrees
Features: Low- to no-light night vision monocular with day/night adaptor; hand-held or able to mount on firearm or helmet; off/on/momentary/constant IR activation; available accessories include 3X and 5X mil-spec Afocal night lenses, remote pressure switch, and iPhone camera adaptor kit
MSRP $4549.99

NIKON MONARCH 2000

Type: Rangefinder
Weight: 6.1 oz.
Length: 3.8 in.
Power: 6X
Obj. Dia.: 21mm
Field of View: 39.3 ft.
Eye Relief: 18mm
Features: Featuring Nikon's Advanced ID (Incline/Decline) technology accurate to 89.1 degrees; maximum reflective yardage of 2000; focusing diopter; OLED display; distant target priority mode
MSRP $299.95

NIKON PROSTAFF 1000, 1000I

Type: Rangefinder
Weight: 4.6 oz.
Length: 3.6 in.
Power: 6X
Obj. Dia.: 20mm
Field of View: 31.4 ft.
Eye Relief: 16.7mm
Features: Maximum reflective ranging to 1000 yards; 100i includes ID incline/decline technology
MSRP . . . . $169.95–$199.95

SHIELD SIGHTS RMSW

Type: Reflex sight
Power: 1X
Field of View: Unlimited
Eye Relief: Unlimited
Features: Model stands for Reflex Mini Sight Waterproof; gasket sealed and watertight to 20 meters for up to thirty minutes; hard-coated S1O2 polymer lens; 4 MOA or 8 MOA dot
MSRP $499.00

SHIELD SIGHTS SMS2

Type: Reflex sight
Power: 1X
Field of View: Unlimited
Eye Relief: Unlimited
Features: Updated "2.0" version of the original Shield Mini Sight (SMS); available with 1 MOA, 4 MOA, 8 MOA, or 65/1 MOA ring/dot
MSRP . . . . $206.45–$267.17

SIGHTMARK CORE SHOT A-SPEC FMS, A-SPEC LQD

Type: Reflex sight
Weight: 4.4 oz.
Length: 2.3 in.
Power: 1X
Obj. Dia.: 28X18mm
Field of View: Unlimited
Eye Relief: Unlimited
Features: Features include 100 MOAs of windage and elevation; ability to handle recoil up to .50 BMG; AR red lens coating; 1400 hours battery life; 5 MOA dot; eight brightness settings
MSRP . . . . $156.00–$180.00

SIGHTMARK ULTRA SHOT A-SPEC

Type: Reflex sight
Weight: 10.8 oz.
Length: 4.33 in.
Power: 1X
Obj. Dia.: 33X24mm
Field of View: Unlimited
Eye Relief: Unlimited

Features: The A stands for Advanced. Features include: scratch-resistant wide-angle lens; aluminum hood and shield; 120 MOA windage and elevation adjustments in 1 MOA clicks; recoil-rated up to .338-caliber; one-hour shutoff; battery life of 2000 hours
MSRP $148.98

SIGHTMARK ULTRA SHOT M-SPEC FMS, M-SPEC LQD

Type: Reflex sight
Weight: 9.6 oz.
Length: 4.01 in.
Power: 1X
Obj. Dia.: 33X24mm
Field of View: Unlimited
Eye Relief: Unlimited
Features: Useful across law enforcement, hunting, and target competition disciplines, this rugged reflex sight's feature includes: waterproof to 40 feet; ability to handle recoil up to .50 BMG; 12-hour auto off with five minute motion activation shutoff/on; 65 MOA dot; 120 MOA of windage and elevation adjustment in 1 MOA clicks; 2000 hours of battery life; integrated sunshade; quick-detach option with the LQD version
MSRP . . . . $229.97–$249.97

SIGHTMARK ULTRA SHOT R-SPEC

Type: Reflex sight
Weight: 10.7 oz.
Length: 4.33 in.
Power: 1X
Obj. Dia.: 33X24mm
Field of View: Unlimited
Eye Relief: Unlimited
Features: The R stands for Range. Features include: 10 brightness settings; 120 MOA of windage and elevation adjustment with 1 MOA clicks; choice of four each red or green reticles; one-hour auto shutoff
MSRP $159.99

SIG SAUER KILO1400BDX 6X20MM

SIG SAUER KILO1800BDX 6X22MM

SIG SAUER KILO2200BDX 7X25MM

SIG SAUER KILO2400BDX 7X25MM

SIG SAUER LIMA365

SIG SAUER ROMEO8H

SIG SAUER ROMEO8T

TEINER TOR FUSION

STEINER TOR FUSION

SIG SAUER KILO1400BDX 6X20MM

Type: Rangefinder
Weight: 5 oz.
Length: 3.9 in.
Power: 6X
Obj. Dia.: 20mm
Exit Pupil: 6.5 degreea
Eye Relief: 15mm
Features: Ultralightweight, extended range rangefinder with SIG's BDX--Ballistic Data Xchange--technology. Paired with SIG's SIERRA3BDX rifle scope, the rangefinder sends ballistic data via Bluetooth to the scope and illuminates a holdover and wind hold dot in the reticle; BDX app is downloadable to Android or iOS devices; line of sight or angle modified range estimates; readings in MIL or MOA; diopter adjustment; ranges include 3400 yards to reflective objects, 1600 yards to trees, and 1300 yards to deer-sized game; circle reticle; up to 1600 yards reflective ranging
MSRP **$299.99**

SIG SAUER KILO1800BDX 6X22MM

Type: Rangefinder
Weight: 7.8 oz.
Length: 4.1in.
Power: 6X
Obj. Dia.: 22mm
Exit Pupil: 6 degrees
Eye Relief: 17mm
Features: Similar to the KILO1400BDX but with a slightly bigger aperture and eye relief; circle reticle; up to 2000 yards reflective ranging
MSRP **$479.99**

SIG SAUER KILO2200BDX 7X25MM

Type: Rangefinder

Weight: 7.5 oz.
Length: 4.4 in.
Power: 7X
Obj. Dia.: 25mm
Exit Pupil: 6.78 degrees
Eye Relief: 15mm
Features: Similar to the KILO1400BDX but at 7X and with a circle plus Milling grid reticle; ten illumination settings; gray body; up to 3400 yards reflective ranging
MSRP **$599.99**

SIG SAUER KILO2400BDX 7X25MM

Type: Rangefinder
Weight: 7.5 oz.
Length: 4.4 in.
Power: 7X
Obj. Dia.: 25mm
Exit Pupil: 6.78 degrees
Eye Relief: 15mm
Features: Similar to the other rangefinders in the KILO BDX series but at 7X and with a circle plus Milling grid reticle; ten illumination settings; OD green body; up to 3400 yards reflective ranging
MSRP **$959.99**

SIG SAUER LIMA365

Type: Laser
Features: Designed specifically for SIG's P365 compact handgun, the rail-mounted laser is available in either red or green
MSRP . . . . **$179.99–$239.99**

SIG SAUER ROMEO8H

Type: Red-dot
Power: 1X
Obj. Dia.: 38mm
Eye Relief: Unlimited
Features: Similar to the 8T, but with a 2 MOA red ballistic circle dot
MSRP **$599.99**

SIG SAUER ROMEO8T

Type: Red-dot
Power: 1X
Obj. Dia.: 38mm
Eye Relief: Unlimited
Features: Intended for use on MSR rifle platforms and on shotguns; 2 MOA/65 MOA circle reticle; MOTAC motion activated illumination power up/down; LED illumination for daytime use; four integrated user-selectable reticles; lens covers; ½ hex bolt mount; 100,000 hours battery life; waterproof and fog-proof
MSRP **$719.99**

STEINER DRS 1X

Type: Reflex sight
Weight: 10.4 oz.
Length: 3.88 in.
Power: 1X
Features: Housed in a magnesium body, this solid battle sight offers a choice of three reticle options; seven illumination settings; 2X AA battery power; waterproof, shockproof, and fog-proof; 50 MOA windage and elevation adjustment
MSRP **$749.99**

STEINER TOR FUSION

Type: Laser
Features: A rail-mounted combo white light and aiming laser; laser available in red or green; left and right activation buttons; mil-spec engineering; anodized aluminum housing; dustproof; splash-proof; windage and elevation adjustment screws; auto-mode that senses motion like draw from a holster and automatically turns on the laser; boost mode forces unit to maximum output
MSRP **$399.00**

NEW Products: Optics

STEINER TOR MICRO

STEINER TOR MINI

TRIJICON RMR HRS

TRUGLO TRUTEC 20MM

TRUGLO TRUTEC 30MM

TRUGLO TRUTEC 30MM WITH LASER

TRUGLO TRUTEC EXTREME 30MM WITH CANTILEVER MOUNT

TRUGLO TRUTEC MICRO SUB-COMPACT

STEINER TOR MICRO

Type: Laser
Features: Steiner classifies this rail-mounted laser unit as sub-miniature and "combat ready"; both red and green direct diode operation for utilization in extreme cold; universal rail mount that fits all Picatinny and Weaver rails; left and right side activation buttons
MSRP **$199.00**

STEINER TOR MINI

Type: Laser
Features: Similar to the Micro, but intended for rail mounting forward of the trigger guard. Red and green lasers available; low, medium, high, and high pulse modes plus setting memory; auto-on senses movement such as retrieval from a nightstand safe and automatically activates laser; ambidextrous use
MSRP **$299.00**

TRIJICON RMR HRS

Type: Reflex sight
Weight: 1.2 oz.
Length: 1.77 in.
Power: 1X
Features: Housing of forged aluminum; similar version to RMR Type 2 HRS chosen by the USSOCOM; hard-anodized coyote brown coating designed to reduce detection
MSRP **$739.00**

TRUGLO TRUTEC 20MM

Type: Red-dot
Power: 1X
Obj. Dia.: 20mm
Eye Relief: Unlimited
Features: 2 MOA reticle; Quick Touch power-on lets the user tap anywhere on the optic to turn it on; multiple brightness settings; one option has both high and low mounts, the second has a quick-detach mount
MSRP . . . . **$211.49–$247.99**

TRUGLO TRUTEC 30MM

Type: Red-dot
Power: 1X
Obj. Dia.: 30mm
Eye Relief: Unlimited
Features: 2 MOA reticle; quick detach mounting system; flip-up lens covers; waterproof and fog-proof; programmable on/off
MSRP **$223.99**

TRUGLO TRUTEC 30MM WITH LASER

Type: Red-dot
Power: 1X
Obj. Dia.: 30mm
Eye Relief: Unlimited
Features: Similar to the standard TruTec 1X30, but with built-in red or green laser
MSRP . . . . **$258.99–$352.99**

TRUGLO TRUTEC EXTREME 30MM WITH CANTILEVER MOUNT

Type: Red-dot
Power: 1X
Obj. Dia.: 30mm
Eye Relief: Unlimited
Features: A red-dot with a built-in super-durable cantilever mount for extra height; motion-sensing "wake up"; programmable automatic sleep mode; multiple brightness settings; flip up lens covers
MSRP **$247.99**

TRUGLO TRUTEC MICRO SUB-COMPACT

Type: Reflex sight
Power: 1X
Obj. Dia.: 23X17mm
Eye Relief: Unlimited
Features: Ten brightness settings; compatible with most pistol optics mounting plates/platforms; shock-, water-, and fog-resistant; includes ABS hardshell cover; aluminum body
MSRP **$235.99**

SIGHTS

TRIJICON FIBER SIGHTS

WILLIAMS GUN SIGHT COMPANY AR-15 FOLDING TACTICAL SIGHT

XS SIGHTS DXT

XS SIGHTS DXT2 BIG DOT NIGHT SIGHTS

XS SIGHTS DXW

TRIJICON FIBER SIGHTS

Features: Front post is .110-inch wide with a .060-inch-diameter fiber; rear sight is blacked out with a .125-inch square notch, is steeply hooked for one-handed slide manipulation as needed, and has rounded edges to reduce snagging; red front installed, red and green replacements included
MSRP. **$89.99**

WILLIAMS GUN SIGHT COMPANY AR-15 FOLDING TACTICAL SIGHT

Features: CNC high-grade machined aluminum construction; upright lock; fit any Picatinny-style rail; windage and elevation adjustments
MSRP. . . . . **N/A**

XS SIGHTS DXT

Features: Defensive Express Tritium available in Big Dot or Standard Dot

versions for the CZ P10C, Kimber Micro 9 and 380, and BerettaPico
MSRP. **$123.00**

XS SIGHTS DXT2 BIG DOT NIGHT SIGHTS

Features: Available in orange or yellow, the sight design naturally allows the shooter to focus on the front sight; dot absorbs light and glows when conditions aren't dark enough to sustain the visible glow of tritium; fits all GLOCKs, Smith & Wesson Shields and compact and full-size M&Ps, SIG Sauer P320, P226, and P229, Springfield Armory XDs, and the FNH FN509
MSRP. **$132.00**

XS SIGHTS DXW

Features: Defensive Express White Rear available in Big Dot or Standard Dot versions for the CZ P10C, Kimber Micro 9 and 380, and Beretta Pico
MSRP. **$97.67**

NEW Products: **Ammunition**

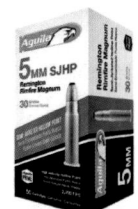

AGUILA 5MM REMINGTON SJHP

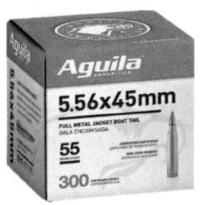

AGUILA 5.56X45MM

ALLEGIANCE HOG STRIKE

ALLEGIANCE ONE STRIKE

ALLEGIANCE SILENT STRIKE

AGUILA 5MM REMINGTON SJHP

Features: The unusual 5mm necked rimfire round in a semi-jacketed hollowpoint; 2200 fps velocity
Available in: 5mm Remington (30 gr.)
Box of: 50
MSRP. **$29.99**

AGUILA 5.56X45MM

Features: Bulk packs of 300 rounds with full metal jacket boattails
Available in: 5.56x45mm (55 gr.)
Box of: 300
MSRP. **$119.99**

ALLEGIANCE HOG STRIKE

Features: A frangible round with a thick solid core that penetrates tough

game hides and fragments into soft fluid tissue and creates devastating wound channels
Available in: .300 BLK, 5.56 NATO, .223 Rem., .308 Win.
Box of: 20
MSRP. . . . .**$29.00–$40.00**

ALLEGIANCE ONE STRIKE

Features: A frangible offering intended for use where metal enclosures or crowds are a concern; HET High Energy Transfer frangible core; fragments on light barriers
Available in: 9mm (70 gr.), 5.56 NATO (55 gr., 80 gr.), 7.62x39 NATO (140 gr.), .300 AAC (140 gr.)
Box of: 20
MSRP. . . . .**$24.00–$36.00**

ALLEGIANCE SILENT STRIKE

Features: A subsonic, frangible round made of compressed tungsten powder and with a high-density core that will penetrate even thick clothing; fragmentation of core occurs both horizontally and vertically upon hitting fluid-filled tissue
Available in: 9mm (135 gr.), .45 ACP (230 gr.), 5.56 NATO/.223 Rem. (110 gr., 130 gr.), 7.62x39 (200 gr.), .300 AAC (140 gr., 200 gr.)
Box of: 20
MSRP. . . . .**$36.00–$46.66**

NEW Products: Ammunition

BLACK HILLS HONEYBADGER

BOSS SHOTSHELLS UNMUZZLED

BROWNING LONG RANGE PRO

BROWNING TSS TUNGSTEN TURKEY

CCI BLAZER .22 LR BULK PACK

CCI BLAZER 9MM

CCI CLEAN-22

CCI QUIET-22 SEMI-AUTO

CCI VNT .17 MACH 2, .22 WMR

DDUPLEKS BROADHEAD DEVASTATOR

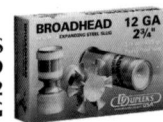

DDUPLEKS BROADHEAD HEXOLIT 32 EXPANDING

BLACK HILLS HONEYBADGER

Features: A unique fluted projectile—not a hollowpoint—designed for self-defense purposes; a .45-70 load is likely suitable for ranch and varmint/predator work
Available in: .38 Spec. +P (100 gr.), .380 ACP (60 gr.), .44 Mag. (160 gr.), .44 Spec. (125 gr.), .45 ACP (235 gr.), .45-70 Gov't. (325 gr.), 9mm (100 gr.)
Box of: 20
MSRP . . . .$25.57–$69.31

BOSS SHOTSHELLS UNMUZZLED

Features: A line of Bismuth shells without the historically high cost; a variety of 3-inch and 2 ¾-inch 12 ga. and 20 ga. loads, with 28 ga. loadings projected for future release; custom shells can be ordered as well
Available in: 12, 20, 28 ga.
Box of: 20
MSRP . . . .$23.00–$33.00

Rifle Ammunition

BROWNING LONG RANGE PRO

Features: Designed specifically for the hottest game in town, long-range shooting; high BCs; high velocity retention; Sierra Tipped MatchKing bullets
Available in: .30-06 Spfd. (195-gr.), .300 Win. Mag. and .300 WSM (195 gr.), .308 Win. (168 gr.), 6.5 Creedmoor (130 gr.)
Box of: 20
MSRP . . . . N/A

Shotshells

BROWNING TSS TUNGSTEN TURKEY

Features: Super-dense loads for gobbler season; shot sizes BB, 6, 5, and 4 across magnum 12- and 20 ga. and .410-bore loads; duplex loads are also to be made available in smaller shot size combos
Available in: 12 ga. (3 ½ in., 3 in.), 20 ga. (3 in.), .410-bore (3 in.)
Box of: 10
MSRP . . . . N/A

CCI BLAZER .22 LR BULK PACK

Features: A 525-count box of lead roundnose for hours of plinking fun
Available in: .22 LR (38 gr.)
Box of: 525
MSRP $29.95

CCI BLAZER 9MM

Features: Designed for high-volume training; FMJ bullet in a reloadable brass case
Available in: 9mm (147 gr.)
Box of: 50
MSRP $17.95

CCI CLEAN-22

Features: A coated polymer bullet leaves no residue behind while reducing traditional copper and lead fouling, even in suppressors; sub-sonic and high-velocity loads; will cycle in semiautomatics
Available in: .22 LR Sub-Sonic (1070 fps), .22 LR High-Velocity (1235 fps)
Box of: 100
MSRP $9.95

CCI QUIET-22 SEMI-AUTO

Features: Reduced report in a round that reliably cycles semiautomatics; noise reduced with or without suppressors; low velocity
Available in: .22 LR (45 gr., 735 fps)
Box of: 50
MSRP $5.95

CCI VNT .17 MACH 2, .22 WMR

Features: Special Speer VNT bullet design for varmint hunters favoring these speedy specialty rimfire rounds; polymer tip and thin jacket; nickel-plated cases
Available in: .17 Mach 2 (17 gr.), .22 WMR (30 gr.)
Box of: 50
MSRP . . . .$10.95–$15.95

DDUPLEKS BROADHEAD DEVASTATOR

Features: Expanding slug with polymer bearing bands that prevent slug contact with the barrel, so safe for use in both rifled and smoothbore barrels; one-piece wad column; six-piece fragmentation after hit; eco-friendly for use in areas that prohibit lead projectile
Available in: 20 ga. (2 ¾ in.)
Box of: 5
MSRP $8.99

DDUPLEKS BROADHEAD HEXOLIT 32 EXPANDING

Features: Expanding slug with polymer bearing bands that prevent slug contact with the barrel, so safe for use in both rifled and smoothbore barrels; one-piece wad column; six-piece fragmentation after hit; eco-friendly for use in areas that prohibit lead projectiles
Available in: 12 ga. (2 ¾ in.)
Box of: 5
MSRP $12.99

DDUPLEKS KAVIAR SLUG

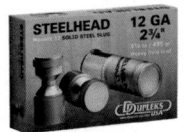
DDUPLEKS STEELHEAD MONOLIT 32

DDUPLEKS STEELHEAD PEN-TRACK

ENVIRON-METAL/ HEVI-SHOT HEVI-DUTY CENTERFIRE

ENVIRON-METAL/ HEVI-SHOT HEVI-SNOW

ENVIRON-METAL/HEVI-SHOT HEVI-X

FEDERAL PREMIUM .450 BUSHMASTER

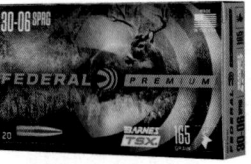
FEDERAL PREMIUM BARNES TSX (TRIPLE-SHOCK X)

FEDERAL PREMIUM BYOB

FEDERAL PREMIUM BERGER HYBRID HUNTER

DDUPLEKS KAVIAR SLUG

Features: Home-defense frangible hollowpoint slug made of a combination of pellets and polyethylene; reduced recoil; also suitable for use on steel targets; designed for smoothbore, suitable for rifled bores
Available in: 12 ga. (2¾ in.)
Box of: 5
MSRP . . . . N/A

DDUPLEKS STEELHEAD MONOLIT 32

Features: A solid steel hunting slug suitable for both rifled and smooth bores; obstacle penetrating; one-piece wad; flat fore-front; self-stabilizing
Available in: 12 ga. (2 ¾ in.)
Box of: 5
MSRP $8.49

DDUPLEKS STEELHEAD PEN-TRACK

Features: A solid steel hunting slug for big game with a waisted body; flat ogive for superb energy transfer; suitable for smoothbore and rifled barrels
Available in: 20 ga. (2 ¾ in.)
Box of: 5
MSRP $6.99

Handgun Ammunition

ENVIRON-METAL/HEVI-SHOT HEVI-DUTY CENTERFIRE

Features: Steel-safe frangible projectiles; non-toxic

Available in: .380 ACP, .357 Mag., .38 Spec. 9mm, .40 S&W, 10mm, .45 ACP
Box of: 50
MSRP . . . .$17.99–$42.99

Shotgun Ammunition

ENVIRON-METAL/HEVI-SHOT HEVI-SNOW

Features: A high-speed, non-toxic load for skies full of snow geese
Available in: 12 ga. (3 in., 3 ½ in.); Shot sizes: 1, 2, BB, BBB
Box of: 25
MSRP . . . .$15.99–$22.08

ENVIRON-METAL/HEVI-SHOT HEVI-X

Features: A tungsten-based load for waterfowl hunters in Hevi Metal's Deadlier at Distance line; allows hunters to shoot two shot sizes smaller than normal to put more pellets on target
Available in: 12 ga. (3 in.), 20 ga. (3 in.); Shot size: 6
Box of: 25
MSRP . . . .$27.99–$33.99

Rifle Ammunition

FEDERAL PREMIUM .450 BUSHMASTER

Features: Three new loads for this trending cartridge include Fusion softpoint, Non-Typical softpoint, and Power-Shok softpoint
Available in: .450 Bushmaster (300 gr.)
Box of: 20
MSRP . . . .$33.95–$37.95

FEDERAL PREMIUM BARNES TSX (TRIPLE-SHOCK X)

Features: One of Federal's most popular hunting designs resurrected. Deep hollowpoint, monolithic bullet design has more than 99% weight retention
Available in: .223 Rem., .224 Valkyrie, .243 Win., .25-06 Rem., 6.5 Creedmoor, .270 Win., .270 WSM, 7mm-08 Rem., .308 Win., .30-30 Win., .30-06 Spfd., 7mm Rem. Mag., .300 WSM, .300 Win. Mag.
Box of: 20
MSRP . . . .$33.95–$52.95

FEDERAL PREMIUM BERGER HYBRID HUNTER

Features: Features a low-drag bullet profile with a hybrid tangent/secant ogive design. Very high BC; Gold Medal primers; nickel-plated brass
Available in: .243 Win., 6.5 Creedmoor, .270 Win., .270 WSM, 7mm Rem. Mag., .280 Ackley Improved, .308 Win., .30-06 Spfd., .300 Win., .300 WSM
Box of: 20
MSRP . . . .$37.95–$49.95

FEDERAL PREMIUM BYOB

Features: Bulk rimfire in "Bring Your Own Bucket" packs
Available in: .17 HMR (17 gr.) Speer TNT; .22 LR (36 gr.) CPHP; .22 WMR (50 gr.) JHP
Box of: 250 (17 HMR, .22 WMR); 450, 825, 1,375 (.22 LR)
MSRP . . . .$30.95–$86.95

NEW Products: **Ammunition**

FEDERAL PREMIUM GOLD MEDAL 6.5 CREEDMOOR, 6MM CREEDMOOR

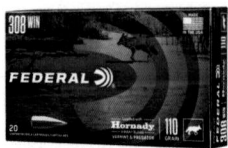

FEDERAL PREMIUM VARMINT & PREDATOR

FEDERAL PREMIUM HST 10MM AUTO

FEDERAL PREMIUM SYNTECH ACTION PISTOL

FEDERAL PREMIUM SYNTECH DEFENSE

FEDERAL PREMIUM SYNTECH PCC (PISTOL-CALIBER CARBINE)

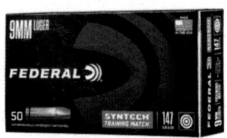

FEDERAL PREMIUM SYNTECH TRAINING MATCH

FEDERAL PREMIUM BALLISTICLEAN FRANGIBLE BUCKSHOT, SLUG

FEDERAL PREMIUM BLACK CLOUD TSS

FEDERAL PREMIUM GOLD MEDAL 6.5 CREEDMOOR, 6MM CREEDMOOR

Features: Federal capitalizes on the hot Creedmoor trend with a Sierra MatchKing on the 6.5 model and a Berger Hybrid on the 6mm. Both have extremely high BC; Federal Gold Medal match primers; Federal brass
Available in: 6.5 Creedmoor (140 gr.), 6mm Creedmoor (105 gr.)
Box of: 20
MSRP . . . .$33.95–$36.95

FEDERAL PREMIUM VARMINT & PREDATOR

Features: A line of coyote and prairie dog ammo priced for high-volume shooters; V-Max bullets; Federal brass and primer
Available in: .204 Ruger (32 gr.), .22-250 Rem. (40 gr.), .223 Rem. (40 gr., 53 gr.), 6.5 Creedmoor (95 gr.), .308 Win. (110 gr.)
Box of: 20
MSRP . . . .$15.95–$24.95

Handgun Ammunition

FEDERAL PREMIUM HST 10MM AUTO

Features: A full-power 10mm self-defense load; hollowpoint that expands with reliability after barrier penetration
Available in: 10mm Auto (200 gr.)
Box of: 20
MSRP $34.95

FEDERAL PREMIUM SYNTECH ACTION PISTOL

Features: Declared the official ammunition of USPSA; loaded to meet power factor requirements while reducing recoil; total synthetic jacket (TSJ) reduces barrel fouling; lead-free primers; offers reduced splashback on steel plates
Available in: 9mm (150 gr.), .40 S&W (205 gr.), .45 ACP (220 gr.)
Box of: 50
MSRP . . . .$18.95–$30.95

FEDERAL PREMIUM SYNTECH DEFENSE

Features: Hollowpoint design separates into three segments for additional trauma, while the core continues penetration; Catalyst lead-free primer; polymer jacket reduces fouling
Available in: 9mm (138 gr.), .40 S&W (175 gr.), .45 ACP (205 gr.)
Box of: 20
MSRP . . . .$19.95–$24.95

FEDERAL PREMIUM SYNTECH PCC (PISTOL-CALIBER CARBINE)

Features: A 9mmm load specifically developed for reliable functionality in pistol-caliber carbines; minimizes splashback so a great choice for competitors; synthetic jacket reduces fouling; lead-free Catalyst primer
Available in: 9mm (130 gr.)
Box of: 50
MSRP $19.95

FEDERAL PREMIUM SYNTECH TRAINING MATCH

Features: Provides the same velocities, trajectories, and point of impact's as Federal's Personal Defense HST and Tactical HST loadings, but with a Catalyst lead-free primer and synthetic bullet jacket that reduces fouling; purple bullet color makes use as a training round easily identifiable
Available in: 9mm (124 gr., 147 gr.), .40 S&W (180 gr.), .45 ACP (230 gr.)
Box of: 50
MSRP . . . .$19.95–$31.95

Shotgun Ammunition

FEDERAL PREMIUM BALLISTICLEAN FRANGIBLE BUCKSHOT, SLUG

Features: Non-lead buckshot or slug backed by the lead-free Catalyst primer; designed for training with performance identical to duty loads
Available in: 12 ga. (2 ¾ in.); Shot sizes: nine-pellet 00 or 325 gr. slug
Box of: 25
MSRP $39.99

FEDERAL PREMIUM BLACK CLOUD TSS

Features: A new and improved duplex Black Cloud with Heavyweight Tungsten Super Shot pellets (60%) and Flitestopper Steel (40%) backed by Flitecontrol Flex wad; Catalyst lead-free primer
Available in: 12 ga. 3 in. in 1 ¼-ounce load in No. 7 TSS/BB FS Steel or No. 9 TSS/No. 3 FS Steel
Box of: 10
MSRP $37.95

FEDERAL PREMIUM GOLD MEDAL GRAND PLASTIC

FEDERAL PREMIUM HEAVYWEIGHT TSS

FEDERAL PREMIUM SHORTY

FEDERAL PREMIUM TOP GUN SPORTING

FEDERAL PREMIUM UPLAND STEEL

FIOCCHI RANGE DYNAMICS

FIOCCHI RANGE DYNAMICS

FIOCCHI SCIROCCO II EXTREME RIFLE

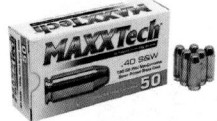

GRASSO HOLDINGS/ GH AMMUNITION MAXXTECH

GRASSO HOLDINGS/ GH AMMUNITION TULAMMO RIFLE WITH BRASS-JACKETED BULLETS

FEDERAL PREMIUM GOLD MEDAL GRAND PLASTIC

Features: A payload premium lead target load with less recoil; two-piece SoftCell wad with integral base; rigid PrimerLock head; 1335 fps
Available in: 12 ga. 2 ¾ in. 24-gram load in No. 7.5 or 9
Box of: 25
MSRP. $11.95

FEDERAL PREMIUM HEAVYWEIGHT TSS

Features: Four duplex loads of HEAVYWEIGHT TSS (Tungsten Super Shot) and a single-size fine-shot TSS load provide superior pellet counts-- more than double the pellet count of a No. 5 load in the same weight
Available in: 12 ga. (3 ½ in. 2 ½-ounce TSS No. 7/9 or No. 8/10); 20 ga. (3 in. 1 5/8-ounc TSS No. 7/9 or No. 8/10); 20 ga. (3 in. 1 ½-ounce TSS No. 9)
Box of: 5
MSRP. . . . .$39.95–$63.95

FEDERAL PREMIUM SHORTY

Features: Just 1¾-inches long, perfect for use in short-chambered older guns and offers performance similar to 2 ¾-inch shells
Available in: 12 ga.; Shot size: #4 Buck, rifled slug, 8
Box of: 10
MSRP. . . . . $5.95–$11.95

FEDERAL PREMIUM TOP GUN SPORTING

Features: A dedicated sporting clays series of loads meant to speed velocities and minimize recoil; with an eight-segment crimp

Available in: 12 ga. (2 ¾ in. 1-ounce No. 7.5, 8); 20 ga. (2 ¾ in. 7/8-ounce 7.5, 8); 28 ga. (2 ¾ in. ¾-ounce No. 7.5, 8, 9); .410-bore (2 ½ in. ½-ounce No. 7.5, 8, 9)
Box of: 25
MSRP. . . . . $8.95–$13.95

FEDERAL PREMIUM UPLAND STEEL

Features: Quail, woodcock, pheasant and other upland game on lands with traditional ammo restrictions are now easier to add to the dinner table with these high-velocity steel loads
Available in: 12 ga. (2 ¾ in. 1 1/8-ounce No. 6, 7.5); 20 ga. (2 ¾ in. ¾-ounce No. 5, 7.5)
Box of: 25
MSRP. . . . . $8.95–$9.95

Handgun Ammunition

FIOCCHI RANGE DYNAMICS

Features: Training and target load sold in bulk; reloadable brass cases
Available in: 9mm (1150 gr.)
Box of: 200
MSRP. . . . . N/A

Rifle Ammunition

FIOCCHI RANGE DYNAMICS

Features: Training and target loads for rifle shooters, most calibers sold in bulk
Available in: .223 Rem., .300 BLK, .308 Win.
Box of: 20, 50
MSRP. . . . . N/A

FIOCCHI SCIROCCO II EXTREME RIFLE

Features: Big-game hunters get a dedicated cartridge modeled on the company's Extrema Rifle One loadings, but with polymer tipped Scirocco II boattail projectiles from Swift
Available in: .308 Win. (150 gr.), 6.5 Creedmoor (123 gr.)
Box of: 20
MSRP. . . . . N/A

GRASSO HOLDINGS/GH AMMUNITION MAXXTECH

Features: Economical brass-cased ammunition for range practice; Boxer primed, full metal jacket except for the lead .22 LR rimfire
Available in: .380 ACP, 9mm, .40 S&W, .45 ACP, .22 LR, .223 Rem.
Box of: 50/100 (pistol), 20/50 (rifle), 250 (.22 LR)
MSRP. . . . .

GRASSO HOLDINGS/GH AMMUNITION TULAMMO RIFLE WITH BRASS-JACKETED BULLETS

Features: Russian-made steel-cased ammo designed to be range-friendly by minimizing spark risks with a non-steel, brass-jacketed projectile; legal in all 50 states; Berdan primers
Available in: .223 Rem., .30 Carbine, .308 Win., 5.45x39mm, 7.62x39, 7.62x54R
Box of: 20
MSRP. . . . . N/A

NEW Products: Ammunition

HONOR DEFENSE HI-PERFORMANCE HOLLOW POINT

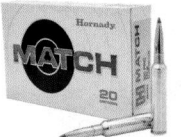

HORNADY 300 PRC MATCH

HORNADY 300 PRC PRECISION HUNTER

HORNADY OUTFITTER

INCEPTOR ARX PREFERRED DEFENSE

KENT CARTRIDGE FASTEEL 2.0

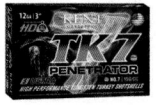

KENT CARTRIDGE TK7 PENETRATOR

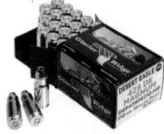

MAGNUM RESEARCH .429 DE MAGNUM

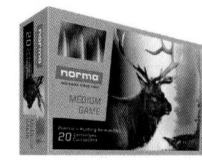

NORMA BONDSTRIKE EXTREME

NORMA MHP

HONOR DEFENSE HI-PERFORMANCE HOLLOW POINT

Features: Previously available only to military and law enforcement, now available to the consumer market; handgun/pistol-caliber carbine rounds with a drilled hollowpoint that's frangible in soft tissue, is lead free, and housed in virgin brass; passes FBI light and heavy clothing, wallboard, plywood, and bare gel protocols
Available in: .380 ACP, 9mm, 10mm, .357 SIG, .40 S&W, .45 ACP
Box of: 20
MSRP . . . . **starting at $13.99**

HORNADY 300 PRC MATCH

Features: PRC stands for Precision Rifle Cartridge. Based on the .375 Ruger, this magnum round features a ELD Match bullet
Available in: .300 PRC (225 gr.)
Box of: 20
MSRP **$44.99**

HORNADY 300 PRC PRECISION HUNTER

Features: The hunting counterpoint to the Match offering with a ELD -X bullet
Available in: .300 PRC (212 gr.)
Box of: 20
MSRP **$44.99**

HORNADY OUTFITTER

Features: Dedicated hunting line of rifle cartridges featuring: corrosion-resistant, waterproof nickel-plated cases; monolithic copper alloy GMX bullets

Available in: .243 Win., 6.5 Creedmoor, .270 Win., .270 WSM, 7mm WSM, 7mm Rem. Mag., .308 Win., .30-06 Spfd., .300 WSM, .300 Win. Mag., .375 H&H Mag., .375 Ruger
Box of: 20
MSRP . . . . **$35.99–$69.99**

INCEPTOR ARX PREFERRED DEFENSE

Features: Non-expanding projectile of a copper/polymer matrix for special critical defense use; 1780 fps, 633 ft.-lb.
Available in: 10mm (90 gr.)
Box of: 20
MSRP **$17.99**

KENT CARTRIDGE FASTEEL 2.0

Features: Zinc-plated shots; nickel-plated case heads; high-performance wad ensures consistent patterns in the coldest conditions; 12 ga. 3 ½-, 3-, 2¾-inch in a range of BB to No. 6; 20 ga. 3-inch in Nos. 2, 3, and 4
Available in: 12 ga., 20 ga.
Box of: 25
MSRP . . . . **N/A**

KENT CARTRIDGE TK7 PENETRATOR

Features: A dedicated turkey load of No. 7 tungsten pellets offering high pellet count and manageable recoil. Available in a 3-inch 12 ga. load with a 1 5/8-ounce payload or a 3-inch 20 ga. load with a 1 3/8-ounce payload, both at 1100 fps.
Available in: 12 ga., 20 ga.
Box of: 5
MSRP . . . . **N/A**

MAGNUM RESEARCH .429 DE MAGNUM

Features: Designed specifically for Magnum Research's new 429 DE Mark XIX pistol; Starline brass; more energy and velocity than a .44 Mag.
Available in: .429 DE (240 gr.) softpoint, (210 gr.) hollowpoint
Box of: 20
MSRP **$42.00**

Rifle Ammunition

NORMA BONDSTRIKE EXTREME

Features: Long-range hunting application; polymer tip match-style boattail projectiles with proprietary bonding produce extreme wound channels; initial offerings all in 180 gr.
Available in: .308 Win., .30-06 Spfd., .300 Win. Mag., .300 WSM, .300 RUM
Box of: 20
MSRP . . . . **N/A**

Handgun Ammunition

NORMA MHP

Features: High-expansion self-defense round with an all copper monolithic hollowpoint
Available in: 9mm (108 gr.)
Box of: 20
MSRP **$22.48**

PMC SFX

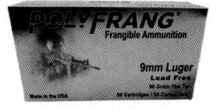

POLYFRANG HANDGUN

POLYFRANG RIFLE

REMINGTON HOG HAMMER RIFLE

REMINGTON HYPERSONIC BONDED

REMINGTON PETERS PREMIER BLUE HIGH VELOCITY RIFLE

REMINGTON PREMIER SCIROCCO BONDED

REMINGTON SUBSONIC RIFLE

REMINGTON PREMIER MAGNUM RIMFIRE

REMINGTON GOLDEN SABER BONDED

PMC SFX

Features: A personal-defense load with "hyper-expanding" hollowpoint. Replaces the old Starfire line and meets current law enforcement ammo protocols
Available in: 9mm (124 gr.), .45 ACP
Box of: 20
MSRP . . . . **N/A**

POLYFRANG HANDGUN

Features: US-made lead-free and frangible cartridges for 9mm or .40 S&W; reduces splashback on steel targets; safe for use with suppressors
Available in: 9mm (90 gr.), .40 S&W (115 gr.)
Box of: 50
MSRP . . . . **$30.50–$33.00**

POLYFRANG RIFLE

Features: US-made lead-free and frangible cartridges; reduces splashback on steel targets; safe for use with suppressors; .223 comes 50 rounds to the box
Available in: .223 Rem/5.56 NATO. (45 gr.), .308/7.62x39mm (125 gr.)
Box of: 20, 50
MSRP . . . . **$39.80–$63.30**

Rifle Ammunition

REMINGTON HOG HAMMER RIFLE

Features: Designed specifically for today's wild boar hunters with an all-copper Barnes TSX bullet; Accu-Groove reduces fouling; four-petal design expands to double the original diameter upon impact
Available in: .223 Rem., 6.5 Creedmoor, .270 Win., .300 BLK, .30-30 Win., .30-06 Spfd., .308 Win., .45-70 Gov't.
Box of: 20
MSRP . . . . **$26.16–$46.09**

REMINGTON HYPERSONIC BONDED

Features: Super-flat trajectories via a Core-Lokt Ultra Bonded projectile; souped up velocities; pointed soft point profile
Available in: .223 Rem., .243 Win., .270 Win., 7mm Rem. Mag., .30-06 Spfd., .300 Win. Mag., .308 Win.
Box of: 20
MSRP . . . . **$26.74–$40.87**

REMINGTON PETERS PREMIER BLUE HIGH VELOCITY RIFLE

Features: Retro packaging housing reasonably priced rifle ammo in a variety of popular calibers wearing Blue-Tipped boattails or Core-Lokt pointed softpoints
Available in: .243 Rem., 6.5 Creedmoor, 7mm Rem. Mag., .30-06 Spfd., .300 Win. Mag., .308 Win., .30-30 Win., .444 Marlin, .45-70 Gov't.
Box of: 20
MSRP . . . . **$22.05–$$48.53**

REMINGTON PREMIER SCIROCCO BONDED

Features: A hunting round with a polymer-tipped boattail whose core is bonded to the jacket; deep penetration and high weight retention
Available in: .243 Win., .270 Win., 7mm Rem. Mag., 7mm RUM, .30-06 Spfd., .300 WSM, .300 RUM Power Level III, .308 Win.
Box of: 20
MSRP . . . . **$43.50–$62.07**

REMINGTON SUBSONIC RIFLE

Features: A round resulting from the partnership of AAC and Remington; designed to work ideally with silencer-equipped firearms; special heel design reduces lead residue and fouling
Available in: .300 BLK
Box of: 20
MSRP **$19.46**

Rimfire Ammunition

REMINGTON PREMIER MAGNUM RIMFIRE

Features: Repackaged and repriced in 2019; .17 HMR in AccuTip; .22 Win. Mag. In Accutip, jacketed hollowpoint, or pointed softpoint
Available in: .17 HMR, .22 Win. Mag.
Box of: 50
MSRP . . . . **$11.29–$12.95**

Handgun Ammunition

REMINGTON GOLDEN SABER BONDED

Features: A personal-defense round with a lead core hot-bonded to a brass jacket for super weight retention; nickel-plated cases; waterproof primers; flash-diminishing powders
Available in: 9mm, 9mm +P, .357 SIG, .40 S&W, .45 ACP
Box of: 20
MSRP **$26.72**

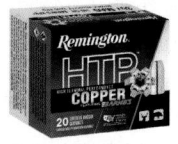

REMINGTON HTP COPPER

REMINGTON HOG HAMMER HANDGUN

REMINGTON SUBSONIC HANDGUN

REMINGTON PETERS PREMIER BLUE FIELD & TARGET

REMINGTON PETERS PREMIER BLUE HIGH VELOCITY STEEL

REMINGTON PREMIER EXPANDER SABOT SLUGS

RIO TARGET LOAD LOW RECOIL

RIO VINTAGE 1896 HELICE

RIO VINTAGE 1896 PAPER

RIO WING & TARGET LITE, HIGH VELOCITY

REMINGTON HOG HAMMER HANDGUN

Features: For wild boar hunters who pursue the hunt via handgun; Barnes all-copper XPB projectiles; six-petal expansion upon penetration
Available in: .357 Mag., 10mm, .41 Rem. Mag., .44 Rem. Mag., .45 LC, .454 Casull
Box of: 20
MSRP . . . .$22.13–$37.05

REMINGTON HTP COPPER

Features: Similar to the Hog Hammer rounds
Available in: .357 Mag., 10mm, .41 Rem. Mag., .44 Rem. Mag., .45 LC, .454 Casull
Box of: 20
MSRP . . . .$22.13–$37.05

REMINGTON SUBSONIC HANDGUN

Features: A round resulting from the partnership of AAC and Remington; designed to work ideally with silencer-equipped firearms; special heel design reduces lead residue and fouling
Available in: 9mm, .45 ACP
Box of: 50
MSRP . . . .$14.38–$22.59

Shotgun Ammunition

REMINGTON PETERS PREMIER BLUE FIELD & TARGET

Features: With handsome retro packaging; blue hulls; 12 ga. 2 ¾- inch shells in 2 ¾ or 3 DE; Nos. 7.5, 8
Available in: 12 ga.
Box of: 25
MSRP $7.77

REMINGTON PETERS PREMIER BLUE HIGH VELOCITY STEEL

Features: Eye-catching vintage packaging; six-crimp hulls; Kleanbore priming; all 12 ga. 3-inch shells in BB, 2, 3, or 4 at 1,400 fps
Available in: 12 ga.
Box of: 25
MSRP $13.42

REMINGTON PREMIER EXPANDER SABOT SLUGS

Features: Utilizes Barnes Expander slug; 12 ga. 2 ¾- and 3-inch loads, both in max DE
Available in: 12 ga.
Box of: 5
MSRP . . . .$14.69–$16.87

RIO TARGET LOAD LOW RECOIL

Features: A sound choice for new shooters; 12 ga. 2 ¾-inch 1-ounce, 2 ½ DE, 1,135 fps, Nos. 7, 7.5, 8, and 9
Available in: 12 ga.
Box of: 25
MSRP . . . . N/A

RIO VINTAGE 1896 HELICE

Features: Designed specifically for the challenging game of Helice; three 12 ga. 1-ounce 2 ¾-inch loads, one at 3 DE and 1,250 fps, one at Max DE and 1,300 fps, and a third at Max DE in a high-velocity 1,350 fps, all in Nos. 7.5 and 8
Available in: 12 ga.
Box of: 10
MSRP . . . . N/A

RIO VINTAGE 1896 PAPER

Features: Nothing beats the smell of a paper-hulled shotgun shell. Rio's new line of five loads uses single-based powders for minimal fouling; unique dust-stopping membrane on primers; Kraft paper hulls; premium lead shot. Five 12 ga. 2 ¾-inch loadings: Paper Light 1 1/8 ounce, 2 ¾ DE, 1,150 fps , No. 7.5, 8; Paper 1 1/8 ounce, 3 DE, 1,200 fps, No. 7.5, 8, 9; Paper HC 1 1/8 ounce, 3 ¼ DE, 1,235 fps, No. 7.5, 8; Paper Light 1 ounce, 2 ¾ DE, 1,200 fps, No. 7.5, 8, 9; and Sporting 1-ounce, 3 DE, 1,250 fps, No. 7.5, 8
Available in: 12 ga.
Box of: 25
MSRP . . . . N/A

RIO WING & TARGET LITE, HIGH VELOCITY

Features: A soft-shooting load offered in a Lite version with a 12 ga. 2 ¾- inch 1-ounce load at 1,150 fps and a High Velocity with the same payload at 1,350 fps; Nos. 7.5, 8
Available in: 12 ga.
Box of: 15
MSRP . . . . N/A

SIG SAUER ELITE BALL

SIG SAUER SBR ELITE COPPER DUTY

SIG SAUER 365 ELITE FMJ

SIG SAUER 365 ELITE V-CROWN

SIG SAUER ELITE MATCH9

SIG SAUER SIG ELITE RANGE M17

SIG SAUER SIG ELITE CARRY M17

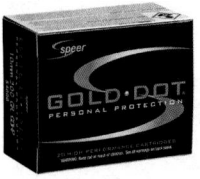

SPEER GOLD DOT 10MM

STEINEL AMMUNITION .500 AUTO MAX

TB AMMUNITION, LLC GPM QUADRA-SHOCK

Rifle Ammunition

SIG SAUER ELITE BALL

Features: Intended for training purposes with a full metal jacket projectile. Available in: 55-grain .223 Rem. with a muzzle velocity of 3,240 fps and 1,282 ft.-lb. of energy; 150-grain .308 Win. with a muzzle velocity of 2,900 fps and 2802 ft-lb. of energy
Available in: .223 Rem., .308 Win.
Box of: 20
MSRP . . . .$15.95–$26.95

SIG SAUER SBR ELITE COPPER DUTY

Features: A supersonic load developed for use in short-barreled rifles; all-copper bullet reduces fouling; black oxide case identifies the round specifically for SBR (sub-9-inch barrel) use; flash-reducing propellants
Available in: .300 BLK (120 gr.)
Box of: 20
MSRP . . . . N/A

Handgun Ammunition

SIG SAUER 365 ELITE FMJ

Features: Training ammo designed specifically for short-barreled handguns; offers reduced recoil; 1050 fps; 282 ft.-lb. energy
Available in: 9mm (115 gr.)
Box of: 50
MSRP $18.95

SIG SAUER 365 ELITE V-CROWN

Features: Carry ammo designed specifically for short-barreled handguns; offers reduced recoil; 1050 fps; 282 ft.-lb. energy
Available in: 9mm (115 gr.)
Box of: 20
MSRP $20.95

SIG SAUER ELITE MATCH9

Features: Designed for competitive handgun practitioners, specifically those shooting minor power factors; low recoil; coated nickel cases; velocities range from 860 to 900 fps
Available in: 9mm (147 gr.)
Box of: 50
MSRP $24.50

SIG SAUER SIG ELITE RANGE M17

Features: Military-grade ammunition for 9mm handguns and carbine rifles capable of handling +P pressures. Muzzle velocity 1198 fps; muzzle energy 395 ft.-lb. Designed for training
Available in: 9mm +P
Box of: 50
MSRP $18.95

SIG SAUER SIG ELITE CARRY M17

Features: Military-grade ammunition for 9mm handguns and carbine rifles capable of handling +P pressures. Muzzle velocity 1198 fps; muzzle energy 395 ft.-lb. Designed with a stacked hollowpoint for maximum weight retention and expansion
Available in: 9mm +P
Box of: 20
MSRP $20.95

SPEER GOLD DOT 10MM

Features: Attending the resurrection of the long-dormant 10mm is this power load from Speer.
Available in: 10mm (200 gr.)
Box of: 20
MSRP $34.95

STEINEL AMMUNITION .500 AUTO MAX

Features: A jacketed hollowpoint designed for use in Big Horn Armory's AR500 rifle
Available in: .500 Auto Max (350 gr.)
Box of: 20
MSRP $41.99

TB AMMUNITION, LLC GPM QUADRA-SHOCK

Features: An economical lead-free alternative in a variety of rifle and pistol calibers; non-frangible bullets
Available in: .223 Rem., .270 Win., .30-06 Spfd., .30-30 Win., .300 AAC, .308 Win., .380 ACP, .40 S&W, .45 ACP, 9mm
Box of: 20, 50
MSRP . . . . N/A

NEW Products: **Ammunition**

WINCHESTER DEER SEASON SHOTGUN SLUG

WINCHESTER XPERT SNOW GOOSE

WINCHESTER XTENDED RANGE BISMUTH

WINCHESTER .350 LEGEND

WINCHESTER DEER SEASON COPPER IMPACT XP

WINCHESTER SUPER SUPPRESSED (CENTERFIRE RIFLE)

WINCHESTER SUPER SUPPRESSED (RIMFIRE)

WINCHESTER USA READY

WINCHESTER WWII VICTORY SERIES (RIFLE)

Shotgun Ammunition

WINCHESTER DEER SEASON SHOTGUN SLUG

Features: A new species-dedicated shotgun slug for whitetail hunters; 1 1/8-ounce rifled slug; 1600 fps muzzle velocity; rear-stabilized wad
Available in: 12 ga.
Box of: 5
MSRP . . . . **N/A**

WINCHESTER XPERT SNOW GOOSE

Features: Continuing the trend of ammo designed for specific species, XPERT Snow Goose uses features from Winchester's XPERT Steel and Blind Side lines, with XPERT Steel Shot and the Diamond Cut Wad; 12 ga. 3-inch BB, No. 1, No 2 1,475 fps; 12 ga. 3 ½-inch BB, No. 1. No. 2 1550 fps
Available in: 12 ga.
Box of: 25
MSRP . . . . **N/A**

WINCHESTER XTENDED RANGE BISMUTH

Features: A fresh non-lead alternative with the hard hits bismuth provides; patented Shot-Lok wad protects the shot from deformation during barrel travel; 12 ga. 3-inch 1 5/8-ounce No. 5 at 1200 fps is primarily a turkey load, but suitable for a variety of ducks as well
Available in: 12 ga.
Box of: 10
MSRP . . . . **N/A**

Rifle Ammunition

WINCHESTER .350 LEGEND

Features: An all-new, straight-walled cartridge providing another option for hunters in states with this rifle ammunition restriction; sports more energy than the .30-30, .300 BLK, and .223, but with les recoil than the bigger straightwall.450 Bushmaster; available in the Deer Season XP, USA, SuperX, PowerMax Bonded, and SuperSuppressed lines
Available in: .350 Legend
Box of: 20
MSRP . . . . **N/A**

WINCHESTER DEER SEASON COPPER IMPACT XP

Features: Species-dedicated round for whitetail hunters featuring a wide polymer tip with a hollow nose; solid copper construction; streamlined, boattail profile
Available in: .243 Win. (85 gr.), .270 Win. (130 gr.), .300 Win. Mag. (150 gr.), .30-06 Spfd. (150 gr.), .308 Win. (150 gr.)
Box of: 20
MSRP . . . . **N/A**

WINCHESTER SUPER SUPPRESSED (CENTERFIRE RIFLE)

Features: Optimized for suppressed rifles and specialty handguns with a fully encapsulated bullet backed by a brass disc that reduces fouling; reduced noise with subsonic speeds
Available in: .350 Legend (265 gr.), .300 BLK (200 gr.), .308 Win. (168 gr.)
Box of: 20
MSRP . . . . **N/A**

WINCHESTER SUPER SUPPRESSED (RIMFIRE)

Features: Designed for suppressed .22 LR rifles and handguns, featuring a black copperplated bullet with a roundnose profile; reduced muzzle flash; subsonic performance in both handguns and rifles
Available in: .22 LR (45 gr.)
Box of: 100
MSRP . . . . **N/A**

WINCHESTER USA READY

Features: Intended for competition and training; offered in a variety of common rifle and pistol cartridges; match grade primers; flat-nose or open-tip bullets depending on caliber
Available in: .223 Rem. (62 gr.), .300 BLK (125 gr.), .308 Win. (168 gr.), 6.5 Creedmoor (125 gr.), .45 ACP (230 gr.), .40 S&W (165 gr.), 9mm (115 gr.)
Box of: 20
MSRP . . . . **N/A**

WINCHESTER WWII VICTORY SERIES (RIFLE)

Features: Intended to be a collector's item; standard FMJ ball; in special cartons and wood boxes
Available in: .30-06 (150 gr.)
Box of: 20
MSRP . . . . **N/A**

Handgun Ammunition

WINCHESTER SUPER SUPPRESSED (CENTERFIRE HANDGUN/PCC)

Features: Optimized for suppressed handguns and PCCs with a fully encapsulated bullet backed by a brass disc that reduces fouling
Available in: 9mm (147 gr.), .45 ACP (230 gr.)
Box of: 50
MSRP . . . . N/A

WINCHESTER WWII VICTORY SERIES (HANDGUN)

Features: Intended to be a collector's item;standard ball; period-correct loading for a muzzle velocity of 850 fps; special headstamp; packed in specialty carton and in wood boxes
Available in: .45 ACP (230 gr.)
Box of: 50
MSRP . . . . N/A

WINCHESTER
SUPER SUPPRESSED
(CENTERFIRE
HANDGUN/PCC)

WINCHESTER WWII VICTORY
SERIES (HANDGUN)

NEW Products: **Bullets**

CUTTING EDGE BULLETS

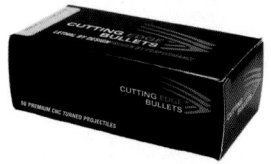

AMERICAN RESERVE MUNITIONS/GO WEST TRADING PREDATOR COMPONET BULLETS

Features: Designed by competitor and Army veteran Stephen Damron, Predator bullets are designed for long-range shooting with closed-tip or open-tip all-brass construction that solves the aerodynamic issues of air flow over a projectile of varying profile heights and widths, a problem known as "parasitic chaotic air flow" and which occurs behind the bullet and results in drag
Available in: .30 (176 gr., 205 gr.), .338 (236 gr.)
Box of: 50
MSRP . . . .$49.50–$79.80

CUTTING EDGE BULLETS LAZER

Features: A tipped hollowpoint; lead-free, made from solid copper bar stock; high BC; some weights available as SINGLE FEED profile
Available in: .308 (165 gr., 180 gr., 200 gr.), .338 (225 gr., 250 gr.. 265 gr., 275 gr., 300 gr.), .375 (325 gr., 350 gr., .375 gr., .400 gr., 425 gr.), .408 (425 gr., 450 gr., 475 gr.), .416 (450 gr., 475 gr., 500 gr., 525 gr., 550 gr.)
Box of: 50
MSRP . . . .$82.51–$152.88

CUTTING EDGE BULLETS MAXIMUS

Features: A cross of the company's high-trauma Raptor bullet and high-BC MTH bullet; deep penetration; 4 to 8 blades (velocity dependent) break off after hit for extreme trauma; SealTite band; lead-free copper construction; some sizes available in SINGLE FEED profile; mostly rifle designs but some handgun/PCC configurations available)
Available in: .264 (105 gr., 125 gr.), .277 (90 gr., 125 gr., 135 gr.), .284/7mm (132 gr.. 152 gr.), .308 (125 gr., 150 gr., 180 gr.), .338 (175 gr., 225 gr., 260 gr.), .358 (180 gr., .275 gr.), .375 (175 gr., 250 gr., 300 gr.), .408 (400 gr.), .416 (325 gr., 400 gr.), .458 (260 gr.), .44/.429 (.210 gr., 250 gr., 275 gr., 300 gr. boattail) .45 (250 gr.), .45/.451 (300 gr.)

Box of: 50
MSRP . . . .$48.44–$78.00

CUTTING EDGE BULLETS MTAC

Features: MTAC stands for "Match/Tactical" and is designed specifically for use in AR-type rifles; lead-free construction from solid copper bar stock; larger-than-caliber SealTite band prevents fliers and gas blow-by and decreases copper fouling; some weights available as SINGLE FEED profile
Available in: .224 (55 gr., 79 gr.), .243 (102 gr.), .243/6mm (90 gr.), .264/6.5mm (133 gr., 143 gr.), .277 (120 gr., 125 gr.), .284/7mm (157 gr., 192 gr.), .308 (132 gr., 155 gr., 168 gr., 182 gr.), .338 (227 gr., .254 gr., 267 gr., 277 gr., 302 gr.), .3745/.3655 (402 gr., 427 gr.), .375 (352 gr., 377 gr., 402 gr., 427 gr., 452 gr.), .408 (395 gr., 420 gr.), .416 (422 gr., 446 gr., 452 gr., 472 gr., 475 gr., 500 gr., 525 gr., 550 gr.), .509/.499 (802 gr.), .510 (720 gr., 762 gr., 802 gr., 902 gr., 1002 gr.)
Box of: 50
MSRP . . . .$36.34–$199.20

NEW Products: **Bullets**

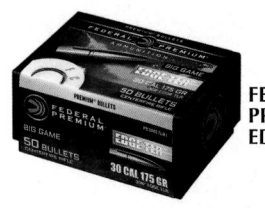

FEDERAL PREMIUM EDGE TLR

FEDERAL PREMIUM FUSION COMPONENT BULLETS

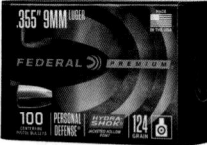

FEDERAL PREMIUM HYDRA-SHOK COMPONENT BULLETS

SPEER IMPACT COMPONENT BULLETS

TB AMMUNITION, LLC CTX FRANGIBLE BULLETS

FEDERAL PREMIUM EDGE TLR

Features: Billed as an "all-range" hunting bullet; copper shank; polymer tip; AccuChannel groove reduces drag
Available in: .284 (155 gr.), .308 (175 gr., 200 gr.), .277 (136 gr.)
Box of: 50
MSRP . . . .**$38.95–$49.95**

FEDERAL PREMIUM FUSION COMPONENT BULLETS

Features: One of today's premier hunting projectiles with an electo-chemically applied copper jacket, boat-tail, and skived pre-programmed nose
Available in: .264 (140 gr.), .277 (130 gr., 150 gr.), .284 (140 gr., 160 gr., 175 gr.), .308 (150 gr., 180 gr.), .338 (200 gr., 225 gr.)
Box of: 50 (.308, .338), 100 (.264, .277, .284)
MSRP . . . .**$20.95–$38.95**

FEDERAL PREMIUM HYDRA-SHOK COMPONENT BULLETS

Features: The orignial bullet first introduced in 1989 in fully loaded factory rounds, now available as a component bullet

Available in: .357 (129 gr., 158 gr.); .355 (124 gr., 147 gr.); .400 (165 gr., 180 gr.); .451 (185 gr., 230 gr.) 100 (.355, .357), 50 (.400, .451)
MSRP . . . .**$16.95–$31.95**

SPEER IMPACT COMPONENT BULLETS

Features: Molecularly fused jacket improves weight retention and accuracy; Slipstream polymer tip
Available in: .264 (140 gr.), .308 (172 gr., 190 gr.)
Box of: 50
MSRP . . . .**$25.95–$26.95**

TB AMMUNITION, LLC CTX FRANGIBLE BULLETS

Features: Frangible, lead-free component bullets in flat- and hollowpoint profiles for pistol calibers, taper-point or roundnose for rifle calibers; select buckshot and and slugs also available
Available in: .380 (75 gr.), 9mm (90 gr., 100 gr.), .357 (110 gr.), .357 SIG (100 gr.), .40 (105 gr., 120 gr.), .44 (172 gr.), .45 (140 gr., 155 gr.), .223 (42 gr., 55 gr.), 6.8mm (95 gr.), .308/7.62X39 (125 gr.), .50 (600 gr.), 12 ga. (325 gr. slug, 00 Buck, No. 4 Buck)
Box of: 500, 700
MSRP . . . .**$66.80–$225.43**

NEW Products: **Muzzleloading Components**

POWERBELT

UMAREX/INCEPTOR AMMUNITION

POWERBELT

Features: Designed specifically for the CVA Paramount long-range bolt-action muzzleloader; 280-grain; .452 BC; best used in 1:22 twist
Type: ELR
Available in: .45
Box of: N/A
MSRP: . . . . **N/A**

UMAREX/INCEPTOR AMMUNITION

Type: Speedbelt ARX
Features: Utilizes the lead-free, copper/polymer matrix Inceptor ARX projectile in a .50-caliber bullet; designed to be used in front of a 100-grain blackpowder charge
Available in: .50
Box of: 15
MSRP: **$24.95**

Accuracy International

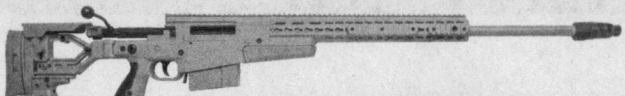

ACCURACY INTERNATIONAL AXMC

AXMC

Action: Semiautomatic
Stock: Synthetic
Barrel: 27 in.
Sights: None
Weight: 15 lb.
Caliber: .300 Win. Mag., .308 Win., .338 Lapua
Magazine: 10 rounds
Features: Multi-caliber, allowing users to switch calibers with a change of barrel, bolt, and magazine; AI's patent-pending Quicklok quick-release barrel; detachable magazine has a left-side cutout that eases insertion into the rifle; Cerakote finishes in Elite Sand, Elite Midnight, AI Dark Earth, AI Green, AI Pale Brown; other barrel lengths available on request; custom options available
MSRP.........$8174.00–$8687.00

Adcor Defense

ADCOR DEFENSE ELITE

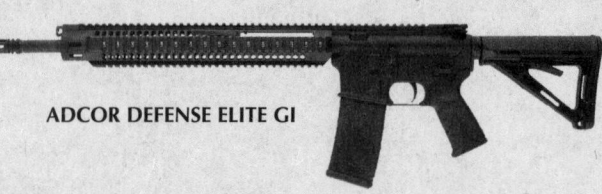

ADCOR DEFENSE ELITE GI

ELITE

Action: Semiautomatic
Stock: Synthetic
Barrel: 16 in.
Sights: None
Weight: 10 lb.
Caliber: 7.62x39, .300 BLK
Magazine: 30 rounds
Features: Gas piston action, billet upper and lower, free-floating chrome-lined barrel and forward charging handle are standard. Choice of Quad or Key Mod rails; black, Flat Dark Earth, Olive Drab Green, or Patriot Brown
MSRP.........$2295.00–$2545.00

ELITE GI

Action: Semiautomatic
Stock: Synthetic
Barrel: 16 in., 18 in.
Sights: None
Weight: 6 lb. 13 oz.–6 lb. 15 oz.
Caliber: .223
Magazine: 31 rounds

Features: A gas impingement version of Adcor's popular gas pistol Elite; billet upper and lower; two barrel lengths to choose from, either length available with or without a forward-charging handle; choice of quad or Key-Mod rail; finishes in black, Flat Dark Earth, Olive Drab Green, and Patriot Brown
Black:.................$1995.00
Colors:................$2145.00

American Spirit Arms

AMERICAN SPIRIT ARMS 18" SIDE CHARGING RIFLE

AMERICAN SPIRIT ARMS 9MM COMPETITION RIFLE "BASIC"

18" SIDE CHARGING RIFLE

Action: Semiautomatic
Stock: Synthetic
Barrel: 18 in.
Sights: None
Weight: 8 lb. 13 oz.
Caliber: .556 NATO
Magazine: Detachable box
Features: Mil-Std 1913 rail; barrel threaded for flash suppressor; nitrided carrier; 12 in. Samson evolution rail; ergo grip; Choice of ASA 4 or 3 lb. single-stage trigger; A2 flash hider; VLTOR collapsible buttstock with Ergo grip. Optional flip-up sights, Samson bipod stud, and 15-in. Samson Evolution rail available.
MSRP.................$1499.99

9MM COMPETITION RIFLE "BASIC"

Action: Semiautomatic
Stock: Synthetic
Barrel: 16 in.
Sights: None
Weight: N/A
Caliber: 9mm
Magazine: 17 rounds
Features: A2 flash hider; Faxon lightweight contour barrel; six-position adjustable Magpul MOE stock; Std Mil-Spec trigger; 1913 rail; upper receiver is side-charging, lower designed to take GLOCK 17 magazines
MSRP.................$1349.00

RIFLES

American Spirit Arms

AMERICAN SPIRIT ARMS 9MM G9 GLOCK MAG COMPATIBLE AR15

9MM G9 GLOCK MAG COMPATIBLE AR15

Action: Semiautomatic
Stock: Synthetic
Barrel: 16 in.
Sights: None
Weight: N/A
Caliber: 9mm

Magazine: 17 rounds
Features: ASA side charging upper receiver; Mil-Std 1913 rail; M-LOK rail; dedicated 9mm Glock magazine lower; six-position collapsible Magpul MOE stock; Glock 17 magazine and hard carrying case
MSRP $1349.99

American Tactical Imports

AMERICAN TACTICAL OMNI HYBRID MAXX

OMNI HYBRID MAXX

Action: Semiautomatic
Stock: Synthetic
Barrel: 16 in.
Sights: None
Weight: 6 lb. 4 oz., 6 lb. 8 oz.
Caliber: .223 Rem./5.56 NATO, .22 LR, .300 BLK

Magazine: Detachable box, 30 round
Features: Retractable stock; metal-reinforced polymer lower and upper receiver; Picatinny rail
.22 LR: $329.95
.223 Rem./5.56
    NATO: . . . . $479.95–$499.95
.300 BLK: $499.95

Anschütz (J.G. Anschütz)

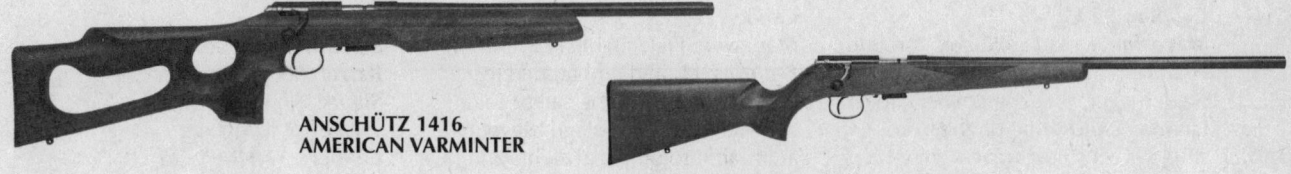

ANSCHÜTZ 1416 AMERICAN VARMINTER

ANSCHÜTZ 1416 D HB CLASSIC

1416 AMERICAN VARMINTER

Action: Bolt
Stock: Thumbhole walnut
Barrel: 18 in.
Sights: None
Weight: 5 lb. 10 oz.
Caliber: .22 LR
Magazine: 5 rounds
Features: 64 bolt-action repeater; 5098 two-stage trigger; blued finish; hex-key bolts; medium-weight barrel threaded ½ in. x 28 tpi; no iron sight provision; counter-bored crown
MSRP $1749.00

1416 D HB CLASSIC

Action: Bolt
Stock: Walnut
Barrel: 23 in.
Sights: None
Weight: 6 lb. 7 oz.
Caliber: .22 LR
Magazine: Detachable box, 5 rounds
Features: Heavy barrel; lacquered walnut wood stock (optional beaver-tail); pistol grip; black buttplate; studs for sling swivel; lateral sliding safety
MSRP $1199.00

Anschütz (J.G. Anschütz)

ANSCHÜTZ 1416 D HB THUMBHOLE

ANSCHÜTZ 1517 D HB

ANSCHÜTZ 1710 D HB

ANSCHÜTZ 1710 HB GRS SPORTER/VARMINT

ANSCHÜTZ 1727 F

1416 D HB THUMBHOLE
Action: Bolt
Stock: Walnut
Barrel: 23 in.
Sights: None
Weight: 6 lb. 7 oz.
Caliber: .22 LR
Magazine: Detachable box, 5 rounds
Features: Luxus repeating rifle; single-stage trigger; black buttplate; carved German checkering on the pistol grip; sling swivel studs; wave-style V-block dovetail rail for telescopic sight
MSRP $1649.00

1517 D HB, 1517 D HB BEAVERTAIL
Action: Bolt
Stock: Walnut, hardwood
Barrel: 22 in.
Sights: None
Weight: 6 lb.–6 lb. 6 oz.
Caliber: .17 HMR
Magazine: Detachable box, 4 rounds
Features: Single- or two-stage adjustable trigger; optional beavertail stock
Classic stock: $1249.00
Beavertail: $1199.00

1710 D HB
Action: Bolt
Stock: Walnut
Barrel: 23 in.
Sights: Open
Weight: 7 lb. 11 oz.
Caliber: .22 LR
Magazine: Detachable box, 5 rounds
Features: Drilled and tapped for scope mounts; sliding safety catch; two-stage or single-stage trigger; adjustable folding leaf sights and pear front adjustable ramp; Meistergrade has engraved forestock and trigger guard; black plastic buttplate
MSRP: $2295.00

1710 HB GRS SPORTER/VARMINT
Action: Bolt
Stock: GRS Sporter/Varmint
Barrel: 23 in.
Sights: None
Weight: 9 lb.
Caliber: .22 LR
Magazine: 5 rounds
Features: Standard 1710 HB barreled action; two-stage 5109/2 trigger; GRS Sporter/Varmint stock; bottom metal included, as well as hex-keyed action screws
MSRP $2495.00

1727 F
Action: Bolt
Stock: Walnut German stock
Barrel: 18 in., 22 in.
Sights: None
Weight: 7 lb. 11 oz.
Caliber: .17 HMR, .22 LR
Magazine: Internal, 4 rounds
Features: Unique straight-pull bolt combines with traditional German-shaped stock in walnut; .22 LR is available in both barrel lengths, .17 HMR in 22-in only; 18-in. .22 LR features a threaded, tapered heavy weight barrel, 22-in. .22LR available left-hand.
.22 LR 18 in.: $3595.00
.22 LR 23 in.: $3495.00
.17 HMR: $3495.00

Anschütz (J.G. Anschütz)

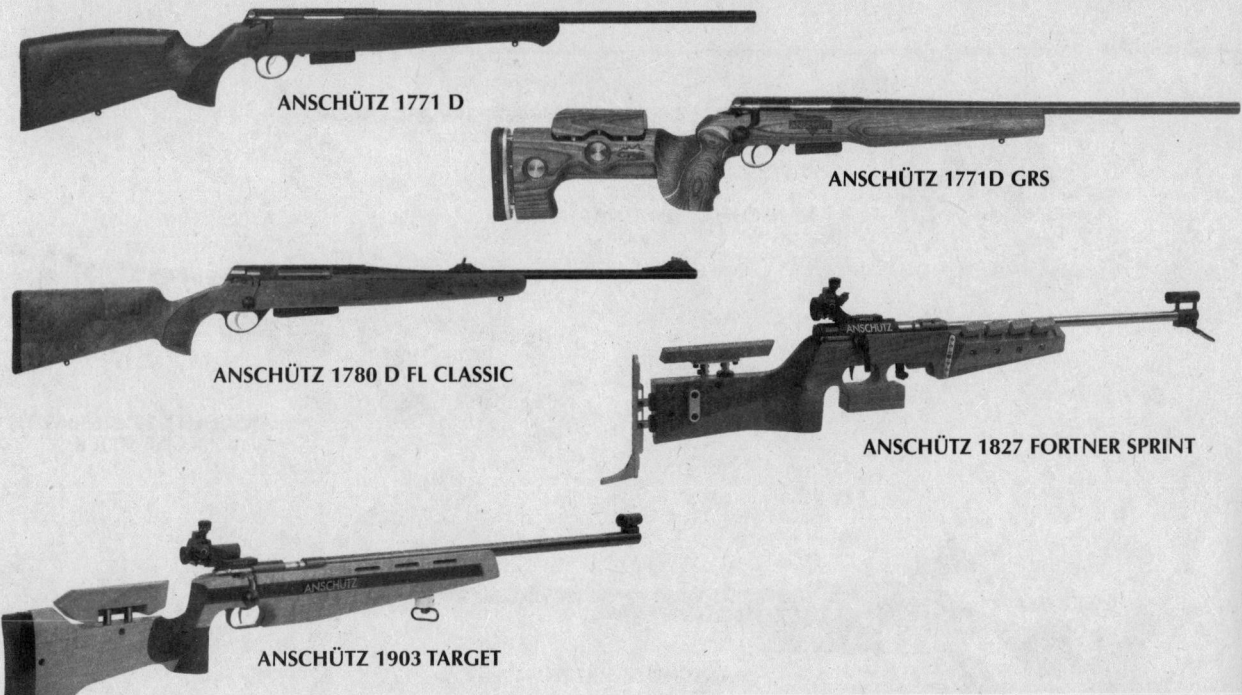

ANSCHÜTZ 1771 D

ANSCHÜTZ 1771D GRS

ANSCHÜTZ 1780 D FL CLASSIC

ANSCHÜTZ 1827 FORTNER SPRINT

ANSCHÜTZ 1903 TARGET

1770 D

Action: Bolt
Stock: Walnut
Barrel: 22 in.
Sights: Drilled and tapped for scopes
Weight: 7 lb. 7 oz.
Caliber: .223 Rem.
Magazine: Detachable, 3-shot, in-line
Features: Six locking lug action for strength and reliability; adjustable, single-stage match trigger; hand checkered stock with oval cheekpiece and rubber buttpad; detachable sling swivel studs
MSRP. $2495.00

1771 D

Action: Bolt
Stock: Germany-styled walnut
Barrel: 21.5 in.
Sights: None
Weight: 7 lb. 7 oz.
Caliber: .22 Hornet, .222 Rem., .223 Rem., .204 Ruger
Magazine: 4 rounds
Features: 1771 bolt action repeater; six front locking lugs; blued finish; heavy barrel; no iron sight provision
MSRP. $2243.00

1771D GRS

Action: Bolt
Stock: Laminated birch
Barrel: 22 in.
Sights: None
Weight: 8 lb. 6 oz.
Caliber: .204 Ruger, .222 Rem., .223 Rem., .300 BLK
Magazine: Detachable box, 4 rounds
Features: Butt plate speed lock adjustment; GRS-rubber butt plate; cheek piece speed lock adjustment; ergonomical and gripping forend; precision barrel
MSRP. $3300.00

1780 D FL CLASSIC

Action: Bolt
Stock: Walnut
Barrel: 23 in.
Sights: Drilled and tapped for scopes
Weight: 7 lb. 2 oz.
Caliber: .308 Win., .30-06 Spfd., 8x57 IS, 9.3x62 Mauser
Magazine: Detachable box, 5 rounds
Features: Single-stage trigger; fast acquisition sight; sliding safety catch; available in a variety of stock options, including wood Monte Carlo, German, thumbhole and classic stocks, and classic stocks in soft grip wood orange camo, wood green camo, and black
MSRP. $3495.00

1827 FORTNER SPRINT

Action: Bolt
Stock: Biathlon, walnut
Barrel: 22 in.
Sights: None
Weight: 8 lb. 2 oz.
Caliber: .22 LR
Magazine: Detachable box, 5 rounds
Features: Combination of an extra light 1827 Fortner barreled action with the stock of the 1827 model; lacquered walnut stock with stippled checkering; heavy, cylindrical match barrel; match stage two or single trigger
MSRP. $3995.00

1903 TARGET

Action: Bolt
Stock: Hardwood
Barrel: 26 in., heavy
Sights: None
Weight: 9 lb. 11 oz.
Caliber: .22 LR
Magazine: None
Features: A match rifle for small bore shooters; anatomically perfect walnut stock with vertically adjustable cheek piece; optional aluminum, hook, or rubber buttplate; aluminum accessories rail
MSRP. $1499.00

Anschütz (J.G. Anschütz)

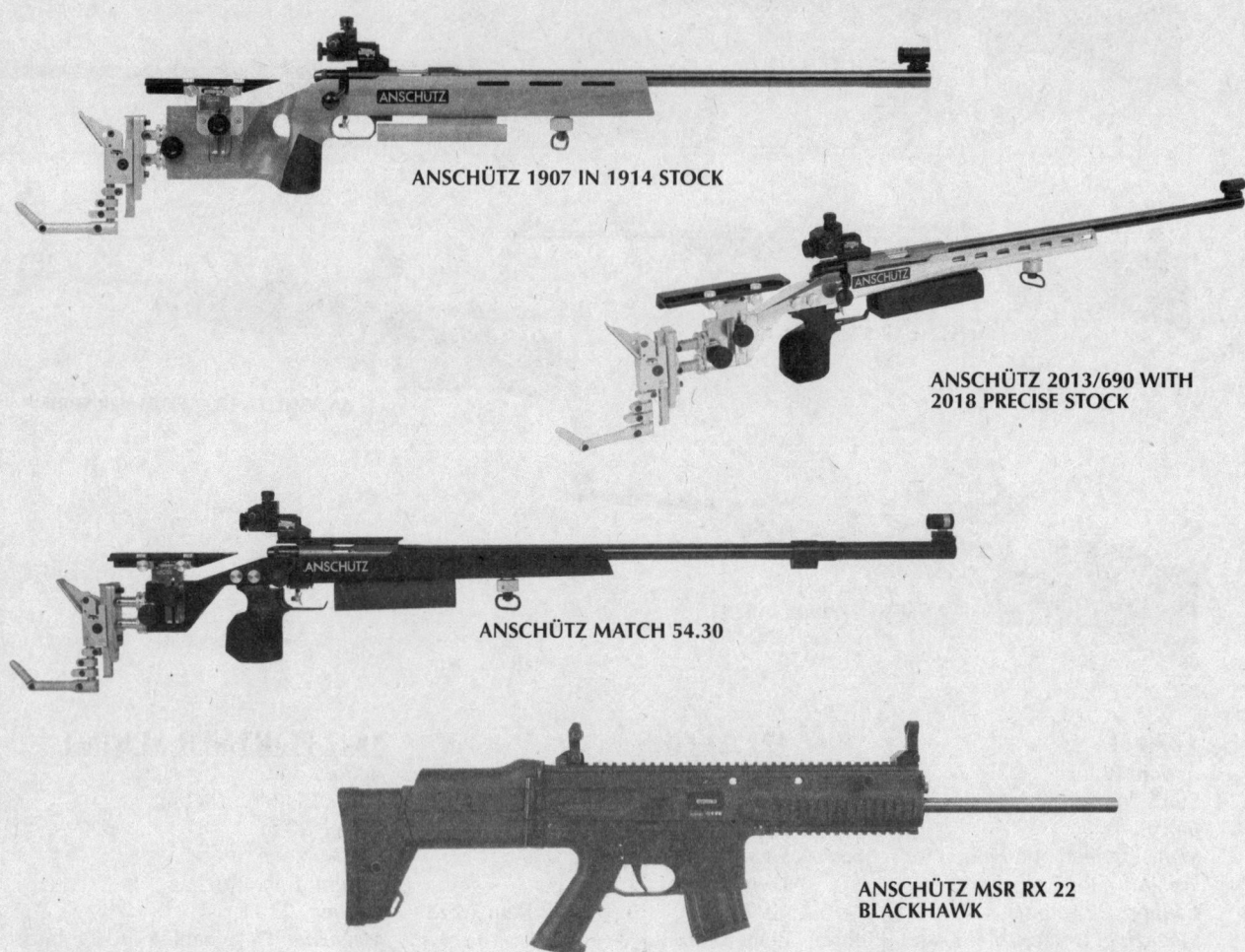

ANSCHÜTZ 1907 IN 1914 STOCK

ANSCHÜTZ 2013/690 WITH 2018 PRECISE STOCK

ANSCHÜTZ MATCH 54.30

ANSCHÜTZ MSR RX 22 BLACKHAWK

1907 IN 1914 STOCK

Action: Bolt
Stock: Walnut
Barrel: 32.28 in.
Sights: None
Weight: 10 lb. 12 oz.
Caliber: .22 LR
Magazine: None
Features: Match 54 action; heavy, cylindrical barrel; match two-stage or single-stage trigger; safety signal pin
MSRP $3650.00

2013/690 WITH 2018 PRECISE STOCK

Action: Bolt
Stock: Aluminum
Barrel: 27.17 in.
Sights: None
Weight: 13 lb.
Caliber: .22 LR
Magazine: None
Features: Single loader; two-stage trig-ger; optional buttplate; new backend offers large range of adjustment for small shooters
MSRP $5695.95

MATCH 54.30

Action: Barreled
Stock: Aluminum or walnut
Barrel: 26 in.
Sights: None
Weight: 11 lb. 3 oz.
Caliber: .22 LR
Magazine: 8 rounds
Features: Improved ergonomics; reduced weight of firing pin for increase in velocity and shorter lock time; newly designed target chamber for better accuracy; threaded receiver and barrel connection; available in aluminum or walnut stock
MSRP . . . . $3775.00–$5135.00

MSR RX 22 BLACKHAWK

Action: Semiautomatic
Stock: Laminated wood, plastic
Barrel: 16.5 in.
Sights: None
Weight: 7 lb.
Caliber: .22 LR
Magazine: Detachable box, 10 rounds
Features: Folding stock; aluminum grooved Picatinny rail for accessories; six possible positions for cocking lever; optional buttplate and sight set; black, desert, aluminum colors available
MSRP $899.99

ARMALITE AR-10 DEF 10

ARMALITE AR-10 COMPETITION RIFLE

ARMALITE AR-31 .308 BOLT ACTION RIFLE

ARMALITE AR-50 .50 BMG PRECISION BOLT ACTION RIFLE

AR-10 DEF 10

Action: Semiautomatic
Stock: Synthetic
Barrel: 16 in.
Sights: Front
Weight: 7 lb. 14 oz.
Caliber: 7.62 NATO, .308 Win.
Magazine: 10, 20 rounds
Features: No-frills rifle built for sporting or defensive use; mid-length gas system, six-position collapsible stock, forged flat top with Mil-Std 1913 rail, 7075 forged aluminum lower and receiver, standard charging handle, single-stage trigger are standard; supplied with one 20-round Magpul Pmag; Colorado-compliant version comes with 10-round Magpul Pmag
MSRP $1099.00

AR-10 COMPETITION RIFLE

Action: Semiautomatic

Stock: Synthetic
Barrel: 13 in., 18 in.
Sights: None
Weight: 8 lb. 3 oz.–8 lb. 14 oz.
Caliber: .308 Win./7.62 NATO
Magazine: Detachable box, 25 rounds
Features: Picatinny rail; Armalite tunable brake pinned and welded; 12-in. free-floating handguard; stock adjustable for length-of-pull and comb height; ambidextrous safety and charging handle
MSRP $2199.00

AR-31 .308 BOLT-ACTION RIFLE

Action: Bolt
Stock: Synthetic
Barrel: 24 in.
Sights: None
Weight: 14 lb. 2 oz.
Caliber: .308 Win.
Magazine: 10 rounds

Features: A short-action version of Armalite's AR-30A1; double-lapped chrome moly barrel; single-stage trigger; AR-31 stock adjustable for length of pull and cheekpiece height; steel V-Block bedding system; Armalite muzzle brake
MSRP $3460.00

AR-50 .50 BMG BOLT-ACTION RIFLE

Action: Bolt
Stock: Synthetic
Barrel: 33 in.
Sights: None
Weight: 33 lb. 3 oz.
Caliber: .50 BMG
Magazine: None
Features: Chromoly barrel; muzzle-brake; 15 minute rail; single-stage trigger
MSRP $3359.00

Arsenal, Inc.

ARSENAL, INC. SAM7R

ARSENAL, INC. SAM7SFK SBR

ARSENAL, INC. SAM7UF

ARSENAL, INC. SLR-104FR

ARSENAL, INC. SLR-104UR

ARSENAL, INC. SLR-107R

SAM7R

Action: Semiautomatic
Stock: Polymer
Barrel: 16.25 in.
Sights: Scope rail
Weight: 8 lb.
Caliber: 7.62x39 Warsaw
Magazine: Detachable box, 10 rounds
Features: Milled receiver; chrome-lined, hammer-forged barrel; muzzle brake; cleaning rod; intermediate length US-made 10 in. trapdoor buttstock
MSRP $1349.00

SAM7SFK SBR

Action: Semiautomatic
Stock: Polymer
Barrel: 8.5 in.
Sights: Front sight/gas block combo, peep rear
Weight: 7 lb. 2 oz.
Caliber: 7.62x39mm
Magazine: 30 rounds
Features: Ambidextrous safety lever; receiver, bolt, and bolt carrier are hot-die hammer-forged; barrel is cold hammer-forged; side rail, sights, ambidextrous safety, flash hider are standard; peep rear sight
MSRP $2499.99

SAM7UF

Action: Semiautomatic
Stock: Metal underfolding
Barrel: 16.25 in.
Sights: Adjustable
Weight: 7 lb. 8 oz.
Caliber: .7.62x39 Warsaw
Magazine: Detachable box, 10 rounds
Features: Milled and forged receiver; chrome lined hammer forged barrel; muzzle nut, bayonet/accessory lug; reinforced underfolding buttstock; black polymer pistol grip and handguards; stainless steel heat shield
MSRP $1299.00

SLR-104FR

Action: Semiautomatic
Stock: Synthetic
Barrel: 16.25 in.
Sights: Adjustable
Weight: 6 lb. 2 oz.
Caliber: 5.45x39 Warsaw
Magazine: Detachable box, 30 rounds
Features: Left-sided folding stock; muzzle brake; bayonet and accessory lugs; scrope rail; sling; two-stage trigger; available in 5.56 NATO and 7.62x39 Warsaw
MSRP $1099.00

SLR-104UR

Action: Semiautomatic
Stock: Synthetic
Barrel: 16.25 in.
Sights: Fixed
Weight: 6 lb.
Caliber: 5.45x39 Warsaw
Magazine: Detachable box, 30 rounds
Features: Stamped receiver; short gas system; front sight block/gas block combination; black polymer furniture; stainless steel heat shield; left-side folding polymer stock; two stage trigger; scope rail
MSRP $1299.00

SLR-107R

Action: Semiautomatic
Stock: Polymer
Barrel: 16.25 in.
Sights: Front sight, 800m rear
Weight: 7 lb. 5 oz.
Caliber: 7.62x39mm
Magazine: 5 rounds
Features: Manufactured in Las Vegas with a Bulgarian-made stamped receiver; anti-slap double-stage trigger; Warsaw-length buttstock with a cleaning kit compartment; stainless steel heat shield, side rail, and slings; available in black, Plum, Desert Sand, or OD Green
MSRP $969.99

RIFLES

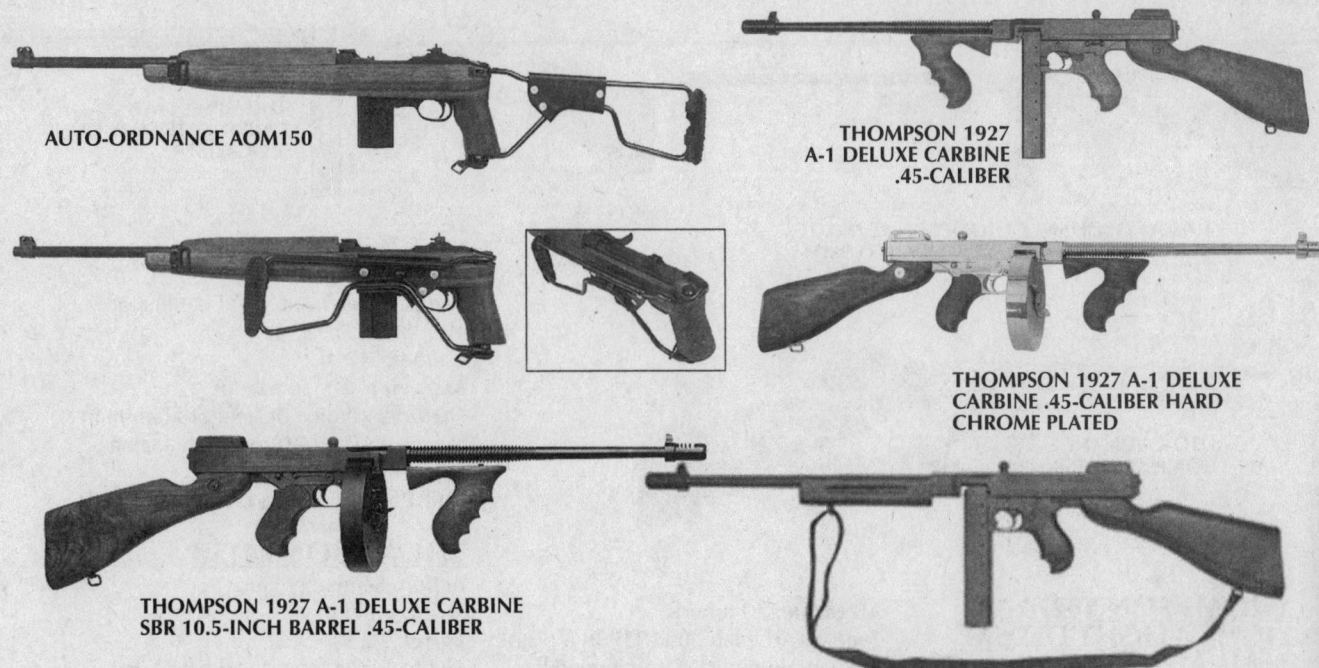

AUTO-ORDNANCE AOM150

THOMPSON 1927 A-1 DELUXE CARBINE .45-CALIBER

THOMPSON 1927 A-1 DELUXE CARBINE .45-CALIBER HARD CHROME PLATED

THOMPSON 1927 A-1 DELUXE CARBINE SBR 10.5-INCH BARREL .45-CALIBER

THOMPSON 1927 A-1 "COMMANDO" CARBINE .45-CALIBER

AOM150

Action: Semiautomatic
Stock: Walnut; handguard
Barrel: 18 in.
Sights: Blade front; flip style rear
Weight: 5 lb. 6 oz.
Caliber: .30
Magazine: Detachable stick, 15 rounds
Features: Folding stock; Parkerized finish
MSRP. $1137.00

THOMPSON 1927 A-1 DELUXE CARBINE .45-CALIBER

Action: Semiautomatic
Stock: Walnut, vertical foregrip
Barrel: 16.5 in.
Sights: Blade front, open rear adjustable
Weight: 13 lb.
Caliber: .45 ACP
Magazine: 20 rounds
Features: Finned barrel with compensator; blued steel receiver; magazine options range from 10- and 0-round sticks to 50- and 100-round drums; violin case is an option
MSRP. . . . . $1551.00–$1984.00

THOMPSON 1927 A-1 DELUXE CARBINE .45-CALIBER HARD CHROME PLATED, GOLD PLATED

Action: Semiautomatic
Stock: Walnut
Barrel: 16.5 in.
Sights: Blade front, open rear adjustable
Weight: 13 lb.
Caliber: .45 ACP
Magazine: One each round 50 drum and 20 stick magazines
Features: Finned barrel; fixed stock with vertical foregrip
MSRP. $3431.00

THOMPSON 1927 A-1 DELUXE CARBINE SBR 10.5-INCH BARREL .45-CALIBER

Action: Semiautomatic
Stock: Walnut, vertical foregrip
Barrel: 10.5 in.
Sights: Blade front, open rear adjustable
Weight: 12 lb.
Caliber: .45 ACP
Magazine: 20, 30 rounds
Features: NFA short-barrel rifle with a finned and compensated barrel; 20- or 30-round stick magazines; optional detachable buttstock
MSRP. . . . .$2088.00–$2709.00

THOMPSON 1927 A-1 "COMMANDO" CARBINE .45-CALIBER

Action: Semiautomatic
Stock: Black finish stock and forend
Barrel: 16.5 in.
Sights: Blade front, open rear adjustable
Weight: 13 lb.
Caliber: .45 ACP
Magazine: Detachable stick, 30 rounds
Features: Frame and receiver made from solid steel; compensator; black nylon sling
MSRP. $1479.00

Auto-Ordnance

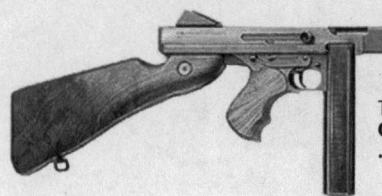

THOMPSON M1 CARBINE "TOMMY GUN" .45-CALIBER

AUTO-ORDNANCE THOMPSON 1927 A-1C LIGHTWEIGHT DELUXE SEMI-AUTO 9MM

AUTO-ORDNANCE THOMPSON M1SB

THOMPSON 1927A-1C LIGHTWEIGHT DELUXE SEMI-AUTO 9MM

Action: Semiautomatic
Stock: Walnut
Barrel: 16.5 in.
Sights: Blade front, adjustable open rear
Weight: 13 lb.
Caliber: 9mm
Magazine: 20 rounds
Features: The famous 1927 in a pistol caliber; aluminum frame; finned barrel with compensator; comes with one 20-round magazine
MSRP $1364.00

THOMPSON M1 CARBINE "TOMMY GUN" .45-CALIBER

Action: Semiautomatic
Stock: Walnut, vertical foregrip
Barrel: 16.5 in.
Sights: Blade front, fixed battle rear
Weight: 11 lb. 8 oz.
Caliber: .45 ACP
Magazine: 10, 30 rounds
Features: Choice of steel or aluminum receiver; 10- or 30-round stick magazines; no vertical fore-grip
MSRP . . . . $1318.00–$1457.00

THOMPSON M1SB

Action: Semiautomatic
Stock: Walnut, vertical foregrip
Barrel: 10.5 in.
Sights: Blade front, fixed battle rear
Weight: 10 lb. 8 oz.
Caliber: .45 ACP
Magazine: Detachable stick, 30 rounds
Features: Will not accept drum magazines; frame and receiver made from solid steel
MSRP $2088.00

Barrett

BARRETT FIELDCRAFT

BARRETT 82A1

BARRETT M107A1

FIELDCRAFT

Action: Bolt
Stock: Carbon fiber
Barrel: 18 in., 21 in., 24 in.
Sights: None
Weight: 5 lb. 1 oz.–5 lb. 12 oz.
Caliber: .243 Win., .22-250 Rem., 6.5 Creedmoor, 7mm-08 Rem., .308 Win., .25-06 Rem., .270 Win., .30-06 Spfd., 6.5x55 Swede, 6mm Creedmoor
Magazine: 4 rounds
Features: Carbon fiber stock bedded to action; short or long action scaled to specific caliber; bolts made of 410 heat-treated steel and NP3 coated; 416 stainless steel barrels and receivers
Standard: $1879.00
Threaded: $1929.00

M107A1

Action: Semiautomatic
Stock: Synthetic
Barrel: 20 in., 29 in.
Sights: Flip-up iron sights
Weight: 30 lb. 14 oz.
Caliber: .50 BMG
Magazine: Detachable box, 10 rounds
Features: Chrome-lined barrel, Flat Dark Earth stock finish; suppressor-ready muzzlebrake; pelican case; M1913 optics rail; detachable adjust-able lightweight bipod legs; light-weight monopod; black, Flat Dark Earth, OD Green, or Tungsten Grey Cerakote receiver finishes
MSRP $12281.00

MODEL 82A1

Action: Semiautomatic
Stock: Synthetic
Barrel: 20 in., 29 in.
Sights: Flip-up iron sights or Leupold scope
Weight: 30 lb. 14 oz.
Caliber: .416, .50 BMG
Magazine: Detachable box, 10 rounds
Features: Pelican case; detachable adjustable bipod legs; cleaning kit; carry handle; muzzlebrake; Picatinny rail; chrome-lined barrel; manganese phosphate finish or Cerakote receiver finishes in Flat Dark Earth, Burnt Bronze, Tungsten Grey, or OD Green
MSRP . . . . $9119.00–$9463.00

Barrett

BARRETT 95

BARRETT 99

BARRETT MRAD

BARRETT REC7

BARRETT REC7 D1

MODEL 95

Action: Semiautomatic
Stock: Synthetic
Barrel: 29 in.
Sights: Flip-up iron sights
Weight: 25 lb.
Caliber: .50 BMG
Magazine: Detachable box, 5 rounds
Features: Pelican case; detachable adjustable bipod legs; cleaning kit; Picatinny rail
MSRP $6671.00

MODEL 99

Action: Bolt
Stock: Synthetic
Barrel: 29 in., 32 in.
Sights: None
Weight: 25 lb.
Caliber: .416 Barrett, .50 BMG
Magazine: None
Features: Picatinny rail; pelican case; detachable adjustable bipod; cleaning kit; available in black anodized or Cerakote Flat Dark Earth receiver
MSRP . . . . $3967.00–$4222.00

MRAD

Action: Bolt action repeater
Stock: Synthetic
Barrel: 17 in., 20 in., 22 in., 24 in., 26 in.

Sights: None
Weight: 12 lb. 15 oz.–14 lb. 8 oz.
Caliber: .300 Win. Mag., .308 Win. Mag., .338 Lapua Mag., 7mm Rem. Mag., 6.5 Creedmoor, .260 Rem.
Magazine: Detachable box, 10 rounds
Features: Fluted, carbon fiber, or heavy barrel; multi-role brown finish stock; folding stock; adjustable cheekpiece and buttplate; includes two 10-round magazines, two sling loops, and three adjustable accessory rails; receivers in black anodized or in Cerakote Tungsten Grey, Flat Dark Earth, OD Green, or Burnt Bronze
MSRP . . . . $6000.00–$6975.00

REC7

Action: Semiautomatic
Stock: Synthetic
Barrel: 11.5 in., 16 in., 18 in.
Sights: Flip up front and rear
Weight: 6 lb. 2 oz.–7 lb. 15 oz.
Caliber: 5.56 NATO, 6.8 SPC
Magazine: 10, 20, 30 rounds
Features: Gas piston semi-auto with enhanced KeyMod rail, Magup MOE six-position buttstock, two-position gas plug, one-piece piston, and oversized trigger guard; 6.8 SPC only available in 16-inch carbine-profile barrel; 5.56 has all barrel profiles, with 16-inch in either a carbine- or

flyweight profile; 18-inch is DMR profile; 11.5 is NFA regulated; Cerakote receivers in Black, Flat Dark Earth, OD Green, Tungsten Grey, or Burnt Bronze
MSRP . . . .$2199.00–$2799.00

REC7 D1

Action: Semiautomatic
Stock: Synthetic
Barrel: 16 in. and 18 in. (6.8 SPC and 5.56 NATO), 10.25 in. and 16 in. (.300 BLK)
Sights: None
Weight: 5 lb. 8 oz.–6 lb. 3 oz.
Caliber: 16 in. and 18 in. (6.8 SPC and 5.56 NATO), 10.25 in. and 16 in. (.300 BLK)
Magazine: 10, 20, 30 rounds
Features: Hand-built, lightweight, direct impingement; Magpul MOE six-position stock, Barrett designed 15-in. KeyMod handguard, Bravo Company Gunfighter charging handle, and ALG Defense ACT trigger; bolt carrier group plated in nickel boron finish; Black, Flat Dark Earth, OD Green, Tungsten Grey, or Burnt Bronze Cerakote.
MSRP $1899.00

RIFLES

Benelli USA

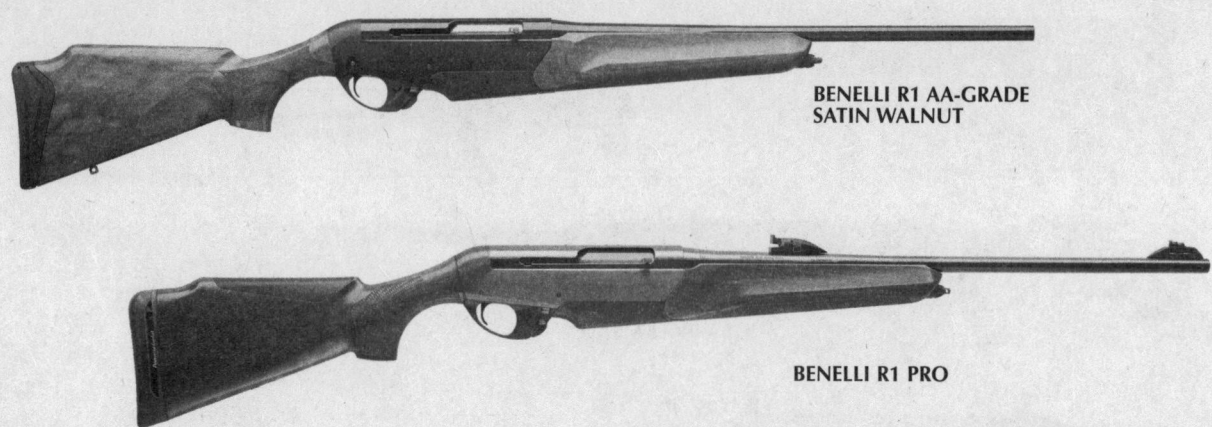

BENELLI R1 AA-GRADE SATIN WALNUT

BENELLI R1 PRO

R1 BIG GAME

Action: Semiautomatic
Stock: AA-grade satin walnut, synthetic or Realtree APG
Barrel: 22 in., 24 in.
Sights: None
Weight: 7 lb. 2 oz.–7 lb. 5 oz.
Caliber: .30-06 Spfd., .300 Win. Mag., .338 Win. Mag.
Magazine: Detachable box, 3+1 or 4+1 rounds
Features: Picatinny rail; synthetic and APG finish come with GripTight coating; raised comb; auto-regulating gas-operated system
Walnut: **$1149.00**
ComforTech: **$1349.00**

R1 PRO BIG GAME

Action: Semiautomatic
Stock: Walnut
Barrel: 22 in.
Sights: Fiber optic front, adjustable rear
Weight: 7 lb. 3.2 oz.
Caliber: .30-06 Spfd.
Magazine: 4 rounds
Features: Includes Benelli's Progressive Comfort technology; AA walnut satin finish stock; receiver drilled and tapped for scope mount, Picatinny rail and shim kit included; CRIO treated barrel
MSRP **$1499.00**

Beretta USA

BERETTA USA ARX100

BERETTA CX4 STORM

ARX100

Action: Semiautomatic
Stock: Telescopic folding
Barrel: 16 in.
Sights: Removable back-up sights
Weight: 6 lb. 13 oz.
Caliber: 5.56 NATO (other barrels available)
Magazine: 30 rounds
Features: Cold hammer forged barrel can be replaced with barrels in different lengths and calibers; case ejection switches from right to left at a button push; completely ambidextrous; technopolymer receiver; contains no pins and can be disassembled without the use of tools; optional .300 Black Out kit available
MSRP **$1950.00**

CX4 STORM

Action: Single-action
Stock: Synthetic
Barrel: 16.6 in.
Sights: Front sight post
Weight: 5 lb. 12 oz.
Caliber: 9mm
Magazine: 10, 15 rounds
Features: Picatinny rail; allows for reverse ejection and extraction; ideal for left-handed shooters; adjustable length-of-pull; easy to accessorize; takes Beretta series 92 pistol magazines
MSRP **$699.00**

BERGARA B-14 BMP

BERGARA B-14 HMR

BERGARA B-14 HUNTER

BERGARA B-14 RIDGE

BERGARA B-14 TIMBER

B-14 BMP

Action: Bolt
Stock: Bergara BMP chassis (machined aluminum)
Barrel: 24 in. (6.5 Creedmoor); 20 in. (.308 Win.)
Sights: None
Weight: 10 lb. 2 oz.–11 lb.
Caliber: 6.5 Creedmoor, .308 Win.
Magazine: 5 rounds
Features: Drilled and tapped for Remington 700 scope mounts; removable buttstock adjustable for cheekpiece and LOP, allowing for a standard AR-style stock and buffer tube to be installed; detachable magazine, threaded muzzle
MSRP . . . . **starting at $1699.00**

B-14 HMR

Action: Bolt
Stock: Bergara BMP HMR molded with mini-chassis
Barrel: 20 in. (.308 Win.), 22 in. (6.5 Creedmoor)
Sights: None
Weight: 9 lb. 2.4 oz.–9 lb. 4 oz.
Caliber: 6.5 Creedmoor, .308 Win., .22-250 Rem., .300 Win. Mag.
Magazine: 5 rounds
Features: Field or competition use;

buttstock has adjustable cheekpiece and LOP spacers, integrated mini-chassis; one-piece Bergara B-14 action, Bergara Performance trigger, AICS detachable magazine, threaded muzzle and thread protector
MSRP . . . . **$1150.00–$1179.00**

B-14 HUNTER

Action: Bolt
Stock: Glass fiber-reinforced polymer
Barrel: 22 in. (short actions), 24 in. (long actions)
Sights: None
Weight: 7 lb.–7 lb. 2 oz.
Caliber: .30-06 Spfd., .300 Win. Mag., .270 Win., .308 Win., 6.5 Creedmoor, 7mm Rem. Mag., .243 Win., .22-250 Rem., 7mm-08 Rem.
Magazine: 3, 4 rounds
Features: Stock has Soft Touch coating for better purchase; drilled and tapped for Remington 700-style bases; barrel is matte blue
MSRP $825.00

B-14 RIDGE

Action: Bolt
Stock: Glass fiber-reinforced polymer
Barrel: 18, 22, 24 in.
Sights: None
Weight: 7 lb. 3 oz.–7 lb. 15 oz.

Caliber: .300 Win. Mag., .30-06 Spfd., .270 Win., .308 Win., .243 Win., 6.5 Creedmoor, 7mm Rem. Mag., .22-250 Rem., 7mm-08
Magazine: 3, 4 rounds
Features: Stock has Soft Touch coating for better purchase; drilled and tapped for Remington 700-style bases; barrel is a #5 profile of 4140 CrMo steel in matte blue and threaded for suppressor or muzzle brake use; choice of hinged floor plate or detachable magazine; .308 and 6.5 Creedmoor available in an 18-inch Special Purpose Short Barrel
MSRP $865.00

B-14 TIMBER

Action: Bolt
Stock: Walnut
Barrel: 22 in. (short actions), 24 in. (long actions)
Sights: None
Weight: 7 lb. 5 oz.–7 lb. 9 oz.
Caliber: .300 Win. Mag., .30-06 Spfd., .270 Win., .308 Win., .243 Win., 6.5 Creedmoor, .243 Win., 7mm-08 Rem.
Magazine: 3, 4 rounds
Features: Monte Carlo cheekpiece; drilled and tapped for Remington 700-style bases; barrel is a #3 profile of 4140 CrMo steel in matte blue; integral epoxy resin pillars surround the action screws in the stock
MSRP $945.00

Bergara

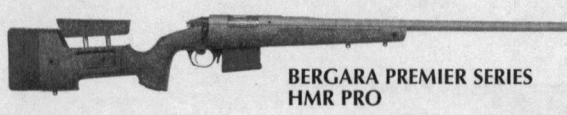

BERGARA B-14 WOODSMAN

BERGARA PREMIER SERIES HMR PRO

BERGARA PREMIER SERIES MOUNTAIN

BERGARA PREMIER SERIES APPROACH

BERGARA PREMIER SERIES LRP

B-14 WOODSMAN

Action: Bolt
Stock: Walnut
Barrel: 22 in., 24 in.
Sights: None
Weight: 7 lb. 2 oz.–7 lb. 6 oz.
Caliber: .270, .30-06 Spfd., .300 Win. Mag., .308, 6.5 Creedmoor, 7mm Rem., Mag.
Magazine: Detachable box
Features: Coned bolt nose and breech ensuring consistently smooth feeding; sliding plate extractor for proper alignment; stocks are bedded with integral pillars for stability and enhanced accuracy; factory drilled and tapped to fit Remington 700 style rings and bases.
MSRP . . . . starting at $945.00

PREMIER SERIES APPROACH

Action: Bolt
Stock: Synthetic
Barrel: 20, 22, 24, 26 in.
Sights: None
Weight: 8 lb. 3 oz.–8 lb. 10 oz.
Caliber: 6.5 Creedmoor, .308 Win., 6mm Creedmoor, .450 Bushmaster; .22-250 Rem., 6.5 PRC, 7mm Rem. Mag., .300 PRC, .300 Win. Mag., 7mm-08 Rem.

Features: Hand-laid fiberglass stock in a mottled gray and tan; barrel is threaded; a #5 taper profile; bronze Cerakote finish; TriggerTech Frictionless Release Technology; integral QD cup sling; swivel mounts
MSRP $1960.00

PREMIER SERIES HMR PRO

Action: Bolt
Stock: Synthetic
Barrel: 20, 22, 24, 26 in.
Sights: None
Weight: 9 lb. 5 oz.–9 lb. 13 oz.
Caliber: 6.5 Creedmoor, .308 Win., .22-250 Rem., 6mm Creedmoor, .450 Bushmaster; 6.5 PRC, 7mm Rem. Mag., .300 Win. Mag., 7mm-08 Rem.
Magazine: 5, 7 rounds
Features: Stainless one-piece bolt with a cone-shaped nose and a spring-loaded sliding plate extractor; bolt shroud is fully nitrided and self-lubricating; free-floating #5 taper barrel in gray Cerakote; full-length mini chassis; stock adjustable for comb height and length of pull; threaded barrel; detachable AICS-style magazine
MSRP $1715.00

PREMIER SERIES LRP

Action: Bolt
Stock: Aluminum chassis
Barrel: 20, 24, 26, 28 in.
Sights: None
Weight: 9 lb. 5 oz.–9 lb. 11 oz.
Caliber: .308 Win., 6.5 Creedmoor, 6mm Creedmoor: .300 Win. Mag.
Magazine: 5 rounds
Features: Aluminum chassis that is CNC machined from solid 6061 T6 aluminum; AR15-style grip; adjustable length of pull; adjustable comb height; butt plate can be canted to give a precise fit to the shooter in virtually any shooting position; threaded muzzle (5/8X24); Dead Air Armament Key Lock muzzle brake/suppressor mount
MSRP $2000.00

PREMIER SERIES MOUNTAIN

Action: Bolt
Stock: Carbon fiber
Barrel: 22 in.; .24 in. .300 Win. Mag.
Sights: None
Weight: 6 lb. 3 oz.–6 lb. 6 oz.
Caliber: .308 Win., 6.5 Creedmoor, .300 Win. Mag., .280 Ackley Improved, .30-06 Sprg., .270 Win.
Magazine: 3 (magnum), 4 rounds
Features: Proprietary Bergara Premier action with nonrotating gas shield, coned bolt nose, and sliding plate extractor; 416 stainless steel barrel with Cerakote finish; Timney trigger, two-position safety; sub 1.0 MOA accuracy guaranteed
MSRP $2190.00

Big Horn Armory

BIG HORN ARMORY AR500

BIG HORN ARMORY AR500

Action: Semiautomatic
Stock: Synthetic
Barrel: 18 in.
Sights: None
Weight: 9 lb. 8 oz.
Caliber: .500 Auto Max
Magazine: 10 rounds
Features: Adjustable gas block; Picatinny rail; flash suppressor; adjustable buttstock; includes a hard case
MSRP $1999.00

BLASER USA K95 STUTZEN BARONESSE

BLASER USA CLASSIC SPORTER

BLASER R8 INTUITION

BLASER R8 JAEGER

BLASER R8 PROFESSIONAL

BLASER R8 PROFESSIONAL SUCCESS

K95 STUTZEN BARONESSE

Action: Single shot
Stock: Walnut
Barrel: 19.75 in.
Sights: None
Weight: 5 lb. 11 oz.
Caliber: .243 Win., 6.5x57R, 6.5x55 SE, .270 Win., 7x65R, 7x57 R, .308 Win., .30-06 Spfd., 8x57 IRS
Magazine: None
Features: Octagonal barrel standard, barrels are interchangeable; available from grade Lexus; split forearm for continuous precision even in extreme weather; black forearm tip; range of ornamentation and game engravings
MSRP $2066.00

R8 CLASSIC SPORTER

Action: Bolt
Stock: Turkish walnut
Barrel: Variable
Sights: None
Weight: Variable
Caliber: Variable
Magazine: Variable
Features: Manual cocking bolt; interchangeable caliber system; trigger magazine housing combination; Prince of Wales grip
MSRP $4699.00

R8 INTUITION

Action: Bolt
Stock: Wood (various grades)
Barrel: Varies
Sights: Varies
Weight: N/A
Caliber: All common short-action,

long-action, and magnum centerfire calibers from .204 Ruger to .338 Lapua.
Magazine: 1, 2, 3, 4, 5 rounds by caliber
Features: Designed specifically for women with a shorter length of pull and a buttstock designed to fit a woman's unique anatomy, including a higher comb, slimmer pistol grip, and a reduction of distance between the trigger and the grip; available in all R8 wood stock configurations
MSRP . . . . $4385.00 and up

R8 JAEGER

Action: Straight-pull bolt-action
Stock: Walnut, pistol grip
Barrel: 20.5 in., 23 in., 25.75 in.
Sights: None
Weight: 6 lb. 6 oz.
Caliber: .222 Rem. to .338 Win. Mag.
Magazine: Detachable box, 3 rounds with lock
Features: Cold-hammer-forged barrels and chambers; black forearm tip; synthetic stock in dark green or walnut, straight comb; manual cocking system; integrated trigger/magazine unit; original Blaser saddle mount
MSRP $4386.00

R8 PROFESSIONAL

Action: Straight-pull bolt-action
Stock: Matte dark green synthetic stock, pistol grip
Barrel: 20.5 in., 23 in., 25.75 in.
Sights: None
Weight: 6 lb. 6 oz.
Caliber: .222 Rem. to .338 Win. Mag.

Magazine: Detachable box, 3 rounds with lock
Features: Shatter-proof, synthetic dark green stock; detachable magazine/trigger unit; single-stage trigger; quick-release scope mount; ergonomically optimized pistol grip; kickstop optional; precision trigger; black forearm tip; integrated receiver
MSRP $3787.00

R8 PROFESSIONAL SUCCESS

Action: Bolt
Stock: Synthetic
Barrel: 22.8 in., 25.6 in.
Sights: Open
Weight: 7 lb.
Caliber: .222 Rem., .204 Ruger, .223 Rem., .22–250 Rem., .243 Win., 6XC, 6.5x55 Swedish, 6.5x57, 6.5x65 RWS, .270 Win., 7x64 Brenneke, .308 Win., .30-06 Spfd., 8x57 IS, 8.5x63, 9.3x57, 9.3x62 Mauser, 6.5x68, 7.5x55 Suisse, 8x68 S, .257 Wby. Mag., .270 Wby. Mag., .270 WSM, 7mm Blaser Mag., 7mm Rem. Mag., .300 Blaser Mag., .300 Win. Mag., .300 Wby. Mag., .300 WSM, .338 Blaser Mag., .338 Win. Mag., .375 Blaser Mag., .375 H&H
Magazine: 3+1, 4+1, 5+1 rounds
Features: Blaser precision trigger; radial locking system; ergonomically optimized stock in dark green or dark brown and elastomer grips; double loading option; leather model available
MSRP $4337.00

Brownells

BROWNELLS BRN-10A

BROWNELLS BRN-16A1

BROWNELLS BRN-10B

BROWNELLS BRN-601

BROWNELLS XBRN16E1

BROWNELLS XBRN-177E2

BRN-10A
Action: Semiautomatic
Stock: Synthetic
Barrel: 20 in.
Sights: Standard AR-15-style front, period-style rear
Weight: 8 lb.
Caliber: .308 Win.
Magazine: 20 rounds
Features: Based on the Stoner rifle in use from 1955-1960; open three-prong Dutch flash hider; a heavy-contour fluted barrel; trigger-style charging handle under the carry handle; 7075-T6 aluminum receiver; brown retro stock and forearm; aluminum magazine included
MSRP $1699.99

BRN-10B
Action: Semiautomatic
Stock: Synthetic
Barrel: 20 in.
Sights: Standard AR-15-style front, period-style rear
Weight: 8 lb.
Caliber: .308 Win.
Magazine: 20 rounds
Features: Based on the Stoner rifle in use from 1955-1960; closed-prong Portuguese flash hider; trigger-style charging handle; 7075-T6 aluminum

receiver; black retro stock and forearm; aluminum magazine included
MSRP $1599.99

BRN-16A1
Action: Semiautomatic
Stock: Synthetic
Barrel: 20 in.
Sights: Standard AR-15-style front, period-style rear
Weight: 6 lb. 13 oz.
Caliber: 5.56 NATO
Magazine: 20 rounds
Features: Direct impingement rifle; matte gray anodized; three-prong A1 flash hider, 1:12 chrome bore barrel; based off the original in use from 1967-1982
MSRP $1299.99

BRN-601
Action: Semiautomatic
Stock: Synthetic
Barrel: 20 in.
Sights: Standard AR-15-style front, period-style rear
Weight: 6 lb. 11 oz.
Caliber: 5.56 NATO
Magazine: 20 rounds
Features: Based on 1959–1964 model; slickside upper; 1:12 chrome-bore barrel; a three-prong "duckbill" flash hider; green stock and pistol grip; waffle magazine
MSRP $1299.99

XBRN16E1
Action: Semiautomatic
Stock: Synthetic
Barrel: 20 in.
Sights: Standard AR-15-style front, period-style rear
Weight: 6 lb. 11 oz.
Caliber: 5.56 NATO
Magazine: 20 rounds
Features: Based on 1964–1967 model; chrome bolt carrier group with forward assist; anodized matte gray finish; black stock and forend; three-prong flash hider; lower receiver has a partial "magazine fence"
MSRP $1299.99

XBRN-177E2
Action: Semiautomatic
Stock: Synthetic
Barrel: 12.7 in.
Sights: Standard AR-15-style front, period-style rear
Weight: 5 lb. 11 oz.
Caliber: 5.56 NATO
Magazine: 20 rounds
Features: Based on model used from 1967–1982; adjustable buttstock and short, maneuverable barrel; Mil-Spec phosphate/chrome bolt carrier group; AXM177 three-prong flash hider with a grenade ring; full "magazine fence"
MSRP $1299.99

RIFLES

BROWNING AB3 COMPOSITE STALKER

BROWNING AB3 HUNTER

BROWNING AB3 MICRO STALKER

BROWNING BAR MARK II SAFARI WITH BOSS

BROWNING BAR MK 3

BROWNING BAR MK 3 DBM

AB3 COMPOSITE STALKER

Action: Bolt
Stock: Synthetic
Barrel: 22 in., 26 in.
Sights: None
Weight: 6 lb. 9 oz.–7 lb. 3 oz.
Caliber: .243 Win., .270 Win., .270 WSM, .30-06 Spfd., .300 Win. Mag., .300 WSM, .308 Win., 6.5 Creedmoor, 7mm Rem. Mag., 7mm-08 Rem.
Magazine: Detachable box, 4 rounds
Features: Inflex Technology recoil pad; top tang safety; blued barrel and action
MSRP. $599.99

AB3 HUNTER

Action: Bolt
Stock: Satin
Barrel: 22 in.
Sights: Drilled and tapped for sights
Weight: 6 lb. 11 oz.–7 lb. 6 oz.
Caliber: .243 Win., .270 Win., .270 WSM, .30-06 Spfd., .300 Win. Mag., .300 WSM, .308 Win., 6.5 Creedmoor, 7mm Rem. Mag., 7mm-08 Rem.
Magazine: Detachable box
Features: 5-round mag capacity; steel barrel; polished finish
MSRP. $669.99

AB3 MICRO STALKER

Action: Bolt
Stock: Composite
Barrel: 20 in.
Sights: None
Weight: 6 lb. 6 oz.–6 lb. 8 oz.
Caliber: .243 Win., 6.5 Creedmoor, 7mm-08 Rem., .308 Win.
Magazine: 5 rounds
Features: Intended for smaller-statured hunters; 13 in. length of pull; Pachmayr Decelerator recoil pad; drilled and tapped for scope mounts
MSRP. $599.99

BAR MARK II SAFARI WITH BOSS

Action: Gas-operated semiautomatic
Stock: Walnut
Barrel: 22 in., 24 in.
Sights: None
Weight: 8 lb. 1.6 oz.–8 lb. 3 oz.
Caliber: .270 Win., .30-06 Spfd., .300 Win. Mag., .338 Win. Mag.
Magazine: Detachable box
Features: Checkered, select gloss finish walnut stock; steel receiver with blued finish and scroll engraving; drilled and tapped for scope mounts; multi-lug rotary bolt; recoil pad sling swivel studs installed
MSRP. . . . . $1419.99–$1549.99

BAR MK 3

Action: Semiautomatic
Stock: Walnut
Barrel: 22 in., 23 in., 24 in.
Sights: None
Weight: 7 lb. 2 oz.–7 lb. 11 oz.
Caliber: .243 Win., .270 Win., .270 WSM, .30-06 Spfd., .300 Win. Mag., .300 WSM, .308 Win., 7mm Rem. Mag., 7mm-08 Rem.
Magazine: Detachable rotary, 3 or 4 rounds
Features: Completely new styling; fine oil-finished walnut; precision alloy receiver; hammer-forged barrel; drilled and tapped for scope; gold trigger guard engraving
MSRP. . . . . $1299.99–$1389.99

BAR MK 3 DBM (DETACHABLE BOX MAGAZINE)

Action: Semiautomatic
Stock: Composite
Barrel: 18 in.
Sights: None
Weight: 6 lb. 10 oz.
Caliber: .308 Win.
Magazine: 10 rounds
Features: Detachable box magazine with a magwell instead of the standard hinged floor plate design; QD swivel cups (QD sling swivels included); 1913 Picatinny rail scope bases; hammer-forged barrel
MSRP. $1499.99

RIFLES

Browning

BROWNING BAR MK 3 STALKER

BROWNING BLR LIGHTWEIGHT '81

BROWNING BLR LIGHTWEIGHT '81
STAINLESS TAKEDOWN

BROWNING BLR
LIGHTWEIGHT STAINLESS
WITH PISTOL GRIP

BROWNING T-BOLT GRAY
LAMINATED TARGET/VARMINT
STAINLESS, SUPPRESSOR READY

BAR MK 3 STALKER, MOSSY OAK BREAK-UP COUNTRY

Action: Semiautomatic
Stock: Composite
Barrel: 22 in., 23 in., 24 in.
Sights: None
Weight: 6 lb. 10 oz.–7 lb. 8 oz.
Caliber: .243 Win., 7mm-08 Rem., .308 Win., .270 Win., .30-06 Spfd., 7mm Rem. Mag., .300 Win. Mag., .300 WSM, .270 WSM
Magazine: 3, 4 rounds
Features: Composite stock with contemporary design; shim-adjustable for cast and drop at comb; gas-piston operation; lightweight aluminum alloy receiver drilled and tapped for scope mounts; hinged floor plate with detachable box magazine
Standard Stalker: . . $1299.99–$1389.99
Mossy Oak: . . . . $1399.99–$1539.99

BLR LIGHTWEIGHT '81

Action: Lever
Stock: Walnut, straight grip
Barrel: 20 in., 22 in., 24 in.
Sights: None
Weight: 6 lb. 8 oz.–7 lb. 12 oz.
Caliber: .22-250 Rem., .223 Rem., .243 Win., .270 Win., .270 WSM, .30-06 Spfd., .300 Win. Mag., .300 WSM, .308 Win., .325 WSM, .358 Win., .450 Mar, 7mm Rem. Mag., 7mm WSM, 7mm-08 Rem.
Magazine: Detachable box
Features: Aircraft-grade alloy receiver; drilled and tapped for scope mounts;

crowned muzzle; adjustable sights; gloss finish walnut stock; recoil pad
MSRP. . . . . **$959.99–$1039.99**

BLR LIGHTWEIGHT '81 STAINLESS TAKEDOWN

Action: Lever-action
Stock: Laminate, straight grip
Barrel: 20 in., 22 in., 24 in.
Sights: Open
Weight: 6 lb. 8 oz.–7 lb. 12 oz.
Caliber: .223 Rem., .22-250 Rem., .243 Win., 7mm-08 Rem., .308 Win., .358 Win., .270 Win., .30-06 Spfd., 7mm Rem. Mag., .300 WSM, .300 Win. Mag., .270 WSM, .450 Marlin
Magazine: Detachable box
Features: Aircraft-grade alloy receiver; drilled and tapped for scope mounts; stainless steel barrel with matte finish; gray laminate wood stock in satin finish; recoil pad; separates for storage or transportation; optional Scout-style scope mount; TRUGLO/Marble's fiber optic front sight
MSRP. . . . . **$1259.99–$1339.99**

BLR LIGHTWEIGHT STAINLESS WITH PISTOL GRIP

Action: Lever-action
Stock: Walnut, pistol grip
Barrel: 20 in., 22 in., 24 in.
Sights: None
Weight: 6 lb. 8 oz.–7 lb. 12 oz.
Caliber: .223 Rem., .22-250 Rem., .243 Win., 7mm–08 Rem., 7mm Rem. Mag., .308 Win., .358 Win., .270

Win., .30-06 Spfd., .300 Win. Mag., .300 WSM, .270 WSM, 7mm WSM, .450 Marlin, .325 WSM
Magazine: Detachable box
Features: Aircraft-grade alloy receiver; drilled and tapped for scope mounts; steel barrel with matte finish; crowned muzzle; adjustable sights; gloss finish walnut stock with pistol grip; sling swivel studs installed; recoil pad
MSRP. . . . . **$1119.99–$1199.99**

T-BOLT GRAY LAMINATED TARGET/VARMINT STAINLESS, SUPPRESSOR READY

Action: T-bolt
Stock: Laminate
Barrel: 22 in.
Sights: None
Weight: 5 lb. 10 oz.
Caliber: .22 LR, .22 WMR, .17 HMR
Magazine: 10 rounds
Features: Gray laminate stock with a Monte Carlo comb; a free-floating barrel with a medium target profile and recessed crown; semi-match grade chamber; adjustable trigger; installed sling swivels; threaded for suppressor use; thread protector included
MSRP. . . . . **$939.99–$979.99**

BROWNING X-BOLT ECLIPSE HUNTER

BROWNING X-BOLT ECLIPSE TARGET

BROWNING X-BOLT ECLIPSE VARMINT

BROWNING X-BOLT HELL'S CANYON LONG RANGE

BROWNING X-BOLT HELL'S CANYON SPEED

X-BOLT ECLIPSE HUNTER
Action: Bolt
Stock: Wood laminate
Barrel: 22 in., 23 in., 24 in., 26 in.
Sights: None
Weight: 6 lb. 7 oz.–7 lb. 8 oz.
Caliber: .25-06 Rem., .243 Win., .270 Win., .270 WSM, .30-06 Spfd., .300 Win. Mag., .300 WSM, .308 Win., 6.5 Creedmoor, 6mm Creedmoor, 7mm Rem. Mag., 7mm-08 Rem.
Magazine: Detachable box, 4 rounds
Features: Inflex Technology recoil pad
MSRP . . . . $1229.99–$1259.99

X-BOLT ECLIPSE TARGET
Action: Bolt
Stock: Satin
Barrel: 28 in.
Sights: None
Weight: 10 lb.–10 lb. 3 oz.
Caliber: .308 Win., 6mm Creedmoor, 6.5 Creedmoor
Magazine: Detachable box
Features: Steel barrel; short action; drilled and tapped for scope
MSRP $1429.99

X-BOLT ECLIPSE VARMINT
Action: Bolt
Stock: Satin
Barrel: 26 in.
Sights: None
Weight: 9 lb. 5 oz.– 9 lb. 6 oz.
Caliber: .204 Ruger., .223 Rem., .22-250 Rem.
Magazine: Detachable box
Features: Steel barrel; super short action; steel barrel
MSRP $1429.99

X-BOLT HELL'S CANYON LONG RANGE
Action: Bolt
Stock: Composite
Barrel: 26 in.
Sights: None
Weight: 7 lb. 3 oz.–7 lb. 8 oz.
Caliber: 6.5 Creedmoor, .270 WSM., .300 WSM, .26 Nosler, 7mm Rem. Mag., .300 Win. Mag., .28 Nosler, 6mm Creedmoor, 6.5 PRC, .30 Nosler, .300 RUM
Magazine: 4 rounds
Features: Heavy sporter contour barrel for increased long-range accuracy; exclusive A-TACS AU camouflage with DuraTouch Armor Coating; free-floated, fluted barrel and receiver metal are in burnt bronze Cerakote; barrel is threaded for suppressor use; bolt unlock button, Inflex recoil pad 60-degree short bolt lift, and detachable rotary magazine
MSRP . . . . $1259.99–$1319.99

X-BOLT HELL'S CANYON SPEED
Action: Bolt
Stock: Composite
Barrel: 22 in., 23, in. 26 in.
Sights: None
Weight: 6 lb. 5 oz.–6 lb. 13 oz.
Caliber: .26 Nosler, .243 Win., .270 Win., .270 WSM, .30-06 Spfd., 300 Win. Mag., .300 WSM, .308 Win., 6mm Creedmoor, .28 Nosler, 6.5 Creedmoor, 7mm Rem. Mag., 7mm-08 Rem., 6.5 PRC, .30 Nosler
Magazine: Detachable rotary, 3 or 4 rounds
Features: A-TACS AU (Arid/Urban) camouflage; Dura-Touch finish; composite stock; Cerakote finish; fluted; sporter barrel with threaded muzzle brake; detachable rotary magazine; short throw bolt; adjustable trigger; Inflex Technology recoil pad
MSRP . . . .$1229.99–$1299.99

Browning

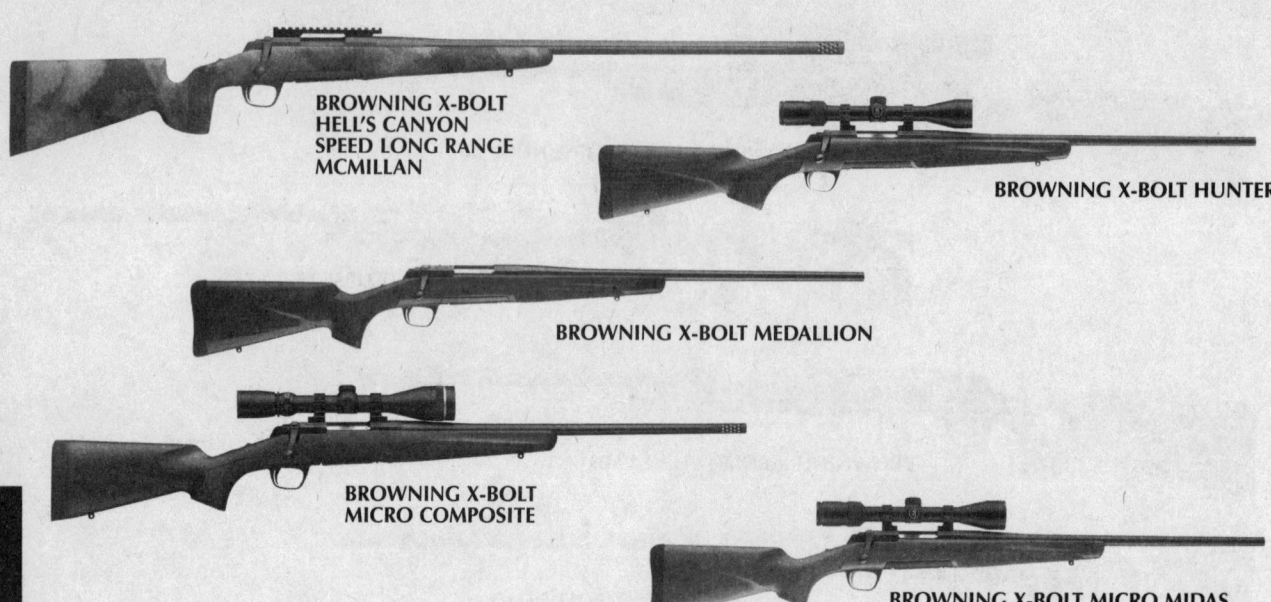

BROWNING X-BOLT HELL'S CANYON SPEED LONG RANGE MCMILLAN

BROWNING X-BOLT HUNTER

BROWNING X-BOLT MEDALLION

BROWNING X-BOLT MICRO COMPOSITE

BROWNING X-BOLT MICRO MIDAS

X-BOLT HELL'S CANYON SPEED LONG RANGE MCMILLAN

Action: Bolt
Stock: Composite
Barrel: 26 in.
Sights: None
Weight: 7 lb. 7 oz.–7 lb. 12 oz.
Caliber: 6mm Creedmoor, 6.5 Creedmoor, .300 WSM, .26 Nosler, 7mm Rem. Mag., .28 Nosler, .300 Win. Mag., 6.5 PRC, .30 Nosler, .300 RUM
Magazine: 3, 4 rounds
Features: The McMillan Game Scout stock (high comb, vertical pistol grip) has a palm swell and textured grip panels, in Browning's A-TACS AU (arid/urban) camo; free-floating, hand-chambered barrel has a threaded muzzle brake mounted on suppressor-ready threads and wears a target crown; receiver is glass-bedded; magazine is detachable; top-side optics rail; adjustable feather trigger
MSRP . . . .$2189.99–$2259.99

X-BOLT HUNTER

Action: Bolt
Stock: Satin finish walnut stock
Barrel: 22 in., 23 in., 24 in., 26 in.
Sights: None
Weight: 6 lb. 13 oz.–7 lb.
Caliber: .223 Rem., .243 Win., 7mm-08 Rem., .308 Win., .25-06 Rem., .270 Win., .280 Rem., .30-06 Spfd., 7mm Rem. Mag., .375 HH Mag., .388 Win. Mag., .300 Win. Mag., .300 WSM, .270 WSM, 7mm WSM, .325 WSM, .223 Rem., .22-250 Rem.
Magazine: Detachable rotary box
Features: Adjustable feather trigger; top-tang safety with bolt unlock button; sling swivel studs installed; Inflex technology recoil pad
MSRP . . . . $899.99–$979.99

X-BOLT MEDALLION

Action: Bolt
Stock: Walnut
Barrel: 22 in., 23 in., 24 in., 26 in.
Sights: Open
Weight: 6 lb. 6 oz.–7 lb.
Caliber: .223 Rem., .22-250 Rem., .243 Win., .308 Win., .25-06 Rem., .270 Win., .280 Rem., .30-06 Spfd., 6.5 Creedmoor, 6mm Creedmoor, 7mm Rem. Mag., .300 Win. Mag., .338 Win. Mag., .300 WSM, .270 WSM, 7mm WSM, .325 WSM, .375 H&H Mag.
Magazine: Detachable rotary box
Features: Gloss finish walnut stock, rosewood forend grip and pistol cap; Inflex technology recoil pad; adjustable feather trigger; drilled and tapped for scope mounts; left-hand option
Right-hand: . . . . . . $1039.99–$1099.99
Left-hand: . . . . $1069.99–$1139.99

X-BOLT MICRO COMPOSITE

Action: Bolt
Stock: Composite
Barrel: 20 in.
Sights: None
Weight: 6 lb. 5 oz.
Caliber: .243 Win., 6mm Creedmoor, 6.5 Creedmoor, 7mm-08 Rem., .308 Rem.
Magazine: 4 rounds
Features: Shorter length of pull at 13 in.; stock is a non-glare composite in black and with textured gripping surfaces and a palm swell; free-floating barrel features a threaded muzzle brake, thread protector, target crown, and light sporter contour; sling swivel studs; Pachmayr Decelerator recoil pad
MSRP $959.99

X-BOLT MICRO MIDAS

Action: Bolt
Stock: Walnut
Barrel: 20 in.
Sights: None
Weight: 6 lb. 1 oz.–6 lb. 6 oz.
Caliber: .243 Win., 7mm-08 Rem., .270 WSM, .300 WSM, .308 Win., .22-250 Rem., 6.5 Creedmoor, 6mm Creedmoor
Magazine: Detachable rotary magazine
Features: Drilled and tapped for scope mounts, low-luster blued finish, free-floating barrel; adjustable feather trigger; top-tang safety; left-hand option
MSRP . . . . $859.99–$899.99

BROWNING X-BOLT PRO

BROWNING X-BOLT PRO LONG RANGE

BROWNING X-BOLT STAINLESS STALKER

BROWNING X-BOLT RMEF WHITE GOLD

X-BOLT PRO

Action: Bolt
Stock: Carbon fiber wrap
Barrel: 22 in., 23 in., 26 in.
Sights: None
Weight: 6 lb. 1 oz.–6 lb. 10 oz.
Caliber: 6.5 Creedmoor, .308 Win., .30-06 Spfd., .300 Win. Mag., .28 Nosler, .300 WSM, .26 Nosler, 7mm Rem. Mag., .270 Win., 6mm Creedmoor, 6.5 PRC, .30 Nosler, .300 RUM
Magazine: 3, 4 rounds
Features: "Semi-custom" rifle; stock has a compressed foam core wrapped 360-degrees with carbon fiber; barrel is a lightweight sporter profile; threaded muzzle brake; spiral-fluted bolt with an oversized knob; Burnt Bronze Cerakote finish
MSRP . . . . $2099.99–$2189.99

X-BOLT PRO LONG RANGE

Action: Bolt
Stock: Carbon fiber wrap
Barrel: 26 in.

Sights: None
Weight: 6 lb. 1 oz.–6 lb. 10 oz.
Caliber: 6.5 Creedmoor, .308 Win., .30-06 Spfd., .300 Win. Mag., .28 Nosler, .300 WSM, .26 Nosler, 7mm Rem. Mag., .270 Win., 6mm Creedmoor, 6.5 PRC, .30 Nosler, .300 RUM
Magazine: 3, 4 rounds
Features: Pro Long Range barrel with heavy sporter contour, fluted, free-floating, and threaded muzzle brake; Burnt Bronze Cerakote finish
MSRP . . . .$2159.99–$2229.99

X-BOLT RMEF WHITE GOLD

Action: Bolt
Stock: Walnut
Barrel: 26 in.
Sights: None
Weight: 7 lb.
Caliber: .300 Win. Mag.
Magazine: Detachable rotary box
Features: Monte Carlo stock; stainless steel barrel and receiver, receiver etched in gold; raised cheekpiece; Inflex technology recoil pad; adjustable feather trigger; top-tang safety
MSRP $1579.99

X-BOLT STAINLESS STALKER

Action: Bolt
Stock: Composite
Barrel: 22 in., 23 in., 24 in., 26 in.
Sights: None
Weight: 6 lb. 3 oz.–6 lb. 13 oz.
Caliber: .243 Win., 7mm-08 Rem., .308 Win., .25-06 Rem., .270 Win., .280 Rem., .30-06 Spfd., 6.5 Creedmoor, .300 H&H Mag., 7mm Rem. Mag., .300 Win. Mag., .388 Win. Mag., .300 WSM, .270 WSM, 7mm WSM, .325 WSM, .223 Rem., .22-250 Rem., 6mm Creedmoor
Magazine: Detachable rotary box
Features: Composite stock in matte black with textured gripping surfaces; Dura-Touch armor coating; adjustable feather trigger; top-tang safety; bolt unlock button; palm swell
MSRP . . . .$1159.99–$1199.99

Bushmaster Firearms

Rifle: $1299.00
Carbine: $1299.00

ACR DMR (DESIGNATED MARKSMAN RIFLE)

Action: Semiautomatic
Stock: Synthetic
Barrel: 18.5 in.
Sights: None
Weight: 10 lb. 6.4 oz.
Caliber: 5.56 NATO
Magazine: 20 rounds
Features: Modular rifle designed for instant changeout of barrels and calibers; AAC 51T flash hider; heavy barrel treated with Melonite; two-position gas piston operating system; Magpul PR52 stock; Geissele trigger
MSRP $2569.00

BUSHMASTER .450 RIFLE & CARBINE

BUSHMASTER ACR DMR (DESIGNATED MARKSMAN RIFLE)

.450 RIFLE & CARBINE

Action: Semiautomatic
Stock: Synthetic, A2 pistol grip
Barrel: 16 in. (carbine), 20 in. (rifle)
Sights: None
Weight: 8 lb. 2 oz. (carbine), 8 lb. 8 oz. (rifle)
Caliber: .450 Bushmaster

Magazine: Detachable box, 5 rounds
Features: Chromoly steel barrels; free-floating aluminum forends; forged aluminum receivers; solid A2 buttstock with trapdoor storage compartment; Pictatinny rail; black web sling included; shipped in lockable hard plastic case with orange safety block

Bushmaster Firearms

BUSHMASTER MINIMALIST-SD

BUSHMASTER XM-15 MOE 16" MID-LENGTH

BUSHMASTER XM-15 STANDARD 16" HEAVY BARREL CARBINE A2

BUSHMASTER MINIMALIST-SD .450 BUSHMASTER SD CARBINE

BUSHMASTER XM-15 QUICK RESPONSE CARBINE (QRC)

BUSHMASTER XM-15 STANDARD 16-IN. A3 PATROLMAN'S CARBINE WITH QUAD-RAIL

RIFLES

MINIMALIST-SD
Action: Semiautomatic
Stock: Synthetic
Barrel: 16 in.
Sights: None
Weight: 6 lb.
Caliber: .300 BLK, 5.56 NATO
Magazine: 30 rounds
Features: Ultralightweight MSR; AAC SquareDrop rail and handguard; Mission First Tactical minimalist stock, grip and magazine; ALG Advanced Combat Trigger (ACT) with 5.5-lb. pull; and AAC 51T flash hider
MSRP **$1169.00**

MINIMALIST-SD .450 BUSHMASTER SD CARBINE
Action: Semiautomatic
Stock: Synthetic
Barrel: 16 in., 20 in.
Sights: None
Weight: N/A
Caliber: .450 Bushmaster
Magazine: 5 rounds
Features: Proprietary twin port muzzle brake; Magpul grip; ALG Defense fire control group; 16-in. barrel has B5 Sopmod stock; 20-in. barrel has Hunter stock with recoil pad
MSRP **$1299.00**

PREDATOR RIFLE COMPLIANT
Action: Semiautomatic
Stock: Synthetic, ambidextrous pistol grip
Barrel: 20 in.
Sights: None
Weight: 8 lb.
Caliber: 5.56 NATO

Magazine: Detachable box, 5 rounds (accepts all M16/AR 15 type)
Features: Non-chrome lined fluted barrel with 1:8 twist; two-stage trigger; Magpul MOE stock; one five-round magazine supplied
MSRP **$1159.00**

XM-15 MOE 16-IN. MID-LENGTH
Action: Semiautomatic
Stock: Synthetic
Barrel: 16 in.
Sights: Magpul MSBUS rear flip sight
Weight: 6 lb. 2 oz.
Caliber: .308 Win., 7.62 NATO
Magazine: Detachable box, 20 rounds
Features: Receiver length Picatinny rail; Magpul MOE polymer mid-length handguard; Magpul MOE adjustable buttstock with strong A-frame design; rubber buttplate; Magpul MOE vertical grip; MOE enhanced trigger guards; shipped in lockable hard case with yellow safety block; stock comes in black, Flat Dark Earth, or OD green
MSRP **$1099.00**

XM-15 QUICK RESPONSE CARBINE (QRC)
Action: Semiautomatic
Stock: Synthetic
Barrel: 16 in.
Sights: Mini red-dot
Weight: 6 lb.
Caliber: 5.56 NATO
Magazine: 30 rounds
Features: AR-15-style rifle has superlight contour, chrome-moly, Melonite-coated barrel, six-position collapsible stock, and A2 birdcage flash hider; supplied with quick-detach mini red-

dot optic and one 30-round Magpul PMag
MSRP **$769.00**

XM-15 STANDARD 16-IN. A3 PATROLMAN'S CARBINE WITH QUAD-RAIL
Action: Semiautomatic
Stock: Synthetic
Barrel: 16 in.
Sights: None
Weight: 8 lb. 5 oz.
Caliber: 5.56 NATO
Magazine: Detachable box, 30 rounds
Features: Chrome-lined barrel; A2 birdcage-type suppressor; free-float quad rail forend; six-position telestock for light weight and quick handling; ships with lockable hard case and yellow safety block
MSRP **$1099.00**

XM-15 STANDARD 16-IN. HEAVY BARREL CARBINE A2
Action: Semiautomatic
Stock: Synthetic
Barrel: 16 in.
Sights: Open
Weight: 6 lb. 3 oz.
Caliber: 5.56 NATO
Magazine: Detachable box, 30 rounds (accepts all M16/AR15 type)
Features: 16-in. chrome-lined HBAR-profile heavy barrel with A2 flash hider; M16 bolt carrier, M4 feed ramp, six-position stock
MSRP **$895.00**

Bushmaster Firearms

BUSHMASTER XM-15 STANDARD TARGET MODEL RIFLE A2

XM-15 STANDARD TARGET MODEL A2, A3
Action: Semiautomatic
Stock: Synthetic

Barrel: 20 in
Sights: None
Weight: 8 lb. 7 oz.
Caliber: 5.56 NATO, .223 Rem.

Magazine: Detachable box, 30 rounds (accepts all M16 / AR15 type)
Features: A2 upper receiver 300–800 meter rear sight system; chromoly steel or polished stainless steel barrels; shipped in a lockable hard case with orange safety block
A2:....................$969.00
A3:....................$999.00

C&H Precision Weapons

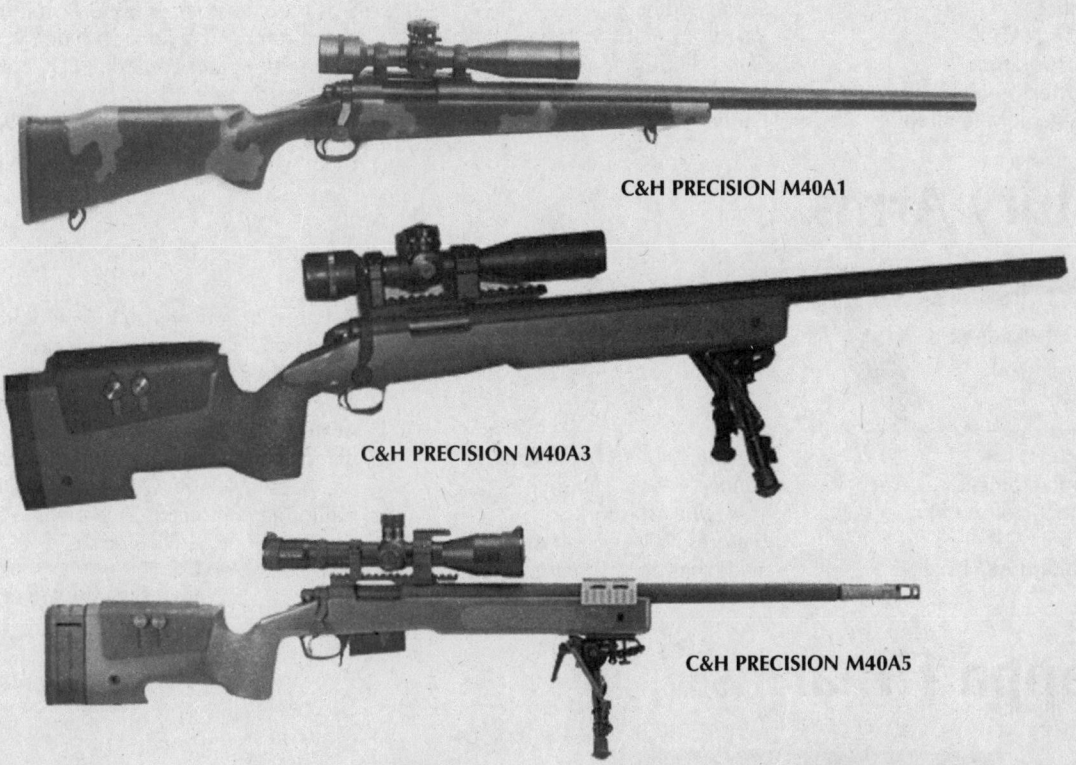

C&H PRECISION M40A1

C&H PRECISION M40A3

C&H PRECISION M40A5

M40A1
Action: Bolt
Stock: Synthetic
Barrel: 25 in.
Sights: None
Weight: N/A
Caliber: .308 Win., 7.62 NATO
Magazine: N/A
Features: USMC stainless steel contour barrel; McMillan M40A1-HTG stock in forest camo; USMC spec. trigger guard custom made from Winchester model 70 steel trigger guard and floor plate; matte black finish
MSRP.................$3825.00

M40A3
Action: Bolt
Stock: Synthetic
Barrel: 25 in.
Sights: None
Weight: N/A
Caliber: .308 Win., 7.62 NATO
Magazine: N/A
Features: USMC stainless steel contour barrel; McMillan A4 stock with adjustable saddle cheek and spacer system in olive drab green; DD Ross trigger guard; matte black finish
MSRP................. $4225.00

M40A5
Action: Bolt
Stock: Synthetic
Barrel: 25 in.
Sights: None
Weight: N/A
Caliber: .308 Win., 7.62 NATO
Magazine: Detachable box, 5 rounds
Features: USMC stainless steel contour barrel with Surefire muzzle brake/suppressor adapter; McMillan A4 stock with adjustable saddle cheek, spacer system, and PGW PVS-22 night vision mount, in olive drab green; Badger Ordnance M5 DBM with five round magazine; matte black finish
MSRP.................$4625.00

Caracal

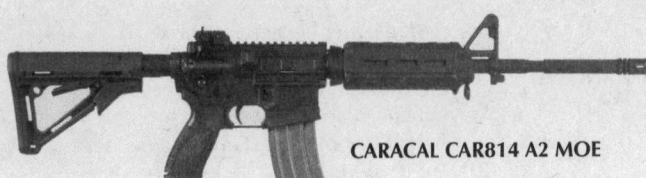

CARACAL CAR814 A2 MOE

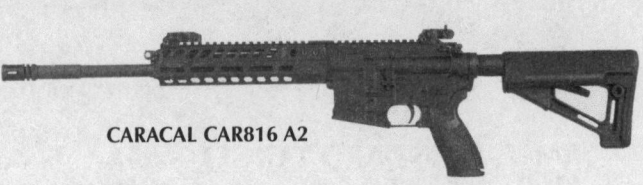

CARACAL CAR816 A2

CAR814 A2 MOE

Action: Semiautomatic
Stock: Synthetic
Barrel: 11.5, 14.5, 15 in.
Sights: A2 front sight, flip-up rear
Weight: 7 lb.
Caliber: 5.56 NATO
Magazine: 30 rounds
Features: Direct impingement gas-operated system; Magpul MOE

M-LOK handguard; Magpul CTR mil-spec carbine stock; Caracal grip
MSRP **$999.00**

CAR816 A2

Action: Semiautomatic
Stock: Synthetic
Barrel: 11.5, 14.5, 16 in.
Sights: Flip-up front and rear
Weight: 7 lb. 6.4 oz.
Caliber: 5.56 NATO

Magazine: 30 rounds
Features: Short-stroke push rod gas piston system; three-position adjustable gas valve; Caracal handguard; full-length 1913 Picatinny rail; Modified M4 barrel contour; Magpul STR Carbine stock or SBA3 Pistol Brace stock; A2-style flash hider; select-fire option available; EDT Sharp Shooter trigger
MSRP . . . . **$1849.00–$1969.00**

Century Arms

CENTURY ARMS C39V2

C39V2

Action: Semiautomatic
Stock: Synthetic or wood
Barrel: 10.6 in., 12.4 in.
Sights: Standard AKM sights

Weight: 7 lb. 15 oz.–8 lb. 3 oz.
Caliber: 7.62 x 39mm
Magazine: 30 rounds
Features: 100 percent American made; barrel 1:10 twist; larger

T-shaped magazine catch; bolt hold-open notch on the safety selector; front sight gas block and birdcage-style flash hider; bolt carrier tail heat treated to ensure maximum performance and life; accepts all standard AK mags; available with MOE, MOE California compliant, Zhukov-S, Tactical Wood, or California-compliant wood stock
MSRP . . . . **$899.99–$1084.99**

Chiappa Firearms

CHIAPPA FIREARMS 1886 LEVER ACTION DELUXE

CHIAPPA FIREARMS LA322 KODIAK CUB TAKE DOWN

1886 LEVER ACTION DELUXE

Action: Lever
Stock: Walnut
Barrel: 26 in.
Sights: Dovetail front, buckhorn rear
Weight: 9 lb.
Caliber: .45-70 Govt.
Magazine: 8 rounds
Features: High-grade current production of Browning's classic 1886 rifle;

color case finished receiver; select walnut; checkering at wrist and forend; octagonal barrel
MSRP $1880.00

LA322 KODIAK CUB TAKE DOWN

Action: Lever action
Stock: English-style black soft touch
Barrel: 18.5 in.
Sights: Hooded front, adjustable rear
Weight: 5 lb. 8 oz.

Caliber: .22 LR
Magazine: 15 rounds
Features: Matte hard chrome finish that is durable and corrosion-resistant; black soft touch coating makes the stock easier to grip and protects from the elements; easy take down
MSRP $754.00

RIFLES

Chiappa Firearms

CHIAPPA FIREARMS LA322 TAKEDOWN DELUXE

CHIAPPA FIREARMS LA322 TAKEDOWN STANDARD

CHIAPPA FIREARMS LITTLE BADGER

CHIAPPA FIREARMS M1-9

CHIAPPA FIREARMS M1-22

CHIAPPA FIREARMS M6

LA322 TAKEDOWN DELUXE

Action: Lever action
Stock: Walnut
Barrel: 18.5 in.
Sights: Hooded front, adjustable rear
Weight: 5 lb. 8 oz.
Caliber: .22 LR
Magazine: 15 rounds
Features: A takedown lever-action rimfire with a dovetail groove for scope mounting; pistol grip wood stock; blacked chrome receiver; blued barrel
MSRP $576.00

LA322 TAKEDOWN STANDARD

Action: Lever action
Stock: English-style wood
Barrel: 18.5 in.
Sights: Hooded front, adjustable rear
Weight: 5 lb. 8 oz.
Caliber: .22 LR
Magazine: 15 rounds
Features: 3/8-inchdovetail on top of receiver for scope mounting; takedown design; straight wood stock; blued metalwork
MSRP $389.00

LITTLE BADGER

Action: Single shot
Stock: Metal foldable
Barrel: 16.5 in.

Sights: Adjustable rear
Weight: 3 lb. 8 oz.
Caliber: .22 LR, .22WMR, .17 HMR
Magazine: None
Features: Single barrel; foldable rifle; extremely light for comfortable carry; folds to 16.5 in. total length; nylon carry bag and special cartridge holder available
MSRP . . . . $216.00–$229.00

M1-9

Action: Semiautomatic
Stock: Polymer, wood
Barrel: 18 in.
Sights: Winged front, sliding rear
Weight: 5 lb. 14.4 oz.–6 lb. 4.8 oz.
Caliber: 9mm
Magazine: 10 rounds
Features: Classic M1 carbine taking Beretta 9mm magazines; metals matte blue; two magazines included
Polymer: $559.00
Wood: $636.00

M1-22

Action: Semiautomatic
Stock: Polymer
Barrel: 18 in.
Sights: Adjustable rear
Weight: 5 lb. 8 oz.

Caliber: .22 LR
Magazine: Detachable box, 10 rounds
Features: The M1 carbine is a lightweight, easy-to-use semiautomatic carbine that became a standard firearm for the U.S. military during World War II, the Korean War, and the Vietnam War, and was produced in several variants
Polymer: $309.00
Wood: $428.00

M6

Action: Lever
Stock: Polypropylene closed cell foam
Barrel: 18.5 in.
Sights: Fiber optic front, military adjustable rear
Weight: 5 lb. 12.8 oz.–6 lb.
Caliber: 12 ga./.22 LR, 20 ga./.22 LR, 12 ga./.22 WMR, 20 ga./.22 WMR
Magazine: 2 rounds
Features: Combo gun, shotgun barrel top, .22 rimfire barrel bottom; folding stock, interchangeable choke tubes, and dedicated triggers for each barrel; cleaning kit and 4–8 additional rounds stored in the stock
MSRP . . . . $680.00–$929.00

Chiappa Firearms

CHIAPPA FIREARMS MFOUR-22 GEN II PRO CARBINE, RIFLE

CHIAPPA FIREARMS RAK-22

MFOUR-22 GEN II PRO CARBINE, RIFLE
Action: Semiautomatic
Stock: Synthetic
Barrel: 16 in.
Sights: None
Weight: 5 lb. 11.2 oz.
Caliber: .22 LR

Magazine: 28 rounds
Features: Fully equipped MSR in .22 LR; eight-position Picatinny rail; six-position adjustable buttstock; heavy barrel profile; two magazines
MSRP . . . . $473.00–$569.00

RAK-22
Action: Semiautomatic

Stock: Wood
Barrel: 17.25 in.
Sights: Adjustable
Weight: 6 lb.
Caliber: .22 LR
Magazine: Detachable box, 10 rounds
Features: Steel blued receiver and barrel
MSRP $665.00

Chipmunk Rifles

CHIPMUNK RIFLES CHIPMUNK

CHIPMUNK
Action: Bolt
Stock: Walnut, laminated
Barrel: 16.125 in.
Sights: Target

Weight: 2 lb. 8 oz.
Caliber: .22 LR
Magazine: None
Features: Designed with younger shooters in mind; single-shot; manual-cocking action; receiver-mounted rear sights; metal with blued finish or stainless steel; post sight on ramp front, fully adjustable peep rear; adjustable trigger; extendable butt-plate and front rail; available in black, walnut, deluxe walnut, camo laminate, and brown laminate
Standard: . . . . $209.00–$270.00
Barracuda: . . . . $258.00–$294.00

Christensen Arms

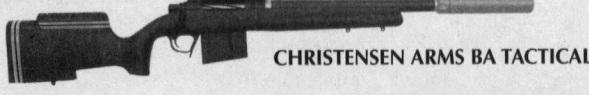

CHRISTENSEN ARMS BA TACTICAL

CHRISTENSEN ARMS CA-10 DMR

BA TACTICAL
Action: Bolt
Stock: Hand-laid fiberglass
Barrel: 16 in., 20 in., 22 in., 24 in., 26 in., 27 in.
Sights: None
Weight: 7 lb. 11 oz.–8 lb. 2 oz.
Caliber: .223 Rem., .300 Win. Mag., .308 Win., 6.5 Creedmoor, .338 Lapua, .300 Norma, .338 Norma
Magazine: Detachable box, 5 rounds
Features: Integral full-length rail incorporates a 20 MOA taper; front stud with five flush cups; adjustable cheek piece via inserts; stainless steel side-port muzzle brake
MSRP $2795.00

CA-10 DMR
Action: Semiautomatic
Stock: Synthetic
Barrel: 18 in., 20 in., 22 in., 24 in.
Sights: None
Weight: 7 lb. 13 oz.–8 lb. 3 oz.
Caliber: .243 Win., .308 Win., 6.5 Creedmoor, .260 Rem.
Magazine: Detachable box
Features: Picatinny rail; OSS suppressor; ambidextrous magazine release; Magpul stock; various finishes available
MSRP $3245.00

RIFLES

Christensen Arms

CHRISTENSEN ARMS CA-10 G2

CHRISTENSEN ARMS CA-15 G2

CHRISTENSEN ARMS ELR

CHRISTENSEN ARMS MESA

CHRISTENSEN ARMS MODERN PRECISION RIFLE

RIFLES

CA-10 G2

Action: Semiautomatic
Stock: Synthetic
Barrel: 18 in., 20 in.
Sights: None
Weight: 7 lb. 12.8 oz.–8 lb. 3.2 oz.
Caliber: 6.5 Creedmoor, .308 Win.
Magazine: N/A
Features: Upper and lower of billet 7075 aluminum; integrated undercut trigger guard on lower, aerograde carbon fiber handguard on an upper with KeyMod or M-Lok configurations; match chamber and trigger; direct impingement system; Magpul adjustable STR stock; 416R stainless barrel wrapped in steel aerograde carbon fiber; Titanium side baffle brake; choice of stainless steel or carbon-fiber-wrapped stainless steel barrel
SS: $2595.00
Carbon-fiber-wrapped: . . . $2995.00

CA-15 G2

Action: Semiautomatic
Stock: Synthetic
Barrel: 16 in.
Sights: None
Weight: 5 lb. 12.8 oz.
Caliber: .223 Wylde
Magazine: N/A
Features: Custom-built AR optimized for weight and accuracy; newly designed matched receiver with a contour-matching carbon fiber handguard; single-stage match trigger; match chamber; flared magwell; button rifled, threaded, and carbon fiber-wrapped barrel; BCM Gunfighter

adjustable stock; stainless steel flash hider; in stainless steel or carbon fiber
Stainless steel: $1749.00
Carbon fiber: $2295.00

ELR

Action: Bolt
Stock: Hand-laid carbon fiber
Barrel: 26 in.–27 in.
Sights: None
Weight: 7 lb. 8 oz.
Caliber: .26 Nosler, .28 Nosler, .30 Nosler, 30-06 Spfd., .300 RUM, .300 Win. Mag., .300 WSM, .308 Win., 6.5 Creedmoor, 6.5-284, .338 Lapua, 7mm Rem. Mag., .33 Nosler
Magazine: 4 rounds
Features: Machined aluminum hinged floorplate; dual front studs with flush cups; adjustable cheek piece via inserts; titanium side-port muzzle brake
MSRP $2795.00

MESA

Action: Bolt
Stock: Carbon fiber composite
Barrel: 20 in., 22 in., 24 in., 26 in.
Sights: None
Weight: 6 lb. 8 oz.–6 lb. 11.2 oz.
Caliber: 6.5 Creedmoor, 7mm-08 Rem., 7mm Rem. Mag., .308 Win., .300 Win. Mag., .28 Nosler, .450 Bushmaster
Magazine: 3 (magnum), 4 rounds
Features: Featherweight contour barrel with removable stainless radial muzzle brake and tungsten Cerakote

finish; skeletonized bolt handle; Limbsaver recoil pad; Invar pillars and spot bedding; match chamber and trigger; and button rifled, free-floating barrel
MSRP $1295.00

MODERN PRECISION RIFLE

Action: Bolt
Stock: Billet aluminum
Barrel: 16 in., 20 in., 22 in., 24 in., 26 in., 27 in.
Sights: None
Weight: 6 lb. 14 oz.–8 lb. 2 oz.
Caliber: 6.5 PRC, 6.5 Creedmoor, .308 Win., .300 Win. Mag. .300 Norma, .338 Lapua
Magazine: N/A
Features: 416 stainless steel barrel is carbon fiber wrapped; removable stainless side-baffle brake in a black nitride finish; barrel is hand lapped, button rifled and free floating; chassis is 7075 billet aluminum with an adjustable carbon fiber cheek riser and adjustable length of pull; six Q/D flush cup mounts; carbon fiber handguard with M-LOK; V-Block bedding; monopod mount ready via Picatinny rail; match chamber; skeletonized bolt handle; twin lug spiral fluted bolt; flat match-grade trigger; 20 MOA of rail
Short action: $2295.00
Long action: $2395.00

Christensen Arms

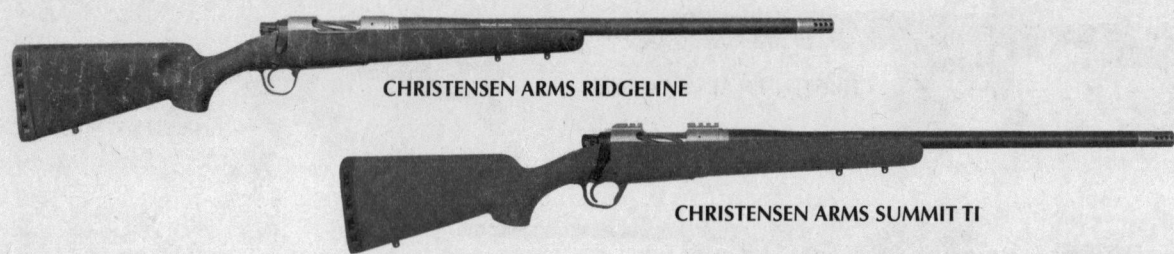

CHRISTENSEN ARMS RIDGELINE

CHRISTENSEN ARMS SUMMIT TI

RIDGELINE
Action: Bolt
Stock: Hand-laid fiberglass with carbon fiber reinforced stock
Barrel: 20 in., 24 in., 26 in.
Sights: None
Weight: 6 lb. 5 oz.–6 lb. 11 oz.
Caliber: .22-250 Rem., .243 Win., 26 Nosler, .270 Win., .270 WSM, .28 Nosler, .280 Ackley, .30 Nosler, 30-06 Spfd., .300 RUM, .300 Win. Mag., .300 WSM, .308 Win., 6.5 Creedmoor, 6.5-284, 7mm Rem. Mag., 7mm-08 Rem, .450 Bushmaster
Magazine: 4 rounds
Features: Carbon fiber–wrapped barrel; a spiral fluted bolt; scalloped bolt knob; dual front studs; SUB MOA accuracy; bedded recoil lug and invar pillar inserts; machined aluminum hinged floorplate
MSRP $1995.00

SUMMIT TI
Action: Bolt
Stock: Aerograde carbon fiber
Barrel: 24 in.–27 in.
Sights: None
Weight: 5 lb. 8 oz.–6 lb.
Caliber: 25-06 Rem., 26 Nosler, .270 Win., .270 WSM, .28 Nosler, .280 Ackley, .30 Nosler, 30-06 Spfd., .300 RUM, .300 Win. Mag., .300 WSM, 6.5 Creedmoor, 6.5-284, .308 Win., .338 Lapua, .375 H&H, 7mm Rem. Mag.
Magazine: 3 rounds
Features: 416R stainless steel, aerograde carbon fiber-wrapped barrel is hand lapped and button rifled and sports a removable radial titanium muzzle brake; trued receiver has integrated Picatinny rail; fully adjustable match trigger, Nitride-treated bolt with fluted knob, enlarged ejection port, full-length bedding with carbon fiber pillars are standard; sporter or thumbhole stock
MSRP $5495.00

Cimarron Firearms Co.

CIMARRON 1860 HENRY CIVILIAN

CIMARRON 1873 SADDLE RIFLE

1860 HENRY CIVILIAN
Action: Lever
Stock: Walnut
Barrel: 24 in.
Sights: Open
Weight: 9 lb. 2 oz.
Caliber: .44 WCF, .45 LC
Magazine: Under-barrel tube, 12 rounds
Features: Reproduction of 1860 Civil War Henry rifle; includes military sling swivels; frame comes in charcoal blue or original finish
MSRP $1496.40

1873 SADDLE RIFLE
Action: Lever
Stock: Wood
Barrel: 18 in.
Sights: Open
Weight: 8 lb.
Caliber: .357 Mag., .45 Colt, .44 WCF
Magazine: Fixed tube
Features: Full octagon barrel; straight stock with checkered forearm and stock
MSRP $1397.80

RIFLES

CIMARRON 1876 CENTENNIAL

CIMARRON 1876 CROSSFIRE CARBINE

CIMARRON 1885 HIGH WALL SPORTING RIFLE

CIMARRON 1886 RIFLE

CIMARRON MODEL 71 CLASSIC

CIMARRON PEDERSOLI SHARPS BUSINESS RIFLE

1876 CENTENNIAL

Action: Lever
Stock: Walnut
Barrel: 28 in.
Sights: Open
Weight: 9 lb. 15 oz.–10 lb. 2 oz.
Caliber: .45-60, .45-75, .40-60, .50-95
Magazine: Under-barrel tube, 12 rounds
Features: Originally dubbed the "Centennial Model" because of its introduction during America's 100th anniversary of the Declaration of Independence from British rule, and featured at Philadelphia's Centennial Exposition, this enlarged version of the famed 1873 Winchester was designed to handle stronger loads than its predecessor; finished in a standard blue octagonal barrel, tubular magazine, barrel band and foreend, with a color case hardened receiver, lever, trigger, hammer and butt plate
MSRP . . . . **$1704.27–$1948.70**

1876 CROSSFIRE CARBINE

Action: Lever
Stock: Walnut
Barrel: 22 in.
Sights: None
Weight: 8 lb. 15 oz.
Caliber: .45-60, .45-75
Magazine: Under-barrel tube, 8 rounds
Features: Gun was glorified in the movie *Crossfire Trail*; case-hardened stock with standard blued finish
MSRP **$1898.82**

1885 HIGH WALL SPORTING RIFLE

Action: Dropping block
Stock: Walnut, pistol grip
Barrel: 30 in.

Sights: Open
Weight: 9 lb. 4 oz.–10 lb. 6 oz.
Caliber: .45-70 Govt., .40-65, .38-55, .45-90, .30-40 KRAG, .348 Win., .405 Win.
Magazine: None
Features: Reproduction of the Winchester single-shot hunting rifle popular in 1880s; standard blued finish on octagonal barrel; single- or double-set triggers
Standard: . . . . . . **$1094.60–$1129.70**
Deluxe: . . . . **$1246.70–$1270.10**

1886 RIFLE

Action: Lever
Stock: Walnut
Barrel: 26 in.
Sights: None
Weight: 8 lb.–9 lb.
Caliber: .45-70 Govt.
Magazine: Under-barrel tube, 7+1, 8+1 rounds
Features: Made by Armi Sport in Italy; color case-hardened receiver and buttplate; octagonal barrel; standard blued finish; carbine version available
Standard: **$1610.70**
Deluxe: **$1986.25**

MODEL 71 CLASSIC

Action: Lever
Stock: Walnut
Barrel: 24 in.
Sights: Open
Weight: 8 lb. 11 oz.
Caliber: .348 Win., .45-70 Gov't.
Magazine: Fixed tube
Features: Blued receiver; pistol grip stock
.348 Win:. **$1846.48**
.45-70 Gov't.: **$1751.10**

PEDERSOLI SHARPS BUSINESS RIFLE

Action: Sharps
Stock: Wood
Barrel: 32 in.
Sights: Adjustable
Weight: 11 lb. 14 oz.
Caliber: .45-70 Govt.
Magazine: N/A
Features: Octagonal barrel; color case hardened framel; walnut stock and forearm; standard blue finish; double set triggers
MSRP **$1541.25**

Colt's Manufacturing Company

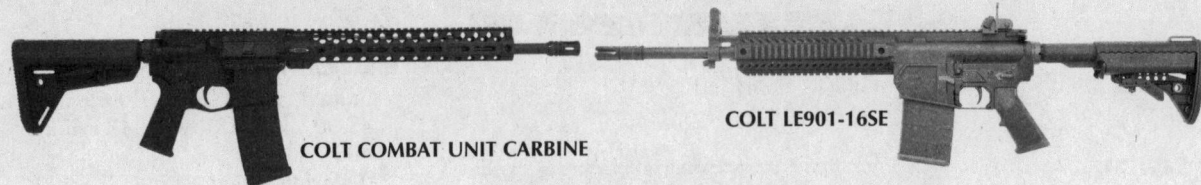

COLT COMBAT UNIT CARBINE

COLT LE901-16SE

COMBAT UNIT CARBINE
Action: Semiautomatic
Stock: Synthetic
Barrel: 16.1 in.
Sights: None
Weight: 6 lb. 7 oz.
Caliber: 5.56 NATO
Magazine: 30 rounds
Features: M-LOK capable handguard and flat top upper receiver ready for the addition of optical sights and accessories; mid-length gas system; lightweight profile barrel; extended handguard; black Magpul MOE SL buttstock; black pistol grip
MSRP. **$1299.00**

LE6940
Action: Semiautomatic
Stock: Combat-style, synthetic
Barrel: 16.1 in.
Sights: Flip-up front flip-up rear
Weight: 6 lb. 11 oz.
Caliber: 5.56 NATO
Magazine: Detachable box, 20, 30 rounds
Features: Incorporates a continuous Picatinny rail from the rear of the upper receiver to the front sight, free-floating chrome-line barrel, folding locking front sight, Magpul MBUS rear sight, integrated quad-rail; single-stage trigger, direct gas impingement system are standard
MSRP. **$1399.00**

Connecticut Valley Arms (CVA)

CVA SCOUT V2

SCOUT V2
Action: Break-open single-shot
Stock: Synthetic
Barrel: 25 in.
Sights: None
Weight: 5 lb. 13 oz.
Caliber: .444 Mag.
Magazine: N/A
Features: Fluted stainless steel barrel; ambidextrous stock; reversible hammer spur; CrushZone recoil pad; black stock with stainless steel barrel
MSRP. **$393.50**

Cooper Firearms of Montana

COOPER FIREARMS MODEL 21 VARMINT EXTREME

COOPER FIREARMS MODEL 21 VARMINTER (LAMINATE STOCK]

MODEL 21 CLASSIC
Action: Bolt
Stock: AA Claro Walnut
Barrel: 24 in.
Sights: None
Weight: 6 lb.–7 lb. 12 oz.
Caliber: .17 Rem., .20 VarTag, .20 Tactical, .204 Ruger, .221 Fireball, .22 Rem., .222 Rem. Mag., .222 Rem., .223 Rem. AI, 6X45, 6X47, .300 BLK,
Features: Hand-rubbed oil-finished stock with four-panel hand checkering, Pachmayer recoil pad, chrome-moly premium match grade Wilson Arms barrel, steel grip cap are standard
Right-hand: **$2495.00**
Left-hand: **$2695.00**

MODEL 22 CLASSIC
Action: Bolt
Stock: AA Claro Walnut
Barrel: N/A
Sights: None
Weight: N/A
Caliber: .More than 30 calibers available, from .22 BR to .338 Federal
Magazine: None
Features: Hand-rubbed oil-finished stock with four-panel hand checkering, Pachmayer recoil pad, chrome-moly premium match grade Wilson Arms barrel, steel grip cap are standard
Right-hand: **$2495.00**
Left-hand: **$2695.00**

RIFLES

Cooper Firearms of Montana

COOPER FIREARMS MODEL 51

COOPER FIREARMS MODEL 52 WESTERN CLASSIC

COOPER FIREARMS OF MONTANA MODEL 52 OPEN COUNTRY

COOPER FIREARMS OF MONTANA MODEL 52 TIMBERLINE

COOPER FIREARMS MODEL 57M CLASSIC

MODEL 51

Action: Bolt
Stock: AA Claro Walnut
Barrel: 24 in.
Sights: None
Weight: 6 lb. –7 lb. 12 oz.
Caliber: .17 Rem., .20 Tactical, .204 Ruger, .222 Rem., .222 Rem. Mag., .223 Rem., .223 Rem. AI, 6X45, 6X47, .300 BLK
Magazine: None
Features: Longer barrel standard on all varmint models; fully adjustable single-stage trigger; Sako style extraction machined from solid bar stock
Right-hand: $2495.00
Left-hand: $2745.00

MODEL 52 OPEN COUNTRY

Action: Bolt
Stock: Composite
Barrel: N/A
Sights: None
Weight: N/A
Caliber: N/A
Magazine: N/A
Features: Drop box magazine; topside Picatinny rail; proof barrels; muzzle brakes; double swing swivels at the forend; Green, Dark Grey, or Black/Grey spiderwebbed stock; metalwork available with or without Cerakote color options
MSRP $3795.00
Cerakote: $4155.00

MODEL 52 TIMBERLINE

Action: Bolt
Stock: Composite
Barrel: N/A
Sights: None
Weight: N/A
Caliber: N/A
Magazine: N/A
Features: Tan stock with black spiderwebbing; raised comb; fluted bolt; Proof barrel with muzzle brake
MSRP $2595.00

MODEL 52 WESTERN CLASSIC

Action: Bolt
Stock: AAA+ Claro Walnut
Barrel: 24 in.
Sights: None
Weight: 6 lb. 12 oz.–8 lb.
Caliber: More than 30 calibers available from .257 Wtby. Mag. to .375 H&H
Magazine: 3 rounds
Features: Stock has shadowline beaded cheekpiece, African ebony tip, and western fleur wraparound checkering. Steel grip cap, sling swivels, and case coloring on selected metal work are standard
Right-hand: $3995.00
Left-hand: $4245.00

MODEL 54 CLASSIC

Action: Bolt
Stock: AA Claro Walnut
Barrel: 24 in.

Sights: None
Weight: 6 lb.–7 lb. 12 oz.
Caliber: .22-250 Rem., .22-250 AI, .243 Win., .243 Win. AI, .250 Savage, .250 Savage AI, .260 Rem., 6.5 Creedmoor, 6.5-57 Lapua, 7mm-08, .300 Savage, .308 Win., .338 Federal, .358 Win.
Magazine: 3 rounds
Features: Three-rear locking lug bolt action magazine fed repeater; center-fire action, also available in stainless steel; Sako style extraction machined from solid bar stock; plunger style ejector machined form solid bar; fully adjustable single-stage trigger
Right-hand: $2495.00
Left-hand: $2754.00

MODEL 57-M CLASSIC

Action: Bolt
Stock: AA Claro walnut
Barrel: 24 in,
Sights: None
Weight: 6 lb.–7 lb. 12 oz.
Caliber: .17 HMR, .22 LR, .22 WMR
Magazine: 4, 5 rounds
Features: Hand-rubbed oil-finished stock with four-panel hand checkering, Pachmayer recoil pad, chrome-moly premium match grade Wilson Arms barrel, steel grip cap are standard
Right-hand: $2495.00
Left-hand: $2695.00

Cooper Firearms of Montana

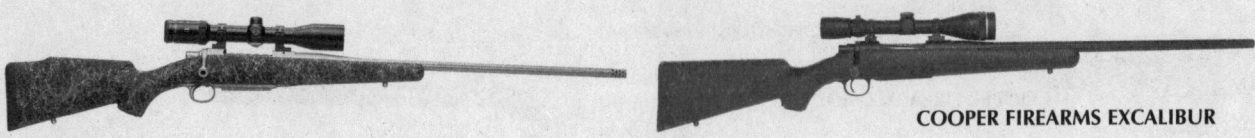

COOPER FIREARMS MODEL 92 BACKCOUNTRY

COOPER FIREARMS EXCALIBUR

MODEL 92 BACKCOUNTRY

Action: Bolt
Stock: Composite
Barrel: 24 in.
Sights: None
Weight: 5 lb. 12 oz.
Caliber: All standard long-action calibers and magnums up to .338 caliber
Magazine: 3 rounds
Features: Lightweight Cooper Model 92 all-stainless steel action (Chromoly available on request); detachable magazine; Jewell trigger; Wilson Arms fluted barrel with muzzle brake; guaranteed ½-MOA accuracy
MSRP **$2995.00**

MODEL TRP-3

Action: Bolt
Stock: Wood; synthetic
Barrel: 26 in.
Sights: None
Weight: 8 lb.
Magazine: N/A
Caliber: A wide variety of calibers across three Cooper platforms
Features: Available in the Model 21, Model 22, and Model 57-M platforms; choice of wood or synthetic stock; adjustable single-stage trigger; matte stainless steel barrel with straight taper
MSRP . . . . **$2455.00–$2755.00**

"VARIATIONS"

1. Classic

AA Claro walnut; steel grip; four-panel hand checkering; oil finish; matte metal finish; no options; available in all Cooper models

2. Custom Classic

AAA Claro walnut stock, shadowline beaded cheekpiece, African ebony tip, and western fleur wraparound checkering; sling swivel studs and chorome-moly premium match-grade Wilson Arms barrel are standard; all metal work has high gloss finish; available in all models

3. Excalibur

Hand-laid synthetics with Kevlar reinforcing material surrounding an aircraft-grade aluminum bedding block. Spiral fluted bolt, chrome-moly premium match grade Wilson Arms fluted barrel are standard; all metal work is matte finish; available for models 51, 52, and 54

4. Jackson Game

AA+ Claro walnut stock, rollover cheekpiece, semi-beavertail forearm. VE hand checkered grip in crossover multi-point pattern; stainless steel premium match grade Wilson Arms barrel; laminate version available; available for Models 51, 52, and 54

5. Jackson Hunter

Hand-laid synthetics with Kevlar reinforcing material surrounding an aircraft-grade aluminum bedding block; stainless steel premium match grade Wilson Arms barrel is standard; all metal work is matte finish; available for models 51, 52, 54, and 57-M

6. Jackson Squirrel

AA+ Claro walnut stock with rollover cheekpiece and semi-beavertail forearm. Grip has VE hand checkering in a crossover multi-point pattern; stainless steel premium match Wilson Arms barrel; also available in laminate; all metal work is matte finish; available in Model 57-M only

7. Mannlicher

AAA+ Claro walnut, shadowline beaded cheekpiece, African ebony tip, western fleur wraparound hand checking, chrome-moly premium match grade Wilson Arms octagonal barrel; all metal work is high gloss finish; available in all models

8. Montana Varminter

AA+ Claro walnut stock, hand-check-ered grip, stainless steel straight taper premium match grade Wilson Arms barrel; all metal work is matte finish; available in models 21, 22, 38, 51, 52, 54, and 57-M

9. Phoenix

Hand-laid synthetics with Kevlar reinforcing material surrounding an aircraft-grade aluminum bedding block; spiral fluted bolt, chrome-moly premium match grade Wilson Arms fluted barrel are standard; all metal work is matte finish; available for models 21, 22, 38, 51, 54; left-hand options only in models 21 and 38

10. Schnabel

Available in models 52, 54, 56, and 57; AA+ Claro walnut; raised comb; slim taper forearm; multi-point two panel hand checkering; oil finish; standard grade sling swivel studs; Pachmayr pad; steel grip cap; chromoly premium match grade barrel; metal work is matte finished; available in Models 51, 52, 54, 57-M, 58, and muzzleloader

11. Varminter

AA Claro walnut stock, hand checkered grip, stainless steel straight taper premium match grade Wilson Arms barrel; all metal work is matte finish; available in Models 21, 22, 38, 51, 52, 54, and 57-M

12. Varmint Extreme

AAA Claro walnut stock, hand checkered grip in a crossover western fleur pattern; stainless steel straight taper matte finish premium match grade Wilson Arms barrel; all blued steel is high gloss finish; available in models 21, 22, 38, 51, 52, 54, and 57-M

13. Western Classic

AAA+ Claro walnut, shadowline beaded cheekpiece, African ebony tip, western fleur wraparound hand checking, chrome-moly premium match grade Wilson Arms octagonal barrel; all metal work is high gloss finish, selected metal work is highlighted with case coloring

RIFLES

CZ-USA (Ceska Zbrojovka)

CZ-USA 512 SEMI-AUTOMATIC

CZ-USA 527 VARMINT

CZ-USA CZ 527 AMERICAN SYNTHETIC
SUPPRESSOR-READY

CZ-USA 550 SAFARI MAGNUM

CZ-USA 557 LEFT HAND

CZ-USA 750 SNIPER

CZ–USA SCORPION EVO 3
S1 CARBINE

512 SEMI-AUTOMATIC

Action: Semiautomatic
Stock: Lacquered beech wood
Barrel: 20.7 in.
Sights: Adjustable
Weight: 5 lb. 14 oz.
Caliber: .22 LR, .22 WMR
Magazine: Detachable box, 5 rounds
Features: Aluminum alloy upper receiver and fiberglass reinforced polymer lower half; dual guide rods; hammer-forged CZ barrel; integral 11mm dovetail for mounting optics
MSRP . . . . $480.00–$510.00

527 SERIES

Action: Bolt
Stock: Walnut
Barrel: 18.5 in.–24 in.
Sights: Open
Weight: 5 lb. 14 oz.–7 lb. 13 oz.
Caliber: .223 Rem., .204 Ruger, 7.62x39, 6.5 Grendel, .222 Rem., .22 Hornet, .17 Hornet; Carbine .223 Rem., 7.62x39; FS .223 Rem.; Lux .223 Rem., .22 Hornet, .222 Rem.; Lux left-hand .223 Rem.; Varmint .223 Rem., .204 Ruger, .17 Hornet
Magazine: Detachable box, 5 rounds
Features: Hammer-forged barrel; controlled round feed; single-set trigger; each model comes in a variety of calibers and a different stock
American: . . . . $733.00–$787.00
Carbine: $733.00
Lux: . . . . $733.00–$778.00
M1 American: $665.00
Varmint: $725.00

527 AMERICAN SYNTHETIC SUPPRESSOR-READY

Action: Bolt
Stock: Synthetic
Barrel: 16.5 in.
Sights: None
Weight: 5 lb. 14 oz.
Caliber: .300 BLK, 7.62x39
Magazine: 5 rounds
Features: Threaded 5/8×24 for a suppressor; 13.5 in. length of pull; cold hammer-forged barrel; two-position safety; single set trigger; detachable magazine; integral 16mm scope bases
MSRP $748.00

550 SAFARI MAGNUM

Action: Bolt
Stock: Walnut
Barrel: 25 in.
Sights: Express sights
Weight: 9 lb. 6 oz.
Caliber: 416 Rigby, .458 Win. Mag.
Magazine: 5 rounds
Features: Known worldwide as the 602 BRNO; hammer-forged barrel; single-set trigger; controlled round feed and fixed ejector make the rifle reliable enough for heavy and dangerous game; express sights (1 standing, 2 folding); select Trukish walnut stock with classic safari shape
MSRP . . . . $1215.00–$1318.00

557 LEFT HAND

Action: Bolt
Stock: Turkish walnut
Barrel: 24 in.
Sights: None
Weight: 7 lb. 14 oz.
Caliber: .30-06 Spfd., .308 Win.
Magazine: 4 rounds
Features: Integrated dovetail mounts; hinged floorplate; fully adjustable trigger; unique checking on the forend
MSRP $865.00

750 SNIPER

Action: Bolt
Stock: Synthetic thumbhole
Barrel: 26 in.
Sights: Open
Weight: 11 lb. 14 oz.
Caliber: .308 Win.
Magazine: Detachable box, 10 rounds
Features: Adjustable comb; underside of forend is fitted with a 220mm-long rail for bipod attachment; muzzle-brake; thread protector; mirage shield; blued barrel; single-stage trigger
MSRP $1999.00

SCORPION EVO 3 S1 CARBINE

Action: Semiautomatic
Stock: Synthetic
Barrel: 16.2 in.
Sights: Low-profile fully adjustable aperture and post, 4 rear aperture sizes
Weight: 7 lb.
Caliber: 9mm
Magazine: 10 or 30 rounds
Features: 16.2 in. barrel fitted with either a compensating muzzle brake or a faux suppressor built specifically for CZ-USA by SilencerCo; newly designed forend covered in M-LOK attachment points to keep the profile slim while still being big enough to swallow most pistol-caliber suppressors; top Picatinny rail; low-profile aluminum adjustable sights; ambidextrous controls; swappable non-reciprocating charging handle; adjustable trigger
MSRP . . . . $999.00–$1079.00

Dakota Arms

DAKOTA MODEL 10

DAKOTA MODEL 76 CLASSIC

DAKOTA MODEL 97

DAKOTA SHARPS

DAKOTA VARMINTER

MODEL 10
Action: Falling block
Stock: Walnut
Barrel: 23 in.
Sights: None
Weight: 6 lb.–7 lb.
Caliber: .22 LR to .300 Win., .338 to .375 H&H Mag.
Magazine: None
Features: Point wrap checkering; scope ring bases installed; custom length of pull; barrel break in
MSRP . . . . from $5260.00
Deluxe: . . . . from $6690.00

MODEL 76 CLASSIC
Action: Bolt
Stock: Walnut
Barrel: 23 in.
Sights: None
Weight: 6 lb. 8 oz.–9 lb. 8 oz.
Caliber: Classic: .257 Roberts, .260 Rem., .270 Win., .280 Rem., .30-06 Spfd., .300 Dakota, .300 Win. Mag., .300 WSM, .308 Win., .330 Dakota, .416 Rem., 7mm Rem. Mag., 7mm-08 Rem.; Safari: .300 H&H, .375 Dakota, .416 Rem., 7mm Dakota; African: .338 Win. Mag., .375 H&H, .416 Rem., .404 Jeffery, .416 Rigby, .450 Dakota, .458 Lott
Magazine: Box, 4 rounds
Features: Barrel break in; custom

length of pull; optional engraving; point panel checkering; Dakota swivel studs; 1-inch recoil pad; straddle floor plate; right- or left-hand configurations; Safari model has front island sight with flip-up night sight; African model has quarter rib sights with banded front sights and flip-up night sights
Classic: . . . .**from $6030.00**
Safari: . . . .**from $8010.00**
African: . . . .**from $8890.00**

MODEL 97
Action: Bolt
Stock: Fiberglass, composite, walnut
Barrel: 22 in. (short action), 25 in. (long action)
Sights: None
Weight: 7 lb.
Caliber: All-Weather: .30-06 Spfd., .338 Win. Mag., .375 H&H, 7mm Rem. Mag., 7mm-08 Rem.; Long Range: .280 Rem., .338 Win. Mag., 7mm Rem. Mag., 7mm-08 Rem.
Magazine: Blind box
Features: Stainless Douglas barrel; black composite stock with two inletted Ken Howell swivel studs; stainless trigger bow
All-weather: . . . .**from $4050.00**
Deluxe: . . . .**from $4820.00**
Long Range: . . . .**from $3720.00**

SHARPS
Action: Falling block
Stock: Walnut
Barrel: 26 in.
Sights: Open
Weight: 8 lb. 4 oz.
Caliber: .17 HMR, .22 Hornet, .30-30 Win., .30-40 Krag., .375 H&H
Magazine: None
Features: Octagon barrel; steel buttplate; single blade rear sight with front bead; matte blued metal finish
Sharps: . . . .**from $4490.00**
Miller: . . . .**from $5590.00**

VARMINTER
Action: Bolt
Stock: Walnut
Barrel: 22 in.
Sights: None
Weight: 8 lb. 4 oz.
Caliber: .17 VarTag, .17 Rem., .17 Tactical, .20 PPC, .204 Ruger, .221 Rem. Fireball, .22 PPC, .223 Rem., 6mm PPC, 6.5 Grendel
Magazine: None
Features: Available in walnut sporter-style stock or XXX walnut varmint style stock with semi-beavertail forend; checkered grip; recessed target crown; vapor hone matte bead blast finish on stainless; stainless barrel
MSRP . . . .**from $2840.00**
All-weather, Deluxe: . .**from $3390.00**

Daniel Defense

DANIEL DEFENSE DD5V1

DANIEL DEFENSE DD5V2

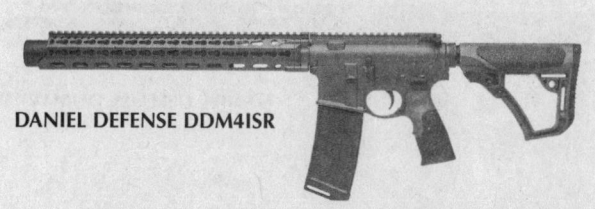

DANIEL DEFENSE DDM4ISR

DANIEL DEFENSE DDM4V4S

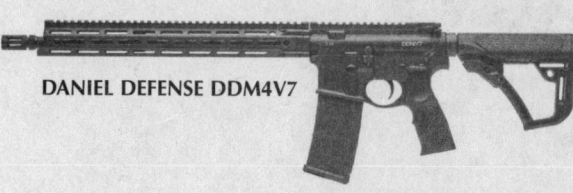

DANIEL DEFENSE DDM4V7

DD5V1

Action: Semiautomatic
Stock: Synthetic
Barrel: 16 in.
Sights: None
Weight: 8 lb. 5 oz.
Caliber: .308 Win./7.62x51 mm
Magazine: 20 rounds
Features: Four-bolt connection system utilizing a unique barrel extension; optimized upper receiver; improved bolt carrier group; ambidextrous controls; configurable modular charging handle; cold hammer-forged barrel; Geissele SSA two-stage trigger for precise fire control; DD Superior Suppression Device; 15 in. Picatinny top rail; black, Mil-Spec+, or Daniel Defense Tornado finishes
MSRP . . . .$3044.00–$3198.00

DD5V2

Action: Semiautomatic
Stock: Synthetic
Barrel: 18 in.
Sights: None
Weight: 8 lb. 9.6 oz.
Caliber: .308 Win.
Magazine: 20 rounds Magpul PMAG
Features: Four-bolt connection system utilizing a unique barrel extension; ambidextrous controls; configurable modular charging handle; cold-ham-
mer-forged barrel; Geissele SSA two-stage trigger; DD Superior Suppression Device; 15-in. Picatinny top rail; available in black, Daniel Defense Deep Woods green, and M-LOK version in black
MSRP . . . . $3044.00–$3198.00

DDM4ISR

Action: Semiautomatic
Stock: Synthetic
Barrel: 9 in.
Sights: None
Weight: 7 lb. 9 oz.
Caliber: .300 BLK
Magazine: DD magazine
Features: Integrally suppressed weapon system optimized for the .300 BLK cartridge; cold-hammer-forged barrel is fluted, has a target crown; standard pistol length gas system; direct impingement; MFR XL 15.0 rail with KeyMod attachments on sides and bottom; Mil-Spec with enhanced flared magwell; rear receiver QD swivel attachment point; available in black, Daniel Defense Deep Woods green, and Mil Spec + Cerakote in a bronze finish
MSRP . . . . $3135.00–$3294.00

DDM4V4S

Action: Semiautomatic
Stock: Synthetic

Barrel: 11.5 in.
Sights: None
Weight: 5 lb. 14 oz.
Caliber: 5.56 NATO
Magazine: Detachable box, 30 rounds
Features: Lightweight, ergonomic rail system affords ample room for securely mounting multiple accessories and offers the longest possible sight radius with iron sights; three removable high-temperature-resistant Daniel Defense Rail Panels for a secure, comfortable grip while also protecting the support hand from heat; compatibility with a wide variety of muzzle devices and sound suppressors; free-floating, cold hammer-forged barrel
MSRP $1826.00

DDM4V7

Action: Semiautomatic
Stock: Synthetic
Barrel: 16 in.
Sights: None
Weight: 6 lb. 3 oz.
Caliber: 5.56 NATO
Magazine: Detachable box, 30 rounds
Features: M-LOK attachment technology with Daniel Defense MFR XS 15.0 rail; DD improved flash suppressor; mid-length gas system; uninterrupted 1913 Picatinny rail; black, Mil Spec+, or Daniel Defense Tornado finishes; available in black or hybrid paint scheme called Rattlecan
MSRP . . . . $1729.00–$1902.00

Daniel Defense

DANIEL DEFENSE DDM4V7LW

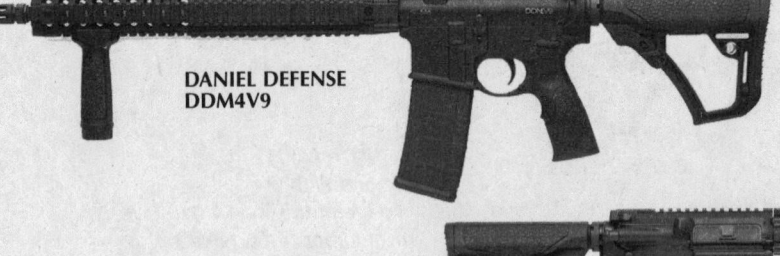

DANIEL DEFENSE DDM4V7 S

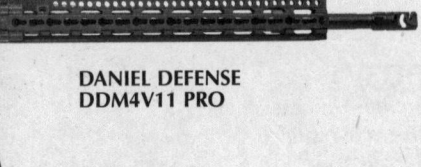

DANIEL DEFENSE DDM4V7 PRO

DANIEL DEFENSE DDM4V9

DANIEL DEFENSE DDM4V11 PRO

RIFLES

DDM4V7 LW

Action: Semiautomatic
Stock: Synthetic
Barrel: 16 in.
Sights: None
Weight: 6 lb. 1 oz.
Caliber: 5.56 NATO
Magazine: Detachable box, 30 rounds
Features: M-LOK attachment technology with Daniel Defense MFR XS 15.0 rail; DD improved flash suppressor; mid-length gas system; uninterrupted 1913 Picatinny rail; available in black or hybrid paint scheme called Rattlecan
MSRP . . . . **$1729.00–$1902.00**

DDM4V7 PRO

Action: Semiautomatic
Stock: Synthetic
Barrel: 18 in.
Sights: None
Weight: 7 lb. 6.4 oz.
Caliber: 5.56 NATO
Magazine: DD magazine
Features: Designed for multi-gun competitors; 18-in. Strength-to-Weight

(S2W), cold-hammer-forged barrel; rifle-length gas system; Muzzle Climb Mitigator; Geissele Automatics Super Dynamic 3 Gun trigger; MFR XS 15.0 rail with M-LOK attachment system; larger Vltor BCM Gunfighter Mod 4 Charging Handle latch; DD buttstock and pistol grip
MSRP **$1999.00**

DDM4V7 S

Action: Semiautomatic
Stock: Synthetic
Barrel: 11.5 in.
Sights: None
Weight: 5 lb. 9.6 oz.
Caliber: 5.56 NATO
Magazine: DD magazine
Features: Short-barreled rifle featuring M-LOK attachment technology; free-floating, cold-hammer-forged barrel; carbine-length gas system; free-floating MFR XS 10.0 rail; M-LOK attachment points that run along seven positions; uninterrupted 1913 Picatinny rail on top
MSRP **$1729.00**

DDM4V9

Action: Semiautomatic
Stock: Synthetic
Barrel: 16 in.
Sights: None
Weight: 6 lb. 10 oz.
Caliber: 5.56 NATO
Magazine: Detachable box, 30 rounds
Features: Daniel Defense stock, pistol and vertical grips, flash suppressor, and M4 rail
MSRP **$1826.00**

DDM4V11 PRO

Action: Semiautomatic
Stock: Synthetic
Barrel: 18 in.
Sights: None
Weight: 7 lb. 8 oz.
Caliber: 5.56 NATO
Magazine: Detachable box, 30 rounds
Features: Picatinny rails; muzzle climb mitigator; freefloat rail; Geissele automatics super dynamic 3-gun trigger; flared magazine well
MSRP **$1999.00**

Davide Pedersoli & C.

DAVIDE PEDERSOLI 1874 SHARPS OLD WEST

DAVIDE PEDERSOLI 1886 HUNTER LIGHT

DAVIDE PEDERSOLI 1886 SPORTING CLASSIC

DAVIDE PEDERSOLI 1886 SPORTING RIFLE

DAVIDE PEDERSOLI MODEL 86/71 LEVER ACTION BOARBUSTER CAMO

DAVIDE PEDERSOLI MODEL 86/71 BOARBUSTER MARK II

RIFLES

1874 SHARPS OLD WEST MAPLE

Action: Dropping block
Stock: Maple
Barrel: 30 in.
Sights: None
Weight: 11 lb. 7 oz.
Caliber: .45-70 Govt.
Magazine: None
Features: Optional Creedmoor and tunnel sights; brass plate on right side of butt stock can be personalized; forend has wedge plates; pistol grip cap is made of hardened steel
MSRP $2345.00

1886 HUNTER LIGHT

Action: Lever
Stock: Walnut
Barrel: 22 in.
Sights: Ramped front, buckhorn rear
Weight: 7 lb. 2 oz.
Caliber: .45-70 Govt., .444 Marlin
Magazine: 3 rounds
Features: Lighter, shorter version of standard 1886 lever-action; designed to accommodate a left side-mounted Creedmoor sight; barrel is broach rifled; sling swivels included
MSRP $1815.00

1886 SPORTING CLASSIC

Action: Lever
Stock: American walnut

Barrel: 26 in.
Sights: Blade front sight, semi-buckhorn rear
Weight: 9 lb. 4 oz.
Caliber: .45-70 Gov't.
Magazine: 8 rounds
Features: Straight English stock of American walnut; case hardened receiver; blued round barrel; crescent buttplate; receiver can accept a peep sight
MSRP $2140.00

1886 SPORTING RIFLE

Action: Lever
Stock: Wood
Barrel: 26 in.
Sights: Adjustable rear, fixed front
Weight: 9 lb. 13 oz.
Caliber: .45-70 Govt.
Magazine: N/A
Features: PMG quality barrel; forged and CNC machined frame; American selected walnut stock; blade front sight and adjustable rear sight; drilled and tapped to assemble the aperture bolt sight
MSRP $1995.00

MODEL 86/71 LEVER ACTION BOARBUSTER

Action: Lever
Stock: Walnut
Barrel: 19 in.
Sights: Drilled and tapped for scopes

Weight: 7 lb. 4 oz.
Caliber: .444 Marlin, .45-70 Govt.
Magazine: 5 rounds
Features: Barrel equipped with European Picatinny style base with integral rear sight; half cock safety on hammer; safety slide catch at the rear of the frame; checkered pistol grip stock and forend are made from walnut; also available in soft touch orange camo color; metal parts are blued; drilled and tapped for sights
MSRP . . . . $1950.00–$1985.00

MODEL 86/71 LEVER ACTION BOARBUSTER MARK II

Action: Lever
Stock: Synthetic
Barrel: 19 in.
Sights: Superluminova front and rear
Weight: 7 lb. 4 oz.
Caliber: .444 Marlin, .45-70
Magazine: 5 rounds
Features: Adjustable comb synthetic stock Cerakoted metalwork in bronze; ample rail for optics
MSRP $2650.00

Davide Pedersoli & C.

DAVIDE PEDERSOLI MODEL 86/71 LEVER ACTION CLASSIC

DAVIDE PEDERSOLI MODEL 86/71 LEVER ACTION STAINLESS STEEL

DAVIDE PEDERSOLI MODEL 86/71 LEVER ACTION WILDBUSTER

DAVIDE PEDERSOLI KODIAK MARK IV

MODEL 86/71 LEVER ACTION CLASSIC

Action: Lever
Stock: Walnut
Barrel: 24 in.
Sights: Drilled and tapped for scopes
Weight: 8 lb. 3 oz.
Caliber: .348 Win., .45-70 Govt.
Magazine: 5 rounds
Features: Last "big frame" rifle for Winchester; drilled and tapped for scopes; broach rifled barrel and magazine are blued finished; checkered walnut pistol grip; frame is forged and CNC-machined, with a blued finish on the standard version and case-hardened frame and buttcap on the Premium model with select walnut stock and forend
Standard Classic: $1820.00–$1840.00
Premium: **$1960.00**

MODEL 86/71 LEVER ACTION STAINLESS STEEL

Action: Lever
Stock: Synthetic
Barrel: 19 in.
Sights: Adjustable rear, fixed front
Weight: 7 lb. 15 oz.
Caliber: .45-70 Govt.
Magazine: N/A
Features: PMG barrel, broach rifled; fiber optic front sight and Weaver/Picatinny base with integrated rear sight; stock is made of American walnut covered with a camouflage film; microcell thick butt plate and swivel stud
MSRP **$2465.00**

MODEL 86/71 LEVER ACTION WILDBUSTER

Action: Lever
Stock: Walnut
Barrel: 24 in.
Sights: Drilled and tapped for scopes
Weight: 8 lb. 3 oz.
Caliber: .45-70 Govt.
Magazine: 5 rounds
Features: Ramp rear sight; walnut forend and pistol grip stock with checkered buttplate; blued finish on metal parts; drilled and tapped for scopes
MSRP **$1775.00**

KODIAK MARK IV

Action: Breech loading
Stock: Walnut
Barrel: 22 in., 24 in.
Sights: Open
Weight: 9 lb. 11 oz.–10 lb. 5 oz.
Caliber: .450 NE, .45-70 Govt. 8x57JRS, 9.3x74R
Magazine: None
Features: Double-leave rear sight in a dovetail; tapered round barrels made of blued steel; select walnut stock with checkering and oil finish; available with an interchangeable 20-gauge barrel in all calibers except the .450 NE
Rifle calibers only: . . . **$6095.00–$8180.00**
With 20-gauge barrel: . **$8285.00–$8340.00**

Davide Pedersoli & C.

DAVIDE PEDERSOLI ROLLING BLOCK MISSISSIPPI CLASSIC

DAVIDE PEDERSOLI ROLLING BLOCK TARGET

DAVIDE PEDERSOLI SHARPS 1877 OVERBAUGH LONG RANGE

DAVIDE PEDERSOLI SHARPS LITTLE BESTY

DAVIDE PEDERSOLI SHARPS SMALL GAME

ROLLING BLOCK MISSISSIPPI CLASSIC

Action: N/A
Stock: Wood
Barrel: 26 in.
Sights: Adjustable rear, fixed front
Weight: 7 lb. 8 oz.
Caliber: .357 Mag, .38-55, .45 Colt
Magazine: N/A
Features: High carbon steel barrel is broach rifled; alloy frame is embellished with a engraving; old silver colour finishing; equipped with a blade front sight and an adjustable rear sight, drilled to assemble the Creedmoor sight; stock and forend are made of American walnut with brass fittings
MSRP $1020.00

ROLLING BLOCK TARGET

Action: Dropping block
Stock: Walnut
Barrel: 30 in.
Sights: Open
Weight: 10 lb. 9 oz.
Caliber: .357 Mag., .45–70 Govt.
Magazine: None
Features: Octagonal, conical blued barrel; case-hardened color frame is equipped with ramp rear sight adjustable in elevation; steel buttplate and trigger guard; straight stock and forend made of walnut with oil finish; Deluxe grade also available
Standard Target: $1245.00
Deluxe Target: $2580.00

SHARPS 1877 OVERBAUGH LONG RANGE

Action: Sharps
Stock: Walnut
Barrel: 30 in.
Sights: Blade front, military-style rear
Weight: 8 lb. 4.8 oz.
Caliber: .45-70 Govt.
Magazine: N/A
Features: Designed to meet the 10-lb. weight limitations in NRA competition; forged frame and parts; oil-finished American walnut stock with checkering; double set triggers are standard; rifle is drilled and tapped for Creedmoor sights
MSRP $2150.00

SHARPS LITTLE BETSY

Action: N/A
Stock: Wood
Barrel: 24 in.
Sights: Creedmoor
Weight: 7 lb. 10 oz.
Caliber: .17 HRM, .22LR, .22 Hornet, .357 Mag, .30-30 Win.
Magazine: N/A
Features: Forged and CNC machined frame features a floral engraving; stock is made of American walnut; barrel PMG quality features a matt blue finish; sights includes a tunnel front sight and the folding Creedmoor sight; with double set trigger
MSRP . . . . $1770.00–$1930.00

SHARPS SMALL GAME

Action: Sharps
Stock: Walnut
Barrel: 24 in.
Sights: Brass bead front, buckhorn rear
Weight: 7 lb. 9.6 oz.
Caliber: .22 LR, .22 Hornet
Magazine: N/A
Features: Lighter, slimmer version of standard 1874 Sharps; half-octagon, half-round barrel styling; overall length is under 42 in.; match barrel and double-set triggers
.22 LR: $1535.00
.22 Hornet: $1560.00

Del-Ton

DEL-TON ECHO 7.62X39

DEL-TON ECHO 316H OR

DEL-TON DTI EVOLUTION

DEL–TON DTI EXTREME DUTY 316

ECHO 7.62X39
Action: Semiautomatic
Stock: Synthetic
Barrel: 16 in.
Sights: Adjustable front sight
Weight: 6 lb. 10 oz.
Caliber: 7.62x39
Magazine: Detachable box, 30 rounds
Features: Carbine gas system; phosphated under F-marked front sight base; chrome-lined carrier interior; carbine-length hand guards; aluminum delta ring; single heat shield
MSRP. **$753.42**

ECHO 316H OR
Action: Semiautomatic
Stock: M4 five-position
Barrel: 16 in.

Sights: None
Weight: 6 lb. 10 oz.
Caliber: 5.56 NATO
Magazine: Detachable box, 30 rounds
Features: Single rail gas block; CAR handguards with single heat shields; A2 flash hider; forged 7075 T6 aluminum upper and lower receivers
MSRP. **$816.44**

DTI EVOLUTION
Action: Semiautomatic
Stock: Magpul CTR Mil-Spec
Barrel: 16 in.
Sights: Folding front, flip rear
Weight: 7 lb. 3 oz.
Caliber: 5.56 NATO
Magazine: Detachable box, 30 rounds
Features: Chrome-lined barrel;

Samson Evolution free-float rail; Quick Flip Dual Aperture rear sight; Magpul MOE+ grip
Standard:. **$1319.05**

DTI EXTREME DUTY 316
Action: Semiautomatic
Stock: M4 reinforced fiber
Barrel: 16 in.
Sights: Samson quick flip dual aperture rear sight
Weight: 6 lb. 6.4 oz.
Caliber: 5.56 NATO
Magazine: Detachable box
Features: Hammer forged CMV chrome-lined barrel; H-buffer
MSRP. **$1119.05**

DoubleStar Corp.

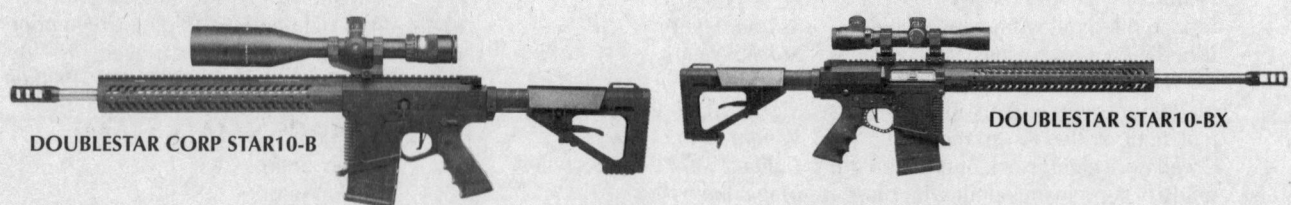

DOUBLESTAR CORP STAR10-B

DOUBLESTAR STAR10-BX

STAR10-B
Action: Semiautomatic
Stock: Synthetic
Barrel: 18 in.
Sights: None
Weight: 9 lb. 13 oz.
Caliber: .308 cal
Magazine: 20 rounds
Features: Hogue pistol grip; Wilson air gauged stainless steel barrel

(fluted); Samson Evolution handguard; brass deflector and dust cover; integrated trigger guard
MSRP. **$2549.99**

STAR10-BX
Action: Semiautomatic
Stock: Synthetic
Barrel: 22 in.
Sights: None
Weight: 10 lb.

Caliber: .260 Rem., 6.5 Creedmoor
Magazine: 20 rounds
Features: Direct impingement; stainless steel free-floating barrel; Bullseye muzzle brake; 15-in. Samson .309 Evolution handguard; brass deflector; dust cover; enhanced magazine well; CMC flat trigger group set to 3.5 pounds; ACE Hammer stock
MSRP. **$2549.99**

DPMS Panther Arms

DPMS AP4 CARBINE

DPMS CARBINE 16

DPMS GII AP4

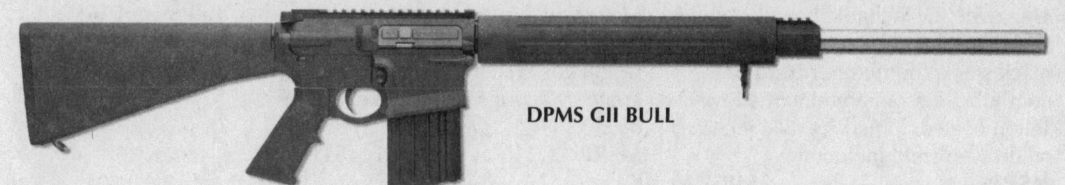

DPMS GII BULL

AP4 CARBINE
Action: Semiautomatic
Stock: Synthetic
Barrel: 16 in.
Sights: Open
Weight: 7 lb. 2 oz.
Caliber: 5.56 NATO
Magazine: Detachable box, 30 rounds
Features: Chromoly steel barrel with A2 Flash hider; A3 aircraft aluminum alloy receiver with detachable carrying handle; adjustable rear sight and A2 front sight assembly; black AP4–6 position, telescoping fiber reinforced polymer stock; oval, carbine length GlacierGuards
MSRP................. **$959.00**

CARBINE
Action: Semiautomatic
Stock: Synthetic
Barrel: 16 in.
Sights: Open
Weight: 6 lb. 14 oz.
Caliber: 5.56 NATO
Magazine: Detachable box, 30 rounds
Features: Chromoly steel barrel with flash hider; A3 aircraft aluminum alloy receiver with detachable carrying handle; adjustable rear sight and A2 front sight assembly; DPMS Pardus black stock; oval, carbine length GlacierGuards
MSRP................. **$869.00**

GII AP4
Action: Semiautomatic
Stock: Synthetic
Barrel: 16 in.
Sights: F marked front sight base
Weight: 7 lb. 4 oz.
Caliber: 7.62 NATO
Magazine: Detachable box
Features: A2 pistol grip; cancellation brake; 34.25 in. collapsed; six position collabsible stock; muzzle brake; receiver mounted Picatinny rail
MSRP................. **$1499.00**

GII BULL
Action: Semiautomatic
Stock: Synthetic
Barrel: 24 in.
Sights: None
Weight: 10 lb.
Caliber: 7.62 NATO
Magazine: Detachable box
Features: 416 stainless steel bull barrel; A2 MII Spec buttstock; receiver mounted Picatinny rail
MSRP................. **$1299.00**

DPMS Panther Arms

DPMS LR-204

DPMS RECON

DPMS SWEET 16

LR-204

Action: Semiautomatic
Stock: Synthetic
Barrel: 24 in.
Sights: None
Weight: 10 lb. 4 oz.
Caliber: .204 Ruger
Magazine: Detachable box, 30 rounds
Features: Fluted barrel; standard A2 black stock; aluminum ribbed free-float tube; aircraft aluminum alloy, Teflon coated, forged A3 style receiver; nylon web sling included
MSRP $1059.00

RECON

Action: Semiautomatic
Stock: Synthetic
Barrel: 16 in.
Sights: Magpul BUIS
Weight: 9 lb.
Caliber: 5.56 NATO
Magazine: Detachable box, 30 rounds
Features: Bead-blasted stainless, mid length gas system; semi-auto trigger group; Magpul MOE stock in Teflon black
MSRP $1196.00

SWEET 16, BULL 20, BULL 24

Action: Semiautomatic
Stock: Synthetic
Barrel: 16 in., 20 in., 24 in.
Sights: None
Weight: 7 lb. 14 oz.–9 lb. 13 oz.
Caliber: .223 Rem.
Magazine: Detachable box, 30 rounds
Features: Aircraft aluminum alloy, A3 style flattop receiver coated in black Teflon; aluminum trigger guard; black standard A2 Zytel Mil-Spec stock; aluminum ribbed free-float tube; Nylon web sling included
Bull Sweet 16: $939.00
Bull 20:. $969.00
Bull 24:. $999.00

DRD Tactical

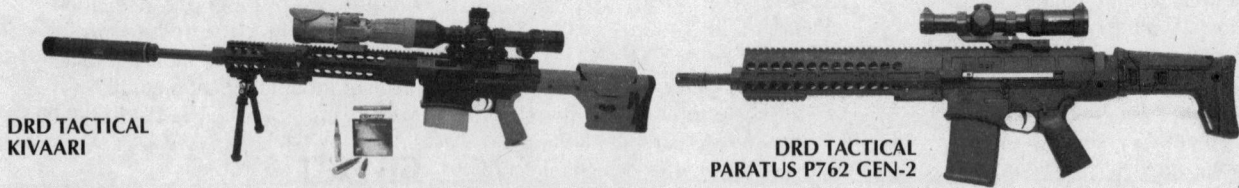

DRD TACTICAL KIVAARI

DRD TACTICAL PARATUS P762 GEN-2

KIVAARI

Action: Semiautomatic
Stock: Synthetic
Barrel: 24 in.
Sights: None
Weight: 13 lb. 9 oz.
Caliber: .338 Lapua, .300 Norma Mag.
Magazine: 10 rounds
Features: Billet aircraft aluminum receiver; direct gas operated action; fully adjustable Magpul PRS stock is mated with 17-in. QD Magpul M-LOK rail; SilencerCo QD muzzle brake; ambidextrous safety; Wilson Combat two-stage match trigger; choice of hard case or Tactical-Tailor Trekker backpack; available in anodized black, Cerakote Flat Dark Earth, or NiB Battle Worn finishes
Black, Flat Dark Earth: $5000.00
NiB Battle Worn: $5650.00

PARATUS P762 GEN-2

Action: Semiautomatic
Stock: Synthetic
Barrel: 16 in.
Sights: None
Weight: 9 lb. 3 oz.
Caliber: 7.62x51 NATO, 6.5 Creedmoor
Magazine: 20 rounds
Features: Compact enough when disassembled to be stowed in a briefcase or backpack; adjustable Magpul folding stock; Mil-Std 1913 rail; direct gas operated; rifle may be fired with the stock in the folded position; in black or NiB Battle Worn finishes.
Black: $3300.00
NiB Battle Worn: $3850.00

Excel Arms

EXCEL ARMS ACCELERATOR RIFLE

EXCEL ARMS X-5.7R

EXCEL ARMS X-22R

ACCELERATOR RIFLE
MR-22, MR-5.7

Action: Semiautomatic
Stock: Polymer composite, pistol grip
Barrel: 18 in.
Sights: Standard includes Red/Green dot optic
Weight: 8 lb.
Caliber: .22 WMR, .17 HMR
Magazine: Detachable box, 9 rounds
Features: Corrosion-resistant 17-4 stainless steel, including its fluted barrel; features manual and firing pin safeties, a last-round fired hold open bolt, flat-top accessory rail. A number of options are available:
Basic: supplied with one 9-round magazine; Standard: supplied with two 9-round magazines and red-dot optic; Limited Edition Zanders: supplied with two 9-round magazines, grey shroud, and two side-mounted Picatinny rails; P1 Package: supplied with two 9-round magazines, nylong sling, detachable sling swivels, detachable iron sights; P2 Package:

same as P1 Package, but with 3-9x40 scope and scope rings instead of iron sights; P3 Package: same as Package 1, but with the addition of a 6 in.–9-in. bipod; P4 Package: same as P2 Package, but with the addition of a 6-in.–9-in. bipod

Basic MR-22:	**$575.00**
Basic MR 5.7:	**$719.00**
Package P-2 MR-22:	**$750.00**
Package P-2 MR 5.7:	**$898.00**
Package P-5 MR-22:	**$1055.00**

X-5.7R

Action: Semiautomatic
Stock: Synthetic
Barrel: 18 in.
Sights: None
Weight: 6 lb. 4 oz.
Caliber: 5.7x28mm
Magazine: Detachable box, 25, 10 10, 20 rounds
Features: CNC-machined aluminum; Picatinny rail; tactical AR styling; collapsible stock; tapped holes in the

hand guard for mounting accessory rails

20-round:	**$795.00**
10-round featureless California compliant:	**$810.00**

X-22R

Action: Semiautomatic
Stock: Synthetic
Barrel: 18 in.
Sights: None
Weight: 4 lb. 12 oz.
Caliber: .22 LR HV
Magazine: Detachable box, 25 rounds (10 rounds optional)
Features: CNC-machined aluminum frame; optional 3–9x40 scope; tapped holes in hand guard for mounting accessory rails; integral weaver base to mount scopes, sights, and optics

Basic:	**$504.00**
Scoped:	**$594.00**
10 RD:	**$504.00**

FN America

FN AMERICA BALLISTA

BALLISTA

Action: Bolt
Stock: Collapsible
Barrel: 26 in.
Sights: N/A, scope compatible
Weight: 15 lb.
Caliber: .308 Win., .300 Win. Mag., .338 Lapua Mag.
Magazine: Detachable box, 8 or 15

rounds (.308 Win.), 6 or 10 rounds (.300 Win. Mag.), 5 or 8 rounds (.338 Lapua)
Features: Modular, multi-caliber designed for long-range precision work; aluminum alloy receiver; adjustable trigger; ambidextrous stock; vibration-isolated aluminum alloy receiver; Picatinny rail
MSRP **$7499.00**

FN America

FN AMERICA FN 15 COMPETITION

FN AMERICA FN 15 DMR II

FN AMERICA FN 15 TACTICAL .300 BLK II

FN AMERICA FN M249S PARA

FN AMERICA FN SPR A5M XP

FN AMERICA SCAR 17S CARBINE

FN 15 COMPETITION

Action: Semiautomatic
Stock: Synthetic
Barrel: 18 in.
Sights: None
Weight: 8 lb. 2 oz.
Caliber: 5.56x45mm
Magazine: 30 rounds
Features: Alloy-steel, cold-hammer forged, and chrome-lined match-grade barrel with muzzle break; Mega Arms 16 in. rail system with M-LOK; Magpul MOE furniture; Timney Competition single stage trigger; ergonomic safety lever and magazine release
MSRP **$2249.00**

FN 15 DMR II

Action: Semiautomatic
Stock: Synthetic
Barrel: 18 in.
Sights: None
Weight: 7 lb.
Caliber: 5.56 NATO
Magazine: 30 rounds
Features: Direct impingement; FN Rail System with M-LOK that allows accessories to be mounted without any shift to zero; cold-hammer-forged, chrome lined, and free floating barrel; hard anodized aluminum flat-top receiver; match-grade Timney trigger; Magpul MOE grip; STR buttstock; Surefire ProComp 556 muzzle brake
Standard: **$1999.00**
California-compliant: **$2099.00**

FN 15 TACTICAL .300 BLK II

Action: Semiautomatic
Stock: Synthetic
Barrel: 16 in.
Sights: None
Weight: 6 lb. 14.5 oz.
Caliber: .300 BLK
Magazine: 30 rounds
Features: Direct impingement; FN Rail System with M-LOK that allows accessories to be mounted without any shift to zero; cold-hammer-forged, chrome lined, and free floating barrel; FN Combat trigger; hard anodized aluminum flat-top receiver; Magpul MOE grip; MOE SL buttstock; Surefire ProComp 762 muzzle brake
MSRP **$1599.00**

FN M249S PARA

Action: Semiautomatic
Stock: Metal
Barrel: 16.1 in.
Sights: Graduated 1000-meter front and rear combo
Weight: 17 lb.
Caliber: 5.56 NATO
Magazine: 30, 200 rounds
Features: Semiauto version of the full-auto M249 Para light machine gun; originally developed by FN Herstal as the FN MINIMI and adopted by the U.S. military in 1988; features signature 16-in. FN cold-hammer-forged, chrome-lined barrel in a quick-change configuration; formed steel frame receiver with claw extractor and fixed, pivoting ejector that ejects to the side; rotating, telescoping stock assembly with a hydraulic recoil buffer system; operates from a closed bolt and will accept both magazine and linked ammunition belts; Picatinny top rail and integral Mil-Std bipod
Black: **$8799.00**

FN SPR A5M XP

Action: Bolt
Stock: McMillan fiberglass
Barrel: 20 in., 24 in.
Sights: None
Weight: 11 lb. 5 oz.–11 lb. 13 oz.
Caliber: .300 WSM, .308 Win.
Magazine: Detachable box, 4 or 5 rounds
Features: Threaded tactical bolt knob; barrel threaded muzzle; Picatinny rail; external claw extractor with controlled round feeding; integral recoil lug; three-position safety; knurled bolt handle
MSRP **$2899.00**

SCAR 16S, 17S

Action: Gas-operated semiautomatic
Stock: Polymer
Barrel: 16.25 in.
Sights: Adjustable, folding, removable
Weight: 8 lb.
Caliber: .308 Win., 7.62 NATO
Magazine: Detachable box, 10, 20 rounds
Features: Fully adjustable stock; Picatinny rail plus three accessory rails for attaching a variety of sights and lasers; free-floating, cold-hammer-forged barrel; available in black or Flat Dark Earth tactical, telescoping, side-folding polymer stock
16S: **$3299.00**
17S: **$3569.00**

RIFLES

**FRANCHI MOMENTUM,
MOMENTUM COMBO**

MOMENTUM, MOMENTUM COMBO

Action: Bolt
Stock: Synthetic
Barrel: 22 in., 24 in.
Sights: None
Weight: 6 lb. 11 oz.–7 lb. 13 oz.
Caliber: .243 Win., 6.5 Creedmoor,

.270 Win., .308 Win., .30-06 Spfd.,
.300 Win. Mag.
Magazine: 3, 4 rounds
Features: Franchi's first ever rifle; black synthetic stocks; free-floating barrels; 60-degree bolt throws; adjustable triggers,; barrels are available plain or threaded for suppressor use; scoped combo wears a Burris Fullfield 3-9X40mm scope; non-scoped models accept two-piece Remington 700 bases
MSRP..................**$609.00**
Scoped combo:.........**$729.00**

Heckler & Koch

HECKLER & KOCH MR556A1

HECKLER & KOCH MR762A1

**HECKLER & KOCH MR762A1
LONG RIFLE PACKAGE II**

MR556A1

Action: Semiautomatic
Stock: Synthetic
Barrel: 14 in., 16.5 in.
Sights: Troy microsights
Weight: 8 lb. 10 oz.
Caliber: 5.56 NATO, .223 Rem.
Magazine: Detachable box, 30 rounds
Features: Free-floating Picatinny rail; gas operated piston system
MSRP................$3399.00

MR762A1

Action: Semiautomatic
Stock: Synthetic
Barrel: 16.5 in.
Sights: None
Weight: 9 lb. 15 oz.
Caliber: 7.62 NATO
Magazine: Detachable box, 10, 20 rounds
Features: Match rifle features; direct descendant of HK416/417 series, but made for civilians; uses a piston and a solid operating "pusher" rod in place of the common gas tube normally used in AR-style rifles; cold-hammer-forged barrel; adjustable stock
MSRP................$3999.00

MR762A1 LONG RIFLE PACKAGE II

Action: Semiautomatic
Stock: Synthetic
Barrel: 16.5 in.
Sights: 3–9x40mm scope
Weight: 10 lb. 7 oz.
Caliber: 7.62 NATO
Magazine: Detachable box, 10, 20 rounds
Features: Rifle; Leupold 3–9 VX-R Patrol scope and mount; HK G28 buttstock; LaRue Tactical BRM-S bipod; ERGO Pistol Grip; Blue Force Gear sling; Manta rail covers; OTIS cleaning kit; a 10- and 20-round magazine; Model 1720 Pelican case
**Without scope
 and mount:** $6399.00
With scope and mount:...$6899.00

RIFLES

Henry Repeating Arms

HENRY REPEATING ARMS .30–30

HENRY REPEATING ARMS .45-70 LEVER ACTION

HENRY REPEATING ARMS .45-70 LEVER ACTION OCTAGON

HENRY REPEATING ARMS ALL-WEATHER LEVER ACTION

HENRY REPEATING ARMS BIG BOY, BIG BOY CARBINE COLOR CASE HARDENED

HENRY REPEATING ARMS BIG BOY CLASSIC

RIFLES

.30-30 LEVER ACTION

Action: Lever
Stock: Walnut
Barrel: 20 in.
Sights: Open
Weight: 7 lb.
Caliber: .30-30 Win.
Magazine: Under-barrel tube, 5 rounds
Features: Steel round barrel: deluxe checkered American walnut with rubber buttpad; XS Ghost Rings sights; blued steel receiver, drilled and tapped for easy scope mounting. Brass octagon barrel: straight-grip American walnut with buttplate; marble fully adjustable semi-buckhorn rear sight, with diamond insert, beaded front sight; brass receiver, drilled and tapped for easy scope mounting
Steel: **$893.00**
Brass: **$998.00**

.45-70 LEVER ACTION

Action: Lever
Stock: Walnut
Barrel: 18.43 in.
Sights: Closed rear, blade front
Weight: 7 lb. 1 oz.
Caliber: .45-70 Govt.
Magazine: Under-barrel tube, 4 rounds
Features: Pistol-grip American walnut with buttplate; blued steel drilled and tapped for easy scope mounting; XS Ghost Rings rear sight with blade front
MSRP **$893.00**

.45-70 LEVER ACTION OCTAGON

Action: Lever
Stock: Wood
Barrel: 22 in.
Sights: Adjustable
Weight: 8 lb. 2 oz.
Caliber: .45-70 Govt.
Magazine: 4 rounds
Features: Straight-grip American Walnut stock with brass buttplate; fully adjustable semi-buckhorn rear, and brass beaded front sight; brass drilled and tapped for a Weaver 63B mount
MSRP **$998.00**

ALL-WEATHER LEVER ACTION

Action: Lever
Stock: Stained hardwood
Barrel: 18.43 in., 20 in.
Sights: Adjustable semi-buckhorn rear, brass bead front
Weight: 7 lb.–7 lb. 1 oz.
Caliber: .30-30, .45-70
Magazine: Under-barrel tube, 4 or 5 rounds
Features: Adjustable buckhorn/bead sights; straight-grip in the .30-30 and pistolgrip in the .45-70; hard chrome plating on all metal surfaces (except springs and sights); durable industrial-grade coating on hardwood furniture; low-gloss look that won't spook game
MSRP **$1050.00**

BIG BOY, BIG BOY CARBINE COLOR CASE HARDENED

Action: Lever
Stock: American walnut
Barrel: 20 in. (standard), 16 in. (carbine)
Sights: Brass bead front, fully adjustable semi-buckhorn rear with diamond insert
Weight: 7 lb. (standard), 6 lb. 8 oz. (carbine)
Caliber: .357 Mag., .44 Mag., .45 Colt
Magazine: 10 rounds (standard), 7 rounds (carbine)
Features: Updated version of Big Boy rifle; octagon barrels; carbine gets a large loop
MSRP **$1045.00**

BIG BOY CLASSIC

Action: Lever
Stock: Walnut
Barrel: 20 in.
Sights: Open
Weight: 8.68 lb.
Caliber: .41 Mag., .327 Fed. Mag., .44 Mag., .45 Colt, .357 Mag.
Magazine: Under-barrel tube, 10 rounds
Features: Adjustable marble semi-buckhorn rear with white diamond insert and brass beaded front sight; solid top brass receiver, brass buttplate and brass barrel band; straight-grip American walnut stock; octagonal barrel
MSRP **$945.00**

Henry Repeating Arms

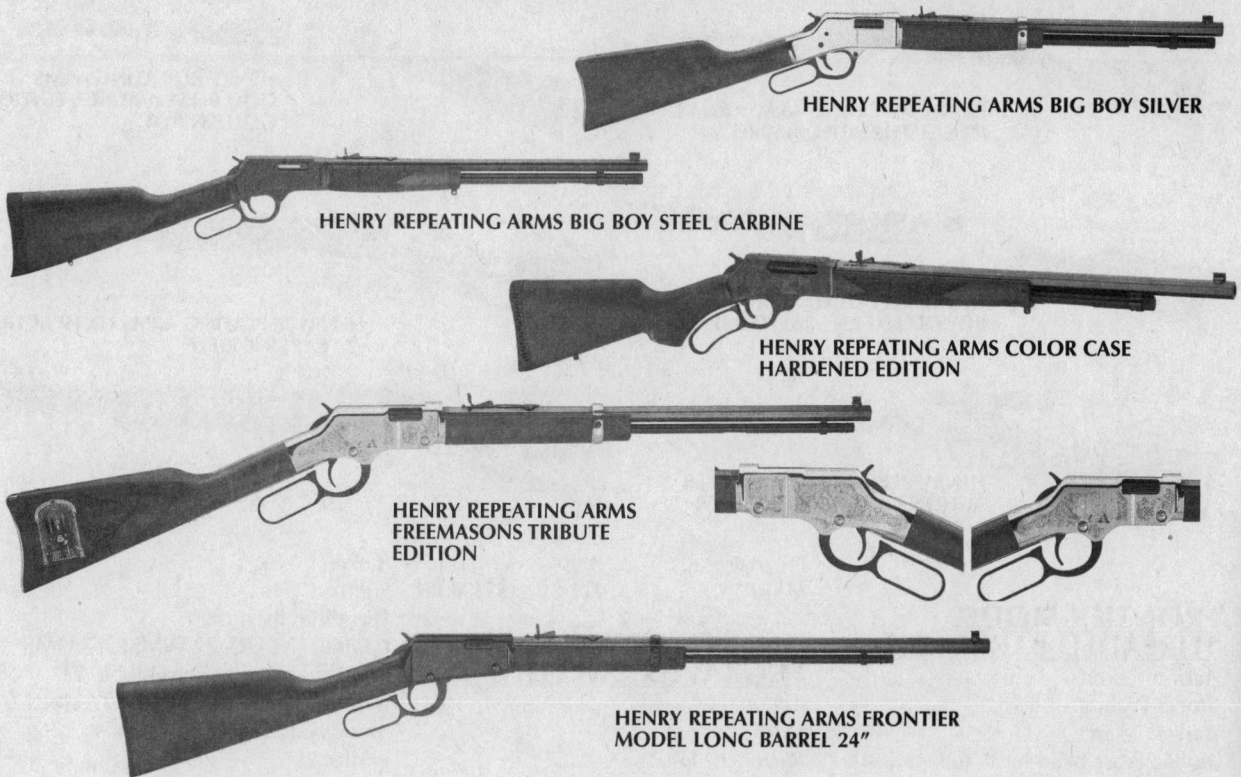

HENRY REPEATING ARMS BIG BOY SILVER

HENRY REPEATING ARMS BIG BOY STEEL CARBINE

HENRY REPEATING ARMS COLOR CASE HARDENED EDITION

HENRY REPEATING ARMS FREEMASONS TRIBUTE EDITION

HENRY REPEATING ARMS FRONTIER MODEL LONG BARREL 24"

BIG BOY SILVER

Action: Lever
Stock: Walnut
Barrel: 20 in.
Sights: Semi-buckhorn rear, brass bead front
Weight: 8 lb. 11 oz.
Caliber: .44 Magnum, .45 Colt, .357 Mag/.38 Spl.
Magazine: Under-barrel tube, 10 rounds
Features: Nickel plating; octagon barrel; buckhorn/bead sights; drilled and tapped scope option; straight stock wrist; carbine-style buttplate; okay for left-handed shooters
MSRP **$1040.00**

BIG BOY STEEL CARBINE

Action: Lever
Stock: Checkered walnut
Barrel: 16.5 in.
Sights: Adjustable semi-buckhorn rear with adjustable white diamond insert, brass bead front
Weight: 6 lb. 9 oz.
Caliber: .44 Magnum, .45 Colt, .357 Mag/.38 Spl., .327 Fed., .41 Mag.
Magazine: Under-barrel tube, 7 rounds
Features: Sliding transfer bar safety

system in its hammer; lighter steel frame; ventilated rubber recoil pad; sling swivel studs; rifle-style fore-end cap; glove-friendly oversized lever
MSRP **$893.00**

COLOR CASE HARDENED EDITION

Action: Lever
Stock: Walnut
Barrel: 20 in., 22 in.
Sights: Semi-buckhorn rear, brass bead front
Weight: 8 lb. 2 oz.–8 lb. 8 oz.
Caliber: .30-30, .45-70
Magazine: Under-barrel tube, 4 or 5 rounds
Features: Deep bluing, dark walnut, and mottled case colors achieved through a genuine case-hardening process; octagonal barrels; transfer bar safety; sling swivel studs; drilled and tapped frame; ventilated rubber recoil pad; okay for left-handed shooters
MSRP **$1045.00**

FREEMASONS TRIBUTE EDITION

Action: Lever
Stock: Walnut
Barrel: 20 in.

Sights: Adjustable semi-buckhorn rear with adjustable white diamond insert, brass bead front
Weight: 6 lb. 12 oz.
Caliber: .22 S/L/LR
Magazine: 16 rounds (long range), 21 rounds (short)
Features: Receiver engraving with 24K gold plating; engraved/painted stock; depicts our first president in full Masonic regalia
MSRP **$1071.00**

FRONTIER MODEL LONG BARREL 24"

Action: Lever
Stock: Walnut
Barrel: 24 in.
Sights: Brass bead front, fully adjustable semi-buckhorn rear with adjustable white diamond insert
Weight: 7 lb.
Caliber: .22 LR, .22 Mag.
Magazine: 12, 16, 21 rounds by caliber
Features: Merge of Henry's Lever Octagon and Frontier models; octagonal barrel adds weight, rigidity, and stability; grooved receiver for scope mounting
.22 LR: **$499.00**
.22 Mag.: **$599.00**

Henry Repeating Arms

HENRY REPEATING ARMS FRONTIER MODEL THREADED BARREL 24"

HENRY REPEATING ARMS GOD BLESS AMERICA EDITION GOLDEN BOY

HENRY REPEATING ARMS GOLDEN BOY DELUXE ENGRAVED 3RD EDITION

HENRY REPEATING ARMS LEVER ACTION .22 CARBINE RIFLE

HENRY REPEATING ARMS LEVER ACTION OCTAGON FRONTIER

HENRY REPEATING ARMS MARE'S LEG

FRONTIER MODEL THREADED BARREL 24"

Action: Lever
Stock: Walnut
Barrel: 24 in.
Sights: Brass bead front, fully adjustable semi-buckhorn rear with adjustable white diamond insert
Weight: 7 lb.
Caliber: .22 LR, .22 Mag.
Magazine: 12, 16, 21 rounds by caliber
Features: Similar to the standard Frontier Long Barrel 24-in. model but with a ½x28 threads for suppressor use
.22 LR: $527.00
.22 Mag.: $626.00

GOD BLESS AMERICA EDITION GOLDEN BOY

Action: Lever
Stock: American walnut
Barrel: 20 in.
Sights: Brass bead front, fully adjustable semi-buckhorn rear with diamond insert
Weight: 6 lb. 12 oz.
Caliber: .22 LR
Magazine: 16 rounds
Features: Nickel receiver is engraved on both sides with floral scrollwork; right side features 24k gold banner reading "Home of the Free Because of the Brave" and gold American flag; left side features the Liberty Bell and a bald eagle in gold; the right side of the stock has a painted rendition of the Statue of Liberty's raised arm and torch; the forend has painted engrav-

ing that reads "God Bless America"
MSRP. $1208.00

GOLDEN BOY DELUXE ENGRAVED 3RD EDITION

Action: Lever
Stock: Walnut
Barrel: 20 in.
Sights: Fully adjustable rear, brass-beaded front
Weight: 6 lb. 12 oz.
Caliber: .22 LR, .22 WMR, .17 HMR
Magazine: Under-barrel tube, 16 rounds (LR), 12 rounds (Short)
Features: American walnut stock; adjustable buckhorn rear sight, beaded front sight; brasslite receiver, brass buttplate, and blued barrel
.22 LR: $1575.00
.22 WMR: $1627.00
.17 HMR: $1654.00

LEVER ACTION .22 CARBINE RIFLE

Action: Lever
Stock: Walnut
Barrel: 16.13 in.
Sights: Open
Weight: 4 lb. 8 oz.
Caliber: .22 LR
Magazine: 15 rounds (.22 LR), 17 rounds (.22 L), 18 rounds (.22 S), 21 rounds (.22)
Features: Straight-grip American walnut stock; adjustable rear, hooded front sight; blued round barrel and lever
MSRP. $394.00

LEVER ACTION OCTAGON FRONTIER

Action: Lever
Stock: Walnut

Barrel: 20 in.
Sights: Open
Weight: 6 lb. 4 oz.
Caliber: .22 LR, .22 WMR, .17 HMR
Magazine: Under-barrel tube, 21 rounds (.22 S), 16 rounds (.22 LR); 12 rounds (.22 Mag.); 11 rounds (.17 HMR)
Features: American walnut; marble fully adjustable semi-buckhorn rear with reversible white diamond insert and brass beaded front sight; blued barrel and lever
.22 LR: $473.00
.22 WMR: $578.00
.17 HMR: $578.00

MARE'S LEG

Action: Lever
Stock: Walnut
Barrel: 12.5 in.–12.9 in.
Sights: Open
Weight: 4 lb. 7 oz.–5 lb. 13 oz.
Caliber: .22 LR, .22 WMR, .357 Mag., .44 Mag., .45 Colt
Magazine: 5–10 rounds depending on caliber
Features: .45 Colt: American walnut; marble fully adjustable semi-buckhorn rear with reversible white diamond insert and brass beaded front sights; brasslite receiver, brass buttplate, and blued barrel; .22 S/L/LR: American walnut; fully adjustable rear, with hooded front sight; blued metal barrel and lever
.22 Magnum: $473.00
.22 LR: $462.00
.45 Colt, .44 Mag.,
    .357 Mag.: $1024.00

Henry Repeating Arms

HENRY REPEATING ARMS
MINI BOLT YOUTH

HENRY REPEATING ARMS THE
ORIGINAL HENRY RIFLE

HENRY REPEATING ARMS
PUMP ACTION OCTAGON

HENRY REPEATING ARMS SECOND
AMENDMENT TRIBUTE EDITION

HENRY REPEATING ARMS SINGLE
SHOT RIFLE IN STEEL & BRASS

HENRY REPEATING ARMS STAND FOR
THE FLAG EDITION GOLDEN BOY

MINI BOLT YOUTH

Action: Bolt
Stock: Synthetic
Barrel: 16.25 in.
Sights: Open
Weight: 3 lb. 4 oz.
Caliber: .22 LR, .22 S
Magazine: None
Features: Single-shot; one-piece fiberglass synthetic stock in orange or black; Williams fire sights; stainless steel receiver and barrel; black or Muddy Girl Camo stock finishes
MSRP...................$289.00

ORIGINAL HENRY RIFLE

Action: Lever
Stock: Walnut
Barrel: 24.5
Sights: Folding ladder rear
Weight: 9 lb.
Caliber: .44-40, .45 Colt
Magazine: Under-barrel tube, 13+1 rounds
Features: True to original specifications; first time the Original Henry has been offered in the U.S. by an American manufacturer in 150 years
MSRP.................$2415.00

PUMP ACTION OCTAGON

Action: Pump
Stock: Walnut
Barrel: 19.75 in.
Sights: Open
Weight: 6 lb.
Caliber: .22 LR, .22 WMR
Magazine: Under-barrel tube, 15

rounds (.22 LR), 12 rounds (.22 WMR)
Features: American walnut stock; adjustable rear, beaded front sight; blued octagonal barrel
.22 LR: $578.00
.22 WMR: $620.00

SECOND AMENDMENT TRIBUTE EDITION

Action: Lever
Stock: Walnut
Barrel: 20 in.
Sights: Brass bead front, fully adjustable semi-buckhorn rear with adjustable white diamond insert
Weight: 6 lb. 12 oz.
Caliber: .22 LR
Magazine: 12, 16, 21 rounds by caliber
Features: Hi-gloss silver-toned finish on receiver cover, barrel band, and carbine-style buttplate; cover is embellished on both side flats with 19th century floral engraving set off by 24K gold-plated and raised-relief symbology that includes on its right side a flintlock rifle above the now-famous FROM MY COLD DEAD HANDS statement made by Charlton Heston (NRA president from 1998–2003) at the 2000 NRA convention, and on the smaller panel the NRA seal; the left side shows a gold American eagle in flight, the Second Amendment in a gold shield, and the Bill of Rights in a gold scroll
MSRP............... $1154.00

SINGLE SHOT RIFLE IN STEEL & BRASS

Action: Break-open single-shot
Stock: Walnut

Barrel: 22 in.
Sights: Brass bead front, fully adjustable folding leaf rear
Weight: 6 lb. 15 oz.
Caliber: .223 Rem., .243 Win., .308 Win., .44 Mag., .45-70 Govt. (brass version .44 Mag./.45-70 Govt. only).
Magazine: N/A
Features: Centerfire top-lever rifle; matte finish on steel frame or a high-polished finish on hardened brass frame; steel models get curved pistol grip and rubber recoil pad; brass version have straight English grip and and brass buttplate; top lever is ambidextrous
Brass:................. $576.00
Steel: $448.00

STAND FOR THE FLAG EDITION GOLDEN BOY

Action: Lever
Stock: American walnut
Barrel: 20 in.
Sights: Brass bead front, fully adjustable semi-buckhorn rear with diamond insert
Weight: 6 lb. 12 oz.
Caliber: .22 LR
Magazine: 16 rounds
Features: Bright nickel receiver 90 percent covered with a Cerakote American flag; on the stock's right side, a man pays homage to the flag with his hand over his heart, surrounded by a circle bearing the opening line from the National Anthem
MSRP.................$1208.00

Henry Repeating Arms

HENRY REPEATING ARMS STEEL
WILDLIFE EDITION

HENRY REPEATING ARMS THE LONG
RANGER WITH SIGHTS

HENRY REPEATING ARMS
U.S. SURVIVAL AR-7

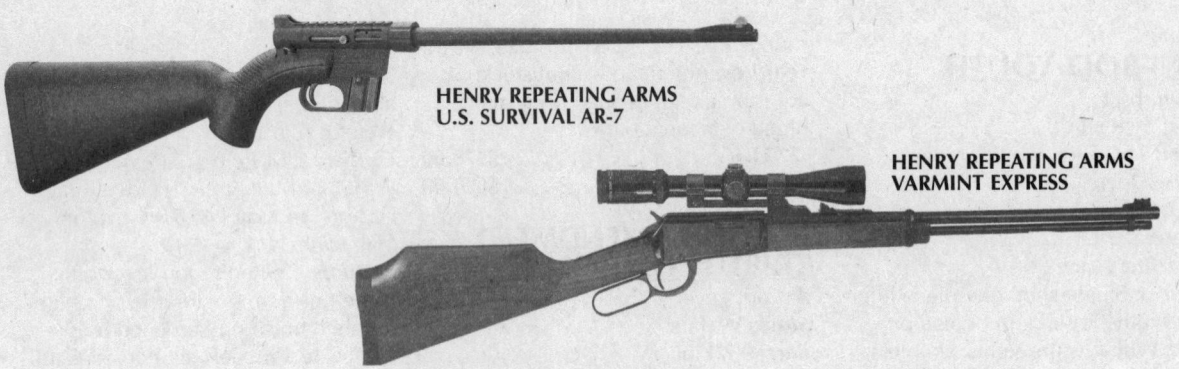

HENRY REPEATING ARMS
VARMINT EXPRESS

STEEL WILDLIFE EDITION
Action: Lever
Stock: Walnut
Barrel: 18.43 in., 20 in.
Sights: Semi-buckhorn rear, brass bead front
Weight: 7 lb.–7 lb. 1 oz.
Caliber: .30-30, .45-70
Magazine: Under-barrel tube, 4 or 5 rounds
Features: Swivel studs; engraved receiver with 24K gold plating; lighter steel frame; straight-wristed walnut stock with checkering fore and aft; black rubber recoil pad; frame drilled and tapped for scope mounts; center-fire in-hammer transfer bar; American vine, scroll, and braided borders surrounding a circular buck's head portrait in 24K gold relief on the right side behind the ejection port and an oval-framed leaping buck on the left
.30-30: **$1496.00**
.45-70 Gov't.: **$1523.00**

THE LONG RANGER
Action: Lever
Stock: Walnut
Barrel: 20 in.
Sights: Ramp ivory bead front, fully adjustable folding rear
Weight: 7 lb.
Caliber: .223 Rem.. .243 Win., .308 Win. 6.5 Creedmoor
Magazine: 4 rounds
Features: Henry's first long-range hunting rifle; exposed hammer and forged steel lever; geared action that drives a machined and chromed steel bolt with a six-lug rotary head into a rear extension of the barrel; side-ejection from alloy receiver; drilled and tapped for scope mounts; laser-cut checkering; available with or without sights
MSRP **$1066.00**

US SURVIVAL AR-7
Action: Semiautomatic
Stock: ABS Plastic
Barrel: 16 in.
Sights: Adjustable rear, blade front

Weight: 3 lb. 8 oz.
Caliber: .22 LR
Magazine: Detachable box, 8 rounds
Features: ABS plastic in black; Teflon coated receiver and coated steel barrel; in black or choice of True Timber-Kanati or Viper Western full-coverage camo
Black: **$305.00**
Camo: **$368.00**

VARMINT EXPRESS
Action: Lever
Stock: Walnut
Barrel: 20 in.
Sights: Open
Weight: 5 lb. 12 oz.
Caliber: .17 HMR
Magazine: Under-barrel tube, 11 rounds
Features: Checkered American walnut stock; Williams fire sights; blued round barrel and lever
MSRP **$578.00**

Hi-Point Firearms

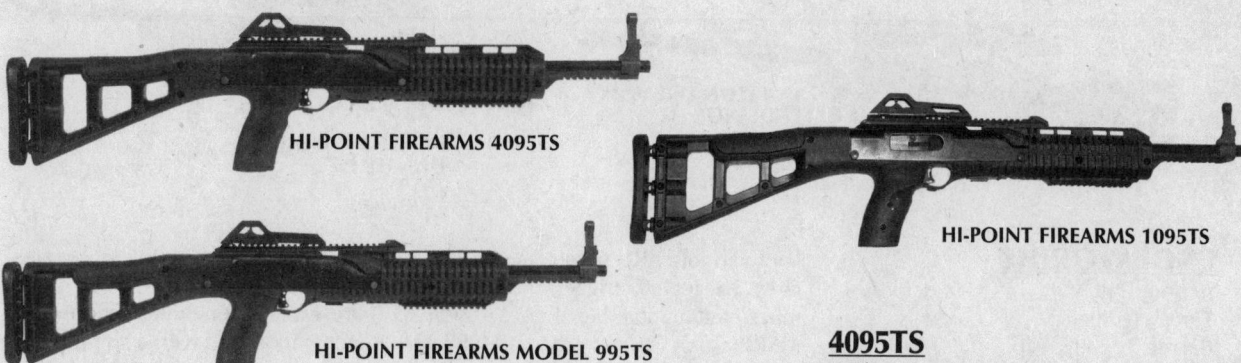

HI-POINT FIREARMS 4095TS

HI-POINT FIREARMS 1095TS

HI-POINT FIREARMS MODEL 995TS

RIFLES

995TS

Action: Blow-back semiautomatic
Stock: Black, skeleton-style, all-weather molded polymer
Barrel: 16.5 in.
Sights: Adjustable
Weight: 7 lb.
Caliber: 9mm
Magazine: Detachable box, 10 rounds
Features: Sling, swivels, and base mount included; last round lock-open latch; multiple Picatinny rails; internal recoil buffer; also available in digital tan, pink, and woodland camos
MSRP . . . . $315.00–$481.00

1095TS

Action: Semiautomatic
Stock: Synthetic
Barrel: 17.5 in.
Sights: Fully adjustable front, rear
Weight: 7 lb.
Caliber: 10mm
Magazine: 10 rounds
Features: Skeletonized stock; fully adjustable front and rear sights; a raised soft-rubber cheekpiece; sling swivels; scope base; accessory rails; threaded barrel; available in black, Flat Dark Earth, and hydro-dipped Realtree Edge camo
Black: $389.99
Realtree Edge: $439.00
Flat Dark Earth: $445.00

4095TS

Action: Semiautomatic
Stock: Polymer
Barrel: 17.5 in.
Sights: Adjustable
Weight: 7 lb.
Caliber: .40 S&W
Magazine: 9 rounds
Features: All-weather; black polymer skeletonized stock sling; swivels and scope base internal recoil buffer in stock weaver style rails; fully adjustable sights ("ghost ring" rear peep and post front); quick on/off thumb safety; grip-mounted clip release; also available in digital tan, pink, and woodland camos
MSRP . . . . $325.00–$495.00

HM Defense

HM DEFENSE AVENGER M308

AVENGER M308 TUNGSTEN

Action: Semiautomatic
Stock: Synthetic
Barrel: 18 in.
Sights: None

Weight: 8 lb. 15 oz.
Caliber: .308 Win.
Magazine: 10 rounds
Features: Rifle-length gas system; Chrome-moly steel barrel threaded; 15-inch free-floating Picatinny rail

with Magpul's M-LOK mounting system; three-pound Velocity trigger; custom charging handle; Black, Midnight Tungsten, and Flat Dark Earth Cerakote finishes available
MSRP $1895.00

Horizon Firearms

HORIZON FIREARMS ENDEAVOR HZ

HORIZON FIREARMS HUNTER HZ

ENDEAVOR HZ

Action: Bolt
Stock: Synthetic
Barrel: 22 in., 24 in.
Sights: None
Weight: N/A
Caliber: 6.5 Creedmoor, 6mm Creedmoor, 6.5 PRC, .26 Nosler, .28 Nosler, 7mm Rem. Mag., .300 Win. Mag., .22 Creedmoor
Magazine: N/A
Features: Horizon Stiller action; Proof Research barrel; spiral-fluted bolt; Tac knob; an iota KRUX stock in citadel Grey; TriggerTech trigger; threaded muzzle; guaranteed to shoot ½-MOA
MSRP $4999.00

HUNTER HZ

Action: Bolt
Stock: Synthetic
Barrel: 24 in., 25 in.
Sights: None
Weight: N/A
Caliber: 6.5 Creedmoor, .22 Creedmoor, 6.5 PRC, .28 Nosler, 7mm Rem., Mag., .300 Win. Mag.
Magazine: N/A
Features: Horizon Stiller action; Benchmark barrel with a spiral-fluted bolt; six-groove progressive-fluted barrel; Small Tac bolt knob; TriggerTech trigger; threaded muzzle; stock is an iota KREMLIN in Sentinel Green
MSRP $4599.00

Howa by Legacy Sports

HOWA APC CHASSIS RIFLE

HOWA HOGUE RIFLE

APC CHASSIS RIFLE

Action: Bolt
Stock: Aluminum
Barrel: 20 in., 24 in., 26 in.
Sights: None
Weight: 10 lb. 13 oz.–11 lb.
Caliber: .223 Rem., .308 Win., .22-250 Rem., 6mm Creedmoor, 6.5 Creedmoor, .243 Win.
Magazine: 10 rounds
Features: APC stands for Australian Precision Chassis; a Hogue overmolded grip; LUTH-AR MBA-4 buttstock; an AmmoBoost detachable mag; a free-floating handguard with M-LOK slots; Picatinny rail; a threaded barrel in a heavy #6 profile; available as a scope-ready combo with bases and rings; in black or Multicam/Flat Dark Earth
MSRP . . . . $1149.00–$1359.00
Scope package: . . . $1439.00–$1659.00

HOGUE RIFLES

Action: Bolt
Stock: Synthetic
Barrel: 20 in., 22 in., 24 in.
Sights: None
Weight: 7 lb. 12 oz.
Caliber: .223 Rem., .22-250 Rem., .243 Win., 6.5 Creedmoor, 7mm-08 Rem., .308 Win., .25-06 Rem., .270 Win., .30-06 Spfd., 7mm Rem. Mag., .300 Win. Mag., 6mm Creedmoor
Magazine: Internal box
Features: Stainless or blued barrel; Hogue overmolded stock comes in black or green and with a Hogue recoil pad; hinged floor plate; sling; swivel studs; two=stage HACT trigger; sling swivel studs
Standard barrel: . . . **$529.00–$539.00**
Lightweight barrel: **$539.00**
Heavy threaded barrel: . . . . **$569.00–$609.00**

Howa by Legacy Sports

HOWA HS PRECISION RIFLE

HOWA KRG BRAVO

HOWA KUIU RIFLE

HOWA MINI ACTION

HS PRECISION RIFLE
Action: Bolt
Stock: HS precision
Barrel: 22 in., 24 in.
Sights: None
Weight: 7 lb. 9 oz.–8 lb. 2 oz.
Caliber: .223 Rem., .22-250 Rem., .243 Win., 6.5 Creedmoor, 7mm-08 Rem., .308 Win., .25-06 Rem., .270 Win., .30-06 Spfd., 7mm Rem. Mag., .300 Win. Mag., 6mm Creedmoor,
Magazine: 3, 4 rounds
Features: HOWA 1500 barreled action set in an aluminum bedding block with hand-laminated stock of Kevlar, fiberglass, carbon fiber molded around it; two-stage HACT trigger; a threaded barrel is optional; in gray/black, tan/black, or green/black stock finishes
MSRP . . . . $1099.00–$1229.00

KRG BRAVO
Act*ion*: Bolt
Stock: Aluminum
Barrel: 20 in., 24 in., 26 in.
Sights: None
Weight: 9 lb. 9 oz.–10 lb. 3 oz.

Caliber: 6mm Creedmoor, 6,5 Creedmoor, .308 Win.
Magazine: 10 rounds
Features: Accepts AICS detachable magazines; available in black or Flat Dark Earth; threaded barrel
MSRP . . . . $1279.00–$1313.00

KUIU RIFLE
Action: Bolt
Stock: Synthetic
Barrel: 20 in., 22 in., 24 in.
Sights: None
Weight: 7 lb.–8 lb.
Caliber: .223 Rem., .22-250 Rem., .243 Win., 6mm Creedmoor, 6.5 Creedmoor, 7mm-08 Rem., .308 Win., .25-06 Rem., .270 Win., .30-06 Spfd., 7mm Rem. Mag., .300 Win. Mag.
Magazine: 5 rounds
Features: KUIU camo on Hogue pillar-bedded stock and recoil pad; Cerakote Gun Metal finish on barrel and action; KUIU Vias or Verde camo finishes
MSRP . . . . $749.00–$759.00

MINI ACTION
Action: Bolt
Stock: Synthetic
Barrel: 20 in., 22 in.
Sights: None
Weight: 5 lb. 11 oz.–6 lb. 10 oz.
Caliber: .223 Rem., 7.62X39, 6.5 Grendel, .300 BLK,
Magazine: Detachable box, 10 rounds
Features: HOWA's Mini Action is only 6 in. long and weighs just 10.2 oz., 3 oz. and almost a full inch less than a standard short action and two ounces nearly 1.5 in. less than a long-action; barrels in lightweight (#1), standard (#2), and heavy (#6) options, as well as stocks in black, OD Green, Kryptek Highlander, Multicam and Yote camo finishes; package includes Nikko Stirling 3-9x40mm scope and one-piece base and rings
MSRP . . . . $589.00–$829.00

H-S Precision

H-S PRECISION HTR

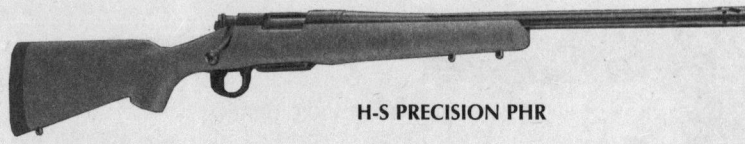

H-S PRECISION PHR

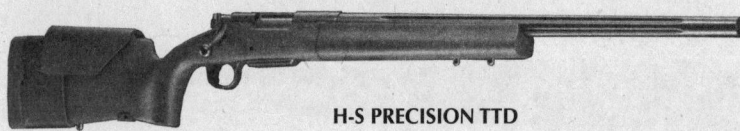

H-S PRECISION TTD

HTR (HEAVY TACTICAL RIFLE)

Action: Bolt
Stock: Synthetic
Barrel: 20 in., 22 in., 24 in., 26 in., 28 in.
Sights: None
Weight: 10 lb. 12 oz.–11 lb. 4 oz.
Caliber: Any standard SAAMI, LR calibers
Magazine: Detachable box, 3, 10 rounds
Features: Pro-Series 2000; fully adjustable synthetic stock comes in a wide range of colors combinations including sand, black, olive, gray, and spruce green; heavy fluted barrel
MSRP **$3999.00**

PHR (PROFESSIONAL HUNTER RIFLE)

Action: Bolt
Stock: Synthetic
Barrel: 20 in., 22 in., 24 in., 26 in., 28 in.
Sights: None
Weight: 7 lb. 12 oz.–8 lb. 4 oz.
Caliber: All popular magnum calibers up to .458 Lott
Magazine: Detachable box, 3, 4 rounds
Features: Pro-Series 2000; cheekpiece and built-in recoil reduction system; steel barrel; optional muzzlebrake; synthetic stock comes in a wide range of color combinations including sand, black, olive, gray, and spruce green; left-hand available for additional cost
MSRP **$3799.00**

TTD (TACTICAL TAKE-DOWN RIFLE)

Action: Bolt
Stock: Composite
Barrel: 22 in., 24 in.
Sights: None
Weight: 11 lb. 4 oz.–11 lb. 12 oz.
Caliber: Available in all standard SA SAAMI and LR calibers
Magazine: Detachable box, 3, rounds
Features: Stainless steel barrel and floor plate; synthetic stock with full length bedding block chassis system; metal parts are finished in matte black Teflon; wide variety of stock colors including sand, black, olive, gray, and spruce green
MSRP **$6499.00**

Isreal Weapons Industry (IWI)

ISRAEL WEAPON INDUSTRIES (IWI) X95

X95

Action: Semiautomatic
Stock: Polymer
Barrel: 16.5 in.
Sights: Folding front blade with tritium insert, aperture rear
Weight: 7 lb. 15 oz.
Caliber: .300 BLK, .223 Rem., 5.45X39mm, 9mm
Magazine: 30 rounds
Features: Bullpup with a long-stroke gas-piston action and a closed rotating bolt; improved fire control pack; ambidextrous mag release; Picatinny rail; pistol grip is modular; in black or Flat Dark Earth; conversion kits for 9mm and 5.56 NATO available
MSRP . . . . **N/A**

Iver Johnson

IVER JOHNSON 1911A1
CARBINE

1911A1 CARBINE
Action: Semiautomatic
Stock: Walnut
Barrel: 16.125 in.
Sights: Blade front, notch rear

Weight: 4 lb.
Caliber: .45 ACP
Magazine: 8, 28 rounds
Features: Detachable walnut stock; barrel has a black oxide finish; walnut pistol grips with checkering and the Iver Johnson logo; 28-round drum magazine is available; includes one eight-round magazine
MSRP $728.00

Jarrett Rifles

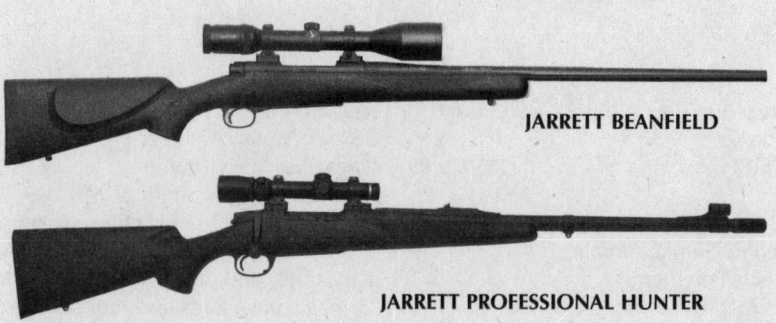

JARRETT BEANFIELD

JARRETT PROFESSIONAL HUNTER

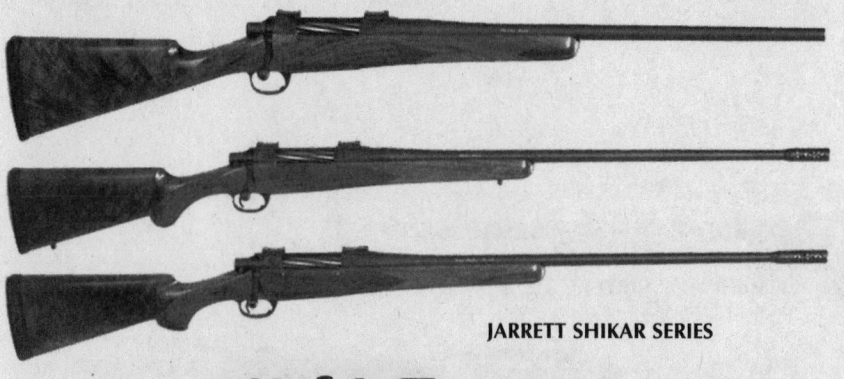

JARRETT SHIKAR SERIES

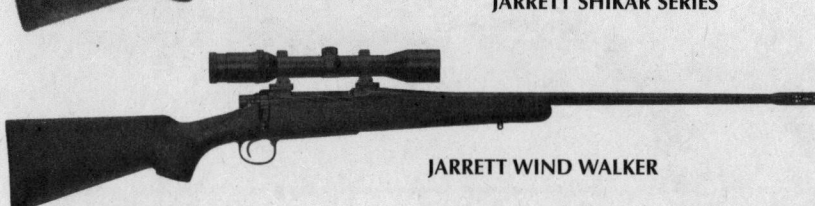

JARRETT WIND WALKER

Magazine: Comes with 40 rounds
Features: Includes 40 rounds of soft pointed bullets and solids created custom for each gun; ballistics printout and last three targets the gun shot also provided; optional scopes; .416 Rem. comes with Jarrett Tri-Lock receiver
MSRP . . . . starting at $11700.00

SHIKAR SERIES
Action: Bolt
Stock: Wood
Barrel: N/A
Sights: None
Weight: 8 lb.
Caliber: Any long action, standard or magnum caliber
Magazine: N/A
Features: Muzzle brake; decelerator pad; hand checkering; trap door plate; Shilen or Jewell trigger; aged American black walnut stock; Jarrett Tri-Lock left or right hand receiver
MSRP . . . . starting at $10,320.00

WIND WALKER
Action: Bolt
Stock: Synthetic
Barrel: Up to 24 in.
Sights: None
Weight: 7 lb. 8 oz.
Caliber: Any popular short-action
Magazine: Comes with 20 rounds
Features: Jarrett Tri-Lock action; muzzlebrake; Tally scope mounting system; phenolic resin metal finish with choice of stock colors; ballistic print out included
MSRP . . . . starting at $8320.00

BEANFIELD
Action: Bolt
Stock: Synthetic
Barrel: Various lengths available
Sights: None
Weight: Varies depending on options
Caliber: Any popular standard or magnum chambering
Magazine: Comes with 20 rounds
Features: Can build rifle on any receiver provided; optional caliber, stock style, color, muzzlebrake, barrel size, and taper; includes load data and 20 rounds of custom ammo
MSRP . . . . .starting at $6050.00

PROFESSIONAL HUNTER
Action: Bolt
Stock: Synthetic or walnut
Barrel: Various lengths available
Sights: None
Weight: Varies depending on options
Caliber: .375 H&H, .416 Rem., .416 Rigby, .450 Rigby

Kel-Tec

KEL-TEC RFB

KEL-TEC SUB-2000

RFB

Action: Semiautomatic
Stock: Synthetic
Barrel: 18 in., 24 in.
Sights: None
Weight: 8 lb.–8 lb. 11 oz.
Caliber: 7.62 NATO
Magazine: Detachable box, 10 or 20 rounds
Features: Picatinny rail; short-stroke gas piston operation; A2-style flash hider
MSRP $1929.09

SUB-2000

Action: Semiautomatic
Stock: Polymer
Barrel: 16.1 in.
Sights: Target
Weight: 4 lb.
Caliber: 9mm, .40 S&W
Magazine: 10+1 rounds
Features: Accepts Smith & Wesson M&P an SIG P226 magazines in 9mm or .40 S&W, Beretta 92 and 96 magazines, and Glock 17, 19, 22, and 23 magazines; folds away for storage and transportation
MSRP $500.00

Kimber

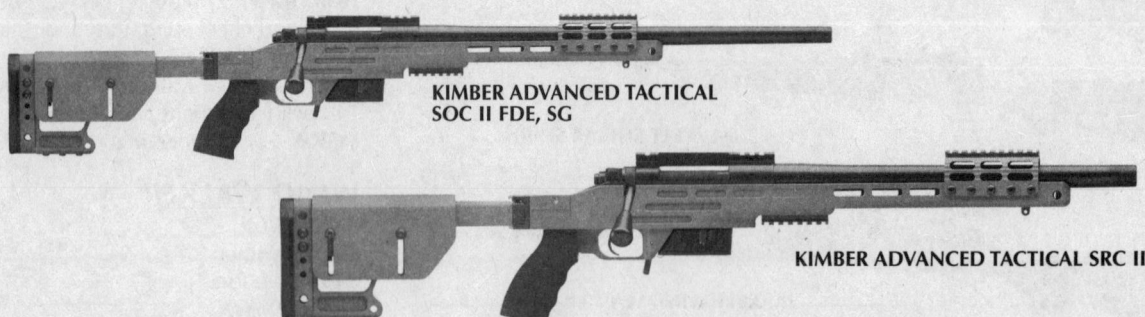

KIMBER ADVANCED TACTICAL SOC II FDE, SG

KIMBER ADVANCED TACTICAL SRC II

ADVANCED TACTICAL SOC II FDE, SG

Action: Bolt
Stock: Aluminum
Barrel: 22 in.
Sights: None
Weight: 11 lb.
Caliber: 6.5 Creedmoor, .308 Win.
Magazine: 5 rounds
Features: Sub .5-MOA accuracy guarantee; match grade chamber; threaded barrel; side-folding stock adjustable for length and comb height; night vision mount; M-LOK rail; 1913 Mil-Spec tripod mount; Mauser claw extractor; in Flat Dark Earth (FDE) or anodized black (SG) stocks; barrels and action are finished in matte black Kim Pro II; SOC stands for Special Operations Capable
MSRP $2449.00

ADVANCED TACTICAL SRC II

Action: Bolt
Stock: Aluminum
Barrel: 16 in.
Sights: None
Weight: 10 lb.
Caliber: .308 Win.
Magazine: 5 rounds
Features: Similar to the SOC II, but with a shorter, suppressor-ready barrel; SRC stands for Suppressor Ready Compact
MSRP $2449.00

KIMBER MODEL 84M ADIRONDACK

KIMBER MODEL 84M HUNTER

KIMBER HUNTER (BLACK)

KIMBER HUNTER (BOOT CAMPAIGN)

KIMBER MODEL 84M OPEN COUNTRY

KIMBER MONTANA

RIFLES

MODEL 84M ADIRONDACK

Action: Bolt
Stock: Synthetic
Barrel: 18 in.
Sights: None
Weight: 4 lb. 13 oz.
Caliber: .308 Win., 7mm-08 Rem., 6.5 Creedmoor, .300 BLK
Magazine: Internal, 4 rounds
Features: Kevlar/carbon fiber stock with Optifade Forrest finish; recoil pad; fluted barrel threaded for muzzle break/suppressor
MSRP **$1768.00**

MODEL 84M HUNTER

Action: Bolt
Stock: FDE composite
Barrel: 22 in., 24 in.
Sights: None
Weight: 5 lb. 10 oz.
Caliber: .243 Win., .257 Roberts, 6.5 Creedmoor, .270 Win., .280 Ackley Imp., 7mm-08 Rem., .308 Win., .30-06 Spfd.
Magazine: 3 rounds
Features: Lightweight stock; match-grade adjustable trigger; match-grade chamber; sporter contour stainless barrel; removable box magazine; available in Flat Dark Earth stocks with either blue or stainless hardware, or in the Hunter (Boot Campaign) with a Kryptek Highlander stock and blue hardware
MSRP **$891.00**

MODEL 84M HUNTER (BLACK)

Action: Bolt
Stock: Composite
Barrel: 22 in., 24 in.
Sights: None
Weight: 5 lb. 11 oz.
Caliber: .243 Win., .308 Win., 6.5 Creedmoor, .270 Win., .30-06 Spfd.
Magazine: 3, 4 rounds
Features: Sporter contour barrel; match grade chamber; pillar bedding; 1 in. Kimber recoil pad; Mauser claw extractor; stainless steel barrel is finished in a matte black Kimber Pro II
MSRP **$945.00**

MODEL 84M HUNTER (BOOT CAMPAIGN)

Action: Bolt
Stock: Composite
Barrel: 22 in., 24 in.
Sights: None
Weight: 5 lb. 11 oz.
Caliber: .243 Win., .308 Win., 7mm-08 Rem., .270 Win., .280 Ackley Imp., .30-06 Spfd., .25-06 Rem., 6.5 Creedmoor
Magazine: 3
Features: Similar to the Hunter (Black) model; additional caliber options; a stock wearing Kryptek Highlander camo
MSRP . . . . **$990.00–$1005.00**

MODEL 84M OPEN COUNTRY

Action: Bolt
Stock: Reinforced carbon fiber
Barrel: 24 in.
Sights: None
Weight: 6 lb. 15 oz.
Caliber: 6.5 Creedmoor, .308 Win.
Magazine: 5 rounds
Features: Fluted barrel; match-grade chamber; pillar bedding; stock has Gore Optifade Open Country soft touch treatment; also available in a solid Granite stock
MSRP **$2269.00**

MODEL 8400 MAGNUM MONTANA

Action: Bolt
Stock: Reinforced carbon fiber
Barrel: 22 in., 24 in., 26 in.
Sights: None
Weight: 5 lb. 2 oz.–6 lb. 13 oz.
Caliber: .300 Win. Mag., .300 WSM, .270 Win., .30-06 Spfd., .280 Ackley Improved, .308 Win., 7mm-08 Rem., 6.5 Creedmoor
Magazine: 4, 5 rounds
Features: A Montana rifle with Kimber enhancements; match-grade chamber; threaded barrel; sling swivel studs; pillar bedding; sporter contour stainless barrel with satin finish; adjustable trigger; green stock; stainless hardware
MSRP **$1427.00**

Kimber

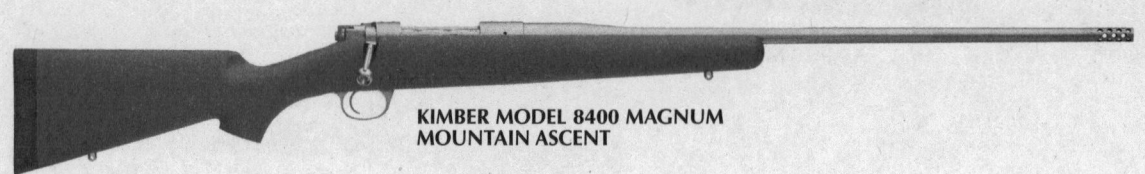

KIMBER MODEL 8400 MAGNUM MOUNTAIN ASCENT

MODEL 8400 MAGNUM MOUNTAIN ASCENT

Action: Bolt
Stock: Reinforced carbon fiber
Barrel: 22 in., 24 in., 26 in.
Sights: None
Weight: 4 lb. 13 oz.–6 lb. 7 oz.
Caliber: .280 Ackley Improved, .270 Win., .30-06 Spfd., .308 Win., .300 WSM, .270 WSM, .300 Win. Mag., 7mm Rem. Mag., 7mm-08 Rem., 6.5 Creedmoor
Magazine: 4 rounds
Features: Stainless fluted barrel with muzzle brake and thread protector; adjustable trigger; 1-inch Pachmayr Decelerator pad; three-position M70-type safety; Mauser claw extractor; match-grade chamber; 84M action; Moss Green stock
MSRP $2040.00

Knight's Armament Company

KNIGHT'S ARMAMENT SR-15 E3 CARBINE MOD 2 M-LOK

KNIGHT'S ARMAMENT SR-15 E3 LPR MOD 2 M-LOK

KNIGHT'S ARMAMENT SR-15 E3 MOD 2 M-LOK

KNIGHT'S ARMAMENT SR-30 M-LOK

SR-15 E3 CARBINE MOD 2 M-LOK

Action: Semiautomatic
Stock: Synthetic
Barrel: 14.5 in.
Sights: Adjustable
Weight: 6 lb. 6.4 oz.
Caliber: 5.56mm NATO
Magazine: 30 rounds
Features: Free-floated barrel inside a URX4 M-LOK handguard; improved E3 round-lug bolt design; ambidextrous bolt release, selector lever, and magazine release; drop-in two-stage trigger; 3-prong flash eliminator
MSRP $2575.56

SR-15 E3 LPR MOD 2 M-LOK

Action: Semiautomatic
Stock: Synthetic
Barrel: 18 in.
Sights: Adjustable
Weight: 7 lb. 6.4 oz.
Caliber: 5.56mm NATO
Magazine: 30 rounds
Features: Free-floated barrel inside a URX4 M-LOK handguard; improved E3 round-lug bolt design; ambidextrous bolt release, selector lever, and magazine release; drop-in two-stage trigger; 3-prong flash eliminator
MSRP $2700.56

SR-15 E3 MOD 2 M-LOK

Action: Semiautomatic
Stock: Synthetic
Barrel: 16 in.
Sights: Adjustable
Weight: 6 lb. 9 oz.
Caliber: 5.56mm NATO
Magazine: 30 rounds
Features: Free-floated barrel inside a URX4 M-LOK handguard; improved E3 round-lug bolt design; ambidextrous bolt release, selector lever, and magazine release; drop-in two-stage trigger; 3-prong flash eliminator
MSRP $2450.56

SR-30 M-LOK

Action: Semiautomatic
Stock: Synthetic
Barrel: 9.5 in.
Sights: Adjustable
Weight: 6 lb. 3 oz.
Caliber: .300 BLK (7.62x35mm)
Magazine: 30 rounds
Features: QDC-compatible flash hider will mount any of the KAC 7.62mm QDC suppressors; ambidextrous controls; two-stage match trigger; M-Lok accessory mounting system
MSRP $2631.94

RIFLES

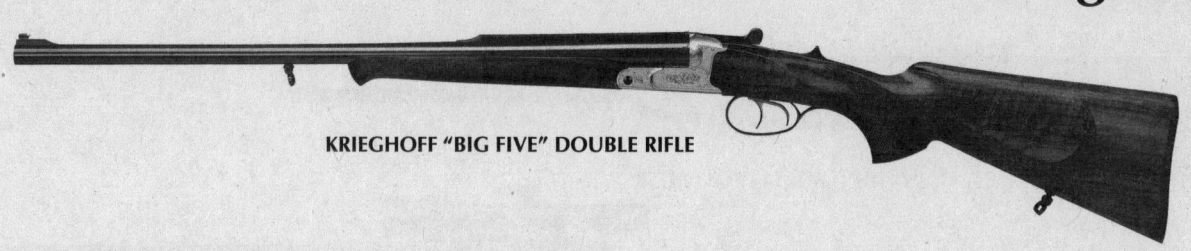

KRIEGHOFF "BIG FIVE" DOUBLE RIFLE

"BIG FIVE" DOUBLE RIFLE

Action: Hinged breech
Stock: Walnut
Barrel: 23.5 in.
Sights: Open
Weight: 9 lb. 8 oz.–10 lb. 8 oz.
Caliber: .375 H&H Mag., .375
Flanged Magnum N.E., .450/.400 NE, .500/.416 N.E., .470 N.E., .500 N.E.
Magazine: None
Features: Double triggers; V-shaped rear sight with a white, vertical middle line and a pearl front sight; optional Super-Express sight; Monte Carlo style cheekpiece; European walnut stock with small game scene engraving; steel trigger and floor plate; straight comb and large recoil pad
MSRP . . . .**starting at $13995.00**

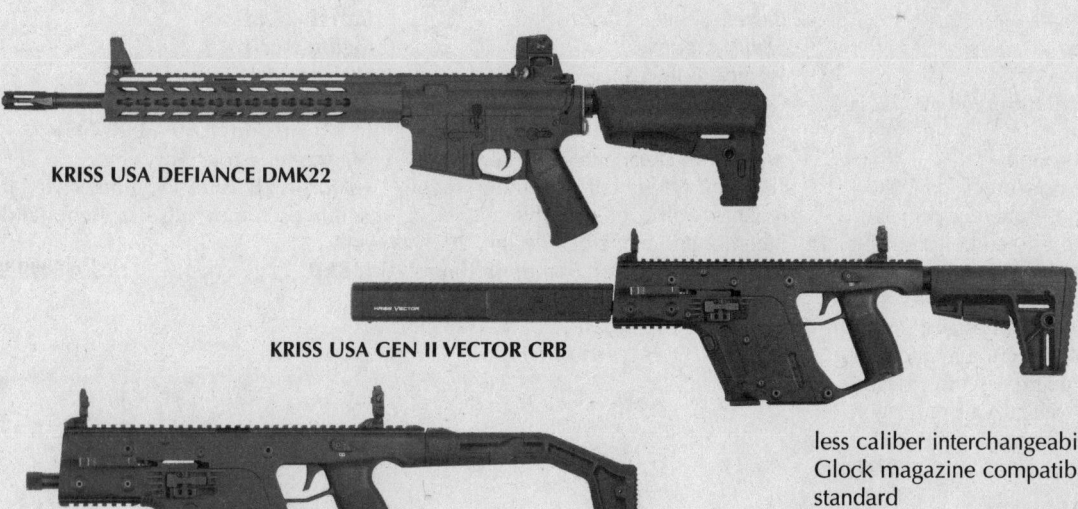

KRISS USA DEFIANCE DMK22

KRISS USA GEN II VECTOR CRB

KRISS USA VECTOR GEN II SBR

DEFIANCE DMK22

Action: Semiautomatic
Stock: Synthetic
Barrel: 16 in.
Sights: Adjustable
Weight: N/A
Caliber: .22 LR
Magazine: 10 or 15 rounds
Features: Full-metal construction; compatible with aftermarket barrels, magazines, stocks, pistol grips, handguards, and some AR-15 trigger upgrades; available in black, Flat Dark Earth, OD Green, Alpine, and LVOA Black (LVOA version has extended LVOA-C rail from War Sport Manufacturing, LLC)
MSRP **$699.99**

VECTOR GEN II CRB

Action: Semiautomatic
Barrel:16 in., 18.6 in.
Sights: Low-profile folding front and rear
Weight: 8 lb.
Caliber: 9mm, 9x21, .45 ACP, 10mm, .40 S&W, .357 SIG
Magazine: Glock magazines
Features: Patented Kriss Super V recoil mitigation system, ambidextrous short-throw safety lever, Mil-Std 1913 Picatinny rails top and bottom, tool-less caliber interchangeability and Glock magazine compatibility are standard
MSRP . . . .**$1499.00–$1619.00**

VECTOR GEN II SBR

Action: Semiautomatic
Stock: Polymer
Barrel: 5.5 in.
Sights: Custom flip-up iron
Weight: 5 lb. 10 oz.
Caliber: .45 ACP, 9mm, 9x21, 10mm, .40 S&W, .357 SIG
Magazine: Glock magazines
Features: Gen II iteration has side-folding stock, Kriss's Super V recoil management system, tool-less caliber interchangeability, Glock magazine compatibility, and a barrel threaded for attachments. Available in black, Flat Dark Earth, OD Green, Combat Grey, and Alpine finishes
MSRP . . . .**$1549.00–$1569.00**

Lazzeroni Arms, Inc.

LAZZERONI L2012LT-MTLR

LAZZERONI L2012SP-XTLR

LAZZERONI L2012TH-XTLR

L2012LT-MTLR

Action: Bolt
Stock: Graphite/composite
Barrel: 26 in.
Sights: None
Weight: 7 lb. 5 oz.
Caliber: 7.82 (.308) Warbird, 7.21 (.284) Firebird
Magazine: 4 rounds
Features: All new precision CNC-machined chromoly receiver; one-piece diamond-fluted bolt shaft; stainless steel match-grade button-barrel; custom molded hand-bedded graphite/composite stock designs; precision-machined aluminum alloy floor plate/trigger guard assembly; jewel competition trigger; Vais muzzlebrake; Limbsaver recoil pad
MSRP.................**$5999.99**

L2012SP-XTLR

Action: Bolt
Stock: Graphite/composite
Barrel: 28 in.
Sights: None
Weight: 8 lb. 13 oz.
Caliber: 7.82 (.308) Warbird, 7.21 (.284) Firebird, 8.59 (.338) Titan
Magazine: Detachable box, 4 rounds
Features: Heavy barrel contour; recoil reducing roll-over cheekpiece incorporated into stock design; 20 MOA Picatinny rail; 34mm or 30mm rings
MSRP.................**$7499.99**

L2012TH-XTLR

Action: Bolt
Stock: Graphite/composite
Barrel: 25 in.
Sights: None
Weight: 7 lb. 11 oz.
Caliber: 7.82 (.284) Warbird, 7.21 (.284) Firebird, 8.59 (.338) Titan
Magazine: 4 rounds
Features: 20 MOA Picatinny style rail; 34mm or 30mm ring sets; right hand only
MSRP.................**$6999.99**

Lewis Machine & Tool Company

LEWIS MACHINE & TOOL LM8PDW556

LM8PDW556, LM8PDW300

Action: Semiautomatic
Stock: Synthetic
Barrel: 16 in.
Sights: Adjustable flip up front and rear
Weight: 7 lb. 3.2 oz.
Caliber: 5.56x45 NATO, .300 Blackout
Magazine: 30 rounds
Features: Completely ambidextrous features; flared magazine well; winter trigger guard; ¼ MOA windage adjustable rear sight; SOPMOD buttstock; easily field strips with no special tools
MSRP.....................**$2299.00**

RIFLES

Lithgow Arms

LITHGOW ARMS LA101 CROSSOVER RIMFIRE

LITHGOW ARMS LA105 WOOMERA

LA101 CROSSOVER RIMFIRE

Action: Bolt
Stock: Synthetic, laminate
Barrel: 20.9 in.
Sights: None
Weight: 6 lb. 9.6 oz.–7 lb. 3.2 oz.
Caliber: .22 LR, .22 WMR, .17 HMR
Magazine: N/A
Features: Free-floating barrel; integral molded trigger guard; length of pull adjustment spacers; Cerakote-finished barrel; receiver, bolt handle, and integral scope bases; black synthetic and laminate stock options
MSRP . . . . **$1199.00–$1299.00**

LA105 WOOMERA

Action: Bolt
Stock: Polymer
Barrel: 24 in.
Sights: None
Weight: 11 lb.
Caliber: 6.5 Creedmoor, .308 Win.
Magazine: 10 rounds
Features: Adjustable KRG tactical rifle stock; muzzle brake; Cerakote finish; threaded muzzle; 20 MOA Picatinny rail; in black or Flat Dark Earth finishes
MSRP **$2199.00**

LWRC International

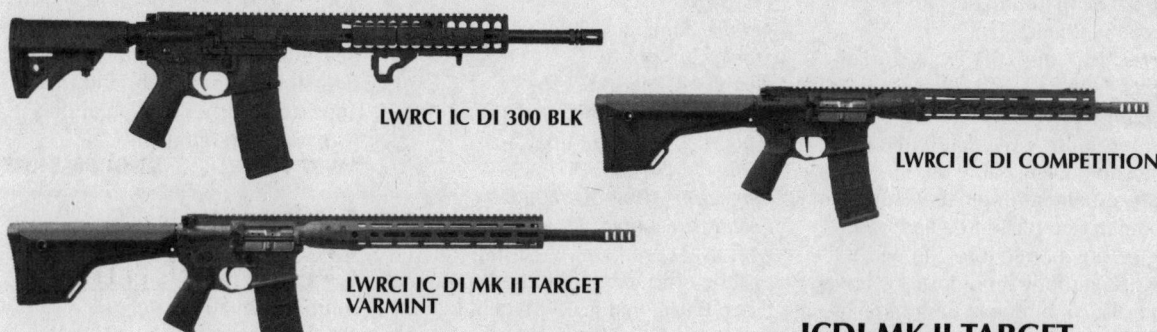

LWRCI IC DI 300 BLK

LWRCI IC DI COMPETITION

LWRCI IC DI MK II TARGET VARMINT

IC DI 300 BLK

Action: Semiautomatic
Stock: Polymer
Barrel: 16.1 in.
Sights: None
Weight: 6 lb. 10 oz.
Caliber: .300 Blackout
Magazine: 30 rounds
Features: Direct impingement AR platform; A2 flash hider; ambidextrous controls; six-position Mil-Spec buffer tube; NiCorr-treated barrel; gas block; gas tube; in black, Patriot Brown, or Gun Metal Gray
MSRP . . . .**$1459.00–$1744.00**

IC DI COMPETITION

Action: Semiautomatic
Stock: Polymer
Barrel: 16.1 in.
Sights: None
Weight: 7 lb.
Caliber: 5.56 NATO
Magazine: 10, 30 rounds
Features: A shorter-barreled direct impingement AR platform; fully ambidextrous controls; sling mount; charging handle; LWRCI's new four-port Ultra Brake and M-LOK free-float handguard; Timney 6675 straight competition trigger; short-throw selector; in black, Flat Dark Earth, OD Green, Patriot Brown, or Tungsten Grey
MSRP . . . .**$1950.50–$2369.32**

ICDI MK II TARGET VARMINT

Action: Semiautomatic
Stock: Polymer
Barrel: 18.1 in.
Sights: None
Weight: 7 lb. 12 oz.
Caliber: .223 Wylde
Magazine: 10, 30 rounds
Features: Direct impingement rifle-length system; Geissele SSA-E two-stage trigger; Magpul MOE rifle stock; a cold hammer-forged NiCorr-treated barrel; DI bolt carrier group; LWRCI's new four-port Ultra Brake; ambidextrous sling mount and charging handle; 14-in. M-LOK free-floating handguard; SnakeSkin pistol grip; in black, Flat Dark Earth, OD Green, Patriot Brown, or Tungsten Grey
MSRP . . . .**$1879.00–$2184.00**

LWRC International

LWRCI IC DI STANDARD

LWRCI IC A5

LWRCI IC SPR

LWRCI REPR MK II

LWRCI R.E.P.R. MK II 6.5 CREEDMOOR ELITE

RIFLES

IC DI STANDARD

Action: Semiautomatic
Stock: Synthetic
Barrel: 16.1 in., 18.1 in.
Sights: None
Weight: 6 lb. 10 oz.
Caliber: 5.56 NATO, .300 Blackout
Magazine: Detachable box
Features: Direct impingement system; modular, one-piece free-float rail; angled ergonomic fore grip with QD sling point; fully ambidextrous lower controls; A2 birdcage flash hider
MSRP . . . . $1289.00–$1674.00

IC A5

Action: Semiautomatic
Stock: Composite
Barrel: 10.5 in., 14.7 in., 16.1 in.
Sights: Skirmish back up iron sights
Weight: 6 lb. 8 oz.–7 lb. 5 oz.
Caliber: .5.56 NATO
Magazine: 10 or 30 rounds
Features: Enhanced Fire Control Group; dual-control fully ambidextrous lower receiver; Magpul MOE grip; NiCorr treated cold hammer-forged barrel; ambidextrous charging handle; Monoforge upper receiver with modular rail system; adjustable two-position gas block; A2 birdcage flash hider
MSRP . . . . $2458.63–$2492.94

IC SPR

Action: Semiautomatic
Stock: Composite
Barrel: 14.7 in., 16.1 in.
Sights: Skirmish back up iron sights
Weight: 7 lb.–7 lb. 5 oz.
Caliber: 5.56 NATO
Magazine: 10 or 30 rounds
Features: Monoforge upper receiver with user-configurable 12-inch rail system; cold hammer-forged spiral fluted barrel that is 20 percent lighter; Enhanced Fire Control Group; advanced trigger guard; adjustable compact stock; compact high-efficiency flash hider; patented short-stroke gas piston system; Magpul MOE grip
MSRP $2396.00

R.E.P.R. MK II

Action: Semiautomatic
Stock: Synthetic
Barrel: 12 in., 16 in., 20 in.
Sights: None
Weight: 9 lb. 4.8 oz.
Caliber: 6.5 Creedmoor, 7.62x39
Magazine: N/A
Features: Rapid Engagement Precision Rifle utilizes patented Short Stroke Gas Piston System; billet 7075 aluminum upper and lower; 12.5-in. modular rail system; gas system normal and suppressed settings; side-mounted non-reciprocating charging handle; NiCorr-treated cold-hammer-forged heavy barrel; Patriot Brown, OD Green, Flat Dark Earth, and black anodized finishes available, plus many custom options
MSRP . . . . $3901.00–$4045.00

R.E.P.R. MK II 6.5 CREEDMOOR, 6.5 CREEDMOOR ELITE

Action: Semiautomatic
Stock: Polymer
Barrel: 22 in.
Sights: Backup iron sights
Weight: 11 lb. 13 oz.
Caliber: 6.5 Creedmoor
Magazine: N/A
Features: Short-stroke gas piston system; 20-position tunable gas block; black nitride-treated heavy barrel; Geissele SSA-E two-stage Precision trigger; Magpul PRS adjustable stock; LWRCI's new four-port Ultra Brake; enhanced trigger guard; backup Skirmish iron sights; carbon fiber-wrapped match barrel from PROOF Research with a 1:8 twist; in black, Flat Dark Earth, OD Green, Patriot Brown, or Tungsten Grey
Standard: $4303.00
Elite: $4823.00

LWRC International

LWRCI SIX A5

LWRCI VALKYRIE 224 DI

SIX A5

Action: Semiautomatic
Stock: Composite
Barrel: 10.5 in., 12.7 in., 14.7 in., 16.1 in.
Sights: Skirmish back up iron sights
Weight: 6 lb. 8 oz.–7 lb. 5 oz.
Caliber: 6.8 SPC II
Magazine: 10 or 30 rounds
Features: Cold hammer-forged barrel; 12-inch user-configurable rail with scallop cut design; compact stock with integral sling attachment point; short-stroke piston operation; Enhanced Fire Control Group; adjustable two-position gas block; ambidextrous charging handle; Magpul MOE grip; enlarged ejection point
MSRP **$2804.00**

VALKYRIE 224 DI

Action: Semiautomatic
Stock: Polymer
Barrel: 20.1 in.
Sights: None
Weight: 8 lb. 2 oz.
Caliber: .224 Valkyrie
Magazine: N/A
Features: Direct impingement, Rifle+1-length system with LWRCI fire control group; LWRCI's news four-port Ultra Brake; NiCorr-treated gas block; cold hammer-forged non-fluted NiCorr-treated barrel; Magpul MOE stock; LWRCI's all-new SnakeSkin Pistol grip provides for sight tool and battery storage; in black, Flat Dark Earth, Olive Drab, Patriot Brown, and Tungsten Grey
MSRP . . . . **$1875.30–$2294.12**

Magnum Research

MAGNUM RESEARCH MAGNUMLITE ULTRA BARREL WITH THREADED MUZZLE

MAGNUMLITE ULTRA BARREL WITH THREADED MUZZLE

Action: Semiatuomatic
Stock: Synthetic
Barrel: 17 in.
Sights: None
Weight: 4 lb. 4 oz.
Caliber: .22 LR
Magazine: 10+1
Features: Ambidextrous lightweight thumbhole stock made of polypropylene with fiber additives; semi palm swell on both sides of the pistol grip; molded-to-fit hard rubber buttplate attached with screws; graphite bull barrel with uni-directional graphite fibers parallel to the bore axis; full floating barrel; French gray anodized finish
MSRP **$596.00**

Marlin Firearms

MARLIN 60

MARLIN 70PSS

MARLIN 336C

MARLIN 336XLR

MARLIN 336SS

60

Action: Semiautomatic
Stock: Laminated hardwood
Barrel: 19 in.
Sights: Open
Weight: 5 lb. 8 oz.
Caliber: .22 LR
Magazine: Under-barrel tube, 14 rounds
Features: Manual and automatic "last-shot" bolt hold-opens; receiver top has serrated, non-glare finish; cross-bolt safety; steel charging handle; Monte Carlo walnut-finished laminated hardwood; Model 60C is blue with walnut-finished hardwood stock; Model 60C is blue with a Realtree HardwoodsTM synthetic stock; Model 60SB is stainless with walnut-finished hardwood stock; Model 60SN is blue with black synthetic stock and also comes as a scope package option; and 60SS is stainless with a laminated black/gray hardwood stock

60:	**$209.00**
60C:	**$246.00**
60SB:	**$265.00**
60SN:	**$201.00**
60SN with scope:	**$217.00**
60SS:	**$316.00**

70PSS

Action: Semiautomatic
Stock: Synthetic
Barrel: 16.25 in.

Sights: Open
Weight: 3 lb. 4 oz.
Caliber: .22 LR
Magazine: Detachable clip, 7 rounds
Features: Automatic "last-shot" bolt hold-open; manual bolt hold-open; Monte Carlo black fiberglass-filled synthetic stock with abbreviated forend; nickel plated swivel studs; molded-in checkering; adjustable open rear sight; front ramp sight with high visibility orange post and cut-away wide-scan hood
MSRP **$345.00**

336C

Action: Lever
Stock: Walnut
Barrel: 20 in.
Sights: Open
Weight: 7 lb.
Caliber: .30-30 Win., .35 Rem.
Magazine: Under-barrel tube, 6 rounds
Features: Deeply blued surfaces; hammer block safety; American black walnut stock with pistol grip and checkering
MSRP **$635.00**

336SS

Action: Lever
Stock: Walnut
Barrel: 20 in.
Sights: Open

Weight: 7 lb.
Caliber: .30-30 Win.
Magazine: Under-barrel tube, 6 rounds
Features: Stainless steel receiver, barrel, lever, and trigger guard; hammer block safety; American black walnut pistol grip stock with fluted comb and cut checkering; rubber rifle buttpad; adjustable semi-buckhorn folding rear, ramp front sight with brass bead and wide-scan hood; solid top receiver tapped for scope mount; offset hammer spur for scope use
MSRP **$779.00**

336XLR

Action: Lever
Stock: Laminated hardwood
Barrel: 24 in.
Sights: Open
Weight: 7 lb.
Caliber: .30-30 Win.
Magazine: Under-barrel tube, 5 rounds
Features: Stainless steel receiver, barrel, lever, and trigger guard plate; black/gray laminated hardwood stock with pistol grip and checkering; deluxe recoil pad; nickel plates swivel studs; adjustable semi-buckhorn folding rear sight and brass bead front sight with wide-scan hood; receiver tapped for scope mount
MSRP **$969.00**

Marlin Firearms

MARLIN 1894

MARLIN 1895

MARLIN 1895GBL

MARLIN 1895SBL.

1894

Action: Lever
Stock: Walnut
Barrel: 20 in.
Sights: Open
Weight: 6 lb. 8 oz.
Caliber: .45 Colt, .44 Mag./.44 Spl.
Magazine: Under-barrel tube, 10 rounds
Features: Lever action with squared finger lever; deeply blued metal surfaces; straight-grip American black walnut stock; hard rubber buttplate; tough Mar-Shield finish; blued steel forend cap; tapered octagon barrel; adjustable marble semi-buckhorn rear sight and marble carbine front sight; solid top receiver tapped for scope mount
MSRP $789.00

1895

Action: Lever
Stock: Walnut
Barrel: 22 in.
Sights: Open
Weight: 7 lb. 8 oz.
Caliber: .45-70 Govt.
Magazine: Under-barrel tube, 4 rounds
Features: Standard 1895 has American black walnut pistol grip stock, 22-in. barrel, and blued metal; 1895CB has American walnut straight grip stock and 26-in. octagonal barrel, and blued metal; 1895CBA has 18.5 tapered octagonal barrel, blued metal and black walnut straight grip stock; 1895G has a black walnut straight grip stock, 18.5-in. barrel, and blued metal; 1895GS has 18.5-in barrel, walnut straight grip stock, and stainless steel metal;1895GSBL has blued metal, 18.5-in. barrel, and green laminate pistol grip stock with black webbing
1895: $745.00
1895CB: $786.00
1895CBA $899.00
1895G: $750.00
1895GS: $896.00

1895GBL

Action: Lever
Stock: Laminate
Barrel: 18.5 in.
Sights: Open
Weight: 7 lb.
Caliber: .45-70 Govt.
Magazine: Full length tubular magazine, 6 rounds
Features: Lever action with big loop finger lever; deeply blued metal surfaces; hammer block safety; American pistol grip two-tone brown laminate stock with cut checkering; ventilated recoil pad; tough Mar-Shield finish; swivel studs; adjustable semi-buckhorn folding rear sight and ramp front sight with brass bead; receiver tapped for scope mount; offset hammer spur for scope use
MSRP $786.00

1895SBL

Action: Lever
Stock: Laminated hardwood
Barrel: 18.5 in.
Sights: Open
Weight: 8 lb.
Caliber: .45-70 Govt.
Magazine: Under-barrel tube, 6 rounds
Features: Lever action with big loop finger lever; deeply blued metal surfaces; stainless steel barrel and receiver; black/gray laminated hardwood with pistol-grip stock and cut checkering; fluted comb; deluxe recoil pad; compact version available
MSRP $1146.00

Marlin Firearms

MARLIN XT-22

XT-22
Action: Bolt
Stock: Hardwood
Barrel: 22 in.
Sights: Open
Weight: 6 lb.
Caliber: .22 LR
Magazine: Detachable clip, 7 rounds

Features: Pro-Fire adjustable trigger; Micro-Groove rifling; blued bolt action; thumb safety; red cocking indicator; Monte Carlo walnut-finished hardwood with swivel studs; full pistol grip; tough Mar-Shield finish; adjustable rear sight and front ramp sights; receiver grooved for scope mount, drilled and tapped for scope bases
MSRP................$239.00

Masterpiece Arms

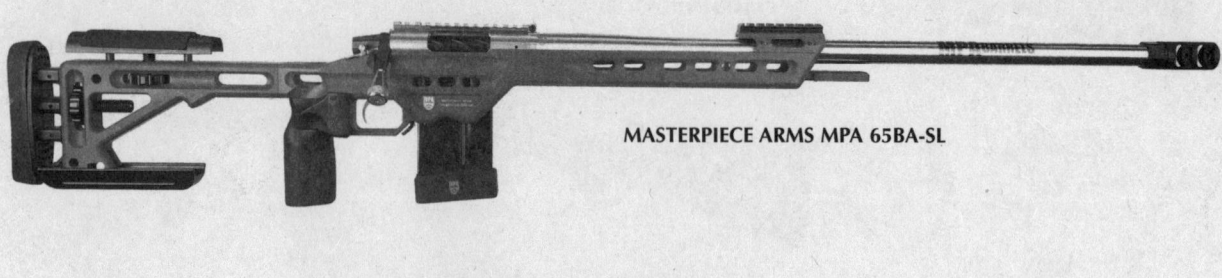

MASTERPIECE ARMS MPA 65BA-SL

MASTERPIECE ARMS MPA .300 NORMA BOLT-ACTION RIFLE

MPA 65BA-SL
Action: Bolt
Stock: Aluminum
Barrel: 24 in.
Sights: None
Weight: 12 lb. 8 oz.
Caliber: 6.5 Creedmoor
Magazine: 10 rounds
Features: Switch-barrel chassis rifle; barrel/caliber can be switched out in less than five minutes with West Texas Ordnance Switch Lug System; Spencer/MPA hand-lapped barrel; Trigger Tech adjustable trigger; built-in bubble level; choice of MPA tactical or competition chassis (tactical gets a monopod); MPA muzzle brake; Curtis Custom Axiom action; 60-degree bolt throw; one-piece spiral fluted bolt; night vision bridge; Cerakote finish; custom Cerakote colors and left-hand action available
MSRP.................$3375.00

MPA .300 NORMA BOLT-ACTION RIFLE
Action: Bolt
Stock: Aluminum
Barrel: 26 in.
Sights: None
Weight: 5 lb. 4 oz.
Caliber: .300 Norma
Magazine: 5 rounds
Features: Chassis rifle with a ½-MOA guarantee; V-bedding; a bubble level built into the adjustable skeleton stock; Spencer Heavy Varmint profile barrel; Curtis spiral fluted one-piece bolt; upper and lower Picatinny rails; MPA muzzle brake; built-tin rear monopod; in black, burnt bronze, flat dark earth, or gunmetal finishes; custom Cerakote finishes add $135.00 for the chassis body, $65.00 for the barreled action
MSRP........ $3375.00–$3525.00

RIFLES

Mauser

MAUSER M12 EXTREME

MAUSER M12 IMPACT

MAUSER M12 TRAIL

MAUSER M18

MAUSER M98 MAGNUM

M12 EXTREME
Action: Bolt
Stock: Wood, Synthetic
Barrel: 22 in., 24.5 in.
Sights: None
Weight: 7 lb.
Caliber: .22-250 Rem., .243 Win.,
6.5x55 Swedish, .270 Win., 7x64
Brenneke, .308 Win., .30-06 Spfd.,
8x57 IS, 9.3x62 Mauser,
7mm Rem., .300 Win. Mag., .338
Win. Mag.
Magazine: 5+1 rounds
Features: 60-degree bolt lift; detachable magazine; open sights available; drilled and tapped for scopes; stock extension available
MSRP **$1561.00**

M12 IMPACT
Action: Bolt
Stock: Synthetic
Barrel: 20 in.
Sights: None
Weight: 6 lb. 12 oz.

Caliber: .243 Win., .308 Win.
Magazine: Detachable box, 5+1 rounds
Features: Three-position SRS firing pin safety; solid-steel 20 MOA Picatinny rail; uncompromising, crisp single-stage trigger; ergonomic extended bolt handle with 60-degree bolt lift; high accuracy thanks to direct locking in the cold hammer-forged barrel; Ilaflon coating for maximum rust protection
MSRP **$1934.00**

M12 TRAIL
Action: Bolt
Stock: Synthetic
Barrel: 18.5 in.
Sights: Three dot hunt drive sights
Weight: 6 lb. 12 oz.
Caliber: .308 Win., 8x57 IS, 9.3x62
Magazine: 5+1 rounds
Features: Removable sling swivel at muzzle; moveable snap-ball sling loop on hear stock; barrel and action surfaces are finished in matte black

Ilaflon; signal orange-grey synthetic camo stock
MSRP **$1903.00**

M18
Action: Bolt
Stock: Polymer
Barrel: 22 in., 24 in.
Sights: None
Weight: 6 lb. 6 oz.–6 lb. 10 oz.
Caliber: .243 Win., .270 Win., .300 Win. Mag., .30-06 Spfd., .308 Win., 6.5 Creedmoor, 6.5 PRC, 7mm Rem. Mag.
Magazine: 5 rounds
Features: All-steel receiver; an all-weather polymer stock with soft-grip inserts; three-position safety; cold-hammer-forged barrel; adjustable trigger; buttstock has a removable cap for small-tool or compact cleaning kit storage
MSRP **$699.00**

M98 MAGNUM
Action: Bolt
Stock: Wood
Barrel: 24.4 in.
Sights: Windage and elevation adjustable two-leaf express sights.
Weight: 9 lb. 7 oz.–10 lb. 1.6 oz.
Caliber: .375 H&H Mag., .416 Rigby
Magazine: 4, 5 rounds
Features: Premium steel construction with plasma nitriding; long extractor; controlled round feed; double recoil lugs; pillar bedding; newly designed horizontal safety; double square bridge system designed for swing-off scope mounts; wood upgrades available; .416 Rigby can option heavy barrel profile
MSRP . . . . **$8331.00–$14,985.00**

McMillan Firearms

MCMILLAN CUSTOM HUNTING RIFLE - LEGACY

CUSTOM HUNTING RIFLES - LEGACY
Action: Bolt
Stock: Nutmeg laminate
Barrel: 22 in., 24 in.
Sights: None
Weight: 6 lb. 8 oz.–7 lb.
Caliber: .223 Rem., .243 Win., .260

Rem., .308 Win., .300 WSM
Magazine: Fixed
Features: Today's Legacy model features McMillan's G31 short-action and a match grade stainless steel barrel with a target crown; five stock options available: McMillan Dynasty, McMillan Hunter, McMillan A3, stan-

dard walnut, XX walnut, and Nutmeg laminate; barreled action and bolt are dressed in black Cerakote; muzzle brake can be optioned; supplied with a rollered travel case
MSRP . . . . **Contact manufacturer**

McMillan Firearms

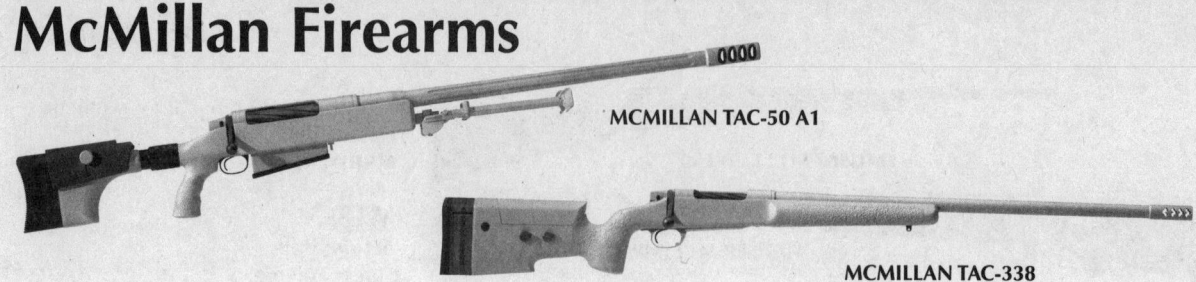

MCMILLAN TAC-50 A1

MCMILLAN TAC-338

TAC-50 A1
Action: Semiautomatic
Stock: Synthetic
Barrel: 29 in.
Sights: Drilled and tapped for scopes
Weight: 26 lb.
Caliber: .50 BMG
Magazine: Detachable box, 5 rounds
Features: McMillan's TAC-50A1 features the company's TAC-50A1 removable stock with an adjustable cheekpiece, Decelerator recoil pad, bipod, and four flush-mount cups with 1.25-in. sling loops; barrel is a 29-in. Navy contour 1:15 twist, free-floating, match grade, hand-lapped, and fluted with a threaded muzzle and threaded McMillan muzzle brake; metal finish made to match stock color, available in black, olive, gray, tan, and Dark Earth
MSRP . . . . . . Contact manufacturer

TAC-338
Action: Bolt
Stock: Composite
Barrel: 27 in.
Sights: None
Weight: 11 lb.
Caliber: .338 Alpha Mag.
Magazine: Detachable box, 1 to 5 rounds
Features: Featuring McMillan's own TAC-338 action designed for the .338 Lapua; the 27-in. barrel has a medium-heavy contour, is match grade and stainless steel, and has a muzzle brake with ¾-24 threads; McMillan's Tactical stock with adjustable cheekpiece, length-of-pull spacers, one stud, and six flush-mount cups with ¼-in. sling loops; 20 MOA 1913 Mil-Std rail is standard; metalwork finished to match the stock, available in black, OD Green, and Flat Dark Earth
MSRP $5699.00

Merkel

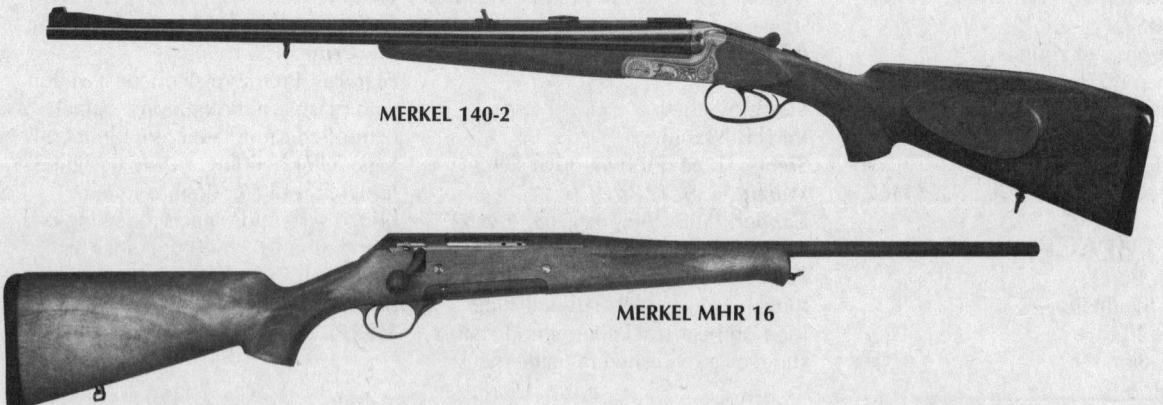

MERKEL 140-2

MERKEL MHR 16

140-2
Action: Side-by-side
Stock: Wood
Barrel: 23.6 in.
Sights: None
Weight: 7 lb. 8 oz.
Caliber: 7x65R, .30-06 Spfd., .30R Blaser, 8x57IRS, 9.3x74R
Magazine: None
Features: Anson & Deeley locks; steel action; Greener-style cross-bolt and double bottom bite; double trigger with front set trigger, optional single trigger; automatic trigger safety; optional with ejectors; hard soldered barrels with muzzle adjustment; engraving English arabesque or game scene "JAGD"; rubber buttplate; pistol grip; cheekpiece and hogback comb
MSRP $13,920.00

MHR 16
Action: Bolt
Stock: Synthetic or wood
Barrel: 22 in., 24 in.
Sights: None
Weight: 6 lb. 9.8 oz.–7 lb. 6 oz.
Caliber: .243 Win., .270 Win., .30-06 Spfd., .300 Win. Mag., .308 Win., 6.5x55, 7mm Rem. Mag., 9.3x62
Magazine: Detachable box, 3+1 rounds
Features: Two-position trigger safety with separate chamber lock; newly designed receiver that is cold-forged and precision machined; 60-degree bolt throw; direct trigger with a weight of just less than three pounds
Synthetic stock: $799.00
Wood stock: $915.00

RIFLES

Merkel

MERKEL RX HELIX

MERKEL RX HELIX EXPLORER

RX HELIX

Action: Straight-pull bolt
Stock: Walnut
Barrel: 20 in., 22 in., 24 in.
Sights: Fixed fiber optic
Weight: 6 lb. 6 oz.
Caliber: .222 Rem., .223 Rem., .243 Win., .270 Win., .300 Win. Mag., .308 Win., 6.5x55 Swedish, 7mm Rem. Mag., 7x64 Brenneke, .30-06 Spfd., 8x57 IS, 9.3x62 Mauser
Magazine: Detachable box, 3, 5 rounds
Features: Fully enclosed action with integral rail; interchangeable barrels and mags for tool-free caliber change in 60 seconds; tang-mounted safety; aluminum action; Weaver mounting rail; European walnut stock; manual cocking system; Elastomer recoil pad; checkering on forend and pistol grip
MSRP. . . . . **$3785.00–$4585.00**

RX HELIX EXPLORER

Action: Straight-pull bolt
Stock: Synthetic
Barrel: 20 in., 22 in., 24 in.
Sights: Fixed fiber optic
Weight: 6 lb.–6 lb. 3 oz.
Caliber: .222 Rem., .223 Rem., 6.5x55 Swedish, .270 Win., 7x64 Brenneke, .308 Win, .30-06 Spfd., 8x57 IS, 9.3x62 Mauser, 7mm Rem. Mag., .300 Win. Mag.
Magazine: Detachable box, 3, 5 rounds
Features: Fully enclosed action with integral rail; interchangeable barrels and mags for tool-free caliber change in 60 seconds; tang-mounted safety; aluminum action; Weaver rail; manual cocking system; Elastomer recoil pad
MSRP. **$2995.00**

Montana Rifle Company

MONTANA RIFLE COMPANY AMERICAN LEGENDS RIFLE (ALR)

AMERICAN LEGENDS RIFLE (ALR)

Action: Bolt
Stock: Black walnut
Barrel: 24 in.
Sights: None
Weight: 7 lb. 2 oz.–7 lb. 5 oz.
Caliber: .243 Win., .25-06 Rem., 6.5 Creedmoor, 6.5 PRC, .270 Win., .270 WSM, .275 Rigby, 7mm Rem. Mag., .300 Win. Mag., .300 WSM, .308 Win., .30-06 Spfd., .338 Win. Mag.
Magazine: N/A
Features: Raised cheekpiece; AA black walnut stock; black forend tip and grip cap; wrap-around checkering; barrel is free-floated, button rifled, and hand-lapped; glass bedded and sports control round feed action; Mauser-style ejector; three-position safety; right or left hand; blue or stainless steel finish
MSRP. . . . . **starting at $1699.00**

Montana Rifle Company

MONTANA RIFLES COLORADO BUCK EDITION (CBE)

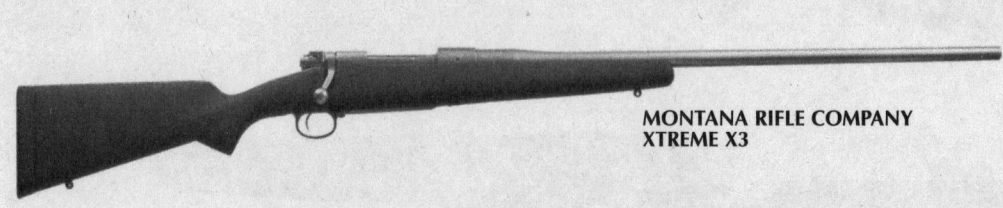

MONTANA RIFLE COMPANY XTREME X3

COLORADO BUCK EDITION (CBE)

Action: Bolt
Stock: Carbon fiber
Barrel: 24 in.
Sights: Leupold VX-6 1–6x24mm CDS turret with Warne ringmounts
Weight: 6 lb. 10 oz.–9 lb. 11 oz.
Caliber: 6.5 Creedmoor, 7mm Rem. Mag., .300 WSM, .308 Win., .338 Norma, .338 Lapua, .375 H&H Mag., .505 Gibbs
Magazine: N/A
Features: satin finished stainless barrel in Tungsten Grey Cerakote with Montana Flats muzzle brake; MRC

1999 action or 1999 double square bridge PH action; aluminum and glass pillar bedded; right- and left-hand in short- and long-actions, right-hand only in PH action; adjustable pre-64-style trigger
MSRP . . . . starting at $2547.00

XTREME X3, XTREME ELITE

Action: Bolt
Stock: Synthetic
Barrel: 24 in., 26 in.
Sights: None
Weight: 6 lb. 10 oz.–6 lb. 15 oz.
Caliber: .243 Win., .25-06 Rem., 6.5 Creedmoor, 6.5 PRC, .26 Nosler, 6.5x284 Norma, 257 Roberts, .26 Nosler, .270 Win., .270 WSM, .275

Rigby, .28 Nosler, 7mm-08 Rem., 7mm WSM, 7mm Rem. Mag., .280 Rem., .280 Ackley Improved, .30 Nosler, .300 Win. Mag., .300 WSM, .300 RUM, .308 Win., .30-06 Spfd., .33 Nosler, .338 Win. Mag., .338 RUM
Magazine: N/A
Features: MRC premium synthetic stock; satin stainless free-floating button rifled, hand-lapped barrel; 1999 action with aluminum pillars and glass bedding; adjustable pre-64 type trigger; Elite version gets a threaded muzzle with thread cap and Montana Flats muzzle brake
MSRP . . . . starting at $1599.00

Mossberg (O. F. Mossberg & Sons)

MOSSBERG 464 LEVER-ACTION CENTERFIRE RIFLE

MOSSBERG 464 SPX LEVER-ACTION RIMFIRE RIFLE

464 LEVER-ACTION CENTERFIRE RIFLE

Action: Lever
Stock: Walnut
Barrel: 20 in.
Sights: Adjustable rifle sights or three-dot adjustable fiber optic
Weight: 6 lb. 12 oz.
Caliber: .30-30 Win.
Magazine: Under-barrel tube, 7–14 rounds
Features: Ejection port designed for cases to clear optics, top tang safety are standard; three-dot adjustable

fiber optic sights or adjustable rifle sights; receiver is drilled and tapped for Weaver #403 bases; pistol grip or straight stock; pistol grip has diamond pattern fine-line checkering on the grip and wrapped around edge-to-edge on the forearm
Straight grip: $558.00
PIstol grip: $518.00

464 SPX LEVER-ACTION RIMFIRE RIFLE

Action: Lever
Stock: Synthetic

Barrel: 18 in.
Sights: Rifle sights
Weight: 6 lb.
Caliber: .22 LR
Magazine: Under-barrel tube, 14 rounds
Features: 6-position adjustable stocks; tri-rail forends with rail covers; adjustable fiber optic sights; flash suppressor and muzzlebrake; top-tang safety; dovetail receiver, Picatinny tri-rail fore-end
MSRP $525.00

Mossberg (O. F. Mossberg & Sons)

MOSSBERG 715T FLAT TOP

MOSSBERG 817

MOSSBERG BLAZE-47

MOSSBERG BLAZE AUTOLOADING RIMFIRE RIFLE GREEN DOT

MOSSBERG MMR PRO

MOSSBERG MMR CARBINE

RIFLES

715T FLAT TOP

Action: Semiautomatic
Stock: Synthetic
Barrel: 16.25 in.
Sights: Mounted front, adjustable rear; rail mount and adjustable front and rear; 30mm red-dot
Weight: 5 lb. 8 oz.
Caliber: .22 LR
Magazine: Detachable box, 11 or 26 rounds
Features: Four versions available with a mounted front sight and adjustable rear: fixed 13-in. length of pull black synthetic; A2 adjustable black synthetic stock; A2 adjustable black synthetic stock; A2 adjustable stock in Moonshine Muddy Girl or Muddy Girl Serenity, rail mount, and adjustable front and rear sights; three versions equipped with a 30mm red dot sight, one fixed stock, and two A2 adjustable stocks all in black
Sights only: . . . . . . $326.00–$438.00
Red dot: $373.00

817

Action: Bolt
Stock: Synthetic or wood
Barrel: 21 in.
Sights: None
Weight: 4 lb. 8 oz.–5 lb.
Caliber: .17 HMR
Magazine: Detachable box, 6 rounds
Features: Factory-mounted Weaver-style scope bases; cross-bolt safety and magazine release buttons; free gun lock included; varmint option has

heavier bull barrel and comes only in the Sport Grip configuration
Wood stock: $274.00
Synthetic stock: $275.00

BLAZE-47

Action: Semiautomatic
Stock: Wood or synthetic
Barrel: 16.5 in.
Sights: Adjustable
Weight: 4 lb. 8 oz.–4 lb. 12 oz.
Caliber: .22 LR
Magazine: 10, 25 rounds
Features: AK-47 lookalike in a rimfire; adjustable fiber optic rear sight; wood stock; 10- or 25-round magazine options
MSRP $420.00

BLAZE AUTOLOADING RIMFIRE RIFLE

Action: Semiautomatic
Stock: Synthetic
Barrel: 16.5 in.
Sights: Fixed
Weight: 3 lb. 8 oz.
Caliber: .22 LR
Magazine: 10, 25 rounds
Features: Free-floating 16.5-inch barrels with fixed front sight; 1:16 twist rate; 3/8-inch dovetail for ease of scope mounting; and blue metal finishes; optional sight systems include adjustable rifle rear sight for windage and elevation; barrel-mounted, top Picatinny rail; scoped combos come with a rail-mounted, Dead Ringer Green Dot adjustable sight featuring four optional reticle configurations; vented forends ; Muddy Girl Serenity camo stock with 10-round mag; black stock with choice of 10-round,

25-round, green dot/25-round, or Youth Bantam with 10-round
MSRP . . . . $210.00–$281.00

MMR CARBINE

Action: Semiautomatic
Stock: Synthetic
Barrel: 16.25 in.
Sights: Rail-mounted adjustable
Weight: 6 lb. 12 oz.
Caliber: 5.56mm NATO/.223 Rem.
Magazine: 10 or 30 rounds
Features: Direct-impingement gas system; 13 in. handguard that combines a comfortable, slim profile with the versatile Magpul M-LOK system and a full-length top rail; Magpul MOE polymer trigger guard; 6-position adjustable or optional fixed length-of-pull stock; free-floating, button-rifled, carbon steel barrel; black phosphate/anodized metal finishes for enhanced durability; CA-compliant versions available
MSRP $938.00

MMR PRO

Action: Semiautomatic
Stock: Synthetic
Barrel: 18 in.
Sights: None
Weight: 7 lb.
Caliber: .223 Rem./5.56 NATO, .224 Valkyrie
Magazine: 30 rounds
Features: Designed for 3-Gun competition; full-length direct impingement gas system; 18-in. free floating stainless barrel with M-LOK 15-in. forend; forward assist; ejection port dust cover; six-position stock; interchangeable FLEX pad
MSRP $1393.00

Mossberg (O. F. Mossberg & Sons)

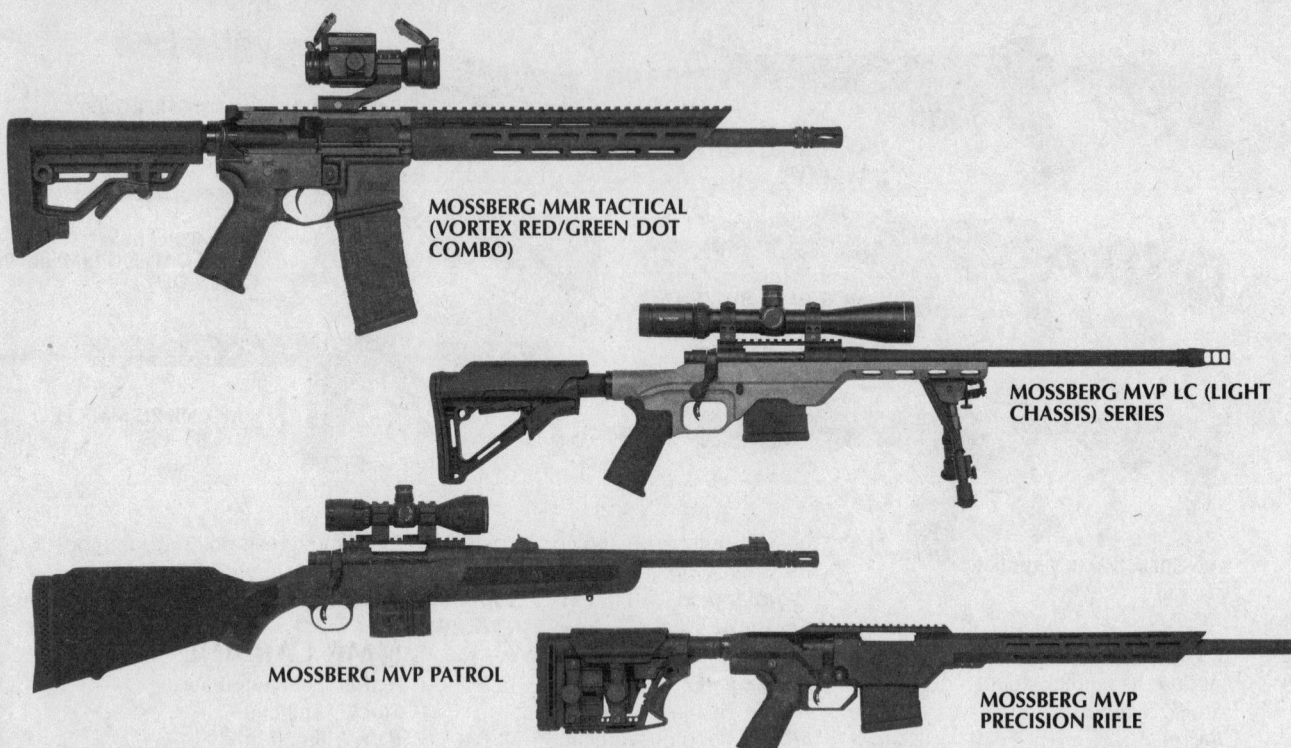

MOSSBERG MMR TACTICAL (VORTEX RED/GREEN DOT COMBO)

MOSSBERG MVP LC (LIGHT CHASSIS) SERIES

MOSSBERG MVP PATROL

MOSSBERG MVP PRECISION RIFLE

MMR TACTICAL (VORTEX RED/GREEN DOT COMBO)

Action: Semiautomatic
Stock: Synthetic
Barrel: 16 in.
Sights: Red/green dot 30mm Vortex optic
Weight: 7 lb.
Caliber: 5.56 NATO/.223
Magazine: 30 rounds
Features: Direct impingement system; phosphate and hard-coat anodized metalwork; barrel gets 13-in. slim forend with M-LOK functionality; JM Pro Drop-In Match Trigger; Magpul MOE grip and trigger guard; an optics-ready version leaves out Vortex scope
MSRP. $1399.00

MVP LC (LIGHT CHASSIS) SERIES

Action: Bolt
Stock: Synthetic
Barrel: 16.25 in., 18.5 in., 22 in.
Sights: None
Weight: 8 lb.–10 lb.
Caliber: 5.56 NATO, 6.5 Creedmoor, 7.62 NATO
Magazine: Detachable box, 11 rounds
Features: Housed in an aluminum,

tan-finished, light chassis stock designed by MDT that provides a modular, ergonomic base; free-floating, medium bull barrel is threaded and comes with a SilencerCo Saker muzzle brake, utilizing the Trifecta quick-detach mounting system (thread cap included); the barrels, constructed of carbon steel, are button-rifled with 16.25-inch length and 1:7 twist rate in the 5.56 NATO (.223 Rem.) chambering and the 7.62 NATO (.308 Win.) sports an 18.5-inch barrel with a 1:10 twist rate; both barrels feature a matte blue finish on all metalwork; Mossberg's Lightning Bolt Action (LBA) Trigger System is user-adjustable from 3 to 7 pounds and is machined from aircraft-grade aluminum and hard-coat anodized to military spec; spiral fluted bolt; oversized tactical-style bolt handle; Picatinny top rail; adjustable bipod; Magpul P-Mag 10-round magazines standard; tan-colored chassis with Magpul accessories added in 2018
MSRP $1050.00

MVP PATROL

Action: Bolt
Stock: Synthetic
Barrel: 16.25 in.
Sights: Adjustable

Weight: 7 lb.–7 lb. 8 oz.
Caliber: 5.56 NATO, 7.62 NATO
Magazine: Detachable box, 10+1 rounds
Features: Picatinny rail; threaded barrel for flash suppressor; Lightning Bolt action adjustable trigger system; Standard Patrol rifles have 16.25-in. barrels and come in black
MSRP. $595.00

MVP PRECISION RIFLE

Action: Bolt
Stock: Aluminum
Barrel: 20 in., 24 in.
Sights: None
Weight: 9 lb. 4 oz. (7.62 NATO), 10 lb. (6.5 Creedmoor)
Caliber: 7.62 NATO, 6.5 Creedmoor, .224 Valkyrie
Magazine: 11 rounds
Features: Mossberg chassis; UTH-AR MBA-3 adjustable stock; Magpul MOE grip; accepts both M1A/M14 and AR10-SR25 magazines; Magpul M-LOK modular mounting system; medium bull barrel is free-floating and threaded; the Mossberg Lightning Trigger System adjusts from three to seven pounds; oversized bolt and trigger guard; 20 MOA Picatinny rail
MSRP. $1407.00

Mossberg (O. F. Mossberg & Sons)

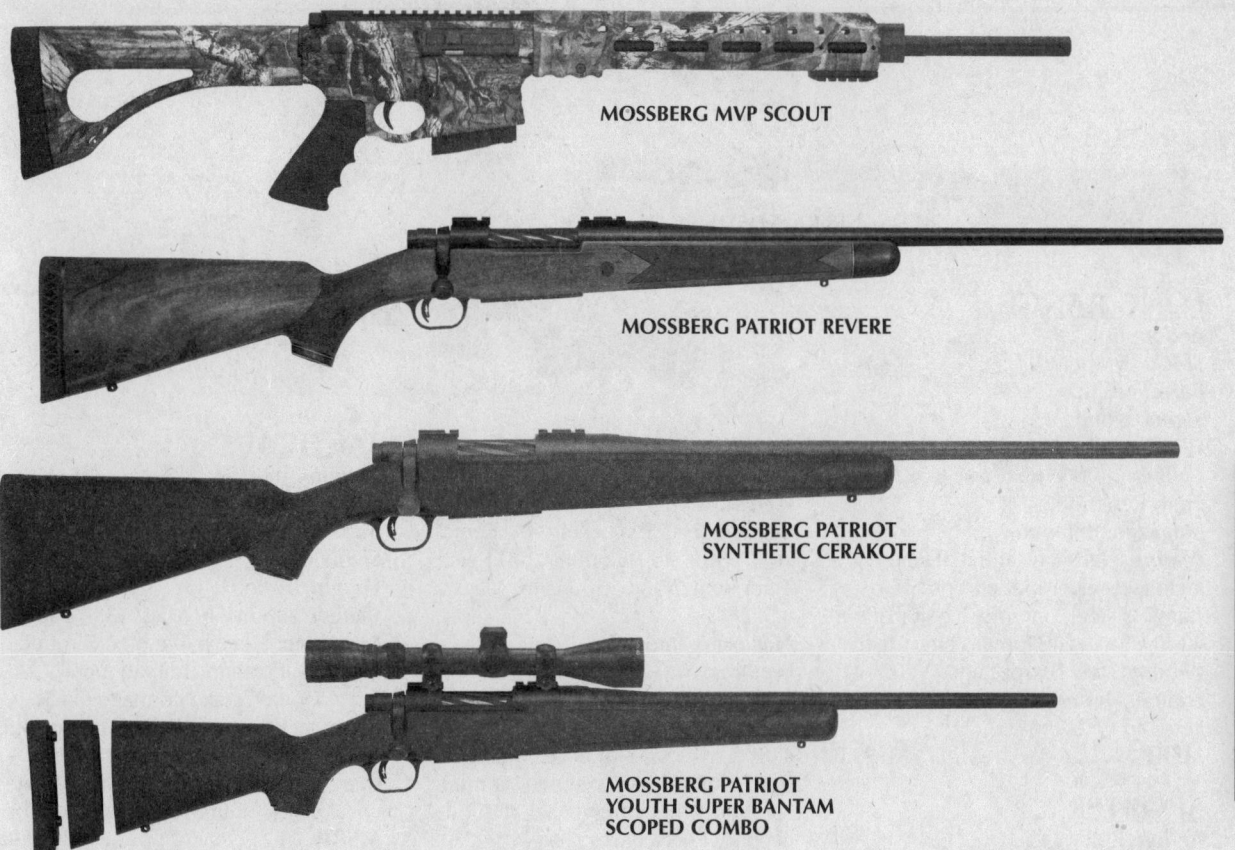

MOSSBERG MVP SCOUT

MOSSBERG PATRIOT REVERE

MOSSBERG PATRIOT
SYNTHETIC CERAKOTE

MOSSBERG PATRIOT
YOUTH SUPER BANTAM
SCOPED COMBO

MVP SCOUT

Action: Bolt
Stock: Synthetic
Barrel: 16.25 in.
Sights: Fiber optic front ghost ring
Weight: 6 lb. 12 oz.
Caliber: 7.62 NATO
Magazine: Detachable box, 11 rounds
Features: Has an 11-inch receiver/barrel-mounted Picatinny rail; an integrated, rail-mounted, Ghost Ring rear sight is paired with a barrel-mounted, fiber optic front sight; two Picatinny side rails, located near the front of the forend; a compact 16 ¼-inch medium bull, carbon steel button-rifled, threaded barrel with an A2-style suppressor, with a 1:10 twist rate; a protective thread cap is provided; an adjustable rifle sling; scoped package includes Vortex 2-7x32 rifle scope
Rifle only: **$623.00**
Vortex scope:. **$780.00**

PATRIOT REVERE

Action: Bolt
Stock: Walnut

Barrel: 24 in.
Sights: None
Weight: 7 lb.
Caliber: 6.5 Creedmoor, .243 Win., .308 Win., .270 Win., .30-06 Spfd., .300 Win. Mag.
Magazine: 4, 5 rounds
Features: Grade #2 European walnut stocks; rosewood forend tip; maple grip spacers; soft-polished blue finishes; flush-mount polymer box magazines; Lightning Bolt Action Trigger System; fine-line checkering; spiral-fluted bolts; checkered bolt handles; Weaver-style bases
MSRP **$823.00**

PATRIOT SYNTHETIC CERAKOTE

Action: Bolt
Stock: Synthetic
Barrel: 22 in.
Sights: None; adjustable
Weight: 6 lb. 8 oz.
Caliber: 6.5 Creedmoor, .243 Win., .308 Win., 7mm-08 Rem., .270 Win., .30-06 Spfd., .22-250 Rem., .25-06 Rem., 7mm Rem. Mag., .300 Win.

Mag., .338 Win. Mag., .375 Ruger
Magazine: 5 rounds
Features: Cerakote Stainless with black synthetic stocks; button-rifled, carbon steel, free-floating fluted barrel; Weaver-style optics bases; spiral-fluted bolts; the Lightning Bolt Action Trigger System
No sights: **$440.00**
Adjustable sights: **$461.00**

PATRIOT YOUTH SUPER BANTAM SCOPED COMBO

Action: Bolt
Stock: Synthetic
Barrel: 20 in.
Sights: 3-9x40mm scope
Weight: 7 lb. 8 oz.
Caliber: .243 Win., 6.5 Creedmoor, 7mm-08 Rem., .308 Win., .243 Win.
Magazine: 5 rounds
Features: Adjustable stock; fluted matte blue barrel; stock in black or choice of Muddy Girl Serenity or Strata camo
MSRP . . . . **$436.00–$473.00**

Nesika

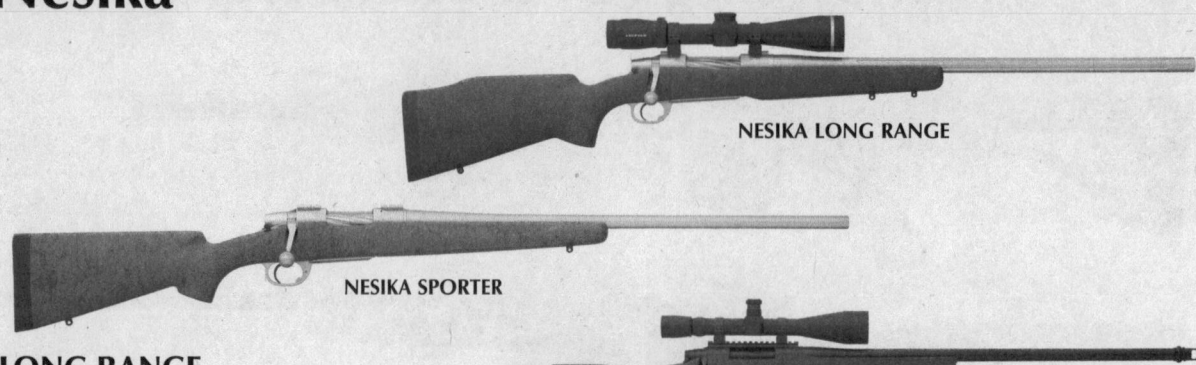

NESIKA LONG RANGE

NESIKA SPORTER

NESIKA TACTICAL

LONG RANGE

Action: Bolt
Stock: Synthetic
Barrel: 26 in.
Sights: None
Weight: 9 lb. 12 oz.
Caliber: .300 Win. Mag., 6.5x284, 7mm Rem. Mag.
Magazine: Internal
Features: Nesika stainless Hunter action; receiver made from 15-5 stainless steel; one-piece bolt from 4340 CM steel; Douglas air-gauged stainless steel barrel; fluted Varmint contour; Timney trigger set at a 3 lbs.; Leupold QRW bases
MSRP $3999.00

SPORTER

Action: Bolt
Stock: Synthetic

Barrel: 24 in., 26 in.
Sights: None
Weight: 8 lb.
Caliber: .260 Rem., 7mm-08 Rem., .308 Win., .30-06 Spfd., .280 Rem., 7mm Rem. Mag., .300 Win. Mag., 6.5x284
Magazine: Internal
Features: Nesika stainless Hunter action; receiver made from 15-5 stainless steel; one-piece bolt from 4340 CM steel; Douglas air-gauged stainless steel barrel; fluted Varmint contour; Timney trigger set at a 3 lbs.; Leupold QRW bases
MSRP $3499.00

TACTICAL

Action: Bolt
Stock: Synthetic
Barrel: 26 in., 28 in.
Sights: None
Weight: 13 lb. 12 oz.
Caliber: .300 Win. Mag., .338 Lapua
Magazine: Detachable box, 5 rounds
Features: Picatinny rail; all metal coated with Cerakoted matte black finish; tactical hand laid-up composite stock with aluminum bedding block, spacer adjuster system, and adjustable cheekpiece; Timney trigger set at 3 lbs.
MSRP $4499.00

New Ultra Light Arms

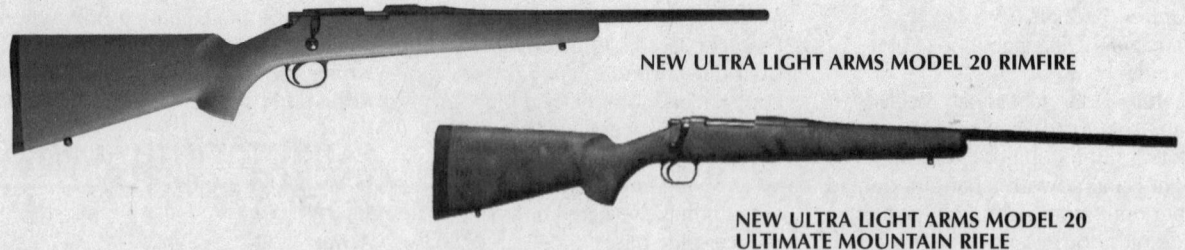

NEW ULTRA LIGHT ARMS MODEL 20 RIMFIRE

NEW ULTRA LIGHT ARMS MODEL 20 ULTIMATE MOUNTAIN RIFLE

MODEL 20 RIMFIRE

Action: Bolt
Stock: Kevlar/graphite composite
Barrel: 22 in.
Sights: None
Weight: 5 lb. 4 oz.
Caliber: .22 LR
Magazine: None or detachable box, 5 rounds
Features: Single-shot or repeater; drilled and tapped for scope; recoil

pad; sling swivels; color stock options; left-hand models available for no extra charge
Single shot: $1800.00
Repeater: $1850.00

MODEL 20 ULTIMATE MOUNTAIN RIFLE

Action: Bolt
Stock: Kevlar/graphite composite
Barrel: 22 in.

Sights: None
Weight: 5 lb.
Caliber: .308 Win., .243 Win., 6mm Rem., .257 Roberts, 7mm-08, .284 Win.
Magazine: Detachable box
Features: Available in left-hand; choice of stock colors; 20-oz. action; two-position safety
MSRP $3500.00
Left-hand: $3600.00

RIFLES

Nosler

NOSLER M48 CUSTOM RIFLE

NOSLER M48 HERITAGE

NOSLER M48 LONG-RANGE

NOSLER M48 LONG-RANGE CARBON

M48 CUSTOM RIFLE

Action: Bolt
Stock: Walnut
Barrel: 24 in., 24.75 in.
Sights: Open
Weight: 8 lb. 4 oz.–8 lb. 12 oz.
Caliber: .30 Nosler, .300 WSM, .280 Ack. Imp., .338 Win. Mag.
Magazine: Internal, 3, 4 rounds
Features: Leupold Custom Shop; match-grade stainless, fully free-floated hand lapped barrel; three-stage safety; glass pillar-bedded fancy walnut stock; custom case cruzer by Pelican; custom leather sling
MSRP . . . . starting at $2595.00

M48 HERITAGE

Action: Bolt
Stock: Wood
Barrel: 24 in.–26 in.
Sights: None
Weight: 7 lb. 4 oz.–7 lb. 13 oz.
Caliber: .22 Nosler, .243 Win., 6.5 Creedmoor, 6.5-284 Norma, .26 Nosler, .270 Win., .280 AI, 7mm Rem. Mag., .28 Nosler, .308 Win., .30-06 Spfd., .300 WSM, .300 Win. Mag., .30 Nosler, .338 Win. Mag., .33 Nosler
Magazine: N/A
Features: Nosler Model 48 Custom action; stainless match-grade barrel; fancy walnut stock with heckering; hinged floor-plate; two-position Rocker safety; Cerakote all-weather finish
MSRP $2035.00

M48 LONG-RANGE

Action: Bolt
Stock: Manners MCS-T
Barrel: 26 in.
Sights: None
Weight: N/A
Caliber: 6.5 Creedmoor, .26 Nosler, .28 Nosler, .300 Win. Mag., .30 Nosler, .33 Nosler
Magazine: 3, 4 rounds
Features: Custom Nosler 48 bedded action; aluminum pillars; free-floating Shilen stainless steel barrel; machined action rails; single stage Timney trigger
MSRP $2675.00

NOSLER M48 LONG-RANGE CARBON

Action: Bolt
Stock: Carbon Fiber
Barrel: 26 in.
Sights: None
Weight: 7 lb.
Caliber: 6.5 Creedmoor, .26 Nosler, .28 Nosler, .300 Win. Mag., .30 Nosler, .33 Nosler
Magazine: 3, 4 rounds
Features: Proof Research carbon-fiber-wrapped match-grade barrel; Manners MCS carbon-fiber stock in Elite Midnight Camo; action and bottom metal in Cerakote Sniper Grey; glass and aluminum pillar bedding; threaded muzzle; muzzle brake is available
MSRP $3190.00

Noveske

Features: Noveske's Gen III rifles come in a wide variety of barrel lengths, handguard and stock configurations, rails, and sight options. Current Gen III models includes OMW (One More Wave); Light Recce; Diplomat; Switchblock; 6.5 Grendel; Varmageddon; N6; Afghan; Infidel; Leonidas Switchblock N6; Leonidas Switchblock
MSRP . . . . $2350.00–$4175.00

NOVESKE GEN 3 SERIES

GEN 3 SERIES

Action: Semiautomatic
Stock: Synthetic
Barrel: 7.5 in.–18 in.
Sights: Adjustable
Weight: N/A
Caliber: .300 BLK, 5.56 NATO, 6.5 Creedmoor, 6.5 Grendel; .22 Nosler, 7.62X51 NATO,
Magazine: Detachable box, 30 rounds

Patriot Ordnance Factory

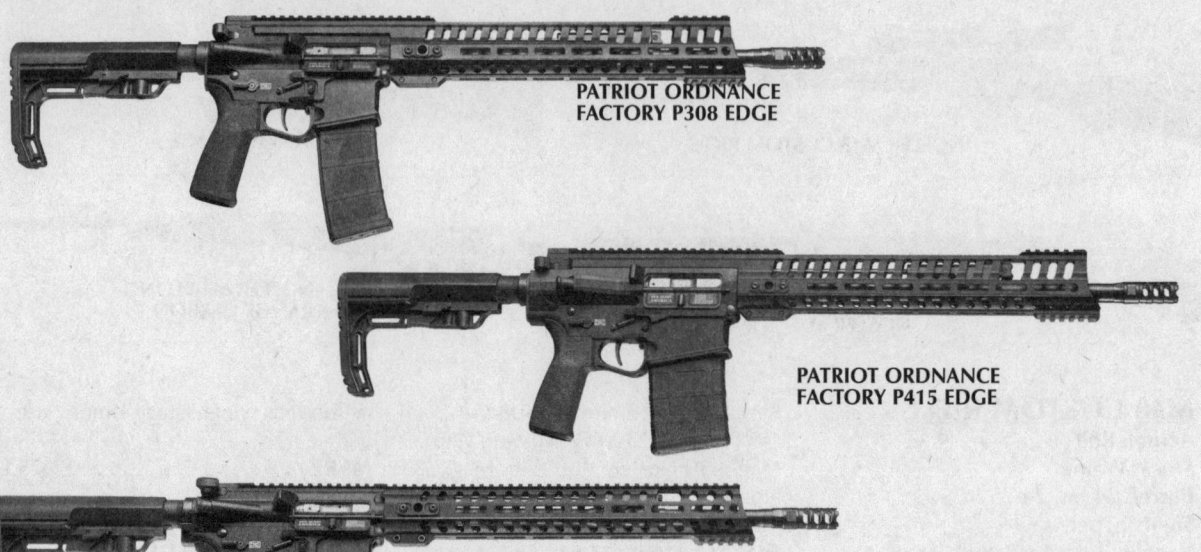

PATRIOT ORDNANCE FACTORY P308 EDGE

PATRIOT ORDNANCE FACTORY P415 EDGE

PATRIOT ORDNANCE FACTORY RENEGADE PLUS

PATRIOT ORDNANCE FACTORY REVOLUTION

P308 EDGE

Action: Semiautomatic
Stock: Synthetic
Barrel: 16.5 in.
Sights: None
Weight: 8 lb. 4 oz.
Caliber: .308 Win.
Magazine: N/A
Features: Short-stroke gas piston action; five-position adjustable gas block; nitride heat-treated barrel; 14 ½-in. M-LOK rail; triple port muzzle break; seven-position anti-tilt buffer tube; chrome-plated bolt; Mission First Tactical furniture; E2 Dual Extraction Technology chamber; POF drop-in trigger group; black, NP3, Burnt Bronze, and Tungsten finishes
MSRP . . . . **$2399.99–$2549.99**

P415 EDGE

Action: Semiautomatic
Stock: Synthetic
Barrel: 16.5 in.
Sights: None
Weight: 7 lb.
Caliber: 5.56 NATO, .300 Blackout
Magazine: N/A
Features: Short-stroke gas piston action; nitride heat-treated barrel; 14 ½-in. M-LOK rail; triple port muzzle break; six-position anti-tilt buffer tube; chrome-plated bolt; Mission First Tactical furniture; E2 Dual Extraction Technology chamber; POF drop-in trigger group; black, NP3, Burnt Bronze, and Tungsten finishes
MSRP . . . . **$1999.99–$2149.99**

RENEGADE PLUS

Action: Semiautomatic
Stock: Synthetic
Barrel: 16.5 in. (5.56 NATO), 18.5 in. (.223 Wylde)
Sights: None
Weight: 6 lb. 6 oz. (5.56 NATO), 7 lb. 11 oz. (.223 Wylde)
Caliber: 5.56 NATO, .300 Blackout
Magazine: Detachable box
Features: M-LOK compatible Renegade rail; heat sink barrel nut; Dictator 9-position adjustable gas block with straight gas tube; nitride heat-treated barrel; Gen 4 POF-USA ambidextrous billet lower receiver and POF-USA Ultimate Bolt Carrier Group; flat 3.5 lb match-grade trigger with KNS Precision anti-walk pins; NP3 coated for maximum protection and reliability; integrated gas key (no screws required)
MSRP . . . . **$1899.99–$1999.99**

REVOLUTION

Action: Semiautomatic
Stock: Synthetic
Barrel: 14.5, 16.5. 20 in.
Sights: None
Weight: 7 lb. 4 oz.–9 lb. 4 oz.
Caliber: .308 Win., 6.5 Creedmoor
Magazine: N/A
Features: A .308/6.5 Creedmoor that handles like a 5.56; Edge handguard with four built-in QD mounts; five-position gas operating system; single stage match grade trigger; 6.5 Creedmoor available in 20-inch barrel only; both calibers available in black or burnt bronze finishes
MSRP . . . . **$2669.00–$2729.99**

Primary Weapons Systems

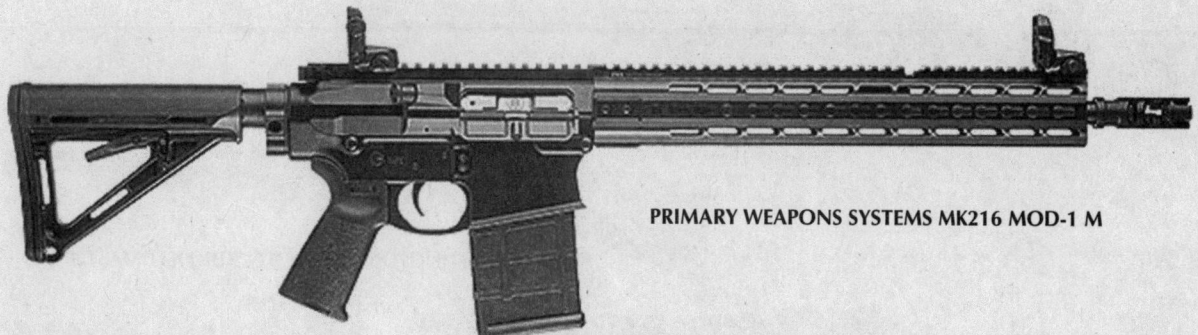

PRIMARY WEAPONS SYSTEMS MK216 MOD-1 M

MK216 MOD-1 M
Action: Semiautomatic
Stock: Synthetic
Barrel: 16 in.
Sights: Adjustable

Weight: 8 lb. 10 oz.
Caliber: .308 Win., 7.62 NATO
Magazine: Detachable box, 10 or 20 rounds
Features: FSC muzzle brake and

suppressor; Picatinny rail; adjustable stock
MSRP.................**$2199.95**

Proof Research

PROOF RESEARCH SWITCH

SWITCH
Action: Bolt
Stock: Synthetic
Barrel: 20 in., 24 in.
Sights: None
Weight: 6 lb. 12 oz.–7 lb. 4 oz.
Caliber: .223 Rem., 6.5 Creedmoor, 6mm Creedmoor, .260 Rem., .308 Win., base calibers carbon fiber bar-

rels; .22-250 Rem., .223 Rem., .243 Win., .260 Rem., .308 Win., 6.6 Creedmoor, 6mm Creedmoor, 7mm-08 Rem. in additional carbon fiber or steel barrels
Magazine: 5 rounds
Features: User can switch out one of four carbon fiber base barrels with other barrels of short-action caliber,

requiring only a change in the bolt face, not the entire bolt; additional barrels from Proof Research are available in carbon fiber or steel; carbon fiber stock; TriggerTech adjustable trigger; Big Horn Arms bolt with a mechanical ejector; 20-MOA Picatinny rail; threaded muzzle
MSRP.................**$3999.99**

PTR Industries

PTR INDUSTRIES 32 KFR PTR 200

32 KFR PTR 200
Action: Semiautomatic
Stock: Synthetic
Barrel: 16 in.
Sights: Fixed
Weight: 9 lb. 5 oz.

Caliber: 7.62X39
Magazine: 10, 30 rounds
Features: H&K Navy-type polymer trigger group housing, HK 91-length handguards, cocking tube, welded scope mount, paddle magazine

release, delayed blowback roller lock system are standard; now with 5/8-24 barrel threading.
MSRP.........**$1336.00–$1418.00**

Remington Arms Company

REMINGTON MODEL 552 BDL SPEEDMASTER

REMINGTON MODEL 572 BDL FIELDMASTER

REMINGTON MODEL 597 HB

REMINGTON MODEL 597
MOSSY OAK PINK

REMINGTON MODEL
597 SYNTHETIC

MODEL 552 BDL SPEEDMASTER

Action: Semiautomatic
Stock: Walnut
Barrel: 22 in.
Sights: Open
Weight: 5 lb. 12 oz.
Caliber: .22 S, L, LR
Magazine: Under-barrel tube
Features: Adjustable iron sights for open sight plinking; grooved receiver for scope mounts; high-gloss American walnut stock and forend checkering; richly blued carbon-steel barrel; positive cross-bolt safety
MSRP $707.00

MODEL 572 BDL FIELDMASTER

Action: Pump
Stock: Walnut
Barrel: 21 in.
Sights: Open
Weight: 5 lb. 12 oz.
Caliber: .22 S, L, LR
Magazine: Under-barrel tube
Features: Smooth classic side action; high-gloss American walnut stock and forend with cut checkering; richly blued carbon-steel barrel; adjustable iron sights for open slight plinking;

receiver grooved for scope mounts; positive cross-bolt safety
MSRP $723.00

MODEL 597 HB

Action: Semiautomatic
Stock: Synthetic
Barrel: 22 in.
Sights: None
Weight: 5 lb. 12 oz.
Caliber: .22 LR
Magazine: Detachable clip, 10 rounds
Features: Heavy barrel with rugged green synthetic stock; bolt-guidance system features twin tool-steel guide rails; Teflon nickel plated sear and hammer; patented drop-out staggered stack, detachable metal magazine; last-shot "hold open" bolt; scope rail
MSRP $254.00

MODEL 597 PINK CAMO, KRYPTEK THREADED

Action: Semiautomatic
Stock: Synthetic
Barrel: 20 in.
Sights: Fiber optic front
Weight: 5 lb. 8 oz.
Caliber: .22 LR
Magazine: Detachable box, 10

rounds
Features: Matte blue barrel with Mossy Oak Pink synthetic stock; bolt-guidance system features twin tool-steel guide rails; Teflon nickel plated sear and hammer; patented drop-out staggered stack, detachable metal magazine; last-shot "hold open" bolt; scope rail
MSRP $306.00

597 SYNTHETIC

Action: Semiautomatic
Stock: Synthetic
Barrel: 22 in.
Sights: Open
Weight: 5 lb. 8 oz.
Caliber: .22 LR, .22 WMR
Magazine: Detachable clip, 10 rounds
Features: Bolt-guidance system features twin, tool-steel guide rails; sear and hammer are Teflon/nickel-plated; non-glare matte finish; adjustable big game iron sights; last-shot "hold open" bolt for added safety
MSRP . . . . $213.00–$257.00

Remington Arms Company

REMINGTON MODEL 700 ADL 200TH ANNIVERSARY OMMEMORATIVE

REMINGTON MODEL 700 AWR (AMERICAN WILDERNESS RIFLE)

REMINGTON MODEL 700 BDL

REMINGTON MODEL 700 CDL

REMINGTON MODEL 700 CDL SF

MODEL 700 ADL 200TH ANNIVERSARY COMMEMORATIVE

Action: Bolt
Stock: Walnut
Barrel: 24 in., 26 in.
Sights: Fixed
Weight: 7 lb. 6 oz.–7 lb. 10 oz.
Caliber: .243 Win., .270 Win., .30-06 Spfd., .300 Win. Mag.
Magazine: 3 or 4 rounds
Features: A-grade walnut stock with fleur de lis checkering; medallion in grip; X-Mark Pro externally adjustable trigger
MSRP **$695.00**

MODEL 700 AWR (AMERICAN WILDERNESS RIFLE)

Action: Bolt
Stock: Grayboe fiberglass composite
Barrel: 24 in.
Sights: None
Weight: 7 lb. 6 oz.
Caliber: .270 Win., .30-06 Spfd., 7mm Rem., Mag., .300 Win. Mag., .300 RUM, .338 RUM
Magazine: 3, 4 rounds
Features: Black Cerakote finish on a free-floated 5R rifled barrel; stainless steel action; X-Mark Pro trigger is externally adjustable
MSRP **$1150.00**

MODEL 700 BDL

Action: Bolt
Stock: Walnut
Barrel: 22 in., 24 in.
Sights: Open
Weight: 7 lb. 4 oz.–7 lb. 8 oz.
Caliber: .243 Win., .270 Win., .30-06 Spfd., 7mm Rem. Mag.
Magazine: Internal
Features: Adjustable X-Mark Pro Trigger system; walnut stock with black forend cap; Monte Carlo comb with raised cheekpiece and skipline cut checkering; hinged magazine floor plate; sling swivel studs; hooded ramp front sight and adjustable rear sight; cylindrical receiver machined from solid-steel bar
MSRP . . . . **$994.00–$1024.00**

MODEL 700 CDL

Action: Bolt
Stock: Walnut
Barrel: 24 in., 26 in.
Sights: None
Weight: 7 lb. 5 oz.–7 lb. 10 oz.
Caliber: .243 Win., .25-06 Rem., .270 Win., 7mm-08 Rem., 7mm Rem. Mag., .300 Win. Mag., .30-06 Spfd.
Magazine: Internal
Features: Adjustable X-Mark Pro Trigger system; cylindrical receiver machined from solid-steel bar stock; walnut stock with oil finish
MSRP . . . . **$1029.00–$1059.00**

MODEL 700 CDL SF

Action: Bolt
Stock: American walnut
Barrel: 22 in., 24 in., 26 in.
Sights: None
Weight: 7 lb. 6 oz.–7 lb. 10 oz.
Caliber: 6.5 Creedmoor, .257 Wby. Mag., .270 Win., .270 WSM, 7mm-08 Rem., 7mm Rem. Mag., .30-06 Spfd., .300 WSM, .25-06 Rem.
Magazine: 3, 4 rounds
Features: Recessed bolt face; counterbored breech; integral extractor; externally adjustable trigger; 416 stainless steel fluted barrel
MSRP . . . . **$1180.00–$1272.00**

Remington Arms Company

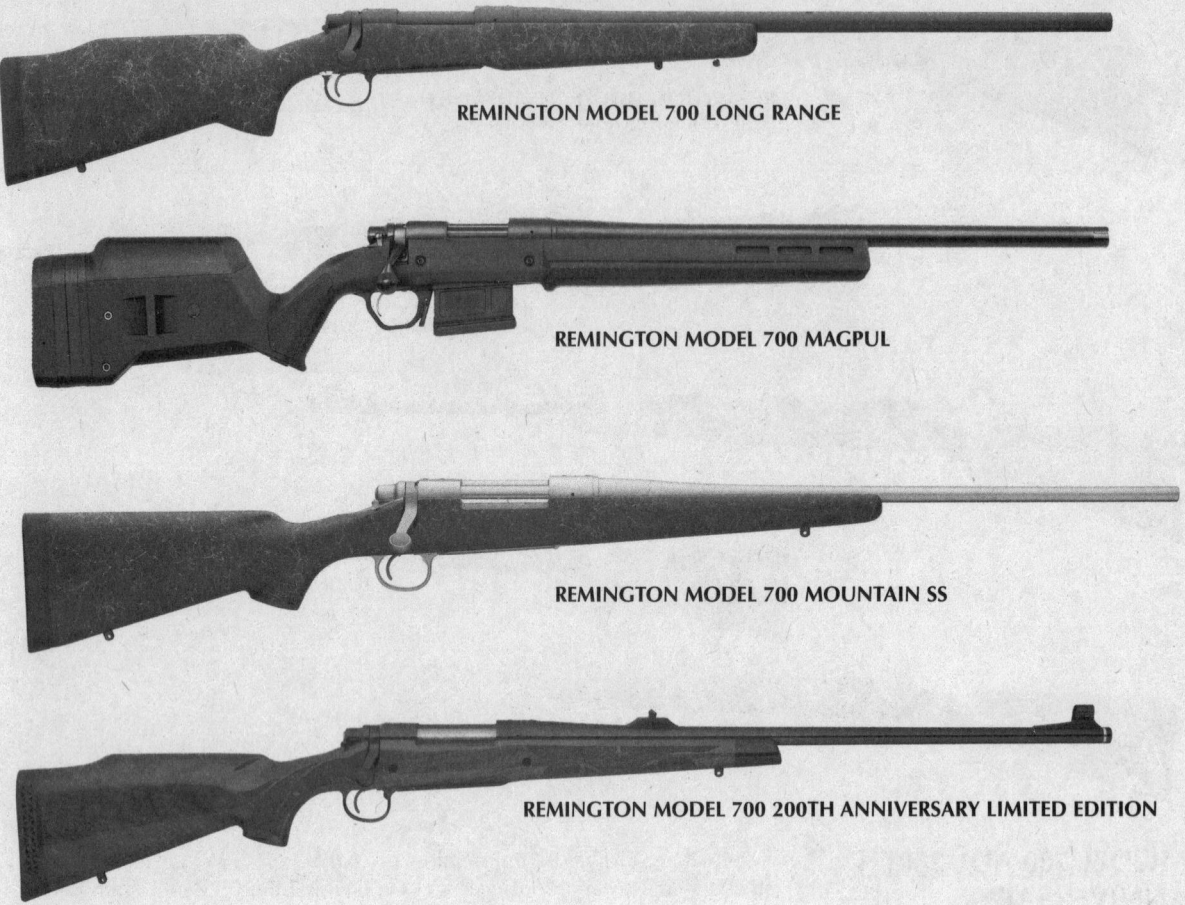

REMINGTON MODEL 700 LONG RANGE

REMINGTON MODEL 700 MAGPUL

REMINGTON MODEL 700 MOUNTAIN SS

REMINGTON MODEL 700 200TH ANNIVERSARY LIMITED EDITION

MODEL 700 LONG RANGE

Action: Bolt
Stock: Synthetic
Barrel: 26 in.
Sights: None
Weight: 9 lb.
Caliber: .25-06 Rem., .30-06 Spfd., .300 Rem. Ultra Mag., .300 Win. Mag., 7mm Rem. Mag.
Magazine: Internal, 4 or 3 (Mag.) rounds
Features: Bell and Carlson M40 tactical stock; heavy varmint barrel with matte finish; X-Mark Pro externally adjustable trigger system
MSRP.................**$879.76**

MODEL 700 MAGPUL

Action: Bolt
Stock: Magpul
Barrel: 22 in.
Sights: None
Weight: 8 lb. 12 oz.
Caliber: .260 Rem., .308 Win., 6.5 Creedmoor, .300 Win. Mag.
Magazine: 5 rounds
Features: Reinforced polymer Magpul

Hunter stock with anodized aluminum bedding block; adjustable length of pull kit; comb height adjustment inserts; detachable magazine; carbon fiber threaded steel barrel with Cerakote finish
MSRP.................**$1175.00**

MODEL 700 MOUNTAIN SS

Action: Bolt
Stock: Synthetic
Barrel: 22 in.
Sights: Drilled and tapped for scopes
Weight: 6 lb. 8 oz.
Caliber: .25-06 Rem., .270 Win., .280 Rem., .30-06 Spfd., 7mm-08 Rem., .308 Win.
Magazine: Internal
Features: Bell & Carson aramid fiber reinforced stock; X-Mark Pro trigger system; cylindrical receiver design; sling swivel studs; stainless steel barrel and action; hinged magazine floor plate
MSRP.................**$1152.00**

MODEL 700 200TH ANNIVERSARY LIMITED EDITION

Action: Bolt
Stock: Walnut
Barrel: 24 in.
Sights: Fixed
Weight: 7 lb. 8 oz.
Caliber: 7mm Rem. Mag.
Magazine: 3 rounds
Features: C-grade walnut stock with fleur de lis checkering; classic American-style engraving and 24k gold inlay portraying founder Eliphalet Remington; steel floorplate; medallion in grip; limited to quantity of 2016; special serial number; New England custom sights; custom box
MSRP.................**$2399.00**

Remington Arms Company

REMINGTON MODEL 700 SENDERO SF II

REMINGTON MODEL 700 SPS LEFT-HAND

REMINGTON MODEL 700 SPS CAMO

REMINGTON ARMS MODEL 700 SPS COMPACT

REMINGTON ARMS MODEL 700 SPS STAINLESS

RIFLES

MODEL 700 SENDERO SF II

Action: Bolt
Stock: Composite
Barrel: 26 in.
Sights: None
Weight: 8 lb. 8 oz.
Caliber: .25-06 Rem., .264 Win. Mag., 7mm Rem. Mag., .300 Win. Mag., .300 Rem. Ultra Mag.
Magazine: Internal
Features: Composite stock in black with gray webbing, reinforced with aramid fibers; features contoured beavertail forend with ambidextrous finger grooves and palm swells; heavy contour barrels are fluted for rapid cooling; full-length aluminum bedding stocks; twin front swivel studs for sling and bipod; concave target-style barrel crown
MSRP.................**$1502.00**

MODEL 700 SPS

Action: Bolt
Stock: Synthetic
Barrel: 24 in., 26 in.
Sights: None
Weight: 7 lb.–7 lb. 10 oz.
Caliber: .223 Rem., .243 Win., .260 Rem., .270 Win., .270 WSM, 7mm-08 Rem., 7mm Rem. Mag., .30-06 Spfd., .300 WSM, .300 Win. Mag., .308 Win., .300 RUM, 6.5 Creedmoor
Magazine: Internal box
Features: Black ergonomic synthetic stock; carbon steel sight drilled and tapped for scope mounts; exterior metal-work features matte blued finish; hinged floor plate; swivel studs
MSRP.................**$731.00**

MODEL 700 SPS CAMO

Action: Bolt
Stock: Synthetic
Barrel: 20 in., 22 in., 24 in.
Sights: None
Weight: 7 lb.–7 lb. 6 oz.
Caliber: .270 Win., .30-06 Spfd., 7mm Rem. Mag., .300 Win. Mag.
Magazine: None
Features: Hammer-forged barrel; X-Mark Pro externally adjustable trigger system; SuperCell recoil pad; synthetic stock in Mossy Oak Break-Up Infinity pattern; Hogue over-molded grips; receivers tapped and drilled
MSRP.................**$809.00**

MODEL 700 SPS COMPACT

Action: Bolt
Stock: Synthetic
Barrel: 20 in.
Sights: None
Weight: 7 lb.
Caliber: .243 Win., 7mm-08 Rem.
Magazine: 4 rounds
Features: Available in right- and left-handed; drilled and tapped for scope mounts; X-Mark Pro adjustable trigger; length of pull less than 12.5 in.
MSRP.................**$731.00**

MODEL 700 SPS STAINLESS

Action: Bolt
Stock: Synthetic
Barrel: 24 in., 26 in.
Sights: None
Weight: 7 lb. 4 oz.–7 lb. 10 oz.
Caliber: .223 Rem., .22-250 Rem., .243 Win., .25-06 Rem., .270 Win., .270 WSM, 7mm-08 Rem., 7mm Rem. Mag., 7mm Rem. Ultra Mag., .30-06 Spfd., .300 WSM, .300 Win. Mag., .308 Win., .300 Rem. Ultra Mag.
Magazine: 3, 4, 5 rounds
Features: All-weather stainless steel barrel and receiver bead-blasted to cut down reflection; drilled and tapped; swivel studs; overmolded grip panels; X-Mark Pro adjustable trigger
MSRP.................**$838.00**

Remington Arms Company

REMINGTON MODEL 700 SPS TACTICAL

REMINGTON MODEL 700 SPS TACTICAL AAC-SD

REMINGTON MODEL 700 SPS VARMINT

REMINGTON MODEL 700 TACTICAL CHASSIS

REMINGTON ARMS MODEL 700 VARMINT SF

RIFLES

MODEL 700 SPS TACTICAL

Action: Bolt
Stock: Synthetic
Barrel: 16.5, 20 in.
Sights: None
Weight: 7 lb. 4 oz.–7 lb. 11 oz.
Caliber: .223 Rem., .300 BLK, .308 Win.
Magazine: Detachable box
Features: Ergonomic tactical stock in black; sling swivel studs; carbon steel barrel is drilled and tapped for sights; metal features blued finish; X-Mark Pro adjustable trigger; SuperCell recoil pad; semi-beavertail forend; hinged floor plate
MSRP . . . . **$788.00–$842.00**

MODEL 700 SPS TACTICAL AAC-SD

Action: Bolt
Stock: Synthetic
Barrel: 20 in.
Sights: None
Weight: 7 lb. 5 oz.
Caliber: .308 Win., 6.5 Creedmoor
Magazine: Internal box
Features: Heavy barrel with threaded muzzle; accepts AAC and other threaded flash hiders, muzzlebrakes and suppressors; Hogue overmolded hillier green pillar bedded stock; X-Mark Pro adjustable trigger; optional Leupold Mark IV scope
MSRP **$842.00**

MODEL 700 SPS VARMINT

Action: Bolt
Stock: Synthetic
Barrel: 26 in.
Sights: None
Weight: 8 lb. 8 oz.
Caliber: .204 Ruger, .223 Rem., .22-250 Rem., .243 Win., .308 Win.
Magazine: Internal
Features: Ergonomic black synthetic stock has a vented beavertail forend; non-reflective matte blued finish on barrel and receiver; hinged floor plate; sling swivel studs; drilled and tapped for scope mounts
MSRP **$761.00**

MODEL 700 TACTICAL CHASSIS

Action: Bolt
Stock: Synthetic
Barrel: 24 in., 26 in.
Sights: None
Weight: 11 lb. 12 oz.–12 lb. 4 oz.
Caliber: .300 Win. Mag., .308 Win., .338 Lapua Mag.
Magazine: Detachable box
Features: MDT TAC21 tactical chassis constructed out of aluminum anodized to Mil-Spec Type III; top full-length Picatinny rail; stainless steel barreled action with black cerakote finish; Magpul MAG307 PRS adjustable stock and pistol grip; target tactical bolt handle; AAC 51-T ratchet mount muzzle brake; X-Mark Pro externally adjustable trigger
MSRP . . . . **$2900.00–$3500.00**

MODEL 700 VARMINT SF

Action: Bolt
Stock: Synthetic
Barrel: 26 in.
Sights: None
Weight: 8 lb. 8 oz.
Caliber: .22-250 Rem., .223 Rem., .220 Swift, .308 Win.
Magazine: 4, 5 rounds
Features: Long, heavy-contour fluted barrel with a target-style crown; dual swivel studs up front and one at the rear; SuperCell recoil pad; X-Mark Pro adjustable trigger
MSRP **$991.00**

Remington Arms Company

REMINGTON MODEL 700 VLS

REMINGTON MODEL 700 VTR

REMINGTON ARMS MODEL 700 VTR SS

REMINGTON ARMS MODEL 700 XCR COMPACT TACTICAL

REMINGTON ARMS MODEL 700 XCR TACTICAL

MODEL 700 VLS

Action: Bolt
Stock: Laminate
Barrel: 26 in.
Sights: Target
Weight: 9 lb. 6 oz.
Caliber: .204 Ruger, .22-250 Rem., .223 Rem., .243 Win., .308 Win.
Magazine: Internal
Features: Varmint laminated stock; Monte Carlo cheekpiece; beavertail shape forend; blued, satin finish metal; concave target-style barrel crown
MSRP $1056.00

MODEL 700 VTR

Action: Bolt
Stock: Synthetic
Barrel: 22 in.
Sights: None
Weight: 7 lb. 10 oz.
Caliber: .22-250 Rem., .223 Rem., .260 Rem., .308 Win.
Magazine: Internal
Features: Integral muzzle brake; Picatinny rail; detachable bipod; stainless steel barrel available
MSRP $930.00

MODEL 700 VTR SS

Action: Bolt
Stock: Synthetic
Barrel: 22 in.
Sights: None
Weight: 7 lb. 10 oz.
Caliber: .223 Rem., .308 Win.
Magazine: 4, 5 rounds
Features: Oversized bolt handle; triangular barrel contour; machined-in muzzle brake; top-side Picatinny rail; X-Mark Pro adjustable trigger; bipod included
MSRP $980.00

MODEL 700 XCR COMPACT TACTICAL

Action: Bolt
Stock: Composite
Barrel: 20 in.
Sights: None
Weight: 7 lb. 8 oz.
Caliber: .308 Win.
Magazine: 4 rounds
Features: H.S. Precision Aramid fiber-reinforced stock in O.D. Green; 416 stainless free-floating barrel with LTR-style fluting finished in Black TryNite PVD; four-round magazine with a hinged floorplate; externally adjustable X-Mark Pro trigger
MSRP $1540.00

MODEL 700 XCR TACTICAL

Action: Bolt
Stock: Composite
Barrel: 26 in.
Sights: None
Weight: 8 lb. 8 oz.
Caliber: .308 Win., .300 Win. Mag., .338 Lapua Mag.
Magazine: 3, 4, 5 rounds
Features: Bell & Carlson tactical stock in OD Green and with black webbing; full-length aluminum bedding block and a beavertail forend; barrel is a varmint contour with a dish-style crown; .338 Lapua includes five-round detachable magazine and an OPS, Inc., muzzle brake
.308 Win., .300 Win.Mag.: . . . $1540.00
.338 Lapua: $2515.00

Remington Arms Company

REMINGTON MODEL 783 SCOPED

REMINGTON MODEL 7600

REMINGTON MODEL 7600 200TH
ANNIVERSARY LIMITED EDITION

REMINGTON R-25 GII

REMINGTON MODEL
SEVEN CDL

MODEL 783 SCOPED
Action: Bolt
Stock: Black synthetic
Barrel: 20 in., 22 in., 24 in.
Sights: None
Weight: 8 lb. 4 oz.–8 lb. 10 oz.
Caliber: .22-250 Rem., .223 Rem.,
.243 Win., .270 Win., .30-06 Spfd.,
.300 Win. Mag., .308 Win., 7mm
Rem. Mag., 6.5 Creedmoor
Magazine: 3–5 rounds
Features: CrossFire trigger system;
carbon steel magnum contour button
rifled barrel; pillar-bedded stock and
free-floated barrel; SuperCell recoil
pad; available in Mossy Oak Break-
Up Country in .223, .243, .308, and
.30-06 only; both stock options come
with a pre-mounted and bore-sighted
3-9x40mm scope; 6.5 Creedmoor
available only in camo model
Black:. **$399.00**
Camo: **$451.00**

MODEL 7600
Action: Pump
Stock: Wood
Barrel: 18.5 in., 22 in.
Sights: Open
Weight: 7 lb. 8 oz.
Caliber: .270 Win.,
.30-06 Spfd., .308 Win.
Magazine: Detachable box, 4 rounds
Features: Free-floated barrel; Monte
Carlo walnut stock with satin finish as
standard; metal work has black non-
reflective finish; iron sights and drilled
and tapped receiver for scope
mounts; rotary-bolt lock-up
MSRP. **$918.00**

MODEL 7600 200TH ANNIVERSARY LIMITED EDITION
Action: Pump
Stock: Walnut
Barrel: 22 in.
Sights: Fixed
Weight: 7 lb. 8 oz.
Caliber: .30-06 Spfd.
Magazine: 4 rounds
Features: C-grade walnut stock with
fleur de lis checkering; classic
American-style engraving and 24k
gold inlay portraying founder
Eliphalet Remington; steel floorplate;
medallion in grip; limited to quantity
of 2016; special serial number; New
England custom sights; custom box
MSRP. **$1999.00**

MODEL R-25 GII
Action: Semiautomatic
Stock: Synthetic
Barrel: 18 in.
Sights: None
Weight: 7 lb. 10 oz.
Caliber: 7.62x51mm
Magazine: 4 rounds
Features: Stainless steel, Teflon-coated
barrel, target crown muzzle; fixed,
lightweight stock with SuperCell
Recoil pad, available in Mossy Oak
Breakup Infinity; Hogue pistol grip;
carbon fiber vented free float hand-
guard; two stage match trigger
MSRP. **$1697.00**

MODEL SEVEN CDL
Action: Bolt
Stock: Walnut
Barrel: 20 in.
Sights: Open
Weight: 6 lb. 8 oz.
Caliber: .243 Win., .260 Rem.,
7mm-08 Rem., .308 Win.
Magazine: Internal box
Features: SuperCell recoil pad;
American walnut CDL stock with sat-
in-finished barrel; compact design for
fast handling; cylindrical receiver;
available in Rem. short-action mag-
num and Winchester short magnum
MSRP. **$1039.00**

Remington Arms Company

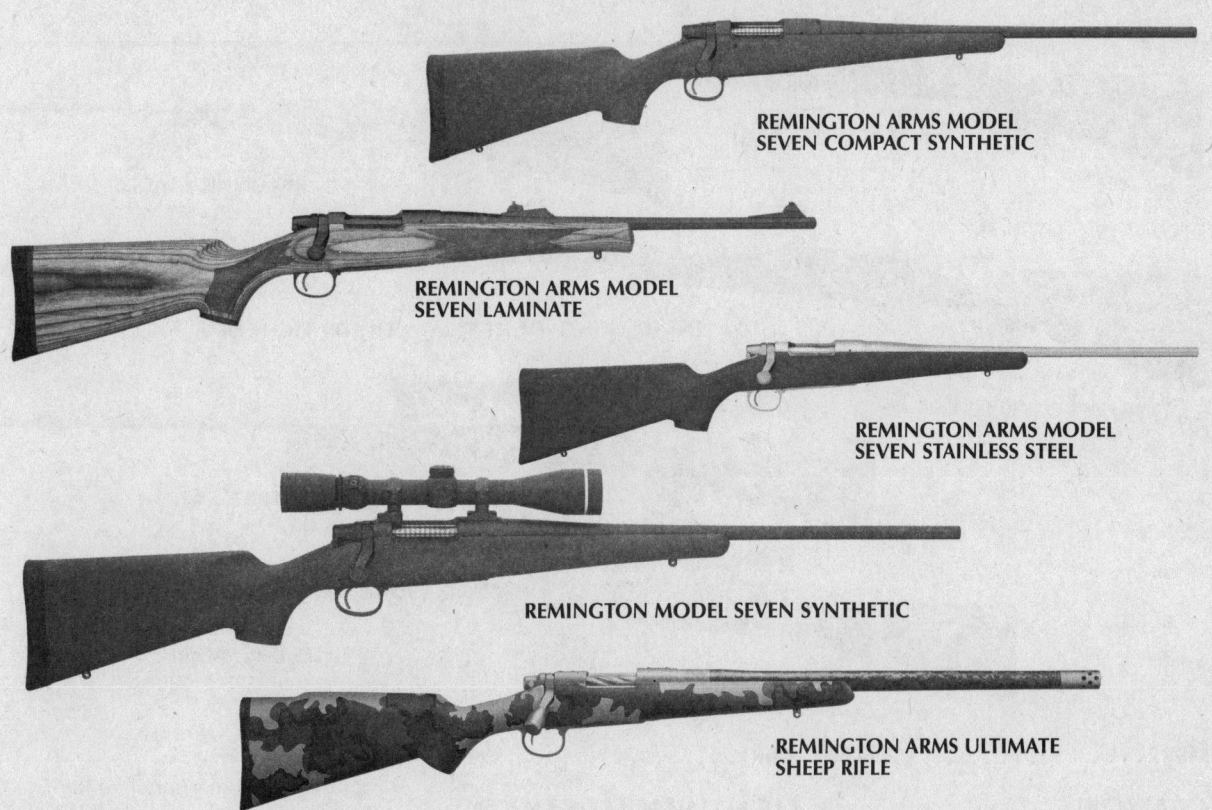

REMINGTON ARMS MODEL SEVEN COMPACT SYNTHETIC

REMINGTON ARMS MODEL SEVEN LAMINATE

REMINGTON ARMS MODEL SEVEN STAINLESS STEEL

REMINGTON MODEL SEVEN SYNTHETIC

REMINGTON ARMS ULTIMATE SHEEP RIFLE

MODEL SEVEN COMPACT SYNTHETIC

Action: Bolt
Stock: Synthetic
Barrel: 18.5 in.
Sights: None
Weight: 6 lb. 2 oz.
Caliber: .243 Win., 7mm-08 Rem.
Magazine: 4 rounds
Features: Compact for easy handling; designed for smaller-statured shooters; X-Mark Pro adjustable trigger
MSRP $731.00

MODEL SEVEN LAMINATE

Action: Bolt
Stock: Laminate
Barrel: 18.5 in.
Sights: Rifled sights
Weight: 6 lb. 8 oz.
Caliber: .223 Rem., .243 Win., 7mm-08 Rem., .308 Win.
Magazine: 4, 5 rounds
Features: Chestnut laminate stock; SuperCell recoil pad; X-Mark Pro adjustable trigger; rifled sights
MSRP $1039.00

MODEL SEVEN STAINLESS STEEL

Action: Bolt
Stock: Synthetic
Barrel: 20 in.
Sights: None
Weight: 6 lb. 8 oz.
Caliber: .223 Rem., .243 Win., .260 Rem., 7mm-08 Rem., .308 Win., .300 WSM, 6mm Rem.
Magazine: 4, 5 rounds
Features: Light contour barrel; X-Mark Pro adjustable trigger; satin-finished stainless barrel and action
MSRP $838.00

MODEL SEVEN SYNTHETIC

Action: Bolt
Stock: Synthetic
Barrel: 18 in., 20 in.
Sights: None
Weight: 6 lb. 2 oz.–6 lb. 8 oz.
Caliber: .243 Win., .260 Rem., 7mm-08 Rem., .308 Win.
Magazine: Internal
Features: Synthetic black stock; compact design for fast handling; cylindrical receiver design
MSRP $731.00

ULTIMATE SHEEP RIFLE

Action: Bolt
Stock: Carbon fiber
Barrel: 20 in.
Sights: None
Weight: 5 lb. 9 oz.
Caliber: 6.5 Creedmoor, customer choice
Magazine: N/A
Features: Choice of standard short-action calibers with a titanium action or magnum short-action calibers in a stainless action; carbon fiber-wrapped Proof Research barrel; cut rifled; Light Sendero contour and with threaded custom muzzle brake; Cerakoted action in Titanium and with custom Kuiu engraving; Manners carbon fiber EH8 stock in a custom Cerakoted Kuiu Vias pattern developed by Scalpel Arms; Long Rifles, Inc., custom bipod rail; Badger Ordnance mini bolt knob with Kuiu engraving, triple-pinned and timed; Badger Ordnance M16-type extractor; Timney 510 trigger; aluminum floor plate, firing pin, and bolt shroud; the floorplate with Kuiu engraving

Rifles Inc.

RIFLES INC. CANYON

RIFLES INC. CLASSIC

RIFLES INC. LIGHTWEIGHT STRATA, LIGHTWEIGHT 70

RIFLES INC. MASTER'S SERIES

RIFLES INC. SAFARI

MSRP $5895.00

CANYON
Action: Bolt
Stock: McMillan HTG
Barrel: 24 in.
Sights: None
Weight: 10 lb.
Caliber: Most popular calibers
Magazine: Internal
Features: Blind or hinged floor plate; customer-supplied Rem. 700 action; match grade stainless steel Lilja number 6 barrel; optional muzzlebrake; matte stainless metal finish, optional black Teflon; adjustable cheekpiece; custom buttpad
MSRP $3500.00

CLASSIC
Action: Bolt
Stock: Laminated fiberglass
Barrel: 24 in.–26 in.
Sights: None
Weight: 6 lb. 8 oz.
Caliber: All popular chamberings up to .375 H&H
Magazine: Internal
Features: Customer-supplied Rem. 700 action; match grade stainless steel Lilja barrel; blind or hinged floor plate; matte stainless metal finish, optional Black Teflon finish; black laminated fiberglass, pillar glass bedded stock

MSRP $2900.00

LIGHTWEIGHT STRATA, LIGHTWEIGHT 70
Action: Bolt
Stock: Laminate
Barrel: 22 in.–26 in.
Sights: None
Weight: 4 lb. 8 oz.–5 lb. 12 oz.
Caliber: All popular chamberings up to .375 H&H
Magazine: Internal
Features: Customer-supplied Rem. 700 action; match grade stainless steel Lilja barrel; fluted bolt and hollowed-handle; blind or hinged floor plate; matte stainless metal finish, optional black Teflon finish; hand-laminated blend of Kevlar/graphite and boron, pillar glass bedded stock; Titanium Strata has hand-laminated graphite stock with pillar glass bedded; custom buttpad; Quiet Slimbrake II muzzlebrake
Lightweight Strata: $3200.00
Lightweight 70: $3100.00

MASTER'S SERIES
Action: Bolt
Stock: Laminated fiberglass
Barrel: 24 in.–27 in.
Sights: None
Weight: 7 lb. 12 oz.
Caliber: All popular chamberings up to .375 H&H

Magazine: Internal
Features: Customer-supplied Rem. 700 action; match grade stainless steel Lilja number 5 barrel; hinged floor plate; matte stainless metal finish, optional black Teflon finish; black laminated fiberglass, pillar glass bedded stock; optional muzzlebrake
MSRP $3200.00

SAFARI
Action: Bolt
Stock: Laminated fiberglass
Barrel: 23 in.–25 in.
Sights: Optional Express Sights
Weight: 8 lb. 8 oz.
Caliber: .375 H&H, .416 Rem. Mag., and other large game cartridges
Magazine: 4 rounds
Features: Customer-supplied Winchester Model 70 Classic action; lapped and face trued bolt; match grade stainless steel Lilja barrel; Quiet Slimbrake II muzzlebrake; hinged floor plate or optional drop box; matte stainless finish, optional black Teflon; double laminated fiberglass, pillar glass bedded stock; Pachmayr decelerator; optional barrel band
MSRP $3500.00

RIFLES

ROCK RIVER ARMS LAR-6.8
COYOTE CARBINE

ROCK RIVER ARMS LAR-6.8 X-1

ROCK RIVER ARMS LAR-8 PREDATOR HP MID-LENGTH

ROCK RIVER ARMS LAR-8 PREDATOR HP

LAR-6.8 COYOTE CARBINE

Action: Semiautomatic
Stock: Synthetic
Barrel: 16 in.
Sights: None
Weight: 7 lb.
Caliber: 6.8 SPC II
Magazine: 1 round
Features: Smith Vortex flash hider; chromoly barrel; RRA two-stage match trigger
MSRP $1310.00

LAR-6.8 X-1

Action: Semiautomatic
Stock: Synthetic
Barrel: 18 in.
Sights: None
Weight: 7 lb. 13 oz.
Caliber: 6.8 SPC II
Magazine: Detachable box, 25 rounds
Features: RRA Beast of Hunter

muzzle brake; available in black or tan; available with A2 or CAR stocks
MSRP . . . . $1595.00–$1655.00

LAR-8 PREDATOR HP

Action: Semiautomatic
Stock: Synthetic
Barrel: 20 in.
Sights: None
Weight: 8 lb. 10 oz.
Caliber: .308 Win., 7mm-08 Rem., .243 Win.
Magazine: Detachable box
Features: Forged A4 receiver with forward assist and port door; stainless steel barrel; gas block sight Base; two-stage trigger; Hogue rubber grip; RRA aluminum free-float tube; A2 buttstock or operator stock
MSRP . . . . $1950.00–$2000.00

LAR-8 PREDATOR HP MID-LENGTH

Action: Semiautomatic
Stock: Synthetic
Barrel: 16 in.
Sights: None
Weight: 8 lb. 14.4 oz.–9 lb. 3.2 oz.
Caliber: .308 Win.
Magazine: N/A
Features: Forged LAR-8 lower and A4 upper; stainless steel barrel has 1:10 twist, is fluted, bead-blasted, and cryogenically treated; available with or without muzzle brake; two-stage match trigger with winter trigger guard; RRA Operator CAR or A2 buttstock; RRA LAR-8 DLX rifle-length free-floating handguard with three short accessory rails; Hogue pistol grip
MSRP . . . . $1900.00–$1950.00

Rock River Arms

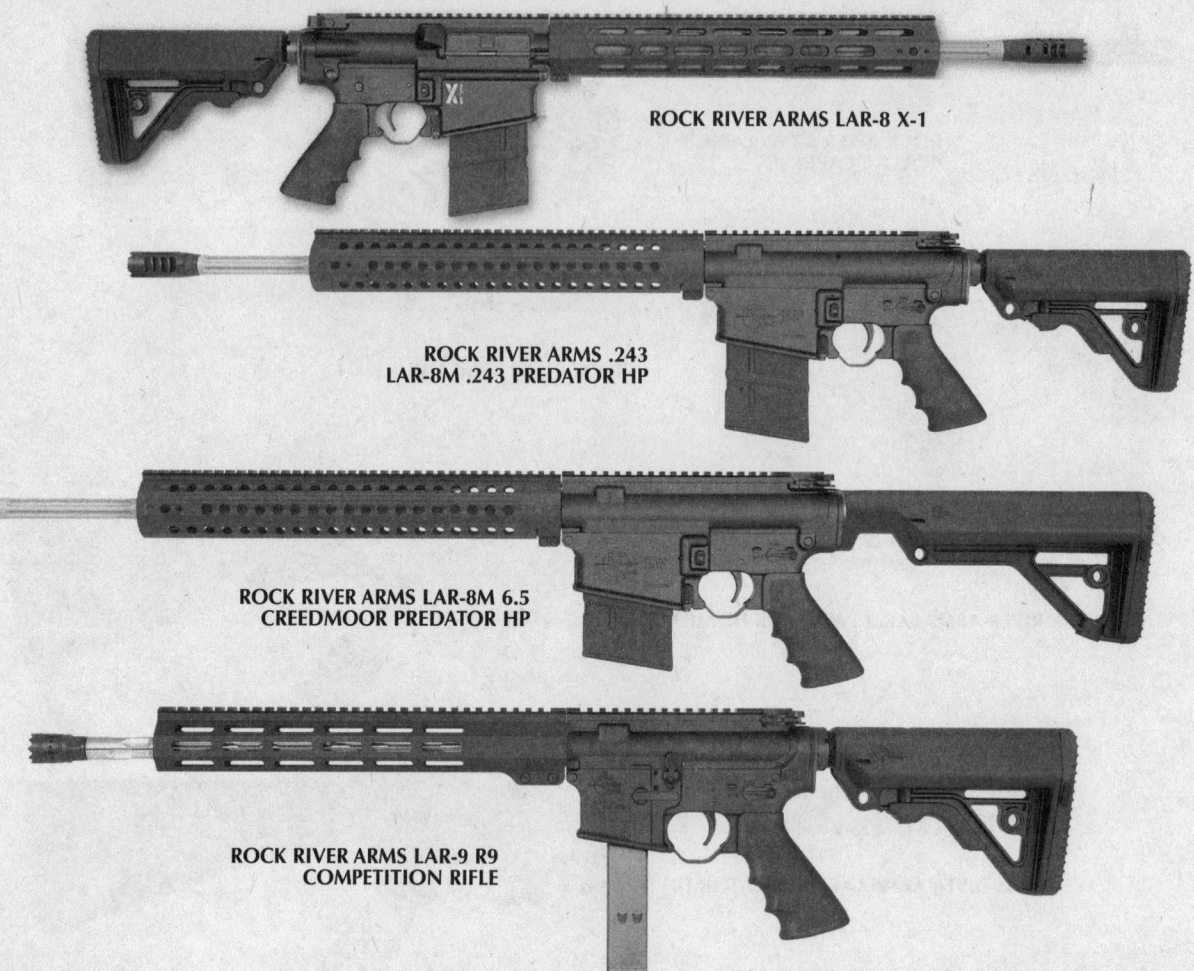

ROCK RIVER ARMS LAR-8 X-1

ROCK RIVER ARMS .243
LAR-8M .243 PREDATOR HP

ROCK RIVER ARMS LAR-8M 6.5
CREEDMOOR PREDATOR HP

ROCK RIVER ARMS LAR-9 R9
COMPETITION RIFLE

LAR-8 X-1

Action: Semiautomatic
Stock: Synthetic
Barrel: 18 in.
Sights: None
Weight: 9 lb. 8 oz.
Caliber: .308 Win., 7.62 NATO
Magazine: Detachable box, 20 rounds
Features: RRA Beast of Hunter muzzle brake; available in black or tan; available with A2 or CAR stocks
MSRP . . . . **$1845.00–$1895.00**

LAR-8M .243 PREDATOR HP

Action: Semiautomatic
Stock: Synthetic
Barrel: 20 in.
Sights: None
Weight: 9 lb. 3.2 oz.–9 lb. 8 oz.
Caliber: .243 Win.
Magazine: N/A
Features: Rifle features a forged, multi-caliber marked LAR-8M lower and a forged A4 upper; stainless steel barrel has 1:10 twist, is fluted, and cryogenically treated; Rock River's Operator muzzle brake available; low-profile gas block; two-stage match trigger with a winter trigger guard; RRA Operator A2 or CAR stock; RRA LAR-8 DLX free-floating rifle-length handrail with three short accessory rails; Hogue pistol grip
MSRP . . . . **$1950.00–$2000.00**

LAR-8M 6.5 CREEDMOOR PREDATOR HP

Action: Semiautomatic
Stock: Synthetic
Barrel: 20 in.
Sights: None
Weight: 9 lb. 3.2 oz.–9 lb. 6.4 oz.
Caliber: 6.5 Creedmoor
Magazine: N/A
Features: Rifle features a forged, multi-caliber marked LAR-8M lower and a forged A4 upper; barrel has 1:8 twist, is bead blasted, and cryogenically treated; Rock River's Operator muzzle break available; low-profile gas block; two-stage match trigger with a winter trigger guard; RRA Operator A2 stock; RRA LAR-8 DLX free-float handrail with three short accessory rails; Hogue pistol grip
MSRP . . . . **$1950.00–$2020.00**

LAR-9 R9 COMPETITION

Action: Semiautomatic
Stock: Synthetic
Barrel: 16 in.
Sights: None
Weight: 7 lb. 6.4 oz.
Caliber: 9mm
Magazine: N/A
Features: Forged LAR-9 lower with integral Magwell and a forged A4 upper; barrel has 1:10 twist, is chain-link fluted, and cryogenically treated; wears a 9mm Mini-Break; two-stage match trigger; RRA Operator CAR stock; RRA Lightweight Extended Mid-Length handguard; Hogue pistol grip
MSRP **$1475.00**

ROCK RIVER ARMS LAR-15
BTB CARBINE

ROCK RIVER ARMS DELTA CAR

ROCK RIVER ARMS LAR-15
FES LIGHT PREDATOR2L

LAR-15 BTB CARBINE

Action: Semiautomatic
Stock: Synthetic
Barrel: 16 in.
Sights: RRA NSP flip up front and rear
Weight: 7 lb.
Caliber: 5.56 NATO
Magazine: 20 rounds
Features: Forged A4 upper; Rock River Arms' forged LAR-15 lower; over-molded pistol grip; single-stage trigger; drop-in rail; six-position stock; flip-up sights front and rear; includes two magazines; available in black or tan
MSRP. **$825.00**

LAR-15 DELTA CAR

Action: Semiautomatic
Stock: Synthetic
Barrel: 16 in.
Sights: None
Weight: 7 lb.–7 lb. 4.8 oz.
Caliber: 5.56 NATO, .223 Rem.
Magazine: Detachable box, 30 rounds
Features: Delta Quad Rail two piece drop-in and gas system, available in CAR or Mid-length; low profile gas block; Ergo SureGrip; two stage trigger
MSRP. **$1850.00**

LAR-15 FES LIGHT PREDATOR2L

Action: Semiautomatic
Stock: Synthetic
Barrel: 16 in.
Sights: None
Weight: 6 lb. 14 oz.
Caliber: .223 Wylde
Magazine: 20 rounds
Features: Free-floating, extended length, top rail handguard; FES muzzle brake; lightweight fluted steel barrel; mid-length gas system with low-profile gas block; Rock River's Operator stock; two-stage trigger; Winter trigger guard; BCM GUNFIGHTER charging handle; furniture is black; receiver and lower can be upgraded to Rock River's ROCKote Gunmetal Gray
MSRP. **$1800.00**
ROCKote Gunmetal
   Gray receiver:. **$1910.00**

Rock River Arms

ROCK RIVER ARMS LAR-15
FES PREDATOR2 GHOST
CAMO

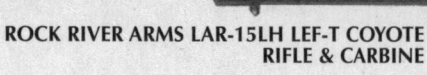

ROCK RIVER ARMS LAR-15LH LEF-T COYOTE
RIFLE & CARBINE

ROCK RIVER ARMS LAR-15M VARMINT A4

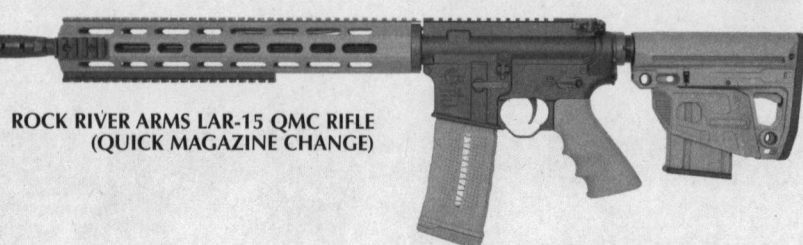

ROCK RIVER ARMS LAR-15 QMC RIFLE
(QUICK MAGAZINE CHANGE)

LAR-15 FES PREDATOR2 GHOST CAMO

Action: Semiautomatic
Stock: Synthetic
Barrel: 16 in.
Sights: None
Weight: 7 lb. 10 oz.
Caliber: .223 Wylde
Magazine: 20 rounds
Features: FES stands for Fred Eichler Series; Ghost Camo stock; handguard emblazoned with paw prints; Rock River's FES muzzle brake; Operator CAR stock; chrome two-stage trigger; FES extended free-floating handguard with full-length rail; Cryo-treated fluted barrel; Hogue rubber pistol grip; Rock River's Winter trigger guard; BCM GUNFIGHTER charging handle
MSRP **$2225.00**

LAR-15LH LEF-T COYOTE RIFLE & CARBINE

Action: Semiautomatic
Stock: Synthetic A2
Barrel: 16 in., 20 in.
Sights: None
Weight: 7 lb.-8 lb. 6.4 oz.
Caliber: 5.56 NATO, .223 Rem.
Magazine: Detachable box, 20 rounds
Features: Smith Vortex Flash Hider; Hogue free float tube; Hogue grip; two stage trigger
Carbine: **$1445.00**
Rifle: **$1500.00**

LAR-15M VARMINT A4

Action: Semiautomatic
Stock: Synthetic
Barrel: 20 in.
Sights: None
Weight: 9 lb. 1.6 oz.
Caliber: .204 Ruger
Magazine: N/A
Features: Forged, multi-caliber marked LAR-15M lower and A4 upper; stainless steel bull barrel has 1:12 twist, is fluted, air gauged, and cryogenically treated; low-profile gas block; two-stage match trigger with a winter trigger guard; A2 buttstock; RRA TRO-STD free-floating handrail with octagonal top rail providing one STD and two short accessory rails; Hogue pistol grip
MSRP **$1400.00**

LAR-15 QMC RIFLE (QUICK MAGAZINE CHANGE)

Action: Semiautomatic
Stock: Synthetic
Barrel: 16 in.
Sights: None
Weight: 7 lb. 14.4 oz.
Caliber: 5.56 NATO
Magazine: 10, 30 rounds
Features: Forged LAR-15 lower and forged A4 upper with a BCM Gunfighter charging handle; chrome moly HBAR carbine barrel with a 1:9 twist; Rock River Beast muzzle brake; two-stage match trigger; winter trigger guard; RRA MAG CAR buttstock; RRA TRO-STD free-floating handguard rail featuring an octagonal top rail with one STD and two short accessory rails
MSRP . . . . **$1400.00–$1450.00**

Rock River Arms

ROCK RIVER ARMS LAR-15 R3 COMPETITION RIFLE

ROCK RIVER ARMS LAR-15 X-1

ROCK RIVER ARMS LAR-47 CAR A4

ROCK RIVER ARMS LAR-47 DELTA CARBINE

LAR-15 R3 COMPETITION RIFLE
Action: Semiautomatic
Stock: Synthetic A2 or CAR
Barrel: 18 in.
Sights: None
Weight: 7 lb. 9.6 oz.
Caliber: 5.56 NATO, .223 Rem.
Magazine: Detachable box, 30 rounds
Features: RRA tuned and ported muzzle brake; low profile gas block; two stage trigger; Hogue Rubber grip
MSRP . . . . $1355.00–$1365.00

LAR-15 X-1
Action: Semiautomatic
Stock: Synthetic
Barrel: 18 in.
Sights: None
Weight: 7 lb. 13 oz.
Caliber: 5.56 NATO, .223 Rem.
Magazine: Detachable box, 30 rounds
Features: RRA Beast of Hunter muzzle brake; available in black or tan; available with A2 or CAR stocks
MSRP . . . . $1035.00–$1555.00

LAR-47 CAR A4
Action: Semiautomatic
Stock: Synthetic
Barrel: 16 in.
Sights: None
Weight: 6 lb. 6 oz.
Caliber: 7.62x39 Warsaw
Magazine: Detachable box, 30 rounds, standard AK-47 mag
Features: RRA 6-postion tactical CAR stock; A2 pistol grip; CAR hand-guards; RRA two-stage trigger; A2 flash hider; ambidextrous mag release
MSRP $1270.00

LAR-47 DELTA CARBINE
Action: Semiautomatic
Stock: Synthetic
Barrel: 16 in.
Sights: None
Weight: 7 lb. 12 oz.
Caliber: 7.62x39 Warsaw
Magazine: Detachable box, 30 rounds, standard AK-47 mag
Features: RRA 6-position delta CAR stock; RRA delta pistol grip; RRA 2-piece quad rail; RRA delta muzzlebrake; RRA two-stage trigger; ambidextrous mag release
MSRP $1545.00

Rock River Arms

ROCK RIVER ARMS LAR-47 X-1

ROCK RIVER ARMS LAR-300 AAC X-1

ROCK RIVER ARMS LAR-458 CAR A4

ROCK RIVER ARMS LAR-458 X-1

RIFLES

ROCK RIVER ARMS LAR-PDS CARBINE

LAR-47 X-1
Action: Semiautomatic
Stock: Synthetic
Barrel: 18 in.
Sights: None
Weight: 8 lb. 3 oz.
Caliber: 7.62 Warsaw
Magazine: Detachable box
Features: Available in black or tan; RRA Operator A2 Stock; RRA Beast muzzle brake
MSRP.........$1600.00–$1660.00

LAR-300 X-1
Action: Semiautomatic
Stock: Synthetic
Barrel: 18 in.
Sights: None
Weight: 7 lb. 14 oz.
Caliber: .300 BLK
Magazine: Detachable box

Features: Stainless steal cryo treated barrel; RRA two stage trigger; RRA beast muzzle break; A2 or CAR stock
MSRP........ $1585.00–$1645.00

LAR-458 CAR A4
Action: Semiautomatic
Stock: Synthetic
Barrel: 16 in.
Sights: None
Weight: 7 lb. 10 oz.
Caliber: .458 SOCOM
Magazine: Detachable box
Features: Forged A4 receiver; A2 flash hider; chromoly bull barrel; varmint gas block with sight rail; RRA two-stage trigger; RRA aluminum free-float tube; A2 pistol grip; A2 buttstock
MSRP..................$1145.00

LAR-458 X-1
Action: Semiautomatic
Stock: Synthetic
Barrel: 18 in.
Sights: None
Weight: 8 lb. 12 oz.
Caliber: .458 SOCOM
Magazine: Detachable box, 30 rounds
Features: RRA Beast of Hunter muzzle brake; available in black or tan; available with A2 or CAR stocks
MSRP........ $1595.00–$1655.00

LAR PDS CARBINE RIBBED, TRI-RAIL
Action: Semiautomatic
Stock: Synthetic
Barrel: 16 in.
Sights: None
Weight: 7 lb. 6 oz.
Caliber: .223 Rem.
Magazine: Detachable box
Features: Ambidextrous non-reciprocating charging handle; A2 flash hider; RRA two-stage trigger; Hogue rubber grip; tri-rail handguard available
Ribbed: $1595.00
Tri-Rail $1750.00

ROSSI M92 .44-40 WIN.

M92

Action: Lever
Stock: Wood
Barrel: 20 in., 24 in.
Sights: None
Weight: 5 lb.–7 lb.

Caliber: .45 LC
Magazine: Under-barrel tube, 10+1 or 12+1 rounds
Features: Round barrel with a variety of metal finishes: blued, blued/case-hardened, blued/brass, and stainless; authentic curved buttplate with finish matched to receiver
MSRP . . . . $629.00–$659.00

Ruger (Sturm, Ruger & Co.)

RUGER 10/22 CARBINE

RUGER 10/22 TAKEDOWN

RUGER 10/22 TARGET LITE

10/22 CARBINE

Action: Semiautomatic
Stock: Synthetic or hardwood
Barrel: 18.5 in.
Sights: Gold bead front sight, adjustable rear
Weight: 5 lb.
Caliber: .22 LR
Magazine: Detachable rotary, 10 rounds
Features: Stock comes in black synthetic, green modular synthetic, Go Wild Camo Rock Star synthetic, or hardwood; extended magazine release; push-button manual safety; combination scope base adapter; hammer-forged barrel; polymer trigger housing; aluminum receiver; contoured buttpad; barrel band; modular stock version has topside Picatinny rail; hardwood version available as a kit with hard case and Taylor Targets animal spinner silhouette target; black stock available with stainless hardware, blue hardware, or blued hardware with a Weaver 3–9X40mm Dual-X scope factory mounted

Wood/black synthetic: $309.00
Black synthetic with
   stainless: $339.00
Black synthetic with scope: . . $399.00
Go Wild camo: $399.00
Green modular stock: $399.00
Target kit: $399.00

10/22 TAKEDOWN

Action: Semiautomatic
Stock: Black synthetic
Barrel: 16.12 in.–18.5 in.
Sights: Gold bead front, adjustable rear
Weight: 4 lb. 9.6 oz.–5 lb. 5 oz.
Caliber: .22 LR
Magazine: Detachable rotary, 10 rounds
Features: Built of alloy steel with satin black finish; easy takedown and reassembly; detachable rotary magazine; extended magazine release; combination scope base adapter; push-button manual safety; available in three configurations: black synthetic stock with 18.5-in. stainless barrel; black synthetic stock with 16.4-in. threaded barrel with flash suppressor in blue; black synthetic Ruger modular stock with 16.12-in. satin black threaded, fluted target barrel

Stainless: $439.00
Blued with flash
   suppressor: $459.00
Blued threaded/fluted: $629.00

10/22 TARGET LITE

Action: Semiautomatic
Stock: Laminate
Barrel: 16.13 in.
Sights: None
Weight: 5 lb.
Caliber: .22 LR
Magazine: 10 rounds
Features: Laminated thumbhole stock adjustable for length of pull; vented forearm; cold hammer-forge barrel; scope base adapter that works with Weaver-style and .22 tip-off mounts; metal has a satin blue finish
MSRP $649.00

Ruger (Sturm, Ruger & Co.)

RUGER AMERICAN RIFLE

RUGER AMERICAN RIFLE PREDATOR, PREDATOR WITH VORTEX CROSSFIRE II RIFLESCOPE

RUGER AMERICAN RIFLE RANCH

RUGER AMERICAN RIFLE WITH GO WILD CAMO

RUGER AMERICAN RIFLE WITH VORTEX CROSSFIRE II RIFLESCOPE

AMERICAN RIFLE

Action: Bolt
Stock: Synthetic
Barrel: 22 in.
Sights: Drilled and tapped for scopes
Weight: 6 lb. 2 oz.–6 lb. 4 oz.
Caliber: .22-250 Rem., .223 Rem., 6.5 Creedmoor, 7mm-08 Rem., .243 Win., .270 Win., .30-06 Spfd., .308 Win.
Magazine: Detachable rotary, 4 rounds
Features: Ruger Marksman adjustable trigger; ergonomic, lightweight stock; soft rubber recoil pad; three-lug 70 degree bolt; Power Bedding positively locates the receiver and free-floats the barrel; hammer-forged barrel; tang safety; round rotary magazine
MSRP $489.00

AMERICAN RIFLE PREDATOR, PREDATOR WITH VORTEX SCOPE

Action: Bolt
Stock: Synthetic
Barrel: 22 in.
Sights: None
Weight: 6 lb. 9 oz.
Caliber: .22-250 Rem., 6.5 Creedmoor, .308 Win., .243 Win., 7mm-08 Rem., 6.5 Grendel, .223 Rem., 6mm Creedmoor, .204 Ruger
Magazine: 10 rounds
Features: Moss Green synthetic stock; Ruger Marksman Adjustable Trigger and Power Bedding; threaded barrel; unscoped model has installed Picatinny rail; scoped model comes with a Vortex Crossfire II 4-12x44mm scope factory mounted and the Dead-Hold BDC reticle
Rifle only: . . . . $529.00–$569.00
With scope: . . . . . . $639.00–$699.00

AMERICAN RIFLE RANCH

Action: Bolt
Stock: Synthetic
Barrel: 16.1 in.
Sights: None
Weight: 6 lb.–6 lb. 8 oz.
Caliber: 5.56 NATO, .300 BLK, .450 Bushmaster, 7.62X39
Magazine: Detachable rotary, 3–5 rounds
Features: Ruger Marksman Adjustable trigger offers a pull weight that is adjustable between 3 and 5 pounds; ergonomic, lightweight flat dark earth composite stock with modern forend contouring and grip serrations and swivel studs; soft rubber recoil pad; Power Bedding positively locates the receiver and free-floats the barrel for outstanding accuracy; threaded barrel is cold hammer-forged; tang safety; rotary magazine; factory installed one-piece aluminum scope rail
MSRP . . . . $529.00–$599.00

AMERICAN RIFLE WITH GO WILD CAMO

Action: Bolt
Stock: Synthetic
Barrel: 22 in.
Sights: None
Weight: 6 lb. 9 oz.
Caliber: 7mm-08 Rem., .243 Win., 6.5 Creedmoor, .308 Win., .30-06 Spfd., .450 Bushmaster, .300 Win. Mag.
Magazine: 3 rounds
Features: Go Wild I-M Brush camo; action and barrel in Bronze Cerakote; Picatinny rail; muzzle brake; Ruger's Marksman Adjustable Trigger and Power Bedding
MSRP $629.00

AMERICAN RIFLE WITH VORTEX SCOPE

Action: Bolt
Stock: Synthetic
Barrel: 22 in.
Sights: None
Weight: 7 lb. 3 oz.
Caliber: .223 Rem.
Magazine: 5 rounds
Features: Vortex 3-9x40mm Crossfire II scope (Dead-Head BDC reticle) already mounted; Ruger Marksman Adjustable Trigger and Power Bedding; a cold hammer forged barrel
MSRP $639.00

RIFLES

Ruger (Sturm, Ruger & Co.)

RUGER AMERICAN RIMFIRE TARGET

RUGER AMERICAN RIMFIRE WITH WOOD STOCK

RUGER AR-556

RUGER AR-556 MULTI-PURPOSE RIFLE (MPR)

RUGER GUIDE GUN

AMERICAN RIMFIRE TARGET

Action: Bolt
Stock: Laminate
Barrel: 18 in.
Sights: None
Weight: 6 lb. 8 oz.–6 lb. 11 oz.
Caliber: .17 HMR, .22 LR, .22 WMR
Magazine: 9, 10 rounds
Features: Black laminate stock has Alexander Henry forend; Ruger Marksman Adjustable trigger; aluminum Picatinny rail; cold-hammer-forged bull barrel with installed knurled thread protector
Standard stock: **$499.00**
Thumbhole stock: **$559.00**

AMERICAN RIMFIRE WOOD STOCK

Action: Bolt
Stock: Wood

Barrel: 22 in.
Sights: Fiber optic front, adjustable rear
Weight: 6 lb. 2 oz.
Caliber: .22 LR
Magazine: 10 rounds
Features: Extended magazine release; patent-pending Power Bedding integral bedding block system; Ruger Marksman Adjustable trigger offers a crisp release with a pull weight that is user adjustable between 3 and 5 lb.; wood stock with checkering on the grip and forend and a rubber buttpad for a comfortable length of pull; cold hammer-forged barrel
MSRP **$459.00**

AR-556

Action: Semiautomatic
Stock: Synthetic
Barrel: 16.1 in.
Sights: Adjustable
Weight: 6 lb. 8 oz.
Caliber: .223 Rem./5.56 NATO
Magazine: Detachable box, 30 rounds

Features: The milled gas block is located at a carbine length (M4) position; multiple attachment points include a QD socket and bayonet lug; front sight post is elevation adjustable, and a front sight tool is included; A-2 Style F-Height allows co-witness with many optics; Ruger Rapid Deploy folding rear sight provides windage adjustability; six-position telescoping M4-style buttstock and Mil-Spec buffer tube; barrel is cold hammer-forged; Ruger flash suppressor; matte black oxide finish on the exterior of the bolt carrier
MSRP . . . . **$799.00–$849.00**

AR-556 MULTI-PURPOSE RIFLE (MPR)

Action: Semiautomatic
Stock: Synthetic
Barrel: 18 in.
Sights: Adjustable post front, adjustable Ruger rapid deploy rear
Weight: 6 lb. 8 oz.
Caliber: 5.56 NATO, .450 Bushmaster
Magazine: 10, 30 rounds
Features: M-LOK accessory-compatible 15-in. free-floating handguard; Ruger's Elite 452 AR trigger; rifle-length gas system; contoured barrel that reduces overall weight; low-profile gas block; stock is adjustable; long topside Picatinny rail
5.56 NATO: **$899.00**
.450 Bushmaster: **$1099.00**

GUIDE GUN

Action: Bolt
Stock: Green Mountain laminate
Barrel: 20 in.
Sights: Bead front, adjustable rear
Weight: 8 lb.-8 lb. 2 oz.
Caliber: .300 Win. Mag., .338 Win. Mag., .30-06 Spfd., .375 Ruger, .416 Ruger
Magazine: 3, 4 rounds
Magazine: 3 rounds (4 rounds in .30-06 Spfd.)
Features: LC6 Trigger; Mauser-type extractor; muzzle brake system; three-position safety; manner-forged barrel; integral scope mounts; stainless steel bolt; swivel studs;
MSRP **$1279.00**

Ruger (Sturm, Ruger & Co.)

RUGER GUNSITE SCOUT RIFLE

RUGER HAWKEYE LONG-RANGE TARGET

RUGER HAWKEYE PREDATOR

RUGER M77 HAWKEYE

RUGER MINI-14 RANCH RIFLE

RUGER MINI-14 TACTICAL

GUNSITE SCOUT RIFLE
Action: Bolt
Stock: Laminate; synthetic; wood
Barrel: 16.50 in.
Sights: Post front sight, adjustable rear
Weight: 7 lb.
Caliber: .308 Win., .450 Bushmaster
Magazine: Detachable box, 10 rounds
Features: Flash suppressor, Picatinny rail; recoil pad; accurate sighting system; integral scope mounts; Mauser-type extractor; developed with Gunsite and features their logo
MSRP . . . . $1139.00–$1199.00

HAWKEYE LONG-RANGE TARGET
Action: Bolt
Stock: Laminate
Barrel: 24 in.
Sights: None
Weight: 10 lb. 11 oz.
Caliber: .300 Win. Mag., 6.5 Creedmoor, 6.5 PRC
Magazine: 5 rounds
Features: Heavy contour barrel; Ruger's Precision Rifle Muzzle Brake; two-stage target trigger; controlled round feed; fixed-blade ejecto;, a 20 MOA rail that screws down on top of

Ruger's own integral mounts; adjustable laminate stock
MSRP $1279.000

HAWKEYE PREDATOR
Action: Bolt
Stock: Laminate
Barrel: 22 in., 24 in.
Sights: None
Weight: 7 lb. 11 oz.–8 lb. 2 oz.
Caliber: .22-250 Rem., .223 Rem., .204 Ruger, .6.5 Creedmor
Magazine: 4 rounds
Features: Non-rotating, Mauser-type controlled round feed extractor; hinged solid-steel floorplate; cold hammer-forged barrel; patented integral scope mounts
MSRP . . . . $1139.00–$1159.00

HAWKEYE STANDARD
Action: Bolt
Stock: Walnut
Barrel: 22 in., 24 in.
Sights: None
Weight: 7 lb.–8 lb. 3 oz.
Caliber: .204 Ruger, .223 Rem., .243 Win., .270 Win., 7mm Rem. Mag., 7mm-08 Rem., .30-06 Spfd., .300 Win. Mag., .308 Win.
Magazine: 3–5 rounds
Features: American walnut stock;

alloy steel, satin blued barrel; LC6 trigger; positive floor plate latch; integral scope mounts; three-position safety
MSRP $979.00

MINI-14 RANCH RIFLE
Action: Semiautomatic
Stock: Hardwood, synthetic
Barrel: 18.5 in.
Sights: Blade front sight, adjustable rear
Weight: 6 lb. 12 oz.–7 lb.
Caliber: 5.56 NATO, .223 Rem.
Magazine: 5 rounds, or detachable box, 20 rounds
Features: Stock comes in hardwood or black synthetic; Garand style action; hammer-forged barrel; sighting system; integral scope mounts; flat buttpad; integral sling swivels on hardwood or black synthetic stocks
MSRP . . . . $999.00–$1139.00

MINI-14 TACTICAL
Action: Semiautomatic
Stock: Synthetic
Barrel: 16.1 in.
Sights: Adjustable
Weight: 6 lb. 12 oz.–7 lb. 4 oz.
Caliber: 5.56 NATO, .223 Rem., .300 BLK
Magazine: Detachable box, 5, 20 rounds
Features: Black synthetic stock; blued barrel with a flash suppressor; adjustable ghost ring rear sight, non-glare protected-post front sight
MSRP . . . . $1089.00–$1169.00

Ruger (Sturm, Ruger & Co.)

RUGER MINI THIRTY RIFLE

RUGER NO. 1

RUGER PC (PISTOL CALIBER) CARBINE

RUGER PRECISION RIFLE

RUGER PRECISION RIMFIRE

MINI THIRTY RIFLE

Action: Semiautomatic
Stock: Synthetic
Barrel: 16.12 in., 18.5 in.
Sights: Blade front sight, adjustable rear
Weight: 6 lb. 11 oz.
Caliber: 7.62x39 Warsaw
Magazine: 5 rounds, or detachable box, 20 rounds
Features: Garand style action, hammer-forged barrel; sighting system; integral scope mounts; black synthetic stock; sling swivels; stainless steel or alloy steel barrel in matte or blued finish as well as a newer version in stainless steel with a 16.12-in. barrel
MSRP . . . . $1069.00–$1169.00

NO. 1

Action: Single-shot
Stock: American walnut
Barrel: 20 in.
Sights: Blade front and rear
Weight: 7 lb. 1 oz.
Caliber: .450 Marlin, .308 Win., .450 Bushmaster
Magazine: 1 round
Features: Falling-block breech mechanism rifle includes a sliding tang safety; Ruger's patented scope mounting system; ejector that can be adjusted to perform as an extractor only; caliber changes from year to year and rifle is available in limited quantities; for 2019 the .450 Bushmaster is in a gray laminate stock with stainless hardware, the .450 Marlin is in a traditional wood stock with blued metalwork, and the .308 is in a special 50th Anniversary edition with an engraved receiver
.450 Bushmaster: **$1899.00**
.450 Marlin: **$1899.00**
.308 Win.: **$2299.00**

PC (PISTOL CALIBER) CARBINE

Action: Semiautomatic
Stock: Synthetic
Barrel: 16.12 in.
Sights: Protected blade front, adjustable ghost ring rear
Weight: 6 lb. 12 oz.
Caliber: 9mm
Magazine: 10, 17 rounds
Features: Interchangeable magwell that lets the operator use a variety of Ruger or Glock magazines; buttstock is adjustable for length of pull via included spacers; magazine release and charging handle are both reversible; dead blow action with a tungsten weight both shortens the overall bolt trave, reduces felt recoil and muzzle rise
MSRP $649.00

PRECISION RIFLE

Action: Bolt
Stock: Synthetic
Barrel: 20 in., 24 in.
Sights: None
Weight: 9 lb. 12 oz.–10 lb. 12 oz.
Caliber: .308 Win., 6.5 Creedmoor, 6mm Creedmoor, ,338 Lapua, .300 Win. Mag.
Magazine: 10 rounds
Features: Cold hammer-forged chrome-moly steel barrel with 5R rifling at minimum bore and groove dimensions, minimum, headspace and centralized chamber; Samson Evolution KeyMod handguard; 20 MOA Picatinny rail; in-line recoil path manages recoil directly from the rear of the receiver to the buttstock; patent-pending multi-magazine interface functions interchangeably with M110, SR25, DPMS, and Magpul-style magazines and AICS magazines (works with some M14 magazines); Ruger Marksman Adjustable trigger
MSRP . . . . $1599.00–$2099.00

PRECISION RIMFIRE

Action: Bolt
Stock: Synthetic
Barrel: 18 in.
Sights: None
Weight: 6 lb. 12 oz.
Caliber: .22 LR, .22 WMR, .17HMR
Magazine: 10, 15 rounds
Features: One-piece molded chassis is mated with an oversized bolt; adjustable bolt throw to prevent short stroking; Ruger's Marksman Adjustable trigger; reversible safety; glass-filled nylon buttstock is fully adjustable; Picatinny rail bag rider for monopod use; a molded in window allows squeeze bag attachment
MSRP $529.00

Sako

SAKO 85 BAVARIAN CARBINE

SAKO 85 BLACK WOLF

SAKO 85 CARBONLIGHT

SAKO 85 CARBON WOLF

SAKO 85 CLASSIC

85 BAVARIAN CARBINE
Action: Bolt
Stock: Walnut
Barrel: 22.5, 24.3 in.
Sights: Rifled sights
Weight: N/A
Caliber: .308 Win., .270 Win., .30-06 Spfd., .300 Win. Mag., 6.5 Creedmoor
Features: Featuring a full Mannlicher stock with Schnabel fore-tip and Bavarian cheekpiece/comb; iron sights; sling swivel studs; single set trigger
MSRP: $2225.00

85 BLACK WOLF
Action: Bolt
Stock: Walnut and synthetic
Barrel: 24 in.
Sights: None
Weight: 8 lb. 12 oz.–9 lb. 4 oz.
Caliber: .308 Win., .30-06 Spfd., .300 Win. Mag., 7mm Rem. Mag., 6.5 Creedmoor
Magazine: 5, 6 rounds
Features: Wide forend with two studs for bipod mounting; buttstock has a push-button adjustable comb; pistol

grip has a vertical, slab-sided design
MSRP. $2325.00

85 CARBONLIGHT
Action:Bolt
Stock: Carbon fiber
Barrel: 20 in.
Sights: None
Weight: 5 lb. 5 oz.
Caliber: .308 Win., .260 Rem., 7mm-08 Rem.
Magazine: Detachable box, 5 rounds
Features: Fluted barrel; stainless steel action; stainless steel barrel; single stage trigger; single set trigger available
MSRP. $3175.00

85 CARBON WOLF
Action: Bolt
Stock: Carbon fiber
Barrel: 24 in.
Sights: None
Weight: 7 lb. 4 oz.–7 lb. 11 oz.
Caliber: .308 Win., .30-06 Spfd., .300 Win. Mag., 7mm Rem. Mag., 6.5 Creedmoor
Magazine: 5, 6

Features: Carbon fiber stock with a RTM technology and a soft-touch coating; stock is adjustable for length of pull and cheek-piece height
MSRP. $3600.00

85 CLASSIC
Action: Bolt
Stock: Walnut
Barrel: 22.4 in., 24.4 in.
Sights: Open
Weight: 7 lb.–7 lb. 12 oz.
Caliber: .308 Win., .25-06 Rem., .270 Win., .30-06 Spfd., .300 Win. Mag., .338 Win. Mag., .375 H&H, .270 WSM, .300 WSM, 7mm Rem. Mag.
Magazine: Detachable box, S/M 6 rounds, SM/L 5 rounds
Features: Comes in short actions Extra Short (XS), Short (S) and Short Magnum (SM), medium action (M), and long action (L); straight, classic walnut stock with rosewood forend tip and pistol grip cap; integral rails for scope mounts; free-floating barrel is cold-hammer-forged; adjustable single-stage trigger
MSRP. $2275.00

SAKO 85 FINNLIGHT

SAKO 85 FINNLIGHT II STAINLESS

SAKO 85 GREY WOLF (AKA 85 HUNTER LAMINATED STAINLESS)

SAKO 85 KODIAK

SAKO 85 LONG RANGE

85 FINNLIGHT

Action: Bolt
Stock: Synthetic
Barrel: 20.25, 22.4, 24.3 in.
Sights: None
Weight: 6 lb. 3 oz.–6 lb. 13 oz.
Caliber: (Short): .22-250 Rem., .243 Win., .260 Rem., .7mm-08 Rem., .308 Win.; (SM) .270 Win. Short Mag., .300 Win. Short Mag.; (Medium): .25-06 Rem., 6.5x55 Swedish, .270 Win., .30-06 Spfd.; (Long) 7mm Rem. Mag., .300 Win. Mag.
Magazine: Detachable box, S/M 6 rounds, SM/L 5 rounds
Features: Comes in short actions Short (S) and Short magnum (SM), Medium action (M), and Long action (L); single-stage trigger; two-way Sako safety locks both trigger and bolt handle; black synthetic stock with soft gray grip areas; pistol grip stock; integral rails for scope mounts; free-floating barrel is cold-hammer-forged of stainless steel
MSRP $1800.00

85 FINNLIGHT II STAINLESS

Action: Bolt
Stock: Fiberglass

Barrel: 20 in., 23 in., 24 in.
Sights: None
Weight: 6 lb. 3 oz.–6 lb. 13 oz.
Caliber: .22-250 Rem., .243 Win., .308 Win., .25-96 Rem., .270 Win., .30-06 Spfd., .260 Rem., .300 Win. Mag., .270 WSM, .300 WSM, 6.5x55 Swedish Mauser, 7mm-08 Rem., 7mm Rem. Mag., 6.5 Creedmoor
Magazine: 4, 5 rounds
Features: Fiberglass stock with RTM technology; fully adjustable cheekpiece; improved gripping surfaces; barrel finished in Cerakote
MSRP $2475.00

85 GREY WOLF

Action: Bolt
Stock: Laminated
Barrel: 23 in., 24 in.
Sights: None
Weight: 6 lb. 6 oz.–7 lb. 8 oz.
Caliber: .270 Win., .30-06 Spfd., .300 Win. Mag., .270 WSM, .300 WSM, 7mm Rem. Mag.
Magazine: 4, 5 rounds
Features: Gray matte-lacquered laminate stock; stainless hardware throughout; single stage trigger is standard, single set trigger optional; detachable magazine
MSRP . . . . $1725.00–$1775.00

85 KODIAK

Action: Bolt
Stock: Laminated hardwood
Barrel: 12.25 in.
Sights: Open
Weight: 7 lb. 15 oz.
Caliber: .375 H&H
Magazine: Detachable box, 5 rounds
Features: Adjustable single-stage trigger; barrel band for front swivel; integral dovetail rails for secure scope mounting; straight stock made of gray matte-lacquered laminated hardwood and reinforced with two cross-bolts; free-floating "bull" barrel
MSRP $1950.00

85 LONG RANGE

Action: Bolt
Stock: Wood
Barrel: 26 in.
Sights: None
Weight: 9 lb. 12 oz.
Caliber: .300 Win. Mag., .338 Lapua Mag.
Magazine: Detachable box, 4+1 rounds
Features: Flush design muzzle brake; designed for long range hunting
MSRP $2875.00

Sako

SAKO TRG 22

SAKO TRG 22 A1, 42A1

SAKO TRG M10

TRG 22
Action: Bolt
Stock: Synthetic
Barrel: 20 in., 26 in., 27.1 in.
Sights: None
Weight: 10 lb. 4 oz.–10 lb. 12 oz.
Caliber: .308 Win., 6.5 Creedmoor
Magazine: Detachable box, 5, 7, 10 rounds
Features: Double-stage trigger; two-way Sako safety locks both trigger and bolt handle; base of stock is made of polyurethane with aluminum skeleton; adjustable cheekpiece and buttplate; Ambidextrous stock in green or desert tan color; includes integral dovetail on receiver and is drilled and tapped for Picatinny rail mounting
MSRP. $3500.00

TRG 22A1, 42A1
Action: Bolt
Stock: Aluminum
Barrel: 26 in., 27 in.
Sights: None
Weight: 11 lb. 11 oz.–13 lb. 3 oz.
Caliber: .308 Win., .260 Rem., 6.5 Creedmoor, .300 Win. Mag., .338 Lapua
Magazine: 5, 7, 10 rounds
Features: Adjustable folding stock with two hinge points that eliminate wobble; M-LOK forend for accessory attachments; threaded muzzles; phosphatized steel parts; detachable magazine; muzzle brake and Picatinny or Weaver rail is standard on some models, optional on others
MSRP. . . . . $6400.00–$7400.00

TRG M10
Action: Bolt
Stock: Synthetic
Barrel: 20–27 in.
Sights: None
Weight: 13 lb. 4 oz.–14 lb. 5 oz.
Caliber: .308 Win., .300 Win. Mag., .338 Lapua
Magazine: Detachable box, 8 or 11 rounds
Features: Threaded muzzle; muzzle break available; phosphatized steel parts; stainless steel barrel; double stage trigger; Picatinny or Weaver rail; fully adjustable rear stock; ambidextrous controls
MSRP. $11,275.00

Savage Arms

SAVAGE ARMS 10/110 STEALTH EVOLUTION

SAVAGE ARMS 10 GRS

10 STEALTH EVOLUTION
Action: Bolt
Stock: Synthetic
Barrel: 20 in., 24 in., 26 in.
Sights: None
Weight: 10 lb. 12 oz.–11 lb. 2 oz.
Caliber: .223 Rem., 6mm Creedmoor, 6.5 Creedmoor, .308 Win.
Magazine: 10 rounds, 5 rounds magnum calibers
Features: Heavy fluted barrel; bronze Cerakote finish; Savage's zero-tolerance headspacing; AccuTrigger; 5R

barrel rifling across six calibers all designed for long-range work; Magpul's PRS Gen3 adjustable buttstock allows for precise user fit; full-length top rail has room for optics, lights, other sights, and accessories
MSRP. $1799.00

10 GRS
Action: Bolt
Stock: Synthetic
Barrel: 26 in.
Sights: None

Weight: 9 lb. 8 oz.
Caliber: 6.5 Creedmoor, 6mm Creedmoor, .308 Win.
Magazine: 4 rounds
Features: Long-range bolt rifle with a GRS adjustable stock that's fiberglass reinforced synthetic; threaded muzzle; fluted heavy barrel; Savage's AccuTrigger
MSRP. $1449.00

SAVAGE ARMS 12 VARMINT SERIES 12 BTCSS

SAVAGE ARMS 110 BEAR HUNTER

SAVAGE ARMS 110 ENGAGE HUNTER XP

SAVAGE ARMS 110 HUNTER

SAVAGE ARMS 110 LONG RANGE HUNTER

12 VARMINT SERIES 12 BTCSS

Action: Bolt
Stock: Laminate
Barrel: 26 in.
Sights: None
Weight: 10 lb.
Caliber: .204 Ruger, .223 Rem., .22-250 Rem.
Magazine: Detachable box, 4 rounds
Features: Drilled and tapped for scope mounts; stainless steel barrel with high luster finish; AccuTrigger; wood laminate with thumbhole and satin finish
MSRP................$1293.00

110 BEAR HUNTER

Action: Bolt
Stock: Synthetic
Barrel: 23 in.
Sights: None
Weight: 8 lb. 6 oz.
Caliber: .300 Win. Mag., .300 WSM, .338 Federal, .338 Win. Mag., .375 Ruger
Magazine: 2 rounds
Features: AccuFit System Accustock; four ¼-in. length-of-pull spacers and five 1/8-in. comb risers, all easily swappable; stainless steel finish; hinged floorplate magazine; straight

fluted barrel; stock in Mossy Oak Breakup Country.
MSRP..................$999.00

110 ENGAGE HUNTER XP

Action: Bolt
Stock: Synthetic
Barrel: 22 in.
Sights: None
Weight: 7 lb. 4 oz.
Caliber: .243 Win., 6.5 Creedmoor, 7mm-08 Rem., .308 Win., .260 Rem., .270 WSM, .300 WSM, .338 Federal, .25-06 Rem., .270 Win., 6.5X284 Norma, .30-06 Spfd., 7mm Rem. Mag., .300 Win. Mag., .280 Ackley Improved
Magazine: 4 rounds
Features: Adjustable stock for length of pull; user-adjustable AccuTrigger; detachable box magazine; Weaver Grand Slam bases and rings; Bushnell Engage 3–9x40mm drop-compensating reticle scope mounted and bore sighted
MSRP..................$639.0

110 HUNTER

Action: Bolt
Stock: Synthetic
Barrel: 22 in., 24 in.
Sights: None
Weight: 7 lb. 2 oz.–7 lb. 5 oz.

Caliber: .204 Ruger, .22-250 Rem., .223 Rem., .243 Win., .25-06 Rem., .270 Win., .280 Ackley Imp., .30-06 Spfd., .300 Win Mag., .308 Win., 7mm Rem. Mag., 7mm-08 Rem., 6.5 Creedmoor
Magazine: 3, 4 rounds
Features: AccuFit System Accustock; four ¼-inch length-of-pull spacers and five 1/8-inch comb risers, all easily swappable; black matte finish; detachable box magazine
MSRP..................$749.00

110 LONG RANGE HUNTER

Action: Bolt
Stock: Synthetic
Barrel: 26 in.
Sights: None
Weight: 8 lb.
Caliber: .260 Rem., .280 Ackley Imp., .300 Win. Mag., .300 WSM, .308 Win., .338 Federal, 6.5 Creedmoor, 6.5x284 Norma, 7mm Rem., Mag.
Magazine: 3, 4 rounds
Features: AccuFit System Accustock; four ¼-inch length-of-pull spacers and five 1/8-inch comb risers, all easily swappable; black matte finish barrel; hinged floorplate magazine; muzzle brake
MSRP..................$1119.00

Savage Arms

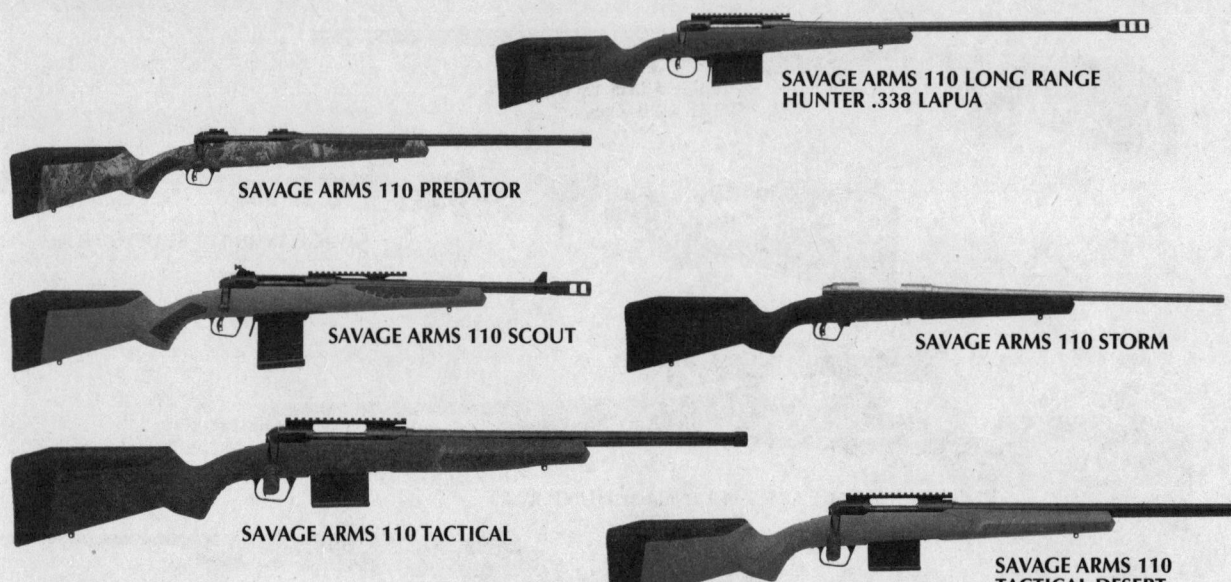

SAVAGE ARMS 110 LONG RANGE HUNTER .338 LAPUA

SAVAGE ARMS 110 PREDATOR

SAVAGE ARMS 110 SCOUT

SAVAGE ARMS 110 STORM

SAVAGE ARMS 110 TACTICAL

SAVAGE ARMS 110 TACTICAL DESERT

110 LONG RANGE HUNTER .338 LAPUA

Action: Bolt
Stock: Synthetic
Barrel: 26 in.
Sights: None
Weight: 8 lb. 14 oz.
Caliber: .338 Lapua
Magazine: 5 rounds
Features: AccuFit System Accustock; four ¼-inch length-of-pull spacers and five 1/8-inch comb risers, all easily swappable; black matte finish barrel; detachable box magazine; muzzle brake
MSRP. $1325.00

110 PREDATOR

Action: Bolt
Stock: Synthetic
Barrel: 22 in., 24 in.
Sights: None
Weight: 8 lb. 4 oz.–8 lb. 11 oz.
Caliber: .204 Ruger, .22-250 Rem., .223 Rem., .243 Win., .260 Rem., 6.5 Creedmoor, .308 Win.
Magazine: 4 rounds
Features: AccuFit System Accustock; four ¼-inch length-of-pull spacers and five 1/8-inch comb risers, all easily swappable; black matte finish barrel; detachable box magazine; stock in Realtree Max-1 camo stock; two-piece Weaver-style bases
MSRP. $910.00

110 SCOUT

Action: Bolt
Stock: Synthetic

Barrel: 16.5 in.
Sights: Adjustable iron
Weight: 7 lb. 11 oz.
Caliber: .223 Rem., .308 Win., .338 Federal, .450 Bushmaster
Magazine: 10 rounds
Features: AccuFit System Accustock; four ¼-inch length-of-pull spacers and five 1/8-inch comb risers, all easily swappable; black matte finish barrel; detachable Magpul AICS box magazine; Flat Dark Earth stock; adjustable iron sights; forward-mounted accessory/optic rail
MSRP. $829.00

110 STORM

Action: Bolt
Stock: Synthetic
Barrel: 22 in., 24 in.
Sights: None
Weight: 7 lb. 2 oz.–7 lb. 5 oz.
Caliber: .22-250 Rem., .223 Rem., .243 Rem., .25-06 Rem., .270 Win., .270 WSM, .280 Ackley Imp., .30-06 Spfd., 300 Win. Mag., .300 WSM, .308 Win., .338 Federal, .338 Win. Mag., 6.5 Creedmoor, 6.5x284 Norma, 7mm Rem., Mag., 7mm-08 Rem.,
Magazine: 3, 4 rounds
Features: AccuFit System Accustock; four ¼-inch length-of-pull spacers and five 1/8-inch comb risers, all easily swappable; matte stainless steel barrel finish; detachable box magazine; left-hand versions available in nine calibers
MSRP. $865.00

110 TACTICAL

Action: Bolt
Stock: Synthetic
Barrel: 20 in., 24 in.
Sights: None
Weight: 8 lb. 11 oz.–8 lb. 14 oz.
Caliber: .308 Win., 6.5 Creedmoor
Magazine: 10 rounds
Features: AccuFit System Accustock; four ¼-inch length-of-pull spacers and five 1/8-inch comb risers, all easily swappable; matte black barrel finish; detachable box magazine; threaded heavy barrel with end cap; an oversized bolt; a 20 MOA EGW accessory/optic rail; left-hand versions available
MSRP. $799.00

110 TACTICAL DESERT

Action: Bolt
Stock: Synthetic
Barrel: 24 in., 26 in.
Sights: None
Weight: 8 lb. 14 oz.–9 lb.
Caliber: 6.5 Creedmoor, 6mm Creedmoor
Magazine: 10 rounds
Features: AccuFit System Accustock; four ¼-inch length-of-pull spacers and five 1/8-inch comb risers, all easily swappable; a matte black barrel finish; detachable box magazine; Flat Dark Earth stock; threaded heavy barrel with end cap; oversized bolt; 20 MOA EGW accessory/optic rail
MSRP. $799.00

Savage Arms

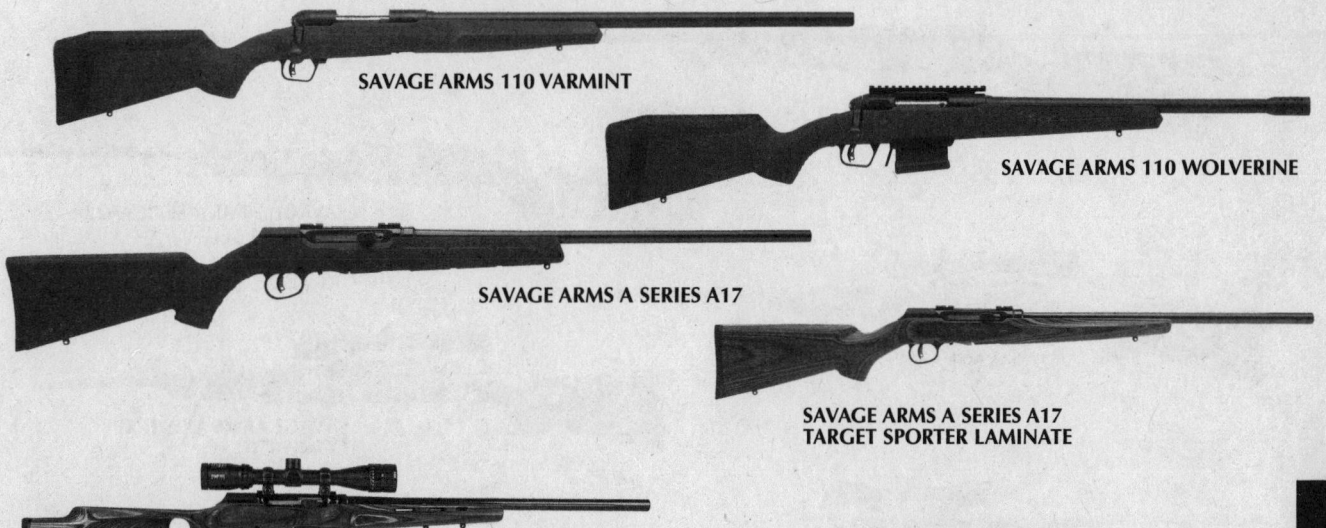

SAVAGE ARMS 110 VARMINT

SAVAGE ARMS 110 WOLVERINE

SAVAGE ARMS A SERIES A17

SAVAGE ARMS A SERIES A17 TARGET SPORTER LAMINATE

SAVAGE ARMS A SERIES A17 TARGET THUMBHOLE

SAVAGE ARMS A SERIES A17 XP

110 VARMINT

Action: Bolt
Stock: Synthetic
Barrel: 26 in.
Sights: None
Weight: N/A
Caliber: .204 Ruger, .22-250 Rem.,
.223 Rem.,
Magazine: 4 rounds
Features: AccuFit System Accustock;
four ¼-inch length-of-pull spacers
and five 1/8-inch comb risers, all easily swappable; matte black barrel finish; detachable box magazine
MSRP $759.00

110 WOLVERINE

Action: Bolt
Stock: Synthetic
Barrel: 18 in.
Sights: None
Weight: 7 lb. 14 oz.
Caliber: .450 Bushmaster
Magazine: 4 rounds
Features: AccuFit System Accustock;
four ¼-inch length-of-pull spacers
and five 1/8-inch comb risers, all easily swappable; matte black barrel finish; detachable Magpul AICS box
magazine; one-piece 20 MOA accessory/optic rail; muzzle brake
MSRP $909.00

A SERIES A17

Action: Semiautomatic
Stock: Synthetic
Barrel: 22 in.
Sights: Drilled and tapped for scope
mounts
Weight: 5 lb. 7 oz.
Caliber: .17 HMR
Magazine: Detachable rotary
Features: Carbon steel barrel; high
luster barrel finish; Delayed Blowback
Action, Hard Chromed Bolt with Dual
Controlled Round Feed, Case
Hardened Receiver, Button-Rifled
Barrel
MSRP $479.00

A SERIES A17 TARGET SPORTER LAMINATE

Action: Semiautomatic
Stock: Wood laminate
Barrel: 22 in.
Sights: None
Weight: N/A
Caliber: .17 HMR
Magazine: Detachable rotary, 10
rounds
Features: Delayed blowback action;
hard chromed bolt with dual controlled round feed; case hardened
receiver; button-rifled barrel
MSRP $579.00

A SERIES A17 TARGET THUMBHOLE

Action: Semiautomatic
Stock: Wood laminate
Barrel: 22 in.
Sights: None
Weight: N/A
Caliber: .17 HMR
Magazine: Detachable rotary, 10
rounds
Features: Grey laminate thumbhole
stock; delayed blowback action; hard
chromed bolt with dual controlled
round feed; case hardened receiver;
button-rifled barrel
MSRP $639.00

A SERIES A17 XP

Action: Semiautomatic
Stock: Synthetic
Barrel: 22 in.
Sights: 3.5–10x36mm Bushnell
Rimfire Optics A17 scope
Weight: N/A
Caliber: .17 HMR
Magazine: Detachable rotary, 10
rounds
Features: Delayed blowback action;
hard chromed bolt with dual controlled round feed; case hardened
receiver; button-rifled barrel
MSRP $589.00

Savage Arms

SAVAGE ARMS A SERIES A22

SAVAGE ARMS A SERIES A22 MAGNUM

SAVAGE ARMS AXIS II XP

SAVAGE ARMS AXIS II XP COMPACT

SAVAGE ARMS AXIS II XP STAINLESS STEEL

SAVAGE ARMS B SERIES (B17 F, B22 F, B22 MAGNUM F)

A SERIES A22

Action: Semiautomatic
Stock: Synthetic
Barrel: 21 in.
Sights: Adjustable
Weight: 5 lb. 10 oz.
Caliber: .22 LR
Magazine: 10 rounds
Features: Modeled after the A17, but chambered for .22 LR; straight blow-back action; steel billet receiver; user-adjustable AccuTrigger
MSRP $284.00

A SERIES A22 MAGNUM

Action: Semiautomatic
Stock: Synthetic
Barrel: 21 in.
Sights: None
Weight: 5 lb. 9 oz.
Caliber: .22 WMR
Magazine: Detachable rotary, 10 rounds
Features: Delayed blowback action; hard chromed bolt with dual controlled round feed; case hardened receiver; button-rifled barrel
MSRP $479.00

AXIS II XP

Action: Bolt
Stock: Synthetic
Barrel: 22 in.

Sights: None
Weight: 6 lb. 8 oz.
Caliber: .22-250 Rem., .223 Rem., .243 Win., .25-06 Rem., .270 Win., .30-06 Spfd., .308 Win., 6.5 Creedmoor, 7mm-08 Rem.
Magazine: 4 rounds
Features: Carbon steel, button-rifled barrel; user-adjustable AccuTrigger; detachable box magazine; factory-mounted and bore-sighted 3–9x40mm Bushnell Banner scope
MSRP $495.00

AXIS II XP COMPACT

Action: Bolt
Stock: Synthetic
Barrel: 20 in.
Sights: None
Weight: 6 lb. 3 oz.
Caliber: .243 Win.
Magazine: 4 rounds
Features: Shorter length of pull; carbon steel, button-rifled barrel; user-adjustable AccuTrigger; detachable box magazine; factory-mounted and bore-sighted 3–9x40mm Bushnell Banner scope
MSRP $495.00

AXIS II XP STAINLESS

Action: Bolt
Stock: Synthetic
Barrel: 22 in.

Sights: None
Weight: 6 lb. 8 oz.
Caliber: .223 Rem., .22-250 Rem., 6.5 Creedmoor, .243 Win., 7mm-08 Rem., .308 Win., .30-06 Spfd., .270 Win.
Magazine: 4 rounds
Features: Carbon steel, button-rifled barrel; user-adjustable AccuTrigger; detachable box magazine; factory-mounted and bore-sighted 3–9x40mm Bushnell Banner scope; stainless-finish barrel, receiver, and bolt
MSRP $589.00

B SERIES

Action: Bolt
Stock: Synthetic
Barrel: 16.25 in., 21 in.
Sights: None
Weight: 5 lb. 8 oz.–6 lb.
Caliber: .17 HMR, .22 LR, .22 WMR
Magazine: 10 rounds
Features: In 2019, the series boasts a total of 21 guns; three available calibers; wood and synthetic stocks; some left-hand models; G models get a raised cheekpiece and vertical pistol grip on a hardwood stock and a fore-end with grooves for improved gripping surface; compact models has 12.5-inch length of pull; all have sling swivel studs and adjustable triggers
MSRP . . . . $285.00–$445.00

SAVAGE ARMS LONG RANGE SERIES MODEL 10 SAVAGE ASHBURY PRECISION

SAVAGE ARMS MAGNUM SERIES 93 BRJ

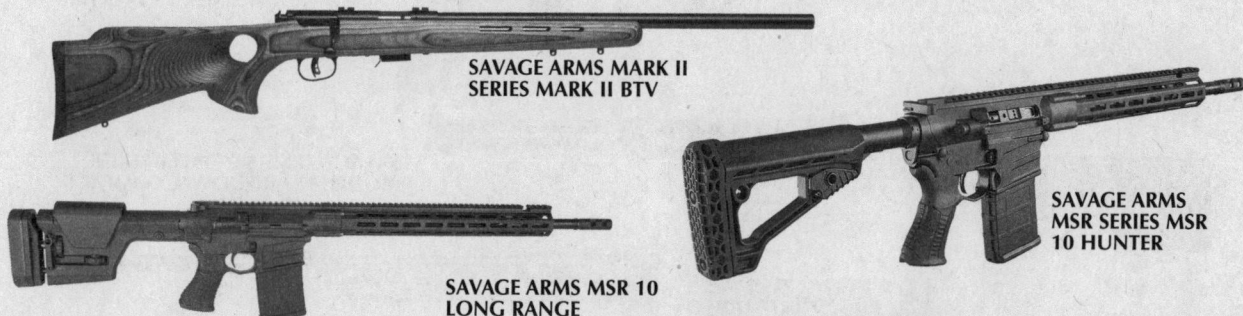

SAVAGE ARMS MARK II SERIES MARK II BTV

SAVAGE ARMS MSR SERIES MSR 10 HUNTER

SAVAGE ARMS MSR 10 LONG RANGE

SAVAGE ARMS MSR SERIES MSR 15 PATROL

LONG RANGE SERIES MODEL 10 SAVAGE ASHBURY PRECISION

Action: Semiautomatic
Stock: Synthetic
Barrel: 24 in.
Sights: None
Weight: 10 lb. 5 oz.
Caliber: 6.5 Creedmoor, .308 Win.
Magazine: 5 rounds
Features: A long-range chassis rifle with a factory blueprinted Model 10 barreled action mated to Ashbury's SABER MRCS-AR folding chassis
MSRP $1829.00

MAGNUM SERIES 93 BRJ

Action: Bolt
Stock: Wood laminate
Barrel: 21 in.
Sights: None
Weight: 7 lb.
Caliber: .22 WMR
Magazine: Detachable box, 5 rounds
Features: Carbon steel barrel in blued satin finish; wood laminate stock; AccuTrigger
MSRP $542.00

MARK II SERIES MARK II BTV

Action: Bolt
Stock: Wood laminate
Barrel: 21 in.

Sights: None
Weight: 6 lb. 8 oz.
Caliber: .22 LR
Magazine: Detachable box, 5 rounds
Features: Carbon steel barrel with blued satin finish; wood laminate stock with thumbhole; AccuTrigger
MSRP $469.00

MSR SERIES MSR 10 HUNTER

Action: Semiautomatic
Stock: Synthetic
Barrel: 16.125 in.
Sights: None
Weight: 7 lb. 13 oz.–8 lb.
Caliber: 6.5 Creedmoor, .308 Win.
Magazine: 20 rounds
Features: Light, compact sporting platform with 5R rifled upgraded barrel; target chamber; BLACKHAWK! AR Blaze trigger; Melonite QPQ finish
MSRP $1505.00

MSR SERIES MSR 10 LONG RANGE

Action: Semiautomatic
Stock: Synthetic
Barrel: 20 in.

Sights: None
Weight: 9 lb. 12 oz.
Caliber: 6.5 Creedmoor, .308 Win.
Magazine: 10 rounds
Features: Long distance capabilities built on a compact frame; non-reciprocating side-charging handle; fluted heavy barrel; BLACKHAWK! two-stage target trigger; Magpul PRS adjustable stock; target chamber
MSRP $2325.00

MSR SERIES MSR 15 PATROL

Action: Semiautomatic
Stock: Synthetic
Barrel: 16.125 in.
Sights: Custom gas block front, BLACKHAWK! flip-up rear
Weight: 6 lb. 8 oz.
Caliber: .223 Rem.
Magazine: 30 rounds
Features: BLACKHAWK! pistol grip, forend, and buttstock; .223 Wylde target chamber; 5R rifling
MSRP $885.00

Savage Arms

RIFLES

SAVAGE ARMS MSR SERIES MSR 15 RECON

SAVAGE ARMS MSR 15 VALKYRIE

SAVAGE ARMS SPECIALTY SERIES MODEL 42 TAKEDOWN, COMPACT

SAVAGE ARMS TARGET SERIES 12 BENCHREST

SAVAGE ARMS TARGET SERIES 112 MAGNUM TARGET

MSR SERIES MSR 15 RECON

Action: Semiautomatic
Stock: Synthetic
Barrel: 16.125 in.
Sights: BLACKHAWK! flip-up
Weight: 7 lb.
Caliber: .223 Rem., 5.56x45mm
Magazine: 30 rounds
Features: BLACKHAWK! AR Blaze trigger; free-floating forend; upgraded Savage barrel with a 223 Wylde target chamber; 5R rifling; Melonite QPQ finish
MSRP **$1009.00**

MSR SERIES MSR 15 VALKYRIE

Action: Semiautomatic
Stock: Aluminum
Barrel: 18 in.
Sights: None
Weight: 7 lb. 12 oz.
Caliber: .224 Valkyrie
Magazine: 30 rounds

Features: Aluminum UBR Gen 2 butt-stock; Hogue pistol grip; two-stage trigger; adjustable gas block with mid-length system; muzzle brake with a Class 3 thread; Elite Series Cerakote on the upper and lower
MSRP **$1529.00**

SPECIALTY SERIES MODEL 42 TAKEDOWN, COMPACT

Action: Over/under
Stock: Synthetic
Barrel: 20 in.
Sights: Adjustable
Weight: 6 lb.
Caliber: .22 LR, .410
Magazine: 2 rounds
Features: Carbon steel barrel; matte barrel finish; break-open combination gun, .22 LR over .410
MSRP **$509.00**

TARGET SERIES 12 BENCHREST

Action: Bolt, single shot

Stock: Wood laminate
Barrel: 29 in.
Sights: None
Weight: 12 lb. 12 oz.
Caliber: .308 Win., 6.5-284 Norma, 6 Norma BR
Magazine: None
Features: Drilled and tapped for scope mounts; stainless steel barrel with high luster finish; wood laminate stock with satin finish; AccuTrigger
MSRP **$1699.00**

TARGET SERIES 112 MAGNUM TARGET

Action: Bolt
Stock: Wood laminate
Barrel: 26 in.
Sights: None
Weight: 12 lb.
Caliber: .338 Lapua Mag.
Magazine: Single shot
Features: Carbon steel barrel; matte barrel finish
MSRP **$1195.00**

Savage Arms

SAVAGE ARMS LIGHTWEIGHT VARMINT SERIES 25 LIGHTWEIGHT VARMINTER

SAVAGE ARMS LIGHTWEIGHT VARMINT SERIES 25 WALKING VARMINTER

VARMINT SERIES 25 LIGHTWEIGHT VARMINTER

Action: Bolt
Stock: Wood laminate
Barrel: 24 in.
Sights: None
Weight: 8 lb. 4 oz.
Caliber: .17 Hornet, .204 Ruger, .22 Hornet, .223 Rem.
Magazine: Detachable box, 4 rounds

Features: Drilled and tapped for scope mounts; carbon steel barrel with blued satin finish; wood laminate stock with satin finish
MSRP **$784.00**

VARMINT SERIES 25 WALKING VARMINTER

Action: Bolt
Stock: Synthetic
Barrel: 22 in.

Sights: None
Weight: 6 lb. 14 oz.
Caliber: .17 Hornet, .204 Ruger, .22 Hornet, .222 Rem., .223 Rem.
Magazine: Detachable box, 4 rounds
Features: Matte black synthetic stock; matte black carbon steel barrel; AccuTrigger
MSRP **$629.00**

Sero

GM6 LYNX

GM6 LYNX

Action: Semiautomatic
Stock: N/A
Barrel: 28.7 in.
Sights: None
Weight: 25 lb. 6 oz.
Caliber: .50 BMG
Magazine: 5 rounds
Features: Hungarian-made .50 BMG bullpup; "unique barrel recoil technology" knocks the punch down to half of any other comparable rifle; a match-grade Lothar Walther barrel; long-recoil action; an effective range of 1500 meters
MSRP **$14,999.00**

Shaw Custom Rifles

SHAW CUSTOM RIFLES ERS10, ERS15

SHAW CUSTOM RIFLES MARK X

ERS10, ERS15

Action: Semiautomatic
Stock: Synthetic
Barrel: 16 in., 18 in., 20 in. (ERS15), 20 in. (ERS10)
Sights: None
Weight: Varies
Caliber: 5.56 NATO, .308, .300 Blackout (ERS15).308, 6.5 Creedmoor (ERS10)
Magazine: N/A
Features: Barrels have continuous twist fluted profiles and can be matte or polished finish; the handguard is either a Magpul MOE or a T-Mod rail heat shield; 7075-T6 forged aluminum upper/lowers; uppers with an M4 feed ramp and finished in black anodized, dry film lube, or Cerakote; lowers in anodized black or Cerakote; button-rifled barrel with an H-bar profile, one-piece hard anodized T-Mod heat shield
ERS 10: . . . . **starting at $995.00**
ERS 15: . . . . **starting at $903.00**

MARK X

Action: Bolt
Stock: Walnut
Barrel: Varies
Sights: None
Weight: Varies
Caliber: Customer choice
Magazine: Varies
Features: Customizable in thousands of combinations; choice of two barrel profiles; more than 80 caliber choices; Grade 5 walnut stocks; integral scope mount bases machined into the receiver; hybrid push/controlled-round feeding; Savage's AccuTrigger; numerous upgrades offered
MSRP . . . . **starting at $1400.00**

SIG Sauer

SIG SAUER MCX RATTLER SBR

SIG SAUER S100 ATACAMA

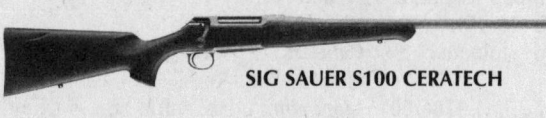

SIG SAUER S100 CERATECH

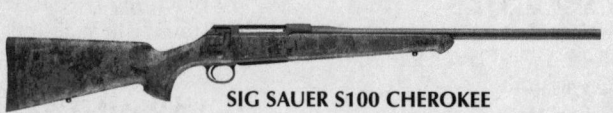

SIG SAUER S100 CHEROKEE

SIG SAUER S100 FIELDSHOOT

SIG SAUER S100 PANTERA

MCX RATTLER SBR

Action: Semiautomatic
Stock: Aluminum
Barrel: 5.5 in.
Sights: None
Weight: 5 lb. 11 oz.
Caliber: .300 Blackout
Magazine: 30 rounds
Features: Takes AR mags; PDW upper and Ultra Thin Folding Aluminum Stock; M-LOK handguard is free-floating; action is gas piston
MSRP **$2727.00**

SAUER S100 ATACAMA

Action: Bolt
Stock: Synthetic
Barrel: 22 in., 24 in.
Sights: None
Weight: N/A
Caliber: .223 Rem., .243 Win. .270 Win., 7mm-08 Rem., 6.5x55 SE, 6.5 Creedmoor, 6.5 PRC, .308 Win., .30-06 Spfd., 8x57 IS, 9.3x62, 7mm Rem. Mag., .300 Win Mag.
Magazine: N/A
Features: Schnabel forend in soft-touch tan/white Digi-Camo; bolt knob, steel receiver, barrel are in Cerakote Desert Sand; adjustable trigger; optional threaded muzzle; optional Hexalock Picatinny rail
MSRP . . . . **$1200.00–$1300.00**

SAUER S100 CERATECH

Action: Bolt
Stock: Synthetic
Barrel: 22 in., 24 in.
Sights: None
Weight: N/A
Caliber: .223 Rem., .243 Win. .270 Win., 7mm-08 Rem., 6.5x55 SE, 6.5 Creedmoor, 6.5 PRC, .308 Win., .30-06 Spfd., 8x57 IS, 9.3x62, 7mm Rem. Mag., .300 Win Mag.
Magazine: N/A
Features: Adjustable trigger; detachable magazine; ERGO MAX Stock; cold hammer forged barrel; receiver and barrel are in Cerakote Grey Ice
MSRP **$899.00**

SAUER S100 CHEROKEE

Action: Bolt
Stock: Synthetic
Barrel: 22 in., 24 in.
Sights: None
Weight: N/A
Caliber: .223 Rem., .243 Win. .270 Win., 7mm-08 Rem., 6.5x55 SE, 6.5 Creedmoor, 6.5 PRC, .308 Win., .30-06 Spfd., 8x57 IS, 9.3x62, 7mm Rem. Mag., .300 Win Mag.
Magazine: N/A
Features: Schnabel forend in soft-touch green/gold Digi-Camo; bolt, steel receiver, and barrel are in Cerakote Tundra Green; adjustable trigger; optional threaded muzzle
MSRP **$1100.00**

SAUER S100 FIELDSHOOT

Action: Bolt
Stock: Wood
Barrel: 24 in.
Sights: None
Weight: N/A
Caliber: .223 Rem., 6.5 Creedmoor, 6.5 PRC, .308 Win.
Magazine: N/A
Features: Oiled wood stock is adjustable for vertical height and length of pull; adjustable cheekpiece; vented forend is trim and has a bipod adaptor; barrel has a varmint match profile; bolt knob is an oversized cone design; threaded muzzle
MSRP **$1599.99**

SAUER S100 PANTERA

Action: Bolt
Stock: Laminated wood
Barrel: 20 in., 22 in.
Sights: None
Weight: N/A
Caliber: .223 Rem., 6.5 Creedmoor, 6.5 PRC, .308 Win., .39-06 Spfd., .300 Win. Mag.
Magazine: N/A
Features: Threaded fluted barrel treated in Cerakote Black Recon; adjustable cheek piece; vented forend is trim and has a bipod adaptor; threaded muzzle
MSRP **$1599.99**

RIFLES

SAUER S101 ARTEMIS

SAUER S101 CLASSIC

J. P. SAUER & SOHN S404 CLASSIC

SIG SAUER SIG516 PATROL

SAUER S101 ARTEMIS

Action: Bolt
Stock: Wood
Barrel: 20 in.
Sights: Adjustable
Weight: 6 lb. 6 oz.
Caliber: .243 Win., .270 Win., .308 Win., 7x64 Brenneke, .30-06 Spfd., 8x57IS, 9.3x62 Mauser
Magazine: 5+1 rounds
Features: Designed for individuals with small hands and frames; walnut ERGO MAX stock; laserline stock grain; exclusive jeweled bolt; DURA SAFE direct firing pin safety; walnut bolt knob; super crisp 2-lb. trigger pull; fully adjustable iron sights
MSRP $2052.00

SAUER S101 CLASSIC

Action: Bolt
Stock: Walnut
Barrel: 22 in., 24 in.
Sights: Adjustable open sights optional
Weight: 6 lb. 12 oz.
Caliber: .22-250 Rem., .243 Win., .270 Win., .308 Win., .30-06 Spfd., 6.5x55 Swedish, 7x64 Brenneke, 8x57IS, 9.3x62 Mauser, 7mm Rem. Mag., .300 Win. Mag., .338 Win. Mag.
Magazine: 5+1 rounds (standard), 4+1 rounds (magnum)

Features: 60-degree bolt lift; six locking lugs; available in standard and magnum calibers; matte black finish; DURA SAFE firing pin safety; EVER REST action bedding; ambidextrous stock
MSRP $1770.00

SAUER S404 CLASSIC

Action: Bolt
Stock: Wood
Barrel: 20–24.4 in.
Sights: Adjustable
Weight: 7 lb.–7 lb. 3 oz.
Caliber: .243 Win., 6.5x55 Swedish, .270 Win., 7x64 Brenneke, .308 Win., .30-06 Spfd., 8x57IS, 9.3x62 Mauser, 7mm Rem. Mag., .300 Win. Mag., 8x68 S, .338 Win. Mag., .375 H&H Mag.
Magazine: 2–3 rounds
Features: ERGO LUX stock in grade-5 figured walnut; aviation-grade high-alloy aluminum receiver; perfectly placed ergonomic manual cocking slide on the bolt shroud; easily replaceable bolt head makes switching from standard to magnum calibers a snap; twin ejectors for a precisely perpendicular ejection pattern; 6-lug bolt locks directly into the barrel; jeweled bolt body; SAUER Quattro trigger with choice of four trigger pull weights: 550 g (1.2 lbs), 750 g (1.7 lbs), 1000 g (2.2 lbs) and 1250 g (2.7 lbs); infinitely adjustable trigger blade with 8 mm (0.3 in) adjustment range for length of pull and a left-to-right swivel range of 5 degrees; SAUER Universal Mount (SUM) integral to with receiver for an extremely low build height; SAUER universal key (SUS) integrated into the front sling swivel for forend and buttstock removal, barrel removal or replacement, and selection of trigger pull weight; MagLock magazine safety
MSRP $4884.00

SIG516 PATROL

Action: Semiautomatic
Stock: Tactical synthetic
Barrel: 16 in.
Sights: None
Weight: 7 lb. 5 oz.
Caliber: 5.56 NATO
Magazine: Detachable box, 30 rounds
Features: Gas piston operating system; three-position gas regulator; free-floating military grade chrome-lined barrel; Picatinny flat top upper; aircraft grade aluminum upper and lower receiver with hard coat anodize finish.
Black: $1888.00
Flat Dark Earth: $2024.00

SIG Sauer

SIG SAUER SIG716G2 PATROL

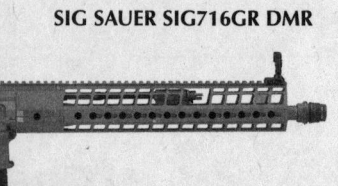

SIG SAUER SIG716GR DMR

SIG716G2 PATROL

Action: Semiautomatic
Stock: Tactical synthetic
Barrel: 16 in.
Sights: None
Weight: 9 lb. 5 oz.
Caliber: 7.62 NATO
Magazine: Detachable box, 20 rounds
Features: Second generation is a short-stroke gas piston operating system with a free-floating barrel, aluminum fore-end, telescoping stock, and M1913 Mil-Std rail; one 20-round polymer AR-10 mag included; available in Cerakote or hard coat aniodized receiver finish
MSRP . . . . **starting at $2385.00**

SIG716GR DMR

Action: Semiautomatic
Stock: Synthetic
Barrel: 16 in.
Sights: None
Weight: 8 lb. 3 oz.
Caliber: 6.5 Creedmoor, 7.62 NATO
Magazine: 20 rounds
Features: Taper-Lok muzzle brake; aluminum KeyMod handguard with continuous M1913 top rail; two-position adjustable gas valve; two-stage match trigger; sub-MOA performance; available in black (7.62 only) or Flat Dark Earth Cerakote (both calibers)
MSRP . . . . **starting at $2749.00**

Smith & Wesson

SMITH & WESSON M&P 10 6.5 CREEDMOOR

SMITH & WESSON M&P10 OPTIC READY

M&P10 6.5 CREEDMOOR

Action: Semiautomatic
Stock: Synthetic
Barrel: 20 in.
Sights: None
Weight: 9 lb.
Caliber: 6.5 Creedmoor
Magazine: 10 rounds
Features: MSR flattop platform; threaded muzzle with thread protector; two-stage match trigger; 15-in. free-floating Troy Alpha M-LOK handguard; 2-in. aluminum M-LOK accessory rail; Magpul MOE stock; gas-operated
MSRP **$2035.00**

M&P10 OPTIC READY

Action: Gas-operated semiautomatic
Stock: Synthetic
Barrel: 22 in.
Sights: None
Weight: 7 lb. 11 oz.
Caliber: .308 Win., 7.62 NATO
Magazine: Detachable box, 20 rounds
Features: Ambidextrous magazine catch; bolt catch; reversible, ambidextrous safety selector; S&W enhanced flash hider; gas block with integral Picatinny rail; QD sling swivel attachment point (bottom of gas block); 5R rifling
MSRP **$1619.00**

RIFLES

Smith & Wesson

SMITH & WESSON M&P 10
SPORT OPTICS READY

SMITH & WESSON M&P15

SMITH & WESSON M&P15 300 WHISPER

SMITH & WESSON M&P 15
COMPETITION

SMITH & WESSON M&P15
MOE SL MID MAGPUL
SPEC SERIES

M&P 10 SPORT OPTICS READY

Action: Semiautomatic
Stock: Synthetic
Barrel: 16. in.
Sights: None
Weight: 8 lb.
Caliber: .308 Win.
Magazine: 20 rounds
Features: Mid-length gas system; ambidextrous safety; bolt and magazine releases; mid-length handguard; A2 suppressor; chromed firing pin; six-position telescoping stock; gas block with Picatinny rail; barrel is finished inside and out with Armornite
MSRP **$1049.00**

M&P15

Action: Semiautomatic
Stock: Synthetic
Barrel: 16 in.
Sights: Troy adjustable front post, folding rear battle sight
Weight: 6 lb. 12 oz.
Caliber: 5.56 NATO, .223 Rem.
Magazine: Detachable box, 30 rounds

Features: Six-position telescopic black stock; chrome-lined gas key and bolt carrier; flash suppressor compensator; two-position safety lever
MSRP **$1269.00**

M&P15 300 WHISPER

Action: Semiautomatic
Stock: Synthetic
Barrel: 16 in.
Sights: None
Weight: 6 lb. 6 oz.
Caliber: .300 Whisper
Magazine: Detachable box, 10 rounds
Features: Sub-sonic and super-sonic capabilities; 4140 chromoly steel barrel; forged 7075 aluminum receivers coated with Realtree APG finish; gas-operated rifle; single-stage trigger; integral one-piece trigger guard; six-position collapsible CAR stock; optics ready; available in black or full-coverage Realtree APG camo
MSRP **$1119.00**

M&P15 COMPETITION

Action: Semiautomatic
Stock: Synthetic
Barrel: 18 in.

Sights: None
Weight: 7 lb. 6 oz.
Caliber: 5.56 NATO
Magazine: 30 rounds
Features: Performance Center muzzle brake; two-stage match trigger; 15-in. free-floating Troy Alpha M-LOK handguard; 2-in. aluminum M-Lok rail; VLTOR I-Mod stock; Hogue pistol grip; aluminum frame; gas-operated
MSRP **$1579.00**

M&P15 MOE SL MID MAGPUL SPEC SERIES

Action: Semiautomatic
Stock: Synthetic
Barrel: 16 in.
Sights: M4-A2 post front, folding Magpul rear
Weight: 6 lb. 8 oz.
Caliber: 5.56 NATO
Magazine: Detachable box, 30 rounds
Features: Mid-length operating system, patent-pending flash hider; available in black and dark earth finish; Magpul designed forged lower receiver with flared magazine; one-piece integrated trigger guard; Melonite finish on barrel; MOE six-position collapsible buttstock; available in black or Stealth Gray
MSRP **$1239.00**

Smith & Wesson

SMITH & WESSON
M&P15 SPORT II

SMITH & WESSON M&P 15T
WITH M-LOK, M&P 15T WITH
M-LOK AND CRIMSON TRACE
LINQ SYSTEM

SMITH & WESSON
M&P15-22 SPORT,
SPORT M-LOK

SMITH & WESSON M&P15 VTAC
II VIKING TACTICS

SMITH & WESSON M&P
15-22 SPORT ROBIN'S EGG
BLUE PLATINUM FINISH

M&P15 SPORT II

Action: Semiautomatic
Stock: Synthetic
Barrel: 16 in.
Sights: Adjustable front, Magpul MBUS rear
Weight: 6 lb. 7 oz.
Caliber: 5.56 NATO
Magazine: 30+1 rounds
Features: Forged, integral trigger guard; Armornite finish (durable corrosion-resistant finish); chromed firing pin; forward assist; dust cover; available in Colorado- and California-compliant versions, MOE M-LOK, and as Optics Ready variant with or without M-LOK handguard
MSRP **$739.00**

M&P 15T WITH M-LOK, WITH M-LOK AND CRIMSON TRACE LINQ SYSTEM

Action: Semiautomatic
Stock: Synthetic
Barrel: 16 in.
Sights: Magpul MBUS flip-up front and rear
Weight: 6 lb. 11.2 oz.
Caliber: 5.56 NATO
Magazine: 30 rounds
Features: Gas-operated semiautomatic; 13-in. M&P modular free-float rail system; M-LOK capability; 2-in. M-LOK Picatinny rail; lightweight barrel with 5R rifling; Crimson Trace LiNQ System combo green laser and light available
With M-LOK only: **$1189.00**
With Crimson Trace: **$1499.00**

M&P15 VTAC II VIKING TACTICS

Action: Semiautomatic
Stock: Synthetic
Barrel: 16 in.
Sights: None
Weight: 6 lb. 4 oz.
Caliber: 5.56 NATO
Magazine: Detachable box, 30 rounds
Features: Mid-length operating system, patent-pending flash hider; 4150 CMV steel barrel with Melonite finish; VTAC/Troy Extreme TRX handguard that reduces heat transfer; packaged with 2-inch adjustable Picatinny rails; Geissele Super V trigger
MSRP **$1949.00**

M&P15-22 SPORT, SPORT M-LOK

Stock: Synthetic
Barrel: 16.5 in.
Sights: Folding Magpul MBUS front and rear
Weight: 4 lb. 12 oz.
Caliber *.22 LR*
Capacity: 10, 25 rounds
Features: Updated version of the original M&P 15-22, with a slightly shorter barrel; six-position collapsible stock, 10-in. slim handguard, M-LOK compatible, functioning charging handle, shell deflector, two-position receiver-mounted safety, and Armonite barrel finish are standard; available in black, Kryptek, and Muddy Girl finishes; California-compliant version available in black only
MSRP . . . . **$449.00–$499.00**

M&P 15-22 SPORT ROBIN'S EGG BLUE PLATINUM FINISH

Action: Semiautomatic
Stock: Synthetic
Barrel: 16.5 in.
Sights: MBUS folding front and rear
Weight: 5 lb.
Caliber: .22 LR
Magazine: 25 rounds
Features: carbon steel barrel; folding sights; six-position CAR stock; 2-in. M-LOK rail panel; M&P handguard with Magpul's M-LOKTM
MSRP **$499.00**

Springfield Armory

SPRINGFIELD ARMORY LOADED M1A

SPRINGFIELD ARMORY M1A SOCOM 16

SPRINGFIELD ARMORY M1A SOCOM 16 CQB

SPRINGFIELD ARMORY NATIONAL MATCH M1A

SPRINGFIELD ARMORY SAINT 5.56 NATO

SPRINGFIELD ARMORY SAINT EDGE

LOADED M1A

Action: Semiautomatic
Stock: Synthetic
Barrel: 22 in.
Sights: Adjustable
Weight: 11 lb. 4 oz.
Caliber: 7.62 NATO, 6.5 Creedmoor
Magazine: 10 rounds
Features: 1:11 inch barrel twist; match grade aperture with ½ MOA adjustment for windage and 1 MOA for elevation; FDE precision adjustable stock
MSRP . . . . $1847.00–$2045.00

M1A SOCOM 16

Action: Semiautomatic
Stock: Composite
Barrel: 16.25 in.
Sights: Tritium front sight
Weight: 8 lb. 13 oz.
Caliber: 7.62 NATO, .308 Win
Magazine: Detachable box, 10 rounds
Features: Muzzlebrake; forward mounted scope base; two-stage military trigger; composite black or green stock
MSRP . . . . $1987.00–$2422.00

M1A SOCOM 16 CQB

Action: Semiautomatic
Stock: Synthetic
Barrel: 16.25 in.
Sights: XS Post with tritium insert front, adjustable rear
Weight: 9 lb. 3 oz.
Caliber: .308 Win., 7.62x51mm NATO

Magazine: 10 or 20 rounds
Features: Adjustable buttstock; five-position length and two-position adjustable cheek piece; standard AR-type commercial buffer tube; AK-style pistol grip; accepts any standard AK-style replacement; M-Lok compatible system; fixed top rail
MSRP . . . . $2121.00–$2420.00

NATIONAL MATCH M1A

Action: Semiautomatic
Stock: Walnut
Barrel: 22 in.
Sights: National Match front military post sight; rear National Match hooded aperture
Weight: 9 lb. 13 oz.
Caliber: 7.62 NATO, .308 Win.
Magazine: Detachable box, 10 rounds
Features: Glass bedded; NM gas cylinder; NM recoil spring guide; NM flash suppressor; walnut stock; stainless steel or carbon barrel; two-stage military trigger
MSRP . . . . $2485.00–$2542.00

SAINT

Action: Semiautomatic
Stock: Synthetic
Barrel: 16 in.
Sights: Standard post front, Springfield Armory low profile flip-up dual aperture rear
Weight: 6 lb. 11 oz.
Caliber: 5.56 NATO

Magazine: 30 rounds
Features: Type III aircraft-grade 7075 T6 aluminum upper and lower receivers are joined using the Accu-Tite system; 16-inch chrome moly vanadium barrel treated with Melonite; 1:8-inch twist; mid-length gas system paired with a heavier carbine "H" heavy tungsten buffer; Bravo Company Mod 0 pistol grip and Bravo Company buttstock; QD and fixed sling swivels; Bravo PKMT two-piece handguard; aluminum heat shields; black or Flat Dark Earth; California-compliant in black only
Standard: $919.00
California-compliant: $998.00

SAINT EDGE

Action: Semiautomatic
Stock: Synthetic
Barrel: 16 in.
Sights: Flip-up front and rear
Weight: 6 lb. 3 oz.
Caliber: 5.56 NATO
Magazine: 30 rounds
Features: Mid-length multi-mode adjustable gas block; Bravo Company M3 pistol grip; Mod 0 SOPMOD buttstock; Springfield mid-size charging handle; free-floating full-length aluminum handguard; Tungsten Carbine H heavy buffer; flip-up sights are Springfield Armory's low-profile, dual-aperture rear; Springfield multiport muzzle brake
MSRP $1299.00

Springfield Armory

SPRINGFIELD ARMORY SAINT WITH FREE-FLOAT HANDGUARD

SPRINGFIELD ARMORY SCOUT SQUAD

SPRINGFIELD ARMORY STANDARD M1A

SAINT WITH FREE-FLOAT HANDGUARD

Action: Semiautomatic
Stock: Synthetic
Barrel: 16 in.
Sights: SA low-profile flip-up dual-aperture rear, ½-MOA windage/elevation-adjustable flip-up front
Weight: 6 lb. 9 oz.
Caliber: 5.56 NATO
Magazine: 30 round
Features: Aluminum M-LOK free-floating handguard with SA locking tabs; direct-impingement mid-length gas system; six-position Bravo Company stock; a low-profile gas block; Springfield's nickel-boron-coated GI trigger; Mil-Spec carbine receiver extension; a carbine "H" heavy tungsten buffer assembly; Type II hard coat-anodized 7075 T6 aluminum upper and lower; includes a hard case and one 30-round Magpul PMAG Gen M3 magazine
MSRP . . . . $1073.00–$1135.00

SCOUT SQUAD

Action: Semiautomatic
Stock: Walnut, composite
Barrel: 18 in.
Sights: National Match front military post sight; rear military aperture
Weight: 9 lb. 5 oz.
Caliber: 7.62 NATO, .308 Win.
Magazine: Detachable box, 10 rounds
Features: Mounted optical sight base; muzzle stabilizers; black or green fiberglass composite, American walnut stock or Mossy Oak camo stock; two-stage military trigger
MSRP . . . . $1850.00–$1987.00

STANDARD M1A

Action: Semiautomatic
Stock: Composite or walnut
Barrel: 22 in.
Sights: National Match military front post, adjustable rear aperture sight
Weight: 9 lb. 5 oz.
Caliber: 7.62 NATO, .308 Win.
Magazine: Detachable box, 10 rounds
Features: Stocks available in Highlander camo, solid Flat Dark Earth, walnut, or black composite; parkerized carbon steel barrels; two-stage military trigger
MSRP . . . . $1685.00–$1788.00

Stag Arms

STAG ARMS MODEL 3GUN ELITE

MODEL 3GUN ELITE

Action: Semiautomatic
Stock: Synthetic
Barrel: 18 in.
Sights: None
Weight: N/A
Caliber: 5.56 NATO, .223 Rem.
Magazine: Detachable box, 30 rounds
Features: A2 flash hider; Picatinny rail; Magpul ACS buttstock; aluminum enhanced trigger guard; manganese phosphate-coated chrome-lined bolt carrier group; Stag 3G compensator; Geissele Super 3-Gun trigger
Right-hand: $1399.99
Left-hand: $1499.99

STEYR ARMS AUG A3 M1

STEYR ARMS PRO TACTICAL HEAVY BARREL .308

STEYR ARMS SCOUT

STEYR ARMS SSG 08

STEYR ARMS ZEPHYR II

AUG A3 M1
Action: Semiautomatic
Stock: Synthetic
Barrel: 16 in.
Sights: None
Weight: 7 lb. 11 oz.–8 lb. 13. oz.
Caliber: 5.56 NATO, .223 Rem.
Magazine: Detachable box, 30 rounds
Features: Bullpup rifle has adjustable short-stroke gas piston, hard Eloxalcoated aircraft aluminum receiver, chrome-lined CHF barrel with muzzle brake, two-position trigger-blocking safety; short rail, high rail, and optics configurations; available in white/ black, OD Green, or MUD; choice of short, long, or extended rails; choice of 1.5X or 3X optic
MSRP . . . . $2195.00–$2838.00

PRO TACTICAL HEAVY BARREL
Action: Bolt
Stock: Synthetic
Barrel: 15, 20, 26 in.
Sights: None
Weight: N/A
Caliber: 6.5 Creedmoor, .308 Win.
Magazine: N/A

Features: Heavy contour threaded barrel with Mannox finish; tactical bolt knob; 20 MOA Picatinny rail; and stock spacers; two-stage magazine securing mechanism; note the 6.5 Creedmoor Steyr listed with green stock but picture looks like a tan stock, so buyers should research if this is important to them
.308 Win.: . . . . . . $1490.00–$1885.00
6.5 Creedmoor: . .$1650.00–$1750.00

SCOUT
Action: Bolt
Stock: Synthetic
Barrel: 19 in.
Sights: None
Weight: 6 lb. 10 oz.
Caliber: .308 Win., 7mm-08 Rem.
Magazine: Detachable box, 5 rounds (optional 10 round magazine)
Features: Weaver scope mounting rail; set trigger or direct trigger; synthetic stock in black or gray wood imitation; optional bipod integrated into forearm; matte black or stainless steel finish on barrel
MSRP $1787.00

SSG 08
Action: Bolt
Stock: Synthetic
Barrel: 20, 23.6, 25.6 in.
Sights: None
Weight: 5 lb. 8 oz.–5 lb. 11 oz.
Caliber: .300 Win. Mag., .308 Win., .338 Lapua
Magazine: Detachable box, 10 rounds
Features: Direct trigger; Mannox TM system; high grade aluminum folding stock; adjustable cheekpiece and buttplate with height marking; ergonomic exchangeable pistol grip; UIT rail and Picatinny rail; muzzlebrake; Versa-Pod
MSRP . . . .$6195.00–$7149.00

ZEPHYR II
Action: Bolt
Stock: Walnut
Barrel: 19.7 in.
Sights: None
Weight: 5 lb. 13 oz.
Caliber: .17 HMR, .22 LR, .22 WMR
Magazine: 5 rounds
Features: Trim, European walnut stock; fish scale checkering; tang safety; detachable magazine; available with threaded barrel
MSRP . . . .$1075.00–$1099.00

Tactical Rifles

TACTICAL RIFLES CLASSIC SPORTER

TACTICAL RIFLES TACTICAL LONG RANGE

CLASSIC SPORTER

Action: Chimera bolt
Stock: Walnut
Barrel: 22 in.
Sights: None
Weight: 8 lb. 14 oz.
Caliber: .308 Win., .260 Rem., 6.5 Creedmoor and Lapua, .243 Win., 7mm-08 Rem. (short action), .25-06,.30-06 Spfd., .270 Win., .300 Win. Mag., 7mm Rem. Mag. (long action)
Magazine: 4+1 rounds
Features: Chimera action is constructed from stainless steel with a hand-fitted spiral-groove bolt and "Magnum" extractor; Picatinny rail; XXX grade English walnut stock with 22 lpi checkering at grip and forearm; extreme environment matte black finish
MSRP **$5895.00**

TACTICAL LONG RANGE

Action: Bolt, 700 Rem.
Stock: Synthetic
Barrel: 18 in.-26 in.
Sights: None
Weight: 12 lb.–13 lb. 6 oz.
Caliber: 7.62 NATO, .308 Win., .260 Rem., 6.5 Creedmoor, 6.5 Lapua, .243 Win., 7mm-08, .30-06 Spfd., .270 Win., .25-06; other calibers can be custom ordered
Magazine: Detachable box, 5 or 10 rounds
Features: Ergonomic thumbhole stock comes in black or green; raised cheekpiece; free-floating chromoly match grade barrel; ambidextrous sling swivel studs; soft rubber recoil pad; Picatinny rail; aluminum block chassis stock system; optional bipod
MSRP **$3450.00**

Taylor's & Co. Firearms

TAYLOR'S & CO. 1860 HENRY LEVER ACTION RIFLE

TAYLOR'S & CO. 1873 RIFLE - CHECKERED STRAIGHT STOCK

1860 HENRY LEVER ACTION RIFLE

Action: Lever
Stock: Walnut
Barrel: 24.25 in.
Sights: Open
Weight: 9 lb. 3 oz.
Caliber: .44-40 Win., .45 LC
Magazine: Under-barrel tube, 9–13 rounds
Features: Brass frame; octagonal barrel with blued finish; includes sling swivels
MSRP . . . . **$1463.00–$1811.00**

1873 RIFLE - CHECKERED STRAIGHT STOCK

Action: Lever
Stock: Walnut
Barrel: 20 in.
Sights: Open
Weight: 8 lb. 8 oz.
Caliber: .357 Mag., .45 LC
Magazine: Under-barrel tube, 10+1 rounds

Features: Case-hardened frame; straight stock with checkering; available with full octagon barrel
MSRP **$1383.00**

RIFLES

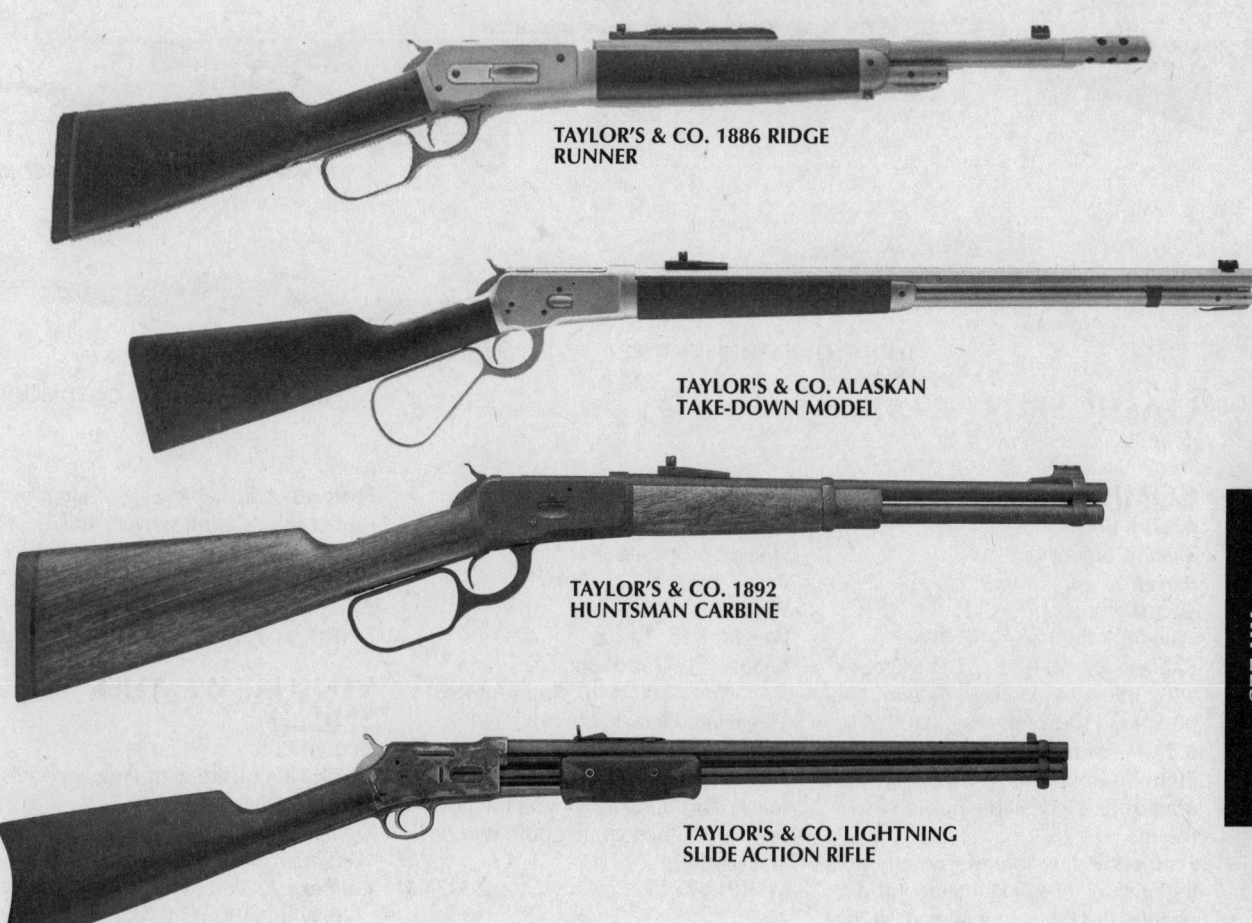

TAYLOR'S & CO. 1886 RIDGE RUNNER

TAYLOR'S & CO. ALASKAN TAKE-DOWN MODEL

TAYLOR'S & CO. 1892 HUNTSMAN CARBINE

TAYLOR'S & CO. LIGHTNING SLIDE ACTION RIFLE

1886 RIDGE RUNNER

Action: Lever
Stock: Wood or synthetic
Barrel: 18.5 in.
Sights: Skinner rear peep sight, fiber optic front
Weight: 7 lb. 13 oz.
Caliber: .45-70 Govt.
Magazine: 4, 8 rounds
Features: Available in two versions, either matte blue or matte chrome metal work. Stock is wood with soft-touch rubber overmold; Integrated Skinner rear peep sight, Weaver rail, front fiber optic sight, D-shaped lever, muzzle brake, and half-octagonal barrel are standard
Blue: **$1728.00**
Chrome: **$1830.00**

1892 ALASKAN TAKE-DOWN MODEL

Action: Lever
Stock: Synthetic
Barrel: 16 in., 20 in.
Sights: Skinner rear
Weight: 6 lb. 10 oz.
Caliber: .357 Mag., .44RM, .45 LC
Magazine: Under-barrel tube, 10 rounds
Features: Matte chrome finish; soft touch stock
MSRP . . . .**$1412.00–$1483.00**

1892 HUNTSMAN CARBINE

Action: Lever
Stock: Walnut
Barrel: 16 in.
Sights: Fiber optic front, adjustable rear
Weight: 6 lb.
Caliber: .357 Mag. .44 Mag. .45 LC
Magazine: 8 rounds
Features: Based on an antique platform; modern sights; short, nimble barrel; reduced weight
MSRP **$1273.00**

LIGHTNING SLIDE ACTION RIFLE

Action: Slide
Stock: Walnut
Barrel: 20, 24, 26 in.
Sights: Open
Weight: 6 lb. 6 oz.–6 lb. 14 oz.
Caliber: .357 Mag., .45 LC
Magazine: 10 rounds
Features: Features an inertia firing pin and unloading latch in four versions: Carbine Standard with a 20-inch round barrel; Rifle Standard with a 20-inch round barrel; and Rifle Premium with a 20- or 24-inch octagonal barrel
Carbine Standard: **$1531.00**
Rifle Standard Round: **$1564.00**
Rifle Premium 20-inch: . . .**$1802.00**
Rifle Premium 24-inch: . . .**$1821.00**

Thompson/Center Arms

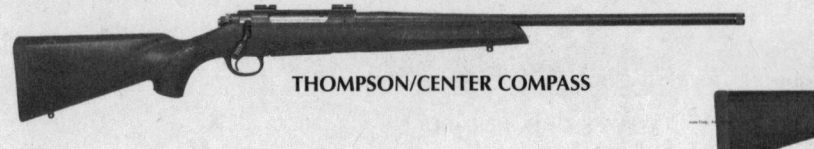

THOMPSON/CENTER COMPASS

THOMPSON/CENTER VENTURE COMPACT

THOMPSON/CENTER VENTURE
PREDATOR

THC
WEATHER SHIELD 6.5 CREEDMOOR

COMPASS

Action: Bolt
Stock: Composite
Barrel: 22 in., 24 in.
Sights: None
Weight: 7 lb. 4 oz.–7 lb. 8 oz.
Caliber: .22-50 Rem., .204 Ruger, .223/5.56, .243 Win., .270 Win., .30-06 Spfd., .300 Win. Mag., .308 Win., 6.5 Creedmoor, 7mm Rem. Mag., 7mm-08 Rem.
Magazine: Detachable box, 5+1 rounds
Features: Adjustable trigger; ergonomic, lightweight stock; textured grip panels; soft rubber recoil pad; aluminum pillar bedding system that positively locates the receiver and free-floats the barrel for outstanding accuracy; easy-to-use three-position safety; rotary magazvine fits flush with the stock and provides smooth feeding; drilled and tapped receiver for scope mounting with bases included
MSRP **$399.00**

VENTURE COMPACT

Action: Bolt
Stock: Composite
Barrel: 20 in.
Sights: None
Weight: 6 lb. 12 oz.
Caliber: .22-250 Rem., .223 Rem., .243 Win., .308 Win., 7mm-08 Rem.
Magazine: Detachable box, 3+1 rounds
Features: Adjustable trigger; included spacer and buttpad; Hogue traction inlays; Melanite coated bolt; two position safety
MSRP **$537.00**

VENTURE PREDATOR

Action: Bolt
Stock: Composite
Barrel: 22 in., 24 in.
Sights: Bases for mounting scopes
Weight: 6 lb. 12 oz.
Caliber: 7mm-08 Rem., .243 Rem., .22-250 Rem., .308 Win.
Magazine: Detachable box, 3+1

rounds
Features: Adjustable trigger; Hogue rubber inlays; sling swivel studs; Weather Shield bolt handle; full-coverage Realtree AP HD Snow or Advantage HD Max-1
MSRP **$638.00**

VENTURE WEATHER SHIELD

Action: Bolt
Stock: Composite with Hogue panels
Barrel: 22 in.
Sights: None
Weight: 7 lb.
Caliber: .22-250 Rem., 6.5 Creedmoor, .270 Win., .300 Win. Mag., .308 Win., .30-06 Spfd., 7mm Rem. Mag., 7mm-08 Rem.
Magazine: 3 rounds
Features: Weaver-style bases factory installed; adjustable trigger; detachable magazine; Hogue Overmolded panels; nitride-coated bolt; Weather Shield finish
MSRP **$578.00**

Tikka

TIKKA T1X MTR

T1X MTR

Action: Bolt
Stock: Synthetic
Barrel: 20 in.
Sights: None
Weight: 5 lb. 5 oz.

Caliber: .22 LR, .17 HMR
Magazine: 10 rounds
Features: Detachable magazine; threaded muzzle; modular stock with grip adjustable for angle
MSRP **$499.00**

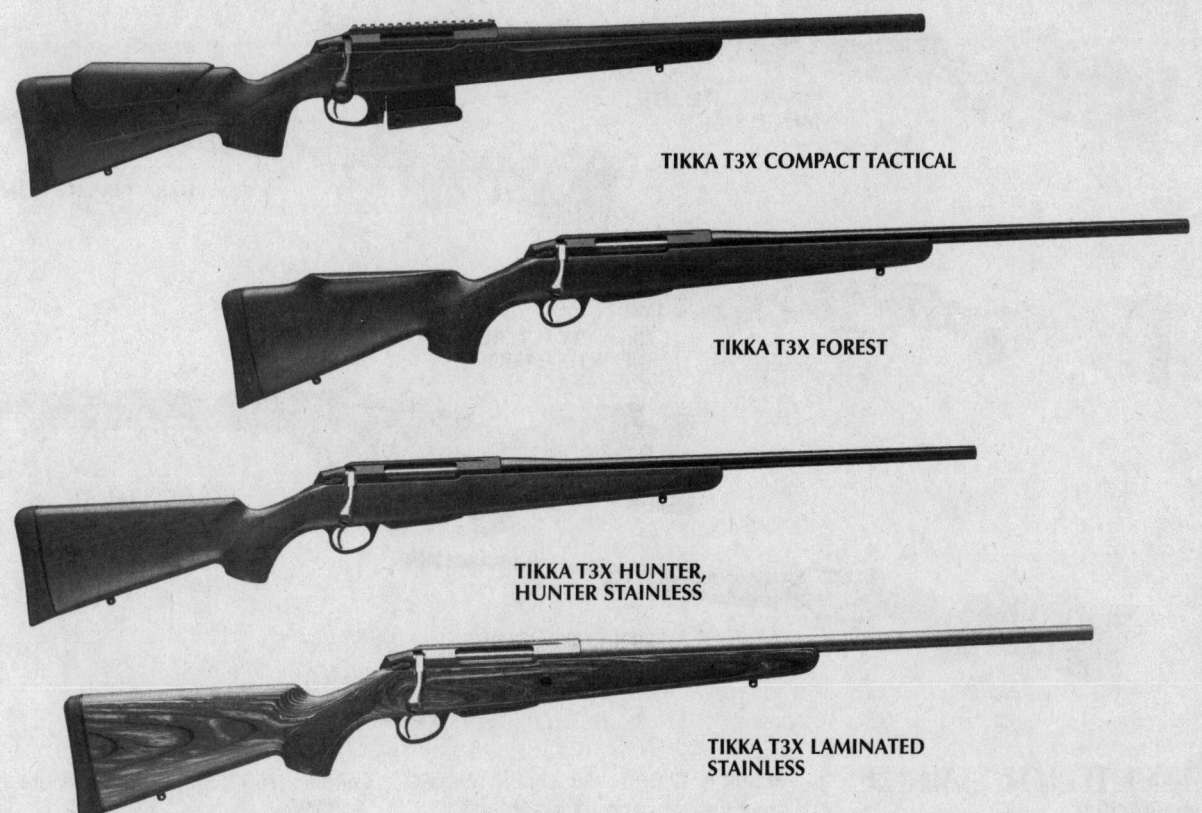

TIKKA T3X COMPACT TACTICAL

TIKKA T3X FOREST

TIKKA T3X HUNTER, HUNTER STAINLESS

TIKKA T3X LAMINATED STAINLESS

T3X COMPACT TACTICAL

Action: Bolt
Stock: Synthetic
Barrel: 20 in.
Sights: None
Weight: 5 lb. 14.4 oz.
Caliber: .308 Win., .260 Rem., 6.5 Creedmoor
Magazine: 3, 4 rounds
Features: Designed specifically for low-recoiling centerfire rifle rounds; 30mm spacer and larger recoil pad to further improve fit and reduce felt recoil; black synthetic stock; stainless steel barrel; single-stage adjustable trigger; integral 17mm rail; drilled and tapped for scope mounts; blue or stainless metal finishes
Blue: **$1150.00**
Stainless: **$1275.00**

T3X FOREST

Action: Bolt
Stock: Synthetic
Barrel: 20 in., 22.4 in., 24.4 in.
Sights: Optional open
Weight: 6 lb. 9.8 oz.–7 lb.
Caliber: .270 Win., .300 Win. Mag., .308 Win., .30-06 Spfd., 7mm Rem. Mag.

Magazine: 3, 4 rounds
Features: Designed for hunter using scopes with large variable optics that require higher mounting; modular synthetic stock has interchangeable pistol grip and optional attachment point that allows the user to change the width of the forend; asymmetrical grip pattern provides solid grip in adverse conditions; stocks without cheekpieces have foam insert that lowers stock-generated noise; widened ejection port improves cycling; extra top-side receiver screw permits Picatinny rail mounting; set and standard triggers available
MSRP **$1000.00**

T3X HUNTER, HUNTER STAINLESS

Action: Bolt
Stock: Walnut
Barrel: 22.4 in.
Sights: None
Weight: 6 lb. 12.8 oz.
Caliber: .243 Win., 6.5x55mm, .270 Win., .308 Win., .30-06 Spfd., 7mm-08 Rem., 7mm Rem. Mag. 6.5 Creedmoor
Magazine: 3 rounds
Features: Classic walnut stock has improved checkering and enhanced recoil pad; stainless finish barrel is fluted and has hand-cut target crown; receiver has widened ejection port; integral 17mm rail drilled and tapped to accept standard scope mounts or Picatinny rail
Blue right-hand: **$875.00**
Blue left-hand: **$925.00**
Stainless: **$1100.00**

T3X LAMINATED STAINLESS

Action: Bolt
Stock: Laminate
Barrel: 22.4 in., 24.3 in.
Sights: None
Weight: 6 lb. 9.6 oz.–7 lb.
Caliber: .243 Win., .260 Rem., .270 Rem., .270 WSM, .308 Win., .30-06 Spfd., 7mm Rem. Mag, .300 WSM, 6.5 Creedmoor
Magazine: N/A
Features: Weather-resistant gray laminate stock; cold-hammer-forged stainless steel free-floating barrel with hand-cut target crown; receiver has widened ejection port; integral 17mm rail drilled and tapped to accept standard scope mounts or Picatinny rail
MSRP . . . .**$1050.00–$1100.00**

Tikka

TIKKA T3X LITE, LITE STAINLESS

TIKKA T3X LITE COMPACT

TIKKA T3X SUPERLITE, SUPERLITE CAMO

TIKKA T3X TAC A1

TIKKA T3X VARMINT

T3X LITE, LITE STAINLESS

Action: Bolt
Stock: Synthetic
Barrel: 22 in., 24 in.
Sights: None
Weight: 7 lb. 3 oz.
Caliber: .223 Rem., .22-250 Rem., .243 Win., .25-06 Rem., .270 Win., .270 WSM, .300 Win. Mag., .300 WSM, .30-06 Spfd., .308 Win., 7mm-08 Rem., 7mm Rem. Mag., 6.5 Creedmoor
Magazine: 3, 4 rounds
Features: Weather-resistant rifle; modular stock that allows for grip angle adjustment; new recoil pad; improved textured gripping surfaces; stock's foam insert reduces noise; left-hand models available
MSRP . . . . **$725.00–$775.00**
Stainless: . . . . **$850.00–$1000.00**

T3X LITE COMPACT

Action: Bolt
Stock: Synthetic
Barrel: 20 in.
Sights: None
Weight: 6 lb. 10 oz.
Caliber: .204 Ruger, .22-250 Rem., .223 Rem., .243 Win., .308 Win., 7mm-08 Rem., 6.5 Creedmoor
Magazine: 3, 4 rounds
Features: Stock comes with a 1-in. spacer and a thick recoil pad; length

of pull is 12.5 in.; detachable magazine; textured grip panels; blued hardware
MSRP **$725.00**

T3X SUPERLITE, SUPERLITE CAMO

Action: Bolt
Stock: Synthetic
Barrel: 22.4 in.
Sights: None
Weight: 6 lb.
Caliber: .243 Win., .308 Win., .270 Win., .30-06 Spfd., 7mm Rem. Mag., 6.5 Creedmoor, .300 Win. Mag., 7mm-08 Rem.
Magazine: 3 rounds
Features: Enhanced gripping areas; new recoil pad; stock's foam insert reduces noise; black stock model is exclusive to Sportsmen's Warehouse; Camo model is available only through Cabela's; both models have a single-stage adjustable trigger, fluted barrels
MSRP **$799.00**
Camo: **$1029.00**

T3X TAC A1

Action: Bolt
Stock: Aluminum rear stock and middle chassis
Barrel: 16 in., 20 in., 24 in.
Sights: None
Weight: 10 lb. 5.7 oz.–11 lb. 4 oz.

Caliber: .260 Rem., 6.5 Creedmoor, .308 Win.
Magazine: 10 rounds
Features: Long-range chassis rifle; aluminum rear stock with height- and angle-adjustable cheekpiece; adjustable-height recoil pad; Picatinny rail for monopod attachment; aluminum middle chassis with modular, removable forend connector; AR-15 buffer tube-compatible interface; AR-15 pistol grip compatible slot; barrel is threaded and mid-contour; trigger is two-stage and adjustable; detachable magazine; two-way safety with bolt release lever; topside Picatinny rail
MSRP . . . . **$1899.00–$1999.00**

T3X VARMINT

Action: Bolt
Stock: Synthetic
Barrel: 23.7 in.
Sights: None
Weight: 7 lb. 8 oz.
Caliber: .223 Rem., .22-250 Rem. 6.5 Creedmoor
Magazine: 5, 6 rounds
Features: Raised Varmint cheekpiece aids in alignment with larger scopes; free-floating barrel; wide forend perfect for sandbag use
MSRP **$950.00**

TNW Firearms

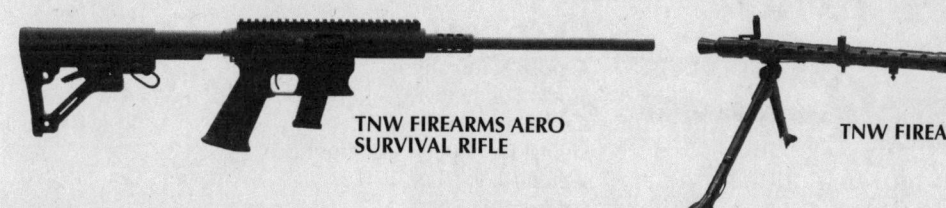

TNW FIREARMS AERO SURVIVAL RIFLE

TNW FIREARMS MG34

AERO SURVIVAL RIFLE

Action: Semiautomatic
Stock: Synthetic
Barrel: 16.25 in.
Sights: None
Weight: 5 lb.
Caliber: .22 LR, 9mm, 10mm, .40 S&W, .357 SIG, .45 ACP
Magazine: 10, 15, 24, 29, 31 rounds by caliber
Features: Specialty survival/home-defense rifle; removable barrel and collapsible AR stock; calibers can eas-ily be converted; TNW offers barrel threading services for suppressor use; black, Tiger Green, Pink Attitude, Dark Earth, and OD Green finishes
Single caliber: **$699.00**
3-caliber package: **$1199.00**

MG34

Action: Semiautomatic
Stock: Synthetic
Barrel: 24.5 in.
Sights: None
Weight: 10 lb.
Caliber: 8mm
Magazine: 50 rounds
Features: Semiauto version of the German lightweight machine gun that saw service in the Spanish Civil War; belt-fed rifle fires from a closed bolt position; available with a modified grip that meets California restrictions and 10-round belt for states with mag-azine/belt capacity restrictions
MSRP **$4699.00**

Troy Industries

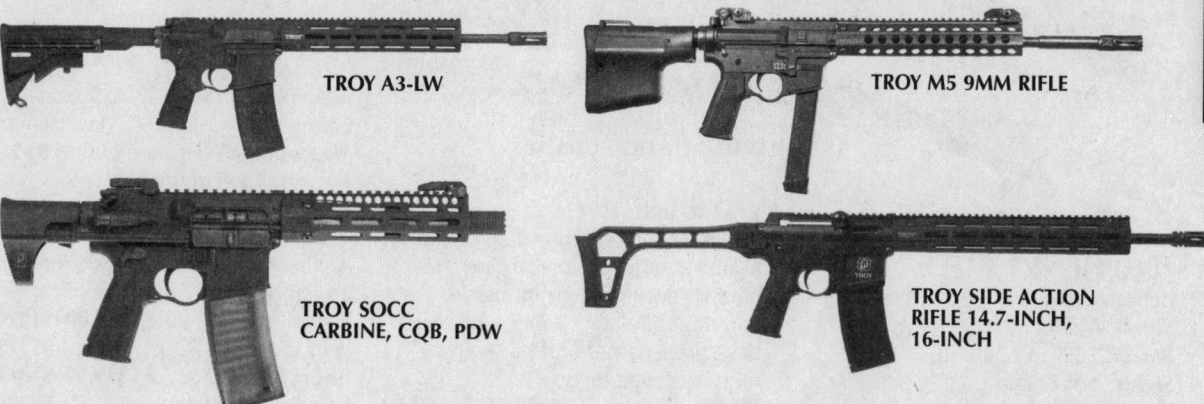

TROY A3-LW

TROY M5 9MM RIFLE

TROY SOCC CARBINE, CQB, PDW

TROY SIDE ACTION RIFLE 14.7-INCH, 16-INCH

A3-LW

Action: Semiautomatic
Stock: Synthetic
Barrel: 16 in.
Sights: None
Weight: 5 lb. 9.6 oz.
Caliber: 5.56 NATO
Magazine: N/A
Features: Chrome-lined lightweight barrel; 13-in. Troy M-LOK BattleRail; Troy Medieval Flash suppressor; Mil-Spec trigger
MSRP $849.00

M5 9MM RIFLE

Action: Semiautomatic
Stock: Polymer
Barrel: 16 in.
Sights: Standard rear and M4 front folding battlesights
Weight: 6 lb. 7 oz.
Caliber: 9mm
Magazine: 17 rounds
Features: Upper receiver designed to prevent over insertion of Glock maga-zines; Troy Medieval muzzle brake; lightweight Troy BattleAx CQB stock
MSRP . . . . $1199.00–$1299.00

SIDE ACTION RIFLE 14.7-INCH, 16-INCH

Action: Manual side-action
Stock: Synthetic
Barrel: 14.7 in., 16 in.
Sights: None
Weight: 5 lb. 8 oz.–6 lb. 3 oz.
Caliber: .223 Rem.
Magazine: 10 rounds
Features: Ambidextrous manually-operated side-action MSR with a left-folding stock; A2 flash hider; target bolt knob; Troy SOCC battle rail
MSRP $899.00

SOCC CARBINE, CQB, PDW

Action: Semiautomatic
Stock: SOCC Airborne
Barrel: 14.5 in. (Carbine), 10.5 in. (CQB), 7.5 in. (PDW)
Sights: SOCC front and rear folding
Weight: 6 lb. 12 oz.
Caliber: 5.56 NATO
Magazine: N/A
Features: Special Operations Compatible Carbines are available in three configurations; all feature G2S Geissele triggers, SOCC charging han-dles and rails, and Troy's own mulit-position SOCC Airborne Stock
MSRP $1599.00

Troy Industries

TROY USAF GUU-5/P

USAF GUU-5/P

Action: Semiautomatic
Stock: Synthetic
Barrel: 16 in.
Sights: Front peep, A1 drum rear
Weight: 5 lb. 8 oz.
Caliber: 5.56 NATO
Magazine: N/A
Features: MSR platform with traditional looks; forged upper with carry handle; no forward assist; chrome-lined lightweight steel barrel; carbine handguard with single heat shield; A2 flash suppressor; A-frame gas block
MSRP $999.00

Uberti

UBERTI 1860 HENRY RIFLE

UBERTI 1866 YELLOWBOY

UBERTI 1873 COMPETITION

UBERTI 1873 CARBINE

**UBERTI 1873 SHORT RIFLE
LIMITED EDITION DELUXE**

1860 HENRY RIFLE

Action: Lever
Stock: Walnut
Barrel: 18.5 in., 24.5 in.
Sights: Adjustable
Weight: 9 lb.
Caliber: .45 Colt, .44-40 Win.
Magazine: Under-barrel tube, 8+1 or 13+1 rounds
Features: Several versions: Trapper has 18.5-in barrel, brass frame/buttplate, and case-hardened lever, Rifle has 24.5-in. barrel, brass frame/buttplate, and case-hardened receiver; Steel Rifle has 24.5-in. barrel, case-hardened frame/lever, blue buttplate
MSRP . . . . $1499.00–$1579.00

1866 YELLOWBOY

Action: Lever
Stock: Walnut
Barrel: 19 in., 20 in., 24.25 in.
Sights: Adjustable
Weight: 8 lb. 3 oz.
Caliber: .45 Colt, .44-40 Win., .38 Spl.
Magazine: Under barrel tube, 10+1 or

13+1 rounds
Features: Three versions, all calibers available in all three: Carbine, 19-in. barrel; Short Rifle, 20-in. barrel; Sporting Rifle, 24.25-in. barrel. All have brass frames and buttplates, case-hardened levers
MSRP . . . . $1239.00–$1269.00

1873 COMPETITION

Action: Lever
Stock: Wood
Barrel: 20 in.
Sights: Adjustable
Weight: 8 lb.
Caliber: .357 Mag., .45 Colt
Magazine: Under-barrel tube, 10+1 rounds
Features: Octagonal barrel; A-grade walnut; lever lock; side loading gate for ease of loading
MSRP $1499.00

1873 RIFLE & CARBINE

Action: Lever
Stock: Walnut
Barrel: 16.1 in., 18 in., 19 in., 20 in., 24.5 in.
Sights: Adjustable

Weight: 7 lb. 3 oz.–8 lb. 3 oz.
Caliber: .45 Colt, .357 Mag., .44-44
Magazine: Under-barrel tube, 9+1, 10+1 or 13+1 rounds
Features: Octagonal barrel on rifle; round barrel on carbine and trapper; A-grade walnut with checkered pistol grip and forend
Carbine: . . . . $1309.00–$1419.00
Half Octagon Rifle: $1379.00
Short Rifle: . . . . . $1339.00–$1349.00
Special Sporting: $1339.00
**Special Sporting
   Short: . . . . $1449.00–$1459.00**
Sporting: . . . . $1339.00–$1349.00
Trapper: $1329.00

1873 SHORT RIFLE
LIMITED EDITION DELUXE

Action: Lever
Stock: Walnut
Barrel: 20 in.
Sights: Rifle sights
Weight: 8 lb. 3 oz.
Caliber: .45 Colt
Magazine: 10 rounds
Features: Case-hardened steel receiver with hand-chased engraving; A-grade walnut; case-hardened loop; blue octagon barrel; side-loading gate; crescent buttplate
MSRP $1929.00

Uberti

UBERTI 1874 SHARPS RIFLE

UBERTI 1876 CENTENNIAL

UBERTI 1885 HIGH-WALL SINGLE-SHOT
SPECIAL SPORTING MODEL

UBERTI SPRINGFIELD TRAPDOOR CARBINE

UBERTI SPRINGFIELD TRAPDOOR ARMY

1874 SHARPS RIFLE
Action: Falling block
Stock: Walnut
Barrel: 32 in., 34 in.
Sights: Creedmoor Sight
Weight: 10 lb. 4 oz.–11 lb.
Caliber: .45-70 Govt.
Magazine: None
Features: Blued octagonal barrel; checkered walnut stock; case-hardened; double-set trigger; pewter forend cap
Special: **$2429.00**
Deluxe: **$3809.00**
Down Under: **$3169.00**
Buffalo Hunter: **$3059.00**

1876 CENTENNIAL
Action: Lever
Stock: Walnut
Barrel: 28 in.
Sights: Adjustable
Weight: 10 lb.
Caliber: .45-60, .45-75, .50-95
Magazine: Under-barrel tube, 11+1 rounds
Features: Case-hardened frame and lever; blued buttplate; octagonal

barrel; straight stock
.45-60: **$1689.00**
.45-75: **$1689.00**
.50-95: . . . . **1709.00 MSR**

1885 HIGH-WALL SINGLE-SHOT
Action: Falling block
Stock: Walnut
Barrel: 28 in., 30 in., 32 in.
Sights: Adjustable
Weight: 9 lb. 5 oz. (carbine), 10 lb.
Caliber: .45-70, .45-120
Magazine: None
Features: Case-hardened frame and lever; blued buttplate; octagonal barrel; carbine model has round barrel; carbine and sporting rifle have straight stock
Big Game: **$1229.00**
Carbine Straight Stock: . . . **$1069.00**
Sporting Rifle Straight Stock: . . . . **$1149.00–$1199.00**
Special Sporting: . **$1279.00–$1349.00**

SPRINGFIELD TRAPDOOR ARMY
Action: Hinged breech
Stock: Walnut

Barrel: 32.5 in.
Sights: Adjustable
Weight: 8 lb. 13 oz.
Caliber: .45-70 Govt.
Magazine: None
Features: Blued steel, case-hardened breechblock and buttplate
MSRP **$2389.00**

SPRINGFIELD TRAPDOOR CARBINE
Action: Hinged breech
Stock: Walnut
Barrel: 22 in.
Sights: Adjustable
Weight: 7 lb. 5 oz.
Caliber: .45-70 Govt.
Magazine: None
Features: Blued steel, case-hardened breechblock and buttplate; fitted with sliding ring and bar for cavalryman to carry it clipped to carbine sling
MSRP **$2070.00**

Volquartsen Firearms

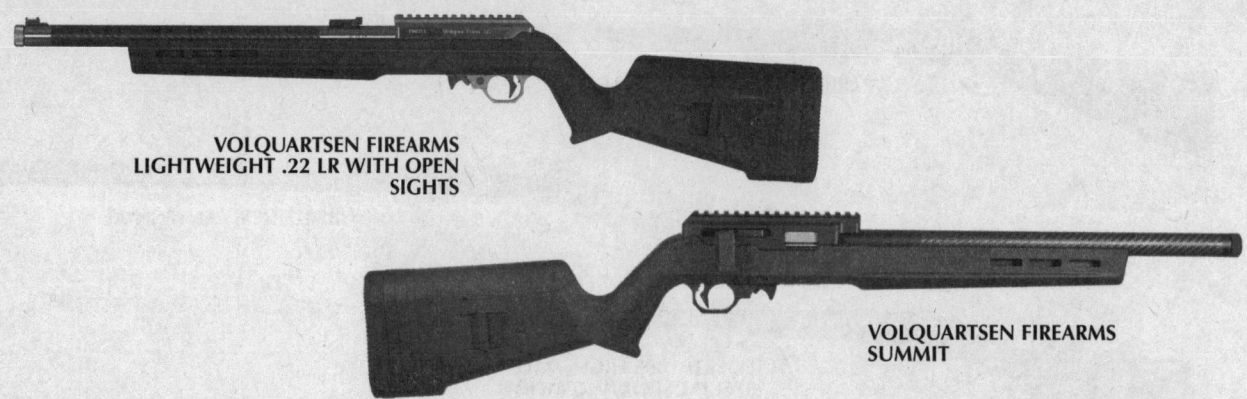

VOLQUARTSEN FIREARMS LIGHTWEIGHT .22 LR WITH OPEN SIGHTS

VOLQUARTSEN FIREARMS SUMMIT

LIGHTWEIGHT .22 LR WITH OPEN SIGHTS

Action: Semiautomatic
Stock: Synthetic
Barrel: 16.5 in.
Sights: HiViz fiber optic front, TL tritium rear
Weight: 6 lb.
Caliber: .22 LR
Magazine: 10 rounds
Features: CNC-machined stainless steel receiver; carbon fiber THM tension barrel; TG2000 trigger guard; Magpul X-22 Hunter stock; black, OD Green, or Flat Dark Earth stock colors
MSRP $1523.00

SUMMIT

Action: Bolt
Stock: Synthetic
Barrel: N/A
Sights: None
Weight: 5 lb. 13 oz.
Caliber: .22 LR, .17 Mach 2
Magazine: N/A
Features: Lightweight Magpul stock adjustable for length of pull; carbon fiber barrel; 1.75-pound trigger; ample rail on the top for optics; threaded barrel accommodates suppressor use; a variety of colored stocks from Magpul and in laminated thumbhole configurations, plus a Hogue stock option and an ambidextrous stock with a tapered stainless barrel

Magpul stock: $1150.00
Hogue stock: $1135.00
Thumbhole stock: $1383.00
Ambidextrous stock: $1378.00

Weatherby

WEATHERBY MARK V ACCUMARK, ACCUMARK RC

WEATHERBY MARK V ALTITUDE

MARK V ACCUMARK, ACCUMARK RC

Action: Bolt
Stock: Composite
Barrel: 24 in., 26 in., 28 in. by caliber
Sights: None
Weight: 7 lb. 4 oz.–8 lb. 8 oz.
Caliber: .240 Wby. Mag., .257 Wby. Mag., 6.5 Creedmoor, 6.5-3000 Wby. Mag., .270 Win., .270 Wby. Mag., 7mm Rem. Mag., 7mm Wby. Mag., .308 Win., .30-06 Spfd., .300 Win. Mag., .300 Wby. Mag., .30-378 Wby. Mag., .338-378 Wby. Mag., .340 Wby Mag., .338 Lapua
Magazine: 2, 3, 4, 5 rounds by caliber

Features: Overhauled Mark V line; enhanced ergonomic stock; reduced grip diameter with added palm swell; overall weight reduction; LXX Trigger; fluted #3 contour barrel; Accubrake available
Accumark: . . . . . $2300.00–$2600.00
Accumark RC: . . $2700.00–$3000.00
.338 Lapua: $2600.00
Left-hand: . . . . . $2400.00–$2700.00

MARK V ALTITUDE

Action: Bolt
Stock: Composite
Barrel: 22 in., 24 in., 26 in., 28 in.
Sights: None
Weight: 5 lb. 12 oz.–6 lb. 12 oz.
Caliber: .240 Wby. Mag., .257 Wby. Mag., 6.5 Creedmoor, 6.5-3000 Wby. Mag., .270 Win., .270 Wby. Mag., 7mm Wby. Mag., .308 Win., .30-06 Spfd., .300 Wby. Mag.
Magazine: 3, 5 rounds
Features: Fluted bolt body; LXX trigger; six-lug standard actions/nine-lug magnum actions; fluted stainless steel hand-lapped barrel with a recessed target crown and Tungsten Cerakote finish; hand-laminated carbon fiber stock has been designed with a slimmer forend and wrist, a right-hand palm swell, and a raised Monte Carlo comb, all in Kryptek Altitude camo
MSRP . . . . $3000.00–$3200.00

Weatherby

WEATHERBY MARK V ARROYO,
ARROYO RC

WEATHERBY MARK V
CAMILLA SUBALPINE

WEATHERBY MARK V DELUXE, CAMILLA DELUXE

MARK V ARROYO, ARROYO RC

Action: Bolt
Stock: Composite
Barrel: 24 in., 26 in., 28 in. by caliber
Sights: None
Weight: 7 lb. 4 oz.–8 lb. 8 oz.
Caliber: .240 Wby. Mag., .257 Wby. Mag., 6.5 Creedmoor, 6.5-3000 Wby. Mag., .270 Wby. Mag., 7mm Wby. Mag., .300 Win. Mag., .300 Wby. Mag., .30-378 Wby. Mag., .338 Lapua, .338-378 Wby. Mag.
Magazine: 2, 3, 4, 5 rounds by caliber
Features: Overhauled Mark V line; enhanced ergonomic stock; reduced grip diameter with added palm swell; overall weight reduction; LXX Trigger; fluted #3 contour free-floating barrel; KUIU camo stock and two-tone Brown Sand/Flat Dark Earth Cerakote; Accubrake available
Arroyo: . . . . **$2800.00–$3000.00**
Arroyo RC: . . . . . **$3200.00–$3400.00**

MARK V CAMILLA SUBALPINE

Action: Bolt
Stock: Composite
Barrel: 22 in., 24 in.
Sights: None
Weight: 5 lb. 12 oz.
Caliber: .240 Wby Mag., .270 Win., 6.5 Creedmoor, .308 Win., .30-06 Spfd.
Magazine: 4, 5 rounds
Features: Hand-laminated composite stock with an aluminum bedding block; handlapped chrome-moly barrel with a field crown; LXX trigger; six-lug action; the stock, designed for women, wears Gore's Optifade Subalpine camo; barrel and action in Flat Dark Earth Cerakote finish
MSRP **$2700.00**

MARK V DELUXE, CAMILLA DELUXE

Action: Bolt
Stock: Walnut
Barrel: 24 in., 26 in., 28 in.
Sights: None
Weight: 6 lb. 12 oz.–10 lb.
Caliber: .270 Win., .308 Win., .30–06 Spfd., .257 Wby. Mag., .270 Wby. Mag., 7mm Wby. Mag., .300 Wby. Mag., .340 Wby. Mag., .378 Wby. Mag., .416 Wby. Mag., .460 Wby. Mag., .240 Wby. Mag., 6.5 Creedmoor, 6.5-300 Wby Mag.
Magazine: 2+1, 3+1, 5+1 rounds
Features: Weatherby overhauled the Mark V in 2018 with ergonomically enhanced stocks that include reduced grip diameter and lighter overall weight, an improved LXX trigger with a wider face, and the company's sub-MOA accuracy gurantee; also new to the Deluxe line is the addition of the Camilla Deluxe, the upgraded sister to the previous Vanguard Camilla, with a six-lug action and a stock designed to better fit the female form
Deluxe: . . . . **$2700.00–$3600.00**
Camilla Deluxe: **$2700.00**

Weatherby

WEATHERBY MARK V LAZERMARK

WEATHERBY MARK V OUTFITTER, OUTFITTER RC, OUTFITTER FDE

WEATHERBY MARK V SAFARI

WEATHERBY MARK V SPORTER

WEATHERBY MARK V TACMARK

MARK V LAZERMARK

Action: Bolt
Stock: Walnut
Barrel: 26 in.
Sights: None
Weight: 8 lb. 8 oz.
Caliber: .257 Wby. Mag., .270 Wby. Mag., .300 Wby. Mag.
Magazine: 3+1 rounds
Features: Adjustable trigger; hand-selected, raised comb Monte Carlo stock with laser-carved oak leaf pattern; blued metalwork in high luster finish; Pachmayr decelerator pad
MSRP $2800.00

MARK V OUTFITTER, OUTFITTER RC, OUTFITTER FDE

Action: Bolt
Stock: Composite
Barrel: 22 in., 24 in., 26 in., 28 in. by caliber
Sights: None
Weight: 5 lb. 8 oz.–6 lb. 12 oz.
Caliber: .240 Wby. Mag., .257 Wby. Mag., 6.5 Creedmoor, 6.5-300 Wby. Mag., .270 Win., .270 Wby. Mag., 7mm Wby. Mag., .308 Win., .30-06 Spfd., .300 Wby. Mag.
Magazine: 3, 4, 5 rounds by caliber
Features: Overhauled Mark V line; enhanced ergonomic stock; reduced grip diameter with added palm swell; LXX Trigger; fluted barrel; High Desert camo stock and Armor Black Cerakote; Accubrake available;

Cerakote Flat Dark Earth metalwork on the FDE variant available
Outfitter: . . . . . . $2800.00–$3000.00
Outfitter RC: . . . $3200.00–$3400.00
Outfitter FDE: . . $2800.00–$3000.00
Outfitter FDE RC: . . $3300.00–$3500.00

MARK V SAFARI

Action: Bolt
Stock: Walnut
Barrel: 24 in., 26 in., 28 in. by caliber
Sights: Post and hood front, classic adjustable rear
Weight: 8 lb. 12 oz.–10 lb.
Caliber: .257 Wby. Mag., .270 Wby. Mag., 7mm Wby. Mag., .300 Wby. Mag., .340 Wby. Mag., .375 H&H Mag., .375 Wby. Mag., .378 Wby. Mag., .416 Wby. Mag., .460 Wby. Mag.
Magazine: 2, 3 rounds by caliber
Features: Overhauled Mark V line; enhanced ergonomic stock; reduced grip diameter with added palm swell; overall weight reduction; LXX Trigger; #2, #3, or #4 contour barrel depending on caliber; AAA fancy French walnut stock with ebony forend and hand-cut fleur-de-lis pattern checkering; Damascened bolt and follower; floorplate is engraved with "Safari Custom"; left-hand versions, Accubrake available
MSRP . . . . $6900.00–$7300.00

MARK V SPORTER

Action: Bolt
Stock: Walnut

Barrel: 24 in., 26 in.
Sights: None
Weight: 8 lb.
Caliber: .257 Wby. Mag., .270 Wby. Mag., 7mm Wby. Mag., .300 Win. Mag., .300 Wby. Mag.
Magazine: 3+1 rounds
Features: Adjustable trigger; raised comb Monte Carlo walnut stock with satin finish; features fine line diamond point checkering and rosewood forend and grip cap; bead blasted, blued metalwork with low luster finish; Pachmayr decelerator pad
MSRP $1800.00

MARK V TACMARK

Action: Bolt
Stock: Composite
Barrel: 28 in.
Sights: None
Weight: 11 lb. 4 oz.
Caliber: .30-378 Wby. Mag., .338 Lapua, .338-378 Wby. Mag., 6.5-300 Wby. Mag., .300 Win. Mag., .300 Wby. Mag.
Magazine: 5 rounds
Features: Overhauled Mark V line; enhanced ergonomic stock; reduced grip diameter with added palm swell; overall weight reduction; LXX Trigger; fluted free-floating barrel; fully adjustable composite stock with CNC-machined aluminum bedding plate; Accubrake
MSRP $4100.00

WEATHERBY MARK V TACMARK ELITE

WEATHERBY MARK V TERRAMARK, TERRAMARK RC

WEATHERBY MARK V ULTRA LIGHTWEIGHT

WEATHERBY VANGUARD BACK COUNTRY

WEATHERBY MARK V WEATHERMARK

MARK V TACMARK ELITE

Action: Bolt
Stock: Composite
Barrel: 28 in.
Sights: None
Weight: 11 lb. 12 oz.
Caliber: .30-378 Wby. Mag., .338 Lapua, .338-378 Wby. Mag., 6.5-300 Wby. Mag., .300 Win. Mag., .300 Wby. Mag.
Magazine: 5 rounds
Features: Overhauled Mark V line; enhanced ergonomic stock; reduced grip diameter with added palm swell; overall weight reduction; LXX Trigger; hand-lapped Krieger Custom match-grade, cut-rifled, free-floating #3 contour barrel; hand-lapped action; fully adjustable composite stock with CNC-machined aluminum bedding plate; DD Ross tactical bolt knob; muzzle brake has 90-degree lateral dispersion ports; Range Certified model comes with Oehler Ballistic Imaging System printout signed and certified by Ed or Adam Weatherby
MSRP $6200.00

MARK V TERRAMARK, TERRAMARK RC

Action: Bolt
Stock: Composite
Barrel: 24 in., 26 in., 28 in. by caliber
Sights: None
Weight: 7 lb. 4 oz.–8 lb. 8 oz.

Caliber: .240 Wby. Mag., .257 Wby. Mag., 6.5 Creedmoor, 6.5-300 Wby. Mag., .270 Wby. Mag., 7mm Wby. Mag., .300 Win. Mag., .300 Wby. Mag., .30-378 Wby. Mag., .338-378 Wby. Mag., .338 Lapua
Magazine: 2, 3, 4, 5 rounds by caliber
Features: Overhauled Mark V line; enhanced ergonomic stock; reduced grip diameter with added palm swell; overall weight reduction; LXX Trigger; fluted #3 contour free-floating barrel; Range Certified version comes with Oehler Ballistic Imaging System printout signed and certified by Ed or Adam Weatherby; Flat Dark Earth Cerakote finish; Accubrake available
Terramark: . . . . . $2800.00–$3000.00
Terramark RC: . . $3200.00–$3400.00
.338 Lapua: $3000.00
.338 Lapua RC: $3500.00

MARK V ULTRA LIGHTWEIGHT

Action: Bolt
Stock: Composite
Barrel: 22 in., 24 in., 26 in., 28 in. by caliber
Sights: None
Weight: 5 lb. 12 oz.–6 lb. 12 oz.
Caliber: .240 Wby. Mag., .257 Wby. Mag., 6.5 Creedmoor, 6.5-3000 Wby. Mag., .270 Win., .270 Wby. Mag., 7mm Rem. Mag., 7mm Wby. Mag., .308 Win., .30-06 Spfd., .300 Win.

Mag., .300 Wby. Mag.
Magazine: 3, 4, 5 rounds by caliber
Features: Overhauled Mark V line; enhanced ergonomic stock; reduced grip diameter with added palm swell; overall weight reduction; LXX Trigger; six lugs in standard calibers, nine in magnum; fluted barrel; Accubrake available
Right-hand: . . . . $2300.00–$2400.00
Left-hand: . . . . . $2400.00–$2500.00

MARK V WEATHERMARK

Action: Bolt
Stock: Composite
Barrel: 24 in., 26 in., 28 in. by caliber
Sights: None
Weight: 6 lb. 4 oz.–8 lb. 4 oz.
Caliber: .240 Wby. Mag., .257 Wby. Mag., 6.5-300 Wby. Mag., .270 Win., .270 Wby. Mag., 7mm Rem. Mag., 7mm Wby. Mag., .308 Win., .30-06 Spfd., .300 Win. Mag., .300 Wby. Mag., .30-378 Wby. Mag., .338-378 Wby. Mag., .340 Wby. Mag., .375 H&H Mag.
Magazine: 2, 3, 5 rounds by caliber
Features: Overhauled Mark V line; enhanced ergonomic stock; reduced grip diameter with added palm swell; overall weight reduction; LXX Trigger; non-fluted barrel in #1, #2, or #3 contour depending on caliber; Tactical Gray Cerakote finish; Accubrake available
MSRP $1700.00

VANGUARD BACK COUNTRY

Action: Bolt
Stock: Monte Carlo composite
Barrel: 24 in.
Sights: None
Weight: 6 lb. 12 oz.
Caliber: .240 Wby. Mag., .270 Win., .257 Wby. Mag., .30-06 Spfd., .300 Win. Mag., .300 Wby. Mag., .308 Win.
Magazine: 5+1 or 3+1 rounds
Features: SUB-MOA guarantee; chrome moly metalwork with Cerakote Tactical Grey finish; pillar-bedded stock; two-stage trigger; 3-position safety; auxiliary trigger sear; Pachmayr Decelerator pad
MSRP $1429.00

RIFLES

Weatherby

WEATHERBY VANGUARD
CAMILLA

WEATHERBY VANGUARD
DANGEROUS GAME RIFLE

WEATHERBY VANGUARD
FIRST LITE

WEATHERBY VANGUARD
SPORTER

WEATHERBY VANGUARD
SPORTER DBM

VANGUARD CAMILLA

Action: Bolt
Stock: Turkish walnut
Barrel: 20 in.
Sights: None
Weight: 6 lb. 4 oz.
Caliber: 6.5 Creedmoor, .243 Win., .308 Win., 7mm-08 Rem.
Magazine: 4, 5 rounds
Features: SUB-MOA accuracy guarantee; "creep-free," match-quality, two-stage trigger; three-position safety; slimmer grip angle; shorter, slimmer forearm and grip with right side palm swell for better balance and fit; fleur de lis checkering pattern; recoil pad has been given a negative angle, reduced in size, and the toe canted away from the body to better fit a woman's shoulder
MSRP. $849.00

VANGUARD DANGEROUS GAME RIFLE

Action: Bolt
Stock: Composite
Barrel: 24 in.
Sights: Adjustable rear, hooded front
Weight: 7 lb. 12 oz.
Caliber: .375 H&H
Magazine: 3+1 rounds

Features: Guaranteed SUB-MOA accuracy; hand-laminated, raised comb, Monte Carlo composite stock with full-length aluminum bedding plate, matte gel coat finish, and spiderweb accents; matte, bead blasted, blued finish; NECG adjustable rear sight and Williams Gun Sight Company hooded front sight
MSRP. $1299.00

VANGUARD FIRST LITE

Action: Bolt
Stock: Composite
Barrel: 26 in., 28 in.
Sights: None
Weight: 7 lb. 8 oz.
Caliber: .240 J244. Mag., .257 Wby. Mag., 6.5-3000 Wby. Mag., .270 Win., .308 Win., .30-06 Spfd., .300 Win. Mag. .300 Wby. Mag.
Magazine: 3, 5 rounds
Features: Stock finished in First Lite Fusion camo; stock has texturing at the grip and forearm; Flat Dark Earth Cerakote finish on the barrel and action; one-piece machined fluted bolt body; #2 contour fluted barrel with Accubrake; adjustable match-grade two-stage trigger
MSRP. $1090.00

VANGUARD SPORTER

Action: Bolt
Stock: Walnut
Barrel: 24 in.
Sights: None
Weight: 7 lb. 4 oz.–7 lb. 8 oz.
Caliber: .223 Rem., .22-250 Rem., .243 Win., .25-06 Rem., .270 Win., 7mm-08 Rem., .308 Win., .30-06 Spfd., .257 Wby. Mag., 7mm Rem. Mag., .300 Win. Mag., .300 Wby. Mag.
Magazine: 3+1, 5+1 rounds
Features: Two-stage trigger; raised comb, Monte Carlo stock with satin urethane finish; hand-selected A fancy grade Turkish walnut; rosewood forend; low luster, matte blued metalwork; fine line diamond point checkering; low density recoil pad
MSRP. $849.00

VANGUARD SPORTER DBM

Action: Bolt
Stock: Walnut Monte Carlo
Barrel: 24 in.
Sights: None
Weight: 7 lb. 4 oz.
Caliber: .25-06 Rem., .270 Win., .30-06 Spfd.
Magazine: Detachable box, 3 rounds
Features: Rosewood forend; raised comb; satin urethane finish; matte blued metalwork; adjustable trigger
MSRP. $849.00

Weatherby

WEATHERBY VANGUARD SYNTHETIC

WEATHERBY VANGUARD SYNTHETIC DBM

WEATHERBY VANGUARD WEATHERGUARD

VANGUARD SYNTHETIC

Action: Bolt
Stock: Synthetic
Barrel: 24 in.
Sights: None
Weight: 7 lb. 4 oz.
Caliber: .25-06 Rem., .30-06 Spfd., .223 Rem.,.240 Wby. Mag., .243 Win., .257 Wby. Mag., .300 Wby. Mag., .300 Win. Mag., .308 Win., .338 Win. Mag., 7mm Rem. Mag., and 7mm-08 Rem., 6.5 Creedmoor, .22-250 Rem., .270 Win., 6.5-300 Wby. Mag.
Magazine: Internal, 6+1 rounds
Features: Lightweight, composite Monte Carlo Griptonite stock; matte bead blasted blued finish; three-position safety.
MSRP **$649.00**

VANGUARD SYNTHETIC DBM

Action: Bolt
Stock: Injection-molded Monte Carlo
Barrel: 24 in.
Sights: None
Weight: 7 lb. 4 oz.
Caliber: .240 Wby., .25-06 Rem., .270 Win., .30-06 Spfd.
Magazine: Detachable box, 3 rounds
Features: Matte bead blasted blued metalwork; low density recoil pad; two-stage trigger
MSRP **$649.00**

VANGUARD WEATHERGUARD

Action: Bolt
Stock: Monte Carlo Griptonite
Barrel: 24 in.

Sights: None
Weight: 7 lb. 12 oz.
Caliber: .25-06 Rem., .22-250 Rem., .30-06 Sfpd., .223 Rem., .240 Wby Mag., .243 Win., .257 Wby Mag., .270 Win., .300 Win. Mag., .300 Wby Mag., .308 Win., 7mm Rem. Mag., 7mm-08 Rem., 6.5 Creedmoor
Magazine: 3+1 or 5+1 rounds
Features: Guaranteed SUB-MOA accuracy; Monte Carlo Griptonite stock features pistol grip, forend inserts, and right-side palm swell (aids shooter's comfort and control); tactical grey Cerakote finish for exceptional weather and corrosion resistance; fluted bolt body; three-position safety; hinged floorplate; cold hammer-forged barrel; match quality two-stage trigger
MSRP **$749.00**

Webley & Scott

WEBLEY & SCOTT EMPIRE

WEBLEY & SCOTT XOCET RIMFIRE

EMPIRE

Action: Bolt
Stock: Walnut
Barrel: 22 in.
Sights: None
Weight: 7 lb. 13 oz.–9 lb.

Caliber: .243 Win., .270 Win., .308 Win., .30-06 Spfd., 7mm-08
Magazine: Detachable box, 5 rounds
Features: Cold hammer-forged barrel provides top accuracy; two-stage trigger; fully jeweled bolt and knurled

handle; pillar-bedded, Hogue over-molded stock with cheek weld
MSRP **$799.00**

XOCET RIMFIRE RIFLE

Action: Bolt
Stock: Synthetic
Barrel: 19 in.
Sights: None
Weight: 7 lb. 9 oz.
Caliber: .17 HMR, .22 WMR, .22 LR
Magazine: Detachable box, 10 rounds
Features: Carbon/kevlar composite bull barrel or carbon-steel standard barrel; threaded barrel with knurled cap; skeletonized trigger; Picatinny rail; sling swivel studs
MSRP . . . . **$439.00–$499.00**

Wilson Combat

WILSON COMBAT .458 HAM'R TACTICAL HUNTER

WILSON COMBAT RECON TACTICAL

WILSON COMBAT SUPER SNIPER

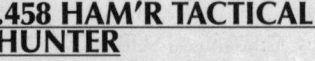

WILSON COMBAT URBAN SUPER SNIPER

RIFLES

.458 HAM'R TACTICAL HUNTER

Action: Semiautomatic
Stock: Synthetic
Barrel: 18 in.
Sights: None
Weight: 7 lb. 11 oz.
Caliber: .458 Ham'r
Magazine: 7, 9 rounds
Features: .458 Ham'r caliber sports 3,000 ft-lbs of energy; hybrid-length receiver has a mid-length gas system; SLR Rifleworks adjustable gas block; Wilson's TTU M2 4# trigger; custom-length buffer; Rogers/Wilson Super-Stoc; fluted match-grade Wilson barrel; collapsible stock; Armor-Tuff Mil-Spec hard-anodized brown/green camo; other color schemes available; optional scope package with a Leupold VX-R 2–7x333mm FireDot

and 30mm Ultralight AR rings can be added for $590.00
MSRP $2905.00

RECON TACTICAL

Action: Semiautomatic
Stock: Synthetic tactical
Barrel: 16 in.
Sights: Optional rail
Weight: 7 lb.
Caliber: .308 Win., .338 Fed., 6.5 Creedmoor,.204 Ruger, 5.56 NATO, 6.8 SPC, .300 BLK, 7.62x40 WT, .458 SOCOM
Magazine: Detachable box, 30 rounds
Features: Match grade medium weight stainnless steel barrel; forged 7075 upper (flat top) and lower receiver; mid-length gas system with low-profile gas block; Wilson Combat T.R.I.M. rail; ergo pistol grip
MSRP . . . . starting at $2250.00

SUPER SNIPER

Action: Semiautomatic
Stock: Synthetic, telescoping
Barrel: 20 in.
Sights: None
Weight: 10 lb. 11 oz.
Caliber: .223 Wylde, .260 Rem., 6mm Creedmoor, 6,5 Grendel; .224 Valkyrie
Magazine: 10 rounds, 20 rounds
Features: Barrel is precision button rifled from 416-R stainless steel; 1:10 twist; Picatinny rail; BILLet-AR machined aluminum upper and lower receivers; 12 inch or 14 inch free-floating TRIM rail; available with a fluted or non-fluted barrel
MSRP . . . . .starting at $2250.00

URBAN SUPER SNIPER

Action: Semiautomatic, mid-length gas system with low-profile gas block
Stock: Synthetic, telescoping
Barrel: 18 in.
Sights: None
Weight: 7 lb. 5 oz.
Caliber: 6.8 SPC
Magazine: 10, 20, or 30 rounds
Features: Medium heavy-weight, fluted, stainless steel premium match-grade barrel; 1:8 twist; Picatinny rail; 10.4 inch free-floating TRIM rail
MSRP . . . . .starting at $2225.00

Winchester Repeating Arms

WINCHESTER REPEATING ARMS MODEL 70 ALASKAN

MODEL 70 ALASKAN

Action: Bolt
Stock: Walnut
Barrel: 25 in.
Sights: Open
Weight: 8 lb. 8 oz.

Caliber: .30-06 Spfd., .300 Win. Mag. .338 Win. Mag., .375 HH Mag.
Magazine: None
Features: Satin finish Monte Carlo walnut stock with cut checkering; folding adjustable rear sight with

hooded gold bead front sight; recessed target crown
MSRP . . . . $1399.99–$1439.99

Winchester Repeating Arms

WINCHESTER REPEATING ARMS MODEL
70 COYOTE LIGHT SR

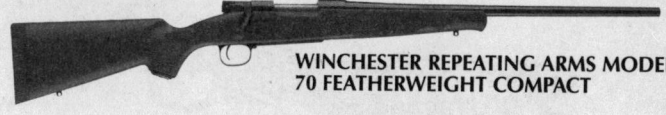

WINCHESTER REPEATING ARMS MODEL
70 FEATHERWEIGHT COMPACT

WINCHESTER REPEATING ARMS MODEL
70 FEATHERWEIGHT HIGH GRADE MAPLE

WINCHESTER REPEATING ARMS
MODEL 70 SAFARI EXPRESS

WINCHESTER REPEATING ARMS MODEL
70 SUPER GRADE MAPLE

WINCHESTER REPEATING
ARMS MODEL 94 CARBINE

MODEL 70 COYOTE LIGHT SR

Action: Bolt
Stock: Composite
Barrel: 24 in.
Sights: None
Weight: 7 lb. 8 oz.
Caliber: .22-250 Rem., .243 Win., .308 Win., .300 WSM, .270 WSM, .325 WSM, 6.5 Creedmoor
Magazine: 3, 5 rounds
Features: Bipod mounting studs; matte-blued receiver and medium-heavy fluted stainless barrel mount threaded for suppressor; Pachmayr Decelerator; MOA trigger system;
MSRP . . . . $1269.99–$1309.99

MODEL 70 FEATHERWEIGHT COMPACT

Action: Bolt
Stock: Walnut
Barrel: 20 in.
Sights: None
Weight: 6 lb. 8 oz.
Caliber: 6.5 Creedmoor 7mm-08 Rem., .308 Win.
Magazine: 5 rounds
Features: Pachmayr decelerator recoil pad; action is drilled and tapped for optics
MSRP $1099.99

MODEL 70 FEATHERWEIGHT HIGH GRADE MAPLE

Action: Bolt
Stock: Maple
Barrel: 22 in.
Sights: None

Weight: 6 lb. 12 oz.–7 lb.
Caliber: 308 Win. .270 Win., .30-06 Spfd.
Magazine: 5 rounds
Features: Gloss-finished AAAA maple stock with cut checkering and a schnabel forearm; MOA Trigger System; pre-64 action; controlled round feed; controlled ejection
MSRP $1329.99

MODEL 70 SAFARI EXPRESS

Action: Bolt
Stock: Satin-finished checkered walnut with deluxe cheekpiece
Barrel: 24 in.
Sights: Hooded-blade front and express-style rear
Weight: 9 lb.
Caliber: .375 H&H Mag., .416 Rem. Mag., .458 Win. Mag.
Magazine: 3 rounds
Features: Pre-'64 type claw extractor; Pachmayr decelerator recoil pad; barrel band front swivel base; dual recoil lugs and three-position safety; MOA trigger system; matte blued finish; two steel cross-bolts and one-piece steel trigger guard and hinged floor plate
MSRP $1559.99

MODEL 70 SUPER GRADE MAPLE

Action: Bolt
Stock: Maple

Barrel: 24 in., 26 in.
Sights: None
Weight: 7 lb. 12 oz.–8 lb. 6 oz.
Caliber: .243 Win., .308 Win., .270 Win., .30-06 Spfd., .264 Win. Mag., 7mm Rem. Mag., .300 Win. Mag.
Magazine: 3, 5 rounds
Features: Gloss-finished AAA maple stock with ebony forend tip; Shadowline cheekpiece; Super Grade engraved hinged floorplate; jeweled bolt body; knurled bolt handle; pre-64 action with MOA Trigger System; hammer-forged, free-floating steel barrel with target crown
MSRP . . . . $1669.99–$1699.99

MODEL 94 CARBINE

Action: Lever
Stock: Walnut
Barrel: 20 in.
Sights: Adjustable semi-buckhorn rear, Marble Arms front
Weight: 6 lb. 8 oz.
Caliber: 6.5 Creedmoor 7mm-08 Rem., .308 Win.
Magazine: Under-barrel tube
Features: Triple-checked button rifled barrel; round locking bolt trunnions; top-tang safety; rebounding hammer; bolt relief cut; steel loading gate; articulated cartridge stop; available knurled hammer spur extension
MSRP $1199.99

Winchester Repeating Arms

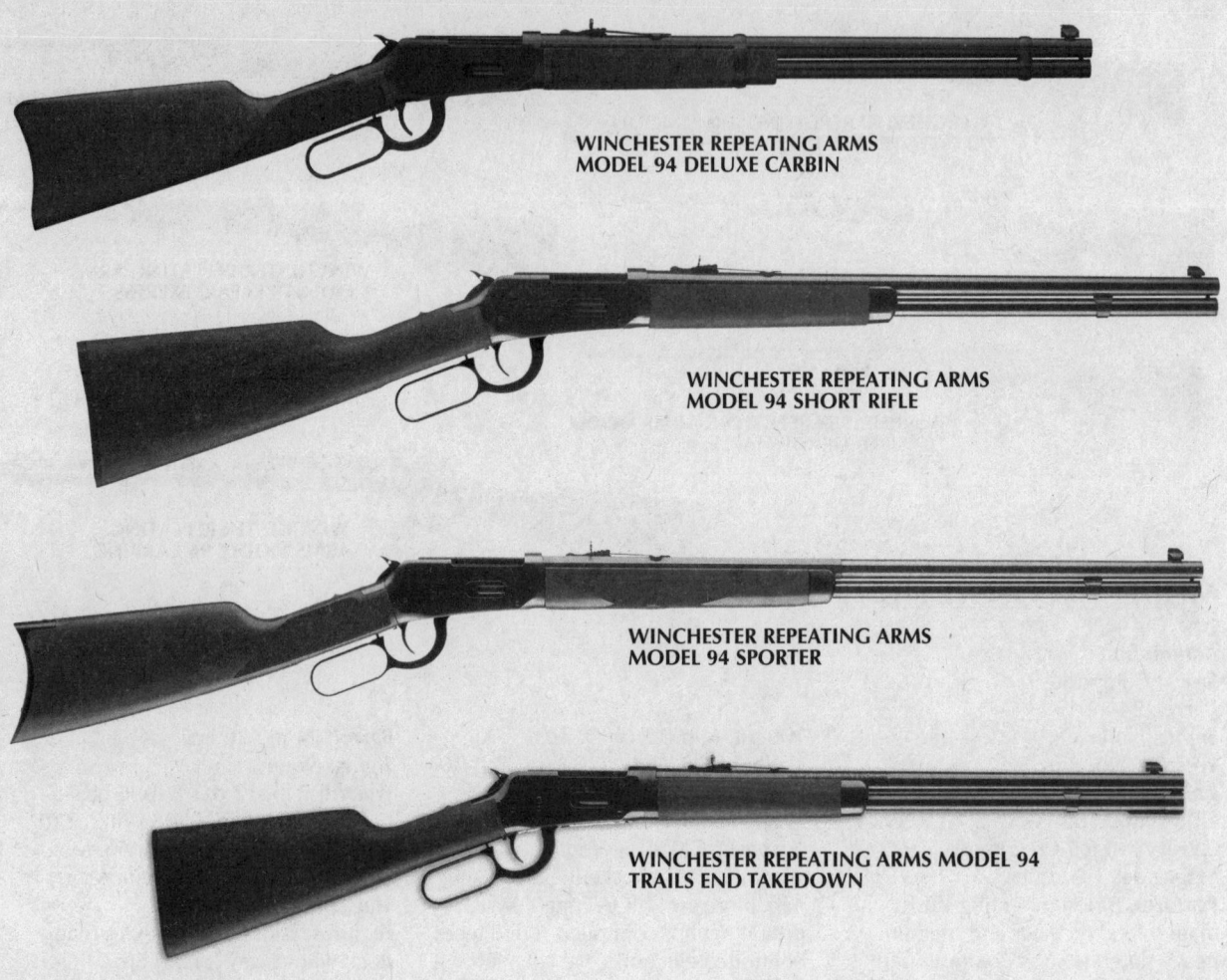

WINCHESTER REPEATING ARMS MODEL 94 DELUXE CARBIN

WINCHESTER REPEATING ARMS MODEL 94 SHORT RIFLE

WINCHESTER REPEATING ARMS MODEL 94 SPORTER

WINCHESTER REPEATING ARMS MODEL 94 TRAILS END TAKEDOWN

MODEL 94 DELUXE CARBINE

Action: Lever
Stock: Walnut
Barrel: 20 in.
Sights: Marble Arms iron sights
Weight: 6 lb. 8 oz.–6 lb. 12 oz.
Caliber: .38-55 Win.
Magazine: 7 rounds
Features: Limited edition; grade IV/V checkered walnut stock and forend; gloss blued steel; left-side saddle ring; hammer spur; receiver is drilled and tapped for scope mounting
MSRP **$1329.99**

MODEL 94 SHORT RIFLE

Action: Lever
Stock: Walnut
Barrel: 20 in.
Sights: Front, adjustable rear
Weight: 6 lb. 12 oz.
Caliber: .30-30 Win., .450 Marlin, .25-35 Win., .38-55 Win., .32 WCF
Magazine: Under-barrel tube, 7 rounds
Features: Straight grip; rifle-style forearm and black grip cap; semi-buckhorn rear sights, Marble Arms gold-bead front sight; drilled and tapped for optics
MSRP **$1229.99**

MODEL 94 SPORTER

Action: Lever
Stock: Walnut
Barrel: 24 in.
Sights: Marble Arms front, adjustable rear
Weight: 7 lb. 8 oz.
Caliber: .25-35 Win., .30-30 Win., .38-55 Win., .32 WCF
Magazine: Under-barrel tube, 8 rounds
Features: Half-round, half-octagon blued barrel; straight grip stock with a crescent butt and finely checkered blued-steel buttplate with double-line bordering; drilled and tapped for optics
MSRP **$1399.99**

MODEL 94 TRAILS END TAKEDOWN

Action: Lever
Stock: Walnut
Barrel: 20 in.
Sights: Adjustable
Weight: 6 lb. 12 oz.
Caliber: .30-30 Win., .38-55 Win., .450 Marlin
Magazine: Under-barrel tube, 6 rounds
Features: Walnut stock and forearm with satin finish and straight-grip styling; blued steel receiver and barrel; Marble Arms front sight with semi-buckhorn rear sight; Pachmayr Decelerator recoil pad (450 model)
MSRP **$1459.99**

Winchester Repeating Arms

WINCHESTER REPEATING ARMS MODEL 1866 SHORT RIFLE

WINCHESTER REPEATING ARMS MODEL 1873 CARBINE

WINCHESTER REPEATING ARMS MODEL 1873 SHORT RIFLE

WINCHESTER REPEATING ARMS MODEL 1873 SHORT RIFLE COLOR CASE HARDENED

WINCHESTER REPEATING ARMS MODEL 1873 SPORTER OCTAGON COLOR CASE HARDENED

WINCHESTER REPEATING ARMS MODEL 1873 SPORTER OCTAGON COLOR CASE HARDENED

MODEL 1866 SHORT RIFLE

Action: Lever
Stock: Walnut
Barrel: 20 in.
Sights: Marble Arms gold bead front, folding leaf rear
Weight: 7 lb.
Caliber: .38 Spl., .44-40 Win., .45 LC
Magazine: 10, 11 rounds by caliber
Features: Crescent brass buttplate; full-length tube magazine; open top ejection; bright polished blue finish; American walnut straight grip stock
MSRP $1299.99

MODEL 1873 CARBINE

Action: Lever-action
Stock: Black walnut
Barrel: 20 in.
Sights: Marble Arms gold bead front, semi-buckhorn rear
Weight: 7 lb. 4 oz.
Caliber: .357-38, .44-40 Win., .45 Colt
Magazine: 10 rounds
Features: Blued carbine strap buttplate; round barrel; full-length magazine; receiver is drilled and tapped for a tang-mounted rear sight; saddle ring is also in blue
MSRP $1299.99

MODEL 1873 SHORT RIFLE

Action: Lever
Stock: Wood
Barrel: 20 in.
Sights: Adjustable
Weight: 7 lb. 4 oz.
Caliber: .357 Mag., .45 Colt, .44-40 Win.
Magazine: Under-barrel tube, 10 rounds
Features: Walnut straight grip stock with satin oil finish; classic rifle style forearm with blued steel cap; semi-buckhorn rear sight with Marble Arms gold bead front sights; steel loading gate; receiver rear tang drilled and tapped for optional tang-mounted rear sight
MSRP $1299.99

MODEL 1873 SHORT RIFLE COLOR CASE HARDENED

Action: Lever
Stock: Wood
Barrel: 20 in.
Sights: Adjustable
Weight: 7 lb. 4 oz.
Caliber: .357 Mag., .38 Spl., .44-40 Win., .45 Colt
Magazine: 10–11 rounds
Features: Steel receiver, color case hardened; steel loading gate; rear tang is drilled and tapped for scope mount; steel barrel, polished blued finish; full-length magazine tube; grade II/III walnut stock; straight grip; classic rifle-style forearm; steel forend cap; semi-buckhorn rear sight; Marble's gold bead front sight; color case hardened crescent buttplate, lever, forend cap, and loading gate
MSRP $1579.99

MODEL 1873 SPORTER OCTAGON COLOR CASE HARDENED

Action: Lever
Stock: Walnut
Barrel: 24 in.
Sights: Marble Arms gold bead front, semi-buckhorn rear
Weight: 8 lb.
Caliber: .357 Mag., .44-40 Win., .45 Colt
Magazine: 14 rounds
Features: Classic lever has octagon barrel; pistol grip Grade II/III walnut stock; top tang drilled and tapped for tang-mounted rear sight; crescent buttplate; deep-polished blue finish
MSRP $1739.99

Winchester Repeating Arms

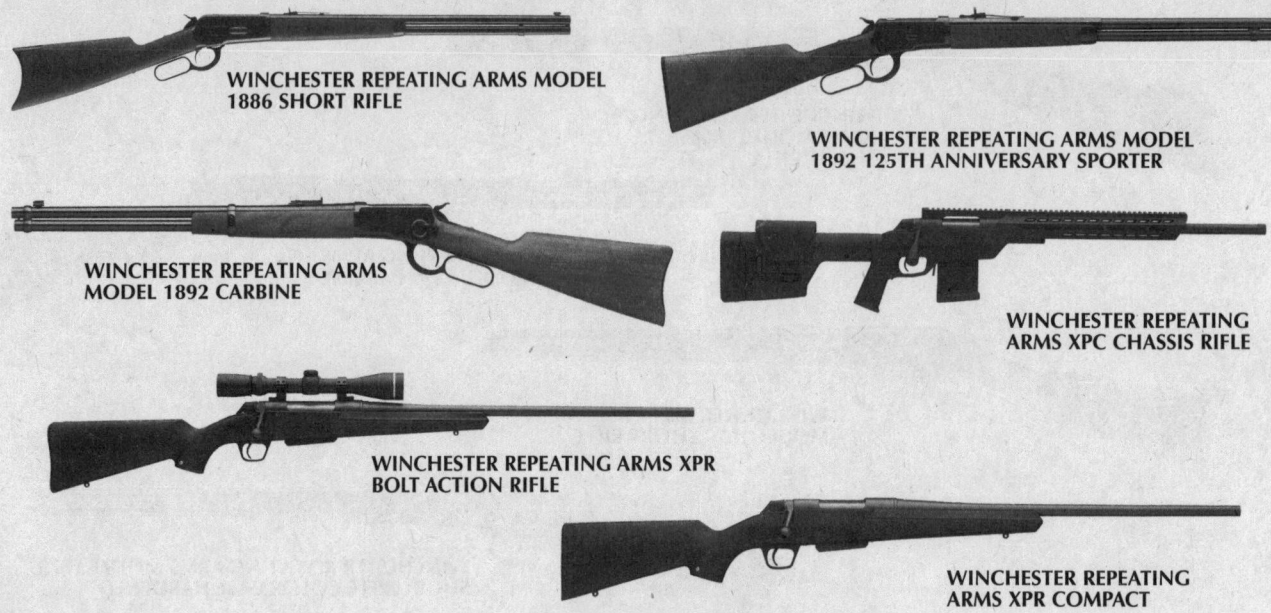

WINCHESTER REPEATING ARMS MODEL 1886 SHORT RIFLE

WINCHESTER REPEATING ARMS MODEL 1892 125TH ANNIVERSARY SPORTER

WINCHESTER REPEATING ARMS MODEL 1892 CARBINE

WINCHESTER REPEATING ARMS XPC CHASSIS RIFLE

WINCHESTER REPEATING ARMS XPR BOLT ACTION RIFLE

WINCHESTER REPEATING ARMS XPR COMPACT

RIFLES

MODEL 1886 SHORT RIFLE

Action: Lever
Stock: Walnut
Barrel: 20 in., 24 in.
Sights: Front with brass bead, adjustable rear
Weight: 8 lb. 6 oz.
Caliber: .45-70 Govt., .45-90 Win.
Magazine: Under-barrel tube, 8 rounds
Features: Deeply blued receiver and lever; end cap and steel crescent buttplate; straight grip
MSRP $1339.99

MODEL 1892 125TH ANNIVERSARY SPORTER

Action: Lever
Stock: Walnut
Barrel: 24 in.
Sights: Front post, folding leaf rear
Weight: 6 lb.
Caliber: .357 Mag., .44 Rem. Mag., .44-40 Win., .45 Colt
Magazine: 13 rounds
Features: Half-octagon/half-round button rifled barrel in gloss blue finish; grade IV/V walnut with top tang safety; scroll engraving on receiver; top tang is drilled and tapped for optional peep sight
MSRP $1799.99

MODEL 1892 CARBINE

Action: Lever-action
Stock: Black walnut
Barrel: 20 in.
Sights: Marble Arms gold bead front, semi-buckhorn rear
Weight: 6 lb.
Caliber: .357 Mag., .44 Rem. Mag., .44-40 Win., .45 Colt
Magazine: 10 rounds
Features: Blued carbine strap buttplate; barrel band; saddle ring; straight-grip stock; top tang is drilled and tapped to add a peep sight
MSRP $1069.99

XPC CHASSIS RIFLE

Action: Bolt
Stock: Composite
Barrel: 20 in., 24 in.
Sights: None
Weight: 10 lb.
Caliber: .308 Win., .243 Win., 6.5 Creedmoor
Magazine: 5, 10 rounds
Features: Designed for long-range work; machined alloy chassis frame; Magpul PRS Gen 3 stock; threaded muzzle; target crown; M-LOK rail; 20 MOA scope base; full-length Picatinny rail; 10-round Magpul P-MAG AICS magazine and five-round MDT metal magazine
MSRP $1599.99

XPR

Action: Bolt
Stock: Composite polymer
Barrel: 24 in., 26 in.
Sights: None
Weight: 7 lb.
Caliber: .243 Win., 7mm-08, .308 Win., .270 WSM, .300 WSM, .325 WSM, .270 Win., .30-06 Spfd., 7mm Rem. Mag., .300 Win. Mag., .338 Win. Mag., 6.5 Creedmoor, .350 Legend
Magazine: Detachable box, 3 rounds
Features: Chromoly steel barrel; matte blue finish; hardened steel components; recessed target-style crown; Inflex recoil pad
MSRP $549.99

XPR COMPACT

Action: Bolt
Stock: Composite
Barrel: 20 in., 22 in., 24 in.
Sights: None
Weight: 6 lb. 12 oz.–7 lb.
Caliber: .243 Win., 6.5 Creedmoor, 7mm-08 Rem., .308 Win., .270 WSM, .300 WSM, .325 WSM, .350 Legend
Magazine: 3 rounds
Features: Shorter 13-in. length of pull; advanced polymer stock in black, matte blue metal finish; detachable box magazine
MSRP $549.99

Winchester Repeating Arms

WINCHESTER REPEATING ARMS XPR HUNTER MOSSY OAK BREAK-UP COUNTRY

WINCHESTER REPEATING ARMS XPR HUNTER MOUNTAIN COUNTRY RANGE

WINCHESTER REPEATING ARMS XPR SPORTER

WINCHESTER REPEATING ARMS XPR HUNTER KUIU VERDE 2.0

WINCHESTER REPEATING ARMS XPR MUDDY GIRL COMPACT

WINCHESTER REPEATING ARMS XPR THUMBHOLE VARMINT SUPPRESSOR READY

XPR HUNTER, HUNTER COMPACT MOSSY OAK BREAK-UP COUNTRY

Action: Bolt
Stock: Composite
Barrel: 24 in.
Sights: None
Weight: 6 lb. 5.44 oz.
Caliber: .270 Win., 30-06 Spfd., .300 Win. Mag., .338 Win. Mag., .243 Win. 7mm-08 Rem., .308 Win., .270 WSM, .300 WSM, .325 WSM, 7mm Rem. Mag., 6.5 Creedmoor; Compact available in .243 Win., 7mm-08 Rem., .308 Win., .270 WSM, .300 WSM, .325 WSM, .350 Legend
Magazine: 3 rounds
Features: Mossy Oak Break-Up Country with Perma-Cote matte black hardware on fullsize, matte gray on Compact; drilled and tapped for scope mounts; free-floating barrel; MOA trigger system; two- position thumb safety; Inflex technology recoil pad; swing swivel studs
MSRP. **$599.99**

XPR HUNTER KUIU VERDE 2.0, VIAS

Action: Bolt
Stock: Composite
Barrel: 22 in., 24 in., 26 in.
Sights: None
Weight: 6 lb. 12 oz.–7 lb. 4 oz.
Caliber: .243 Win., 7mm-08 Rem., .308 Win., .270 WSM, .300 WSM, .325 WSM, .270 Win., .30-06 Spfd., 7mm Rem. Mag., .300 Win. Mag., .338 Win. Mag., 6.5 Creedmoor
Magazine: 3 rounds
Features: XPR rifle featuring steel receiver and free-floating, button rifled barrel in Permacote gray finish; Kuiu's Vias macro or Verde composite patterns on stock; Highlander version has metal in Flat Dark Earth

Permacote and wears Kryptek's Highlander camo
MSRP. **$599.99**

XPR HUNTER MOUNTAIN COUNTRY RANGE

Action: Bolt
Stock: Composite
Barrel: 22 in., 24 in., 26 in.
Sights: None
Weight: 6 lb. 5 oz.–7 lb.
Caliber: .243 Win., 7mm-08 Rem., .308 Win., .270 WSM .300 WSM, .325 WSM, .270 Win., .30-06 Spfd., 7mm Rem. Mag., .300 Win. Mag., .338 Win. Mag., 6.5 Creedmoor
Magazine: 3 rounds
Features: Stock in Mossy Oak Mountain Country Range camo with textured grip panels; a matte-blue barrel and receiver; M.O.A. Trigger System; two-position thumb safety; bolt unlock button; detachable magazine; Inflex recoil pad; sling swivel studs; barrel is button rifled and free-floating with a target crown
MSRP. **$599.99**

XPR MUDDY GIRL COMPACT

Action: Bolt
Stock: Composite
Barrel: 20 in., 22 in.
Sights: None
Weight: 6 lb. 12 oz.–7 lb. 4 oz.
Caliber: .243 Win., 7mm-08 Rem., .308 Win., .270 WSM, .300 WSM, .270 Win., .30-06 Spfd., 6.5 Creedmoor
Magazine: 3 rounds
Features: Shorter 13-in. length of pull; composite stock in Muddy Girl camo with textured grip panels; button-rifled, free-floating barrel in Permacote gray finish; detachable

magazine; MOA Trigger
MSRP. **$599.99**

XPR SPORTER

Action: Bolt
Stock: Walnut
Barrel: 22 in., 24 in., 26 in.
Sights: None
Weight: 6 lb. 12 oz.–7 lb. 4 oz.
Caliber: .243 Win., 6.5 Creedmoor, 7mm-08 Rem., .308 Win., .270 Win., .30-06 Spfd., 7mm Rem. Mag., .300 Win. Mag., .338 Win. Mag., .300 WSM, .270 WSM, .325 WSM, .350 Legend
Magazine: 3 rounds
Features: Button-rifled free-floating barrel; M.O.A. Trigger System; detachable box magazine; Inflex Technology recoil pad; metal is finished in matte black Perma-Cote
MSRP. **$599.99**

XPR THUMBHOLE VARMINT SUPPRESSOR READY

Action: Bolt
Stock: Laminate
Barrel: 24 in.
Sights: None
Weight: 6 lb. 12 oz.
Caliber: .243 Win., 6.5 Creedmoor, .308 Win., .270 Win., .30-06 Spfd., .350 Legend
Magazine: 3 rounds
Features: Laminate thumbhole stock; raised cheekpiece; vented forearm aids cooling; two front sling swivels accommodate sling and bipod simultaneously; metal is matte blue finished; barrel is threaded
MSRP. **$799.99**

Windham Weaponry

WINDHAM WEAPONRY 300 BLACKOUT

WINDHAM WEAPONRY R20FFTM-308

WINDHAM WEAPONRY RMCS-2 (MULTI-CALIBER SYSTEM) RIFLE KIT

300 BLACKOUT

Action: Semiautomatic gas impingment system
Stock: Synthetic, telescoping
Barrel: 16 in.
Sights: None
Weight: 7 lb.
Caliber: .300 BLK, 7.62x35
Magazine: Detachable box, 30+1 rounds
Features: Hogue six-position telescoping buttstock; 1:7 inch twist; Diamondhead VRS-T 13.5 inch free-float forend; two quick detachable sling swivels included; Hogue beavertail pistol grip; hardcoat black anodize receiver finish; Picatinny rail; chrome-lined barrel with Diamondhead T brake
MSRP $1680.00

R20FFTM-308

Action: Semiautomatic
Stock: Synthetic
Barrel: 20 in.
Sights: None
Weight: 9 lb. 0.8 oz.
Caliber: .308 Win.
Magazine: 5+1 rounds

Features: Magpul fixed length buttstock with multiple sling attachments; comfortable rubber recoil pad under which is a handy storage compartment; multiple attachment options for M-Lok accessory rails; internal heat shielding; Hogue overmolded rubber pistol grip; Mil Std 1913 Picatinny rails on both receiver and gas block
MSRP $1438.00

RMCS-2 (MULTI-CALIBER SYSTEM) RIFLE KIT

Action: Semiautomatic
Stock: Synthetic
Barrel: 16 in.
Sights: None
Weight: N/A

Caliber: .223 Rem./5.56 NATO–300 BLK
Magazine: 30 rounds
Features: Two calibers in the same AR platform by simply switching out the barrel; chrome-lined barrels; Mil Std 1913 railed gas block; receivers are CNC machined from forged 7075 T6 aircraft aluminum and finished in hardcoat black anodize; twist rates differ depending on barrel
MSRP $1499.00

Windham Weaponry

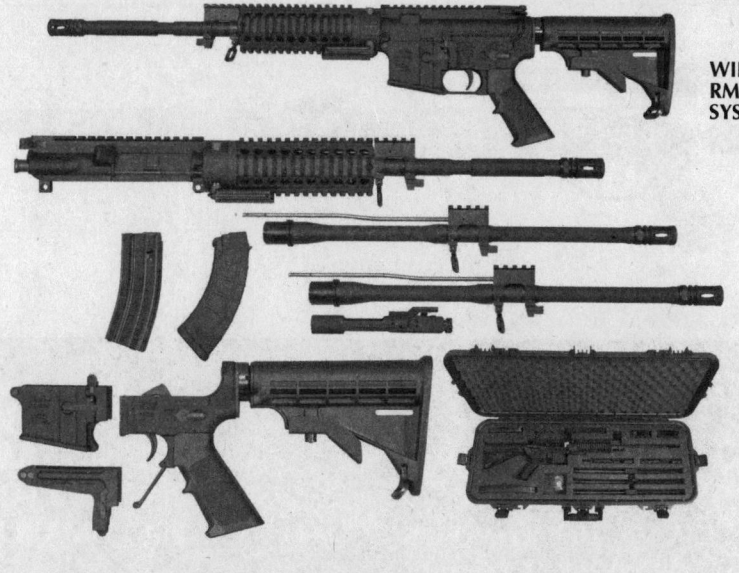

**WINDHAM WEAPONRY
RMCS-3 (MULTI-CALIBER
SYSTEM) RIFLE KIT**

**WINDHAM WEAPONRY
RMCS-4 (MULTI-CALIBER
SYSTEM) RIFLE KIT**

RMCS-3 (MULTI-CALIBER SYSTEM) RIFLE KIT

Action: Semiautomatic
Stock: Synthetic
Barrel: 16 in.
Sights: None
Weight: N/A
Caliber: .223 Rem./5.56 NATO–300 BLK–7.62x36mm
Magazine: Standard 30 rd. for .223 Rem./5.56 NATO; standard Magpul for 7.62x39mm; standard Colt type Mag for 9mm
Features: Two calibers in the same AR platform by simply switching out the barrels and magazine wells; chrome-lined barrels; Mil Std 1913 railed gas block; receivers are CNC machined from forged 7075 T6 aircraft aluminum and finished in hardcoat black anodize; twist rates differ depending on barrel
MSRP. **$2061.00**

RMCS-4 (MULTI-CALIBER SYSTEM) RIFLE KIT

Action: Semiautomatic
Stock: Synthetic
Barrel: 16 in.
Sights: None
Weight: N/A
Caliber: .223 Rem./5.56 NATO–300 BLK–7.62x36mm–9mm
Magazine: Standard 30 rd. for .223 Rem./5.56 NATO; standard Magpul for 7.62x39mm; standard Colt type Mag for 9mm
Features: Two calibers in the same AR platform by simply switching out the barrels and magazine wells; chrome-lined barrels; Mil Std 1913 railed gas block; receivers are CNC machined from forged 7075 T6 aircraft aluminum and finished in hardcoat black anodize; twist rates differ depending on barrel
MSRP. **$2561.00**

AIRGUNS

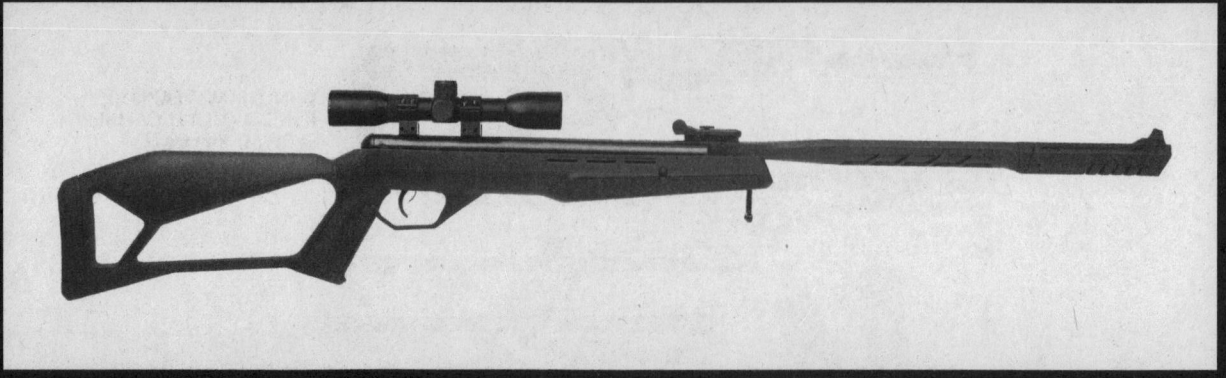

AIRGUNS

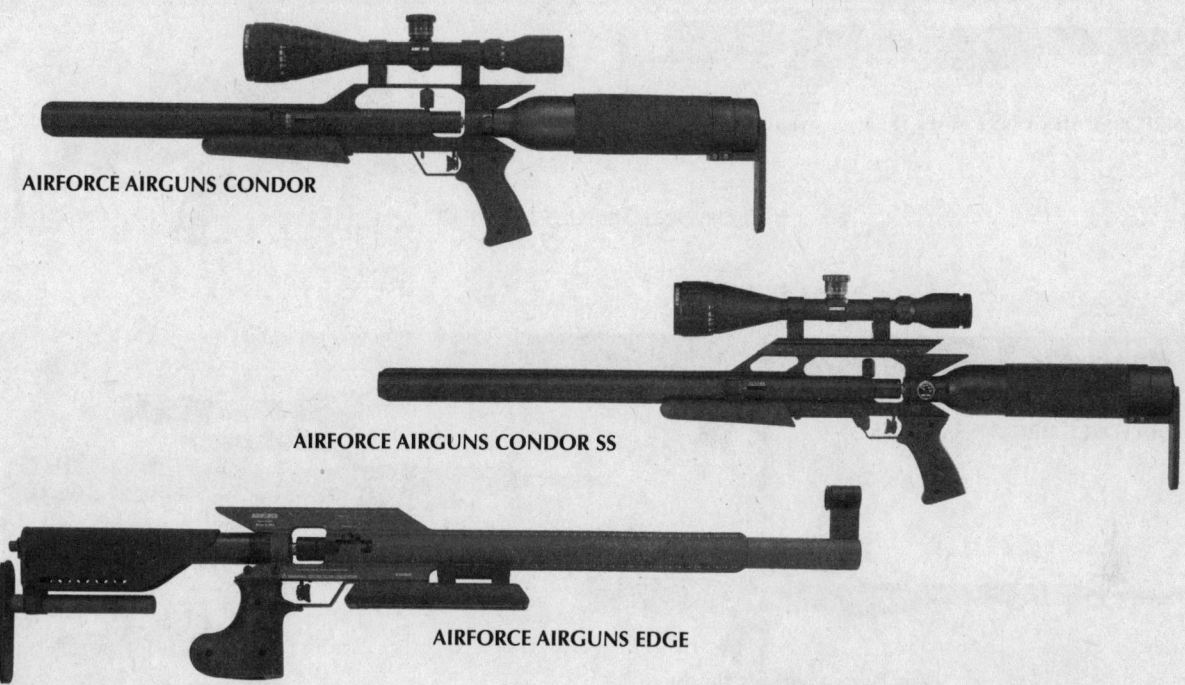

AIRFORCE AIRGUNS CONDOR

AIRFORCE AIRGUNS CONDOR SS

AIRFORCE AIRGUNS EDGE

AIRFORCE AIRGUNS ESCAPE

CONDOR

Power: Pre-charged pneumatic, user adjustable
Stock: Composite
Overall Length: 38.7 in.
Sights: None
Weight: 6 lb. 8 oz.
Caliber: .25, .22, .20, .177
Features: Black, red, or blue composite stock; integral extended scope rail; detachable air tank; Lothar Walther barrel; pressure relief device; adjustable power; scopes optional
Spin-Loc: **$784.95**

CONDOR SS

Power: Compressed air
Stock: Composite
Overall Length: 38.125 in.
Sights: Open or optical may be installed
Weight: 6 lb. 2 oz.
Caliber: .177, .20, .22, .25
Features: CondorSS combines the major attributes of the TalonSS's quiet operation and the Condor's high power levels; new sound reduction technology; 18-inch barrel blue, red, or original black; 600–1300 fps; two-stage trigger; single shot
MSRP. **$814.95**

EDGE

Power: Pre-charged pneumatic
Stock: Composite
Overall Length: 35–40 in.
Sights: TS1 peep sight system
Weight: 6 lb. 2 oz.
Caliber: .177
Features: Ambidextrous cocking knob; regulated air system; adjustable length of pull; adjustable forend; hooded front sight only or front and rear sight available; two-stage adjustable trigger; composite stock in red or blue finish; scopes optional
Front sight only: **$639.95**
Front and rear sights:. **$799.95**

ESCAPE

Power: Compressed air
Stock: Synthetic
Overall Length: 34.5 in.–39 in.
Sights: Open or optical
Weight: 5 lb. 4.8 oz
Caliber: .22, .25
Features: Lothar Walther Barrels; Quick-Detach or Spin-Loc air tanks; lightweight and compact; geared for survival situations; user adjustable length
MSRP. **$729.95**

AIRGUNS

AirForce Airguns

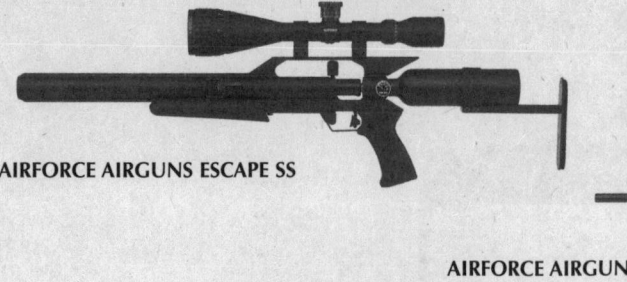

AIRFORCE AIRGUNS ESCAPE SS

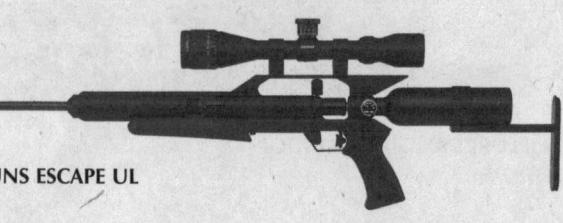

AIRFORCE AIRGUNS ESCAPE UL

AIRFORCE AIRGUNS TALON SS

AIRFORCE AIRGUNS TALON

AIRFORCE AIRGUNS TEXAN

AIRFORCE AIRGUNS TALON P

ESCAPE SS
Power: Compressed air
Stock: Synthetic
Overall Length: 27.75 in.–32.25 in.
Sights: Open or optical
Weight: 4 lb. 4.8 oz
Caliber: .22, .25
Features: Lothar Walther Barrels; Quick-Detach or Spin-Loc air tanks; lightweight and compact; geared for survival situations; user adjustable length; Sound-Loc sound reduction technology installed
MSRP **$719.95**

ESCAPE UL
Power: Compressed air
Stock: Synthetic
Overall Length: 28.5 in.–33 in.
Sights: Open or optical
Weight: 4 lb. 4 oz
Caliber: .22, .25
Features: Lothar Walther Barrels; Quick-Detach or Spin-Loc air tanks; lightweight and compact; geared for survival situations; user adjustable length
MSRP **$642.95**

TALON
Power: Compressed air
Stock: Composite
Overall Length: 32.6 in.

Sights: None
Weight: 5 lb. 8 oz.
Caliber: .25, .22, .20, .177
Features: Lothar Walther barrel; pressure relief device; adjustable power; detachable air tank; black composite stock; scopes optional
MSRP **$674.95**

TALON P
Power: Compressed air
Stock: Composite
Overall Length: 24 in.
Sights: None
Weight: 3 lb. 8 oz.
Caliber: .25
Features: Designed to deliver over 50 ft.-lbs. of energy with a .25-caliber hunting pellet; integral extended scope rail; Lothar Walther barrels; scopes optional
MSRP **$504.95**

TALON SS
Power: Compressed air
Stock: Composite
Overall Length: 32.7 in.
Sights: None
Weight: 5 lb. 4 oz.
Caliber: .25, .22, .20, .177
Features: Improved sound reduction; Lothar Walther barrel; pressure relief device; adjustable power; detachable air tank; black, red, or blue composite

stock; multiple mounting rails; two-stage trigger; innovative muzzle cap that strips away air turbulence and reduces discharge sound levels; scopes optional
MSRP **$688.95**

TEXAN
Power: Compressed air
Stock: Synthetic
Overall Length: 48 in.
Sights: Open or optical
Weight: 8 lb.
Caliber: .257, .308, .357, .457
Features: With the ability to launch .45 caliber projectiles at over 1000 feet per second and generating energy levels of over 500 foot pounds, the Texan takes its place as the world's most powerful production air rifle. Easy to load and simple to use, this Big Bore air rifle will let you focus on hunting with the knowledge you have enough power to get the job done.
MSRP . . . . **$1054.95–$1084.95**

Anschütz (J.G. Anschütz)

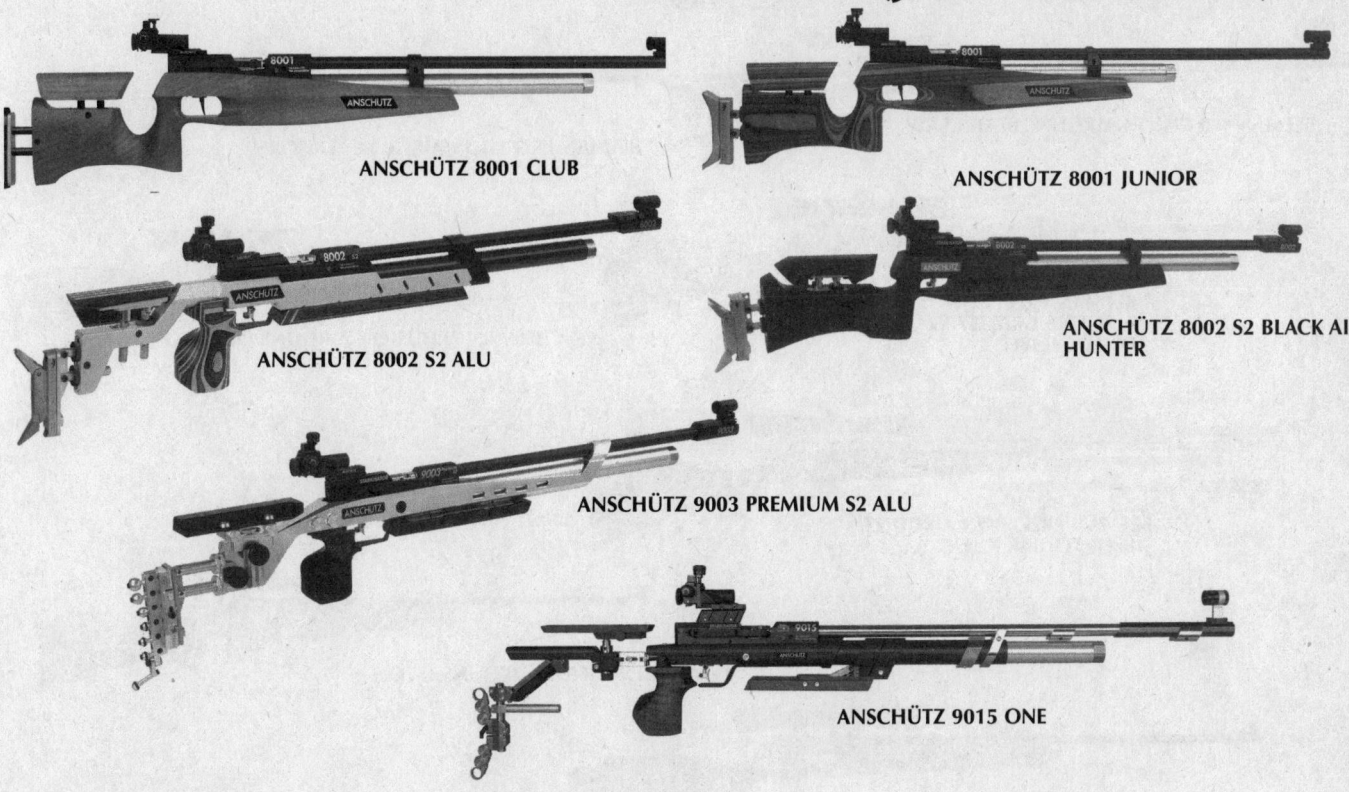

ANSCHÜTZ 8001 CLUB

ANSCHÜTZ 8001 JUNIOR

ANSCHÜTZ 8002 S2 ALU

ANSCHÜTZ 8002 S2 BLACK AIR HUNTER

ANSCHÜTZ 9003 PREMIUM S2 ALU

ANSCHÜTZ 9015 ONE

8001 CLUB
Power: Compressed air
Stock: Walnut
Overall Length: 42.1 in.
Sights: Open, includes sight set 6834
Weight: 8 lb. 6 oz.
Caliber: .177
Features: Walnut stock with stippled checkering and non-stained aluminum or rubber buttplate; adjustable trigger; match grade barrel
MSRP $2000.00

8001 JUNIOR
Power: Compressed air
Stock: Laminate
Overall Length: 37.4 in.
Sights: Open, includes sight set 6834
Weight: 8 lb. 2 oz.
Caliber: .177
Features: Laminated wood in blue and orange with aluminum buttplate stock; cylindrical match grade barrel; comes with accessory box
MSRP $1999.99

8002 S2 ALU
Power: Compressed air
Stock: Aluminum and synthetic pistol grip or laminated wood pistol grip
Overall Length: 42.1 in.
Sights: Open, includes sight set 6834

Weight: 10 lb. 2 oz.
Caliber: .177
Features: Aluminum stock in silver and blue with laminated wood or synthetic pistol grip; blue air cylinder; ProGrip cheekpiece and forend; includes accessory box; aluminum accessory rail
Aluminum: $2325.00
Wood: $2619.99

8002 S2 BLACK AIR HUNTER
Power: Compressed air
Stock: Plastic
Length: 43.3 in.
Sights: Rear, turnable front
Weight: 9 lb. 8 oz.
Caliber: .177
Features: IWA special edition equipped with new Anschütz SOFT-Grip stock, combining the vibration damping and recoil absorbing characteristics of a naturally grown wooden stock with the characteristics of an easy-care and weather-proof plastic stock; match barrel; aluminum buttplate; cheekpiece; two-stage trigger
MSRP $2350.00

9003 PREMIUM S2 PRECISE
Power: Compressed air
Stock: Aluminum

Overall Length: 43.7 in.
Sights: Open, includes sight set 6834
Weight: 9 lb. 15 oz.
Caliber: .177
Features: Silver/black aluminum stock pistol grip; Soft Link shock absorber pads; adjustable forend stock, cheekpiece, and buttplate; includes plastic rifle case; steel match barrel; aluminum accessory rail on stock
MSRP $3900.00

9015 ONE
Power: Barreled action
Stock: Aluminum; stainless steel; carbon
Overall Length: 39 in.–47.2 in.
Sights: Adjustable
Weight: 10.1 lb.
Caliber: .177
Features: New patented 5065 4K trigger with ball bearings and versatile adjustable trigger blade; a stainless steel barrel unit; thin, special coated barrel extension; maintenance free stabilizer; air filter against pollutions; cocking lever mountable left and right; adjustable cheekpiece; scalloped grip
MSRP $3749.99

Beeman Precision Airguns

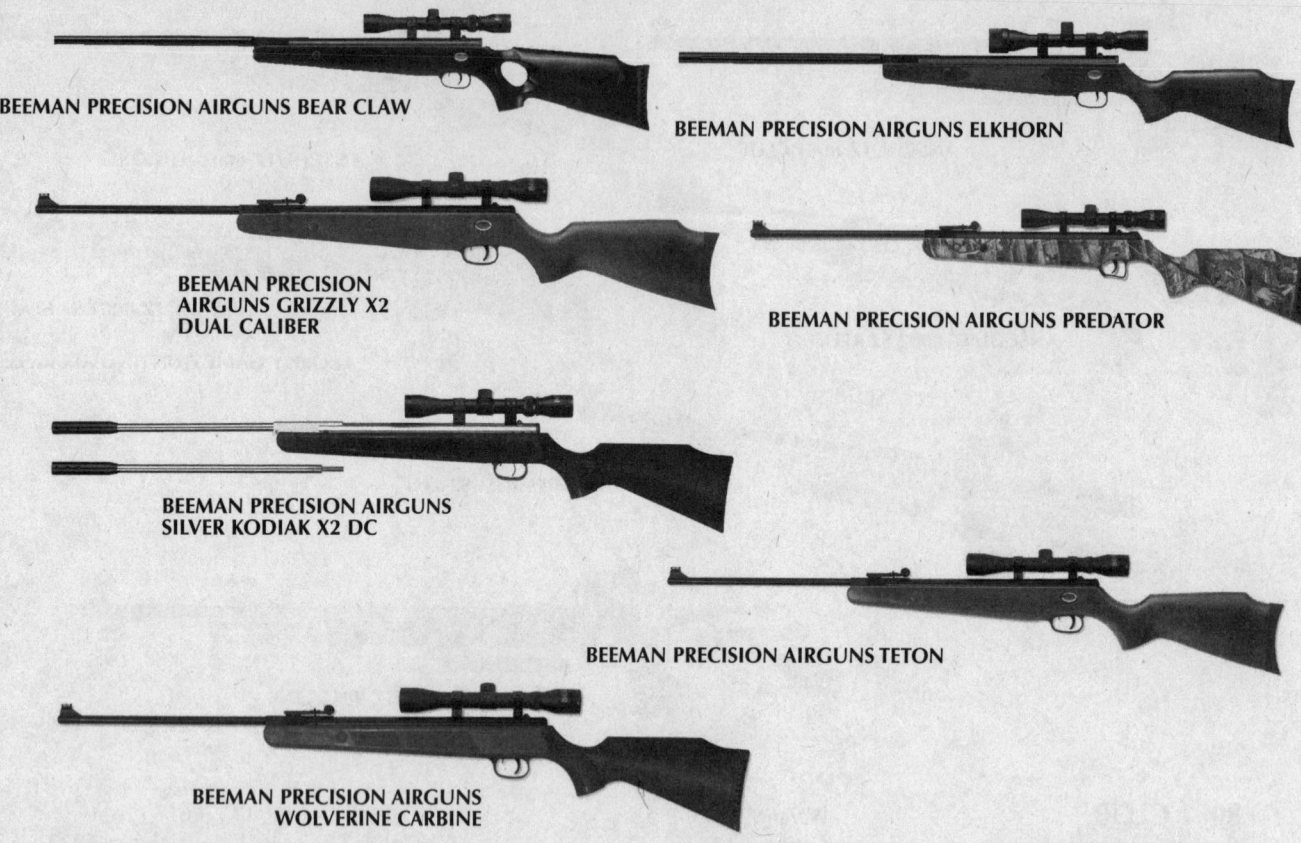

BEEMAN PRECISION AIRGUNS BEAR CLAW

BEEMAN PRECISION AIRGUNS ELKHORN

BEEMAN PRECISION AIRGUNS GRIZZLY X2 DUAL CALIBER

BEEMAN PRECISION AIRGUNS PREDATOR

BEEMAN PRECISION AIRGUNS SILVER KODIAK X2 DC

BEEMAN PRECISION AIRGUNS TETON

BEEMAN PRECISION AIRGUNS WOLVERINE CARBINE

BEAR CLAW
Power: Spring piston
Stock: Wood
Overall Length: 45.5 in.
Sights: Scope
Weight: 8 lb. 8 oz.
Caliber: .177, .22
Features: 3–9x32 scope included; break barrel action; available as dual caliber version
MSRP.................$239.99

ELKHORN
Power: Spring piston
Stock: Wood
Overall Length: 46.5 in.
Sights: Scope
Weight: 9 lb.–10 lb
Caliber: .177, .22
Features: 3–9x32 scope included; break barrel action; fluted barrel
MSRP.................$299.99

GRIZZLY X2 DUAL CALIBER
Power: Spring piston
Stock: Wood
Overall Length: 45.5 in.

Sights: Fixed and scope
Weight: 8 lb. 8 oz.
Caliber: .177, .22
Features: 4x32 scope and fiber optics sights; break barrel action; interchangeable barrels; available with case
MSRP.......... $179.99–$199.99

PREDATOR
Power: Spring piston
Stock: Synthetic
Overall Length: 45.5 in.
Sights: Fixed and scope
Weight: 8 lb. 8 oz.
Caliber: .22
Features: 3–9x32 scope and fiber optic sights; break barrel action
MSRP.................$199.99

SILVER KODIAK X2 DC
Power: Break action, spring piston
Stock: All-weather synthetic
Overall Length: 47.5 in.
Sights: 3–9x32 or 4x32 scope
Weight: 8 lb. 12 oz.
Caliber: .177, .22
Features: Two airguns in one; satin

nickel plated barrel and receiver; ported muzzle brake; 1000 fps max velocity
MSRP.................$168.00

TETON
Power: Spring piston
Stock: Wood
Overall Length: 44.5 in.
Sights: Fixed and scope
Weight: 9 lb.
Caliber: .177, .22
Features: 4x32 scope and fiber optic sights; break barrel action; rifled barrel
MSRP.................$149.99

WOLVERINE CARBINE
Power: Spring piston
Stock: Synthetic
Overall Length: 45.5 in.
Sights: Fixed and scope
Weight: 8 lb. 8 oz.
Caliber: .177, .22
Features: 4x32 scope and fiber optic sights; break barrel action; rifled barrel; rubber recoil pad
MSRP.................$149.99

CROSMAN 1911

CROSMAN AIRMASTER

CROSMAN BENJAMIN ARMADA

CROSMAN BENJAMIN BULLDOG .357 TROPHY GAME HUNTING AIR RIFLE

CROSMAN BENJAMIN DISCOVERY

CROSMAN BENJAMIN FORTITUDE

1911

Power: CO2
Stock: Polymer
Overall Length: 8 in.
Sights: Fixed
Weight: 1 lb. 14 oz.
Caliber: .177
Magazine: 6 rounds
Features: In traditional Colt 1911 style; polymer frame; metal slide; accessory rail; removable metal magazine with two six-round rotary clips; available in blue or stainless finishes
MSRP. **$109.99**

AIRMASTER

Power: Variable pump
Stock: Synthetic
Overall length: 39.75 in.
Sights: Fiber optic front, adjustable rear
Weight: 4 lb. 12 oz.
Caliber: BB, .177
Features: Variable pump; rifled steel barrel; single-stage trigger; crossbolt safety; 4x15mm scope; optional kit includes metal swinging target, 500 pellets, 1,500 BBs, and safety glasses
AirMaster: **$99.99**
AirMaster Kit: **$114.99**

BENJAMIN ARMADA

Power: Multi-shot pneumatic, bolt
Stock: Synthetic

Overall Length: 42 in.
Sights: None
Weight: 7 lb. 5 oz.
Caliber: .177, .22, .25
Features: Modular, versatile design; backwards compatible with Mil-Spec AR-15 grips and stocks; machined receiver featuring 5 inches of Picatinny rail space; delivers over 30 consistent shots per fill (up to 16 in .25 cal); bolt action is reversible; integrated resonance dampener; 10-round magazine delivers fast follow up shots (8-rd magazine in .25 cal); rifled barrel, choked and shrouded; optics and bipod not included
MSRP. **$649.99**

BENJAMIN BULLDOG .357

Power: Multi-shot pneumatic, bolt
Stock: Synthetic
Overall Length: 36 in.
Sights: None
Weight: 7 lb. 11 oz.
Caliber: .357
Features: Bullpup configuration; 26 inches of picatinny rail; Baffle-less SoundTrap shroud for big bore sound suppression; sidelever bolt reversible for left hand shooters; intuitive, easy to load 5-shot magazine; reversible bolt; 10 shots per fill; now available in Realtree Xtra camo, Sportsman's Pack, and Big

Game Hunter's Pack
Black:. **$849.99**
Realtree Xtra:. **$899.99**
Big Game Hunter's Pack:. . .**$1199.99**

BENJAMIN DISCOVERY

Power: Dual fuel compressed air
Stock: Walnut
Overall Length: 39 in.
Sights: Fiber optic front, adjustable rear
Weight: 5 lb. 2 oz.–5 lb. 3 oz.
Caliber: .22, .177
Features: Rifled steel barrel; velocity up to 900 fps; cross-bolt safety; built-in pressure gauge; high pressure pump included
MSRP. **$269.95**

BENJAMIN FORTITUDE

Power: Pre-charged pneumatic
Stock: Synthetic
Overall Length: 23 in.
Sights: None
Weight: 5 lb. 5 oz.
Caliber: .177, .22
Magazine: 10 rounds
Features: Single-stage trigger; 3,000 psi regulated cylinder; 11mm dovetail mount; fully shrouded barrel; on-board pressure gauge
MSRP. **$399.00**

AIRGUNS

Crosman

CROSMAN BENJAMIN IRONHIDE

CROSMAN BENJAMIN TITAN NP

CROSMAN BENJAMIN TRAIL NP2

CROSMAN BENJAMIN VAPORIZER

CROSMAN BUSHMASTER ACR DUAL AMMO AIR RIFLE

CROSMAN CHALLENGER PCP

BENJAMIN IRONHIDE

Power: Gas piston
Stock: Synthetic
Overall Length: N/A
Sights: Fixed front, adjustable open rear
Weight: 10 lb.
Caliber: .177, .22
Magazine: 1 round
Features: Thumbhole-stocked break-barre; two-stage adjustable trigger; SBD Gold Sound Suppression; CenterPoint 3–9x40mm scope
MSRP. $189.99

BENJAMIN TITAN NP

Power: Nitro piston
Stock: Hardwood, synthetic
Length: 43 in., 44.5 in.
Sights: 4x32mm scope included
Weight: 6 lb. 10 oz.–6 lb. 14 oz.
Caliber: .177, .22
Features: Powered by Nitro Piston technology; delivers velocities up to 1200 fps (.177) with alloy pellets; included 4x32mm scope; ambidextrous hardwood stock with thumbhole; two-stage adjustable trigger; ventilated rubber recoil pad; .177- and .22-caliber available in hardwood stock, .22-caliber also available in ambidextrous all-weather synthetic stock
MSRP. . . . . $139.99–$199.99

BENJAMIN TRAIL NP2

Power: NP2 nitro piston
Stock: Synthetic or wood
Overall Length: 46.25 in.
Sights: CenterPoint 3–9x32mm scope
Weight: 8 lb. 5 oz.
Caliber: .22
Features: Break barrel; first to feature new NP2 power system; enhanced Clean Break Trigger; integrated sound suppression system; shoots up to 1200 fps alloy, 900 fps pellet; .22 available in hardwood and Realtree Xtra
Wood: $339.00
Realtree: $279.99

BENJAMIN VAPORIZER

Power: Gas piston
Stock: Synthetic
Overall Length: N/A
Sights: Fixed front sight, adjustable rear
Weight: 10 lb.
Caliber: .177, .22
Magazine: 1 round
Features: Crosman's SBD Gold Sound Suppression; synthetic stock with soft-touch inserts; Picatinny rail; CenterPoint 3–9x40mm scope
MSRP. $259.99

BUSHMASTER ACR DUAL AMMO AIR RIFLE

Power: Variable pump
Stock: Synthetic
Overall length: 33 in.
Sights: Elevation adjustable pin front, windage adjustable dual aperture rear
Weight: 3 lb. 8 oz.
Caliber: BB, .177
Features: Bolt-action air rifle with pump-action powerplant modeled after Bushmaster's ACR (Adaptive Combat Rifle); Picatinny rail; pistol grip stock; five-shot Firepow'r pellet clip; 18-shot internal magazine; 200-shot reservoir
MSRP. $124.99

CHALLENGER PCP

Power: Pneumatic pump and CO2
Stock: Synthetic
Overall Length: 41.5 in.
Sights: Open
Weight: 7 lb. 2 oz.
Caliber: .177
Features: Two-stage match grade adjustable trigger; Lothar Walther barrel; adjustable cheekpiece and butt-piece; black synthetic stock; 11mm scope mount rails; ambidextrous
Without sights: $529.99
Sights: $629.99

AIRGUNS

CROSMAN CLASSIC 2100

CROSMAN DIAMONDBACK

CROSMAN DPMS CLASSIC A4 NITRO PISTON

CROSMAN DPMS SBR

CROSMAN FIRE NP

CROSMAN FURY NP

CROSMAN M4-177

CLASSIC 2100

Power: Pneumatic pump
Stock: Synthetic
Overall Length: 39.75 in.
Sights: Visible impact front, adjustable rear
Weight: 4 lb. 13 oz.
Caliber: .177
Features: Cross-bolt safety; BB up to 755 fps, pellet up to 725 fps
MSRP $69.99

DIAMONDBACK

Power: Gas piston
Stock: Synthetic
Overall Length: N/A
Sights: Fixed front sight, adjustable rear
Weight: N/A
Caliber: .177, .22
Magazine: 1 round
Features: Sturdy pistol grip stock; rifled barrel; SBD Gold Sound Suppression; CenterPoint 4x32mm scope
MSRP $189.99

DPMS CLASSIC A4 NITRO PISTON

Power: Nitro Piston 2
Stock: Synthetic
Overall length: 40 in.
Sights: None

Weight: 5 lb. 12.8 oz.
Caliber: .177
Features: Break-barrel action modeled after DPMS A4 platform; two-stage adjustable trigger; Picatinny rail; CenterPoint 4x32mm scope included
MSRP $219.99

DPMS SBR

Power: CO2
Stock: Synthetic
Overall Length: 26.5 in.
Sights: Flip-up front, windage adjustable rear
Weight: 6 lb. 8 oz.
Caliber: BB
Magazine: 30 rounds
Features: Dual action semiauto/full-auto BB gun on an AR-type platform; adjustable stock; quad rail; blowback bolt
MSRP $199.99

FIRE NP

Power: Nitro piston
Stock: Synthetic
Overall Length: 43.5 in.
Sights: None
Weight: 6 lb.
Caliber: .177
Features: Rifled steel barrel; two-stage, adjustable trigger; CenterPoint 4x32mm scope
MSRP $149.99

FURY NP

Power: Break action Nitro Piston
Stock: Synthetic all-weather
Overall Length: 45 in.
Sights: 4X32mm scope; rifled sights
Weight: 6 lb. 6 oz.
Caliber: .177
Features: Velocities up to 1200 fps; rifled steel barrel; adjustable two-stage trigger; Nitro Piston technology delivers smooth cocking, reduced vibration and shoots with 70 percent less noise
Scope: $139.99
Rifled sights: $89.99

M4-177, M4-177T

Power: Multi-pump pneumatic
Stock: Synthetic
Length: 34 in.
Sights: Adjustable front and rear
Weight: 3 lb. 9 oz.
Caliber: .177
Features: Rifled steel barrel; shoots both pellets and BBs; variable pump action easy to use for right- or lefthanded shooters; Picatinny rails; front and rear sights and stock are removable for upgrades; adjustable stock; velocities up to 660 fps with BBs and 625 fps with 7.9gr, .177 caliber pellets; in black (M4-177) or tan (M4-177T)
Black: $79.99
Tan: $75.00

AIRGUNS

Crosman

CROSMAN MAKO

CROSMAN MARAUDER

CROSMAN MARLIN CLASSIC (BB)

CROSMAN MAXIMUS

CROSMAN MAYHEM

CROSMAN MK45

CROSMAN MTR77NP

MAKO
Power: CO2
Stock: Synthetic
Overall Length: 8.56 in.
Sights: Fiber optic front and rear
Weight: 1 lb. 11 oz.
Caliber: BB
Magazine: 20 rounds
Features: Designed based on the Beretta Model 92; tri-color look; finger grips on the front strap; removable backstraps; accessory rail
MSRP. **$79.99**

MARAUDER
Power: Compressed air
Stock: Wood
Overall Length: 42.8 in.
Sights: None
Weight: 8 lb. 3 oz.
Caliber: .177, .22, .25
Features: Bolt action; ten round magazine; reversable bolt; dovetail mounting rail; available in wood, black synthetic, and Realtree Max1, Realtree Xtra, and Muddy Girl camo stocks
MSRP. . . . . **$539.99–$579.99**

MARLIN CLASSIC (BB)
Power: Spring
Stock: Resin
Overall length: N/A
Sights: Fixed blade front, adjustable notch rear
Weight: 2 lb. 10 oz.
Caliber: BB
Features: Lever-action modeled after traditional Marlin rifle; ratcheting lever; 700-BB reservoir
MSRP. **$49.99**

MAXIMUS
Power: Bolt
Stock: Synthetic
Overall Length: N/A
Sights: Fiber optic front and rear
Weight: N/A
Caliber: .22, .177
Features: Easy filling 2000 PSI reservoir; rifled barrel; up to 30 effective shots per fill
MSRP. **$219.99**

MAYHEM
Power: Nitro Piston 2
Stock: Synthetic
Overall length: 46.5 in.
Sights: Fixed front, windage/elevation adjustable rear
Weight: 7 lb. 6 oz.
Caliber: .177, .22
Features: Break-barrel action with Nitro Piston 2 powerplant; ambidextrous stock with soft-touch inserts;

rifled and shrouded barrel; two-stage trigger; rubber buttpad; sling mounts; Picatinny rail; includes 3-9x40mm AO scope and Crosman's SBD (Silencing Barrel Device)
MSRP. **$339.99**

MK45
Power: CO2
Stock: Synthetic
Overall Length: 7.5 in.
Sights: Fixed blade front, notch rear
Weight: N/A
Caliber: BB
Magazine: 20 rounds
Features: Removable grip makes CO2 cartridge loading easy; tan with a black grip; accessory rail
MSRP. **$49.99**

MTR77NP
Power: Break action Nitro Piston
Stock: Synthetic all-weather
Overall Length: 40 in.
Sights: 4x32mm scope
Weight: 6 lb. 2 oz.
Caliber: .177
Features: Nitro Piston technology delivers smooth cocking, reduced vibration and shoots with 70 percent less noise; sling mounts; storage in false magazine; up to 1200 fps; carry handle and carry handle/scope combo also available
MSRP. . . . . **$199.95–$245.99**

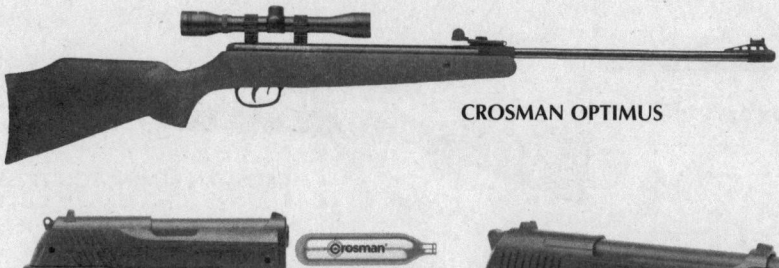

CROSMAN OPTIMUS

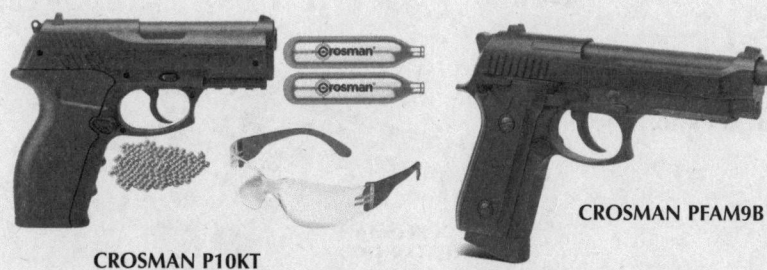

CROSMAN P10KT

CROSMAN PFAM9B

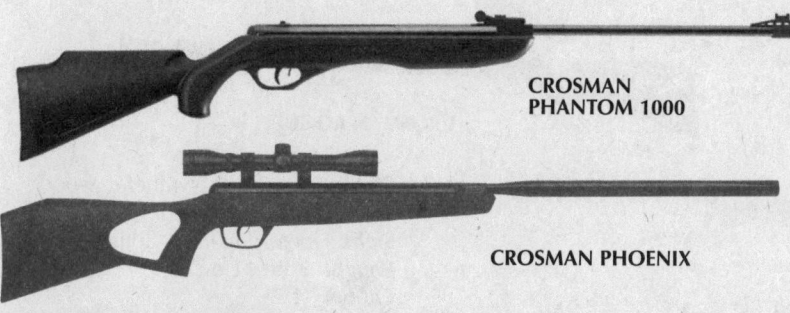

CROSMAN PHANTOM 1000

CROSMAN PHOENIX

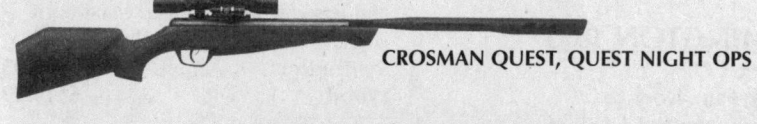

CROSMAN QUEST, QUEST NIGHT OPS

CROSMAN RECRUIT

PHANTOM 1000

Power: Spring piston
Stock: Synthetic
Overall Length: 44.5 in.
Sights: Fiber optic front, adjustable rear
Weight: 6 lb.
Caliber: .177
Features: All-weather, synthetic black stock and forearm; checkered grip and forearm; velocity up to 1000 fps; rifled steel barrel; two-stage adjustable trigger; scoped package available
Rifled sights: **$89.99**
Scope: **$99.99**

PHOENIX

Power: NP2 nitro piston
Stock: Synthetic
Overall Length: 45.8 in.
Sights: CenterPoint 4x32mm scope
Weight: 8 lb.
Caliber: .22, .177
Features: Velocities up to 1400 fps; enhanced two-stage Clean Break Trigger; precision rifled steel barrel; integrated sound suppression system; dovetail rail
MSRP **$199.99**

QUEST, QUEST NIGHT OPS

Power: Gas piston
Stock: Synthetic
Overall Length: 45 in.
Sights: None
Weight: 6 lb.
Caliber: .177, .22
Magazine: 1 round
Features: Two-stage adjustable Clean Break Trigger; SBD Gold Sound Suppression; rifled barrel; Quest includes CenterPoint 4x32mm scope; Quest Night Ops also includes a 90 lumen LED flashlight and Class III red laser
Quest: **$184.99**
Quest Night Ops: **$249.99**

RECRUIT

Power: Pneumatic pump
Stock: Synthetic
Overall Length: 38.25 in.
Sights: Scope
Weight: 2 lb. 15 oz.
Caliber: .177
Features: Adjustable buttstock; adjustable synthetic stock; 11mm dovetail scope rail; cross-bolt safety
MSRP **$79.99**

OPTIMUS

Power: Break action
Stock: Hardwood
Overall Length: 43 in.
Sights: 4x32mm CenterPoint scope
Weight: 6 lb. 8 oz.
Caliber: .177, .22
Features: Ambidextrous hardwood stock; relatively light cocking force and a two-stage adjustable trigger; velocities of up to 1200 fps with alloy pellets; barrel incorporates a micro-adjustable rear sight and fiber optic front sight; .177 also available without scope
MSRP . . . .**$109.99–$139.99**

P10KT

Power: CO2
Stock: Synthetic
Overall Length: 6.9 in.
Sights: Fixed blade front, notch rear
Weight: 1 lb. 1.6 oz.
Caliber: BB
Magazine: 20 rounds
Features: Steel barrel; grip removes for CO2 cartridge replacement; accessory rail
MSRP **$59.99**

PFAM9B

Power: CO2
Stock: Synthetic
Overall Length: 8.5 in.
Sights: Blade front, fixed rear
Weight: 2 lb. 7 oz.
Caliber: BB
Magazine: 20 rounds
Features: Designed based on Beretta's Model 92; full metal construction
MSRP **$129.99**

AIRGUNS

Crosman

CROSMAN REMINGTON 725 VTR

CROSMAN REMINGTON 777SB

CROSMAN REPEATAIR 1077

CROSMAN REMINGTON 1875

CROSMAN REMINGTON RP45

CROSMAN ROGUE

CROSMAN SILVER FOX NITRO PISTON (.22)

REMINGTON 725 VTR
Power: Gas piston
Stock: Synthetic
Overall Length: 48 in.
Sights: None
Weight: 10 lb. 8 oz.
Caliber: .25
Magazine: 1 round
Features: All-weather synthetic stock; two-stage adjustable trigger; Picatinny rail; CenterPoint 3–9x32mm scope
MSRP $259.99

REMINGTON 777SB
Power: Gas piston
Stock: Wood
Overall Length: 44.5 in.
Sights: None
Weight: 6 lb. 12 oz.
Caliber: .177
Magazine: 1 round
Features: High-gloss finish and checkering on wood stock; dovetail mounts; two-stage adjustable trigger; silver-finished bull barrel; CenterPoint 4x32mm scope
MSRP $189.99

REMINGTON 1875
Power: CO2
Stock: Faux ivory
Overall length: 13.125 in.
Sights: Fixed blade front, fixed notch rear
Weight: 2 lb. 4.8 oz.
Caliber: BB, .177
Features: Replica of Remington 1875 revolver; single-action; functional hammer, load gate, and extractor; nickel finish
MSRP $149.99

REMINGTON RP45
Power: CO2
Stock: Synthetic
Overall length: 7.7 in.
Sights: Fixed blade front, fixed notch rear
Weight: 1 lb. 11 oz.
Caliber: BB
Features: Modeled after Remington's RP45 handgun; semiauto repeater; Picatinny rail; slide safety
MSRP $69.99

REPEATAIR 1077
Power: CO2

Stock: All-weather, synthetic, wood
Overall Length: 36.88 in.
Sight: Fiber optic front, adjustable rear
Weight: 3 lb. 11 oz.
Caliber: .177
Features: Exclusive 12-shot rotary pellet clip lets you shoot longer; maximum velocity 625 fps; cross-bolt safety
Synthetic: $69.95
Wood: $114.99

ROGUE
Power: Nitro Piston 2
Stock: Synthetic
Overall length: 48 in.
Sights: Fixed front, adjustable rear
Weight: 7 lb. 6 oz.
Caliber: .177, .22
Features: Break-barrel action with Nitro Piston 2 powerplant; rifled steel barrel; 3-9x32mm scope; Crosman's SBD (Silencing Barrel Device)
MSRP $299.99

SILVER FOX NITRO PISTON
Power: Nitro Piston
Stock: Synthetic
Overall length: 43.5 in.
Sights: None
Weight: 6 lb.
Caliber: .177, .22
Features: Break-barrel action; dovetail mounting rail; two-stage trigger; CenterPoint 4x32mm scope
MSRP $199.99

AIRGUNS

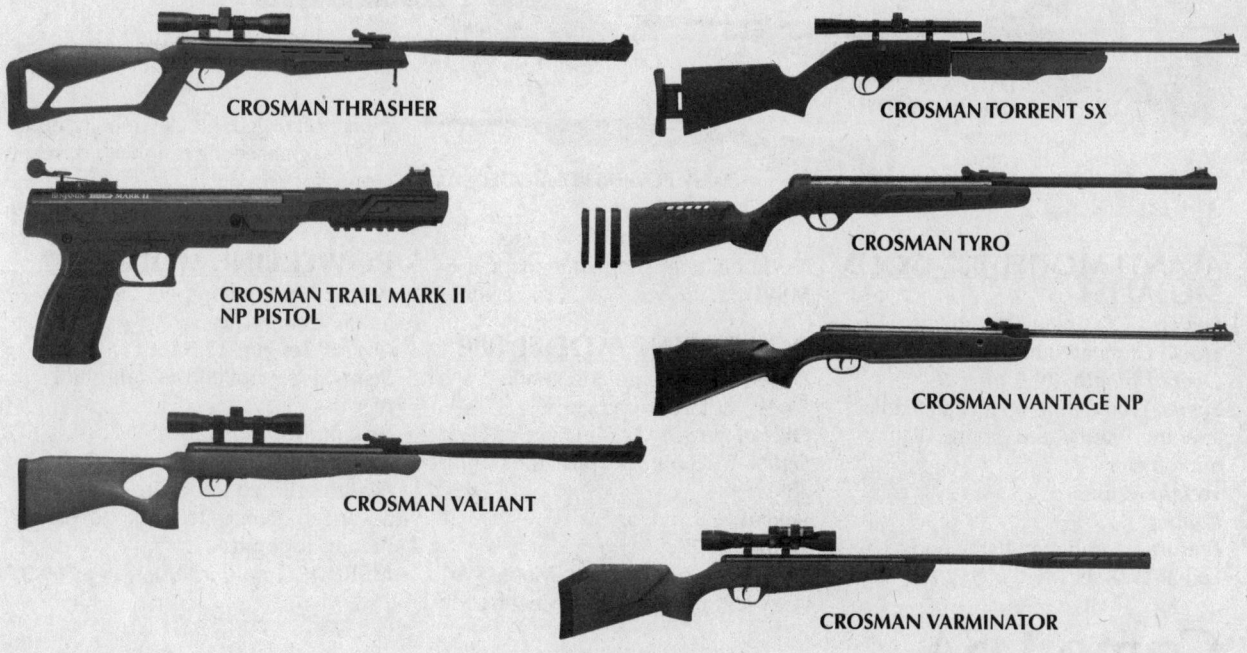

CROSMAN THRASHER

CROSMAN TORRENT SX

CROSMAN TRAIL MARK II
NP PISTOL

CROSMAN TYRO

CROSMAN VANTAGE NP

CROSMAN VALIANT

CROSMAN VARMINATOR

THRASHER
Power: Gas piston
Stock: Synthetic
Overall Length: 45.5 in.
Sights: Fixed front, adjustable rear
Weight: 8 lb. 5 oz.
Caliber: .177, .22
Magazine: 1 round
Features: Skeleton stock; rifled barrel; two-stage adjustable trigger; CenterPoint 4x32mm scope
MSRP **$184.99**

TORRENT SX
Power: Variable pump
Stock: Synthetic
Overall Length: 36.75 in.
Sights: Fiber optic front, adjustable rear
Weight: 2 lb. 15 oz.
Caliber: .177
Features: Lightweight, variable pump BB/pellet rifle; adjustable stock; customized length of pull; up to 695 fps; five-shot clip; olive-drab stock and forearm
MSRP **$49.95**

TRAIL MARK II NP PISTOL
Power: Nitro Piston
Stock: Synthetic
Overall length: N/A
Sights: Fiber optic front, adjustable notch rear
Weight: 3 lb. 7 oz.
Caliber: .177
Features: Break-barrel action; rifled steel barrel; tactical frame; removable cocking aid
MSRP **$114.99**

TYRO
Power: Spring
Stock: Synthetic
Overall Length: 30.5 in.–32.75 in.
Sights: Fiber optic front, adjustable rear
Weight: 5 lb.
Caliber: .177
Magazine: 1 round
Features: Designed for younger shooters; soft shooting; ambidextrous stock with a number of spacers to adjust for length of pull
MSRP **$105.99**

VALIANT
Power: Gas piston
Stock: Wood
Overall Length: N/A
Sights: Fixed front sight, adjustable rear
Weight: 6 lb. 4 oz.
Caliber: .177, .22
Magazine: 1 round
Features: Ambidextrous thumbhole stock of hardwood; two-stage adjustable trigger; CenterPoint 4x32mm scope
MSRP **$219.99**

VANTAGE NP
Power: Break action
Stock: Hardwood
Length: 45 in.
Sights: Fiber optic front, adjustable rear 4x32mm scope included
Weight: 7 lb. 2 oz.
Caliber: .177, .22
Features: Crosman's own version of the Bantage NP; hardwood stock; fiber optic front sight and fully adjustable rear sight; .177-caliber comes with scope; .22-caliber only with fiber optic sights and 11mm dovetail groove for optics mounting
.22-caliber: **$104.99**
.177-caliber: **$160.00**

VARMINATOR
Power: Gas piston
Stock: Synthetic
Overall Length: N/A
Sights: None
Weight: 6 lb. 4 oz.
Caliber: .177
Magazine: 1 round
Features: Gray stock with a raised comb; SBD Gold Sound Suppression; two-stage adjustable trigger; CenterPoint 4x32mm scope
MSRP **$199.99**

AIRGUNS

Daisy

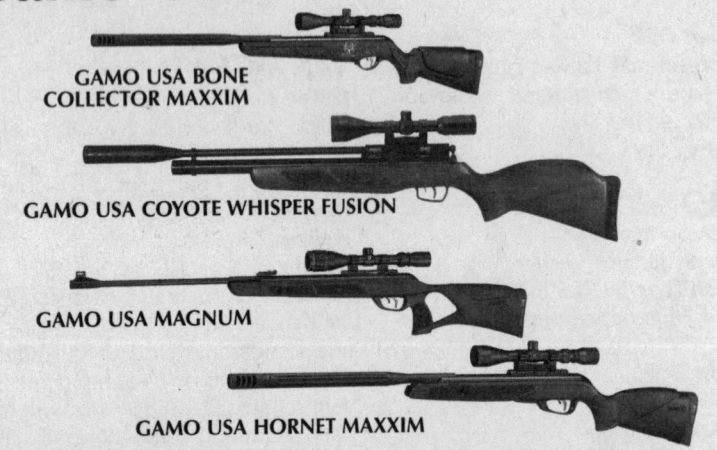

DAISY AVANTI MODEL 887 GOLD MEDALIST

DAISY POWERLINE MODEL 880

DAISY POWERLINE MODEL 901

AVANTI MODEL 887 GOLD MEDALIST
Power: CO2 single shot bolt
Stock: Laminated hardwood
Overall Length: 39.5 in.
Sights: Front globe with changeable aperture inserts, rear diopter with micrometer
Weight: 7 lb. 5 oz.
Caliber: .177
Features: Laminated hardwood stock; Lothar Walther rifled high-grade steel barrel; manual, cross-bolt trigger block; includes scope rail adapter
MSRP $499.99

POWERLINE MODEL 880
Power: Multi-pump pneumatic
Stock: Molded wood grain
Overall Length: 37.6 in.
Sights: TruGlo fiber optic front, adjustable rear
Weight: 3 lb. 11 oz.
Caliber: .177
Features: Wood-grained, Monte Carlo stock and forearm; rifled steel barrel; cross-bolt trigger block; velocity up to 750 fps; engineering resin with dovetail mount for scope
MSRP $49.99

POWERLINE MODEL 901
Power: Multi-pump pneumatic
Stock: Composite
Overall Length: 37.5 in.
Sights: Fiber optic front, adjustable rear
Weight: 3 lb. 11 oz.
Caliber: .177
Features: Rifled steel barrel; black advanced composite stock; dovetail mounts for optics
MSRP $69.99

Gamo USA

GAMO USA BONE COLLECTOR MAXXIM

GAMO USA COYOTE WHISPER FUSION

GAMO USA MAGNUM

GAMO USA HORNET MAXXIM

BONE COLLECTOR MAXXIM
Power: Inert Gas Technology
Stock: Synthetic
Overall length: 45.3 in.
Sights: 3-9X air rifle scope
Weight: 5 lb. 11.5 oz.
Caliber: .177, .22
Features: Designed in collaboration with Michael Waddell, Nick Mundt, and Travis "T Bone" Turner of the "Bone Collector" TV series; single-shot; features a single-cocking system, fluted polymer jacketed steel barrel with Whisper Maxxim technology, two-stage adjustable Custom Action Trigger, all-weather stock, double-sided cheekpiece, and Shock Wave Absorber recoil pad
MSRP $199.99

COYOTE WHISPER FUSION
Power: PCP
Stock: Beechwood
Overall length: 42.9 in.
Sights: None
Weight: 7 lb. 13.6 oz.
Caliber: .177, .22
Features: An entry-level PCP-power plant bolt-action air rifle that boasts a 10-pellet rotary clip, hammer forged rifled barrel, selve-regulating valve, Custom Action Trigger, Shock Wave Absorber, double-sided molded cheekpiece, and Whisper Fusion technology
MSRP $559.99

GAMO MAGNUM
Power: Inert Gas Technology Mach 1
Stock: All-weather synthetic
Overall length: 49.2 in.
Sights: 3-9X air rifle scope
Weight: 6 lb. 14 oz.
Caliber: .177, .22
Features: The power plant system substitutes the traditional spring for a gas cylinder that delivers more power; single-shot, single-cocking air rifle is designed for pest control and features a fluted polymer jacketed steel barrel with Whisper Maxxim technology, two-stage adjustable Custom Action Trigger, double-sided cheekpiece, and Shock Wave Absorber recoil pad
MSRP $299.99

HORNET MAXXIM
Power: Inert Gas Technology
Stock: All-weather synthetic
Overall length: 45.3 in.
Sights: 3-9X air rifle scope
Weight: 5 lb. 11.5 oz.
Caliber: .177, .22
Features: Break-barrel air rifle is single-cocking, allows 10 shots before reloading, has cocking safety system, fluted polymer jacketed steel barrel with Whisper Maxxim technology, two-stage adjustable Custom Action Trigger, Shock Wave Absorber recoil pad, Whisper Maxxim silencing technology and Recoil Reducing Rail
MSRP: $159.99

AIRGUNS

Gamo USA

GAMO USA SWARM MAXXIM

GAMO USA URBAN PCP

GAMO USA VARMINT HUNTER HP

GAMO USA WHISPER CFR

GAMO USA WHISPER FUSION MACH 1

SWARM MAXXIM

Power: Inert Gas Technology
Stock: Synthetic
Overall length: 45.3 in.
Sights: 3-9X air rifle scope
Weight: 5 lb. 10 oz.
Caliber: .177
Features: Break-barrel air rifle is single-cocking, allows 10 shots before reloading, has cocking safety system, fluted polymer jacketed steel barrel with Whisper Maxxim technology, two-stage adjustable Custom Action Trigger, all-weather stock, and Shock Wave Absorber recoil pad
MSRP $199.99

URBAN PCP

Power: PCP
Stock: Synthetic
Overall length: 42.9 in.
Sights: None
Weight: 6 lb. 11.2 oz.
Caliber: .22
Features: Bolt-action air rifle features Whisper Fusion technology multi-shot mechanism, Custom Action Trigger, hammer forged barrel, and thumbhole stock with double-sided molded cheekpiece
MSRP $399.99

VARMINT HUNTER HP

Power: Break action/spring piston
Stock: Synthetic
Length: 43.78 in.
Sights: 4x32mm scope
Weight: 6 lb. 10 oz.
Caliber: .177
Features: Lightweight synthetic stock; match grade fluted barrel; 1400 fps maximum velocity; 4x32mm air rifle scope with laser sight and flashlight; break barrel single cocking system
MSRP $289.95

WHISPER CFR

Power: Single shot/spring piston
Stock: Synthetic
Length: 46.85 in.
Sights: Fiber optic sights, mounted 4x32 standard reticle scope
Weight: 8 lb.

Caliber: .177
Features: First Whisper Air Rifle with a fixed barrel; integrated ND52 noise dampener system; fixed rifled steel barrel; capable of 1100 fps; newly designed recoil pad with 74 percent more recoil absorbing pressure; all-weather synthetic molded stock with thumbhole
MSRP $299.95

WHISPER FUSION MACH 1

Power: IGT Mach 1
Stock: Synthetic
Overall length: 46.5 in.
Sights: Fiber optic front, adjustable rear
Weight: 8 lb.
Caliber: .177, .22
Features: Break-barrel, single-cocking action; single-shot; fluted polymer jacketed steel barrel; Custom Action Trigger; Recoil Reducing Rail; 3-9x40 air rifle scope
MSRP $249.99

Gletcher

M712

Power: CO2
Stock: Wood
Overall length: 23 in.
Sights: Post front, tangent rear
Weight: 3 lb.
Caliber: .177
Features: Reproduction of WWII 1932 broomhandle Mauser; breech mechanism moves when firing; full-auto

GLETCHER M712

functionality and blowback system
MSRP $179.99

M1891

Power: CO2
Stock: Imitation wood
Overall length: 22.43 in.

GLETCHER M1891

Sights: Hooded front post, tangent rear
Weight: 5 lb. 9.6 oz.
Caliber: .177
Features: Reproduction of Russian Civil War "Obrez" model, a sawed-off Mosin-Nagant; mechanism works as in the original; built-in hex key for CO2 cartridge installation
MSRP $199.99

Gletcher

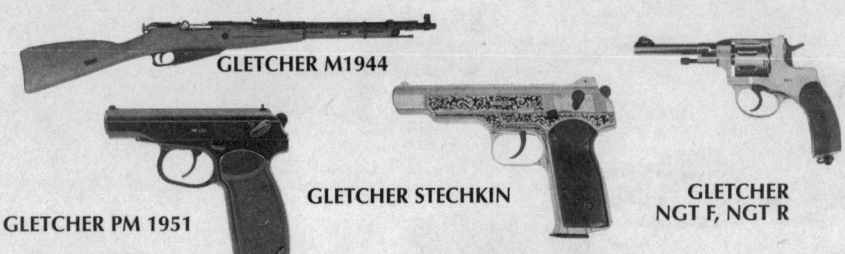

GLETCHER M1944

GLETCHER STECHKIN

GLETCHER NGT F, NGT R

GLETCHER PM 1951

M1944

Power: CO2
Stock: Imitation wood
Overall length: 52.75 in.
Sights: Post front, tangent rear
Weight: 8 lb. 3 oz.
Caliber: .177
Features: Reproduction of M44 Russian Mosin-Nagant carbine; barrel, bolt mechanism, and magazine are metal; action operates like the original firearm; integral folding bayonet; built-in hex wrench for CO2 cartridge installation
MSRP. $299.99

NGT F, NGT R

Power: CO2
Stock: Plastic
Overall length: 9 in.

Sights: Front post, cutout rear
Weight: 1 lb. 8 oz.
Caliber: .177
Features: Reproduction of the Belgian Nagant revolver; steel BBs fired through decorative snap cap "cartridges"; seven-shot true revolving action; blue or silver finishes; rifled barrel options available in both finishes
MSRP. . . . . $134.99–$149.99

PM 1951

Power: CO2
Stock: Plastic
Overall length: 6.3 in.
Sights: Low-profile integral front and rear
Weight: 1 lb. 10 oz.

Caliber: .177
Features: Reproduction of Russian Makarov sidearm; metal body and slide; safety lever; magazine pinky finger extension
MSRP. $99.99

STECHKIN

Power: CO2
Stock: Plastic
Overall length: 8.8 in.
Sights: Low-profile integral front, adjustable rear
Weight: 2 lb. 4.8 oz.
Caliber: .177
Features: Limited edition (100 units) reproduction of Soviet Stretchkin pistol; weight is identical to the firearm version; double-action, with gold finish, engraving on slide and frame; comes in a presentation box
MSRP. $259.99

HatsanUSA

HATSANUSA BARRAGE

HATSANUSA BULLMASTER

BARRAGE

Power: PCP
Stock: Synthetic
Overall length: 19.7 in.
Sights: Fiber optic front and rear
Weight: 10 lb. 1.6 oz.
Caliber: .177, .22
Features: Semiautomatic; fitted with a 500cc air bottle mounted to the forearm; barrel is precision rifled, choked, and fully shrouded; ambidextrous thumbhole stock; Picatinny rail on the forearm; includes magazines for both calibers (.177 mag holds 14 shots, .22 holds 12 shots); TruGlo sights; HatSan's patented anti-knock system that prevents gas discharge and waste if the rifle is knocked or bounced
MSRP. $1039.99

BULLMASTER

Power: PCP
Stock: Synthetic
Overall length: 19.7 in.
Sights: None
Weight: 10 lb. 4.8 oz.
Caliber: .177, .22
Features: Semiautomatic bullpup design; 500cc air bottle mounted to the forearm; barrel is precision rifled, choked, and fully shrouded; includes magazines for both calibers (.177 mag holds 14 shots, .22 holds 12 shots); topside and and under forearm Picatinny rails; elevation adjustable cheekpiece; HatSan's patented anti-knock system that prevents gas discharge and waste if the rifle is knocked or bounced
MSRP. $1039.99

SIG SAUER 1911 MAX
CO2 BB GUN

SIG SAUER 1911
SPARTAN CO2 BB
GUN

SIG SAUER 1911 WE THE
PEOPLE BB PISTOL

SIG SAUER ASP20 SYNTHETIC
STOCK, WOOD STOCK

SIG SAUER P320 AIR
PISTOL, AIR PISTOL
COYOTE TAN

SIG SAUER X-FIVE ASP

1911 MAX CO2 BB GUN

Power: CO2
Stock: Cust Max Michael
Overall length: 8.7 in
Sights: White dot front and rear
Weight: 2 lb. 9.6 oz.
Caliber: BB (4.5mm)
Features: CO2-operated BB gun replication of SIG Max Michael 1911 pistol; accessory rail; skeletonized trigger; cam-lever CO2 loading port; functional grip safety; full blowback metal slide; 16-round magazine; natural alloy finish
MSRP $109.99

1911 SPARTAN CO2 BB GUN

Power: CO2
Stock: Custom Spartan
Overall length: 8.7 in.
Sights: White dot front and rear
Weight: 2 lb. 9.6 oz.
Caliber: BB (4.5mm)
Features: CO2-operated BB gun replication of SIG Spartan 1911 pistol; MOLON LABE engraved slide; custom Spartan grips; skeletonized trigger; cam-lever CO2 loading port; func-

tional grip safety; full blowback metal slide; 16-round magazine; oil-rubbed bronze finish
MSRP $109.99

1911 WE THE PEOPLE BB PISTOL

Power: CO2
Stock: Aluminum
Overall Length: 8.5 in.
Sights: Fixed
Weight: 2 lb. 3 oz.
Caliber: BB
Magazine: 17 rounds
Features: Custom aluminum 50-star grips (25 each side); distressed finish slide and frame
MSRP $119.99

ASP20 SYNTHETIC STOCK, WOOD STOCK

Power: Gas piston
Stock: Synthetic, wood
Overall Length: 45.6 in.
Sights: None
Weight: N/A
Caliber: .177, .22
Magazine: 1 round
Features: Advanced Sport Pellet; suppressed break-barrel single-shot air rifle designed to reduce the force needed to cock the action to 33 pounds; ambidextrous safety located

outside the trigger guard; rifled steel barrel; adjustable MatchLite trigger
Synthetic: $399.99
Wood: $489.99

P320 AIR PISTOL, AIR PISTOL COYOTE TAN

Power: CO2
Stock: Polymer
Overall length: 7.9 in.
Sights: White dot front and rear
Weight: 1 lb. 11 oz.
Caliber: .177
Features: CO2-operated airgun model of SIG's P320 carry gun; rotary magazine holds 30 rounds; rifled steel barrel; manual safety; all-metal slide; black or Coyote Tan finishes
MSRP $119.99

X-FIVE

Power: CO2
Stock: Metal
Overall Length: 8.7 in.
Sights: Adjustable
Weight: 2 lb. 11.2 oz.
Caliber: .177
Magazine: 20 rounds
Features: Advanced Sport Pellet; full blowback, metal-framed CO2 air pistol; cam-lever CO2 housing; ambidextrous safety
MSRP $139.99

AIRGUNS

Stoeger Airguns

STOEGER AIRGUNS S6000-A

STOEGER AIRGUNS S8000-TAC SUPPRESSED

STOEGER AIRGUNS XP4

S6000-A UNDERLEVER

Power: Spring piston
Stock: Wood
Overall Length: 43 in.
Sights: Fiber optic front, adjustable rear
Weight: 6 lb. 13 oz.
Caliber: .177, .22
Magazine: N/A
Features: Spring piston operated via an underlever, which requires less effort to operate than a traditional break barrel; safety is automatic, ambidextrous; available with a 3–9x40 adjustable objective scope; two-stage adjustable trigger
MSRP $199.00
Scoped: $229.00

S8000-TAC SUPPRESSED

Power: Break action/gas-operated
Stock: Synthetic
Overall Length: 42.5 in.
Sights: 4–16x40mm scope
Weight: 8 lb. 14 oz.
Caliber: .177, .22
Features: Airflow control technology and dual-stage noise reduction system; automatic ambidextrous safety; black tactical stock; up to 1200 fps with alloy pellets (.177); adjustable length of pull; integral Picatinny rails
MSRP $249.00

XP4

Power: Single-pump pneumatic
Stock: Synthetic
Overall Length: 9.7 in.
Sights: Fiber optic front, adjustable rear
Weight: 1 lb. 8 oz.
Caliber: .177
Magazine: N/A
Features: Ambidextrous grip design; two-stage trigger; automatic safety; integral rail
MSRP $89.00

UMAREX

BERETTA APX

UMAREX DX17

UMAREX EMBARK

BERETTA APX

Power: CO2
Stock: N/A
Overall length: 7.25 in.
Sights: Fixed front and rear
Weight: 1 lb. 12 oz.
Caliber: BB
Features: Semiautomatic; 20-shot; double-action repeater has realistic recoil action; CO2 cartridge housed in grip; drop-free steel BB magazine; integrated Picatinny rail
MSRP $65.00

DX17

Power: Spring-powered
Stock: Synthetic
Overall length: 9.5 in.
Sights: Fixed fiber optic front, fixed rear
Weight: 1 lb.
Caliber: BB
Features: Single-action air pistol shoots steel BBs; built-in BB reservoir; integrated accessory rail; 15-shot capacity; includes 200 steel BBs
MSRP $18.00

EMBARK

Power: Break-barrel spring piston
Stock: Synthetic
Overall Length: 40 in.
Sights: Fixed open blade front, micrometer adjustable rear
Weight: 4 lb. 7 oz.
Caliber: .177
Magazine: 1 round
Features: An electric-green, ambidextrous thumbhole stock; official air rifle of the Student Air Rifle Program; cocking poundage is 16.25 lbs
MSRP $95.00

UMAREX

UMAREX FORGE

UMAREX GAUNTLET

HECKLER & KOCH USP BLOWBACK

LEGENDS ACE IN THE HOLE

LEGENDS MP

UMAREX MCP KIT

UMAREX OCTANE ELITE

FORGE
Power: T.N.T. Turbo Nitrogen Technology gas piston
Stock: Wood
Overall length: 44.8 in.
Sights: 4x32mm scope
Weight: 7 lb. 13 oz.
Caliber: .177
Features: T.N.T. fast piston system; spring piston break barrel with a single-shot cocking mechanism and automatic safety; adjustable trigger; integrated rail platform; 4x32 airgun scope; rifled barrel; enhanced SilencAir noise dampener
MSRP $161.99

GAUNTLET
Power: Pre-charged pneumatic
Stock: Synthetic
Overall length: 46.75 in.
Sights: N/A
Weight: 8 lb. 8 oz.
Caliber: .177, .22
Features: Bolt-action repeater; removable 3000 psi 13 cubic in. tank; 1100 psi regulator; adjustable stock comb; pressure key release; rotary magazine; single-shot tray
MSRP $320.99

HECKLER & KOCH USP BLOWBACK
Power: CO2
Stock: Synthetic
Overall Length: 7.75 in.
Sights: Fixed front blade, fixed rear
Weight: 2 lb. 2 oz.
Caliber: BB
Magazine: 16 rounds
Features: Replica of H&K's semiautomatic pistol; magazine houses both BBs and the CO2 capsule; blowback action
MSRP $49.21

LEGENDS ACE IN THE HOLE
Power: CO2
Stock: Synthetic
Overall Length: 9 in.
Sights: Blade front, groove rear
Weight: 1 lb. 15 oz.
Caliber: .177
Magazine: 6 rounds
Features: Single-action CO2 revolver; weathered finish; black grips with an embossed spade; speed-draw thumb spur; by Umarex
MSRP $120.95

LEGENDS MP
Power: CO2
Stock: Metal
Overall length: 33 in.
Sights: Fixed front, elevation adjustable rear
Weight: N/A
Caliber: .177
Features: Distinctive German replication; 10-in. barrel; folding stock; full-auto blowback action; 60-shot drop-free steel BB magazine; two CO2 cartridges housed in the magazine
MSRP $228.47

MCP KIT
Power: CO2
Stock: Synthetic
Overall Length: 7.75 in.
Sights: Fixed blade front, fixed rear
Weight: 14.4 oz.
Caliber: BB
Magazine: 19 rounds
Features: Safety glasses; packet of 250 BBs; pair of CO2 cartridges; CO2 is housed in the grip; accessory rail
MSRP $39.99

OCTANE ELITE
Power: ReAxis gas-powered piston
Stock: Synthetic
Overall length: 48.6 in.
Sights: 3-9x40mm scope
Weight: 9 lb. 8 oz.
Caliber: .177, .22
Features: Lockdown rail mounting system; 3-9x40mm airgun scope with adjustable objective; Stopshox anti-recoil system; SilencAir 5 chamber noise dampener; all-weather stock; rifled barrel; single-shot cocking mechanism
MSRP $249.99

AIRGUNS

UMAREX

RUGER YUKON MAGNUM

RWS MODEL 34

RWS MODEL 48 WITH SCOPE

RWS MODEL 54

RWS MODEL 350 MAGNUM

UMAREX SA10

RUGER YUKON MAGNUM

Power: Break-barrel gas piston
Stock: Wood
Overall Length: 48.25 in.
Sights: Fiber optic front, adjustable rear
Weight: 9 lb. 3 oz.
Caliber: .177, .22
Magazine: 1 round
Features: Made by Umarex; ReAxis piston for improved velocities; equipped with a 3–9x42mm scoped premounted on the air rifle's Picatinny rail; two-stage adjustable trigger; SilencAir suppressor; cocking effort is 47 pounds
MSRP **$250.54**

RWS MODEL 34

Power: Break action/spring piston
Stock: Hardwood, synthetic
Overall Length: 45 in.
Sights: 4x32mm scope
Weight: 7 lb. 8 oz.–8 lb.
Caliber: .177, .22
Features: Polished with blued metal-work; full-sized hardwood stock; two-stage adjustable trigger; automatic safety; finely rifled barrel; 34 Pro large muzzlebrake
MSRP **$332.00**
With scope: **$385.99**

RWS MODEL 48

Power: Side lever/spring piston
Stock: Hardwood
Overall Length: 42.5 in.
Sights: Adjustable rear
Weight: 8 lb. 8 oz.
Caliber: .177
Features: Extended breech stock to reduce recoil; fixed barrel system; adjustable trigger; automatic safety; optional RWS 4x32mm scope and mounts
MSRP **$502.85**
With scope: **$567.09**

RWS MODEL 54

Power: Side lever/spring piston
Stock: Hardwood
Overall Length: 43.75 in.
Sights: Adjustable rear
Weight: 9 lb.
Caliber: .177, .22
Features: Adjustable trigger; scope rail; Monte Carlo hardwood stock with cheekpiece and checkering; automatic safety; 1100 fps maximum velocity
MSRP: **$695.45**

RWS MODEL 350 MAGNUM

Power: Break action/spring piston
Stock: Hardwood

Overall Length: 48.3 in.
Sights: 4x32mm scope
Weight: 8 lb. 3 oz.
Caliber: .177, .22
Features: Two-stage trigger; mounted scope rail
MSRP **$492.25**
With scope: **$593.85**

SA10

Power: CO_2
Stock: Synthetic
Overall length: 9.25 in.
Sights: None
Weight: 2 lb. 1 oz.
Caliber: BB, .177
Features: Dual-ammo air pistol accommodating both BBs and .177-caliber pellets; uses one CO_2 cartridge; blowback action; DA/SA trigger; eight-round rotary magazine; integrated accessory rail; gold-colored barrel; includes 1 polymer and three metal bonus magazines
MSRP **$82.95**

UMAREX STRIKE POINT

UMAREX TREVOX

WALTHER
PPS M2

STRIKE POINT
Power: Multi-pump pneumatic
Stock: Synthetic
Overall length: 14 in.
Sights: Fiber optic
Weight: 2 lb. 10 oz.
Caliber: .177, .22
Features: Variable pump power; easy grip pump-action; easy load bolt-action; SilencAir 3 chamber noise dampener
MSRP $53.49

TREVOX
Power: T.N.T. Turbo Nitrogen Technology gas piston
Stock: Synthetic
Overall length: 18.11 in.
Sights: Fiber optic
Weight: 3 lb. 2 oz.
Caliber: .177
Features: Rifled barrel accuracy with an easy-grip; single-stroke cocking mechanism; SilencAir 3 chamber noise dampener; 11mm dovetail cuts for optics mounting; blued finish
MSRP $79.99

WALTHER PPS M2
Power: CO2
Stock: Synthetic
Overall Length: 6.3 in.
Sights: Fixed blade front, fixed rear
Weight: 1 lb. 2 oz.
Caliber: BB
Magazine: 18 rounds
Features: Blowback design; metal parts for added weight; CO2 housing is hidden in the backstrap; from Umarex
MSRP $79.99

SHOTGUNS

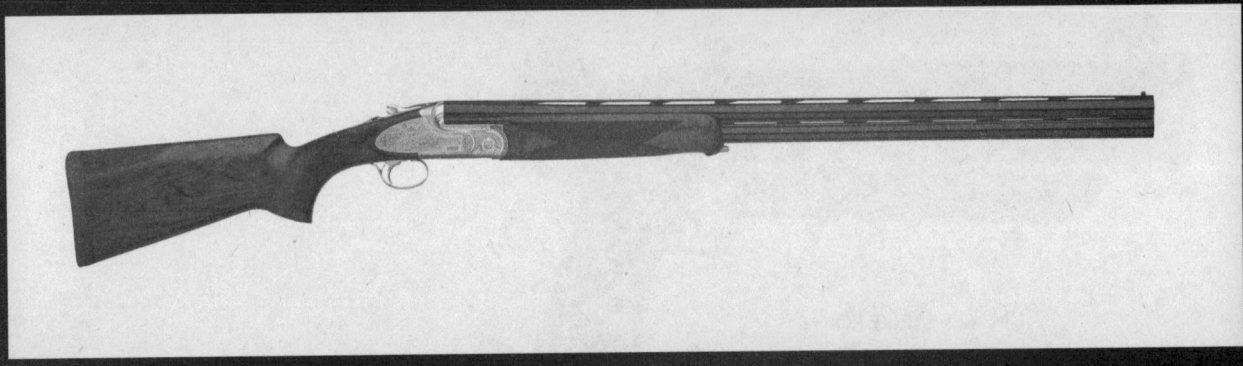

American Tactical

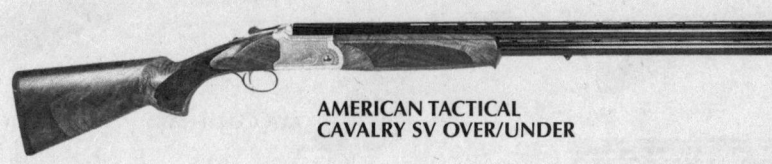

**AMERICAN TACTICAL
CAVALRY SV OVER/UNDER**

CAVALRY SV OVER/UNDER
Action: Over/under
Stock: Turkish walnut
Barrel: 26 in., 28 in.
Chokes: C, IC, M, IM, F
Weight: N/A
Bore/Gauge: 12, 20, 28, .410
Magazine: 2 shells
Features: Brass front bead sights, available with auto ejector, chambered for 3-in. Mag. shells, single selective trigger
MSRP......................**$659.95**

Armscor/Rock Island Armory

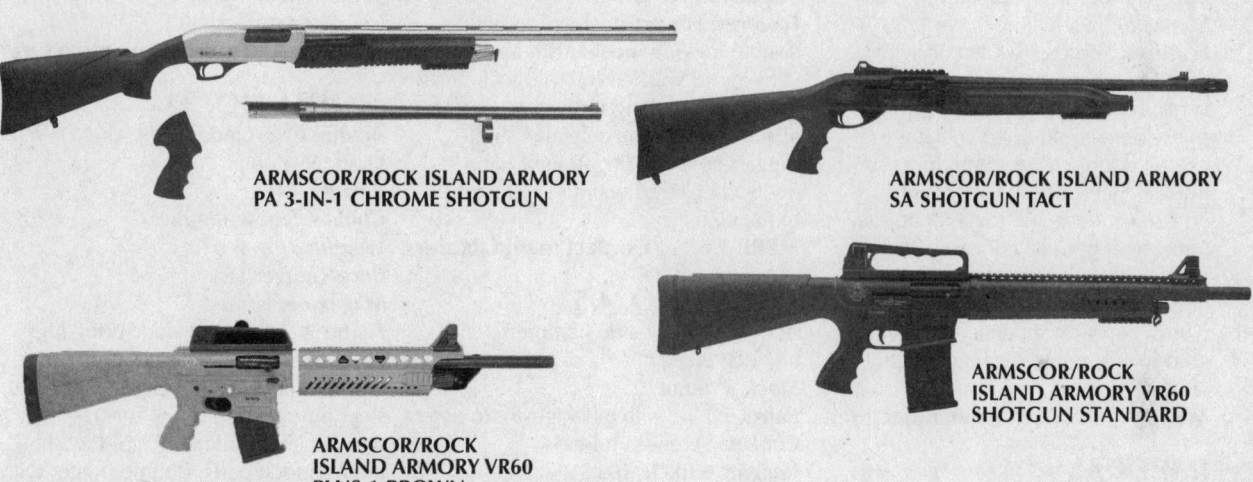

**ARMSCOR/ROCK ISLAND ARMORY
PA 3-IN-1 CHROME SHOTGUN**

**ARMSCOR/ROCK ISLAND ARMORY
SA SHOTGUN TACT**

**ARMSCOR/ROCK
ISLAND ARMORY VR60
PLUS 1 BROWN**

**ARMSCOR/ROCK
ISLAND ARMORY VR60
SHOTGUN STANDARD**

PA 3-IN-1 CHROME SHOTGUN
Action: Pump
Stock: Polymer
Barrel: 18.5 in., 28 in.
Chokes: S, F, M, IC
Weight: 6 lb. 2.7 oz.
Bore/Gauge: 12
Magazine: 4 shells
Features: 28-in. vent rib barrel with removable chokes; 18.5-in. cylinder bored barrel with front post sight; full polymer stock; add-on pistol grip; aluminum receiver; metalwork finished in Marine Chrome
MSRP................**$375.00**

SA SHOTGUN TACT
Action: Semiautomatic
Stock: Polymer
Barrel: 18.5 in.
Chokes: F, M, IC
Weight: 7 lb.

Bore/Gauge: 12
Magazine: 4 shells
Features: Economical shotgun for home-defense or 3-Gun competition; flash hider at the muzzle; fiber optic front sight, rear sight; Picatinny rail; aluminum receiver in black chrome finish; polymer stock with pistol grip
MSRP................. **$399.00**

VR60 PLUS 1 BROWN
Action: Semiautomatic
Stock: Polymer
Barrel: 20 in.
Chokes: F, M, IC
Weight: 8 lb.
Bore/Gauge: 12
Magazine: 5 shells
Features: AR-type platform; conventional gas operation; aluminum receiver; polymer pistol grip stock with molded cheekpiece; A2-type front sight; removable A2-type carry

handle; ventilated handguard; Picatinny rail; left-side manual safety; chambered for 2 ¾- or 3-in. shells; brown, red, or black finishes
MSRP.................**$549.00**

VR60 SHOTGUN STANDARD
Action: Semiautomatic
Stock: Polymer
Barrel: 20 in.
Chokes: F, M, IC
Weight: 7 lb. 6.2 oz.
Bore/Gauge: 12
Magazine: 5 shells
Features: AR-platform semiautomatic; conventional gas-operated action; removable carry handle; full-length Picatinny rail
MSRP.................**$499.00**

AYA (Aguirre y Aranzabal)

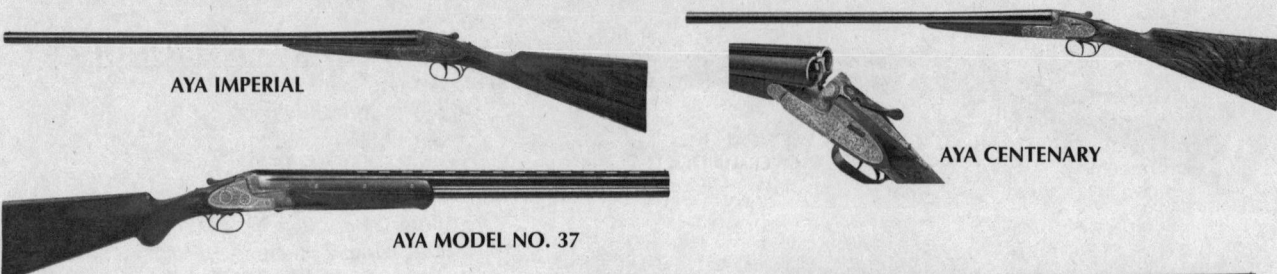

AYA IMPERIAL

AYA CENTENARY

AYA MODEL NO. 37

AYA MODEL NO. 4/53

CENTENARY

Action: Side-by-side
Stock: Wood
Barrel: 28 in.
Chokes: N/A
Weight: 6 lb. 12 oz.
Bore/Gauge: 12, 16, 20, 28, .410
Magazine: 2 shells
Features: Forged steel action with double locking mechanism and gas vents; hardened steel intercepting safety sears; gold lined cocking indicators; double trigger with hinged front trigger; optional selective or non-selective single trigger; chopper lump steel barrels; concave rib; straight hand, finely chequered oil finished walnut stock; exhibition wood; custom Centenary engraving, gold inlays; initial oval; automatic safety
MSRP . . . . . . Contact manufacturer

IMPERIAL

Action: Side-by-side hammerless sidelock
Stock: Walnut
Barrel: 28 in., with other lengths to order

Chokes: Screw-in tubes
Weight: 6 lb. 12 oz.
Bore/Gauge: 12, 16, 20, 28, .410
Magazine: None
Features: Forged steel action with double locking mechanism and gas vents; gold washed internal lock parts; gold lined cocking indicators; optional selective or non-selective single trigger; concave rib; straight hand, finely checkered walnut stock; gold initial oval
MSRP . . . . . . Contact manufacturer

MODEL NO. 4/53

Action: Side-by-side hammerless boxlock ejector
Stock: Walnut
Barrel: 28 in., with other lengths to order
Chokes: Screw-in tubes
Weight: 6 lb. 10 oz.
Bore/Gauge: 12, 16, 20, 28, .410
Magazine: None
Features: Double locking mechanism with replaceable hinge pin; disk set firing pins; double trigger; chopper lump barrels with concave rib; light scroll engraving; metal finish available in hardened, old silver, or white finish; automatic safety
MSRP . . . . . . Contact manufacturer

MODEL NO. 37

Action: Over/under sidelock
Stock: Walnut
Barrel: 28 in.
Chokes: Screw-in tubes
Weight: 7 lb. 8 oz.
Bore/Gauge: 12
Magazine: None
Features: Double underlocking lugs and double crossbolt; chopper lump chrome nickel steel barrels; hardened steel intercepting safety sears; gold line cocking indicators; gold washed internal lock parts; double trigger with hinged front trigger; fine rose and scroll, game scene, or bold relief engraving on action plates; full pistol grip walnut stock
MSRP . . . . . . Contact manufacturer

Barrett Sovereign

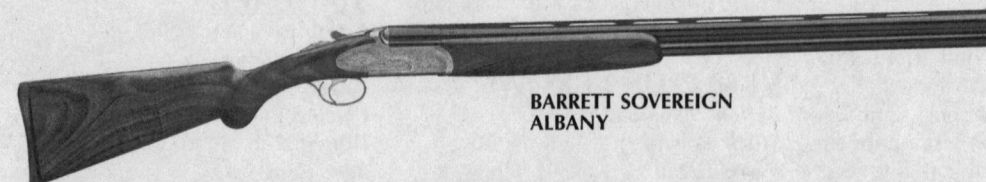

BARRETT SOVEREIGN
ALBANY

ALBANY

Action: Over/under
Stock: Turkish walnut
Barrel: 26 in., 28 in., 30 in.
Chokes: Five tubes
Sights: Front bead

Weight: 6 lb. 3 oz.–7 lb. 13 oz.
Bore/Gauge: 12, 20
Magazine: 2 shells
Features: Automatic ejectors; 30mm forcing cones; rounded forend; Prince of Wales grip; classic checkering; box lock design with intricate scroll

engraving on the receiver and side-plates; 12 ga. and 20 ga. are chambered for 3-in. shells and have all three barrel lengths available; 28 ga. chambers 2.75-in. shells and is available only with 28-in. barrels
MSRP . . . . $5700.00–$6150.00

Barrett Sovereign

BARRETT SOVEREIGN BELTRAMI

BARRETT SOVEREIGN B-XPRO

BARRETT SOVEREIGN RUTHERFORD

BELTRAMI
Action: Side-by-side
Stock: Walnut
Barrel: 26 in., 28 in., 30 in.
Chokes: F, IM, M, IC, C
Weight: N/A
Bore/Gauge: 12, 20, 28
Magazine: 2 shells
Features: Grade 3A Turkish walnut stock in straight English configuration; steel box lock receiver with coin-finished, engraved sideplates; tapered solid ribs; steel-shot rated barrels; 12- and 20-ga. models have splinter forends and 3-in. chambers, 28-ga. has semi-beavertail forend and 2 ¾-in. chamber; single non-selective trigger
MSRP . . . . $6150.00–$6550.00

B-XPRO
Action: Over/under
Stock: Walnut
Barrel: 30 in., 32 in.
Chokes: Extended (F, IM, M, IC, C)
Weight: 8 lb. 3 oz.–8 lb. 4 oz.
Bore/Gauge: 12
Magazine: 2 shells
Features: A+ walnut stock with pistol grip; 10mm-7mm tapered vent rib; fiber optic front bead; 3-in. chambers; rounded forend; box lock action; receiver has coin-finished engraving; single selective trigger; automatic ejectors
MSRP $3075.00

RUTHERFORD
Action: Over/under
Stock: Walnut
Barrel: 26 in., 28 in.
Chokes: F, IM, M, IC, C
Weight: 6 lb. 4 oz.–7 lb. 9 oz.
Bore/Gauge: 12, 16, 20, 28
Magazine: 2 shells
Features: Round body box lock; stock is A+ walnut; receiver is coin finished and engraved; single selective trigger; automatic ejectors; Prince of Wales grip; 30mm forcing cones; 6mm vent rib; 12-, 16-, and 20-ga. have 3-in. chambers, 28-ga. is 2 ¾-in.
MSRP . . . . $2200.00–$2520.00

Benelli USA

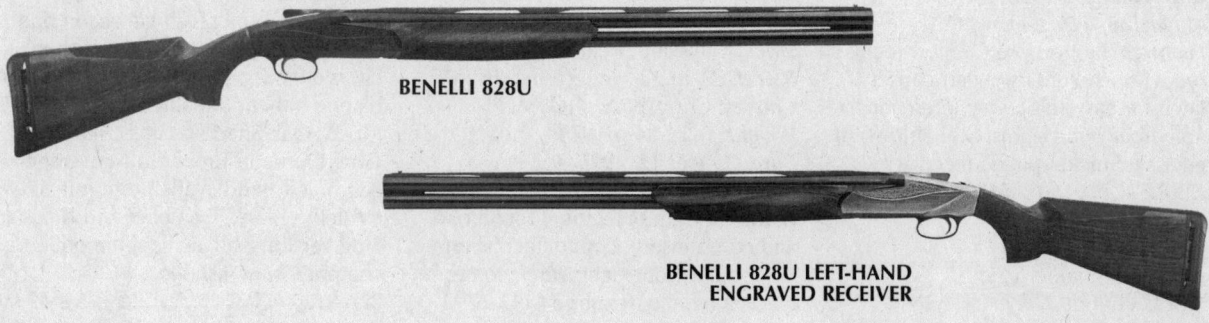

BENELLI 828U

BENELLI 828U LEFT-HAND ENGRAVED RECEIVER

828U
Action: Over/under
Stock: Wood
Barrel: 26 in., 28 in.
Chokes: C, IC, M, IM, F, wrench
Weight: 6 lb. 8 oz.
Bore/Gauge: 12
Magazine: 2 shells
Features: Patented steel locking system and plate; easily removable trigger group receiver; adjustable drop and cast; ergonomic opening lever; impulse activated ejectors; available with the receiver in either black anodized finish or engraved nickel finish
MSRP . . . . $2699.00–$3199.00

828U LEFT-HAND ENGRAVED RECEIVER
Action: Over/under
Stock: Walnut
Barrel: 26 in., 28 in.
Chokes: Crio (C, IC, M, IM, F)
Weight: 6 lb. 8 oz.–6 lb. 9.6 oz.
Bore/Gauge: 12
Magazine: 2 shells
Features: Left-hand stock orientation with engraved nickel-plated receiver
MSRP $3199.00

Benelli USA

BENELLI ETHOS

BENELLI ETHOS SPORT

BENELLI M2 FIELD 12 GA.

BENELLI M2 FIELD 20 GA.

ETHOS
Action: Inertia-operated semiautomatic
Stock: Walnut
Barrel: 26 in., 28 in.
Chokes: C, IC, M, IM, F
Weight: 5 lb.–6 lb. 5 oz.
Bore/Gauge: 12, 20, 28
Magazine: 4+1 shells
Features: Progressive Comfort recoil reduction system; two-part carrier latch for easy reloading; interchangerable fiber optic sights; available with engraved nickel-plated receiver
MSRP . . . . **$1999.00–$2149.00**

ETHOS SPORT
Action: Semiautomatic
Stock: Walnut
Barrel: 28 in., 30 in.
Chokes: Five Extended Crio (C, IC, M, IM, F)
Sights: Interchangeable fiber optic front, mid-rib bead
Weight: 5 lb. 6 oz.–6 lb. 11 oz.
Bore/Gauge: 12, 20, 28
Magazine: 4 shells
Features: Cycles loads from featherweight to heavy without interruption; stocks are AA walnut satin finished;

receivers are nickel-plated and anodized with light engraving; red, green, and yellow fiber optic sight inserts; stock shim kit; hard case
MSRP **$2269.00**

M2 FIELD 12 GA.
Action: Inertia operated semiautomatic
Stock: Synthetic, Realtree APG
Barrel: 21 in., 24 in., 26 in., 28 in.
Chokes: Crio Chokes (IC, M, F)
Weight: 6 lb. 14 oz.–7 lb. 3 oz.
Bore/Gauge: 12
Magazine: 3+1 shells
Features: ComforTech gel recoil pad and comb insert; ComforTech shim kit; red bar front sight; stock comes in black synthetic, Realtree MAX-5, Mossy Oak Shadow Grass Blades, or Gore Optifade Timber full-coverage camo; left-hand available in full-size model in black or Max-5; Compact and Rifled Slug versions; all 12-gauge models chamber 3-inch shells
Black: **$1449.00**
Realtree Max-5, Mossy Oak Shadow Grass Blades, Gore Optifade Timber: **$1559.00**
Compact: **$1449.00**
Rifled slug: **$1559.00**

M2 FIELD 20 GA.
Action: Inertia operated semiautomatic
Stock: Synthetic
Barrel: 24 in., 26 in.
Chokes: Crio Chokes (IC, M, F)
Weight: 5 lb. 13 oz.–6 lb. 8 oz.
Bore/Gauge: 20
Magazine: 3+1 shells
Features: ComforTech gel recoil pad and comb insert; ComforTech shim kit; red bar front sight; stock comes in black synthetic, Realtree MAX-5, Mossy Oak Shadow Grass Blades, or Gore Optifade Timber full-coverage camo; left-hand available in full-size model in black; Compact and Rifled Slug versions; all 12-gauge models chamber 3-inch shells
Black: **$1449.00**
Realtree Max-5, Mossy Oak Shadow Grass Blades, Gore Optifade Timber: **$1559.00**
Compact: **$1449.00**
Rifled slug: **$1559.00**

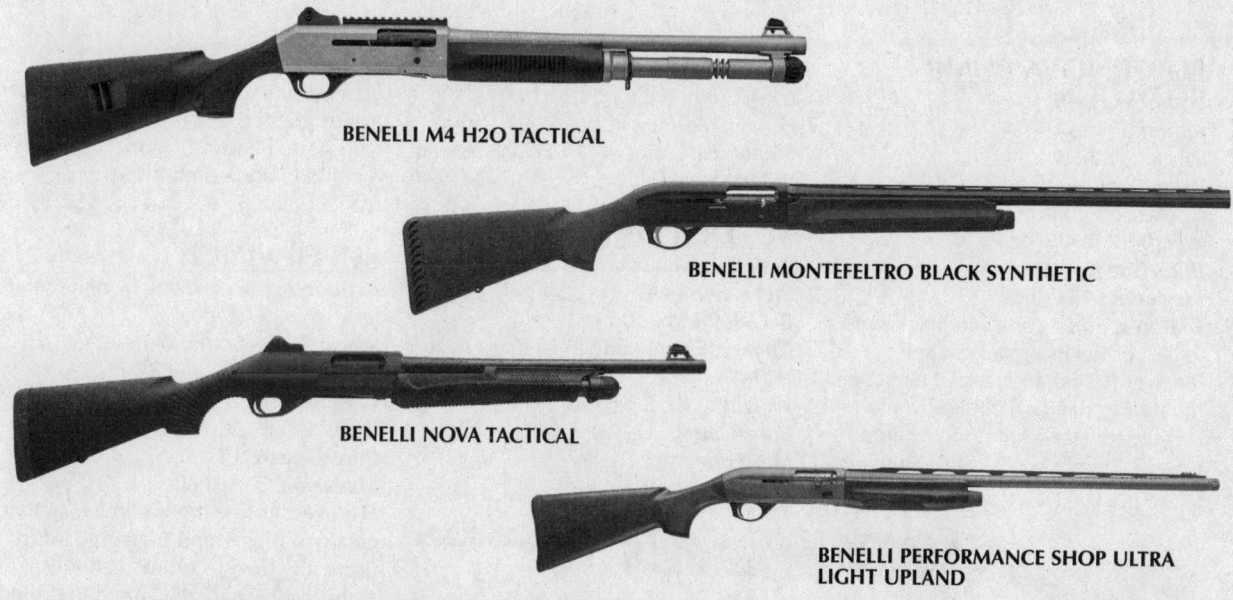

BENELLI M4 H2O TACTICAL

BENELLI MONTEFELTRO BLACK SYNTHETIC

BENELLI NOVA TACTICAL

BENELLI PERFORMANCE SHOP ULTRA LIGHT UPLAND

BENELLI SUPER BLACK EAGLE 3

M4 H2O TACTICAL

Action: Pump
Stock: Synthetic
Barrel: 18.5 in.
Chokes: M
Weight: 7 lb. 12.8 oz.
Bore/Gauge: 12
Magazine: 5 shells
Features: Titanium Cerakote finish on barrel, receiver, and magazine tube; black Cerakote on bolt; internal components receive corrosion-resistant coatings; ghost ring sights; Picatinny rail; standard or pistol grip stocks
Standard rifled sights: **$439.00**
Standard ghost ring sights: . . . **$449.00**
H2O: **$669.00**

MONTEFELTRO

Action: Semiautomatic
Stock: Synthetic, walnut
Barrel: 24 in., 26 in., 28 in., 30 in.
Chokes: IC, M, F
Weight: 5 lb. 5 oz.–5 lb. 10 oz. (20 ga.); 6 lb. 15 oz.–7 lb. 3 oz. (12 ga.)
Bore/ Gauge: 12, 20
Magazine: 4 +1 shells
Features: A traditionally styled semi-auto field gun in 12- or 20-ga. with a low-profile rib, slim fore-end, and a lightweight anodized receiver; inertia driven system; Sporting 12-ga. has a 30-inch barrel and walnut stock; field 12-ga. has choice of 26- or 28-inch

barrel with either walnut stock or black synthetic stock (non-Comfort Tech); left-hand 12-ga. choice of 26- or 28-inch barrel in walnut stock only; 20-ga. and Compact 20-ga. in walnut stock only with 24- or 26-inch barrel; all walnut stocks are satin-finished
MSRP: **$1129.00**

NOVA TACTICAL

Action: Pump
Stock: Synthetic
Barrel: 18.5 in.
Chokes: Fixed cylinder choke
Weight: 7 lb. 3 oz.
Bore/Gauge: 12
Magazine: 4+1 shells
Features: Available with ghost-ring or open rifle sights; push-button shell stop; grooved grip surface stocks in black synthetic stock; available with H2O technology, including a matte nickel-plated metal work
Standard rifled sights: **$439.00**
Standard ghost ring sights: . . **$449.00**
H2O: **$669.00**

PERFORMANCE SHOP ULTRA LIGHT UPLAND

Action: Semiautomatic
Stock: Walnut
Barrel: 24 in. (20-ga.), 26 in. (12-ga.)
Chokes: Crio (C, IC, M), 3 Rob Roberts Custom Triple Threat

BENELLI PERFORMANCE SHOP ULTRA LIGHT UPLAND

Weight: 5 lb. 3.2 oz. (20-ga.), 6 lb. 1.6 oz. (12-ga.)
Bore/Gauge: 12, 20
Magazine: 2 shells
Features: Alloy receivers; shortened magazine tubes; carbon fiber ribs; enlarged bolt handles and bolt release buttons; lengthened forcing cones; EDM porting; Burnt Bronze Cerakote finish
MSRP **$2799.00**

SUPER BLACK EAGLE 3

Action: Semiautomatic
Stock: Synthetic
Barrel: 26 in., 28 in.
Chokes: Crio (C, IM, F), Extended Crio (IC, M)
Weight: 7 lb.–7 lb. 3 oz.
Bore/Gauge: 12
Magazine: 2 shells
Features: Inertia-driven action with 3 ó -in. chamber; Easy Locking System; oversized safety, bolt handle, and bolt release button; new magazine cap, trigger, stock, and forend designs; enlarged loading port; Easy Fitting System shim kit allows for eight different drop and cast configurations; ComforTech stock; Combtech cheek pad; Crio-treated barrel; black synthetic, Realtree Max-5, GORE OPTIFADE Timber, or Mossy Oak Bottomlands or Shadow Grass Blades; red bar front sight, midbead; receiver drilled and tapped for 93A Weaver scope mounts
Black: **$1899.00**
Camo: **$1999.00**

SHOTGUNS

Benelli USA

SUPERNOVA PUMP SHOTGUN

Action: Pump
Stock: Synthetic
Barrel: 24 in., 26 in., 28 in.
Chokes: Standard choke (IC, M, F)
Weight: 7 lb. 13 oz.–8 lb.
Bore/Gauge: 12
Magazine: 4+1 shells
Features: Stock comes in black synthetic or Realtree Max-5 camo; receiver drilled and tapped for scope mounting; standard chokes; vented recoil pad; standard model chambers up to 3 ½-inch shells; rifled slug ver-

sion chambers only up to 3-in. shells, comes only with a 24-in. barrel, and is available only in black
Standard: . . . . $559.00–$669.00
Rifled slug: $839.00

SUPERSPORT

Action: Inertia operated semiautomatic
Stock: Synthetic
Barrel: 28 in., 30 in.
Chokes: Extended Crio Chokes(C, IC, M, IM, F)
Weight: 6 lb. 5 oz.–7 lb. 5 oz.
Bore/Gauge: 12, 20
Magazine: 4+1 shells

Features: Stock comes in black SuperSport carbon fiber finish; red bar front sight and metal bead mid sight; Crio ported barrels; ComforTech gel recoil pad and comb insert
MSRP. **$2199.00**

SUPER VINCI

Action: Inertia operated semiautomatic
Stock: Synthetic, Realtree APG
Barrel: 26 in., 28 in., 30 in.
Chokes: Crio Chokes (C, IC, M, IM, F)
Weight: 6 lb. 14 oz.–7 lb. 2 oz.
Bore/Gauge: 12
Magazine: 3+1 shells
Features: In-line inertia driven system; enlarged trigger and trigger guard for use with gloves; ComforTech Plus recoil pad; QuadraFit shim kit; drilled and tapped for scopes; available in black, Realtree Max-5. or Mossy Oak Shadow Grass Blades or Gore Optifade Concealment Marsh; all models chamber up to 3 ½-inch shells
MSRP. . . . . **$1599.00–$1699.00**

ULTRA LIGHT

Action: Inertia operated semiautomatic
Stock: Walnut
Barrel: 24 in., 26 in.
Chokes: Crio Chokes (IC, M, F)
Weight: 5 lb. 3 oz.–6 lb. 2 oz.
Bore/Gauge: 12, 20, 28
Magazine: 2+1 shells
Features: Weather-coated walnut stock; red bar front sight and metal bead mid sight; gel recoil pad; option of checkered Montefeltro forend or ultra light forend
MSRP. . . . . **$1669.00–$1799.00**

VINCI

Action: Inertia operated semiautomatic
Stock: Synthetic
Barrel: 26 in., 28 in.
Chokes: Crio Chokes (C, IC, M, IM, F)
Weight: 6 lb. 13 oz.–6 lb. 14 oz.
Bore/Gauge: 12
Magazine: 3+1 shells
Features: Stock in black, or Realtree MAX-5 camo; red bar front sight and metal bead mid sight; drilled and tapped for scope mounting; ComforTech Plus recoil pads
MSRP: . . . . **$1349.00–$1449.00**

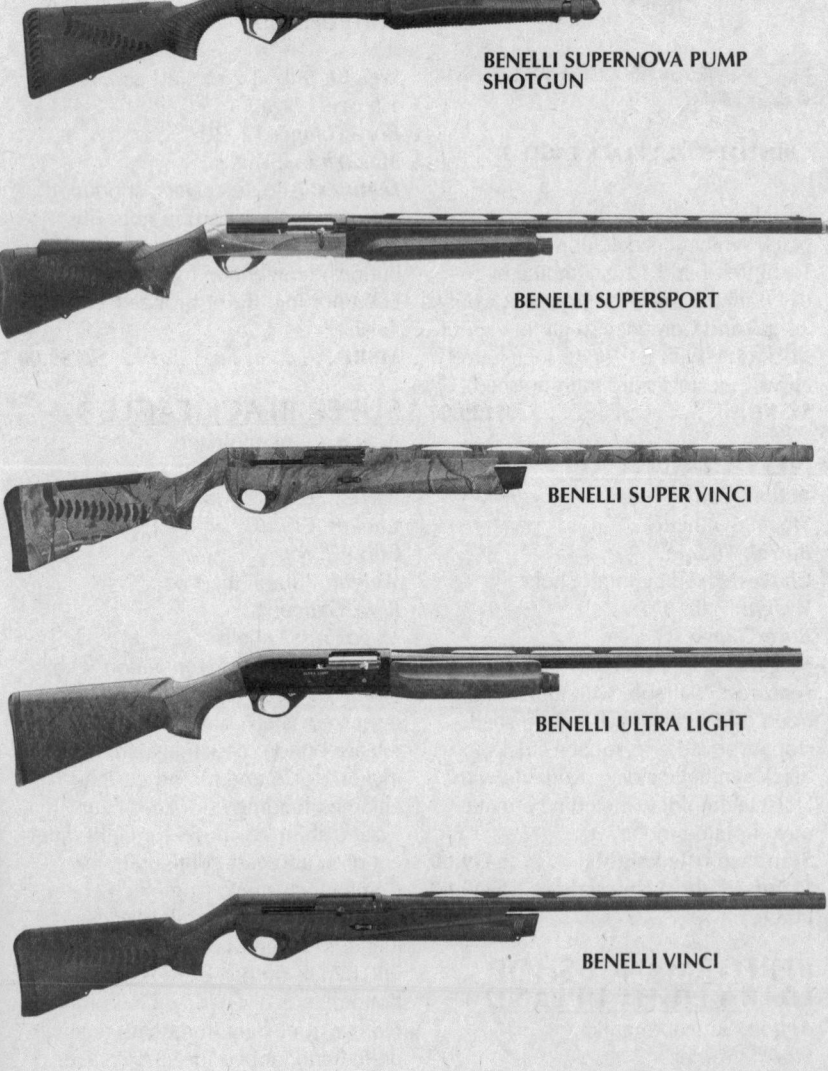

BENELLI SUPERNOVA PUMP SHOTGUN

BENELLI SUPERSPORT

BENELLI SUPER VINCI

BENELLI ULTRA LIGHT

BENELLI VINCI

Beretta USA

BERETTA 486 PARALLELO

BERETTA 686 SILVER PIGEON I

BERETTA 690 FIELD I

BERETTA 1301 COMP

BERETTA 692 SPORTING BLACK

BERETTA 1301 TACTICAL

BERETTA 1301 TACTICAL
FDE, MARINE, OD GREEN

486 PARALLELO
Action: Side-by-side
Stock: Wood
Barrel: 28 in., 30 in.
Chokes: Fixed, Optima-Choke
Weight: 7 lb.
Bore/Gauge: 12
Magazine: 2 shells
Features: Round action with lavish scroll engraving; new leaf springs, trigger group, barrel technology
MSRP $5350.00

686 SILVER PIGEON I
Action: Over/under
Stock: Walnut
Barrel: 26 in., 28 in., 30 in.
Chokes: MC
Weight: 6 lb. 13 oz.
Bore/Gauge: 12, 20, 28, .410
Magazine: 2 shells
Features: Extensive but refined floral and scroll decoration on the frame; dual-conical locking mechanism; automatic safety; oil finish on checkered walnut stock and forend; metal bead sight
MSRP $2350.00

690 FIELD I
Action: Over/under
Stock: Walnut
Barrel: 28 in.
Chokes: Optima-Choke HP
Weight: 7 lb. 6 oz.
Bore/Gauge: 12, 20, 28, .410
Magazine: 2 shells
Features: Steelium cold-hammer-forged and chrome-lined barrels; oiled Grade 2.5 walnut stock with pistol grip and semi-beavertail forend; receiver has rolled floral pattern engraving
MSRP $2650.00

692 SPORTING BLACK
Action: Over/under
Stock: Walnut
Barrel: 30 in., 32 in.
Chokes: 5 OCHP
Weight: 7 lb. 11 oz.
Bore/ Gauge: 12
Magazine: 2 shells
Features: Steelium Plus barrels; longer forcing cone; Beretta Fast Adjustment System Technology; Adjustable Balance System; adjustable trigger
MSRP . . . . $5250.00–$5750.00

1301 COMP
Action: Gas-operated semiautomatic
Stock: Synthetic
Barrel: 21 in., 24 in.

Chokes: IC
Weight: 7 lb. 2 oz.
Bore/Gauge: 12
Magazine: 5+1 shells
Features: Fiber optic sights; oversized bolt release and handle; Optima Bore HP interchangable choke system
MSRP $1275.00

1301 TACTICAL
Action: Gas-operated semiautomatic
Stock: Synthetic
Barrel: 18.5 in.
Chokes: F
Weight: 7 lb. 2 oz.
Bore/Gauge: 12
Magazine: 5+1 shells
Features: Ghost ring sight; front blade sight; Picatinny rail; oversized bolt release and handle; fixed cylinder choke
MSRP $1275.00

1301 TACTICAL FDE, MARINE, OD GREEN
Action: Semiautomatic
Stock: Synthetic
Barrel: 18.5 in.
Chokes: Optima Bore HP
Sights: Ghost ring
Weight: 6 lb. 6 oz.
Bore/Gauge: 12
Magazine: 5 shells
Features: All-over Flat Dark Earth, all-over OD Green, or two-tone Marine with black stock pieces and stainless metalwork; aluminum receiver that keeps weight down; extended bolt knob; oversized safety and bolt release; ghost ring sights; Picatinny rail
MSRP $1375.00

Beretta USA

BERETTA A300 OUTLANDER

BERETTA A300 OUTLANDER SPORTING

BERETTA A300 OUTLANDER TURKEY

BERETTA A300 OUTLANDER TURKEY XTRA GREEN CAMO

BERETTA A350 EXTREMA MAX-5

BERETTA A400 LITE MAX-5

A300 OUTLANDER

Action: Gas-operated semiautomatic
Stock: Synthetic, camo, walnut
Barrel: 28 in.
Chokes: MC3
Weight: 7 lb. 10 oz.
Bore/Gauge: 12
Magazine: 3+1 shells
Features: Gas operation with compensating exhaust valve and self-cleaning piston; adjustable shim system on stock; aluminum alloy receiver; crossbolt safety with ergonomics; front metal bead sight; oiled wood stock finish
MSRP **$900.00**

A300 OUTLANDER SPORTING

Action: Semiautomatic
Stock: Wood
Barrel: 30 in.
Chokes: Three MobilChoke Victory (IC, M, F)
Sights: Front and mid-rib beads
Weight: N/A
Bore/Gauge: 12
Magazine: 3 shells
Features: High-grade wood with checkering pattern; gas-operated; valve with a self-cleaning cylinder and piston combination
MSRP **$1100.00**

A300 OUTLANDER TURKEY

Action: Semiautomatic
Stock: Synthetic
Barrel: 24 in.
Chokes: 3 chokes (F, M, IC)
Weight: 7 lb. 9 oz.
Bore/Gauge: 12
Magazine: 3+1 shells
Features: TRUGLO fiber optic sights; Realtree XTRA camo finish; adjustable drop cast; reliable/clean gas operating system; sling attachment
MSRP **$900.00**

A300 OUTLANDER TURKEY XTRA GREEN CAMO

Action: Semiautomatic
Stock: Synthetic
Barrel: 24 in.
Chokes: Extended TruGlo Turkey Choice choke
Weight: 7 lb. 9.6 oz.
Bore/Gauge: 12
Magazine: 3 shells
Features: Chambered for 3 in.; Truglo fiber optic sights mid-rib and muzzle; adjustable drop and cast; reversible safety; aluminum alloy receiver milled for Beretta Optics Mount; sling swivel studs front and back; Realtree Xtra Green camo
MSRP **$900.00**

A350 EXTREMA MAX-5

Action: Semiautomatic
Stock: Synthetic
Barrel: 28 in.
Chokes: Optima HP
Weight: 7 lb. 2 oz.
Bore/Gauge: 12
Magazine: N/A
Features: Adjustable shim system for drop and right-hand or left-hand configuration; 3.5 in. chamber; steelium barrel; fiber optic bead front sight; sling points; Micro Core recoil pad; Max-5 camo finish
MSRP **$1150.00**

A400 LITE MAX-5

Action: Semiautomatic
Stock: Synthetic
Barrel: 26 in., 28 in.; 30 in. (12-ga. only)
Chokes: Optima-Choke HP
Weight: 6 lb. 9.6 oz.
Bore/Gauge: 12, 20
Magazine: 2 shells
Features: 3-in. chambers; Beretta Blink gas system; stock features Kick-Off Plus system, adjustable shims, and S-Grip checkering pattern for improved grip; safety is crossbolt type and reversible; black or Realtree Max-5 camo; fiber optic front sight
12 ga.: **$1600.00**
20 ga.: **$1700.00**

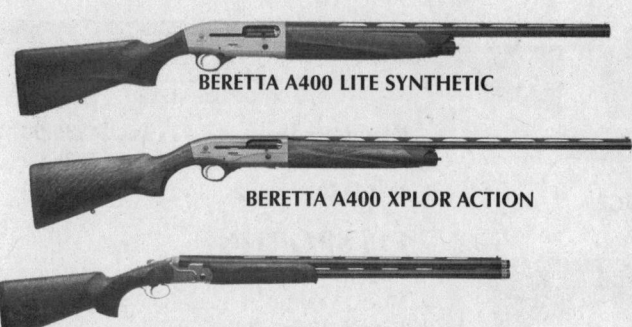

BERETTA A400 LITE SYNTHETIC

BERETTA A400 XPLOR ACTION

BERETTA DT11 SPORTING BLACK

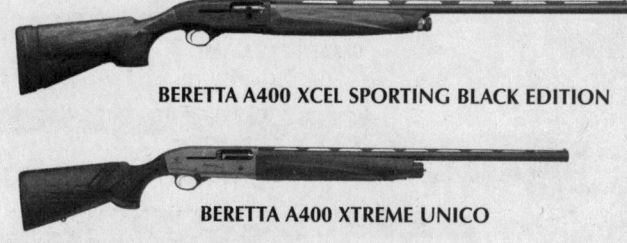

BERETTA A400 XCEL SPORTING BLACK EDITION

BERETTA A400 XTREME UNICO

A400 LITE SYNTHETIC
Action: Semiautomatic
Stock: Walnut and polymer
Barrel: 24 in., 26 in., 28 in., 30 in.
Chokes: OptimaChoke screw-in tube
Weight: 6 lb. 3 oz.–6 lb. 10 oz.
Bore/Gauge: 12, 20
Magazine: 3+1 or 2+1 shells
Features: Steelium barrel design, walnut stock with polymer forend insert, trigger guard and kick-off interface; 3-in. chamber; blink operating system; Micro-Core recoil pad; available with Kick-Off damper system; available in a standard-length 20-ga. (26-, 28-inch barrel) and a Compact 20-ga. (24-, 26-inch barrel), both with 3-inch chambers; Compact does not include the Kick-Off system
12-ga.: $1600.00
20-ga.: $1600.00
Compact 20-ga.: $1500.00

A400 XCEL SPORTING BLACK EDITION
Action: Semiautomatic
Stock: Walnut
Barrel: 30 in.
Chokes: Optima HP Extended Black
Weight: 7 lb. 6.4 oz.
Bore/Gauge: 12

Magazine: 3 shells
Features: 3-in. chambers; MicroCore recoil pad; reversible safety; oversized bolt handle and release; medium weight forend balancing cap; 10mm carbon fiber rib; matte black receiver finish; black weighted forend cap; carbon fiber 10x10 rib
MSRP . . . . $2100.00–$2200.00

A400 XPLOR ACTION
Action: Gas-operated semiautomatic
Stock: Walnut
Barrel: 26 in., 28 in.
Chokes: F
Weight: 5 lb. 8 oz.
Bore/Gauge: 12, 20, 28
Magazine: 3+1 shells
Features: Fiber optic sights; Gun Pod shell counter, cartridge tester, and temperature display; Kick-Off recoil reduction system; Optima Bore interchangable bore system; left-hand available in 12-ga. 3-inch chamber with 28-inch barrel only
MSRP . . . .$1600.00–$1750.00

A400 XTREME UNICO SYNTHETIC, XTREME UNICO CAM MAX-5
Action: Semiautomatic
Stock: Synthetic or camo
Barrel: 26 in., 28 in., 30 in.
Chokes: Optima Bore HP (C, Mod, Full)

Weight: 7 lb. 10 oz.
Bore/Gauge: 12
Magazine: 4+1 or 3+1 shells
Features: Adjustable buttstock shim kits, anti-corosion coatings on the barrel, Beretta's fast-cycling Blink technology, fast-assembly B-Lock fore-end cap, Kick-Off 3/Kick-Off Mega recoil reduction system, and Steelium Optma Bore HP barrels; chamber 3 ½-in. shells; camo version available in Realtree Max-5; left-hand available in either finish but only with 28-in. barrel
Synthetic: . . . . . $1750.00–$1800.00
MAX-5: . . . . $1900.00–$1950.00

DT11 SPORTING BLACK
Action: Over/under
Stock: Walnut
Barrel: 30 in., 32 in.
Chokes: OCHPe
Weight: 9 lb.
Bore/ Gauge: 12
Magazine: 2 shells
Features: Steelium Pro barrel; top rib with hollowed bridges; ergonomic top lever; safety selector switch; increased receiver side wall thickness; select high-quality walnut wood finished in oil; stock and forend can be fitted to customer's measurement; pistol grip and forend are hand-checkered; B-Fast adjustable stock available; left-hand model available in both barrel lengths, but without B-Fast stock option
MSRP . . . . $10999.00–$11300.00

Blaser USA

F3 SPORTING
Action: Over/under
Stock: Walnut
Barrel: 28 in., 30 in., 32 in., 34 in.
Chokes: Briley Spectrum chokes (SK, IC, M., IM, F)
Weight: 7 lb. 5 oz.
Bore/Gauge: 12, 20, 28, .410
Magazine: 2 shells
Features: Sporting stock, forearm with Schnabel; internal block system; ergo-

BLASER F3 SPORTING

nomically optimized, adjustable trigger blade; Triplex Bore design; ejection-ball-system; balancer
Standard: $8650.00
Luxus: $10,248.00
Baron: $12,066.00
Grand Luxe: $13,429.00
Attache: $12,339.00

Baron DeLuxe: $14,076.00
Bonsi Scroll: $14,749.00
Custom I (hand engraved, one animal each side): .$15,273.00
Baronesse: $16,473.00
Heritage: $31,950.00
Custom II, III, IV: . . . . . . Contact manufacturer

Blaser USA

BLASER F16 GAME

BLASER USA F16 GAME HERITAGE

BLASER F16 GAME INTUITION

BLASER F16 SPORTING

BLASER F16 SPORTING INTUITION

BLASER USA F16 GAME GRANDE LUXE

Wood grade 4:	$4289.00
Grande Luxe:	$7726.00
Heritage:	$10,415.00

F16 SPORTING

Action: Over/under
Stock: Walnut
Barrel: 30 in., 32 in.
Chokes: Blaser chokes flush to muzzle
Weight: 7 lb. 8 oz.–8 lb. 6 oz.
Bore/Gauge: 12
Magazine: 2 shells
Features: Balancer system allows the adjustment of the weight distribution to shooter's personal needs; sleak English-style forearm design; crisp trigger pull; Triplex bore design; tapered rib; proven Blaser ejection system; Inertial Block System (IBS) prevents an involuntary second shot or the unintentional triggering of a second shot while maintaining a superb trigger pull; many options available within three grades: Standard, Grande Luxe, and Heritage

Fusion:	$4371.00
Wood grade 3:	$4447.00
Wood grade 4:	$4706.00
Grande Luxe:	$8143.00
Heritage:	$10,832.00

F16 SPORTING INTUITION

Action: Over/under
Stock: Wood grade II
Barrel: 30 in., 32 in.
Chokes: Three flush chokes (¼, ½, ¾)
Weight: 7 lb. 5 oz.–8 lb. 3 oz.
Bore/Gauge: 12
Magazine: 2 shells
Features: Designed specifically for women, with a specially designed buttstock tailored to the female anatomy, including a more slender pistol grip, higher comb, and reduced pitch; non-adjustable trigger; 13.8-in. length of pull; Blaser Comfort recoil pad; adjustable trigger length; prep for barrel balancer and stock balancer; red F16 logo and red fiber optic front bead; many options available, including upgraded wood and barrel balancer weights

Fusion:	$4371.00
Wood grade 3:	$4447.00
Wood grade 4:	$4706.00
Grande Luxe:	$8143.00
Heritage:	$10,832.00

F16 GAME

Action: Over/under
Stock: Walnut
Barrel: 28 in., 30 in.
Chokes: Blaser chokes flush to muzzle
Weight: 6 lb. 13 oz.
Bore/Gauge: 12
Magazine: 2 shells
Features: Sleak English-style forearm design; crisp trigger pull; Triplex bore design; tapered rib; proven Blaser ejection system; Inertial Block System (IBS) prevents an involuntary second shot or the unintentional triggering of a second shot while maintaining a superb trigger pull; many options available within three grades: Standard, Grande Luxe, and Heritage

Fusion:	$3954.00
Wood grade 3:	$4030.00
Wood grade 4:	$4289.00
Grande Luxe:	$7726.00
Heritage:	$10,415.00

F16 GAME GRANDE LUXE

Action: Over/under
Stock: Grade 6 walnut
Barrel: 28 in., 30 in., 32 in.
Chokes: N/A
Sights: Nickel silver front bead
Weight: N/A
Bore/Gauge: 12
Magazine: 2 shells
Features: Grade 6 wood stock; has engravings of either game scenes or an English scroll; available in Game (28-in. or 30-in. barrel) and Sporting configurations (30-in. or 32-in. barrel); Sporting includes Blaser's stock Balancer system

MSRP	$7726.00

F16 GAME HERITAGE

Action: Over/under
Stock: Grade 8 walnut
Barrel: 28 in., 30 in., 32 in.
Chokes: N/A
Sights: Nickel silver front bead, luminescent red
Weight: N/A
Bore/Gauge: 12
Magazine: 2 shells
Features: Grade 8 walnut stock; has engravings of either game scenes or an English scroll on elongated sideplates; available in Game (28-in., 30-in. barrel) and Sporting configurations (30-in., 32-in. barrel); Sporting includes Blaser's stock Balancer system, luminescent red front bead, tapered rib, and an adjustable trigger pull length

MSRP	$10,415.00

F16 GAME INTUITION

Action: Over/under
Stock: Wood grade II
Barrel: 28 in., 30 in.
Chokes: Three flush chokes (¼, ½, ¾)
Weight: 6 lb. 10 oz.
Bore/Gauge: 12
Magazine: 2 shells
Features: Designed specifically for women, with a specially designed buttstock tailored to the female anatomy, including a more slender pistol grip, higher comb, and reduced pitch; non-adjustable trigger; 13.8-in. length of pull; sling swivel (not mounted); silver F16 logo and silver front bead; many options available, including upgraded wood and weight balancer

Fusion:	$3954.00
Wood grade 3:	$4030.00

SHOTGUNS

Browning

BROWNING A5 HUNTER

BROWNING A5 HUNTER HIGH GRADE

BROWNING A5 STALKER

BROWNING A5 SWEET SIXTEEN

BROWNING A5 WICKED WING

A5 HUNTER

Action: Semiautomatic
Stock: Walnut
Barrel: 26 in., 28 in., 30 in.
Chokes: Invector-DS
Weight: 6 lb. 15 oz.
Bore/Gauge: 12
Magazine: None
Features: Strong, lightweight aluminum alloy; black anodized bi-tone finish; flat, ventilated rib; recoil operated Kinematic Drive is ultra-reliable and cycles a wide range of loads; gloss finish walnut with close radius pistol grip; 22 lines-per-inch checkering; shim adjustable for length of pull, cast and drop; Vector Pro lengthened forcing cone; three invector-DS choke tubes; Inflex II technology recoil pad; brass front bead sight; ivory mid-bead sight; included ABS case
3-inch: $1669.99
3 1/2-inch: $1799.99

A5 HUNTER HIGH GRADE

Action: Semiautomatic
Stock: Walnut
Barrel: 26 in., 28 in.
Chokes: Invector-DS (F, M, IC)
Weight: 6 lb. 11 oz.–6 lb. 13 oz.
Bore/Gauge: 12
Magazine: 4 shells
Features: 3-in. chambered gun; gloss finished barrel; receiver with intricate scrollwork, pheasant and mallard engraving; grade 2.5 gloss varnish finish walnut stock with 22 lines-per-inch checkering; lightweight profile barrel; aluminum alloy receiver; recoil-operated Kinematic drive; Vector Pro lengthened forcing cones
MSRP. $1899.99

A5 STALKER

Action: Semiautomatic
Stock: Composite
Barrel: 26 in., 28 in., 30 in.
Chokes: Invector-DS
Weight: 7 lb. 3 oz.–7 lb. 7 oz.
Bore/Gauge: 12
Magazine: None
Features: Strong, lightweight aluminum alloy; flat, ventilated rib; recoil operated Kinematic Drive is ultra-reliable and cycles a wide range of loads; composite with close radius pistol grip; textured gripping surfaces; shim adjustable for cast and drop; matte black finish; Dura-Touch armor coating; Vector Pro lengthened forcing cone; Inflex II technology recoil pad; fiber-optic front sight; included ABS case
3-inch: $1539.99
3 1/2-inch: $1669.99

A5 SWEET SIXTEEN

Action: Semiautomatic
Stock: Turkish walnut
Barrel: 28 in.
Chokes: Invector-DS flush
Weight: 5 lb. 13 oz.
Bore/Gauge: 16
Magazine: 4 shells
Features: Gloss walnut stock; brass bead front sight; humpback receiver; ergo balanced; short recoil-operated Kinematic Drive System; auto-loader shotgun; Invector-DS choke tubes; built on a smaller, lighter receiver for reduced weight
MSRP. $1739.99

A5 WICKED WING

Action: Semiautomatic
Stock: Composite
Barrel: 26 in., 28 in.
Chokes: Extended Invector-DS Banded (F,M,IC)
Weight: 7 lb. 3 oz.–7 lb. 5 oz.
Bore/Gauge: 12
Magazine: 4 shells
Features: Chambered for 3.5-in. shells; Cerakote Burnt Bronze camo receiver and Burnt Bronze barrel with Mossy Oak Shadow Grass Blades stock; Briley extended bolt handle and oversize bolt release; fully chromed bore; recoil operated Kinematic Drive; Vector Pro lengthened forcing cone; fiber-optic front sight and ivory mid-bead
3-inch: $1869.99
3 1/2-inch: $1999.99

Browning

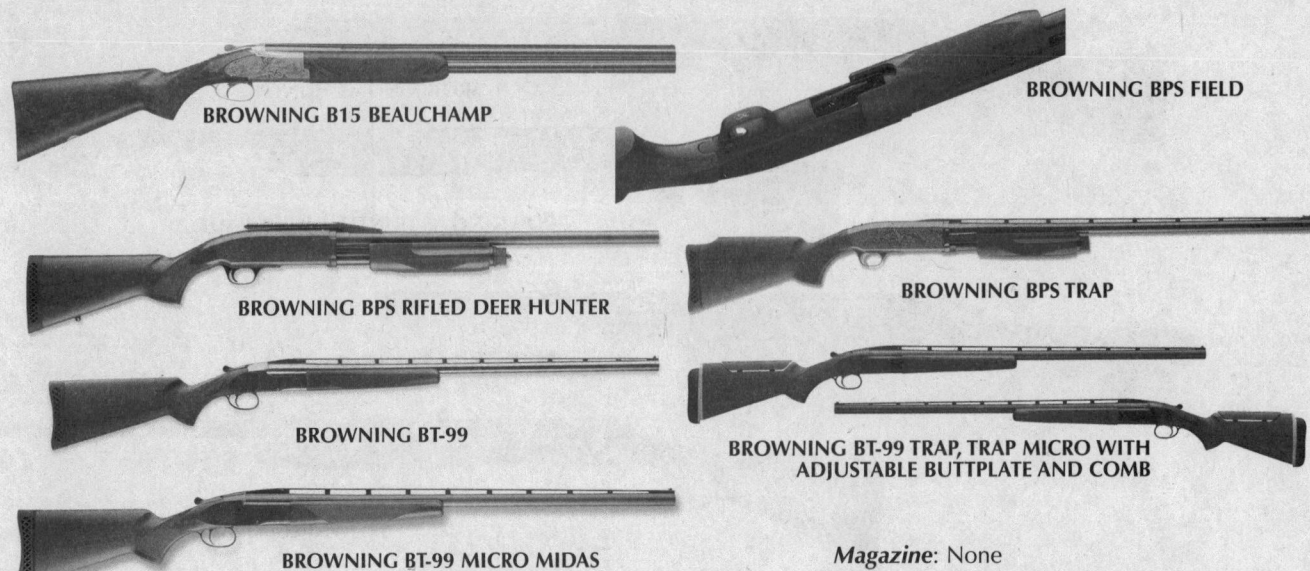

BROWNING B15 BEAUCHAMP

BROWNING BPS FIELD

BROWNING BPS RIFLED DEER HUNTER

BROWNING BPS TRAP

BROWNING BT-99

BROWNING BT-99 TRAP, TRAP MICRO WITH ADJUSTABLE BUTTPLATE AND COMB

BROWNING BT-99 MICRO MIDAS

B15 BEAUCHAMP

Action: Over/under
Stock: Walnut
Barrel: 28 in., 30 in., 32 in.
Chokes: Five Invector DS
Sights: Front bead
Weight: 6 lb. 6 oz.
Bore/Gauge: 20
Magazine: 2 shells
Features: Part of Belgium-produced John M. Browning Collection; offered in four wood grades and three barrel lengths, with various forearms, butt-plates and engraving levels; mechanical triggers; back-bored Vector Pro barrels; full flush-mounted choke set; leather case
MSRP . . . . $12999.99–$20499.99

BPS FIELD

Action: Pump
Stock: Walnut
Barrel: 26 in., 28 in.
Chokes: Three Invector-Plus flush (12, 20 ga.); three standard Invector (16, 28 ga., .410 bore)
Sights: Silver bead
Weight: 6 lb. 15 oz.–7 lb. 11 oz.
Bore/Gauge: 12, 16, 20, 28, .410
Magazine: 4 shells
Features: Matte blue barrel; satin-finished stock; bottom ejection; vent rib; .410-bore is a 3-in. chamber with a 26-in. barrel only; 16, 28 ga. are available in 2.75-in. chamber; 12, 20 ga. in 3-in. chamber
MSRP . . . . $599.99–$639.99

BPS RIFLED DEER HUNTER

Action: Pump
Stock: Walnut
Barrel: 22 in.
Chokes: Screw-in tubes
Weight: 7 lb. 4 oz.–7 lb. 10 oz.
Bore/Gauge: 12, 20
Magazine: None
Features: Satin finish walnut stock; forged and machined steel receiver; thick-walled barrel for slug ammunition only; dual steel action bars
12-ga.: $829.99
20-ga.: $839.99

BPS TRAP

Action: Pump
Stock: Walnut
Barrel: 30 in.
Chokes: Three Invector-Plus choke tubes
Weight: 8 lb. 2 oz.
Bore/Gauge: 12
Magazine: None
Features: Satin finish walnut stock with raised comb; forged and machined steel receiver with engraving; dual steel action bars; top-tang safety; magazine cut-off; HiViz ProComp fiber optic sight with mid-bead
MSRP $839.99

BT-99

Action: Pump
Stock: Walnut
Barrel: 32 in., 34 in.
Chokes: Screw-in tubes
Weight: 8 lb. 3 oz.–8 lb. 5 oz.
Bore/Gauge: 12

Magazine: None
Features: Satin finish walnut stock with beavertail forearm; steel receiver with blued finish; high-post ventilated rib
MSRP $1469.99

BT-99 MICRO MIDAS

Action: Pump
Stock: Walnut
Barrel: 28 in., 30 in.
Chokes: 1 Invector-Plus
Weight: 7 lb. 11 oz
Bore/ Gauge: 12
Magazine: None
Features: Blued finish; high-post ventilated rib barrel; beavertail forearm; scaled down for smaller shooters; Vector-Pro lengthed forcing cone; recoil pad; ivory front and mid-bead sights
MSRP $1469.99

BT-99, BT-99 MICRO WITH ADJUSTABLE BUTTPLATE AND COMB

Action: Single-shot
Stock: Black walnut
Barrel: 30 in., 32 in., 34 in.
Chokes: One Invector-Plus flush
Sights: Ivory bead
Weight: 7 lb. 12 oz.–8 lb. 5 oz.
Bore/Gauge: 12
Magazine: 1 shell
Features: Graco Pro Fit adjustable buttpad plate and comb; barrels and receiver are satin blue; stock is in a satin finish; standard model (32-in., 34-in. barrel); Micro version (30-in., 32-i.n barrel) has shorter length of pull and is 12 ga., 2.75-in. chamber
MSRP $1839.99

BROWNING CITORI 725 FEATHER

BROWNING CITORI 725 FIELD

BROWNING CITORI 725 FIELD GRADE VI

BROWNING CITORI 725 PRO SPORTING WITH PRO FIT ADJUSTABLE COMB

BROWNING CITORI 725 PRO TRAP WITH PRO FIT ADJUSTABLE COMB

CITORI 725 FEATHER

Action: Over/under
Stock: Walnut
Barrel: 26 in., 28 in.
Chokes: 3 Invector-DS
Weight: 5 lb. 14 oz.–6 lb. 9 oz.
Bore/ Gauge: 12, 20
Magazine: 2 shells
Features: Lightweight alloy receiver; low-profile; silver nitride finish; ventilated top rib barrel; Fire Lite Mechanical Trigger system; hammer ejectors; ivory front and mid-bead sights
MSRP $2669.99

CITORI 725 FIELD

Action: Over/under
Stock: Walnut
Barrel: 26, 28 in.
Chokes: Invector-DS
Weight: 6 lb. 7 oz.–7 lb. 8 oz.
Bore/Gauge: 12, 20, 28, .410
Magazine: 2 shells
Features: Steel receiver with silver nitride finish; accented, high-relief engraving; ventilated top rib action; mechanical trigger system; hammer ejectors; top-tang barrel selector/safety; gloss oil finish Grade II/III walnut with close radius pistol grip; Vector

Pro lengthened forcing cones; ivory front and mid-bead sights
12- & 20-gauge: $2519.99
28-gauge & .410-bore: $2589.99

CITORI 725 FIELD GRADE VI

Action: Over/under
Stock: Black walnut
Barrel: 26 in., 28 in.
Chokes: Three Invector-DS flush (F, M, IC)
Sights: Ivory bead
Weight: 7 lb. 4 oz.–7 lb. 6 oz. (12-gauge); 6 lb. 7 oz.–6 lb. 9 oz. (20-gauge)
Bore/Gauge: 12, 20
Magazine: 2 shells
Features: Grade V/VI black walnut with oil gloss finish; silver nitride receiver has scroll leaf engraving, accented with gold; hammer ejectors; Fire Lite mechanical trigger system; Vector Pro lengthened forcing cones; 3-in. chambers; mid-rib bead
MSRP $5999.99

CITORI 725 PRO SPORTING WITH PRO FIT ADJUSTABLE COMB

Action: Over/under

Stock: Wood
Barrel: 30 in., 32 in.
Chokes: F, IM, M, IC, S
Weight: 7 lb. 5 oz.–7 lb. 13 oz.
Bore/Gauge: 12, 20
Magazine: 2 shells
Features: Polished blue barrel finish; grade III/IV black walnut stock with gloss oil finish; HiViz ProComp sights; vented ribs; drilled and tapped for scopes
MSRP $4079.99

CITORI 725 PRO TRAP WITH PRO FIT ADJUSTABLE COMB

Action: Over/under
Stock: Wood
Barrel: 30 in., 32 in.
Chokes: F, LF, M, 2IM
Weight: 8 lb. 8 oz., 8 lb. 11 oz.
Bore/Gauge: 12
Magazine: 2 shells
Features: Polished blue barrel finish; grade III/IV black walnut stock with gloss oil finish; HiViz ProComp sights; vented ribs; drilled and tapped for scopes
MSRP $4079.99

Browning

BROWNING CITORI 725 SPORTING

BROWNING CITORI 725 SPORTING ADJUSTABLE COMB

BROWNING CITORI 725 SPORTING GOLDEN CLAYS

BROWNING CITORI 725 TRAP ADJUSTABLE COMB

BROWNING CITORI 725 TRAP GOLDEN CLAYS

BROWNING CITORI CXS

CITORI 725 SPORTING

Action: Over/under
Stock: Walnut
Barrel: 30, 32 in.
Chokes: Invector-DS
Weight: 6 lb. 4 oz.–7 lb. 10 oz.
Bore/Gauge: 12, 20, 28, .410
Magazine: 2 shells
Features: Steel receiver with silver nitride finish; gold accented engraving; ventilated top and side rib action; mechanical trigger system; hammer ejectors; top-tang barrel selector/safety; gloss oil finish Grade III/IV walnut with close radius pistol grip; Vector Pro lengthened forcing cones; five Invector-DS choke tubes; HiViz Pro-Comp sight and ivory mid-bead
12-, 20-gauge: $3199.99
28-gauge, .410-bore: $3269.99

CITORI 725 SPORTING ADJUSTABLE COMB

Action: Over/under
Stock: Wood
Barrel: 30 in., 32 in.
Chokes: F, IM, M, IC, S
Weight: 7 lb. 13 oz.
Bore/Gauge: 12
Magazine: 2 shells
Features: Steel low-profile receiver with silver nitride finish and gold accented engraving; ventilated barrel with top and side ribs; Fire Lite mechanical trigger system; top-tang barrel selector/safety; gloss oil finish Grade III/IV walnut stock with close radius pistol grip and adjustable comb; HiViz Pro-Comp sight and ivory mid-bead
MSRP $3599.99

CITORI 725 SPORTING GOLDEN CLAYS

Action: Over/under
Stock: Walnut
Barrel: 30 in., 32 in.
Chokes: Extended Invector-DS (F, IM, M, IC, Skeet)
Weight: 7 lb. 13 oz.
Bore/Gauge: 12
Magazine: 2 shells
Features: Unique "Golden Clays" accented gold engraving; Pro Fit adjustable comb; ported barrels with vented top and side ribs; HiViz Pro-Comp fiber optic front side and ivory mid-bead; grade V/VI walnut stock; low-profile silver nitride finish steel receiver; FireLite mechanical trigger
MSRP $5439.99

CITORI 725 TRAP ADJUSTABLE COMB

Action: Over/under
Stock: Wood
Barrel: 30 in., 32 in.
Chokes: F, IM, M
Weight: 8 lb. 8 oz.–8 lb. 11 oz.
Bore/Gauge: 12
Magazine: 2 shells
Features: Steel low-profile receiver with silver nitride finish and gold accented engraving; ventilated barrel with top and side ribs; Fire Lite mechanical trigger system; top-tang barrel selector/safety; gloss oil finish Grade III/IV walnut stock with close radius pistol grip and Monte Carlo or adjustable straight comb; HiViz Pro-Comp sight and ivory mid-bead
MSRP $3819.99

CITORI 725 TRAP GOLDEN CLAYS

Action: Over/under
Stock: Walnut
Barrel: 30 in., 32 in.

Chokes: Extended Invector-DS (F, LF, IM, IM, M)
Weight: 8 lb. 8 oz.–8 lb. 11 oz.
Bore/Gauge: 12
Magazine: 2 shells
Features: 2¾ in. chamber; Fire Lite Mechanical trigger system; hammer ejectors and top-tang barrel selector/safety; gloss grade V/VI walnut stock with close radius pistol grip and right-hand palm swell; receiver has a silver nitride finish and gold-accented engraving; adjustable Monte Carlo comb; Pachmayr Decelerator XLT Trap recoil pad; ventilated top and side ribs; Vector Pro lengthened forcing cones; GraCoil recoil reduction system; Triple Trigger System; HiViz Pro-Comp front sight and ivory mid-bead
MSRP $5859.99

CITORI CXS, CXS WITH ADJUSTABLE COMB

Action: Over/under
Stock: Black walnut
Barrel: 28 in., 30 in., 32 in.
Chokes: Three Invector-Plus Midas (F, M, IC)
Sights: Ivory bead
Weight: 6 lb. 3 oz.–6 lb. 7 oz. (20-gauge); 7 lb. 10 oz.–7 lb. 14 oz. (12-gauge); 7 lb. 14 oz.–8 lb. 2 oz. (12-gauge with adjustable comb)
Bore/Gauge: 12, 20
Magazine: 2 shells
Features: Barrels with a lightweight profile, vented top and side; shoots 50/50 point of impact; Grade II American walnut with a gloss finish; Vector Pro lengthened forcing cones; Triple Trigger system (one trigger included); ivory mid-bead
CXS: $2189.99
With adjustable comb: . . . $2539.99

SHOTGUNS

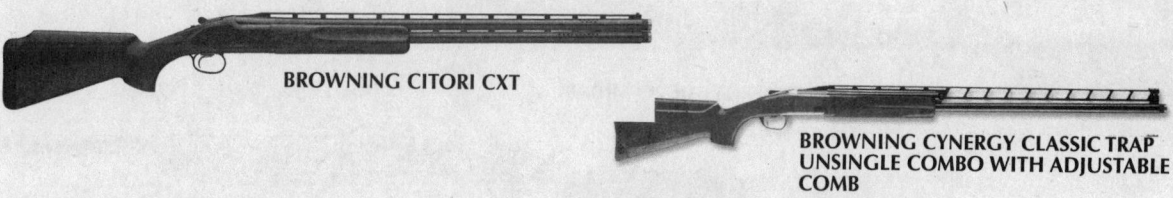

BROWNING CITORI CXT

BROWNING CYNERGY CLASSIC TRAP UNSINGLE COMBO WITH ADJUSTABLE COMB

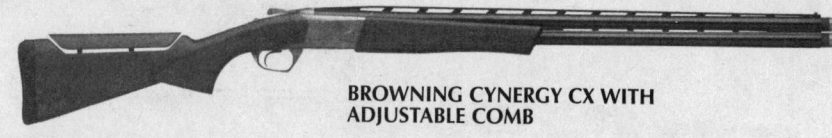

BROWNING CYNERGY CX, CX COMPOSITE

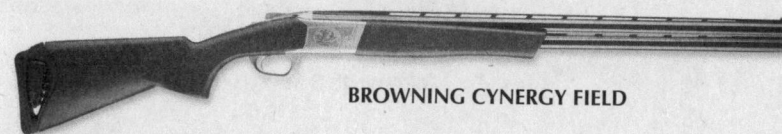

BROWNING CYNERGY CX WITH ADJUSTABLE COMB

BROWNING CYNERGY FIELD

CITORI CXT, CXT WITH ADJUSTABLE COMB

Action: Over/under
Stock: Black walnut
Barrel: 30 in., 32 in.
Chokes: Three Invector-Plus Midas Extended (F, M, IC)
Sights: Ivory bead
Weight: 8 lb. 6 oz.–8 lb. 8 oz. (CXT); 8 lb. 10 oz.–8 lb. 12 oz. (CXT with adjustable comb)
Bore/Gauge: 12
Magazine: 2 shells
Features: Raised comb (in the non-adjustable model); high-post floating rib; point of impact is 70/30; 3-in. chamber
CXT: **$2259.99**
With adjustable comb: . . . **$2659.99**

CYNERGY CLASSIC TRAP UNSINGLE COMBO WITH ADJUSTABLE COMB

Action: Single shot and over/under
Stock: Walnut
Barrel: 32/32 in., 30/34 in., 32/34 in.
Chokes: Four Invector-Plus Midas Grade choke tubes
Weight: 8 lb. 13 oz.–8 lb. 15 oz.
Bore/Gauge: 12
Magazine: 1 or 2 shells
Features: Steel receiver with MonoLock hinge; double- and single-barrel sets included; reverse striker ignition system; impact ejectors; top-tang barrel selector/safety; gloss finish Monte Carlo grade III/IV walnut stock with right-hand palm swell
MSRP **$4359.99**

CYNERGY CX, CX COMPOSITE

Action: Over/under
Stock: Black walnut, composite
Barrel: 30 in., 32 in.
Chokes: Invector-Plus Midas Grade (F, M, IC)
Weight: 7 lb. 14 oz.–8.0 lb. (CX); 7 lb. 11 oz.–7 lb. 13 oz. (CX Composite)
Bore/Gauge: 12
Magazine: 2 shells
Features: Crossover barrel design with a 60/40 POI; ventilated top and side ribs; ivory front and mid-bead sights; steel ultra-low profile receiver with MonoLock Hinge engraved with a silver nitride finish; reverse striker ignition system; mechanical trigger design; Impact Ejectors; top-tang barrel selector/safety; 3-in. chamber; composite version features black rubber overmolding at grip points and adjustable comb
CX: **$1779.99**
CX Composite: **$1709.99**

CYNERGY CX WITH ADJUSTABLE COMB

Action: Over/under
Stock: Black walnut
Barrel: 28 in., 30 in., 32 in.
Chokes: Three Invector-Plus Midas Extended (F, M, IC)
Sights: Ivory bead
Weight: 8 lb. 2 oz.–8 lb. 6 oz.
Bore/Gauge: 12
Magazine: 2 shells
Features: Shoots 60/40 point of impact; adjustable comb; trigger adjustable for length of pull; 0.25-in. stock spacer; reverse striker ignition system; mechanical trigger; impact ejectors; Grade 1 walnut in a satin finish; Vector Pro lengthened forcing cones
MSRP **$2189.99**

CYNERGY FIELD

Action: Over/under
Stock: Walnut
Barrel: 26 in., 28 in.
Chokes: Three Invector-Plus
Weight: 6 lb. 2 oz.–7 lb. 11 oz.
Bore/Gauge: 12, 20
Magazine: 2 shells
Features: Steel receiver with MonoLock hinge; reverse striker ignition system; impact ejectors; oil finish walnut stock; ivory front and mid-bead sights
12-gauge: **$1909.99**
20-gauge: **$1979.99**

Browning

BROWNING CYNERGY MICRO MIDAS

BROWNING GOLD LIGHT 10 GA., MOSSY OAK DUCK BLIND

BROWNING MAXUS HUNTER

BROWNING MAXUS SPORTING

BROWNING MAXUS SPORTING GOLDEN CLAYS

BROWNING MAXUS STALKER

CYNERGY MICRO MIDAS

Action: Over/under
Stock: Wood
Barrel: 24 in., 26 in.
Chokes: F, M, IC
Weight: 6 lb.–6 lb. 2 oz.
Bore/Gauge: 20
Magazine: 2 shells
Features: Matte blued barrel finish; grade I/II black walnut stock with satin finish; ivory bead front sight; Cynergy Inflex recoil pad
MSRP $1909.99

GOLD LIGHT 10 GA.

Action: Gas-operated semiautomatic
Stock: Composite
Barrel: 26 in., 28 in.
Chokes: Three Standard Invector choke tubes
Weight: 9 lb. 9 oz.–9 lb. 10 oz.
Bore/Gauge: 10
Magazine: 4+1 shells
Features: Aluminum alloy receiver; ventilated rib barrel; composite stock and forearm in MO Break-Up Country or MO Shadow Grass Blades; DuraTouch armor coating
MSRP $1779.99

MAXUS HUNTER

Action: Gas-operated semiautomatic
Stock: Composite
Barrel: 26 in., 28 in., 30 in.
Chokes: Three Invector-Plus
Weight: 6 lb. 15 oz.–7 lb. 1 oz.

Bore/Gauge: 12
Magazine: None
Features: Aluminum alloy receiver with durable satin nickel finish; laser engraving of pheasant and mallard on receiver; Inflex technology recoil pad; ivory front bead sight
3-inch: $1589.99
3 1/2-inch: $1739.99

MAXUS SPORTING

Action: Gas-operated semiautomatic
Stock: Walnut
Barrel: 28 in., 30 in.
Chokes: Five Invector-Plus choke tubes
Weight: 7 lb.–7 lb. 1 oz.
Bore/Gauge: 12
Magazine: None
Features: Aluminum alloy receiver with durable satin nickel finish; laser engraving of game birds transforming into clay birds; speed lock forearm; ivory mid bead sight, HiVix Tri-Comp fiber optic front sight
MSRP $1799.99

MAXUS SPORTING GOLDEN CLAYS

Action: Gas-operated semiautomatic
Stock: Walnut
Barrel: 28 in., 30 in.

Chokes: 5 Invector-Plus
Weight: 7 lb. 3 oz.–7 lb. 4 oz.
Bore/ Gauge: 12
Magazine: None
Features: Gold-enhanced engraving; lightweight aluminum alloy; flat, ventilated rib; 3 in. chamber; Power Drive Gas System; Speed Lock Forearm; Vector Pro lengthened forcing cone; HiViz Pro-Comp fiber optic front sight
MSRP $2099.99

MAXUS STALKER

Action: Gas-operated semiautomatic
Stock: Composite
Barrel: 26 in., 28 in.
Chokes: Three Invector Plus choke tubes
Weight: 6 lb. 14 oz.–7 lb. 2.08 oz.
Bore/Gauge: 12
Magazine: None
Features: Magazine cut-off, matte black composite stock with pistol grip; speed lock forearm; textured gripping surfaces; Dura Touch armor coating; Inflex technology recoil pads; lightning trigger system; ventilated rib
3-inch: $1399.99
3 1/2-inch: $1589.99

BROWNING MAXUS ULTIMATE

BROWNING MAXUS WICKED WING

**BROWNING SILVER BLACK LIGHTNING
AND SILVER HUNTER MATTE**

BROWNING SILVER FIELD

MAXUS ULTIMATE
Action: Gas-operated semiautomatic
Stock: Walnut
Barrel: 26 in., 28 in., 30 in.
Chokes: Invector Plus (F, M, IC)
Weight: 7 lb. 1 oz.–7 lb. 4 oz.
Bore/Gauge: 12
Magazine: None
Features: Strong, lightweight aluminum alloy receiver; durable satin nickel finish; laser engraved (pintails on the left-hand side and pheasants on the right); gloss blued finish; ventilated rib; gloss oil finished grade III walnut with close radius pistol grip; speed lock forearm; shim adjustable for length of pull, cast, and drop; Inflex technology recoil pad; brass bead front sight; ABS case included
MSRP $1979.99

MAXUS WICKED WING
Action: Semiautomatic
Stock: Composite

Barrel: 26 in., 28 in.
Chokes: Banded Invector-Plus Extended
Weight: 7.0 lb.–7 lb. 2 oz.
Bore/Gauge: 12
Magazine: 4 shells
Features: 3.5-in. autoloader; A-TACS US, Mossy Oak Bottomlands, or Shadow Grass Blades stocks; Browning's Dura-Touch Armor Coating and burnt bronze Cerakote finish on receiver and barrel; Briley extended bolt handles; oversized bolt release come
3-inch: $1779.99
3 1/2-inch: $1899.99

SILVER BLACK LIGHTNING
Action: Semiautomatic
Stock: Turkish walnut
Barrel: 26 in., 28 in.
Chokes: Invector-Plus (F, M, IC)
Weight: 7 lb. 4 oz.–7 lb. 6 oz.
Bore/Gauge: 12
Magazine: 4 shells
Features: Gloss black and deep blued metal with gloss finish walnut Lightweight aluminum alloy receiver; Active Valve System regulates light and heavy loads; semi-humpback receiver styling; brass front bead; back-bored barrel; matte version features satin finish stock and bi-tone matte black and silver finish on the receiver
MSRP $1139.99

SILVER FIELD
Action: Semiautomatic
Stock: Turkish walnut
Barrel: 26 in., 28 in.
Chokes: Three Invector-Plus flush (F, M, IC)
Sights: Brass bead
Weight: 7 lb. 4 oz.–7 lb. 5 oz. (12-gauge); 6 lb. 5 oz.–6 lb. 6 oz. (20-gauge)
Bore/Gauge: 12, 20
Magazine: 4 shells
Features: Aluminum receiver; matte blue barrel; satin-finished bi-tone receiver; 3-in. chamber; square pistol grip
MSRP . . . . $1069.99–$1139.99

SHOTGUNS

Browning

BROWNING SILVER FIELD COMPOSITE

BROWNING SILVER FIELD
MICRO MIDAS

BROWNING SILVER FIELD MOSSY OAK
SHADOW GRASS BLADES

BROWNING SILVER RIFLED DEER MATTE

SILVER FIELD COMPOSITE

Action: Semiautomatic
Stock: Composite
Barrel: 26 in., 28 in.
Chokes: Three Invector-Plus flush (F, M, IC)
Sights: Brass bead
Weight: 7 lb. 8 oz.–7 lb. 9 oz.
Bore/Gauge: 12
Magazine: 4 shells
Features: Active Valve system for reliable cycling across a variety of loads; stock in a matte black finish; two-tone gray/black receiver emblazoned with Buckmark logo; choice of 3-in. or 3.5-in. chamber
MSRP . . . . $999.99–$1069.99

SILVER FIELD MICRO MIDAS

Action: Semiautomatic
Stock: Turkish walnut
Barrel: 24 in., 26 in.
Chokes: Three Invector-Plus flush (F, M, IC)
Sights: Brass bead

Weight: 7 lb. 3 oz.–7 lb. 5 oz. (12-gauge); 6 lb.–6 lb. 2 oz. (20-gauge)
Bore/Gauge: 12, 20
Magazine: 4 shells
Features: A reduced stock version (13 in.) for young and shorter-statured hunters; two-tone silver and black receiver; Inflex 1 small buttpad with a hard heel insert; 3-in. chamber
MSRP . . . . $1069.99–$1139.99

SILVER FIELD MOSSY OAK SHADOW GRASS BLADES

Action: Semiautomatic
Stock: Composite
Barrel: 26 in., 28 in.
Chokes: Three Invector-Plus flush (F, M, IC)
Sights: Brass bead
Weight: 7 lb. 8 oz.–7 lb. 9 oz.
Bore/Gauge: 12
Magazine: 4 shells
Features: Stock is fully covered in Mossy Oak Shadow Grass Blades; two-tone gray/black receiver wears a Buckmark logo on each side; light-

weight barrel profile makes for fast swinging; Active Valve system produces consistent shooting across a wide variety of loads; 3.5-in. chamber
MSRP $1139.99

SILVER RIFLED DEER MATTE

Action: Semiautomatic
Stock: Turkish walnut
Barrel: 22 in.
Chokes: N/A
Weight: 6 lb. 12 oz.
Bore/Gauge: 20
Magazine: 4 shells
Features: Fully rifled barrel for sabot slugs; top cantilever scope mount; gas operation; 3-in. chamber; satin finish stock
MSRP $1199.99

SHOTGUNS

Caesar Guerini

CAESAR GUERINI ELLIPSE EVO

CAESAR GUERINI INVICTUS I SPORTING

CAESAR GUERINI INVICTUS V SPORTING

CAESAR GUERINI MAGNUS SPORTING

CAESAR GUERINI MAXUM IMPACT

ELLIPSE CURVE, EVO, EVO LIGHT

Action: Round body
Stock: Hand-rubbed oil on walnut
Barrel: 28 in.
Chokes: 5 nickel plated, flush fitting
Weight: 6 lb. 1 oz.–7 lb. 4 oz.
Bore/ Gauge: 12, 20, 28
Magazine: 2 shells
Features: Engraving pattern coated with Invisalloy; brass front bead sight; single (selective optional) trigger; manual safety; tapered, solid top rib; three variants available: the Curve (rose scroll engraving with nude goddess on receiver bottom), Evo (tight scroll engraving with large oak leaf carvings, and Evo Light (a lighter Evo); left-hand and English stocks available
Curve: . . . . $7500.00–$9740.00
EVO, EVO Light: . . .$6850.00–$9085.00

INVICTUS I SPORTING

Action: Over/under
Stock: Wood
Barrel: 30 in., 32 in.
Chokes: 6 MAXIS competition chokes
Weight: 8 lb. 1 oz.–8 lb. 3 oz.
Bore/Gauge: 12
Magazine: 2 shells
Features: White Bradley style front silver center bead; manual safety (auto-

matic optional); DTS-2 trigger system with two trigger pull weight options, take up, over travel and length of pull adjustments
MSRP $7395.00
Left-hand: . . . . add $250.00
Adjustable comb: . . . . add $400.00

INVICTUS V SPORTING

Action: Over/under
Stock: Wood
Barrel: 30 in., 32 in.
Chokes: 6 MAXIS competition chokes
Weight: 8 lb. 1 oz.–8 lb. 3 oz.
Bore/Gauge: 12
Magazine: 2 shells
Features: DPS2 trigger system; factory selective release triggers available in single and double release; contemporary Italian Ornato-style engraving with deep relief game scenes; white Bradley-style front silver center bead
MSRP $9375.00
Left-hand: . . . . add $250.00
Adjustable comb: . . . . add $400.00

MAGNUS SPORTING

Action: Over/under
Stock: Hand-rubbed oil on walnut
Barrel: 30 in., 32 in., 34 in.
Chokes: 6 CCP competition chokes (6 MAXIS for 12 Ga. models)

Weight: 7 lb. 6 oz.–8 lb. 2 oz.
Bore/Gauge: 12, 20, 28, .410
Magazine: 2 shells
Features: Single selective trigger; manual safety; ventilated center rib; available 20/28 gauge combo and 20/28/.410 gauge combo
Standard right-hand: $5770.00
20/28-ga. combo: $8395.00
20/28/.410 combo: $11,195.00
Left-hand stock: . . . . . . add $250.00
Adjustable comb: . . . . add $400.00
Case-hardened receiver: . . . . add $305.00

MAXUM IMPACT

Action: Over/under
Stock: Checkered walnut with adjustable cheekpiece
Barrel: 30 in., 32 in.
Chokes: Maxis choke system
Weight: 7 lb. 11 oz.–8 lb. 7 oz.
Bore/Gauge: 12, 20
Magazine: 2 shells
Features: Engraved receiver; 17mm-tall D.T.S. rib for more upright shooting; 5 in. dual conical forcing cones; selective and non-selective triggers available; left-hand available
MSRP: $9295.00
Left-hand: . . . . add $250.00

Caesar Guerini

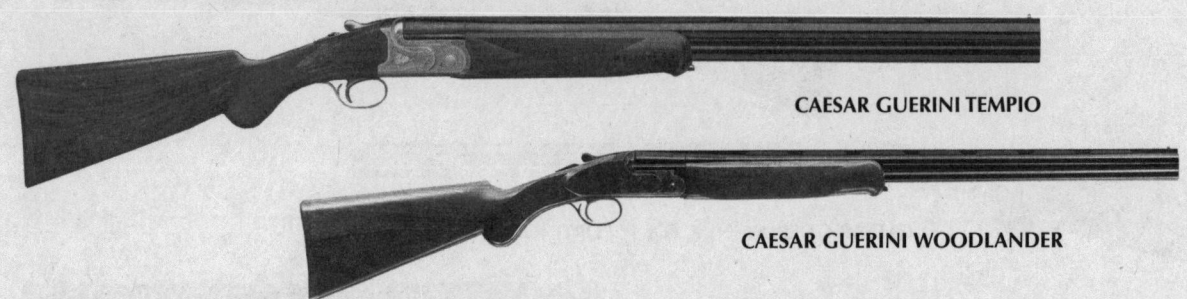

CAESAR GUERINI TEMPIO

CAESAR GUERINI WOODLANDER

TEMPIO

Action: Over/under
Stock: Turkish walnut
Barrel: 26 in., 28 in., 30 in.
Chokes: 5 nickel plated, flush fitting chokes
Weight: 6 lb.–7 lb.
Bore/Gauge: 12, 20, 28, .410
Magazine: 2 shells
Features: Designed to be a sleek and fast pointing shotgun in the field; perfect companion for upland game hunters; low-profile receiver matched with a trim stock, classic Prince-of-Wales grip and schnabel forend make the gun a perfect match for fast game birds; contemporary style of "ornato" style scroll with tasteful gold accents; Invisalloy protective coating

Standard 12-, 20-, 28-ga.:	. $4325.00
Standard .410-bore:	$4515.00
20/28-ga. combo:	$6475.00
20/28/.410 combo:	$8815.00
Left-hand or English stock:	add $250.00

WOODLANDER

Action: Over/under
Stock: English walnut
Barrel: 26 in., 28 in., 30 in.
Chokes: Five precision patterned flush chokes (CYL, IC, M, IM, F)
Weight: 6 lb.–7 lb.
Bore/Gauge: 12, 20, 28, .410
Magazine: 2 shells
Features: Gun reflects passion for fall coverts, autumn foliage, wet gun dogs, and the smell of wood; understated elegance of color case hardening and nicely figured, oil-finished English walnut that speaks of quality from a bygone era; a superior-handling upland game gun that's perfect for tight cover and fast-flushing birds

Standard:	$3795.00
20/28 combo:	$5945.00
20/28/.410 combo:	$8285.00
Left-hand or English stock:	$250.00

Charles Daly/Chiappa Firearms

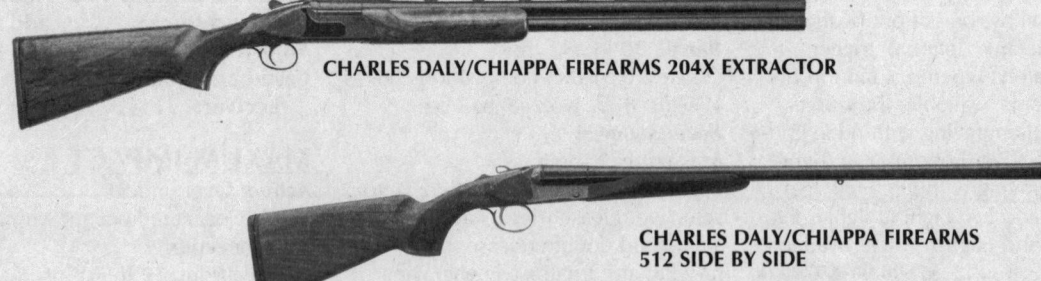

CHARLES DALY/CHIAPPA FIREARMS 204X EXTRACTOR

CHARLES DALY/CHIAPPA FIREARMS 512 SIDE BY SIDE

204X

Action: Over/under
Stock: Walnut
Barrel: 26 in., 28 in.
Chokes: Skeet, IC, MOD, IM, F
Weight: 6 lb. 6 oz.–6 lb. 13 oz.
Bore/Gauge: 20, 12
Magazine: 2 shells
Features: Fiber optic sights; matte black receiver; 12-ga. with walnut stock offered in 26- or 28-in. barrels and 3-in. chambers, Realtree APG camo version has 24-in. barrels and chambers 3 ½-inch shells

Camo:	$880.00
Walnut:	$799.00

512 SIDE BY SIDE

Action: Break-action side-by-side
Stock: Walnut
Barrel: 28 in.
Chokes: Rem-choke in all barrels
Weight: 6 lb. 2 oz.
Bore/Gauge: 12
Magazine: 2 shells
Features: Interchangeable choke tubes in each barrel; white receiver

MSRP	$917.00

Charles Daly/Chiappa Firearms

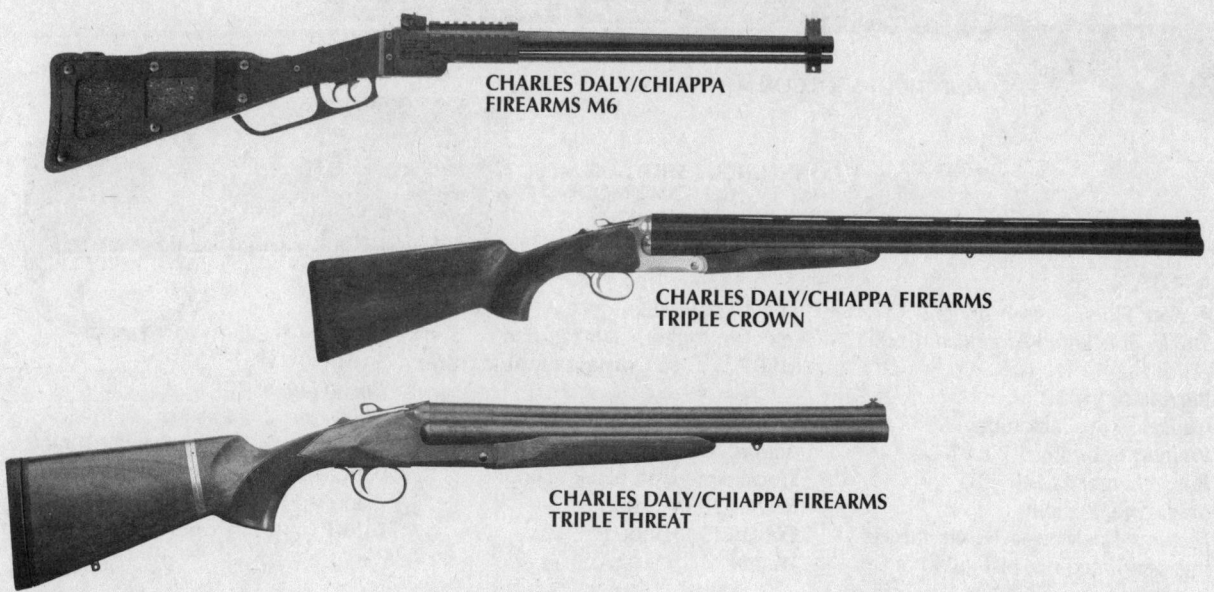

CHARLES DALY/CHIAPPA FIREARMS M6

CHARLES DALY/CHIAPPA FIREARMS TRIPLE CROWN

CHARLES DALY/CHIAPPA FIREARMS TRIPLE THREAT

M6
Action: Over/under
Stock: Foam and steel
Barrel: 18.5 in.
Chokes: N/A
Weight: 6 lb.
Bore/Gauge: 20-ga./.22LR, 12-ga./.22LR, 12-ga./.22WMR, 20-ga./.22WMR
Magazine: 2 shells
Features: Three Picatinny rails; cleaning kit included in stock; folds for transportation; top tang manual safety; adjustable iron type with fiber optics
MSRP . . . . $680.00–$929.00

TRIPLE CROWN
Action: Break-action
Stock: Wood
Barrel: 26 in., 28 in.
Chokes: Rem-choke in all barrels
Weight: 8 lb. 11 oz.
Bore/Gauge: 12, 20, 28
Magazine: 3 shells
Features: Side-by-side and middle arrangement sporting model with three shotgun barrels; chokes in all three barrels; sling swivel studs
MSRP $1929.00

TRIPLE THREAT
Action: Break-action
Stock: Wood
Barrel: 18.5 in.
Chokes: Rem-choke in all barrels
Weight: 8 lb.
Bore/ Gauge: 12, 20
Magazine: 3 shells
Features: Side-by-side and middle arrangement defense model with three shotgun barrels; chokes in all three barrels; sling swivel studs; wooden stock can be partly disassembled
MSRP $1955.00

Cimarron Firearms Co.

CIMARRON 1878 COACH GUN

1878 COACH GUN
Action: Side-by-Side
Stock: Wood
Barrel: 20 in., 26 in.

Chokes: Open
Weight: 8 lb.–8 lb. 15 oz.
Bore/ Gauge: 12
Magazine: 2 shells

Features: 3 in. blue steel real working hammers; available in standard blue
MSRP . . . . $596.70–$622.70

Connecticut Shotgun Mfg. Co.

CONNECTICUT SHOTGUN MFG. CO. A-10

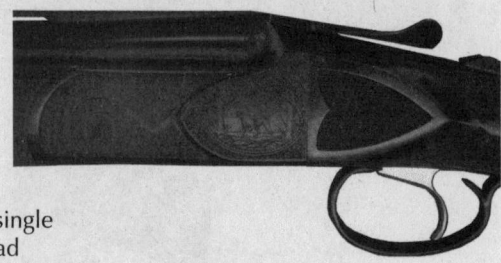

CONNECTICUT SHOTGUN MFG. CO. CSMC MODEL 21

A-10

Action: Sidelock over/under
Stock: Checkered American black walnut
Barrel: 26 in.–32 in.
Chokes: 5 TruLock tubes
Weight: 6 lb. 8 oz.–7 lb. 8 oz.
Bore/Gauge: 12, 20, 28
Magazine: 2 shells
Features: Finely engraved, cut checkering; ventilated rib; pistol grip or straight grip; auto ejectors, single selective trigger; Galazan pad
MSRP . . . . . . **Contact manufacturer**

CSMC MODEL 21

Action: Sidelock over/under
Stock: American black walnut
Barrel: 28 in., 30 in.
Chokes: 5 included
Weight: 7 lb. 9 oz.
Bore/Gauge: 20
Magazine: 2 shells
Features: Available in Standard grade with a blued receiver, a #6 Pigeon grade, and a Grand American grade.
MSRP . . . . . . **Contact manufacturer**

CZ-USA (Ceska Zbrojovka)

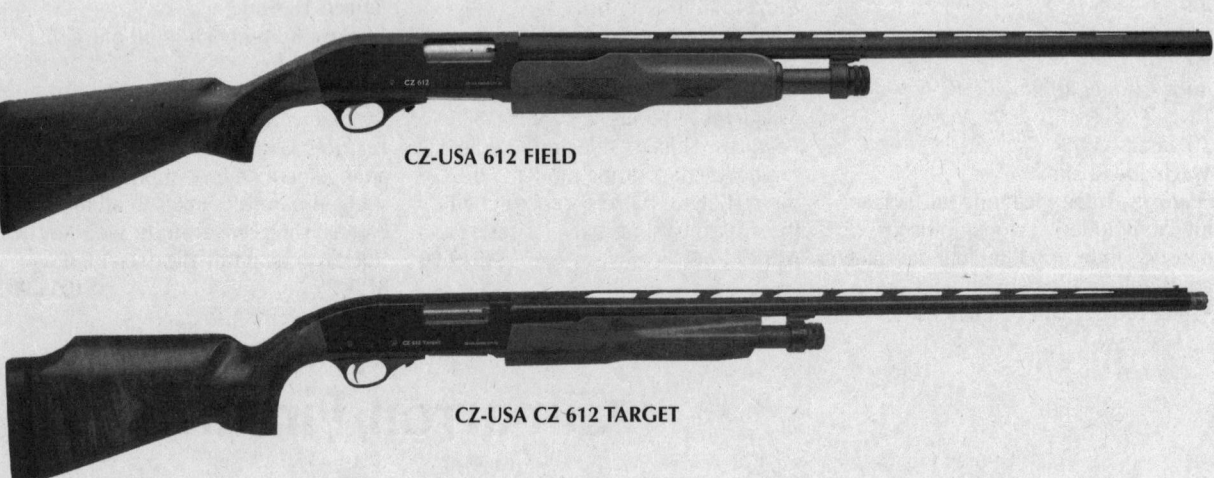

CZ-USA 612 FIELD

CZ-USA CZ 612 TARGET

612 FIELD

Action: Pump
Stock: Walnut
Barrel: 28 in.
Chokes: 3 chokes
Weight: 6 lb. 3 oz.
Bore/Gauge: 12
Magazine: 4+1 shells
Features: Satin chrome finish; capable of shooting 2 ¾-in. and 3-in. shells; supplied with three chokes
MSRP **$389.00**

612 TARGET

Action: Pump
Stock: Turkish walnut
Barrel: 32 in.
Chokes: Extended knurled
Weight: 7 lb. 5 oz.
Bore/Gauge: 12
Magazine: 4 shells
Features: Select grade wood with a glossy oil finish; metal is a deep polished blue; tuned trigger system; raised rib; comfortable Monte Carlo stock; pair of Bradley-style white beads
MSRP **$549.00**

SHOTGUNS

CZ-USA (Ceska Zbrojovka)

CZ-USA CZ 620/628 FIELD SELECT

CZ–USA 712 GREEN G2

CZ-USA 712 G2

CZ-USA 712 TARGET G2

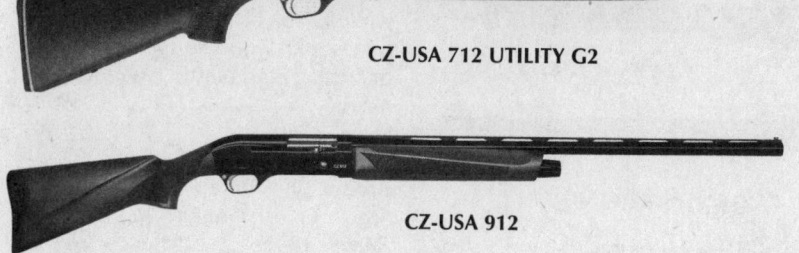

CZ-USA 712 UTILITY G2

CZ-USA 912

Magazine: 4+1 shells
Features: Gas operated aluminum alloy action with target-grade enhancements; chrome-lined barrel; fiber optic front sight on a 10mm stepped rib; Schnabel forend; smooth rounded heel; Monte Carlo buttstock
MSRP $680.00

620/628 FIELD SELECT
Action: Pump
Stock: Turkish walnut
Barrel: 28 in.
Chokes: F, M, C
Weight: 5 lb. 6 oz.
Bore/Gauge: 28 (628); 20 (620)
Magazine: 4 shells
Features: Gauge-specific 7075 aluminum action; deep glossy blue finish; select grade Turkish Walnut; full forend
MSRP $429.00

712 G2
Action: Semiautomatic
Stock: Turkish walnut
Barrel: 26 in., 28 in.
Chokes: 5 included
Weight: 7 lb. 5 oz.–7 lb. 6 oz.
Bore/Gauge: 12
Magazine: 4+1 shells
Features: Accepting 2¾ and 3-inch shells, it is an all-arounder, a great choice for upland game, waterfowl, or clays; barrel is chrome-lined and has a matte black hard chrome exterior

that will resist corrosion for many seasons in the field; G2 stock adds new laser-engraved checkering, right-hand palm swell as well as a barrel lock-ring to make assembly easier
MSRP $499.00

712 GREEN G2
Action: Semiautomatic
Stock: Turkish walnut
Barrel: 28 in.
Chokes: 5 chokes
Weight: 7 lb. 6 oz.
Bore/Gauge: 12
Magazine: 4+1 shells
Features: Green anodized receiver; laser-cut checkering; healthy palm swell; smooth gas-operating system
MSRP $518.00

712 TARGET G2
Action: Gas-operated semiautomatic
Stock: Walnut
Barrel: 30 in.
Chokes: Interchangeable chokes (F, M, IC)
Weight: 7 lb. 10 oz.
Bore/Gauge: 12

712 UTILITY G2
Action: Semiautomatic
Stock: Synthetic
Barrel: 20 in.
Chokes: Screw-in chokes (F, IM, M, IC, C)
Weight: 6 lb. 10 oz.
Bore/Gauge: 12
Magazine: 4+1 shells
Features: 3-in. chamber cross-bolt safety; black synthetic stock; matte chrome black barrel
MSRP $499.00

912
Action: Recoil-operated semiautomatic
Stock: Walnut
Barrel: 28 in.
Chokes: 5 interchangeable choke tubes
Weight: 7 lb. 5 oz.
Bore/Gauge: 12
Magazine: 4+1 shells
Features: Fiber optic front bead; features a gloss black finish on metalwork; cross-bolt safety; chrome-lined barrel; aluminum frame
MSRP $544.00

CZ-USA (Ceska Zbrojovka)

CZ-USA CZ ALL-AMERICAN

CZ–USA ALL AMERICAN TRAP COMBO

CZ–USA DRAKE

CZ-USA REAPER MAGNUM

CZ–USA REDHEAD PREMIER

CZ–USA SCTP STERLING

CZ–USA SHARP-TAIL

ALL-AMERICAN
Action: Over/under
Stock: Turkish walnut
Barrel: 30 in., 32 in.
Chokes: Extended black
Weight: 8 lb. 8 oz.
Bore/Gauge: 12
Magazine: 2 shells
Features: CNCed throughout; drop-in replacement parts (including locking blocks for those who shoot tens of thousands of rounds a year); four-way comb; adjustable buttplate hardware; barrels have lengthened forcing cones and are ported; 3-in. chambers
MSRP $2572.00

ALL-AMERICAN TRAP COMBO
Action: Over/under
Stock: Turkish walnut
Barrel: 32 in.
Chokes: 1 Skeet, 1 IC, 2 M, 1 IM, 2 F
Weight: 8 lb. 8 oz.
Bore/Gauge: 12
Magazine: 2 shells
Features: Comes with a single-shot un-single with a dial-adjustable aluminum rib (adjustable from 50/50 up

to 90/10 point of impact) and a standard set of barrels with stepped rib (50/50 point of impact); surface hardened CNC-milled action; firing pins that ride in bushings; replaceable locking blocks; adjustable parallel comb; competition trigger; auto ejectors
MSRP $3471.00

DRAKE
Action: Over/under
Stock: Turkish walnut
Barrel: 28 in.
Chokes: 5 chokes
Weight: 6 lb.–7 lb. 6 oz.
Bore/Gauge: 12, 20, 28 ga., .410-bore
Magazine: 2 shells
Features: CNC action; extractor operation; single selectable trigger; .410-bore has fixed Improved Cylinder/Modified chokes; left-hand Southpaw model available in 12- and 20-gauge.
12-, 20-gauge: $655.00
28-gauge, .410-bore: $702.00

REAPER MAGNUM
Action: Over/under

Stock: Polymer
Barrel: 26 in.
Chokes: Five extended
Sights: Front bead
Weight: 7 lb.
Bore/Gauge: 12
Magazine: 2 shells
Features: Dressed in Realtree Xtra Green with a black receiver; topside Picatinny rail for optics mounting; mechanical trigger
MSRP $993.00

REDHEAD PREMIER
Action: Over/under
Stock: Turkish walnut
Barrel: 26 in., 28 in.
Chokes: 5 flush-mount
Weight: 6 lb. 14 oz.
Bore/Gauge: 12, 20
Magazine: 2 shells
Features: The tried-and-true Redhead also gets CZ's new 1-piece CNCed receiver; laser-cut checkering, solid mid-ribs, pistol grip, and a classy white bead; silver receiver and ejectors that kick out the spent shells automatically, hard plastic case included
MSRP $959.00

SCTP STERLING
Action: Over/under
Stock: Turkish walnut
Barrel: 28 in.
Chokes: Five flush chokes (C, IC, M, IM, F)
Sights: None
Weight: 7 lb. 8 oz.
Bore/Gauge: 12
Magazine: 2 shells
Features: Stock designed to fit female and young shooters; silver receiver is finished in two-tone satin and gloss chrome; the barrels are gloss black chrome; stock features laser stippling; 3-in. chambers; left-hand Southpaw model available
MSRP $1361.00

SHARP-TAIL
Action: Side-by-side
Stock: Wood
Barrel: 28 in.
Chokes: 5 flush interchangeable
Weight: 6 lb.– 7 lb. 5 oz.
Bore/Gauge: 12, 20, 28, .410
Magazine: 2 shells
Features: Black hard chrome barrel finish; color case hardened receiver finish; semi-beavertail forend; extractor; manual safety
MSRP . . . . $999.00–$1229.00

SHOTGUNS

CZ-USA (Ceska Zbrojovka)

CZ-USA SHARP-TAIL COACH

CZ-USA SUPREME FIELD

CZ-USA CZ SWAMP MAGNUM

CZ–USA UPLAND STERLING SOUTHPAW

CZ-USA UPLAND STERLING

CZ-USA UPLAND ULTRALIGHT

CZ–USA WINGSHOOTER ELITE

SHARP-TAIL COACH
Action: Side-by-side
Stock: Turkish walnut
Barrel: 20 in.
Chokes: Fixed chokes (C/C)
Sights: Front bead
Weight: 6 lb. 11 oz.
Bore/Gauge: 12, 20
Magazine: 2 shells
Features: Semi-beavertail forearm for a solid grip; single selectable trigger; extractors
MSRP **$1006.00**

SUPREME FIELD
Action: Over/under
Stock: Grade III Turkish walnut
Barrel: 28 in.
Chokes: Five extended
Sights: Front bead
Weight: 6 lb.–7 lb. 14 oz.
Bore/Gauge: 12, 20, 28
Magazine: 2 shells
Features: Grade III walnut; polished nickel chrome receiver with border engraving; ejectors; solid mid-rib; sharp checkering
MSRP **$1784.00**

SWAMP MAGNUM
Action: Over/under

Stock: Polymer
Barrel: 30 in.
Chokes: Extended black
Weight: 7 lb. 2 oz.
Bore/Gauge: 12
Magazine: 2 shells
Features: Only over/under in CZ's line with an automatic safety, which engages every time the action is opened; polymer stocks in either black or camo; all metal work blacked out; chambered for 3 ½ in.
Black: **$952.00**
Camo: **$1075.00**

UPLAND STERLING
Action: Over/under
Stock: Turkish walnut
Barrel: 28 in.
Chokes: 5 screw-in
Weight: 7 lb. 8 oz.
Bore/ Gauge: 12
Magazine: 2 shells
Features: Built on a new platform featuring a CNC-milled steel receiver, resulting in mechanical components that operate with clockwork precision and consistency; Turkish walnut stock features a stippled grip area on the wrist and forend
MSRP **$999.00**

UPLAND STERLING SOUTHPAW
Action: Over/under
Stock: Turkish walnut with laser stippling
Barrel: 30 in.
Chokes: 5 flush-mount
Weight: 7 lb. 8 oz.
Bore/Gauge: 12
Magazine: 2 shells
Features: Cast on for left-handed shooters; shares most of the other features of the Upland Sterling, but with a more universal 29-inch barrel; a mechanical trigger and safety with selectable barrels; a regular right-handed top lever latch; plastic case
MSRP **$1038.00**

UPLAND ULTRALIGHT, ULTRALIGHT GREEN
Action: Over/under
Stock: Turkish walnut
Barrel: 26 in., 28 in.
Chokes: F, IM, M, IC, C
Weight: 6 lb.
Bore/Gauge: 12, 20
Magazine: 2 shells
Features: Lightweight, black alloy receiver; vent rib; matte-blued model available in 12-gauge only; green model features a unique green anodized receiver and is available in 12- or 20-gauge, both with 28-in. barrels
Ultralight: **$762.00**
Ultralight Green: **$786.00**

WINGSHOOTER ELITE
Action: Over/under
Stock: Turkish walnut
Barrel: 28 in.
Chokes: 5 flush-mount
Weight: 7 lb. 6 oz.
Bore/Gauge: 12, 20
Magazine: 2 shells
Features: Replaces the Wingshooter; new CNCed 1-piece receiver; fully hand-engraved side-plates, reminiscent of custom-grade Super Scroll; single selectable trigger, solid mid-ribs, ejectors, and two-tone chromed finish; laser-cut checkering, solid mid-ribs, pistol grip stock, white bead; hard plastic case
MSRP **$1059.00**

Dickinson Arms

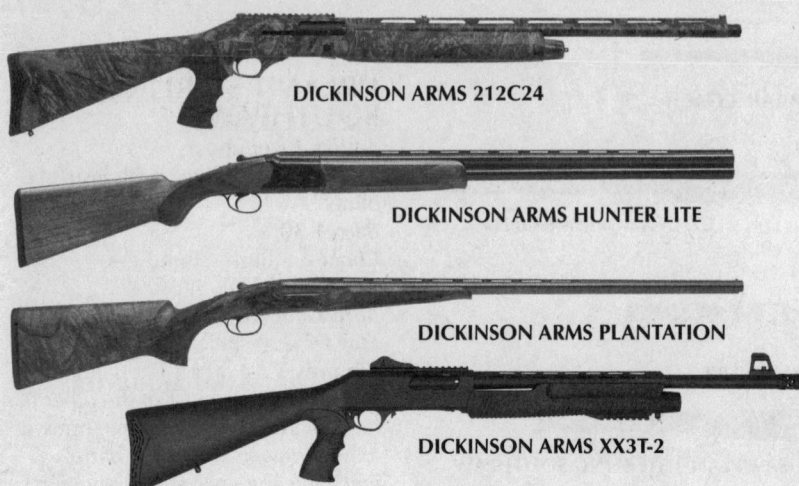

DICKINSON ARMS 212C24

DICKINSON ARMS HUNTER LITE

DICKINSON ARMS PLANTATION

DICKINSON ARMS XX3T-2

212C24

Action: Semiautomatic
Stock: Synthetic
Barrel: 24 in.
Chokes: One extended choke
Sights: Fiber optic front and rear
Weight: 7 lb.
Bore/Gauge: 12
Magazine: 4 shells
Features: Picatinny rails; finger-grooved pistol grip; full-coverage Mossy Oak Obsession camo; hard-sided carrying case
MSRP $440.00

HUNTER LIGHT

Action: Over/under
Stock: Turkish walnut

Barrel: 24 in., 26 in., 28 in., 30 in.
Chokes: Interchangeable
Sights: Front bead
Weight: 6 lb.
Bore/Gauge: 12, 16, 20, 28, .410
Magazine: 2 shells
Features: Receivers with light engraving in either a black or black and white receivers; single selective triggers; automatic ejectors; choice of English, Prince of Wales, or pistol grips; either standard or beavertail forends
MSRP $499.00

PLANTATION

Action: Side-by-side
Stock: Turkish walnut
Barrel: 24 in., 26 in., 28 in., 30 in.

Chokes: Fixed, thin-walled interchangeable
Sights: Front bead
Weight: 7 lb.
Bore/Gauge: 12, 16, 20, 28, .410
Magazine: 2 shells
Features: Premier Grade Turkish walnut stocks and case hardened receivers; 25 percent coverage English scroll engraving; choice of oil or satin finished stocks; double or single triggers; English, Prince of Wales, or pistol grips; manual or auto safeties; automatic ejectors and extractors; high-rib version is available
MSRP $2100.00

XX3T-2

Action: Pump
Stock: Synthetic
Barrel: 18.5 in.
Chokes: None
Sights: Front post, ghost ring rear
Weight: 6 lb.
Bore/Gauge: 12
Magazine: 5 shells
Features: Muzzle brake; Picatinny rails top side and under the forearm; pistol grip stock with overmolds in gripping areas; heat shield; 3-in. chamber
MSRP $249.99

Fabarm

FABARM AXIS ALLSPORT QUICK
RELEASE RIB (QRR)

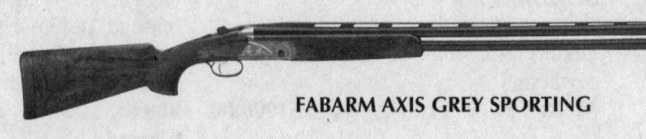

FABARM AXIS GREY SPORTING

AXIS ALLSPORT QUICK RELEASE RIB (QRR)

Action: Over/under
Stock: Wood
Barrel: 30–32 in.
Chokes: 5 Exis HP
Weight: 8 lb. 6 oz.
Bore/Gauge: 12
Magazine: 2 shells
Features: Quick Release Rib design allows configuration for varying shooting styles and disciplines; standard offering includes two 10mm high ramp style ribs—one with a 50/50 percent point-of-impact and a second

for a higher 65/35 percent; includes Tribore free floating barrels for improved balance and performance; 97mm Exis HP hyperbolic choke tubes; integrated recoil reducer; adjustable trigger; Triwood enhanced stock finish; Micro Metric adjustable stock comb
Standard: $4500.00
Left-hand stock: . . . . . . add $150.00

AXIS GREY SPORTING

Action: Over/under
Stock: Triwood
Barrel: 30 in., 32 in.

Chokes: Five EXIS HP Competition tubes
Sights: Front bead
Weight: 8 lb. 4 oz.
Bore/Gauge: 12
Magazine: 2 shells
Features: Protective Triwood finish; greyed receiver with scroll engraving and gold game bird scenes; vent rib; separated barrels; available with adjustable stock.
MSRP $3695.00
Left-hand stock: . . . . . . add $150.00
Adjustable stock: . . . . . add $370.00

SHOTGUNS

FABARM AXIS GREY TRAP

FABARM AXIS RS12 SPORTING

FABARM AXIS RS12 TRAP

FABARM ELOS D2

FABARM ELOS N2 SPORTING

FABARM L4S INITIAL HUNTER

FABARM L4S SERIES

AXIS GREY TRAP

Action: Over/under
Stock: Triwood
Barrel: 32 in., 34 in.
Chokes: Five EXIS HP Competition tubes
Sights: Front bead
Weight: 8 lb. 14 oz.
Bore/Gauge: 12
Magazine: 1, 2 shells
Features: High rib adjustable for point of impact; available in an over/under, as an single-shot configuration, or a combination
Over/under or Unsingle:. . . $4995.00
Combo: $6725.00
Left-hand stock:. . . . . . add $150.00

AXIS RS12 SPORTING

Action: Over/under
Stock: Wood
Barrel: 30 in., 32 in.
Chokes: 5 Exis HP
Weight: 8 lb. 4 oz.
Bore/Gauge: 12
Magazine: 2 shells
Features: Axis free-floating barrels feature Tribore HP tapered bores that lower recoil and reduce the need for excessively long forcing cones; blued action; Fabarm Micro Metric adjustable comb and left hand stocks available
Standard: $3375.00
Left-hand: . . . . add $150.00
Adjustable stock: . . . . . add $370.00

AXIS RS12 TRAP

Action: Over/under
Stock: Wood
Barrel: 32 in., 34 in. (unsingle)
Chokes: 5 Exis HP

Weight: 8 lb. 14 oz.
Bore/Gauge: 12
Magazine: 1 or 2 shells
Features: Free-floating over-and-under barrels; adjustable ribs on all barrels; tapered bores; integrated recoil reducer; adjustable comb; optional release triggers; 97mm Exis HP hyperbolic choke tubes; adjustable trigger; Triwood enhanced stock finish
Over/under or Unsingle:. . . $4500.00
Combo: $6340.00
Left-hand stock: . . . . . . add $150.00

ELOS D2

Action: Over/under
Stock: Wood
Barrel: 28 in.
Chokes: Five INNER HP chokes
Sights: Front bead
Weight: 5 lb. 8 oz.–6 lb. 8 oz.
Bore/Gauge: 12, 20, 28
Magazine: 2 shells
Features: A lightweight upland bird gun; stainless receiver with scroll and game birds engravings
MSRP. $2665.00
Left-hand stock:. . . . . . add $150.00

ELOS N2 SPORTING

Action: Over/under
Stock: Wood
Barrel: 30 in., 32 in.
Chokes: Five EXIS HP Competition tubes
Sights: Front bead
Weight: 7 lb. 7 oz.
Bore/Gauge: 12
Magazine: 2 shells
Features: Micro-meter adjustable comb; vented barrel separation; adjustable competition trigger

MSRP: $2850.00
Left-hand stock:. . . . . . add $150.00

L4S DELUXE HUNTER, GREY HUNTER

Action: Semiautomatic
Stock: Wood
Barrel: 26 in., 28 in.
Chokes: 3 Inner HP
Weight: 6 lb. 5 oz.–6 lb. 13 oz.
Bore/Gauge: 12
Magazine: 4 shells
Features: Stock shim system for adjusting fit; Tribore HP tapered barrels; available in three grades: Initial Hunter (black action), Grey Hunter (silver action with game scene), and Deluxe Hunter (silver action with detailed game scene with gold inlays and upgraded wood); Initial Hunter available in left-hand
Deluxe Hunter: $2255.00
Grey Hunter: $1825.00

L4S INITIAL HUNTER

Action: Semiautomatic
Stock: Turkish walnut
Barrel: 26 in., 28 in.
Chokes: 3 inner HP
Weight: 6 lb. 5 oz.–6 lb. 13 oz
Bore/Gauge: 12
Magazine: 4 shells
Features: Pulse Piston system; TRIBORE HP tapered barrels; innovative new design that allows the fore-end to be removed without disassembling the shotgun; gas-operating system that significantly reduces recoil; stock shim system for adjusting fit; left-hand versions available in both barrel lengths; model chambers 3-in. shells
Right-hand: $1325.00
Left-hand: $1515.00

SHOTGUNS

Fabarm

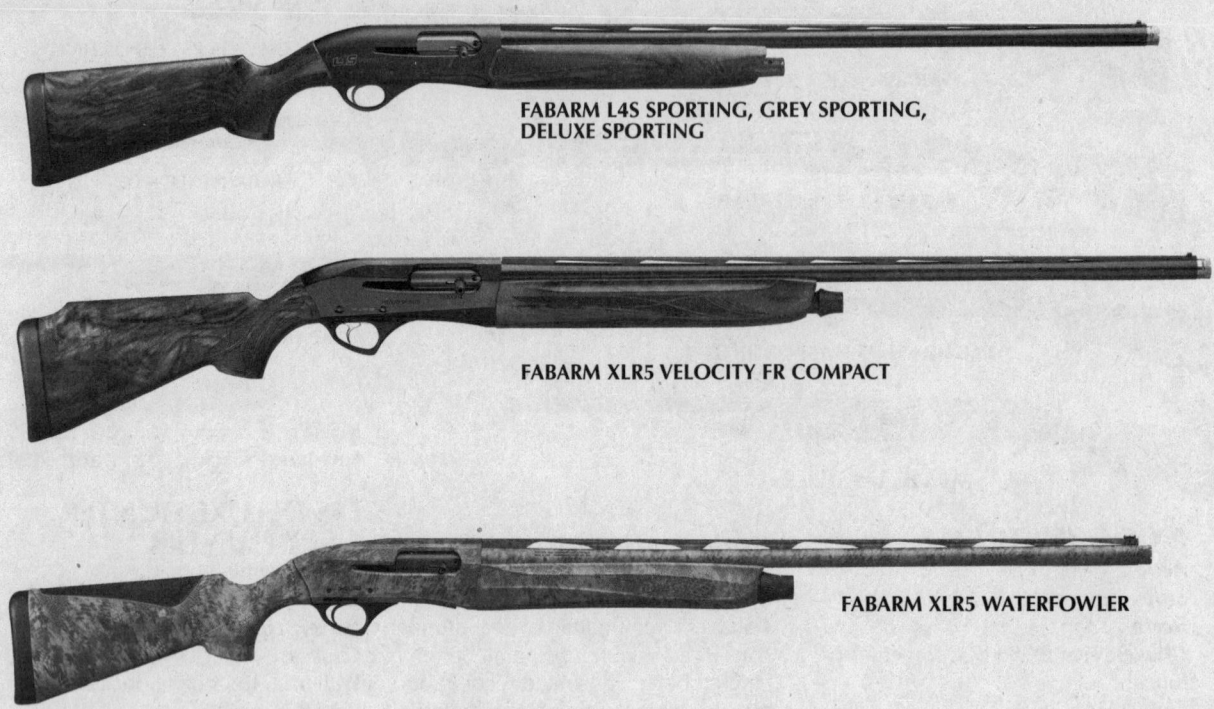

FABARM L4S SPORTING, GREY SPORTING, DELUXE SPORTING

FABARM XLR5 VELOCITY FR COMPACT

FABARM XLR5 WATERFOWLER

L4S SPORTING, GREY SPORTING, DELUXE SPORTING

Action: Semiautomatic
Stock: Walnut
Barrel: 28 in., 30 in., 32 in.
Chokes: Five EXIS HP Competition tubes
Sights: White bead
Weight: 7 lb. 3 oz.
Bore/Gauge: 12
Magazine: 4 shells
Features: Designed around the 2.75-in.,12 ga. shell; Fabarm's tapered Tribore that improves patterns and velocities; oversized bolt handle and bolt release; highlights in bright red; stock can accept Kinetik recoil reducer; available left-handed; Grey and Deluxe include engraving and gold inlays of game birds
Sporting right-hand: $1950.00
Sporting left-hand: $2140.00
Grey: $2355.00
Deluxe: $2765.00

XLR5 VELOCITY FR COMPACT

Action: Semiautomatic
Stock: Wood
Barrel: 28 in., 30 in.
Chokes: 5 Exis HP
Weight: 7 lb. 6 oz.
Bore/Gauge: 12
Magazine: 5 shells
Features: Tapered Tribore HP barrel; oversized bolt handle; oversized bolt release; three optional magazine cap weights to adjust the balance point; barrel features a tapered top rib; stock features Triwood enhanced finish
MSRP: $2155.00

XLR5 WATERFOWLER

Action: Semiautomatic
Stock: Synthetic
Barrel: 28 in., 30 in.
Chokes: 3 inner HP, 1 EXIS DK
Weight: 7 lb.
Bore/Gauge: 12
Magazine: 5 shells
Features: Pulse Piston system; TRIBORE HP barrel design for reduced recoil and improved pattern performance; special competition choke tube, the EXIS DK, tuned for non-toxic ammo in the most popular pellet sizes; a top rib increases the sighting plain by 4 in. and allows the shooter to see down the rib with a more comfortable head-up posture; chrome plated barrel extension and bores; left-hand versions available in both barrel lengths; model chambers 3-in. shells; in True Timber Viper camo stock with OD green receiver or a left-hand-only version in full-coverage Kryptec Banshee camo
Right-hand: $1795.00
Left-hand: $1985.00

Fausti USA

FAUSTI USA CALEDON L4

FAUSTI USA CLASS

FAUSTI USA ITALYCO

FAUSTI USA MAGNIFICENT

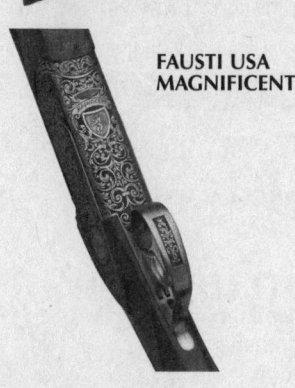

FAUSTI USA MAGNIFICENT

CALEDON
Action: Over/under
Stock: Walnut
Barrel: 26 in., 28 in., 30 in.
Chokes: Fixed or interchangeable choke tubes
Weight: 5 lb. 12 oz.–7 lb. 4 oz.
Bore/Gauge: 12, 16, 20, 28, .410
Magazine: 2 shells
Features: Single selectable trigger; A+ Turkish walnut stock with oil finish; laser-engraved lower receiver; automatic ejectors; metallic bead sight
MSRP . . . . **$1999.00–$2569.00**

CLASS
Action: Over/under
Stock: Walnut
Barrel: 26 in., 28 in., 30 in.
Chokes: Fixed or interchangeable choke tubes
Weight: 5 lb. 12 oz.–7 lb. 5 oz.
Bore/Gauge: 12, 16, 20, 28, .410
Magazine: 2 shells
Features: Features automatic ejectors; metallic bead; single-selectable trigger; 14–3/8-in. length of pull; timeless AA walnut oil-polished stock; Prince of Wales style stock; receiver laser-engraved with flushing quail
MSRP . . . . **$2549.00–$3099.00**

ITALYCO
Action: Over/under
Stock: Wood
Barrel: 23–32 in.
Chokes: Fixed
Weight: N/A
Bore/Gauge: 12 (2 ¾ in., 3 in.), 16 (2 ¾ in.), 20 (2 ¾ in., 3 in.), 28 (2 ¾ in.), .410 (3 in.)
Magazine: 2 shells

Features: Single selective trigger (double trigger available); automatic ejector (manual ejector available); box lock round body; pistol grip with steel grip cap or Prince of Wales or English
MSRP . . . . . . **Contact manufacturer**

MAGNIFICENT
Action: Over/under
Stock: Walnut
Barrel: 26 in., 28 in., 30 in.
Chokes: Fixed or interchangeable choke tubes
Weight: 5 lb. 12 oz.–7 lb. 6 oz.
Bore/Gauge: 12, 16, 20, 28, .410
Magazine: 2 shells
Features: AAA+ walnut stock with oil finish; precision scroll engraving accompanies Aphrodite, the Greek goddess of love and beauty, on the receiver; the Crest of the city of Brescia, Italy, where all Fausti shotguns are produced, is on the underside of the receiver; single selectable trigger; automatic ejectors; metallic bead sight
MSRP: . . . . **$4999.00–$5559.00**

Fox by Savage Arms

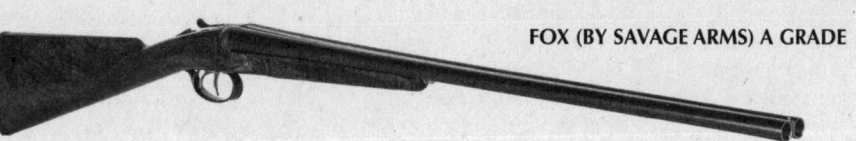

FOX (BY SAVAGE ARMS) A GRADE

A GRADE
Action: Side-by-side
Stock: American black walnut
Barrel: 26 in., 28 in.
Chokes: IM, M, F
Sights: Front brass bead

Weight: N/A
Bore/Gauge: 12, 20
Magazine: 2 shells
Features: Splinter forend; checkered stock; straight grip; case-colored receiver; three interchangeable

chokes; double triggers; 14.5-in. length of pull; hard polymer case
MSRP **$4999.00**

Franchi

FRANCHI AFFINITY 3

FRANCHI AFFINITY 3 COMPACT

FRANCHI AFFINITY 3.5

FRANCHI AFFINITY CATALYST

FRANCHI AFFINITY LEFT-HAND

FRANCHI INSTINCT CATALYST

AFFINITY 3
Action: Semiautomatic
Stock: Synthetic, walnut
Barrel: 26 in., 28 in.
Chokes: Three chokes (F, IC, M)
Sights: Fiber optic bar front sight
Weight: 5 lb. 15 oz.–6 lb. 15 oz.
Bore/Gauge: 12, 20
Magazine: 4 shells
Features: Drop at heel is adjustable; in black, Realtree Max-5, or Mossy Oak Bottomland synthetic stocks or A-grade satin-finished walnut; chambers 3-inch shells
MSRP . . . . $789.00–$899.00

AFFINITY 3 COMPACT
Action: Semiautomatic
Stock: Synthetic
Barrel: 24 in., 26 in.
Chokes: Three chokes (F, IC, M)
Sights: Fiber optic bar front sight
Weight: 5 lb. 15 oz.–6 lb. 11 oz.
Bore/Gauge: 12, 20
Magazine: 4 shells
Features: A hunting semiautomatic for youth, women, and shorter-statured shooters; length of pull and drop at heel are adjustable; chambers 3-inch shells; both gauges available in full-coverage Realtree Max-5; 20 ga. available in all-black
MSRP . . . . $849.00–$959.00

AFFINITY 3.5
Action: Semiautomatic
Stock: Synthetic
Barrel: 26 in., 28 in.
Chokes: Three chokes (F, IC, M)
Sights: Fiber optic bar front sight
Weight: 6 lb. 15 oz.–7 lb.
Bore/Gauge: 12
Magazine: 4 shells
Features: Chambers 3.5-in. shells; adjustable drop at heel; 26-in. barrel model available in black synthetic or Realtree Max-5; 28-in. barrel model available in Realtree Max-5 or Mossy Oak Bottomland
Black: $959.00
Camo: $1069.00

AFFINITY CATALYST
Action: Semiautomatic
Stock: Walnut
Barrel: 28 in.
Chokes: IC, M, F
Weight: 6 lb. 10 oz.
Bore/Gauge: 12
Magazine: 4+1 shells
Features: Drop, cast, pitch, and length-of-pull are all tailored to a woman's build; fiber optic red-bar front sight
MSRP $969.00

AFFINITY LEFT-HAND
Action: Semiautomatic
Stock: Synthetic
Barrel: 28 in.
Chokes: Three chokes (F, IC, M)
Sights: Fiber optic bar front sight
Weight: 6 lb. 15 oz.
Bore/Gauge: 12
Magazine: 4 shells
Features: Drop at heel is adjustable; in black, Realtree Max-5, or Mossy Oak Bottomland synthetic stocks or A-grade satin-finished walnut; chambers 3-inch shells
MSRP $789.00

INSTINCT CATALYST
Action: Over/under
Stock: Walnut
Barrel: 28 in.
Chokes: IC, M, F
Weight: 7 lb. 3 oz.
Bore/Gauge: 12
Magazine: 2 shells
Features: Redesigned stock with a drop, cast, pitch, length-of-pull, and grip length that better align with a woman's body; red, fiber optic front sights; auto ejectors; automatic safety
MSRP $1469.00

SHOTGUNS

Franchi

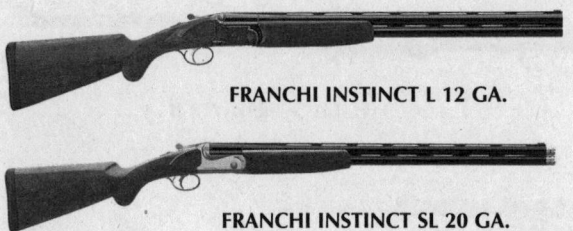

FRANCHI INSTINCT L 12 GA.

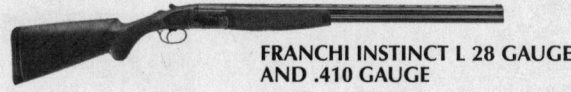

FRANCHI INSTINCT L 28 GAUGE
AND .410 GAUGE

FRANCHI INSTINCT SL 20 GA.

INSTINCT L

Action: Over/under
Stock: Walnut
Barrel: 26 in., 28 in.
Chokes: Interchangeable (IC, M, F)
Weight: 6 lb. 2 oz.–6 lb. 6 oz.
Bore/Gauge: 12, 20, 28, .410
Magazine: 2 shells
Features: Ventilated raised rib; red fiber optic front sight; blued and color-case-hardened finish on the receiver, with gold inlay; A-grade walnut stock in Prince-of-Wales style with cut checkering on the forend and pistol grip; satin oil finish; single gold-plated trigger; chrome-lined barrels proofed for steel shot; hard-shell custom-fitted gun case included
MSRP . . . . **$1299.00–$1569.00**

INSTINCT SL

Action: Over/under
Stock: Walnut
Barrel: 26 in., 28 in.
Chokes: Interchangeable (IC, M, F)
Weight: 5 lb. 6 oz.–5 lb. 11 oz.
Bore/Gauge: 12, 16, 20
Magazine: 2 shells
Features: Vent rib; red fiber optic front bead; aluminum alloy receiver; blued barrels; AA-grade satin walnut stock in Prince-of-Wales style with cut checkering and oil finish; tang-mounted automatic safety; custom-fitted, hard-shell gun case included
MSRP . . . . **$1599.00–$1729.00**

Henry Repeating Arms Co.

HENRY REPEATING ARMS
LEVER ACTION .410
SHOTGUN

HENRY REPEATING ARMS SINGLE SHOT
SHOTGUN IN STEEL & BRASS

LEVER ACTION .410 SHOTGUN

Action: Lever
Stock: Walnut
Barrel: 20 in., 24 in.
Chokes: None
Weight: 7 lb. 5 oz.–7 lb. 8 oz.
Bore/Gauge: .410
Magazine: 5 shells
Features: Available in standard and carbine barrel lengths; brass bead front sight; pistol grip stock; long version has a smooth Full constriction; carbine length has a smooth Cylinder constriction
MSRP . . . . **$893.00–$947.00**

SINGLE SHOT SHOTGUN IN STEEL & BRASS

Action: Break-open single-shot
Stock: Walnut
Barrel: 26 in., 28 in.
Chokes: 1 (varies with gauge)
Weight: 6 lb. 10 oz.–6 lb. 12 oz.
Bore/Gauge: 12, 20, .410
Magazine: 1 shell
Features: Sharing the same action as the single-shot rifle but chambered for 12-ga. 20-ga., and .410-bore shotshells; front brass bead; steel models have pistol grip, brass models sport a straight grip; Rem-Choke style threaded chokes
Steel: **$448.00**
Brass: **$576.00**

Israel Weapon Industries (IWI)

ISRAEL WEAPON INDUSTRIES
(IWI) TAVOR TS 12

TAVOR TS 12

Action: Semiautomatic
Stock: Synthetic
Barrel: 18.5 in.
Chokes: One
Sights: None
Weight: 8 lb.
Bore/Gauge: 12
Magazine: 15 shells
Features: Triple-magazine bullpup semiauto shotgun; each magazine can hold a maximum of four 3-in. or five 2.75-in. 12-ga. shells and can be both fed and unloaded from either side; available in black, Flat Dark Earth, and OD Green
MSRP **$1399.00**

Ithaca Gun Company

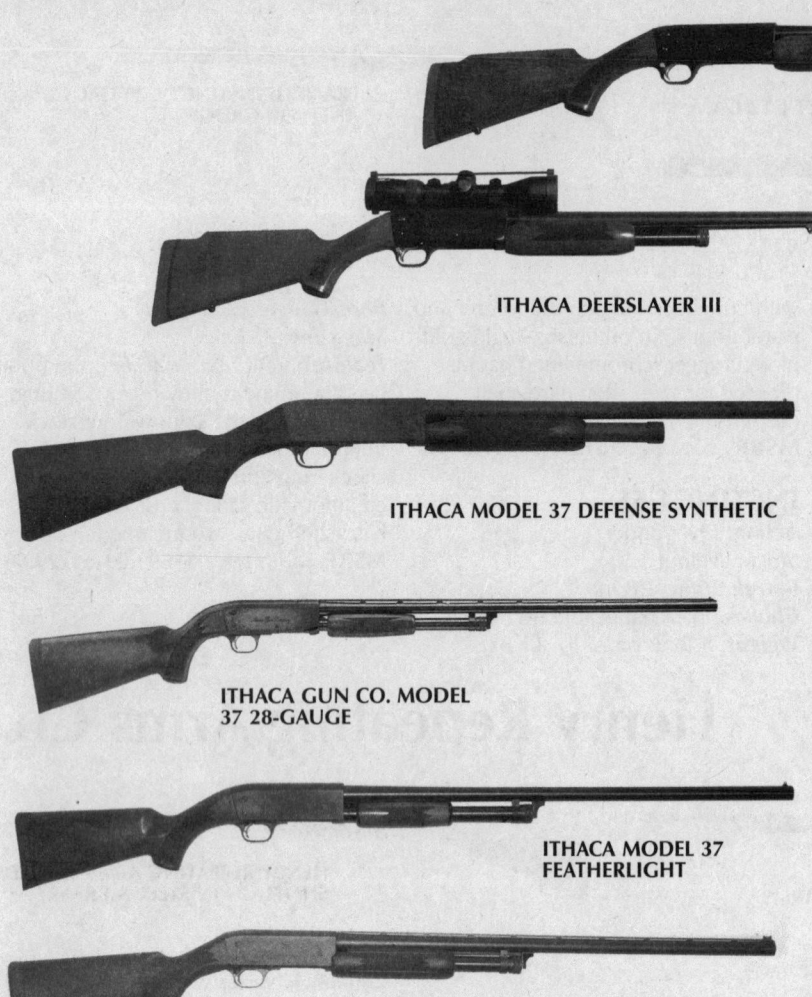

ITHACA DEERSLAYER II

ITHACA DEERSLAYER III

ITHACA MODEL 37 DEFENSE SYNTHETIC

ITHACA GUN CO. MODEL 37 28-GAUGE

ITHACA MODEL 37 FEATHERLIGHT

ITHACA MODEL 37 WATERFOWL

DEERSLAYER II

Action: Pump
Stock: Walnut
Barrel: 24 in.
Chokes: None
Weight: 6.8 lb.–8 lb. 6 oz.
Bore/Gauge: 12, 20
Magazine: 4+1 shells
Features: Solderless barrel system; thumbhole or standard black walnut Monte Carlo stock; fat deluxe checkered forend; sling swivel studs; Pachmayr 750 Decelerator recoil pad; matte blued finish on barrel; gold-plated trigger; Marble Arms rifle sights; drilled and tapped for Weaver #62 scope rail
MSRP . . . . $1150.00–$1500.00

DEERSLAYER III

Action: Pump
Stock: Walnut

Barrel: 20 in., 26 in., 28 in.
Chokes: None
Weight: 8.1 lb.–9 lb. 8 oz.
Bore/Gauge: 12, 20
Magazine: 4+1 shells
Features: Heavy-walled, fluted, fixed barrel in blue matted finish; walnut Monte Carlo stock with optional thumbhole; Pachmayr 750 Decelerator recoil pad; sling swivel studs; gold-plated trigger; Weaver #62 rail pre-installed on receiver
MSRP . . . . $1350.00–$1700.00

MODEL 37 28-GAUGE

Action: Pump
Stock: Walnut
Barrel: 24 in., 26 in., 28 in.
Chokes: N/A
Sights: Bead
Weight: N/A
Bore/Gauge: 28

Magazine: 4 shells
Features: Choice of A, AA, or AAA walnut; chrome finish with light engraving at the edges of the receiver; available in blue
Blue: . . . . $1145.00–$1495.00
Chrome: . . . . . . $1945.00–$2395.00

MODEL 37 DEFENSE

Action: Pump
Stock: Walnut
Barrel: 18.5 in., 20 in.
Chokes: None
Weight: 6.5 lb.–7 lb. 2 oz.
Bore/Gauge: 12, 20
Magazine: 4+1 or 7+1 shells
Features: Choice of walnut or black synthetic stock; 3 in. chamber; matte blued finish barrel; Pachmayr decelerator recoil pad
MSRP . . . . $784.00–$855.00

MODEL 37 FEATHERLIGHT

Action: Pump
Stock: Walnut
Barrel: 26 in., 28 in., 20 in.
Chokes: 3 Briley Choke tubes (F, M, IC, and wrench)
Weight: 6.1 lb.–7 lb. 10 oz.
Bore/Gauge: 12, 16, 20, 28
Magazine: 4+1 rounds
Features: Solderless shells system; classic game scene engraving; black walnut stock with semi-pistol butt stock; TruGlo red front sight; Pachmayr 752 Decelerator recoil pad
MSRP . . . . $895.00–$1495.00

MODEL 37 WATERFOWL

Action: Pump
Stock: Camo, synthetic black
Barrel: 28 in., 30 in.
Chokes: Briley choke tubes
Weight: 7 lb. 3 oz.–7 lb. 6 oz.
Bore/ Gauge: 12, 20
Magazine: 4+1 shells
Features: 3 in. chamber; gold plated trigger; gamescene engraving; permaguard protection
MSRP $865.00

Iver Johnson Arms

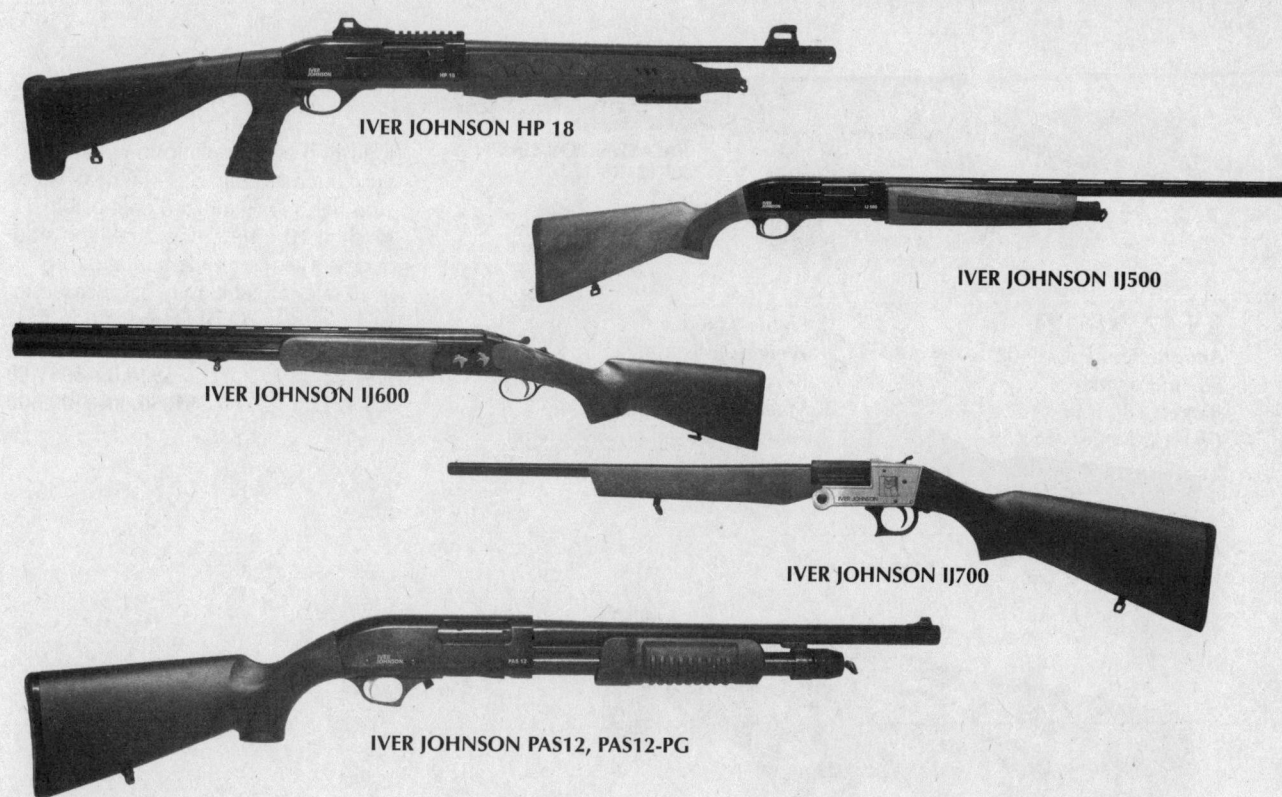

IVER JOHNSON HP 18

IVER JOHNSON IJ500

IVER JOHNSON IJ600

IVER JOHNSON IJ700

IVER JOHNSON PAS12, PAS12-PG

HP 18

Action: Semiautomatic
Stock: Synthetic
Barrel: 18.5 in.
Chokes: N/A
Weight: 6 lb. 6 oz.
Bore/Gauge: 12, 20
Magazine: 5+1 shells
Features: High grade alloy receiver for reduced weight; two-piece detachable pistol grip stock; rubber buttpad on the stock to help reduce felt recoil; Picatinny rail on top of the receiver, with a fully adjustable white dot rear sight; fiber optic front sight; finger grooves on the forend to ensure a solid grip while firing; muzzle break externally threaded onto the barrel; 12-ga. available in black or Digital Tan, 20-ga. in black only
Black:. **$385.00**
Digital Tan 12-ga.:. **$486.00**

IJ500

Action: Semiautomatic
Stock: Walnut
Barrel: 28 in.
Chokes: 3 internally threaded choke tubes (F, IM, M)
Weight: 7 lb. 2 oz.
Bore/Gauge: 12

Magazine: 5+1 shells
Features: Front brass bead sight; checkered stock and forend; chambered for 2 ¾" and 3" shotshells. —12-ga. now available in synthetic stock in Max-4 camo.
Wood stock: **$385.00**
Max-4 camo: **$486.00**

IJ600

Action: Over/under
Stock: Walnut
Barrel: 28 in.
Chokes: 5 internal (F, IM, M, IC, C)
Weight: 6 lb. 1 oz.–7 lb. 5 oz.
Bore/Gauge: 12, 20, .410
Magazine: N/A
Features: Vent rib on top and bottom barrel; extractors on both barrels; engraved receiver with birds accented in gold colored coating; selector switch located on the safety for choosing which barrel fires first; checkered stock and forend; sling swivel on barrel and stock; 20 gauge has a scaled down receiver, stock, and forend
MSRP. **$527.00**

IJ700

Action: Break-open single-shot

Stock: Walnut
Barrel: 18 in., 26 in.
Chokes: None
Weight: 4 lb. 8 oz.–4 lb. 14 oz.
Bore/Gauge: .410
Magazine: 1 shell
Features: Silver receiver; blued barrel; single extractor; sling swivels
MSRP. **$180.00**

PAS12, PAS12-PG

Action: Pump
Stock: Synthetic
Barrel: 18 in.
Chokes: N/A
Sights: Blade front
Weight: 6 lb.
Bore/Gauge: 12
Magazine: 4 shells
Features: Lightweight alloy frame; chambers 3-in. shells; forend is grooved and belled on the back end to ensure proper stroking of the action; PAS12 is available with or without a muzzle brake; PAS12 PG is equipped with a pistol grip; PAS12 standard barrel is available in all-over satin nickel
PAS12: **$257.00**
PAS12-PG: . . . . **$277.00–$439.00**

Kalashnikov USA

**KALASHNIKOV USA
KS-12, KS-12T**

KS-12, KS-12T
Action: Semiautomatic
Stock: Polymer
Barrel: 18.25 in.
Chokes: None

Sights: Fixed
Weight: 8 lb. 8 oz.
Bore/Gauge: 12
Magazine: 5 shells
Features: Based on historical

Kalashnikov rifle platform goes shotgun; threaded barrel; T–Tactical–version has a skeletonized collapsible stock, a 10-round magazine, and side accessory rails on the handguard; available in black; may be released in OD Green and Flat Dark Earth in the future
KS-12: . . . . $936.00–$961.00
KS-12T:. . . . . $1050.00–$1099.00

Kel-Tec

KEL-TEC KSG

KEL-TEC KSG-25

KEL-TEC KSG-NR

KSG
Action: Pump
Stock: Glass reinforced nylon
Barrel: 18.5 in.
Chokes: Cylinder bore
Weight: 6 lb. 14.4 oz.-8 lb. 8 oz.
Bore/Gauge: 12 gauge (3 in.)
Magazine: 6+6+1
Features: KSG receiver is made from hardened steel and includes the magazine tubes which have been welded in place; pump action feeds from either the left or right tube
MSRP. $990.00

KSG-25
Action: Pump
Stock: Synthetic
Barrel: 30 in.
Chokes: None
Weight: 9 lb. 4 oz.
Bore/Gauge: 12
Magazine: 21, 25 shells
Features: Magpul MBUS and an RVG vertical grip on the pump; 3-in. chambers; holds a full box of 2 ¾-in. or 3-in. shells
MSRP. $1400.00

KSG-NR
Action: Pump
Stock: Polymer
Barrel: 18.5 in.
Chokes: Choke adapter
Weight: 6 lb. 13 oz.
Bore/Gauge: 12
Magazine: 4+4+1
Features: Shortened forend and magazine tubes; integral vertical foregrip; built-in flashlight
MSRP. $1299.00

Krieghoff

KRIEGHOFF K-20 SPORTER

KRIEGHOFF K-20 PRO-SPORTER

KRIEGHOFF K-80 ACS

KRIEGHOFF K-80 SPORTER

KRIEGHOFF KX-6

Chokes: Steel or Titanium choke tubes (C, S, IC, LM, M, LIM, IM, F, SF)
Weight: 8 lb. 4 oz.
Bore/Gauge: 12
Magazine: 2 shells
Features: White pearl front sight and metal center bead; nickel-plated steel receiver with satin grey finish; single select trigger; top-tang push button safety; fine-checkered Turkish walnut
From: . . . . $11295.00–$17995.00

K-80 ACS COMBO
Action: Single barrel
Stock: Walnut
Barrel: 30 in., 32 in., 34 in.
Chokes: 8 factory steel choke tubes
Weight: 8 lb. 12 oz.
Bore/Gauge: 12
Magazine: 2 shells
Features: White pearl front bead and metal center bead sight; case-hardened action, nickel-plated steel receiver with nitride silver finish; single selective trigger; Combo is a an over/under and Unsingle.
From: $17995.00

KX-6
Action: Single-shot trap
Stock: Walnut
Barrel: 34 in.
Chokes: IM, LIM, F
Weight: 8 lb. 12 oz.
Bore/Gauge: 12
Magazine: 1 shell
Features: White pearl front sight and metal center bead; case hardened, long lasting black nitro carbonized finish; semiautomatic ejector; adjustable tapered rib; readily available add-ons include adjustable butt-plate, installed release trigger, and upgraded titanium choke tubes
MSRP . . . . **starting at $6495.00**

K-20 PRO-SPORTER
Action: Over/under
Stock: Walnut
Barrel: 30 in., 32 in.
Chokes: Titanium choke tubes
Weight: 8 lb.
Bore/Gauge: 20, 28, .410
Magazine: 2 shells
Features: Higher rib and stock allows shooter to keep their head more erect, increasing sight range, allowing for quicker target acquisition, reduced neck fatigue, and perceived recoil; high rib easily adjustable
Single gauge: $12395.00
Two-gauge set: $17725.00
Three-gauge set: $22995.00

K-20 SPORTER
Action: Over/under
Stock: Walnut

Barrel: 30 in., 32 in.
Chokes: 5 choke tubes (C, S, IC, LM, M, LIM, IM, F)
Weight: 7 lb. 8 oz.
Bore/Gauge: 20, 28, .410
Magazine: 2 shells
Features: Top-tang push safety button; classic scroll engraving; white pearl front bead and metal center bead; single-selective mechanical trigger; hand-checkered select European walnut stock with satin epoxy finish
Single gauge: . . **starting at $11995.00**
2-gauge set: . . . **starting at $16925.00**
3-gauge set: . . . **starting at $21795.00**

K-80
Action: Over/under
Stock: Walnut
Barrel: 30 in., 32 in., 34 in.

K-Var

K-VAR VEPR 12

VEPR 12
Action: Semiautomatic
Stock: Synthetic
Barrel: 19 in.

Chokes: Cylinder
Weight: 6 lb. 14 oz.
Bore/Gauge: 12
Magazine: 5+1 shells
Features: AK safety selector with

levers on both sides for easy operation; ability to insert magazines straight into the magazine well without canting; RPK-style windage adjustable rear sights; windage and elevation adjustable front sights integrated to the gas block; Picatinny rail incorporated into the hinged dust cover; left-side folding tubular buttstock with cheek rest and sling loop
MSRP $1199.00

Ljutic

LJUTIC ADJUSTABLE RIB MONO GUN

LJUTIC MONO GUN

LJUTIC PRO 3

ADJUSTABLE RIB MONO GUN
Action: Single barrel
Stock: Walnut
Barrel: 34 in.
Chokes: Fixed or Ljutic SIC
Weight: 10 lb.
Bore/Gauge: .740, 12
Magazine: 1 shell
Features: "One Touch" adjustable rib allows you to change your point-of-impact; adjustable comb stock
MSRP: $8500.00

MONO GUN
Action: Single barrel
Stock: Walnut
Barrel: 32 in.–34 in.
Chokes: Optional screw in chokes (Fixed, Ljutic SIC, Briley SIC)
Weight: 10 lb.
Bore/Gauge: .740, 12
Magazine: 1 shell
Features: Comes with American walnut wood; optional roll over combs and cheek pieces; various upgrades available
Mono: $7495.00
Stainless: $8495.00

PRO 3
Action: Single barrel
Stock: Walnut
Barrel: 34 in.
Chokes: 4 Briley Series 12 chokes
Weight: 9 lb.
Bore/Gauge: .740, 12
Magazine: 1 shell
Features: Aluminum baseplate; interchangeable two-pad system; adjustable comb; English or American walnut stock; screw in hinge pin; stainless or blued barrel
Blued barrel: $8495.00
Stainless: $8995.00

Merkel

MERKEL 147EL

147EL
Action: Side-by-side
Stock: Wood
Barrel: 27 in., 28 in.

Chokes: Steel-shot proofed chokes
Weight: 6 lb. 3 oz.
Bore/Gauge: 12, 16 ga.
Magazine: None

Features: English stock finished with fine hand-cut checkering at buttplate; silver monogram plate; steel action is gray nitrated; Anson & Deeley locks; Greener-style cross bolt and double bottom bite; double trigger; automatic safety
12-gauge: $8885.00
16-gauge: $9315.00

Mossberg (O. F. Mossberg & Sons)

MOSSBERG 500 ATI TACTICAL

500 ATI TACTICAL
Action: Pump
Stock: Synthetic
Barrel: 18.5 in.
Chokes: Cylinder

Weight: 6 lb. 12 oz.
Bore/Gauge: 12
Magazine: 5 shells
Features: ATI TacLite six-position adjustable buttstock; Scorpion Recoil ATI Akita fore-end; heat shield; top-

side and muzzle-end rails; three-shell side-saddle; in Flat Dark Earth or Destroyer Gray
MSRP: $588.00

SHOTGUNS

Mossberg (O. F. Mossberg & Sons)

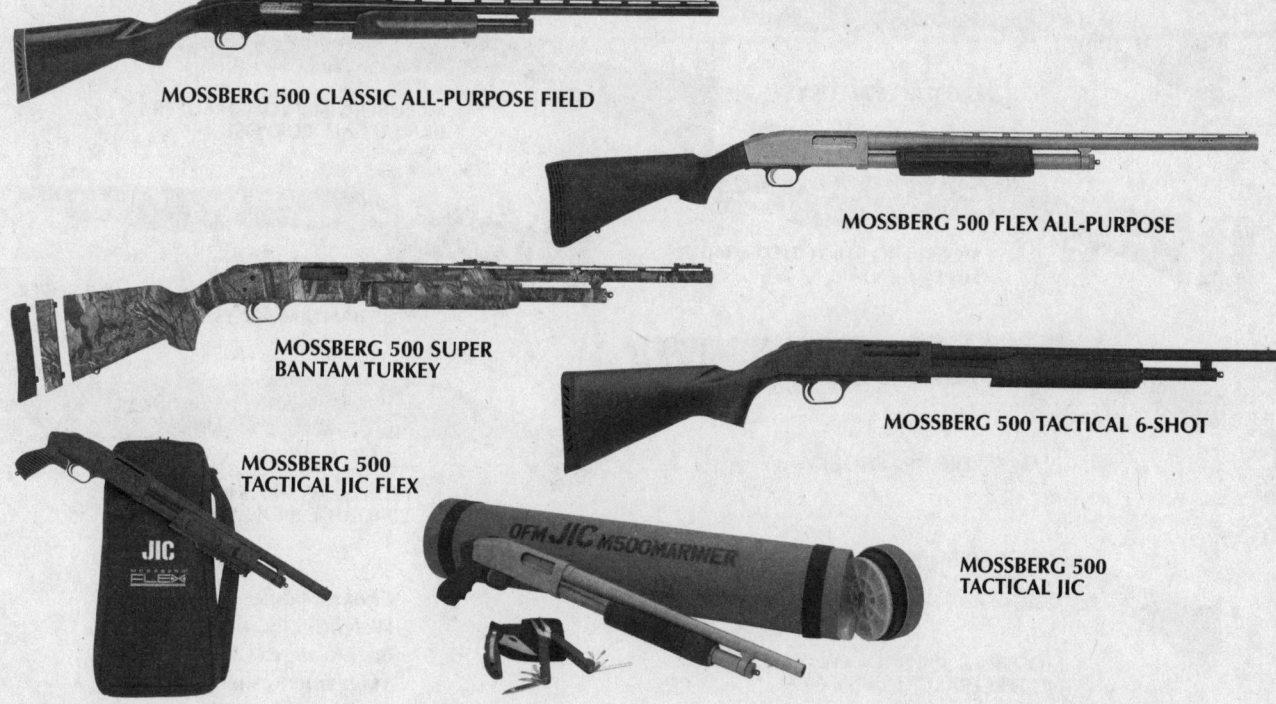

MOSSBERG 500 CLASSIC ALL-PURPOSE FIELD

MOSSBERG 500 FLEX ALL-PURPOSE

MOSSBERG 500 SUPER BANTAM TURKEY

MOSSBERG 500 TACTICAL JIC FLEX

MOSSBERG 500 TACTICAL 6-SHOT

MOSSBERG 500 TACTICAL JIC

500 CLASSIC ALL-PURPOSE FIELD

Action: Pump
Stock: Walnut, synthetic
Barrel: 28 in.
Chokes: Interchangeable Accu-Choke tubes
Weight: 7 lb. 8 oz.
Bore/Gauge: 12
Magazine: 5 shells
Features: High-gloss walnut stock and forend; fine checkering on the pistol grip and wrapping around the underside of the forend; classic red recoil pad with white Pachmayr line spacer; distinctive jeweled bolt, gold trigger, and high polished blued metal finish; non-binding twin action bars; anodized aluminum receiver; vent rib Accu-Choke barrel; ambidextrous top-mounted safety; available in MO Break-up Infinity
MSRP $480.00

500 FLEX ALL-PURPOSE

Action: Pump
Stock: Synthetic
Barrel: 28 in.
Chokes: Accu-Set
Weight: 7 lb. 8 oz.
Bore/Gauge: 12
Magazine: 5 shells
Features: Matte metal finishes; stock with medium recoil pad; stock and forend constructed of synthetic with black matte finish; twin bead sights
MSRP $489.00

500 SUPER BANTAM TURKEY

Action: Pump
Stock: Synthetic
Barrel: 22 in.
Chokes: Interchangeable Accu-Choke (X-full and wrench)
Weight: 5 lb. 4 oz.
Bore/Gauge: 20
Magazine: 6 shells
Features: Adjustable synthetic stock in Mossy Oak Obsession; adjustable fiber optic sights; drilled and tapped for scopes; gun lock
MSRP $486.00

500 TACTICAL 6-SHOT

Action: Pump
Stock: Synthetic
Barrel: 18.5 in.
Chokes: None
Weight: 5 lb. 8 oz.–6 lb. 12 oz.
Bore/Gauge: 12, 20 ga., .410-bore
Magazine: 6 shells
Features: Fixed Cylinder bore; matte blue finish; bead front sight; additional pistol grip supplied
12-gauge: $484.00
20-gauge: $485.00
.410-bore: $466.00

500 TACTICAL JIC

Action: Pump
Stock: Synthetic
Barrel: 18.5 in.
Chokes: Cylinder bore chokes
Weight: 5 lb. 8 oz.
Bore/Gauge: 12
Magazine: 6 shells
Features: Bead sight; Marinecote metal finish; comes with multi-tool, survival knife and cordura carrying case; gun lock; swivel studs; black synthetic stock; only pump-action shotguns to pass all U.S. Military Mil-Spec 3443 standards; available with matte blued metalwork
Blue: $500.00
Marinecote: $647.00

500 TACTICAL JIC FLEX

Action: Pump
Stock: Synthetic
Barrel: 18.5 in.
Chokes: C
Weight: 5 lb. 8 oz.
Bore/Gauge: 12
Magazine: 6 shells
Features: Bead sights; FLEX pistol grip; 3-in. barrel with matte black finish
MSRP $507.00

SHOTGUNS

Mossberg (O. F. Mossberg & Sons)

MOSSBERG 500 TURKEY

MOSSBERG 500 YOUTH SUPER BANTAM ALL-PURPOSE

MOSSBERG 510 YOUTH MINI SUPER BANTAM

MOSSBERG 510 YOUTH MINI SUPER BANTAM ALL-PURPOSE FIELD

MOSSBERG 590 SHOCKWAVE

MOSSBERG 590 SHOCKWAVE 20-GAUGE (NON-NFA)

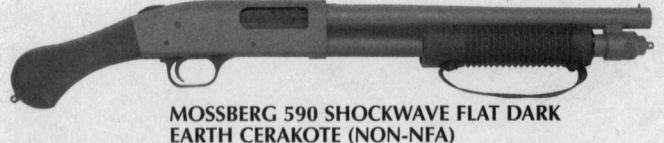

MOSSBERG 590 SHOCKWAVE FLAT DARK EARTH CERAKOTE (NON-NFA)

500 TURKEY

Action: Pump
Stock: Synthetic
Barrel: 20, 22, 26 in.
Chokes: X-Factor; none
Weight: 6 lb. 8 oz.–7 lb.
Bore/Gauge: 12, 20 ga., .410-bore
Magazine: 5, 6 shells
Features: 12-gauge has 20-inch barrel, X-Factor ported choke tube, adjustable fiber optic sights, full-coverage Mossy Oak Obsession; 20-gauge has 22-inch barrel, X-Factor choke, adjustable fiber optic sights, full-coverage Mossy Oak Obsession; .410-bore has 26-inch barrel, fixed Full choke, front fiber optic sight, full-coverage Mossy Oak Bottomland
MSRP: $500.00

500 YOUTH SUPER BANTAM ALL-PURPOSE

Action: Pump
Stock: Synthetic
Barrel: 22 in.
Chokes: Accu-Set
Sights: Bead
Weight: 5 lb. 4 oz.
Bore/Gauge: 20
Magazine: 6 shells
Features: Designed for youth and people with a shorter length of pull; Muddy Girl Serenity camo adjustable stock; Accu-Set chokes; vent rib
MSRP. $458.00

510 YOUTH MINI SUPER BANTAM

Action: Pump
Stock: Synthetic
Barrel: 18.5 in.
Chokes: None
Sights: Bead
Weight: 5 lb.
Bore/Gauge: 20, .410-bore
Magazine: 4 shells
Features: Designed for youth and people with a shorter length of pull; Muddy Girl Serenity camo; adjustable stock; vent rib on the fixed-choke Modified barrel
MSRP. $469.00

510 YOUTH MINI SUPER BANTAM ALL-PURPOSE FIELD

Action: Pump
Stock: Synthetic
Barrel: 18.5 in.
Chokes: Accu-set, Fixed-Mod.
Weight: 5 lb.
Bore/Gauge: 20, .410
Magazine: 3 (.410) or 4 (20 Ga.) shells
Features: Feature shim-adjustable synthetic stocks in black or MO Break-Up Country; all have vent ribs
MSRP. . . . . $419.00–$470.00

590 SHOCKWAVE

Action: Pump
Stock: Synthetic
Barrel: 14 in.

Chokes: None
Weight: 5 lb. 4.8 oz.
Bore/Gauge: 12
Magazine: 6 shells
Features: Features unique Raptor pistol grip
MSRP. $455.00

590 SHOCKWAVE 20-GAUGE

Action: Pump
Stock: Synthetic
Barrel: 14.375 in.
Chokes: None
Sights: Front bead
Weight: 4 lb. 14 oz.
Bore/Gauge: 20
Magazine: 6 shells
Features: Bird's head Raptor pistol grip; strapped forend for additional stability; no NFA paperwork needed
MSRP. $455.00

590 SHOCKWAVE FLAT DARK EARTH CERAKOTE

Action: Pump
Stock: Synthetic
Barrel: 14.375 in.
Chokes: None
Sights: Bead
Weight: 5 lb. 5 oz.
Bore/Gauge: 12
Magazine: 6 shells
Features: Flat Dark Earth Cerakote treatment; Raptor pistol grip; corn-cob forend; forend hand strap; barrel is Cylinder bore; no NFA paperwork needed
MSRP. $504.00

Mossberg (O. F. Mossberg & Sons)

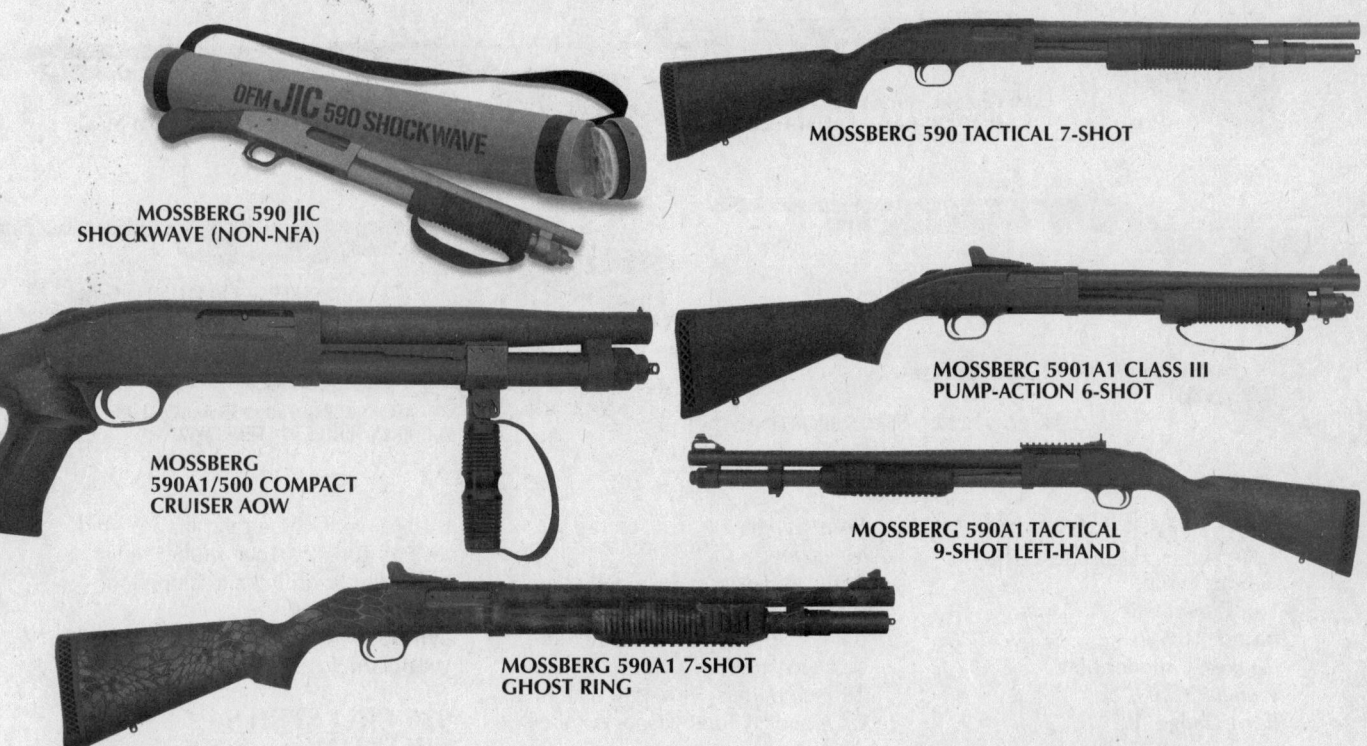

MOSSBERG 590 JIC SHOCKWAVE (NON-NFA)

MOSSBERG 590 TACTICAL 7-SHOT

MOSSBERG 590A1/500 COMPACT CRUISER AOW

MOSSBERG 5901A1 CLASS III PUMP-ACTION 6-SHOT

MOSSBERG 590A1 TACTICAL 9-SHOT LEFT-HAND

MOSSBERG 590A1 7-SHOT GHOST RING

590 SHOCKWAVE JIC

Action: Pump
Stock: Synthetic
Barrel: 14.375 in.
Chokes: None
Sights: Bead
Weight: 5 lb. 5 oz.
Bore/Gauge: 12
Magazine: 6 shells
Features: Mossberg's Shockwave in the Just in Case package; water-resistant carry tube; non-reflective Cerakote Stainless finish on the metal
MSRP $647.00

590 TACTICAL 7-SHOT

Action: Pump
Stock: Synthetic
Barrel: 18.5 in.
Chokes: Cylinder
Weight: 7 lb. 4 oz.
Bore/Gauge: 12
Magazine: 7 shells
Features: Front bead sight; matte blue metal barrel with Heatshield; black synthetic stock; top-mounted safety for amidextrous operation; tri-rail forend
MSRP $455.00

590A1/500 COMPACT CRUISER AOW

Action: Pump
Stock: Synthetic
Barrel: 7.5 in., 10.25 in.
Chokes: None
Weight: 4 lb. 14.4 oz.–5 lb. 4.8 oz.
Bore/Gauge: 12
Magazine: 4, 3 shells
Features: Mossberg's classic pumps in Compact Cruiser versions; dual extractors; twin action bars; anti-jam elevators
500: $735.00
590A1: $805.00

5901A1 CLASS III PUMP-ACTION 6-SHOT

Action: Pump
Stock: Synthetic
Barrel: 14 in.
Chokes: None
Sights: Bead, ghost ring
Weight: 6 lb. 12 oz.
Bore/Gauge: 12
Magazine: 6 shells
Features: fore-end with hand strap; Parkerized finish, 3-inch chamber; heavy-walled Cylinder barrel; Compact Synthetic has 13-in. length of pull and ghost ring sights; Parkerized finish; ghost ring sights; Plus-4 shell-holder stock
MSRP 714.00

590A1 TACTICAL 7-SHOT GHOST RING

Action: Pump
Stock: Synthetic
Barrel: 18.5 in.
Chokes: Cylinder
Weight: 6 lb. 12 oz.–7 lb. 8 oz.
Bore/Gauge: 12
Magazine: 7 shells
Features: Mil-Spec construction; heavy-walled barrel; metal trigger guard and safety buttons; ghost ring or bead sight; comes with Cylinder choke tube and takes other AccuChoke tubes
MSRP $650.00

590A1 TACTICAL 9-SHOT LEFT-HAND

Action: Pump
Stock: Synthetic
Barrel: 20 in.
Chokes: Cylinder bore
Weight: 7 lb.
Bore/Gauge: 12
Magazine: 9 shells
Features: Feature black synthetic stocks; non-binding twin action bars; positive steel-to-steel lock-up and anti-jam elevator; dual extractors; ambidextrous top-mounted safety
MSRP $692.00

Mossberg (O. F. Mossberg & Sons)

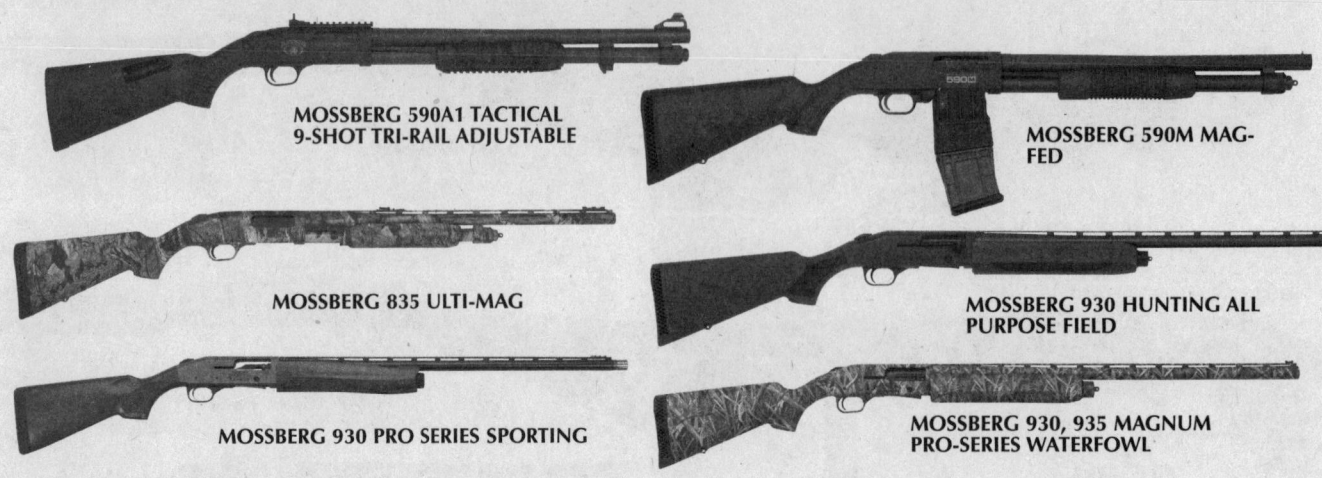

MOSSBERG 590A1 TACTICAL 9-SHOT TRI-RAIL ADJUSTABLE

MOSSBERG 590M MAG-FED

MOSSBERG 835 ULTI-MAG

MOSSBERG 930 HUNTING ALL PURPOSE FIELD

MOSSBERG 930 PRO SERIES SPORTING

MOSSBERG 930, 935 MAGNUM PRO-SERIES WATERFOWL

590A1 TACTICAL 9-SHOT TRI-RAIL ADJUSTABLE

Action: Pump
Stock: Synthetic
Barrel: 18.5 in.
Chokes: Cylinder bore
Weight: 7 lb. 8 oz.
Bore/Gauge: 12
Magazine: 9 shells
Features: Six-position adjustable stock with a tri-rail forend; ghost ring sights; Parkerized finish; speedfeed, black stock; heavy barrel wall; Blackwater logo
MSRP $879.00

590M MAGFED

Action: Pump
Stock: Synthetic
Barrel: 18.5 in.
Chokes: none; Accu-Choke
Sights: Bead; ghost ring
Weight: 7 lb. 12 oz.–8 lb.
Bore/Gauge: 12
Magazine: 10 shells
Features: Detachable double-stack magazine; magazine tube is inactive and serves as support for the pumping action of the fore-end and rails; basic version gets a fixed Cylinder bore with a front bead; heat-shield option gets heat shield, ghost ring sights, a Cylinder Accu-Choke only
Stadard: $721.00
Heat shield: $801.00

835 ULTI-MAG

Action: Pump
Stock: Synthetic
Barrel: 20 in., 24 in., 28 in.
Chokes: Ulti-full tube chokes, Accu-Mag Set, or Modified Tube
Weight: 7 lb. 8 oz.–7 lb. 12 oz.

Bore/Gauge: 12
Magazine: 5 shells
Features: Features 3 ½-inch chambers; dual extractors; over-bored and ported barrels. Variations include Turkey/Waterfowl combo (24- and 28-inch barrels) in Mossy Oak Break-Up Country; Turkey/Deer combo with dual combs and two barrels (one Ulti-Full barrel, one fully rifled barrel with cantilever scope mount, both 24-inch) in Mossy Oak Break-Up Country; Turkey With Marble Arms Bullseye fiber optic sights, 24-inch barrel with Ulti-Full choke, Mossy Oak Obsession; Waterfowl with 28-inch barrel, Accu-Set chokes, fiber optic front sight, Mossy Oak Shadow Grass Blades; All-Purpose Field with choice of 26-inch barrel (Accu-Mag chokes, X-Factor ported turkey choke, Mossy Oak New Bottomland) or 26-inch barrel (Accu-Mag chokes, black stock, matte blued metal)
All-Purpose Field Camo: . . .$603.00
All-Purpose Field Black: $444.00
Turkey With Marble Arms:. . .$542.00
Waterfowl: $518.00
Turkey/Deer Combo: $570.00
Turkey/Waterfowl Combo: . . .$570.00

930 HUNTING ALL PURPOSE FIELD

Action: Semiautomatic
Stock: Synthetic; walnut
Barrel: 28 in.
Chokes: Accu-Set (F, M, IC)
Sights: Fiber optic
Weight: 7 lb. 8 oz.–7 lb. 12 oz.
Bore/Gauge: 12
Magazine: 5 shells
Features: Black-stocked version with a 28-in. vent rib barrel; full-coverage Mossy Oak Bottomland shooter with

a 26-in. vent rib barrel, plus a ported XX-Full Turkey X-Factor tube; sling swivel studs; drilled and tapped for optics mounting
Synthetic stock: $560.00
Wood stock: $706.00

930 PRO SERIES SPORTING

Action: Semiautomatic
Stock: Walnut
Barrel: 28 in.
Chokes: 3 chokes (F, M, IC)
Weight: 7 lb. 12 oz.
Bore/Gauge: 12
Magazine: 5 shells
Features: Chambered in 2 ¾ in. and 3 in.; engraved Cerakote receiver; beveled loading gate; Briley extended chokes; vented rib ported barrel; boron nitride-coated gas piston, piston rings, magazine tube, hammer, and sear prevents corrosion and facilitates cleaning
MSRP. $1061.00

930, 935 MAGNUM PRO-SERIES WATERFOWL

Action: Semiautomatic
Stock: Synthetic
Barrel: 28 in.
Chokes: 3 chokes (F, M, IC)
Weight: 7 lb. 12 oz.
Bore/Gauge: 12
Magazine: 5 shells
Features: Synthetic stock covered in Mossy Oak Shadowgrass Blades; over-bored vent rib barrel; Stock Drop System; Pro Series Waterfowl engraved receivers. 930 model has 3-in. chamber, 935 has 3.5-in chamber
930: $770.00
935: $875.00

SHOTGUNS

Mossberg (O. F. Mossberg & Sons)

MOSSBERG 930 TACTICAL 8 SHOT

MOSSBERG 935 MAGNUM TURKEY

MOSSBERG MAVERICK 88-SECURITY FLAT DARK EARTH

MOSSBERG MAVERICK 88-SECURITY WITH TOP FOLDING STOCK

MOSSBERG SA-20 ALL-PURPOSE FIELD

MOSSBERG SA-20 YOUTH BANTAM WALNUT, SYNTHETIC

930 TACTICAL 8-SHOT

Action: Semiautomatic
Stock: Synthetic
Barrel: 18.5 in.
Chokes: None
Weight: 6 lb. 12 oz.
Bore/Gauge: 12
Magazine: 8 shells
Features: The popular 930 tactical autoloader gets an extended eight-shot magazine
MSRP **$612.00**

935 MAGNUM TURKEY

Action: Semiautomatic
Stock: Synthetic
Barrel: 22 in.
Chokes: Vent rib. overbored
Weight: 7 lb. 8 oz.
Bore/Gauge: 12
Magazine: 5 shells
Features: Chambers 3 ½-inch shells; over-bored barrels; dual vent system; Quick Empty magazine release button; stock spacer system; drilled and tapped receivers; X-Factor choke; adjustable fiber optic sights; standard stock option in Mossy Oak Bottomland or pistol grip stock in Mossy Oak Obsession
Standard stock: **$756.00**
Stock with pistol grip: **$924.00**

MAVERICK 88-SECURITY FLAT DARK EARTH

Action: Pump
Stock: Synthetic

Barrel: 18.5 in., 20 in.
Chokes: None
Sights: Bead
Weight: 6 lb. 4 oz.
Bore/Gauge: 12
Magazine: 6, 8 shells
Features: Six rounds in the 18.5-in. barrel, eight in the 20-in. barrel; Flat Dark Earth stock and forend; chambers 3-in. rounds
MSRP **$245.00**

MAVERICK 88-SECURITY WITH TOP FOLDING STOCK

Action: Pump
Stock: Glass-reinforced polymer
Barrel: 18.5 in.
Chokes: None
Sights: Bead
Weight: 6 lb.
Bore/Gauge: 12
Magazine: 6 shells
Features: Top-folding stock by Advanced Technology International; chambers 3-in. rounds
MSRP **$259.00**

SA-20 ALL-PURPOSE FIELD

Action: Semiautomatic
Stock: Walnut
Barrel: 26 in.
Chokes: 5 chokes (C, IC, M, IM, F)
Weight: 5 lb. 12 oz.
Bore/Gauge: 20
Magazine: 5 shells

Features: Smooth cycling gas-operated system; bead sight; blue finish on barrel; available in walnut or synthetic stocked All-Purpose Field, pink Muddy Girl synthetic stock, a Turkey version in Mossy Oak Obsession, railed versions with and without pistol grips in black synthetic stock, and in a 13-in. length of pull Youth Bantam version with a black synthetic stock
Synthetic: **$588.00**
Wood: **$675.00**

SA-20 YOUTH BANTAM WALNUT, SYNTHETIC

Action: Semiautomatic
Stock: Walnut, synthetic
Barrel: 24 in.
Chokes: Five tubes (F, IM, M, IC, C)
Sights: Bead
Weight: 5 lb. 8 oz. (synthetic), 6 lb. 4 oz. (walnut)
Bore/Gauge: 20
Magazine: 5 shells
Features: Easy recoiling, semiautomatic youth shotgun with shortened stock and barrel; chambers 3-in. shells; synthetic stock has metal with a matte blue finish; high-gloss walnut stock has polished blue metalwork
Synthetic: **$588.00**
Walnut: **$675.00**

Mossberg (O. F. Mossberg & Sons)

MOSSBERG INTERNATIONAL SA-28 ALL PURPOSE FIELD

MOSSBERG SA-28 YOUTH BANTAM
WALNUT, SYNTHETIC

MOSSBERG SILVER RESERVE II FIELD

SA-28 ALL PURPOSE FIELD

Action: Semiautomatic
Stock: Walnut
Barrel: 26 in.
Chokes: Sport Set
Weight: 6 lb. 8 oz.
Bore/Gauge: 28
Magazine: 5 shells
Features: Lightweight field gun in 2 ¾-in.; front bead; high-polish blue metal; high-gloss walnut stock
MSRP. $675.00

SA-28 YOUTH BANTAM ALL-PURPOSE FIELD

Action: Semiautomatic
Stock: Synthetic
Barrel: 24 in.
Chokes: Five tubes (F, IM, M, IC, C)
Sights: Bead
Weight: 5 lb. 8 oz.
Bore/Gauge: 28
Magazine: 5 shells
Features: Easy recoiling, semiautomatic youth shotgun with shortened stock and barrel; chambers 2¾-inch shells
MSRP: $588.00

SILVER RESERVE II FIELD

Action: Over/under
Stock: Walnut, satin
Barrel: 26 in., 28 in.
Chokes: 5, Field set or fixed mod–fixed full
Weight: 6 lb. 8 oz.–7 lb. 8 oz.
Bore/Gauge: 12, 20, 28, .410
Magazine: 2 shells
Features: Corrosion-resistant chrome-lined chambers and barrels, tang-mounted safties with integrated barrel selector, dual locking lugs, and wrap-around receiver engraving; variations include: Combo 12/20 Field, Combo 20/28 Field; all single gauges with extractors
Combos: $1162.00
Single gauge:. $773.00

Perazzi

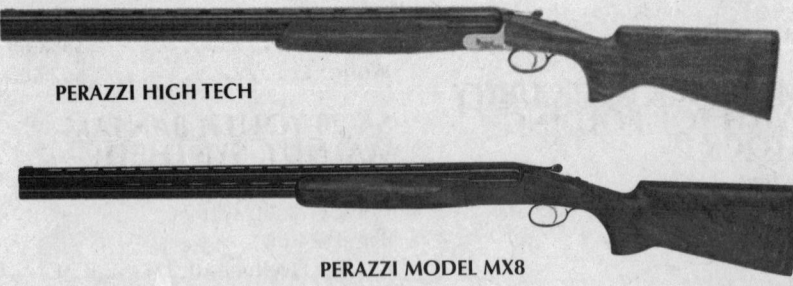

PERAZZI HIGH TECH

PERAZZI MODEL MX8

HIGH TECH

Action: Over/under
Stock: Wood
Barrel: 27–31 in.
Chokes: Can be specified or made interchangeable
Weight: N/A
Bore/Gauge: 12
Magazine: 2 shells
Features:High Tech has a sporty and futuristic look; a large logo engraved in black smoke color on both sides of the receiver, under clear varnish, in contrast to the rest of the receiver; hinge pins are engraved with a checkered design; action is two-tone and varnished "in the white" only in the areas where the logo appears; frame has a greater weight than other Perazzi models and it is distributed within the median line between the grip of the hands, which both improves the fluidity of handling and further reduces recoil; divergent rib that goes from 7mm wide at the action to 10mm at the front end of the barrels allows you to greatly speed up your perception of the target and also expands your field of vision.
MSRP . . . Contact retailers for pricing

MX8 SPORTING CLAYS

Action: Over/under
Stock: Walnut
Barrel: 29 in., 30 in., 31 in.
Chokes: Interchangeable chokes
Weight: 7 lb. 5 oz.
Bore/Gauge: 12, 20
Magazine: 2 shells
Features: Custom walnut stock with beavertail forend; half-ventilated side ribs on barrel; removable trigger with flat or coil springs; blue or nickel plating; Sporting, Skeet and Trap models; 28 Ga. and .410 models also available
MSRP . . . . Contact retailers for pricing

SHOTGUNS

Remington Arms Company

REMINGTON MODEL 11-87
SPORTSMAN FIELD

REMINGTON MODEL 870 200TH ANNIVERSARY
COMMEMORATIVE

REMINGTON MODEL
870 DM

REMINGTON MODEL 870 EXPRESS

REMINGTON MODEL 870 EXPRESS HARDWOOD
HOME DEFENSE

MODEL 11-87 SPORTSMAN FIELD

Action: Semiautomatic
Stock: Walnut
Barrel: 26 in., 28 in.
Chokes: Rem. modified choke
Weight: 7 lb. 4 oz.–8 lb. 4 oz.
Bore/Gauge: 12, 20
Magazine: None
Features: Solid walnut stock and forend with satin finish and fleur-de-lis checkering; nickel-plated bolt and gold-plated trigger; vent rib with dual bead sights
MSRP $815.92

MODEL 870 200TH ANNIVERSARY COMMEMORATIVE

Action: Pump
Stock: Walnut
Barrel: 28 in.
Chokes: Vent Rib Rem Choke
Weight: 7 lb.
Bore/Gauge: 12
Magazine: 4 shells

Features: A-grade walnut stock with fleur de lis checkering; matte black finish; medallion in grip
MSRP $599.00

MODEL 870 DM

Action: Pump
Stock: Synthetic
Barrel: 18.5 in.
Chokes: None
Sights: Front bead
Weight: 7 lb. 8 oz.
Bore/Gauge: 12
Magazine: 3, 6 shells
Features: A fast-cycling pump fed with via a detachable magazine; tactical stock with molded grip areas for enhanced purchase; slim, ribbed forend; barrel is Cylinder bore
MSRP $529.00

MODEL 870 EXPRESS

Action: Pump
Stock: Hardwood, synthetic, laminate, or camo
Barrel: 18 in.–28 in.

Chokes: Modified Remington choke, extra full Rem.
Weight: 5 lb. 12 oz.–7 lb. 8 oz.
Bore/Gauge: 12, 20
Magazine: 2–7 shells depending on model
Features: Single bead sight; standard express finish on barrel and receiver; rubber recoil pad; twin action bars ensure smooth, reliable non-binding action; solid steel receiver; optional thumbhole stock in some models
Express: . . . . $417.00–$468.00
Deer: $417.00
Turkey Camo: $492.00

MODEL 870 EXPRESS HARDWOOD HOME DEFENSE

Action: Pump
Stock: Hardwood
Barrel: 18.5 in.
Chokes: Cylinder bore
Weight: 7 lb. 8 oz.
Bore/Gauge: 12
Magazine: 4 shells
Features: Traditional dark stain hardwood stock; accepts standard 870 replacement barrels without modification; single bead front sight
MSRP . . . . $420.00–$443.00

Remington Arms Company

REMINGTON MODEL 870 EXPRESS SUPER
MAGNUM TURKEY WATERFOWL

REMINGTON MODEL 870 EXPRESS
SYNTHETIC TACTICAL

REMINGTON MODEL 870 SHURSHOT
SYNTHETIC TURKEY

REMINGTON MODEL 870 SP MARINE
MAGNUM

REMINGTON MODEL 870 SPS SUPER SLUG

REMINGTON MODEL
870 TAC-14

REMINGTON MODEL 870 WINGMASTER

MODEL 870 EXPRESS SUPER MAGNUM

Action: Pump
Stock: Hardwood, synthetic, or camo
Barrel: 26 in.
Chokes: Wingmaster HD Waterfowl and Turkey Extra Full Rem chokes
Weight: 7 lb. 4 oz.
Bore/Gauge: 12
Magazine: None
Features: Synthetic stock available in full Mossy Oak Bottomland or Duck Blind camo; HiVix fiber-optics; SuperCell recoil pad; drilled and tapped receiver
Express Super Mag: **$469.00**
Synthetic: **$469.00**
Turkey/Waterfowl: **$629.00**
Waterfowl Camo: **$629.00**

MODEL 870 EXPRESS SYNTHETIC TACTICAL

Action: Pump
Stock: Synthetic
Barrel: 18.5 in.
Chokes: Screw-in tube
Weight: 7 lb. 8 oz.
Bore/Gauge: 12
Magazine: 4–7 shells
Features: Synthetic stock available in A-tacs digitized camo; Tactical Rem. choke SpeedFeed IV; pistol grip stock; SuperCell recoil pad; adjustable XS Ghost Ring sight rail with removable with bead front sight; Picatinny-style rail
Express Tactical: **$420.00**
7-Shot: **$443.00**

MODEL 870 SHURSHOT SYNTHETIC TURKEY

Action: Pump
Stock: Synthetic
Barrel: 21 in.
Chokes: Screw-in tubes
Weight: 7 lb. 6 oz.
Bore/Gauge: 12
Magazine: 4 shots
Features: Ambidextrous Shurshot pistol-grip synthetic stock; rubberized overmolding; SuperCell recoil pad; receiver is drilled and tapped; Weaver rail; sling swivels; Mossy Oak camo
MSRP **$536.00**

MODEL 870 SP MARINE MAGNUM

Action: Pump
Stock: Synthetic
Barrel: 18 in.
Chokes: Cylinder chokes
Weight: 7 lb. 8 oz.
Bore/Gauge: 12
Magazine: 6 shells
Features: Single-bead front sight; padded Cordura; sling swivels; electroless nickel plating covers all metal; twin action bars ensure smooth, reliable non-binding action
MSRP **$841.00**

MODEL 870 SPS SUPER SLUG

Action: Pump
Stock: Synthetic

Barrel: 25.5 in.
Chokes: Wingmaster HD extended Rem Choke
Weight: 7 lb. 14 oz.
Bore/Gauge: 12
Magazine: None
Features: Mossy Oak Tree Stand camo; features ShurShot synthetic pistol grip stock; adjustable TruGlo fiber-optic sights; receiver drilled and tapped for scope mounts
MSRP **$829.00**

MODEL 870 TAC-14

Action: Pump
Stock: Synthetic
Barrel: 14 in.
Chokes: None
Sights: Front bead
Weight: 5 lb. 9 oz.
Bore/Gauge: 12, 20
Magazine: 4 shells
Features: Self-defense shotgun; Raptor grip; Magpul M-LOK forend; Cylinder bore; black oxide-finished receiver
12-gauge: **$443.05**
20-gauge: **$464.00**

MODEL 870 WINGMASTER

Action: Pump
Stock: Walnut
Barrel: 25 in., 26 in., 28 in.
Chokes: Screw-in or fixed
Weight: 5 lb. 12 oz.–7 lb.
Bore/Gauge: 12, 20, 28, .410
Magazine: 4 shots
Features: Twin action bars for non-binding action; receiver machined from solid billet of steel; highly polished and richly blued receiver; wide array of barrel and choke options
MSRP . . . . **$847.00–$962.00**

SHOTGUNS

Remington Arms Company

REMINGTON MODEL 870 WINGMASTER 200TH ANNIVERSARY LIMITED EDITION

REMINGTON MODEL 1100 200TH ANNIVERSARY LIMITED EDITION

REMINGTON MODEL 1100 CLASSIC TRAP

REMINGTON MODEL 1100 SPORTING SERIES

REMINGTON MODEL 870 WINGMASTER CLASSIC TRAP

REMINGTON MODEL 1100 AMERICAN CLASSIC

REMINGTON MODEL 1100 COMPETITION SYNTHETIC

MODEL 870 WINGMASTER 200TH ANNIVERSARY LIMITED EDITION

Action: Pump
Stock: Walnut
Barrel: 26 in.
Chokes: Vent Rib Rem Choke
Weight: 7 lb.
Bore/Gauge: 12
Magazine: 4 shells
Features: C-grade walnut stock with fleur de lis checkering; classic American-style engraving and 24k gold inlay portraying founder Eliphalet Remington; steel floorplate; medallion in grip; limited to quantity of 2016; special serial number; rifle sights; custom box
MSRP $1499.00

MODEL 870 WINGMASTER CLASSIC TRAP

Action: Pump
Stock: Walnut
Barrel: 30 in.
Chokes: Screw-in tube, Rem. Choke
Weight: 8 lb. 4 oz.
Bore/Gauge: 12
Magazine: None
Features: American walnut, Monte Carlo stock; forend with deep cut checkering and a high-gloss finish; twin bead sights; three specialized trap Rem. choke tubes; twin action bars ensure smooth, reliable non-binding action; choke vent rib barrel
MSRP $1120.00

MODEL 1100 200TH ANNIVERSARY LIMITED EDITION

Action: Semiautomatic
Stock: Walnut
Barrel: 28 in.
Chokes: None
Weight: 8 lb.
Bore/Gauge: 12
Magazine: 4 shells
Features: C-grade walnut stock with fleur de lis checkering; classic American-style engraving and 24k gold inlay portraying founder Eliphalet Remington; steel floorplate; medallion in grip; limited to quantity of 2016; special serial number; rifle sights; custom box
MSRP $1999.00

MODEL 1100 AMERICAN CLASSIC

Action: Semiautomatic
Stock: Walnut
Barrel: 28 in.
Chokes: Rem choke
Sights: Front and mid-rib beads
Weight: 7 lb. (20-gauge), 8 lb. (12-gauge)
Bore/Gauge: 12, 20
Magazine: 4 shells
Features: B-grade walnut stock with a scroll-engraved high gloss blue receiver wearing gold accents
MSRP $1682.00

MODEL 1100 CLASSIC TRAP

Action: Semiautomatic
Stock: Walnut
Barrel: 30 in.
Chokes: Screw-in tubes
Weight: 8 lb. 4 oz.
Bore/Gauge: 12
Magazine: None
Features: American walnut stock with cut-checkering; bead blasted top and bottom radius; blued finish on receiver and barrel; gold triggers and gold embellishments on receiver
MSRP $1334.00

MODEL 1100 COMPETITION SYNTHETIC

Action: Semiautomatic
Stock: Synthetic
Barrel: 30 in.
Chokes: 5 extended Briley (Target) choke tubes (Skeet, IC, LM, M, Full)
Weight: 8 lb. 4 oz.
Bore/Gauge: 12
Magazine: None
Features: Nickel-Teflon finish on receiver and all internal parts; barrel has 10mm target-style rib; adjustable comb and cast adjustment options; high-gloss blued barrel; fully adjustable target-style stock with recoil reduction; synthetic polymer stock and forend finished with carbon graphite appearance; twin target-style bead sights
MSRP $1305.00

MODEL 1100 SPORTING SERIES

Action: Semiautomatic
Stock: Walnut
Barrel: 27 in., 28 in.
Chokes: Four Rem choke
Sights: Front and mid-rib beads
Weight: 6 lb. 4 oz.–8 lb.
Bore/Gauge: 12, 20, 28, .410-bore
Magazine: 4 shells
Features: Walnut stocks with a high gloss finish; high-polish blue receivers and barrels; gold-plated triggers; 12 ga. and 20 ga. have a light-contour rib; 28 ga. and .410-bore have a standard vent rib
Light-contour rib: 1254.00
Vent rib: $1315.00

Remington Arms Company

REMINGTON V3 FIELD SPORT SYNTHETIC

REMINGTON V3 FIELD SPORT WALNUT

REMINGTON VERSA MAX COMPETITION TACTICAL

REMINGTON VERSA MAX SPORTSMAN

REMINGTON VERSA MAX MO DUCK BLIND

REMINGTON VERSA MAX TACTICAL

REMINGTON VERSA MAX WATERFOWL PRO

V3 FIELD SPORT SYNTHETIC

Action: Semiautomatic
Stock: Synthetic
Barrel: 26 in., 28 in.
Chokes: Modified
Weight: 7 lb. 4 oz.
Bore/Gauge: 12
Magazine: 3+1 shells
Features: Reliably cycles 12-gauge rounds from 2" to 3" magnum; Versaport gas system regulates cycling pressure based on shell length; light contoured barrel with ventilated rib; twin bead sights; synthetic and synthetic camo available in Mossy Oak Break-Up Country, Mossy Oak Shadow Grass Blades, and Realtree Timber
Black stock: $895.00
Camo stock: $995.00

V3 FIELD SPORT WALNUT

Action: Semiautomatic
Stock: Walnut
Barrel: 26 in., 28 in.
Chokes: Rem choke
Sights: Front and mid-rib beads
Weight: 7 lb. 4 oz.
Bore/Gauge: 12
Magazine: 3 shells
Features: Remington's VersaPort system that regulates gas pressure; satin-finished walnut stock; SuperCell recoil pad; magazine cutoff
MSRP $995.00

VERSA MAX COMPETITION TACTICAL

Action: Semiautomatic
Stock: Synthetic
Barrel: 22 in.

Chokes: IC, M, IM, LM, F
Weight: 8 lb.
Bore/Gauge: 12
Magazine: 8 shells
Features: Enlarged feeding port; "welded" style carrier; enlarged bolt closure button, safety and cocking handle; adjustable XS rear rifle sight; two-shot carbon fiber extension (10+1 shells); QD sling swivel cups on stock and forend
MSRP $1733.00

VERSA MAX SPORTSMAN

Action: Semiautomatic
Stock: Synthetic
Barrel: 26 in., 28 in.
Chokes: Modified Pro Bore Flush Mount; Pro Bore Wingmaster Turkey TXF Extended
Weight: 7 lb. 12 oz.
Bore/Gauge: 12
Magazine: 3+1 or 2+1 shells
Features: VersaPort Gas System; 4140 hammer-forged barrel; SuperCell Recoil Pad. Three versions: Sportsman has black synthetic stock, matte black metalwork, ivory bead; Turkey Camo has full-coverage Mossy Oak Obsession and HiViz fiber optic sights; second camo version in full-coverage Mossy Oak Duck Blind with bead sight
Black: $1066.00
Mossy Oak Obsession: $1222.00
Mossy Oak Duck Blind: . . . $1222.47

VERSA MAX SYNTHETIC

Action: Semiautomatic
Stock: Synthetic
Barrel: 26 in., 28 in.
Chokes: 5 Flush Mount Pro Bore chokes (F, M, IM, LB, IC)
Weight: 7 lb. 12 oz.
Bore/Gauge: 12
Magazine: 3+1 or 2+1 shells

Features: Remington patented gas piston system; black synthetic stock and fore-end with gray over-molded grips; optional full-coverage Mossy Oak Duck Blind or Realtree AP HD camo stocks; drilled and tapped receiver; enlarged trigger guard opening and larger safety for easier use with gloves; TriNyte Barrel and nickel Teflon-plated internal components
Black stock: $1456.00
Camo stock: $1664.00

VERSA MAX TACTICAL

Action: Semiautomatic
Stock: Synthetic
Barrel: 22 in.
Chokes: IC and Tactical ProBore tube
Weight: 7 lb. 12 oz.
Bore/Gauge: 12
Magazine: 8+1 shells
Features: Ventilated rib; fiberoptic HiViz front sight; receiver is drilled and tapped for optics; Picatinny rail; recoil pad; size bolt-release button; oversized trigger guard for easy operation when wearing gloves
MSRP $1456.00

VERSA MAX WATERFOWL PRO

Action: Semiautomatic
Stock: Synthetic
Barrel: 28 in.
Chokes: Extended
Sights: Hi-Viz fiber optic, mid-rib bead
Weight: 7 lb. 12 oz.
Bore/Gauge: 12
Magazine: 3 shells
Features: Chambers up to 3.5-in. shells; Remington's self-cleaning VersaPort system cycles all loads without changing internal components; drilled and tapped; overmold grip panels; oversized bolt handle; safety button; bolt release button; Mossy Oak Shadow Grass Blades
MSRP $1765.00

Savage Arms

SAVAGE ARMS 220 SLUG GUN   STEVENS 301 SINGLE-SHOT

SAVAGE 301 SINGLE-SHOT COMPACT   SAVAGE ARMS STEVENS 320 FIELD GRADE

SAVAGE ARMS STEVENS 320 FIELD GRADE COMPACT

SAVAGE ARMS STEVENS 320 FIELD GRADE MUDDY GIRL

220 SLUG GUN

Action: Bolt
Stock: Synthetic
Barrel: 22 in.
Sights: None
Weight: 7 lb. 8 oz.
Caliber: 20 Ga.
Magazine: 2 shells
Features: Detachable box magazine; adjustable AccuTrigger; button-rifled barrels; left-hand version in black synthetic stock and matte black metalwork; right-hand version in Mossy Oak Break-Up stock and matte stainless metalwork or Mossy Oak Break-Up Infinity with matte black metalwork

Black left-hand: **$629.00**
Camo/stainless right-hand: . . **$799.00**
Camo/black right-hand: **$779.00**

STEVENS 301 SINGLE-SHOT

Action: Single-shot
Stock: Synthetic
Barrel: 26 in. (12-ga.); 22, 24 in. (20-ga.); 22, 26 in. (.410-bore)
Chokes: None
Sights: Front bead
Weight: N/A
Bore/Gauge: 12, 20, .410-bore
Magazine: 1 shell
Features: Break-action single-shot

with a receiver-side safety; synthetic stock; carbon steel barrel
MSRP **$175.00**

STEVENS 301 SINGLE-SHOT COMPACT

Action: Single-shot
Stock: Synthetic
Barrel: 22 in. (Compact); 26 in. (Standard)
Chokes: Interchangeable
Sights: Bead
Weight: 5 lb. 4 oz. (Compact); 5 lb. 8 oz. (Standard)
Bore/Gauge: 12, 20, .410-bore
Magazine: 1 shell
Features: Interchangeable chokes; two-position safety; 3-in. chambers; compact available only in the 20 ga. and .410-bore
MSRP **$173.00**

STEVENS 320 FIELD GRADE

Action: Pump
Stock: Synthetic
Barrel: 26 in., 28 in.
Chokes: M
Weight: 6 lb. 15.2 oz.–7 lb. 7.2 oz.
Bore/Gauge: 12, 20
Magazine: 5 shells
Features: Base model has black synthetic stock; Waterfowl model has stock in Mossy Oak Shadow Grass blades and matte blue metalwork,

mid-length fore-end and fiber-optic front sight;
Black stock: **$238.00**
Waterfowl: **$273.00**

STEVENS 320 FIELD GRADE COMPACT

Action: Pump
Stock: Synthetic
Barrel: 22 in.
Chokes: N/A
Weight: 7 lb.
Bore/Gauge: 20
Magazine: 2 shells
Features: Carbon steel barrel; compact size and light recoil make it the ideal shotgun for introducing young people to the shooting sports
MSRP **$238.00**

STEVENS 320 FIELD GRADE MUDDY GIRL

Action: Pump
Stock: Synthetic
Barrel: 22 in., 26 in.
Chokes: M
Weight: 6 lb. 15.2 oz.–7 lb. 4 oz.
Bore/Gauge: 20
Magazine: 5 shells
Features: Designed for youth and women with shorter length of pull (13.25 in.); bottom load; right-eject pump; dual rails; rotary bolt; Muddy Girl camo
MSRP **$273.00**

Savage Arms

SAVAGE ARMS STEVENS 320 SECURITY

SAVAGE ARMS STEVENS 555

SAVAGE ARMS STEVENS 555 ENHANCED

STEVENS 320 SECURITY

Action: Pump
Stock: Synthetic
Barrel: 18.5 in.
Chokes: M
Weight: 6 lb. 13.6 oz.–7lb.
Bore/Gauge: 12, 20
Magazine: 5 shells
Features: Intended for home and personal defense, five versions available: heat shield with top-side optics rail; ghost ring with pistol grip stock; ergonomic stock with bead sight; ergonomic stock with ghost ring sights; bead sight and pistol grip
MSRP: . . . . $236.00–$276.00

STEVENS 555

Action: Over/under
Stock: Wood
Barrel: 28 in.
Chokes: 5 interchangeable chokes
Weight: 6 lb.
Bore/Gauge: 12, 20, 28, .410
Magazine: 2 shells
Features: Lightweight alloy receiver, Turkish walnut stock & forearm, single selective trigger, mechanical triggers, extractors, manual safetys
MSRP. $692.00

STEVENS 555 ENHANCED

Action: Over/under
Stock: Walnut

Barrel: 28 in. (12-ga.); 26 in. (20- and 28-ga, .410)
Chokes: SK, IC, M, IM, F
Weight: 5 lb. 8 oz.–6 lb.
Bore/Gauge: 12, 20, 28, .410
Magazine: 2 shells
Features: Lightweight aluminum receiver is scaled to gauge; imperial walnut stock; automatic shell ejectors; laser-engraved filigree decoration on the receiver
MSRP. $865.00

SRM Arms

SRM ARMS MODEL 1216

MODEL 1216

Action: Semiautomatic
Stock: Synthetic
Barrel: 18 in.

Chokes: N/A
Weight: 7 lb. 4 oz.
Bore/Gauge: 12
Magazine: 16 shells

Features: Picatinny rail combined with a three face handguard rail; ambidextrous receiver and controls; quad-tube, revolving detachable magazine
MSRP. $1553.00

SHOTGUNS

STOEGER COACH GUN

STOEGER CONDOR

STOEGER CONDOR COMBO

STOEGER CONDOR COMPETITION

STOEGER CONDOR OUTBACK

STOEGER DOUBLE DEFENSE
OVER/UNDER

COACH GUN

Action: Side-by-side
Stock: Walnut, hardwood
Barrel: 20 in.
Chokes: Fixed chokes (IC, M)
Weight: 6 lb. 5 oz.–7 lb.
Bore/Gauge: 12, 20, .410
Magazine: 2 shells
Features: A-grade satin or black finished hardwood stock; brass bead sights; nickel or blued metal finish
MSRP . . . . $449.00–$549.00

CONDOR

Action: Over/under
Stock: Walnut
Barrel: 22 in., 24 in., 26 in., 28 in.
Chokes: Screw-in and fixed chokes on 12 Ga., 20 Ga., 28 Ga. (IC, M), 16 Ga. (M, F), .410 (F&F)
Weight: 5 lb. 8 oz.–7 lb. 6 oz.
Bore/Gauge: 12, 16, 20, 28, .410
Magazine: 2 shells
Features: Walnut stock; brass bead sight; single trigger; auto-ejectors
Condor Field: . . . . $449.00–$649.00
Condor Supreme: $619.00

Condor Youth:. $449.00
Condor Longfowler: $449.00

CONDOR COMBO

Action: Over/under
Stock: Walnut
Barrel: 26 in., 28 in.
Chokes: IC, M
Weight: 6 lb. 9.6 oz.–7 lb. 3.2 oz.
Bore/Gauge: 12, 20
Magazine: 2 shells
Features: Two-gauge combo has barrels for 12- and 20-ga.; satin finished walnut stock; 3-in. chambers; brass front bead
MSRP $649.00

CONDOR COMPETITION

Action: Over/under
Stock: Walnut
Barrel: 30 in.
Chokes: Screw-in (IC, M, F)
Weight: 7 lb. 5 oz.–7 lb. 13 oz.
Bore/Gauge: 12, 20
Magazine: 2 shells
Features: Walnut stock; brass bead with silver mid-bead sight; single

selective trigger; automatic ejector; ported barrel
MSRP $669.00

CONDOR OUTBACK

Action: Over/under
Stock: Walnut, hardwood
Barrel: 20 in.
Chokes: Screw-in (IC, M)
Weight: 6 lb. 8 oz.–7 lb.
Bore/Gauge: 12, 20
Magazine: 2 shells
Features: Notched rear sight and fixed blade front sight; shell extractor; single trigger; A-grade satin walnut or black finished hardwood
MSRP . . . . $469.00–$499.00

DOUBLE DEFENSE OVER/UNDER

Action: Over/under
Stock: Hardwood
Barrel: 20 in.
Chokes: Screw-in chokes (IC/IC fixed)
Weight: 6 lb. 3 oz.–6 lb. 8 oz.
Bore/Gauge: 12, 20
Magazine: 2 shells
Features: Black hardwood stock; green fiber optic front sight; ported barrels; two Picatinny rails; single trigger design; tang-mounted automatic safety
MSRP $449.00

SHOTGUNS

Stoeger Industries

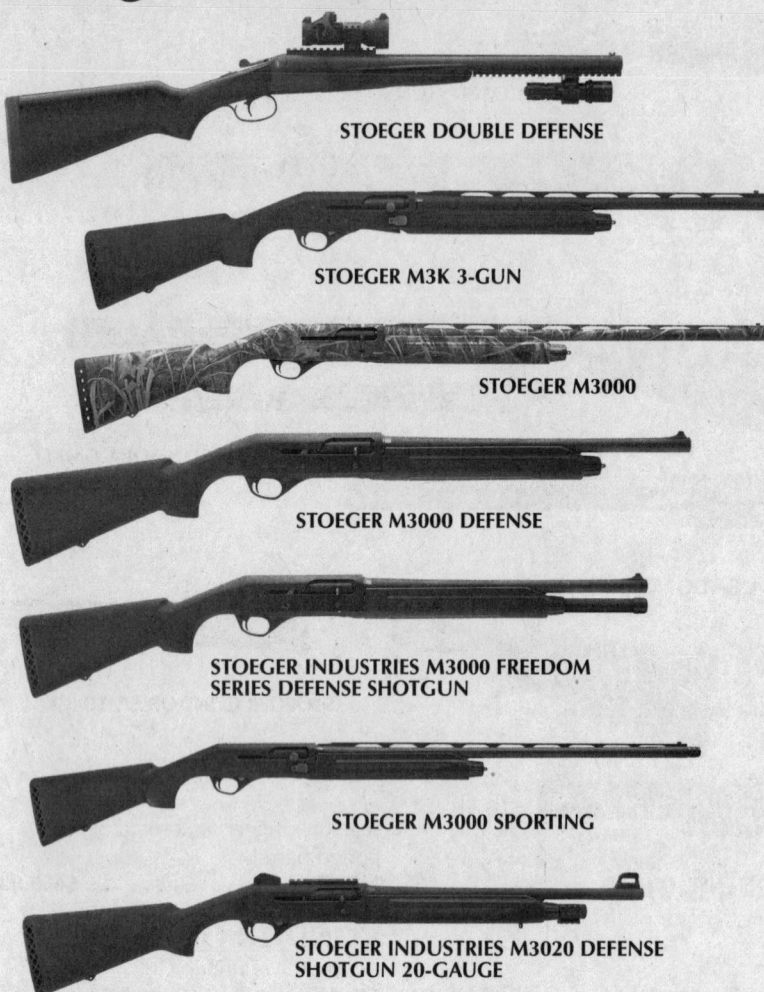

STOEGER DOUBLE DEFENSE

STOEGER M3K 3-GUN

STOEGER M3000

STOEGER M3000 DEFENSE

STOEGER INDUSTRIES M3000 FREEDOM
SERIES DEFENSE SHOTGUN

STOEGER M3000 SPORTING

STOEGER INDUSTRIES M3020 DEFENSE
SHOTGUN 20-GAUGE

DOUBLE DEFENSE SIDE-BY-SIDE

Action: Side-by-side
Stock: Hardwood
Barrel: 20 in.
Chokes: Screw-in chokes (IC/IC fixed)
Weight: 6 lb. 8 oz.
Bore/Gauge: 12, 20
Magazine: 2 shells
Features: Black hardwood stock; fiber optic front sight; ported barrels; two Picatinny rails; single trigger design; tang-mounted automatic safety
MSRP $489.00

M3K 3-GUN, FREEDOM SERIES 3-GUN

Action: Semiautomatic, inertia-driven
Stock: Synthetic
Barrel: 24 in.
Chokes: XC, IC, M
Weight: 7 lb. 5 oz.
Bore/Gauge: 12
Magazine: 4+1

Features: Fiber optic sights; based on the M3000 line of shotguns; 3-gun ready; oversized anodized aluminum bolt release, oversized safety, and extended tactical-style anodized aluminum bolt handle; elongated carrier and enlarged, beveled loading port for quicker and easier reloading
MSRP . . . . $669.00–$699.00

M3000

Action: Semiautomatic
Stock: Black synthetic, Realtree APG, Realtree APG SteadyGrip, Realtree Max-5
Barrel: 24 in.
Chokes: IC, M, XFT, wrench
Weight: 7 lb. 5 oz.
Bore/ Gauge: 12
Magazine: 4+1 shells
Features: Intertia Driven; red-bar front sight; drilled and tapped; shim kit; 3 in. loads
MSRP . . . . $559.00–$669.00

M3000 DEFENSE

Action: Semiautomatic
Stock: Synthetic
Barrel: 18.5 in.
Chokes: Cylinder fixed
Weight: 7 lb.
Bore/Gauge: 12
Magazine: 4 shells
Features: 3-in. chamber; blade front sight; field or pistol grip stock
Pistol grip: $619.00
Standard: $559.00

M3000 FREEDOM SERIES DEFENSE

Action: Semiautomatic
Stock: Synthetic
Barrel: 18.5 in.
Chokes: None
Sights: Blade front sight
Weight: 6 lb. 10 oz.–7 lb.
Bore/Gauge: 12
Magazine: 7 shells
Features: A super self-defense shotgun with a seven-round magazine, blade front sight, fixed Cylinder choke. Includes a stock shim kit included. Available with a pistol grip stock.
MSRP $619.00
Pistol grip: $669.00

M3000 SPORTING

Action: Semiautomatic
Stock: Synthetic
Barrel: 30 in.
Chokes: SK1, SK2, IC
Weight: 7 lb. 8 oz.
Bore/Gauge: 12
Magazine: 4 shells
Features: Built for clay game competition; 3-in. chamber; fiber optic front sight; extended choke tubes
MSRP $669.00

M3020 DEFENSE SHOTGUN 20-GAUGE

Action: Semiautomatic
Stock: Synthetic
Barrel: 18.5 in.
Chokes: None
Sights: Ghost ring sights
Weight: 5 lb. 8 oz.
Bore/Gauge: 20
Magazine: 4 shells
Features: Self-defense shotgun; fixed Cylinder choke; ghost ring sights; chambers 3-in. shells
MSRP $619.00

SHOTGUNS

Stoeger Industries

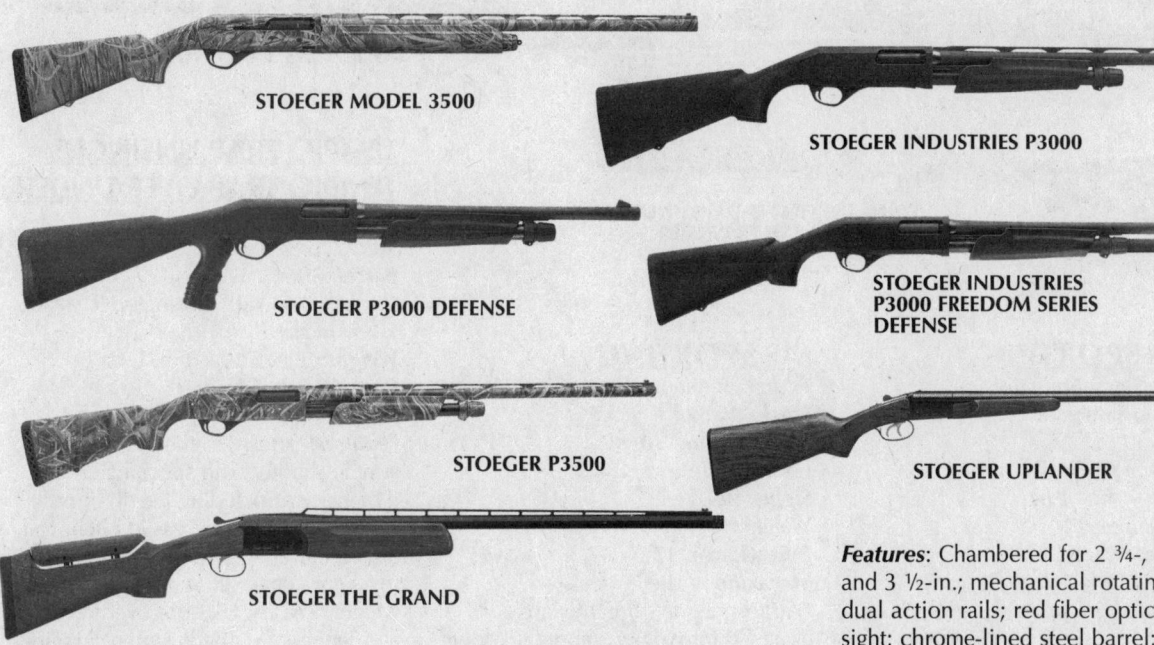

STOEGER MODEL 3500

STOEGER INDUSTRIES P3000

STOEGER P3000 DEFENSE

STOEGER INDUSTRIES
P3000 FREEDOM SERIES
DEFENSE

STOEGER P3500

STOEGER UPLANDER

STOEGER THE GRAND

M3500
Action: Semiautomatic
Stock: Synthetic
Barrel: 24 in., 26 in., 28 in.
Chokes: Screw-in choke tubes (C, IC, M, F, XFT) and wrench
Weight: 7 lb. 7 oz.–7 lb. 10 oz.
Bore/Gauge: 12
Magazine: 4+1 shells
Features: Synthetic stock comes in black or camo finish in Realtree Max-5 or Mossy Oak Bottomland; one Mossy Oak Bottomland version offered with Burnt Bronze Cerakote metalwork; satin walnut stock version available; inertia drive system; recoil reducer; red-bar front sight; Weaver scope base; includes shim kit
Black synthetic: $669.00
Camo or walnut stock: $769.00
Camo with Cerakote:. $799.00

P3000
Action: Pump
Stock: Synthetic
Barrel: 18.5 in., 26 in., 28 in.
Chokes: M inner choke
Weight: 6 lb. 6 oz.–6 lb. 14 oz.
Bore/Gauge: 12
Magazine: 4+1 shells
Features: Chambered for 2 ¾- and 3-in. shells; in black or Realtree Max-5 camo in long barrel options; 18.5-in. barrel option only in black synthetic but with choice of pistol grip or standard buttstock
MSRP . . . . $289.00–$339.00

P3000 DEFENSE
Action: Pump
Stock: Synthetic, wood
Barrel: 18.5 in.
Chokes: Cylinder fixed
Weight: 6 lb. 8 oz.
Bore/Gauge: 12
Magazine: 4 shells
Features: Blade front sight; 3-in. chamber; field or pistol grip stock
Pistol grip, wood: $339.00
Standard: $289.00

P3000 FREEDOM SERIES DEFENSE
Action: Pump
Stock: Synthetic
Barrel: 18.5 in.
Chokes: None
Sights: Blade front sight
Weight: 6 lb. 4 oz.
Bore/Gauge: 12
Magazine: 7 shells
Features: A pump self-defense shotgun with added capacity; fixed Cylinder choke
MSRP $339.00

P3500
Action: Pump
Stock: Synthetic
Barrel: 26 in., 28 in.
Chokes: M
Weight: 6 lb. 14 oz.–7 lb.
Bore/Gauge: 12
Magazine: 4 shells

Features: Chambered for 2 ¾-, 3-, and 3 ½-in.; mechanical rotating bolt; dual action rails; red fiber optic front sight; chrome-lined steel barrel; black or Realtree Max-5
Black:. $339.00
Camo: $389.00

THE GRAND
Action: Break-action
Stock: Wood
Barrel: 30 in.
Chokes: M, IM, F
Weight: 9 lb.
Bore/Gauge: 12
Magazine: 1 shell
Features: Single-barrel target gun designed for shooting trap; stepped ventilated rib and fiber optic front sight; automatic safety that engages when the lever is activated to open the action
MSRP. $629.00

UPLANDER
Action: Side-by-side
Stock: Walnut
Barrel: 22 in. (youth), 26 in., 28 in., 28 in.
Chokes: Screw-in and fixed tubes
Weight: 6 lb. 8 oz.–7 lb. 8 oz.
Bore/Gauge: 12, 16, 20, 28, .410
Magazine: 2 shels
Features: Brass bead sights; A-grade satin walnut stock; tang-mounted safety; single or double triggers; extractors included
Uplander Field: $449.00
Uplander Supreme: $549.00
Uplander Youth: $449.00
Uplander Longfowler: $449.00

Syren USA

SYREN L4S SPORTING

SYREN ELOS SPORTING

SYREN TEMPIO TRAP UNSINGLE AND TEMPIO TRAP OVER/UNDER

ELOS SPORTING

Action: Semiautomatic
Stock: Turkish walnut
Barrel: 30 in.
Chokes: 5 EXIS HP
Weight: 7 lb. 14 oz.
Bore/Gauge: 12
Magazine: 4+1 shells
Features: Turkish walnut stock enhanced by a proprietary TRIWOOD finish, which adds grain and water resistance; TRIBORE HP barrels for the ultimate in ballistic performance; adjustable trigger; lefthand option; 32-in. barrels can be optioned for additional charge
MSRP. $2795.00
Left-hand: . . . . add $150.00

L4S SPORTING

Action: Semiautomatic
Stock: Walnut
Barrel: 28 in., 30 in.
Chokes: N/A
Sights: Bead
Weight: N/A
Bore/Gauge: 12
Magazine: 4 shells
Features: Syren's firearms are designed for women shooters; Monte Carlo comb; slimmed pistol grip; drop and cast dimensions that are better suited to the female form; lefthand model available
MSRP. $1950.00
Left-hand: $2140.00

TEMPIO TRAP UNSINGLE, TEMPIO TRAP OVER/UNDER

Action: Over/under
Stock: Turkish walnut
Barrel: 30 in., 32 in.
Chokes: 3 MAXIS (unsingle); 5 MAXIS (over/under)
Weight: 8 lb. 5 oz.–8 lb. 6 oz.
Bore/Gauge: 12
Magazine: 2 shells
Features: Stock designed to fit the female shooter with specialized dimensions, including length of pull, smaller grip, and increased pitch; calibrated barrel and stock weight; DTS trigger system with two trigger pull weight options, take up, over travel, and length of pull adjustments; hand-polished coin finish with Invisalloy protective finish; 30-in. barreled over/under, 32-in. barrel Unsingle, and combo with both barrel sets
MSRP. $6895.00
Combo: $9680.00
Left-hand: . . . . add $250.00

Taylor's & Co. Firearms

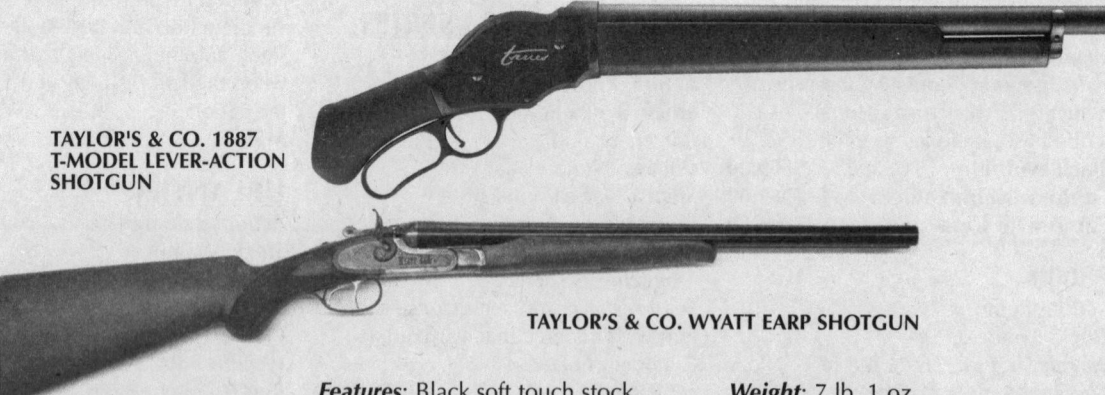

TAYLOR'S & CO. 1887 T-MODEL LEVER-ACTION SHOTGUN

TAYLOR'S & CO. WYATT EARP SHOTGUN

1887 T-MODEL LEVER-ACTION SHOTGUN

Action: Lever
Stock: Synthetic
Barrel: 18.5 in.
Chokes: None
Weight: 7 lb.
Bore/Gauge: 12
Magazine: 5+1 shells

Features: Black soft touch stock, matte blued finish; Bootleg Model
MSRP. $1312.00

WYATT EARP SHOTGUN

Action: Side-by-side
Stock: Walnut checkered pistol grip
Barrel: 20.06 in.
Chokes: N/A

Weight: 7 lb. 1 oz.
Bore/ Gauge: 12
Magazine: 2 shells
Features: Easily opened with one hand for fast shell loading; case-hardened frame stamped with 'Wyatt Earp'; chromed barrel bores with blued finish
MSRP. $1535.00

SHOTGUNS

Thompson/Center Arms

THOMPSON/CENTER PRO HUNTER TURKEY

PRO HUNTER TURKEY
Action: Hinged-breech single-shot
Stock: AP camo with Flextech
Barrel: 24 in. or 26 in.
Chokes: T/C extra full

Weight: 6 lb. 4 oz.–6 lb. 12 oz.
Bore/Gauge: 12, 20
Magazine: 1 shell
Features: Fiber optic sights; 14 in. length pull
MSRP $892.00

TriStar Sporting Arms

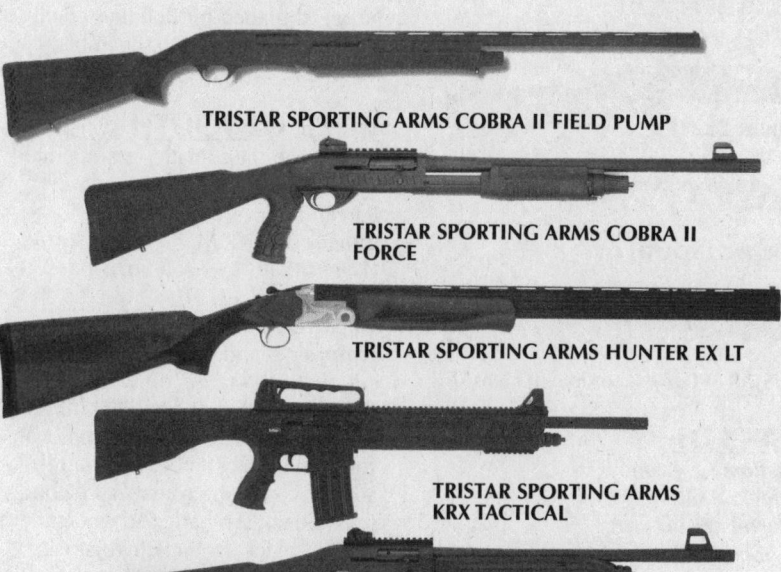

TRISTAR SPORTING ARMS COBRA II FIELD PUMP

TRISTAR SPORTING ARMS COBRA II FORCE

TRISTAR SPORTING ARMS HUNTER EX LT

TRISTAR SPORTING ARMS KRX TACTICAL

TRISTAR SPORTING ARMS RAPTOR A-TAC

Barrel: 26 in.
Chokes: SK, IC, M, IM, F
Weight: 4 lb. 13 oz.–6 lb. 13 oz.
Bore/ Gauge: 12, 20, 28
Magazine: 2 shells
Features: Aluminum alloy receiver; steel hinge and firing pins; chambered for 3 in.; fiber optic sight
MSRP $670.00

KRX TACTICAL
Action: Semiautomatic
Stock: Synthetic
Barrel: 20 in.
Chokes: Extended tactical choke
Weight: 7 lb. 6.4 oz.
Bore/Gauge: 12
Magazine: 5 shells
Features: AR-platform with a 3-in. chamber; controls similar to those of an actual AR; gas-operated; full-length Picatinny rail; removable carry handle; bridge front sight; injection-molded stock and forearm; two detachable magazines
Black: $595.00
Flat Dark Earth: $625.00

RAPTOR A-TAC
Action: Semiautomatic
Stock: Synthetic
Barrel: 20 in.
Chokes: N/A
Weight: 7 lb.
Bore/Gauge: 12
Magazine: 5 shells
Features: Gas-operated; bridge-front sight with fiber optic bead; Picatinny rail mounted on of the receiver with a ghost ring sight installed; fixed pistol grip stock, swivel studs, and a tactical style operating handle; comes with an Extended Tactical Beretta/Benelli style choke; available in Kryptec Typhon and digital camo finishes
MSRP $430.00

COBRA II FIELD PUMP
Action: Pump
Stock: Synthetic
Barrel: 24 in., 26 in., 28 in.
Chokes: 3 Berretta-style choke (IC, M, F)
Weight: 5 lb. 10 oz.–7 lb.
Bore/Gauge: 12, 20
Magazine: None
Features: Replaces the previous Cobra lineup; fiber optic front sight, extended fore-end for easy manipulation, sling swivel studs; Synthetic Pump is a 12- or 20-gauge with a 28-inch barrel in all black; Camo model comes in a 12- or 20-gauge with a standard stock in Realtree Max-5 (3-inch chamber), a pistol grip stock 12-gauge in Advantage Timber, (3-inch chamber), or as a regular stock 12-gauge in Realtree Max-5 with a 3 ½-inch chamber; Youth model comes in 20-gauge in black synthetic or Realtree Max-5

Black: $275.00
Camo: . . . . $335.00–$365.00
Youth: . . . . $275.00–$335.00

COBRA II FORCE
Action: Pump or semiautomatic
Stock: Black synthetic
Barrel: 20 in.
Chokes: External Ported Cylinder choke
Weight: 7 lb. 6.4 oz.
Bore/ Gauge: 12
Magazine: N/A
Features: Capable of operating in pump or semiautomatic mode; 3 in. chamber; picatinny rail; ghost ring sight; raised front bridge sight with fiber optic bead; fixed rubber pistol grip; military sling swivels and swivel studs
MSRP $320.00

HUNTER EX LT
Action: Over/under
Stock: Wood

TriStar Sporting Arms

TRISTAR SPORTING ARMS SETTER S/T

TRISTAR SPORTING ARMS TT-15

TRISTAR SPORTING ARMS TT-15 DT

TRISTAR SPORTING ARMS VIPER G2 LH

TRISTAR SPORTING ARMS VIPER G2 YOUTH

TRISTAR SPORTING ARMS VIPER MAX

SETTER S/T
Action: Over/under
Stock: Walnut
Barrel: 26 in., 28 in.
Chokes: 3-Beretta style tubes (IC, M, F)
Weight: 6 lb. 3 oz.–7 lb. 3 oz.
Bore/Gauge: 12, 20, 28, .410
Magazine: 2 shells
Features: Fiber optic front sight; high-gloss wood; single selective trigger; extractors; ventilated rib
12-, 20-gauge: $535.00
28-gauge, .410-bore: $565.00

TT-15
Action: Over/under, top-single, top-unsingle, or combo
Stock: Turkish walnut
Barrel: 30 in., 32 in., 34 in.
Chokes: 3 or 5 extended Benelli/Beretta chokes
Weight: 7 lb. 13 oz.–8 lb. 14 oz.
Bore/Gauge: 12
Magazine: 1 shell, 2 shells
Features: Monte Carlo stock; fully adjustable comb; elegant hand-engraved receiver with nickel finish; fitted with high-standing 3-point adjustable rib, auto-ejectors, and fiber optic front sight
MSRP . . . .$1040.00–$1420.00

TT-15 DT
Action: Over/under
Stock: Walnut
Barrel: 32 in.
Chokes: 5 Beretta Mobil (F, IM, M, IC, SK)
Weight: 8 lb. 11.2 oz.
Bore/Gauge: 12
Magazine: 2 shells
Features: The newest addition to TriStar's TT-15 line of dedicated trap guns; back-bored barrels; 2 ¾-in. chambers; adjustable high trap rib; four-way fully adjustable buttstock; red fiber optic front sight. Supplied with color-coded, extended Beretta Mobil Chokes
MSRP $1495.00

VIPER G2 BRONZE
Action: Semiautomatic
Stock: Turkish walnut
Barrel: 26, 28 in.
Chokes: Three Beretta-style chokes
Sights: Fiber optic front sight
Weight: 5 lb. 3 oz.–6 lb. 13 oz.
Bore/Gauge: 12, 20, 28, .410
Magazine: 5 shells
Features: High-grade Turkish walnut stock and Cerakote Bronze receiver; tight checkering; shim kits; vent rib with a matte sighting plane; 20-ga. has a 26-in. barrel and chambers

2.75-in; other models have 28-in. barrels and 3-in. chambers.
MSRP . . . . $795.00–$825.00

VIPER G2 LH
Action: Semiautomatic
Stock: Synthetic
Barrel: 28 in.
Chokes: IC, M, F
Weight: 6 lb. 14.4 oz.
Bore/ Gauge: 12
Magazine: N/A
Features: Chrome lined chambers; barrels threaded for Beretta/Benelli style choke tubes; 3 in. chambers
MSRP . . . . $595.00–$685.00

VIPER G2 YOUTH
Action: Semiautomatic, gas-operated
Stock: Synthetic
Barrel: 26 in.
Chokes: SK, IC, M, F
Weight: 5 lb. 11 oz.–6 lb. 3 oz.
Bore/Gauge: 12, 20
Magazine: 5 shells
Features: Manual E-Z Load magazine cut-off; raised target rib w/ matted sight plane; middle bead and fiber pptic sight; quick shot plug removal; chrome-lined chamber and barrel; adjustable comb; available in wood stock, black synthetic, Advantage Timber, black synthetic two-stock combo, and a black synthetic stock Sport model with red metallic finish on receiver and magazine cap
MSRP . . . . $565.00–$640.00

VIPER MAX
Action: Semiautomatic
Stock: Synthetic
Barrel: 28 in., 30 in.
Chokes: Beretta Mobil (SK, IC, M, F)
Weight: 7 lb. 6.4 oz.
Bore/Gauge: 12
Magazine: 4 shells
Features: Gas-operated; 3 ó -in. chamber; heavy and light load pistons; extra piston can be stored in the forearm for instant in-the-field change-out; fiber optic front sight; sling swivel studs; magazine cut-off; Quick Shot plug removal; chrome-lined barrel and chamber; black synthetic stock with black metalwork, Mossy Oak Max-5 full-coverage camo, or Mossy Oak Shadow Grass Blades stock with bronze metalwork
MSRP: . . . . $655.00–$765.00

UTAS UTS-15 BLACK

UTAS XTR-12

UTS-15

Action: Pump
Stock: Polymer
Barrel: 18.5 in.
Chokes: N/A
Weight: 6 lb. 15 oz.
Bore/ Gauge: 12
Magazine: 15 shells
Features: Unique pump action chambers up to 3-in. shells, features dual
seven-round magazines with alternat-
ing or slectible feed, cartridge counter
magazine followers, integrated topside Picatinny rail, spring-assisted pin
ejector, quick-removal fire control
housing, fiber-reinforced buttplate,
internally mounted point-and-shoot
high-intensity lens focused LED spot-
light, and adjustable laser sight; finishes in Flat Dark Earth, Burnt Bronze,
Tungsten grey, OD Green, and Muddy
Girl pink camo
MSRP . . . .$1099.00–$1299.00

XTR-12

Action: Semiautomatic
Stock: Synthetic
Barrel: 20 in.
Chokes: N/A
Weight: 8 lb. 8 oz.
Bore/Gauge: 12
Magazine: 5 shells
Features: Compact forend features a
full-length top rail; machined from
7075 aluminum with standard mil-
spec fire control parts; AR-style adjust-
able butt stock; available in matte
black, burnt bronze, flat dark earth,
OD green, or tungsten finishes
MSRP . . . .$1099.00–$1199.00

Weatherby

WEATHERBY ELEMENT DELUXE

WEATHERBY ELEMENT SYNTHETIC

WEATHERBY ORION I

ELEMENT DELUXE

Action: Semiautomatic
Stock: Walnut
Barrel: 26 in., 28 in.
Chokes: IC, M, F
Weight: 6 lb.–6 lb.12 oz.
Bore/Gauge: 12, 20, 28
Magazine: 3+1 or 4+1 shells
Features: Fiber optic front sight; "AA"
grade American walnut stock; aircraft
grade aluminum; chrome-lined bores;
drop-out trigger system; dual purpose
bolt release; chrome-plated bolt; inertia-operated action; chrome-lined barrel; ventilated top rib; integral multi
choke system with three application
specific tubes (IC, Mod, Full)
MSRP $1099.00

ELEMENT SYNTHETIC

Action: Semiautomatic
Stock: Synthetic
Barrel: 26 in., 28 in.
Chokes: 4 application specific chokes
(IC, Mod, Full, Long Range Steel)
Weight: 6 lb. 4 oz.–6 lb. 12 oz.
Bore/Gauge: 12, 20
Magazine: 4+1 shells
Features: Griptonite stock features pis-
tol grip and forend inserts gray/black
design color; matte, bead blasted finish
MSRP $749.00

ORION I

Action: Over/under
Stock: Walnut
Barrel: 30 in.
Chokes: IC, M, F
Weight: 7 lb.
Bore/Gauge: 12
Magazine: 2 shells
Features: Brass front sights; ambidex-
trous top tang safety; automatic ejec-
tors; low profile receiver; chrome-
lined bores; matte ventilated top rib
with brass bead front sight; traditional
boxlock action; integral multi choke
system with three application specific
tubes (IC, Mod, Full)
MSRP $1099.00

SHOTGUNS

Weatherby

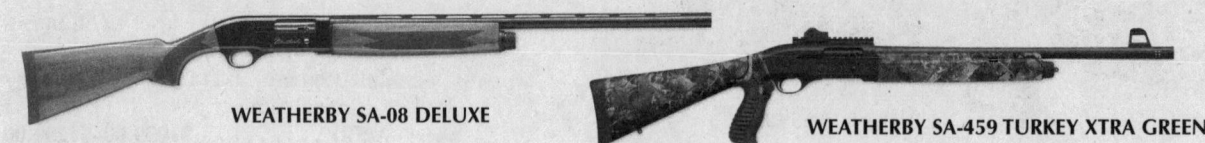

WEATHERBY SA-08 DELUXE

WEATHERBY SA-459 TURKEY XTRA GREEN

SA-08 DELUXE
Action: Semiautomatic
Stock: Walnut
Barrel: 26 in., 28 in.
Chokes: Screw in tubes (IC, M, F)
Weight: 6 lb.–6 lb. 12 oz.
Bore/Gauge: 12, 20
Magazine: None
Features: Walnut stock with high–gloss finish and metalwork; vented top rib dissipates heat and aids in target acquisition; dual valve system
MSRP $849.00

SA-459 TURKEY XTRA GREEN
Action: Gas-operated semiautomatic
Stock: Synthetic
Barrel: 21.25 in.
Chokes: Interchangeable tubes (X-F)
Weight: 6 lb. 4 oz.–6 lb. 12 oz.
Bore/Gauge: 12, 20
Magazine: 4+1 or 5+1 shells
Features: Trimmer forend for easier handling; swivel studs; Mil-Spec Picatinny rail for mounting optics; LPA-style ghost ring rear sight that is adjustable for windage and elevation; front blade sight with fiber optic insert; over-size hourglass-shaped bolt handle for quick and positive chambering; pistol grip stock
MSRP $799.00

Winchester Repeating Arms

WINCHESTER REPEATING ARMS MODEL 101 FIELD

WINCHESTER REPEATING ARMS MODEL 101 DELUXE FIELD

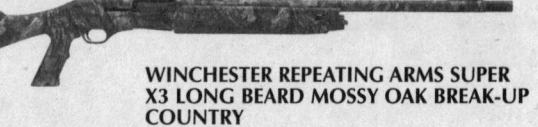

WINCHESTER REPEATING ARMS SUPER X3 LONG BEARD MOSSY OAK BREAK-UP COUNTRY

WINCHESTER REPEATING ARMS SX3 ULTIMATE SPORTING ADJUSTABLE

MODEL 101
Action: Over/under
Stock: Walnut
Barrel: 26 in., 28 in., 30 in., 32 in.
Chokes: Invector-Plus choke system, 3 tubes
Weight: 6 lb. 12 oz.–7 lb. 6 oz.
Bore/Gauge: 12
Magazine: 2 shells
Features: Solid brass bead front sight on Field; Truglo front sight on Sporting; deep relief receiver engraving; high-gloss grade II/III walnut stock; vented Pachmayr Decelerator pad with classic white line spacer
Field: $1899.99
Sporting: $2379.99

MODEL 101 DELUXE FIELD
Action: Over/under
Stock: Walnut
Barrel: 26 in., 28 in.
Chokes: Invector-Plus (F, M, IC)
Weight: 6 lb. 12 oz.

Bore/Gauge: 12
Magazine: 2 shells
Features: Grade III European walnut stock; detailed engraving on steel receiver; back-bored, hard-chromed barrels; front bead; 3-in. chambers
MSRP $1999.99

SUPER X3 LONG BEARD MOSSY OAK BREAK-UP COUNTRY
Action: Semiautomatic
Stock: Synthetic
Barrel: 24 in.
Chokes: Invector-Plus Briley Extra-Full Long Beard
Weight: 7 lb. 8 oz.
Bore/Gauge: 12, 20
Magazine: 4 shells
Features: Synthetic pistol grip stock with textured gripping surfaces; TruGlo front sight; adjustable rear sight; back-bored barrel with hard chrome plated bore and chamber; cantilever scope mount; Quadra-Vent ports; drop-out trigger assembly
MSRP $1269.99

SUPER X3 ULTIMATE SPORTING ADJUSTABLE
Action: Semiautomatic
Stock: Walnut
Barrel: 28 in., 30 in., 32 in.
Chokes: Extended Signature Invector-Plus Choke Tubes
Weight: 7 lb. 6 oz.
Barrel: 30 in.
Magazine: 4 shells
Features: Adjustable comb; cut checkering; matte nickel-plated receiver; signature Red Briley bolt handle, bolt release button, and magazine cap; back-bored technology; ported Perma-Cote gray barrel; vent rib; Tru-Glo fiber optic sight with white mid-bead; hard chrome-plated chamber and bore; active valve system; Pachmayr Decelerator recoil pad; ambidextrous crossbolt safety; drop-out trigger group
MSRP $1869.99

SHOTGUNS

Winchester Repeating Arms

WINCHESTER REPEATING ARMS SUPER X3 WATERFOWL HUNTER

WINCHESTER REPEATING ARMS SX4 UNIVERSAL HUNTER

WINCHESTER REPEATING ARMS SXP BLACK SHADOW

WINCHESTER REPEATING ARMS SX4 NWTF CANTILEVER TURKEY HUNTER

WINCHESTER REPEATING ARMS SX4 WATERFOWL HUNTER

WINCHESTER REPEATING ARMS SXP BLACK SHADOW DEER 20-GAUGE

SUPER X3 WATERFOWL HUNTER

Action: Semiautomatic
Stock: Synthetic
Barrel: 26 in., 28 in.
Chokes: Invector-Plus tube
Weight: 6 lb. 10 oz.–7 lb. 2 oz.
Barrel: 28 in.
Magazine: None
Features: .742 Back-Bored technology; hard chrome chamber and bore; vent rib; TruGlo Long Bead fiber optic front sight; Active Valve Gas System; Quadra-Vent Ports; ambidextrous crossbolt safety; available in full-coverage Mossy Oak Shadow Grass Blades, Mossy Oak Bottomlands, Realtree Max-5 (20-ga.)
MSRP . . . . $1139.99–$1199.99

SX4 NWTF CANTILEVER TURKEY HUNTER

Action: Semiautomatic
Stock: Composite
Barrel: 24 in.
Chokes: One Invector-Plus Extended
Sights: TruGlo fiber optic front, adjustable rear
Weight: 7 lb. 8 oz.
Bore/Gauge: 12
Magazine: 4 shells
Features: Created with input from the National Wild Turkey Federation; 3.5-in. chamber; back-bored barrels; reengineered stock with gripping surfaces; Quadra-Vent ports; cantilever optics mount; drop-out trigger group; stock spacers and one Extra-Full turkey choke are included; full-coverage Mossy Oak Obsession
MSRP $1069.99

SX4 UNIVERSAL HUNTER

Action: Semiautomatic
Stock: Composite
Barrel: 24 in., 26 in., 28 in.
Chokes: Three Invector-Plus flush (F, M, IC)
Sights: TruGlo Long Bead fiber optic
Weight: 6 lb. 8 oz.–7 lb. 2 oz.
Bore/Gauge: 12, 20
Magazine: 4 shells
Features: Full-coverage Mossy Oak Break-Up Country; chambers 3.5-in. shells; Winchester's Active Valve; Quadra Vent ports; stock spacers; oversized bolt handles and release buttons
MSRP $1069.99

SX4 WATERFOWL HUNTER

Action: Semiautomatic
Stock: Synthetic
Barrel: 26 in., 28 in.
Chokes: Invector-Plus (F, M, IC)
Weight: 6 lb. 10 oz.–7 lb. 2 oz.
Bore/Gauge: 12, 20
Magazine: 4 shells
Features: Improved stock ergonomics with smaller pistol grip and textured gripping surfaces; back-bored barrels; vent rib; Active Valve gas system; Quadra-Vent ports; drop-out trigger group; oversized bolt handle; stock spacers; ambidextrous crossbolt safety; Mossy Oak Bottomlands, Mossy Oak Shadow Grass Blades, Realtree Max-5, and Realtree Timber camo finishes; 3- and 3 ½-inch chambers in 12-gauge; 3-inch chamber 20-gauge
MSRP . . . . $939.99–$1069.99

SXP BLACK SHADOW

Action: Pump
Stock: Synthetic
Barrel: 26 in., 28 in.
Chokes: Invector Plus
Weight: 6 lb. 12 oz.–7 lb.
Bore/Gauge: 12, 20
Magazine: 4 shells
Features: Hard chrome chamber and bores; drop-out trigger group for easy cleaning; synthetic stock with non-glare black matte finish on barrel and receiver
MSRP . . . . $379.99–$399.99

SXP BLACK SHADOW DEER

Action: Pump
Stock: Synthetic
Barrel: 22 in.
Chokes: None
Weight: 6 lb. 10 oz.
Bore/Gauge: 12, 20
Magazine: 4 shells
Features: Rotary-bolt pump; fully rifled barrel; alloy receiver; TruGlo fiber optic front sight; adjustable rear sight; three-shot Speed Plug adaptor; drop-out trigger; ambidextrous crossbolt safety; drilled and tapped for scope mounts
12-gauge: $549.99
20-gauge: $519.99

SHOTGUNS

Winchester Repeating Arms

WINCHESTER REPEATING ARMS SXP DARK EARTH DEFENDER

WINCHESTER REPEATING ARMS SXP DEFENDER

WINCHESTER REPEATING ARMS SXP EXTREME DEER HUNTER

WINCHESTER REPEATING ARMS SXP FIELD COMPACT

WINCHESTER REPEATING ARMS SXP LONG BEARD

WINCHESTER REPEATING ARMS SXP NWTF TURKEY HUNTER

SXP DARK EARTH DEFENDER

Action: Pump
Stock: Synthetic
Barrel: 18 in.
Chokes: Fixed cylinder
Weight: 6 lb. 4 oz.
Bore/Gauge: 12, 20
Magazine: 5 shells
Features: Aluminum alloy receiver; 3-in. chamber; front brass bead with removable TruGlo fiber optic sight; finished in Dark Earth
MSRP . . . . $379.99–$399.99

SXP DEFENDER

Action: Pump
Stock: Composite
Barrel: 18 in.
Chokes: Fixed cylinder choked barrel
Weight: 6 lb.–6 lb. 5 oz.
Bore/Gauge: 12, 20
Magazine: 5+1 shells
Features: Uses Foster-type slugs; non-glare metal surfaces with a tough black composite stock; deeply grooved forearm for control and stability
MSRP . . . . $349.99–$379.99

SXP EXTREME DEER

Action: Pump
Stock: Synthetic

Barrel: 22 in.
Chokes: None
Weight: 7 lb.
Bore/Gauge: 12
Magazine: 4 shells
Features: Rotary-bolt pump with fully rifled barrel; alloy receiver; TruGlo fiber optic front sight; adjustable rear sight; three-shot Speed Plug adaptor; drop-out trigger; ambidextrous crossbolt safety; drilled and tapped for scope mounts; 3-in. chamber; synthetic pistol grip stock has textured grip surfaces, two interchangeable cheek pieces, and two length-of-pull spacers
MSRP $559.99

SXP FIELD COMPACT

Action: Pump
Stock: Satin finish
Barrel: 24 in., 26 in., 28 in.
Chokes: Three Invector-Plus chokes
Weight: 6 lb. 4 oz.–6 lb. 10 oz.
Bore/ Gauge: 12, 20
Magazine: None
Features: Aluminum alloy receiver; matte black finish; hard chrome chamber and bore; Speed plug system; brass bead front sight; Inflex technology recoil pad
MSRP . . . . $399.99–$429.99

SXP LONG BEARD

Action: Pump
Stock: Composite
Barrel: 24 in.
Chokes: Invector-Plus flush, extra full
Weight: 6 lb. 14 oz.–7 lb.
Bore/Gauge: 12, 20
Magazine: 4 shells
Features: TRUGLO fiber optic sights; two user-interchangeable combs and height adjust spacers; hard chrome-plated chamber and bore; easily operated crossbolt safety; inflex technology recoil pad; in full-coverage Mossy Oak Obsession or Mossy Oak Break-Up Country; 12-gauge available in both 3- and 3½-inch chamber versions; 20-gauge chambers 3-inch shells
MSRP . . . . $529.99–$559.99

SXP NWTF TURKEY HUNTER

Action: Pump
Stock: Synthetic
Barrel: 24 in.
Chokes: Invector Plus
Weight: 6 lb. 4 oz.–6 lb. 10 oz.
Bore/Gauge: 12, 20
Magazine: 4 shells
Features: Hard chrome chamber and bores; drop-out trigger group for easy cleaning; Invector Plus Extra-Full Turkey Choke Tube; crossbolt safety; Inflex technology recoil pad; synthetic stock with textured gripping surfaces in Mossy Oak Break-Up Country or Mossy Oak Obsession; 12-gauge with 3 ½-inch chamber, 20-gauge with 3-inch chamber
MSRP $519.99

Winchester Repeating Arms

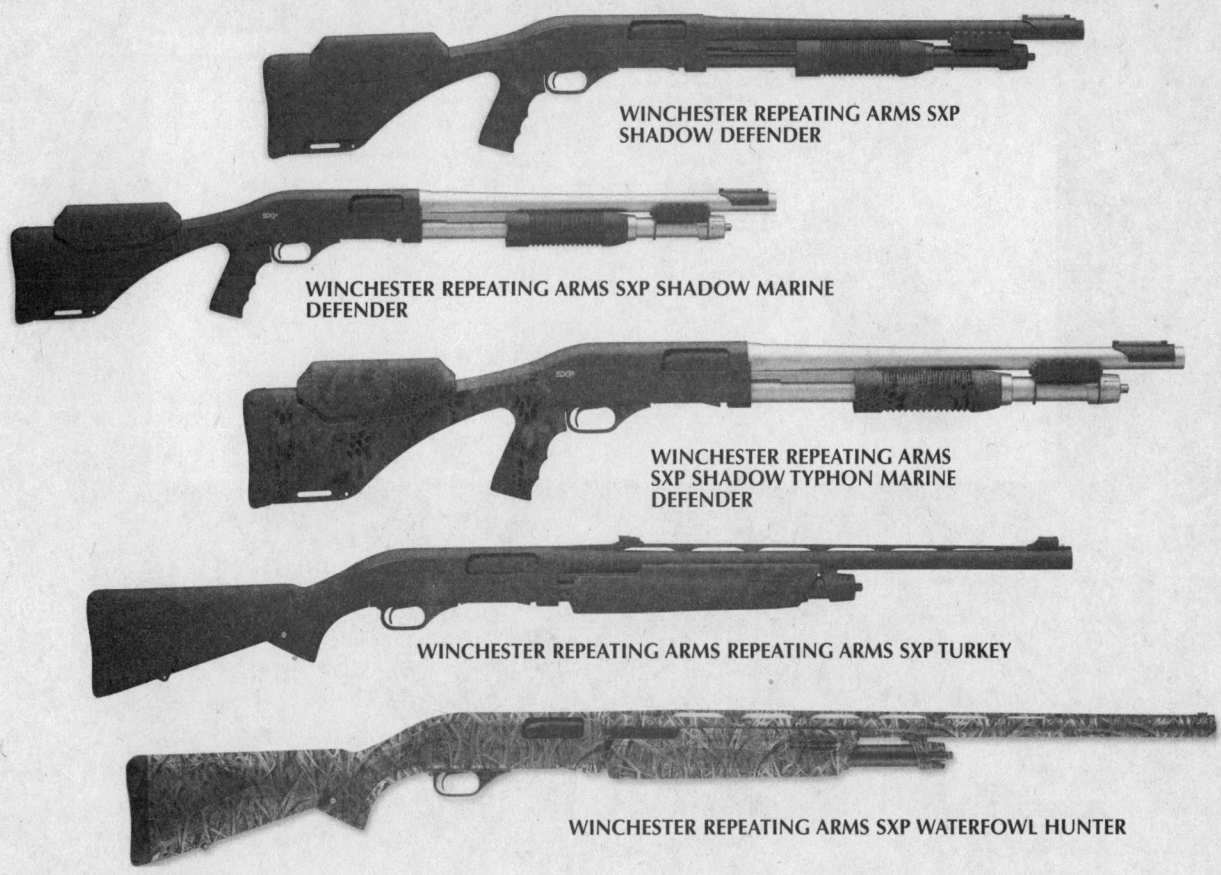

WINCHESTER REPEATING ARMS SXP SHADOW DEFENDER

WINCHESTER REPEATING ARMS SXP SHADOW MARINE DEFENDER

WINCHESTER REPEATING ARMS SXP SHADOW TYPHON MARINE DEFENDER

WINCHESTER REPEATING ARMS REPEATING ARMS SXP TURKEY

WINCHESTER REPEATING ARMS SXP WATERFOWL HUNTER

SXP SHADOW DEFENDER

Action: Pump
Stock: Synthetic
Barrel: 18 in.
Chokes: One Invector-Plus flush
Sights: TruGlo fiber optic
Weight: 7 lb. 8 oz.
Bore/Gauge: 12, 20
Magazine: 5 shells
Features: Pistol grip stock with textured gripping surfaces; two interchangeable comb modules; two length-of-pull spacers; ribbed forend; TruGlo fiber optic front sight; accessory rail; 3-in. chamber; one Cylinder choke tube
MSRP . . . . $449.99–$469.99

SXP SHADOW MARINE DEFENDER

Action: Pump
Stock: Synthetic
Barrel: 18 in.
Chokes: Invector-Plus (C)
Weight: 7 lb. 8 oz.
Bore/Gauge: 12, 20
Magazine: 5 shells
Features: Hard chrome plating on most exterior metal surfaces and bore; alloy receiver is drilled and tapped for scope mounts; 3-in. chamber; syn-thetic pistol grip stock has textured grip surfaces; two interchangeable cheek pieces; two length-of-pull spacers
MSRP . . . . $499.99–$519.99

SXP SHADOW TYPHON MARINE DEFENDER

Action: Pump
Stock: Synthetic
Barrel: 18 in.
Chokes: Invector-Plus (C)
Weight: 7 lb. 8 oz.
Bore/Gauge: 12, 20
Magazine: 5 shells
Features: Hard chrome plating on most exterior metal surfaces and bore; alloy receiver is drilled and tapped for scope mounts; 3-in. chamber; syn-thetic pistol grip stock has textured grip surfaces; two interchangeable cheekpieces; two length-of-pull spacers; stock in dipped Kryptek Typhon camo
MSRP . . . . $499.99–$529.99

SXP TURKEY

Action: Pump
Stock: Synthetic
Barrel: 24 in.

Chokes: Invector-Plus Extra Full Turkey
Weight: 6 lb. 4 oz. (20-ga.), 6 lb. 10 oz. (12-ga.)
Bore/Gauge: 12, 20
Magazine: 4 shells
Features: Hard chrome plated cham-ber and bore; back-bore technology; TruGlo fiber optic adjustable sights; 12-ga. has 3 ½-in. chamber; 20-ga. has 3-in. chamber
MSRP $439.99

SXP WATERFOWL HUNTER

Action: Pump
Stock: Synthetic
Barrel: 26 in., 28 in.
Chokes: Invector Plus
Weight: 6 lb. 8 oz.–7 lb.
Bore/Gauge: 12, 20
Magazine: 4 shells
Features: Hard chrome chamber and bores; drop-out trigger group; synthetic stock with textured gripping surfaces; in full-coverage Mossy Oak Shadow Grass Blades or Bottomlands or Realtree Max-5 or Timber
MSRP . . . . $459.99–$499.99

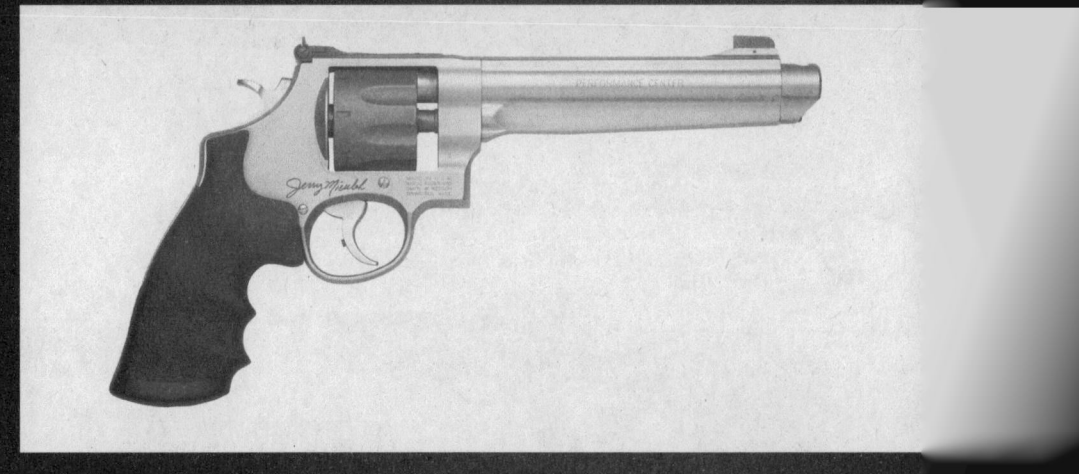

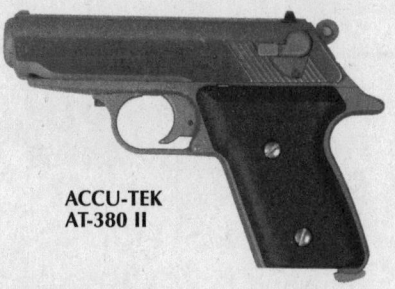

ACCU-TEK AT-380 II

ACCU-TEK HC-380

ACCU-TEK LT-380

AT-380 II

Action: Semiautomatic
Grips: Composite
Barrel: 2.8 in.
Sights: Target
Weight: 23.5 oz.
Caliber: .380 ACP
Capacity: 6+1 rounds
Features: Stainless steel construction; adjustable rear sight; one hand manual safety blocks; stainless steel magazine
MSRP **$289.00**

HC-380

Action: Semiautomatic
Grips: Composite
Barrel: 2.8 in.
Sights: Target
Weight: 26 oz.
Caliber: .380 ACP
Capacity: 13 rounds
Features: Adjustable rear sight; black checkered grip; one-hand manual safety block; includes two magazines and cable lock
MSRP **$330.00**

LT-380

Action: SA semiautomatic
Grips: Composite
Barrel: 2.8 in.
Sights: Adjustable rear sight
Weight: 15 oz.
Caliber: .380 ACP
Capacity: 6 rounds
Features: Aluminum frame; stainless steel slide; exposed hammer; manual safety; European type magazine release
MSRP **$324.00**

American Derringer

AMERICAN DERRINGER LM4 SIMMERLING

AMERICAN DERRINGER LM5

AMERICAN DERRINGER MODEL 1

LM4 SIMMERLING

Action: Hinged breech
Grips: Mesquite, Rosewood, custom
Barrel: 2 in.
Sights: Open, fixed
Weight: 24 oz.
Caliber: .45 ACP
Capacity: 5 rounds
Features: Vest pocket pistol; first round carried in the chamber; only 1in. thick; stainless steel
MSRP . . . . . . **Contact manufacturer**

LM5

Action: Hinged breech
Grips: Rosewood
Barrel: 2 in.
Sights: Open, fixed
Weight: 15 oz.
Caliber: .25 ACP
Capacity: 5
Features: Stainless steel; cam lock safety
MSRP . . . . . . **Contact manufacturer**

MODEL 1

Action: Hinged breech
Grips: Rosewood or stag
Barrel: 3 in.
Sights: Fixed, open
Weight: 15 oz.
Caliber: .45 Colt, .410, .45-70, .45 ACP, .45 Win. Mag., .44-40 Win., .44 Mag., .44 Spl., .41 Mag., .40 S&W, .380 ACP, .38 Spl., .38 Super, .357 Mag., .32-20, .32 Mag. S&W Long, .30-30 Win., .30 Carbine, .22 LR, .22 WMR, 10mm, 9mm, .223
Capacity: 2 rounds
Features: Single-action; automatic barrel selection; manually operated hammer-block safety
MSRP . . . . . . **Contact manufacturer**

American Derringer

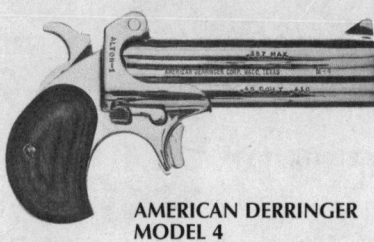

AMERICAN DERRINGER MODEL 4

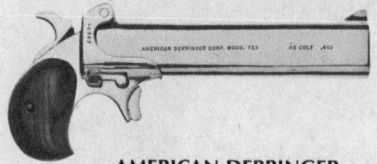

AMERICAN DERRINGER MODEL 6

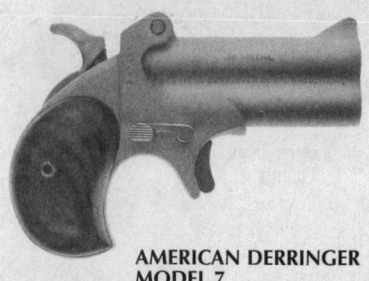

AMERICAN DERRINGER MODEL 7

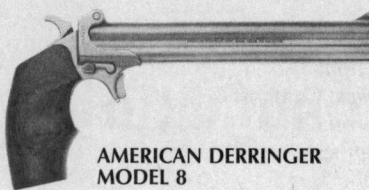

AMERICAN DERRINGER MODEL 8

MODEL 4

Action: Hinged breech
Grips: Rosewood
Barrel: 4.1 in
Sights: Fixed open
Weight: 16.5 oz.
Caliber: .375 Mag., 357 Max., .45-70 Govt.,
.45 Colt/.410, .44 Mag.
Capacity: 2 rounds
Features: Satin or high polish stainless steel finish; single-action; automatic barrel selection; manually operated hammer-block type safety
MSRP . . . . . . Contact manufacturer

MODEL 6

Action: Hinged breech
Grips: Rosewood, walnut, black
Barrel: 6 in.
Sights: Fixed open
Weight: 21 oz.
Caliber: .22 WMR, .357 Mag., .45 ACP, .45 Colt/.410
Capacity: 2 rounds
Features: Satin or high polish stainless steel finish; single-action; automatic barrel selection; manually operated hammer-block type safety
MSRP . . . . . . Contact manufacturer

MODEL 7 LIGHTWEIGHT & ULTRA LIGHTWEIGHT

Action: Hinged breech
Grips: Blackwood
Barrel: 3 in.
Sights: Fixed open
Weight: 7.5 oz.
Caliber: .44 Spl., .380 ACP, .38 Spl., .32 Mag./.32 S&W Long, .22 LR, .22 Mag.

Capacity: 2 rounds
Features: Grey matte finish; single-action; automatic barrel selection; manually operated hammer-block type safety
MSRP . . . . . . Contact manufacturer

MODEL 8

Action: Hinged breech
Grips: Rosewood, walnut, black
Barrel: 6 in.
Sights: Optional Adco red dot scope
Weight: 24 oz.
Caliber: .45 Colt/.410
Capacity: 2 rounds
Features: Satin or high polish stainless steel finish; single-action; automatic barrel selection; manually operated hammer-block type safety
MSRP . . . . . . Contact manufacturer

American Tactical Imports

AMERICAN TACTICAL IMPORTS FIREPOWER XTREME HYBRID 45ACP FXH-45 1911

AMERICAN TACTICAL IMPORTS FIREPOWER XTREME 45ACP G1 1911 (FX SERIES)

FIREPOWER XTREME HYBRID 45ACP FXH-45 1911 (FX SERIES)

Action: SA semiautomatic
Grips: Polymer
Barrel: 5 in.
Sights: Fixed
Weight: 27.5 oz.
Caliber: .45 ACP
Capacity: 8 rounds
Features: Polymer frame with 2 metal inserts for added stability and durability; steel match grade barrel and a custom designed steel slide; ergonomic frame with built-in finger grooves; accepts Glock front and rear sights, including aftermarket night sights
MSRP $599.95

FIREPOWER XTREME 45ACP G1 1911 (FX SERIES)

Action: Semiautomatic
Grips: Mahogany
Barrel: 4.25 in.
Sights: Fixed
Weight: 33.5 oz.
Caliber: .45 ACP
Capacity: 7+1 rounds
Features: Steel parts; black matte military-style fixed front and rear sights; military-style slide stop and thumb safety, solid mahogany grip panels
MSRP $449.95

American Tactical Imports

AMERICAN TACTICAL IMPORTS FX FIREPOWER XTREME 45ACP MILITARY 1911 (FX SERIES)

FIREPOWER XTREME 45ACP MILITARY 1911 (FX SERIES)

Action: Semiautomatic
Grips: Mahogany
Barrel: 5 in.
Sights: Fixed
Weight: 37 oz.
Caliber: .45 ACP
Capacity: 7+1 rounds

Features: Steel parts; black matte military-style fixed front and rear sights; military-style slide stop and thumb safety, solid mahogany grip panels
MSRP $449.95

Anderson Manufacturing

AM-15 EXT 5.56 7.5-INCH PISTOL

Action: Semiautomatic
Grips: Synthetic
Barrel: 7.5 in. extended barrel
Sights: None
Weight: 4 lb. 14 oz.
Caliber: .223 Rem./5.56 NATO
Capacity: Detachable box, 30 rounds
Features: Picatinny rail; Anderson Knight Stalker flash hider; Magpul grip; available treated with proprietary no lube RF85 treatment
MSRP . . . . $613.95–$909.99

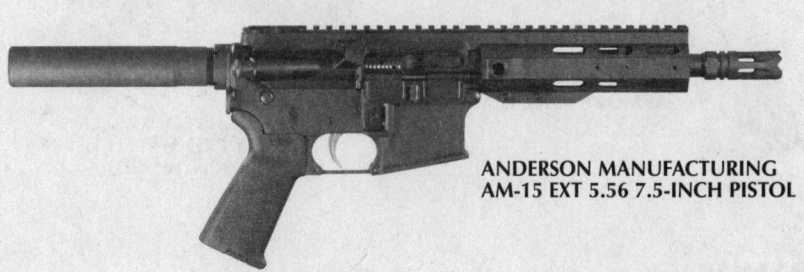

ANDERSON MANUFACTURING
AM-15 EXT 5.56 7.5-INCH PISTOL

AREX (Fime Group)

AREX (FIME GROUP) REX ZERO 1CP

AREX (FIME GROUP) REX ZERO 1S

REX ZERO 1CP

Action: Semiautomatic
Grips: Polymer
Barrel: 3.85 in.
Sights: White dot
Weight: 25.2 oz.
Caliber: 9mm, 9x21
Capacity: 17 rounds
Features: Produced in Slovenia, this is the company's first entry into the U.S. market; DA/SA semiauto with a short-recoil, modified Browning linkless locking design; combo slide stop/decocker; hard anodized T7075 aluminum frame; nitrocarburized steel slide and cold-hammer-forged barrel; ambidextrous safety and magazine release; loaded chamber indicator; Picatinny rail; oversized trigger guard for use with gloves
MSRP . . . . $595.08–$630.72

REX ZERO 1S

Action: Semiautomatic
Grips: Polymer
Barrel: 4.3 in.
Sights: White dot
Weight: 29 oz.
Caliber: 9mm, 9x21
Capacity: 17 rounds
Features: Produced in Slovenia, this is the company's first entry into the U.S. market; DA/SA semiauto with short-recoil, modified Browning linkless locking design; combo slide stop/decocker; hard anodized T7075 aluminum frame; nitrocarburized steel slide and cold-hammer-forged barrel; ambidextrous safety and magazine release; loaded chamber indicator; Picatinny rail; oversized trigger guard for use with gloves
MSRP . . . . $595.08–$630.72

Armscor/Rock Island Armory

HANDGUNS

ARMSCOR/ROCK ISLAND ARMORY BABY ROCK

ARMSCOR/ROCK ISLAND ARMORY GI STANDARD FS HC-45ACP

ARMSCOR/ROCK ISLAND ARMORY GI STANDARD MS-45ACP

ARMSCOR/ROCK ISLAND ARMORY MAPP TCM9R

ARMSCOR/ROCK ISLAND ARMORY PRO MATCH ULTRA 6-IN-10MM

ARMSCOR/ROCK ISLAND ARMORY PRO MATCH ULTRA HC

BABY ROCK

Action: Semiautomatic
Grips: Rubber
Barrel: 4 in.
Sights: Fixed
Weight: 1 lb. 8 oz.
Caliber: .380 ACP
Capacity: 7 rounds
Features: Parkerized frame; front post, Novak-style rear sight
MSRP.................**$460.00**

GI STANDARD FS HC-45ACP

Action: Semiautomatic
Grips: Rubber
Barrel: 5 in.
Sights: Fixed
Weight: 2 lb. 9 oz.
Caliber: .45 ACP
Capacity: 10 rounds
Features: Parkerized frame; 1:16 in. twist; 4–6 lb. trigger pull
MSRP.................**$608.00**

GI STANDARD MS-45ACP

Action: Semiautomatic
Grips: Wood
Barrel: 4.25 in.
Sights: Fixed
Weight: 2 lb. 6 oz.

Caliber: .45 ACP
Capacity: 8 rounds
Features: Parkerized frame; 1:16 in. twist; 4–6 lb. trigger pull
MSRP.................**$537.00**

MAPP TCM9R

Action: Semiautomatic
Grips: Polymer
Barrel: 3.8 in.
Sights: Integrated front post, LPA MPS2 adjustable rear
Weight: 35.5 oz.–37.1 oz.
Caliber: TCM9R
Capacity: 16 rounds
Features: Brings Armscor centerfire, bottlenecked .22-caliber, 9mm length cartridge to the company's MAPP platform; DA/SA; Parkerized finish on frame and slide
MSRP.................**$429.00**

PRO MATCH ULTRA 6-IN. 10MM

Action: Semiautomatic
Grips: Rubber
Barrel: 6 in.
Sights: Dovetail mounted fiber optic front, LPA TRT1 adjustable rear
Weight: 2 lb. 8 oz.
Caliber: 10mm

Capacity: 8 rounds
Features: Parkerized frame; orange fiber-optic front sight, tactical adjustable rear sight; comes with 9mm conversion kit; 1:16 twist; 4–6 lb. trigger pull; ambidextrous safety; combat hammer; extended beavertail
MSRP.................**$1168.00**

PRO MATCH ULTRA HC-10MM, HC-40S&W

Action: Semiautomatic
Grips: G10
Barrel: 5 in., 6 in.
Sights: Dovetail mounted fiber-optic front, LPA TRT-type rear
Weight: 2 lb. 14 oz.
Caliber: .40 S&W, 10mm
Capacity: 17 rounds
Features: Parkerized frame; orange fiber-optic front sight, tactical adjustable rear sight; comes with 9mm conversion kit; 1:16 twist; 4–6 lb. trigger pull; ambidextrous safety; combat hammer; extended beavertail
.40 S&W:..............**$1077.00**
10mm:................**$1322.00**

Armscor/Rock Island Armory

ARMSCOR/ROCK ISLAND ARMORY ROCK ULTRA CCO

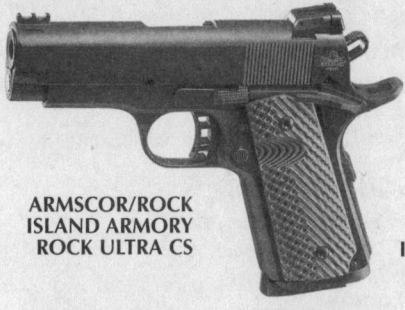

ARMSCOR/ROCK ISLAND ARMORY ROCK ULTRA CS

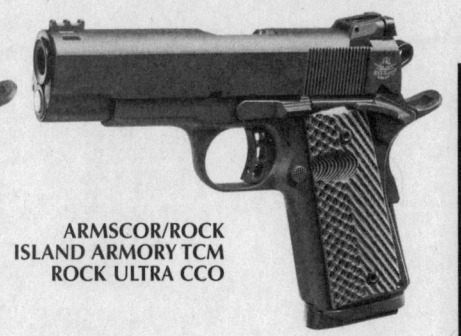

ARMSCOR/ROCK ISLAND ARMORY TCM ROCK ULTRA CCO

ARMSCOR/ROCK ISLAND ARMORY TCM ROCK ULTRA CS-L

ARMSCOR/ROCK ISLAND ARMORY XT 22 MAGNUM

ROCK ULTRA CCO
Action: Semiautomatic
Grips: G10
Barrel: 4.25 in.
Sights: Dovetail fiber optic front, LPA MPS1-type adjustable rear
Weight: N/A
Caliber: .45 ACP
Capacity: 8 rounds
Features: Officer's grip; aluminum frame; Commander-length slide; full-length guide rod; button-rifled barrel; skeletonized hammer; trigger with overtravel; frame has black oxide finish; slide is parkerized
MSRP $760.00

ROCK ULTRA CS
Action: Semiautomatic
Grips: Rubber
Barrel: 3.62 in.

Sights: Dovetail standard front, low-profile, snag-free rear
Weight: 46.4 oz.
Caliber: .45 ACP
Capacity: 7 rounds
Features: Traditional 70-series 1911 design in a compact concealed carry package; snag-free features; checkered rubber grips; all-over parkerized matte finish
MSRP $731.00

TCM ROCK ULTRA CCO
Action: Semiautomatic
Grips: G10
Barrel: 4.25 in.
Sights: Dovetail fiber optic front, LPA MPS1-type adjustable rear
Weight: N/A
Caliber: .22 TCM9R/9mm
Capacity: 8 rounds

Features: Officer's grip; aluminum frame; Commander-length slide; full-length guide rod; button-rifled barrel; skeletonized hammer; beveled magazine well; drop-in 9mm accessory barrel
MSRP $845.00

TCM ROCK ULTRA CS-L
Action: Semiautomatic
Grips: G10
Barrel: 3.62 in.
Sights: Dovetail fiber optic front, LPA MPS1-type adjustable rear
Weight: 46.4 oz.
Caliber: .22 TCM9R/9mm
Capacity: 8 rounds
Features: Aluminum frame with a short barrel; drop-in 9mm accessory barrel
MSRP $837.00

XT 22 MAGNUM
Action: Semiautomatic
Grips: Rubber
Barrel: 5 in.
Sights: Fixed
Weight: 2 lb. 3 oz.
Caliber: .22 Mag.
Capacity: 22 rounds
Features: Parkerized frame; single action
MSRP $598.00

Arsenal, Inc.

ARSENAL, INC. SAM7K

SAM7K
Action: Semiautomatic
Grips: Black polymer
Barrel: 10.5 in.
Sights: Peep rear
Weight: 128 oz.
Caliber: 7.62x39 Warsaw
Capacity: 5 rounds
Features: Milled receiver; short gas system; front sight block; gas block system; chrome-lined hammer-forged barrel; ambidextrous safety lever; scope rail; sling included
MSRP . . . .$999.99–$1199.99

Auto-Ordnance

**AUTO-ORDNANCE
1911BKO**

1911BKO
Action: Semiautomatic
Grips: Brown checkered plastic, checkered wood grips
Barrel: 5 in.
Sights: Blade front, rear drift adjustable sight
Weight: 39 oz.
Caliber: .45 ACP
Capacity: 7+1 rounds
Features: Single-action 1911 Colt design; WWII parkerized; stainless steel or blued metal finish
MSRP $673.00

Avidity Arms (By Eagle Imports)

**AVIDITY ARMS (BY
EAGLE IMPORTS) PD10**

PD10
Action: Semiautomatic
Grips: Polymer
Barrel: 4 in.
Sights: Ameriglo Luma Glow front, I.C.E. Claw Emergency Manipulation
Weight: 18.8 oz.
Caliber: 9mm
Capacity: 10 rounds
Features: Personal Defense (PD) carry gun; ergonomic polymer frame; safety trigger; stainless steel slide with a black nitride finish; loaded chamber indicator
MSRP $499.00

Beretta USA

92A1
Action: Semiautomatic
Grips: Plastic
Barrel: 4.9 in.
Sights: 3-Dot System
Weight: 34.4 oz.
Caliber: 9mm, .40 S&W
Capacity: 12 or 17 rounds, restricted capacity 10 rounds
Features: Removable front sight; Picatinny rail, internal recoil buffer; captive recoil spring assembly
MSRP $775.00

92FSR_22 SNIPER GRAY
Action: Semiautomatic
Grips: Plastic
Barrel: 4.9 in.
Sights: Dovetailed front and rear
Weight: 26.08 oz.
Caliber: .22 LR
Capacity: 10, 15 rounds
Features: DA/SA .22 LR version of maker's famed 9mm; open slide design; reversible magazine release; ambidextrous decocker/safety; combat trigger guard; 1913 Picatinny rail; Sniper Gray frame finish
MSRP $450.00

92FSR_22 SUPPRESSOR READY KIT
Action: Semiautomatic
Grips: Plastic
Barrel: 4.9 in.
Sights: Suppressor-height front and rear
Weight: 26.08 oz.
Caliber: .22 LR
Capacity: 10, 15 rounds
Features: DA/SA .22 LR version of maker's famed 9mm; open slide design; reversible magazine release; ambidextrous decocker/safety; combat trigger guard; 1913 Picatinny rail; suppressor-height sights; extended threaded barrel with thread protector and mock suppressor
MSRP $495.00

BERETTA 92A1

**BERETTA 92FSR_22
SNIPER GRAY**

**BERETTA 92FSR_22
SUPPRESSOR
READY KIT**

BERETTA 3032 TOMCAT INOX

BERETTA APX RDO

BERETTA M9A1

BERETTA APX COMBAT

BERETTA BU-9 NANO

BERETTA APX FDE

BERETTA M9

3032 TOMCAT INOX

Action: Semiautomatic
Grips: Plastic
Barrel: 2.5 in.
Sights: Fixed, open
Weight: 14.5 oz.
Caliber: .32 ACP, .380 ACP
Capacity: 7+1 round
Features: Double-action; tip-up barrel latch; Inox has stainless steel slide and barrel; titanium alloy frame in black or gray; double- or single-trigger
MSRP **$485.00**

APX COMBAT

Action: Semiautomatic
Grips: Polymer
Barrel: 4.9 in.
Sights: Drift-adjustable front and rear, optics plates
Weight: 33.3 oz.
Caliber: 9mm
Capacity: 10, 17 rounds
Features: Striker-fired DA/SA pistol; threaded barrel; slide cut out to accept four different optics mounting plates for reflex red dot sights from Burris, Trijicon, Leupold, and C-More; interchangeable backstraps
MSRP **$775.00**

APX FDE

Action: Semiautomatic
Grips: Polymer
Barrel: 4.9 in.
Sights: Drift-adjustable
Weight: 33.3 oz.
Caliber: 9mm
Capacity: 10, 15, 17 rounds
Features: Developed for law enforcement and military personnel; easy-to-find controls; under frame accessory rail; three interchangeable backstraps; slide stop is ambidextrous; mag release is reversible; in all-over Flat Dark Earth
MSRP **$595.00**

APX RDO

Action: Semiautomatic
Grips: Polymer
Barrel: 4.9 in.
Sights: Drift-adjustable front and rear, optics plates
Weight: 33.3 oz.
Caliber: 9mm, .40 S&W
Capacity: 10, 15, 17 rounds
Features: Striker-fired DA/SA pistol; slide cut out to accept four different optics mounting plates for reflex red dot sights from Burris, Trijicon, Leupold, and C-More; interchangeable backstraps
MSRP **$725.00**

BU-9 NANO

Action: Semiautomatic
Grips: Technopolymer
Barrel: 3.07 in.
Sights: 3-dot low profile
Weight: 17.67 oz.

Caliber: 9mm
Capacity: 6+1 rounds
Features: Interchangeable sights; ambidextrous magazine release button; serialized sub-chassis; patent-pending striker deactivator; technopolymer grip frame; three variations available include black, pink, Flat Dark Earth
MSRP **$450.00**

M9

Action: Semiautomatic
Grips: Plastic
Barrel: 4.9 in.
Sights: Dot-and-Post system
Weight: 33.3 oz.
Caliber: 9mm
Capacity: 15 rounds, restricted capacity 10+1 rounds
Features: Has distinctive military style markings; chrome-lined bore; double-action; automatic firing pin block; ambidextrous manual safety; lightweight forged aluminum alloy frame w/ combat-style trigger guard
MSRP **$675.00**

M9A1

Action: Semiautomatic
Grips: Plastic
Barrel: 4.9 in.
Sights: 3-Dot System
Weight: 33.9 oz.
Caliber: 9mm
Capacity: 15+1 rounds, restricted capacity 10+1 rounds
Features: Picatinny rail; magazine well bevel; sand-resistant magazine
MSRP **$750.00**

Beretta USA

BERETTA PICO

BERETTA PX4 STORM COMPACT

BERETTA PX4 COMPACT CARRY

BERETTA PX4 STORM FULL SIZE

BERETTA U22 NEOS

PICO

Action: Semiautomatic
Grips: Technopolymer
Barrel: 2.7 in.
Sights: Front and rear adjustable
Weight: 11.5 oz.
Caliber: .380 ACP
Capacity: 6+1 rounds
Features: Stainless steel sub-chassis engraved with serial number; snag-free slide and frame; barrel can be replaced with a .32 ACP barrel; dovetail quick-change sights; frames available in flat dark earth, light aqua blue, black, or purple
MSRP. **$300.00**

PX4 STORM COMPACT

Action: Semiautomatic
Grips: Plastic
Barrel: 3.2 in.
Sights: 3-Dot System
Weight: 27.3 oz.
Caliber: 9mm, .40 S&W
Capacity: 12 or 15 rounds; full size magazines 9mm: 17 or 20 rounds, .40 S&W: 14 or 17 rounds; restricted capacity 10 rounds
Features: Ambidextrous side stop lever; integral Picatinny rail; bruiton

non-reflective black coating; visible automatic firing pin block
MSRP. **$650.00**

PX4 STORM COMPACT CARRY

Action: DA/SA
Grips: Synthetic
Barrel: 3.2 in.
Sights: High-visibility night sights
Weight: 27.3 oz.
Caliber: 9mm
Capacity: 15 rounds
Features: Rotating barrel; grey Cerakote slide; Picatinny rail; competition trigger; double stack magazine; Talon grips; reversible magazine release; lightweight polymer frame; stealth levers decock only
MSRP. **$899.00**

PX4 STORM FULL SIZE

Action: Semiautomatic
Grips: Plastic
Barrel: 4 in.
Sights: 3-Dot System
Weight: 27.7 oz.
Caliber: 9mm, .40 S&W
Capacity: 14 or 17 rounds, restricted

capacity 10 rounds
Features: Picatinny rail; innovative locked-breech with a rotating barrel system; visible automatic firing pin block; ambidextrous safety; reversible magazine release; available in Inox finish; California-compliant model available with and without night sights
MSRP. **$650.00**
Tritium night sights:. **$749.00**
Inox: **$700.00**

U22 NEOS

Action: Semiautomatic
Grips: Plastic
Barrel: 4.5 in., 6 in.
Sights: Target
Weight: 31.7–36.2 oz.
Caliber: .22 LR
Capacity: 10+1 rounds
Features: Single-action; removable colored grip inserts; deluxe model features adjustable trigger, replaceable sights; optional 7.5 in. barrel
Standard:. **$325.00**
Inox: **$350.00**

BERSA BP
CONCEALED CARRY
SERIES

BERSA THUNDER
9 PRO XT

BERSA THUNDER 380

BERSA THUNDER 380
COMBAT PLUS

BERSA THUNDER 380
CONCEALED CARRY

BP CONCEALED CARRY SERIES

Action: Short reset DAO
Grips: Integral to frame
Barrel: 3.3 in.
Sights: Interchangeable front and rear
Weight: 21.5 oz.
Caliber: 9mm, .380 ACP, .40 S&W
Capacity: 6+1 or 8+1 rounds
Features: Bersa polymer concealed carry; high impact polymer frame; Picatinny rail, polygonal rifling, and loaded chamber indicator; ambidextrous magazine release; striker fired; micro-polished bore with sharp, deep rifling; 3-dot sight system; integral locking system; automatic firing pin safety; 9mm available in matte black, duotone, or frames in olive drab, flat dark earth or urban gray; .40 S&W availble in matte black; .380 ACP available in matte black and duotone; some limited edition 9mm in matte black or duotone available with turquoise blue frame
MSRP $429.00

THUNDER 9 PRO XT

Action: DA/SA
Grips: Checkered black polymer
Barrel: 4.96 in.
Sights: Fiber optic front sight, adjustable rear
Weight: 33.9 oz.

Caliber: 9mm
Capacity: 10–17 rounds
Features: Dovetailed front fiber optic sight; windage and elevation adjustable rear sights; ambidextrous controls for easy handling; 5-inch competition barrel fitted to slide for maximum precision; Cerakote finish to protect against abrasion, wear, and corrosion
MSRP $835.00

THUNDER 380

Action: Semiautomatic
Grips: Black polymer
Barrel: 3.5 in.
Sights: 3-Dot system
Weight: 20 oz.
Caliber: .380 ACP
Capacity: 7+1 rounds
Features: Combat style trigger guard; extended slide release; micro-polished bore with sharp, deep rifling; integral locking system; available in matte, matte with pink rubber wraparound grips, duotone, or Cerakote nickel
MSRP . . . . starting at $294.00

THUNDER 380 COMBAT PLUS

Action: DA/SA
Grips: Olive rubber wrap-around
Barrel: 3.5 in.

Sights: Dovetail front, notched-bar dovetail rear
Weight: 20.5 oz.
Caliber: .380 ACP
Capacity: 8+1, 15+1
Features: Decocker for safer conceal carry; flat-bottom 8 shot magazine; integral locking system for the ultimate in safety; micro-polished bore with sharp, deep rifling for greater accuracy; slim side release for a lower profile; u-shaped combat rear sight for optimum sighting in low-light situations
MSRP . . . . starting at $302.00

THUNDER 380 CONCEALED CARRY

Action: Semiautomatic
Grips: Black polymer
Barrel: 3.2 in.
Sights: Blade front and notched-bar dovetailed rear
Weight: 16.4 oz.
Caliber: .380 ACP
Capacity: 8+1 rounds
Features: Extra low profile sights; combat style trigger guard; slim slide release; integral locking system; available with Crimson Trace laser
MSRP . . . . starting at $307.00

Bersa

BERSA (BY EAGLE IMPORTS) TPR9C DUOTONE, MATTE

BERSA (BY EAGLE IMPORTS) TPR40C

BERSA (BY EAGLE IMPORTS) TPR45C DUOTONE, MATTE

TPR9C DUOTONE, MATTE

Action: Semiautomatic
Grips: Polymer
Barrel: 3.25 in.
Sights: Interchangeable Sig Sauer-type front and rear
Weight: 23 oz.
Caliber: 9mm
Capacity: 10, 13 rounds
Features: Compact DA/SA for concealed carry; Browning Petter locking action that enhances reliability
MSRP . . . . starting at $465.00

TPR40C

Action: Semiautomatic
Grips: Polymer
Barrel: 3.6 in.
Sights: Interchangeable Sig Sauer-type front and rear
Weight: 23 oz.
Caliber: 40 S&W
Capacity: 10 rounds
Features: Compact DA/SA for concealed carry; Browning Petter locking action that enhances reliability; in all black only
MSRP . . . . starting at $465.00

TPR45C DUOTONE, MATTE

Action: Semiautomatic
Grips: Polymer
Barrel: 3.6 in.
Sights: Interchangeable Sig Sauer-type front and rear
Weight: 27 oz.
Caliber: .45 ACP
Capacity: 10 rounds
Features: Compact DA/SA for concealed carry; Browning Petter locking action that enhances reliability; available in all black or as a Duotone with a stainless slide
MSRP . . . . starting at $465.00

Bond Arms

BOND ARMS BACKUP

BOND ARMS, INC. BULLPUP 9

BOND ARMS CENTURY 2000

BACKUP

Action: SA semiautomatic
Grips: Rubber
Barrel: 2.5 in.
Sights: Blade front, fixed rear
Weight: 18.5 oz.
Caliber: .357 Mag., .38 Spl., .40 S&W, .45 ACP, .45 Colt
Capacity: 2 rounds
Features: Interchangable barrels; rebounding hammer; retracting firing pins; crossbolt safety
MSRP $540.00

BULLPUP 9

Action: Semiautomatic
Grips: Rosewood
Barrel: 3.35 in.
Sights: Dovetail drift-adjustable non-illuminated three-dot
Weight: 17.5 oz.
Caliber: 9mm Luger
Capacity: 7 rounds
Features: Based on the XR-9 by Boberg Arms; Bond Arms purchased the patents and rights to that gun in 2016, basing its new Bullpup on it
MSRP $1099.00

CENTURY 2000

Action: SA
Grips: Custom laminated black ash or rosewood
Barrel: 3.5 in.
Sights: Blade front, fixed rear
Weight: 21 oz.
Caliber: .357 Mag./.38 Spl., .410/.45 LC
Capacity: 2 rounds
Features: Interchangeable barrels; automatic extractor; rebounding hammer; retracting firing pins; crossbolt safety; spring-loaded cammed locking lever; trigger guard; stainless steel with satin polish finish
MSRP $567.00

BOND ARMS MAMA BEAR

BOND ARMS MINI 45

BOND ARMS, INC. PT2A (PROTECT THE SECOND AMENDMENT)

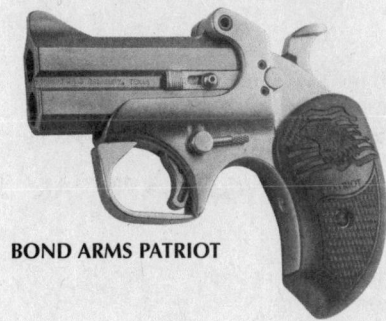

BOND ARMS PATRIOT

BOND ARMS GIRL MINI

BOND ARMS SNAKE SLAYER

MAMA BEAR

Action: SA
Grips: Pink wood
Barrel: 2.5 in.
Sights: Blade front, fixed rear
Weight: 18.5 oz.
Caliber: .357 Mag, .38 Spl.
Capacity: 2 rounds
Features: Stainless steel double barrel and frame; automatic spent casing extractor; rebounding hammer; retracting ring pins; crossbolt safety; spring-loaded, cammed locking lever; laser-carved American Flag and bald eagle grips
MSRP.................$541.00

MINI 45, GIRL MINI

Action: SA
Grips: Rosewood or pink
Barrel: 2.5 in.
Sights: Blade front, fixed rear
Weight: 18 oz.–19 oz.
Caliber: .45 Colt (Mini 45), .357 Mag. (Girl Mini)
Capacity: 2 rounds
Features: The Bond Mini was developed as a special edition gun that is even easier to conceal and carry, but still packs the same power Bond Arms guns are known for;

comes in two models the Mini .45 and the Girl Mini; Girl Mini has slightly smaller barrel included and pink grips
MSRP.................$534.00

PATRIOT

Action: SA
Grips: Rosewood
Barrel: 3 in.
Sights: Blade front, fixed rear
Weight: 21.5 oz.
Caliber: .45 Colt, .410
Capacity: 2 rounds
Features: Stainless steel double barrel and frame; automatic spent casing extractor; rebounding hammer; retracting ring pins; crossbolt safety; spring-loaded, cammed locking lever; laser-carved American Flag and bald eagle grips
MSRP.................$648.00

PT2A (PROTECT THE SECOND AMENDMENT)

Action: Break-top
Grips: Rosewood
Barrel: 4.25 in.
Sights: Front blade, fixed rear
Weight: 23.5 oz.
Caliber: .45 LC/.410-bore, .357 Mag.

Capacity: 2 rounds
Features: Custom extended rosewood grips; "The Right of the People to Keep and Bear Arms" is emblazoned on right side of top barrel; "shall not be infringed" on right side of bottom barrel; cross-bolt safety; stainless steel barrels; compatibility with all Bond barrels; automatic spent casing extractors; BAD premium leather driving holster
MSRP.................$887.00

SNAKE SLAYER

Action: SA
Grips: Extended custom rosewood
Barrel: 3.5 in.
Sights: Blade front, fixed rear
Weight: 22 oz.
Caliber: .357 Mag./.38 Spl., .410/.45 LC
Capacity: 2 rounds
Features: Interchangeable barrels; automatic extractor; rebounding hammer; retracting firing pins; crossbolt safety; spring-loaded cammed locking lever; trigger guard; stainless steel with satin polish finish
MSRP.................$603.00

Bond Arms

BOND ARMS SNAKE SLAYER IV

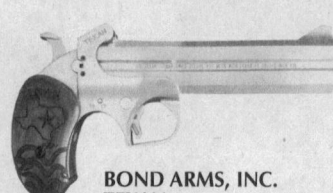

BOND ARMS, INC. TEXAN

BOND ARMS TEXAS DEFENDER

BOND TEXAS RANGER - SPECIAL EDITION

SNAKE SLAYER IV
Action: SA
Grips: Extended custom rosewood
Barrel: 4.25 in.
Sights: Blade front, fixed rear
Weight: 23.5 oz.
Caliber: .357 Mag./.38 Spl., .410/.45 LC
Capacity: 2 rounds
Features: Automatic extractor; interchangeable barrels; rebounding hammer; retracting firing pins; crossbolt safety; spring-loaded cammed locking lever; trigger guard; stainless steel with satin polish finish
MSRP $648.00

TEXAN
Action: Break-top
Grips: Rosewood
Barrel: 6 in.
Sights: Front ramp
Weight: 23.5 oz.
Caliber: .45 LC/.410-bore

Capacity: 2 rounds
Features: Bond's first six-inch production model; patented rebounding hammer; cross-bolt safety; automatic spent casing extractor; spring-loaded cammed locking lever; compatible with all Bond Arms barrels; rosewood grips are extended and engraved
MSRP $700.00

TEXAS DEFENDER
Action: SA
Grips: Custom laminated black ash or rosewood
Barrel: 3 in.
Sights: Blade front and fixed rear
Weight: 20 oz.
Caliber: 45 Colt/.410
Capacity: 2 rounds
Features: Interchangeable barrels; automatic extractor; rebounding hammer; retracting firing pins; crossbolt safety; spring-loaded

cammed locking lever; trigger guard; stainless steel with satin polish finish
MSRP $543.00

TEXAS RANGER - SPECIAL EDITION
Action: SA
Grips: Texas mesquite
Barrel: 3.5 in.
Sights: Blade front, fixed rear
Weight: 22 oz.
Caliber: .410/.45 LC
Capacity: 2 rounds
Features: Bond Arms has been chosen to represent the prestigious Texas Rangers in their historic 200th Anniversary; gun and knife grips are made from real Texas mesquite wood, the Texas Ranger Stars are handmade by Texas inmates in the Texas Department of Corrections, and it is gold engraved on the barrel; custom glass top display case included
MSRP $1355.00

Browning

BROWNING 1911-22 A1 FULL SIZE

BROWNING 1911-22 BLACK LABEL MEDALLION

1911-22 A1 FULL SIZE
Action: Semiautomatic
Grips: Brown composite
Barrel: 4.25 in.
Sights: Fixed
Weight: 15 oz.
Caliber: 22 LR
Capacity: 10+1 rounds
Features: Alloy frame in matte blued finish; stainless steel barrel block with matte blued finish; blowback action; single-action trigger; detachable magazine; manual thumb safety; grip safety
MSRP $599.99

1911-22 BLACK LABEL MEDALLION
Action: Semiautomatic
Grips: Rosewood
Barrel: 3.625 in., 4.25 in.
Sights: Combat white dot
Weight: 13 oz., 15 oz.
Caliber: .22LR
Capacity: 10 rounds
Features: Available in full-size or compact 85-percent scale of 1911 package; checkered grips; extended slide release; machined aluminum slide; ambidextrous thumb safety; skeletonized trigger and hammer
MSRP $669.99

BROWNING 1911-380 BLACK LABEL

BROWNING 1911-380 BLACK LABEL MEDALLION PRO COMPACT

BROWNING 1911-380 BLACK LABEL PRO

BROWNING 1911-380 BLACK LABEL PRO STAINLESS FULL SIZE WITH RAIL

BROWNING 1911-380 BLACK LABEL PRO STAINLESS COMPACT

BROWNING BUCK MARK FIELD TARGET

1911-380 BLACK LABEL

Action: Semiautomatic
Grips: Synthetic
Barrel: 4.25 in.
Sights: Fixed
Weight: 18 oz.
Caliber: .380 ACP
Capacity: 8 rounds
Features: Combat sights; matte black finish; single-stack magazine
MSRP...................$669.99

1911-380 BLACK LABEL MEDALLION PRO COMPACT

Action: Semiautomatic
Grips: Laminate
Barrel: 3.625 in. (compact), 4.25 in. (full-size)
Sights: Steel three-dot combat or steel bar-dot combat night sights
Weight: 16 oz. (compact), 18 oz. (full-size)
Caliber: .380 ACP
Capacity: 8 rounds
Features: 85 percent-scale 1911 pistol; compact and full-size versions; stainless steel slide and rosewood laminate grips; ambidextrous manual thumb safety; extended slide release beavertail grip safety; two magazines; Commander hammer; target crown; grips are grooved and checkered
MSRP...................$799.99
Night sights: $879.99

1911-380 BLACK LABEL PRO

Action: Semiautomatic
Grips: Synthetic
Barrel: 4.25 in.
Sights: Combat white dot
Weight: 18 oz.
Caliber: .380 ACP
Capacity: 8 rounds
Features: High strength/lightweight composite frame; machined steel slide; target crown; extended ambidextrous manual safety; skeletonized hammer
MSRP...................$799.99

1911-380 BLACK LABEL PRO STAINLESS COMPACT, COMPACT WITH RAIL

Action: Semiautomatic
Grips: G-10 composite
Barrel: 3.625 in.
Sights: Combat white dot, night sights
Weight: 16 oz.; 18 oz. (with rail)
Caliber: .380 ACP
Capacity: 8 rounds
Features: Stainless slide; black-and-white G-10 composite grips; composite aluminum frame; extended slide release; Commander hammer; two magazines; ABS case; night sights optional
Standard:...............$799.99
With rail: $829.99

1911-380 BLACK LABEL PRO STAINLESS FULL SIZE WITH RAIL

Action: Semiautomatic
Grips: Textured G10
Barrel: 4.25 in.
Sights: Steel three-dot combat or steel bar-dot combat night sights
Weight: 18 oz.
Caliber: .380 ACP
Capacity: 8 rounds
Features: 85 percent-scale 1911 pistol; 1913 Picatinny rail; composite frame; ergonomic and skeletonized controls; two magazines; fully machined 7075 aluminum sub-frame and slide rails; target crown; satin silver finish
MSRP...................$829.99

BUCK MARK FIELD TARGET, FIELD TARGET SUPPRESSOR READY

Action: Semiautomatic
Grips: Laminate cocobolo
Barrel: 5.5 in.
Sights: Pro Target adjustable
Weight: 38 oz.
Caliber: .22 LR
Capacity: 10 rounds
Features: Suppressor-ready; full-length Picatinny rail on top; barrel profile is heavy bull
Field Target:............$579.99
Suppressor-ready: $599.99

Browning

BROWNING BUCK MARK LITE UFX

BROWNING BUCK MARK PLUS CAMPER UFX SR

BROWNING BUCK MARK PLUS UDX

BROWNING BUCK MARK PLUS UDX, STAINLESS UDX, ROSEWOOD UDX

BUCK MARK LITE UFX

Action: Semiautomatic
Grips: Ultragrip FX
Barrel: 5.5 in.
Sights: Pro-Target adjustable rear, Marble Arms violet fiber-optic front
Weight: 35 oz.
Caliber: .22 LR
Capacity: 10 rounds
Features: Blowback action; steel barrel with aluminum alloy outer sleeve; alloy frame; matte black finish with Buckmark symbol in silver on top side of barrel; ambidextrous grip; black rubber overmolding
MSRP **$589.99**

BUCK MARK PLUS CAMPER UFX SR

Action: Semiautomatic
Grips: Ultragrip FX
Barrel: 6 in.
Sights: TruGlo/Marble Arms fiber optic front, white outline Pro Target rear
Weight: 34 oz.
Caliber: .22 LR
Capacity: 10 rounds
Features: Suppressor-ready; Browning ambidextrous Ultragrip FX grips; long tapered bull barrel with a matte finish; topside Picatinny rail for optics mounting; pistol rug
MSRP **$499.99**

BUCK MARK PLUS PRACTICAL URX

Action: Semiautomatic
Grips: Ultragrip RX ambidextrous
Barrel: 5.5 in.
Sights: Pro-target adjustable rear; Truglo/Marble's fiber-optic front
Weight: 34 oz.
Caliber: .22 LR

Capacity: 10+1 rounds
Features: Tapered bull barrel with matte blued finish; matte gray finish receiver
MSRP **$479.99**

BUCK MARK PLUS UDX, STAINLESS UDX, ROSEWOOD UDX

Action: Semiautomatic
Grips: Laminate
Barrel: 5.5 in.
Sights: TruGlo fiber optic front; white outline Pro-Target rear
Weight: 34 oz.
Caliber: .22 LR
Capacity: 10 rounds
Features: Wood laminate UDX grips (Utragrip Deluxe); stainless steel frame and slabside barrel with polished flats; SA trigger; Picatinny top rail for optics; grip frame machined with finger grooves that match up to textured wood grips; slab-side barrel has high-polished flats
Stainless: **$599.99**
Buckmark UDX, Rosewood: . . .**$549.99**

B&T (Brügger & Thomet)

B&T (BRÜGGER & THOMET) USWA1

USWA1

Action: Semiautomatic
Grips: Polymer
Barrel: 4.33 in.
Sights: Aimpoint NANO
Weight: 40.8 oz.
Caliber: 9mm
Capacity: 17, 19, 30 rounds

Features: Swiss-made with unique design; interchangeable grip panels; Aimpoint NANO red dot sight; APL tac light; sling; cleaning kit; hard case; optional stock kit is available with all the attendant NFA paperwork and taxes
MSRP . . . . . . **contact manufacturer**

Bushmaster

BUSHMASTER SQUAREDROP

SQUAREDROP

Action: Semiautomatic
Grips: Synthetic
Barrel: 7 in., 9 in., 10 in.
Sights: None
Weight: N/A
Caliber: .223, .300 Blackout
Capacity: 30 rounds

Features: AR pistol; Mil-Std uppers and lowers; SquareDrop rail; SB tactical arm brace; FNC-treated 4150 chrome-moly steel barrels
MSRP **$1399.00**

CABOT GUNS THE AMERICAN JOE COMMANDER

CABOT GUNS THE DRAKO GARRA

CABOT GUNS THE GENTLEMAN'S CARRY

CABOT GUNS THE ICON

CABOT GUNS VINTAGE CLASSIC

THE AMERICAN JOE COMMANDER

Action: Semiautomatic
Grips: Aluminum
Barrel: 4.25 in.
Sights: Cabot reverse dovetail white-dot front, low-mount fixed rear
Weight: 33.5 oz.
Caliber: .45 ACP
Capacity: 8 rounds

Features: The original American Joe now in Commander-length slide; "Tire Tread" USA engraving at front of slide; wing and spiderweb engraving designed by Joe Faris covering the rest of the slide; special flag grips
MSRP . . . . starting at $4500.00

THE DRAKO GARRA

Action: Semiautomatic
Grips: Ebony
Barrel: 5 in.
Sights: Gold bead Cabot reverse dovetail front, low-mount fixed rear
Weight: N/A
Caliber: 9mm, .45 ACP
Capacity: 8 rounds
Features: 1911 with "claw mark" front and rear slide cocking serrations in negative/positive relief that extends to the frame; Cabot's radiused, precision-fit trigger with an all-new electric-discharge wire cut design of twin claws; hand-polished ebony grips; mammoth grips optional; night sights available
MSRP . . . . starting at $5295.00

THE GENTLEMAN'S CARRY

Action: Semiautomatic
Grips: Walnut
Barrel: 4.25 in.
Sights: Reverse dovetail tritium front, Warren-style U-notch tritium rear
Weight: N/A
Caliber: .45 ACP, 9mm
Capacity: 8 rounds
Features: Rhombus-cut checkering on the frontstrap and mainspring housing; bobtail cut frame; Carry Cut slide and slide serrations; hand-polished ramp' Cabot's Idiot Scratch-Proof slide star; aluminum trigger skeletonized with a tristar pattern; checkered walnut grips with inlaid Cabot medallion
MSRP $4795.00

THE ICON

Action: Semiautomatic
Grips: Stainless steel
Barrel: 4.25 in., 5 in.
Sights: Reverse dovetail front, Cabot ACE fixed rear
Weight: N/A
Caliber: .45 ACP, 9mm
Capacity: 8 rounds
Features: Made from U.S. sourced stainless steel; choice of Government-length or Commander-length national match-grade barrels with reverse crowns; 24 lines-per-inch rhombus cut checkering on the mainspring housing and frontstrap; Cabot's beavertail safety grip; barrel bushing; mainspring housing with rhombus cuts; Idiot Scratch Proof takedown lever; full-length guide rod; stainless steel monochrome grips
MSRP $4995.00

VINTAGE CLASSIC

Action: Semiautomatic
Grips: Walnut
Barrel: 5 in.
Sights: Gold bead Cabot reverse dovetail front, low-mount fixed rear
Weight: N/A
Caliber: .45 ACP
Capacity: 8 rounds
Features: Cabot frame and slide from 416 stainless steel billet; proprietary hardening and vintage "classic" finish; Cabot Trinity Stripes rear slide serrations; beveled magazine well; lowered and flared ejection port; Cabot aluminum TriStar trigger; match-grade hand-fit barrel; rhombus-cut front strap and mainspring housing checkering; sight and grip options
MSRP . . . . starting at $3995.00

Canik USA

CANIK USA TP9SFX

TP9SFX

Action: SA
Grips: Plastic
Barrel: 5.2 in.
Sights: Industry-standard dovetail sight cuts & four red dot interface plates; removable red dot over
Weight: 29.92 oz.
Caliber: 9mm Luger

Capacity: 20+1 rounds
Features: Improved single action trigger with 3.5–4 lb. pull; lightening cuts on slide to reduce muzzle rise; reversible ambidextrous cocking lever; adjustable length reversible magazine catch; Picatinny rail; Tungsten grey Cerakote over phosphate
MSRP $549.99

Caracal USA

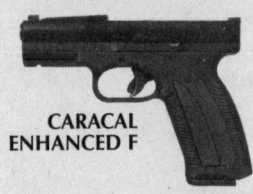

CARACAL ENHANCED F

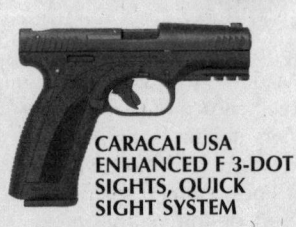

CARACAL USA ENHANCED F 3-DOT SIGHTS, QUICK SIGHT SYSTEM

ENHANCED F

Action: Semiautomatic
Grips: Polymer
Barrel: 4 in.
Sights: Three-dot
Weight: 28 oz.
Caliber: 9mm
Capacity: 10, 18 rounds
Features: Striker-fired polymer frame; integrated trigger safety; firing pin safety; drop safety; rail interface for light and laser mounting; full-length steel slide guide; fully supported chamber; cold-hammer-forged barrel; available Quick Sight option
MSRP $599.00

ENHANCED F 3-DOT SIGHTS, QUICK SIGHT SYSTEM

Action: Semiautomatic
Grips: Polymer
Barrel: 4 in.
Sights: Three-dot dovetail
Weight: 28 oz.
Caliber: 9mm
Capacity: 10, 18 rounds
Features: Cocking indicator; drop and firing pin safeties; Quick Sight version has a slide places both front and rear sights on a single focal plane; available with a threaded barrel; available in black, tan, and OD green finishes
MSRP . . . . $599.00–$699.00

Charter Arms

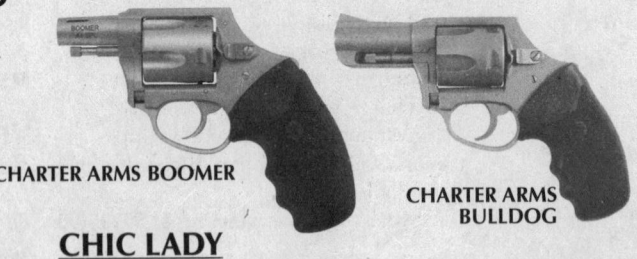

CHARTER ARMS BOOMER

CHARTER ARMS BULLDOG

CHARTER ARMS CHIC LADY DAO

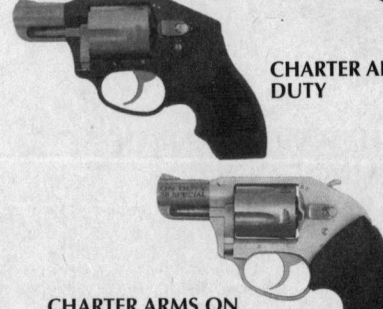

CHARTER ARMS OFF DUTY

CHARTER ARMS ON DUTY

BOOMER

Action: DAO revolver
Grips: Rubber
Barrel: 2 in. tapered
Sights: None
Weight: 20 oz.
Caliber: .44 Spl.
Capacity: 5 rounds
Features: Designed specifically for concealed carry; DAO hammer; full rubber combat grips; matte stainless finish; tapered barrel for reduced kick
MSRP $443.00

BULLDOG

Action: DA revolver
Grips: Rubber; Crimson Trace lasergrips
Barrel: 2.5 in., 3 in. or 5 in. in target model
Sights: Fixed, adjustable rear on Target model
Weight: 21 oz.
Caliber: .44 Spl.
Capacity: 5 rounds
Features: A larger concealed carry revolver, with DA/SA exposed hammer; available configurations include: Blue Standard; Tiger; Classic with 3-in. barrel, no underlug, exposed crane, and full wood grips; black Nitride; On Duty semi-concealed hammer in all stainless; Stainless Standard; Stainless DAO with concealed hammer; matte stainless with Crimson Trace laser grips; and Target with ramp front sight and adjustable rear
MSRP . . . . $409.00–$690.00

CHIC LADY

Action: DA/SA, DAO revolver
Grips: Rubber
Barrel: 2 in.
Sights: Fixed
Weight: 12 oz.
Caliber: .38 Spl.
Capacity: 5 rounds
Features: High-polish stainless-steel pink anodized aluminum frame; frame based on Undercover Lite models; DA/SA explosed hammer version also available with Crimson Trace laser grips
MSRP . . . . $425.00–$672.00

OFF DUTY

Action: DA revolver
Grips: Crimson Trace lasergrip
Barrel: 2 in.
Sights: Serrated front, rear notch
Weight: 12 oz.
Caliber: .38 Spl. +P
Capacity: 5 rounds
Features: Lightweight, concealed hammer DAO concealed carry revolver of aircraft-grade aluminum and stainless steel; finishes include: black frame/high-polished stainless barrel and cylinder; black frame/matte stainless barrel and cylinder; matte aluminum frame/matte gray barrel and cylinder
MSRP . . . . $404.00–$436.00

ON DUTY

Action: DA revolver
Grips: Rubber; Crimson Trace lasergrips
Barrel: 2 in.
Sights: Fixed
Weight: 12 oz.
Caliber: .357 Mag., .38 Spl. +P
Capacity: 5 rounds
Features: Unique semi-concealed hammer design; constructed of heat-treated aluminum; allows single-action and double-action operations while minimizing the risk of snagging the hammer on clothing; standard or Crimson Trace grip
MSRP $402.00

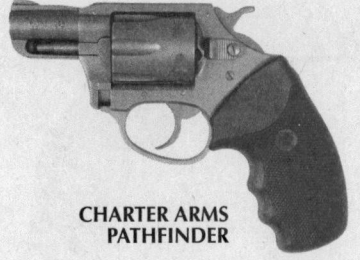

CHARTER ARMS PATHFINDER

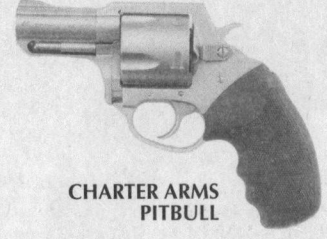

CHARTER ARMS PITBULL

CHARTER ARMS PITBULL 9MM BLACKNITRIDE FINISH

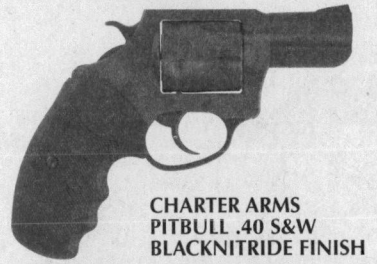

CHARTER ARMS PITBULL .40 S&W BLACKNITRIDE FINISH

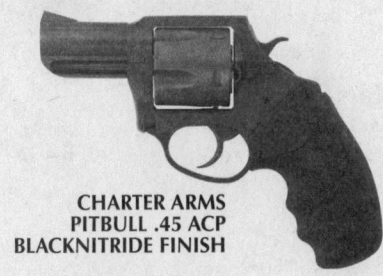

CHARTER ARMS PITBULL .45 ACP BLACKNITRIDE FINISH

CHARTER ARMS MAG PUG

PATHFINDER

Action: DA revolver
Grips: Rubber; Crimson Trace lasergrips
Barrel: 2 in., 4.2 in.
Sights: Fixed, adjustable rear on Target model
Weight: 12 oz.–24 oz.
Caliber: .22 LR, .22 Mag.
Capacity: 6 rounds
Features: Choice of stainless steel or aluminum frames, has exposed hammer for DA/SA operation; aluminum frame Lite models in .22 Mag only available in brushed silver frame with matte blue barrel and cylinder; pink frame with matte silver cylinder and barrel; lavender frame with matte silver barrel and cylinder; and matte black frame with matte stainless barrel and cylinder; steel frame models are in .22 LR and .22 WMR, with choice of barrel lengths, all in all stainless
MSRP . . . . $365.00–$409.00

PITBULL

Action: DA/SA
Grips: Rubber
Barrel: 2.5 in.
Sights: Fixed
Weight: 22 oz.
Caliber: .40 S&W, 9mm,.45 ACP
Capacity: 5 rounds
Features: Unique design provides a dual coil spring assembly located in the extractor which allows for the insertion and retention of rimless cartridges, so no moon clips are required
MSRP . . . . $489.00–$502.00

PITBULL 9MM BLACKNITRIDE FINISH

Action: DA/SA revolver
Grips: Rubber
Barrel: 2.2 in.

Sights: Fixed
Weight: 22 oz.
Caliber: 9mm
Capacity: 5 rounds
Features: Rimless cartridge extractor assembly system; dual coil spring assembly located in the extractor; nitride adds hardness to the finish and reduces friction and wear; scratch-resistant surface; extended life in the rifling and chambers
MSRP $522.00

PITBULL .40 S&W BLACKNITRIDE FINISH

Action: DA/SA revolver
Grips: Rubber
Barrel: 2.3 in.
Sights: Fixed
Weight: 20 oz.
Caliber: .40 caliber
Capacity: 5 rounds
Features: Dual coil spring assembly located in the extractor; nitride adds hardness to the finish and reduces friction and wear; scratch-resistant surface; extended life in the rifling and chambers
MSRP $509.00

PITBULL .45 ACP BLACKNITRIDE FINISH

Action: DA/SA revolver
Grips: Rubber
Barrel: 2.5 in.
Sights: Fixed
Weight: 22 oz.
Caliber: .45 ACP
Capacity: 5 rounds
Features: Rimless cartridge extractor assembly system; dual coil spring assembly located in the extractor; nitride adds hardness to the finish and reduces friction and wear; scratch-resistant surface; extended life in the rifling and chambers
MSRP $509.00

MAG PUG

Action: DA revolver
Grips: Rubber; Crimson Trace lasergrips
Barrel: 2.2 in., 4.2 in.
Sights: Fixed, adjustable rear on Target model
Weight: 23 oz.
Caliber: .357 Mag.
Capacity: 5 rounds
Features: Traditional spurred hammer and full-size grips; optional Crimson Trace grip; stainless steel frame; blued and stainless finish
Standard: $394.00
Crimson: $609.00
Green/black stripe: $456.00
Stainless 4.2-in. barrel: $470.00
SS DAO: $395.00

Charter Arms

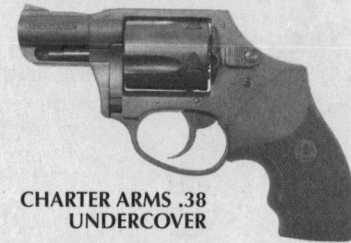

CHARTER ARMS .38 UNDERCOVER

CHARTER ARMS UNDERCOVER BLACKNITRIDE FINISH

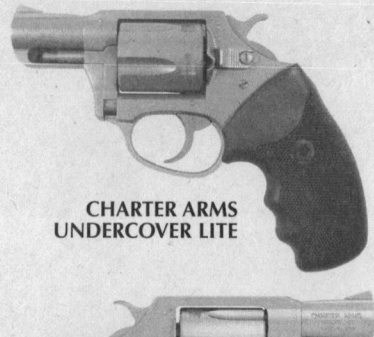

CHARTER ARMS UNDERCOVER LITE

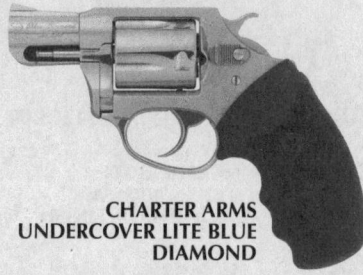

CHARTER ARMS UNDERCOVER LITE BLUE DIAMOND

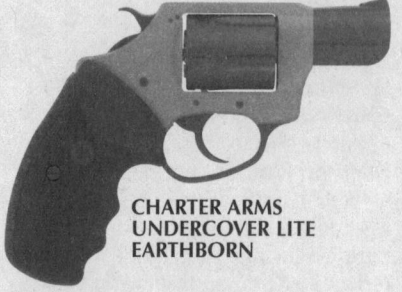

CHARTER ARMS UNDERCOVER LITE EARTHBORN

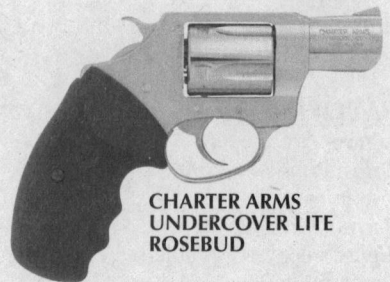

CHARTER ARMS UNDERCOVER LITE ROSEBUD

UNDERCOVER

Action: DA revolver
Grips: Checkered compact rubber or Crimson Trace lasergrips
Barrel: 2 in.
Sights: Fixed
Weight: 16 oz.
Caliber: .38 Spl. +P
Capacity: 5 rounds
Features: Stainless steel frame; blued, stainless, tiger & black, DAO available; compact and lightweight, this revolver is ideal for concealed carry situations; 3-point cylinder lock-up
MSRP . . . . $346.00–$404.00

UNDERCOVER BLACKNITRIDE FINISH

Action: DA/SA revolver
Grips: Rubber
Barrel: 2 in.
Sights: Fixed
Weight: 16 oz.
Caliber: .38 Spl.
Capacity: 5 rounds
Features: Compact and lightweight; ideal for concealed carry due to 2 in. barrel and superior safety features; nitride adds hardness to the finish and reduces friction and wear; scratch-resistant surface; extended life in the rifling and chambers
MSRP $379.00

UNDERCOVER LITE

Action: DA revolver
Grips: Rubber, compact
Barrel: 2 in.
Sights: Fixed
Weight: 12 oz.
Caliber: .38 Spl. +P
Capacity: 5 rounds
Features: Frame is constructed from aircraft-grade aluminum and steel; traditional spurred hammer; optional DAO (double action trigger); many finishes and special editions available
MSRP . . . . $397.00–$473.00

Chiappa Firearms

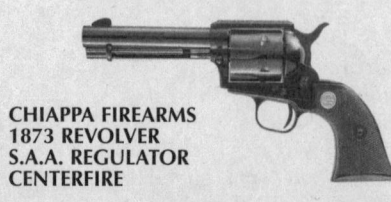

CHIAPPA FIREARMS 1873 REVOLVER S.A.A. REGULATOR CENTERFIRE

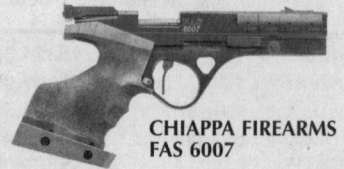

CHIAPPA FIREARMS FAS 6007

1873 REVOLVER S.A.A. REGULATOR CENTERFIRE

Action: SA revolver
Grips: Black polymer
Barrel: 4.75 in.
Sights: Fixed front
Weight: 32 oz.
Caliber: .38 Spl.
Capacity: 6 rounds
Features: Centerfire cartridge; perfect for competition or plinking
MSRP $443.00

FAS 6007

Action: Semiautomatic
Grips: Wood

Barrel: 5.63 in.
Sights: Two-position front, adjustable rear
Weight: 37.6 oz.
Caliber: .22 LR
Capacity: 5 rounds
Features: Developed in collaboration with Olympic shooters; adjustable palm rest; a rear sight with an adjustable window; adjustable grip; outside access set screws for hammer and hammer weight; modular weights; adjustable trigger; shock buffer
MSRP $1630.00

Chiappa Firearms

CHIAPPA FIREARMS RHINO 30 DS HUNTER, 60 DS HUNTER

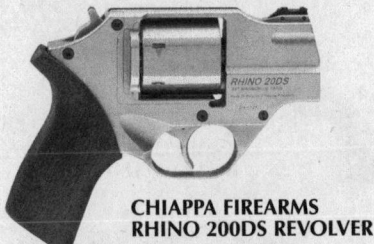

CHIAPPA FIREARMS RHINO 200DS REVOLVER

CHIAPPA FIREARMS SAA 17-10

RHINO 30 DS HUNTER, 60 DS HUNTER

Action: Revolver
Grips: Walnut
Barrel: 3 in., 6 in.
Sights: Fiber optic front, adjustable rear
Weight: 28.8 oz.–32 oz.
Caliber: .357 Mag.
Capacity: 6 rounds
Features: Frame and barrel in "Hunter" OD Green Cerakote; barrels have vent ribs; stippled walnut grips with finger grooves; Rhino's distinct flat-sided cylinder; long-barrel version has accessory rail; includes three moon clips
30DS Hunter: **$1237.00**
60DS Hunter: **$1326.00**

RHINO 200DS REVOLVER

Action: Revolver
Grips: Wood
Barrel: 6 in.
Sights: Front blade; adjustable rear
Weight: 37 oz.
Caliber: .357, .40 S&W, .357 Mag/9mm combo
Capacity: 6 rounds
Features: Rhino barrel is aligned with the bottom most chamber, which lowers the center of gravity and yields a centerline of the bore more in line with the shooter's arm allowing for the most natural "point ability" while engaging a target; reduces both recoil and muzzle flip which insures subsequent shots are on target faster; frame available in chrome, black, or gold finish
MSRP . . . . **$1040.00–$1213.00**

SAA 17-10

Action: SA revolver
Grips: Plastic
Barrel: 7.5 in.
Sights: Adjustable
Weight: 34 oz.
Caliber: .17 HMR
Capacity: 10 rounds
Features: Black frame
MSRP **$249.00**

Christensen Arms

CHRISTENSEN ARMS 1911 A5, A5-TR, A4

1911 A5, A5-TR, A4

Action: Semiautomatic
Grips: G10
Barrel: 4 in., 5 in.
Sights: Raised night sights, suppressor sights
Weight: 32 oz. (A4), 35.2 oz. (A5), 38.4 oz. (A5-TR)
Caliber: 9mm
Capacity: 9 rounds

Features: Aluminum frame machined from 7075 billet aluminum; A5s have raised night sights, A4 has 4-in. threaded barrel and suppressor height sights as well as tactical rail and flared magwell
MSRP **$1995.00**

Cimarron Firearms Co.

CIMARRON 1872 OPEN TOP NAVY

CIMARRON 1911

1872 OPEN TOP NAVY

Action: SA revolver
Grips: Walnut
Barrel: 4.75, 5.5, 7.5 in.
Sights: Fixed, open
Weight: 40 oz.
Caliber: .44 Spl.; .44 Colt, .44 Russian

Capacity: 6 rounds
Features: Forged, color case-hardened frame; Army or Navy grip; charcoal blued, standard blued, or original barrel finish
MSRP . . . . **$518.70–$531.67**

1911

Action: Semiautomatic
Grips: Walnut
Barrel: 5 in.
Sights: Open, fixed
Weight: 39.52 oz.
Caliber: .45 ACP
Capacity: 8+1 rounds
Features: Correct historical markings; diamond checkered walnut grips; nickel, polished blued, and parkerized finish; optional WWI-style lanyard magazine
MSRP . . . . **$570.00–$799.50**

Cimarron Firearms Co.

CIMARRON 1911 WILD BUNCH COMBO

1911 WILD BUNCH COMBO

Action: Semiautomatic
Grips: Diamond checkered walnut
Barrel: 5 in.
Sights: Fixed
Weight: 39.52 oz.
Caliber: .45 ACP
Capacity: 8+1 rounds
Features: Correct historical markings; the original 1911 frame with a Type 1 smooth mainspring housing; combo includes the 1911 in polished blue finish and the Tanker shoulder holster, a reproduction of the rig used by William Holden in the movie The Wild Bunch
MSRP **$955.50**

BAD BOY

Action: Revolver
Grips: Wood
Barrel: 6 in., 8 in.
Sights: Ramp front, adjustable rear
Weight: N/A
Caliber: .44 Mag.
Capacity: 6 rounds
Features: Model P pre-war frame single action; octagonal barrel; flat top; adjustable rear sight
MSRP **$704.90**

BISLEY MODEL

Action: SA revolver
Grips: Walnut
Barrel: 4.75 in., 5.5 in., 7.5 in.
Sights: Fixed, open
Weight: 42–45 oz.
Caliber: .45 LC, .44 Spl., .44 WCF, .357 Mag.
Capacity: 6 rounds
Features: Reproduction of the original Colt Bisley; forged, color case-hardened frame; blued, charcoal blued, or nickel finish
MSRP **$651.60**

ELIMINATOR 8

Action: SA
Grips: Wood
Barrel: 4.75 in.
Sights: Fixed
Weight: N/A
Caliber: .357 Mag., .45 LC
Capacity: N/A
Features: Octagonal barrel; short stroke; checkered walnut Army grip; Cimarron low wide hammer; US

action job; case hardened pre-war frame; standard blue finish;
MSRP **$760.50**

FRONTIER

Action: SA
Grips: Ivory
Barrel: 4.75 in., 7.5 in.
Sights: Fixed
Weight: 4 lb. 8 oz.
Caliber: .45 Colt
Capacity: N/A
Features: Old silver frame; standard blue finish; laser engraved; nickel frame and finish available
MSRP . . . . **$542.33–$741.23**

HOLY SMOKER

Action: SA revolver
Grips: Walnut
Barrel: 4.75 in.
Sights: Open, fixed
Weight: 36 oz.
Caliber: .45 Colt
Capacity: 6 rounds
Features: Revolver made famous in *3:10 to Yuma* film; standard blued finish; case-hardened pre-war frame; gold-plated sterling silver cross inlayed on both sides of one-piece walnut grip
MSRP **$744.87**

LIGHTNING

Action: SA revolver
Grips: Walnut
Barrel: 3.5 in., 4.75 in., 5.5 in., 6.5 in.
Sights: Fixed, open
Weight: 28.5–30.75 oz.
Caliber: .38 Spl., .22 LR, .41 Colt, .32-20 Win./.32 H&R Dual Cylinder
Capacity: 6 rounds
Features: Forged, pre-war color case-hardened frame; charcoal blued, standard blued, or original barrel finish; walnut stock smooth or checkered
MSRP . . . . **$564.98–$664.92**

CIMARRON FIREARMS BAD BOY

CIMARRON BISLEY MODEL

CIMARRON ELIMINATOR 8

CIMARRON FRONTIER

CIMARRON HOLY SMOKER

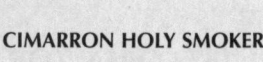

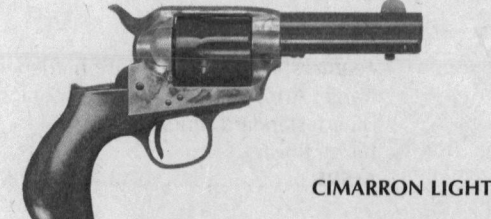

CIMARRON LIGHTNING

Cimarron Firearms Co.

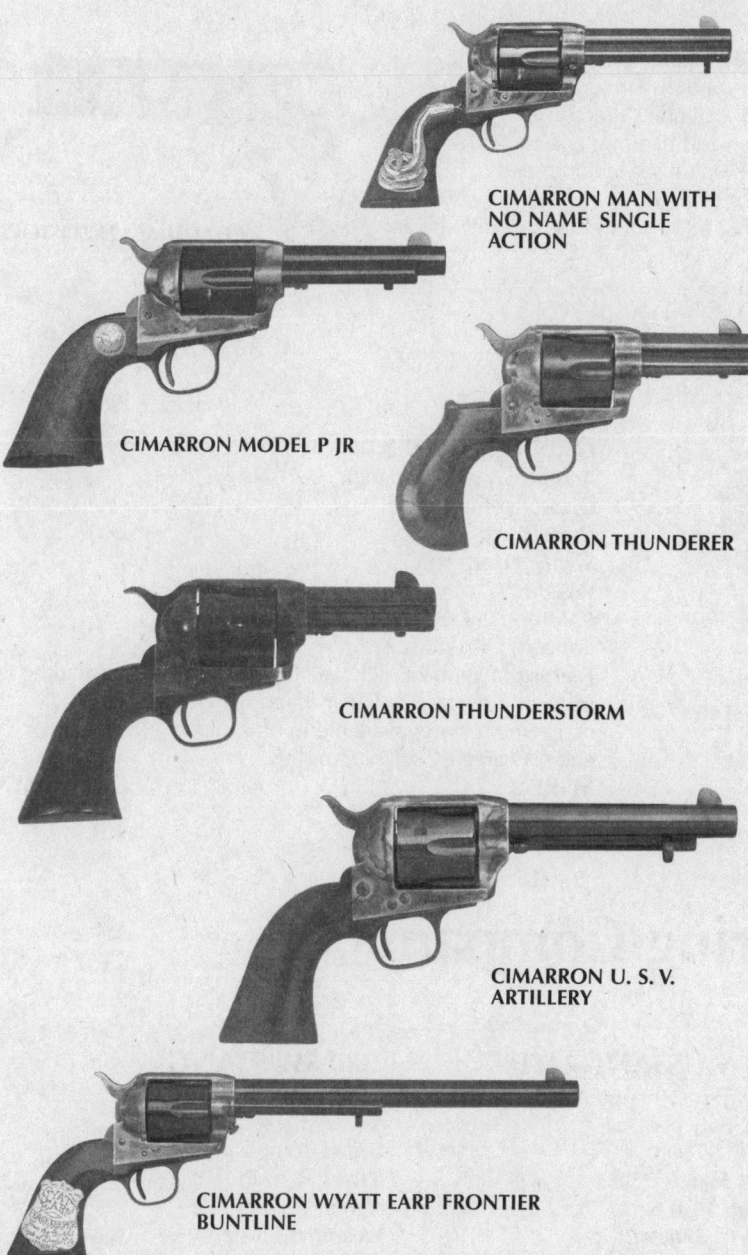

CIMARRON MAN WITH NO NAME SINGLE ACTION

CIMARRON MODEL P JR

CIMARRON THUNDERER

CIMARRON THUNDERSTORM

CIMARRON U. S. V. ARTILLERY

CIMARRON WYATT EARP FRONTIER BUNTLINE

THUNDERER
Action: SA revolver
Grips: Walnut, ivory, mother of pearl or black hard rubber
Barrel: 3.5 in. w/ ejector, 4.75 in., 5.5 in., 7.5 in.
Sights: Fixed, open
Weight: 38–43.60 oz.
Caliber: .45 LC, .44 Spl., .44 WCF, .357 Mag., .45 LC/.45 ACP Dual Cylinder
Capacity: 6 rounds
Features: Designed in 1990 by Cimarron founder & president "Texas Jack" Harvey; forged, color case-hardened frame; blued, charcoal blued or stainless finish
MSRP . . . . $588.97–$766.19

THUNDERSTORM
Action: SA revolver
Grips: Walnut
Barrel: 3.5 in., 4.75 in.
Sights: Front, rear
Weight: 35.7 oz.–39.68 oz.
Caliber: .45 Colt, .357 Mag./.38 Spl.
Capacity: 6 rounds
Features: Checkered grips; stainless steel or standard blued finishes; wide front sights and deep rear notch; smooth action and hand-knurled hammer; available in Model P or Thunderer versions
MSRP . . . . $800.80–$975.00

U. S. V. ARTILLERY
Action: SA revolver
Grips: Walnut
Barrel: 5.5 in.
Sights: Fixed, open
Weight: 40 oz.
Caliber: .45 LC
Capacity: 6 rounds
Features: Old model case-hardened with US Artillery markings; stock is a solid piece of walnut with RAC Cartouche; blued, charcoal blued, or original finish
MSRP . . . . $603.33–$632.94

MAN WITH NO NAME SINGLE ACTION
Action: SA revolver
Grips: Walnut
Barrel: 4.75 in., 5.5 in.
Sights: Open, fixed
Weight: 42.56 oz.–44.16 oz.
Caliber: .45 Colt
Capacity: 6 rounds
Features: Model P in .45 Colt; sterling silver snake on both sides of walnut grip
MSRP $758.20

MODEL P JR.
Action: SA revolver
Grips: Walnut
Barrel: 3.5 in., 4.75 in., 5.5 in.
Sights: Fixed, open
Weight: 35.2 oz.
Caliber: .38 Spl., .22 LR, .32-20 Win./.32 H&R Dual Cylinder
Capacity: 6 rounds
Features: Fashioned after the 1873 Colt SAA but on a smaller scale; color case-hardened frame
MSRP . . . . $491.70–$648.93

WYATT EARP FRONTIER BUNTLINE
Action: SA revolver
Grips: Walnut
Barrel: 10 in.
Sights: Open, fixed
Weight: 43.04 oz.
Caliber: .45 LC
Capacity: 6 rounds
Features: Revolver made famous in the film *Tombstone*; one-piece walnut grips with silver inlaid medallion; choice of blue or case hardened finishes
MSRP . . . . $873.83–$904.64

Citadel by Legacy Sports

M-1911
Action: Semiautomatic
Grips: Cocobolo
Barrel: 3.5 in., 5 in.
Sights: Fixed
Weight: 33.6–37.6 oz.
Caliber: 9mm, .45 ACP
Capacity: 7 or 8 rounds

Features: Choice of Government or Officer models with a Series 70 firing system; extended slide stop, skeletonized hammer and trigger, matte blue finish; includes two magazines
MSRP. $599.00

CITADEL M-1911 PISTOLS

Cobra Pistols

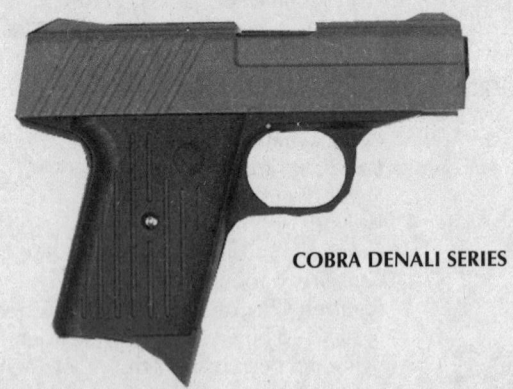

COBRA DENALI SERIES

DENALI SERIES
Action: SA semiautomatic
Grips: Synthetic
Barrel: 2.8 in.
Sights: Fixed
Weight: 17 oz.
Caliber: .380 ACP
Capacity: 5 rounds
Features: Compact, lightweight, and easily concealed; features a durable polymer frame with a pushbutton magazine release; available in black, tactical tan, satin, and OD green Cerakote finishes
MSRP. $199.93

Colt's Manufacturing Company

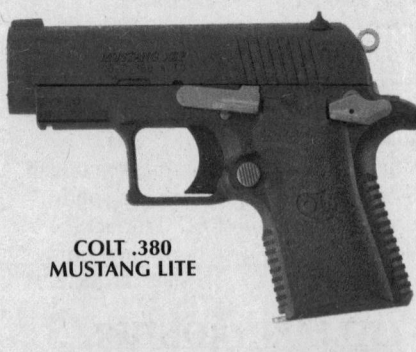

COLT .380 MUSTANG LITE

.380 MUSTANG LITE
Action: SA semiautomatic
Grips: Polymer
Barrel: 2.75 in.
Sights: Fixed
Weight: 11.8 oz.
Caliber: .380 ACP
Capacity: 6 rounds
Features: Polymer grip frame with tactical grip profile; texturing on front and back straps; front and rear dovetail sights; aluminum alloy frame also available
MSRP. $599.00

.380 MUSTANG POCKETLITE
Action: SA semiautomatic
Grips: Composite
Barrel: 2.75 in.
Sights: High-profile
Weight: 12.5 oz.
Caliber: .380 ACP
Capacity: 6+1 rounds
Features: Aluminum alloy frame with a CNC-machined stainless steel slide and barrel; thumb safety and firing-pin-block safety; solid aluminum trigger; lowered ejection port; electroless nickeled aluminum receiver
MSRP. $699.00

COLT .380 MUSTANG POCKETLITE

Colt's Manufacturing Company

COBRA, CLASSIC COBRA

COLT COMBAT UNIT RAIL GUN

COLT COMPETITION PISTOL

COLT CUSTOM COMPETITION PISTOL

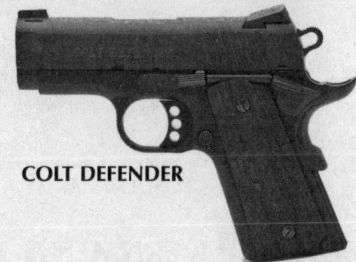

COLT DEFENDER

COLT GOLD CUP TROPHY

COLT COMPETITION SS

COBRA, CLASSIC COBRA

Action: Revolver
Grips: Rubber
Barrel: 2 in.
Sights: Fiber optic front
Weight: 25 oz.
Caliber: .38 Spl.
Capacity: 6 rounds
Features: DA revolver with all-steel contruction; small frame and barrel ideal for concealed carry; Hogue Overmolded grip has been moved rearward to manage recoil on standard model; Classic version has medallion wood grips, brass front bead, and polished cylinder
Cobra: $699.00
Classic Cobra: $749.00

COMBAT UNIT RAIL GUN

Action: Semiautomatic
Grips: G10
Barrel: 5 in.
Sights: Novak night sight front, Novak Low Mount Carry rear
Weight: 40 oz.
Caliber: 9mm, .45 ACP
Capacity: 8 rounds (.45 ACP), 9 rounds (9mm)
Features: Upgraded duty-ready 1911 with 1913 Picatinny rail; checkered and scalloped gray G10 grips;

designed with Special Forces trainers Daryl Holland and Ken Hackathorn
MSRP $1499.00

COMPETITION PISTOL

Action: SA
Grips: G10 grips
Barrel: 5 in.
Sights: Fiber optic front, Novak adjustable rear
Weight: 36 oz.
Caliber: .38 Super, .45 ACP, 9mm
Capacity: 8 or 9 rounds
Features: Dual spring recoil system; undercut trigger guard; upswept beavertail grip safety; National Match barrel
Standard: $899.00
SS 9mm, .45 ACP: $999.00
SS .38 Super: $1049.00
Titanium: $999.00

CUSTOM COMPETITION PISTOL

Action: Semiautomatic
Grips: G10
Barrel: 5 in.
Sights: Novak fiber optic front, Bomar-style rear
Weight: N/A
Caliber: .45 ACP
Capacity: 8 rounds
Features: Hand-assembled by Colt's

Custom Shop gunsmiths; blended magwell; frontstrap checkering; stainless steel slide and frame; wide slide serrations front and rear
MSRP $2499.00

DEFENDER

Action: Semiautomatic
Grips: Rubber finger-grooved
Barrel: 5 in.
Sights: White dot carry front and rear
Weight: 30 oz.
Caliber: .45 ACP, 9mm
Capacity: 7+1 rounds, 8+1 rounds
Features: Beveled magazine well; black skeletonized aluminum trigger; Series 80 firing system; beavertail grip and standard thumb safety; stainless steel slide, Teflon coated receiver; aluminum alloy frame
MSRP $999.00

GOLD CUP TROPHY

Action: Semiautomatic
Grips: Black composite
Barrel: 5 in.
Sights: Dovetail front, adjustable rear
Weight: 39 oz.
Caliber: 9mm, .45 ACP
Capacity: 8+1 rounds
Features: Beveled magazine well; beavertail grip safety; Colt competition blue G10 grips; wide aluminum 3-Hole trigger adjustable for over travel; stainless steel frame finish and material; enhanced hammer. National Match version appears in blue and adds target sights, National Match barrel, wood grips with inset gold Colt medallion
MSRP $1699.00
National Match: $1299.00

Colt's Manufacturing Company

COLT LIGHTWEIGHT COMMANDER

COLT SERIES 70 GOVERNMENT

COLT SINGLE ACTION ARMY

LIGHTWEIGHT COMMANDER

Action: SA
Grips: G10 grips
Barrel: 4.25 in.
Sights: Novak sights
Weight: 29.4 oz.
Caliber: .45 ACP, 9mm
Capacity: 8 or 9 rounds
Features: Shorter profile and lower weight than a traditional full-size Government model; dual spring recoil system; undercut trigger guard; upswept beavertail grip safety
MSRP . . . . $999.00\

M45A1 MARINE PISTOL

Action: Semiautomatic
Grips: G10
Barrel: 5 in.
Sights: Novak night sights
Weight: 40 oz.
Caliber: .45 ACP
Capacity: 7 rounds
Features: Selected by the US Marine Corps as their Close Quarters Battle Pistol; available in Decobond Brown finish; checkered Desert Tan G10 grip panels; underside Picatinny rail
MSRP $1699.00

RAIL GUN

Action: Semiautomatic
Grips: Double diamond rosewood or blackened rosewood
Barrel: 5 in.
Sights: White dot, Novak rear
Weight: 39 oz.
Caliber: .45 ACP, 9mm
Capacity: 8+1 rounds
Features: Stainless steel, blackened receiver and brushed slide, blackened receiver and slide frame finish options; stainless steel frame material; Colt upswept beavertail with palm swell; enhanced hammer; Picatinny rail; National Match barrel; single-slide tactical thumb safety
MSRP $1199.00

SERIES 70 GOVERNMENT

Action: Semiautomatic
Grips: Double diamond rosewood
Barrel: 5 in.
Sights: Fixed
Weight: 39 oz.
Caliber: .45 ACP
Capacity: 7+1 rounds
Features: Spur hammer; single-action; blued finish; stainless steel frame; short steel trigger; original series 70 firing system with titanium firing pin
MSRP $899.00

SINGLE ACTION ARMY

Action: SA revolver
Grips: Black composite eagle
Barrel: 4.75 in., 7.5 in.
Sights: Fixed
Weight: 46 oz.
Caliber: .357 Mag., .45 Colt
Capacity: 6 rounds
Features: Case-colored frame; transfer bar; second generation style cylinder bushing; blued or nickel finish
MSRP $1799.00

COLT M45A1 MARINE PISTOL

COLT RAIL GUN

CZ-USA (Ceska Zbrojovka)

CZ-USA 75 B

CZ–USA 75 B Ω CONVERTIBLE

CZ–USA 75 B Ω URBAN GREY SUPPRESSOR-READY

CZ-USA 75 COMPACT

CZ–USA 75 P-01 Ω CONVERTIBLE

CZ–USA 75 P-01 Ω URBAN GREY SUPPRESSOR-READY

CZ-USA 75 SP-01

75 B
Action: Semiautomatic
Grips: Plastic
Barrel: 4.6 in.
Sights: Fixed, 3-dot system
Weight: 35.2 oz.
Caliber: 9mm
Capacity: 10, 16 rounds
Features: Steel frame; high-capacity double column magazines; hammer forged barrels; ergonomic grip and controls; DA/SA; firing pin block safety; black polycoat finish
MSRP . . . . $631.00–$643.00

75 B Ω CONVERTIBLE
Action: DA/SA
Grips: Plastic
Barrel: 4.6 in.
Sights: Fixed
Weight: 35.2 oz.
Caliber: 9mm Luger
Capacity: 10, 16 rounds
Features: Swappable safety/decocker; interlocking trigger design for easy disassembly and reassembly without tools
MSRP $587.00

75 B Ω URBAN GREY SUPPRESSOR-READY
Action: DA/SA
Grips: Plastic
Barrel: 5.2 in.
Sights: High titrium three dot
Weight: 42.1 oz.
Caliber: 9mm Luger
Capacity: 10, 18 rounds
Features: Threaded barrels; high suppressor sights with tritium lamps; swappable safety/decocker; interlocking trigger design for easy disassembly and reassembly without tools
MSRP $655.00

75 COMPACT
Action: Semiautomatic
Grips: Plastic
Barrel: 3.8 in.
Sights: Fixed, 3-dot system
Weight: 32.48 oz.
Caliber: 9mm Luger
Capacity: 10, 14 rounds
Features: Black polycoat, dual tone, satin nickel frame finishes; manual safety; steel frame; high capacity double column magazines; hammer forged barrels
MSRP . . . . $646.00–$658.00

75 P-01 Ω CONVERTIBLE
Action: DA/SA
Grips: Rubber
Barrel: 3.8 in.
Sights: Fixed
Weight: 28 oz.

Caliber: 9mm Luger
Capacity: 10, 14 rounds
Features: Swappable safety/decocker; interlocking trigger design for easy disassembly and reassembly without tools; compact size and reduced weight ideal for discrete carry
MSRP $646.00

75 P-01 Ω URBAN GREY SUPPRESSOR-READY
Action: DA/SA
Grips: Rubber
Barrel: 4.5 in.
Sights: High titrium three dot
Weight: 30.1 oz.
Caliber: 9mm Luger
Capacity: 10, 16 rounds
Features: Swappable safety/decocker; threaded barrels; high suppressor sights with tritium lamps; extended capacity magazine; interlocking trigger design for easy disassembly and reassembly without tools; compact size and reduced weight ideal for discrete carry
MSRP $673.00

75 SP-01
Action: Semiautomatic
Grips: Rubber
Barrel: 4.6 in.
Sights: 3-Dot tritium night
Weight: 38.4 oz.
Caliber: 9mm Luger
Capacity: 10, 18 rounds
Features: Based upon the Shadow Target; decocking lever; safety stop on hammer; firing pin safety; steel frame
MSRP $700.00

CZ-USA (Ceska Zbrojovka)

CZ-USA 75 SP-01 PHANTOM

CZ–USA 75 SP-01 SHADOW TARGET II

CZ–USA 75 TACTICAL SPORT ORANGE

CZ–USA 75 SP-01 TACTICAL URBAN GREY SUPPRESSOR-READY

CZ-USA 75 TS CZECHMATE

CZ-USA 97 B

75 SP-01 PHANTOM

Action: Semiautomatic
Grips: Polymer, interchangeable
Barrel: 4.6 in.
Sights: Three-dot
Weight: 29.4 oz.
Caliber: 9mm
Capacity: 18 rounds
Features: Essentially a polymer-framed SP-01 Tactical; same fiber-reinforced polymer formula used in P-09 and P-07 frames; interchangeable backstraps and mag compatibility with the standard 75 platform; ambidextrous decocking lever; firing pin block safety
MSRP $636.00

75 SP-01 SHADOW TARGET II

Action: DA/SA
Grips: Thin aluminum checkered
Barrel: 4.61 in.
Sights: Adjustable target rear, fiber optic front
Weight: 38.4 oz.
Caliber: 9mm Luger
Capacity: 18 rounds
Features: Competition-ready Pre-B style SP-01 Shadow, featuring a CZ Custom trigger job with the new short reset single-action trigger, fully-adjustable rear sight, fiber optic front sight, stainless steel guide rod, lighter springs for competition (11 lb recoil and 13 lb main springs), extended

magazine release, drop-free magazines and checkered aluminum grips; created by champion shooter Angus Hobdell's CZ Custom Shop to have trigger pulls of 3.0-4.0 lbs in SA and 7.5-8.5 lbs in DA
MSRP $1687.00

75 SP-01 TACTICAL URBAN GREY SUPPRESSOR-READY

Action: DA/SA
Grips: Rubber
Barrel: 5.2 in.
Sights: High titrium three dot
Weight: 42.1 oz.
Caliber: 9mm Luger
Capacity: 10, 18 rounds
Features: Threaded barrels; high suppressor sights with tritium lamps; extended capacity magazine; ambidextrous decocker; 1913 accessory rail on the dust cover; rubber grip panels; corrosion-resistant black polycoat finish; extended beavertail
MSRP $745.00

75 TACTICAL SPORT ORANGE

Action: SA
Grips: Thin aluminum
Barrel: 5.4 in.
Sights: Adjustable
Weight: 48 oz.
Caliber: 9mm Luger; .40 S&W
Capacity: 10, 16, 20 rounds
Features: Ambidextrous manual safety; slimmer trigger guard; improved grip geometry; thumb stop;

long slide; full-length dust cover; light pull and short reset
MSRP $1837.00

75 TS CZECHMATE

Action: Semiautomatic
Grips: Aluminum
Barrel: 5.4 in.
Sights: Fixed, C-more red dot
Weight: 48 oz.
Caliber: 9mm
Capacity: 20, 26 rounds
Features: Built upon a modified version of the CZ 75 TS frame; interchangeable parts allow the user to quickly configure the gun for both roles; features a single-action trigger mechanism; red-dot sight; includes spare barrel; includes three 20-round magazines and one 26-round magazine; all-steel pistol is finished in black matte
MSRP $3416.00

97 B

Action: Semiautomatic
Grips: Plastic
Barrel: 4.8 in.
Sights: Fixed
Weight: 40 oz.
Caliber: .45 ACP
Capacity: 10 rounds
Features: Manual safety; cold hammer-forged barrel; single- or double-action
MSRP $729.00

HANDGUNS

CZ-USA (Ceska Zbrojovka)

CZ-USA 2075 RAMI

CZ-USA ACCUSHADOW 2

CZ-USA P-01

CZ–USA P-07

CZ-USA P-07 OD GREEN

CZ-USA P-07 SUPPRESSOR-READY

CZ–USA P-07 URBAN GREY SUPPRESSOR-READY

CZ–USA P-09

CZ-USA P-09 OD GREEN

2075 RAMI

Action: Semiautomatic
Grips: Rubber
Barrel: 3 in.
Sights: Fixed
Weight: 25.6 oz.
Caliber: 9mm Luger
Capacity: 10, 14 rounds
Features: Operates in selective DA and SA mode depending on shooter's preferences; firing pin block; manual safety; double-stack magazine; black polycoat alloy frame; cold hammer forged
MSRP . . . . $632.00–$644.00

ACCUSHADOW 2

Action: Semiautomatic
Grips: Polymer
Barrel: 4.89 in.
Sights: Fiber optic front, HAJO rear
Weight: 46.5 oz.
Caliber: 9mm
Capacity: 17 rounds
Features: Steel frame; new quarter-turn bushing; short-reset trigger; hand-fit disconnector; custom hammer; safety is ambidextrous
MSRP $2138.00

P-01

Action: Semiautomatic
Grips: Rubber
Barrel: 3.8 in.
Sights: Fixed
Weight: 28.8 oz.
Caliber: 9mm Luger
Capacity: 10, 14 rounds
Features: Decocking lever; safety stop on hammer; firing pin safety; black polycoat frame finish; black or pink grips; single- or double-action
MSRP . . . . $646.00–$658.00

P-07

Action: DA/SA semiautomatic

Grips: Synthetic
Barrel: 3.8 in.
Sights: Fixed
Weight: 27 oz.
Caliber: 9mm
Capacity: 10, 15 rounds
Features: Ambidextrous safety or decocker; firing pin block
MSRP $510.00

P-07 OD GREEN

Action: Semiautomatic
Grips: Polymer
Barrel: 3.75 in.
Sights: Tritium night sights
Weight: 27.7 oz.
Caliber: 9mm
Capacity: 10, 15 rounds
Features: OD Green polymer frame; tritium nights sights; double-stack magazine
MSRP $539.00

P-07 SUPPRESSOR-READY

Action: Semiautomatic
Grips: Polymer
Barrel: 4.36 in.
Sights: High tritium thee-dot
Weight: 28.7 oz.
Caliber: 9mm
Capacity: 17 rounds
Features: Updated version of the CZ 75 P-07 Duty; interchangeable backstraps; nitrided finish on the slide; frame has been dehorned; interchangeable safety and decocker; muzzle is threaded ½×28 to accept suppressors
MSRP $539.00

P-07 URBAN GREY SUPPRESSOR-READY

Action: DA/SA
Grips: Stippled
Barrel: 4.5 in.
Sights: High titrium three dot
Weight: 28 oz.

Caliber: 9mm Luger
Capacity: 10, 17 rounds
Features: Swappable safety/decocker; threaded barrels; high suppressor sights with tritium lamps; extended capacity magazine; interlocking trigger design for easy disassembly and reassembly without tools; nitrated slide finish; increased corrosion resistance; small, medium, and large backstraps; integrated 1913 Picatinny rail on the dust cover; snag-free hammer; forward cocking serrations
MSRP $559.00

P-09

Action: DA/SA semiautomatic
Grips: Synthetic
Barrel: 4.53 in. or 5.23 in. (suppressor model)
Sights: Fixed
Weight: 30 oz.
Caliber: 9mm Luger
Capacity: 19 rounds
Features: Ambidextrous safety or decocker; firing pin block
MSRP $530.00

P-09 OD GREEN

Action: Semiautomatic
Grips: Polymer
Barrel: 4.54 in.
Sights: Tritium night sights
Weight: 31 oz.
Caliber: 9mm
Capacity: 10, 19 rounds
Features: OD Green polymer frame; night sights; ambidextrous decocker that can be converted to a manual safety; three backstrap sizes for a custom grip fit
MSRP $603.00

CZ-USA (Ceska Zbrojovka)

CZ–USA P-09 URBAN GREY SUPPRESSOR-READY

CZ-USA P-10 C

CZ-USA P-10 C URBAN GREY SUPPRESSOR-READY

CZ–USA SCORPION EVO 3 S1 PISTOL

CZ-USA SCORPION EVO 3 S1 PISTOL WITH FLASH CAN AND FOLDING BRACE

CZ-USA SCORPION EVO 3 S2 PISTOL MICRO WITH BRACE

CZ-USA CZ SCORPION EVO 3 S1 PISTOL W/ FLASH CAN

CZ-USA SHADOW 2 BLACK & BLUE

P-09 URBAN GREY SUPPRESSOR-READY

Action: DA/SA
Grips: Stippled
Barrel: 5.2 in.
Sights: High titrium three dot
Weight: 30.4 oz.
Caliber: 9mm Luger
Capacity: 21+1 rounds
Features: Threaded barrels; high suppressor sights with tritium lamps; Omega trigger system; swappable safety/decocker; 1913 Picatinny rail
MSRP $629.00

P-10 C

Action: Semiautomatic
Grips: Polymer
Barrel: 4.02 in.
Sights: Metal three-dot
Weight: 26 oz.
Caliber: 9mm
Capacity: 10, 12 rounds
Features: Striker-fired pistol; ergonomically designed with a mild palm swell, deep beavertail, and three interchangeable backstraps; trigger engineered to break at 4–4.5 lb.with a short reset; fiber-reinforced polymer frame with nitride finish
MSRP $499.00

P-10 C URBAN GREY SUPPRESSOR-READY

Action: Semiautomatic
Grips: Polymer
Barrel: 4.61 in.
Sights: High metal night sights
Weight: 26 oz.
Caliber: 9mm
Capacity: 10, 17 rounds
Features: Urban gray frame and

darker gray slide; threaded barrel is suppressor-ready; high sights
MSRP $559.00

SCORPION EVO 3 S1 PISTOL

Action: SA
Grips: Polymer
Barrel: 7.72 in.
Sights: Low-profile fully adjustable aperture and post, 4 rear aperture sizes
Weight: 5 lb.
Caliber: 9mm Luger
Capacity: 10+1 rounds, 20+1 rounds
Features: Scorpion sub-gun, imported as a pistol; blowback-operated; 11-in. Picatinny rail; ambidextrous controls; non-reciprocating charging handle is swappable and reach to the trigger is adjustable; arm brace adapter adds an AR-style pistol buffer tube to the rear of the action, enabling the use of an arm brace; barrel threaded at 18x1 to accept the factory flash hider and also at ½x28 underneath flash hider for easy addition of suppressor or after market muzzle device
MSRP . . . . $884.00–$911.00

SCORPION EVO 3 S1 PISTOL W/FLASH CAN

Action: Semiautomatic
Grips: Polymer
Barrel: 7.72 in.
Sights: Post front, low-profile fully adjustable aperture rear
Weight: 91.2 oz.
Caliber: 9mm
Capacity: 10, 20 rounds
Features: Extended forend; M-LOK attachment points; boosted the sight radius; dual threads of 18×1 and

½×28 provide options
MSRP $979.00

SCORPION EVO 3 S1 PISTOL WITH FLASH CAN AND FOLDING BRACE

Action: Semiautomatic
Grips: Polymer
Barrel: 7.72 in.
Sights: Post front, low-profile fully adjustable rear
Weight: 104 oz.
Caliber: 9mm
Capacity: 10, 20 rounds
Features: ATF-legal pistol unless brace is attached; Adjustable grips; flash can is removable for suppressor installation; rail space for lights and optics
MSRP $1047.00

SCORPION EVO 3 S2 PISTOL MICRO WITH BRACE

Action: Semiautomatic
Grips: Polymer
Barrel: 4.12 in.
Sights: Post front, low-profile fully adjustable rear
Weight: 88 oz.
Caliber: 9mm
Capacity: 10, 20 rounds
Features: ATF-legal pistol unless brace is attached; NoOsprey false suppressor from SilencerCo
MSRP $1211.00

SHADOW 2 BLACK & BLUE, URBAN GREY

Action: Semiautomatic
Grips: Aluminum
Barrel: 4.89 in.
Sights: Fiber optic front, HAJO rear
Weight: 46.5 oz.
Caliber: 9mm
Capacity: 17 rounds
Features: Higher beavertail; undercut trigger guard; contoured slide; increased weight at the dust cover/rail helps keep muzzle down; steel frame with nitride finish; blue aluminum grips checkered to match front and backstraps; reversible mag release three-position adjustable
MSRP $1349.00

Dan Wesson Firearms

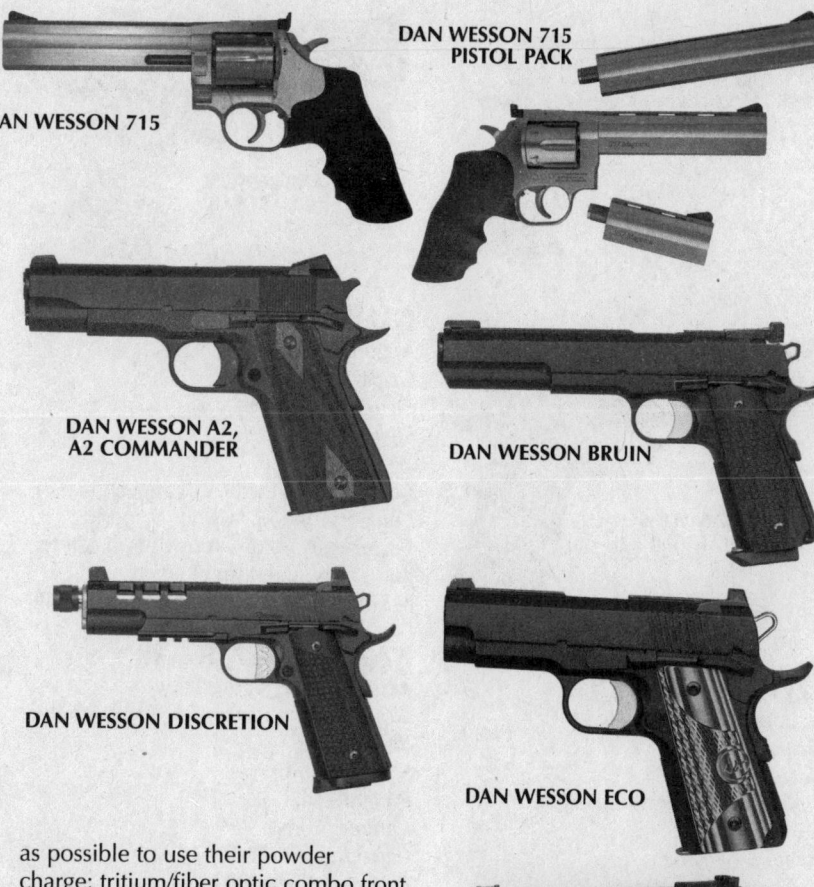

DAN WESSON 715

DAN WESSON 715 PISTOL PACK

DAN WESSON A2, A2 COMMANDER

DAN WESSON BRUIN

DAN WESSON DISCRETION

DAN WESSON ECO

DAN WESSON ELITE SERIES CHAOS

715

Action: DA semiautomatic
Grips: Rubber
Barrel: 6 in.
Sights: Fixed
Weight: 46 oz.
Caliber: .357 Mag.
Capacity: 6 rounds
Features: Adjustable target rear sight; six inch heavy barrel with ventilated rib; stainless steel construction
MSRP **$1558.00**

715 PISTOL PACK

Action: DA/SA
Grips: Rubber
Barrel: 4 in., 6 in., 8 in.
Sights: Adjustable
Weight: N/A
Caliber: .357 Mag., .38 Spl.
Capacity: 6 rounds
Features: Swappable barrel assemblies and grips; tensioned barrel; forward crane latch ensures proper cylinder/barrel alignment; clockwise-rotating cylinder reduces stress on the crane
MSRP **$1999.00**

A2, A2 COMMANDER

Action: Semiautomatic
Grips: Wood
Barrel: 5 in., 4.25 in.
Sights: Fixed front and rear
Weight: 40 oz.
Caliber: .45 ACP
Capacity: 8 rounds
Features: Dan Wesson's vision of a 3rd Generation military 1911; lowered and flared ejection port; modern combat sights; match barrel; tactical beavertail; extended thumb safety; frame and slide are forged steel finished in a bead-blasted matte blue; Commander-length option available
MSRP **$1363.00**

BRUIN

Action: SA
Grips: Synthetic
Barrel: 6.3 in.
Sights: Adjustable titrium with titrium/fiber optic front
Weight: 42.9 oz.
Caliber: 10mm Auto; .45 ACP
Capacity: 8 or 9 rounds
Features: Long slide for a long sight radius; 6.3 in. barrel within allows full-power 10mm loads as much time

as possible to use their powder charge; tritium/fiber optic combo front sight to make sure the front glows day or night
MSRP . . . . **$2064.00–$2194.00**

DISCRETION

Action: SA
Grips: Synthetic
Barrel: 5.75 in.
Sights: High tactical ledge titrium
Weight: N/A
Caliber: .45 ACP; 9mm Luger
Capacity: 8 or 10 rounds
Features: Suppressor ready; match-grade stainless barrel; aggressively ported slide; serrated trigger; competition-inspired hammer
MSRP **$2142.00**

ECO

Action: SA semiautomatic
Grips: Composite
Barrel: 3.5 in.
Sights: Fixed tritium
Weight: 25 oz.
Caliber: 9mm, .45 ACP
Capacity: 7+1 rounds
Features: Single-stack Officer's size 1991; aluminum alloy frame; undercut trigger guards; 25 lpi checkering; mainspring housing is

aluminum with 25 lpi checkering; Ed Brown high rise grip safety; forged steel slide; tritium night sights with tactical ledge rear sight; flush cut ramped bull barrel with target crown
9mm: **$1623.00**
.45 ACP: **$1662.00**

ELITE SERIES CHAOS

Action: SA semiautomatic
Grips: Synthetic
Barrel: 5 in.
Sights: Adjustable
Weight: 51 oz.
Caliber: 9mm Luger
Capacity: 21 rounds
Features: Ambidextrous thumb safety; grip safety; double-stack magazine; Picatinny rail; fiber optic sights
MSRP **$3829.00**

Dan Wesson Firearms

DAN WESSON ELITE SERIES FURY

DAN WESSON GUARDIAN

DAN WESSON RAZORBACK RZ-10

DAN WESSON SPECIALIST

ELITE SERIES FURY

Action: Semiautomatic
Grips: G10
Barrel: 5.5 in.
Sights: High front night sight, RMR red dot rear
Weight: 48.5 oz.
Caliber: 9mm, 10mm
Capacity: 18 rounds (9mm), 14 rounds (10mm)
Features: Double-stack, suppressor-ready; single-action equipped; super-short reset Elite Series trigger; skeletonized hammer; underside accessory rail; ambidextrous thumb safety
MSRP. $4899.00

GUARDIAN

Action: SA semiautomatic
Grips: Wood
Barrel: 4.25 in.
Sights: Fixed
Weight: 29 oz.
Caliber: 9mm Luger, .38 Super, .45 ACP
Capacity: 8 (.45 ACP) or 9 rounds
Features: Ambidextrous thumb safety; grip safety; fixed night sights
MSRP. . . . . $1558.00–$1619.00

RAZORBACK RZ-10

Action: SA semiautomatic
Grips: Diamond-checkered cocobolo
Barrel: 5 in.
Sights: Fixed
Weight: 38.4 oz.
Caliber: 10mm
Capacity: 9 rounds
Features: Razorback is back in 2012 in limited quantities; serrated Clark-style target rib; 1911 model; stainless steel frame; manual thumb safety, grip safety
MSRP. $1480.00

SPECIALIST

Action: SA semiautomatic
Grips: G10 VZ Operator II grips
Barrel: 5 in.

Sights: Fixed tritium
Weight: 37 oz.
Caliber: .45 ACP, 9mm Luger
Capacity: 8+1 or 10 rounds
Features: Full size single-stack pistol; matte stainless steel or black Duty finishes; forged slide and frame; Clark-style serrated rib with tritium dual-colored night sights stacked in a straight eight-type pattern; tactical ledge rear sight with single rear amber dot and green front with white target ring; Picatinny rail; undercut trigger guard with 25 lpi front strap checkering; ambidextrous thumb safety; two magazines with bumper pads included
SS: $1701.00
Black: $2012.00

Daniel Defense

DANIEL DEFENSE DDM4 V7P

DDM4 V7P

Action: Semiautomatic
Grips: Synthetic
Barrel: 10.3 in.
Sights: None

Weight: 87 oz.
Caliber: 5.56 NATO
Capacity: N/A
Features: Chrome-moly vanadium steel barrel; carbine-length gas

system; Daniel Defense flash suppressor; SB Tactical SBO pistol brace; MFR 9.0 rail
MSRP. $1902.00

Dark Storm Industries

**DARK STORM INDUSTRIES
DS-9 HAILSTORM**

DS-9 HAILSTORM
Action: Semiautomatic
Grips: Synthetic
Barrel: 7.5 in.
Sights: None
Weight: 62 oz.
Caliber: 9mm
Capacity: 17 rounds
Features: An AR-platform pistol caliber; CAA Stock Saddle Cheek Riser; Thordsen Enhanced Buffer Tube; QD sling sockets; aluminum upper and lower; narrow-profile barrel shroud; Hogue pistol grip; DSI's Conical Muzzle Blast Deflector; includes one 17-round magazine and takes all GLOCK 17, 19, and 26 9mm mags
MSRP **$1195.00**

Davide Pedersoli & C.

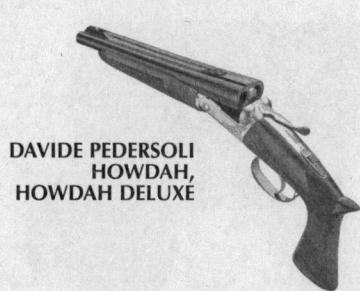

**DAVIDE PEDERSOLI
HOWDAH,
HOWDAH DELUXE**

HOWDAH, HOWDAH DELUXE
Action: Break-open side-by-side
Grips: Walnut
Barrel: 10 in.
Sights: Dovetail front
Weight: 63.5 oz.
Caliber: .45 LC/.410-bore
Capacity: 2 rounds

Features: Based on Ithaca's 1920 Auto & Burglar pistol; case hardened action; oil finished walnut stock; manual extractors; automatic safety on hammers; cartridge chamber allows interchangeable use of .45 LC or .410-bore
MSRP **$1455.00**

Del-Ton

LIMA KEYMOD PISTOL

Action: Semiautomatic
Grips: Synthetic
Barrel: 7.5 in.
Sights: None
Weight: 4 lb. 13 oz.

Caliber: 5.56x45mm
Capacity: 8 rounds
Features: Pistol-length Sampson Evolution keymod free floating rail; Mil-spec; chrome-lined carrier interior
MSRP **$876.71**

**DEL-TON LIMA
KEYMOD PISTOL**

Devil Dog Arms

DDA 1911
Action: Semiautomatic
Grips: NBD
Barrel: 3.5 in., 4.25 in., 5 in.
Sights: Kensight DFS fixed white dot sights
Weight: N/A
Caliber: 9mm, .45 ACP
Capacity: 10 rounds (9mm), 8 rounds (.45 ACP)
Features: First 1911 offerings from this maker; available in full-size, Officer, and Commander versions; two caliber choices; black, Flat Dark Earth, Nickel, or two-tone stainless/black finishes; investment cast 4140 steel frames; 4140 billet steel machined slides with a custom flat-top design; button-rifled 416 stainless barrels with match-fit bushing; three-hole aluminum trigger; optional accessory rail; oversized slide serrations
MSRP . . . . **$999.00–$1149.00**

**DEVIL DOG ARMS
DDA 1911**

DoubleStar Corp.

PHD 1911

Action: SA
Grips: Magpul MOE 1911 grip panels
Barrel: 5 in.
Sights: XS Express titrium front sight, XS Express rear sight
Weight: 33 oz.
Caliber: .45 ACP
Capacity: 8 rounds
Features: Aggressive rear cocking serrations for a sure grip in the harshest of environments; flat-topped and serrated slide to reduce glare; round butt and Wilson combat high-ride beavertail grip safety
MSRP $1369.99

DOUBLESTAR PHD 1911

DoubleTap Defense LLC

DOUBLETAP

Action: DAO semiautomatic
Grips: Synthetic
Barrel: 3 in.
Sights: Front blade
Weight: 12 oz.–14 oz.
Caliber: .45 ACP, 9mm
Capacity: 2+2 rounds
Features: Titanium frame with a MIL-STD finish that resists corrosion; integral grips house additional two spare rounds; ported barrel reduces muzzle flip and recoil; ambidextrous thumb latch to eject spent rounds; quick-change interchangable barrels; comes with one barrel and you can purchase extra conversion kits; firearm and conversion kit available ported and non-ported
Aluminum: . . . .
    $499.00–$569.00
Conversion kits: . . . .
    $199.00–$269.00

DOUBLETAP DEFENSE LLC DOUBLETAP

Eagle Imports

EAGLE IMPORTS MAC 1911 BOBCUT

EAGLE IMPORTS MAC 1911 BULLSEYE

MAC 1911 BOBCUT

Action: SA semiautomatic
Grips: Hardwood
Barrel: 4.25 in.
Sights: Adjustable rear, dovetail front
Weight: 34.58 oz.
Caliber: .45 ACP
Capacity: 8+1 rounds
Features: 4140 steel frame and hammer forged slide; fully adjustable Novak-type rear sight; dovetail front sight with fiber optic; flared and lowered ejection port; enhanced beavertail grip safety; skeletal hammer; combat trigger; stippled front strap serration; throated forged steel barrel
Deep Blue: $902.00
Hard Chrome: $978.00

MAC 1911 BULLSEYE

Action: SA semiautomatic
Grips: Hardwood
Barrel: 6 in.
Sights: Adjustable rear, dovetail front
Weight: 46.91 oz.
Caliber: .45 ACP
Capacity: 8+1 rounds
Features: The largest of the MAC 1911 pistol line; 4140 steel frame and hammer forged slide; fully adjustable Bomar-type rear sight; dovetail front sight; flared and lowered ejection port; enhanced beavertail grip safety; skeletal hammer; combat trigger; checkered front strap serration; ramped match grade bull barrel
Deep Blue: $1219.00
Hard Chrome: $1294.00

EAGLE IMPORTS MAC 1911 CLASSIC

EAGLE IMPORTS SPS PANTERA

EAGLE IMPORTS SPS VISTA LONG AND SHORT

MAC 1911 CLASSIC

Action: SA semiautomatic
Grips: Hardwood
Barrel: 5 in.
Sights: Adjustable rear, dovetail front
Weight: 40.56 oz.
Caliber: .45 ACP
Capacity: 8+1 rounds
Features: 4140 steel frame and hammer forged slide; fully adjustable bomar-type rear sight; dovetail front sight with fiber optic; flared and lowered ejection port; enhanced beavertail grip safety; skeletal hammer; combat trigger; checkered front strap serrations; ramped match grade bull barrel
Deep Blue: **$1045.00**
Hard Chrome: **$1120.00**

SPS PANTERA

Action: SA semiautomatic
Grips: Glass-filled nylon polymer
Barrel: 5 in.
Sights: Adjustable rear, dovetail front
Weight: 36.68 oz.
Caliber: .45 ACP
Capacity: 12+1 rounds
Features: IPSC Standard or Open Competition ready; fully adjustable Bomar-type rear sight, dovetail front sight with fiber optic; light weight polymer trigger; wide front and rear slide serrations; ambidextrous thumb safety; black chrome finish
Blue: **$1730.00**
Black chrome: **$1895.00**
Hard chrome: **$1805.00**

SPS VISTA LONG AND SHORT

Action: SA semiautomatic
Grips: Glass-filled nylon polymer
Barrel: 5 in., 5.5 in.
Sights: Sight mount included
Weight: 41.62 oz.–43.38 oz.
Caliber: 9mm (Short), .38 Super (Long)
Capacity: 21 rounds
Features: Hammer forged steel slide; scope mount for C-MORE optical sight included; checkered front strap serration; ramped match grade threaded barrel; wide magwell; black chrome finish
MSRP **$2450.00**

Ed Brown Products

ED BROWN 18 CLASSIC CUSTOM

ED BROWN 18 EXECUTIVE ELITE

18 CLASSIC CUSTOM

Action: Semiautomatic
Grips: Cocobolo wood
Barrel: 5 in.
Sights: Adjustable rear, cross dovetail front
Weight: 40 oz.
Caliber: .45 ACP
Capacity: 7+1 rounds
Features: Single-action; single-stack government model frame; special mirror finished side; two-piece guide rod for smoother cycling and easier disassembly; stainless or blued finish
MSRP **$3695.00**

18 EXECUTIVE ELITE

Action: Semiautomatic
Grips: Checkered cocobolo wood
Barrel: 5 in.
Sights: Fixed, night
Weight: 38 oz.
Caliber: .45 ACP
Capacity: 7+1 rounds
Features: Single-stack government model frame; matte finished slide for low glare, with traditional square cut serrations on rear of slide only; blued or stainless finish
MSRP . . . . **$3295.00–$3395.00**

Ed Brown Products

ED BROWN PRODUCTS
18 EXECUTIVE TARGET

ED BROWN 18 KOBRA
CARRY

ED BROWN 18
KOBRA CARRY
LIGHTWEIGHT

ED BROWN
PRODUCTS BO/EB ZEV
19 RMR

ED BROWN SIGNATURE EDITION

18 EXECUTIVE TARGET
Action: Semiautomatic
Grips: Wood
Barrel: 5 in.
Sights: Blade front, Trijicon RMR reflex red dot
Weight: 40 oz.
Caliber: 9mm, .38 Super .45 ACP
Capacity: 7, 8 rounds
Features: Checkered wood grips; 25 lines-per-inch checkering on the mainspring housing and frontstrap; rear slide cocking serrations; hundreds of customization options
MSRP. $3880.00

18 KOBRA CARRY
Action: Semiautomatic
Grips: Cocobolo wood
Barrel: 5 in.
Sights: Fixed, night
Weight: 38 oz.
Caliber: .45 ACP
Capacity: 7+1 rounds
Features: Single-stack government model frame; John Browning traditional design; exclusive snakeskin treatment on forestrap and mainspring housing; matte finished slide for low glare; 3-dot night sights with high

visibility white outlines; blued or stainless finish
MSRP. . . . . $2995.00–$3095.00

18 KOBRA CARRY LIGHTWEIGHT
Action: Semiautomatic
Grips: Cocobolo wood
Barrel: 4.25 in.
Sights: Fixed dovetail front night with high visibility white outlines
Weight: 27 oz.
Caliber: .45 ACP
Capacity: 7+1 rounds
Features: Lightweight aluminum frame and Bobtail housing; all other components are steel; exclusive snakeskin treatment on forestrap and housing; matte finished Gen III coated slide for low glare
MSRP. . . . . $3410.00–$3510.00

BO/EB ZEV 19 RMR
Action: Semiautomatic
Grips: G10
Barrel: 4.25 in.
Sights: Tall night sights, Trijicon RMR reflex red dot
Weight: 40 oz.
Caliber: 9mm
Capacity: 8 rounds

Features: A joint venture with ZEV technologies; dimpled barrel; ported slide top and side; FX1 Snakeskin treatment to the frontstrap; threaded suppressor-ready barrel; VZ Alien G10 grips
MSRP. $4995.00

SIGNATURE EDITION
Action: Semiautomatic
Grips: Cocobolo wood
Barrel: 5 in.
Sights: Adjustable rear, cross dovetail front
Weight: 40 oz.
Caliber: .45 ACP
Capacity: 7+1 rounds
Features: The Ed Brown Signature Edition is based on the timeless Classic Custom pistol, with hand relief engraving by our master engraver; single stack government model frame; special mirror finished slide; 50 lpi serrations on back of slide to match serrated adjustable sight; hand relief engraved package; adjustable rear sight buried deep into slide; cross dovetail front sight; blued metal parts
Blued: $7695.00
Stainless: $9995.00

EMF Company, Inc.

EMF 1873 GREAT WESTERN II ALCHIMISTA II

EMF 1873 GREAT WESTERN II DELUXE ENGRAVED SHERIFF

EMF 1873 GREAT WESTERN II ALL BLUE PALADIN

EMF 1873 GREAT WESTERN II BUNTLINE

EMF 1873 GREAT WESTERN II "FREEDOM"

EMF 1873 GREAT WESTERN II PONY EXPRESS

EMF 1873 GREAT WESTERN II CALIFORNIAN

EMF 1873 GREAT WESTERN II LIBERTY

1873 GREAT WESTERN II ALCHIMISTA I, II, III, III STD, III DLX

Action: SA revolver
Grips: Walnut
Barrel: 4.75 in., 5.5 in., 7.5 in.
Sights: Fixed
Weight: 33.6 oz.
Caliber: .357 Mag., .44-40; .45 LC
Capacity: 6 rounds
Features: Standard case-hardening; stainless steel; checkered walnut grips; express grips available ; three variations: Alchimista I has checkered walnut 1860 walnut grips, wide setback trigger, case hardened frame; Alchimista II is similar to I but has lower, wider hammer; Alchimista III STD is similar to the II but with an octagonal barrel and available in STD (case hardened) or DLX (old silver/black) options

Alchimista I: **$630.00**
Alchimista II: **$675.00**
Alchimista III STD: **$715.00**
Alchimista III DLX: **$800.00**

1873 GREAT WESTERN II BUNTLINE

Action: Revolver
Grips: Walnut or Ultra Ivory
Barrel: 12 in.
Sights: Fixed
Weight: N/A
Caliber: .45 LC
Capacity: 6 rounds
Features: Deep color case hardened finish; first version was designed by Colt for Ned Buntline
Walnut grips: **$640.00**
Ultra Ivory grips: **$665.00**

1873 GREAT WESTERN II CALIFORNIAN

Action: SA revolver
Grips: Walnut
Barrel: 4.75 in., 5.5 in., 7.5 in.
Sights: Fixed
Weight: 48 oz.
Caliber: .357 Mag., .44-40 Win., .45 LC
Capacity: 6 rounds
Features: Standard case-hardening; steel frame
MSRP **$565.00**

1873 GREAT WESTERN II DELUXE ENGRAVED SHERIFF

Action: Revolver
Grips: Ultra Ivory
Barrel: 3 in.
Sights: Fixed
Weight: N/A
Caliber: .357 Mag., 45 LC
Capacity: 6 rounds
Features: Manufactured in Italy; stainless steel with factory laser engraving
MSRP **$950.00**

1873 GREAT WESTERN II FREEDOM

Action: SA
Grips: Synthetic
Barrel: 4.75 in., 5.5 in.
Sights: Blade front
Weight: 36.8 oz.
Caliber: .45 ACP, .357
Capacity: 6 rounds
Features: Laser engraving/grips
MSRP **$660.00**

1873 GREAT WESTERN II LIBERTY

Action: Revolver
Grips: Ultra Ivory
Barrel: 4.75 in., 5.5 in.
Sights: Fixed
Weight: N/A
Caliber: .357 Mag., .45 LC
Capacity: 6 rounds
Features: Manufactured in Italy; all blued barrel, cylinder, and frame; factory laser engraved
MSRP **$650.00**

1873 GREAT WESTERN II PALADIN

Action: Revolver
Grips: Ultra Ivory
Barrel: 7.5 in.
Sights: Fixed
Weight: N/A
Caliber: .45 LC
Capacity: 6 rounds
Features: Single action; all blued barrel, cylinder, and frames as seen in Hollywood westerns
MSRP **$610.00**

1873 GREAT WESTERN II PONY EXPRESS

Action: SA revolver
Grips: Walnut express grips
Barrel: 3.5 in.
Sights: Fixed
Weight: 32 oz.
Caliber: .357 Mag., .45 LC
Capacity: 6 rounds
Features: Designed by Dave Anderson, one of the pioneering gunmakers in Cowboy Action Shooting and intended for mounted shooting competitors; available in an Express (bird's head) grip and turned-down hammer or a standard grip and Bisley hammer, both in bright stainless, or in a case hardened version with Express grip
MSRP . . . . **$705.00–$945.00**

European American Armory (EAA)

EUROPEAN AMERICAN
ARMORY BOUNTY HUNTER

EUROPEAN
AMERICAN ARMORY
WITNESS HUNTER

EUROPEAN AMERICAN
ARMORY POLYMER
FULL SIZE

EUROPEAN AMERICAN ARMORY
WITNESS STEEL COMPACT

BOUNTY HUNTER

Action: SA revolver
Grips: Walnut
Barrel: 4.5 in., 6.75 in., 7.5 in.
Sights: Fixed, open
Weight: 39–41 oz.
Caliber: .357 Mag.,.44 Mag., .22
LR/.22 WMR, 45 LC
Capacity: 6 or 8 rounds
Features: Transfer bar safety; steel or
alloy frame; in blued or nickel
finishes
MSRP . . . . **$374.00–$562.00**

WITNESS HUNTER

Action: Semiautomatic
Grips: Rubber
Barrel: 6 in.
Sights: Dovetail front
Weight: 41 oz.

Caliber: 10mm, .45 ACP
Capacity: 10+1 or 15+1 rounds
Features: Single-action with over
travel stop; extended manual safety;
super sight; cone barrel, slide lockup;
checkered non-slip frame; drilled and
tapped for scope mount; auto-firing
pin block
MSRP **$1372.00**

WITNESS POLYMER FULL SIZE

Action: Semiautomatic
Grips: Rubber
Barrel: 4.5 in.
Sights: 3-Dot
Weight: 33 oz.
Caliber: 9mm, 10mm, .40 S&W, .45
ACP
Capacity: 10+1, 14+1, or 17+1

rounds
Features: Windage adjustable sight;
double- or single-action; polymer
frame; integral accessory rail
MSRP **$589.00**

WITNESS STEEL COMPACT

Action: Semiautomatic
Grips: Rubber
Barrel: 3.6 in.
Sights: Adjustable
Weight: 30 oz.
Caliber: 9mm, .40 S&W, 10mm, .45
ACP
Capacity: 8+1, 12+1, or 14+1 rounds
Features: Wonder finish, windage
adjustable sight; double- or single-
action; polymer or steel frame;
integral accessory rail; matte stainless
finish
MSRP **$699.00**

Fightlite Industries

SCR PISTOL KEYMOD, M-LOK

Action: Semiautomatic
Grips: Synthetic
Barrel: 7.25 in.
Sights: None
Weight: 63 oz.
Caliber: 5.56 NATO, .300 Blackout
Capacity: 10 rounds
Features: Short-barreled, grip stock
rifle-caliber carbine pistol; overall
length of about 20 inches;barrel of
4150 Vanadium that is gas-ferritic
nitrocarbonized and threaded;

hardcoat anodized finish on the
aluminum receiver; choice of KeyMod
or M-LOK handguards
MSRP **$865.00**

FIGHTLITE SCR PISTOL
KEYMOD, M-LOK

FN AMERICA FN 15 PISTOL

FN AMERICA FNS-9

FN AMERICA FN FIVE-SEVEN SERIES

FN AMERICA FNS 9 COMPACT FDE

FN AMERICA FNX-9

FN AMERICA FNX-45 TACTICAL

FN AMERICA FNX-45

FN 15 PISTOL

Action: Semiautomatic
Grips: Synthetic
Barrel: 10.5 in., 12 in.
Sights: None
Weight: 83 oz.–90 oz.
Caliber: 5.56 NATO, .300 Blackout
Capacity: 30 rounds
Features: AR-type pistol with an SBX-K pistol stabilizing brace; FN combat trigger; 9 in. M-LOL rail; carbine-length gas system; A2-style flash hider; Magpul MOE grip; pistol buffer tube kit; forward assist
MSRP. $1599.00

FN FIVE-SEVEN SERIES

Action: SA semiautomatic
Grips: Plastic
Barrel: 4.8 in.
Sights: Adjustable 3-dot
Weight: 20.8 oz.
Caliber: 5.7x28mm
Capacity: 10 or 20 round magazines
Features: Integrated accessory rail for mounting tactical lights or lasers;

reversible magazine button; ambidextrous manual safety levers; hammer-forged, chrome lined barrel; adjustable three-dot target sights available with matte or flat dark earth
MSRP. $1435.00

FNS-9, FNS-40

Action: DA semiautomatic
Grips: Polymer
Barrel: 4 in.
Sights: Night sights
Weight: 25.2 oz.
Caliber: 9mm, .40 S&W
Capacity: 17 (FNS-9) or 14 (FNS-40) rounds
Features: Striker-fired semiautomatic; manual safety levers; stainless steel slide in matte black or silver finish; external extractor with loaded chamber indicator; three-dot night sights; hammer-forged stainless steel barrel; black polymer frame; fully ambidextrous
MSRP. $599.00

FNS-9 COMPACT FDE

Action: Semiautomatic
Grips: Polymer
Barrel: 3.6 in.
Sights: Fixed three-dot
Weight: 23.4 oz.
Caliber: 9mm
Capacity: 10, 12, 17 rounds
Features: Striker-fired compact autoloader; Flat Dark Earth allover

finish; polymer frame with replaceable steel slide rails; stainless steel slide with front and rear cocking serrations; 1913 accessory rail; serrated trigger guard; two interchangeable backstraps with lanyard eyelets
MSRP. $639.00

FNX-9, FNX-40

Action: Semiautomatic
Grips: Interchangeable backstraps with lanyard eyelets
Barrel: 4 in.
Sights: 3-Dot system
Weight: 21.9 oz. (9mm), 24.4 oz. (.40)
Caliber: 9mm, .40 S&W
Capacity: 17 (9mm) or 14 (.40 S&W) rounds
Features: Ergonomic polymer black frame with low bore axis; checkered and ribbed grip panels; stainless steel slide and hammer-forged stainless barrel; DA/SA ambidextrous operating controls
MSRP. $699.00

FNX-45

Action: DA/SA Semiautomatic
Grips: Interchangeable backstraps with lanyard eyelets
Barrel: 4.5 in.
Sights: Fixed 3-dot
Weight: 33.2 oz.
Caliber: .45 ACP
Capacity: 15 rounds
Features: Polymer frame with stainless steel barrel; external extractor with loaded chamber indicator; front and rear cocking serrations; Picatinny rail; manual, ambidextrous safety; available in black
MSRP. $824.00

FNX-45 TACTICAL

Action: DA/SA semiautomatic
Grips: Textured polymer
Barrel: 5.3 in.
Sights: High-profile night sights
Weight: 33.6 oz.
Caliber: .45 ACP
Capacity: 15 rounds
Features: Stainless steel slide; external extractor with loaded chamber indicator; high-profile combat night sights; red-dot sight optional; hammer-forged stainless steel barrel; flat dark earth or black polymer frame; Picatinny rail; fully ambidextrous
MSRP. $1349.00

Freedom Arms

FREEDOM ARMS MODEL 83 PREMIER GRADE

FREEDOM ARMS MODEL 83 RIMFIRE

FREEDOM ARMS MODEL 97 PREMIER GRADE

MODEL 83 PREMIER GRADE

Action: SA revolver
Grips: Hardwood
Barrel: 4.75 in., 6 in., 7.5 in., 10 in.
Sights: Fixed or adjustable
Weight: 52.5 oz.
Caliber: .500 Wyoming Express, .475 Linebaugh, .454 Casull, .44 Rem. Mag., .41 Rem. Mag., .357 Mag.
Capacity: 5 rounds
Features: Adjustable sight models are drilled and tapped for scope mounts; stainless steel, brush finish and impregnated hardwood grips
MSRP . . . . $2743.00–$2848.00

MODEL 83 RIMFIRE

Action: SA revolver
Grips: Hardwood
Barrel: 10 in.
Sights: Adjustable
Weight: 55.5 oz.
Caliber: .22 LR
Capacity: 5 rounds
Features: Drilled and tapped for scope mounts; stainless steel frame; matte finish; match grade chambers
MSRP $2634.00

MODEL 97 PREMIER GRADE

Action: SA revolver
Grips: Laminated hardwood

Barrel: 4.5 in., 5.5 in., 7.5 in., or 10 in.
Sights: Adjustable or fixed
Weight: 39 oz.
Caliber: .45 Colt, .44 Spl., .41 Rem. Mag., .357 Mag., .327 Fed., .224-32 FA, .22 LR, .17 HMR,
Capacity: 5 or 6 rounds
Features: Impregnated hardwood grips; stainless steel frame; brush stainless finish
MSRP . . . .$2309.00–$2339.00

Full Conceal

FULL CONCEAL M3G43

M3S G43

Action: Semiautomatic
Grips: Polymer
Barrel: 3.39 in.
Sights: Fixed
Weight: N/A
Caliber: 9mm
Capacity: 12 rounds
Features: Based on the basic GLOCK 34, but as a folding, pocket-carry 9mm; folds like a flip cell phone with no printing in a pocket; unfolded, it is a plus-capacity sub-compact pistol
MSRP $1049.00

Glock

Glock Compact Models

G19, G19 GEN4, G19 GEN4 MOS

Action: Semiautomatic
Grips: Polymer
Barrel: 4.01 in.
Sights: Fixed
Weight: 23.65 oz.
Caliber: 9mm
Capacity: 10, 15, 17, 33 rounds
Features: Striker-fired, polymer framed pistol with safe action system, trigger safety, hexagonal barrel, DAO action; Gen4 has modular backstrap design, rough-textured grip, enlarged and reversible magazine release, and is available in Glock's MOS—Modular Optic System—configuration, which simplifies mounting of many modern pistol red dot and reflex sight optics

GLOCK COMPACT G19

G19 (California only): $599.00
G19 Gen4: $599.00
G19 Gen4 MOS:. $750.00

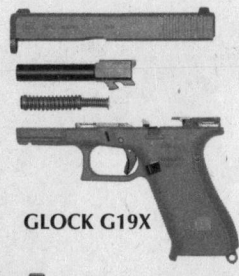

GLOCK G19X

GLOCK G32 GEN4

GLOCK G34 GEN4

**GLOCK G34 GEN5
MODULAR OPTIC
SYSTEM (MOS)**

G19X

Action: Semiautomatic
Grips: Polymer
Barrel: 4 in.
Sights: Fixed
Weight: 31.4 oz.
Caliber: 9mm
Capacity: 17 rounds
Features: GLOCK's first "crossover" pistol; originally developed for military; GLOCK's signature Coyote coloring, including on the factory-colored slide; GLOCK Marksman Barrel; tough nPVD slide coating; ambidextrous slide stop levers; a stock without finger grooves; lanyard loop; Coyote-colored hard case; two 17-round and two 17+2-round magazines unique to the 19X
MSRP...................**$749.00**

G23, G23 GEN4

Action: Semiautomatic
Grips: Polymer
Barrel: 4.01 in.
Sights: Fixed
Weight: 23.65 oz.
Caliber: .40 S&W
Capacity: 10, 15, 22 rounds
Features: Striker-fired, polymer framed pistol with safe action system, trigger safety, hexagonal barrel, DAO action; Gen4 has modular backstrap design, rough-textured grip, enlarged and reversible magazine release
G23 (California only): **$599.00**
G23 Gen4: **$599.00**

G38

Action: Semiautomatic
Grips: Polymer
Barrel: 4.01 in.
Sights: Fixed

**GLOCK
COMPETITION G34**

Weight: 26.83 oz.
Caliber: .45 G.A.P.
Capacity: 8, 10 rounds
Features: Striker-fired, polymer framed pistol with safe action system, trigger safety, hexagonal barrel, DAO action
MSRP...................**$614.00**

Glock Competition Models

G34, G34 GEN4, G34 GEN4 MOS

Action: Semiautomatic
Grips: Polymer
Barrel: 5.31 in.
Sights: Fixed
Weight: 25.77 oz.
Caliber: 9mm
Capacity: 10, 17, 33 rounds
Features: Striker-fired, polymer framed pistol with safe action system, trigger safety, hexagonal barrel, DAO action; Gen4 has modular backstrap design, rough-textured grip, enlarged and reversible magazine release, and is available in Glock's MOS—Modular Optic System—configuration, which simplifies mounting of many modern pistol red dot and reflex sight optics
G34 (CA-only):...........**$679.00**
G34 Gen4: **$679.00**
G34 Gen4 MOS:..........**$840.00**

G34 GEN5 MODULAR OPTIC SYSTEM (MOS)

Action: Semiautomatic
Grips: Polymer
Barrel: 5.31 in.
Sights: Fixed
Weight: 25.7 oz.
Caliber: 9mm
Capacity: 17 rounds
Features: Glock's Modular Optics System (MOS), which allows the mounting of various red dot and

reflex sights without the need to machine the slide for a custom mount; GLOCK's improved nDLC finish; GLOCK Marksman Barrel; improved barrel crown; grip frame without finger grooves
MSRP..................**$899.00**

G35, G35 GEN4, G35 GEN4 MOS

Action: Semiautomatic
Grips: Polymer
Barrel: 5.31 in.
Sights: Fixed
Weight: 27.18 oz.
Caliber: .40 S&W
Capacity: 10, 15, 22 rounds
Features: Striker-fired, polymer framed pistol with safe action system, trigger safety, hexagonal barrel, DAO action; Gen4 has modular backstrap design, rough-textured grip, enlarged and reversible magazine release, and is available in Glock's MOS—Modular Optic System—configuration, which simplifies mounting of many modern pistol red dot and reflex sight optics
G34 (California-only): **$679.00**
G34 Gen4: **$679.00**
G34 Gen4 MOS:..........**$840.00**

G41 GEN4, G41 GEN4 MOS

Action: Semiautomatic
Grips: Polymer
Barrel: 5.31 in.
Sights: Fixed
Weight: 27 oz.
Caliber: .45 ACP
Capacity: 10, 13 rounds
Features: Striker-fired, polymer framed pistol with safe action system, trigger safety, hexagonal barrel, DAO action; Gen4 has modular backstrap design, rough-textured grip, enlarged and reversible magazine release, and is available in Glock's MOS—Modular Optic System—configuration, which simplifies mounting of many modern pistol red dot and reflex sight optics
G41 Gen4 MOS:..........**$840.00**
G41 Gen4: **$729.00**

Glock

GLOCK G40 GEN4

GLOCK STANDARD G17

GLOCK G20 GEN4

GLOCK G21 GEN4

Glock Long Slide Models

G40 GEN4 MOS

Action: Semiautomatic
Grips: Polymer
Barrel: 6.02 in.
Sights: Fixed
Weight: 28.15 oz.
Caliber: 10mm
Capacity: 15 rounds
Features: Striker-fired, polymer framed pistol with safe action system, trigger safety, hexagonal barrel, DAO action; Gen4 has modular backstrap design, rough-textured grip, enlarged and reversible magazine release, and is available in Glock's MOS—Modular Optic System—configuration, which simplifies mounting of many modern pistol red dot and reflex sight optics.
MSRP $840.00

Glock Standard Models

G17, G17 GEN4, G17 GEN4 MOS

Action: Semiautomatic
Grips: Polymer
Barrel: 4.48 in.
Sights: Fixed
Weight: 25.06 oz.
Caliber: 9mm
Capacity: 10, 17, 33 rounds
Features: Striker-fired, polymer framed pistol with safe action system, trigger safety, hexagonal barrel, DAO action; Gen4 has modular backstrap design, rough-textured grip, enlarged and reversible magazine release, and is available in Glock's MOS—Modular Optic System—configuration, which simplifies mounting of many modern pistol red dot and reflex sight optics
G17 (Californa-only): $599.00
G17 Gen4: $599.00
G17 Gen4 MOS: $750.00

G20SF, G20 GEN4

Action: Semiautomatic
Grips: Polymer
Barrel: 4.6 in.
Sights: Fixed
Weight: 30.71 in.
Caliber: 10mm
Capacity: 10, 15 rounds
Features: Striker-fired, polymer framed pistol with safe action system, trigger safety, hexagonal barrel, DAO action; SF designation model has a reduced circumference backstrap. Gen4 has modular backstrap design, rough-textured grip, enlarged and reversible magazine release
G20 Gen4: $687.00
G20SF: $637.00

G21 SF, G21 GEN4

Action: Semiautomatic
Grips: Polymer
Barrel: 4.6 in.
Sights: Fixed
Weight: 29.30 in.
Caliber: .45 ACP
Capacity: 10, 13 rounds
Features: Striker-fired, polymer framed pistol with safe action system, trigger safety, hexagonal barrel, DAO action; SF designation model has a reduced circumference backstrap. Gen4 has modular backstrap design, rough-textured grip, enlarged and reversible magazine release
G21 Gen4: $687.00
G21 SF: $637.00

G22, G22 GEN4

Action: Semiautomatic
Grips: Polymer
Barrel: 4.48 in.
Sights: Fixed
Weight: 25.59 oz.
Caliber: .40 S&W
Capacity: 10, 15, 22 rounds Features: Striker-fired, polymer framed pistol with safe action system, trigger safety,

hexagonal barrel, DAO action; Gen4 has modular backstrap design, rough-textured grip, enlarged and reversible magazine release
MSRP $599.00

G37, G37 GEN4

Action: Semiautomatic
Grips: Polymer
Barrel: 4.48 in.
Sights: Fixed
Weight: 28.95 oz.
Caliber: .45 G.A.P.
Capacity: 10 rounds
Features: Striker-fired, polymer framed pistol with safe action system, trigger safety, hexagonal barrel, DAO action; Gen4 has modular backstrap design, rough-textured grip, enlarged and reversible magazine release
G37 Gen4: $664.00
G37: $614.00

G31, G31 GEN4

Action: Semiautomatic
Grips: Polymer
Barrel: 4.48 in.
Sights: Fixed
Weight: 26.12 oz.
Caliber: .357 SIG
Capacity: 10, 15 round
Features: Striker-fired, polymer framed pistol with safe action system, trigger safety, hexagonal barrel, DAO action; Gen4 has modular backstrap design, rough-textured grip, enlarged and reversible magazine release
MSRP $599.00

GLOCK GEN4 G26

GLOCK G26 GEN5

GLOCK G29 GEN4

GLOCK SUBCOMPACT G26

GLOCK G30S

GLOCK G33 GEN4

GLOCK SUBCOMPACT SLIMLINE G36

Glock Subcompact Models

G26, G26 GEN4

Action: Semiautomatic
Grips: Polymer
Barrel: 3.42 in.
Sights: Fixed
Weight: 21.71 oz.
Caliber: 9mm
Capacity: 10, 15, 17, 33 rounds
Features: Striker-fired, polymer framed pistol with safe action system, trigger safety, hexagonal barrel, DAO action; Gen4 has modular backstrap design, rough-textured grip, enlarged and reversible magazine release
MSRP. $599.00

G26 GEN5

Action: Semiautomatic
Grips: Polymer
Barrel: 3.42 in.
Sights: Fixed
Weight: 21.7 oz.
Caliber: 9mm
Capacity: 10 rounds
Features: GLOCK's improved nDLC finish; GLOCK Marksman Barrel; improved barrel crown; grip frame without finger grooves
MSRP. $699.00

G27, G27 GEN4

Action: Semiautomatic
Grips: Polymer
Barrel: 3.42 in.
Sights: Fixed
Weight: 21.89 oz.
Caliber: .40 S&W
Capacity: 9, 13, 15, 22 rounds
Features: Striker-fired, polymer framed pistol with safe action system, trigger safety, hexagonal barrel, DAO action; Gen4 has modular backstrap design, rough-textured grip, enlarged and reversible magazine release
MSRP. $599.00

G29SF, G29 GEN4

Action: Semiautomatic
Grips: Polymer
Barrel: 3.77 in.
Sights: Fixed
Weight: 26.83 oz.
Caliber: 10mm
Capacity: 10, 15 rounds
Features: Striker-fired, polymer framed pistol with safe action system, trigger safety, hexagonal barrel, DAO action; SF designation model has a reduced circumference backstrap. Gen4 has modular backstrap design, rough-textured grip, enlarged and reversible magazine release
G29 Gen4:. $687.00
G29SF:. $637.00

G30S, G30 FS, G30 GEN4

Action: Semiautomatic
Grips: Polymer
Barrel: 3.77 in.
Sights: Fixed
Weight: 22.95 oz.–26.30 oz.
Caliber: .45 ACP
Capacity: 10 rounds
Features: Striker-fired, polymer framed pistol with safe action system, trigger safety, hexagonal barrel, DAO action; S designation denotes slim slide profile. SF designation model has a reduced circumference backstrap. Gen4 has modular backstrap design, rough-textured grip, enlarged and reversible magazine release
G30S:. $637.00
G30 SF: $637.00
G30 Gen4: $687.00

G33, G33 GEN4

Action: Semiautomatic
Grips: Polymer
Barrel: 3.42 in.
Sights: Fixed
Weight: 21.89 oz.
Caliber: .357 SIG
Capacity: 9, 13, 15 rounds
Features: Striker-fired, polymer framed pistol with safe action system, trigger safety, hexagonal barrel, DAO action; Gen4 has modular backstrap design, rough-textured grip, enlarged and reversible magazine release
MSRP. $599.00

G39

Action: Semiautomatic
Grips: Polymer
Barrel: 3.42 in.
Sights: Fixed
Weight: 24.18 oz.
Caliber: .45 G.A.P.
Capacity: 6, 8, 10 rounds
Features: Striker-fired, polymer framed pistol with safe action system, trigger safety, hexagonal barrel, DAO action
MSRP. $614.00

Glock Subcompact Slimline Models

G36

Action: Semiautomatic
Grips: Polymer
Barrel: 3.77 in.
Sights: Fixed
Weight: 22.42 oz.
Caliber: .45 ACP
Capacity: 6 rounds
Features: Striker-fired, polymer framed pistol with safe action system, trigger safety, hexagonal barrel, DAO action, single-stack magazine
MSRP. $637.00

Glock

GLOCK G42

**GLOCK G43
SINGLE STACK**

G43
Action: Semiautomatic
Grips: Polymer
Barrel: 3.39 in.
Sights: Fixed
Weight: 17.95 oz.
Caliber: 9mm
Capacity:
Features: Striker-fired, polymer framed pistol with safe action system, trigger safety, hexagonal barrel, DAO action, single-stack magazine
MSRP.................$580.00

G42
Action: Semiautomatic
Grips: Polymer
Barrel: 3.25 in.
Sights: Fixed
Weight: 13.76 oz.
Caliber: .380 ACP

Capacity: 6 rounds
Features: Striker-fired, polymer framed pistol with safe action system, trigger safety, hexagonal barrel, DAO action, single-stack magazine
MSRP.................$480.00

Grand Power (By Eagle Imports)

Q100
Action: Semiautomatic
Grips: Polymer
Barrel: 4.3 in.
Sights: Plastic front, drift-adjustable steel rear
Weight: 26.1 oz.
Caliber: 9mm

Capacity: 15 rounds
Features: Rotary locking barrel system; front and rear slide serration; ambidextrous controls; CNC machined steel chassis; four interchangeable grips
MSRP.................$539.00

GRAND POWER (BY EAGLE IMPORTS) Q100

Hämmerli

**HÄMMERLI MODEL
X-ESSE LONG**

MODEL X-ESSE
Action: Semiautomatic
Grips: Composite
Barrel: 4.5 in., 5.9 in.
Sights: Adjustable
Weight: 27.9–31 oz.

Caliber: .22 LR
Capacity: 10 rounds
Features: Single-action, two-stage trigger; universal hi-grip
MSRP................. $879.00

Heckler & Koch

HECKLER & KOCH HK45

HK45
Action: Semiautomatic
Grips: Polymer
Barrel: 4.53 in.
Sights: Fixed
Weight: 31 oz.
Caliber: .45 ACP
Capacity: 10 rounds
Features: DA/SA with control lever; integral Picatinny rail; ambidextrous

controls with dual slide releases; modified Browning linkless recoil operating system; polygonal rifling; open square notch rear sight with contrast points; low profile drift adjustable three-dot sights; available in black, RAL8000 green brown, and olive finishes; supplied with one additional backstrap; night sights optional
MSRP...........$819.00–$919.00

HECKLER & KOCH HK45 COMPACT

HECKLER & KOCH HK45 COMPACT TACTICAL

HECKLER & KOCH HK45 TACTICAL

HECKLER & KOCH MARK 23

HECKLER & KOCH P30

HECKLER & KOCH P30 L

HECKLER & KOCH P30SK

HK45 COMPACT

Action: Semiautomatic
Grips: Synthetic
Barrel: 3.94 in.
Sights: Fixed
Weight: 28.48 oz.
Caliber: .45 ACP
Capacity: 8 or 10 rounds
Features: Picatinny rail molded into the polymer frame dust cover; slim-line grip profiles with user replaceable grip panels; ambidextrous controls with dual slide releases and enlarged magazine release; uses the proven modified Browning linkless recoil operating system; O-ring barrel for precise barrel-to-slide lockup and better accuracy; polygonal rifling for longer barrel life and increased accuracy; improved ergonomic control levers (safety and/or decocking); low profile drift adjustable 3-dot sights; contoured and radiused slide with forward slide (grasping) grooves and anti-glare longitudinal ribs; polymer frame; available in black, RAL8000 green brown, and olive finishes; supplied with one additional backstrap; night sights optional
MSRP . . . . $819.00–$919.00

HK45 COMPACT TACTICAL

Action: DA/SA semiautomatic
Grips: Textured polymer
Barrel: 4.57 in.
Sights: 3-dot
Weight: 29.12 oz.
Caliber: .45 ACP
Capacity: 10 rounds
Features: Proprietary internal mechanical recoil reduction system;

O-ring barrel; cold-hammer-forged barrel; available in black, RAL8000 green brown, and olive finishes; supplied with one additional backstrap; night sights optional
MSRP $999.00

HK45 TACTICAL

Action: Semiautomatic
Grips: Polymer with finger grooves
Barrel: 5.16 in.
Sights: 3-dot tritium night sights
Weight: 31.7 oz.
Caliber: .45 ACP
Capacity: 10 rounds
Features: Polymer frame; recoil-operated with modified Browning locking system; threaded barrel; Picatinny rail; key-based HK Lock-Out system; nine different trigger firing modes; available in black, RAL8000 green brown, and olive finishes; supplied with one additional backstrap; night sights optional
MSRP $999.00

MARK 23

Action: Semiautomatic
Grips: Polymer
Barrel: 5.9 in.
Sights: 3-Dot
Weight: 39.4 oz.
Caliber: .45 ACP
Capacity: 12+1 rounds
Features: Threaded O-ring barrel with polygonal bore profile; match grade trigger; one piece machined steel slide; frame mounted decocking lever and separate ambidextrous safety lever; HK recoil reduction system; ambidextrous magazine release lever
MSRP $2299.00

P30

Action: Semiautomatic
Grips: Polymer
Barrel: 3.86 in.
Sights: Fixed
Weight: 26.08 oz.
Caliber: 9mm, .40 S&W
Capacity: 10, 15 rounds
Features: Corrosion proof fiber-reinforced polymer frame; multiple trigger firing modes; HK recoil reduction system; blued finish; Picatinny rail; ambidextrous magazine release levers and side release
MSRP . . . . $719.00–$819.00

P30 L

Action: Semiautomatic
Grips: Polymer
Barrel: 4.4 in.
Sights: Fixed
Weight: 27.5 oz.
Caliber: 9mm, .40 S&W
Capacity: 10, 13, or 15 rounds
Features: Interchangeable backstraps and side panel grips in small, medium, and large sizes; ambidextrous slide and magazine releases levers; integral Picatinny rail; modular design allows DA trigger or DA/SA system, with a decocking button
MSRP . . . . $719.00–$819.00

P30SK

Action: Semiautomatic
Grips: Rubber
Barrel: 3.27 in.
Sights: Fixed
Weight: 23.99 oz.
Caliber: 9mm
Capacity: 10 rounds
Features: Picatinny rail; interchangeable backstraps and lateral grip panels; available in multiple trigger firing modes including HK's enhanced double action only Law Enforcement Modification (LEM); trigger modes include conventional double action/single action (DA/SA)
MSRP . . . . $719.00–$819.00

Heckler & Koch

HECKLER & KOCH P2000

HECKLER & KOCH SP5K

HECKLER & KOCH USP COMPACT

HECKLER & KOCH USP TACTICAL

HECKLER & KOCH USP

HECKLER & KOCH VP9SK

HECKLER & KOCH VP40

P2000, P2000 SK

Action: Semiautomatic
Grips: Polymer
Barrel: 3.26–3.66 in.
Sights: 3-Dot
Weight: 23.8–25.9 oz.
Caliber: 9mm, .40 S&W
Capacity: 9–13 rounds
Features: LEM trigger system; double-action; pre-cock hammer; ambidextrous magazine release and interchangeable grip straps; mounting rail
MSRP . . . . $799.00–$899.00

SP5K

Action: Semiautomatic
Grips: N/A
Barrel: 4.53 in.
Sights: None
Weight: 67 oz.
Caliber: 9mm
Capacity: 10, 30 rounds
Features: Civilian "sporting pistol" (SP) version of HK's MP5 full-auto; rolling delayed blowback system; overall length 14 in.; elasticized "bungee" sling; Picatinny rail scope mount
MSRP $2699.00

USP

Action: Semiautomatic
Grips: Polymer
Barrel: 4.25–4.41 in.
Sights: 3-Dot
Weight: 27.2–31.36 oz.
Caliber: 9mm, .40 S&W, .45 ACP
Capacity: 12, 13, 15 rounds
Features: Browning-type action with a patented recoil reduction system; double and single action modes; available in nine trigger/firing mode configurations; fiber-reinforced polymer frame; blued finish; ambidextrous magazine release trigger
MSRP . . . . $979.00–$1149.00

USP COMPACT

Action: Semiautomatic
Grips: Polymer
Barrel: 3.58–3.80 in.
Sights: Fixed
Weight: 25.6–28.2 oz.
Caliber: 9mm, .40 S&W, .45 ACP
Capacity: 8, 12, 13 rounds
Features: Corrosion proof fiber-reinforced polymer frame; ambidextrous magazine release lever; grooved target triggers; nine trigger firing modes
MSRP . . . . $999.00–$1199.00

USP TACTICAL

Action: Semiautomatic
Grips: Synthetic
Barrel: 4.86 in.
Sights: Adjustable
Weight: 28.16 oz.
Caliber: 9mm, .40 S&W
Capacity: 10 or 15 rounds
Features: High profile target sights; target sights with micrometer adjustment for windage and elevation; one piece machined, nitro-carburized steel slide; nine trigger firing modes; patented HK recoil reduction system; corrosion resistant "Hostile Environment" blued finish; corrosion proof fiber-reinforced polymer frame; oversized trigger guard for use with gloves; choice of flat and extended floorplate magazines; universal mounting grooves for installing accessories; ambidextrous magazine release lever; extended slide release; extractor doubles as a loaded chamber indicator; patented Lock-Out Safety device
MSRP . . . . $1349.00–$1449.00

VP9, VP9 TACTICAL, VP40

Action: Semiautomatic
Grips: Rubber
Barrel: 4.09 in.
Sights: Fixed
Weight: 26.56 oz.
Caliber: .40 S&W, 9mm

Capacity: 10, 13, 15 rounds
Features: Ergonomic handgun grip design that includes three changeable backstraps and six grip side panels; ambidextrous controls; extended Picatinny rail molded into the polymer frame; captive flat recoil spring; supplied with two additional backstraps and two additional sets of lateral grip plates; night sights optional; specialty versions available with gray, OD Green, or Flat Dark Earth frames; tactical versions add threaded barrels and night sights automatically
MSRP . . . . $719.00–$949.00

VP9SK

Action: Semiautomatic
Grips: Polymer
Barrel: 3.39 in.
Sights: Drift-adjustable front, rear
Weight: 23.07 oz.
Caliber: 9mm
Capacity: 10, 13, 15 rounds
Features: A light subcompact striker-fire with an adjustable grip; slide and magazine release are ambidextrous; grip is finger-grooved and textured; slide has serrations front and rear; accessory rail; magazines are available flush or with a finger rest extension; available in black, Flat Dark Earth, Gray, or OD Green frames
MSRP . . . . $719.00–$819.00

HANDGUNS

Heizer Defense

HEIZER DEFENSE PKO45

PKO45

Action: Semiautomatic
Grips: Stainless steel
Barrel: 2.75 in.
Sights: Low-profile three-dot
Weight: 28 oz.
Caliber: .45 ACP
Capacity: 5, 7 rounds
Features: Uses guide-rod-over-barrel configuration; front strap grip safety; one-groove accessory rail; loaded chamber indicator; available in Ghost Grey, Copperhead, and Tactical Black finishes; company plans to produce the gun in 9mm and .40 S&W
MSRP. $899.00

Heritage Manufacturing

ROUGH RIDER BIG BORE

Action: SA revolver
Grips: Cocobolo wood
Barrel: 4.5 in., 5.5 in.
Sights: Fixed, open
Weight: 38 oz.
Caliber: .45 LC, .357 Mag.
Capacity: 6 rounds
Features: Patterned after 1873 Colt; blued, nickel, stainless and blued/color-case-hardened finishes are available; frame mounted inertia firing pin and transfer bar
MSRP. $467.01

ROUGH RIDER SMALL BORE

Action: SA revolver
Grips: Cocobolo wood
Barrel: 3.5 in., 4.75 in., 6.5 in., 9 in.
Sights: Fixed
Weight: 31 oz.
Caliber: .22 LR, .22 Mag.
Capacity: 6 rounds
Features: Machined barrel is micro-threaded; optional cocobolo grips include white mother of pearl, black mother of pearl, or green camo laminate grips; frame finish comes in smooth silver satin, deep matte black, low gloss black satin or case-hardened finish
Two-cylinder combos: . . . . $225.19–$349.99
Single caliber: . . . . $194.97–$329.99

HERITAGE ROUGH RIDER BIG BORE

HERITAGE ROUGH RIDER SMALL BORE

Hi-Point Firearms

HI-POINT FIREARMS MODEL JHP45 ACP

HI-POINT FIREARMS MODEL CF-380

MODEL CF-380

Action: Semiautomatic
Grips: Polymer
Barrel: 3.5 in.
Sights: 3-Dots adjustable
Weight: 29 oz.
Caliber: .380 ACP
Capacity: 8 or 10 rounds
Features: High-impact polymer frame; black powder coat with chrome rail; durable, easy-grip finish; quick on-off thumb safety; free extra rear peep sight; in black with or without hard case or in hydro-dipped pink camo; available with a built-in Laserlyte laser or with an integral compensator
MSRP. . . . . $179.00–$269.00

MODEL JHP45 ACP & JCP 40 S&W

Action: Semiautomatic
Grips: Polymer
Barrel: 4.5 in.
Sights: 3-Dots adjustable
Weight: 35 oz.
Caliber: .40 S&W, .45 ACP
Capacity: 10 rounds
Features: Polymer frame; quick on-off thumb safety; operations safety sheet; +P rated; free extra rear peep sight; free trigger lock; black finish available as standalone gun or with one of three package choices: with Laserlyte, with hard case, with Galco Kydex holster; camo versions (no packages) available in hydro-dipped Desert Digital, pink, or Woodlands
MSRP. . . . . $219.00–$285.00

Hudson Mfg.

HUDSON MFG. H9

H9

Action: Semiautomatic
Grips: G10 VZ
Barrel: 4.28 in.
Sights: Trijicon HD front, drift-adjustable notch rear
Weight: 34 oz.
Caliber: 9mm
Capacity: 15 rounds

Features: Striker-fired pistol; all-steel construction; configurable safeties; interchangeable grips; ambidextrous operation; accessory rail; front and rear slide serrations; G10 Hogue lower backstrap
MSRP. $1147.00

Israel Weapon Industries (IWI)

GALIL ACE PISTOL 5.56 NATO WITH STABILIZING BRACE

Action: Semiautomatic
Grips: Polymer
Barrel: 8.3 in.
Sights: Adjustable; tritium insert front, two-dot tritium aperture rear
Weight: 121 oz.
Caliber: 5.56 NATO
Capacity: 30 rounds

Features: Galil now in a semiautomatic for commercial distribution; reciprocating charging handle on the pistol's left side; STANAG magazine compatibility; ample Picatinny rails with slide on/off covers; stabilizing, folding shoulder brace; action is a long-stroke gas piston
MSRP. $1849.00

ISRAEL WEAPON INDUSTRIES (IWI) GALIL ACE PISTOL 5.56 NATO WITH STABILIZING BRACE

Iver Johnson Arms, Inc.

IVER JOHNSON 1911 A1 CHROME, CHROME AND PEARL

IVER JOHNSON EAGLE XL

IVER JOHNSON POCKET ACE

1911A1 CHROME

Action: Semiautomatic
Grips: Black Dymondwood, black synthetic pearl
Barrel: 5 in.
Sights: GI fixed dovetail front and rear
Weight: 38 oz.
Caliber: .38 Super, .45 ACP
Capacity: 8 round
Features: Polished chrome finish; black Dymondwood grips or synthetic black pearl grips; slightly beveled magazine well; slide sports rear gripping serrations
.38 Super, .45ACP
   Dymondwood: $763.00
.38 Super, .45 ACP
   black pearl: $776.00
.45 ACP white pearl: $776.00

EAGLE XL

Action: Semiautomatic
Grips: Dymondwood walnut
Barrel: 6 in.
Sights: Adjustable
Weight: 42 oz.
Caliber: .45 ACP, 10mm
Capacity: 8 rounds
Features: Front and rear serrations; extended thumb safety and slide stop; lowered and flared ejection port; beavertail grip safety; three-hole trigger; skeletonized hammer
.45 ACP non-ported: $844.00
.45 ACP ported: $932.00
10mm non-ported: $864.00
10mm ported: $938.00

POCKET ACE

Action: Revolver
Grips: Wood
Barrel: 2 in.
Sights: None
Weight: 7 oz.
Caliber: .22 LR
Capacity: 4 rounds
Features: Four-shot pepperbox; rotating firing pin; sighting grove; wood grips; ambidextrous release lever also functions as a safety
MSRP. $350.00

Iver Johnson Arms, Inc.

IVER JOHNSON THRASHER

THRASHER
Action: Semiautomatic
Grips: Wood
Barrel: 3.125 in.
Sights: Dovetail front, low-profile Novak-style rear
Weight: 30.4 oz.
Caliber: 9mm, .45 ACP
Capacity: 7, 8 rounds
Features: Officer-length slide, longer grip; tops and sides of slide are polished chrome; frame is satin finished; thin-line serrations at front and rear of slide; beveled magazine well; lowered and flared ejection port; available with Trijicon night sights
Standard sights:... $647.00–$884.00
Night sights: ..... $878.00–$995.00

Just Right Carbines

JUST RIGHT CARBINES 9MM TAKEDOWN PISTOL, 9MM QUADRAIL PISTOL

9MM TAKEDOWN PISTOL, 9MM QUADRAIL PISTOL
Action: Semiautomatic
Grips: Synthetic
Barrel: 6.5 in.
Sights: None
Weight: N/A
Caliber: 9mm
Capacity: 10, 15, 17 rounds
Features: Ambidextrous charging handle and ejection; one-piece machined aluminum receiver; M4 pistol buffer tube; threaded barrel; available as a smooth-fronted takedown model or equipped with an accessory quadrail
Takedown:..... starting at $722.00
Quadrail:...... starting at $965.00

Kahr Arms

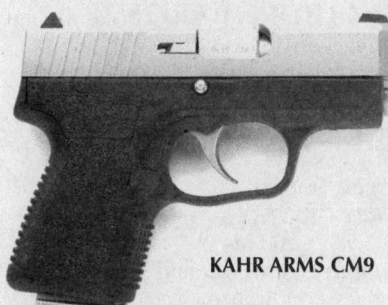

KAHR ARMS CM9

KAHR ARMS CM40

KAHR ARMS CM45

CM9
Action: Semiautomatic
Grips: Textured polymer
Barrel: 3 in.
Sights: Adjustable
Weight: 15.9 oz.
Caliber: 9mm
Capacity: 6+1 rounds
Features: Trigger cocking double-action; lock breech; Browning-type recoil lug; passive striker block; no magazine disconnect; drift adjustable, white bar-dot combat sights; available in Armor Black, Kryptek Camo, or Tungsten with Grip Glove frame, or matte stainless slide with front night sight
MSRP.......... $460.00–$499.00

CM40
Action: Semiautomatic
Grips: Textured polymer
Barrel: 3 in.
Sights: Adjustable
Weight: 17.7 oz.
Caliber: .40 S&W
Capacity: 5+1 rounds
Features: Trigger cocking DAO; lock breech; "Browning-type" recoil lug; passive striker block; no magazine disconnect; black polymer frame, matte stainless steel slide
MSRP...................$460.00

CM45
Action: DAO semiautomatic
Grips: Synthetic
Barrel: 3.24 in.
Sights: Fixed
Weight: 17.3 oz.
Caliber: .45 ACP
Capacity: 5+1 rounds
Features: Trigger cocking DAO; lock breech; "Browning-type" recoil lug; passive striker block; no magazine disconnect; textured grips; drift adjustable white bar-dot combat rear sight; pinned in polymer front sight
MSRP...................$460.00

Kahr Arms

KAHR ARMS CT40

KAHR ARMS CT45

**KAHR ARMS CT380,
CW380 GOLD CERAKOTE
LIMITED EDITION**

KAHR ARMS CT380

**KAHR ARMS CW9
KRYPTEK CAMO**

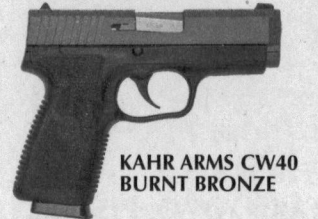

**KAHR ARMS CW40
BURNT BRONZE**

KAHR ARMS CW45

CT40

Action: DAO semiautomatic
Grips: Synthetic
Barrel: 4 in.
Sights: Fixed
Weight: 21.8 oz.
Caliber: .40 S&W
Capacity: 7+1 rounds
Features: Trigger cocking DAO; lock breech; "Browning-type" recoil lug; passive striker block; no magazine disconnect; textured grips; drift adjustable white bar-dot combat rear sight; pinned in polymer front sight; black polymer frame, matte stainless steel slide
MSRP. **$449.00**

CT45

Action: DAO semiautomatic
Grips: Synthetic
Barrel: 4.04 in.
Sights: Fixed
Weight: 23.7 oz.
Caliber: .45 ACP
Capacity: 7+1 rounds
Features: Trigger cocking DAO; lock breech; "Browning-type" recoil lug; passive striker block; no magazine disconnect; textured grips; drift adjustable white bar-dot combat rear sight; pinned in polymer front sight; black polymer frame, matte stainless steel slide
MSRP. **$449.00**

CT380

Action: Semiautomatic
Grips: Synthetic
Barrel: 3 in.

Sights: Fixed
Weight: 11.44 oz.
Caliber: .380 ACP
Capacity: 7+1 rounds
Features: Textured polymer grips; trigger cocking DAO; lock breech; Browning-type recoil lug; passive striker block; no magazine disconnect; drift adjustable white bar-dot combat rear sight; pinned in polymer front sight; available either with a matte stainless slide or with a Tungsten Cerakote slide with or without Grip Glove; matte stainless version also comes as package with an ambidextrous leather belt slide holster and an extra magazine
MSRP. . . . . **$419.00–$439.00**

CT380 GOLD

Action: Semiautomatic
Grips: Textured polymer
Barrel: 3 in. (CT380), 2.58 in. (CW380)
Sights: Pinned polymer front, drift-adjustable white bar rear
Weight: 12.8 oz. (CT380), 11.5 oz (CW380)
Caliber: .380 ACP
Capacity: 7 rounds (CT380), 6 rounds (CW380)
Features: Concealed carry .380 ACP models in a limited edition featuring gold Cerakote coated stainless steel slide
MSRP. **$439.00**

CW9 KRYPTEK CAMO

Action: Semiautomatic
Grips: Polymer

Barrel: 3.6 in.
Sights: Pinned polymer front dot, drift-adjustable two-dot rear
Weight: 15.8 oz.
Caliber: 9mm
Capacity: 7 rounds
Features: Lightweight and slim; Kryptek camo; Cerakote Black Armor slide
MSRP. **$495.00**

CW40 BURNT BRONZE

Action: Semiautomatic
Grips: Polymer
Barrel: 3.6 in.
Sights: Pinned polymer front dot, drift-adjustable two-dot rear
Weight: 16.8 oz.
Caliber: .40 S&W
Capacity: 6 rounds
Features: Lightweight and slim; DAO action; Burnt Bronze Cerakote slide finish
MSRP. **$495.00**

CW45

Action: Semiautomatic
Grips: Textured polymer
Barrel: 3.64 in.
Sights: Adjustable
Weight: 21.7 oz.
Caliber: .45 ACP
Capacity: 6+1 rounds
Features: Trigger cocking double-action; lock breech; Browning-type recoil lug; passive striker block; no magazine disconnect; drift adjustable, white bar-dot combat rear sight, pinned in polymer front sight; black frame; matte stainless steel slide
MSRP. **$449.00**

Kahr Arms

KAHR ARMS CW380

KAHR ARMS CW380 BLACK CARBON FIBER

KAHR ARMS CW380 KRYPTEK CAMO

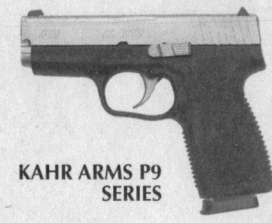
KAHR ARMS P9 SERIES

KAHR ARMS P40 SERIES

KAHR ARMS P45 BLACK WITH NIGHT SIGHTS

KAHR ARMS P380

CW380

Action: DAO semiautomatic
Grips: Black polymer
Barrel: 2.58 in.
Sights: Adjustable white bar-dot combat rear, pinned in polymer front
Weight: 10.2 oz.
Caliber: .380 ACP
Capacity: 6+1 rounds
Features: Lock breech; modified Browning type recoil lug; "safe cam" action; conventional rifled barrel; metal-injection-molded slide stop lever; slide lock after last round; available with front night sight; available configurations include: matte stainless slide/black frame, standard or packaged with a leather belt slide holster and an extra magazine
MSRP . . . . $419.00–$439.00

CW380 BLACK CARBON FIBER

Action: Semiautomatic
Grips: Polymer
Barrel: 2.58 in.
Sights: Pinned polymer front dot, drift-adjustable two-dot rear
Weight: 10.2 oz.
Caliber: .380 ACP
Capacity: 6 rounds
Features: Smallest, lightest Kahr model; black carbon fiber print; matte stainless steel slide
MSRP $439.00

CW380 KRYPTEK CAMO

Action: Semiautomatic
Grips: Polymer
Barrel: 2.58 in.
Sights: Pinned polymer front dot, drift-adjustable two-dot rear

Weight: 10.2 oz.
Caliber: .380 ACP
Capacity: 6 rounds
Features: Smallest, lightest Kahr model; Kryptek Camo treatment on the frame; Cerakote Armor Black on the slide
MSRP $439.00

P9 SERIES

Action: Semiautomatic
Grips: Textured polymer
Barrel: 3.6 in.
Sights: Adjustable
Weight: 16.9 oz.
Caliber: 9mm
Capacity: 7+1 rounds
Features: Trigger cocking DAO; lock breech; Browning-type recoil lug; passive striker block; no magazine disconnect; six versions available: Base P9 with matte stainless slide; with matte stainless slide and night sights; with matte stainless slide, night sights, external thumb safety, and loaded chamber indicator; with matte black slide; with matte black slide and night sights
MSRP . . . . $762.00–$996.00

P40 SERIES

Action: Semiautomatic
Grips: Textured polymer
Barrel: 3.6 in.
Sights: Adjustable
Weight: 18.7 oz.
Caliber: .40 S&W
Capacity: 6+1 rounds
Features: Trigger cocking DAO; lock breech; Browning-type recoil lug; passive striker block; no magazine disconnect; black polymer frame; six versions available: with matte stainless

slide; with matte stainless slide and night sights; with matte black slide; with matte black slide and night sights; with matte stainless slide, external thumb safety, and loaded chamber indicator; and with matte stainless slide, external thumb safety, loaded chamber indicator, and night sights
MSRP $762.00

P45 SERIES

Action: Semiautomatic
Grips: Textured polymer
Barrel: 3.54 in.
Sights: Adjustable
Weight: 18.5 oz.
Caliber: .45 ACP
Capacity: 5+1 or 6+1 rounds
Features: Trigger cocking DAO; lock breech; Browning-type recoil lug; passive striker block; no magazine disconnect; black polymer frame
MSRP . . . . $762.00–$880.00

P380 SERIES

Action: Semiautomatic
Grips: Textured polymer
Barrel: 2.5 in.
Sights: Adjustable
Weight: 11.27 oz.
Caliber: .380 ACP
Capacity: 6+1 rounds
Features: Trigger cocking DAO; lock breech; Browning-type recoil lug; passive striker block; no magazine disconnect; eight versions available: with matte stainless slide; with matte stainless slide and night sights; with matte stainless or black slide; night sights; California-approved variant
MSRP . . . . $710.00–$762.00

Kahr Arms

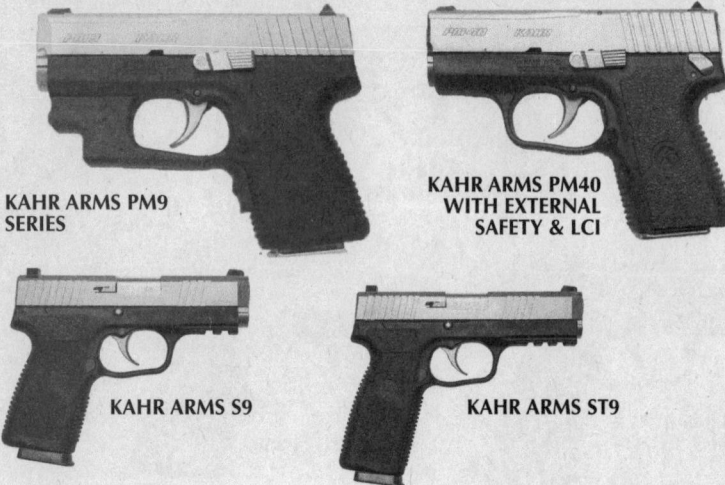

KAHR ARMS PM9 SERIES

KAHR ARMS PM40 WITH EXTERNAL SAFETY & LCI

KAHR ARMS PM45

KAHR ARMS S9

KAHR ARMS ST9

PM9 SERIES

Action: Semiautomatic
Grips: Textured polymer
Barrel: 3 in.
Sights: Adjustable
Weight: 15.9 oz.
Caliber: 9mm
Capacity: 6+1 or 7+1 rounds
Features: Trigger cocking DAO; lock breech; Browning-type recoil lug; passive striker block; no magazine disconnect; eight versions available: with matte stainless slide; with matte stainless slide and night sights; with matte stainless or black slide; night sights; California-approved variant
MSRP **$762.00**

PM40 SERIES

Action: Semiautomatic
Grips: Textured polymer
Barrel: 3 in.
Sights: Adjustable
Weight: 17.7 oz.
Caliber: .40 S&W
Capacity: 5+1 or 6+1 rounds
Features: Trigger cocking DAO; lock breech; Browning-type recoil lug; passive striker block; no magazine disconnect; eight versions available:

with matte stainless slide; with matte stainless slide and night sights; with matte stainless or black slide; night sights; California-approved variant
MSRP **$762.00**

PM45 SERIES

Action: Semiautomatic
Grips: Textured polymer
Barrel: 3.24 in.
Sights: Adjustable
Weight: 19.3 oz.
Caliber: .45 ACP
Capacity: 6+1 rounds
Features: Trigger cocking DAO; lock breech; Browning-type recoil lug; passive striker block; no magazine disconnect; eight versions available: with matte stainless slide; with matte stainless slide and night sights; with matte stainless or black slide; night sights
MSRP **$762.00**

S9

Action: Semiautomatic
Grips: Polymer
Barrel: 3.6 in.
Sights: Pinned polymer front dot, drift-adjustable two-dot rear

Weight: 15.8 oz.
Caliber: 9mm
Capacity: 7 rounds
Features: Intended primarily for concealed carry; stainless slide has grip serrations front and rear; accessory rail in front of the trigger guard; textured frame with ridges on the front and backstraps for improved purchase.; DAO pistol; Browning-type recoil lug; lock breech; passive striker block; no magazine disconnect; includes two magazines with a pinky rest
MSRP **$477.00**

ST9

Action: Semiautomatic
Grips: Polymer
Barrel: 4 in.
Sights: Pinned polymer front dot, drift-adjustable two-dot rear
Weight: 18.5 oz.
Caliber: 9mm
Capacity: 8 rounds
Features: Intended primarily for concealed carry; stainless slide has grip serrations front and rear; accessory rail in front of the trigger guard; textured frame with ridges on the front and backstraps for improved purchase.; DAO pistol; Browning-type recoil lug; lock breech; passive striker block; no magazine disconnect; includes two magazines with a pinky rest
MSRP **$456.00**

Kel-Tec

KEL-TEC P-3AT

P-3AT

Action: Semiautomatic
Grips: Polymer
Barrel: 2.7 in.
Sights: Fixed
Weight: 8.3 oz.
Caliber: .380 ACP

Capacity: 6+1 rounds
Features: Double-action only; steel barrel and slide; aluminum frame; transfer bar
MSRP **$338.18**

KEL-TEC P-11

KEL-TEC P-32

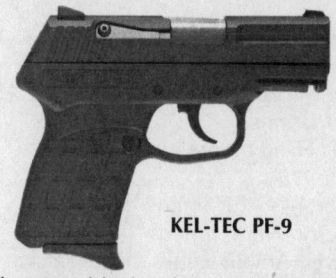

KEL-TEC PF-9

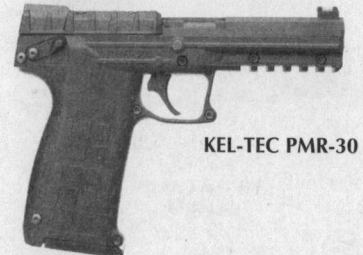

KEL-TEC PMR-30

P-11

Action: Semiautomatic
Grips: Polymer
Barrel: 3.1 in.
Sights: Fixed
Weight: 14 oz.
Caliber: 9mm
Capacity: 10+1 rounds, optional 12 rounds
Features: Double-action only; steel barrel and slide; aluminum frame; locked breech; high-impact polymer DuPont grips
MSRP. **$347.27**

P-32

Action: Semiautomatic
Grips: Polymer
Barrel: 2.7 in.
Sights: Fixed
Weight: 6.6 oz.
Caliber: .32 ACP
Capacity: 7+1 rounds
Features: Steel barrel and slide; locked breech mechanism
MSRP. **$325.45**

PF-9

Action: Semiautomatic
Grips: Polymer
Barrel: 3.1 in.
Sights: Adjustable
Weight: 12.7 oz.
Caliber: 9mm
Capacity: 7+1 rounds
Features: Firing mechanism is double-action only with an automatic

hammer block safety; grips available in black, grey, and olive drab; rear sight is a new design and is adjustable for windage
MSRP. **$356.36**

PMR-30

Action: SA Semiautomatic
Grips: Nylon
Barrel: 4.3 in.
Sights: Picatinny accessory rail under barrel
Weight: 13.6 oz.
Caliber: .22 WMR
Capacity: 30 rounds
Features: Blowback/locked breech system; lightweight but full sized; urethane recoil buffer; disassembles for cleaning with removal of one pin
MSRP. **$454.55**

Kimber

KIMBER AEGIS ELITE CUSTOM, CUSTOM (OI)

KIMBER AEGIS ELITE PRO, PRO (OI)

KIMBER AEGIS ELITE ULTRA

AEGIS ELITE CUSTOM, CUSTOM (OI)

Action: Semiautomatic
Grips: G-10
Barrel: 5 in.
Sights: Venom reflex red dot sight
Weight: 38 oz.
Caliber: .45 ACP, 9mm
Capacity: 8, 9 rounds
Features: Full-size 1911; textured green/black/gray G-10 grips; full-length guide rod; 24 lines-per-inch frontstrap checkering; stainless steel frame in satin silver; matte black Kim Pro II finish on the stainless steel slide; cross-hatched slide serrations front and back; round heel frame; OI

is Optics included
MSRP. . . . . **$1021.00–$1415.00**

AEGIS ELITE PRO, PRO (OI)

Action: Semiautomatic
Grips: G-10
Barrel: 4 in.
Sights: Venom reflex red dot sight
Weight: 38 oz.
Caliber: .45 ACP, 9mm
Capacity: 7, 9 rounds
Features: Mid-size 1911; textured green/black/gray G-10 grips; full-length guide rod; 24 lines-per-inch frontstrap checkering; stainless steel frame in satin silver; stainless steel slide in matte black Kim Pro II finish; cross-hatch serrations at the rear of

the slide; round heel frame; OI is Optics included
MSRP. . . . . **$1021.00–$1415.00**

AEGIS ELITE ULTRA

Action: Semiautomatic
Grips: G-10
Barrel: 3 in.
Sights: Green and red fiber optic
Weight: 25 oz.
Caliber: .45 ACP, 9mm
Capacity: 7, 8 rounds
Features: Compact version in the Aegis Elite series; cross-hatch serrations only at the rear of the slide
MSRP. . . . . **$1021.00–$1041.00**

Kimber

AMETHYST ULTRA II

Action: Semiautomatic
Grips: Micarta thin grips
Barrel: 3 in.
Sights: Fixed titrium night sights
Weight: 25 oz.
Caliber: .45 ACP, 9mm
Capacity: 7 or 8 rounds
Features: Ambidextrous thumb safety; full-length guide rod; amethyst purple PVD coating on small parts and fine engraving; front strap serrations and checkering; ramped barrel; tactical wedge titrium night sights; purple ball-milled Micarta thin grips
MSRP **$1652.00**

CAMP GUARD 10

Action: Semiautomatic
Grips: Rosewood
Barrel: 5 in.
Sights: Tactical wedge
Weight: 38 oz.
Caliber: 10mm
Capacity: 8 rounds
Features: Designed in partnership with Rocky Mountain Elk Foundation for use in the backcountry; stainless steel frame, slide, and barrel; front strap checkering at 30 lines per inch
MSRP **$1228.00**

CLASSIC CARRY PRO

Action: SA semiautomatic
Grips: Solid ivory G10
Barrel: 4 in.
Sights: Fixed low-profile, 3-dot
Weight: 35 oz.
Caliber: .45 ACP
Capacity: 8 rounds
Features: Deep charcoal blued finish; steel frame and slide; match grade bull barrel; serrated flat top slide; night sights; front strap checkering
MSRP **$1785.00**

CUSTOM II (TWO-TONE II)

Action: Semiautomatic
Grips: Smooth/checkered rosewood
Barrel: 5 in.
Sights: Fixed, low profile
Weight: 38 oz.
Caliber: .45 ACP, 9mm
Capacity: 7 or 9 rounds
Features: Brushed polished carbon slide; stainless frame; full-length guide rod; sainless steel match-grade barrel
9mm: **$857.00**
.45 ACP: **$837.00**

CUSTOM TLE/RL II (EM)

Action: Semiautomatic
Grips: G10
Barrel: 5 in.
Sights: Fixed low-profile
Weight: 39 oz.
Caliber: .45 ACP
Capacity: 7 rounds
Features: Tactical Law Enforcement family; matte black-finished steel frame and slide; match-grade stainless bushing; 1913 Picatinny rail
MSRP **$1164.00**

CUSTOM TLE/RL II (TFS)

Action: Semiautomatic
Grips: G10
Barrel: 5 in.
Sights: Fixed
Weight: 39 oz.
Caliber: .45 ACP, 9mm
Capacity: 7 rounds
Features: Threaded for suppression; Meprolight Tritium 3-dot night sight; Picatinny rail
.45 ACP: **$1175.00**
9mm: **$1195.00**

ECLIPSE TARGET

Action: Semiautomatic
Grips: G10
Barrel: 5 in.
Sights: Kimber adjustable bar/dot tritium night sights
Weight: 38 oz.
Caliber: .38 Super, .45 ACP
Capacity: 8 rounds
Features: Front strap checkering at 30 lines per inch; aluminum trigger; match-grade bushing; brush-polished flats on a charcoal gray finish
.45 ACP: **$1393.00**
.38 Super: **$1361.00**

KIMBER AMETHYST ULTRA II

KIMBER CAMP GUARD 10

KIMBER CLASSIC CARRY PRO

KIMBER CUSTOM II (TWO-TONE II)

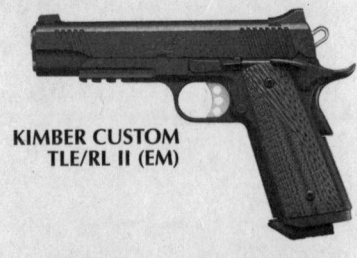

KIMBER CUSTOM TLE/RL II (EM)

KIMBER CUSTOM TLE/ RL II (TFS)

KIMBER ECLIPSE TARGET

KIMBER GOLD MATCH II

KIMBER HERO CUSTOM

KIMBER K6S CDP

KIMBER K6S DC

KIMBER K6S STAINLESS 3-INCH

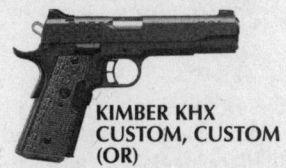

KIMBER KHX CUSTOM, CUSTOM (OR)

KIMBER KHX PRO, PRO (OR)

KIMBER KHX ULTRA

GOLD MATCH II

Action: Semiautomatic
Grips: Rosewood double diamond
Barrel: 5 in.
Sights: Kimber adjustable
Weight: 38 oz.
Caliber: .45 ACP
Capacity: 8 rounds
Features: Premium aluminum, match grade trigger; full length guide rod; steel frame with highly polished blued finish; stainless steel, match grade barrel
MSRP. $1393.00

HERO CUSTOM

Action: Semiautomatic
Grips: Composite
Barrel: 5 in.
Sights: Green and red fiber optic
Weight: 38 oz.
Caliber: .45 ACP
Capacity: 7 rounds
Features: Full-size 1911; Desert Tan Kim Pro II finish on the frame; matte black Kim Pro II finish on the slide; composite checkered grips in Kryptek Highlander camo; match grade stainless steel barrel and bushing; aluminum three-hole trigger; the American flag is engraved in tan on the slide
MSRP. $987.00

K6S CDP, CDP (LG)

Action: DA only
Grips: Rosewood
Barrel: 2 in.
Sights: Night sights
Weight: 23 oz.
Caliber: .357 Mag.
Capacity: 6 rounds
Features: Snub-nose small grip revolver; stainless steel frame with a black DLC over-brushed finish; serrated backstrap; night sights;

brushed stainless finish on the barrel; lightly fluted cylinder; CDP stands for Custom Defense Package; (LG) indicates Crimson Trace laser grips
CDP: $1155.00
CDP (LG): $1510.00

K6S DC, DC (LG)

Action: DA only
Grips: G-10
Barrel: 2 in.
Sights: Night sights
Weight: 23 oz.
Caliber: .357 Mag.
Capacity: 6 rounds
Features: Snub-nose small grip revolver; black and gray G-10 grips; black DLC finish overbrushed on all metal parts; DC stands for Deep Cover (LG) indicates Crimson Trace laser grips
CDP: $1155.00
CDP (LG): $1485.00

K6S STAINLESS

Action: DAO
Grips: Rubber
Barrel: 2 in.
Sights: Low-profile removable dovetail sights
Weight: 23 oz.
Caliber: .357 Mag.
Capacity: 6 rounds
Features: Stainless steel barrel; low-profile removable front and rear dovetail sights; smooth no-stack double action trigger; superior ergonomic grip contour; serrated backstrap
(LG): $1177.00
(NS): $919.00

K6S STAINLESS 3-INCH

Action: DA only
Grips: Walnut
Barrel: 3 in.
Sights: White dot
Weight: 25.1 oz.

Caliber: .357 Mag.
Capacity: 6 rounds
Features: Snub-nose small grip revolver; full crane shroud; longer barrel and grip than other K6s models; brushed stainless steel finish; smooth walnut grips
MSRP. $899.00

KHX CUSTOM, CUSTOM (OR)

Action: Semiautomatic
Grips: G-10
Barrel: 5 in.
Sights: Fiber optics
Weight: 38 oz.
Caliber: .45 ACP, 9mm
Capacity: 7, 9 rounds
Features: Full-size 1911; "snakeskin" textured Hogue Magrip G-10 grip panels; textured gripping areas on the slide; Stiplex front strap stippling; OR stands for "optics ready"; milled slide
Custom:. . . . . . . $1259.00–$1279.00
Custom (OR):. . . $1087.00–$1108.00

KHX PRO, PRO (OR)

Action: Semiautomatic
Grips: G-10
Barrel: 4 in.
Sights: Fiber optics
Weight: 38 oz.
Caliber: .45 ACP, 9mm
Capacity: 7, 9 rounds
Features: Hogue Magrip G-10 grip with a built-in red laser; G-10 mainspring housing; OR stands for "optics ready"; milled side
Pro: . . . . $1259.00–$1279.00
Pro (OR): . . . . . . $1087.00–$1108.00

KHX ULTRA

Action: Semiautomatic
Grips: G-10
Barrel: 3 in.
Sights: Fiber optics
Weight: 38 oz.
Caliber: .45 ACP, 9mm
Capacity: 7, 8 rounds
Features: G-10 mainspring housing; Hogue Enhanced Magrip G-10 grips with a built-in red laser; slide grip texturing appears only at the rear
MSRP. . . . . $1259.00–$1279.00

Kimber

KIMBER MASTER CARRY PRO

KIMBER MICRO 9 BEL AIR

KIMBER MICRO 9 CDP (LG)

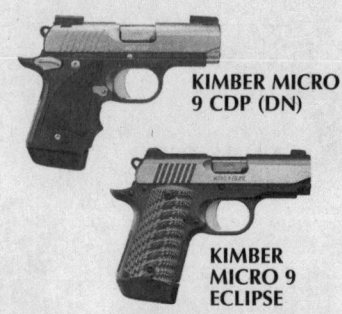

KIMBER MICRO 9 CDP (DN)

KIMBER MICRO 9 ECLIPSE

KIMBER MICRO 9 COVERT

KIMBER MICRO 9 DESERT NIGHT (DN)

KIMBER MICRO 9 DESERT TAN (LG)

KIMBER MICRO 9 NIGHTFALL (DN)

MASTER CARRY PRO

Action: Semiautomatic
Grips: Crimson Trace Lasergrips
Barrel: 3in. (Ultra), 5 in.
Sights: Fixed low profile
Weight: 25 oz.–31 oz.
Caliber: .45 ACP, 9mm
Capacity: 7 or 8 rounds
Features: Aluminum, round-heel frame; satin silver finish; dovetailed night sights; recessed slide-stop pin; serrated mainspring housing; stainless steel slide
.45 ACP: **$1477.00**
9mm: **$1497.00**

MICRO 9 BEL AIR

Action: Semiautomatic
Grips: Ivory micarta
Barrel: 3.15 in.
Sights: Three-dot white
Weight: 15.6 oz.
Caliber: 9mm
Capacity: 6 rounds
Features: Kimber's unique Bel Air Blue finish on the aluminum frame; mirror-polished stainless slide; stainless steel barrel; bull-length guide rod; single-action
MSRP **$864.00**

MICRO 9 CDP (DN)

Action: Semiautomatic
Grips: Rubber
Barrel: 3.15 in.
Sights: TruGlo TFX Pro day/night sights
Weight: 15.6 oz.
Caliber: 9mm
Capacity: 7 rounds
Features: Satin silver finish on an aluminum frame; Hogue wrap-around grips; matte black frame; Carry Melt treatment; full-length guide rod; Charcoal Gray Kim Pro II steel slide
MSRP **$973.00**

MICRO 9 CDP (LG)

Action: Semiautomatic
Grips: Rosewood Crimson Trace laser grips
Barrel: 3.15 in.
Sights: Three-dot tritium night sights
Weight: 15.6 oz.
Caliber: 9mm
Capacity: 6 rounds
Features: Custom Defense Package of features, including: ambidextrous thumb safety; front strap checkering at 30 lines per inch; Carry Melt treatment rounds; smooth edges for snag-free carry
MSRP **$1142.00**

MICRO 9 COVERT

Action: Semiautomatic
Grips: Crimson Trace laser grips
Barrel: 3.15 in.
Sights: Tritium night sights
Weight: 15.6 oz.
Caliber: 9mm
Capacity: 7 rounds
Features: Charcoal gray finish on an aluminum frame; Urban Camouflage Crimson Trace laser grips; full-length guide rod; charcoal gray Kim Pro II finish on the stainless steel slide
MSRP **$973.00**

MICRO 9 DESERT NIGHT (DN)

Action: Semiautomatic
Grips: Rubber
Barrel: 3.15 in.
Sights: TruGlo TFX Pro day/night sights
Weight: 15.6 oz.
Caliber: 9mm
Capacity: 7 rounds

Features: Desert Tan finish on an aluminum frame; Hogue wrap-around grips; matte black steel slide; full-length guide rod; matte black stainless slide; DN designates day/night sights
MSRP **$755.00**

MICRO 9 DESERT TAN (LG)

Action: Semiautomatic
Grips: Crimson Trace laser grips
Barrel: 3.15 in.
Sights: White-dot
Weight: 15.6 oz.
Caliber: 9mm
Capacity: 6 rounds
Features: Super slim, super lightweight concealed carry pistol; stainless barrel; bull-length guide rod; aluminum frame; single-action
MSRP **$790.00**

MICRO 9 ECLIPSE

Action: Semiautomatic
Grips: G-10
Barrel: 3.15 in.
Sights: Tritium night sights
Weight: 15.6 oz.
Caliber: 9mm
Capacity: 7 rounds
Features: Charcoal gray finish on an aluminum frame; stainless steel slide with polished flats; checkered gray G-10 grips; round-heel frame; 30 lines-per-inch front strap checkering; full-length guide rod; tritium night sights
MSRP **$788.00**

MICRO 9 NIGHTFALL (DN)

Action: Semiautomatic
Grips: Rubber
Barrel: 3.15 in.
Sights: TruGlo TFX Pro day/night sights
Weight: 15.6 oz.
Caliber: 9mm
Capacity: 7 rounds
Features: Satin silver finish on an aluminum frame; Hogue wrap-around grips; all-over matte black finish
MSRP **$755.00**

KIMBER MICRO 9 SAPPHIRE

KIMBER MICRO 9 STAINLESS (DN)

KIMBER MICRO 9 TLE

KIMBER MICRO 9 TWO-TONE (DN)

KIMBER MICRO AMETHYST

KIMBER MICRO COVERT

KIMBER MICRO DESERT NIGHT

KIMBER MICRO ECLIPSE

MICRO 9 SAPPHIRE

Action: Semiautomatic
Grips: G10
Barrel: 3.15 in.
Sights: Three-dot tritium night sights
Weight: 15.6 oz.
Caliber: 9mm
Capacity: 6 rounds
Features: Brilliant blue PVD finish on slide; coordinated blue and black G10 grips; slide has scroll engraving enhancements; aluminum frame; stainless steel barrel; bull-length guide rod; single-action
MSRP **$1061.00**

MICRO 9 STAINLESS (DN)

Action: Semiautomatic
Grips: Rubber
Barrel: 3.15 in.
Sights: TruGlo TFX Pro day/night sights
Weight: 15.6 oz.
Caliber: 9mm
Capacity: 7 rounds
Features: Satin silver finish on an aluminum frame; Hogue wrap-around grips; full-length guide rod; satin silver finish on the stainless steel slide; DN designates day/night sights
MSRP **$755.00**

MICRO 9 TLE

Action: Semiautomatic
Grips: G-10
Barrel: 3.15 in.
Sights: Tritium night sights
Weight: 15.6 oz.
Caliber: 9mm
Capacity: 7 rounds

Features: Matte black finish on an aluminum frame and stainless steel slide; checkered tan-and-black G-10 grips; round-heel frame; 30 lines-per-inch front strap checkering; full-length guide rod; tritium night sights; TLE stands for Tactical Law Enforcement
MSRP **$788.00**

MICRO 9 TWO-TONE (DN)

Action: Semiautomatic
Grips: Rubber
Barrel: 3.15 in.
Sights: TruGlo TFX Pro day/night sights
Weight: 15.6 oz.
Caliber: 9mm
Capacity: 7 rounds
Features: Satin silver finish on an aluminum frame; Hogue wrap-around grips; matte black steel slide; full-length guide rod; matte black stainless steel slide; DN designates day/night sights
MSRP **$755.00**

MICRO AMETHYST

Action: Semiautomatic
Grips: G10
Barrel: 2.75 in.
Sights: Three-dot tritium night sights
Weight: 13.4 oz.
Caliber: .380 ACP
Capacity: 6 rounds
Features: Concealed carry gun in vibrant purple PVD finish; engraved scroll accents; aluminum frame; stainless steel barrel; bull-length guide rod; single-action
MSRP **$1014.00**

MICRO COVERT

Action: Semiautomatic
Grips: Crimson Trace laser grips
Barrel: 2.75 in.
Sights: Tritium night sights
Weight: 13.4 oz.
Caliber: .380 ACP
Capacity: 9 rounds

Features: Charcoal gray finish on an aluminum frame; Urban Camouflage Crimson Trace laser grips; full-length guide rod; Carry Melt treatment; charcoal gray Kim Pro II finish on the stainless steel slide
MSRP **$919.00**

MICRO DESERT NIGHT

Action: Semiautomatic
Grips: G10
Barrel: 2.75 in.
Sights: Three-dot white
Weight: 13.4 oz.
Caliber: .380 ACP
Capacity: 6 rounds
Features: Concealed carry gun; Desert Tan KimPro finish; black-finished slide; stainless steel slide and barrel; bull-length guide rod
MSRP **$626.00**

MICRO ECLIPSE

Action: Semiautomatic
Grips: Rosewood
Barrel: 2.75 in.
Sights: Tactical wedge tritium night sights
Weight: 13.4 oz.
Caliber: .380 ACP
Capacity: 9 rounds
Features: Matte black finish on an aluminum frame; satin silver finish on the slide; Carry Melt treatment; thin ball-milled rosewood grips; round-heel frame; 30 lines-per-inch front strap checkering; full-length guide rod; tactical wedge night sights
MSRP **$679.00**

Kimber

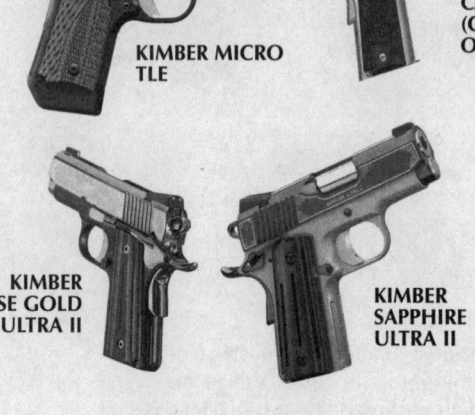

KIMBER MICRO STAINLESS ROSEWOOD

KIMBER MICRO TLE

KIMBER PRO CARRY HD II (CALIFORNIA ONLY)

KIMBER PRO COVERT

KIMBER PRO RAPTOR II

KIMBER ROSE GOLD ULTRA II

KIMBER SAPPHIRE ULTRA II

KIMBER STAINLESS II

MICRO STAINLESS ROSEWOOD

Action: Semiautomatic
Grips: Rosewood
Barrel: 2.75 in.
Sights: Fixed
Weight: 13.4 oz.
Caliber: .380 ACP
Capacity: 6 rounds
Features: Mild recoil; smooth trigger pulls; full-length guide rod; aluminum frame with anodized finish; ramped barrel
MSRP $597.00

MICRO TLE

Action: Semiautomatic
Grips: G-10
Barrel: 2.75 in.
Sights: Tritium night sights
Weight: 13.4 oz.
Caliber: .380 ACP
Capacity: 9 rounds
Features: Matte black finish on an aluminum frame and stainless steel slide; checkered tan-and-black G-10 grips; round-heel frame; 30 lines-per-inch front strap checkering; full-length guide rod; tritium night sights; TLE stands for Tactical Law Enforcement
MSRP $734.00

PRO CARRY HD II (CALIFORNIA ONLY)

Action: Semiautomatic
Grips: Synthetic
Barrel: 4 in.
Sights: Fixed, low profile
Weight: 35 oz.

Caliber: .38 Super, .45 ACP
Capacity: 7 rounds
Features: Aluminum frame with satin silver finish; stainless stell slide; steel match-grade barrel; double-diamond textured grips
.38 Super: $1094.00
.45 ACP: $1046.00

PRO COVERT

Action: Semiautomatic
Grips: Urban Camouflage Crimson Trace laser grips
Barrel: 4 in.
Sights: Tactical wedge tritium night sights
Weight: 28 oz.
Caliber: .45 ACP
Capacity: 7 rounds
Features: Carry Melt treatment; 30 lines per inch checkering on front strap; Charcoal Gray and KimPro II finish; aluminum frame
MSRP $1427.00

PRO RAPTOR II

Action: SA semiautomatic
Grips: Zebra wood, scale pattern
Barrel: 4 in.
Sights: Tactical wedge 3-dot
Weight: 35 oz.
Caliber: .45 ACP
Capacity: 8 rounds
Features: Available in all stainless or all blue; match grade barrel; ambidextrous thumb safety; full-length guide rod
Blue: $1192.00
Stainless: $1313.00

ROSE GOLD ULTRA II

Action: Semiautomatic

Grips: G10
Barrel: 3 in.
Sights: Tactical wedge
Weight: 25 oz.
Caliber: .45 ACP
Capacity: 7 rounds
Features: Personal defense gun; finished in Rose Gold PVD coating; solid aluminum trigger; aluminum round-heel frame; ambidextrous thumb safety; ball-milled front strap
MSRP $1652.00

SAPPHIRE ULTRA II

Action: SA semiautomatic
Grips: G-10 thin grips
Barrel: 3 in.
Sights: Tactical Wedge night sights
Weight: 25 oz.
Caliber: 9mm, .45 ACP
Capacity: 8 rounds
Features: Highly-polished stainless steel slide and small parts are finished with bright blue PVD finish accented with fine engraving; blue/black ball-milled G-10 thin grips and short trigger; ambidextrous thumb safety; Tactical Wedge night sights
MSRP $1652.00

STAINLESS II

Action: Semiautomatic
Grips: Synthetic
Barrel: 5 in.
Sights: Fixed, low profile
Weight: 38 oz.
Caliber: .45 ACP
Capacity: 7 or 9 rounds
Features: Aluminum frame with satin silver finish; stainless stell slide; steel match-grade barrel; double-diamond textured grips
MSRP $998.00

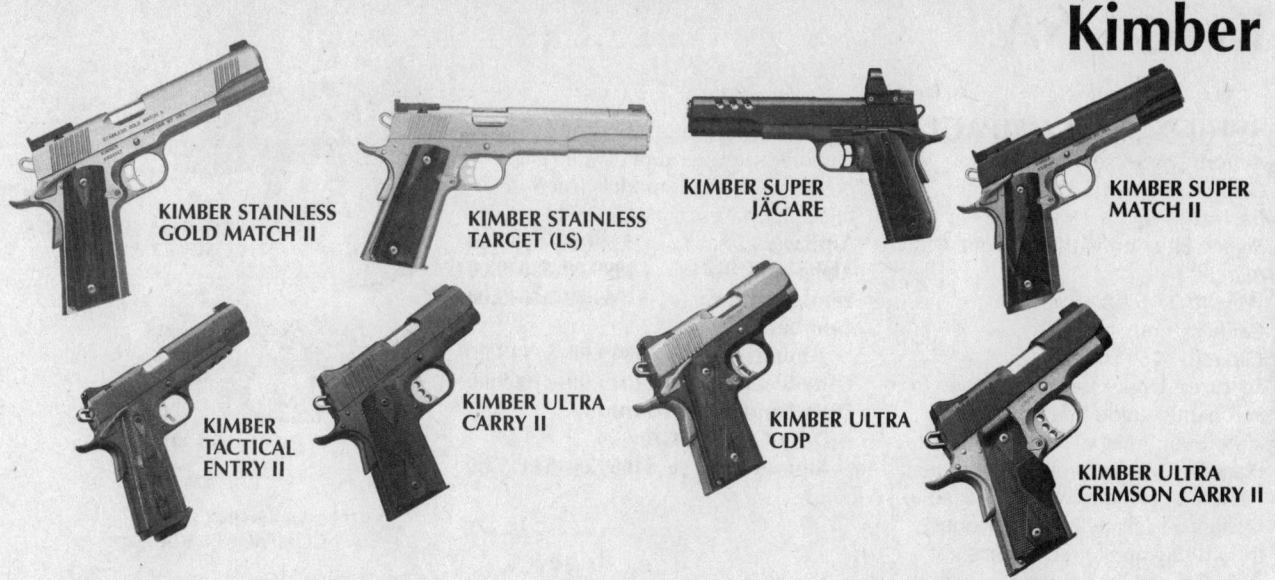

KIMBER STAINLESS GOLD MATCH II

KIMBER STAINLESS TARGET (LS)

KIMBER SUPER JÄGARE

KIMBER SUPER MATCH II

KIMBER TACTICAL ENTRY II

KIMBER ULTRA CARRY II

KIMBER ULTRA CDP

KIMBER ULTRA CRIMSON CARRY II

STAINLESS GOLD MATCH II

Action: Semiautomatic
Grips: Rosewood
Barrel: 5 in.
Sights: Adjustable
Weight: 38 oz.
Caliber: .45 ACP
Capacity: 8 rounds
Features: Ambidextrous thumb safety; full-length guide rod; stainless steel frame with satin silver finish; stainless steel match-grade barrel
MSRP $1574.00

STAINLESS TARGET (LS)

Action: Semiautomatic
Grips: Rosewood
Barrel: 6 in.
Sights: Kimber adjustable
Weight: 42 oz.
Caliber: .45 ACP, 10mm
Capacity: 7, 8 rounds
Features: Full-size 1911 with a longer slide for bull's-eye or other precision competition; slide and frame are finished in a satin silver; LS stands for Long Slide
MSRP . . . . $1055.00–$1075.00

SUPER JÄGARE

Action: Semiautomatic
Grips: Micarta
Barrel: 6 in.
Sights: DeltaPoint Pro optic
Weight: 42 oz.
Caliber: 10mm
Capacity: 8 rounds
Features: Designed for close-range big-game and varmint hunting; stainless steel frame and slide; frame has round heel and high cut trigger guard; finished in KimPro and

Charcoal Gray; slide has carbon coating and Super Carry pattern on its flat top; Carry Melt treatment; match-grade bushing; solid aluminum trigger
MSRP $2688.00

SUPER MATCH II

Action: Semiautomatic
Grips: Walnut
Barrel: 5 in.
Sights: Adjustable
Weight: 38 oz.
Caliber: .45 ACP
Capacity: 8 rounds
Features: Ambidextrous thumb safety; full-length guide rod; stainless steel frame with satin silver finish; front strap checkering and checkering under trigger guard
MSRP $2313.00

TACTICAL ENTRY II

Action: SA semiautomatic
Grips: Laminated double diamond, Kimber logo
Barrel: 5 in.
Sights: Meprolight tritium 3-dot night, fixed
Weight: 40 oz.
Caliber: .45 ACP
Capacity: 7 rounds
Features: Ambidextrous thumb safety; full-length guide rod; stainless steel frame and slide; matte gray Kim Pro II frame finish
MSRP $1490.00

ULTRA CARRY II

Action: SA semiautomatic
Grips: Black synthetic double diamond
Barrel: 3 in.
Sights: Fixed, low profile

Weight: 25 oz.
Caliber: .45 ACP
Capacity: 7 rounds
Features: Black matte finish; aluminum frame; steel slide; full-length guide rod
MSRP $919.00

ULTRA CDP

Action: Semiautomatic
Grips: Rosewood double diamond
Barrel: 3 in.
Sights: Meprolight tritium 3-dot night, fixed
Weight: 25 oz.
Caliber: .45 ACP
Capacity: 7 rounds
Features: Ambidextrous thumb safety, Carry Melt treatment, aluminum frame with charcoal gray KimPro II finish, stainless slide is flat-topped with satin silver finish
MSRP $1194.00

ULTRA CRIMSON CARRY II

Action: SA semiautomatic
Grips: Rosewood double diamond, Crimson Trace lasergrips
Barrel: 3 in.
Sights: Fixed low profile
Weight: 25 oz.
Caliber: .45 ACP
Capacity: 7 rounds
Features: Full-length guide rod; aluminum frame in satin silver finish; steel match grade barrel; aluminum match grade trigger
MSRP $1180.00

Kriss USA

SPHINX SDP COMPACT

Action: DA/SA semiautomatic
Grips: Composite
Barrel: 3.7 in., 4.35 in.
Sights: Fiber optic/tritium front, tritium rear
Weight: 27.5 oz.
Caliber: 9mm
Capacity: 15+1 rounds
Features: Upper frame machined from aeronautic-grade hard-anodized aluminum; integral recoil buffer; Picatinny rail; polymer lower frame; interchangeable grip sizes available; Defiance sights feature fiber optic/tritium day-night green front sight with tritium two-dot red rear sight; internal firing pin safety, drop safety, hammer safety, and integrated slide-position safety; all models listed in this entry have Cerakote finish

Alpha: . . . . $949.00–$999.00
Alpha Wolf, Black:. . . $999.00–$1049.00
Sand, Krypton: . . . $1049.00–$1099.00
Combat Grey,
 Alpine: . . . . . .$1049.00–$1119.00
Duty Black: . . . . .$1019.00–$1069.00
Duty Sand, Duty Krypton,
 Duty Combat Grey,
 Alpine: . . . .$1069.00–$1119.00

KRISS USA SPHINX SDP COMPACT ALPHA

KRISS USA SPHINX SDP COMPACT BLACK

Les Baer Custom

LES BAER 1911 BLACK BAER 9MM

1911 BLACK BAER 9MM

Action: SA
Grips: Black recon
Barrel: 4.25 in.
Sights: Fixed rear combat night sight, dovetail front night sight
Weight: N/A
Caliber: 9mm
Capacity: 9 rounds
Features: Compact size suitable for comfortable concealed carry; slide fitted to frame; rear serrated slide; speed trigger with crisp 4 lb. pull; tactical extended combat safety; Dupont S coating on complete pistol for maximum corrosion resistance
MSRP $2981.00

Llama (by Eagle Imports)

LLAMA MAX-1

LLAMA MICROMAX

MAX-1

Action: Semiautomatic
Grips: G10
Barrel: 5.5 in.
Sights: Mil-Spec
Weight: 36.96 oz.
Caliber: .38 Super, .45 ACP
Capacity: 9 rounds
Features: 1911-type pistol; steel frame; blue or hard-chrome finishes for .38 Super; .45 ACP available only in blue
MSRP . . . . **starting at $565.00**

MICROMAX

Action: Semiautomatic
Grips: Polymer
Barrel: 3.75 in.
Sights: Dovetail fiber optic front, Novak-style rear
Weight: 22.9 oz.
Caliber: .380 ACP
Capacity: 7 rounds
Features: 1911-style frame; beavertail grip safety; lowered and flare ejection port; combat hammer and trigger that are both skeletonized; forged steel barrel; ambidextrous thumb safety; slide serrations
MSRP $468.00

MAGNUM RESEARCH BABY DESERT EAGLE III SERIES

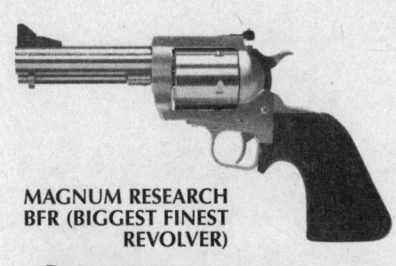

MAGNUM RESEARCH BFR (BIGGEST FINEST REVOLVER)

MAGNUM RESEARCH DESERT EAGLE 1911

MAGNUM RESEARCH DESERT EAGLE 1911 C STAINLESS

MAGNUM RESEARCH DESERT EAGLE 1911 G STAINLESS

MAGNUM RESEARCH DESERT EAGLE 1911 U STAINLESS

MAGNUM RESEARCH DESERT EAGLE BLACK TIGER STRIPE

MAGNUM RESEARCH DESERT EAGLE CASE HARDENED

MAGNUM RESEARCH DESERT EAGLE COMBO CALIBER PACKAGE

BABY DESERT EAGLE III SERIES

Action: Semiautomatic
Grips: Rubber
Barrel: 3.85 in., 4.43 in.
Sights: Fixed
Weight: 25 oz.–37.9 oz.
Caliber: 9mm, .40 S&W, .45 ACP
Capacity: 10 or 13 Rounds
Features: Polymer or steel frame; available in full size or semi-compact; Weaver rail; double action/single action; ambidextrous, slide-mounted safety and decocker; three dot combat sights
Polymer: **$646.00**
Steel: **$691.00**

BFR (BIGGEST FINEST REVOLVER)

Action: SA revolver
Grips: Rubber, optional wood
Barrel: 5 in., 6.5 in., 7.5 in., 10 in.
Sights: Adjustable rear, fixed front
Weight: 57.6–85 oz.
Caliber: Long Cylinder: .30-30 Win., .444 Marlin, .45 LC/.410, .45-70 Govt., .450 Marlin, .44 Mag., .460 S&W Mag., .500 S&W Mag.; Short Cylinder: .22 Hornet, .454 Casull, .480 Ruger/.475 Linebaugh, .50AE, .500 JRH

Capacity: 5 rounds
Features: Both long and short-cylinder models are made of stainless steel; barrels are stress-relieved and cut rifled; current production revolvers are shipped with rubber grips and Weaver style scope mount
MSRP . . . . **$1219.00–$1391.00**

DESERT EAGLE 1911 SERIES

Action: SA semiautomatic
Grips: Checkered wood
Barrel: 3 in., 5 in., 4.3 in.
Sights: Fixed
Weight: 36 oz. (5 in. barrel), 32 oz. (4.3 in. barrel), 25.8 oz. (3-in. barrel)
Caliber: .45 ACP
Capacity: 6, 8 rounds
Features: Seven variants comprise this series: C has 4.33-in. barrel, allover stainless or blue finish; G has 5.05-in. barrel, allover stainless or blue finish; U Stainless has a 3-in. barrel, allover stainless or blue finish; GR is in allover blue only, with 5.05-in barrel, and accessory rail
MSRP . . . . **$831.00–$1019.00**

DESERT EAGLE BLACK TIGER STRIPE

Action: Semiautomatic
Grips: Hard rubber
Barrel: 6 in.
Sights: Fixed combat style
Weight: 70 oz.–71 oz.

Caliber: .50 AE, .44 Mag.
Capacity: 8 rounds
Features: Desert Eagle in unique black tiger stripe finish
MSRP **$1999.00**

DESERT EAGLE CASE HARDENED

Action: Semiautomatic
Grips: Walnut, Hogue
Barrel: 6 in.
Sights: Fixed combat-type
Weight: 72.4 oz.
Caliber: .357 Mag., .44 Mag., .50 AE
Capacity: 7, 8, 9 rounds
Features: Gold trigger; walnut grips with the engraved Desert Eagle logo; includes a pair of Hogue grips
MSRP **$2368.00**

DESERT EAGLE COMBO CALIBER PACKAGE

Action: Semiautomatic
Grips: Polymer
Barrel: 6 in.
Sights: Fixed combat-type
Weight: 69.8 oz.–70.6 oz.
Caliber: .44 Mag./.50 AE
Capacity: 7, 8 rounds
Features: Magnum Research's first combo package; comes assembled as a .44 Mag. with an 8-round magazine; .50 AE barrel with a .50 AE 7-round magazine included; both barrels have a Weaver-style rail on top
MSRP **$1949.00**

Magnum Research

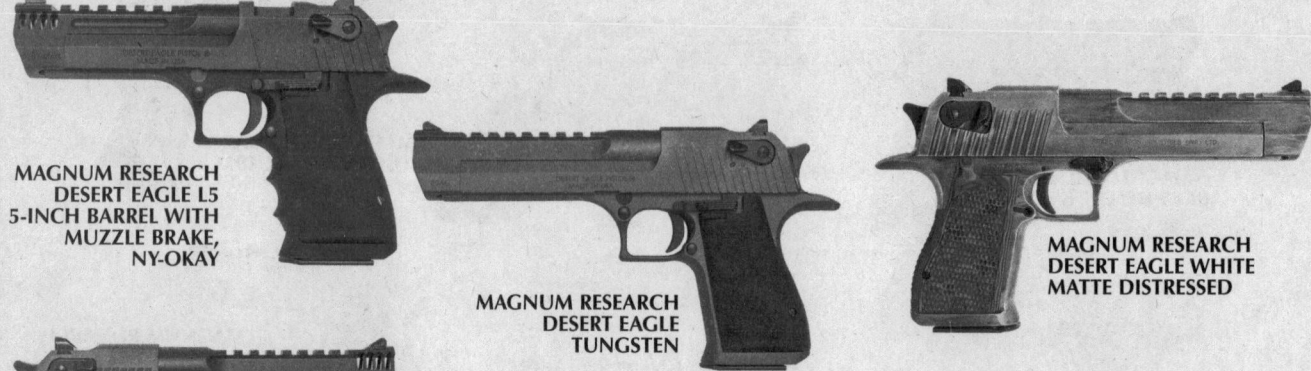

MAGNUM RESEARCH
DESERT EAGLE L5
5-INCH BARREL WITH
MUZZLE BRAKE,
NY-OKAY

MAGNUM RESEARCH
DESERT EAGLE
TUNGSTEN

MAGNUM RESEARCH
DESERT EAGLE WHITE
MATTE DISTRESSED

MAGNUM RESEARCH
DESERT EAGLE WITH
INTEGRAL MUZZLE
BRAKE

DESERT EAGLE L5 5-INCH BARREL WITH MUZZLE BRAKE, NY-OKAY

Action: SA semiautomatic
Grips: Plastic composite
Barrel: 5 in.
Sights: Fixed combat
Weight: 2 lb. 9 oz.
Caliber: .50 AE, .44 Mag., .357 Mag.
Capacity: 9 rounds
Features: Black aluminum frame; black slide/barrel with integral muzzle brake and full Weaver-style accessory rail
MSRP $1864.00

DESERT EAGLE TUNGSTEN

Action: SA semiautomatic
Grips: Plastic composite
Barrel: 6 in.
Sights: Fixed combat
Weight: 4 lb. 6.6 oz.
Caliber: .44 Magnum, .50 A.E.
Capacity: 8 rounds
Features: Tungsten Cerakote finish; high-quality carbon steel barrel; frame and slide with full Weaver-style accessory rail
MSRP $1782.00

DESERT EAGLE WHITE MATTE DISTRESSED

Action: Semiautomatic
Grips: Hard rubber
Barrel: 6 in.
Sights: Fixed combat style

Weight: 70 oz.–71 oz.
Caliber: .50 AE, .44 Mag.
Capacity: 8 rounds
Features: Desert Eagle in unique White Matte Distressed finish
MSRP $1999.00

DESERT EAGLE WITH INTEGRAL MUZZLE BRAKE

Action: Semiautomatic
Grips: Hard rubber
Barrel: 6 in.
Sights: Fixed combat style
Weight: 71 oz.–74 oz.
Caliber: .50 AE, .44 Mag., .357 Mag.
Capacity: 8 rounds
Features: Three-port integral muzzle brakel; Weaver-style accessory rail; black or stainless finish
MSRP . . . . $1741.00–$2143.00

MG Arms

MG ARMS WRAITHE

WRAITHE

Action: Semiautomatic
Grips: Custom G10
Barrel: 4.5 in.
Sights: Night or fixed
Weight: 18 oz.–20 oz.
Caliber: .45 ACP, 9mm
Capacity: 8+1, 9+1 rounds
Features: Aluminum alloy bobtail frame; custom grip panels; high ride beavertail safety; two Wilson magazines included, available in olive drab, black or desert tan
MSRP $2895.00

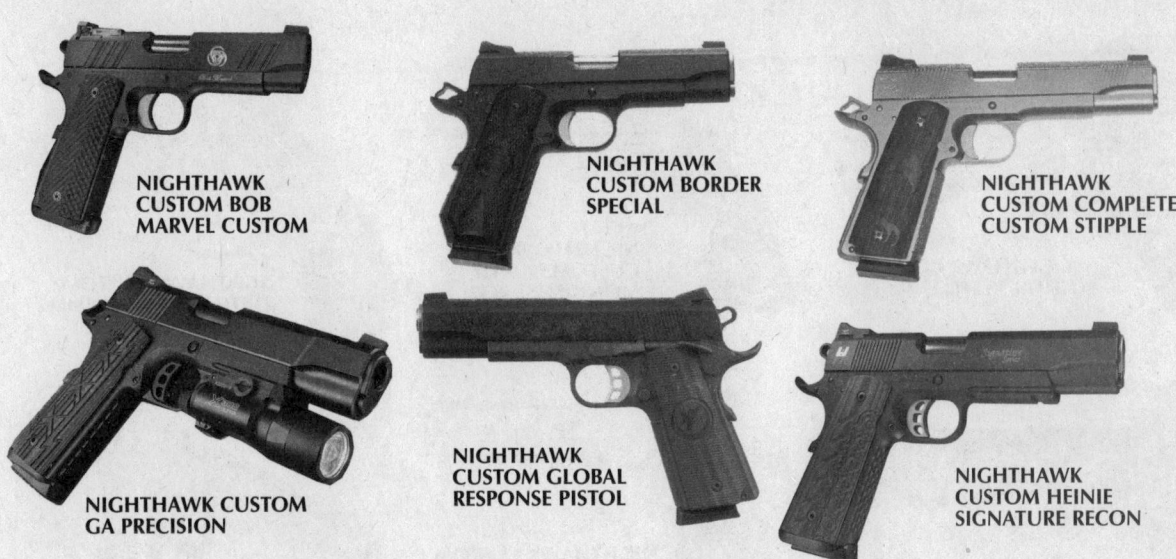

NIGHTHAWK CUSTOM BOB MARVEL CUSTOM

NIGHTHAWK CUSTOM BORDER SPECIAL

NIGHTHAWK CUSTOM COMPLETE CUSTOM STIPPLE

NIGHTHAWK CUSTOM GA PRECISION

NIGHTHAWK CUSTOM GLOBAL RESPONSE PISTOL

NIGHTHAWK CUSTOM HEINIE SIGNATURE RECON

BOB MARVEL CUSTOM

Action: Semiautomatic
Grips: Custom Mil Tac
Barrel: 4.25 in.
Sights: Novak tritium night sight front, tritium adjustable rear
Weight: 38 oz.
Caliber: 9mm, .45 ACP
Capacity: 8+1 rounds
Features: Incorporates new Nighthawk/Marvel Everlast Recoil System allowing for at least 10,000 rounds before a spring change is necessary and reduced recoil and muzzle flip
MSRP . . . . starting at $4399.00

BORDER SPECIAL

Action: Semiautomatic
Grips: Cocobolo
Barrel: 4.25 in.
Sights: Gold bead post front, Heinie Black Slant-Pro rear
Weight: 34.1 oz.
Caliber: .45 ACP
Capacity: 8 rounds
Features: Built on concealed carry cut; Commander-sized frame and slide; frame and mainspring housing dehorned for carry; match-grade barrel; ultra high-cut front strap; fluted barrel hood; Elite Midnight Cerakote finish; optional black, two-tone, or all-stainless upgrades available
MSRP . . . . starting at $3699.00

COMPLETE CUSTOM STIPPLE

Action: Semiautomatic

Grips: Cocobolo
Barrel: 5 in.
Sights: Nighthawk tritium front, Heinie 2-Dot Slant-Pro tritium rear
Weight: 38.8 oz.
Caliber: .45 ACP
Capacity: 8 rounds
Features: Aggressively stippled on top and rear of slide, front strap, mainspring housing, hammer top, slide stop, mag release, recoil spring plug, thumb safety, and grip safety pad; heavy French border; round butt mainspring housing; beveled frame; front and rear cocking serrations; bead-blasted stainless finish with polished flats
MSRP . . . . starting at $4299.00

GA PRECISION

Action: Semiautomatic
Grips: Checkered G10 grips
Barrel: 5 in.
Sights: Night sights
Weight: 38.92 oz.
Caliber: .45 ACP
Capacity: 8 rounds
Features: Fitted and hand-lapped frame and slide; skeletonized aluminum trigger with an adjustable overtravel stop; extended magazine release; single-sided extended safety; precisely fitted beavertail grip safety with a speed bump
MSRP . . . . starting at $3699.00

GLOBAL RESPONSE PISTOL (GRP)

Action: SA Semiautomatic

Grips: Micarta gator grips
Barrel: 5 in.
Sights: Night
Weight: 39 oz.
Caliber: .45 ACP
Capacity: 8 rounds
Features: 1911 design; Lanyard loop integrated into the mainspring housing; forged slide stop axle is cut flush with the frame; Heinie Slant-Pro Night Sights, Novak Low Mount Night Sights, or Novak Extreme Duty Adjustable Night Sights are standard; Perma Kote finish in black, sniper gray, green, coyote tan, titanium blued, and hard chrome
MSRP . . . . starting at $3099.00

HEINIE SIGNATURE

Action: Semiautomatic
Grips: Thin proprietary G10
Barrel: 4.25 in., 5 in.
Sights: Tritium front night sight, Heinie Slant-Pro Rear
Weight: 38 oz.–40 oz.
Caliber: 9mm, .45 ACP
Capacity: 7+1 or 8+1 rounds
Features: Features a proprietary thinned frame and mainspring housing that are scalloped to provide a positive grip without the abrasion felt from checkering; new G10 pattern grips are thinned to make concealed carry even easier, and feature a relieved area on the side to allow easy access to the magazine release
Competition
5-inch: . . . . starting at $3699.00
Recon: . . . . starting at $3799.00

Nighthawk Custom

NIGHTHAWK CUSTOM HEINIE KESTREL

NIGHTHAWK CUSTOM/KORTH MONGOOSE .357

NIGHTHAWK CUSTOM/ KORTH SKY HAWK 9MM

NIGHTHAWK CUSTOM/ KORTH SUPER SPORT .357

NIGHTHAWK CUSTOM NHC CLASSIC

NIGHTHAWK CUSTOM PREDATOR T5

KESTREL
Action: Semiautomatic
Grips: Ultra-Thin Alumagrips
Barrel: 4.25 in.
Sights: Heinie Slant pro straight eight night sights
Weight: 34.25 oz.
Caliber: .45 ACP, 9mm
Capacity: 7-10 rounds
Features: Reduced overall frame circumference; magazine well beveled for insertion; hand serrated rear of slide; Heinie Signature scalloped front strap and mainspring housing; tactical checkered extended magazine release; standard black nitride finish with stainless controls and optional stainless steel upgrade
MSRP . . . . .starting at **$3699.00**

KORTH MONGOOSE .357
Action: Revolver
Grips: Hogue
Barrel: 3 in., 4 in., 5.25 in., 6 in.
Sights: Gold bead front post, adjustable rear
Weight: 37.6 oz.
Caliber: .357 Mag.
Capacity: 6 rounds
Features: Partnership with German manufacturer Korth; revolver has an AISI 4140 aluminum frame; skeletonized high-speed hammer; easy access cylinder release; optional

9mm cylinder designed for use without moon clips
MSRP . . . . **starting at $3499.00**

KORTH SKY HAWK 9MM
Action: Revolver
Grips: Hogue
Barrel: 2 in., 3 in.
Sights: Ramp front, adjustable rear
Weight: 19.7 oz.
Caliber: 9mm
Capacity: 6 rounds
Features: Partnership with German manufacturer Korth; 7075 aluminum frame; designed for use without moon clips
MSRP . . . . **starting at $1699.00**

KORTH SUPER SPORT .357
Action: Revolver
Grips: Hogue
Barrel: 6 in.
Sights: Fully adjustable front and rear
Weight: 58.24 oz.
Caliber: .357 Mag.
Capacity: 6 rounds
Features: Partnership with German manufacturer Korth; Lothar Walther cold-forged polygonal barrel; five-way adjustable DA mechanism; Roller Trigger; Picatinny rails; optional 9mm/.38 Spl. conversion cylinder available
MSRP . . . . **starting at $4799.00**

NHC CLASSIC
Action: Semiautomatic
Grips: Cocobolo
Barrel: 5 in.
Sights: Gold bead front post, Heinie Black Ledge rear
Weight: 36.9 oz.
Caliber: .45 ACP
Capacity: 8 rounds
Features: Custom offering; slide top has been flattened and accented with arrow pattern and French border; curved slide stop; round butt mainspring housing; frame dehorning; ultra high-cut front strap; stainless finish with script engraving at slide rear; threaded barrel upgrade available
MSRP . . . . **starting at $3899.00**

PREDATOR T5
Action: Semiautomatic
Grips: Synthetic
Barrel: 5 in.
Sights: Fixed
Weight: 40.3 oz.
Caliber: 9mm, 10mm, .45 ACP
Capacity: N/A
Features: Stainless steel frame standard; black nitride finish; Nighthawk two-piece magwell; tritium dot front sight; Heinie Slant Pro Straight Eight Tritium rear sight; single-side safety; thinned cocobolo with double diamond checkering
MSRP . . . . **starting at $3799.00**

NIGHTHAWK CUSTOM SILENT HAWK SUPPRESSOR READY

NIGHTHAWK CUSTOM T3

NIGHTHAWK CUSTOM T4

NIGHTHAWK CUSTOM THE BULL

NIGHTHAWK CUSTOM TRI-CUT CARRY 9MM

SILENT HAWK 9MM

Action: Semiautomatic
Grips: G10 grips
Barrel: 4.25 in.
Sights: Tritium tall suppressor night sights
Weight: 36.91 oz.
Caliber: 9mm
Capacity: 8 rounds
Features: Commander Recon frame and Commander slide; custom checkering on front strap of frame; one piece mainspring housing and magwell; hand serrated rear of the slide; custom slide cocking serrations to match osprey silencer; thick barrel bushing and matching smooth spring plug; nitride black out finish; G10 black and gray spiral cut grips with mag release cut-out
MSRP . . . . starting at $4299.00

T3, T3 THIN

Action: SA semiautomatic
Grips: G10 grips
Barrel: 4.25 in.
Sights: Heinie Straight Eight Slant-Pro, night
Weight: 40 oz.
Caliber: .45 ACP, 9mm
Capacity: 7 rounds

Features: Frame based on Officer model; extended magazine well; Heinie Slant-Pro Straight Eights Night Sights are standard; mainspring housing and rear of slide are horizontally serrated to match; top of slide serrated to reduce glare; Nighthawk Custom lightweight aluminum trigger that has been blacked-out using Perma Kote; available in black, gun metal grey, green coyote tan, titanium blued, and hard chrome Perma Kote or stainless steel model; T3 Thin model appears in two-tone with a blued slide and stainless frame, has reduced grip circumference with a thinned front strap, flat mainspring housing, and thin alien grips
T3: . . . . starting at $3499.00
T3 Stainless: . . . starting at $3699.00
T3 Thin: . . . . . . starting at $3699.00

T4

Action: Semiautomatic
Grips: Slim
Barrel: 3.8 in.
Sights: Fixed
Weight: 34.3 oz.
Caliber: 9mm
Capacity: 9 or 10 rounds
Features: Thinned aluminum frame and mainspring housing
MSRP . . . . starting at $3499.00

THE BULL

Action: Semiautomatic
Grips: Carbon fiber
Barrel: 5 in.
Sights: Nighthawk tritium front, Heinie Ledge Straight Eight tritium rear
Weight: 38.8 oz.
Caliber: .45 ACP
Capacity: 8 rounds
Features: Government frame with French border; bow tie plug; match-grade bull barrel; frame dehorning; Elite Smoke Cerakote finish
MSRP . . . . starting at $3799.00

TRI-CUT CARRY 9MM

Action: Semiautomatic
Grips: Aluminum
Barrel: 4.25 in.
Sights: Nighthawk tritium front, Heinie Ledge Straight Eight tritium rear
Weight: 34.7 oz.
Caliber: 9mm
Capacity: 10 rounds Features: Commander-sized frame with custom tri-cut angled design; pneumatic stippling; slide ports; flat-faced Nighthawk Custom trigger; angled mag release
MSRP . . . . starting at $4499.00

Nighthawk Custom

NIGHTHAWK CUSTOM TURNBULL VIP 1

NIGHTHAWK CUSTOM VIP (VERY IMPRESSIVE PISTOL)

NIGHTHAWK CUSTOM WAR HAWK COMPACT

NIGHTHAWK CUSTOM WAR HAWK GOVERNMENT

NIGHTHAWK CUSTOM WAR HAWK RECON

TURNBULL VIP 1, TURNBULL VIP 2

Action: Semiautomatic
Grips: Mastodon ivory
Barrel: 5 in.
Sights: Gold bead front, Heinie solid black Slant-Pro rear
Weight: 37.4 oz.
Caliber: .45 ACP
Capacity: 8 rounds
Features: Very Impressive Pistol is a collaboration between Nighthawk Custom and Doug Turnbull; mastodon ivory grips; custom display case; all-over charcoal blue finish; VIP II has case-hardened frame
VIP I: . . . . **starting at $7499.00**
VIP II: . . . . **starting at $7199.00**

VIP (VERY IMPRESSIVE PISTOL)

Action: Semiautomatic
Grips: Giraffe bone
Barrel: 5 in.
Sights: Heinie black rear, 14k gold bead front
Weight: 39.78 oz.
Caliber: .45 ACP
Capacity: 8 rounds
Features: Custom vertical front strap and mainspring serrations; 14k plated gold bead front sight and crowned barrel; deep hand engraving featured throughout; antiqued nickel finish; custom cocobolo hardwood presentation case
MSRP . . . . **starting at $7999.00**

WAR HAWK COMPACT

Action: Semiautomatic
Grips: Synthetic
Barrel: 4.25 in.
Sights: Fixed
Weight: 34.7 oz.
Caliber: 9mm, .45 ACP
Capacity: N/A
Features: Unique tri-cut slide with bold angles; serrated arrow style slide top; heavy bevel on bottom of slide; hand serrated rear of slide; barrel is crowned and beveled with the bushing; one-piece fully machined 20 LPI checkered mainspring housing/magwell; high-cut front strap; hightweight solid aluminum match grade trigger; thin G10 in hyena brown; Heinie Slant Pro Straight Eight Tritium night sights; Nighthawk Custom/Marvel EVERLAST recoil system; War Hawk logo engraved on slide; stainless steel frame standard; black nitride finish
MSRP . . . . **starting at $3999.00**

WAR HAWK GOVERNMENT

Action: Semiautomatic
Grips: Synthetic
Barrel: 5 in.
Sights: Fixed
Weight: 39.6 oz.
Caliber: 9mm, .45 ACP
Capacity: N/A

Features: Unique multi-faceted slide; serrated arrow style slide top; heavy bevel on bottom of slide; hand serrated rear of slide; barrel is crowned and beveled with the bushing; one-piece fully machined 20 LPI checkered mainspring housing/magwell; high-cut front strap; lightweight aluminum medium solid match trigger; aggressive G10 hyena brown grips; red fiber optic front sights; Tritium dot front sight upgrade available; Jardine Hook rear sight; tactical magazine catch; Nighthawk Custom/Marvel EVERLAST recoil system; War Hawk logo engraved on slide
MSRP . . . . **starting at $3999.00**

WAR HAWK RECON

Action: Semiautomatic
Grips: Synthetic
Barrel: 5 in.
Sights: Fixed
Weight: 39.6 oz.
Caliber: 9mm, .45 ACP
Capacity: N/A
Features: Integrated recon accessory rail; unique multi-faceted slide; serrated arrow style slide top; heavy bevel on bottom of slide; hand serrated rear of slide; barrel is crowned and beveled with the bushing; one-piece fully machined 20 LPI checkered mainspring housing/magwell; high cut front strap; lightweight aluminum medium solid match trigger; aggressive G10 hyena brown grips; red fiber optic front sight; Tritium dot front sight upgrade available; Jardine rear hook sight; extended tactical mag catch; Nighthawk Custom/Marvel EVERLAST recoil system; War Hawk logo engraved on slide
MSRP . . . . **starting at $4999.00**

North American Arms

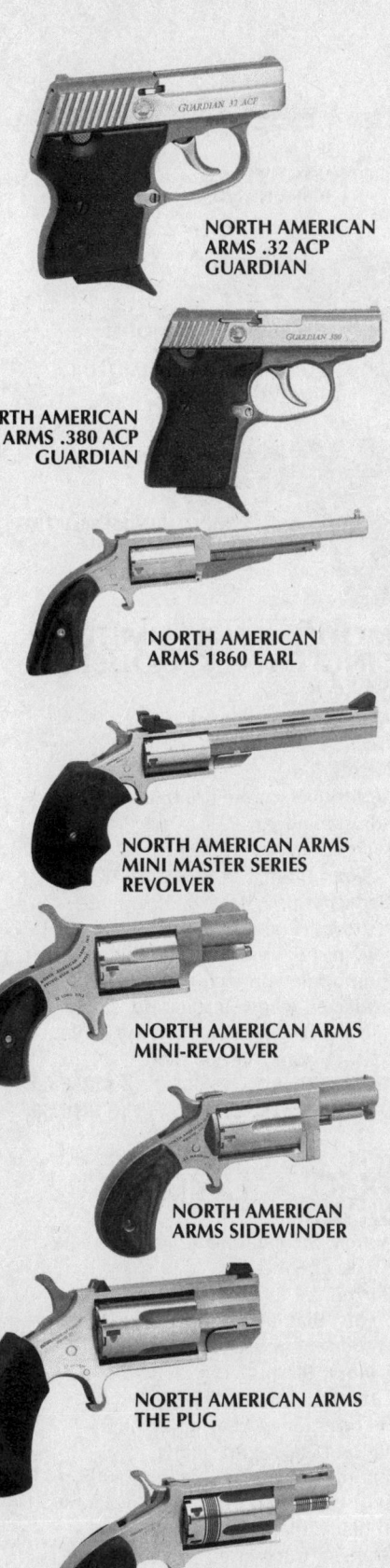

NORTH AMERICAN ARMS .32 ACP GUARDIAN

NORTH AMERICAN ARMS .380 ACP GUARDIAN

NORTH AMERICAN ARMS 1860 EARL

NORTH AMERICAN ARMS MINI MASTER SERIES REVOLVER

NORTH AMERICAN ARMS MINI-REVOLVER

NORTH AMERICAN ARMS SIDEWINDER

NORTH AMERICAN ARMS THE PUG

NORTH AMERICAN ARMS THE WASP

.32 ACP/.25 NAA GUARDIAN

Action: DAO semiautomatic
Grips: Polymer
Barrel: 2.5 in.
Sights: Fixed, open
Weight: 13.5 oz.
Caliber: .32 ACP, .25 NAA
Capacity: 6+1 rounds
Features: Stainless steel; double action only; optional Integral Locking System (ILS)
Standard (either caliber):. . .$409.00
ILS (.32 ACP only):. $437.00

.380 ACP/.32 NAA GUARDIAN

Action: DAO semiautomatic
Grips: Composite
Barrel: 2.49 in.
Sights: Fixed, open
Weight: 18.72 oz.
Caliber: .380 ACP, .32 NAA
Capacity: 6+1 rounds
Features: Stainless steel; double action only; optional Integral Locking System (ILS)
Standard (either caliber): $456.00
ILS (.380 ACP only): $486.00

1860 EARL

Action: SA revolver
Grips: Rosewood
Barrel: 3, 4, 6 in.
Sights: Stainless steel post front sight
Weight: 9.7 oz.
Caliber: .22 Mag.
Capacity: 5 rounds
Features: Replica of 1860s Hogleg, with faux loading lever and pin, octagonal barrel, rosewood grips; available with .22 LR conversion cylinder
3-inch, 4-inch: $298.00
6-inch: $398.00
3- or 4-inch with conversion cylinder:. $332.00
6-inch with conversion cylinder:. $344.00

MINI MASTER SERIES REVOLVER

Action: SA revolver
Grips: Rubber
Barrel: 4 in.
Sights: Fixed or adjustable
Weight: 10.7 oz.
Caliber: .22 LR, .22 Mag.
Capacity: 5 rounds
Features: Conversion cylinder or adjustable sights available
Fixed sights:. $298.00
W/ conversion cylinder:. . . $332.00

W/ adjustable sights: $328.00
W/ conversion and adjustable sights: $363.00

MINI-REVOLVER

Action: SA revolver
Grips: Laminated rosewood
Barrel: 1.2 in., 1.625 in.
Sights: Fixed, open
Weight: 4 oz.–6.2 oz.
Caliber: .22 Short, .22 LR, .22 Mag.
Capacity: 5 rounds
Features: Features NAA's safety cylinder so mini-revolver can be carried fully loaded; .22 LR available with folding "holster grip." .22 Mag available ported or with folding "holster grip"
.22: $226.00
.22 LR: . . . . $226.00–$256.00
.22 Mag:. . . . . $236.00–$301.00

SIDEWINDER

Action: Revolver
Grips: Laminated rosewood
Barrel: 1 in., 2.5 in., 4. in.
Sights: Stainless steel post
Weight: 6.7 oz.
Caliber: .22 Mag.
Capacity: 5 rounds
Features: Features NAA's safety cylinder; stainless steel frame; available .22 LR conversion
MSRP . . . . $350.00–$508.00

THE PUG

Action: Revolver
Grips: Rubber
Barrel: 1 in.
Sights: Tritium and white dot
Weight: 6.4 oz.
Caliber: .22 Mag.
Capacity: 5 rounds
Features: Oversized pebble-textured rubber grips enable the handler to keep a firm grip
White dot sight:. $328.00
Tritium sight: $347.00

THE WASP

Action: SA revolver
Grips: Rubber pebble finish
Barrel: 1.125 in., 1.625 in.
Sights: Stainless post
Weight: 5.9 oz.–7.2 oz.
Caliber: .22 Mag.
Capacity: 5 rounds
Features: Stainless steel frame; vent rib barrel; skeleton hammer; .22 LR conversion cylinders available; brushed sides, matte contours, black inlay
MSRP . . . . $266.00–$301.00

Remington Arms Company

MODEL 1911 R1

Action: Semiautomatic
Grips: Double diamond walnut
Barrel: 5 in.
Sights: Fixed
Weight: 38.5 oz.
Caliber: .45 ACP
Capacity: 7 rounds
Features: Short trigger; double diamond walnut grips; modern enhancements include a lowered and flared ejection port; beveled magazine well; loaded chamber indicator; high-profile fixed sights in a three-white-dot pattern; match grade stainless-steel barrel; available in stainless steel
MSRP. **$774.00**
Stainless: **$837.00**

MODEL 1911 R1 10MM HUNTER

Action: Semiautomatic
Grips: VZ Operator II G10
Barrel: 6 in.
Sights: Fully adjustable match sights
Weight: 41 oz.
Caliber: 10mm
Capacity: 8 rounds
Features: Long-slide SA 1911-type handgun; extended beavertail safety; wide rear and front slide cocking serrations
MSRP. **$1310.00**
Flat Dark Earth: **$1340.00**

MODEL 1911 R1 200TH ANNIVERSARY COMMEMORATIVE

Action: Semiautomatic
Grips: Walnut
Barrel: 5 in.
Sights: Fixed
Weight: 38.5 oz.
Caliber: .45 Auto
Capacity: 7+1 rounds
Features: Commemorative engraved medalions in grip and grip cap; classic GI-style thumb safety, grip safety, and hammer; stainless steel match-grade barrel; includes 2 magazines; satin black oxide finish on frame
MSRP. **$835.00**

MODEL 1911 R1 200TH ANNIVERSARY LIMITED EDITION

Action: Semiautomatic
Grips: Walnut
Barrel: 5 in.
Sights: Fixed

REMINGTON MODEL R1 STAINLESS

REMINGTON MODEL 1911 R1 200TH ANNIVERSARY COMMEMORATIVE

REMINGTON MODEL 1911 R1 COMMANDER

REMINGTON ARMS R51

Weight: 38.5 oz.
Caliber: .45 Auto
Capacity: 7+1 rounds
Features: C-grade walnut grips; classic American-style engraving and 24k gold inlay; limited to quantity of 2016; special serial number; bicentennial box with Remington historical timeline
MSRP. **$1649.00**

MODEL 1911 R1 COMMANDER

Action: Semiautomatic
Grips: Wood
Barrel: 4.25 in.
Sights: Fixed
Weight: 38.5 oz.
Caliber: .45 ACP
Capacity: 7+1 rounds
Features: Oversized, flared ejection port; carbon steel frame and slide; 3-dot sights; GI style grip safety; GI style short trigger; black oxide finish; walnut double diamond grips
MSRP. **$744.00**

REMINGTON MODEL 1911 R1 10MM HUNTER

REMINGTON MODEL 1911 R1 200TH ANNIVERSARY LIMITED EDITION

REMINGTON MODEL 1911 R1 LIMITED SINGLE STACK, DOUBLE STACK

MODEL 1911 R1 LIMITED SINGLE STACK, DOUBLE STACK

Action: Semiautomatic
Grips: VZ Operator G10
Barrel: 5 in.
Sights: Fiber optic front, fully adjustable rear
Weight: 38 oz.–48 oz.
Caliber: 9mm, .40 S&W, .45 ACP
Capacity: 8, 9, 16, 18, 19 rounds
Features: Competition-ready SA 1911-style pistol; ambidextrous extended thumb safety; match-grade barrel; oversized magwell standard; single and double stack versions available; semi-custom Tomasie model
Single-Stack: **$1250.00**
Double-Stack: **$1310.00**

R51, R51 CRIMSON TRACE, R51 SMOKE/SILVER

Action: Semiautomatic
Grips: Polymer
Barrel: 3.4 in.
Sights: Blade front, dovetail rear
Weight: 22.6 oz.
Caliber: 9mm
Capacity: 7 rounds
Features: Snag-free sights; single-action trigger; grip safety; ambidextrous mag release; low bore axis; checkered front strap; available in black, black with a built-in Crimson Trace laser, and a no-laser bi-tone smoke/silver version
MSRP. **$448.00**
Crimson Trace: **$648.00**
Smoke/Silver: **$460.00**

Remington Arms Company

REMINGTON RP9

REMINGTON RM380

REMINGTON RM380 MICRO WITH CRIMSON TRACE

REMINGTON ARMS RP45

RM380

Action: Semiautomatic
Grips: Glass-filled nylon
Barrel: 2.9 in.
Sights: Fixed
Weight: 12.2 oz.
Caliber: .380 ACP
Capacity: 6+1 rounds
Features: Fully functional slide stop; all metal construction; DOA trigger; ambidextrous magazine release; checkered front strap and undercut trigger guard; optimized grip handle; 10-pound trigger pull
MSRP $328.36

RM380 MICRO CRIMSON TRACE

Action: Semiautomatic
Grips: Glass-filled nylon
Barrel: 2.9 in.
Sights: Fixed
Weight: 12.2 oz.
Caliber: .380 ACP
Capacity: 6+1 rounds
Features: Fully functional slide stop; all metal construction; DOA trigger; ambidextrous magazine release; checkered front strap and undercut trigger guard; optimized grip handle; 10-pound trigger pull; trigger-guard mounted red Crimson Trace laser
MSRP $638.00

RP9

Action: Semiautomatic
Grips: Polymer
Barrel: 4.5 in.
Sights: Drift-adjustable front and rear
Weight: 26.4 oz.
Caliber: 9mm
Capacity: 10, 18 rounds
Features: Single-action with short tactile reset; ambidextrous slide control; rear sight "fighting surface" enables one-handed racking; undercut trigger guard; PVD finish on slide and barrel; night sight option available
MSRP $418.09
Night sights: $504.00

RP45

Action: Semiautomatic
Grips: Polymer
Barrel: 4.5 in.
Sights: Tritium three-dot night sights
Weight: 26.4 oz.
Caliber: .45 ACP
Capacity: 10, 15 rounds
Features: Lightweight double-stack .45; undercut trigger guard;PVD finish on slide and barrel; three interchangeable backstraps; ambidextrous slide control; night sights; accessory rail; single-action trigger with a short reset
MSRP . . . . $418.09–$504.00

Rock River Arms

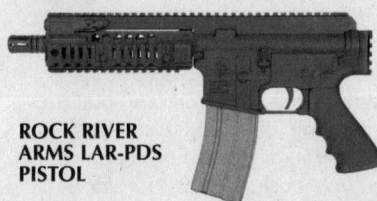

ROCK RIVER ARMS 1911 POLY

ROCK RIVER ARMS LAR-PDS PISTOL

1911 POLY

Action: SA semiautomatic
Grips: Polymer
Barrel: 5 in.
Sights: Dovetail front and rear
Weight: 32.6 oz.
Caliber: .45 ACP
Capacity: 7 rounds
Features: Chromoly barrel; polymer frame and mainspring housing; steel frame insert; steel slide; parkerized finish on metal; RRA overmolded grips; aluminum speed trigger; beavertail grip safety; RRA dovetail front and rear sights
MSRP $1025.00

LAR-PDS PISTOL

Action: Gas-operated semiautomatic
Grips: Hogue rubber
Barrel: 8 in. chromoly
Sights: Picatinny rail
Weight: 80 oz.
Caliber: 5.56 NATO
Capacity: 30 rounds
Features: Forged lower; Hogue rubber grip; A2 flash hider; two-position regulator; not compatible with suppressors; one version has injection-molded ribbed handguard, second version has an aluminum tri-rail handguard
Ribbed handguard: $1245.00
Tri-rail handguard: $1395.00

Ruger (Sturm, Ruger & Co.)

RUGER 22 CHARGER TAKEDOWN

RUGER 22/45 LITE

RUGER AMERICAN PISTOL

RUGER EC9

RUGER GP100

RUGER GP100 7-ROUND .327 FEDERAL

RUGER GP100 MATCH CHAMPION

22 CHARGER

Action: Semiautomatic
Grips: Synthetic
Barrel: 10 in.
Sights: None
Weight: 3 lb. 4 oz.
Caliber: .22 LR
Capacity: 15 rounds
Features: Cold hammer-forged barrel; threaded barrel; Picatinny rail; A2-style grip; adjustable bipod
Standard: **$309.00**
Takedown: **$419.00**

22/45 LITE

Action: Semiautomatic
Grips: Synthetic
Barrel: 4.4 in.
Sights: Adjustable
Weight: 22.7 oz.
Caliber: .22 LR
Capacity: 6 rounds
Features: Zytel polymer grip frame; threaded barrel; ccontoured ejection port; loaded chamber indicator; available in black or bronze anodized finishes
MSRP **$559.00**

AMERICAN PISTOL

Action: Semiautomatic
Grips: Ergonomic wrap-around
Barrel: 4.2 in., 4.5 in.

Sights: Three dot
Weight: 30 oz.–31.5 oz.
Caliber: 9mm Luger, .45 ACP
Capacity: 10 or 17 rounds
Features: Trigger features a short takeup with positive reset; recoil-reducing barrel cam; low-mass slide; Novak LoMount Carry three-dot sights; modular wrap-around grip system for adjusting palm swell and trigger reach; ambidextrous slide stop and magazine release; safety features include internal, automatic sear block system, integrated trigger safety and no trigger pull required for takedown
MSRP **$579.00**

EC9

Action: Semiautomatic
Grips: Glass-filled nylon
Barrel: 3.12 in.
Sights: Integral
Weight: 17.2 oz.
Caliber: 9mm
Capacity: 7 rounds
Features: Lightweight carry gun is a striker-fired semiautomatic with a checkered grip frame; integral trigger safety; magazine disconnect; external safety; finger rest magazine
MSRP **$299.00**

GP100

Action: DA revolver
Grips: Black hogue monogrip
Barrel: 3 in., 4.2 in., 6 in.
Sights: Ramp front, fixed or adjustable rear
Weight: 36 oz.–45 oz.
Caliber: .327 Fed Mag., .357 Mag., .44 Spl.
Capacity: 5, 6, 7 rounds

Features: Satin stainless or blued finish; stainless steel or alloy steel frame; cushioned rubber grip; transfer bar; triple-locking cylinder
MSRP . . . .**$769.00–$829.00**

GP100 .22 LR

Action: DA revolver
Grips: Cushioned rubber with wood insert
Barrel: 5.5 in.
Sights: Fiber optic front, adjustable rear
Weight: 42 oz
Caliber: .22 LR
Capacity: 10 rounds
Features: Triple-locking cylinder locked into the frame at the front, rear, and bottom; patented grip frame design easily accommodates a wide variety of custom grips; takedown of integrated subassemblies requires no special tools and allows for easy maintenance and assembly; patented transfer bar mechanism provides an unparalleled measure of security against accidental discharge
MSRP **$829.00**

GP100 7-ROUND .327 FEDERAL

Action: DA/SA
Grips: Rubber
Barrel: 4.2 in.
Sights: Ramp front, adjustable rear
Weight: 40 oz.
Caliber: .327 Federal
Capacity: 7 rounds
Features: Cylinder locks into the frame at the front, rear and bottom, improving alignment and reliability; grip frame design accommodates multiple custom grips; transfer bar mechanism
MSRP **$899.00**

Ruger (Sturm, Ruger & Co.)

RUGER GP100 7-ROUND .357 MAG.

RUGER GP100 .22 LR

RUGER LC380

RUGER LCP

RUGER LCP II

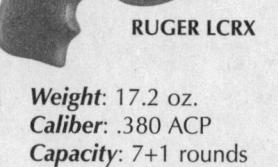

RUGER LCRX

RUGER MARK IV HUNTER

GP100 7-ROUND .357 MAG.
Action: DA/SA
Grips: Rubber with hardwood inserts
Barrel: 2.5 in., 4.2 in., 6 in.
Sights: Fiber optic front, adjustable rear
Weight: 36 oz., 40 oz., 43.5 oz.
Caliber: .357 Mag.
Capacity: 7 rounds
Features: Cylinder locks into the frame at the front, rear and bottom, improving alignment and reliability; adjustable sights at the rear with a fiber optic front; three barrel lengths
MSRP $899.00

GP100 MATCH CHAMPION
Action: DA revolver
Grips: Wood
Barrel: 4.2 in.
Sights: Fixed or adjustable
Weight: 38 oz.
Caliber: .357 Mag.
Capacity: 6 rounds
Features: Hogue stippled hardwood; fiber optic front site; triple-locking cylinder; easy takedown; features a slab-sided, half-lug barrel
MSRP $969.00

LC380
Action: Semiautomatic
Grips: Black, glass-filled nylon
Barrel: 3.12 in.
Sights: Adjustable 3-dot

Weight: 17.2 oz.
Caliber: .380 ACP
Capacity: 7+1 rounds
Features: Hardened alloy steel slide; checkered grip frame; finger grip extension floorplate; three safeties and loaded chamber indicator; blued finish; California-approved version available
MSRP $539.00

LCP
Action: Semiautomatic
Grips: Glass-filled nylon
Barrel: 2.75 in.
Sights: Integral, Viridian E-Series red laser
Weight: 9.9 oz.
Caliber: .380 ACP
Capacity: 6+1 rounds
Features: Alloy steel barrel and slide; blued finish; fixed/LaserMax CenterFire sights; black, high performance, glass-filled nylon grips; standard model is all black and is available with a built-in laser; Moon Shine camo frames in Harvest moon or Toxic patterns; 10th Anniversary Limited Edition is engraved with that sentiment and has a stainless slide and skeletonized trigger
Standard: $259.00
With laser: $349.00
Harvest Moon or Toxic
  camo: $299.00
10th Anniversary Ltd. Ed.: . . . $299.00

LCP II
Action: Semiautomatic
Grips: Glass-filled nylon
Barrel: 2.75 in.
Sights: Fixed front and rear
Weight: 10.6 oz.
Caliber: .380 ACP
Capacity: 6 rounds
Features: Updated from the original;

improved sights and trigger; last round hold open; larger grip surface
Standard: $349.00
With laser: $439.00
Reduced Moon Shine Camo
  Toxic, Harvest Moon: $399.00

LCR
Action: DA/SA
Grips: Rubber
Barrel: 1.87 in.
Sights: Adjustable
Weight: 13.5 oz.–17.2 oz.
Caliber: .38 Spl. +P, 22 LR, 22 WMR, .327 Fed. Mag., .357 Mag., 9mm Luger
Capacity: 5–8 rounds
Features: Hogue Tamer monogrip; adjustable black blade rear sight; lonbond Diamondblack cylinder finish
MSRP . . . . $579.00–$669.00

LCRX
Action: DA/SA revolver
Grips: Rubber
Barrel: 1.87 in.–3 in.
Sights: Fixed
Weight: 13.5 oz.
Caliber: .22 LR, .22 WMR, .38 Spec. +P, .327 Fed. Mag., .357 Mag., 9mm
Capacity: 5 rounds
Features: High-strength stainless steel cylinder features an lonbond Diamondblack finish; Grip Peg allows a variety of grip styles to be installed; external hammer that allows for single-action mode; also available with Crimson Trace lasergrips
MSRP . . . . $579.00–$669.00

MARK IV HUNTER
Action: SA semiautomatic
Grips: Checkered laminate
Barrel 6.88 in.
Sights: Fiber optic front sight, adjustable rear
Weight: 44 oz.
Caliber: .22 LR
Capacity: 10 rounds
Features: Stainless steel frame with satin finish; fluted bull barrel; one-button takedown; drop-free magazine
MSRP . . . . $769.00–$799.00

Ruger (Sturm, Ruger & Co.)

RUGER MARK IV HUNTER

RUGER MARK IV STANDARD

RUGER MARK IV TACTICAL

RUGER MARK IV TARGET WITH THREADED BULL BARREL

RUGER NEW BEARCAT

RUGER NEW MODEL SUPER BLACKHAWK

RUGER REDHAWK WITH SLEEVE AND SHROUD BARREL

MARK IV STANDARD

Action: Semiautomatic
Grips: Synthetic
Barrel: 4.75 in., 6 in.
Sights: Fixed blade front, fixed notch rear
Weight: 28.2–30.1 oz.
Caliber: .22 LR
Capacity: 10 rounds
Features: Tapered barrel; naturally pointing grip angle; ambidextrous safety; bolt stop; drop-free magazines; magazine disconnect; one-button takedown
MSRP.................**$449.00**

MARK IV TACTICAL

Action: Semiautomatic
Grips: Synthetic
Barrel: 4.4 in.
Sights: Fixed blade front, adjustable rear
Weight: 34.6 oz.
Caliber: .22 LR
Capacity: 10 rounds
Features: Threaded barrel; Picatinny rails both top and bottom; drop-free magazines; magazine disconnect
MSRP.................**$569.00**

MARK IV TARGET

Action: Semiautomatic
Grips: Laminate, synthetic
Barrel: 5.5 in.
Sights: Fixed front, adjustable rear
Weight: 35.6 oz.–42.8 oz.

Caliber: .22 LR
Capacity: 10 rounds
Features: Latest version of Ruger's esteemed .22-caliber SA handguns; one-piece CNC-machined frame; ambidextrous manual safety; drop-free mag design; magazine disconnect; one-button takedown; two magazines; blued or stainless steel options
Blued: .... **$529.00–$569.00**
Stainless steel: .... **$689.00–$699.00**

MARK IV TARGET WITH THREADED BULL BARREL

Action: Semiautomatic
Grips: Synthetic
Barrel: 5.5 in.
Sights: Fixed front, adjustable rear
Weight: 42.8 oz.
Caliber: .22 LR
Capacity: 10 rounds
Features: Threaded bull barrel; includes two drop-free magazines
MSRP.................**$699.00**

NEW BEARCAT

Action: SA revolver
Grips: Hardwood
Barrel: 4.2 in.
Sights: Blade front, integral notch
Weight: 24 oz.
Caliber: .22 LR
Capacity: 6 rounds
Features: Alloy steel with blued finish or stainless steel frame with satin

stainless finish; decorative cylinder; transfer bar mechanism; features one piece frame reminiscent of old Remington Civil War-era revolvers
Alloy Steel: **$639.00**
SS: **$689.00**

NEW MODEL SUPER BLACKHAWK

Action: SA revolver
Grips: Hardwood, laminate
Barrel: 4.62 in., 5.5 in., 7.5 in., 10.5 in.
Sights: Ramp front, adjustable rear
Weight: 45–55 oz.
Caliber: .44 Rem. Mag.
Capacity: 6 rounds
Features: Alloy steel or stainless steel frame; blued or satin stainless finish; transfer bar mechanism; western-style grip; Bisley Hunter variation has 7.5-in. barrel, black laminate grips
Standard: .... **$829.00–$859.00**
Hunter: **$959.00**
Bisley Hunter: **$959.00**

REDHAWK WITH SLEEVE AND SHROUD BARREL

Action: DA/SA
Grips: Hardwood
Barrel: 4.2 in., 5.5 in.
Sights: Color insert front blade, white outline adjustable rear
Weight: 44 oz., 49 oz.
Caliber: .357 Mag., .45 ACP, .44 Mag.
Capacity: 8 rounds
Features: Two cold hammer-forged sleeve and shroud barrel models; satin stainless finish; colored front sight insert is easily replaced
MSRP................. **$1079.00**

Ruger (Sturm, Ruger & Co.)

RUGER SECURITY-9

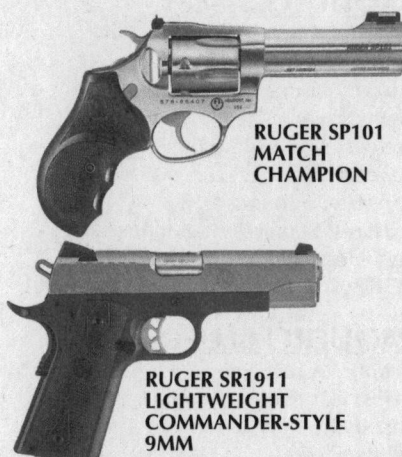

RUGER SP101 MATCH CHAMPION

RUGER SR1911 LIGHTWEIGHT COMMANDER-STYLE 9MM

RUGER SINGLE-SIX .17 HMR

RUGER SR22 RIMFIRE PISTOL

RUGER SP101

RUGER SR1911

SECURITY-9

Action: Semiautomatic
Grips: Glass-filled nylon
Barrel: 4 in.
Sights: Drift-adjustable front and rear
Weight: 23.7 oz.
Caliber: 9mm
Capacity: 10, 15 rounds
Features: Aluminum chassis; full-length rails; blued alloy steel slide; Ruger's Secure Action found on the LCP II; textured grip frame; supplied with two magazines
Standard: $379.00
**With Viridian E-Series
  red laser**: $439.00
With Hogue grip: $399.00

SINGLE-SIX

Action: SA revolver
Grips: Black checkered hard rubber
Barrel: 6.5, 7.5 in.
Sights: Ramp or front bead, adjustable rear
Weight: 35, 45 oz.
Caliber: .17 HMR, .22 LR
Capacity: 6 rounds
Features: cold hammer-forged barrel; checkered hard-rubber grips; .17 HMR is in blue; .22 LR is in stainless and has integral scope mount grooves
.17 HMR: $629.00
.22 LR: $879.00

SP101

Action: DA/SA
Grips: Wood and rubber
Barrel: 2.25 in.–4.2 in.
Sights: Fixed
Weight: 25 oz.–30 oz.
Caliber: .22 LR, .38 Spl +P, .327 Fed. Mag., .357 Mag., 9mm
Capacity: 6 rounds
Features: Features a light-gathering front sight, windage and elevation adjustable rear sight; triple-locking cylinder; easy takedown
MSRP . . . . $719.00–$769.00

SP101 MATCH CHAMPION

Action: DA/SA
Grips: Hardwood
Barrel: 4.2 in.
Sights: Fiber optic front, adjustable rear
Weight: 30 oz.
Caliber: .357 Mag.
Capacity: 5 rounds
Features: Target crown barrel; checkered hardwood grips; full-lug barrel
MSRP $859.00

SR22

Action: DA semiautomatic
Grips: Polymer
Barrel: 3.5 in., 4.5 in.
Sights: Adjustable 3-dot
Weight: 17.5 oz.
Caliber: .22 LR
Capacity: 10 rounds
Features: 3-dot sight system has fixed front sight and adjustable rear sight; polymer frame and two interchangeable rubberized grips; underside Picatinny rail; aluminum slide; ambidextrous manual thumb safety/decocking lever; ambidextrous

magazine release; Talo Distributor exclusives were offered in purple, black, flat dark earth, red titanium Cerakote, yellow Cerakote, and turquoise Cerakote finishes
MSRP $439.00
Silver: $469.00
Threaded Barrel: $479.00
**Moon Shine Camo Toxic,
  Reduced Moon Shine
  Camo Harvest Moon**: $479.00
4.5-inch barrel: $459.00

SR1911

Action: Semiautomatic
Grips: G10, Wood
Barrel: 4.25 in., 5 in.
Sights: Fixed, adjustable
Weight: 29.3 oz.–39 oz.
Caliber: .45 ACP
Capacity: 7+1 rounds, 8+1 rounds
Features: Anodized aluminum frame; stainless steel barrel; standard recoil guide system and flat mainspring housing; rear slide serrations allow for positive grip; now available as a Target model with checkered G10 grips, low-glare stainless finish, and Bomar-style adjustable sights
MSRP . . . . $939.00–$1019.00

SR1911 LIGHTWEIGHT COMMANDER-STYLE

Action: Semiautomatic
Grips: G10
Barrel: 4.25 in.
Sights: Novak drift-adjustable three-dot
Weight: 29.3 oz.
Caliber: .45 ACP, 9mm
Capacity: 9 rounds
Features: Classic 1911 70-series style in Commander-length slide
MSRP $979.00

Ruger (Sturm, Ruger & Co.)

RUGER SR1911 OFFICER-STYLE

RUGER SR1911 TARGET

RUGER VAQUERO BLUED

RUGER SUPER REDHAWK

RUGER VAQUERO BISLEY

SR1911 OFFICER-STYLE, LIGHTWEIGHT OFFICER-STYLE

Action: Semiautomatic
Grips: G-10
Barrel: 3.6 in.
Sights: Drift-adjustable three-dot Novak
Weight: 27.2, 31 oz.
Caliber: 9mm
Capacity: 8 rounds
Features: 9mm is the lightweight version, .45 ACP in the standard; anodized aluminum frame; checkered G10 grips; low-glare stainless finish
MSRP $979.00

SR1911 TARGET

Action: Semiautomatic
Grips: G10
Barrel: 5 in.

Sights: Bomar-style adjustable
Weight: 39 oz.–40.4 oz.
Caliber: 9mm, 10mm, .45 ACP
Capacity: 8 rounds
Features: Classic 1911 70-series style; oversized ejection port; skeletonized aluminum trigger
MSRP $1019.00

SUPER REDHAWK

Action: DA revolver
Grips: Black Hogue Tamer monogrip
Barrel: 2.5 in., 7.5 in., 9.5 in.
Sights: Ramp front, adjustable rear
Weight: 53 oz.–58 oz.
Caliber: 10mm, .44 Mag., .454 Casull, .480 Ruger
Capacity: 6 rounds
Features: Satin stainless finish; triple-locking cylinder; integral scope system; corrosion-resistant; extended

frame; dual chambering; transfer bar; Alaskan model has short 2.5-in. barrel
MSRP . . . . $1159.00–$1189.00

VAQUERO BISLEY

Action: SA revolver
Grips: Simulated ivory
Barrel: 5.5 in.
Sights: Fixed
Weight: 41 oz.–45 oz.
Caliber: .45 Colt, .357 Mag.
Capacity: 6 rounds
Features: Stainless steel frame with high-gloss stainless finish
MSRP $899.00

VAQUERO BLUED

Action: SA revolver
Grips: Hardwood
Barrel: 4.62 in., 5.5 in.
Sights: Fixed
Weight: 40 oz.–43 oz.
Caliber: .45 Colt, .357 Mag.
Capacity: 6 rounds
Features: Blued finish alloy steel; reverse Indexing Pawl; ejector rod head; transfer bar mechanism; internal lock
MSRP $829.00

SIG Sauer

SIG SAUER 1911 SPARTAN FULL-SIZE

SIG SAUER 1911 TWO-TONE ULTRA COMPACT

SIG SAUER WE THE PEOPLE FULL-SIZE

1911 SPARTAN FULL-SIZE, SPARTAN CARRY

Action: SAO semiautomatic
Grips: Hogue Spartan
Barrel: 4.2 in., 5 in.
Sights: SIGLite
Weight: 41.6 oz.

Caliber: .45 ACP
Capacity: 8 rounds
Features: Oil-rubbed bronze Nitron finish; gold inlay engraving; 1911 design and ergonomic feel; ancient Greek inscription on slide and grip supposedly spoken by Spartan King Leonidas: "Molon labe," or "Come and take it"
MSRP $1397.00

1911 TWO-TONE ULTRA COMPACT

Action: SA semiautomatic
Grips: Black diamondwood, rosewood
Barrel: 3.3 in.
Sights: Low-pro night sights
Weight: 28 oz.
Caliber: .45 ACP
Capacity: 6+1 rounds
Features: Smallest SIG 1911 yet; stainless slide over alloy frame; unique recoil system; 26 lpi front strap

checkering; skeletonized trigger; Nitron (all black with black diamondwood grips) and Two-Tone (natural stainless slide over black hardcoat anodized aluminum frame; rosewood grips)
MSRP $1119.00

1911 WE THE PEOPLE FULL-SIZE

Action: Semiautomatic
Grips: Aluminum
Barrel: 5 in.
Sights: SIGLITE
Weight: 41.6 oz.
Caliber: .45 ACP
Capacity: 7 rounds
Features: Embellished 1911; distressed finish; custom aluminum grips that sport 25 stars on each side; 13 stars across the pistol's top side; the slide engravings of "WE THE PEOPLE" and "1776"
MSRP $1481.00

SIG SAUER 1911 XO FULL-SIZE

SIG SAUER P210 TARGET

SIG SAUER P220 HUNTER FULL-SIZE

SIG SAUER P220 NITRON FULL-SIZE

SIG SAUER P225-A1 NITRON COMPACT

SIG SAUER P226

SIG SAUER P226 LEGION FULL-SIZE

HANDGUNS

1911 XO FULL-SIZE

Action: Semiautoamatic
Grips: Ergo XT
Barrel: 5 in.
Sights: Contrast
Weight: 41.6 oz.
Caliber: .45 ACP
Capacity: 8 rounds
Features: SIG's Nitron finish in either black or stainless, match-grade barrel, hammer, sear set, and trigger, beavertail safety, extended thumb safety, firing pin safety, and hammer intercept notch; California-compliant variant availble
MSRP **$1010.00**

P210 TARGET

Action: Semiautomatic
Grips: Walnut
Barrel: 4.8 in.
Sights: Adjustable
Weight: 36.9 oz.
Caliber: 9mm
Capacity: 8 rounds
Features: Ergonomic walnut grips; frontstrap stippling; sleek controls; target trigger; reversed rail design; single-action-only; the slide is Nitron-coated to reduce wear
MSRP **$1699.00**

P220 HUNTER FULL-SIZE

Action: DA/SA
Grips: Hogue G10 grips
Barrel: 5 in.
Sights: Adjustable rear, fiber optic front
Weight: 39.4 oz.
Caliber: 10mm
Capacity: 8 rounds
Features: Kryptek stainless steel slide and frame; match-grade barrel
MSRP **$1629.00**

P220 NITRON FULL-SIZE

Action: Semiautomatic
Grips: Polymer, laminated or custom shop wood
Barrel: 4.4 in.
Sights: Siglite night
Weight: 30.4 oz.–31.2 oz.
Caliber: 10mm, .45 ACP
Capacity: 8 rounds
Features: Nitron finish, light-weight alloy frame; accessory rail; California- and Massachusetts-compliant variation available
MSRP **$1087.00**

P225-A1 NITRON COMPACT

Action: DA/SA
Grips: Checkered G10 with medallion or checkered wood
Barrel: 3.6 in.
Sights: SIGLITE
Weight: 30.5 oz.
Caliber: 9mm
Capacity: 8 rounds
Features: Enhanced trigger; fully machined stainless steel slide with Nitron finish; hard coat anodized frame; two-piece grips with the SIG mark medallion
MSRP **$1032.00**

P226

Action: DA/SA Semiautomatic
Grips: One-piece ergo grip, extreme model features Hogue custom G10 grips, custom wood
Barrel: 4.4 in.
Sights: Contrast, Siglite night optional
Weight: 23.7 oz.–42.2 oz.
Caliber: 9mm, .357 SIG, .40 S&W
Capacity: 9mm: 10, 15, 20 rounds; .357 SIG: 10 or 12 rounds, .40 S&W: 10 or 12 rounds

Features: Select has custom brown G10 Select grips, Elite slide with front cocking serrations, accessory rail; Stainless Elite has extended beavertail, Elite slide, short reset trigger, front strap checkering, SIGLITE night sights; RX Full Size has tall SIGLITE night sights, accessory rail, and comes with a ROMEO1 reflex sight; Tacops has a Truglo front sight paired with SIGLITE rear, extended beavertail frame, short reset trigger, rail, Nitron finish, and polymer Magwell grips; Nitron Full-Size has SIGLITE night sights, Nitron finish, and a one-piece grip; Emperor Scorpion has a PVD-coated frame and slide in Flat Dark Earth, black G10 grips, front cocking serrations, SIGLITE night sights, and short reset trigger

Select:	**$1195.00**
Stainless Elite Full-Size:	**$1413.00**
RX Full-Size:	**$1201.00**
Tacops Full-Size:	**$1304.00**
Nitron Full-Size:	**$1087.00**
Emperor Scorpion:	**$1282.00**

P226 LEGION FULL-SIZE, LEGION RX FULL-SIZE

Action: DA/SA
Grips: Checkered G10 grips
Barrel: 4.4 in.
Sights: X-ray blacked-out day/night rear
Weight: 34 oz.
Caliber: .357 SIG, .40 S&W, 9mm
Capacity: 10, 12, 15 rounds
Features: Legion gray PVD finish; enhanced action with SRT; low-profile slide catch and decocking levers; reduced and contoured beavertail; RX version gets G10 grips, tall night sights, P-SAIT trigger, and carbon steel barrel and is in 9mm only

Legion Full-Size:	**$1413.00**
Legion RX Full-Size:	**$1636.00**

SIG Sauer

SIG SAUER P226 MK25

SIG SAUER P229 LEGION RX COMPACT

SIG SAUER P238 STAND MICRO-COMPACT

SIG SAUER P320 FDE COMPACT

SIG SAUER P320 TACOPS CARRY

P226 MK25 FULL-SIZE

Action: SA/DA semiautomatic
Grips: Polymer
Barrel: 4.4 in.
Sights: SIGLITE night sights
Weight: 34 oz.–35 oz.
Caliber: 9mm
Capacity: 10 or 15 rounds
Features: New designation of the Navy's P226 9mm variant issued to U. S. Navy SEALs; still with phosphated internals; (three) 15 round magazines; classic two-piece polymer grips; anchor engraved on slide; Picatinny rail; actual UID scanable serial number label; packaged with FDE grip band and a certificate of authenticity; available in black Nitron or in Desert Tan Nitron; black version can be had with threaded barrel
MSRP................$1187.00

P229

Action: Semiautomatic
Grips: FDE polymer
Barrel: 3.9 in.
Sights: Contrast, Siglite night optional
Weight: 34.4 oz.
Caliber: 9mm, .40 S&W, .357 SIG
Capacity: 9mm: 10, 13 rounds; .357 SIG: 10, 12 rounds, .40 S&W: 10, 12 rounds
Features: Mid-size 9mm double-stack pistol comes in several versions: Legion Compact SAO is a single-action only with accessory rail, P-SAIT trigger, Cerakote Elite Legion Gray finish, XRAY3 day/night sights, X-Five undercut trigger guard; Select Compact has custom brown Select G10 grips, SIGLITE night sights, Nitron finish; Legion RX Compact has the Cerakote Legion Gray finish, XRAY3 sights, ROMEO1 reflex sight, P-SAIT trigger; Legion Compact is

similar to the RX Compact, but without the factory-mounted reflex sight; Emperor Scorpion Full-Size has PVD-coated slide and frame in Flat Dark Earth, black G10 grips, SIGLITE night sights, SRT trigger; RX gets a ROMEO1 reflex sight, SIGLITE night sites, polymer E2 grip, accessory rail; M11 A-1 Army Compact has green anodized frame, Nitron finish, SIGLITE night sights; Nitron Compact has rail, Nitron finish, one-piece grip, SIGLITE night sights; M11-A1 Compact is similar to Army version, but with a black hard-coat anodized frame, short reset trigger, no rail; Enhanced Elite California Compliant has short reset trigger, rail, front cocking serrations, SIGLITE night sights

Legion Compact SAO:	$1413.00
Select Compact:	$1195.00
Legion RX Compact:	$1636.00
Legion Compact:	$1413.00
Emperor Scorpion Full-Size:	$1282.00
RX:	$1310.00
M11 A-1 Army Compact:	$1174.00
Nitron Compact:	$1087.00
M11-A1 Compact:	$1119.00
Enhanced Elite California Compliant:	$1234.00

P238

Action: SA semiautomatic
Grips: Fluted polymer, Rosewood Tribal, Pearl, Tribal Engraved Aluminum, Hogue pink rubber
Barrel: 2.7 in.
Sights: Siglite night
Weight: 15.2 oz.
Caliber: .380 ACP (9mm Short)
Capacity: 6 rounds
Features: Ultra compact, single-action-only (miniature 1911 design) .380 carry pistol. Sixteen variants in 2019 with a variety of different grips, slide and frame finishes, magazine styles, and sight configurations

Legion Micro-Compact:	$850.00
Stand Micro-Compact:	$738.00
BRG Micro-Compact:	$706.00
Select Micro-Compact:	$738.00
Texas Flag:	$760.00

Rose Gold:	$932.00
We The People:	$728.00
ASE Micro-Compact:	$740.00
Emperor Scorpion Micro-Compact:	$801.00
SAS Micro-Compact:	$738.00
Army Micro-Compact:	$692.00
Black Pearl Micro-Compact:	$798.00
Blackwood Micro-Compact:	$715.00
Desert Micro-Compact:	$738.00
Rainbow Micro-Compact:	$738.00
Spartan Micro-Compact:	$1013.00
Rosewood Micro-Compact:	$715.00
Nitron Micro-Compact:	$679.00
Nightmare Micro-Compact:	$738.00
HD Micro-Compact California-Compliant:	$898.00

P320

Action: DAO semiautomatic
Grips: Synthetic
Barrel: 3.6 in.–4.7 in.
Sights: Fixed
Weight: 25 oz.–29.4 oz.
Caliber: .40 S&W, 9mm, .357 SIG, .45 ACP
Capacity: 10–17 rounds
Features: Expansive line of subcompact, compact and full-size modular striker-fired pistols with three-point takedown and interchangeable grip sets; with four new introductions for 2019, total model count in this series stands at 16, with a variety of finish, grip, barrel length, frame size, sight, rail, and magazine options

M17-Commemorative:	$1122.00
XCompact:	$804.00
X-Five Coyote:	$1005.00
X-Carry Coyote:	$804.00
M17:	$768.00
M17 Bravo:	$768.00
X-VTAC:	$918.00
RX Compact:	$887.00
RX Full-Size:	$887.00
TACOPS Carry:	$830.00
FDE Compact:	$679.00
Nitron Carry:	$679.00
LIMA Compact:	$884.00
Nitron Compact:	$597.00
Nitron Full-Size:	$679.00
Nitron Subcompact:	$679.00

SIG SAUER P365 NITRON MICRO COMPACT

SIG SAUER P238 NITRON

SIG SAUER P938 BLACKWOOD

SIG SAUER MCX RATTLER PCB

SIG SAUER SP2022 NITRON FULL-SIZE

P365 NITRON MICRO COMPACT

Action: Semiautomatic
Grips: Polymer
Barrel: 3.1 in.
Sights: SIGLITE night sights
Weight: 17.8 oz.
Caliber: 9mm
Capacity: 10 rounds
Features: A striker-fired micro-compact carry pistol; rated for 9mm +P; flush mag; finger rest extension mag; a 12-round magazine is available
MSRP $599.99

P938

Action: SA semiautomatic
Grips: Synthetic or wood
Barrel: 3 in.
Sights: SIGLITE night sights, TFO front on Equinox
Weight: 16 oz.
Caliber: 9mm
Capacity: 6+1, 7+1 rounds
Features: 9mm version of the P238 family, with similar aesthetics; 16 variants with a wide variety of finishes and grips available for 2019,

including a threaded-barrel (TB) suppressor-ready model
Legion Micro-Compact: $904.00
Select Micro-Compact: $815.00
Navy Micro-Compact: $747.00
Stand Micro-Compact: $815.00
Rose Gold: $986.00
We The People: $772.00
Emperor Scorpion TB Micro-
Compact: $978.00
ASE Micro-Compact: $820.00
SAS Micro-Compact: $815.00
Nightmare Micro-Compact: . . $815.00
Extreme Micro-Compact Massachusetts-
Compliant: $815.00
Blackwood Micro-Compact: . . $793.00
BRG Micro-Compact: $815.00
Combat Micro-Compact: . . . $815.00
Target Micro-Compact: $651.00
Nitron Micro-Compact: $719.00

MCX RATTLER PCB

Action: Semiautomatic
Grips: N/A
Barrel: 5.5 in.
Sights: None
Weight: 82 oz.
Caliber: .300 Blackout
Capacity: 30 rounds
Features: Pistol version of Sig's short-

barreled rifle takes standard AR mags; sports PDW upper; three-position telescoping PSB pistol brace; M-LOK handguard is free-floating; action is gas piston
MSRP $2719.00

SP2022

Action: Semiautomatic
Grips: Polymer
Barrel: 3.9 in., 4.4 in.
Sights: Siglite
Weight: 29 oz.
Caliber: 9mm, .40 S&W
Capacity: 10 or 15 rounds (9mm), 10 or 12 rounds (.40 S&W)
Features: SIG's original full-size polymer pistol, available in three versions: Two-Tone Full-Size, stainless slide, black frame, SIGLITE night sights (9mm); FDE Full-Size, allover Flat Dark Earth finish, SIGLITEs (9mm, .40 S&W)
Nitron Full-Size: $568.00
FDE Full-Size: $638.00

Smith & Wesson

SMITH & WESSON
MODEL 10

SMITH & WESSON
MODEL 27 CLASSICS

SMITH & WESSON
MODEL 29 CLASSICS

SMITH & WESSON MODEL
36 CLASSICS

SMITH & WESSON
MODEL 57 CLASSICS

SMITH & WESSON
MODEL 60

SMITH & WESSON MODEL 60
LADYSMITH

SMITH & WESSON
MODEL 66

REVOLVERS

MODEL 10

Action: SA/DA revolver
Grips: Wood
Barrel: 4 in.
Sights: Black blade, fixed
Weight: 36 oz.
Caliber: .38 S&W Spl. +P
Capacity: 6 rounds
Features: Carbon steel frame; carbon steel cylinder; blued finish; medium size frame; exposed hammer
MSRP $739.00

MODEL 27 CLASSICS

Action: SA/DA revolver
Grips: Checkered square butt walnut
Barrel: 4 in., 6.5 in.
Sights: Pinned serrated ramp front; Micro adjustable with cross serrations
Weight: 48.5 oz.
Caliber: .357 Mag., .38 S&W Spl. +P
Capacity: 6 rounds
Features: Carbon steel frame; bright blued or blued finish
MSRP . . . . $1019.00–$1059.00

MODEL 29 CLASSICS

Action: Revolver
Grips: Checkered square butt walnut;
6 in. model features Altamont Service walnut grips
Barrel: 4 in., 6.5 in.
Sights: Red ramp, micro adjustable rear
Weight: 48.5 oz.
Caliber: .44 Mag., .44 S&W Spl.
Capacity: 6 rounds
Features: Carbon steel frame in blue; blued with machine engraving and grips with enhanced carvings also available in 4-inch barrel only
MSRP . . . . $999.00–$1169.00

MODEL 36 CLASSICS

Action: Revolver
Grips: Wood
Barrel: 1.8 in.
Sights: Integral front, fixed rear
Weight: 19.5 oz.
Caliber: .38 S&W Spl. +P
Capacity: 5 rounds
Features: Small sized frame; exposed hammer; carbon steel frame and cylinder; blued finish; single or double action
MSRP $749.00

MODEL 57 CLASSICS

Action: DA N-frame revolver
Grips: Checkered square-butt walnut
Barrel: 6 in.
Sights: Pinned red ramp front, micro adjustable white outline rear;
Weight: 4.8 oz.
Caliber: .41 Mag.
Capacity: 6 rounds
Features: Bright blued or nickel finish; carbon steel frame; classic style thumbpiece; color case wide spur hammer; color case wide serrated target trigger
MSRP $1009.00

MODEL 60, MODEL 60 LADYSMITH

Action: Revolver
Grips: Synthetic, wood
Barrel: 2.125 in., 3 in.
Sights: Black blade front, adjustable rear
Weight: 21.4 oz.–23.2 oz.
Caliber: .357 Mag., .38 S&W Spl. +P
Capacity: 5 rounds
Features: Satin stainless finish; single- or double-action; stainless steel fame and cylinder. Lady Smith has finger-grooved wood grips designed for smaller hands, brushed stainless finish, and is engraved with "Lady Smith" on the frame.
2.125-in. barrel: $729.00
3-in. barrel: $759.00
Lady Smith: $759.00

MODEL 66

Action: DA/SA revolver
Grips: Synthetic
Barrel: 4.25 in.
Sights: Adjustable
Weight: 36.9 oz.–37.4 oz.
Caliber: .38 S&W Spl. +P, .357 Mag.
Capacity: 6 rounds
Features: Full top strap and barrel serration; ball-detent lock-up; two-piece barrel; matte stainless finish
MSRP $849.00

SMITH & WESSON MODEL 66 COMBAT MAGNUM

SMITH & WESSON MODEL 69

SMITH & WESSON MODEL 69 COMBAT MAGNUM

SMITH & WESSON MODEL 442 ENGRAVED

SMITH & WESSON MODEL 360 FLAT DARK EARTH GRIPS

SMITH & WESSON PERFORMANCE CENTER MODEL 460XVR 14-IN BARREL WITH BIPOD

SMITH & WESSON MODEL 586

MODEL 66 COMBAT MAGNUM

Action: Revolver
Grips: Synthetic
Barrel: 2.75 in.
Sights: Red ramp front, white outline adjustable rear
Weight: 33.5 oz.
Caliber: .357 Mag., .38 Spl. +P
Capacity: 6 rounds
Features: K-frame revolver; full top strap and barrel serration; ball detent lockup; two-piece barrel; full-length extractor rod
MSRP **$849.00**

MODEL 69

Action: DA/SA revolver
Grips: Synthetic
Barrel: 2.75 in., 4.25 in.
Sights: Adjustable
Weight: 34.4 oz.–37.4 oz.
Caliber: .44 Mag., .44 Spl.
Capacity: 5 rounds
Features: Full top strap and barrel serration; ball-detent lock-up; two-piece barrel
MSRP **$849.00**

MODEL 69 COMBAT MAGNUM

Action: Revolver
Grips: Synthetic
Barrel: 2.75 in.
Sights: Red ramp front, white outline adjustable rear
Weight: 34.4 oz.
Caliber: .44 Mag.
Capacity: 5 rounds
Features: Full top strap and barrel serration; ball detent lockup; two-piece barrel; full-length extractor rod
MSRP **$849.00**

MODEL 360 FLAT DARK EARTH GRIPS

Action: Revolver
Grips: Synthetic
Barrel: 1.875 in.
Sights: Red ramp front, notch fixed rear
Weight: 14.9 oz.
Caliber: .357 Mag.
Capacity: 5 rounds
Features: Scandium alloy frame; stainless steel barrel; stainless steel unfluted cylinder with a PVD finish; synthetic grips in Flat Dark Earth; "Airweight" engraved on the frame's right side
MSRP **$770.00**

MODEL 442 ENGRAVED

Action: DA revolver
Grips: Engraved wood
Barrel: 1.875 in.
Sights: Integral front, fixed rear
Weight: 14.2 oz.
Caliber: .38 S&W Spl. +P
Capacity: 5 rounds
Features: Aluminum alloy frame; stainless barrel/cylinder; matte black
MSRP **$749.00**

MODEL 460XVR, PERFORMANCE CENTER 460XVR, PERFORMANCE CENTER HIVIZ 460XVR

Action: SA/DA revolver
Grips: Synthetic
Barrel: 3.5 in., 7 in., 8.38-in., 10.5 in., 12 in., 14 in.
Sights: Vary with model
Weight: 72.02 oz.–79.3 oz.
Caliber: .460 S&W Mag., .45 LC, .454 Casull, .460 S&W Mag.
Capacity: 5 rounds
Features: Highest muzzle velocity revolver in the world, gain-twist rifling; HIVIZ gets muzzle brake, integral scope base, unfluted cylinder, HIVIZ fiber optic front sight and adjustable white outline rear, PC-tuned action, full underlug on 7.5-in. barrel; 14-in. Barrel with Bipod gets bipod, black ramp front sight, adjustable rear sight, muzzle brake, top and bottom accessory/optics rails, chrome hammer, chrome trigger with trigger stop, PC-tuned action (.460 S&W Mag); 12-inch barrel has sling swivels and integrated Picatinny topside rail, removeable Patridge front sight; 10.5-inch barrel has interchangeable fiber optic front sight, adjustable rear sight, muzzle brake, graduated underlug, sling swivels; 3.5-inch barrel has unfluted cylinder, HiViz green fiber optic front and adjustable rear sights; Model 460XVR has 8.38-inch barrel, removeable compensator, gain twist barrel, interchangeable front sight and adjustable rear, full underlug
HIVIZ: **$1779.00**
XVR: **$1369.00**
14-in. barrel and bipod: . . . **$1559.00**
12-in. barrel: **$1689.00**
10.5-in. barrel: **$1629.00**
3.5-in. barrel: **$1609.00**

MODEL 586

Action: SA/DA revolver
Grips: Wood
Barrel: 4 in., 6 in.
Sights: Adjustable
Weight: 46.3 oz.
Caliber: .357 Mag., .38 S&W Spl. +P
Capacity: 6 rounds
Features: Carbon steel frame and cylinder with blued finish; adjustable white outline rear sight and red ramp front sight; square-butt design; checkered wood grips
MSRP **$839.00**

Smith & Wesson

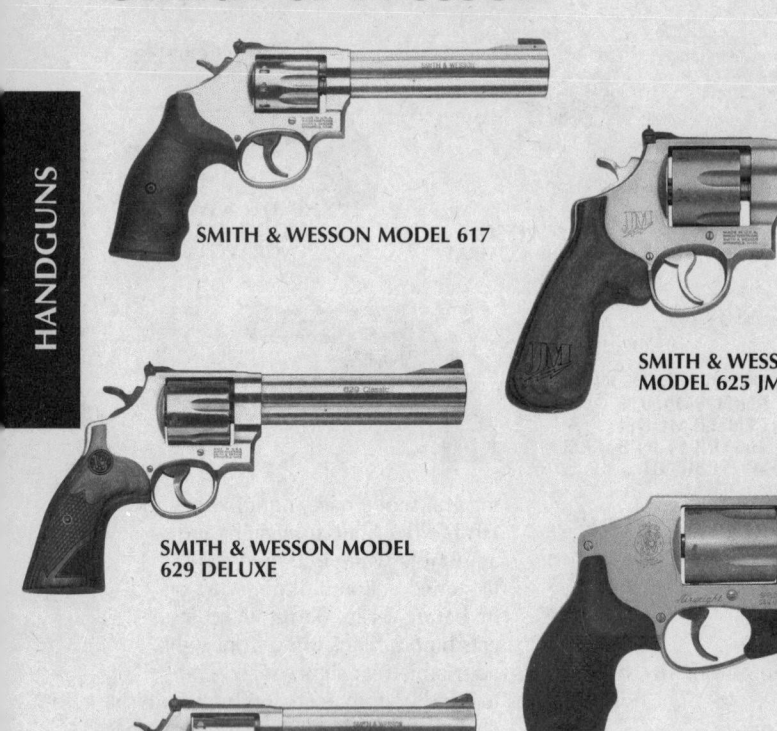

SMITH & WESSON MODEL 617

SMITH & WESSON MODEL 625 JM

SMITH & WESSON MODEL 629 DELUXE

SMITH & WESSON MODEL 629

SMITH & WESSON MODEL 642 LASERMAX

SMITH & WESSON MODEL 686

MODEL 617
Action: SA/DA revolver
Grips: Synthetic
Barrel: 4 in., 6 in.
Sights: Partridge front, adjustable rear
Weight: 38.9 oz.–44.1 oz.
Caliber: .22 LR
Capacity: 10 rounds
Features: Stainless steel frame and cylinder with satin stainless finish; medium size frame with exposed hammer
MSRP $829.00

MODEL 625 JM
Action: SA/DA revolver
Grips: Jerry Miculek wood
Barrel: 4 in.
Sights: Gold bead partridge front, adjustable rear
Weight: 40.3 oz.
Caliber: .45 ACP
Capacity: 6 rounds
Features: JM model named for champion professional S&W team shooter Jerry Miculek, features Jerry

Miculek wood grip, Miculek-style .265-in. wide grooved speed trigger, allover bead-blast matte finish, full underlug
MSRP $979.00

MODEL 629, 629 CLASSIC
Action: SA/DA revolver
Grips: Synthetic
Barrel: 4, 5, 6 in.
Sights: Red ramp, adjustable white outline
Weight: 44.3 oz.
Caliber: .44 Mag, .44 S&W Spl.
Capacity: 6 rounds
Features: Stainless steel frame and cylinder with satin stainless finish; exposed hammer
4-inch: $949.00
5-inch Classic: $989.00
6-inch: $949.00
6-inch Classic: $989.00

MODEL 629 DELUXE
Action: Revolver
Grips: Wood
Barrel: 3 in., 6.5 in.
Sights: Red ramp front, white outline

adjustable rear
Weight: 39.6 oz. (3-in. barrel), 51.2 oz. (6.5-in. barrel)
Caliber: .44 Mag., .44 S&W Spl.
Capacity: 6 rounds
Features: N-frame revolver; all-stainless construction; textured wood grips
3-in. barrel: $999.00
6.5-in. barrel: $1029.00

MODEL 642 LASERMAX
Action: DAO
Grips: Synthetic
Barrel: 1.88 in.
Sights: Fixed front, integral rear
Weight: 15.5 oz.
Caliber: .38 S&W Special +P
Capacity: 5 rounds
Features: Enables positive target acquisition and enhances accuracy in low-light conditions; no-snag, hammerless design; rapid target acquisition of the LaserMax sighting system; matte silver finish
MSRP $539.00

MODEL 686
Action: Revolver
Grips: Synthetic
Barrel: 4.125, 6 in.
Sights: Varies with model
Weight: 44.8 oz.
Caliber: .357 Mag.
Capacity: 6 rounds
New Features: L-frame six-shot revolver in satin stainless finish; red ramp front sight, adjustable white outline rear, synthetic grips, full underlug
MSRP $829.00

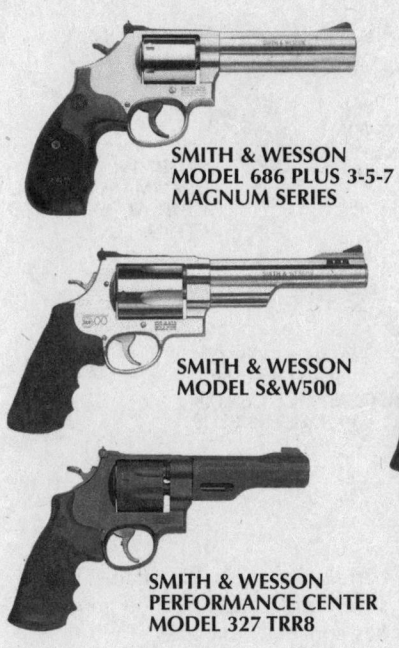

SMITH & WESSON MODEL 686 PLUS 3-5-7 MAGNUM SERIES

SMITH & WESSON MODEL S&W500

SMITH & WESSON PERFORMANCE CENTER MODEL 327 TRR8

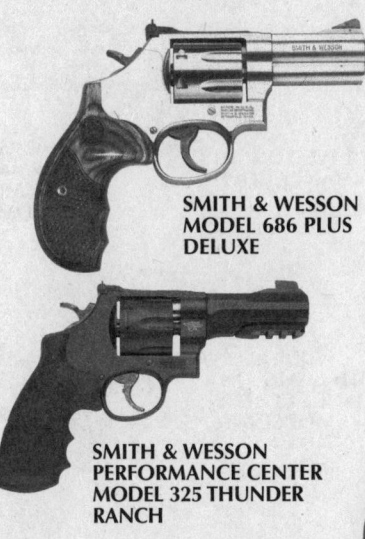

SMITH & WESSON MODEL 686 PLUS DELUXE

SMITH & WESSON PERFORMANCE CENTER MODEL 325 THUNDER RANCH

SMITH & WESSON MODEL GOVERNOR

SMITH & WESSON PERFORMANCE CENTER MODEL 327

MODEL 686 PLUS 3-5-7 MAGNUM SERIES

Action: Revolver
Grips: Wood
Barrel: 3 in., 5 in., 7 in.
Sights: Red ramp front, white outline adjustable rear
Weight: 37.4 oz. (3-in. barrel), 37.4 oz. (5-in. barrel)
Caliber: .357 Mag.
Capacity: 7 rounds
Features: Collector's Model 686 L-frame; custom black/silver wood grips bearing "357"; cylinder is unfluted
MSRP..................$899.00

MODEL 686 PLUS DELUXE

Action: Revolver
Grips: Wood
Barrel: 3 in.
Sights: Red ramp front, white outline adjustable rear
Weight: 36.8 oz. (3-in. barrel), 44.9 oz. (6-in. barrel)
Caliber: .357 Mag.
Capacity: 7 rounds
Features: S&W's classic 686 L-frame revolver; all stainless steel
MSRP..................$899.00

MODEL GOVERNOR

Action: SA/DA revolver
Grips: Synthetic, Crimson Trace
Barrel: 2.75 in.
Sights: Tritium front, fixed rear
Weight: 30.3 oz.
Caliber: .45 Colt, .45 ACP, .410

Capacity: 6 rounds
Features: Patented heat-treated scandium frame; PVD coated cylinder; matte silver finish; furnished with two full moon clips and three two-shot moon clips for use with .45 ACP
MSRP..................$809.00

MODEL S&W500

Action: SA/DA revolver
Grips: Synthetic
Barrel: 3.5 in., 4 in., 6.5 in., 7.5 in., 8.38-in., 10.5 in.
Sights: Vary with model
Weight 55.6 oz.–79.6 oz.
Caliber: .500 S&W Mag.
Capacity: 5 rounds
Features: First X-frame developed by S&W and debuted in 2003; most powerful production revolver in the world; removable high-efficiency compensator; HIVIZ red dot interchangeable front sight
6.5-in. barrel:...........$1299.00
8.38-in. barrel:...$1299.00–$1369.00
4-in. barrel:...........$1369.00
Performance Center 10.5-in. barrel:........$1599.00
Performance Center HIVIZ 3.5-in. barrel:....$1609.00
Performance Center 7.5-in. barrel:........$1579.00

PERFORMANCE CENTER MODEL 325 THUNDER RANCH

Action: SA/DA revolver
Grips: Synthetic
Barrel: 4 in.
Sights: Interchangeable gold bead front; adjustable rear

Weight: 31 oz.
Caliber: .45 ACP
Capacity: 6 rounds
Features: Scandium alloy frame; stainless steel cylinder; matte black; accommodates accessory rail
MSRP..................$1329.00

PERFORMANCE CENTER MODEL 327

Action: Revolver
Grips: Wood
Barrel: 2 in.
Sights: Orange ramp front sight, integral "U" rear
Weight: 23.1 oz.
Caliber: .357 Mag., .38 S&W Spl. +P
Capacity: 8 rounds
Features: Color case with overtravel stop; color case tear drop with pinned sear; exposed hammer; matte black finish; scandium alloy frame and titanium alloy cylinder; smooth DA with Wolff Mainspring
MSRP..................$1309.00

PERFORMANCE CENTER MODEL 327 TRR8

Action: SA/DA revolver
Grips: Synthetic
Barrel: 5 in.
Sights: Interchangeable front; adjustable V-notch rear
Weight: 35.3 oz.
Caliber: .357 Mag., .38 S&W Spl. +P
Capacity: 8 rounds
Features: Scandium alloy frame; stainless steel cylinder; matte black; exposed hammer; equipment rails
MSRP..................$1329.00

Smith & Wesson

SMITH & WESSON
PERFORMANCE CENTER
MODEL 586 L-COMP

SMITH & WESSON
PERFORMANCE CENTER
MODEL 625

SMITH & WESSON
PERFORMANCE
CENTER MODEL
629 V-COMP

SMITH & WESSON
PERFORMANCE CENTER
MODEL 637 ENHANCED
ACTION

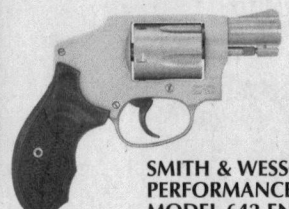

SMITH & WESSON
PERFORMANCE CENTER
MODEL 642 ENHANCED
ACTION

SMITH & WESSON
PERFORMANCE CENTER
MODEL 686

SMITH & WESSON
PERFORMANCE
PERFORMANCE CENTER
MODEL 686 PLUS

PERFORMANCE CENTER MODEL 586 L-COMP

Action: Revolver
Grips: Rosewood
Barrel: 3 in.
Sights: Tritium night front, adjustable black board rear
Weight: 37.5 oz.
Caliber: .357 Mag.
Capacity: 7 rounds
Features: L-frame with ported full-lug barrel; Performance Center-tuned action carbon steel construction
MSRP **$1208.00**

PERFORMANCE CENTER MODEL 625

Action: SA/DA revolver
Grips: Altamont laminate, red, white & blue
Barrel: 4 in.
Sights: Gold bead S&W interchangeable front; Black adjustable rear
Weight: 42 oz.
Caliber: .45 ACP
Capacity: 6 rounds
Features: Performance Center version sports Altamont red-white-and-blue laminate grips, stainless steel frame and cylinder with satin stainless finish],deep cut broached rifling, chamfered charge holes, custom teardrop hammer, interchangeable gold bead front sight, adjustable black rear sight, ¾ underlug
MSRP **$1079.00**

PERFORMANCE CENTER MODEL 629 V-COMP

Action: SA/DA revolver
Grips: Synthetic

Barrel: 4 in.
Sights: Adjustable orange dovetail front, adjustable black rear
Weight: 43.8 oz.
Caliber: .44 Mag., .44 S&W Spl.
Capacity: 6 rounds
Features: Stainless steel frame and cylinder with matte finish; removable compensator and cap muzzle protector; chamfered charge holes; ball detent lock-up; chromed hammer and trigger with overtravel stop
MSRP **$1559.00**

PERFORMANCE CENTER MODEL 637 ENHANCED ACTION

Action: Revolver
Grips: Wood
Barrel: 1.875 in.
Sights: Integral ramp front
Weight: 15 oz.
Caliber: .38 Spl. +P
Capacity: 5 rounds
Features: J-frame with Performance Center-tuned action; stainless steel barrel; aluminum alloy frame; matte silver finish; custom wood grips
MSRP **$525.00**

PERFORMANCE CENTER MODEL 642 ENHANCED ACTION

Action: Revolver
Grips: Wood
Barrel: 1.875 in.
Sights: Integral ramp front
Weight: 15 oz.
Caliber: .38 Spl. +P
Capacity: 5 rounds
Features: J-frame with Performance Center-tuned action; stainless steel

barrel; aluminum alloy frame; matte silver finish; custom wood grips; DAO has concealed hammer
MSRP **$525.00**

PERFORMANCE CENTER MODEL 686

Action: Revolver
Grips: Wood
Barrel: 2.5 in.
Sights: Red ramp front, *adjustable rear*
Weight: 34.1 oz.
Caliber: .357 Mag.
Capacity: 7 rounds
Features: Unfluted cylinder; Performance Center-tuned action; custom teardrop hammer; precision crowned barrel; cylinder cut for moon
MSRP **$1089.00**

PERFORMANCE CENTER MODEL 686 PLUS

Action: Revolver
Grips: Synthetic
Barrel: 5 in.
Sights: Interchangeable blade front, adjustable rear
Weight: 38.4 oz.
Caliber: .357 Mag.
Capacity: 7 rounds
Features: Slanted half-underlug; unfluted cylinder; vent rib; Performance Center-tuned action; custom teardrop hammer; speed-release cylinder thumbpiece; includes an orange front blade, which can be subbed out for the user's choice
MSRP **$966.00**

Smith & Wesson

SMITH & WESSON
PERFORMANCE CENTER
MODEL 929

SMITH & WESSON
PERFORMANCE CENTER
PRO SERIES MODEL 442
MOON CLIP

SMITH & WESSON
PERFORMANCE CENTER
PRO SERIES MODEL 627

SMITH & WESSON
PERFORMANCE CENTER
PRO SERIES MODEL 986

SMITH & WESSON
PERFORMANCE CENTER PRO
SERIES MODEL 640

SMITH & WESSON
PERFORMANCE CENTER
PRO SERIES MODEL 686 SSR

PERFORMANCE CENTER MODEL 929

Action: DA/SA revolver
Grips: Synthetic
Barrel: 6.5 in.
Sights: Adjustable
Weight: 44.2 oz.
Caliber: 9mm
Capacity: 8 rounds
Features: Removable compensator; titanium cylinder; Jerry Miculek signature; chrome teardrop hammer; chrome trigger with stop
MSRP $1189.00

PERFORMANCE CENTER MODEL 986

Action: Revolver
Grips: Wood
Barrel: 2.5 in.
Sights: Red ramp front, adjustable rear
Weight: 31.7 oz.
Caliber: 9mm
Capacity: 7 rounds
Features: L-frame 9mm with unfluted cylinder; custom barrel with recessed crown; trigger overstop travel; bossed mainspring; Performance Center-tuned action; stainless steel barrel and frame; titanium cylinder; moon clips
MSRP $1129.00

PERFORMANCE CENTER PRO SERIES MODEL 442 MOON CLIP

Action: DA revolver
Grips: Synthetic
Barrel: 1.87 in.
Sights: Integral front, fixed rear
Weight: 15 oz.
Caliber: .38 S&W Spl. +P
Capacity: 5 rounds
Features: Aluminum alloy frame; stainless steel cylinder; matte black finish; internal hammer; cylinder cut for moon clips
MSRP $499.00

PERFORMANCE CENTER PRO SERIES MODEL 627

Action: SA/DA revolver
Grips: Synthetic
Barrel: 2.625 in., 4 in., 5 in.
Sights: varies with model
Weight: 37.8 oz.–46.7 oz.
Caliber: .357 Mag.
Capacity: 8 rounds
Features: Performance Center Pro Series with 4-in. barrel has matte silver finish, chamfered charge holes, custom barrel with recessed precision crown, bossed mainspring, Hogue grips, interchangeable front sight, adjustable rear; Performance Center V-Comp variant has 5-in. barrel, removable compensator, two-tone black frame and barrel/matte stainless cylinder and controls, Hogue grips, adjustable orange dovetail front sight, adjustable rear sight, chrome hammer, chrome trigger with trigger stop; two variants known simply as Performance Center Model 627: 1) Has 2.625-in. barrel, unfluted cylinder, wood gripsdovetail red ramp front sight, adjustable white outline rear, ball detent lockup, chrome flashed custom tear drop hammer, chrome flashed trigger with stop, cylinder cut for moon clips; 2) Performance Center 5-in. barrel similar to Pro Series with tapering underlug, but with both wood and synthetic grips, gold bead front sight, adjustable rear sight, matte silver finish
MSRP $999.00

PERFORMANCE CENTER PRO SERIES MODEL 640

Action: DA revolver
Grips: Synthetic
Barrel: 2.1 in.
Sights: Black blade front, fixed rear
Weight: 23 oz.
Caliber: .357 Mag.
Capacity: 5 rounds
Features: Stainless steel frame, barrel, and cylinder, front and rear dovetail tritium night sights, concealed hammer, cylinder cut for moon clips, satin stainless finish
MSRP $839.00

PERFORMANCE CENTER PRO SERIES MODEL 686 SSR

Action: Revolver
Grips: Wood
Barrel: 4 in.
Sights: Interchangeable front, adjustable rear
Weight: 38.3 oz.
Caliber: .357 Mag., .38 S&W Spl. +P
Capacity: 6 rounds
Features: Stainless steel frame and barrel with satin finish; exposed hammer; chamfered charge holes; bossed mainspring; ergonomic grip to force high-hand hold; custom barrel with recessed precision crown
MSRP $999.00

PERFORMANCE CENTER PRO SERIES MODEL 986

Action: DA/SA revolver
Grips: Synthetic
Barrel: 5 in.
Sights: Adjustable
Weight: 34.9 oz.
Caliber: 9mm
Capacity: 7 rounds
Features: Titanium, fluted cylinder; precision crowned barrel; cylinder cut for moonclips
MSRP $1149.00

HANDGUNS

Smith & Wesson

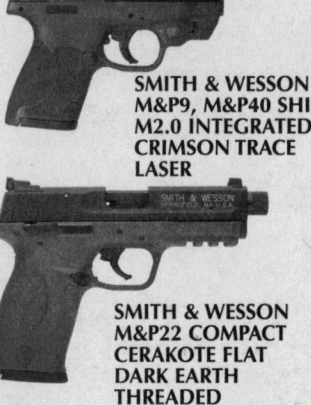

SMITH & WESSON M&P9, M&P40 SHIELD M2.0 INTEGRATED CRIMSON TRACE LASER

SMITH & WESSON M&P9, M&P40 M2.0 NO THUMB SAFETY FLAT DARK EARTH

SMITH & WESSON M&P9, M&P40 SHIELD M2.0 LASERGUARD PRO GREEN LASER/LIGHT COMBO

SMITH & WESSON M&P22 COMPACT CERAKOTE FLAT DARK EARTH THREADED

SMITH & WESSON M&P BODYGUARD 380

SMITH & WESSON M&P BODYGUARD 380 ENGRAVED

SMITH & WESSON M&P BODYGUARD 380 CRIMSON TRACE INTEGRAL LASER FLAT DARK EARTH

SEMIAUTOMATIC

M&P9, M&P40 SHIELD M2.0 INTEGRATED CRIMSON TRACE LASER

Action: Semiautomatic
Grips: Polymer
Barrel: 3.1 in.
Sights: Steel three-dot white
Weight: 18.8 oz.
Caliber: 9mm, .40 S&W
Capacity: 7, 8 rounds
Features: Super-compact striker-fired pistol; built-in Crimson Trace Laser in green or red
Green laser:. **$549.00**
Red laser:. **$499.00**

M&P9, M&P40 M2.0 NO THUMB SAFETY FLAT DARK EARTH

Action: Semiautomatic
Grips: Polymer
Barrel: 5 in.
Sights: White three-dot
Weight: 26.9 oz.
Caliber: 9mm, .40 S&W
Capacity: 15, 17 rounds
Features: Armonite finish; unique rear slide serrations; improved M2.0 trigger; accessory rail; no loaded chamber indicator
MSRP. **$599.00**

M&P9, M&P40 SHIELD M2.0 LASERGUARD PRO GREEN LASER/LIGHT COMBO

Action: Semiautomatic
Grips: Polymer
Barrel: 3.1 in.
Sights: Steel three-dot white
Weight: 22 oz.
Caliber: 9mm, .40 S&W

Capacity: 7, 8 rounds
Features: An ultra-compact firearm; integrated combination Laserguard green laser; tactical light
MSRP. **$649.00**

M&P22 COMPACT CERAKOTE FLAT DARK EARTH THREADED

Action: Semiautomatic
Grips: Polymer
Barrel: 3.5 in.
Sights: White three-dot
Weight: 15.3 oz.
Caliber: .22 LR
Capacity: 10 rounds
Features: Reduced scale version of full-size M&P pistols; ambidextrous manual safety; reversible magazine release; Picatinny accessory rail; magazine safety; threaded barrel; two magazines
MSRP. **$429.00**

M&P BODYGUARD 380

Action: DA semiautomatic
Grips: Synthetic
Barrel: 2.75 in.
Sights: Adjustable
Weight: 11.85 oz.
Caliber: .380 ACP
Capacity: 6+1 rounds
Features: Stainless steel drift adjustable sights; ergonomic grip; high-strength polymer frame; external takedown lever and slide stop; manual thumb safety; double action fire control (2nd strike compatibility); available in Flat Dark Earth with or without integral Crimson Trace laser; in Armornite finish without thumb safety, without thumb safety but with integral Crimson Trace laser, with thumb safety (no other enhancements), and with thumb safety and choice of Crimson Trace

green Laserguard; and with an engraved stainless slide
Standard:. **$379.00**
Standard, no thumb safety:. .**$379.00**
Crimson Trace red:. **$449.00**
Crimson Trace red, no thumb safety:. **$449.00**
Crimson Trace green Laserguard:. **$519.00**

M&P BODYGUARD 380 ENGRAVED

Action: Semiautomatic
Grips: Polymer
Barrel: 2.75 in.
Sights: Drift adjustable front and rear
Weight: 12 oz.
Caliber: .380 ACP
Capacity: 6 rounds
Features: Ultra-compact carry gun; DAO; custom machine-engraved matte silver slide
MSRP. **$385.00**

M&P BODYGUARD 380 FLAT DARK EARTH

Action: Semiautomatic
Grips: Polymer
Barrel: 2.75 in.
Sights: Drift adjustable front and rear, Crimson Trace laser
Weight: 12.5 oz.
Caliber: .380 ACP
Capacity: 6 rounds
Features: Ultra-compact carry gun; black matte slide; polymer frame in Flat Dark Earth
Standard:. **$379.00**
Crimson Trace Red:. **$449.00**

**SMITH & WESSON
PERFORMANCE CENTER
SW1911 PRO SERIES
9MM**

**SMITH & WESSON
SD9, SD40 FLAT DARK
EARTH FRAME FINISH**

**SMITH & WESSON
SD9, SD40 GRAY
FRAME FINISH**

**SMITH &
WESSON SD9 VE**

**SMITH & WESSON
SW22 VICTORY**

**SMITH & WESSON
SW1911 ENGRAVED**

PERFORMANCE CENTER SW1911 PRO SERIES 9MM

Action: Semiautomatic
Grips: Synthetic
Barrel: 3 in.
Sights: Fixed white three-dot
Weight: 26.2 oz.
Caliber: 9mm, .40 S&W
Capacity: 8 rounds
Features: Scandium alloy frame; stippled synthetic grips; serrated mainspring housing; rear slide serrations; skeletonized hammer and trigger; full-length guide rod; ambidextrous safety; oversized external extractor
MSRP $1330.00

SD9, SD40 FLAT DARK EARTH FRAME FINISH

Action: Semiautomatic
Grips: Synthetic
Barrel: 4 in.
Sights: White three-dot
Weight: 22.3 oz.
Caliber: 9mm, .40 S&W
Capacity: 14, 16 rounds
Features: Self-Defense Trigger textured grip; accessory rail; slide serrations front; gray frame with matte black slide
MSRP $389.00

SD9, SD40 GRAY FRAME FINISH

Action: Semiautomatic
Grips: Synthetic

Barrel: 4 in.
Sights: White three-dot
Weight: 22.3 oz.
Caliber: 9mm, .40 S&W
Capacity: 14, 16 rounds
Features: Self-Defense Trigger textured grip; accessory rail; slide serrations front; frame is in Flat Dark Earth
MSRP $389.00

SD9 VE AND SD40 VE

Action: Striker Fired
Grips: Textured polymer
Barrel: 4 in.
Sights: White dot front, fixed 2-dot rear
Weight: 22.7 oz.
Caliber: 9mm, .40 S&W
Capacity: 10+1, 14+1, 16+1 rounds
Features: Lightweight polymer frame; front and rear slide serrations; Self Defense Trigger; ergonomic grip; Picatinny rail; two-tone finish Standard and low capacity
Massachusetts-compliant: . . . $389.00
California-compliant: $409.00
HiViz sights: $429.00
Grey finish: $389.00

SW22 VICTORY

Action: SA
Grips: Polymer
Barrel: 5.5 in.
Sights: Green fiber optic front,

adjustable fiber optic rear
Weight: 36 oz.
Caliber: .22 LR
Capacity: 10+1 rounds
Features: Removable interchangeable match-grade barrel; steel reinforced polymer thumb safety; Picatinny-style rail; adjustable trigger stop; textured grip panels with finger cuts for easy magazine removal; Kryptek Highlander finish or stainless with threaded barrel
**Standard, low capacity, Massachusetts-
compliant:** $389.00
California-compliant: $409.00
HiViz sights: $429.00
**Grey or Flat Dark Earth
frame:** $389.00

SW1911 ENGRAVED

Action: SA
Grips: Wood laminate E-Series
Barrel: 5 in.
Sights: White dot front, white 2-dot rear
Weight: 39.1 oz.
Caliber: .45 ACP
Capacity: 8+1 rounds
Features: Glass bead finish; machine scroll engraving; engraved, wooden presentation case
MSRP $1219.00

Springfield Armory

SPRINGFIELD ARMORY 911 .380 ACP

SPRINGFIELD ARMORY 1911 EMP

SPRINGFIELD ARMORY 1911 EMP 4-INCH CONCEALED CARRY CONTOUR

SPRINGFIELD ARMORY 1911 EMP LIGHTWEIGHT CHAMPION

SPRINGFIELD ARMORY 1911 LOADED

SPRINGFIELD ARMORY 1911 MIL-SPEC

911

Action: Semiautomatic
Grips: G10, Hogue
Barrel: 2.7, 3 in.
Sights: ProGlo tritium front, white outline tritium rear
Weight: 12.6–15.3 oz.
Caliber: .380 ACP, 9mm
Capacity: 6, 7 rounds
Features: Lightweight, aluminum-framed Carry gun with full-length guide rod, G10 grips, Octo-Grip texture on frontstrap and mainspring housing, night sights, ambidextrous extended thumb safety, trigger is set to five pounds. 9mm models available in Nitride with green G10 grips, Hogue rubber grips, or grip laser; Stainless with stainless slide, black frame and gray grips or grip laser. .380 models add all-over Desert Flat Dark Earth with Hogue grips; Cerakote Desert Flat Dark Earth frame with black nitride slide, black Sand Dune G10 grips; Platinum with clear hard-coat frame, Concrete Cerakote slide, engineered ivory grip panels; Titanium with all-over Cerakote Titanium finish, Blacked Out G10 grips; Cerakote Titanium frame with black nitride slide, black chevron G10 grips; Vintage Blue Cerakote frame with stainless slide, engineered ivory grips
9mm: . . . . $639.00–$659.00
9mm with grip laser: $849.00
.380: . . . . $629.00–$729.00
.380 with grip laser: $809.00

1911 EMP

Action: Semiautomatic
Grips: Thin line cocobolo wood
Barrel: 3 in.
Sights: Fixed low profile combat rear, dovetail
Weight: 26 oz.–33 oz.
Caliber: 9mm, .40 S&W
Capacity: 3–9 (9mm) or 3–8 (.40 S&W) rounds
Features: Forged stainless steel, satin finish; dual spring recoil system with full length guide rod
Black: $1104.00
Bi-Tone: $1249.00

1911 EMP 4-INCH CONCEALED CARRY CONTOUR

Action: Semiautomatic
Grips: G10
Barrel: 4 in.
Sights: Fiber optic front, low-profile combat rear
Weight: 30.5 oz.
Caliber: 9mm
Capacity: 9 rounds
Features: Longer barrel; frame trimmed for concealment; bevel-cut mainspring housing; contouring to prevent snagging and printing; stainless steel match-grade bull barrel; fully supported feed ramp; satin slide; black hard coat anodized aluminum alloy frame; Posi-Lok texturing on rear and front straps; premium carry case; three magazines
MSRP $1220.00

1911 EMP 4-INCH LIGHTWEIGHT CHAMPION

Action: SA semiautomatic
Grips: Cocobolo
Barrel: 4 in.
Sights: Three dot iron w/ fiber optic front and white dot rear
Weight: 31 oz. (9mm), 37 oz. (.40 S&W)
Caliber: 9mm, .40 S&W
Capacity: 9, 10 rounds
Features: Ambidextrous safety levers; match-grade barrel; Posi-Lock grip texture to the front strap; forged aluminum alloy frame with black hardcoat anodized finish
MSRP $1177.00

1911 LOADED

Action: Semiautomatic
Grips: Synthetic
Barrel: 5 in.
Sights: Fixed combat, 3-dot tritium
Weight: 34–43 oz.
Caliber: .45 ACP
Features: Forged steel; integral accessory rail; GI-style recoil system. Six versions include Marine Corps Operator with gray G10 grips and Olive Drab Armory Kote frame and Black Armory Kote slide; MC Operator with Olive Drab Armory Kote frame, Black Armory Kote slide, and wraparound Pachmayr grips; LB Operator with all-over Black Armory Kote and black G10 grips; Lightweight Operator with a black hard coat anodized forged aluminum frame, cocobolo grips; Parkerized with a Parkerized forged carbon steel frame/slide, cocobolo grips, no rail; Stainless Steel with matte rounds and polished flats, cocobolo grips, no rail
Marine Corps Operator: . . $1308.00
MC Operator: $1308.00
LB Operator: $1409.00
Lightweight Operator: $1210.00
Parkerized: $950.00
Stainless Steel: $1004.00

1911 MIL-SPEC

Action: Semiautomatic
Grips: Cocobolo wood and black plastic
Barrel: 5 in.
Sights: Fixed combat, 3-dot
Weight: 39 oz.
Caliber: .45 ACP
Capacity: 2–7 rounds
Features: Forged stainless steel, matte rounds with polished flats; GI style recoil system
Parkerized: $780.00
Stainless: $872.00

SPRINGFIELD ARMORY 1911 RANGE OFFICER

SPRINGFIELD ARMORY 1911 RANGE OFFICER CHAMPION

SPRINGFIELD ARMORY 1911 RANGE OFFICER ELITE CHAMPION

SPRINGFIELD 1911 RANGE OFFICER ELITE COMPACT

SPRINGFIELD ARMORY 1911 RANGE OFFICER ELITE OPERATOR

SPRINGFIELD 1911 RANGE OFFICER ELITE TARGET

SPRINGFIELD ARMORY 1911 TRP

1911 RANGE OFFICER

Action: Semiautomatic
Grips: Cocobolo
Barrel: 5 in.
Sights: Adjustable
Weight: 41 oz.
Caliber: .45 ACP, 9mm
Capacity: 9 rounds
Features: Designed for competitive shooters, with GI-style recoil system, national match stainless barrel with fully supported ramp, Cross Cannon double diamond cocobolo grips, fiber optic front sight in shielded tube, flat mainspring housing, aluminum match trigger, skeletonized hammer
Parkerized: **$942.00**
Stainless: **$1057.00**
Parkerized with rail: **$1042.00**

1911 RANGE OFFICER CHAMPION

Action: Semiautomatic
Grips: Wood
Barrel: 4 in.
Sights: Fixed
Weight: 30 oz.
Caliber: .45 ACP
Capacity: 7 rounds
Features: Grips are Cross Cannon double diamond cocobolo; fiber optic front and low profile combat rear; dual spring recoil system with full length guide rod
MSRP **$924.00**

1911 RANGE OFFICER ELITE CHAMPION

Action: Semiautomatic
Grips: G10
Barrel: 4 in.
Sights: Fiber optic front, Tactical Rack white dot rear
Weight: 31.5 oz., .30 oz.
Caliber: 9mm, .45 ACP

Capacity: 9, 7 rounds
Features: Steel barrel; fully supported ramp; full-size frame of aluminum alloy; slim-line G-10 grips; Black-T surface treatment; Gen 2 trigger; ambidextrous safety; forged steel slide; includes two magazines
9mm: **$1044.00**
.45 ACP: **$1030.00**

1911 RANGE OFFICER ELITE COMPACT

Action: Semiautomatic
Grips: G10
Barrel: 4 in.
Sights: Fiber optic front, Tactical Rack white dot rear
Weight: 29.5 oz., 28.5 oz.
Caliber: 9mm, .45 ACP
Capacity: 8, 6 rounds
Features: Steel barrel; fully supported ramp; full-size frame of aluminum alloy; G-10 grips; Black-T surface treatment; Gen 2 trigger; ambidextrous safety; forged steel slide; includes two magazines
9mm: **$1044.00**
.45 ACP: **$1030.00**

1911 RANGE OFFICER ELITE OPERATOR

Action: Semiautomatic
Grips: G10
Barrel: 5 in.
Sights: Fiber optic front, Tactical Rack white dot rear
Weight: 41 oz.
Caliber: 9mm, .45 ACP, 10mm
Capacity: 9, 7 rounds
Features: Steel barrel; fully supported ramp; full-size frame of aluminum alloy; G-10 grips; Black-T surface treatment; Gen 2 trigger; GI recoil system; ambidextrous safety; forged steel slide; includes two magazines
9mm: **$1159.00**
10mm, .45 ACP: **$1145.00**

1911 RANGE OFFICER ELITE TARGET

Action: Semiautomatic
Grips: G10
Barrel: 5 in.
Sights: Fiber optic front, fully adjustable target rear
Weight: 41 oz.
Caliber: 9mm, .45 ACP
Capacity: 9, 7 rounds
Features: Steel barrel; fully supported ramp; full-size frame of aluminum alloy; G-10 grips; Black-T surface treatment; Gen 2 trigger; GI recoil system; ambidextrous safety; forged steel slide; includes two magazines
9mm: **$1061.00**
.45 ACP: **$1048.00**

1911 TRP

Action: Semiautomatic
Grips: G10 composite
Barrel: 5 in.
Sights: Front tritium 3-dot, fixed low profile combat rear, dovetail
Weight: 42–45 oz.
Caliber: .45 ACP
Capacity: 2–7 rounds
Features: Forged National Match frames, National Match barrels, three-dot low-profile combat tritium sights, two-piece National Match guide rod, G10 grips. Five versions include: Black Armory Kote with gray/black grips; Stainless Steel with black grips; Operator with gray/black grips and rail; Operator Tactical Gray with gray/black grips and rail; Operator Black Armory Kote with black grips and full-length under-rail
Black Armory Kote: **$1648.00**
Stainless Steel: **$1648.00**
Operator, Operator Tactical Gray: **$1730.00**
Operator Blacl Armory Kote: **$1730.00**

Springfield Armory

SPRINGFIELD ARMORY 1911 TRP 10MM

SPRINGFIELD ARMORY XD (M)

SPRINGFIELD ARMORY XD MOD.2 4-IN. SERVICE MODEL

SPRINGFIELD ARMORY SAINT PISTOL

SPRINGFIELD ARMORY XD MOD.2 3-IN. SUB-COMPACT

SPRINGFIELD ARMORY XD-E 3.3 SINGLE STACK

1911 TRP 10MM

Action: Semiautomatic
Grips: G10
Barrel: 5, 6 in.
Sights: Three-dot tritium SA Tactical *rear, three-dot tritium adjustable rear*
Weight: 40–45 oz.
Caliber: 10mm
Capacity: 8 rounds
Features: Tactical Response Pistol; forged steel frame and slide in the corrosion-resistant Black-T finish; match-grade stainless barrel; fully supported ramp with bushings; Springfield's Gen 2 Speed Trigger; accessory rail; Octo-Grip stippling on the frontstrap and mainspring housing; V2 Alien G10 grips in Dirty Olive; 5-inch version has the SA Tactical rear sight/3-dot trititum; 6-inch has a fully adjustable rear/3-dot tritium; both have under rails
5-inch: **$1790.00**
6-inch: **$1842.00**

SAINT PISTOL

Action: Semiautomatic
Grips: Synthetic
Barrel: 7.5, 9 in.
Sights: None
Weight: 88–89 oz.
Caliber: 5.56 NATO, .300 Blackout
Capacity: 10, 30 rounds
Features: Forged 7075 T6 aluminum upper and lower; direct impingement pistol-length gas port; low-profile pinned gas block; SB Tactical stock; SBX-K forearm brace; GI-style charging handle; Bravo Company Mod 3 pistol grip; Springfield's own nickel-boron-coated G1 trigger; 1:7 twist Melonite-treated barrel; heavy Tungsten Carbine H buffer assembly; aluminum M-LOK free-floating handguard with locking tabs and a forward hand stop; rail space over the receiver and at the barrel end for sights, optics, and accessories; .300 Blackout is in black and has 9-inch barrel; 5.56 NATO has 7.5-inch barrel and is in all-over Desert Flat Dark Earth
5.56 NATO: **$1059.00**
.300 Blackout: **$1015.00**

XD-E 3.3 SINGLE STACK

Action: Semiautomatic
Grips: Synthetic
Barrel: 3.3 in.
Sights: Fiber optic front, two-dot combat rear
Weight: 23–25 oz.
Caliber: 9mm, .45 ACP
Capacity: 6, 7, 8, 9 rounds
Features: Compact concealed carry pistol; hammer-forged steel barrel treated with Melonite; a true double/single-action with an exposed hammer; added grip texture
9mm: **$542.00**
.45 ACP: **$580.00**

XD (M)

Action: DA semiautomatic
Grips: Polymer
Barrel: 3.8 in., 4.5 in., 5.25 in.
Sights: Three-dot
Weight: 27.5 oz.–32 oz.
Caliber: 9mm, .40 S&W, .45 ACP, 10mm
Features: "M" features include carrying case, two magazines, paddle holster, magi loader, double magi pouch and three interchangeable backstraps and two magazines; "allterrain" texture and deep slide serrations are standard; 3.8-inch model in 9mm only; 4.5-inch in 9mm, .40 S&W, .45 ACP, 10mm; 4.5 Threaded Barrel in .45 ACP only; 4.5 OSP Threaded Barrel in 9mm only and equipped with Venom reflex red dot sight; 5.25-inch Competition in 9mm, .45 ACP, and 10mm
3.8-, 4.5-inch: . . . . . **$623.00–$652.00**
Threaded Barrel (.45 ACP): . .**$673.00**
OSP Threaded Barrel (9mm): . .**$958.00**
Competition: . . . . . **$753.00–$779.00**

XD MOD.2 3-IN. SUB-COMPACT

Action: Semiautomatic
Grips: Polymer
Barrel: 3 in.
Sights: Fiber optic front, low-profle combat rear
Weight: 26–27oz.
Caliber: .9mm
Capacity: 13, 16 rounds
Features: Ultra-compact carry gun has Melonite finish steel barrel and slide, full-length guide rod; available in
MSRP **$559.00**

XD MOD.2 4-IN. SERVICE MODEL

Action: Semiautomatic
Grips: Polymer
Barrel: 4 in.
Sights: Fiber optic front, low-profle combat rear
Weight: 27.5 oz. (9mm), 30 oz. (.45 ACP)
Caliber: 9mm, .45 ACP
Capacity: 13, 16 rounds
Features: Polymer frame with GripZone texture; available in black; striker status indicator; loaded chamber indicator; forged steel slide with Melonite finish; accessory rail in front of trigger guard; internal firing pin block
9mm: **$559.00**
.45 ACP: **$588.00**

Steyr Arms

STEYR ARMS C-A1

STEYR ARMS L-A1

C-A1
Action: Striker-fired semiautomatic
Grips: Textured polymer
Barrel: 3.6 in.
Sights: Fixed triangular/trapezoid;

TrugloTFX
Weight: 25.6 oz.
Caliber: 9mm, .40 S&W
Capacity: 12, 17 rounds
Features: Polymer frame; trigger, internal striker, internal gun-lock

safeties; polygonal rifling; black matte Mannox finish; Picatinny rail
Trapezoid sights: **$575.00**
Truglo TFX sights: **$750.00**

L-A1
Action: Semiautomatic
Grips: Synthetic
Barrel: 4.5 in.
Sights: Fixed triangular/trapezoid; TrugloTFX
Weight: 28.6 oz.
Caliber: 9mm, .40 S&W
Capacity: 12 or 17 rounds
Features: Rectangular sights with or without Trilux, match sights; full size service pistol; matte finish
Trapezoid sights: **$575.00**
Truglo TFX sights: **$750.00**

STI International

STI INTERNATIONAL DVC-C H.O.S.T.

STI INTERNATIONAL DVC-O

STI INTERNATIONAL DVC-S

DVC-C, DVC-C H.O.S.T.
Action: Semiautomatic
Grips: 2011 DVC
Barrel: 3.9 in.
Sights: Low-profile tritium front, fixed ledge rear
Weight: N/A
Caliber: 9mm
Capacity: 15 rounds
Features: Light and narrow aluminum 2011 frame for concealability; grip stippled by Extreme Shooters; slide lightening cuts; black DLC-coated frame and slide; copper-colored barrel
MSRP **$2999.00**

DVC-O
Action: Semitautomatic

Grips: Synthetic
Barrel: 5 in.
Sights: None
Weight: 48 oz.
Caliber: .38 Super, 9mm
Capacity: 15, 17, 20, 26 rounds
Features: 2.5 lb. trigger; Dawson toolless guide rod; hard chrome finish; titanium nitride finish barrel and compensator; reversible, dual detent slide racker; mounted C-More 6 MOA dot sight
MSRP **$3999.00**

DVC-S
Action: Semiautomatic
Grips: Gen II 2011
Barrel: 4.15 in.

Sights: C-More RTS2
Weight: N/A
Caliber: .38 Super, 9mm
Capacity: 21, 27 rounds
Features: Compensated barrel; frame and slide are in hard chrome; black DVC grips are stippled; Dawson Precision Tool-less guide rod and Ice magwell; available in finish combinations of hard chrome with black Diamond-Like Coating (DLC) barrel, black DLC with gold TiN barrel, or all-over black DLC; includes two 140mm (21 rounds) magazine and one 170mm (27 rounds) magazine; C-More sight is frame-mounted
MSRP **$3999.00**

Taurus

TAURUS 44

TAURUS 82

TAURUS .380 AUTO REVOLVER

TAURUS 605

TAURUS 608

TAURUS 692

TAURUS 856

REVOLVERS

44

Action: Revolver
Grips: Soft rubber
Barrel: 4 in., 6.5 in., 8.4 in.
Sights: Fixed
Weight: 45–57 oz.
Caliber: .44 Mag.
Capacity: 6 rounds
Features: Transfer bar; ported barrel; matte stainless steel finish; double and single-action
4-, 6.5-inch barrel: **$647.72**
8.4-inch barrel: **$663.97**

82

Action: Revolver
Grips: Rubber
Barrel: 4 in.
Sights: Fixed
Weight: 36.5 oz.
Caliber: .38 Spl. +P
Capacity: 6 rounds
Features: Transfer bar; steel construction with blued finish; single/double-action trigger
MSRP **$520.62**

.380 AUTO REVOLVER

Action: Revolver
Grips: Rubber
Barrel: 1.75 in.
Sights: Adjustable rear
Weight: 15.5 oz.
Caliber: .380 ACP
Capacity: 5 rounds
Features: Double-action trigger; fully enclosed hammer; blued or matte stainless finish; bobbed hammer
Blue: **$478.49**
Stainless: **$513.79**

605

Action: Revolver
Grips: Rubber
Barrel: 2 in.
Sights: Fixed
Weight: 24 oz.
Caliber: .357 Mag
Capacity: 5 rounds
Features: Transfer bar safety; steel construction with blued or stainless finish; single-double action trigger
Matte stainless: **$409.66**
Matte black oxide: **$392.94**

608

Action: Revolver
Grips: Rubber
Barrel: 4 in., 6.5 in.
Sights: Fixed front, adjustable rear
Weight: 44 oz.–51 oz.
Caliber: .357 Mag
Capacity: 8 rounds
Features: Matte stainless steel finish; transfer bar; large frame; steel frame; Taurus security system; porting
MSRP **$759.73**

692

Action: Revolver
Grips: Rubber
Barrel: 3 in., 6.5 in.
Sights: Fixed front, adjustable rear
Weight: 35.27 oz., 45.85 oz.
Caliber: .357 Mag., 9mm
Capacity: 7 rounds
Features: User can swap out .38 Special/.357 Mag. cylinder for one in 9mm; unfluted cylinder and porting; 6.5-in. barrel has a vent rib; matte blue or matte stainless finish
Blue: **$639.45**
Stainless: **$691.95**

856, 856UL

Action: Revolver
Grips: Rubber
Barrel: 2 in.
Sights: Serrated ramp front, notch rear
Weight: 16 oz., 22 oz.
Caliber: .38 Spec.
Capacity: 6 rounds
Features: Snub-nosed .38; ribbed rubber grips; matte blue, matte stainless, matte natural anodized and black oxide finishes; UL model is Ultralight 16 oz.; both versions +P rated
Blue: **$363.63**
Stainless: **$378.79**
Matte natural: **$378.79**
Ultra Light black oxide: **$461.00**

TAURUS JUDGE

TAURUS RAGING HUNTER

TAURUS RAGING BULL 444

TAURUS RAGING JUDGE 513

TAURUS TRACKER 17

TAURUS TRACKER 44

TAURUS TRACKER 627

TAURUS TRACKER 992

JUDGE

Action: DA/SA revolver
Grips: Taurus rubber grips
Barrel: 3 in.
Sights: Red fiber optic, fixed
Weight: 29–36.8 oz.
Caliber: .45 Colt/.410
Capacity: 5 rounds
Features: Firing pin block, transfer bar safety; compact frame; matte stainless steel finish; steel construction
MSRP . . . . **$511.37–$629.02**

RAGING BULL 444

Action: Revolver
Grips: Rubber w/cushioned insert
Barrel: 6.5 in., 8.38 in.
Sights: Partridge front, adjustable rear
Weight: 53 oz.–63 oz.
Caliber: .44 Mag.
Capacity: 6 rounds
Features: Steel construction with blued or stainless steel finish; transfer bar; dual lockup cylinder; porting; Taurus security system
MSRP **$899.83**

RAGING HUNTER

Action: Revolver
Grips: Rubber
Barrel: 8.375 in.
Sights: Fixed front, adjustable rear
Weight: 55 oz.
Caliber: .44 Mag.
Capacity: 6 rounds
Features: Optics rail; a steel sleeved barrel in an aluminum housing,
porting, and cushioned grip inserts in all-over matte black or a two-tone with a stainless frame
All blue: **$910.27**
Stainless/blue: **$919.55**

RAGING JUDGE 513

Action: DA/SA revolver
Grips: Rubber with soft cushion insert
Barrel: 3 in., 6.5 in.
Sights: Fiber optic front, fixed rear
Weight: 60.6 oz.–73 oz.
Caliber: .410/.45 Colt, .454 Casull
Capacity: 6 rounds
Features: Stainless steel finish; "Raging Bull" backstrap for added cushioning
MSRP **$1167.75**

TRACKER 17

Action: Revolver
Grips: Rubber with ribs
Barrel: 6.5 in.
Sights: Fixed front, adjustable rear
Weight: 47 oz.
Caliber: .17 HMR
Capacity: 7 rounds
Features: Matte stainless steel or blued finish; transfer bar; steel frame; *porting*
Blue: **$530.63**
Stainless: **$582.87**

TRACKER 44

Action: Revolver
Grips: Rubber with ribs
Barrel: 4 in.
Sights: Fixed front, adjustable rear
Weight: 35 oz.
Caliber: .44 Mag.
Capacity: 5 rounds
Features: Matte stainless steel or blued finish; transfer bar; steel frame; barrel porting; vent rib
Blue: **$566.65**
Stainless: **$582.80**

TRACKER 627

Action: Revolver
Grips: Rubber with ribs
Barrel: 4, 6.5 in.
Sights: Fixed front, adjustable rear
Weight: 35–40 oz.
Caliber: .357 Mag.
Capacity: 6 rounds
Features: Matte stainless steel medium frame revolver; barrel porting; 6.5-inch barrel has topside vent rib
MSRP **$576.53**

TRACKER 992

Action: SA/DA revolver
Grips: Taurus Ribber
Barrel: 4 in., 6.5 in.
Sights: Adjustable
Weight: 55 oz.
Caliber: .22 LR
Capacity: 9 rounds
Features: The versatile Tracker 992 easily transforms from .22 LR to .22 Magnum in seconds with its breakthrough removable cylinder; perfect for plinking, target practice, or varmint hunting
Blue: **$639.45**
Stainless: **$691.95**

Taurus

TAURUS 22 POLY

TAURUS 92

TAURUS 1911 COMMANDER

TAURUS·1911 OFFICER

TAURUS MILLENIUM G2

TAURUS SPECTRUM

TAURUS TH9, TH9C

SEMIAUTOMATICS

22 POLY

Action: DA semiautomatic
Grips: Polymer
Barrel: 2.3 in.
Sights: Fixed
Weight: 11.3 oz.
Caliber: .22 LR
Capacity: 8+1
Features: Polymer/blued steel construction; blued steel finish; tip-up barrel
Blue slide: **$282.58**
Stainless slide: **$299.30**

92

Action: Semiautomatic
Grips: Checkered rubber
Barrel: 5 in.
Sights: Fixed-1 dot front, fixed-2 dots rear
Weight: 34 oz.
Caliber: 9mm
Capacity: 10+1 or 17+1 rounds
Features: Blued, stainless steel finish; steel/alloy construction; firing pin block, hammer decocker, manual safety
Blue: **$433.40**
Stainless: **$550.12**

1911 COMMANDER

Action: Semiautomatic
Grips: Synthetic
Barrel: 4.2 in.
Sights: Novak drift adjustable front and rear
Weight: 38 oz.

Caliber: .45 ACP
Capacity: 8 rounds
Features: Matte black finish; checkered black grips, extended beavertail; easy to customize
MSRP **$639.95**

1911 OFFICER

Action: Semiautomatic
Grips: Synthetic
Barrel: 3.5 in.
Sights: Novak drift adjustable front and rear
Weight: 34.5 oz.
Caliber: .45 ACP
Capacity: 6 rounds
Features: Matte black finish; checkered black grips; shortest model in the 1911 line
MSRP **639.95**

MILLENIUM G2

Action: Semiautomatic
Grips: Polymer
Barrel: 3.2 in.
Sights: Adjustable
Weight: 22 oz.
Caliber: 9mm, .40 S&W
Capacity: 10, 12 rounds
Features: Loaded chamber indicator; blue finish; Taurus Security System; accessory rail
9mm blue: **$316.89**
9mm stainless: **$332.82**
.40 S&W blue: **$310.56**
.40 S&W stainless: **$327.16**

SPECTRUM

Action: Semiautomatic
Grips: Soft-touch overmold
Barrel: 2.8 in.
Sights: Integral low-profile front and rear
Weight: 10 oz.
Caliber: .380 ACP
Capacity: 6 rounds
Features: Ultralight striker-fired micropistol; soft-touch overmold grip; rear slide inserts; slide serrations; soft-edged frame; reversible magazine release; highly customizable color options
MSRP . . . . **$292.21–$307.67**
With laser: **$354.04**

TH9, TH9C

Action: Semiautomatic
Grips: Synthetic
Barrel: 3.54 in., 4.27 in.
Sights: Novak drift adjustable front and rear
Weight: 28.2 oz., 25 oz.
Caliber: 9mm
Capacity: 13, 19 rounds
Features: Lightweight polymer frame DA/SA; dual trigger safety system; ambidextrous controls; underbarrel Picatinny rail; interchangeable backstrap
MSRP **$376.95**

Taylor's & Co. Firearms

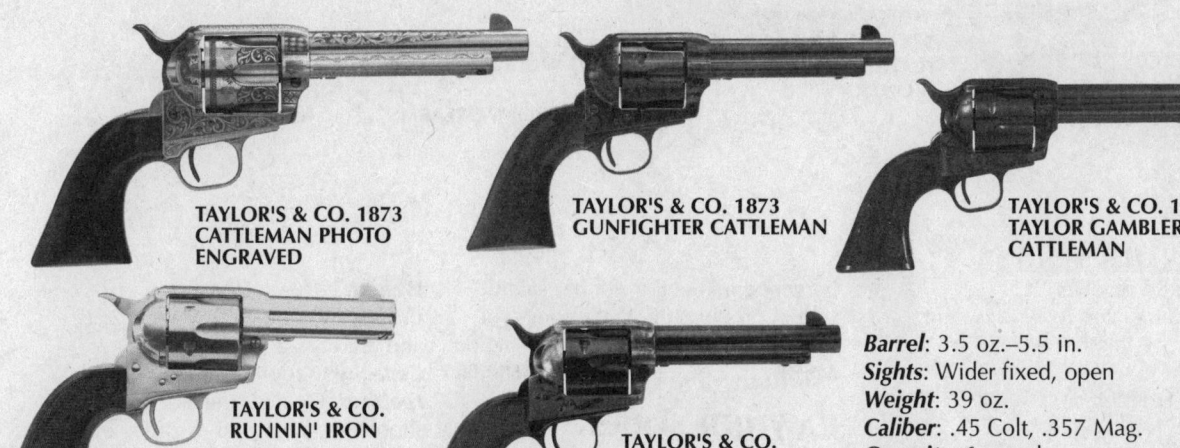

TAYLOR'S & CO. 1873 CATTLEMAN PHOTO ENGRAVED

TAYLOR'S & CO. 1873 GUNFIGHTER CATTLEMAN

TAYLOR'S & CO. 1873 TAYLOR GAMBLER CATTLEMAN

TAYLOR'S & CO. RUNNIN' IRON

TAYLOR'S & CO. SMOKE WAGON

1873 CATTLEMAN PHOTO ENGRAVED

Action: SA revolver
Grips: Walnut
Barrel: 4.75 in., 5.5 in., 7.5 in.
Sights: Fixed
Weight: 2 lb. 4 oz.–3 lb. 6 oz.
Caliber: .357 Mag., .45 LC
Capacity: 6 rounds
Features: White, heat-treated steel finish with charcoal blued screws; laser-engraved and hand chased; forged frame
MSRP . . . . $925.00–$959.00

1873 GUNFIGHTER CATTLEMAN

Action: SA revolver
Grips: Walnut
Barrel: 5.5 in.
Sights: Fixed
Weight: 2 lb. 5 oz.
Caliber: .357 Mag., .45 Colt
Capacity: 6 rounds

Features: Special Army-sized grip; steel trigger guard and backstrap; blued finish with case-hardened frame; forged frame
Smooth grips: $574.00
Checkered grips: $609.00

1873 TAYLOR GAMBLER CATTLEMAN

Action: SA revolver
Grips: Walnut
Barrel: 5.5 in.
Sights: Fixed
Weight: 2 lb. 5 oz.
Caliber: .357 Mag., .45 Colt
Capacity: 6 rounds
Features: Checkered walnut grip; blued color case-hardened frame
MSRP $604.00

RUNNIN' IRON

Action: SA revolver
Grips: Checkered walnut

Barrel: 3.5 oz.–5.5 in.
Sights: Wider fixed, open
Weight: 39 oz.
Caliber: .45 Colt, .357 Mag.
Capacity: 6 rounds
Features: Designed for the sport of mounted shooting; stainless or blued with low, wide hammer spur; checkered, one-piece gunfighter style grips in walnut or black polymer; wide trigger and extra clearance at front and rear of cylinder
MSRP . . . . $633.00–$805.00
Short Stroke: . . . . . $675.00–$847.00

SMOKE WAGON

Action: SA revolver
Grips: Checkered wood
Barrel: 3.5 in., 5.5 in.
Sights: Open rear sight groove, wide angle front sight blade
Weight: 40 oz.
Caliber: .357 Mag., .45 Colt, .44-40 Win.
Capacity: 6 rounds
Features: Low profile hammer; custom tuning, custom hammer and base pin springs; jig-cut positive angles on trigger and sears; wire bolt and trigger springs
MSRP $608.00
Short Stroke: $649.00

TNW Firearms

AERO SURVIVAL PISTOL

Action: Semiautomatic
Grips: Synthetic
Barrel: 8 in.
Sights: Flip-up front and rear
Weight: 88 oz.
Caliber: 9mm, 10mm, .40 S&W, .45 ACP, .357 SIG
Capacity: Varies with magazine
Features: Reduced SBR version of TNW's Aero Survival Rifle; compact, lightweight, and easily disassembled; takes Glock-style magazines; hard black anodized or variegated finishes

in pink/black or green/black; some restricted state versions available
MSRP $699.00
Multi-Caliber Package: . . . $1199.00

TNW FIREARMS AERO SURVIVAL PISTOL

Traditions Firearms

**TRADITIONS FIREARMS
FRONTIER**

**TRADITIONS FIREARMS
RAWHIDE**

FRONTIER SERIES
Action: SA revolver
Grips: Simulated ivory or walnut
Barrel: 3.5 in., 4.75 in., 5.5 in., 7.5 in.
Sights: Front blade
Weight: N/A
Caliber: .357 Mag., .44 Mag., .45 Colt, .44-40 Win.
Capacity: 6 rounds
Features: 1873 single action revolvers; deep bluing and nickel frames and barrel or color case hardened frame; transfer bar safety system provides the highest lever of safety offered in an 1873 single action
MSRP . . . . $499.00–$659.00

RAWHIDE SERIES
Action: SA revolver
Grips: Walnut
Barrel: 4.75 in., 5.5 in., 7.5 in.
Sights: Front blade
Weight: N/A
Caliber: .45 Colt, .357 Mag., .22 LR, and .22 LR/.22 Mag.
Capacity: 6 rounds
Features: Quality single action shooter features at an affordable price; matte black finish that provides excellent corrosion resistance; transfer bar system provides the highest level of safety offered in an 1873 single action
MSRP . . . . $459.00–$504.00

Trailblazer Firearms

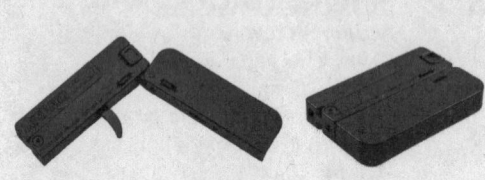

**TRAILBLAZER FIREARMS
LIFECARD .22LR**

LIFECARD .22LR
Action: Single-shot
Grips: Aluminum
Barrel: 3 in.
Sights: None
Weight: 7 oz.
Caliber: .22LR
Capacity: 1 round
Features: Half-inch thick; barrel, bolt, and trigger are 4140 pre-hardened steel; handle is aluminum billet; folds to size of a stack of credit cards; full-size handle when unfolded; firearm will not fire when closed
MSRP $399.00

TriStar Sporting Arms

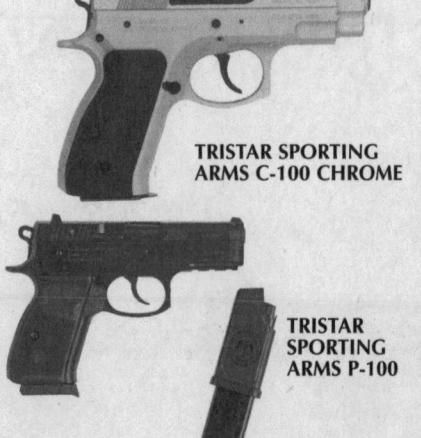

**TRISTAR SPORTING
ARMS C-100 CHROME**

**TRISTAR
SPORTING
ARMS P-100**

C-100
Action: DA/SA semiautomatic
Grips: Polymer
Barrel: 3.9 in.
Sights: Rear dovetail, fixed front
Weight: 24.48 oz.–26.08 oz.
Caliber: 9mm
Capacity: 11, 15 rounds
Features: Produced to NATO specs; rear snag-free dovetail sights; fixed blade front sight; black polycoat finish; black polymer checkered grips; includes two magazines and a hard plastic case
Black Cerakote: $460.00
Tungsten Cerakote: $480.00

P-100
Action: Semiautomatic
Grips: Polymer
Barrel: 3.7 in.
Sights: Fixed front, rear dovetail
Weight: 2 lb. 5 oz.
Caliber: 9mm
Capacity: Detachable box, 11–15 rounds
Features: Steel frame and steel slide; double/single action; rear snag free dovetail sights and fixed blade front sight; Picatinny rail built into frame; Cerakote finish and black polymer checkered grips
MSRP $490.00

TriStar Sporting Arms

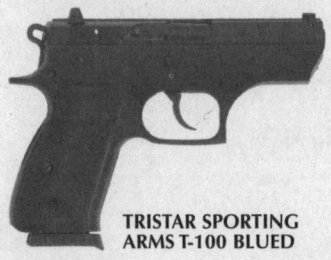

TRISTAR SPORTING ARMS T-100 BLUED

TRISTAR SPORTING ARMS P-120

P-120
Action: DA/SA semiautomatic
Grips: Polymer
Barrel: 4.7 in.
Sights: Rear dovetail, fixed front
Weight: 29.9 oz.
Caliber: 9mm

Capacity: 17 rounds
Features: Originally created for military use; constructed from steel alloy; blued or chrome finish; rear snag-free dovetail sights; fixed blade front sight; includes two magazines, cleaning kit, gun lock, and a black carrying case
Chrome: $510.00
Black Cerakote: $490.00

T-100
Action: DA/SA semiautomatic
Grips: Polymer
Barrel: 3.7 in.
Sights: Rear dovetail, fixed front
Weight: 26.24 oz.
Caliber: 9mm
Capacity: 15 rounds
Features: Compact pistol perfect for concealed carry; constructed from steel alloy; blued or chrome finish; rear snag-free dovetail sights; fixed blade front sight; includes two magazines, cleaning kit, gun lock, and a black carrying case
MSRP. $460.00

Turnbull Restoration, Inc.

TURNBULL RESTORATION COMMANDER HERITAGE MODEL 1911

TURNBULL RESTORATION COMMANDER MODEL 1911

TURNBULL RESTORATION GOVERNMENT HERITAGE MODEL 1911

TURNBULL RESTORATION GOVERNMENT MODEL 1911

COMMANDER HERITAGE MODEL 1911
Action: Semiautomatic
Grips: Double-diamond walnut
Barrel: 4.25 in.
Sights: Titrium Kensights
Weight: 34.5 oz.
Caliber: .45 ACP
Capacity: 7 rounds
Features: Beavertail grip safety; steel parts, blue finished slide; color case hardened frame; checkered front strap
MSRP. . . . . . Contact manufacturer

COMMANDER MODEL 1911
Action: Semiautomatic
Grips: Double-diamond walnut
Barrel: 4.25 in.
Sights: Titrium Kensights
Weight: 34.5 oz.
Caliber: .45 ACP
Capacity: 7 rounds

Features: Beavertail grip safety; steel parts, blue finished slide; blued frame; checkered front strap
MSRP. . . . . . Contact manufacturer

GOVERNMENT HERITAGE MODEL 1911
Action: Semiautomatic
Grips: Double-diamond walnut
Barrel: 5 in.
Sights: Titrium Kensights
Weight: 38 oz.
Caliber: .45 ACP
Capacity: 7 rounds
Features: Beavertail grip safety; steel parts, blue finished slide; color case hardened frame; checkered front strap
MSRP. . . . . . Contact manufacturer

GOVERNMENT MODEL 1911
Action: Semiautomatic
Grips: Double-diamond walnut
Barrel: 5 in.
Sights: Titrium Kensights
Weight: 38 oz.
Caliber: .45 ACP
Capacity: 7 rounds
Features: Beavertail grip safety; steel parts, blue finished slide; blued frame; checkered front strap
MSRP. . . . . . Contact manufacturer

Uberti

1851 NAVY CONVERSION

Action: SA revolver
Grips: Walnut
Barrel: 4.75 in., 5.5 in., 7.5 in.
Sights: Fixed, open
Weight: 42 oz.
Caliber: .38 Spl.
Capacity: 6 rounds
Features: Case-hardened frame octagonal barrel; brass backstrap and trigger guard; conversion revolver frames are retro-fitted with loading gates to accommodate metallic cartridges like the originals
MSRP **$589.00**

1860 ARMY CONVERSION

Action: SA revolver
Grips: Walnut
Barrel: 4.75 in., 5.5 in., 8 in.
Sights: Fixed, open
Weight: 42 oz.
Caliber: .38 Spl., .45 Colt
Capacity: 6 rounds
Features: Case-hardened frame; round barrel; steel backstrap and trigger guard; conversion revolver frames are retro-fitted with loading gates to accommodate metallic cartridges like the originals
MSRP **$619.00**

1871–1872 OPEN-TOP CONVERSION

Action: SA revolver
Grips: Walnut
Barrel: 4.75 in., 5.5 in., 7.5 in.
Sights: Fixed, open
Weight: 42 oz.
Caliber: .38 Spl., .45 Colt
Capacity: 6 rounds
Features: 1872 model has steel backstrap and trigger guard; 1871 model has brass backstrap and trigger guard; case-hardened frame; round barrel; blued finish conversion revolver frames are retro-fitted with loading gates to accommodate metallic cartridges like the originals
1871 Navy: **$549.00**
1871 Army: **$579.00**

1873 CATTLEMAN

Action: SA revolver
Grips: Walnut
Barrel: 4.75 in., 5.5 in., 7.5 in.
Sights: Fixed, open
Weight: 37 oz.
Caliber: .45 Colt

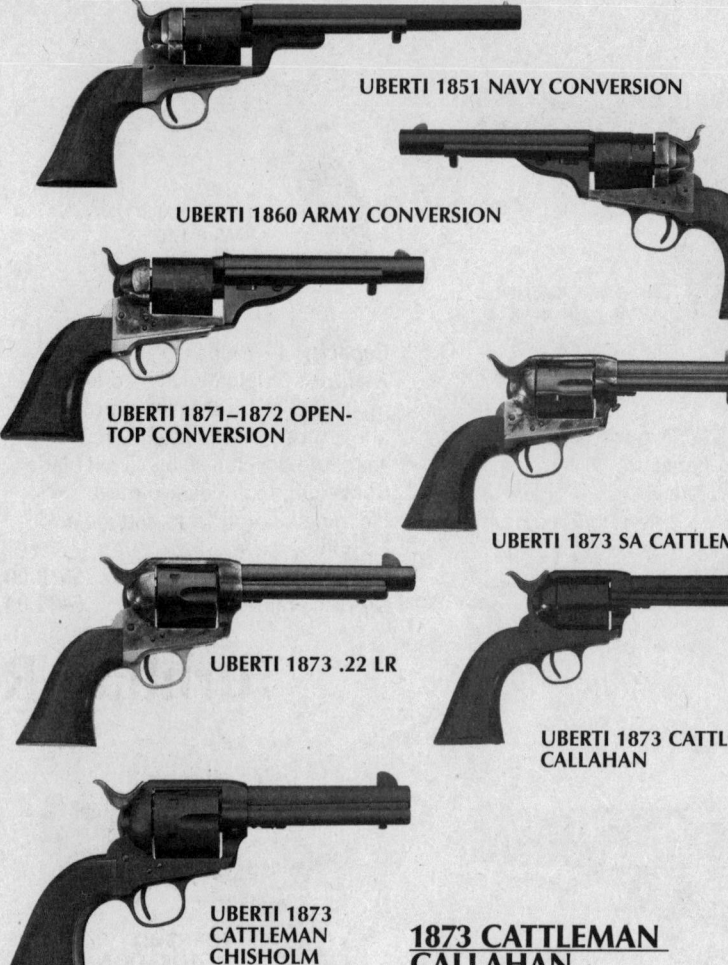

UBERTI 1851 NAVY CONVERSION

UBERTI 1860 ARMY CONVERSION

UBERTI 1871–1872 OPEN-TOP CONVERSION

UBERTI 1873 SA CATTLEMAN

UBERTI 1873 .22 LR

UBERTI 1873 CATTLEMAN CALLAHAN

UBERTI 1873 CATTLEMAN CHISHOLM

Capacity: 6 rounds
Features: Case-hardened frame; brass or steel backstrap and trigger guard; blued, nickel or stainless steel finish; fluted cylinder
Charcoal Blue: . . . . **$669.00–$719.00**
Nickel: **$689.00**
Stainless: . . . .**$679.00–$739.00**

1873 CATTLEMAN .22 LR

Action: SA revolver
Grips: Walnut
Barrel: 4.75 in., 5.5 in., 7.5 in.
Sights: Fixed, open
Weight: 36.8 oz.
Caliber: .22 LR
Capacity: 6 and 12 round models
Features: Ideal for cowboy-action shooting practice; light recoil; six-shot comes with brass or steel backstrap and trigger guard; available in six- or twelve-shot; case-hardened frame; blued finish
Six-shot: **$539.00**
Twelve-shot: **$589.00**

1873 CATTLEMAN CALLAHAN

Action: SA revolver
Grips: Walnut, black or mother-of-pearl synthetic
Barrel: 4.75 in., 6 in., 7.5 in.
Sights: Fixed
Weight: 42 oz.
Caliber: .44 Mag.
Capacity: 6 rounds
Features: Blued, stainless, case-hardened or Old West finish; target model has angled front target sight and adjustable notched rear blade
MSRP **$639.00**

1873 CATTLEMAN CHISHOLM

Action: SA revolver
Grips: Checkered walnut
Barrel: 4.75 in., 5.5 in.
Sights: Fixed, open
Weight: 37 oz.
Caliber: .45 Colt
Capacity: 6 rounds
Features: Complete matte finished steel; fluted barrel
MSRP **$599.00**

UBERTI 1873 CATTLEMAN CODY MATCHING SET

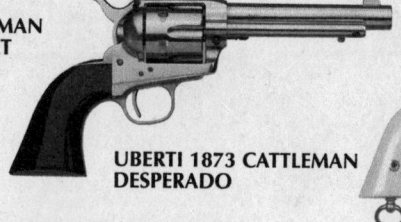

UBERTI 1873 CATTLEMAN DESPERADO

UBERTI FIREARMS 1873 SINGLE ACTION ARMY OUTLAW FRANK

UBERTI FIREARMS 1873 SINGLE ACTION CATTLEMAN NEW MODEL DOC

UBERTI FIREARMS 1873 SINGLE ACTION CATTLEMAN NEW MODEL JESSE

UBERTI 1873 EL PATRÓN COWBOY MOUNTED SHOOTER (CMS)

UBERTI 1875 FRONTIER

1873 CATTLEMAN CODY MATCHING SET

Action: SA revolver
Grips: Walnut
Barrel: 5.5 in.
Sights: Fixed, open
Weight: 37 oz.
Caliber: .45 Colt
Capacity: 6 rounds
Features: Fluted barrel; blued case-hardened frame; steel backstrap; trigger guard; the set shares matching serial numbers; available in nickel and ivory-style grip
MSRP $1778.00

1873 CATTLEMAN DESPERADO

Action: SA revolver
Grips: Bison horn style
Barrel: 4.75 in., 5.5 in.
Sights: Fixed, open
Weight: 37 oz.
Caliber: .45 Colt
Capacity: 6 rounds
Features: Full nickel-plated steel; fluted barrel
MSRP $889.00

1873 SINGLE ACTION ARMY OUTLAW FRANK

Action: Revolver

Grips: Ivory-style
Barrel: 7.5 in.
Sights: Metal blade front, receiver notch rear
Weight: 44.8 oz.
Caliber: .45 Colt
Capacity: 6 rounds
Features: Replica of the 1875 Remington carried by outlaw Jesse James' brother Frank James; all-over nickel-plating; ivory-style grips; lanyard ring
MSRP $969.00

1873 SINGLE ACTION CATTLEMAN NEW MODEL DOC

Action: Revolver
Grips: Bison horn
Barrel: 5.5 in.
Sights: Metal blade front, receiver notch rear
Weight: 36.8 oz.
Caliber: .45 Colt
Capacity: 6 rounds
Features: Based on gambler and gunslinger Doc Holliday's revolver; short-barreled, nimble single-action 1873; all-over nickel-plating and pearl-style grips in a bird's-head design
MSRP $869.00

1873 SINGLE ACTION CATTLEMAN NEW MODEL JESSE

Action: Revolver
Grips: Pearl-style
Barrel: 4.75 in.
Sights: Metal blade front, receiver notch rear
Weight: 35.2 oz.
Caliber: .45 Colt

Capacity: 6 rounds
Features: Based on Jesse James' 1873 Colt; fluted cylinder; all-over polished blue finish; dark bison-horn grips
MSRP $759.00

1873 CATTLEMAN EL PATRÓN COWBOY MOUNTED SHOOTER (CMS)

Action: SA revolver
Grips: Checkered walnut
Barrel: 3.5 in., 4 in.
Sights: EasyView
Weight: 37 oz.
Caliber: .45 Colt, .357 Mag.
Capacity: 6 rounds
Features: Blued or stainless steel finish; optional case-hardened frame; fluted barrel; fitted with U.S.-made Wolff springs; numbered cylinders
MSRP $669.00

1875 OUTLAW & FRONTIER

Action: SA revolver
Grips: Walnut
Barrel: 5.5 in. (Frontier), 7.5 in.
Sights: Fixed, open
Weight: 40–45 oz.
Caliber: .45 Colt
Capacity: 6 rounds
Features: Case-hardened or full nickel plated steel frame; steel backstrap and trigger guard; fluted cylinder
Outlaw case-hardened frame: $609.00
Outlaw full nickel-plating: . . $729.00
Frontier case-hardened frame: $609.00

Uberti

UBERTI 1890 SA POLICE REVOLVER

UBERTI BIRD'S HEAD

UBERTI BISLEY

UBERTI FIREARMS EL PATRON GRIZZLY PAW

UBERTI USA SHORT STROKE SASS PRO NICKEL

UBERTI 1873 STALLION TARGET

UBERTI TOP BREAK REVOLVER

1890 SINGLE ACTION POLICE REVOLVER

Action: SA revolver
Grips: Walnut with lanyard ring
Barrel: 5.5 in.
Sights: Fixed, open
Weight: 42 oz.
Caliber: .45 Colt, .357 Mag.
Capacity: 6 rounds
Features: Blued steel frame, backstrap and trigger guard; fluted cylinder
MSRP $619.00

BIRD'S HEAD

Action: SA revolver
Grips: Walnut
Barrel: 3.5 in., 4 in., 4.75 in., 5.5 in.
Sights: Fixed, open
Weight: 35 oz.
Caliber: .38 Spl., .45 Colt, .357 Mag.
Capacity: 6 rounds
Features: Case-hardened frame; steel backstrap and trigger guard; blued finish; bird head shape grip; Bird's Head Stallion Old West Defense is chambered in .38 Spl., has full matte finish, 3.5-in. barrel
Standard: . . . . $579.00–$589.00
Stallion Old West Defense: . . $589.00

BISLEY

Action: SA revolver
Grips: Bisley target style walnut

Barrel: 4.75 in., 5.5 in., 7.5 in.
Sights: Fixed, open
Weight: 40 oz.
Caliber: .45 Colt, .357 Mag.
Capacity: 6 rounds
Features: Case-hardened frame; steel backstrap and trigger guard; blued finish; fluted cylinder
MSRP $619.00

EL PATRON GRIZZLY PAW

Action: Revolver
Grips: Walnut
Barrel: 4.75 in., 5.5 in.
Sights: EasyView sights
Weight: 36.8 oz.
Caliber: .357 Mag., .45 Colt
Capacity: 6 rounds
Features: Made for those with larger hands ("grizzly paws"); checkered walnut 1860 Army grips; blued barrel and cylinder; blued, case-hardened frame; cylinder has numbered chambers
MSRP $659.00

SHORT STROKE SASS PRO NICKEL

Action: Revolver
Grips: Simulated ivory
Barrel: 4.75 in., 5.5 in.
Sights: Blade front
Weight: 36.8 oz.
Caliber: .357 Mag., .44 Mag.
Capacity: 6 rounds

Features: Single-action short-stroke SASS competition revolver; low, wide, and checkered hammer; custom-grade mainspring; wider rear channel Easy View sights; shortened hammer travel; mirror nickel finish
MSRP $909.00

STALLION

Action: SA revolver
Grips: Walnut
Barrel: 4.75 in., 5.5 in., 6.5 in.
Sights: Fixed, open
Weight: 32 oz.
Caliber: .22 LR, .22 LR/Mag.
Capacity: 6 or 10 round
Features: Case-hardened frame; brass or steel backstrap and trigger guard; blued finish; fluted cylinder
Stallion: . . . . $489.00–$579.00
Stallion Target: $639.00
Stallion 10-Shot: $529.00

TOP BREAK REVOLVERS

Action: SA revolver
Grips: Walnut or pearl-style
Barrel: 3.5 in., 5 in., 7 in.
Sights: Fixed, open
Weight: 40 oz.
Caliber: .45 Colt, .38 Spl., .44-40 Win.
Capacity: 6 rounds
Features: Full nickel plated steel or blued steel frame and blackstrap; case-hardened trigger guard; fluted cylinder
No. 3 Russian New Model blued frame: . . . . . . $1189.00–$1199.00
No. 3 Russian New Model full nickel-plating: $1599.00
1875 No. 3 2nd Model blued frame: $1179.00
1875 No. 3 2nd Model full nickel-plating: $1589.00

WALTHER CCP (CONCEALED CARRY PISTOL)

WALTHER CREED

WALTHER P22

WALTHER P99AS

WALTHER P99AS COMPACT

WALTHER PKK/S

WALTHER PPK/S .22

WALTHER PPQ M2 .45 ACP

CCP (CONCEALED CARRY PISTOL)

Action: Semiautomatic
Grips: Synthetic
Barrel: 3.54 in.
Sights: Adjustable
Weight: 22.33 oz.
Caliber: 9mm
Capacity: 8+1 rounds
Features: Available in black or stainless steel; interchangeable front sight with white dot; adjustable rear sight; reversible magazine release
Black: **$469.00**
Stainless: **$489.00**
Viridian Red Laser: **$499.00**

CREED

Action: Semiautomatic
Grips: None
Barrel: 4 in.
Sights: Three-dot, low profile
Weight: 26.6 oz.
Caliber: 9mm
Capacity: 16, 10 rounds
Features: Economically priced, polymer frame; DAO pre-set trigger pistol; firing pin and drop safeties; ambidextrous magazine release button; 1913 Picatinny rail
MSRP **$379.00**

P22

Action: DA/SA semiautomatic
Grips: Polymer
Barrel: 3.42 in., 5 in.
Sights: 3-dot adjustable low-profile
Weight: 17 oz., 22 oz.
Caliber: .22 LR
Capacity: 10 rounds
Features: Threaded barrel, interchangeable with target barrel; loaded chamber indicator; external slide stop; 3 safeties; two magazine styles; ergonomic grip; ambidextrous magazine release lever; available with integrated laser-set; available in black, nickel, and military finish; now available with laser, Target models with 5-in. barrels available in black, Flat Dark Earth, or nickel
MSRP . . . . **$319.00–$459.00**

P99AS

Action: DA semiautomatic
Grips: Black polymer frame and grips
Barrel: 4 in. stainless steel with Tenifer finish
Sights: Front and rear tritium night
Weight: 24 oz.–25.6 oz.
Caliber: 9mm, .40 S&W
Capacity: 15 (9mm) or 12 (.40 S&W) rounds
Features: The first pistol with a firing pin block combines advantages of a traditional DA pull with SA trigger and a decocking button safety integrated into slide, allowing users the ability to decock the striker, preventing inadvertent firing in both DA and SA mode
MSRP . . . . **starting at $629.00**

P99AS COMPACT

Action: Striker-fired semiautomatic
Grips: Polymer
Barrel: 3.5 in.
Sights: 3-dot adjustable low-profile
Weight: 20.8 oz.–22.4 oz.
Caliber: 9mm, .40 S&W
Capacity: 10 (9mm) or 8 (.40 S&W) rounds
Features: Flat-bottom magazine buttplate, finger rest magazine buttplate; molded with a Weaver-style rail; interchangeable backstraps; hammerless striker system and integral safety devices come standard
MSRP . . . . **starting at $629.00**

PPK AND PPK/S

Action: DA/SA semiautomatic
Grips: Polymer
Barrel: 3.3 in.
Sights: Fixed, open
Weight: 22.4 oz. (PPK), 24 oz. (PPK/S)
Caliber: .380 ACP
Capacity: 6 (PPK) or 7 (PPK/S) rounds
Features: Firing pin safety; manual safety with decocking function; double- and single-action trigger; extended beaver tail; nickel plated or blued finish
MSRP **$749.00**

PPK/S .22

Action: DA/SA semiautomatic
Grips: Polymer
Barrel: 3.3 in.
Sights: Fixed, open
Weight: 24 oz.
Caliber: .22 LR
Capacity: 10 rounds
Features: Manual safety; top strap waved to reduce glare; internal slide stop; iconic PPK/S frame; beaver tail extension; nickel plated or black finish
MSRP . . . . **$399.00–$429.00**

PPQ M2 .45 ACP

Action: Striker-fired semiautomatic
Grips: Ergonomic polymer
Barrel: 4.25 in.
Sights: Three dot polymer
Weight: 28 oz.
Caliber: .45 ACP
Capacity: 12 rounds
Features: Custom Picatinny accessory rail; quick-defense trigger; ergonomic, non-slip, cross-directional grip surface; three safeties; Tenifer coating on slide and barrel; front and rear slide serrations; ambidextrous slide stop
MSRP . . . . **$699.00–$749.00**

Walther Arms

WALTHER PPQ M2

WALTHER PPQ SC

WALTHER PPQ Q4 TAC

WALTHER PPS M2

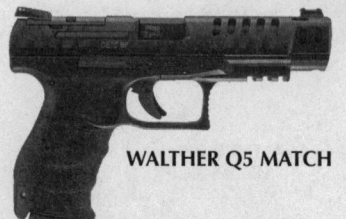

WALTHER Q5 MATCH

PPQ M2 9MM

Action: Striker-fired semiautomatic
Grips: Polymer
Barrel: 4 in., 4.1 in., 4.6 in., 5 in.
Sights: 3-dot adjustable low-profile
Weight: 24 oz. (9mm), 25.6 oz. (.40 S&W)
Caliber: 9mm
Capacity: 15 (9mm), 15/17 (9mm Navy SD) or 11 (.40 S&W) rounds
Features: Quick defense trigger; three safeties; ergonomic grip with checkered trigger guard; ambidextrous slide stop and magazine release button; Tenifer coated slide and barrel with matte finish
MSRP . . . . **$649.00–$749.00**

PPQ Q4 TAC

Action: Semiautomatic
Grips: Synthetic
Barrel: 4.6 in.
Sights: Fiber optic front sight, adjustable target rear
Weight: 26 oz.
Caliber: 9mm

Capacity: 15, 17 rounds
Features: Ambidextrous slide stop and mag release; texturing on the grip; wide trigger guard with serrations for additional purchase; ergonomic and finger-grooved grip; magazine with finger rest; adjustable target sight to the rear paired with an easy-find fiber optics front; interchangeable backstraps for a custom fit; threaded barrel for suppressor add-ons; slide has been milled to be optics ready
MSRP **$749.00**

PPQ SC

Action: Semiautomatic
Grips: Synthetic
Barrel: 3.5 in.
Sights: Three-dot, windage-adjustable rear
Weight: 21.2 oz.
Caliber: 9mm
Capacity: 10, 15 rounds
Features: Sub-Compact is easy to conceal; unique grip texturing; wide trigger guard with serrations on the front for extra purchase; accessory rail; low-profile snag-resistant sights; interchangeable backstraps; ambidextrous slide release; slide has a Tenifer coating
MSRP . . . . **$649.99–$699.00**

PPS M2

Action: Striker-fired semiautomatic

Grips: Ergonomic polymer
Barrel: 3.18 in.
Sights: Three dot metal
Weight: 21.1 oz.
Caliber: 9mm
Capacity: 6, 7, 8 rounds
Features: Front and rear slide serrations; smooth, light trigger; ergonomic, non-slip, cross-directional grip surface; cocking indicator; chamber viewport; slide stop; magazine release conveniently placed for thumb operation; three magazine options; LE (Law Enforcement) variation comes equipped with phosphoric sights and three magazines
MSRP . . . . **469.00–$699.00**

Q5 MATCH

Action: Semiautomatic
Grips: Synthetic
Barrel: 5 in.
Sights: Fiber optic front sight, adjustable target rear
Weight: 27.9 oz.
Caliber: 9mm
Capacity: 15 rounds
Features: Optics-ready slide; Picatinny rail; Walther ergonomic grip; ported slide; blue Quick Defense trigger; front and rear slide serrations; ambidextrous slide stop
Standard Match: **$1499.00**
PRO Match: **$1650.00**

Windham Weaponry

**WINDHAM WEAPONRY
300 BLACKOUT PISTOL**

300 BLACKOUT PISTOL

Action: Semiautomatic gas impingment system
Grips: Rubber

Barrel: 9 in.
Sights: None
Weight: 4 lb. 14 oz.
Caliber: .300 BLK

Capacity: Detachable box, 30+1 rounds
Features: Quick-detach swing swivel; 1:7 inch twist; Picatinny rail; hardcoat black anodize reciever finish with laser caliber identification; chrome-Lined barrel with A2-type flash suppressor
MSRP **$1081.00**

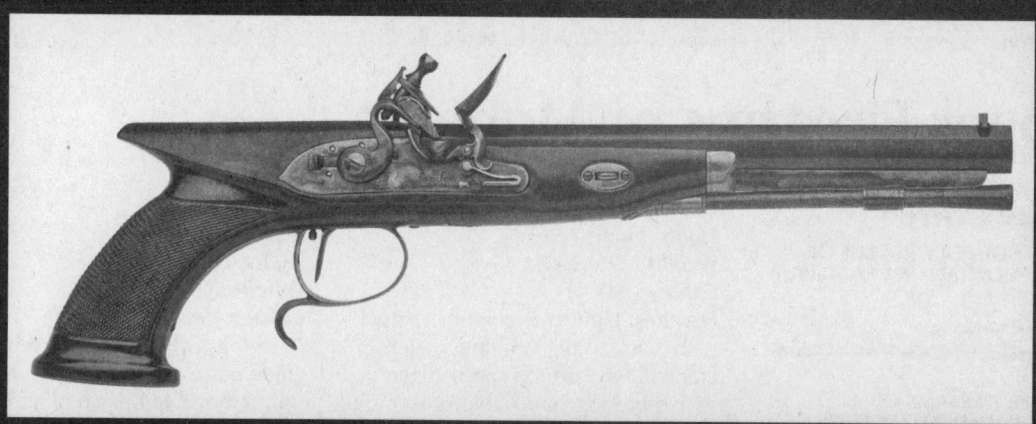

Cimarron Firearms

**CIMARRON FIREARMS
1851 NAVY**

1851 NAVY
Action: Revolver
Stock: Wood

Barrel: 7.5 in.
Sights: Front blade, groove
Weight: 2 lb. 11 oz.
Caliber: .36, .44
Features: Reproduction of the 1851 cap-and-ball revolver originally

known as the Percussion Peacemaker; frame is engraved and finished in a case-hardened old silver finish; walnut grips are checkered; barrel is octagonal
Oval triggerguard: . . $346.45–$446.45
**Laser engraved oval
 triggerguard**: $422.50
London:. $378.43

Cooper Firearms of Montana

**COOPER FIREARMS OF
MONTANA ML EXCALIBUR**

**COOPER FIREARMS OF
MONTANA MUZZLELOADER**

ML EXCALIBUR
Action: Bolt/inline
Stock: Composite

Barrel: 26 in.
Sights: None
Weight: 7 lb. 13 oz.
Caliber: .50
Features: Light gray composite stock with black spiderwebbing; match grade fluted barrel; Timney trigger; sealed breech; removable breech plug
MSRP. $1995.00

MUZZLELOADER
(CUSTOM SHOP)
Action: Bolt/inline

Stock: Wood
Barrel: N/A
Sights: None
Weight: N/A
Caliber: .50
Features: Wilson Arms 1:28 match grade barrel; Easton aluminum ramrod; removable breech plug; Timney trigger; available in Cooper's Classic, Custom Classic, Western Classic, and Schnabel configurations
MSRP. . . . . .POR

CVA (Connecticut Valley Arms)

CVA ACCURA MR

CVA ACCURA PR NITRIDE

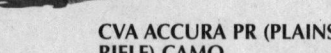

**CVA ACCURA PR (PLAINS
RIFLE) CAMO**

Black Nitride:. $493.50
Nitride Realtree Max-1 HD:. . . .$546.00

ACCURA MR
Lock: Break-action in-line
Stock: Synthetic
Barrel: 25 in.
Sights: Scope mount
Weight: 6 lb. 6 oz.
Bore/Caliber: .50
Features: Aluminum frame; quick release breech plug; trigger guard actuated breeching action; Bergara barrel; neutral center of gravity trigger; premium SoftTouch stock with rubber grip panels; WeatherGuard barrel finish on the stainless steel barrel; Realtree Max-1 or black stock finishes; Quake Claw sling included; DuraSight Dead-On scope mount

ACCURA PR (PLAINS
RIFLE) CAMO
Action: Break-action
Stock: Synthetic
Barrel: 28.in.
Sights: None
Weight: 6 lb. 14.4 oz.
Caliber: .50
Features: 416 stainless steel, fluted, nitride-treated Bergara barrel; break-action is easy opening; disassembly can be performed by removing a single screw; Quick Release breech plug; reversible hammer spur; adjustable trigger; Palm Saver ramrod; Quake Claw sling; CrushZone recoil pad; ambidextrous soft-touch stock; drilled and tapped for scope mounts; DuraSight DEAD-ON one-piece

mount; Realtree Max-1 camo; several available combo packages include a Konus scope and soft case
MSRP. . . . . $551.00–$701.00

ACCURA PR NITRIDE
Action: Break-action
Stock: Synthetic
Barrel: 25 in.
Sights: None
Weight: 7 lb. 2 oz.
Caliber: .50
Features: 416 stainless steel, fluted, nitride-treated Bergara barrel; break-action is easy opening; disassembly can be performed by removing a single screw; Quick Release breech plug; reversible hammer spur; adjustable trigger; Palm Saver ramrod; Quake Claw sling; CrushZone recoil pad; ambidextrous stock; drilled and tapped for scope mounts; DuraSight DEAD-ON one-piece mount
MSRP. . . . . $501.00–$650.00

BLACK POWDER

CVA (Connecticut Valley Arms

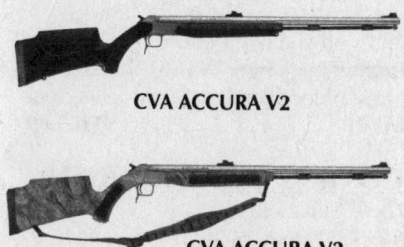

CVA ACCURA V2

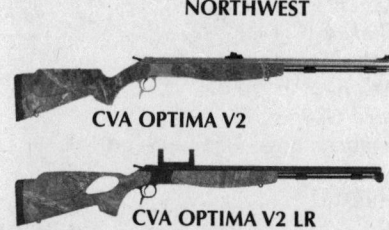

CVA ACCURA V2 NORTHWEST

CVA OPTIMA V2

CVA OPTIMA V2 LR

CVA WOLF

ACCURA V2

Lock: Break-action muzzleloading
Stock: Composite stock in standard or thumbhole
Barrel: 27 in.
Sights: DuraSight fiber optic
Weight: 7 lb. 5 oz.
Bore/Caliber: .50
Features: 416 stainless Bergara barrel; quick-release breech plug; CrushZone recoil pad; drilled and tapped for scope mount; SoftTouch coating and rubber grip panels; Quake Claw sling; with a variety of configuration choices, including standard or thumbhole stock, black or Realtree APG finishes, scope mount or fiber optic sights, black or stainless Nitride finished barrels
MSRP . . . . $563.00–$712.00

ACCURA V2 NORTHWEST

Lock: Break-action muzzleloading
Stock: Synthetic
Barrel: 27 in.
Sights: Fiber optics
Weight: 7 lb. 5 oz.

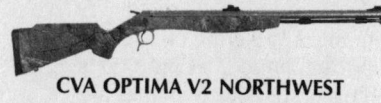

CVA OPTIMA V2 NORTHWEST

CVA WOLF NORTHWEST

Bore/Caliber: .50
Features: Meets open-breech/ignition requirements of Idaho, Oregan, and Washington; CrushZone recoil pad; quick release breech plug; standard stocks, in Realtree APG
MSRP $532.00

OPTIMA V2

Lock: Break-action muzzleloading
Stock: Realtree Xtra Green or black
Barrel: 26 in.
Sights: Fiber optic sights or mount
Weight: 6 lb. 10 oz.
Bore/Caliber: .50
Features: Modeled on Accura V2; stainless steel barrel; quick release breech plug; ambidextrous stock, thumbhole stock option; includes DuraSight Dead-On scope mount and ramrod
MSRP . . . . $303.00–$461.00

OPTIMA V2 LR

Action: Break-action
Stock: Synthetic
Barrel: 26 in.
Sights: None
Weight: 6 lb. 10 oz.
Caliber: .50
Features: Breech lever trigger-guard actuation; Optima's trigger and internal parts; finger-removable Quick-Release breech plug; CrushZone recoil pad; PalmSaver ramrod; reversible hammer spur; DuraSight Dead-On scope mount; stainless steel barrel or Nitride treated; Realtree Xtra Green stock
MSRP . . . . $371.00–$533.00

OPTIMA V2 NORTHWEST

Lock: Break-action muzzleloading
Stock: Synthetic
Barrel: 26 in.
Sights: Fiber optics
Weight: 6 lb. 10 oz.
Bore/Caliber: .50
Features: Meets open-breech/ignition requirements of Idaho, Oregan, and Washington; CrushZone recoil pad; quick release breech plug; stainless steel hardware and Realtree Xtra Green standard stock
MSRP $343.50

WOLF

Lock: Break-action in-line
Stock: Synthetic
Barrel: 24 in.
Sights: DuraSight fiber optic; includes 3–9x40mm duplex scope
Weight: 6 lb. 4 oz.
Bore/Caliber: .50
Features: Bullet-guiding muzzle; new tool-free QR breech plug system; ambidextrous compact or standard stock in black or camo; CrushZone recoil pad; reversible hammer spur; blued or stainless barrel
MSRP . . . . $303.00–$409.00

WOLF NORTHWEST

Lock: Break-action muzzleloading
Stock: Synthetic
Barrel: 24 in.
Sights: Fiber optics
Weight: 6 lb. 4 oz.
Bore/Caliber: .50
Features: Meets open-breech/ignition requirements of Idaho, Oregan, and Washington; CrushZone recoil pad; quick release breech plug
MSRP $236.50

BLACK POWDER

Davide Pedersoli & C.

DAVIDE PEDERSOLI 1763 LEGER (1766) CHARLEVILLE

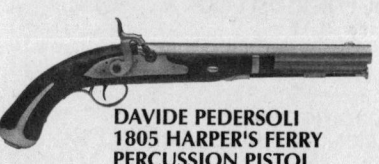

DAVIDE PEDERSOLI 1805 HARPER'S FERRY PERCUSSION PISTOL

1763 LEGER (1766) CHARLEVILLE

Action: Dropping block
Stock: Walnut
Barrel: 44.7 in.
Sights: Open
Weight: 10 lb. 2 oz.
Caliber: .69
Magazine: None
Features: Creedmoor sight; tunnel front sight; replica of French infantry musket
MSRP $1250.00

1805 HARPER'S FERRY PERCUSSION PISTOL

Lock: Percussion cap
Stock: American walnut
Barrel: 10.06 in.
Sights: Bead front
Weight: 2 lb. 10.6 oz.
Bore/Caliber: .54
Features: Brass furniture; smooth bore; chromed and satin finished barrel; old silver case hardened lock
MSRP $545.00

Davide Pedersoli & C.

1854 LORENZ INFANTRY RIFLE TYPE II
Action: Percussion
Stock: Walnut
Barrel: 37 in.
Sights: N/A
Weight: 9 lb.
Caliber: .54
Features: Conceived by the Austrian Lieutenant Joseph Lorenz; official production started in 1854, replacing the Augustin rifle among Austrian troops; used in Italy during the second Independence War, as well as in the Balkans; then largely exported to America, equipping both the Union and the Confederate armies, becoming one of the most used rifles during the American Civil War
MSRP $1650.00

1860 VOLUNTEER
Action: Percussion
Stock: Walnut
Barrel: 33 in.
Sights: Tunnel front, Creedmoor rear
Weight: 8 lb. 13 oz.
Caliber: .451
Features: The British N.R.A., for the first time, organized a national event held at Wimbledon in 1860, inspiring Pedersoli's Volunteer Rifle; broach rifled with an optimal twist for target shooting at 100-150 meters; oil-finished, hand-checkered stock
MSRP $1800.00

BAKER CAVALRY SHOTGUN
Lock: Percussion
Stock: Walnut
Barrel: 11.25 in.
Sights: None
Weight: 5 lb. 12 oz.
Bore/Caliber: 20 Ga.
Features: Single trigger back action, side-by-side shotgun; reproduces a gun made by London gunsmith Ezekiel Baker in 1850; case-hardened
MSRP $1220.00

BOUTET 1ER EMPIRE
Lock: Flintlock
Stock: Hardwood
Barrel: 10 in.
Sights: Fixed
Weight: 2 lb. 14 oz.
Bore/Caliber: .45
Features: Napoleon wrote with flattering appreciation about the style and prestige of the Boutet guns, which Pedersoli now proudly introduces

with fine checkering on sides; metal buttplate; ramrod has horn tip; single set trigger; on lock two lines are engraved with MANUF RE/a Versailles.
MSRP $1350.00

CONTINENTAL TARGET PISTOL
Action: Percussion, flintlock
Stock: Walnut
Barrel: 11 in.
Sights: Front, windage adjustable rear
Weight: 2 lb. 3 oz.
Caliber: .45, .44
Features: Reproduction of target pistol of Central European style; set trigger; octagonal barrel; chrome finished; .44-caliber is a smoothbore
Percussion: $560.00
Flintlock: $645.00

COOK & BROTHER ARTILLERY CARBINE
Lock: Caplock
Stock: Walnut
Barrel: 24 in.
Sights: None
Weight: 6 lb. 10 oz.
Bore/Caliber: .58
Features: Inspired by English model

guns; originally produced by Cook & Brother beginning in 1861; brass garnitures; blued barrel; case-hardened lock
MSRP $1165.00

COOK & BROTHER RIFLE
Lock: Muzzleloading
Stock: Walnut
Barrel: 33 in.
Chokes: IC, M, F
Sights: Fixed
Weight: 8 lb. 10 oz.
Bore/Gauge: .58
Features: Brass garnitures; brown colour barrel
MSRP $1250.00

DERRINGER PHILADELPHIA
Lock: Percussion
Stock: Walnut
Barrel: 3.06 in.
Sights: None
Weight: 8.6 oz.
Bore/Caliber: .45
Features: Originally manufactured by John Henry Derringer; brass furniture; case-hardened lock; original markings on the lock: Derringer/Philadelphia
MSRP $525.00

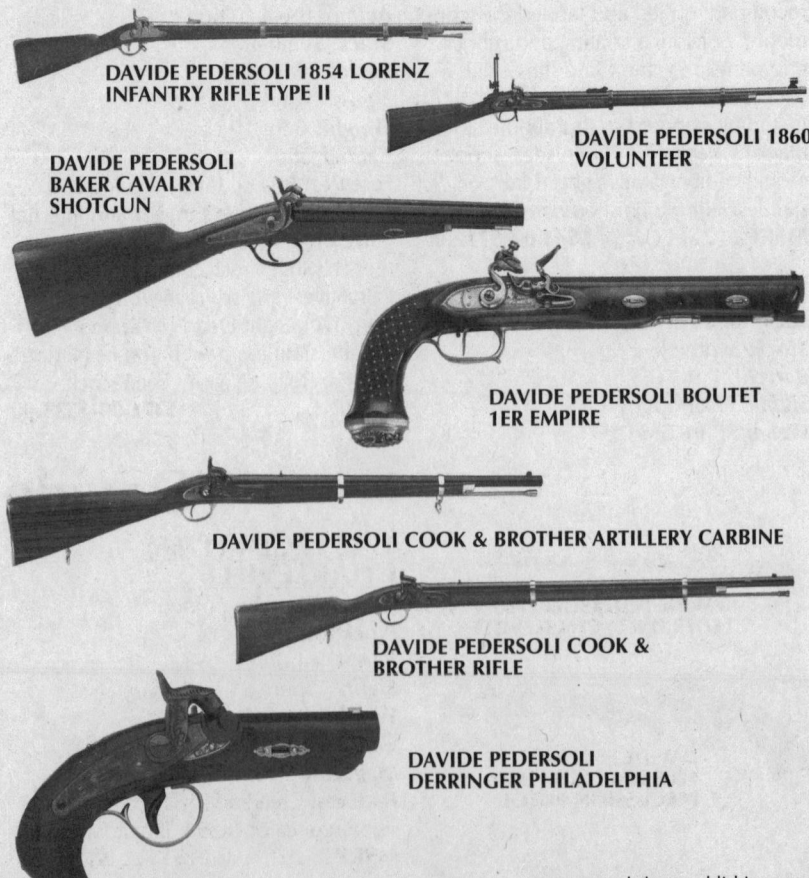

DAVIDE PEDERSOLI 1854 LORENZ INFANTRY RIFLE TYPE II

DAVIDE PEDERSOLI 1860 VOLUNTEER

DAVIDE PEDERSOLI BAKER CAVALRY SHOTGUN

DAVIDE PEDERSOLI BOUTET 1ER EMPIRE

DAVIDE PEDERSOLI COOK & BROTHER ARTILLERY CARBINE

DAVIDE PEDERSOLI COOK & BROTHER RIFLE

DAVIDE PEDERSOLI DERRINGER PHILADELPHIA

Davide Pedersoli & C.

DAVIDE PEDERSOLI ENFIELD 3 BAND P1853 RIFLE MUSKET

DAVIDE PEDERSOLI ENFIELD 3 BAND P1853 WHITWORTH WITH HEXAGONAL RIFLING

DAVIDE PEDERSOLI GIBBS SHORT RANGE RIFLE

DAVIDE PEDERSOLI GIBBS SHOTGUN

DAVIDE PEDERSOLI HAWKEN HUNTER RIFLE

DAVIDE PEDERSOLI HOWDAH HUNTER PISTOL

DAVIDE PEDERSOLI KODIAK EXPRESS MK VI

ENFIELD 3 BAND P1853 RIFLE MUSKET

Lock: Percussion
Stock: Walnut
Barrel: 39 in.
Sights: Adjustable rear
Weight: 8 lb. 13 oz.
Bore/Caliber: .577
Features: Ladder rear sight with a slider assembled on a base with steps; steel barrel bands; brass furniture; ramrod tip is shaped with characteristic jag slot; barrel is blued and lock case-hardened
MSRP $1250.00

ENFIELD 3 BAND P1853 WHITWORTH WITH HEXAGONAL RIFLING

Lock: Percussion cap
Stock: American walnut
Barrel: 36 in.
Sights: Creedmoor sight, tunnel front sight
Weight: 9 lb. 7.4 oz.
Bore/Caliber: .451
Features: Hammer-forged browned finish hexagonal barrel; lock parts with light colour case hardened finish
MSRP $1975.00

GIBBS SHORT RANGE RIFLE

Action: Percussion
Stock: Walnut
Barrel: 32 in.
Sights: Tunnel front, Creedmoor rear
Weight: 10 lb. 9.6 oz.
Caliber: .45
Features: Modeled on the original Gibbs; equipped with a barrel made for target shooting at 100-150 meters
MSRP $2025.00

GIBBS SHOTGUN

Lock: Percussion
Stock: Walnut

Barrel: 32.3 in.
Sights: None
Weight: 8 lb. 9 oz.
Bore/Caliber: 12 Ga.
Features: Octagonal to round barrel; case-hardened color-finished lock; grip and forend caps with ebony inserts; pistol grip stock
MSRP $1625.00

HAWKEN HUNTER RIFLE

Lock: Percussion, flintlock
Stock: Wood
Barrel: 28.4 in.
Chokes: IC, M, F
Sights: Adjustable rear, fixed front
Weight: 8 lb. 10 oz.
Bore/Gauge: .50, .54
Features: Blade front sight and a dovetail slot to equip it with the rear sight; ghost ring aperture sight is mounted to the tang; American walnut stock features a microcell thick butt plate; double set triggers
Percussion: $755.00
Percussion left-hand: $785.00
Flintlock: $815.00
Flintlock left-hand: $840.00

HOWDAH HUNTER PISTOL

Lock: Caplock
Stock: Walnut
Barrel: 11.25 in.
Sights: None
Weight: 5 lb. 1 oz.
Bore/Caliber: .45 LC, .45/.410, .50, .58
Features: Engraved locks with wild animal scenes; case-hardened color finish; checkered walnut pistol grip with steel butt cap
Shotgun: $870.00
.50-caliber: $980.00
.58-caliber: $995.00
Combo 20-gauge/.50-
caliber: $980.00

KODIAK EXPRESS MK VI

Lock: Percussion
Stock: Hardwood
Barrel: 24.25 in.
Sights: Creedmore
Weight: 10 lb. 2 oz.
Bore/Caliber: .50, .54, .58
Features: A very manageable gun, perfectly balanced; particularly suitable for wild boar hunting; practical rubber buttplate; half pistol grip stock; equipped with ghost sights
MSRP $1460.00

Davide Pedersoli & C.

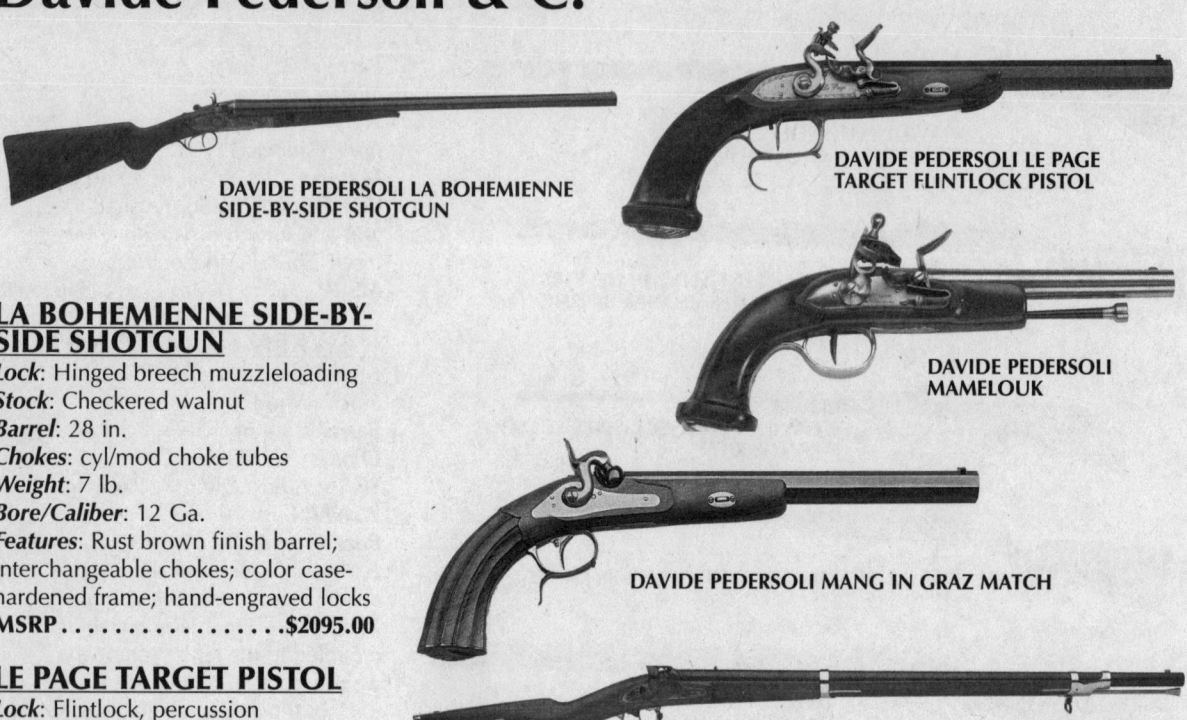

DAVIDE PEDERSOLI LA BOHEMIENNE SIDE-BY-SIDE SHOTGUN

DAVIDE PEDERSOLI LE PAGE TARGET FLINTLOCK PISTOL

DAVIDE PEDERSOLI MAMELOUK

DAVIDE PEDERSOLI MANG IN GRAZ MATCH

DAVIDE PEDERSOLI MISSISSIPPI US MODEL 1841

DAVIDE PEDERSOLI MORTIMER TARGET RIFLE

DAVIDE PEDERSOLI PLAINS SHOTGUN "THE FAST BACK VACTION"

LA BOHEMIENNE SIDE-BY-SIDE SHOTGUN

Lock: Hinged breech muzzleloading
Stock: Checkered walnut
Barrel: 28 in.
Chokes: cyl/mod choke tubes
Weight: 7 lb.
Bore/Caliber: 12 Ga.
Features: Rust brown finish barrel; interchangeable chokes; color case-hardened frame; hand-engraved locks
MSRP $2095.00

LE PAGE TARGET PISTOL

Lock: Flintlock, percussion
Stock: Walnut
Barrel: 10.5 in.
Sights: Adjustable
Weight: 2 lb. 10 oz.
Bore/Caliber: .31, .36, .44 (percussion); .44, .45 (flintlock)
Features: Smoothbore .45 available; adjustable single-set trigger; brightly polished lock with a roller frizzen spring
Percussion: $955.00
Flintlock: $1270.00

MAMELOUK

Lock: Flintlock
Stock: Hardwood
Barrel: 7.6 in.
Sights: Fixed
Weight: 1 lb. 10 oz.
Bore/Caliber: N/A
Features: Like all the firearms equipping Napoleon's Imperial Guards, the Mameluke pistols were made at the Manufacture of Versailles under the technical management of Nicolas-Noël Boutet; the trigger guard, buttcap, screw washers of the lock, and ramrod tip are brass
MSRP $700.00

MANG IN GRAZ MATCH

Lock: Percussion
Stock: Walnut
Barrel: 11.4 in.
Sights: Fixed
Weight: 2 lb. 10 oz.
Bore/Caliber: .38, .44
Features: Fluted grip; octagonal, rifled barrel in brown rust finish; adjustable single set trigger; breech plug shows a typical mask of the period; barrel and tang enriched with gold inlays
MSRP $1850.00

MISSISSIPPI US MODEL 1841

Lock: Percussion
Stock: Walnut
Barrel: 33 in.
Sights: Open rear
Weight: 9 lb. 8 oz.
Bore/Caliber: .54, .58
Features: Considered the best-looking ordnance rifle of its period; brass furniture; browned barrel; notched rear sight; case-hardened lock; ramrod with brass tip
MSRP $1280.00

MORTIMER TARGET RIFLE

Lock: Flintlock
Stock: English-style European walnut
Barrel: 36.4 in.
Sights: Target
Weight: 10 lb. 2 oz.
Bore/Caliber: .54
Features: Case-colored lock; stock has cheekpiece and hand checkering; 7-groove barrel
MSRP $1930.00

PLAINS SHOTGUN "THE FAST BACK ACTION"

Lock: Caplock
Stock: Walnut
Barrel: 27.5 in., 28.5 in.
Sights: None
Weight: 7 lb. 5 oz.–7 lb. 8 oz.
Bore/Caliber: 12, 20 Ga.
Features: Single trigger; side-by-side shotgun; fast second shot, thanks to back action lock reducing minor residues of black powder in lock parts
MSRP $1310.00

Davide Pedersoli & C.

DAVIDE PEDERSOLI RICHMOND 1862, TYPE III

DAVIDE PEDERSOLI SIDE-BY-SIDE SHOTGUN CLASSIC STANDARD, DELUXE

DAVIDE PEDERSOLI SPRINGFIELD MODEL 1861 US

DAVIDE PEDERSOLI SWISS MATCH STANDARD FLINTLOCK

DAVIDE PEDERSOLI TATHAM & EGG PISTOL

DAVIDE PEDERSOLI TRADITIONAL HAWKEN TARGET RIFLE

DAVIDE PEDERSOLI ZOUAVE US MODEL 1863

RICHMOND 1862, TYPE III

Lock: Percussion
Stock: Walnut
Barrel: 39.75 in.
Sights: None
Weight: 9 lb. 14 oz.
Bore/Caliber: .58
Features: Manufactured based on the U.S. 1855 Model with the Maynard tape ignition system; except for the lock's profile, the brass buttplate, and the stock nose cap, the gun's appearance resembles the U.S. Model 1861
MSRP. **$1190.00**

SIDE-BY-SIDE SHOTGUN CLASSIC, CLASSIC EXTRA DELUXE

Action: Percussion
Stock: Walnut
Barrel: 28.5 in.
Sights: Brass bead
Weight: 7 lb.
Caliber: 12 ga.
Features: Standard has a walnut stock, case-hardened receiver, and blued barrels; deluxe has wood, scroll-engraved receiver in a coin finish and rust-brown barrels
Classic: . . . . **$930.00–$1095.00**
Extra Deluxe: **$4860.00**

SPRINGFIELD MODEL 1861 US

Lock: Caplock
Stock: Walnut

Barrel: 40 in.
Sights: None
Weight: 9 lb. 14 oz.
Bore/Caliber: .58
Features: More efficient than earlier smooth bored muskets used by both sides in the American Civil War; satin finish barrel; stock with three bands; coin-colored finish on the steel furniture
MSRP. **$1225.00**

SWISS MATCH STANDARD FLINTLOCK

Lock: Flintlock
Stock: Walnut
Barrel: 30.8 in.
Sights: Adjustable
Weight: 16 lb. 5 oz.
Bore/Caliber: .40
Features: Octagonal conical profile barrel with rust brown finish; lock is case-hardened; steel ramrod; double-set trigger; steel hook buttplate
MSRP. **$3465.00**

TATHAM & EGG PISTOL

Lock: Flintlock
Stock: Walnut
Barrel: 10.06 in.
Sights: Adjustable rear
Weight: 2 lb. 6.7 oz.
Bore/Caliber: .45 smooth
Features: Ergonomic grip; set trigger; PMG-quality trigger; case-hardened metal parts
MSRP. **$1360.00**

TRADITIONAL HAWKEN TARGET RIFLE

Lock: Percussion, flintlock
Stock: Wood
Barrel: 28.4 in.
Chokes: IC, M, F
Sights: Adjustable rear, fixed front
Weight: 8 lb. 10 oz.
Bore/Gauge: .50, .54
Features: Double set trigger; adjustable buckhorn rear sight; American walnut stock is enriched with a brass patch box; left-handed version available
Percussion: **$710.00**
Percussion left-hand: **$740.00**
Flintlock: **$765.00**
Flintlock left-hand: **$785.00**

ZOUAVE US MODEL 1863

Lock: Percussion
Stock: Hardwood
Barrel: 33 in.
Sights: Front, rear
Weight: 9 lb. 4 oz.
Bore/Caliber: .58
Features: Intended for the U.S. Artillery Department and never distributed to any Civil War army division; features brass furnitures; ramrod with a tulip tip; three-leaf rear sight; two sling swivels; the lock shows the Eagle stamp and the U.S. letters in front of the hammer
MSRP. **$1250.00**

Dixie Gun Works

DIXIE GUN WORKS 1853 ENFIELD THREE-BAND

DIXIE GUN WORKS PEDERSOLI SCREW BARREL PISTOL

DIXIE GUN WORKS SHARPS NEW MODEL 1859 MILITARY CARBINE

DIXIE GUN WORKS SPANISH MUSKET

1853 ENFIELD THREE-BAND RIFLE MUSKET

Lock: Traditional caplock
Stock: Walnut
Barrel: 39 in.
Sights: Fixed
Weight: 10 lb. 4 oz.
Bore/Caliber: .58
Features: Color case-hardened lock; single trigger; single swivels; steel ramrod
Smoothbore: $750.00
Rifled: $895.00

PEDERSOLI SCREW BARREL PISTOL

Lock: Traditional caplock
Stock: European walnut
Barrel: 3 in.
Sights: None
Weight: 12 oz.
Bore/Caliber: .44
Features: Color case-hardened lock; single folding trigger; combination nipple/barrel wrench included
MSRP. $225.00

SHARPS NEW MODEL 1859 MILITARY CARBINE

Lock: Dropping block
Stock: Walnut
Barrel: 22 in.
Sights: Adjustable open
Weight: 8 lb.
Bore/Caliber: .54
Features: Steel furniture; color case-hardened; single trigger; single barrel band; saddle bar with ring
MSRP. $1400.00

SPANISH MUSKET

Lock: Flintlock muzzleloading
Stock: Full, European walnut 56 in.
Barrel: 44.75 in.
Sights: Steel stud front
Weight: 10 lb.
Bore/Caliber: .68 round ball
Features: Brass buttplate, trigger guard, and barrel bands; bright steel sideplates; steel ramrod
MSRP. $1400.00

EMF Company, Inc.

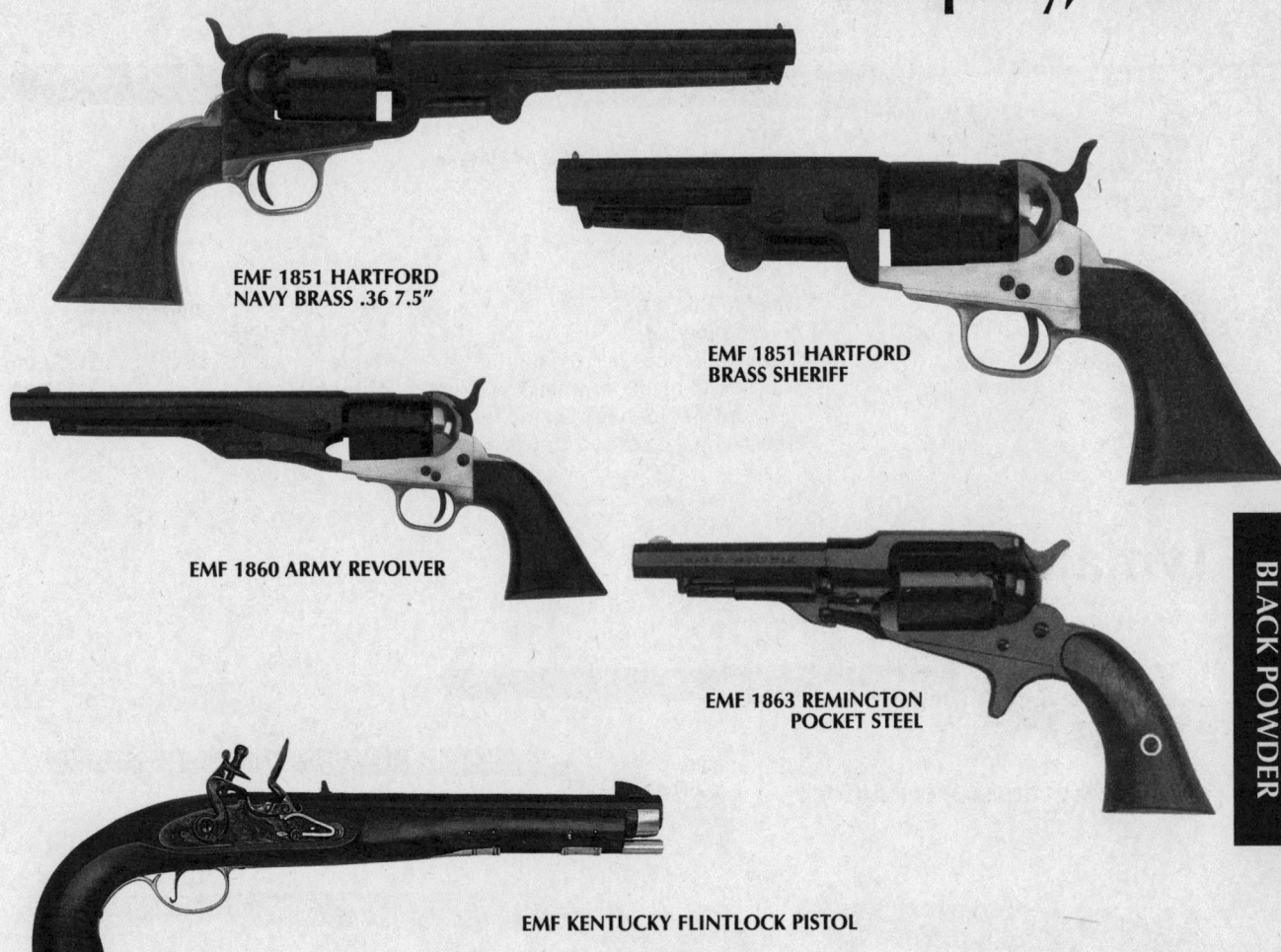

EMF 1851 HARTFORD NAVY BRASS .36 7.5"

EMF 1851 HARTFORD BRASS SHERIFF

EMF 1860 ARMY REVOLVER

EMF 1863 REMINGTON POCKET STEEL

EMF KENTUCKY FLINTLOCK PISTOL

BLACK POWDER

1851 HARTFORD NAVY BRASS

Lock: Caplock revolver
Stock: Walnut
Barrel: 7.5 in.
Sights: Fixed
Weight: 40 oz.
Bore/Caliber: .36, .44
Features: Brass, case-hardened stainless steel frame
MSRP **$280.00**

1851 HARTFORD BRASS SHERIFF

Lock: Caplock revolver
Stock: Walnut
Barrel: 5.5 in.
Sights: None
Weight: 32 oz.
Bore/Caliber: .380 Blank
Features: Brass, case-hardened stainless steel frame; blued barrel
MSRP **$280.00**

1860 ARMY REVOLVER

Lock: Caplock revolver
Stock: Walnut
Barrel: 8 in.
Sights: Fixed
Weight: 41.6 oz.
Bore/Caliber: .44
Features: Case-hardened frame; blued barrel
Brass: **$330.00**
Case-hardened: **$360.00**
Old West steel: **$380.00**
Steel/Ultra Ivory: **$390.00**
Old Silver: **$415.00**
London: **$370.00**

1863 REMINGTON POCKET STEEL

Lock: Caplock revolver
Stock: Walnut
Barrel: 3.5 in.
Sights: Fixed
Weight: 21 oz.
Bore/Caliber: .36
Features: Steel frame, blued barrel
MSRP **$370.00**

KENTUCKY PISTOL

Lock: Flintlock
Stock: Walnut
Barrel: 10.375 in.
Sights: Fixed
Weight: 37 oz.
Bore/Caliber: .45, .50
Features: Classic American pistol during the American Revolution and a favorite of pioneers; case-hardened frame; octagonal rifled blued barrel, polished brass fittings
Percussion: . . . . . . **$435.00–$507.00**
Flintlock: . . . . **$410.00–$500.00**

EMF Company, Inc.

EMF MISSOURI RIVER HAWKEN

MISSOURI RIVER HAWKEN

Lock: Caplock muzzleloading
Stock: Maple or walnut
Barrel: 30 in.
Sights: Open

Weight: 9 lb. 4 oz.
Bore/Caliber: .45, .50
Features: Replica percussion rifle; available in maple or walnut stock in rust brown color finish; barrel features an octagonal cross-section; case-hard-ened color lock; equipped with a double-set trigger
Maple: $1377.00
Walnut: $1230.00

Lyman

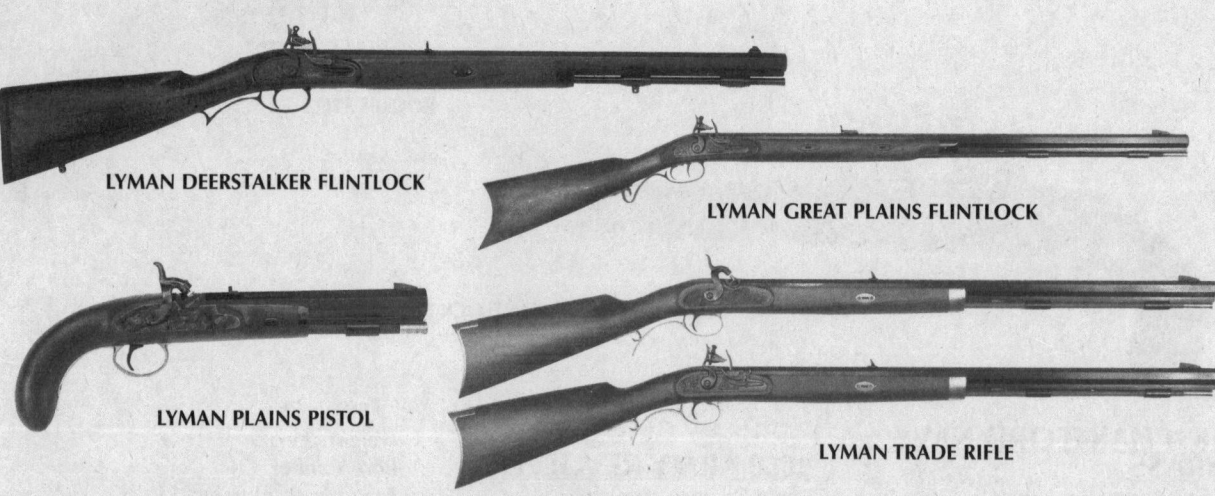

LYMAN DEERSTALKER FLINTLOCK

LYMAN GREAT PLAINS FLINTLOCK

LYMAN PLAINS PISTOL

LYMAN TRADE RIFLE

DEERSTALKER RIFLE

Lock: Traditional cap or flint
Stock: Walnut
Barrel: 24 in.
Sights: Fiber optic front and rear
Weight: 10 lb. 6 oz.
Bore/Caliber: .50, .54
Features: Quiet single trigger; metal blackened to avoid glare; black rubber recoil pad; left-hand available
MSRP. . . . . $599.95–$699.95

GREAT PLAINS RIFLE

Lock: Traditional cap or flint
Stock: Walnut
Barrel: 32 in.
Sights: Adjustable open
Weight: 11 lb. 10 oz.

Bore/Caliber: .50, .54
Features: Double-set triggers; Hawken style percussion "snail" with clean-out screw; separate ram-rod entry thimble and nose cap; left-hand available
MSRP. . . . . $669.95–$899.95

PLAINS PISTOL

Lock: Percussion, flintlock
Stock: Walnut
Barrel: 6 in.
Sights: Fixed
Weight: 3 lb. 2 oz.
Bore/Caliber: .50, .54
Features: Blackened iron furni-ture; polished brass trigger guard and ramrod tips; hooked patent breech takes down quickly for easy cleaning

Percussion: $426.25
Percussion kit .50-caliber: . . . $355.25

TRADE RIFLE

Lock: Traditional cap or flint
Stock: Walnut
Barrel: 28 in.
Sights: Adjustable open
Weight: 10 lb. 13 oz.
Bore/Caliber: .50, .54
Features: Brass furniture; originally developed for the early Indian fur trade
MSRP. . . . . $599.95–$649.95

Shiloh Rifle

SHILOH RIFLE 1874 CREEDMOOR TARGET RIFLE

SHILOH RIFLE 1874 QUIGLEY

SHILOH RIFLE 1877 #1 SHILOH
ENGLISH RIFLE

1874 CREEDMOOR TARGET RIFLE

Lock: Blackpowder cartridge
Stock: Walnut
Barrel: 32 in.
Sights: V aiming rear; blade front
Weight: 9 lb.
Bore/Caliber: All popular black powder cartridges from .38-55 to .50-90
Features: Pistol grip; single trigger; AA finish on American black walnut; polished barrel; octagon barrel; pewter tip
MSRP $3105.00

1874 QUIGLEY

Lock: Falling block
Stock: Walnut
Barrel: 34 in.
Sights: Semi buckhorn rear, midrange vernier tang, #111 globe aperture front
Weight: 12 lb. 8 oz.
Bore/Caliber: .45-70 Govt. or .45-110
Features: Military buttstock; patchbox; heavy octagonal barrel; pewter tip; Hartford collars; double set triggers; antique or standard color finish; gold inlay initials in gold oval
MSRP $3533.00

1877 #1 SHILOH ENGLISH RIFLE

Lock: Muzzleloading
Stock: Wood
Barrel: 26 in.–34 in.
Sights: Adjustable
Weight: N/A
Bore/Caliber: .38-55, .40-50BN, .40-50ST, .40-65, .40-70ST, .40-70BN, .40-90BN, .45-70, .45-90, .45-100
Features: Standard pistol grip; standard forearm; standard color cased; full or semi buckhorn rear sight; blade front sight; single trigger
MSRP $2250.00

Taylor's & Co. Firearms

TAYLOR'S & CO. 1842 SMOOTHBORE MUSKET

TAYLOR'S & CO. 1847 WALKER

1842 SMOOTHBORE MUSKET

Lock: Percussion
Stock: Walnut
Barrel: 42 in.
Sights: Military style
Weight: 9 lb. 12 oz.
Bore/Caliber: .69

Features: The Springfield replica has all the features of the original, including a one-piece, oil-finished walnut stock; original-style barrel bands; and completely interchangeable parts; the percussion lock has a V-style mainspring; features the lock with stamping noting 1842 and Springfield; NSSA approved, with certificate of authenticity and a brass medallion

featuring the model and serial number
Smoothbore: $1034.00

1847 WALKER

Lock: Caplock revolver
Stock: Walnut
Barrel: 9 in.
Sights: Fixed
Weight: 4 lb. 12 oz.
Bore/Caliber: .44
Features: Blued finish; round barrel
Antique finish: $599.00
Case-hardened frame /blued: $473.00
Charcoal blue finish: $559.00
Kit: $416.00

Taylor's & Co. Firearms

TAYLOR'S & CO. 1848 DRAGOONS

TAYLOR'S & CO. LE MAT CAVALRY

1848 DRAGOONS

Lock: Caplock revolver
Stock: Walnut
Barrel: 7.5 in.
Sights: Fixed
Weight: 4 lb.–4 lb. 14 oz.
Bore/Caliber: .44
Features: First used by the U.S. Army's Mounted Rifles 1st Cavalry in 1833 and they went on to see considerable use during the 1850 and during the Civil War; blued finish; six-round capacity; available in 1st, 2nd, and 3rd models, as well as the Whitney variation

1st, 2nd, 3rd: $465.00
Whitneyville: $473.00

LE MAT CAVALRY

Lock: Caplock revolver
Stock: Walnut
Barrel: 8 in.
Sights: Fixed
Weight: 5 lb.
Bore/Caliber: .44 or 20 Ga.
Features: Blued steel finish; nine-shot .44 caliber revolver with a 20 Ga. single-shot barrel was a favorite among Confederate cavalry troops; case-hardened hammer and trigger; lanyard ring; trigger guard with spur

MSRP $1170.00

Thompson/Center Arms

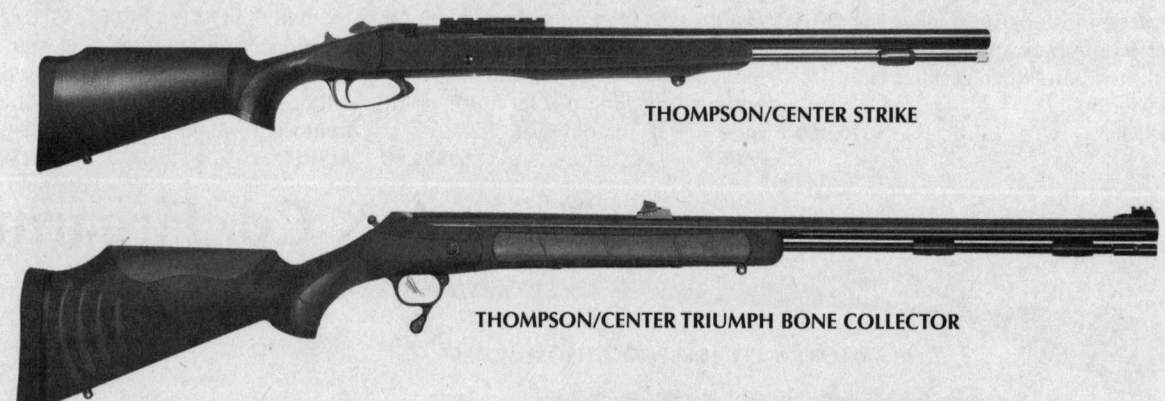

THOMPSON/CENTER STRIKE

THOMPSON/CENTER TRIUMPH BONE COLLECTOR

STRIKE

Lock: Adapt Breech system
Stock: Composite or walnut
Barrel: 24 in.
Sights: None
Weight: 7 lb. 8 oz.
Bore/Caliber: .50
Features: The Adapt Breech system moves the threads to the outside of the barrel, eliminating seized breech plugs and simplifying the cleaning process; Armornite corrosion-protectant metal finish on both inside and outside of barrel; Stealth Striker ambidextrous cocking system; match-grade trigger; finishes include black composite, walnut, or composite G2 camo

MSRP . . . . $499.00–$599.00

TRIUMPH BONE COLLECTOR

Lock: In-line
Stock: Composite, black or Realtree AP HD camo
Barrel: 28 in.
Sights: Adjustable fiber optic
Weight: 6 lb. 8 oz.
Bore/Caliber: .50
Features: Blued, stainless, and weather shield finish; speed breech XT

MSRP . . . . $638.00–$720.00

Traditions Firearms

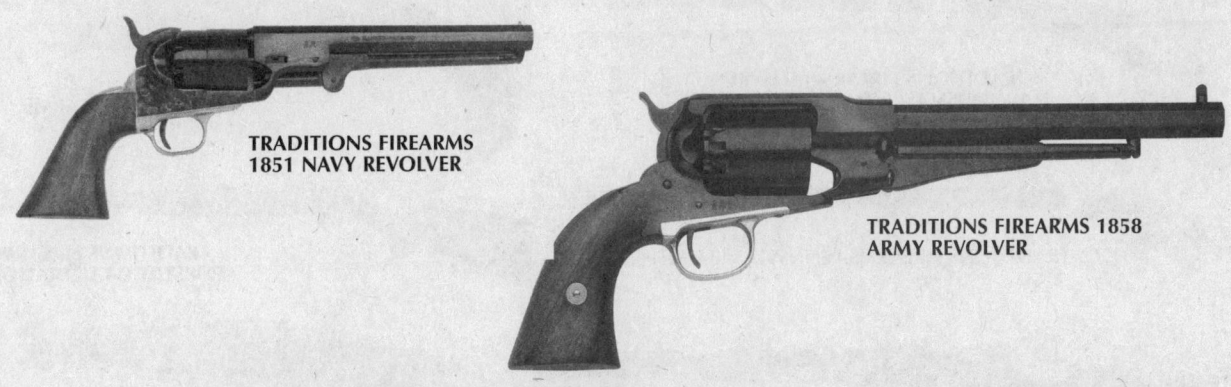

TRADITIONS FIREARMS 1851 NAVY REVOLVER

TRADITIONS FIREARMS 1858 ARMY REVOLVER

TRADITIONS FIREARMS 1860 ARMY REVOLVER

TRADITIONS FIREARMS BUCKSTALKER

TRADITIONS FIREARMS DEERHUNTER RIFLE

1860 ARMY REVOLVER
Lock: Caplock
Stock: Simulated ivory, walnut
Barrel: 8 in.
Sights: Fixed
Weight: 2 lb. 12 oz.
Bore/Caliber: .44
Features: Blued barrel; steel frame; brass guard; hammer/blade sights
MSRP . . . . $289.00–$349.00

BUCKSTALKER
Lock: Break-action muzzleloading
Stock: Synthetic
Barrel: 24 in.
Sights: Tru-Glo fiber optics
Weight: 7 lb. 8 oz.
Bore/Caliber: .50
Features: Dual safety system; nickel guard coating; synthetic black or G1 Vista camo stock; nickel or blued finish barrel; Monte Carlo stock; drilled and tapped for a scope; sling swivel studs
MSRP . . . . $219.00–$369.00

DEERHUNTER RIFLE
Lock: Traditional cap or flint
Stock: Synthetic or hardwood
Barrel: 24 in.
Sights: Lite Optic adjustable
Weight: 6 lb.
Bore/Caliber: .32, .50, .54
Features: Octagonal performance barrels; blued or nickel barrel finish; percussion models are drilled and tapped to accept scope mounts; non-slip recoil pad; stock comes in black synthetic, Mossy Oak Tree Stand camo, or hardwood
MSRP . . . . $269.00–$399.00

1851 NAVY REVOLVER
Lock: Caplock revolver
Stock: Walnut
Barrel: 7.5 in.
Sights: Fixed
Weight: 2 lb. 8 oz.
Bore/Caliber: .44
Features: Octagonal barrel and lever-style loader; brass, antiqued, or old silver frame and guard
MSRP . . . . $249.00–$429.00

1858 ARMY REVOLVER
Lock: Caplock
Stock: Walnut
Barrel: 8 in.
Sights: Fixed
Weight: 2 lb. 12 oz.
Bore/Caliber: .44
Features: Octagonal barrel and lever style loader; steel, brass, or stainless steel frame and guard; top strap and post sights
MSRP . . . . $289.00–$359.00

Traditions Firearms

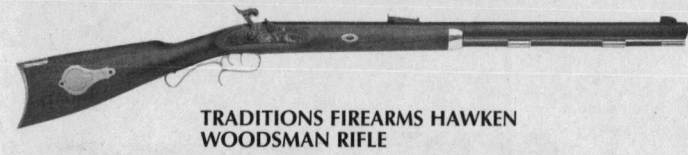

TRADITIONS FIREARMS HAWKEN WOODSMAN RIFLE

TRADITIONS FIREARMS KENTUCKY PISTOL

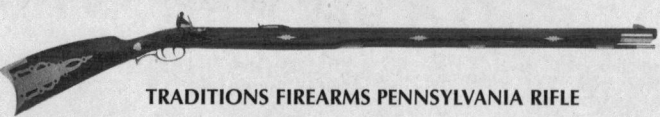

TRADITIONS FIREARMS PENNSYLVANIA RIFLE

TRADITIONS FIREARMS PURSUIT G4 ULTRALIGHT

TRADITIONS FIREARMS TRACKER 209

TRADITIONS FIREARMS TRAPPER PISTOL

TRADITIONS FIREARMS VORTEK STRIKERFIRE

HAWKEN WOODSMAN RIFLE

Lock: Traditional cap or flint
Stock: Hardwood
Barrel: 28 in.
Sights: Adjustable rear hunting
Weight: 7 lb. 13 oz.
Bore/Caliber: .50
Features: Hooked breech for easy barrel removal; double-set triggers in an oversized glove-fitting trigger guard; inletted solid brass patch box; left-hand model available; octagonal blued barrel
Flintlock: **$544.00**
Percussion: **$499.00**

KENTUCKY PISTOL

Lock: Traditional caplock
Stock: Hardwood
Barrel: 10 in.
Sights: Fixed
Weight: 2 lb. 8 oz.
Bore/Caliber: .50
Features: Brass furniture; case-colored sidelock and brass ramrod thimble
MSRP **$254.00**

PENNSYLVANIA RIFLE

Lock: Traditional cap or flint
Stock: Walnut
Barrel: 20 in.
Sights: Adjustable primitive style rear
Weight: 8 lb. 8 oz.
Bore/Caliber: .50
Features: Brass stock inlay ornamentation and toe plate; cheekpiece; solid brass patch box
Flintlock: **$865.00**
Percussion: **$834.00**

PURSUIT G4 ULTRALIGHT

Lock: Muzzleloading
Stock: Synthetic
Barrel: 26 in.
Chokes: IC, M, F
Sights: Fixed front, adjustable rear
Weight: 5 lb. 12 oz.
Bore/Gauge: .50
Features: Wider forend for better grip and hand position; Accelerator Breech Plug; Ultralight Chromoly Tapered, Fluted Barrel with Premium CeraKote Finish; LT-1 Alloy Frame; dual safety system - internal hammer block safety and trigger block safety; speed load system; Quick-T Ramrod Handle; soft touch camo stocks; Quick Relief Recoil Pad; Williams Fiber Optic Metal Sights; fast action release button; 1:28" twist rifling; extended ambidextrous hammer extension; drilled and tapped for a scope; sling swivel studs; 209 shotgun primer ignition; solid aluminum ramrod
MSRP . . . . **$389.00–$486.00**

TRACKER 209

Lock: In-line
Stock: Synthetic, camo
Barrel: 22 in.
Sights: Light optic adjustable
Weight: 6 lb. 8 oz.
Bore/Caliber: .50
Features: Removable 209 primer ignition; projectile alignment system; in-line bolt with a quiet thumb safety; removable breech plug system; rugged synthetic ramrod
MSRP **$184.00**

TRAPPER PISTOL

Lock: Traditional cap or flint
Stock: Hardwood
Barrel: 9.75 in.
Sights: Primitive-style adjustable rear
Weight: 2 lb. 14 oz.
Bore/Caliber: .50
Features: Octagonal blued barrel; double set triggers
Flintlock: **$385.00**
Percussion: **$344.00**

VORTEK STRIKERFIRE

Lock: Break-action muzzleloading
Stock: Soft Touch synthetic
Barrel: 28 in.
Sights: Fiber optic
Weight: N/A
Bore/Caliber: .50
Features: This patent-pending rifle takes in-line muzzleloaders to the next level by taking away the external hammer and using an internal StrikerFire System; to cock the gun, simply slide the striker button forward until it locks and fire; the recessed de-cocking buttons allows for quick and quiet de-cocking of the firearm and the gun is also equipped with an automatic de-cocking mechanism—when the gun is opened, it is automatically de-cocked; also includes: two-stage trigger; CeraKote finish; Realtree Xtra, black, Mossy Oak Break-Up Country; most options available with 3-9x40mm Traditions Duplex scopes
MSRP: . . . . **$464.00–$699.00**

BLACK POWDER

Traditions Firearms

VORTEK ULTRALIGHT
Lock: Hinged breech muzzleloading
Stock: Synthetic black Hogue over-mold, Realtree AP camo, or Reaper Buck camo
Barrel: 28 in.
Sights: Fixed, green
Weight: 6 lb. 4 oz.
Bore/Caliber: .50

TRADITIONS FIREARMS VORTEK ULTRALIGHT

Features: Drop-out trigger assembly; recoil pad; 3-pound factory trigger; frame and barrel have CeraKote finish
MSRP . . . . **$464.00–$529.00**

Uberti

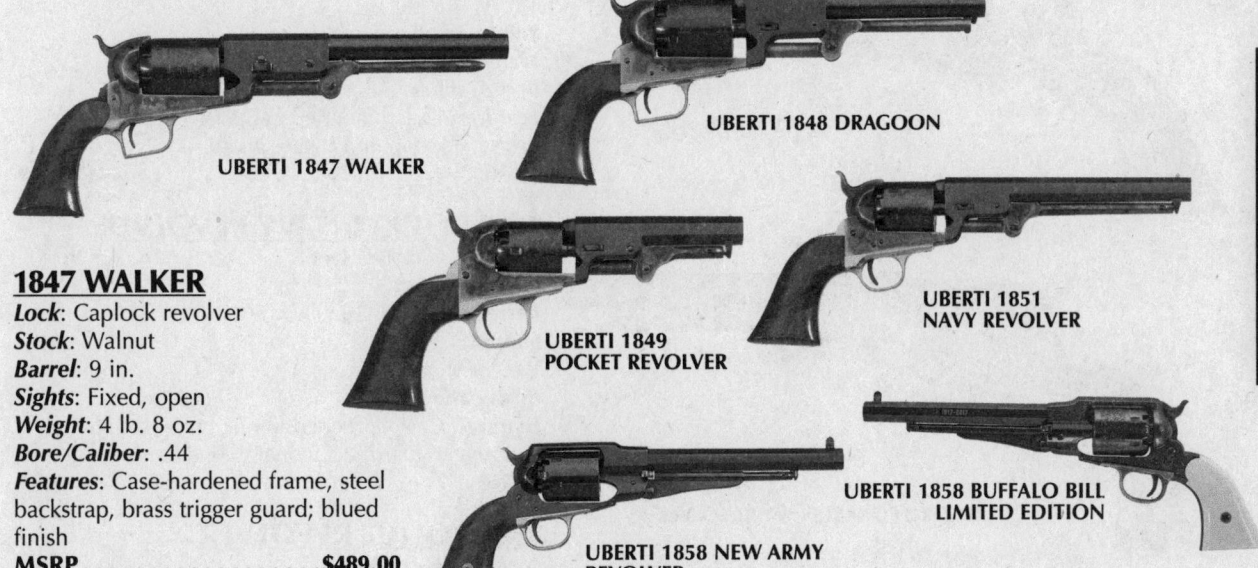

UBERTI 1847 WALKER

UBERTI 1848 DRAGOON

UBERTI 1849 POCKET REVOLVER

UBERTI 1851 NAVY REVOLVER

UBERTI 1858 NEW ARMY REVOLVER

UBERTI 1858 BUFFALO BILL LIMITED EDITION

1847 WALKER
Lock: Caplock revolver
Stock: Walnut
Barrel: 9 in.
Sights: Fixed, open
Weight: 4 lb. 8 oz.
Bore/Caliber: .44
Features: Case-hardened frame, steel backstrap, brass trigger guard; blued finish
MSRP **$489.00**

1848 DRAGOON
Lock: Caplock revolver
Stock: Walnut
Barrel: 7.5 in.
Sights: Fixed, open
Weight: 4 lb. 2 oz.
Bore/Caliber: .44
Features: Case-hardened frame; steel or brass backstrap and trigger guard; engraved
MSRP **$479.00**

1849 POCKET REVOLVER
Lock: Caplock revolver
Stock: Walnut
Barrel: 4 in.
Sights: Fixed, open
Weight: 1 lb. 8 oz.
Bore/Caliber: .31
Features: Case-hardened frame; brass backstrap and trigger guard; blued octagonal barrel; engraved
MSRP **$389.00**

1851 NAVY REVOLVER
Lock: Caplock revolver
Stock: Walnut
Barrel: 7.5 in.
Sights: Fixed, open
Weight: 2 lb. 10 oz.
Bore/Caliber: .36
Features: Color case-hardened frame; oval or squareback trigger guard; brass or steel backstrap and trigger guard; octagonal barrel (Leech-Rigdon model has round barrel)
MSRP . . . . **$359.00–$389.00**

1858 BUFFALO BILL LIMITED EDITION
Action: Revolver
Stock: Simulated ivory
Barrel: 8 in.
Sights: Front post
Weight: 2 lb.11 oz.
Caliber: .44

Features: Six-round cap-and-ball .44 caliber 1858 revolver commemorating the 100th year anniversary of the passing of William Frederick "Buffalo Bill" Cody; hand-chased engraving over the entire metal surface; brass trigger; blue barrel; color case hammer; gold inscriptions on barrel; 500 produced
MSRP **$989.00**

1858 NEW ARMY REVOLVER
Lock: Caplock revolver
Stock: Walnut
Barrel: 8 in.
Sights: Fixed, open
Weight: 2 lb. 11 oz.
Bore/Caliber: .44
Features: Blued or stainless steel frame and backstrap; brass trigger guard; octagonal barrel
Blue: **$409.00**
Stainless: **$509.00**

Uberti

UBERTI 1860 ARMY REVOLVER

UBERTI 1861 NAVY REVOLVER

UBERTI 1862 POCKET NAVY REVOLVER

UBERTI 1862 POLICE REVOLVER

UBERTI 1885 HIGH WALL BIG GAME SINGLE SHOT

1860 ARMY REVOLVER

Lock: Caplock revolver
Stock: Walnut
Barrel: 7.5 in.
Sights: Fixed, open
Weight: 2 lb. 10 oz.
Bore/Caliber: .44
Features: Case-hardened frame, steel backstrap, brass trigger guard; blued, round barrel
MSRP **$389.00**

1861 NAVY REVOLVER

Lock: Caplock revolver
Stock: Walnut
Barrel: 7.5 in.
Sights: Fixed, open
Weight: 2 lb. 10 oz.
Bore/Caliber: .36
Features: Case-hardened frame, steel or brass backstrap and trigger guard
MSRP **$389.00**

1862 POCKET NAVY REVOLVER

Lock: Caplock revolver
Stock: Walnut
Barrel: 5.5 in., 6.5 in.
Sights: Fixed, open
Weight: 1 lb. 11 oz.
Bore/Caliber: .36
Features: Case-hardened frame; brass backstrap and trigger guard; octagonal, blued barrel
MSRP **$409.00**

1862 POLICE REVOLVER

Lock: Caplock revolver
Stock: Walnut
Barrel: 5.5 in., 6.5 in.
Sights: Fixed, open
Weight: 1 lb. 10 oz.
Bore/Caliber: .36
Features: Case-hardened frame; brass backstrap and trigger guard; fluted round barrel
MSRP **$409.00**

1885 HIGH WALL BIG GAME SINGLE SHOT

Lock: Falling block
Stock: Walnut
Barrel: 22 in.
Sights: Fixed front, adjustable dovetail rear
Weight: 6 lb. 11 oz.
Bore/Caliber: .45-70
Features: Stock and forend designed for use with modern sporting optics; Picatinny rail; accurate 22-inch blued barrel; crisp trigger; satin walnut stock with checkered fore end and pistol grip; soft rubber butt pad to lessen felt recoil
MSRP **$1229.00**

SCOPES

ATN Corp.

ATN THOR 4 SERIES

ATN X-SIGHT 4K PRO

ATN X-SIGHT 4K BUCKHUNTER

ATN X-SIGHT II HD SERIES

THOR 4 SERIES
Available in: 1.25–5x, 2–8x, 4.5–18x, 7–28x, 1-10x, 1.5–15x, 2.5–25x, 4–40x
Weight: 31 oz.–37 oz.
Length: 13.1–14.8 in.
Power: 1.25–5x, 2–8x, 4.5–18x, 7–28x, 1-10x, 1.5–15x, 2.5–25x, 4–40x
Main Dia.: 30mm
Eye Relief: 3.5 in.
Features: Thermal vision Smart HD scopes; Gen4 sensor that will display in black hot, white hot, or color modes; can record and stream video; Smart rangefinder; ballistic calculator that displays target profile and environmental conditions; 3D gyroscope; 3D accelerometer; recoil-activated video; e-barometer; microphone; SD card; HD display
MSRP . . . .$1999.00–$4799.00

X-SIGHT 4K PRO
Available in: 3–14x, 5–20x
Weight: 33.6 oz.
Length: 13.8 in.
Power: 3–14x, 5–20x
Main Dia.: 30mm
Eye Relief: 3.5 in.
Features: Smart scope with day and night capabilities; video records in 1080 Full HD; built-in rangefinder that lets you zero in one shot; ballistic calculator; recoil-activated and streaming video capabilities; a built-in compass; Smooth Zoom
3–14x: $699.00
5–20x: $799.00

X-SIGHT 4K BUCKHUNTER
Available in: 3–14x, 5–20x
Weight: 33.6 oz.
Length: 13.8 in.
Power: 3–14x, 5–20x
Main Dia.: 30mm
Eye Relief: 3.5 in.
Features: Smart scope; video records in 1080 Full HD; built-in rangefinder; ballistic calculator; recoil-activated and streaming video capabilities; a built-in compass; Smooth Zoom
3–14x: $599.00
5–20x: $699.00

X-SIGHT II HD SERIES
Available in: 3–14x, 5–20x
Weight: 34.4 oz.
Length: 11.56 in.
Power: 3–14x, 5–20x
Obj. Dia.: 50mm
Field of View: 460 ft.@1000 yds.
Eye Relief: 2.5 in.
Features: Day and night rifle scope with incredible digital viewing clarity; video records in 1080 Full HD; built-in rangefinder; ballistic calculator; recoil-activated and streaming video capabilities; a built-in compass; Smooth Zoom; Profile Manager to store ballistic and zeroing data; Bluetooth/Wi-Fi connectivity to the ATN Obsidian app
3–14x: $599.00
5–20x: $699.00

Barska

AR6 1–6X24MM
Weight: 17.6 oz.
Length: 11 in.
Power: 1–6X
Obj. Dia.: 24mm
Main Dia.: 30mm
Exit Pupil: 4–11mm
Field of View: 75.78–12.79 ft @ 100 yds

Twilight Factor: 4.9–12
Eye Relief: 3.7 in.
Features: Water- and fogproof; red or green illuminated reticle; dual cantilever ring scope mount, flip-up scope caps
MSRP $239.99

BARSKA AR6 1–6X24MM

British Small Arms Co. (BSA)

BRITISH SMALL ARMS CO. 17 SUPERMAG SERIES 4.5–14X44MM

17 SUPERMAG SERIES 4.5–14X44MM
Weight: 21.7 oz.
Length: 13.9 in.

Power: 4.5–14X
Obj. Dia.: 44mm
Main Dia.: 1 in.
Exit Pupil: 6.6–2.3mm

Field of View: 16.6–4.8 ft @ 100 yds
Twilight Factor: 14.07–24.82
Eye Relief: 4 in.
Features: Shock-, water-, and fogproof; adjustable parallax; red, green, or blue glass-etched reticle; designed for use with .17 WSM; 6–24x44 also available
MSRP . . . . $139.95–$159.95

OPTICS

BURRIS 2–7X SCOUT SCOPE

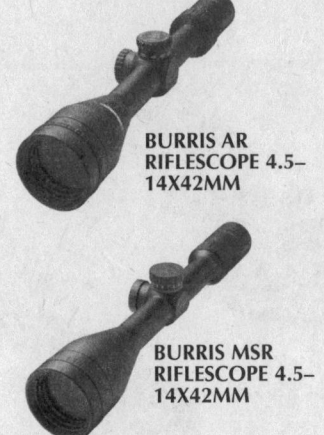

BURRIS AR RIFLESCOPE 4.5–14X42MM

BURRIS DROPTINE RIFLESCOPE 4.5–14X42MM

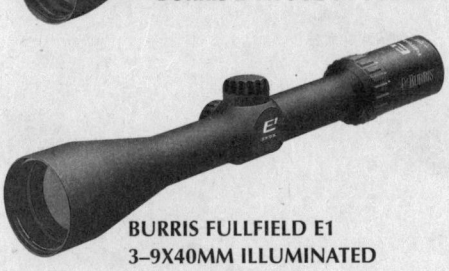

BURRIS FULLFIELD E1 3–9X40MM ILLUMINATED

BURRIS MSR RIFLESCOPE 4.5–14X42MM

BURRIS MTAC 1.5-6X42MM

2–7X SCOUT SCOPE

Weight: 13 oz.
Length: 9.7 in.
Power: 2–7X
Obj. Dia.: 32mm
Main Dia.: 1 in.
Exit Pupil: 16–4.6mm
Field of View: 21–7 ft @ 100 yds
Twilight Factor: 8–15
Eye Relief: 11–21 in.
Features: Ballistic Plex reticle; fully multi-coated; variable power; low mounting capabilities; black matte finish; Scout also available in a fixed-power 2.75x20mm
MSRP . . . . **$299.00–$479.00**

AR RIFLESCOPE 4.5–14X42MM

Weight: 18 oz.
Length: 13 in.
Power: 4.5–14X
Obj. Dia.: 42mm
Main Dia.: 1 in.
Exit Pupil: 9–3mm
Field of View: 22–7.5 ft @ 100 yds
Twilight Factor: 13.75–24.25
Eye Relief: 3.1 in.–3.8 in.
Features: Shock-, water-, and fog-proof; nitrogen filled; C4 Wind MOA reticle; adjustable parallax; anti-reflection device included; 5.56 and 7.62 calibrated custom clickers included
MSRP **$479.00**

DROPTINE RIFLESCOPE 4.5–14X42MM

Weight: 18 oz.

Length: 13 in.
Power: 4.5–14X
Obj. Dia.: 42mm
Main Dia.: 1 in.
Exit Pupil: 9–3mm
Field of View: 22–7.5 ft @ 100 yds
Twilight Factor: 13.75–24.25
Eye Relief: 3.1 in.–3.8 in.
Features: Nitrogen filled; multi-coated lenses; Ballistic Plex reticle or G2B Mil-Dot reticle; adjustable parallax; 2–7x35, 3–9x40, and 3–9x50 also available
MSRP . . . . **$203.00–$311.00**

FULLFIELD E1 3–9X40MM ILLUMINATED

Weight: 12 oz.
Length: 11.4 in.
Power: 3–9X
Obj. Dia.: 40mm
Main Dia.: 1 in.
Exit Pupil: 17–5mm
Field of View: 45–13 ft @ 100 yds
Twilight Factor: 10.95–18.97
Eye Relief: 3.1–4.1 in.
Features: A series of cascading dots to the left and right of the reticle help compensate for crosswinds. The dots represent a 10 mph crosswind (+/- 1.5-in. at 400 yds) for most hunting cartridges. For a 5 mph crosswind, halve the distance between dot and reticle. For 20 mph crosswind, simply double the distance. Also available in 2–7x35, 3–9x50, 4.5–14x42, and 6.5–20x50
MSRP . . . . **$239.00–$599.00**

MSR RIFLESCOPE 4.5–14X42MM

Weight: 18 oz.
Length: 13 in.
Power: 4.5–14X
Obj. Dia.: 42mm
Main Dia.: 1 in.
Exit Pupil: 9–3mm
Field of View: 22–7.5 ft @ 100 yds
Twilight Factor: 13.75–24.25
Eye Relief: 3.1–3.8 in.
Features: Shock-, water-, and fog-proof; nitrogen filled; multi-coated lenses; Ballistic Plex reticle; adjustable parallax; 3–9x40 also available
MSRP . . . . **$239.00–$323.00**

MTAC 1.5-6X42MM

Weight: 15.5 oz.
Length: 12.2 in.
Power: 1.5–6X
Obj. Dia.: 46mm
Main Dia: 30mm
Exit Pupil: 27–7mm
Twilight Factor: N/A
Eye Relief: 3.1–3.8 in.
Features: Features glare-resistant glass, snag-free profile, solid one-piece tube, internal double spring tension assembly, .5-MOA clicks, finger-adjustable mil-rad target knobs, night-vision technology compatibility, 10 brightness settings. Choice of Ballistic CQ or Ballistic AR reticles
MSRP **$479.00**

OPTICS

Burris

BURRIS PREDATOR QUEST RIFLESCOPE 4.5–14X42MM

BURRIS RT-6

BURRIS VERACITY RIFLESCOPE 2–10X42MM

BURRIS T.M.P.R. 3, T.M.P.R. 5

BURRIS XTR II 2–10X42MM

PREDATOR QUEST RIFLESCOPE 4.5–14X42MM
Weight: 18 oz.
Length: 13 in.
Power: 4.5–14X
Obj. Dia.: 42mm
Main Dia.: 1 in.
Exit Pupil: 9–3mm
Field of View: 22–7.5 ft @ 100 yds
Twilight Factor: 13.75–24.25
Eye Relief: 3.1 in.–3.8 in.
Features: Shock-, water-, and fog-proof; nitrogen filled; Hi-Lume multi-coated lenses; Ballistic Plex E1 reticle (illuminated optional); adjustable parallax; anti-reflection device included; camo or matte black
MSRP **$395.00**

RT-6
Weight: 17.4 oz.
Length: 10.3 in.
Power: 1–6x24mm
Obj. Diameter: 24mm
Exit Pupil: 11.5 mm–5.2mm
Eye Relief: 3.3–4 in.
Field of View: 18.5–106 in.
Features: Intended for 3-gun competition; illuminated reticle; integrated adjustable throw lever; eleven brightness levels; tube is 30mm; ballistic AR mil reticle with trajectory compensation to 600 yards
MSRP **$419.00**

VERACITY RIFLESCOPE 2–10X42MM
Weight: 22.7 oz.
Length: 13.5 in.
Power: 2–10X
Obj. Dia.: 42mm
Main Dia.: 30mm
Exit Pupil: 21–4.2mm
Field of View: 52–10.5 ft @ 100 yds
Twilight Factor: 9.17–20.49
Eye Relief: 3.5 in.–4.25 in.
Features: Ballistic E1 FFP MOA reticle with PTC technology; E1 Hunter knobs; parallax adjustment; 3–15x50, 4–20x50, and 5–25x50 also available
MSRP . . . . **$719.00–$1079.00**

T.M.P.R. 3, T.M.P.R. 5
Available in: 3x, 5x
Weight: 18.2 oz.
Length: 5.6 in.
Power: 3x, 5x
Obj. Dia.: 32mm
Field of View: 40 ft.
Eye Relief: 2.2 in.
Features: Modular combo optics package for law enforcement, self-defense, and action sports use; prism optic in 3x or 5x; Ballistic AR reticle; Burris' FastFire M3 red dot sight; Burris T.M.P.R. red laser; components may be purchased individually; ballistic reticle is illuminated digitally at seven levels with a choice of red, blue, or green viewing options; prism is night-vision compatible with three settings and three color choices; CR123 battery; quick-detach mounting base
3x: . . . . **$839.00–$1259.00**
5x: . . . . **$899.00–$1319.00**

XTR II 2–10X42MM
Weight: 22.7 oz.
Length: 13.5 in.
Power: 2–10X
Obj. Dia.: 42mm
Main Dia.: 34mm
Exit Pupil: 12–4.2mm
Field of View: 52–10.5 ft @ 100 yds
Twilight Factor: 9.17–20.49
Eye Relief: 3.5 in.–4.25 in.
Features: Hi-Lume multi-coated lenses; Zero Click Stop technology; G2B Mil-Dot illuminated FFP reticle; adjustable parallax; 3–15x50, 4–20x50, 5–25x50, 1-5x24, 1.5-8x28, 8-40x50mm, and 1-8x24mm also available
MSRP . . . . **$959.00–$1499.00**

Bushnell Outdoor Products

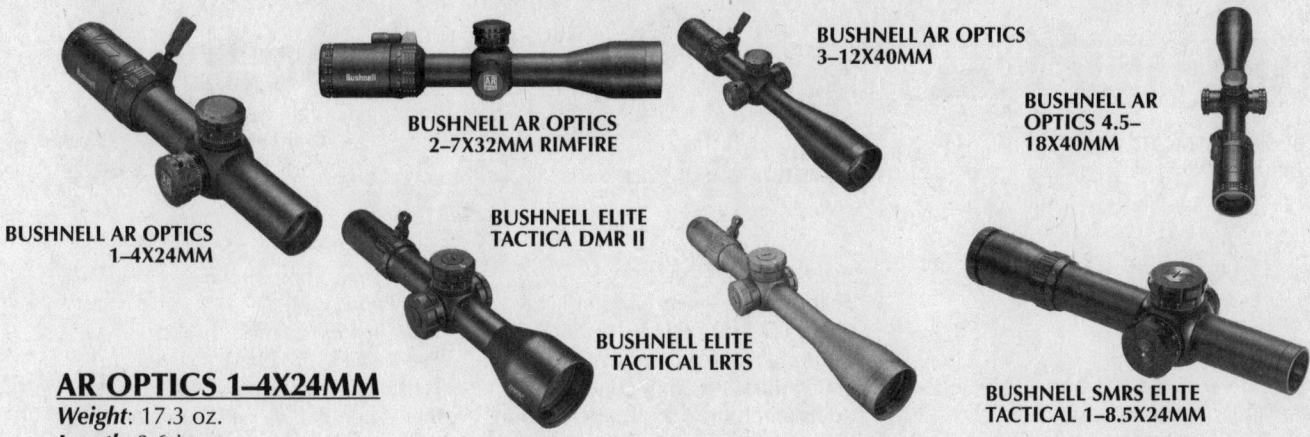

BUSHNELL AR OPTICS
2–7X32MM RIMFIRE

BUSHNELL AR OPTICS
3–12X40MM

BUSHNELL AR
OPTICS 4.5–
18X40MM

BUSHNELL AR OPTICS
1–4X24MM

BUSHNELL ELITE
TACTICA DMR II

BUSHNELL ELITE
TACTICAL LRTS

BUSHNELL SMRS ELITE
TACTICAL 1–8.5X24MM

AR OPTICS 1–4X24MM

Weight: 17.3 oz.
Length: 3.6 in.
Power: 1–4X
Obj. Dia.: 24mm
Main Dia.: 30mm
Exit Pupil: 13–6mm
Field of View: 110–36 ft @ 100 yds
Twilight Factor: 4.9–9.8
Eye Relief: 3.6 in.
Features: Designed for tactical applications; choice of three first focal plane reticles, BTR-300 AAC, Drop-Zone 223, and illuminated BTR-1; fully multi-coated glass; anti-reflective coating on all air-to-glass surfaces; 120 MOA elevation, 140 MOA windage adjustment ranges
Drop-Zone 223: **$199.99**
BTR-300 AAC, BTR-1: **$379.99**

AR OPTICS 2–7X32MM RIMFIRE

Weight: 19.6 oz.
Length: 11.3 in.
Power: 2–7X
Obj. Dia.: 32mm
Main Dia.: 1 in.
Exit Pupil: 13.5–4.6mm
Field of View: 50–17 ft @ 100 yds
Twilight Factor: 8–15
Eye Relief: 3.7 in.
Features: Target turrets; Drop Zone-22 reticle in the second focal plane; fully multi-coated optics; matte finish; 50 MOA elevation, 85 MOA windage adjustment range; Rainguard
MSRP **$199.99**

AR OPTICS 3–12X40MM

Weight: 21.3 oz.
Length: 12 in.
Power: 3–12X
Obj. Dia.: 40mm
Main Dia.: 1 in.
Exit Pupil: 13.7–3.7mm
Field of View: 33–11 ft @ 100 yds
Twilight Factor: 11–21.9

Eye Relief: 3.7 in.
Features: Target turrets; side parallax FOCUS; Drop Zone 223 reticle in the second focal plane; fully multicoated optics; 50 MOA elevation, 85 MOA windage adjustment range; Rainguard
MSRP **$209.99**

AR OPTICS 4.5–18X40MM

Weight: 21.5 oz.
Length: 12.4 in.
Power: 4.5–18X
Obj. Dia.: 40mm
Main Dia.: 1 in.
Exit Pupil: 8.6–2.3mm
Field of View: 22–7.3 ft @ 100 yds
Twilight Factor: 13.4–26.8
Eye Relief: 3.7 in.
Features: Target turrets; side parallax FOCUS; fully multi-coated optics; Drop-Zone second focal plane reticles available calibrated for 6.5 Creedmoor, .224 Valkyrie, .308 Win., and .223; 50 MOA elevation, 80 MOA windage adjustment range; Rainguard
MSRP **$229.99**

ELITE TACTICAL DMR II, DMR II PRO

Weight: 34 oz.
Length: 13.2 in.
Power: 3.5–21x50mm
Obj. Diameter: 50mm
Exit Pupil: 10.4–2.4mm
Eye Relief: 3.74 in.
Field of View: 25.3–5.1 ft @ 100 yds
Features: Throwhammer lever allows instant magnification changes; EXO Barrier Protection repels water, dust, and other debris; IPX7 Waterproof construction; DMR II model offered with first focal plane G3, G3 illuminated or Horus H59 reticles; DMR II Pro gets upgraded ED Prime glass and

first focal plane G3 reticle (no illumination); 100 MOA elevation, 60 MOA windage adjustment range
DMR II: **$1599.99**
DMR II Pro: **$1999.99**

ELITE TACTICAL LRTS

Weight: 27.3 oz.–28 oz.
Length: 13.1 in.–14.3 in.
Power: 3–12x44mm, 4.5–18x44mm
Obj. Diameter: 44mm
Exit Pupil: 12.1–2.5mm
Eye Relief: 3.74–3.94 in.
Field of View: 34.8–6 ft @ 100 yds
Features: LRTS is Long Range Tactical Scope; argon-purged for fog-proofing; Ranguard HD treatment; IPX7 Waterproofing; one version in black has a first focal plane illuminated G3 reticle; second version in Flat Dark Earth has a first focal plane G3 reticle (non-illuminated)
3–12X: **$1349.99**
4.5–18X: **$1499.99**

ELITE TACTICAL SMRS 1–8.5X24MM

Weight: 23 oz.
Length: 10.2 in.
Power: 1–8.5X
Obj. Dia.: 24mm
Main Dia.: 34mm
Exit Pupil: 13.2–3.2mm
Field of View: 105–14 ft @ 100 yds
Twilight Factor: 4.9–14.3
Eye Relief: 3.5 in.
Features: Argon-purged for fog-proofing; EXO barrier protection; IPX7 waterproof construction; windage locking; zero stop; Rainguard HD treatment; Ultra Wide Band coatings; illuminated BTR-2 reticle in the first focal plane
MSRP **$1749.99**

Bushnell Outdoor Products

**BUSHNELL TACTICAL SMRS II
1–6.5X24MM**

**BUSHNELL ELITE
TACTICAL XRS II**

BUSHNELL ENGAGE

**BUSHNELL TAC
OPTICS LRS**

TACTICAL SMRS II 1–6.5X24MM
Weight: 23 oz.
Length: 10.5 in.
Power: 1–6.5x24mm
Obj. Diameter: 24mm
Exit Pupil: 11.4–3.7mm
Eye Relief: 3.74 in.
Field of View: 107.1–16.8 ft @ 100 yds
Features: Argon-purged for fog-proofing; EXO barrier protection; Throwhammer lever for quick magnification changes; elevation and windage locking; Rainguard HD treatment; Ultra Wide Band coatings; Close Quarters BDC reticle in the second focal plane
MSRP $1349.99

ELITE TACTICAL XRS II
Available in: 4.5–30x50mm
Weight: 37.8 oz.
Length: 14.5 in.
Power: 4.5–30x
Obj. Dia.: 50mm
Main Dia.: 34mm
Exit Pupil: 9.3mm–1.6mm
Field of View: 24–3.6 ft.@100 yd.

Eye Relief: 3.74 in.
Features: Designed for long-range work; ED Prism Glass; Bushnell's EXO Barrier glass treatment that repels oil, water, dust and other contaminants; adjustments are 10 MILs per revolution; locking diopter feature ensures consistent focus; windage turret has a lock; elevation turret includes a RevLimiter Zero Stop that prevents the user from turning it past zero; first focal plane reticle/housing color combos in illuminated G3/gun metal gray, Horus H59/black, Horus Tremor3/matte black, or non-illuminated G3 in either black or Flat Dark Earth
MSRP: $2299.99

ENGAGE
Available in: 2–7x36mm, 3–9x40mm, 3–9x50mm, 4–12x40mm, 6–18x50mm, 2.5–10x44mm, 3–12x42mm, 4–16x44mm, 6–24x50mm
Weight: 11.4–23.7 oz.
Length: 12.8–14.3 in.
Power: 2–7x, 3–9x, 4–12x, 6–18x, 2.5–10x, 3–12x, 4–16x, 6–24x
Obj. Dia.: 36mm, 40mm, 50mm, 44mm, 42mm
Main Dia.: 1 in., 30mm
Exit Pupil: varies
Field of View: varies
Eye Relief: 3.5–4 in.
Features: New Deploy MOA reticle that is compatible with a range of calibers; locking turrets; toolless zero reset; EXO lens barrier; some models have side focus
MSRP . . . . $239.95–$479.95

TAC OPTICS LRS
Available in: 4.5–30x50mm, 5–15x40, 6–24x50, 10x40
Weight: 15 oz.–27 oz.
Length: 11.8 in.–14.3 in.
Power: 4.5–30x, 5–15x, 6–24x, 10x
Obj. Dia.: 50mm, 40mm
Main Dia.: 30mm, 1 in.
Exit Pupil: Varies with model
Field of View: Varies with model
Eye Relief: 3.4 in.–3.8 in.
Features: Mil-Dot reticle; 50–120 MOA of elevation; 50–85 MOA windage adjustment; side parallax correction; includes two sunshades
MSRP . . . . $319.99–$1149.99

Cabela's

**CABELA'S RIMFIRE
RIFLESCOPE
3–9X40MM**

CABELA'S LEVER
ACTION
3–9X40MM

LEVER ACTION 3–9X40MM
Weight: 14.64 oz.
Length: 13 in.
Power: 3–9X
Obj.Dia.: 40mm
Main Dia.: 1 in.
Exit Pupil: 13.33–4.44mm
Field of View: 30.55–9.6 ft @ 100 yds
Twilight Factor: 10.95–18.97
Eye Relief: 5.5 in.
Features: Ballistic glass reticles specifically engineered for use with a

particular Hornady LEVERevolution round; tube is machined aluminum and lenses are multi-coated; windage and elevation are adjustable in ¼ MOA clicks; in .45-70 Govt., .44 Mag., and .30-30 Win. reticles
MSRP $99.99

RIMFIRE RIFLESCOPE 3–9X40MM
Weight: 13.4 oz.
Length: 12 in.

Power: 3–9X
Obj.Dia.: 40mm
Main Dia.: 1 in.
Exit Pupil: 13.33–4.44mm
Field of View: 37.7–12.4 ft @ 100 yds
Twilight Factor: 10.95–18.97
Eye Relief: 4 in.
Features: For hunting, target shooting, or plinking with a rimfire rifle; parallax-free at 50 yards; multi-coated glass optics; extended eye relief and an expanded exit pupil; low-profile windage and elevation turrets; Duplex reticle; also available in 2-7x32, 4X
MSRP . . . . $49.99–$79.99

OPTICS

Carl Zeiss Sports Optics

CARL ZEISS SPORTS OPTICS CONQUEST V4

CARL ZEISS SPORTS OPTICS VICTORY V8

CONQUEST V4
Available in: 1–4x24mm, 3–12x56mm, 4–16x44mm, 6–24x50mm
Weight: 16.6 oz. (1–4x), 21.5 oz. (3–12x), 22.6 oz. (4–16x), 24.4 oz. (6–24x)
Length: 10.08 in. (1–4x), 14.5 in. (3–12x), 14 in. (4–16), 14.5 in. (6–24x)
Power: 1–4x, 3–12x, 4–16x, 6–24x
Obj. Dia.: 24mm, 56mm, 44mm, 50mm
Main Dia.: 30mm
Exit Pupil: 11.9–24mm (1–4x), 9.2–4.7mm (3–12x), 8.5–2.8mm (4–16x), 7.5–2.1mm (6–24x)
Field of View: 114–28.5 ft.@100 yd. (1–4x), 38–9.5 ft.@100 yd. (3–12x), 28.5–7.1 ft.@100 yd. (4–16x), 19–4.8 ft.@100 yd. (6–24x)

Twilight Factor: 3.5–9.8 (1–4x), 9.1–25.9 (3–12x), 11.5–26.5 (4–16x), 16.4–34.6 (6–24x)
Eye Relief: 3.5 in.
Features: Multiple reticles available, all second focal plane: 1–4x #60 illuminated center dot, ZQAR (on external turret option), 3–12x Z-Plex, Plex illuminated, 4–16x Z-Plex, ZMOA-2, 6–24x ZBR-1, ZMOA-1
MSRP . . . . $999.99–$1333.32

VICTORY V8
Available in: 1–8x30mm, 1.8–14x50mm, 2.8–20x56mm, 4.8–35x60mm
Weight: 21 oz.–34 oz.
Length: 12 in.–15.75 in.
Power: 1–8X, 1.8–13.5X, 2.8–20X, 4.8–35X
Obj. Dia.: 30mm, 50mm, 56mm, 60mm

Main Dia.: 36mm
Exit Pupil: 9.9–3.9mm, 10.3–3.7mm, 9.8–2.8mm, 9.9–1.4mm
Field of View: 110–15 ft @ 100 yds, 63–8.5 ft @ 100 yds, 42–5.7 ft @ 100 yds, 24–3.3 ft @ 100 yds
Twilight Factor: 3.1–15.5; 5.1–26; 7.9–33; 13.6–45.8
Eye Relief: 3.75 in.
Features: Largest zoom range; interaction of 92 percent transmission; fluoride lens elements and SCHOTT HT glass ensures outstanding image quality and target resolution; large exit pupils and extremely large fields of view ensure fast target acquisition, an excellent overview of the hunting situation, no shadowing, and an immediate round image; compact design; generous adjustment range of 100 clicks enables you to stay on target at distances up to 600 yds; a fiber optic thinner than a human hair provides the finest illuminated dot in the world, resulting in 0.1188 in. subtension at 100 yds
MSRP . . . . $3055.54–$4444.43

C-More Systems

C3 1–6X24MM COMPETITION
Available in: 1–6x24mm
Weight: 22 oz.
Length: 10.5 in.

C-MORE SYSTEMS C3 1–6X24MM COMPETITION

Power: 1–6X
Obj. Dia.: 24mm
Main Dia.: 30mm
Exit Pupil: 12–4.1mm
Field of View: 108.3–19.8 ft @ 100 yds
Twilight Factor: N/A
Eye Relief: 4.25 in.

Features: Lockable windage and elevation turrets; TJ1I competition ballistic reticle with 1.5 in. illuminated red dot; 11 entensity settings; nitrogen filled; waterproof, fogproof, and shockproof; quick-zoom power adjustment ring; coated optics
MSRP $1999.99

Crosman/CenterPoint

CROSMAN/CENTERPOINT 1–4X24MM

CROSMAN/CENTERPOINT 4–12X44MM

1–4X24MM
Weight: N/A
Length: N/A
Power: 1–4x24mm
Obj. Diameter: 24mm
Exit Pupil: N/A
Eye Relief: N/A
Field of View: N/A
Features: Fully multi-coated lenses; nitrogen purged; turret caps
MSRP $179.99

4–12X44MM
Weight: N/A
Length: N/A
Power: 4–12x44mm
Obj. Diameter: 44mm
Exit Pupil: 11–3.7mm
Eye Relief: 4.4–3.6 in.
Field of View: N/A
Features: First focal plane; side parallax adjustment; nitrogen purged; turret caps; 25.4mm tube
MSRP $224.99

OPTICS

Crosman/CenterPoint

4–16X56MM
Weight: N/A
Length: N/A
Power: 4–16x56mm
Obj. Diameter: 56mm
Exit Pupil: 8.0–2.4mm
Eye Relief: 3.1–2.8 in.

Field of View: 12.8–3.6 yds
Features: Mil-dot reticle; side parallax adjustment; fully multi-coated lenses; second focal plane; 30mm tube
MSRP **$199.99**

CROSMAN/CENTERPOINT
4–16X56MM

EoTech

VUDU SERIES
Available in: 1–6x24mm, 2.5–10x44mm, 3.5–18x50mm
Weight: 19.75 oz.–33.23 oz.
Length: 10.63 in.–14.84 in.
Power: 1–6X, 2.5–10X, 3.5–18X
Obj. Dia.: 24mm–50mm
Main Dia.: 30mm, 34mm
Exit Pupil: 11.4–4mm, 11.4–4.4mm, 10–2.4mm
Field of View: 105.8–17.7 ft @ 100 yds, 44–11 ft @100 yds, 30–6 ft @100 yds

Twilight Factor: N/A
Eye Relief: 3.15–4 in., 3.43–3.94 in., 3.39–3.94 in.
Features: Allows for fast target engagement at low power; at higher power provides the resolution and accuracy required to tackle longer shots; extremely clear XC High-Density glass; first focal plane optical design; oversized and precision-machined turrets; EZ Chek zero stop feature; side-mounted parallax adjustment
MSRP . . . . **$1399.00–$1799.00**

EOTECH VUDU SERIES

GPO

GPO GPOTAC   GPO PASSION 3X   GPO PASSION 8X

GPOTAC
Weight: N/A
Length: 10.6 in.–15.5 in.
Power: 1–6x24mm, 1–8x24mm
Obj. Diameter: 24mm
Exit Pupil: Varies with model/magnification
Eye Relief: 3.54–4.33 in.
Field of View: Varies with model/magnification
Features: 1–8x model has a 34mm tube, 1–6x has a 30mm. Features of both include, iControl illumination with a custom Mil-Spec Horseshoe reticle, Double HD objective lenses, and oversized target turrets. These are first focal plane scopes.
1–6x: **$1699.99**
1–8x: **$1899.99**

PASSION 3X
Weight: 13.8 oz.–18.2 oz.
Length: 11.7 in.–13.2in.
Power: 3–9x40imm, 3–9x42mm, 4–12x42mm, 4–12x50i, 6–18x50mm

Obj. Diameter: 40mm, 42 mm
Exit Pupil: Varies with model/magnification
Eye Relief: 3.54–3.74 in.
Field of View: Varies with model/magnification
Features: Entry-level scopes; 1-in. tubes; generous eye relief; fast focus ocular lenses; proprietary lens coatings; metal turret caps; clicks are ¼-MOA; with or without illuminated reticles
MSRP . . . . **$399.99–$699.99**

PASSION 4X
Weight: 22.6 oz.–23.3 oz.
Length: 13.4 in. (3–12x56mm), 15.5 in. (6–24x50mm)
Power: 3–12x56mm, 6–24x50mm
Obj. Diameter: 50mm, 56mm
Exit Pupil: 19–4.7mm
Eye Relief: 3.54 in.
Field of View: 37–14 ft @ 100 yds
Features: Entry-level scopes; 30mm tubes; generous eye relief; fast focus ocular lenses; proprietary lens coatings; metal turret caps; clicks are .36-in. in the 3-12x model, ¼-MOA in the 6-24x model; 3-12x models come with standard or illuminated G4 reticle; 6-24X has Plex reticle; parallax free at 100m for 3-12x; 6-24mm has side-adjustment parallax correction
MSRP . . . . **$599.99–$999.99**

PASSION 6X
Weight: 18.7 oz.–27.5 oz.
Length: 10.6 in. (1–6x24mm), 15 in. (both 2.5–15x models)
Power: 1–6x24mm, 2.5–15x50mm, 2.5–15x56mm
Obj. Diameter: 24mm, 50mm, 56mm
Exit Pupil: Varies with model/magnification
Eye Relief: 3.94 in. (1–6x24mm), 3.74 in. (both 2.5–15x models)
Field of View: Varies with model/magnification
Features: Entry-level scopes; 30mm tubes; generous eye relief; fast focus ocular lenses; proprietary lens coatings; metal turret caps; clicks are .36-in.; illuminated G4 reticles; 1-6x model is parallax free at 100 meters, while both 2.5-15x models features side-adjustment parallax correction
MSRP . . . . **$1249.99–$1399.99**

OPTICS

GPO

PASSION 8X
Weight: 18 oz.
Length: 10.7 in.
Power: 1–8x24mm
Obj. Diameter: 24mm
Exit Pupil: 24–3mm
Eye Relief: 3.54 in.
Field of View: 108–14 ft @ 100 yds

Features: Premium optic; 30mm tube; generous eye relief; Super Zoom technology; proprietary lens coatings; PassionTrac quick-zero target turrets; G4 illuminated reticle; clicks are .36-in.; optic is parallax free at 100 meters
MSRP. $1599.99

GPO PASSION 6X

Kahles

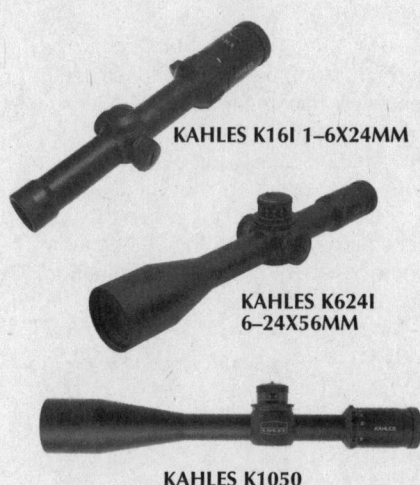
KAHLES K16I 1–6X24MM

KAHLES K624I 6–24X56MM

KAHLES K1050 10–50X56MM

K16I 1–6X24MM
Weight: 16.9 oz.
Length: 10.9 in.
Power: 1–6X
Obj. Dia.: 24mm

Main Dia.: 30mm
Exit Pupil: 9.65–3.81mm
Field of View: 127–20.1 ft @ 100 yds
Twilight Factor: 4.9–12
Eye Relief: 3.74 in.
Features: Rear focal plane; illuminated; integrated magnification throw lever allows for instant magnification changes even in the most adverse environmental conditions
MSRP. $1999.99

K624I 6–24X56MM
Weight: 33.5 oz.
Length: 15.9 in.
Power: 6–24X
Obj. Dia.: 56mm
Main Dia.: 34mm
Exit Pupil: 9.3–2.3mm
Field of View: 20–5.1 ft @ 100 yds
Twilight Factor: 18.33–36.66

Eye Relief: 3.54 in.
Features: Front focal plane; illuminated; adjustable parallax; specifically engineered for long range precision
MSRP. $2999.99

K1050 10–50X56MM
Weight: 31.4 oz.
Length: 16.9 in.
Power: 10–50X
Obj. Dia.: 56mm
Main Dia.: 30mm
Exit Pupil: 15.1–5mm
Field of View: 9.5–2 ft @ 100 yds
Twilight Factor: 23.66–52.92
Eye Relief: 3.75 in.
Features: Rear focal plane; adjustable parallax; ultra-precise 1/8 MOA adjustments constructed of hardened steel
MSRP. $2899.00

Konus

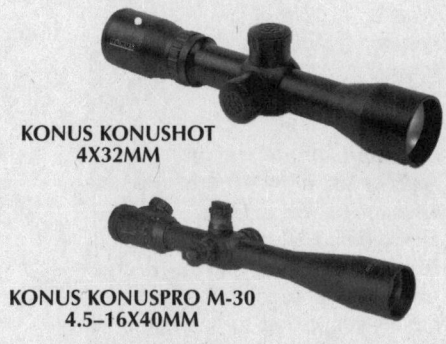
KONUS KONUSHOT 4X32MM

KONUS KONUSPRO M-30 4.5–16X40MM

KONUSHOT SERIES
Weight: 12.6 oz., 11.2 oz., 13.7 oz.
Length: 12.2 in., 12.2 in., 13.3 in.
Power: 3–9X, 3–12X
Obj. Dia.: 32mm, 40mm
Main Dia.: 1 in.

Exit Pupil: 8mm, 10.7–3.9mm, 13.3–3.3mm
Field of View: 25.5 ft @ 100 yds, 33.54–11.56 ft @ 100 yds, 27.4–6.9 ft @ 100 yds
Twilight Factor: 11.31, 9.8–16.97, 10.95–21.91
Eye Relief: 3.4 in., 3 in., 3 in.
Features: Shock-, water-, and fog-proof; nitrogen filled
3–9X: $109.99
3–12X: $119.99

KONUSPRO M-30 SERIES
Weight: 17.6 oz., 21.1 oz., 28.9 oz., 31.7 oz., 30.6 oz., 32.3 oz.
Length: 11.6 in., 12.8 in., 16.4 in., 17.6 in., 18.4 in.

Power: 1–4X, 1.5–6X, 6.5–25X, 8.5–32X, 10–40X, 12.5–50X
Obj. Dia.: 24mm, 56mm, 44mm, 52mm, 52mm
Main Dia.: 30mm
Exit Pupil: 12–6mm, 18–7.3mm, 6.8–1.8mm, 6.1–1.6mm, 4.4–1.15mm, 5.2–1.4mm
Field of View: 100–25 ft @ 100 yds, 64–15.7 ft.@100 yds, *17–4.5 ft @100 yds, 13–3.3 ft @ 100 yds, 9.7–2.5 ft@100 yds, 11–2.8 ft @ 100 yds*
Features: Engraved reticle in second focal plane; shock-, water-, and fog-proof; nitrogen filled; illuminated reticle; adjustable parallax
MSRP. . . . . $278.49–$719.99

OPTICS

Konus

KONUS KONUSPRO PLUS 3–12X50MM

KONUSPRO PLUS SERIES

Weight: 24.3 oz., 25.7 oz.
Length: 13.8 in., 16.4 in.
Power: 3–12X, 6–24X
Obj. Dia.: 50mm
Main Dia.: 1 in.
Exit Pupil: 16.6–42mm, 8.3–2.1mm
Field of View: 31.4–8.1 ft @ 100 yds, 16.2–4.45 ft @ 100 yds
Eye Relief: 3 in., 3.4 in.
Features: engraved reticle in second focal plane; shock-, water-, and fog-proof; nitrogen filled; illuminated reticle
MSRP . . . . $339.99–$349.99

Leapers, Inc.

LEAPERS/UTG T8 SERIES

UTG T8 SERIES

Available in: 1–8x28mm (Circle Dot & QD rings, Mil-dot, or Mil-dot & QD rings), 2–16x44mm
Weight: 18 oz.–22.6 oz.
Length: 10.2 in.–12.4 in.
Power: 1–8X, 2–16X
Obj. Dia.: 28mm, 44mm
Main Dia.: 30mm
Exit Pupil: 26.5–3.4mm, 22–2.7mm
Field of View: 99.5–13 ft @ 100 yds, 44.5–6.3 ft @ 100 yds
Twilight Factor: N/A
Eye Relief: 3.35–5 in., 3.5–4.1 in.
Features: Completely sealed and nitrogen filled; shockproof, fogproof, and rainproof; multi emerald–coated lenses for maximum light and edge-to-edge clarity; innovative EZ-TAP Illumination Enhancing (IE) System with red/green dual-color mode and 36 colors in multi-color mode to accommodate all weather/light conditions; one-click high-tech illumination memory feature
1–8X: $199.97
2–16X: $229.97

Leatherwood/Hi-Lux

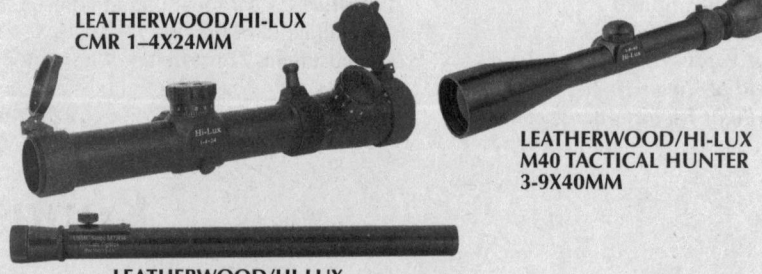

LEATHERWOOD/HI-LUX CMR 1–4X24MM

LEATHERWOOD/HI-LUX M40 TACTICAL HUNTER 3-9X40MM

LEATHERWOOD/HI-LUX M73G4 2.5X16MM

CLOSE MEDIUM RANGE (CMR 4) 1–4X24MM

Weight: 16.5 oz.
Length: 10.2 in.
Power: 1–4X
Obj.Dia.: 24mm
Main Dia.: 30mm
Exit Pupil: 11.1–6mm
Field of View: 94.8–26.2 ft @ 100 yds
Twilight Factor: 4.89–9.79
Eye Relief: 3 in.
Features: Zero-locking turrets; large external target-style windage and elevation adjustment knobs; power-ring extended lever handle for power change; CMR ranging reticle for determining range and also BDC hold over value good for .223, .308, and other calibers; red illuminated reticle; turrets adjustable in ½ MOA clicks
MSRP $395.00

M40 TACTICAL HUNTER 3-9X40MM

Weight: 16.2 in.
Length: 12.5 in.
Power: 3–9X
Obj. Dia.: 40mm
Main Dia.: 1 in.
Exit Pupil: 13.3–4.4mm
Field of View: 37.7–12.6 ft @ 100 yds
Twilight Factor: 10.95–18.97
Eye Relief: 3.25 in.
Features: Built with the same ranging system that Marine Corps snipers relied on in Vietnam, only improved; auto-range system and BDC reticle; fully multi-coated lenses; military flip-up lens covers
MSRP $299.00

M73G4 2.5X16MM

Weight: 11.8 in.
Length: 8.3 oz.
Power: 2.5X
Obj. Dia.: 16mm
Main Dia.: ¾ in.
Exit Pupil: 4mm
Field of View: 24.9 ft @ 100 yds
Twilight Factor: 6.33
Eye Relief: 3.54 in.
Features: Built to bring the vintage sniper rifle competition shooter a top quality scope that surpasses the quality of the WWII originals used on the M1903A4 sniper rifles; modern erector tube and quality multi-coated lenses for superior light transmission; offers a minimum total of 60 MOA with either windage or elevation when those adjustments are at center
MSRP $359.00

OPTICS

Leatherwood/Hi-Lux

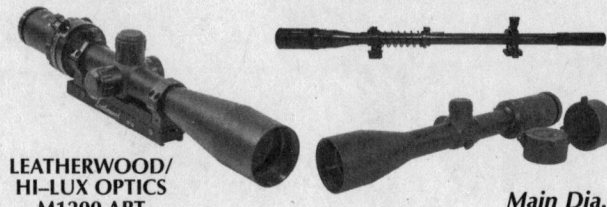

LEATHERWOOD/HI-LUX
M-1000 ART 2.5–10X44MM

LEATHERWOOD/
HI–LUX OPTICS
M1200 ART

LEATHERWOOD/HI-LUX
MALCOLM 8X USMC SNIPER
SCOPE

LEATHERWOOD/HI-LUX TOBY
BRIDGES MUZZLELOADING

LEATHERWOOD/HI-LUX
WM. MALCOLM SERIES
LONG 6X32 INCH

M1000 AUTO RANGING TRAJECTORY (ART) 2.5–10X44MM

Weight: 25.2 oz.
Length: 13.2 in.
Power: 2.5–10X
Obj.Dia.: 44mm
Main Dia.: 1 in.
Exit Pupil: 10.2–4mm
Field of View: 47.2–11.9 ft @ 100 yds
Twilight Factor: 10.5–21
Eye Relief: 3.1 in.
Features: Compensates for the bullet drop automatically by using an external cam system; can be calibrated for most centerfire rifle cartridges–from .223 to .50 BMG; comes with mount and rings; "No-Math Mil-Dot" reticle
MSRP $369.00

M1200 ART

Weight: 29 oz.
Length: 15.5 in.
Power: 6–24X
Obj. Dia.: 50mm
Main Dia.: 30mm
Exit Pupil: 8.5–2mm
Field of View: 12–4 ft @ 100 yds

Twilight Factor: 17.32–34.64
Eye Relief: 3.25 in.
Features: Auto-ranging trajectory; multi-coated lenses; second focal plane; nitrogen gas filled; waterproof; ZRO-LOK system
MSRP $595.00

MALCOLM 8X USMC SNIPER SCOPE

Weight: 25.4 oz.
Length: 22.1 in.
Power: 8X
Obj. Dia.: 31mm
Main Dia.: .75 in.
Exit Pupil: 4.2mm
Field of View: 11 ft @ 100 yds
Twilight Factor: 15.75
Eye Relief: 3.15 in.
Features: Fully multi-coated lens; fine cross reticle; elevation and wind adjustment ¼ MOA per click at the mounts
MSRP $575.00

TOBY BRIDGES SERIES HIGH PERFORMANCE MUZZLELOADING 3–9X40MM MATTE BLACK

Weight: 15.8 oz.
Length: 12.5 in.
Power: 3–9X
Obj.Dia.: 40mm

Main Dia.: 1 in.
Exit Pupil: 13.3–4.4mm
Field of View: 39–13 ft @ 100 yds
Twilight Factor: 10.9–19
Eye Relief: 3.25 in.
Features: The TB/ML scope is designed for in-line ignition muzzleloaders and saboted bullets. It offers multiple reticles for shooting at ranges out to 250 yards.
MSRP $129.00

W. M. MALCOLM SERIES LONG 6X32 INCH

Weight: 32.5 oz.
Length: 30.5 in.
Power: 6X
Obj.Dia.: 16mm
Main Dia.: .75 in.
Exit Pupil: 5.8mm
Field of View: 10 ft @ 100 yds
Twilight Factor: 9.79
Eye Relief: 4 in.
Features: A modern copy of the Model 1855 W. Malcolm riflescopes; early-style mounts for scoping original and replica 19th century breechloading rifles (Sharps, rolling block, high wall, etc.) or late period long-range percussion muzzleloading bullet rifles; ¾-in. (steel) scope tube; interchangeable front extension tubes to mount on rifles with barrels of 30 to 34 inches; also in 3x17-in. and 6x18-in. short Malcolms
MSRP $450.00

Leica Camera AG

VISUS I LW

Weight: 18.3 oz. (2.5–10x42mm), 21.9 oz. (3–12x50mm)
Length: 12.76 in. (2.5–10x42mm), 13.4 in. (3–12x50mm)
Power: 2.5–10x42mm, 3–12x50mm
Obj. Diameter: 42mm, 50mm
Exit Pupil: Varies with model
Eye Relief: 3.9 in.
Field of View: Varies with model
Features: Generous eye relief; 4x zoom; long center tubes; adjustable day/night reticle illumination; choice of L-4 a or L-Ballistic reticles; glossy or matte finishes
MSRP . . . . $1999.99–$2149.00

LEICA MAGNUS I

MAGNUS I

Weight: 19.2 oz.–27.7 oz.
Length: 10.7 in.–14.1 in.
Power: 1–6.3x24mm, 1.5–10x42mm, 1.8–12x50mm, 2.4–16x56mm,
Obj. Diameter: 24mm, 42mm, 50mm, 56 mm
Exit Pupil: Varies with model
Eye Relief: 3.5 in.
Field of View: Varies with model

LEICA VISUS I LW

Features: Zoom factor up to 6.7; bright day/night reticle illumination with brightness control; high contrast images and superior light transmission; new tooless scale zeroing; reduced dot subtensions; improved battery lifetime and exchange; slimmed eyepiece; redesigned illumination activation to prevent accidental on/off
MSRP . . . . $2299.00–$3099.00

OPTICS

Leupold & Stevens

LEUPOLD MARK FX-3
6X42MM

LEUPOLD MARK
5HD 3.6–18X44MM

LEUPOLD MARK
5HD 5–25X56MM

LEUPOLD MARK
6 1–6X20MM

LEUPOLD MARK 6
3–18X44MM

LEUPOLD MARK 8 1.1–
8X24MM CQBSS

LEUPOLD MARK 8
3.5–25X56MM

FX-3 6X42MM
Weight: 15 oz.
Length: 12.2 in.
Power: 6X
Obj.Dia.: 42mm
Main Dia.: 1 in.
Exit Pupil: 7mm
Field of View: 17.3 ft @ 100 yds
Twilight Factor: 15.87
Eye Relief: 4.4 in.
Features: Fixed-power riflescope;
Twilight Light Management System;
rear focal plane Wide Duplex reticle;
¼-MOA clicks
MSRP. $519.99

MARK 5HD 3.6–18X44MM
Available in: 3.6–18x44mm
Weight: 26 oz.
Length: 12.6 in.
Power: 3.6–18x
Obj. Dia.: 44mm
Main Dia.: 35mm
Exit Pupil: 2.4mm
Field of View: 28.4–5.8 ft.@100 yd.
Eye Relief: 3.54–3.82 in.
Features: Lighter than comparable
scopes; 1/10-MIL click adjustments;
side-focus parallax adjustment; choice
of Horus H59, front focal Tremor 3,
TMR illuminated, or TMR reticles;
three full rotations of elevation adjust-
ment; quick-throw lever
MSRP. . . . . $2399.99–$2989.99

MARK 5HD 5–25X56MM
Available in: 5–25x56mm
Weight: 30 oz.
Length: 15.67 in.
Power: 5–25x
Obj. Dia.: 56mm
Main Dia.: 35mm

Exit Pupil: 2.2mm
Field of View: 20.5–4.2 ft.@100 yd.
Eye Relief: 3.58–3.82 in.
Features: Reticle choices include front
focal TMR, first focal plane CCH,
H-59, front focal Tremor 3, TMR illu-
minated, front focal Tremor 3 illumi-
nated, and front focal TMR
MSRP. . . . . $2599.99–$3344.99

MARK 6 1–6X20MM
Weight: 17 oz.
Length: 10.3 in.
Power: 1–6X
Obj. Dia.: 20mm
Main Dia.: 1.34 in.
Exit Pupil: 10.2–3.3mm
Field of View: 103.2–17.4 ft @ 100 yds
Twilight Factor: 4.5–11
Eye Relief: 3.7 in.
Features: Scratch-resistant lenses;
Twilight Max HD Light Management
System; dial illumination control;
side-focus; M5C2 elevation control
dial; 1/10 Mil click adjustments; first
focal plane reticles available in
CMR-W 7.62, CMR-W 5.56, or
TMR-D reticles, all illuminated
MSRP. $2859.99

MARK 6 3–18X44MM
Weight: 23.6 oz.
Length: 11.9 in.
Power: 3–18X
Obj. Dia.: 44mm
Main Dia.: 1.34 in.
Exit Pupil: 10.3–2.4mm
Field of View: 36.8–6.3 ft @ 100 yds
Twilight Factor: 11.5–28.1
Eye Relief: 3.8–3.9 in.
Features: Scratch-resistant lenses;
Twilight Max HD Light Management
System; dial illumination control;

side-focus; M5C2 elevation control
dial; 1/10 Mil click adjustments; first
focal plane reticles available in TMR
(Mk), Tremor 2, and Tremor 3 configurations, all either illuminated and
non-illuminated, as well as a non-illuminated H-59 reticle
MSRP. . . . . $2859.99–$5719.99

MARK 8 1.1–8X24MM CQBSS
Weight: 23.2 oz.
Length: 11.75 in.
Power: 1.1–8x24mm
Obj. Diameter: 24mm
Exit Pupil: N/A
Eye Relief: 3.3–3.7 in.
Field of View: 14.7–92 ft @ 100 yds
Features: Scratch-resistant lenses;
Twilight Max HD Light Management
System; dial illumination control; easy
grip power selector; M5B1 windage/
elevation control; bullet drop com-
pensation; 1/10 Mil click adjustments;
first focal plane reticles available in
H-27D, M-TMR, Mil-Dot, and
CMR-W 7.62 designs, all illuminated
MSRP. . . . . $3899.99–$4939.99

MARK 8 3.5–25X56MM
Weight: 37 oz.
Length: 16 in.
Power: 3.5–25x56mm
Obj. Diameter: 56mm
Exit Pupil: N/A
Eye Relief: 3.3–3.7 in.
Field of View: 4.4–32.5 ft @ 100 yds
Features: Scratch-resistant lenses;
Twilight Max HD Light Management
System; dial illumination control; easy
grip power selector; M5B2 windage/
elevation control; bullet drop com-
pensation; 1/10 Mil click adjustments;
first focal plane reticles available in
Tremor 2, Tremor 3, and TMR (Mk),
all illuminated, plus the non-illumi-
nated Horus H-59
MSRP. . . . . $5589.99–$6109.00

UPOLD RIFLEMAN
3–9X40MM

LEUPOLD VX-3I

LEUPOLD VX-6HD

LEUPOLD
VX-FREEDOM

LEUPOLD
VX-FREEDOM
MUZZLELOADER

LEUPOLD
VX-FREEDOM
RIMFIRE

LEUPOLD VX-R
4–12X40MM

RIFLEMAN 3–9X40MM

Weight: 12.6 oz.
Length: 12.33 in.
Power: 3–9X
Obj.Dia.: 40mm
Main Dia.: 1 in.
Exit Pupil: 12–4.7mm
Field of View: 329–131 ft @ 1000 yds
Twilight Factor: 10.95–18.97
Eye Relief: 4.2–3.7 in.
Features: Fully coated lenses for excellent low light brightness; durable waterproof construction; also in 2–7x33, 4–12x40, and 3–9x50
MSRP **$249.00**

VX-3I

Available in: 1.5-5x20mm, 2.5-8x36mm, 3.5-10x50mm, 3.5-10x40mm, 4.5-14x50mm, 4.5-14x40mm, 6.5-20x40mm, 6.5-20x50mm
Weight: 9.3 oz–20.4 oz.
Length: 9.5 in.–14.4 in.
Power: 1.5–5X, 2.5–8X, 3.5–10x, 4.5–14X, 6.5–20X
Obj. Dia.: 1 in.–2.3 in.
Main Dia.: 1 in.
Exit Pupil: N/A
Field of View: Varies with model
Eye Relief: Varies with model
Features: Twilight Max Light Management System provides maximum brightness in all colors and intensified contrast across the entire field of view; Dual Spring Precision Adjustments perform with match grade precision; easy turn power selector can be quickly turned, even with gloves on
MSRP . . . . **$519.99–$1364.99**

VX-6HD

Weight: 13.4 oz.–23.4 oz.
Length: 11.2 in.–14.6 in.
Power: 1–6x24mm, 2–12x42mm, 3–18x44mm, 3–18x50mm, 4–24x52mm
Obj. Diameter: 24mm, 42mm, 44mm, 50mm, 52mm
Exit Pupil: N/A
Eye Relief: Varies with model
Field of View: Varies with model
Features: Twilight Max Light Management System; CDS-ZL2 dial locks; electronic level; fast-change magnification throw lever; flip-up lens covers; Zero Lock windage adjusment; reversible throw lever for quick-change magnification; Guard Ion lens coating; push-button illumination with power-off motion sensing technology; second generation argon/krypton waterproofing; 2–12X and 3–18X available in Sitka Subalpine camo
MSRP . . . . **$1819.99–$2729.99**

VX-FREEDOM

Available in: 3–9x40mm, 2–7x33mm, 1.5–4x20mm, 3-9x50mm, 4–12x40mm
Weight: 9.6 oz.–14.6 oz.
Length: 9.3 in.–12.39 in.
Power: 3–9x, 2–7x, 1.5–4x, 4–12x
Obj. Dia.: 40mm, 33mm, 20mm, 50mm
Main Dia.: 1 in.
Exit Pupil: Varies with model
Field of View: Varies with model
Eye Relief: Varies with model
Features: Twilight Light Management System; aluminum tubes; scratch-resistant lenses; ¼-MOA finger clicks; rear focal plane reticles. Multiple configurations include: 3–9X40 CDS (Custom Dial System) with Duplex reticle; 3–9X33 EFR (Extended Focal Ring for parallax adjustment) with Duplex reticle; 4–12X40 with Tri-MOA reticle; 1.5–4X28 Scout with Duplex reticle and extended eye relief; 3–9X40 .450 Bushmaster with bullet drop compensation and Duplex reticle; 3–9X50 with Duplex reticle; 1.5–4X20 AR with 1/10 Mil adjustments and AR Ballistic reticle
MSRP . . . . **$259.99–$454.99**

VX-FREEDOM MUZZLELOADER

Available in: 3–9x40mm, 2–7x33mm, 1.5–4x20mm
Weight: 12.2 oz.
Length: 12.39 in.
Power: 3–9x
Obj. Dia.: 40mm
Main Dia.: 1 in.
Exit Pupil: N/A
Field of View: 33.7–13.6 ft.@100 yd. (3–9x), 21.5–10 ft.@100 yd. (2–7x), 74.2–29.4 ft.@100 yd. (1.5–4x)
Eye Relief: 4.17–3.66 in.
Features: Designed for muzzleloader pressures; houses a Sabot Ballistics reticle
MSRP **$389.99**

VX-FREEDOM RIMFIRE

Available in: 2–7x33mm, 3–9x40mm
Weight: 11.1 oz. (2–7x), 12.2 oz. (3–9x)
Length: 11.04 in. (2–7x), 12.39 in (3–9x)
Power: 2–7x, 3–9x
Obj. Dia.: 33mm, 40mm
Main Dia.: 1 in.
Exit Pupil: 5mm (2–7x), 4.7mm (3–9x)
Field of View: 43.8–17.8 ft.@100 yd. (2–7x), 33.7–13.6 ft.@100 yd. (3–9x)
Eye Relief: 4.17–3.7 in. (2–7x), 4.17–3.66 in. (3–9x)
Features: Rimfire MOA reticle; Twilight Light Management System; scratch-resistant lenses
2–7x: **$234.99**
3–9x: **$259.99**

VX-R 4–12X40MM

Weight: 15.1 oz.
Length: 12.4 in.
Power: 4–12X
Obj.Dia.: 40mm
Main Dia.: 30mm
Exit Pupil: 8.6–3.3mm
Field of View: 21.5–10 ft @ 100 yds
Twilight Factor: 14.2–23.1
Eye Relief: 3.7 in.
Features: Fire Dot reticle system with fiber optic technology; DiamondCoat lens coatings; finger click adjustments; index matched lens system; proprietary Motion Sensor Technology; also available in 1.25-4x20, 1.5-5x33, 2-7x33, 3-9x40, 3-9x50, 4-12x50
MSRP . . . . **$649.99–$909.99**

OPTICS

Lucid Optics, LLC

LUCID OPTICS L5 6-24X50 RIFLE SCOPE

LUCID OPTICS L5 4-16X44MM RIFLE SCOPE

LUCID OPTICS L7 1–6X24MM

LUCID OPTICS MLX RIFLE SCOPE

LUCID OPTICS P7 4X COMBAT OPTIC

L5 6-24X50 RIFLE SCOPE

Weight: 24.5 oz.
Length: 15.5 in.
Power: 6–24X
Obj. Dia.: 50mm
Main Dia.: 30mm
Exit Pupil: 8.3–2mm
Field of View: 16.5–4.3 ft @ 100 yds
Twilight Factor: 17.32–34.64
Eye Relief: 4.25–3.25 in.
Features: Sniper-style rifle scope with the new L5 reticle; multi-coated lenses; ⅛ MOA turret click value; water-, fog-, and shockproof; matte black finish; available in STRELOK
MSRP $459.00

L5 4-16X44MM RIFLE SCOPE

Weight: 18 oz.
Length: 13.25 in.
Power: 4–16X
Obj. Dia.: 44mm
Main Dia.: 34mm
Exit Pupil: 11–3mm
Field of View: 25.5–8.5 ft @ 100 yds
Twilight Factor: 13.27–8
Eye Relief: 4.25 in.–3.25 in.
Features: Shock-, water-, and fogproof; adjustable parallax; etched-glass reticle
MSRP $429.00

L7 1–6X24MM

Available in: 1–6x24mm
Weight: 20.40 oz.
Length: 10.75 in.
Power: 1–6X
Obj. Dia.: 34mm
Main Dia.: 30mm
Exit Pupil: 15–4mm
Field of View: 56–20 ft @ 100 yds
Twilight Factor: N/A
Eye Relief: 3.75–4 in.

Features: Edge-to-edge sharp, crisp image resolution through the entire magnification range; Lucid blue reticle illumination; windage and elevation turrets offer 60MOA either side of optical center; selectable magnification lever for fast changes to the zoom function
MSRP $459.00

MLX RIFLE SCOPE

Weight: 26 oz.
Length: 13.89 in.
Power: 4.5–18x44mm
Obj. Diameter: 44mm
Exit Pupil: 2.4–11mm
Eye Relief: 3.1–3.6 in.
Field of View: 8.5–25 ft @ 100 yds
Features: First focal plane scope; one-piece 6063 aluminum 30mm tube; Mil-based reticle; side parallax adjustment; 1/10 Mil tactile and audible click adjustments
MSRP $665.95

P7 4X COMBAT OPTIC

Weight: 19 oz.
Length: 6.5 in.
Power: 4x30mm
Obj. Diameter: 30mm
Exit Pupil: 9mm
Eye Relief: 3.25 in.
Field of View: 25 ft @ 100 yds
Features: Fixed 4x illuminated reticle scope for close-quarters work; one-piece aluminum construction; manual and auto modes of operation; 50 MOA windage and elevation adjustments; re-zeroable turrets; P7 reticle
MSRP $665.95

Meopta USA

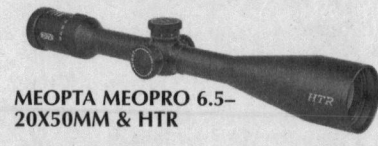

MEOPTA MEOPRO 6.5–20X50MM & HTR

MEOPRO 6.5–20X50MM HTR

Available in: 6.5–20x50mm
Weight: 21.83 oz.

Length: 15.59 in.
Power: 6.5–20X
Obj. Dia.: 50mm
Main Dia.: 1 in.
Exit Pupil: 7.7–2.5mm
Field of View: 17.7–5.7 ft @ 100 yds
Twilight Factor: 18–31.9
Eye Relief: 3.5mm
Features: MeoBright ion-assisted lens multi-coating; fast-focus eyepiece;

third turret mounted parallax control; erector system developed to provide maximum holding force to withstand heavy caliber recoil and eliminate backlash; MeoTrak TRZ elevation and windage turrets; waterproof, fogproof, and shockproof; available reticles are Z-Plex, BDC, McWhorter, and Windmax8
MSRP $949.95

MEOPTA MEOSTAR R1 RD 1.5–6X42MM

MEOPTA MEOSTAR R2 1–6X24MM

MEOPTA ZD 6–24X56MM

MEOSTAR R1 SERIES

Weight: 18.87 oz., 20.6 oz., 15.87 oz., 21.87 oz., 18.27 oz., 24.16 oz.
Length: 12.09 in., 13.54 in., 13.03 in., 14.37 in., 12.91 in., 15.16 in..
Power: 1–4X, 1.5–6X, 3–10X, 3–12X, 4–12X, 4–16X
Power: 1–4X, 1.5–6X, 3–10X, 3–12X, 4–12X, 4–16X, 7X
Obj. Dia.: 22mm, 42mm, 50mm, **56mm, 40mm, 44mm**
Main Dia.: 30mm, 25.4mm
Exit Pupil: 13.5–5.5mm, 14.8–7mm, 16.7–5mm, 14.8–4.6mm, 10–3.3mm, 11–2.8mm, 8mm
Field of View: 117.78–28.22 ft @ 100 yds, 73.49–22.31 ft @ 100 yds, **43.64–13.12 ft @ 100 yds, 36–11.15 ft @ 100 yds, 33.14–11.15 ft @ 100 yds, 16–4.46 ft @ 100 yds, 17.4 ft @ 100 yds**
Twilight Factor: 4.69–9.38, 7.94–15.88, 12.25–22.36, 12.96–25.92, 12.65–21.91, 13.27–26.53, 19.8
Eye Relief: 3.31–3.47 in., 3.23–3.74 in., 3.15–3.23 in., 3.03–3.27 in., 3.58–3.15 in., 3.94–3.15 in., 3.3 in.
Features: Features MeoTrak IITM posi-

click turret adjustments, nitrogen-purged tube, ion-assisted MeoBright and MeoShield lens coatings, MeoQuick fast focus; first and second focal plane models available, some with illuminated reticles
First focal plane models: . . . . . . $999.95–$1199.95
Second focal plane models: . . . . . . $899.95–$1299.95

MEOSTAR R2 SERIES

Weight: 17.64 oz., 20.32 oz., 21.02 oz., 22.93 oz.
Length: 11.69 in. 3.31–3.47 in., 3.23–3.74 in., 3.15–3.23 in., 3.03–3.27 in., 3.58–3.15 in., 3.94–3.15 in.
Power: 1–6X, 1.7–10X, 2–12X, 2.5–15X, 8X56
Obj. Dia.: 24mm, 42mm, 50mm, 56mm
Main Dia.: 30mm
Exit Pupil: varies with model
Field of View: varies with model
Twilight Factor: varies with model
Eye Relief: 3.54 in.
Features: Water- and fogproof; MeoLux ion-assisted multi-coatings

for 99.8 percent light transmission; MeoQuick fast focus adsjutment; MeoClick tactile turret adjustments; MeoTrack windage and elevation controls; second focal plane illuminated reticles in 4C, 4K, BDC-2, and BDC-3 configurations
MSRP . . . . $1479.95–$1599.95

ZD 6–24X56MM

Available in: 6–24x56mm
Weight: 30.6 oz.
Length: 15.2 in.
Power: 6–24X
Obj. Dia.: 56mm
Main Dia.: 30mm
Exit Pupil: 9.1–2.3mm
Field of View: 18–5 ft @ 100 yds
Twilight Factor: 18.3–36.7
Eye Relief: 3.5–3mm
Features: MeoBright ion-assisted lens multi-coating; MeoTrak II elevation and windage control; etched glass reticle; fast-focus eyepiece; waterproof, fogproof, and shockproof; second focal plane illuminated reticle in K-5.56ZD, Mildot Special, Mildot-2, and M223 configurations
MSRP . . . . $1199.95–$1999.95

Minox

MINOX ZE 5I 2–10X50MM

MINOX ZE 5I 3–15X56MM

MINOX ZE 5I 5–25X56MM

ZE 5I 2–10X50MM

Weight: 22.9 oz.
Length: 13.2 in.
Power: 2–10X
Obj. Dia.: 50mm
Main Dia.: 30mm
Exit Pupil: 11.4–5.1mm
Field of View: 55.2–11.5 ft @ 100 yds
Twilight Factor: 10–22.4
Eye Relief: 3.94 in.
Features: Illuminated central red-dot with eleven brightness settings; automatic shut down to conserve battery; German A4, BDC, and Dot reticles available; finished with Minox's M* coating; waterproof; shockproof;

Z-rail mount
MSRP $979.99

ZE 5I 3–15X56MM

Weight: 26.1 oz.
Length: 14.6 in.
Power: 3–15X
Obj. Dia.: 56mm
Main Dia.: 30mm
Exit Pupil: 11.4–3.8mm
Field of View: 36.3–7.6 ft @ 100 yds
Twilight Factor: 13–29
Eye Relief: 3.94 in.
Features: Illuminated central red-dot with eleven brightness settings; automatic shut down to conserve battery; German A4, BDC, and Dot reticles available; finished with Minox's M* coating; Z-rail mount
MSRP $1299.00

ZE 5I 5–25X56MM

Weight: 27.9 oz.
Length: 16.9 in.
Power: 5–25X
Obj. Dia.: 56mm
Main Dia.: 30mm
Exit Pupil: 10.9–2.5mm
Field of View: 21.6–4.5 ft @ 100 yds
Twilight Factor: 16.7–37.4
Eye Relief: 3.94 in.
Features: Illuminated central red-dot with eleven brightness settings; automatic shut down to conserve battery; German A4, BDC, and Dot reticles available; finished with Minox's M* coating; Z-rail mount
MSRP $1425.00

Minox

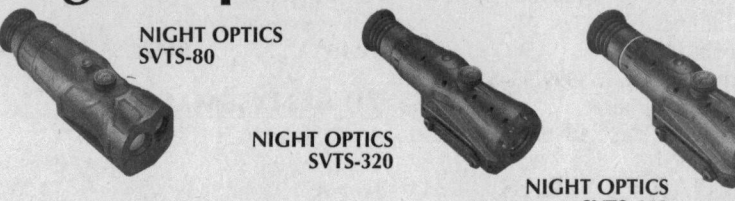

MINOX ZP TAC SERIES 1–8X24MM

ZP TAC SERIES 1–8X24MM
Weight: 24.5 oz.

Length: 11.6 in.
Power: 1–8X
Obj. Dia.: 24mm
Main Dia.: 34mm
Exit Pupil: 10.3–3mm
Field of View: 112.5–14.4 ft @ 100 yds
Twilight Factor: 4.9–13.86
Eye Relief: 3.5 in.

Features: Front focal plane; illuminated reticle; 3–15x50 and 5–25x56 also available
MSRP $3200.00

Night Optics

NIGHT OPTICS SVTS-80

NIGHT OPTICS SVTS-320

NIGHT OPTICS SVTS-640

NIGHT OPTICS SVTS-80
Available in: 1x
Weight: N/A
Length: 10.25 in.
Power: 1x
Eye Relief: 2 in.
Features: Continuous calibration; "Fusion" optic, which provides digital night vision with a thermal overlay; Snap Back post-shot zoom out feature
MSRP $1199.00

NIGHT OPTICS SVTS-320
Available in: 1x, 2x, 4x
Weight: N/A
Length: 9 in.
Power: 1x, 2x, 4x
Eye Relief: 2 in.
Features: Snap Back post-shot zoom out feature; Heat Tracker feature to quickly identify next target; recoil-activated video recording; continuous calibration
MSRP $1999.00

NIGHT OPTICS SVTS-640
Available in: 1x, 3x, 6x
Weight: N/A
Length: 9 in.
Power: 1x, 3x, 6x
Eye Relief: 2 in.
Features: Large core and display resolution; continuous calibration; Snap Back post-shot zoom out feature; Heat Tracker feature to quickly identify next target; recoil-activated video recording
MSRP $3499.00

Nightforce Optics, Inc.

NIGHTFORCE OPTICS ATACR F1 SERIES

NIGHTFORCE OPTICS B.E.A.S.T. 5–25X56MM

ATACR F1 SERIES
Weight: 21, 30, 38 oz.
Length: 10.6, 12.6 in., 15.37 in.
Power: 1–8X, 4–16X, 5–25X, 7–35X
Obj. Dia.: 24mm, 42mm, 56mm
Main Dia.: 30, 34mm
Exit Pupil: 11.2–3.9mm, 10.3–2.7mm, 8.3–2.3mm,
6–1.6mm
Field of View: 96.1–13.1 ft.@100 yds, 26.9–6.9 ft @ 100 yds,
18.7–4.92 ft @ 100 yds, 14.97–3.44 ft @ 100 yards
Eye Relief: 3.74 in., 3.35–3.54 in., 3.26–3.58 in.
Features: Front focal plane; multicoated lenses; eyepiece features enhanced

engraving, an integrated Power Throw Lever (PTL) and an XtremeSpeed thread for making a fast diopter adjustment; adjustments are standard with the patented Nightforce Hi-Speed ZeroStop, and available in .1 Mrad (12 Mils per revolution) or .25 MOA (30 MOA per revolution) Increments. Available reticles as follows: 1–8X first focal plane FC-DM; 4-16X and 5-25X Horus H59 illuminated, Horus Tremor3 illuminated, Mil-C, Mil-R, Mil-XT, MOAR; 7–35X Horus Tremor3 illuminated, Mil-C, Mil-R, MOAR

1–8X:	$2800.00
4-16X:	$2500.00–$2900.00
5-25X:	$3100.00–$3500.00
7-35X:	$3600.00–$4000.00

B.E.A.S.T. 5–25X56MM
Weight: 39 oz.
Length: 15.37 in.
Power: 5–25X
Obj. Dia.: 56mm
Main Dia.: 34mm
Exit Pupil: 8.3–2.3mm
Field of View: 18.7–4.92 ft @ 100 yds
Twilight Factor: 16.7–37.4
Eye Relief: 3.35–3.54 in.
Features: First focal plane precision; 90 percent + light transmission; i4F intelligent four-function elevation control, ZeroStop system; XtremeSpeed adjustments; available reticles include illuminated Horus H59 and Tremor3, plus non-illuminated Mil-R and MOAR
From: . . . . $4100.00–$4500.00

Nightforce Optics, Inc.

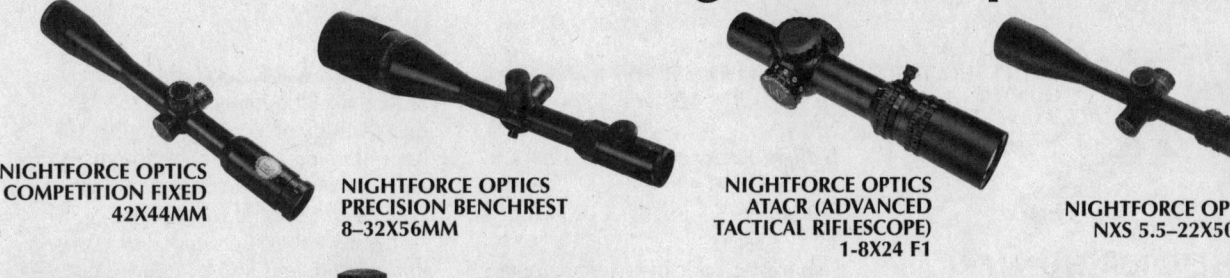

NIGHTFORCE OPTICS COMPETITION FIXED 42X44MM

NIGHTFORCE OPTICS PRECISION BENCHREST 8–32X56MM

NIGHTFORCE OPTICS ATACR (ADVANCED TACTICAL RIFLESCOPE) 1-8X24 F1

NIGHTFORCE OPTICS NXS 5.5–22X50MM

NIGHTFORCE OPTICS NXS 5.5–22X56MM

NIGHTFORCE OPTICS NXS 8–32X56MM

COMPETITION FIXED 42X44MM
Weight: 20.7 oz.
Length: 15.2 in.
Power: 42X
Obj. Dia.: 44mm
Main Dia.: 30mm
Exit Pupil: 1.05mm
Field of View: 2.87 ft @ 100 yds
Twilight Factor: N/A
Eye Relief: 88mm
Features: 1/8 MOA per click, 10 MOA per revolution; premium ED glass; enhanced high-contrast engraving is easier to see with larger numbers than most other riflescopes in its class; 45 minutes of angle of elevation adjustment and 35 minutes of windage adjustment available
MSRP.................$1795.00

PRECISION BENCHREST 8–32X56MM, 12-42X56MM
Weight: 36 oz.
Length: 16.6 in.
Power: 8–32X, 12–42X
Obj.Dia.: 56mm
Main Dia.: 30mm
Exit Pupil: 5.6–1.7mm, 4–1.4mm
Field of View: 9.4–3.1 ft @ 100 yds, 6.7–2.3 ft. @ 100 yds
Twilight Factor: 21.16–42.33
Eye Relief: 2.9 in.
Features: Superior resolution; adjustable objective allows extra-fine focus for parallax adjustment from 25 yards to infinity; target adjustments are calibrated in true 1/8 click) MOA values, and can be re-indexed to zero after sighting in; eyepiece allows for fast reticle focusing; both models have second plane reticles in a choice of NP-R2 or NP-2DD configurations with analog illumination

8-32X:................$1326.00
12-42X:...............$1473.00

NX8 1-8X24 F1
Available in: 1-8x24mm
Weight: 17 oz.
Length: 8.75 in.
Power: 1-8x
Obj. Dia.: 24mm
Main Dia.: 30mm
Exit Pupil: 7.9mm@1x–3.0mm@8x
Field of View: 106 ft.@100 yd.–13.2 ft. @100 yd.
Eye Relief: 3.75 in.
Features: Illuminated daytime reticle with multiple brightness levels; Power Throw Lever that permits fast magnification changes; first focal plane reticle
MSRP.................$1750.00

NXS 5.5–22X50MM
Weight: 31 oz.
Length: 15.1 in.
Power: 5.5–22X
Obj.Dia.: 50mm
Main Dia.: 30mm
Exit Pupil: 9.1–2.3mm
Field of View: 17.5–4.7 ft @ 100 yds
Twilight Factor: 16.58–33.16
Eye Relief: 3.8 in.
Features: Originally developed for the U.S. military's extreme long range shooting and hard target interdiction; 100 MOA of elevation travel make it ideal for use on the .50 BMG, allowing accurate shots to 2000 yards and beyond; slim profile, easily adaptable to a wide range of mounting systems
MSRP.................$2090.00

NXS 5.5–22X56MM
Weight: 32 oz.
Length: 15.2 in.

Power: 5.5–22X
Obj.Dia.: 56mm
Main Dia.: 30mm
Exit Pupil: 10.2–2.5mm
Field of View: 17.5–4.7 ft @ 100 yds
Twilight Factor: 17.54–35.09
Eye Relief: 3.9 in. *Features*: Advanced field tactical riflescope for long-range applications; maximum clarity and resolution across the entire magnification range, exceptional low-light performance; available with ZeroStop technology and 1/8 and . MOA or .1 Mil-Radian adjustments; available with MOAR, MOAR-T, MIL-R, or MIL-DOT reticles
MSRP.................$2090.00

NXS 8–32X56MM
Weight: 34 oz.
Length: 15.9 in.
Power: 8–32X
Obj.Dia.: 56mm
Main Dia.: 30mm
Exit Pupil: 7–1.8mm
Field of View: 12.1–3.1 ft @ 100 yds
Twilight Factor: 21.16–42.33
Eye Relief: 3.8 in.
Features: For long-range hunting, competition, and target shooting; choice of five different reticles for the shooter's chosen application; offered with .125 MOA, .250 MOA or .1 Mil-Radian Hi-Speed adjustments; equipped with ZeroStop; second focal plane reticles available in MOAR, MOAR-T, NP-2DD, MIL-R, or MIL-DOT, all with analog illumination
MSRP.................$2190.00

OPTICS

Nightforce Optics, Inc.

NIGHTFORCE OPTICS SHOOTER HUNTER VARMINTER (SHV) 4–14X56MM

SHOOTER HUNTER VARMINTER (SHV) SERIES

Weight: 20.8 oz., 26.9 oz., 29.1 oz.
Length: 11.6 in., 14.8 in., 15.2 in.
Power: 3–10X, 4–14X, 5–20X
Obj. Dia.: 42mm, 56mm, 56mm
Main Dia.: 30mm
Exit Pupil: 10.7–4.4mm, 12–3.6mm, 8.7–2.5mm

Field of View: 34.9–11 ft @ 100 yds, 24.9–7.3 ft @ 100 yds, 17.9–5 ft @ 100 yds
Twilight Factor: 11.22–20.49, 14.97–28, 16.73–33.47
Eye Relief: 3.5 in., 3.15–3.54 in., 3.15–3.54 in.
Features: European-style fast-focus eyepiece, side parallax adjustment, capped .25-MOA adjustments, and multiple reticle choices, including illuminated options, at a consumer-friendly price point. Numerous reticle choices include: 3–10X second focal plane illuminated Forceplex and the MOAR 30 MOA in both illuminated and non-illuminated; 4–14X50 first

focal plane Mil-R SHV and MOAR SHV, both illuminated; 4–14X56 second focal plane Forceplex and IHR in both illuminated and non-illuminated, and MOAR 30 MOA with illumination; 5–20X second focal plan Forceplex either illuminated or non-illuminated, and MOAR 20 MOA with illumination

3-10X: $900.00
4-14X56mm: . . . . . $950.00–$1128.00
5-20X: . . . . $1195.00–$1345.00
4-14X50mm: $1290.00

Nikko Stirling

NIKKO STIRLING DIAMOND LONG RANGE

NIKKO STIRLING PANAMAX SERIES

NIKKO STIRLING TARGEMASTER SERIES 10–50X60MM

NIKKO STIRLING DIAMOND FPP

DIAMOND FPP

Weight: 24.2 oz.–24 oz.
Length: 13 in.–14.2 in.
Power: 4–16x44mm, 6–24x50mm
Obj. Diameter: 44mm, 50mm
Exit Pupil: N/A
Eye Relief: 3.9 in., 3.5 in.
Field of View: Varies with model
Features: First focal plane (FFP) optics allow for range-finding shot corrections via reticle at any magnification; 30mm main body tube; glass-etched illuminated skeleton HMD or PRR reticles; waterproof, shockproof, nitrogen-filled; fully multi-coated lenses; parallax turret houses illumination
MSRP . . . . $367.00–$392.00

DIAMOND LONG RANGE

Available in: 4–16x50mm, 6–24x50mm, 10-40x56m

Weight: 16.5 oz.
Length: 14.2 in.
Power: 4–16X, 6–24X, 10–40X
Obj. Dia.: 50mm, 56mm
Main Dia.: 30mm
Exit Pupil: N/A
Field of View: 32.1–8 ft @ 100 yds, 21.4–5.4 ft @ 100 yds, 10.5–2.6 ft.@100 yds
Twilight Factor: N/A
Eye Relief: 4.5 in.
Features: Fully multi-coated lens; Zerostop turrets; dual-color red/green illumination settings; 4–16X features LR HMD reticle, 6–24X houses LR Hold Fast reticle
MSRP . . . .$312.00–$328.00

PANAMAX SERIES

Weight: 13.1 oz., 16.6 oz., 19.6 oz.
Length: 12 in., 12.1 in., 12.5 in.

Power: 3–9X, 3–9X, 4–12X
Obj. Dia.: 40mm, 50mm, 50mm
Main Dia.: 1 in.
Exit Pupil: N/A
Field of View: 44.1–14.7 ft @ 100 yds, 44.1–14.7 ft @ 100 yds, 32.9–10.9 ft @ 100 yds
Eye relief: 4 in.
Features: . MOA Increments (7mm @ 100m); centerfire, rimfire and airgun rated; AO models available - adjustable objective from 10 yards up to infinity; HMD or illuminated Black Out (with increased field of view) reticle; fast eye focus; shock- and waterpoof; nitrogen filled; multicoated lenses
MSRP . . . . $112.00–$152.00

TARGETMASTER

Weight: 25 oz.
Length: 15.6 in.
Power: 6–16X
Obj. Dia.: 44mm
Main Dia.: 30mm
Exit Pupil: N/A
Field of View: 25–6 ft @ 100 yds
Features: Adjustable parallax; ETE Mirolux coated lenses; HMD reticle
MSRP $248.00

OPTICS

Nikon

NIKON BLACK FORCE1000

NIKON BLACK FX-1000

NIKON BLACK X1000

NIKON BUCKMASTERS II 3–9X50MM

NIKON M-TACTICAL .223 4–16X42SF BDC 600

NIKON M-TACTICAL .308 4–16X42MM

NIKON M-TACTICAL 1–4X24 MK1-MOA

BLACK FORCE1000

Weight: 16.4 oz.
Length: 10.5 in.
Power: 1–4x24mm
Obj. Diameter: 24mm
Exit Pupil: 6–24mm
Eye Relief: 3.8–4.1 in.
Field of View: 27.2–110.1 ft @ 100 yds
Features: Designed for use with AR platforms; true 1x magnification with 4x zoom designed for both eyes open engagement; tube is 30mm; illuminated Speedforce reticle in the second focal plane
MSRP..................**$399.95**

BLACK FX-1000

Available in: 4–16x50mm, 6–24x50mm
Weight: 23.3 oz. (4–16x), 24.5 oz. (6–24x)
Length: 14.8 in. (4–12x), 15.2 in. (6–24x)
Power: 4–16x, 6–24x
Obj. Dia.: 50mm
Main Dia.: 30mm
Features: First focal plane optics with a proprietary glass-etched reticle; high-speed turrets; built-in return-to-zero stop on the elevation turret; 4–16x available with FX-MOA, FX-MRAD, FX-MOA illuminated, FX-MRAD illuminated reticles; 6–24x available with FX-MOA illuminated or FX-MRAD illuminated; sunshade included
4–16x no illumination:.....**$649.95**
4–16x illuminated:........**$749.95**
6-24x:..................**$799.95**

BLACK X1000

Weight: 23.8 oz.
Length: 14.8 in.
Power: 4–16x50mm
Obj. Diameter: 50mm
Exit Pupil: 3.1–12.5mm
Eye Relief: 3.6–4 in.
Features: Dedicated precision long-range AR-platform scope; available with illuminated X-MOA or X-MRAD reticles or non-illuminated X-MOA reticle in the second focal plane; 6–24X50mm option also available with same reticle configurations
4–16X:..................**$499.95**
6–24X:..................**$649.95**

BUCKMASTERS II 3–9X50MM

Weight: 13.1 oz.
Length: 12.4 in.
Power: 3–9x50mm
Obj. Diameter: 50mm
Exit Pupil: 5.6mm (@9x)
Eye Relief: 3.6 in.
Field of View: 11.3–33.8 ft @ 100 yds
Features: Economy scope has new 50mm objective; 1-in. tube; BDC reticle; ¼-in. click adjustments; also available in 3–9X40mm and 4–12X40mm, both with BDC reticle
3–9X40:..................**$129.95**
3–9X50:..................**$159.95**
4–12X40:.................**$149.95**

M-TACTICAL .223 4–16X42SF BDC 600

Available in: 4–16x42mm
Weight: 20.6 oz.
Length: 13.6 in.
Power: 4–16x
Obj. Dia.: 42mm

Main Dia.: 30mm
Features: A long-range scope specific to .223/5.56 NATO ballistics; side-focus parallax adjustment; knurled turrets; zoom ring; platform-focused ballistics; BDC 600 reticle; quick-focus eyepiece; spring-loaded instant zero reset; ultra-matte finish
MSRP..................**$449.95**

M-TACTICAL .308 4–16X42MM

Weight: 19 oz.
Length: 13.5 in.
Power: 4–16X
Obj. Dia.: 42mm
Main Dia.: 1 in.
Exit Pupil: 10.5–2.6mm
Field of View: 25.2–6.3 ft @ 100 yds
Twilight Factor: 12.96–25.92
Eye Relief: 4–3.7 in.
Features: Available with BDC 800, MK1-MOA, or MK1-MRAD reticles; knurled, zero-reset turrets; quick-focus eyepiece; O-ring *sealed*
MSRP..................**$449.95**

M-TACTICAL 1–4X24 MK1-MOA

Available in: 1–4x24mm
Weight: 16.4 oz.
Length: 10.4 in.
Power: 1–4x
Obj. Dia.: 24mm
Main Dia.: 30mm
Features: MK1-MOA reticle; proprietary glass and multicoating technology; side-focus parallax adjustment; knurled turrets; zoom ring; platform-focused ballistics; quick-focus eyepiece; spring-loaded instant zero reset; ultra-matte finish
MSRP..................**$249.95**

OPTICS

Nikon

**NIKON PROSTAFF P3
3–9X40MM NIKOPLEX**

**NIKON M-TACTICAL
3–12X42SF**

**NIKON P-300 BLK
2–7X32MM BDC SUPERSUB**

**NIKON PROSTAFF 5
2.5–10X50MM MATTE BDC**

M-TACTICAL 3–12X42SF
Available in: 3–12x42mm
Weight: 20.5 oz.
Length: 13.1 in.
Power: 3–12x
Obj. Dia.: 42mm
Main Dia.: 30mm
Features: MK1-MOA or MK1-MRAD reticles; proprietary glass and multi-coating technology; side-focus parallax adjustment; knurled turrets; zoom ring; platform-focused ballistics; quick-focus eyepiece; spring-loaded instant zero reset; ultra-matte finish
MSRP $399.95

P-300 BLK 2–7X32MM BDC SUPERSUB
Weight: 16.1 oz.
Length: 11.5 in.
Power: 2–7X
Obj. Dia.: 32mm
Main Dia.: 1 in.
Exit Pupil: 4.6–16mm
Field of View: 12.7–44.5 ft @ 100 yds
Twilight Factor: 8–15
Eye Relief: 3.8 in.
Features: BDC SuperSub reticle; optimized for use with supersonic and subsonic ammo; Max Adj. 80 MOA; waterproof; fogproof; matte black
MSRP $199.95

PROSTAFF P3 3–9X40MM NIKOPLEX
Weight: 15 oz.
Length: 12.4 in.
Power: 3–9X
Obj.Dia.: 40mm

Main Dia.: 1 in.
Exit Pupil: 13.3–4.4mm
Field of View: 33.8–11.3 ft @ 100 yds
Twilight Factor: 10.95–18.97
Eye Relief: 3.6–3.6 in.
Features: ¼ MOA hand-turn reticle adjustments with "Zero-Reset" turrets; quick-focus eyepiece
MSRP $179.95

PROSTAFF 5 2.5–10X50MM BDC
Weight: 18 oz.
Length: 13.7 in.
Power: 2.5–10X
Obj. Dia.: 50mm
Main Dia.: 1 in.
Exit Pupil: 5–20mm
Field of View: 9.9–40.4 ft @ 100 yds
Twilight Factor: 11.2–22.4
Eye Relief: 4 in.
Features: Hand-turn reticle adjustments with Spring-Loaded Zero-Reset turrets; BDC reticle; multi-coated optics; Max Adj. 70 MOA; waterproof; fogproof; parallax setting
MSRP $229.95

Redfield

REDFIELD REVOLUTION/TAC 3–9X40MM

REDFIELD REVOLUTION 3–9X40MM

REVOLUTION SERIES
Weight: 11.1 oz., 12.6 oz., 14.5 oz., 13.1 oz.
Length: 11 in., 12.3 in., 12.4 in., 12.3 in.
Power: 2–7X, 3–9X, 4–12X
Obj. Dia.: 33mm, 40mm, 50mm
Main Dia.: 1 in.
Exit Pupil: N/A
Field of View: 43.2–17.3 ft @ 100 yds, 32.9–13.1 ft @ 100 yds, 33–13.1 ft @ 100 yds, 19.9–9.4 ft @ 100 yds
Twilight Factor: 8.12–15.2, 10.95–18.97, 12.25–21.21, 12.65–21.91

Eye Relief: 3.7–4.2 in., 3.7–4.2 in., 3.7–4.2 in., 3.7–4.9 in.
Features: Black matte finish and either a 4-Plex or Accu-Range reticle; Illuminator Lens System with premium lenses and vapor-deposition multi-coatings; Accu-Trac windage and elevation adjustment system has resettable stainless steel ¼ MOA finger click adjustments; "Rapid Target Acquisition" (RTA) lockable eyepiece
MSRP . . . . $259.99–$339.99

REVOLUTION/TAC 3–9X40MM
Weight: 12.6 oz.
Length: 12.3 in.
Power: 3–9X
Obj. Dia.: 40mm
Main Dia.: 1 in.
Exit Pupil: 12.1–4.7mm
Field of View: 32.9–13.1 ft @ 100 yds
Twilight Factor: 10.95–18.97
Eye Relief: 3.7 in.–4.2 in.
Features: Shock-, water-, and fogproof; nitrogen filled; vapor deposited, multi-coated illuminator lens system
MSRP $441.95

OPTICS

Schmidt & Bender

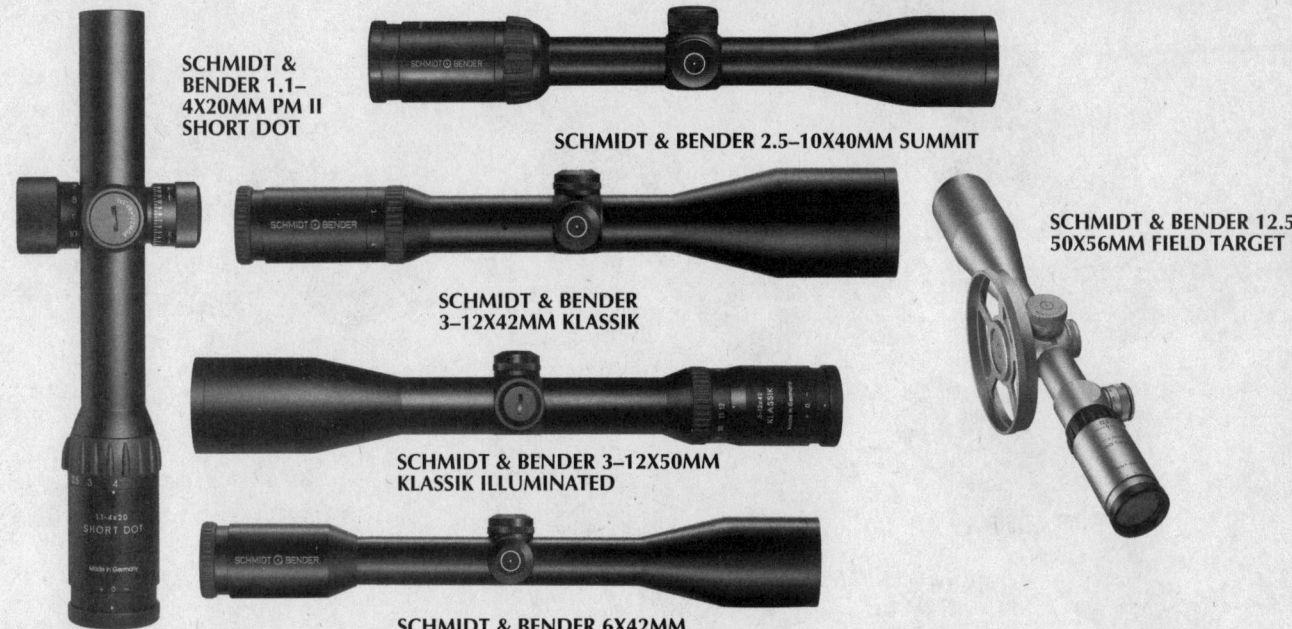

SCHMIDT & BENDER 1.1–4X20MM PM II SHORT DOT

SCHMIDT & BENDER 2.5–10X40MM SUMMIT

SCHMIDT & BENDER 12.5–50X56MM FIELD TARGET II

SCHMIDT & BENDER 3–12X42MM KLASSIK

SCHMIDT & BENDER 3–12X50MM KLASSIK ILLUMINATED

SCHMIDT & BENDER 6X42MM KLASSIK FIXED

1.1–4X20MM PM II SHORT DOT

Weight: 20.11 oz.
Length: 10.6 in.
Power: 1.1–4X
Obj.Dia.: 20mm
Main Dia.: 30mm
Exit Pupil: 14–5mm
Field of View: 96–30 ft @ 100 yds
Twilight Factor: 4.69–8.94
Eye Relief: 3.5 in.
Features: Includes locking turrets and CQB reticle; M855, 75 gr. TAP, and M118LR calibration rings standard; also in 1.5–6x20mm, 1-8x24mm (with dual CC or CC), and 1.5-8x26mm
MSRP $3149.00

2.5–10X40MM SUMMIT

Weight: 16.8 oz.
Length: 13.2 in.
Power: 2.5–10X
Obj.Dia.: 40mm
Main Dia.: 1 in.
Exit Pupil: 16–4mm
Field of View: 40.4–12.3 ft @ 100 yds
Twilight Factor: 14–20
Eye Relief: 3.93 in.
Features: Built for the American market with its 1 inch tube; adjustments are ¼ MOA
MSRP $2068.95

3–12X42MM KLASSIK

Weight: 19.9 oz.
Length: 13.66 in.
Power: 3–12X

Obj.Dia.: 42mm
Main Dia.: 30mm
Exit Pupil: 3.5–14mm
Field of View: 31.5–11.4 ft @ 100 yds
Twilight Factor: 8.5–22.4
Eye Relief: 3.5 in.
Features: Enhanced model 3–12x42 Klassik designed for longer ranges; P3 reticle with bullet-drop compensated elevation knob; adjustments are in ⅓ MOA; third-turret parallax adjustment; also available in 2.5-10x56mm, 3-12x50mm, 4-16x50mm
MSRP $1948.00

3–12X50MM KLASSIK ILLUMINATED

Weight: 21.66 oz.
Length: 13.75 in.
Power: 3–12X
Obj.Dia.: 50mm
Main Dia.: 30mm
Exit Pupil: 4.2–14.4mm
Field of View: 33.3–11.4 ft @ 100 yds
Twilight Factor: 8.5–24.5
Eye Relief: 3.14 in.
Features: All of the Klassik variables have generous objectives for greater light transmission; variety of reticles in illuminated, non-illuminated, and varmint; also in illuminated-reticle 2.5–10x56 and 3–12x42, and in non-illuminated 2.5–10x40, 3–12x42, and 4–16x50
MSRP $2475.00–2612.00

6X42MM KLASSIK FIXED

Weight: 16.67 oz.
Length: 13.7 in.
Power: 6X
Obj.Dia.: 42mm
Main Dia.: 1 in.
Exit Pupil: 7mm
Field of View: 21 ft @ 100 yds
Twilight Factor: 15.8
Eye Relief: 3.14 in.
Features: Fixed 6-power magnification; windage and elevation adjustments are in ⅓ MOA increments.; classic European 8x56 configuration offers maximum light transmission
MSRP $1294.00

12.5–50X56MM FIELD TARGET II

Weight: 40.56 oz.
Length: 16.4 in.
Power: 12.5–50X
Obj.Dia.: 56mm
Main Dia.: 30mm
Exit Pupil: 4.55–1.18mm
Field of View: 10.5–2.7 ft @ 100 yds
Twilight Factor: 26.5–53
Eye Relief: 2.75 in.
Features: High-magnification scope has a shallow depth of field, so the parallax side-focus wheel can be used as a reference for gauging the distance to the target and adjusting the trajectory; extra-large focus wheel to range distances from 7–70m; illuminated reticle with brightness settings adjustable from 1 to 11
MSRP . . . . $3700.00–$4085.00

Schmidt & Bender

SCHMIDT & BENDER PM II DIGITAL BT

SCHMIDT & BENDER PM II HIGH POWER

SCHMIDT & BENDER PM II HIGH POWER DIGITAL BT

SCHMIDT & BENDER PM II ULTRA BRIGHT

SCHMIDT & BENDER POLAR T96

PM II DIGITAL BT

Available in: 5–25x56mm
Weight: 44.62 oz.
Length: 16.7 in.
Power: 5–25x
Obj. Dia.: 56mm
Main Dia.: 34mm
Exit Pupil: 11–2.3mm
Field of View: 5.3–1.5m@100m
Twilight Factor: 16.7–37.4
Eye Relief: 3.54 in.
Features: Bluetooth connection to compatible ballistics computers, rangefinders, and other tools to digitally display relevant information in the scope; reticles available include TReMoR2, H58, H59, MSR, Police, P3L, H2CMR, H37, P4L, Klein, and P4LF
MSRP . . . . $3200.00–$3299.00

PM II HIGH POWER

Available in: 5–45x56mm
Weight: 39.03 oz.
Length: 17 in.
Power: 5–45x
Obj. Dia.: 56mm
Main Dia.: 34mm
Exit Pupil: 8.8–1.2mm
Field of View: 7.8–.9m@100m
Twilight Factor: 16.7–50.2
Eye Relief: 3.54 in.
Features: Developed via a U.S. SOCOM request for a scope to cover extreme distances; reticles available

include TReMoR2, H58, MSR, Police, P3L, H2CMR, H37, P4L, Klein, and P4LF
MSRP . . . . $5400.00–$5900.00

PM II HIGH POWER DIGITAL BT

Available in: 3–27x56mm
Weight: 43.88 oz.
Length: 16 in.
Power: 3–27x
Obj. Dia.: 56mm
Main Dia.: 34mm
Exit Pupil: 8.7–2.1mm
Field of View: 13–1.4m@100m
Twilight Factor: 13–38.9
Eye Relief: 3.54 in.
Features: Bluetooth connection to compatible ballistics computers, rangefinders, and other tools to digitally display relevant information in the scope; reticles available include P4LF, H2CMR, TReMoR2, H37, and H59
MSRP . . . . $4799.00–$4999.00

PM II ULTRA BRIGHT

Available in: 3–12x54mm, 4–16x56mm
Weight: 32.52 oz. (3–12x), 33.79 oz. (4–16x)
Length: 13.8 in. (3–12x), 15.2 in. (4–16x)
Power: 3-12x, 4–16x
Obj. Dia.: 54mm, 56mm
Main Dia.: 34mm

Exit Pupil: 12–4.5mm (3–12x), 12–3.5mm (4–16x)
Field of View: 12.5–3.1m@100m (3–12x), 9.4–2.3m@100m (4–16x)
Twilight Factor: 12.7–25.5 (3–12x), 15–29.9 (4–16x)
Eye Relief: 3.54 in.
Features: More than 96 percent light transmission; "reverse" design is rounder and sports flattened turrets; reticle choices include TReMoR3, P3L, and P4LF; other reticles can be installed at request
MSRP . . . . $3800.00–$4200.00

POLAR T96

Available in: 3–12x54mm, 4–16x56mm
Weight: 23.77–28.57 oz.
Length: 14 in.
Power: 3–12x, 4–16x
Obj. Dia.: 54mm, 56mm
Main Dia.: 34mm
Exit Pupil: 12–4.5mm (3–12x), 12–3.5mm (4–16x)
Field of View: 12.5–3.1m@100m, 9.4–3m@100m
Twilight Factor: N/A
Eye Relief: 3.54 in.
Features: Model is named based on its 96 percent light transmission; dusk-proof reticles; choice of reticle in the first or second focal plane; reticle choices include L7, L4, D7, and D4
MSRP . . . . $2400.00–$2500.00

SIG Sauer

SIG SAUER TANGO4

SIG SAUER TANGO6

SIG SAUER WHISKEY3

SIG SAUER WHISKEY5

TANGO4
Available in: 1–4x24mm, 3–12x42mm, 4–16x44mm, 6–24x50mm
Weight: 20.1 oz.–26.9 oz.
Length: 10 in.–15.6 in.
Power: 1–4X, 3–12X, 4–16X, 6–24X
Obj. Dia.: 24mm–50mm
Main Dia.: 30mm
Exit Pupil: 15.4–6.1mm, 13.3–3.4mm, 22.9–5.1mm, 8–2.1mm
Field of View: 98–24 ft @ 100 yds, 32.8–8.4 ft @ 100 yds, 24.3–6.1 ft @ 100 yds, 16.8–4.2 ft @ 100 yds
Twilight Factor: N/A
Eye Relief: 3.3 in.
Features: Low dispersion glass provides industry-leading optical clarity for any situation; offered in first focal plane with multiple, illuminated reticle options; MOTAC (Motion Activated Illumination) powers up when it senses motion and powers down when it does not; provides for optimum operational safety and enhanced battery life; dependable waterproof (IPX-7 rated for complete immersion up to 1 meter) and fogproof performance; LockDown Zero System features a resettable zero, zero-stop, and auto-locks down at zero
MSRP . . . . $719.99–$1319.99

TANGO6
Available in: 1–6x24mm, 2–12x40mm, 3–18x44mm, 4-24X50mm, 5–30x56mm
Weight: 25.4 oz.–39.5 oz.
Length: 11.1 in.–15.3 in.
Power: 1–6X, 2–12X, 3–18X, 4-24X, 5–30X
Obj. Dia.: 24mm–56mm
Main Dia.: 30mm

Exit Pupil: 11.3–4mm, 11.4–3.3mm, 11.4–2.4mm, 8.8–1.9mm
Field of View: 107–17.7 ft @ 100 yds, 53–8.8 ft @ 100 yds, 35.3–5.9 ft @ 100 yds, 20.2–3.4 ft @ 100 yds
Twilight Factor: N/A
Eye Relief: 3.5–3.9 in.
Features: Offered in first and second focal plane with multiple, illuminated reticle options; HellFire electronic-illuminated reticle system using advanced fiber optic technology to vary the light intensity of the central aiming point in any light condition; HDX optics extra-low dispersion glass combined with high transmittance glass provide industry-leading light transmission and optical clarity for any situation; MOTAC (Motion Activated Illumination) powers up when it senses motion and powers down when it does not; provides for optimum operational safety and enhanced battery life; dependable waterproof (IPX-7 rated for complete immersion up to 1 meter) and fogproof performance; LockDown Zero System features a resettable zero, zero-stop, and is lockable at any location
MSRP . . . . $1679.99–$2999.99

WHISKEY3
Available in: 2–7x32mm, 3–9x40mm, 3–9x50mm, 4–12x40mm, 4–12x50mm
Weight: 14.8 oz.–18.8 oz.
Length: 11.2 in.–14 in.
Power: 2–7X, 3–9X, 4–12X
Obj. Dia.: 32mm–50mm
Main Dia.: 25.4mm
Exit Pupil: 15–4.5mm, 15–4.8mm, 15.1–5.6mm, 10–3.3mm
Field of View: 45.4–13.1 ft @ 100 yds, 33.9–11.3 ft @ 100 yds, 23.6–7.9 ft @ 100 yds

Twilight Factor: N/A
Eye Relief: 3.5 in.
Features: 3X optical zoom offered in second focal plane (SFP) with multiple reticle options; low dispersion glass provides industry-leading optical clarity for any situation; European-style eyepiece for a smooth, fast, and precise reticle adjustment; dependable waterproof (IPX-7 rated for complete immersion up to 1 meter) and fogproof performance
MSRP $359.98

WHISKEY5
Available in: 1–5x20mm, 2-10x42mm, 2.4–12x56mm, 3–15x44mm, 3–15x52mm, 5–25x52mm
Weight: 17.2 oz.–29 oz.
Length: 10.6 in.–14.6 in.
Power: 1–5X, 2–10X, 2.4–12X, 3–15X, 5–25X
Obj. Dia.: 20mm–56mm
Main Dia.: 25.4mm
Exit Pupil: 10.6–4mm, 10.7–4.2mm, 11.6–4.7mm, 10–2.9mm, 10–3.5mm, 8.3–2.1mm
Field of View: 100.4–20.2 ft @ 100 yds, 49.1–9.9 ft @ 100 yds, 43.1–9.3 ft @ 100 yds, 34.1–6.8 ft @ 100 yds, 20.2–4 ft @ 100 yds
Twilight Factor: N/A
Eye Relief: 3.8–4.1 in.
Features: Illuminated and non-illuminated reticles; proprietary HDX optical system provides industry-leading brightness and extreme optical clarity for any situation; offered in second focal plane with multiple reticle options; dependable waterproof (IPX-7 rated for complete water immersion up to 1 meter) and fogproof performance
MSRP . . . . $1079.99–$1679.99

OPTICS

Simmons

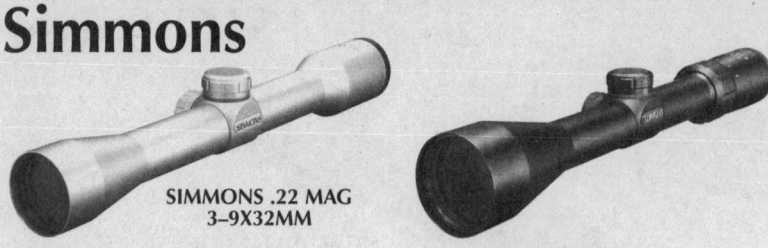

SIMMONS .22 MAG
3–9X32MM

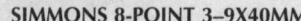

SIMMONS 8-POINT 3–9X40MM

SIMMONS
OPTICS AETEC

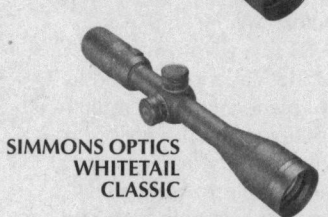

SIMMONS OPTICS
PROTARGET
RIFLESCOPES

SIMMONS OPTICS
WHITETAIL
CLASSIC

.22 MAG 3–9X32MM

Weight: 10 oz.
Length: 12 in.
Power: 3–9X
Obj. Dia.: 32mm
Main Dia.: 1 in.
Exit Pupil: 10.7–3.6mm
Field of View: 31.4–10.5 ft @ 100 yds
Twilight Factor: 9.8–17
Eye Relief: 3.75 in.
Features: One piece tube construction; fully coated optics; waterproof; fogproof; shockproof; Truplex reticle; RF Rings with available Adjustable Objective; also available in 4x32; matte or silver finish
3-9X: . . . . $63.95–$92.45
4X: $52.95

8-POINT 3–9X40MM

Weight: 10 oz.
Length: 13.125 in.
Power: 3–9X
Obj. Dia.: 40mm
Main Dia.: 1 in.
Exit Pupil: 10.7–3.6mm
Field of View: 31.4–10.5 ft @ 100 yds
Twilight Factor: 11–19
Eye Relief: 3.75 in.
Features: TrueZero fingertip adjustments; Quick Target Acquisition; fully coated optics; waterproof; fogproof; recoilproof; Truplex reticle; also available in 4x32, 3–9x32, and 3–9x50; matte finish
MSRP . . . . $64.95–$75.95

AETEC

Available in: 2.8–10x44mm, 4–14x44mm,
Weight: 15.76–23.38 oz.
Length: 11.53–12.51 in.
Power: 2.8–10x, 4–14x
Obj. Dia.: 44mm
Main Dia.: 1 in.
Exit Pupil: 10.4–3.2mm
Field of View: 43–12 ft.@100 yd. (2.8–10x), 30–8.5 ft.@ 100 yd. (4–14x)
Eye Relief: varies
Features: Aspherical Lens technology to prevent image distortion; fully multicoated lenses; waterproof, fogproof, and shockproof; reticle is a standard or illuminated Truplex; the 4–14x has the option of exposed or capped turrets
2.8–10x: . . . . $199.99–$219.99
4–14x: . . . . $229.99–$299.99

PROTARGET RIFLESCOPES

Available in: 2.5–10x40mm, 4–16x40mm, 6–18x40mm
Weight: 20–20.4 oz.
Power: 2.5–10x, 4–16x, 6–18x
Obj. Dia.: 40mm
Main Dia.: 1 in.
Field of View: 31–10.5 ft.@100 yd. (2.5–10x), 33–8.6 ft.@100 yd. (4–16x), 18–6 ft.@100 yd. (6–18x)
Eye Relief: 3.9 in.
Features: Three dedicated rimfire scopes with TruPlex reticles and side parallax adjustment; 3–9x and 6–18x have turrets calibrated for .22 LR; 3–12x's turrets are calibrated for .17 HMR; 3–12x and 6–18x have side focus adjustment; multi-coated glass; matte finish; supplied with rings
MSRP . . . . $99.99–$139.99

WHITETAIL CLASSIC

Available in: 4x32mm, 1–4x20mm, 2–7x32mm, 3–9x40mm, 4–12x40mm, 6–24x50mm
Weight: 13.29–19.4 oz.
Length: 9.76–15.98 in.
Power: 4x, 1–4x, 2–7x, 3–9x, 4–12x, 6–24x
Obj. Dia.: 20, 32, 40, 50mm
Main Dia.: 1 in.
Exit Pupil: varies
Field of View: varies
Eye Relief: varies
Features: Five utilitarian zoom magnifications; second focal plane optics with 1-in. tubes; Black Granite finish and red highlights; waterproof, fogproof, and shockproof
MSRP . . . . $49.99–$119.99

Steiner

STEINER GS3 SERIES
2–10X42MM

GS3 2–10X42MM

Weight: 18 oz.
Length: 13.5 in.
Power: 2–10X
Obj. Dia.: 42mm
Main Dia.: 30mm
Exit Pupil: 16.8–4.2mm
Field of View: 52–10.5 ft @ 100 yds
Twilight Factor: 9.17–20.49
Eye Relief: 3.5 in.–4.25 in.
Features: Rear focal plane; water- and fog-proof; nitrogen filled; 3–15x50, 3–15x56, and 4–20x50 also available
1–5X: $1770.00
3–15X: . . . . $2275.00–$2899.99
5–25X: $2530.00

Steiner

STEINER T5XI SERIES

STEINER NIGHTHUNTER EXTREME SERIES 1–5X24MM

NIGHTHUNTER EXTREME SERIES 1–5X24MM
Weight: 20.4 oz.
Length: 11.5 in.
Power: 1–5X
Obj. Dia.: 24mm
Main Dia.: 30mm
Exit Pupil: 11.5–4.8mm
Field of View: 108–21.5 ft @ 100 yds
Twilight Factor: 4.9–10.95
Eye Relief: 3.54 in.
Features: Rear focal plane; water- and fog-proof; nitrogen filled; illuminated reticle; rubber armoring; 1.6–8x42, 2–10x50, and 3–15x56 also available

1–5X: $2587.49
1.6–8X: $2759.99
2–10X: $3104.99
3–15X: $3219.99

T5XI SERIES
Weight: 19.4 oz., 29.8 oz., 33 oz.
Length: 11.3 in., 13.1 in., 16.6 in.
Power: 1–5X, 3–15X, 5–25X

Obj. Dia.: 24mm, 50mm, 56mm
Main Dia.: 30mm, 34mm, 34mm
Exit Pupil: 11–4.8mm, 12–3.4mm, 11.2–2.3mm
Field of View: 108–21 ft @ 100 yds, 36–7.3 ft @ 100 yds, 21.5–4.3 ft @ 100 yds
Twilight Factor: 4.9–10.95, 12.25–27.39, 16.73–37.42
Eye Relief: 3.5–4.3 in.
Features: The 1-5-24 is designed as a close-combat scope; medium-range 3–15x50 and long-range 5–25x56 scope come with illuminated etched glass featuring the new Special Competition Reticle (SCR) and Second Rotation Indicator that shows each mil of elevation through the indication window on the elevation turret; front focal plane; MOA SCR reticle added as an option in 2018

1–5X: $1770.00
3–15X: .... $2275.00–$2899.99
5–25X: $2530.00

Swarovski Optik

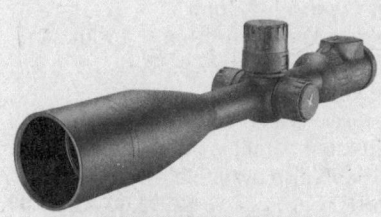

SWAROVSKI OPTIK X5(I) 3.5–18X50MM

SWAROVSKI OPTIK X5(I) 5–25X56 P 1/4 MOA

SWAROVSKI OPTIK Z3 3–10X42MM

X5(I) 3.5–18X50MM
Weight: 28.6 oz.–32.1 oz.
Length: 14.4 in.–14.8 in.
Power: 3.5–18X
Obj. Dia.: 50mm
Main Dia.: 30mm
Exit Pupil: 9.5–2.8mm
Field of View: 30–6.3 ft @ 100 yds
Twilight Factor: 11–30
Eye Relief: 3.7 in.
Features: The X5(i) from SWAROVSKI OPTIK redefines accuracy; new spring retention system and turrets are part of the total package promoting accuracy and offering across the entire adjustment range an accurate impact point adjustment of ¼ MOA in terms of both elevation and windage even in the most extreme situations; use the SUBZERO function to go below the sight-in distance
MSRP $3110.00

X5(I) 5–25X56 P 1/4 MOA
Weight: 32.1 oz.
Length: 14.8 in.
Power: 5–25x56mm
Obj. Diameter: 56mm
Exit Pupil: 2.3–9.5mm
Eye Relief: N/A
Field of View: 4.5–21 ft @ 100 yds
Features: High-luminosity rifle scope with 25x magnification; three reticle options; 30mm tube; 10 illumination brightness settings
MSRP $3332.00

Z3 3–10X42MM
Weight: 12.7 oz.
Length: 12.6 in.
Power: 3–10X
Obj. Dia.: 42mm
Main Dia.: 1 in.
Exit Pupil: 12.6–4.2mm
Field of View: 33–11.7 ft @ 100 yds
Twilight Factor: 11.22–20.49
Eye Relief: 3.5 in.
Features: Z3 riflescopes have a 3x zoom factor and are the lightest riflescopes in the Swarovski Optik line; perfect fit for many of today's lightweight rifles; reticles for the Z3 include the 4A, Plex, BRX, and BRX Heavy
MSRP .... $810.00–$888.00

OPTICS

Swarovski Optik

**SWAROVSKI OPTIK Z5
5–25X52MM**

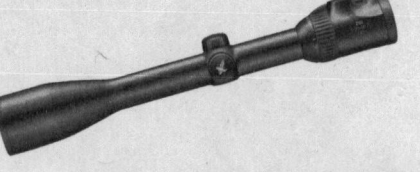

SWAROVSKI OPTIK Z6I 5–30X50MM P

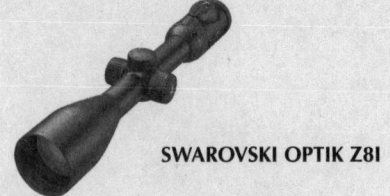

SWAROVSKI OPTIK Z8I

Z5 5–25X52MM

Weight: 17.5 oz.
Length: 14.6 in.
Power: 5–25X
Obj.Dia.: 52mm
Main Dia.: 1 in.
Exit Pupil: 9.6–2.1mm
Field of View: 21.9–4.5 ft @ 100 yds
Twilight Factor: 16.12–36.05
Eye Relief: 3.75 in.
Features: The Z5 Riflescope line features a 5x zoom factor; a third parallax-adjustment turret; and long eye relief; with reticles available in #4, Plex, Fine in the 5–25x, and BRX/BRH; also available with the ballistic turrets; also in 3.5–18x44

5–25X: . . . . $1477.00–$1521.00
3.5–18X: . . . . $1366.00–$1399.00

Z6I 5–30X50MM P

Weight: 22.6 oz.
Length: 15.67 in.
Power: 5–30X
Obj. Dia.: 48.2–50mm
Main Dia.: 30mm
Exit Pupil: 9.5–1.7mm
Field of View: 23.7–3.9 ft @ 100 yds
Twilight Factor: 14.1–38.7
Eye Relief: 3.74 in.
Features: New 2nd Generation scopes feature slimmer design that enables a clearer view of the controls and of the hunting situation; parallax turret also features a lock-in position at the 100 yds mark; more prominent ribbing on the magnification ring; 4A-I, 4W-I reticles available

MSRP . . . . $2321.00–$3077.00

Z8I

Weight: 18.2 oz.–25.6 oz.
Length: 14 in.–14.3 in.
Power: 1–8x24mm, 1.7–13.3x42mm, 2–16x50mm, 2.3–18x56mm
Obj. Diameter: 24, 42, 50, 56mm
Exit Pupil: Varies with model
Eye Relief: N/A
Field of View: Varies with model
Features: Illuminated 8x zoom in a 30mm tube; Flexchange, a switchable reticle; multiple reticles to choose from

1–8x: . . . . $2766.00–$3054.00
1.7–13.3x: $3554.00
2–16x: . . . . $3332.00–$3410.00
2.3–18x: . . . . $3642.00–$3699.00

Tangent Theta

TANGENT THETA PROFESSIONAL MARKSMAN SERIES 5–25X56MM

PROFESSIONAL MARKSMAN SERIES 5–25X56MM

Weight: 40.57 oz.
Length: 16.73 in.
Power: 5–25X
Obj. Dia.: 56mm
Main Dia.: 34mm

Exit Pupil: 11–2.3mm
Field of View: 7.6–1.6m @ 100m
Twilight Factor: 16.73–37.42
Eye Relief: 3.54 in.
Features: Water- and shockproof; adjustable parallax; illuminated reticle; 3–15x50 also available
MSRP . . . . $3999.00–$5321.00

Tract Optics

**TRACT OPTICS
22FIRE**

TRACT OPTICS RESPONSE

22FIRE

Weight: 15.2 oz. (3–9x40mm), 16 oz. (4–12x40mm)
Length: 12.2 in. (3–9x40mm), 13.9 in. (4–12x40mm)
Power: 3–9, 4–12
Obj. Diameter: 40mm
Exit Pupil: Varies with model
Eye Relief: 3.5 in.
Field of View: Varies with model
Features: 22Rifle line designed specifically to maximize accuracy with .22-caliber rifles; Impact BDC or T-Plex reticle; BDC designed for longer-distance work, while T-Plex is suitable for target practice and small-game hunting
3–9x40mm: $174.00
4–12x40mm: $194.00

RESPONSE

Weight: 19.6 oz.
Length: 13.1 in.
Power: 4–16X
Obj. Diameter: 42mm
Exit Pupil: 10.5–2.6mm
Eye Relief: 3.5 in.
Field of View: 22–2.5 ft @ 100 yds
Features: Response line consists of three scopes; intended for use with ARs/MSRs in the .223 reticles and the AR10 platform with the .308 reticle; exposed tactical type turrets; glassetched reticles with windage correction
MSRP $424.00

OPTICS

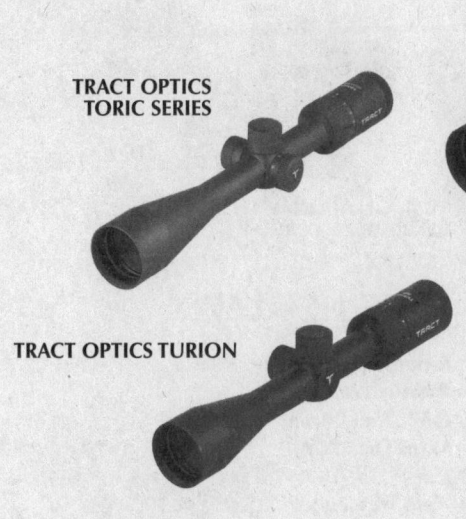

TRACT OPTICS TORIC SERIES

TRACT OPTICS TEKOA

TRACT OPTICS TURION

um optics straight to the customer's door; 1-in., one-piece, Argon-purged tubes; SCHOTT HT (high transmission glass) for superior low light transmission; 4-16x44mm available with BDC or T-Plex reticles and is designed for long-range applications with Tract's HD Optical Technology; 3–12X available only with BDC reticle

3–12X: . . . . $52=74.00
4–16X $594.00

TORIC

Available in: 2–10x42mm, 3–15x42mm, 3–15x50mm
Weight: 18.6 oz.–22.3 oz.
Length: 13.2 in.–13.9 in.
Power: 2–10X, 3–15X, 3–15X
Obj. Dia.: 42mm–50mm
Main Dia.: 1 in.
Exit Pupil: 10.7–4.2mm, 10–2.8mm, 10–3.3mm

TEKOA

Weight: 19.3 oz., 20 oz.
Length: 13.33 in., 13.97 in.
Power: 3–12x42mm, 4–16x44mm
Obj. Diameter: 42mm, 44mm
Exit Pupil: 9.4–3.3mm, 9.3–2.8mm
Eye Relief: 3.5 in.
Field of View: 34.3–8.5 ft.@ 100 yds., 25.7–6.6 ft. @ 100 yds.
Features: Tract Optics delivers premi-

Field of View: 49–9.9 ft @ 100 yds, 34–6.9 ft @ 100 yds, 34.3–6.8 ft @ 100 yds
Twilight Factor: N/A
Eye Relief: 4 in.
Features: Schott HT glass; glass etched BDC and T-Plex reticle (w/ windage correction in the BDC)
2–10X: $694.00
3–15X: $754.00

TURION

Weight: 15.2 oz.
Length: 12.45 in.
Power: 3–9x40mm
Obj. Diameter: 40mm
Exit Pupil: 13.3–4.4mm
Eye Relief: 3.9 in.
Field of View: 33.2–11 ft @ 100 yds
Features: Tract Optics delivers premium optics straight to the customer's door; Impact BDC or T-Plex reticle; Tract's High Definition optical system; SCHOTT HT (high transmission) glass; suitable for use on centerfire rifles, slug shotguns, and muzzleloaders
MSRP $394.00

Trijicon

TRIJICON ACCUPOINT 1–6X24

TRIJICON ACCUPOINT 4–16X50MM

ACCUPOINT SERIES

Weight: 14.4 oz.–26.9 oz.
Length: 10.3 in.–13.8 in.
Power: 1–4X, 1–6x, 2.5–10X, 2.5–12.5X, 3–9X, 5–20X
Obj. Dia.: 24mm–56mm
Main Dia.: 30mm
Exit Pupil: 17.5–5.1mm, 12–4.1mm, 16.3–5.6mm, 10.6–3.3mm, 13.3–4.4mm, 10–2.5mm
Field of View: 97.5–24.2 ft @ 100 yds, 117.5–18.8 ft @ 100 yds, 37.6–10.1 ft @ 100 yds, 41.3–3.8 ft @ 100

yds, 6.45–2.15 ft @ 100 yds, 19.1–5.1 ft @ 100 yds
Twilight Factor: N/A
Eye Relief: 3.2 in., 3.9 in., 2.8–4.1 in, 3.9 in., 3.6 in., 3.8–4.1 in.
Features: Waterproof; rear focal plane; adjustable parallax; titrium and fiber battery-free dual-illuminated; manual brightness adjustment; reticles include BAC Triangle, Standard Cross-Hair with Dot, Mil-Dot Cross-Hair with Dot, and German #4 in red, green, and amber illumination
MSRP . . . . $899.00–$1399.00

ACCUPOINT 4–16X50MM

Available in: 4–16x50mm
Weight: 24.2 oz.
Length: 13.9 in.
Power: 4–16x
Obj. Dia.: 50mm
Main Dia.: 30mm
Exit Pupil: 9.3–3.1mm
Field of View: 25.8–6.4 ft.@100 yd.
Eye Relief: 3.6–3.7 in.
Features: Fiber optic and tritium illuminated reticle; operates without a battery; illumination automatically adjusts to lighting conditions; aircraft-quality aluminum body; available with a standard Duplex crosshair in green, an MOA-Dot crosshair in green, a Mil-Dot crosshair in green, or a BAC triangle post in red, green, or yellow
MSRP $1399.00

OPTICS

Trijicon

ACCUPOWER SERIES

TRIJICON ACCUPOWER SERIES

TRIJICON ACOG WITH .300 BLK RETICLE 3X30MM

Weight: 16.2 oz, 17 oz., 23.6 oz, **23.3 oz., 36 oz., 38.4 oz.**
Length: 10.2 in., 12.3 in., 13.8 in., 14.2 in., 16 in.
Power: 1–4X, 3–9X, 2.5–10X, 4–16X, 4.5–30X, 5–50X
Obj. Dia.: 24mm, 40mm, 56mm, 50mm
Main Dia.: 30mm, 1 in., 30mm, 30mm
Exit Pupil: 15–5mm, 13.3–4.4mm, 16.5–5.6mm, 8.8–1.9mm, 9.3–3.1mm
Field of View: 97.5–24.2 ft @ 100 yds, 35.5–11.8 ft @ 100 yds, 37.9–10.2 ft @ 100 yds, 25.8–6.4 ft @ 100 yds, 24.7–3.7 ft @ 100 yds, 21.2–2.1 ft@100 yds
Eye Relief: 3.5 in., 3.7–3.5 in., 4 in., 3.6–3.7 in., 3.2–3.8 in., 3.5–3.9 in.
Features: Waterproof; illuminated; several reticle options; adjustable parallax; rear focal plane except for 4.5–30X56, which is available in both second and first focal plane configurations.
MSRP . . . . $699.00–$2700.00

ACOG WITH .300 BLK RETICLE 3X30MM

Weight: 11.64 oz.
Length: 6.1 in.
Power: 3X

TRIJICON VCOG 1–6X24MM RIFLESCOPE

Obj. Dia.: 30mm
Main Dia.: N/A
Exit Pupil: 10mm
Field of View: 19.3 ft @ 100 yds
Twilight Factor: 9.5
Eye Relief: 1.9 in.
Features: TA60 Mount; designed for law enforcement and military applications; .300 BLK Ballistic Reticle for subsonic and supersonic rounds; bullet drop compensator; Bindon Aiming Concept (BAC), fiber optics & tritium illuminated; available with amber, green, or red crosshair reticle
MSRP $1407.00

VCOG 1–6X24MM

Weight: 23.2 oz.
Length: 10.05 in.
Power: 1–6X
Obj. Dia.: 24mm
Main Dia.: N/A
Exit Pupil: 10.4–3.8mm
Field of View: 95–15.9 ft @ 100 yds
Twilight Factor: 12
Eye Relief: 4 in.
Features: Designed and built in the U.S.; Mil Spec, hard-coat finish; 90 MOA of windage and elevation adjustment; fully multi-coated lenses; waterproof; seven different reticle choices, between centered crosshair and horseshoe/dot reticle; red illuminated reticle; six brightness settings; matte finish
MSRP . . . . $2800.00–$3050.00

Truglo

TRUGLO TRU-BRITE 30 SERIES

TRUGLO TRU-BRITE XTREME DUAL-COLOR TACTICAL COMPACT 4X32MM

TRU-BRITE 30 SERIES

Available in: 1–4x24mm, 1–6x24mm
Weight: 13.4 oz.–15.1 oz.
Length: 9.88 in.–10.39 in.
Power: 1–4X, 1–6X
Obj. Dia.: 24mm
Main Dia.: 30mm
Exit Pupil: N/A
Field of View: 93.6–23.03 @ 100 yds, 103.71–18.15 ft @ 100 yds
Twilight Factor: N/A
Eye Relief: 3.75 in.
Features: Includes two pre-calibrated BDC turrets in calibers .223 (55 grain) and .308 (168 grain) to engage targets up to 800 yards away; ½ MOA windage/elevation adjustments
MSRP . . . . $176.99–$258.99

TRU-BRITE XTREME DUAL-COLOR TACTICAL COMPACT 4X32MM

Weight: 15.4 oz.
Length: 9.8 in.
Power: 4X
Obj. Dia.: 32mm
Main Dia.: 1 in.
Exit Pupil: N/A
Field of View: 20.79 ft @ 100 yds
Twilight Factor: 11.31
Eye Relief: 5.5 in.
Features: Illuminated reticle; fully coated lenses; durable, scratch-resistant, non-reflective matte finish
MSRP . . . . $87.99–$111.99

OPTICS

Vortex Optics

VORTEX CROSSFIRE II 3–12X56 AO HOG HUNTER

VORTEX CROSSFIRE II SCOUT

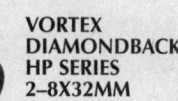
VORTEX DIAMONDBACK HP SERIES 2–8X32MM

VORTEX DIAMONDBACK TACTICAL

VORTEX GOLDEN EAGLE HD

VORTEX RAZOR HD AMG

VORTEX RAZOR HD GEN II-E

VORTEX RAZOR HD GEN II SERIES 4.5–27X56MM

CROSSFIRE II 3–12X56 AO HOG HUNTER
Weight: 21.1 oz.
Length: 14.3 in.
Power: 3–12X
Obj. Dia.: 56mm
Main Dia.: 30mm
Exit Pupil: N/A
Field of View: 36.7–9.2 ft @ 100 yds
Twilight Factor: 12.96–25.92
Eye Relief: 3.5 in.
Features: Second focal plane V-Brite illuminated reticle; single tube piece; aircraft-grade aluminum construction; capped reset turrets; adjustable objective; hard anodized finish
MSRP $369.99

CROSSFIRE II SCOUT
Available in: 2–7x32mm
Weight: 12 oz.
Length: 10.5 in.
Power: 2–7X
Obj. Dia.: 32mm
Main Dia.: 25.4mm
Exit Pupil: N/A
Field of View: 18.3–5.2 ft @ 100 yds
Twilight Factor: N/A
Eye Relief: 9.45 in.
Features: Fully multi-coated; second focal plane reticle; single-piece tube; capped reset turrets
MSRP $199.99

DIAMONDBACK HP 2–8X32MM
Weight: 15.9 oz.
Length: 11.6 in.
Power: 2–8X
Obj. Dia.: 32mm
Main Dia.: 1 in.
Exit Pupil: N/A
Field of View: 41.9–12.2 ft @ 100 yds
Twilight Factor: 8–16
Eye Relief: 4.6 in.
Features: Rear focal plane; shock-,

water-, and fogproof; adjustable parallax; 3–12x42 and 4–16x42 also available
2–8X: $349.00
3–12X: $399.00
4–16X: $429.99

DIAMONDBACK TACTICAL
Weight: 15.9 oz., 16.2 oz., 23.1 oz., 24.6 oz.
Length: 12.5 in., 14.2, 14 in., 14.5 in.
Power: 3–9x40mm, 4–12x40mm, 4–16X44mm, 6–24X50mm
Obj. Diameter: 40mm, 44mm, 50mm
Exit Pupil: N/A
Eye Relief: 3.8 in., 3.9 in.
Field of View: 11.3–3.7 ft @ 100 yds *(3–9x)*, 7.9–23.6 ft @ 100 yds *(4–12x)*, 26.9–6.7 ft @ 100 yds, 18–4.5 ft @ 100 yds
Features: 3–9X and 4–12X have second focal plane reticle (VMR-1); 4–16X and 6–24X have first focal plane reticle (glass-etched EBR-2C MOA); XD lens elements; XR full multi-coatings; fast focus eyepiece; fiber optic turret rotation indicator
3–9X: $379.99
4–12X: $349.99
4–16X: $449.99
6–24X: $499.99

GOLDEN EAGLE HD
Available in: 15–60x52mm
Weight: 29.7 oz.
Length: 16.1 in.
Power: 15–60X
Obj. Dia.: 52mm
Main Dia.: 30mm
Exit Pupil: N/A
Field of View: 6.3–1.7 ft @ 100 yds
Twilight Factor: N/A
Eye Relief: 3.9 in.
Features: Apochromatic objective lens system uses index-matched lenses to correct color across the entire visual spectrum; extra-fine resolution turret
MSRP $1899.99

RAZOR HD AMG
Available in: 6–24x50mm
Weight: 28.8 oz.
Length: 15.2 in.
Power: 6–24X
Obj. Dia.: 50mm
Main Dia.: 30mm
Exit Pupil: N/A
Field of View: 20.4–5.1 ft @ 100 yds
Twilight Factor: N/A
Eye Relief: 3.6 in.
Features: ALO proprietary automated laser optical alignment process; apochromatic objective lens system uses index-matched lenses to correct color across the entire visual spectrum; optically indexed lenses; premium high-density, extra-low dispersion glass; fully multi-coated; first focal plane reticle; illuminated reticle; waterproof, fogproof, and shockproof; side focus adjustment
MSRP $3699.99

RAZOR HD GEN II 4.5–27X56MM
Weight: 48.5 oz.
Length: 14.4 in
Power: 4.5–27X
Obj. Dia.: 56mm
Main Dia.: 34mm
Exit Pupil: N/A
Field of View: 25.3–4.4 ft @ 100 yds
Twilight Factor: 15.87–38.88
Eye Relief: 3.7 in.
Features: Front focal plane; shock-, water-, and fogproof; adjustable parallax; illuminated reticle; glass-etched reticle; 1–6x24 RFP and 3–18x50 also available
1–6X: $1999.99
3–18X: $2499.99
4.5–27X: $2899.99

RAZOR HD GEN II-E
Available in: 1–6x24mm
Weight: 21.5 oz.
Length: 10.1 in.
Power: 1–6x
Obj. Dia.: 24mm
Main Dia.: 30mm
Field of View: 115.2–20.5 ft.@100 yd.
Eye Relief: 4 in.
Features: Optically indexed lens for clarity; XR Plus fully multi-coated

OPTICS

Vortex Optics

VORTEX RAZOR HD LH SERIES

VORTEX VIPER HST SERIES 6–24X50MM

VORTEX VIPER PST GEN II

VORTEX STRIKE EAGLE

VORTEX VIPER PST RFP SERIES 1–4X24MM

VORTEX HS LR RFP SERIES 4–16X44MM

lenses; HD lens elements; second focal plane reticle; illuminated center dot with intensity lock; Armor-Tek finish for reduced external wear; reticles include VRM-2 MOA, VRM-2 MRAD, and JM-1 BDC
MSRP **$1999.99**

RAZOR HD LH SERIES
Available in: 1.5–8x32mm, 2–10x40mm, 3–15x42mm
Weight: 13.4 oz.–16.5 oz.
Length: 11 in.–13.5 in.
Power: 1.5–8X, 2–10X, 3–15X
Obj. Dia.: 32mm–42mm
Main Dia.: 25.4mm
Exit Pupil: N/A
Field of View: 72.2–13.2 ft @ 100 yds, 56.2–10.8 ft @ 100 yds, 35.8–7.1 ft @ 100 yds
Twilight Factor: N/A
Eye Relief: 3.8 in.
Features: Premium extra-low dispersion glass; optically indexed lenses; fully multi-coated; single-piece tube; hard anodized finish; large diameter turrets
1.5–8X: **$949.99**
2–10X: **$999.99**
3–15X: **$1099.99**

STRIKE EAGLE
Available in: 1–6X24mm, 1–8X24mm, 3–18x44mm, 4–24x50mm
Weight: 17.6 oz., 16.5 oz., 23.9 oz., 25.6 oz.
Length: 10.5 in., 10 in., 13.5 in.,14.9 in.
Power: 1–6X, 1–8X, 4–24X, 3–18X,
Obj. Dia.: 24mm, 44mm,
Main Dia.: 30mm
Field of View: 116.5–19.2 ft @ 100 yds, 116,6–14.4 ft @ 100 yds, 34.5–5.7 ft.@100 yds, 26.2–4.3 ft.@100 yds
Eye Relief: 3.5 in., 4.1 in.

Features: Second focal plane; glass-etched, illuminated reticles in a light-weight package and with fast-focus eyepieces; reticle is the EBR-4
1–6X: **$399.99**
1–8X: **$499.99**
3–18X: **$599.99**
4–24X: **$699.99**

VIPER HUNTING SHOOTING LONG RANGE (HS LR) 4–16X50MM
Weight: 19.8 oz.
Length: 13.7 in.
Power: 4–16X
Obj. Dia.: 50mm
Main Dia.: 30mm
Exit Pupil: N/A
Field of View: 27.4–7.4 ft @ 100 yds
Twilight Factor: 13.27–26.53
Eye Relief: 4 in.
Features: Rear focal plane; shock-, water-, and fogproof; adjustable parallax; 4–16X features Dead-Hold BDC reticle; also available in a 6–24X50mm with a first focal plane XLR reticle
4–16X: **$749.99**
6–24X: **$1049.99**

VIPER HUNTING SHOOTING TACTICAL (HST) 6–24X50MM
Weight: 22.6 oz.
Length: 15.5 in.
Power: 6–24X
Obj. Dia.: 50mm
Main Dia.: 30mm
Exit Pupil: N/A
Field of View: 17.8–5.1 ft @ 100 yds
Twilight Factor: 17.32–34.64
Eye Relief: 4 in.
Features: Choice of VMR-1 MRAD or MOA reticles in the second focal plane; shock-, water-, and fogproof; adjustable parallax; 4–16x44 also available
4–16X: **$719.99**
6–24X: **$789.99**

VIPER PRECISION SHOOTING TACTICAL (PST)
Weight: 18.7 oz., 18.8 oz.,
Length: 12 in.
Power: 2.5–10X32mm, 2.5–10X44mm,
Obj. Dia.: 32mm, 44mm
Main Dia.: 30mm
Exit Pupil: N/A
Field of View: 47–10.9 ft @ 100 yds,
Eye Relief: 4 in.
Features: EBR-1 MOA or EBR-1 MRAD glass-etched illuminated reticles available for the 2.5–10X32mm in first focal plane, 2.5–10X44mm in second focal plane, and the 4–16X in second focal plane; one-piece 30mm tubes; hard-anodized finish with scratch-resistant ArmorTek
2.5–10X32mm: **$999.00**
2.5–10X44mm: . . . . **$699.99–$799.99**
4–16X: **$899.00**

VIPER PST GEN II
Weight: 22.7 oz.–31.2 oz.
Length: 10.9 in.–16 in.
Power: 1–6x24mm, 2–10x32mm, 3–15x44mm, 5–25x50mm
Obj. Diameter: 24mm, 32mm, 44mm, 50mm
Exit Pupil: N/A
Eye Relief: 3.4–3.8 in.
Field of View: Varies with model
Features: Extra-low dispersion (XD) glass; multiple anti-reflection coatings on all air-to-glass surfaces; glass-etched, illuminated reticles; Reticle and focal plane options available are: 1–6x VMR-2 MRAD or MOA second focal plane; 2–10x EBR-4 MRAD or MOA first focal plane; 3–15x EBR-4 MOA second focal plane or EBR-2C MRAD or MOA first focal plane; 5–25x EBR-4 MOA second focal plane or EBR-2C MRAD or MOA first focal plane.
1–6x: **$899.99**
2–10x: **$1149.99**
3–15x: . . . . **$1099.99–$1199.99**
5–25x: . . . . **$1199.99–$1299.99**

OPTICS

9000SC

Weight: 7.4 oz.
Length: 6.3 in.
Obj. Dia.: 38mm
Features: Ideal for short length action rifles, semi-automatic firearms, and magnum handguns; ACET technology for longer battery life; available in 2 or 4 MOA dot sizes; two-ring configuration for mounting; waterproof; matte finish
MSRP $747.00

ACO

Weight: 7.8 oz.
Length: 5.1 in.
Power: 1X
Field of View: N/A
Eye Relief: N/A
Features: Developed with the modern sporting rifle owner in mind, the ACO is ready to mount and shoot directly out of the box; 30mm
aluminum alloy sight tube is paired with a rugged fixed height mount designed to provide absolute co-witness with AR-15 backup iron sights; 2 MOA red-dot to allow maximum target acquisition speed and accuracy at all distances; exclusive ACET technology allows for up to one year of constant-on use from a single DL1/3N battery; completely waterproof housing.
MSRP $485.17

MICRO H-1 AND T-1

Weight: 3 oz.
Length: 2.4 in.
Power: 1X
Features: High quality compact red-dot sight; sealed design ensures that

no foreign matter will come between the emitter and the lens; can be mounted on nearly any individual weapon platform including: pistols, carbines, personal defense weapons, and sub-machineguns; also available in 4 MOA red-dot
H-1: . . . . **$707.00–$1087.00**
T-1: . . . . **$788.00–$925.00**

MICRO H-2 AND T-2

Weight: 4.6 oz.–4.8 oz.
Length: 2.7 in.–3.16 in.
Power: 1X
Field of View: N/A
Eye Relief: N/A
Features: Advanced optical lenses for even better light transmission; can be used on shotguns, rifles, handguns or archery tackle; transparent front and rear flip-up lens covers are included; reinforced protection of the turrets for even greater ruggedness; 12 daylight settings; available in 2 MOA dot size; can be "piggybacked" on larger magnifying optics using an adapter.
H-2: . . . . **$820.00–$1200.00**
T-2: . . . . **$860.00–$1150.00**

PRO

Weight: 7.8 oz.
Length: 5.1 in.
Power: 1X
Features: Parallax free optic; 2 MOA dot for accurate target engagement at all distances; four night vision settings and six daylight settings; modular QRP2 mount includes removable spacer that indexes the sight at optimal height for co-witness, with the standard iron sights on AR15/M16/M4 carbine style weapons
MSRP . . . . **$525.65–$619.99**

AIMPOINT 9000SC

AIMPOINT ACO

AIMPOINT MICRO H-1

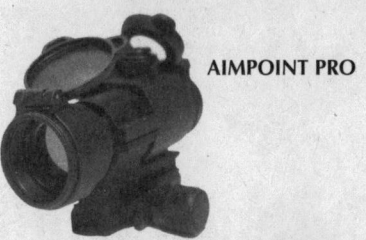

AIMPOINT PRO

AIMPOINT MICRO H-2

OPTICS

British Small Arms Co. (BSA)

BSA TACTICAL WEAPON ILLUMINATED SIGHT

TACTICAL WEAPON ILLUMINATED SIGHT

Weight: 22 oz.
Length: 8.75 in.
Power: 1X
Field of View: 3.7–19.3 ft @ 100 yds
Eye Relief: 2 in.
Features: Fully multicoated optics;

easy one-piece mounting; 5/8-inch Weaver-style rail; illuminated red dot; rubber eye guard; output power: 5mW; wave length: 650 nm; attachable 140 lumen LED flashlight
With flashlight: $139.95

Browning

BROWNING BUCK MARK REFLEX SIGHT

BUCK MARK REFLEX SIGHT
Weight: N/A
Power: 1X
Field of View: 47 ft @ 100 yds
Eye Relief: Unlimited
Features: The Buck Mark has an alumi-num housing, four red reticle patterns, a seven-position brightness rheostat powered by a lithium battery, and mounts on a standard Weaver-styled base
MSRP $69.99

Burris

BURRIS AR-536

BURRIS FASTFIRE 3 RED-DOT REFLEX SIGHT

AR-536
Weight: 18.75 oz.
Length: 5.75 in.
Power: 5X
Obj. Dia.: 36mm
Field of View: 20 ft @ 100 yds
Eye Relief: 2.5–3.5 in.
Features: Ballistic/CQTM lighted reticle; 600 yard range; multi-coated lenses; adjustable diopter; three Picatinny rail mounting points; black matte finish; max adj. 60 MOA; one-year warranty
MSRP . . . . $479.00–$659.00

FASTFIRE 3 RED-DOT REFLEX SIGHT
Weight: 0.9 oz.
Power: 1.07X
Features: Upgraded features such as windage and elevation adjustments that don't require a special tool; 3 or 8 MOA Dot; power button with three levels of brightness; low battery warning indicator and see-through protective cap; ideally suited for use on pistols and AR-15s where fast target acquisition is desired, the FastFire red-dot sight will also match up well with carbines, lever guns, and shotguns; available picatinny mount
MSRP . . . . $287.00–$355.00

Bushnell Outdoor Products

BUSHNELL AR OPTICS ADVANCE

BUSHNELL AR OPTICS CHASE

BUSHNELL AR OPTICS ENRAGE

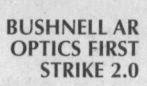

BUSHNELL AR OPTICS FIRST STRIKE 2.0

small enough to fit on a pistol; projects a 5-MOA dot; compact design compatible with a large selection of semiautomatic pistols
MSRP $209.99

AR OPTICS CHASE
Type: Laser
Laser Power Output: Less than 5 mw
Laser Wavelength: 635 nm (red); 525 nm (green)
Features: Creates a continuous laser beam available in red or green; flip-up post; mounts over the bore; waterproof
Red: $301.45
Green: $401.45

AR OPTICS ADVANCE
Weight: N/A
Power: 1x
Features: Micro reflex red dot sight

AR OPTICS ENRAGE
Weight: 9.8 oz.
Power: 1x
Obj. Diameter:
Features: Battery life that lasts twice as long as previous Bushnell red-dots; eight brightness settings lock in with a single click and there's an off setting between each; 2-MOA red-dot is housed in multi-coated optics; optional hi-rise mount
MSRP $209.99

AR OPTICS FIRST STRIKE 2.0
Type: Red dot
Weight: 2.1 oz.
Length: 2.4 in.
Power: 1x
Exit Pupil: 22 mm
Field of View: Unlimited
Eye Relief: Unlimited
Features: Features a brighter dot (five brightness settings) than the last version; longer battery life; side battery compartment that requires no tools to access
MSRP $239.99

Bushnell Outdoor Products

BUSHNELL AR OPTICS HASTE

BUSHNELL AR OPTICS INCINERATE

BUSHNELL AR OPTICS RUSH

BUSHNELL AR OPTICS TRS-26

BUSHNELL ELITE TACTICAL CQTS 2.0

BUSHNELL TAC OPTICS BIG D(OT)

BUSHNELL TAC OPTICS LIL P(RISM)

BUSHNELL TAC OPTICS MINI CANNON

AR OPTICS HASTE

Type: Laser
Laser Power Output: Less than 5 mw
Laser Wavelength: 635 nm (red); 525 nm (green)
Features: Forward grip-mounted under-bore-mounted laser for MSR rifles and pistols; laser available in red or green; laser activates via a single push-button; waterproof; batteries can be replaced without losing zero
Red:.....................$248.95
Green:..................$348.95

AR OPTICS INCINERATE

Weight: 10.2 oz.
Power: 1x
Features: Circle dot reticle, 25-MOA circle, and 2-MOA center dot work with both tactical rifles and shotguns; rear sight is compatible with Glock dovetail sights; eight brightness settings with off setting between each
MSRP....................$209.99

AR OPTICS RUSH

Type: Laser
Laser Power Output: Less than 5 mw
Laser Wavelength: 635 nm (red); 525 nm (green)
Features: High-rise optics mount with an offset laser in red or green; any optic mounting on a Picatinny rail can top this laser

Red:.....................$275.95
Green:..................$375.95

AR OPTICS TRS-26

Type: Red dot
Weight: 13.2 oz.
Power: 1x
Obj. Dia.: 26mm
Field of View: Unlimited
Eye Relief: Unlimited
Features: Compact red dot replacing an older version; brighter, five-setting dot; enhanced battery life; push-button controls
MSRP....................$159.99

ELITE TACTICAL CQTS 2.0

Type: Red dot
Weight: 11 oz.
Length: 4.8 in.
Power: 1x
Obj. Dia.: 32mm
Field of View: Unlimited
Eye Relief: Unlimited
Features: Newer edition of the Close Quarters Tactical Sight; 30mm tube houses a 2.5 dot; users can switch to a circle dot, crosshair dot, or circle/crosshair dot via push-button; 100 MOA of windage and elevation adjustment
MSRP....................$469.99

TAC OPTICS BIG D(OT)

Type: Red dot

Weight: 13.2 oz.
Length: 3 in.
Power: 1x
Obj. Dia.: 37mm
Field of View: Unlimited
Eye Relief: Unlimited
Features: Larger than the typical red dot lense; 5 MOA dot
MSRP....................$319.99

TAC OPTICS LIL P(RISM)

Type: Red dot
Weight: 8 oz.
Length: 2.5 in.
Power: 1x
Field of View: Unlimited
Eye Relief: Unlimited
Features: Bushnell calls it one of the smallest prism sights; houses a BDC reticle
MSRP....................$319.99

TAC OPTICS MINI CANNON

Type: Red dot
Weight: 7.4 oz.
Length: 3 in.
Power: 1x
Obj. Dia.: 25mm
Field of View: Unlimited
Eye Relief: Unlimited
Features: Four reticle options available; change reticle without losing zero
MSRP....................$358.45

Cabela's

CABELA'S TACTICAL REFLEX SIGHT

TACTICAL REFLEX SIGHT

Features: Automatically turns on when cap is lifted; automatic reticle-brightness control; multi-coated optics with 5 MOA center-dot reticle; waterproof; shockproof; mounts to any Picatinny rail; runs for up to 300 hours on one battery
MSRP....................$99.99

OPTICS

Davide Pedersoli & C.

150 UNIVERSAL CREEDMOOR SIGHT, MIDDLE AND LONG RANGE, MODELS USA 465 AND 430

Features: Tang sight with elevation and windage adjustment in the eye piece; for long-distance target shooting both with muzzle-loading and breech-loading rifles; 2.1875–2.3125-in. between two mounting holes; 2- and 3-in. elevation adjustments

USA 430 Long Range: **$215.00**
USA 465 Middle Range: **$215.00**

ENGLISH REAR SIGHT, MODEL USA 428

Features: Rear sight with convex base, with two adjustable and folding leaves

From: **$130.00**

FIBER OPTIC FRONT AND REAR SIGHT, MODEL USA 409

Features: Front sight and rear sight set for muzzleloading rifles (Model 410 for breechloaders); front sight with dovetail base; rear sight with base for octagonal barrel

From: **$125.00**

FOLDING FRONT SIGHT

Features: Globe sight for long-range when raised, or fold down for built-in blade for close range; ball/detent locking mechanism; 3/8-in. dovetail base; 1/2-in. high

From: **$100.00**

GHOST CREEDMOOR SIGHT-USA 422

Features: A tang sight inspired by some models in use in the 1800s, economic, functional, and useful for hunting; adjustable in elevation and windage; can fit several gun types; small eye piece ring enables a quick, instinctive aim at the target; when quickly shouldering the rifle, the open ring provides a clear sight picture with low light condition; distance between the two mounting holes is 1 3/4-in.

From: **$80.00**

"SOULE TYPE" MIDDLE RANGE SET, MODEL USA 170

Features: Wooden-box set including Soule XL Middle Range Sight; tunnel front sight with a micrometric screw for windage adjustment, spirit level, and fifteen interchangeable inserts; professional "Hadley Style" eyepiece with eight varying diameter viewing holes, depending on available light,

on a rotating disk which can be selected without disassembling or loosening the eyepiece, and a rubber ring on the eyepiece; six interchangeable glass bubbles (spirit level) with different colors for varying light conditions; 3-in. elevation adjustment

From: **$755.00**

SPIRIT LEVEL TUNNEL SIGHT ADJUSTABLE WITH 12 INSERTS SET, MODEL USA 425

Features: Spirit level tunnel sight with micrometer adjustment for windage, equipped with twelve interchangeable inserts; also available in 15 and 18 insert sets

From: **$25.00**

U.S. MODEL 1879 SPRINGFIELD TRAPDOOR REAR SIGHT, MODEL USA 473

Features: Sometimes referred to as "Buckhorn" style; used on Trapdoor rifles from 1874 until superseded by Buffington style in 1884; side ramps are graduated to 500 yds and the ladder to 1500 yds; slide has windage adjustment

From: **$80.00**

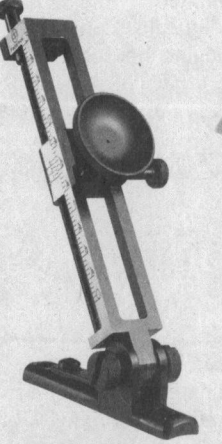

DAVIDE PEDERSOLI
UNIVERSAL CREEDMOOR
SIGHT–430

DAVIDE PEDERSOLI
ENGLISH REAR SIGHT–428

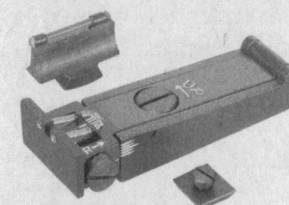

DAVIDE FIBER OPTIC FRONT AND
REAR SIGHT–409

DAVIDE PEDERSOLI
FOLDING FRONT SIGHT

DAVIDE PEDERSOLI
GHOST CREEDMOOR
SIGHT-USA 422

DAVIDE PEDERSOLI "SOULE
TYPE" MIDDLE RANGE SET-170

DAVIDE PEDERSOLI SPIRIT
LEVEL TUNNEL SIGHT
ADJUSTABLE–425

DAVIDE PEDERSOLI U.S.
MODEL 1879 SPRINGFIELD
TRAPDOOR REAR SIGHT–473

EOTECH MODEL 300 BLACKOUT

EOTECH HOLOGRAPHIC HYBRID SIGHT

HOLOGRAPHIC HYBRID SIGHT (HHS)

Power: 3X
Eye Relief: 2.2 in.
Features: The HHS kits combine the speed of the EXPS holographic weapon sight and the extended range versatility of the G33 magnifier; available in three configurations: Sight I houses the EXPS3 red dot; Sight II houses the EXPS2 red dot; and the Sight III houses with the 518.2 red-dot that takes AA batteries
Sight I:.................**$1209.00**
Sight II:...............**$1135.00**
Sight III:..............**$1089.00**

MODEL 300 BLACKOUT

Weight: 9 oz.
Length: 3.8 in.
Power: 1X
Field of View: 90 ft @ 100 yds
Eye Relief: Unlimited
Features: Designed with tactical shooters in mind, this optic offers a two-dot ballistic drop reticle that allows the shooter to zero either subsonic or supersonic rounds in the same reticle pattern; offered in the XPS2 platform, it is the shortest and lightest HWS sight available; its size and weight make it convenient for hunters, military and law enforcement officers to carry; the single compact lithium 123 battery configuration opens up more space on the rail for rear iron sights or magnifiers
MSRP...................**$567.00**

Firefield

FIREFIELD IMPACT XL, XLT

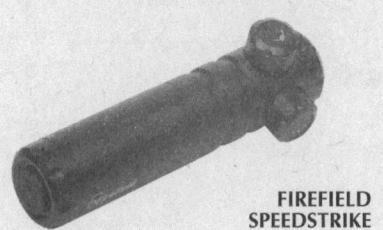

FIREFIELD SPEEDSTRIKE

IMPACT XL, XLT

Type: Red dot
Weight: 5.6, 7.8 oz.
Length: 3.6 in.
Power: 1x
Eye Relief: Unlimited
Battery Life: 25–250 hours (XL); 40–250 hours (XLT)
Features: Multiple reticle options; AR-red coated lenses; parallax correction; ample windage; elevation adjustments; neoprene cover; adjustment tools; XLT has a quick-detach mount, digital controls, and a protective hood
XL:......................**$59.97**
XLT:.....................**$79.97**

SPEEDSTRIKE

Type: Laser
Weight: 6.3 oz.
Length: 4.25 in.
Battery Life: 80 hours (red); 25 hours (green)
Laser Power Output: Less than 5 mw
Laser Wavelength: 632 nm
Features: Available in red or green; modular mount; windage and elevation adjustments can be made without tools; pressure-pad activated
Red:....................**$29.97**
Green:..................**$49.97**

OPTICS

Konus

KONUS SIGHTPRO ATOMIC 2.0

SIGHTPRO ATOMIC 2.0

Weight: 3.8 oz.
Length: 2.4 in.
Power: 1X
Field of View: 76 ft @ 100 yds
Eye Relief: N/A
Features: Illuminated reticle dots; fits both Picatinny and Weaver rails
MSRP.................**$179.99**

Konus

KONUS SIGHTPRO ATOMIC QR

KONUS SIGHTPRO FISSION 2.0

KONUS SIGHTPRO TR

SIGHTPRO ATOMIC QR
Weight: 6.5 oz.
Length: 2.5 in.
Power: 1X

Field of View: N/A
Eye Relief: N/A
Features: Illuminated reticle dots; fits both Picatinny and Weaver rails
MSRP...................$229.99

SIGHTPRO FISSION 2.0
Weight: 1.76 oz.
Length: 1.7 in.
Power: 1X
Field of View: 115 ft @ 100 yds
Eye Relief: N/A
Features: Illuminated reticle dots; fits both Picatinny and Weaver rails
MSRP...................$199.99

SIGHTPRO PTS1
Weight: 14.1 oz.
Length: 12.2 in.
Power: 3X
Obj. Dia.: 32mm
Field of View: 36.6 ft @ 100 yds
Eye Relief: 4.5 in.
Features: Shock-, water-, and fog-proof; illuminated reticle dots; fits both Picatinny and Weaver rails
MSRP.................. **$399.99**

SIGHTPRO TR
Weight: 13 oz.
Length: 4.75 in.
Power: 1X
Field of View: N/A
Eye Relief: N/A
Features: Illuminated reticle dots; four different reticle patterns
MSRP...................$219.99

Lasermax

GRIPSENSE LIGHT AND LASERS
Type: Laser
Weight: 1.5 oz.
Battery Life: At least 4 hours
Laser Power Output: Less than 5 mw
Laser Wavelength: 510–535 nm
Red:....................................**$149.00**
Green:..................................**$169.00**

LASERMAX GRIPSENSE LIGHT AND LASERS

Leapers, Inc.

LEAPERS UTG ITA RED/GREEN CLOSE QUARTERS BATTLE (CQB) T-DOT SIGHT

UTG ITA RED/GREEN CLOSE QUARTERS BATTLE (CQB) T-DOT SIGHT
Weight: 13.1 oz.
Length: 6.1 in.
Power: 1X
Field of View: 85 ft @ 100 yds
Eye Relief: Unlimited
Features: Completely sealed; shock-proof, fogproof; and rainproof; 4

MOA red/green single dot reticle or quick-to-acquire red/green T-dot reticle; premium zero lockable and zero resettable target turrets; TactEdge angled integral sunshade reduces glare off the lens while maintaining superb light transmission clarity
MSRP....................**$67.97**

Leatherwood/Hi-Lux

**LEATHERWOOD/
HI-LUX TAC-DOT**

TAC-DOT
Weight: 2.1 oz.
Length: 2.5 in.
Power: 1X
Obj. Dia.: 21x16mm
Field of View: 30x22 ft @ 100 yds
Eye Relief: N/A
Features: Elevation and windage adjustments are 50 MOA per revolution; special illumination circuit is designed to control the illuminated dot size in a consistent shape and size; dot size is 4 MOA; light sensor will control the brightness of the dot automatically based on the light situation
MSRP $99.00

Leupold & Stevens

LEUPOLD D-EVO

LEUPOLD DELTAPOINT PRO

LEUPOLD LEOPOLD CARBINE OPTIC (LCO)

D-EVO
Weight: 13.8 oz.
Length: 4.6 in.
Power: 6X
Obj. Dia.: 20mm
Field of View: 15.7 ft @ 100 yds
Eye Relief: 3.4 in.
Features: Bullet drop compensation; water- and fogproof; 1/10th MIL click adjustment; 6061-T6 aircraft quality aluminum
MSRP $1299.99

DELTAPOINT PRO
Weight: 1.95 oz.
Length: 1.82 in.
Power: 1X
Field of View: N/A
Eye Relief: Unlimited
Features: Water- and fogproof; DiamondCoat; removable, adjustable rear sight; tool-less, spring actuated battery compartment; illuminated reticle available
MSRP $519.99

LEOPOLD CARBINE OPTIC (LCO)
Weight: 9.5 oz.
Length: 3.6 in.
Power: 1X
Obj. Dia.: 32mm
Field of View: N/A
Eye Relief: Unlimited
Features: Nitrogen filled; water- and fogproof; ½ MOA field click; 6061-T6 aircraft quality aluminum
MSRP $909.99

Lucid Optics, LLC

LUCID HD7 RED DOT SIGHT

HD7 RED DOT SIGHT
Weight: 13 oz.
Length: 5.5 in.
Power: 1X
Obj.Dia.: 34mm
Field of View: 44 ft @ 100 yds
Eye Relief: Unlimited
Features: Third generation unit; integral Picatinny rail and reversible mounting pins for bullpup-style firearms; manual and a Auto- Brightness with twelve brightness settings; four operator-selectable reticles based on a 2 MOA dot with ½ MOA click adjustments; parallax free, it is powered by one AAA battery; the frame is cast aluminum armored in chemical rubber and is available with a 2x screw-in eyepiece; available in tan
Black: $259.00
Tan: $269.00

OPTICS

Meopta USA

MEOPTA MEOMAG3 MAGNIFIER

MEOPTA MEORED 30

MEOPTA MEOSIGHT III 30 IL

MEOMAG3 MAGNIFIER

Type: Magnifier
Weight: 7.48 oz.
Length: 4.65 in.
Power: 3x
Obj. Dia.: 20mm
Exit Pupil: 5.4 mm
Field of View: 7 degrees
Eye Relief: 60mm
Features: Works with both Meopta and other red dot sights on the market; works as a monocular; waterproof, shockproof, and fogproof; Meopta's Fast Opening Lens Covers; optional accessories include fixed, quick-release and hinge mounts, tactical carry pouch, and a hard case
MSRP $999.99

MEORED 30

Weight: 1 oz.
Length: 1.85 in.
Power: 1x
Features: Ultra compact reflex red-dot sight; parallax free and designed for use on handguns with cut-out slides, AR platforms, or shotguns; dot size is 3 MOA; integrated MIL-STD 1913 mount; interface plate accepts a Docter mount; windage adjustment up to 180 MOA; elevation adjustment to 120 MOA; simple on/off button on left side of optic allows the user to adjust brightness level; one CR 2302 battery with a life of up to 300 hours; optic will auto-off after three hours of continuous operation if the on/off button hasn't been activated; MeoBright, MeoDrop, and MeoShield coatings are all featured
MSRP $479.95

MEOSIGHT III 30 IL

Weight: 1.29 oz.
Length: 1.8 in.
Power: 1X
Field of View: N/A
Eye Relief: N/A
Features: Picatinny quick release mount; illuminated reticle; ideal for handguns, shotguns, and tactical weapons
MSRP $349.95

Nikon

P-TACTICAL SPUR

Type: Reflex red dot sight
Weight: 1.1 oz.
Length: 1.8 in.
Power: 1x
Eye Relief: Unlimited
Features: Shockproof; waterproof; Nikon's TRUCOLOR lens coating; ten brightness levels, two of which are night-vision compatible; includes a Picatinny rail mount; five-year warranty
MSRP $219.95

NIKON P-TACTICAL SPUR

Shield Sights

RMSC

Type: Reflex red dot
Weight: .57 oz.
Length: 17 in.
Power: 1x
Features: Reflex Mini Sight Compact; designed specifically for use on subcompact pistols; with a 4 MOA or 8 MOA dot
MSRP $430.00

SHIELD SIGHTS RMSC

OPTICS

SIG Sauer

SIG SAUER JULIET4 MAGNIFIER

SIG SAUER BRAVO4

SIG SAUER ROMEO1

SIG SAUER ROMEO3

SIG SAUER ROMEO4H

SIG SAUER ROMEO4S

JULIET4 MAGNIFIER

Type: Magnifier
Weight: 12.5 oz.
Length: 4.2 in.
Power: 4x
Obj. Dia.: 24mm
Exit Pupil: 6mm
Field of View: 6.25 degrees
Eye Relief: 65mm
Features: Included spacers allow height adjustment; stand-alone or with red dot sight; aircraft grade CNC aluminum housing; quick release mount with recoil lugs; IPX-8 waterproofing of 20 meters per 1 hour; protectors for front thread-in lens and rear flip back lens
MSRP. $479.99

BRAVO4

Weight: 14.8 oz.
Length: 6.25 in.
Power: 4X
Field of View: 53 ft @ 100 yds
Eye Relief: 2.2 in.
Features: MegaView system utilizes an advanced prism and ocular design yielding 43 percent greater field of view than the competitive prismatic battle sights; MOTAC (Motion Activated Illumination) powers up when it senses motion and powers down when it does not; notably flat, distortion-free image for edge-to-edge clarity by means of a combination of low dispersion glass and aspherical lens design; lightweight yet durable magnesium housing with integrated Picatinny top rail for additional accessories such as MRDs and lasers; adjustable eyepiece with +/- 2 diopter correction; IPX-8 waterproof (to 400 mbar or 13 ft)
MSRP. $1199.99

ROMEO1

Weight: 0.8 oz.
Length: 1.8 in.
Power: 1X
Field of View: N/A
Eye Relief: Unlimited
Features: Also available with a universal mount with rear sight dovetail adapters for the most popular handguns on the market; also available with either an M1913 Picatinny or KeyMod Rail interface for use with today's MSR platforms; molded glass aspheric lens with high performance coatings for superior light transmittance and zero distortion; manual illumination controls that remember your last used settings; MOTAC (Motion Activated Illumination) powers up when it senses motion and powers down when it does not; top-loading CR1632 battery, allowing for quick battery replacement without having to remove the sight from the firearm; extremely strong and lightweight aircraft grade CNC magnesium housing waterproof (IPX-7 rated for complete immersion up to 1 meter)
MSRP. . . . . $359.99–$539.99

ROMEO3

Weight: 1.4 oz.
Length: 2.4 in.
Power: 1X
Field of View: N/A
Eye Relief: Unlimited
Features: High transmittance red notch reflector for excellent brightness, light transmittance, and zero distortion; 3 MOA red dot with multiple intensity settings ensures rapid target engagement under a full range of lighting conditions; MOTAC (Motion Activated Illumination) powers up when it senses motion and powers down when it does not; side-loading CR2032 battery, allowing for quick battery replacement without having to remove the sight from the firearm; extremely strong and lightweight aircraft grade CNC Aluminum housing; waterproof (IPX-7 rated for complete water immersion up to 1 meter)
MSRP. $479.99

ROMEO4H

Weight: 3.4 oz.
Power: 1x
Obj. Diameter: 20mm
Features: Designed for a AR-platform pistols, MSRs, and shotguns; four reticle options; side-loading battery has 50,000+ hours of life
MSRP. . . . . $419.99–$479.99

ROMEO4S

Weight: 3.4 oz.
Power: 1x
Obj. Diameter: 20mm
Features: Solar powered red-dot runs in excess of 100,000+ with solar and battery usage; designed for AR-platform pistols, MSRs, and shotguns; lens caps and quick-release mount; four reticle choices
MSRP. $539.99

OPTICS

SIG Sauer

SIG SAUER ROMEO4T

SIG SAUER ROMEO5

SIG SAUER ROMEO7

ROMEO7

Weight: 12.5 oz.
Length: 4.75 in.
Power: 1X
Field of View: N/A
Eye Relief: Unlimited
Features: Low dispersion glass lens design with high-performance coatings for excellent light transmittance and zero distortion; 2 MOA dot is optimal for close quarters battle to mid-range target engagement; MOTAC (Motion Activated Illumination) powers up when it senses motion and powers down when it does not; 62,500 hours of continuous battery life in medium illumination setting; ready to mount with a standard QD mount provided, but can be customized with vertical spacers to fit a variety of systems; dependable waterproof (IPX-7 rated for complete water immersion up to 1 meter)
MSRP $359.99

ROMEO4T

Weight: 3.2 oz.
Power: 1x
Obj. Diameter: 20mm
Features: Solar-powered red dot runs in excess of 100,000+ with solar and battery usage; designed for AR-platform pistols, MSRs, and shotguns; lens caps and quick-release mount; four reticle choices; tactical version designed for harsh environments
MSRP . . . . $659.99–$683.99

ROMEO5

Type: Red dot
Weight: 6 oz.
Length: 2.47 in.
Power: 1x
Obj. Dia.: 20mm
Eye Relief: Infinite
Features: Mounts on any platform; 2 MOA dot; motion-activated illumination; 10 brightness settings; front-mounting AAA battery or side-loading CR2032 battery; waterproof and fogproof; Picatinny low mount and co-witness 1.41-inch riser mount included; torx tool; battery; lens cloth; lens covers; reticles include 2 MOA dot with 65 MOA circle, 2 MOA red dot, 2 MOA green dot with triangle holds
MSRP . . . .$179.99–$599.99

Steiner

STEINER MICRO REFLEX SIGHT (MRS)

STEINER EOPTICS DBAL-RL

STEINER EOPTICS SBAL-PL

MICRO REFLEX SIGHT (MRS)

Weight: 2.5 oz.
Length: N/A
Power: 1X
Field of View: N/A
Eye Relief: Unlimited
Features: Picatinny mount; waterproof; holographic sight; adjustable for windage and elevation; illuminated
MSRP $529.99

EOPTICS DBAL-RL

Type: Laser
Weight: 5.4 oz.
Length: 3.46 in.
Battery Life: 1.75 hours
Laser Power Output: Less than 5 mw
Laser Wavelength: 515–535 nm (green); 635–650 nm (red)
Features: Dual Beam Aiming Laser; includes both a light and a laser, fully programmable and capable of being dimmed in both infrared and visible modes; lasers are in green or red, visible or IR laser; the light is IR illuminator or white light; fully adjustable for windage and elevation; mounts on a standard Picatinny M1913 rail; remote switch operation
MSRP $1342.99

EOPTICS SBAL-PL

Type: Laser
Weight: 4.6 oz.
Length: 3.46 in.
Battery Life: 2 hours
Laser Power Output: Less than 5 mw
Laser Wavelength: 635-650 nm
Features: Single Beam Aiming Laser; red or green laser options; 500 lumen light; custom holsters that accommodate the light accessory are available
MSRP $765.00

OPTICS

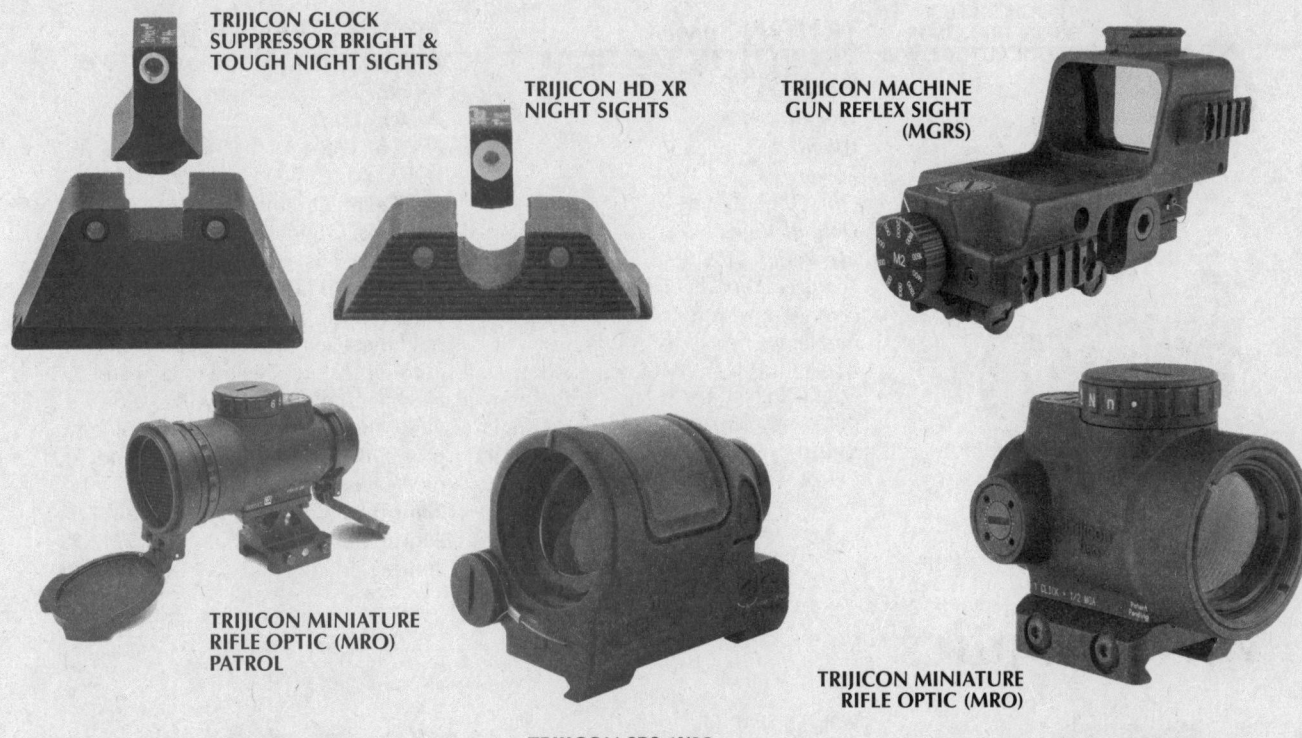

TRIJICON GLOCK SUPPRESSOR BRIGHT & TOUGH NIGHT SIGHTS

TRIJICON HD XR NIGHT SIGHTS

TRIJICON MACHINE GUN REFLEX SIGHT (MGRS)

TRIJICON MINIATURE RIFLE OPTIC (MRO) PATROL

TRIJICON SRS 1X38

TRIJICON MINIATURE RIFLE OPTIC (MRO)

BRIGHT & TOUGH SUPPRESSOR NIGHT SIGHTS

Features: Three-dot iron sights; shock-resistant design; increase night-fire accuracy by as much as 5x; available for a wide variety of Glock, FNH, H&K, SIG Sauer, Smith & Wesson, and Springfield Armory handguns
MSRP **$145.00**

HD XR NIGHT SIGHTS

Type: Night sights
Weight: 1.6 oz.
Length: 1.22 in.
Features: Thin front sight post provides a larger field of view; available for Beretta, FNH, GLOCK, H&K, Sig Sauer, Smith & Wesson, and Springfield Armory handguns; front sight choice of yellow or orange outline
Front sight only: **$99.00**
Front and rear: **$175.00**

MACHINE GUN REFLEX SIGHT (MGRS)

Weight: 66.9 oz.
Length: 8.78 in.
Power: 1x
Features: Created to withstand the constant, violent battering of machine guns; large objective lens with a 3-inch-by-2-inch viewing area; 35 MOA segmented circle reticle; centered 3 MOA dot for precise aiming at close combat to extended ranges; powered by a single CR123A battery that lasts 1000 hours of continuous operation
MSRP **$4499.00**

MINIATURE RIFLE OPTIC (MRO)

Weight: 4.1 oz.
Length: 2.6 in.
Power: 1X
Field of View: N/A
Eye Relief: Unlimited
Features: Large viewing area; adjustable brightness settings; ambidextrous brightness control; easy-to-set adjusters; aircraft-grade aluminum housing; surface-flush adjusters; waterproof to 30 meters; single lithium battery
Green dot: . . . . **$613.00–$663.00**
Red dot: . . . . **$579.00–$639.00**

MINIATURE RIFLE OPTIC (MRO) PATROL

Type: Red dot

Weight: 5.1 oz.
Length: 4.1 in.
Power: 1x
Obj. Dia.: 25mm
Eye Relief: Infinite
Features: Lens covers; Kill Flash feature that eliminates glare; quick-release mount in full height or co-witness configurations; 70 MOAs of adjustment are in 0.5-MOA increments; runs for five years of continuous use on its 2032 battery; available without mount
MSRP . . . . **$849.00–$919.00**

SRS (SEALED REFLEX SIGHT) 1X38

Weight: 13.8 oz.
Length: 3.75 in.
Power: 1X
Obj. Dia.: 38mm
Features: Body length of only 3.75 inches virtually eliminates the "tube effect" common with other, competitive red-dot sights; field of view provides no obstruction to shooters; LED 1.75 MOA aiming point with 10 brightness settings; SRS powered by solar panel and AA battery; parallax free objective lens; available in Colt-Style flattop mount or Quick Release flattop mount
MSRP . . . . **$1150.00–$1250.00**

OPTICS

Truglo

TRUGLO TRITON 30MM TRI-COLOR TACTICAL TG8230GB

TRUGLO TRU-TEC RED DOT

TRITON 30MM TRI-COLOR TACTICAL RED DOT
Weight: 6.4 oz.
Length: 5.2 in.
Power: 1X
Obj. Dia.: 30mm
Field of View: N/A
Eye Relief: N/A
Features: Weaver style mount; multi-coated lenses; tri-color illuminated reticle; two versions: Model #TG8230B has 5 MOA single dot. Model #TG8230GB has 3 MOA center dot and surrounding aiming ring
MSRP $105.99

TRU-TEC RED DOT
Weight: 4.91 oz.–12.9 oz.
Length: 2.4 in.–5.78 in.
Power: 1X
Field of View: 46 ft @ 100 yds, 68 ft @ 100 yds
Eye Relief: Unlimited
Features: Option of 20mm or 30mm objective lens; optional integrated green or red laser with 30mm lens; digital; push-button controls; multiple brightness settings; programmable auto-off feature; click windage and elevation adjustments; wide field of view; shock resistant; waterproof/fogproof; mounts to standard Picatinny or Weaver-style rails
20mm: $211.99
20mm QD: $247.99
30mm: $223.99

Vortex Optics

VORTEX SPARC II

VORTEX CROSSFIRE RED DOT

VORTEX SPITFIRE AR PRISM

VORTEX SPARC AR

CROSSFIRE
Type: Red dot
Weight: 5.2 oz.
Length: 2.5 in.
Power: 1x
Eye Relief: Infinite
Features: Daylight-bright 2 MOA dot; 100 MOA of elevation and windage adjustment; parallax-free viewing
MSRP $219.99

SPARC II
Weight: 5.9 oz.
Length: 3.1 in.
Power: 1X
Field of View: N/A
Eye Relief: N/A
Features: Shock-, water-, and fog-proof; illuminated red dot
MSRP $259.99

SPARC AR
Weight: 7.5 oz.
Length: 2.9 in.
Power: 1X
Field of View: N/A
Eye Relief: Unlimited
Features: Fully multi-coated; bright

red dot highly visible in daylight; ten variable illumination settings; waterproof, fogproof, and shockproof; hard anodized finish; twelve-hour auto-shutdown feature maximizes battery life
MSRP $259.99

SPITFIRE AR PRISM
Weight: 11.2 oz.
Length: 4.3 in.
Power: 1X, 3X
Field of View: 29 ft @ 100 yds
Eye Relief: 3.8 in.
Features: Fully multi-coated; prism-based design; twelve variable illumination settings; waterpoof and shockproof; hard anodized finish; red or green reticle option
MSRP $349.99

Vortex Optics

VORTEX SPITFIRE PRISM

VORTEX STRIKEFIRE II

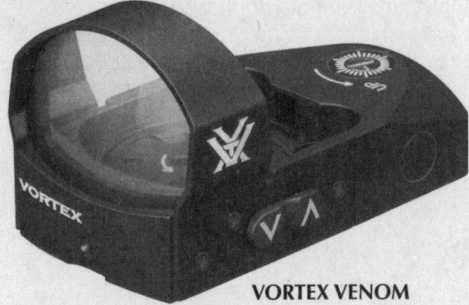

VORTEX VENOM

VORTEX VIPER

SPITFIRE PRISM
Weight: 12.2 oz.
Length: 5.5 in.
Power: 3X
Field of View: 31.5 ft @ 100 yds
Eye Relief: 2.8 in.
Features: Shock-, water-, and fog-proof; illuminated red dot
MSRP **$449.99**

STRIKEFIRE II
Weight: 7.2 oz.
Length: 5.6 in.
Power: 1X
Field of View: N/A

Eye Relief: N/A
Features: Shock-, water-, and fog-proof; illuminated red dot; red/green dot cantilever and low mount models available
MSRP $239.99

VENOM
Weight: 1.1 oz.
Length: 1.9 in.
Power: 1X
Field of View: N/A
Eye Relief: Unlimited
Features: Bright red dot; Picatinny

mount; choice of 3 or 6 MOA dots; machined aluminum housing
MSRP **$329.99**

VIPER
Weight: 1.37 oz.
Length: 1.8 in.
Power: 1X
Field of View: N/A
Eye Relief: Unlimited
Features: Bright red dot; Picatinny mount; 6 MOA dot
MSRP **$329.00**

XS Sights

F8 NIGHT SIGHTS
Type: Sights
Weight: 2.4 oz.
Features: Presents a figure 8 top-to-bottom alignment of front and rear sight; orange ring of the sight absorbs ambient light to glow in low light conditions; wide notch rear allows more light around the front sight for quicker acquisition and also reduces glare in daylight; available for a variety of GLOCK, Sig Sauer, Smith & Wesson, Springfield, and FNH pistols
MSRP **$142.00**

XS SIGHTS F8 NIGHT SIGHTS

ATN Corp.

ATN LASERBALLISTICS 1000, 1500

LASERBALLISTICS 1000, 1500
Type: Rangefinder
Weight: 5.4 oz.
Length: 4.17 in.
Power: 6X
Features: Pairs with ATN's Smart HD Bluetooth scopes; gives the distance to your target in five seconds, then moves the reticle of those scopes accordingly via the mobile app for a shot in under 15 seconds; range is from 5–1000 yds (Model 1000) and 5–1500 yds (Model 1500); waterproof

1000: **$279.00**
1500: **$349.00**

Bushnell Outdoor Products

BUSHNELL ELITE 1 MILE ARC

ELITE 1 MILE ARC
Weight: 12.1 oz.
Power: 7X
Obj. Dia.: 26mm
Range: 5–1760 yd
Features: Waterproof; built-in tripod mount; fully multi-coated lenses
MSRP **$629.00**

Leupold & Stevens

LEUPOLD RX-2800 TBR WITH LASER RANGEFINDER

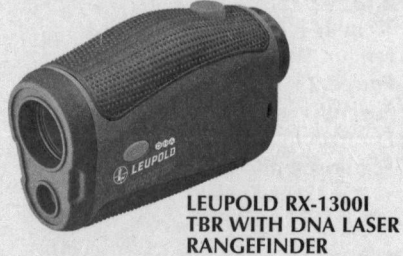

LEUPOLD RX-1300I TBR WITH DNA LASER RANGEFINDER

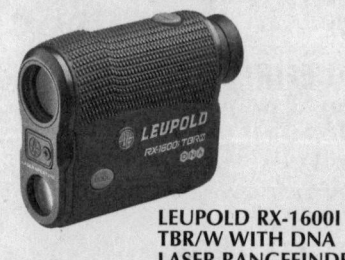

LEUPOLD RX-1600I TBR/W WITH DNA LASER RANGEFINDER

RX-2800 TBR WITH LASER RANGEFINDER
Type: Rangefinder
Weight: 7.3 oz.
Length: 4.3 in.
Power: 7x
Field of View: 318 ft.@1000 yd.
Eye Relief: 16 mm
Features: Powered by Alpha IQ; OLED display; scan mode; trophy scale analysis; True Ballistic Range with Wind
MSRP **$779.99**

RX-1300I TBR WITH DNA LASER RANGEFINDER
Type: Rangefinder
Weight: 7 oz.
Length: 4 in.

Power: 6x
Exit Pupil: 3.9mm
Field of View: 315 ft.@1000 yd.
Eye Relief: 14mm
Features: Ranges from 0.5–1,300 yards; True Ballistic Range to 800 yards; a built-in inclinometer; fully multi-coated lenses; armor coated; CR2 lithium battery; in a black/gray combo or in Mossy Oak Break-Up Country; Leupold's DNA technology that improves accuracy and speed
MSRP **$389.99**

RX-1600I TBR/W WITH DNA LASER RANGEFINDER
Type: Rangefinder
Weight: 7.8 oz.
Length: 3.8 in.

Power: 6x
Exit Pupil: 3.6mm
Field of View: 315 ft.@1000 yd.
Eye Relief: 17mm
Features: Fully multi-coated glass; Leupold's DNA technology that improves accuracy and speed; scan mode; choice of three reticles; line-of-sight distance; trophy scale technology; built-in inclinometer; True Ballistic Range with Wind; fold-down rubber eye cup; quick-set menu; OLED display; available in black/gray, Mossy Oak Break-Up Country, and Mossy Oak Blaze Orange
Black/gray: **$624.99**
Mossy Oak Break-Up: **$649.99**
Mossy Oak Blaze Orange: . . .**$649.99**

BLACK RANGE 4K
Type: Rangefinder
Weight: 6.3 oz.
Length: 4.3 in.
Power: 6x
Obj. Dia.: 21mm
Exit Pupil: 3.5mm
Eye Relief: 18.3mm
Features: Spots from 10 to 4,000 yards in .1-yard increments; displays in meters or yards; ID Technology lets user choose horizontal or line-of-sight distance reading; Tru Target Technology allows the user to choose between First Target and Distant Target modes; Hyper Read Technology returns distances in .3 seconds
MSRP $449.95

NIKON BLACK RANGE 4K

Redfield

REDFIELD RAIDER 650 AND 650A

RAIDER 650 AND 650A
Weight: 5.7 oz.
Power: 6X
Obj. Dia.: 23mm
Range: up to 650 yd
Features: Fully multi-coated optics; high contrast LCD display; light-weight; compact; weatherproof; availabe in Mossy Oak in 650A model
MSRP $274.99

SIG Sauer

SIG SAUER KILO1250

SIG SAUER KILO2400ABS

KILO1250
Weight: 5 oz.
Length: 3.9 in.
Power: 6x
Obj. Diameter: 20mm
Exit Pupil: 3.33mm
Eye Relief: 15mm
Field of View: 34.18 ft @ 100 yds
Features: LightWave DSP Technology ranges up to 1,600 yards; fine line of sight or angle modified range selection; high-transmittance LCD display; user-selectable target modes featuring last or best reading; simple user interface features range or mode buttons only; graphite finish; also available in a 6X configuration
4X: $239.99
6X: $299.99

KILO2400ABS
Weight: 7.5 oz.
Length: 4.2 in.
Power: 7x
Obj. Diameter: 25mm
Exit Pupil: 3.6mm
Eye Relief: 15mm
Field of View: 35.67 ft @ 100 yds
Features: LightWave DSP Technology ranges up to two miles; embedded applied ballistics calculator; integrated temperature, humidity, pressure, and compass; Milling reticle with 2.4 MRAD inner diameter and 3 MRAD outer diameter; user-selectable target modes feature last and best readings; Lumatic OLED display constantly monitors light conditions and adjusts display brightness accordingly; multi-position twist-up eyecup provides custom fit; tripod adaptor; smartphone jack WindMETER; stylus pen; lanyard; three spare batteries; ballistic nylon molle kit; nylon carry pouch; configurable reticle with three viewing options: center aiming circle only, center aiming circle and horizontal milling grid, or center aiming circle with horizontal and vertical milling grids; ranges up to two miles
MSRP $1559.99

OPTICS

AMMUNITION

MUZZLELOADING BULLETS

BULLETS

Alexander Arms

ALEXANDER ARMS .50 BEOWULF 200-GRAIN POLYCASE INCEPTOR ARX PROJECTILES

PRECISION MATCH AMMUNITION

Features: Engineered for precision at extreme distances, with very low standard deviations; Loaded with Barnes match-grade OTM (Open Tip Match) boattail
Available in: 5.56 NATO, .308 Win., .300 Win. Mag., .338 Lapua Mag., 6.5 Creedmoor, 6mm Creedmoor, .260 Rem., .300 BLK
Box 20: . . . . **$24.99–$97.99**

RANGE AR

Features: Higher velocity, flatter trajectory, and ultimate accuracy; factory-fresh brass paired with a lead-free, copper-jacketed, zinc core OTFB (Open Tip Flat Base) provides excellent performance in ARs with quick twist barrels; specialized propellants optimized for ARs of any barrel length
Available in: 5.56x45mm, .300 BLK
Box 20 5.56: **$17.99**
Box 20 .300 AAC: **$19.99**

TAC-XPD AMMUNITION

Features: Loaded with Barnes TAC-XP bullets, the all-copper construction

.50 BEOWULF 200-GRAIN POLYCASE INCEPTOR ARX

Features: Muzzle velocity of 2,500 FPS; high muzzle energy of 2,775 foot-pounds; metal-filled polymer; tri-flute design; hydrodynamic shock during impact; wings fracture away creating secondary fragments and additional wound channels
Available in: .50 Beowulf
Box 20: **$37.02**

and very large, deep hollow-point cavity expand, penetrate, and perform consistently and optimally for personal and home defense
Available in: .357 Mag., .380 ACP, 9mm Luger +P, .40 S&W, .45 ACP +P
Box 20: . . . . **$18.99–$24.99**

VOR-TX AMMUNITION

Features: Provides maximum tissue and bone destruction, pass-through penetration, and devastating energy transfer; multiple grooves in the bullet's shank reduce pressure and improve accuracy; bullets open instantly on contact causing the nose to peel back into four sharp-edged copper petals destroying tissue, bone, and vital organs for a quick, humane kill
Available in: Rifle: .223 Rem., 5.56 NATO, .22-250 Rem., .243 Win., 25-06 Rem. .260 Rem., .270 Win., .270 WSM, 7mm-08 Rem., .280 Rem., 7mm Rem. Mag., .30-30 Win., .300 BLK, .308 Win., .30-06 Spfd., .300 WSM, .300 Win Mag., .300 RUM, .300 Wby. Mag., .338 Win. Mag., .338 Lapua, .35 Whelen, .45-

Barnes Bullets

70 Govt., 9.3x62mm, 7x64 Brenneke, 6.5 Creedmoor
Rifle LR: 6mm Creedmoor, 6.5 Creedmoor, .270 Win., 7mm Rem. Mag., 7mm RUM, .30-06, .300 Win. Mag., .300 RUM, .338 RUM, .375 RUM
Handgun: .357 Mag., 10mm, .41 Rem. Mag., .44 Mag., .45 Colt, .454 Casull
Safari: .375 H&H Mag., .416 Rem. Mag., .416 Rigby, .458 Win. Mag., .458 Lott, .470 Nitro Express, .500 Nitro Express
Euro: 7x64 Brenneke, .308 Win., .30-06 Spfd., 8x57 JS, 9.3x62mm
Rifle: . . . . **$21.79–$112.99**
Rifle LR: . . . .**$36.99–$59.99**
Safari: . . . .**$78.99–$154.99**
Handgun: . . . .**$21.99–$38.99**

BARNES PRECISION MATCH

BARNES VOR-TX

BARNES VOR-TX LR

Black Hills Ammunition

Rifle Ammunition

BLACK HILLS GOLD

Features: Coupling the finest components in the industry with bullets by Barnes; lead-free non-toxic rounds; high-performance hunting ammunition
Available in: .22–250 Rem., .243 Win., .25-06 Rem., .260 Rem., .270 Win., 7mm Rem. Mag., .300 Win. Mag., .308 Win., .30-06 Spfd., .338 Lapua; 6.5 Creedmoor
Box 20: . . . .**$33.15–$117.63**

FACTORY NEW RIFLE

Features: Coupling the finest components in the industry with bullets by manufacturers such as Hornady, Barnes, and Nosler; high-performance hunting ammunition; certain calibers available in Molycoat
Available in: .223 Rem., .308 Win. Match, .300 Win. Mag., .338 Lapua, .338 Norma Mag. , .300 Whisper, 5.56 NATO
Box 20, 50: . . . . **$41.25–$117.06**

REMANUFACTURED

Features: Ammunition designed with the practice shooter in mind, with

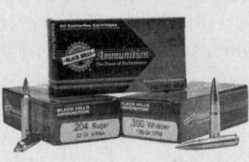

BLACK HILLS FACTORY NEW RIFLE

incredible accuracy for a great price point; the same ammunition used by the U.S. Army Marksmanship Unit in 600 yd matches; has the capability to produce 2-in. groups at 300m
Available in: .223 Rem. (also in Molycoat), .40 S&W
.223 Rem.: . . . . **$29.41–$45.09**
.40 S&W: **$29.00**

Black Hills Ammunition

Handgun Ammunition

COWBOY ACTION

Features: Designed to meet the needs of cowboy-action pistol shooters with its new virgin brass and premium-quality hard-cast bullets; velocities are moderate to provide low recoil and excellent accuracy
Available in: .32 H&R, .32-20 Win., .38 LC, .38 Spl., .38-40 Win., .44-40 Win., .44 Russian, .44 Spl., .44 Colt, .45 Schofield, .45 Colt, .38-55 Win., .357 Mag.
Box 50:............$32.58–$43.99

FACTORY NEW HANDGUN

Features: Used by the U.S. Military in all four branches for its reliability
Available in: .32 H&R Mag., .380 ACP, 9mm Luger, .38 Spl., .357 Mag., .40 S&W, .44 Mag., .45 ACP
Box 20:............$14.57–$53.70

BLACK HILLS COWBOY ACTION

Brenneke USA

28 GAUGE SLUGS

Features: The moderate recoil makes the 28 Ga. a perfect slug for young hunters who will be introduced to slug shooting; 28 Ga. is a multi-talent: small game, home defense, and all around shooting
Available in: 28 Ga. (2¾ in.)
Box 5:...................$11.99

BLACK MAGIC MAGNUM

Features: The Black Magic Magnum and Black Magic Short Magnum are two of the most powerful cartridges available on the market, offering tremendous knockdown power up to 100/60 yds; clean speed coating reduces lead fouling inside the barrel by almost 100 percent
Available in: 12 Ga. (3 in.)
Box 5:...................$12.99

CLASSIC MAGNUM

Features: Invented by Wilhelm Brenneke in 1898, the classic is the ancestor of all modern shotgun slugs; this state-of-the-art slug provides long-range stopping power, consistently flat trajectories, and a patented B.E.T. wad column
Available in: 12 Ga. (2¾ in.), 16 Ga. (2¾ in.)
Box 5:...................$9.99

CLOSE ENCOUNTER

Features: The .410 Close Encounter is the perfect choice if you are a fan of 2½-in. .410/.45 revolvers. They are powerful without having bad recoil, and they have an incredible frontal area and the legendary Brenneke penetration
Available in: .410 (2½ in.)
Box 5:...................$9.29

HEAVY FIELD SHORT MAGNUM GREEN LIGHTNING

Features: The original "Emerald" slug with patented B.E.T wad and famous stopping power; for all barrel types; range up to 100 yds.
Available in: 12 Ga., 20 Ga. (2¾ in.)
MSRP...................$9.99

K.O. SLUG

Features: The KO is an improved Foster-type slug with excellent penetration; range up to 60 yds; for all barrel types
Available in: 12 Ga. (2¾ in.), 20 Ga. (2 ¾ in.)
MSRP...................$6.99

MAGNUM CRUSH

Features: Delivers a force of more than 3.800 ft/lbs, weighs a full 1 ½ oz. / 666 gr. and the flat trajectory is ideal for bigger game; special coating to reduce lead fouling and broad ribs for optimum groove engagement
Available in: 12 Ga. (3 in.)
Box 5:...................$14.49

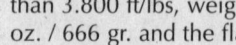

BRENNEKE CLOSE ENCOUNTER

BRENNEKE MAGNUM CRUSH

BRENNEKE HEAVY FIELD SHORT MAGNUM GREEN LIGHTNING SLUGS

Browning Ammunition

BROWNING BPR PERFORMANCE RIMFIRE

BROWNING BPT PERFORMANCE TARGET

BROWNING BXP PERSONAL DEFENSE

BROWNING BXC BIG GAME

BROWNING BXD WATERFOWL

BPR PERFORMANCE RIMFIRE

Features: BPR provides reliability and performance in 22 long rifle ammunition that you can expect from The Best There Is in rimfire ammunition.
Available in: .22 LR
Box of 100: $9.99

BPT PERFORMANCE TARGET

Features: BPT Performance Target is a premium training product that can be used to hone your handgun skills. It is a matched training counterpart to BXP Personal Defense.
Available in: .223 Rem., .38 Spec., .380 ACP, .40 S&W, .45 ACP, 9mm
Box of 50 handgun: . . $13.99–$22.99
Box of 20 .223: $8.61

BPT TARGET LOAD

Features: BPT Performance Target utilizes premium, hard shot to help deliver tight patterns and maximum target breaking energy. The smooth hull allows for a sleek profile and smooth ejection.
Available in: 2¾-inch 12- (No. 7½, 8), 20- (No. 7½), 16- (No. 8) and 28-gauge (No. 7½); 2 ½-inch .410-boren (No. 7½)
MSRP . . . .$9.49–$14.49

BXC BIG GAME

Features: BXC Controlled Expansion Terminal Tip is designed specifically for use on big game like elk, moose, mule deer, and bear. The Terminal Tip and bonded bullet design allow for deep penetration through thick, tough hide and bone. The brass tip, heavy bullet weight, and boat-tail are integral components to delivering precision accuracy, maximum downrange velocity, and long-range, on-target performance.
Available in: .270 Win., .30-06 Spfd., .300 Win. Mag., .300 WSM, .308 Win., 7mm Rem. Mag., 6.5 Creedmoor, .270 WSM
Box of 20: . . . . $37.99–$45.99

BXD UPLAND

Features: BXD Upland Extra Distance launches premium-plated shot at high velocities to achieve premium in-the-field performance. Nickel-plated shot helps keep shot round resulting in high velocity retention and energy transfer as well as tighter downrange patterns.
Available in: 12 (3, 3.5 in.), 20 (3 in.), 16 (2.75 in.); No. 7 and 9 shot
Box of 25: . . . . $17.99–$19.99

BXD WATERFOWL

Features: BXD Waterfowl Extra Distance is launched at high velocities utilizing an optimized long-range wad and plated round steel shot. Combining round steel with a cutting edge wad design results in a lethal combination of energy retention, penetration, and pattern density that is critical in achieving long-range performance. No. 2, 4, and BB shot sizes available in 12-gauge, No. 2 shot only for 20-gauge.
Available in: 12 (3 in., 3.5 in.), 20 (3 in.)
Box of 25: . . . .$19.99–$27.99

BXP PERSONAL DEFENSE

Features: BXP Personal Defense is designed for superior personal defense performance in reliability, expansion, and penetration. The X-Point is designed to shield the hollow point through intermediate barriers.
Available in: .40 S&W, .45 ACP, .380 ACP, 9mm Luger
Box of 20: . . . .$17.99–$20.99

Browning Ammunition

BROWNING BXR DEER

BROWNING BXS DEER

BROWNING BXV PREDATOR & VARMINT

BXR DEER

Features: BXR Rapid Expansion Matrix Tip is designed specifically for use on whitetail, blacktail, mule deer, and antelope. The proprietary matrix tip design allows for high downrange velocity and energy retention while also initiating rapid positive expansion. The jacket and tip combination yields precision accuracy and rapid energy transfer, and generates massive knockdown power.
Available in: .243 Win., .270 Win., .30-06 Spfd., .30-30 Win., .300 Win. Mag., .300 WSM, .308 Win. 6.5

Creedmoor, 7mm Rem. Mag., 7mm-08
Box of 20:..........$21.99–$34.99

BXS DEER

Features: Solid copper expansion sabot slug designed to increase accuracy, penetration, and energy transfer
Available in: Shotshell: 12 (2.75 in., 1 oz. slug), 20 (2.75 in., 0.75 oz. slug). Rifle: .270 Win., .30-06 Spfd., .300 Win. Mag. .300 WSM, .308 Win., 6.5 Creedmoor, 7mm Rem. Mag.

Slugs, box of 5: .....$12.99–$15.99
Rifle, box of 20: .... N/A

BXV PREDATOR & VARMINT

Features: Polymer tip improves BC and results in flatter trajectory and higher downrange velocity
Available in: .223 Win., .243 Win., .22 Hornet, .22-250
Box of 20:..........$19.99–$27.99

CCI Ammunition

.17 HMR VNT

Features: New varmint round; topped with a Speer VNT bullet with a thin jacket and a polymer tip
Available in: .17 HMR (17 gr.)
Box of: 50
MSRP...................$19.99

.22 LR AR TACTICAL

Features: This load is designed specifically for AR-style guns being offered in .22 Long Rifle chambering; rounds get excellent accuracy including 1.5-in. at 100 yds for ten-shot groups; this target bullet has a copper-plated round nose for smooth feeding; CCI case, priming, and bullet lube combined with clean-burning powder
Available in: .22 Long Rifle (40 gr.)
Box of 300:...............$22.99

.22 WIN. MAG. MAXI MAG

Features: A favorite of varmint shooters; 40 gr. TMJ flat nose at 1875 fps, or 40 gr. jacketed HP at 1875 fps; both loads give over 1400 fps from a 6-in. revolver; clean-burning propellants keep actions cleaner; sure-fire CCI priming; reusable plastic box with dispenser lid
Available in: .22 Win. Mag.
Box of 50:...............$10.99

A17 VARMINT TIP

Features: Optimized for feeding and function in the Savage Arms A17 semiautomatic rifle and can be fired through bolt-action .17 HMR firearms; 100 fps faster than other .17 HMR loads of the same weight; Varmint Tip bullet provides rapid expansion; CCI-made and primed case
Available in: .17 HMR
Box of 50:............... $11.99
Box of 2,000: ....$$464.99

A22 MAGNUM GAMEPOINT

Features: GamePoint bullet; designed around Savage's semiautomatic A22 Magnum rifle
Available in: .22 WMR (35 gr.)
Box of 50:............... $13.49
Box of 500:............. $129.99
Box of 2,000: $503.99

BIG 4

Features: Centerfire handgun shotshells with larger No. 4 pellets for extended range and penetration
Available in: 9mm, .38 Spl., .44 Spl., .45 Colt
Box 10:...........$12.99–$15.99

COPPER-22

Features: Non-lead, California-legal bullet; constructed from a unique mix

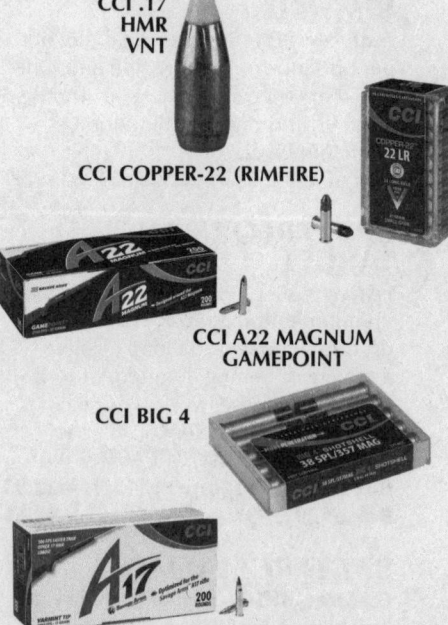

CCI .17 HMR VNT

CCI COPPER-22 (RIMFIRE)

CCI A22 MAGNUM GAMEPOINT

CCI BIG 4

CCI A17 VARMINT TIP

of copper particles and polymer compressed into a potent, 21-grain hollow-point bullet
Available in: .22 LR
Box of 50:................ $7.99
Box of 500:...............$74.99
Box of 5,000: $729.99

AMMUNITION

CCI Ammunition

GREEN TAG

Features: Our first and still most-popular match rimfire product; tight manufacturing and accuracy specs mean you get the consistency and accuracy that the unforgiving field of competition demands; the rimfire match ammo leaves the muzzle sub-sonic which means no buffeting in the transonic zone; clean-burning propellants keep actions cleaner. Sure-fire CCI priming; reusable plastic box with dispenser lid
Available in: .22 LR (40 gr. lead round nose)
Box of 100: $17.99

HMR TNT

Features: A 17-gr. Speer TNT hollow point answers requests from varmint hunters and gives explosive performance over the .17's effective range; clean-burning propellants keep actions cleaner; sure-fire CCI priming; reusable plastic box with dispenser lid
Available in: .17 HMR 17-gr. TNT hollow point or 16-gr. lead-free green TNT solid hollow point
TNT box of 50: $11.99
TNT box of 500: $109.99
Green TNT box of 50: $13.99
Green TNT box of 500: $129.99

LONG HV AND SHORT HV

Features: Designed for rimfire guns that require .22 Long and .22 Short ammunition; clean-burning propellants keep actions cleaner; sure-fire CCI priming; reusable plastic box with dispenser lid
Available in: .22 Short (29 gr. solid lead bullet), .22 Short (27 gr. hollow point bullet), .22 Long (29 gr. solid lead bullet)
Box of 100: $8.99

MINI-MAG

Features: CCI's first rimfire product and still the most popular; Mini-Mag. hollow points are high-velocity products and offer excellent all-around performance for small game and varmints; clean-burning propellants keep actions cleaner; sure-fire CCI priming; reusable plastic box with dispenser lid
Available in: .22 LR (40 gr. gilded round nose or 36 gr. gilded lead hollow point)
Box of 100: $7.99
Box of 5,000: $374.99

MINI-MAG SEGMENTED HOLLOW POINT

Features: New bullet design splits into three equal parts upon impact
Available in: .22 LR (40 gr.)
Box of 50: $6.99
Box of 500: $62.99
Box of 5,000: $612.99

PISTOL MATCH

Features: Designed expressly for high-end semiautomatic match pistols; singe-die tooling and great care in assembly lets you wring the last bit of accuracy from your precision pistol; clean-burning propellants keep actions cleaner; sure-fire CCI priming; reusable plastic box with dispenser lid
Available in: .22 LR (40 gr. lead round nose bullet)
Box of 50: $8.99
Box of 500: $86.99

QUIET-22

Features: Ideal for bolt-action and single shot .22 LR rifles (and perfectly safe in semiautomatics), this new reduced report cartridge generates ¼ the perceived noise level of standard velocity .22 LR
Available in: .22 LR
Box of 50: $3.99
Box of 500: $34.99
Box of 5,000: $338.99

SELECT .22 LR

Features: The .22 Long Rifle Select is built for semiautomatic competition; reliable operation, accuracy, and con-

CCI SUPPRESSOR 22 LONG RIFLE

CCI GREEN TAG

CCI MINI-MAG SEGMENTED HOLLOW POINT

CCI QUIET-22

sistency make Select an ideal choice for competition shooters
Available in: .22 LR
Box of 100: $15.99

SUPPRESSOR 22 LONG RIFLE

Features: Subsonic velocity of 970 fps minimizes sound signature through suppressed firearms; HP bullet; consistent function in semiautomatic firearms; clean-burning powders
Available in: .22 LR
Box of 50: $4.99
Box of 500: $46.99
Box of 5,000: $459.99

CCI MINI-MAG.

AMMUNITION

Cor-Bon

Rifle

DPX RIFLE

Features: This is an optimum load for Law Enforcement; lead-free projectile; reduced recoil due to lighter weight projectile; deep penetration on soft tissue 12–17-in.

Available in: .223 Rem., .243 Win., .260 Rem., .270 WSM, .270 Wby Mag., .270 Win., .30-06 Spfd., .30-30 Win., .300 BLK, .300 H&H Mag., .300 WSM., .300 Wby. Mag., .300 Whisper, .300 Win. Mag., .308 Win., .338 Lapua, .338 RUM, .338 Win. Mag, .340 Wby. Mag., .375 H&H, .444 Marlin, .458 SOCOM, 6.5-284 Norma, 7.62x39mm

Box 20: . . . . $31.90–$129.95

MULTI-PURPOSE RIFLE (MPR)

Features: Features a gilding metal jacket with a specially formulated lead core and a green acetal resin tip, which reduces drag, producing extremely high ballistic coefficient, and also creates more reliable feeding in magazine fed firearms; provides rapid, explosive expansion without excessive penetration; aerodynamic resin tip offers extreme accuracy at long-range precision competition and also improves feeding in magazine fed rifles; reliably expands for humane kills on varmints and deer-size game, giving just the right amount of penetration

Available in: .223 Rem., .22-250 Rem., .243 Win., 30-06 Spfd., .300 Whisper, 300 Win. Mag., .308 Win.

Box 20: . . . . $31.32–$47.09

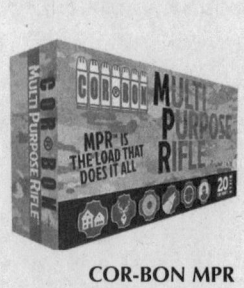

COR-BON MULTI-PURPOSE RIFLE (MPR)

COR-BON MPR

CORBON HUNTER

Handgun

CORBON DPX HANDGUN

CORBON GLASER POW'RBALL

COR-BON GLASER SAFETY SLUG

DPX HANDGUN

Features: DPX is a solid copper hollowpoint bullet that combines the best of the lightweight high-speed JHPs and the heavyweight, deep-penetrating JHPs; the copper bullet construction allows it to conquer hard barriers like auto glass and steel while still maintaining its integrity

Available in: 10mm, .32 ACP, .327 Federal .357 Mag., .357 SIG, .375 JDJ, .38 Spec. +P, .38 Super +P, .380 ACP, .40 S&W, .400 CORBON, .41 Rem. Mag., .44 Mag. .44 Spl., .45 ACP, .45 ACP +P, .45 Colt +P, .454 Casull, .460 S&W, .500 S&W, 9mm, 9mm +P

Box 20: . . . . $26.61–$95.73

GLASER POW'RBALL

Features: Designed for finicky feeding pistols, Pow'Rball is a great choice for your semiauto pistols or revolvers; reliable feeding and consistent reliable expansion; deeper soft tissue penetration; custom scored jacket; proprietary polymer ball and patented lead core

Available in: 10mm, .32 Auto, .358 Mag., .357 SIG, .38 Spl. +P, .38 Super +P, .380 ACP, .40 S&W, .400 CORBON, .45 ACP +P, 9mm +P

Box 20: . . . . $18.11–$25.66

GLASER SAFETY SLUG

Features: Although slug was originally designed for use by Sky Marshals on airplanes, today the slug is recommended for anyone concerned with over-penetration; uses a copper jacket and is filled with a compressed load of either #12 or #6 lead shot, then capped with a round polymer ball that enhances feeding and reloading

Available in: 10mm, .357 Mag., .357 SIG, .38 Spl. +P, .38 Super +P, .380 ACP, .40 S&W, .400 CORBON, .44 Mag., .44 Spl., .45 ACP +P, .45 Colt +P, 9mm +P

Box of 20: . . . . $29.47–$40.31

HUNTER

Features: Bone-breaking loads for the handgun hunter; expanding bullet varieties include Swift A-frame, Swift Scirocco II, Bonded Core Jacketed Soft Point, jacketed soft point, and jacketed hollowpoint; non-expanding bullets include Round Nose Penetrator, hard cast, and full metal jacket

Available in: 10mm, .357 Mag., .41 Rem. Mag., .44 Mag. .45 Colt +P, .454 Casull, ..460 Rowland, .460 S&W,.500 S&W

Box 20: . . . . $25.03–$70.47

AMMUNITION

HEVI DUTY HOME DEFENSE

Features: Frangible, non-toxic, low recoil home defense load
Available in: 12 Ga. (2¾ in.) Shot sizes: 00, 4
Box 25:..................$22.99

HEVI-METAL TURKEY

Features: A layered load that combines premium steel shot with HEVI-Shot pellets; timeless testing of various shot load methods found layering to provide the most pellets on target and the best knockdown performance
Available in: 12 Ga. (3 in., 3½ in.), 20 Ga. (3 in.)
Box 5:..............$9.99–$11.99

HEVI-SHOT CLASSIC DOUBLES

Features: Optimized for your fixed chokes and fine classic doubles; denser than steel but soft like lead which means you get deeper penetration; USFWS-approved non-toxic shot; 45 percent more on target pellets than steel; belted sphere for maximum pellet mass; buffered and nano-treated pellets for tight patterns; weather-resistant crimp
Available in: 12 Ga. (2¾ in., 3 in.), 16 Ga. (2¾ in.), 20 Ga. (2¾ in., 3 in.), .28 Ga. (2¾ in.), .410 (3 in.)
Box 10:............$31.99–$37.99

HEVI-SHOT DEAD COYOTE!

Features: With these HEVI-Shot T-shot loads, you can be deadly at ranges you never thought possible with a 12 gauge; the 3-in. load pounds out 50 perfectly round pellets at 1,350 fps. 10 percent heavier than lead, 54 percent denser than steel; every 50 rounds includes a dry-storage box.
Available in: 12 Ga. (3 in., 3½ in.)
Box of 5:................$34.99
Box of 10 3-inch:..........$64.99
Box of 10 3½-inch:.........$69.99

HEVI-SHOT MAGNUM BLEND

Features: Put more lethal pellets in your pattern with a combination of No. 5, 6, and 7 HEVI-13 shot, and boost your lethal range by 14 to 17 percent; buffered and moly-coated pellets produce a denser pattern than conventional shot; HEVI-13 delivers 40 percent more knockdown energy and up to 40 percent longer range than lead shells
Available in: 10 Ga. (3 ½-in.), 12 Ga. (3 in., 3½ in.) 20 Ga. (3 in.)
Box 5:.............$24.99–$39.99

HEVI-SHOT TRIPLE BEARD

Features: First all lead turkey load from the makers of HEVI-Shot; speed ball technology for reduced deformation on setback, more uniform pellets, and reduced "pancake" effect of lead; Magnum Blend technology; consistent performance in any temperature
Available in: 12 Ga. (3 in., 3 ½ in.), 20 Ga. (3 in.); Shot sizes: 5, 6, 7
MSRP.............$15.99–$19.99

ENVIRON-METAL HEVI-METAL TURKEY

ENVIRON-METAL HEVI-SHOT DEAD COYOTE!

ENVIRON-METAL HEVI-SHOT TRIPLE BEARD

ENVIRON-METAL HEVI DUTY HOME DEFENSE

AMMUNITION

Federal Premium Ammunition

Rifle Ammunition

AMERICAN EAGLE FULL METAL JACKET BOATTAIL

Features: Accurate, non-expanding bullets; flat shooting trajectory, leaves small exit holes in game, and put clean holes in paper; smooth, reliable feeding into semiautomatics
Available in: .223 Rem., .308 Win., .300 BLK, .30-06 Spfd., 5.56 NATO, 6.5 Creedmoor
Box 20: . . . . **$11.95–$31.95**

CAPE-SHOK TROPHY BONDED SLEDGEHAMMER SOLID

Features: Use it on the largest, most dangerous game in the world; Jack Carter design maximizes stopping power; bonded bronze solid with a flat nose that minimizes deflection off bone and muscle for a deep straight wound channel
Available in: .375 H&H Mag., .416 Rigby, .416 Rem. Mag., .458 Win. Mag., .458 Lott, .470 NE
Box 20: . . . . **$115.95–$223.95**

CAPE-SHOK WOODLEIGH HYDRO SOLID

Features: Provides safari hunters superb accuracy, consistent performance, and tremendous impact; special heavy jackets provide excellent weight retention, up to 100 percent for solids
Available in: 9.3x62 Mauser, 9.3x74 R, .370 Sako Mag., .375 H&H Mag., .416 Rigby, .416 Rem. Mag., .458 Win. Mag., 458 Lott, .470 NE, .500 NE
Box 20: . . . . **$90.95–$258.95**

EDGE TLR

Features: Uses the exclusive Slipstream polymer tip to initiate expansion at long range; at close the bullet's copper shank and bonded lead core retain weight for consistent, lethal penetration; long, sleek profile offers an extremely high BC; AccuChannel groove technology improves accuracy and reduces drag
Available in: 6.5 Creedmoor, .270 Win., .270 WSM, 7mm Rem. Mag., .280 Ackley Improved, .308 Win., .30-06 Spfd., .300 Win. Mag., .300 WSM
Box 20: . . . . **$47.95–$59.95**

FUSION RIFLE

Features: This specialized deer bullet electrochemically joins pure copper to an extreme pressure-formed core to ensure optimum performance. The result is high terminal energy on impact that radiates lethal shock throughout the target. This energy is optimized through mass weight retention, a top secretive tip-skiving process and superior bullet integrity.
Available in: .223 Rem., .22-250 Rem., .224 Valkyrie, .243 Win., .25-06 Rem., 6.5 Grendel, 6.5x55 Swedish Mauser, .260 Rem., .270 Win., .270 WSM, 7mm-08, .280 Rem., 7mm Rem. Mag., 7mm WSM, 7.62x39 Soviet, .30-30 Win. 6.5 Creedmoor, .308 Win., .30-06 Spfd., .300 Win. Mag., .300 WSM, .338 Federal, .338 Win. Mag., .35 Whelen, .45-70 Govt.
Box 20: . . . . **$24.95–$62.95**

FUSION MSR

Features: Modern sporting rifles (MSRs) represent a very versatile class of firearms, handling a wide range of ammo and game, often built from the ground up and tricked out with accessories to match specific needs; all-new Fusion MSR loads provide that same degree of customization in ammunition
Available in: .223 Rem., .224 Valkyrie, .300 BLK, 6.8 SPC, .308 Win., .338 Fed.
Box 20: . . . . **$27.95–$37.95**

GOLD MEDAL BERGER HYBRID

Features: Rounds feature a Berger bullet with a high BC to provide flat trajectories, less wind drift, and surgical long-range accuracy; Gold Medal match primers; Federal brass; specially formulated propellants
Available in: 6mm Creedmoor, .300 Win. Mag., .300 Norma Mag.
Box 20: . . . . **$35.95–$61.95**

GOLD MEDAL SIERRA MATCHKING BOATTAIL HOLLOWPOINT

Features: Long ranges are its specialty; excellent choice for everything from varmints to big game animals; tapered, boattail design provides extremely flat trajectories; higher downrange velocity for more energy at the point of impact; reduced wind drift
Available in: .223 Rem., 6.5 Creedmoor, .260 Rem., .308 Win., .30- 06 Spfd., .300 Win. Mag., .338 Lapua Mag.
Box 20: . . . . **$27.95–$117.95**

FEDERAL PREMIUM WOODLEIGH HYDRO SOLID

FEDERAL PREMIUM FUSION RIFLE

FEDERAL PREMIUM GOLD MEDAL BERGER HYBRID

FEDERAL PREMIUM AMERICAN EAGLE SYNTECH

Federal Premium Ammunition

HUNTER MATCH .22 LONG RIFLE

Features: High-velocity long-range round; hollowpoint designed for optimum expansion at 100 yards; nickel-plated case
Available in: .22 LR
Box 50:. **$6.95**

NON-TYPICAL

Features: New line designed for deer hunting; soft-point bullet with a concentric jacket
Available in: .243 Win., 6.5 Creedmoor, .270 Win., .30-30 Win., .308 Win., .30-06 Spfd., .300 Win. Mag., 7mm Rem. Mag. .450 Bushmaster
Box of:. **20**
MSRP. . . . . **$21.95–$36.95**

POWER-SHOK COPPER

Features: Copper-alloy construction; hollow-point design expands consistently; accurate, reliable performance; large wound channels and efficient energy transfer to the target; lead-free; California-legal; federal brass and primers
Available in: .243 Win, .270 Win., .308 Win., .30-06 Spfd., .300 Blackout, .300 Win. Mag., .300 WSM
Box 20:. . . . . **$27.95–$46.95**

V-SHOK SPEER TNT GREEN HOLLOWPOINT

Features: Brings non-tox technology to the Federal Premium V-Shok varmint hunting line; a totally lead-free bullet that couples explosive expansion with match-grade accuracy
Available in: .17 HMR, .22 WMR
Box 20:. . . . . **$16.95–$17.95**

VITAL-SHOK, CAPE-SHOK TROPHY BONDED BEAR CLAW

Features: Ideal for medium to large dangerous game; jacket and core are 100 percent fusion-bonded for reliable bullet expansion from 25 yds to extreme ranges; bullet retains 95 percent of its weight for deep penetration; hard solid copper base tapering to a soft, copper nose section for controlled expansion
Available in: Vital-Shok: 7mm Rem. Mag., .30-06 Spfd., .300 Win. Mag., .338 Win. Mag., .35 Whelen, .375 H&H, .45-70 Gov't.
Cape-Shok: .375 H&H, .416 Rigby, .416 Rem. Mag., .458 Win. Mag., .458 Lott, .470 NE
Vital-Shok:. . . . . **$44.95–$90.95**
Cape-Shok: . . . . **$90.95–$236.95**

VITAL SHOK NOSLER PARTITION

Features: Bullet features a partitioned lead core and shank that allows the front half to mushroom while the rear core remains intact for deep penetration and stopping power
Available in: .22-250 Rem., .243 Win., 6mm Rem., .257 Roberts +P, .25-06 Rem., .270 Win., .270 WSM, 7mm Mauser, 7mm-08, .280 Rem., 7mm Rem. Mag., .30-30 Win., .308 Win. .30-06 Spfd., .300 H&H, .300 Win. Mag., .300 WSM, .338 Win. Mag., .338 RUM, .375 H&H
Box 20:. . . . . **$36.95–$62.95**

VITAL SHOK SIERRA GAMEKING BOATTAIL SOFTPOINT

Features: Proven performer on small game and thin-skinned medium game; aerodynamic tip for a flat trajectory; exposed soft point expands rapidly for hard hits, even as velocity slows at longer ranges

FEDERAL PREMIUM TROPHY BONDED TIP

FEDERAL PREMIUM HUNTER MATCH .22 LONG RIFLE

Available in: .243 Win., .25-06 Rem., .260 Rem., .270 Win., 7-30 Waters, 7mm Rem. Mag., .308 Win., .30-06 Spfd.
Box 20:. . . . . **$32.95–$45.95**

VITAL-SHOK TROPHY BONDED TIP

Features: Built on the Trophy Bonded Bear Claw platform to provide deep penetration and high weight retention; sleek profile, with tapered heel and translucent polymer tip; nickel-plated; available as component and in Federal loaded ammunition
Available in: .223 Rem., .270 Win., .270 WSM, .270 Wby. Mag., 7mm-08 Rem., .280 Rem., 7mm Rem. Mag., 7mm WSM, 7mm Wby. Mag., 7mm STW, .308 Win., .30-06 Spfd., .300 H&H Mag., .300 Wby. Mag., .300 Win. Mag., .300 RUM, .300 Rem. Ultra Mag., .300 WSM, .338 Federal, .338 Win. Mag.
Box 20:. . . . . **$27.95–$81.95**

FEDERAL PREMIUM NON-TYPICAL

FEDERAL PREMIUM POWER-SHOK COPPER

FEDERAL PREMIUM HUNTER MATCH .22 LONG RIFLE

AMMUNITION

Federal Premium Ammunition

FEDERAL PREMIUM HST

**FEDERAL PREMIUM
HYDRA-SHOK DEEP**

**FEDERAL PREMIUM
PERSONAL DEFENSE HST
MICRO .38 SPECIAL +P**

VITAL-SHOK TROPHY COPPER

Features: Tipped bullet cavity for consistent expansion across a broad range of velocities; grooved bullet shank for increased accuracy across a wider range of firearms; copper-alloy design that achieves up to 99 percent weight retention; nickel-plated case
Available in: .223 Rem., .243 Win., .25-06 Rem., .270 Win., 6.5 Creedmoor, .270 WSM, 7mm-08 Rem., .280 Rem., 7mm Rem. Mag., 7mm WSM, .30-30 Win., .308 Win., .30-06 Spfd., .300 Win. Mag., .300 WSM, .338 Fed., .338 Win. Mag., .338 Lapua,
Box 20: . . . . $30.95–$85.95

Handgun Ammunition

AMERICAN EAGLE FULL METAL JACKET

Features: Good choice for range practice and reducing lead fouling in the barrel; jacket extends from the nose to the base, preventing bullet expansion and barrel leading; primarily as military ammunition for recreational shooting
Available in: 5.7X28, .25 ACP, .32 ACP, .327 Federal, .380 ACP, 9mm Luger, .357 SIG, .38 Spl., .40 S&W, 10mm, .45 ACP, .45 G.A.P.
Box 50: . . . . $18.95–$62.95

AMERICAN EAGLE LEAD ROUND NOSE

Features: Great training round for practicing at the range; 100 percent lead with no jacket; excellent accuracy and very economical
Available in: .38 Spl.
MSRP $27.95

AMERICAN EAGLE SYNTECH

Features: Polymer-encapsulated Syntech bullet prevents metal-on-metal contact in the bore, eliminating copper and lead fouling, while extending barrel life; exclusive primer formulation provides reliable, consistent ignition; clean-burning propellants minimize residue and fouling; significantly reduces the required frequency of cleaning; absence of a copper jacket minimizes splash-back on steel targets; less perceived recoil
Available in: .40 S&W, .45 ACP
Box 50 .40 S&W: $24.95
Box 50 .45 ACP: $31.95

CHAMPION LEAD SEMI-WADCUTTER

Features: All-around choice for target practice with a timeless bullet profile that cuts clean holes in targets.
Available in: .22 LR, .22 WMR, .32 H&R Mag., .45 LC, .44 Spec.,
Box of 50 .22 LR: $3.95
Box of 325 .22 LR: $25.95
Box of 525 .22 LR: . . . $28.95–$31.95
Box of 50 .22 WMR: $14.95
Box of 50 .32 H&R: $21.95
Box of 50 .44 Spec.: $33.95
Box of 50 .45 LC: $28.95

FUSION

Features: Bullet weights and velocities have been developed to be lethal on whitetails, without pounding the shooter
Available in: .357 Mag., .41 Rem. Mag.,

.44 Rem. Mag., .454 Casull, .460 S&W, .500 S&W, 50 Action Express
Box 20: . . . . $22.95–$44.95

HYDRA-SHOK DEEP

Features: New version of Hydra-Shok, intended for better results when fired through barriers; 50-percent deeper penetration than original Hydra-Shok
Available in: 9mm, .40 S&W, .45 ACP
Box of: 20
9mm: $27.95
.40 S&W: $31.95
.45 ACP: $33.95

PERSONAL DEFENSE HST

Features: Provides near 100 percent weight retention through most barriers; consistent expansion, optimum penetration, and superior terminal performance, it's specially designed hollow point won't plug while passing through a variety of barriers
Available in: 9mm Luger, .40 S&W, .45 ACP
Box of 20 9mm: $27.95
Box of 20 .40 S&W: $35.95
Box of 20 .45 ACP: $31.95

PERSONAL DEFENSE HST MICRO .38 SPECIAL +P

Features: Designed for subcompact and micro pistol platforms; available in a .38 Special +P with a deeply seated bullet that stabilizes powder burn rates and velocities
Available in: .38 Special +P (130 gr.)
Box of: 20
MSRP $30.95

PERSONAL DEFENSE REVOLVER

Features: Economical personal defense round for revolvers; quick, positive expansion
Available in: .32 H&R Mag., .357 Mag.
Box of 20 .32 H&R: $23.95
Box of 20 .357 Mag: $26.95

PERSONAL DEFENSE SEMI-AUTOMATIC

Features: Ideal personal defense round for semiautomatics; quick, positive expansion; jacket ensures smooth feeding into autoloading firearms
Available in: 9MM, .45 ACP
Box of 20 9mm: $25.95
Box of 20 .45 ACP: $31.95

AMMUNITION

Federal Premium Ammunition

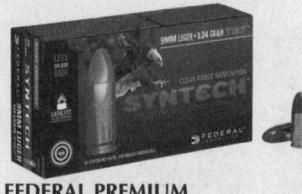

FEDERAL PREMIUM SYNTECH

FEDERAL PREMIUM SYNTECH ACTION PISTOL

FEDERAL PREMIUM TRAIN + PROTECT

FEDERAL PREMIUM 3RD DEGREE WITH HEAVYWEIGHT TSS

FEDERAL BLACK CLOUD FS STEEL CLOSE RANGE

Shotgun Ammunition

3RD DEGREE WITH HEAVYWEIGHT TSS
Features: One of three new turkey loads from Federal; FLITECONTROL FLEX wad opens from the rear and stays with the shot column longer than conventional loads; triplex load of No. 5 copper-plated lead, No. 6 FLITESTOPPER lead pellets, and No. 7 HEAVYWEIGHT TSS pellet that delivers dense pellets more than 40 yards
Available in: 20 ga. (3 in.), 12 ga. (3 in., 3.5 in.)
Box of: 5
12-gauge: . . . . $22.95–$26.95
20-gauge: $22.95

BLACK CLOUD FS STEEL
Available in: 10-gauge 3½-inch No. 2, BB; 12-gauge 3½-inch No. 3, 2, 1, BB, BBB; 12-gauge 3-inch No. 4, 3, 2, 1, BB, BBB; 12-gauge 2¾-inch No. 4, 3, 2, BB; 20-gauge 3-inch No. 4, 3, 2, 1
Box of 25 10-gauge: . . $36.95–$38.95
Box of 25 12-gauge: . . $21.95–$34.95
Box of 25 20-gauge: $25.95

BLACK CLOUD FS STEEL CLOSE RANGE
Features: Engineered to put more pellets on targets 20 to 30 yards away, achieves a full pattern within a very short distance; comprised of 100 percent Flitestopper Steel for the most lethal payload imaginable, produces more open and optimum patterns; crimp and primer sealed
Available in: 12-gauge 2¾-inch No. 3, 3-inch No. 2; 20-gauge 3-inch No. 4, 2
Box of 25 12-gauge: $28.95
Box of 25 20-gauge: $25.95

BLACK CLOUD HIGH VELOCITY
Features: The Black Cloud High Velocity line pumps up the speed and

FEDERAL PREMIUM GOLD MEDAL GRAND PLASTIC

lethal performance for waterfowl hunters everywhere.
Available in: 12-gauge 3-inch No. 4, 3, 2, 1, BB
Box 25: . . . . $27.95–$29.95

GAME-SHOK UPLAND GAME
Available in: 12, 16, 20, 28 Ga. .410 (2¾ in.); Shot sizes: 6, 8, 7.5
Box 25: . . . . $8.95–$11.95

GAME-SHOK UPLAND GAME HI-BRASS
Available in: 12-, 16-, 20-, 28-gauge and .410-bore; shot sizes No. 4, 5, 6, 7.5
Box 25: . . . . $17.95–$20.95

GAME-SHOK UPLAND HEAVY FIELD
Available in: 12, 20, 28 Ga. (2¾ in.); Shot sizes: 4, 5, 6, 7.5
Box 25: . . . . $9.95–$13.95

GOLD MEDAL GRAND PAPER
Available in: 12 Ga. (2¾ in.) only, in 1 1/8-oz. loads of 7.5 or 8, or 1-oz. load of 8
Box of 25: $13.95

GOLD MEDAL GRAND PLASTIC
Available in: 12-gauge 2¾-inch No. 9, 8, 7½; general target shooting and dedicated competition loads available in a variety of velocities and payloads
Box of 25: . . . . $11.95–$12.95

SYNTECH
Available in: 9mm, .40 S&W, .45 ACP
Box of: 50
9mm: $19.95
.40 S&W: $24.95
.45 ACP: $31.95

SYNTECH ACTION PISTOL
Features: Designed for action shooting competitors; flat-nosed bullets help with steel target knockdown while reducing bullet fracturing and splash back; Federal's TSJ–Total Synthetic Jacket–reduces bore fouling; clean powders; Federal's lead-free Catalyst primer
Available in: 9mm (150 gr.), .40 S&W (205 gr.), .45 ACP (.220 gr.)
Box of: 50
MSRP . . . . $18.95–$30.95

TRAIN + PROTECT
Features: New training and self-defense line for 2018; Federal's VHP hollowpoint bullet
Available in: 9mm (115 gr.), .40 S&W (180 gr.), .45 ACP (230 gr.)
9mm: . . . . $27.95–$55.95
.40 S&W: . . . . $33.95–$66.95
.45 ACP: . . . . $33.95–$66.95

Federal Premium Ammunition

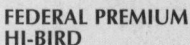

**FEDERAL PREMIUM
HI-BIRD**

**FEDERAL PREMIUM PRAIRIE STORM HIGH
VELOCITY STEEL SHOTSHELLS**

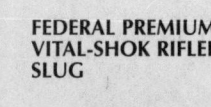

**FEDERAL PREMIUM
VITAL-SHOK RIFLED
SLUG**

**FEDERAL PREMIUM
SPEED SHOK
WATERFOWL**

**FEDERAL PREMIUM
GRAND SLAM**

GRAND SLAM

Features: FLITECONTROL FLEX wad; load of copper-plated lead shot; 20 ga. is available in No. 5 only; 12 ga. is available in 4, 5, and 6; 10 ga. is available in 4 and 5
Available in: 10 ga. (3.5 in.), 12 ga. (2.75 in., 3 in., 3.5 in.), 20 ga. (3 in.)
Box of: 5
MSRP: . . . .**$14.95–$23.95**

HI-BIRD

Features: Two-piece wad features SoftCell technology to decrease perceived recoil and produce more consistent long-range patterns; dense long-range patterns and increased down-range energy
Available in: 12-gauge 2¾-inch No. 8, 7½, 6, 5
Box 25: . . . .**$10.95–$14.95**

PERSONAL DEFENSE SHOTSHELLS

Features: Just as the name implies, buckshot loads for personal-/home-defense use; one of two 12-gauge loads keep shot column tight with Flitecontrol wad; .410 is suitable for revolver use
Available in: .410-bore (3-inch #4 Buck, #000 Buck; 2½-inch No. 4 shot, #000 Buck); 12-gauge (2¾-inch #00 Buck with Flitecontrol or #4 Buck without); 20-gauge (2¾-inch #4 Buck)
Box of 20 .410-bore: . .**$18.95–$20.95**
Box of 5 12-, 20-gauge: **$8.95**

PRAIRIE STORM FS STEEL

Available in: 12-gauge and 20-gauge 3-inch No. 4, 3
Box of 25 12-gauge: **$26.95**
Box of 25 20-gauge: **$24.95**

SPEED-SHOK WATERFOWL

Available in: 10-gauge 3½-inch No. T, BBB, BB, 2; 12-gauge 3½-inch No. T, BBB, BB, 1, 2, 3, 4; 12-gauge 3-inch No. T, BBB, BB, 1, 2, 3, 4, 6; 12-gauge 2¾-inch No. BB, 2, 3, 4, 6; 16-gauge 2¾-inch No. BB, 2, 4; 20-gauge 3-inch No. 1, 2, 3, 4; 20-gauge 2 ¾-inch No. 4, 6, 7
Box of 25 10-gauge: **$33.95**
Box of 25 12-gauge: . . **$16.95–$25.95**
Box of 25 16-gauge: . . **$27.95–$28.95**
Box of 25 20-gauge: . . . **$13.95–$19.95**

STRUT-SHOK

Available in: An economical turkey hunting load with premium lead in 12-gauge 3 ½ or 3-inch, either length in No. 4, 5, or 6
Box of 10 3-inch: **$12.95**
Box of 10 3 ½-inch: **$18.95**

TOP GUN TARGET

Available in: 12- or 20-gauge 2¾-inch in No. 7½, 8, 9; multiple loadings available, including a subsonic load in 12-gauge in No. 7½
Box of 25 subsonic: **$10.95**
Box of 25 target . . . . . **$8.95–$12.95**

TOP GUN TARGET-STEEL

Available in: 12 Ga., 20 Ga. (2¾ in.); Shot size: 7
Box 25: **$10.95**

WING-SHOK HIGH VELOCITY

Features: Pheasant and Quail Forever versions available
Available in: 12-gauge 3-inch No. 6, 5, 4; 12-gauge 2¾-inch No. 7½, 6, 5, 4; 16-gauge 2¾-inch No. 6, 5, 4; 20-gauge 3-inch No. 6, 5, 4;
20-gauge 2¾-inch 7½, 6, 5, 4; 28-gauge 2¾-inch No. 8, 7½, 6
Box of 25 12-gauge: . . . **$21.95–$28.95**
Box of 25 16-gauge: **$27.95**
Box of 25 20-gauge: **$24.95**
Box of 25 28-gauge: **$29.95**

WING-SHOK MAGNUM

Available in: 20-gauge 3-inch No. 6, 5, and 4 or 2 ¾-inch No. 6 and 4
20-gauge: . . . . **$26.95–$27.95**

Shotgun Slugs

POWER-SHOK RIFLED SLUG

Features: Hollow point slug type
Available in: 10 Ga. (3½ in.), 12 Ga. (2¾ in., 3 in.), 16 Ga. (2¾ in.), 20 Ga. (2¾ in.), .410 (2½ in.)
Box 5: . . . .**$6.95–$13.95**

POWER-SHOK SABOT SLUGS

Features: Sabot hollow point slug type
Available in: 12 Ga., 20 Ga. (2¾ in.)
Box 5: **$9.95**

VITAL-SHOK TROPHY COPPER SABOT SLUG

Features: A copper slug that incorporates some of the most advanced technology in the industry; better accuracy, less drop, manageable recoil (similar to a .30-06 Spfd.) and consistent penetration and expansion; unique two-part sabot design achieves accuracy through a clean launch and improved projectile support
Available in: 12 Ga., 20 Ga. (2¾ in., 3 in.)
Box 5: . . . .**$15.95–$17.95**

VITAL-SHOK TRUBALL RIFLED SLUG

Available in: 12, 20 Ga. (2¾ in., 3 in.)
Box 5: . . . .**$5.95–$6.95**

AMMUNITION

Rifle Ammunition

EXTREMA RIFLE HUNTING LINE

Features: Combining the best bullets in the business with our precision-drawn brass cases gives you the best combination of value and performance; uses bullets like the Hornady SST, V Max, and Sierra Game King to provide a combination of accuracy, high ballistic coefficients, and reliable expansion

Available in: .204 Ruger, .223 Rem., .22-50 Rem., .243 Win., .270 Win., 6.5X55 Swedish Mauser, 7mm-08, .300 BLK, .308 Win., .30-06 Spfd., .300 Win. Mag.; .223 Rem. available in 50- and 200-count packages; .204 Ruger available in 50-count package

Box: 20, 50, 200 rounds

20 rounds:	**$14.99–$46.99**
50 rounds:	**$23.99–31.99**
200 rounds:	**$106.99**

SHOOTING DYNAMICS RIFLE LINE

Features: High-quality reloadable brass cases combined with quality full metal jacket, soft point, or flat soft point (for lever guns) make sure your shooting dollar goes further

Available in: .223 Rem., .22-250 Rem., .243 Win., .25-06 Rem., .270 Win., 7mm-08 Rem., .300 BLK, .30 Carbine, .30-30 Win., .308 Win., .30-06 Spfd., .300 Win. Mag., 7.62x39 Soviet; some calibers available in 50-, 500-, or 1,000-count packages

20 rounds:	**starting at $10.99**
50 rounds:	**starting at $33.99**
500 rounds:	**starting at $214.99**
1,000 rounds:	**starting at $489.99**

Handgun Ammunition

COWBOY ACTION LINE

Features: Loaded with brass reloadable cases, noncorrosive primers, smokeless powders, and lead bullets coated with lube to reduce leading in the barrel; velocity is on par with what you would expect from period-correct ammo while keeping the recoil to a minimum for timed Cowboy Action competition and to reduce wear and tear on older guns

Available in: .32 S&W Long, .38 S&W Short, .38 S&W Spl., .357 Mag., .44 Spl., .44-40 Win., .45 Long Colt

MSRP . . . . **$19.99–$39.99**

EXTREMA XTP HANDGUN LINE

Features: Combined with nickel-plated cases for positive feeding and extraction when you need it most, qualified primers and clean powders deliver the maximum performance for the ultimate hunting or self-defense application

Available in: .25 ACP, .32 ACP, .380 ACP, 9mm Luger, .38 Spl., .38 Spl.+P, .357 Mag., .40 S&W, .44 Rem. Mag., .45 ACP

MSRP . . . . **$13.54–$21.66**

SHOOTING DYNAMICS PISTOL & REVOLVER LINE

Features: Combining quality brass cases with consistent primers, clean powders, and full metal jacket, jacketed hollow point, and soft point bullets in many calibers, Fiocchi loads bullets of the same weight to velocities that are comparable with high-quality defensive loads so you get realistic training-recoil impulse and point of aim/impact

Available in: .25 ACP, .32 ACP, .32 S&W Long, .380 ACP, 9mm Luger, 9mm Makarov, 9mm Steyr, 9x21 IMI, .38 Spl., .357 Mag., .38 Super Auto, .40 S&W, .44 Rem. Mag., .44 Spl., .45 ACP

MSRP . . . . **$14.99–$27.99**

Shotgun Ammunition

EXACTA TARGET LOADS

Features: Specifically for competitive shooters; the Target Load Line is the offspring of a fifty year tradition of supporting the world of trap, skeet, and now sporting clays, FITASC, and Compaq

Available in: Steel: 12 Ga., 20 Ga. (2¾ in.), Shot size: 7; Helios: 12 Ga. (2¾ in.), Shot sizes: 7, 7.5

Case of 250 rounds: . . **$109.99–$114.95**

GOLDEN PHEASANT LINE

Features: Golden Pheasant shot shells utilize a special hard, nickel-plated lead shot, based on Fiocchi's strict ballistic tolerances that ensure proven shot consistency and result in deeper penetration, longer ranges, and much tighter patterns

Available in: 12 Ga. (2¾ in., 3 in.), 16 Ga. (2¾ in.), 20, 28 Ga. (2¾ in., 3 in.); Shot sizes: 4, 5, 6, 7.5, 8, 9

250 rounds: . . . . **$139.99–$184.99**

NICKEL-PLATED BUCKSHOT

Features: Harder pellets from the nickel plating mean better patterns, better penetration, and no buffer needed

Available in: 12 Ga. (2¾ in.); Shot sizes: 00, 4

Box of 10: **$7.49**

WATERFOWL STEEL HUNTING

Features: Treated steel pellets, the correct wad, and powders that perform in the cold conditions often encountered in waterfowl hunting deliver the kills a waterfowl hunter wants

Available in: 12 Ga. (2¾ in., 3 in.), 20 Ga. (3 in.); Shot sizes: T, BBB, BB, 1, 2, 3, 4, 5, 6

250 rounds: . . . . **starting at $106.99**

FIOCCHI SHOOTING DYNAMICS PISTOL LINE

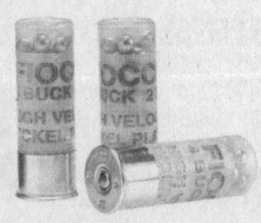

FIOCCHI NICKEL-PLATED BUCKSHOT

GECO

RIFLE AMMUNITION
Features: A range of bullets for training and all types of hunting situations worldwide; GECO offers five different bullet types to cover every hunting situation; GECO PLUS for shooting big game, GECO EXPRESS for the long distance shot, GECO SOFTPOINT as the real all-rounder, GECO SWISS MATCH for .223 competitors, and GECO ZERO, a lead-free line for hunters; made in Germany, which means outstanding accuracy and reliable bullet performance
Available calibers: .223 Rem., .243 Win., .270 WSM, .270 Win., .280 Rem., .30-06 Spfd., .300 Win. Mag., .308 Win., 6.5x55 Swedish Mauser, 7mm Rem. Mag., 7x57, 7x57R, 7x64, 7x65R, 8x57 IRS, 8x57 IS, 9.3x62, 9.3x74R
From:................$20.53

RIMFIRE AMMUNITION
Features: Target shooters can always depend on the cartridges perfect functioning, consistent performance and good precision.; reliable rimfire ammunition to guarantee required standards of accuracy at a favorable price
Available in: .22 LR Rifle, .22 LR Semi-Auto
Box of 500:........$23.00–$29.99

PISTOL AMMUNITION
Features: GECO offers 18 loads with cartridges in nine different calibers; these cover all relevant fields of application like precision shooting, dynamic sport disciplines, hunting, protection, and self-defense.
Available in: .38 Super, .40 S&W,

GECO RIMFIRE AMMUNITION

.45ACP, 6.35 Browning, 7.65 Browning (.32 ACP), 9mm Browning Court (.380 ACP), 9mm, 9mm Makarov, 9x21., .357 Mag., .38 Spl. .357 SIG
Box of 50 :..........$8.99–$30.82

Hornady Manufacturing

Rifle Ammunition

AMERICAN GUNNER RIFLE
Features: The American Gunner line of ammunition is a collection of tried-and-true, versatile loads that are popular with shooters for their target shooting, hunting, or self-defense needs. Made in the USA with premium components, American Gunner ammunition combines generations of ballistics know-how with modern technology. Hornady introduces new rifle calibers to complement the handgun offerings currently available. These rifle options are loaded with match grade hollow point bullets for a broad range of use including self-defense, target shooting, and varmint/small game hunting.
Available in: .223 Rem., 6.5 Creedmoor, .300 BLK, .308 Win.
Box of 50:..........$36.99–$59.99

AMERICAN WHITETAIL
Features: Loaded with Hornady InterLock Bullets, optimized loads specifically for deer hunting, and select propellants for greater consistency

Available in: 6.5 Creedmoor, .243 Win., .25-06 Rem., .270 Win., 7mm-08 Rem., 7mm Rem. Mag, 30-30 Win., .308 Win., 30-06 Spfd., .300 Win. Mag, .300 WSM
Box 20:............$19.99–$31.99

BLACK
Features: Designed to function across a wide variety of platforms including direct impingement, gas piston, suppressed, unsuppressed, inertia, bolt, pump, supersonic, subsonic, rifle, mid-length, carbine, or pistol; seven bullet types; 00 buckshot comes in a box of 10
Available in: 5.45x39, .223 Rem., 5.56 NATO, 6.5 Grendel, .224 Valkyrie, 6mm Creedmoor, 6.8mm SPC, .300 BLK, 7.62x39, .308 Win., .450 Bushmaster
Box 20:............$16.99–$31.99

CRITICAL DEFENSE RIFLE
Features: Corrosion-resistant nickel-plated cases; Critical Defense offers improved expansion with limited penetration in self-defense rifles
Available in: .223 Rem., 5.56 NATO, .30 Carbine, .308 Win.
Box of: 20
MSRP.............$21.99–$34.99

HORNADY AMERICAN WHITETAIL

HORNADY BLACK

HORNADY CRITICAL DEFENSE RIFLE

AMMUNITION

Hornady Manufacturing

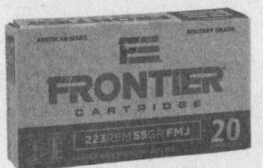

HORNADY FRONTIER   **HORNADY SUPERFORMANCE MATCH**

HORNADY FULL BOAR

HORNADY PRECISION HUNTER

HORNADY SUBSONIC .300 BLACKOUT

CUSTOM

Features: Depending on caliber, Custom ammo is loaded with Hornady SST, InterBond, InterLock, or V-MAX bullets
Available in: .22 Hornet, .218 Bee, .223 Rem., .243 Win., .250 Savage, 6.5 Grendel, .264 Win. Mag., 6.8 SPC, .270 Win., .275 Rigby, 7mm Rem. Mag., .300 BLK
Box 20: . . . . **$24.99–$53.99**

CUSTOM LITE

Features: CustomLite ammunition is recommended for children, women, and anyone new to the game; offer minimum recoil and a reduced muzzle blast; often paired with SST and RN bullets
Available in: .243 Win, .270 Win., 7mm Rem. Mag., 7mm-08 Rem., .308 Win., .30-06 Spfd.
From: . . . . **$28.09–$29.99**

DANGEROUS GAME

Features: These bullets are among the largest offered by Hornady and feature the DGS (Dangerous Game Solid) and the DGX (Dangerous Game eXpanding); made with hard lead/antimony alloy cone and surrounded by a copper-clad steel jacket; straighter penetration comes from a flat meplat that creates more energy than traditional round bullets
Available in: 9.3x62 Mauser, 9.3x74R, .376 Steyr., .375 H&H, .378 H&H Superformance, .375 Ruger, .375 Ruger Superformance, .450–400 Nitro Express, .404 Jeffery, .458 Lott, .470 NE, .500 NE
From: . . . . **$57.99–$159.99**

FRONTIER

Features: Frontier is American made; military grade; brass cases; wide variety of bullet weights and profiles
Available in: .223 Rem., 5.56 NATO, .300 BLK; some profiles available in bulk counts of 150, 500, and 1,000 rounds
Box of 20 . . . . **$7.99–$15.99**

FULL BOAR

Features: Hard hitting Hornady GMX bullets for deep penetration and maximum weight retention; monolithic, copper alloy bullets deliver controlled expansion and 95+ percent weight retention; excellent fit, feed and function in ARs and other semi-autos; California compatible and approved for use in other areas requiring the use of non-traditional bullets
Available in: .223 Rem., .243 Win., .25-06 Rem., 6.5 Creedmoor, 6.8 SPC, .270 Win., 7mm-08 Rem., 7mm Rem. Mag., .300 BLK, .30-30 Win., .308 Win., .30-06 Spfd., .300 Win. Mag.
Box 20: . . . . **$22.99–$49.99**

LEVEREVOLUTION

Features: LEVERevolution bullets travel at a speed of 250 fps and have a faster muzzle velocity than most other conventional lever gun loads; are unbelievably accurate and offer incomparable terminal performance; available in FTX and MonoFlex
Available in: .25-35 Win., .30-30 Win., .307 Win., .308 Marlin Express, .32 Win. Spl., .338 Marlin Express, .348 Win., .35 Rem., .444 Marlin, .45-70 Govt., .450 Marlin
From: . . . . **$25.99–$52.99**

MATCH

Features: Match bullets feature a boattail hollow point design that provides both accuracy and speed; these bullets' jackets feature near-zero wall thickness, which leads to uniformity throughout the jacket; case weight and internal capacity are also consistent throughout Match ammunition
Available in: .223 Rem., .224 Valkyrie, .260 Rem., 6mm Creedmoor, 6.5 Creedmoor, 6.5 PRC, .308 Win., .300 Win. Mag.
From: . . . . **$19.99–$44.99**

PRECISION HUNTER

Features: Best-in-class BCs, match-accurate hunting loads, topped with ELD-X Heat Shield Tip bullets
Available in: .243 Win., 6mm Creedmoor, 25-06 Rem., .257 Wby. Mag., 6.5 Creedmoor, 6.5 PRC, .270 Win., .270 WSM, 7mm-08 Rem., .280 Rem., .280 Ackley Improved, 7mm WSM, 7mm Rem. Mag., .28 Nosler, 7mm Shooting Times Westerner, .308 Win., .30-06 Spfd., .300 Rem. SAUM, .300 Ruger Compact Mgnum, .300 Win. Mag., .300 Wby. Mag., .300 PRC, .300 RUM. .30-378 Wby. Mag., .338 Lapua Mag.
Box 20: . . . . **$34.99–$99.99**

SUBSONIC .300 BLACKOUT

Features: Subsonic .300 Blackout wears a 190-gr. Sub-X (Subsonic eXpanding) bullet; lead core; gilded metal jacket; Flex Tip insert; muzzle velocity is 1,050 fps; muzzle energy is 465 ft-lbs.
Available in: .300 Blackout
Box of: 20
MSRP **$22.99**

SUPERFORMANCE

Features: Superformance bullets are 100–200 fps faster than any other traditional type of bullet on the market today. In addition to their speed, they also offer minimal recoil, muzzle blast, temperature sensativity, and inaccuracies; these bullets are versatile and can be paired with all types of firearms, including semiautomatics, lever guns, and pump actions
Available in: .223 Rem., 5.56 NATO, .243 Win., 6mm Rem., .25-06 Rem., .257 Roberts +P, .260 Rem., , 6.5 Creedmoor, 6.5x55 Swedish, .270 Win., .30-06 Spfd., .300 RCM., .300 Win. Mag., .300 WSM, .338 RCM, .338 Win. Mag., .35 Whelen, .444 Marlin
MSRP . . . . **$25.99–$48.99**

Hornady Manufacturing

SUPERFORMANCE MATCH

Features: Achieves muzzle velocity 100 to 200 fps faster than conventional .308 Win. loads; AMAX or Hornady Boattail Hollowpoint Match bullets featuring AMP (Advanced Manufacturing Process) jackets
Available in: .223 Rem., 5.56 NATO, .308 Win.
Box 20: . . . . **$21.99–$34.99**

Handgun Ammunition

AMERICAN GUNNER HANDGUN

Features: XTP (eXtreme Terminal Performance) bullets are exceptionally accurate and deliver excellent versatility and superior ballistic performance; propellants are matched to each load to ensure optimal pressure, velocity,
volume and consistency from lot to lot; high quality primers and Hornady cases combine to deliver consistent shooting in the field
Available in: .380 ACP, .40 S&W, .45 ACP, 9mm, 9mm +P, .38 Spl., .357 Mag.
Box of 25 . . . .**$17.99**

COWBOY

Features: These swaged bullets flatten instead of fragment when they reach their targets; diamond knurling ensures that the entire surface of the bullet is well-lubed
Available in: .44-40 Win., .45 Colt
Box 20: . . . .**$23.92–$25.60**

CRITICAL DEFENSE HANDGUN

Features: Critical Defense bullets are custom-designed for individual loads, and their shiny silver nickel plating prevents bullet corrosion; Critical Defense ammunition is cannelured and crimped to avoid bullet setback,
and clean burning and stable propellants reduce recoil
Available in: .25 ACP, .32 ACP, .32 NAA, 32 H&R Mag., 9x18mm Makarov, .380 ACP, 9mm Luger, .38 Spl., .38 Spc. Lite, .38 Spl. +P, .357 Mag., .40 S&W, .44 Spl.
Box of 25 . . . .**$22.09–$26.99**

CRITICAL DUTY

Features: Features FlexLock Bullets, crimped and nickel-plated cases, interlocking bands, and a core made of high-antimony lead; these bullets are among the top choices of law enforcement and military professionals and highly reliable
Available in: .357 Mag., .40 S&W, .45 ACP +P, .357 SIG, 9mm, 9mm Luger +P, 10mm Auto
Box of 25 . . . .**$24.99–$25.99**

Shotgun Ammunition

AMERICAN GUNNER SHOTGUN

Features: Reduced recoil rifled slugs or 00 buckshot; rifled slug is 1 oz., 00 buck holds eight high-antimony swaged pellets
Available in: 12 ga.
Box 5 slug: **$9.99**
Box 5 #00 Buck: **$11.99**

AMERICAN WHITETAIL RIFLED SLUG

Features: Rifled slug for smooth-bore barrels; 12 gauge 1-ounce rifled, foster style slug or 325-grain InterLock slug; hollow point, tough lead-alloy core; 1,600 feet per second
Available in: 12 Ga.
Box 5 slug: **$8.99**
Box 5 Interlock: **$12.99**

CUSTOM LITE SHOTGUN SLUGS

Features: Delivers 25 percent less recoil than standard loads; for rifled barrels only; FTX bullet improves ballistic coefficient and aids in expansion; lower recoil and muzzle blast while maintaining accuracy and effectiveness out to 150 yds; innovative sabot design enhances accuracy
Available in: 12 Ga., 20 Ga. (2 ¾ in.)
Box 5: **$12.99**

HEAVY MAGNUM COYOTE

Features: Loaded with 1 ½ oz. of nickel plated lead shot in either a BB or 00 buckshot for close range predators; features Hornady Versatite wad for more impact on target; 1,300 fps
Available in: 12 Ga. (3 in., 00 buckshot or BB)
Box 10: **$14.99**

HEAVY MAGNUM TURKEY

Features: Each 3-in., 12-ga. shotshell contains 1½ oz. of either #4, #5, or #6 nickel-plated lead; each 20-ga. shotshell is loaded with 1 3/8 oz. of #5 nickel-plated lead shot; loads don't require modified shotguns or specialized turkey chokes
Available in: 12 Ga. (3 in.), 20 Ga. (3 in.); Shot sizes: 4, 5, 6 nickel
Box 10: **$14.99**

SST SLUGS

Features: Sharp points at the end of these slugs allow for faster and more accurate shooting; able to reach your target from an impressive 200 yards away; each shot delivers more than 1200 ft.-lbs. of energy
Available in: 12, 20 Ga. (2¾ in)
Box of 5 12-gauge: **$13.99**
Box of 5 20-gauge: **$14.99**

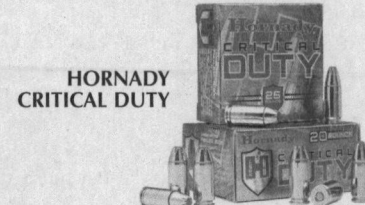

HORNADY CRITICAL DUTY

HORNADY CUSTOM LITE 20-GAUGE SLUG

HORNADY AMERICAN GUNNER SHOTGUN

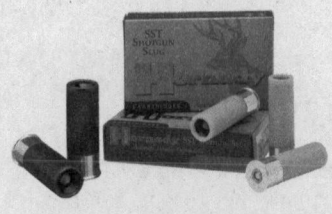

HORNADY SST SLUGS

Hornady Manufacturing

Rimfire Ammunition

VARMINT EXPRESS RIMFIRE .17 HMR
Features: The 17 HMR is one of the most accurate rimfire bullets ever made; polymer tip fragments rapidly and dramatically on impact, and its flat trajectory adds to its accuracy and consistency
Available in: .17 HMR
Box 50: $13.99

VARMINT EXPRESS RIMFIRE .17 MACH 2
Features: These V-MAX bullets are known for their rapid fragmentation and consistent accuracy; these bullets are made in America and hand inspected; paired with Varmint Express products, ignition is fast and easy
Available in: .17 Mach2
Box 50: $9.99

VARMINT EXPRESS RIMFIRE .17 WSM
Features: 20 grain V-Max bullet that provides tack-driving accuracy; muzzle velocity of 3,000 feet per second; fills the gap between the rimfire 17 HMR and centerfire 17 Hornet
Available in: .17 WSM (20 gr.)
Box 50: $16.99

VARMIN EXPRESS RIMFIRE .22 WMR
Features: The .22 WMR guarantees accurate shooting from more than 125 feet; has a muzzle velocity of 2,200 fps and is one of the most requested products Hornady offers; available in 25, 30, and 45 gr.
Available in: .22 WMR
Box 50: $12.59

HORNADY HEAVY MAGNUM COYOTE

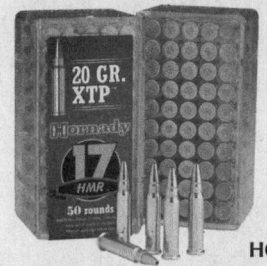

HORNADY 17 HMR

Inceptor Ammunition

INCEPTOR SPORT UTILITY-HANDGUN

SPORT UTILITY-HANDGUN
Features: Lead-free injection-molded copper-polymer projectiles loaded to tight specifications in high-quality brass cases; RNP (Round Nose Precision) profile in handgun cartridges or with the SRR (Short-Range Rifle) in rifle cartridges
Available in: .380 ACP, 9mm, 9mm +P, .38 Spec., .40 S&W, .45 ACO
Box of 50: . . . . $18.99–$30.99

Jarrett Rifles

TROPHY AMMUNITION
Features: Jarrett's high-performance cartridges are in ten round boxes; cases are from Norma with Jarrett's head-stamp
Available in: .243 Win., .270 Win., 7mm Rem. Mag., .30-06 Spfd., .300 WM, .300 Jarrett, .375 H&H, .416 Rem. Mag.
MSRP . . . . $29.12–$82.81

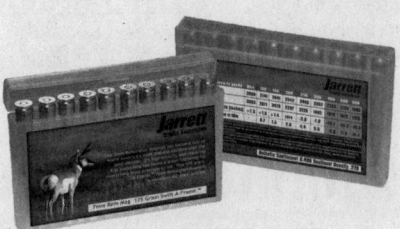

JARRETT TROPHY AMMUNITION

Kent Cartridge

KENT CARTRIDGE BISMUTH UPLAND

BISMUTH UPLAND
Features: Bismuth-based shot is 24 percent denser than steel; safe to use in any choke; doesn't harm barrels; loaded to optimal velocities for max ballistic performance
Available in: 12- and 20-gauge 3- and 2 ¾-inch in No. 5 and 6; 16-gauge 2¾-inch in No. 5 only
Box of: 25
MSRP . . . . $28.99–$40.99

Kent Cartridge

KENT CARTRIDGE BISMUTH WATERFOWL

KENT CARTRIDGE ELITE LOW-RECOIL/TRAINING

KENT CARTRIDGE ELITE PRO TARGET

KENT CARTRIDGE ELITE STEEL TARGET

KENT CARTRIDGE ELITE TARGET

KENT CARTRIDGE FIRST DOVE

KENT CARTRIDGE STEEL DOVE

BISMUTH WATERFOWL

Features: Bismuth-based shot is 24 percent denser than steel; safe to use in any choke; doesn't harm barrels; loaded to optimal velocities for max ballistic performance
Available in: 12-gauge 3½- and 3-inch in No. 3, 4; 12-gauge 2¾-inch in No. 4; 20-gauge 3-inch in No. 3, 4
Box of: 25
MSRP . . . . $31.99–$41.99

ELITE LOW-RECOIL/ TRAINING

Features: The new Elite Low-Recoil/ Training load from Kent comes two ways: a 12-ga. 2.5-in. shell with a 0.75-oz. load, and a 12-ga. 2.75-in. shell with a 0.75-oz. load; loaded with No. 8 to muzzle velocity of 1,200 fps; Kent's Diamond Shot ensures solid break
Available in: 12 ga.

Box of: 25
Case of 250 shells: $72.19

ELITE PRO TARGET

Features: Loaded with Diamond Shot; all 2.75 in. Shot sizes: 7.5, 8, 8.5
Available in: 12, 20 ga.
Box of: 25
Case of 250 shells: $75.49

ELITE STEEL TARGET

Features: Two 12-ga. 2.75-in. loads: a 1-oz. load at 1,290 fps and a 0.75-oz. load at 1,215 fps, both in No. 7
Available in: 12 ga.
Box of: 25
Case of 250 shells: $72.49

ELITE TARGET

Features: Loaded with Diamond Shot; all 2.75 in. Shot sizes: 7.5, 8, 9

Available in: 12, 20 ga.
Box of: 25
Case of 250 shells: $70.49

FIRST DOVE

Features: Consistent patterns; clean-burning powders; in 12-ga. 2.75-in. 1-oz. or 20-ga. 2.75-in. 0.75-oz., both in No. 7.5
Available in: 12, 20 ga.
Box of: 25
Case of 250 shells: $65.49

STEEL DOVE

Features: Two 12-ga. 2.75-in. loads: a 1-oz. and a 1.125-oz.; One 20-ga. 2.75-in. 0.875-oz. load; Shot size: 6
Available in: 12, 20 ga.
Box of: 25
Case of 250 shells: $73.99

Kynoch Ammunition

KYNOCH RIFLE AMMUNITION

RIFLE AMMUNITION

Features: Kynoch hunting ammunition is now standardized on Woodleigh soft nosed and solid bullets, recognized world wide as the most reliable big game bullets currently manufactured; Kynamco offers virtually the whole range of classic British Nitro Express from its purpose-built factory
Available in: .300 Flanged, .303 British, .318 Westley Richards, 9.5X57 Mannlicher, .333 Jeffery Flanged. .350 Rigby, .400/.360 Westley Richards, .375 Flanged 2½-inch, .375 Flanged, .400 Purdey, .405 Winchester, .450/400 3- and 3½-inch, .416 Rigby, .404 Jeffery, .425 Westley Richards, .450 NE, .450 No. 2 NE, .450 Rigby, .577/.450 Martini Henry, .500/.450 NE, .500/.465 NE, .470 NE, .475 No. 2 Eley, .475 No. 2 Jeffery, .476 Westley Richards, .505 Gibbs, .500 Jeffery, .500 NE, .577 NE, .600 NE, .700 NE; currently available in the U.S. from M.W. Reynolds (mwreynolds.com) in Denver, Colorado.
MSRP . . . contact mwreynolds.com

Rifle Ammunition

CENTERFIRE SPORT

Features: Lapua's extremely accurate target shooting cartridges are loaded with the best target bullets—Scenar, FMJBT, D46 and Lock Base; numerous world championships, Olympic championships, and other top competition gold medals, as well as many official world records in different disciplines, are shot with the Lapua cartridges
Available in: .222 Rem., .223 Rem., .243 Win., 6mm BR Norma, 6.5 Creedmoor, 6.5x47 Lapua, 6.5x55 Swedish, 7.62x39, .308 Win., .30-06 Spfd., 7.62x53R, .338 Lapua Mag.
Box 50:. . . . .$32.99–$64.99

NATURALIS 3RD GENERATION

Features: Bullet mushrooming begins immediately on impact; bullet expands symmetrically and without shattering; gives a maximal shock effect to the hunted game; top premium copper bullet; 3rd Generation has updated bullet design with a monolithic pure copper body that can produce weight retention up to 100 percent; new boattail design eases reloading and improves ballistics; controlled expansion is procured via a polymer valve tip
Available in: .222 Rem., .243 Win., 6.5 Creedmoor, 6.5x47 Lapua, 6.5x55 Swedish Mauser, 7x64, 7x65R, .308 Win., .30-06 Spfd., 8x57 JS, 8x57 JRS, 338 Lapua, 9.3X62
Box of 10, 20: . . . .$46.99–$81.99

LAPUA CENTERFIRE SPORT

LAPUA NATURALIS
(3RD GENERATION)

Magtech Ammunition

FIRST DEFENSE HANDGUN

Features: Magtech First Defense rounds are designed with a 100 percent solid copper bullet, unlike traditional hollow points that contain a lead core covered by a copper jacket; First Defense solid copper bullets have no jacket to split or tear away, ensuring every round you fire meets its target with maximum impact and effectiveness
Available in: 9mm Luger, 9mm +P .40 S&W
Box 20:. . . . .$17.49–$21.39

SPORT SHOOTING HANDGUN

Features: The 100 percent solid copper hollow-point projectile features a six-petal hollow-point specifically designed to deliver tight groups, superior expansion, virtually 100 percent weight retention, and increased penetration over jacketed lead-core bullets
Available in: .25 ACP, .32 ACP, .32 S&W, .32 S&W Long, .380 ACP, 9mm, 9mm +P, 9X19 NATO, 9X21mm, .38 S&W, .38 Spec., .38 Spec. +P, .38 Super, .357 Mag., .40 S&W, 10mm Auto, .44040 Win., .44 Spec., .44 Mag., .45 G.A.P., .45 ACP, .454 Casull, .500 S&W
Box of 20, 50: . . . .$10.99–$46.99

MAGTECH
AMMUNITION

Nexus

MATCH GRADE

Features: Proprietary loading process; competition-ready
Available in: .260 Rem., .223 Rem., .338 Lapua, .300 Win. Mag., .300 Norma, .308 Win., 6.5x47 Lapua, 6.5 Creedmoor
Box of 20:. . . . .$22.99–$59.99

AMMUNITION

Norma Ammunition

NORMA AMERICAN
PH ORYX

Rifle Ammunition

AFRICAN PH

Features: Based on many generations of experience of reputable African Professional Hunters, this range of cartridges has been developed to optimize ballistic criteria such as bullet momentum, sectional density and deep, straight-line, bone-breaking penetration; loaded cartridges with Woodleigh softnose and solid bullets
Available in: .375 Flanged Mag. NE, .375 H&H Mag., .404 Jeffery, .416 Rem. Mag., .416 Rigby, .450 Rigby, .458 Lott, .470 NE, .500 Jeffery, .500 NE 3- and 3¼-inch, .505 Mag. Gibbs
Box 10:. . . . . **$59.99–$174.99**

AMERICAN PH KALAHARI

Features: The Kalahari is loaded with selected lots of powder to ensure the highest possible velocity, best possible ballistic coefficient, and lowest wind drift achievable at normal hunting ranges; bullet expansion is controlled and restricted–only the front third of the bullet will expand into six razor-edged petals, leaving the rear part of the bullet unimpeded, guaranteeing deep penetration
Available in: .270 Win., .270 WSM, .280 Rem., .300 Win. Mag., .300 WSM, .30-06 Spfd., .308 Win., 7mm Rem. Mag., 7X64
Box of 20:. . . . . **$46.71–$62.78**

AMERICAN PH ORYX

Features: The Oryx has a thin forward jacket with internal splitting zones; the bonding and the thicker rear jacket wall ensure a high residual weight after impact (often over 90 percent) and excellent penetration
Available in: .243 win., .270 Win., .270 WSM, .280 Rem., .300 Blaser Mag., .300 RUM, .300 Win. Mag., .300 WSM, .30-06 Spfd., .308 Norma Mag., .308 Win., .338 Win. Mag., .35 Whelen, .358 Norma Mag., .375 Blaser Mag., .375 H&H Mag., 6XC, 6.5-284 Norma, 6.5X55 SE, 7mm Blaser Mag., 7mm Rem. Mag., 7X57, 7X57/R, 7X64, 7X65R, 7.5X55 Swiss, 8X57 IRS (JRS), 8X57 IS (JS), 9.3X57, 9.3X62, 9.3X74R
Box 20:. . . . . **$37.96–$62.78**

Nosler

NOSLER SAFARI
AMMUNITION

Rifle Ammunition

MATCH GRADE

Features: Match Grade Ammunition consists of Nosler's precisely-designed Custom Competition bullet along with NoslerCustom Brass; each piece of brass is checked for correct length, neck-sized, chamfered, trued and flash holes are checked for proper alignment; powder charges are meticulously weighed and finished rounds are visually inspected and polished
Available in: .223 Rem., 5.56X45 .22 Nosler, 6mm Creedmoor, 6.5 Creedmoor, 6.5 Grendel, .26 Rem., 6.5-284 Norma, .26 Nosler, .28 Nosler, 6.8 SPC, .30 Nosler, .300 BLK, .308 Win., .300 Win. Mag., .33 Nosler, .338 Lapua Mag., .33 Nosler
Box 20: . . . .**$25.90–$86.45**

SAFARI

Features: Loaded with either the Partition or Nosler Solid and designed for the same point of impact with either bullet, Safari Ammunition provides the ultimate versatility for any dangerous game situation
Available in: .500 Jeffery, 505 Gibbs, 9.3x62 Mauser, .375 Flanged, .375 H&H, .404 Jeffery, .416 Rem. Mag., .416 Rigby, .450 Rigby, .458 Lott, .458 Win. Mag., .470 NE, .500 NE, .500/.416 NE
Box 20:. . . . . **$113.45–$247.90**

AMMUNITION

Nosler

NOSLER TROPHY GRADE VARMINT AMMUNITION

NOSLER VARMAGEDDON AMMUNITION & BULLETS

NOSLER .22 NOSLER TROPHY GRADE/MATCH GRADE

NOSLER DEFENSE HANDGUN

TROPHY GRADE

Features: Manufactured to Nosler's strictest quality standards, Trophy Grade Ammunition uses Nosler Custom Brass and Nosler Bullets to attain optimum performance, no matter where your hunting trip takes you. Whether you want your ammunition loaded with AccuBond, Partition Ballistic Tip or, E-Tip, NoslerCustom Trophy Grade Ammunition will have the right load for the right game.
Available in: .223 Rem., .22 Nosler, 6mm Creedmoor, .243 Win., .25-06 Rem., .257 Roberts, .257 Wby. Mag., 6.5 Creedmoor, 6.5x55 Swedish, .260

Rem., 6.5-284 Norma, .264 Win. Mag., .26 Nosler, .270 Win., .270 WSM, 7mm-08, 7x57 Mauser, .280 Rem., 7mm SAUM, .280 Ackley Improved, 7mm Rem. Mag., 7mm STW, 7mm RUM, .308 Win., .30–06 Spfd., .300 SAUM, .300 H&H, .300 WSM, .300 Win. Mag., .300 Wby. Mag., .30 Nosler, .300 RUM, .325 WSM, .338 Win. Mag., .340 Wby. Mag., .338 RUM, .338 Lapua, .33 Nosler, .35 Whelen, 9.3X62, .375 H&H, .416 Rem. Mag.
Box 20:. . . . . $31.45–$109.45

TROPHY GRADE VARMINT

Features: Trophy Grade VARMINT Ammunition consists of the venerable Ballistic Tip VARMINT bullet or the frangible Ballistic Tip Lead Free along with NoslerCustom Brass
Available in: .204 Ruger, .223 Rem., .22 Nosler, .22-250 Rem.
Box 20:. . . . . $27.45–$47.90

VARMAGEDDON

Features: Featuring a highly accurate polymer tip or hollow point combined with flat base design, Varmageddon products were created for the high-volume varmint shooter who requires the utmost precision; loaded with Nosler Custom Brass, Varmageddon ammunition provides the highest levels of performance for any varmint hunter
Available in: .17 Rem., .204 Ruger, .22 Hornet, .221 Rem. Fireball, .222 Rem., .223 Rem., .22 Nosler, .22-250 Rem., 6mm Creedmoor, .243 Win., 6.5 Grendel, .300 BLK, .308 Win.
Box 20:. . . . . $23.90–$42.10

Handgun Ammunition

DEFENSE HANDGUN

Features: Bonded 'Performance' bullets for higher weight retention and maximum barrier penetration; either jacketed hollow point or polymer tipped configuration
Available in: 9mm Luger +P, .40 S&W
Box of 20 9mm +P:. . . $22.90–$24.90
Box of 20 .40 S&W:. . . $24.90–$26.45

NovX

NOVX ARX ENGAGEMENT EXTREME, +P ENGAGEMENT EXTREME

NOVX RNP CROSSTRAINER, RNP +P CROSS TRAINER

ENGAGEMENT EXTREME, ENGAGMENT EXTREME +P

Features: Lead free; projectiles are a copper-polymer creation; cases are stainless steel; fluted bullet design; 65-gr. 9mm at 1,672 fps/358 ft-lbs standard pressure (1,710 fps/422 ft-lbs in the +P.)
Available in: 9mm, 9mm +P
Box of: 26
MSRP. $27.99
+P:. $28.99

CROSSTRAINER/ COMPETITION

Features: Roundnose design; 65-gr. at *1,600 fps, 347 ft-lbs standard pressure*
Available in 9mm
Box of: 26
MSRP. $27.99

PMC Ammunition

PMC BRONZE LINE - HANDGUN

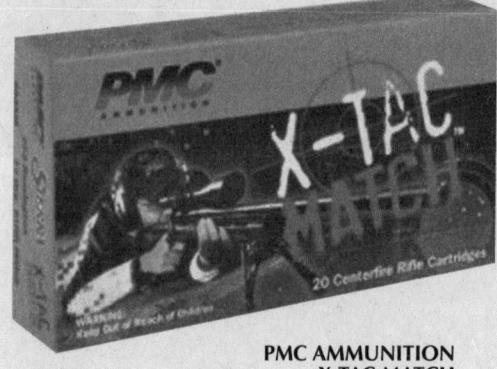

PMC AMMUNITION
X-TAC MATCH

Rifle Ammunition

BRONZE LINE - RIFLE

Features: For shooters and hunters who appreciate affordable quality ammunition, the PMC Bronze Line offers reliable performance for every shooting application; Full Metal Jacket (FMJ) bullet types
Available in: .223 Rem, .223 Soft Point, .308 Soft Point, .308 Win., 7.62x39, .50
Box 20 (Box 10 .50
BMG): . . . .$8.99–$37.99

X-TAC

Features: PMC's exacting adherence to precise specifications of military and law enforcement organizations assures that X-TAC ammunition will perform perfectly in that fraction of a second when a serious threat arises and your life is on the line
Available in: 5.56 NATO, 7.62
Box 20: . . . .$9.99–$20.49

X-TAC MATCH

Features: X-TAC ammo performance comined with Sierra Bullets' ballistics
Available in: .223 Rem., .308 Win., .50
Box 20 (Box 10 .50
BMG): . . . .$16.99–$75.99

Handgun Ammunition

BRONZE LINE - HANDGUN

Features: The same quality and dependability built into our Starfire ammunition is incorporated throughout our extensive line of PMC training ammunition and standard hollow

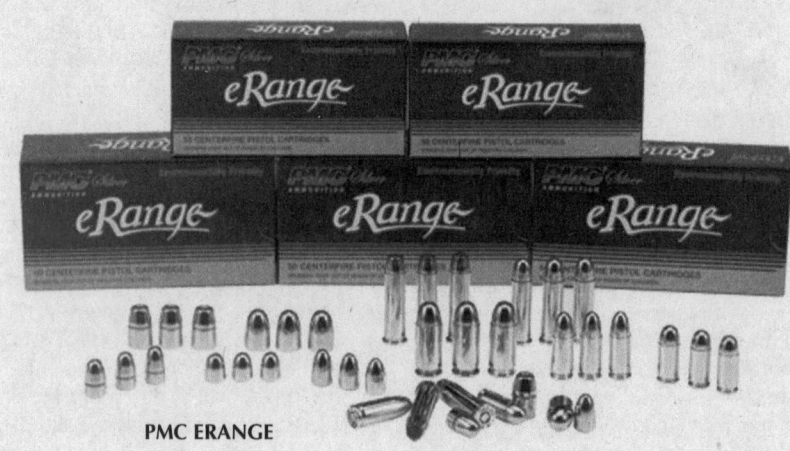

PMC ERANGE

point or soft point ammunition.
Available in: .25 ACP, .32 ACP, .380 ACP, .38 Spl., .38 Super +P, 9mm Luger, .357 Mag., 10mm ACP, .40 S&W, .44 S&W Spl., .44 Rem. Mag., .45 ACP
From: . . . .$9.49–$29.99

ERANGE

Features: PMC's eRange environmentally friendly ammunition utilizes a reduced hazard primer that is the first of this type in the industry, an encapsulated metal jacket (EMJ) bullet which completely encloses the surface of the bullet core with precision made copper alloy, and powder with clean-burning characteristics and smooth fire for increased barrel life
Available in: .380 ACP, .38 Spl., .38

Spl. +P, .357 Mag., 9mm Luger, .40 S&W, .44 Rem., .45 ACP
From: . . . .$17.65–$42.58

GOLD LINE - STARFIRE

Features: The secret of Starfire's impressive performance lies in a unique, patented rib-and-flute hollow point cavity design; upon impact, the pre-notched jacket mouth begins to peel back, separating into five uniform copper petals and allowing expansion to begin
Available in: .380 ACP, .38 Spl. +P, .357 Mag., 9mm Luger, .40 S&W, .44 Rem. Mag., .45 ACP
From: . . . .$8.70–$16.89

Remington Arms Company

Rifle Ammunition

CORE-LOKT

Features: The bonded bullet retains up to 95 percent of its original weight with maximum penetration and energy transfer; features a progressively tapered jacket design, the Core-Lokt Ultra Bonded bullet initiates and controls expansion nearly 2x

Available in: 6mm Rem., .25-06 Rem., .25-20 Win., .250 Savage, 6.5x55 Swedish Mauser, .260 Rem., .264 Win. Mag., .270 Win., .270 WSM, .280 Rem., 7mm-08, 7mm Rem. Mag., 7mm RUM, 7x64, 7mm Mauser, .30 Carbine, .30-30 Win., .30-40 Krag, .30-06 Spfd., .300 Savage, .30 Rem. AR, .300 WSM, .300 Win. Mag., .300 RUM, .300 Wby. Mag., .303 British, 7.62x39, .308 Marlin Express, .308 Win., 8mm Mauser, .32 Win. Spec., .338 Win. Mag., .338 RUM, .35 Rem., .35 Whelen, .444 Marlin, .45-70 Govt., 6.5 Creedmoor, 7mm SA RUM, 6mm Creedmoor

Box 20: . . . . **$17.70–$62.73**

PREMIER ACCUTIP

Features: Featuring precision-engineered polymer tip bullets designed for match-grade accuracy (sub MOA), Premier AccuTip offers an unprecedented combination of super-flat trajectory and deadly down-range performance

Available in: .17 Rem. Fireball, .204 Ruger, .22 Hornet, .222 Rem., .223 Rem., .22-250 Rem., .243 Win., .270 Win., .280 Rem., 7mm Rem. Mag., .30-06 Spfd., .300 Win. Mag., .308 Win., .450 Bushmaster

Box 20: . . . . **$18.94–$43.86**

PREMIER MATCH

Features: Loaded with match-grade bullets, this ammunition employs special loading practices to ensure world-class performance and accuracy with every shot

Available in: 6mm Creedmoor, .223 Rem., 6.5 Creedmoor, 6.8 SPC, .300 BLK, .308 Win.

Box 20: . . . . **$33.34–$38.86**

Handgun Ammunition

ULTIMATE DEFENSE, COMPACT, FULL-SIZE

Features: Designed with the concealed carry permit holder in mind; delivers big gun terminal performance out of shorter barreled pistols and revolvers; engineered to provide optimal penetration and expansion at lower velocities for maximum stopping power

Available in: 9mm, .380 ACP, .38 Spl. +P, .40 S&W, .45 ACP., .45 Colt Full-size line also includes .357 Mag., 9mm +P

Box 20: **$22.52**

Rimfire Ammunition

.22 RIMFIRE TARGET

Features: Whether it's getting young shooters started, practice plinking, small-game hunting, or keeping match shooters scoring high, Remington's rimfire quality stands tall

Available in: .22 LR

Box of 50: **$4.39**
Box of 100: **$8.70**

Shotgun Ammunition

AMERICAN CLAY AND FIELD

Features: Nothing that flies stands a chance against these dual-purpose rounds. Expect the densest, most consistent patterns possible, no matter the day's pursuit. Featuring a premium STS primer, reloadable hull, our patented Power Piston wad, and high-hardness lead shot, they deliver flawless performance and consistent patterning, whether your target is winged or clay.

Available in: 12, 20, 28, .410

MSRP . . . . **$9.33–$11.93**

GUN CLUB TARGET

Features: Loaded with Gun Club Grade Shot, Premier STS Primers, and Power Piston One-Piece Wads, these high-quality shells receive the same care in loading as top-of-the-line Premier STS and Nitro .27 shells

Available in: 12, 20 Ga. (2¾ in.); Shot sizes: 7.5, 8, 9

Box 25: **$7.77**

EXPRESS EXTRA LONG RANGE

Features: Suitable for everything from quail to farm predators

Available in: 12, 16, 20, 28 Ga. (2¾ in.), .410 (2½ in., 3 in.); Shot sizes: 2, 4, 5, 6, 7.5

From: . . . . **$12.43–$20.98**

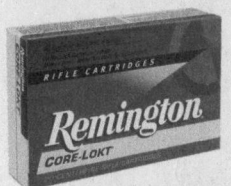

REMINGTON CORE-LOKT

REMINGTON AMMUNITION PREMIER ACCUTIP

REMINGTON AMMUNITION ULTIMATE DEFENSE COMPACT

REMINGTON PREMIER NITRO SPORTING CLAYS

REMINGTON AMMUNITION AMERICAN CLAY AND FIELD

HEAVY DOVE

Features: A sure bet for all kinds of upland game, ShurShot loads have earned the reputation as one of the best-balanced, best-pattering upland field loads available; shells combine an ideal balance of powder charge and shot payload to deliver effective velocities and near-perfect patterns with mild recoil for high-volume upland hunting situations

Available in: 12, 20 Ga. (2¾ in.); Shot sizes: 6, 7.5, 8

From: **$8.50**

HYPERSONIC STEEL

Features: With unprecedented velocity and the highest downrange pattern energies ever achieved, Remington HyperSonic Steel takes lethality to new heights and lengths

Available in: 10 Ga. (3½ in.), 12 Ga. (3 in., 3½ in.), 20 Ga. (3 in.); Shot sizes: BB, BBB, 1, 2, 3, 4

From: . . . . **$23.37–$38.14**

AMMUNITION

Remington Arms Company

REMINGTON ULTIMATE DEFENSE BUCKSHOT

REMINGTON HYPERSONIC STEEL

REMINGTON PREMIER ACCUTIP BONDED SABOT

LEAD GAME

Features: For a wide variety of field gaming, these budget-stretching loads include the same quality components as other Remington shotshells, and are available in four different gauges to match up with your favorite upland shotguns
Available in: 12, 16, 20 Ga. (2¾ in.), .410 (2½ in.); Shot sizes: 6, 7.5, 8
From: . . . . $7.60–$10.23

PREMIER HIGH-VELOCITY MAGNUM COPPER-PLATED TURKEY LOADS

Features: Utilizing a specially-blended powder recipe, Remington's advanced Power Piston one-piece wad, and hardened copper plated shot, these new high-velocity loads result in extremely dense patterns and outstanding knockdown power at effective ranges
Available in: 12 Ga. (3 in., 3½ in.); Shot sizes: 4, 5, 6
From: . . . . $7.22–$15.88

PREMIER MAGNUM COPPER-PLATED TURKEY LOADS

Features: Penetrating power and dense, concentrated patterns; the magnum-grade, Copper-Lokt shot is protected by our Power Piston wad and cushioned with special polymer buffering
Available in: 10 Ga. (3 ½ in.), 12 Ga. (3 in., 3 ½ in.); Shot sizes: 4, 5, 6
Box 5: . . . . $6.27–$10.39
Box of 10: . . . . $12.13–$20.37

PREMIER STS TARGET

Features: STS Target Loads have taken shot-to-shot consistency to a new performance level, setting the standard at all major skeet, trap, and sporting clays shooting across the country, while providing handloaders with unmatched reloading ease and hull longevity; available in most gauges, Premier STS shells are the most reliable, consistent, and reloadable shells you can shoot
Available in: 12, 20, 28 Ga. (2¾ in.), .410 (2½ in.); Shot sizes: 7.5, 8, 8.5, 9
From: . . . . $10.97–$14.99

NITRO PHEASANT

Features: Uses Remington's own Copper-Lokt copper-plated lead shot with high antimony content; hard shot stays rounder for truer flight, tighter patterns, and greater penetration; available in both high-velocity and magnum loadings
Available in: 12, 20 Ga. (2¾ in., 3 in.); Shot sizes: 4, 5, 6
From: . . . . $20.97–$22.21

NITRO-STEEL HIGH-VELOCITY

Features: Greater hull capacity means heavier charges and larger pellets, which makes these loads ideal for large waterfowl; delivers denser patterns for greater lethality and is zinc plated to prevent corrosion
Available in: 10 Ga. (3½ in.), 12 Ga. (2¾ in., 3 in., 3½ in.), 16 Ga. (2¾ in.), 20 Ga. (3 in.); Shot sizes: T, BBB, BB, 1, 2, 3, 4
From: . . . . $20.81–$31.83

NITRO TURKEY

Features: These loads contain Nitro Mag. extra-hard lead shot that is as hard and round as copper-plated shot; will pattern as well as other copper-plated, buffered loads without the higher cost
Available in: 12 Ga. (2¾ in., 3 in., 3½ in.), 20 Ga. (3 in.); Shot sizes: 4, 5, 6
Box of 5: . . . . $4.66–$8.75
Box of 10: . . . . $8.56–$12.73

PHEASANT

Features: For the broadest selection in game-specific Upland shotshells, Remington Upland Loads are the perfect choice with high-velocity and long-range performance for any pheasant hunting situation; standard high-base payloads feature Power Piston one-piece wads
Available in: 12, 16, 20 Ga. (2¾ in.); Shot sizes: 4, 5, 6, 7.5
From: . . . . $11.92–$17.94

SPORTSMAN HI-SPEED STEEL

Features: Sportsman Hi-Speed Steel's sealed primer, high-quality steel shot, and consistent muzzle velocities combine to provide reliability in adverse weather, while delivering exceptional pattern density and retained energy; a high-speed steel load that is ideal for short-range high-volume shooting during early duck seasons or over decoys
Available in: 10 Ga. (3½ in.), 12 Ga. (2¾ in., 3 in., 3½ in.), 20 Ga. (2¾ in.); Shot sizes: BB, 1, 2, 3, 4, 6, 7
From: . . . . $10.50–$30.87

Shotgun Slugs & Buckshot

EXPRESS, EXPRESS MAGNUM BUCKSHOT

Features: A combination of heavy cushioning behind the shot column and a granulated polymer buffering helps maintain pellet roundness for tight, even patterns
Available in: 12 (2¾ in., 3 in., 3½ in.), 20 Ga. (2¾ in.); Shot sizes: 000, 00, 0, 1, 3, 4
Box of 5 Express: $5.37
Box of 4 Express Magnum: . . . .$6.47–$12.29

MANAGED-RECOIL BUCKSHOT

Features: With less felt recoil than full velocity loads, Express Managed-Recoil Buckshot is an ideal close-range performer; less recoil means second shot recovery is quicker, allowing the user to get back on target more easily; loads are buffered for dense patterns, allowing for highly effective performance at up to 40 yards
Available in: 12 Ga. (2¾ in.); Shot size: 00
Box of 5: $5.52

Remington Arms Company

PREMIER ACCUTIP BONDED SABOT

Features: Guided by our new Power Port Tip, the AccuTip Bonded Sabot Slug delivers a degree of accuracy and terminal performance unmatched by any other we tested; yields over 95 percent weight retention thanks to its spiral nose cuts, bonded construction, and high-strength cartridge brass jacket; designed for fully-rifled barrels only
Available in: 12, 20 Ga. (2¾ in., 3 in.)
Box of 5 12-gauge: . . . $15.42–$17.71
Box of 5 20-gauge: $16.87

SLUGGER HIGH VELOCITY

Features: This is the first high-velocity Foster-style lead slug which exits the barrel at 1800 fps, 13 percent faster than standard 1-oz. slugs; the ⁷/₈ oz. Slugger High Velocity delivers 200 ft.-lbs. more energy at 50 yards with flatter trajectory on deer than standard 1-oz. slugs; designed for the avid deer hunter using smooth bore guns
Available in: 12 Ga. (2¾ in., 3 in.), 20 Ga. (2¾ in.)
Box of 5 12-gauge: . . . . .$5.10–$6.81
Box of 5 20-gauge: $4.59

SLUGGER MANAGED-RECOIL RIFLED

Features: Slugger Managed-Recoil Rifled Slugs offer remarkably effective performance but with 45 percent less felt recoil than full velocity Sluggers; with effective energy out of 80 yards, these 1-oz. slugs easily handle the majority of shotgun deer hunting ranges
Available in: 12 Ga. (2¾ in.
Box of 5: $5.41

SLUGGER RIFLED

Features: Remington redesigned their 12-gauge Slugger Rifled Slug for a 25 percent improvement in accuracy; at 1760 fps muzzle velocity, the 3-in. 12-gauge Magnum slug shoot 25 percent flatter than regular 12 gauge slugs
Available in: 12 Ga. (2¾ in., 3 in.), 16 Ga. (2¾ in.), 20 Ga. (2¾ in.), .410 (2½ in.)
Box of 5 12-gauge: . . . . .$5.10–$6.81
Box of 5 16-gauge: $5.22
Box of 5 20-gauge: $4.59
Box of 5 .410-bore: $5.25

ULTIMATE DEFENSE BUCKSHOT

Features: Dense patterns and big knock-down power; short-range patterns through smoothbores are tight; .410-bore loads house four lead 000 buckshot pellets
Available in: 12 ga 3 in., 2 ¾ in., 20 ga. 3 in., .410-bore 2 ½ in., 3 in. 12 ga. in 00 or No. 4 Buck; 20 ga. in No. 3 Buck; .410-bore in 000 Buck
Box of 5 12-gauge: . . . . .$5.26–$6.59
Box of 5 20-gauge: $5.26
Box of 10 .410-bore: . . $12.00–$13.67

Rio Ammunition

RIO AMMUNITION ROYAL PHEASANT

RIO AMMUNITION ROYAL TURKEY BUFFERED MAGNUM

RIO AMMUNITION SPREADER

RIO AMMUNITION VINTAGE 1896 PAPER

ROYAL PHEASANT

Features: A new line of copper-plated upland loads; designed for stopping power and patterns
Available in: 12, 20, 28 ga.
Box of: 25
MSRP . . . .$14.49–$17.79

ROYAL TURKEY BUFFERED MAGNUM

Features: Offered in 12-ga. 3-in. with a Max Dram Equivalent and 1.75 oz. of shot, or a 3.5-in. Max Dram 2-oz. load in your choice of 4, 5, or 6 shot
Available in: 12 ga.

Box of: 10
MSRP $6.29

SPREADER

Features: Velocity of 1,350 fps; 25 percent higher dispersion than other spreader wads
Box of: 10
MSRP $3.99

VINTAGE 1896 PAPER

Features: Shotshell has paper hulls instead of plastic
Box of: 25
MSRP $10.99

SIG Sauer

SIG SAUER MATCH GRADE ELITE MATCH GRADE OTM (OPEN TIP MATCH)

SIG SAUER VARMINT & PREDATOR

ELITE MATCH GRADE OTM (OPEN TIP MATCH)

Features: Engineered to match the ballistics of SIG's V-Crown defensive ammo line as a more affordable match-grade loading
Available in: 6.5 Creedmoor, .30-06 Spfd., .223 Rem., .308 Rem., .300 BLK,
Box of: 20
MSRP . . . .$23.95–$45.95

VARMINT & PREDATOR

Features: Single-based extruded powders; smoke gray-tipped projectiles designed for expansion; match-grade accuracy; flat trajectories
Available in: .223 Rem. (40 gr.), .22-250 Rem. (40 gr.), .243 Win. (55 gr.)
.223 Rem.: $20.95
.22-250 Rem.: $24.95
.243 Win.: $29.95

Speer

GOLD DOT PERSONAL PROTECTION

Features: Well-respected expanding hollowpoint design used by law enforcement and consumers for defensive and personal protection; the .22 WMR round will feed reliably in sub-compact handguns and perform suitable through barrels as short as 2 inches

Available in: .25 ACP, .32 ACP, .327 Fed. Mag., .380 ACP, 9mm, 9mm +P, .357 SIG, .38 Spec. +P, .357 Mag., .40 S&W, 10mm Auto, .44 Spec., .45 ACP, .22 WMR

Box of 20 centerfire: . . . $23.95–$35.95
Box of 50 .22 WMR: $19.95

SPEER GOLD DOT PERSONAL PROTECTION

Weatherby

WEATHERBY MAGNUM

Features: Weatherby Magnum cartridges are loaded with a variety of popular bullet types for a wide range of shooting purposes

Available in: .224, .240, 6.5-300, .257, .270, 7mm, .300, .340, .30–378, .338–378, .375, .378, .416, .460
MSRP . . . . $44.00–$209.00

WEATHERBY 6.5-300 WEATHERBY MAGNUM

Wilson Combat

.458 HAM'R

Features: Wilson's ammo designed for its 2018 .458 Ham'r Tactical Hunter rifle; available in 250-gr. Hornady MFX, 300-gr. Nosler boattail, 300-gr. Xtreme round-nose flat-point, and 300-gr. Barnes TTSX
Available in: .458 Ham'r
Box of: 20
MSRP: . . . . $39.95–$56.95

WILSON COMBAT .458 HAM'R

Winchester Ammunition

WINCHESTER AMMUNITION DEER SEASON XP

WINCHESTER AMMUNITION EXPEDITION BIG GAME

Rifle Ammunition

17 WINCHESTER SUPER MAGNUM

Features: A .27 caliber shellcase necked down to a .17 caliber bullet; surpasses the downrange velocity, energy, trajectory and wind bucking characteristics of both the .17 HMR and .22 WMR; available in Varmint HE, Varmint HV, and VarmintX lines.
Available in: .17 WSM
Box 50: $16.99

BALLISTIC SILVERTIP

Features: Solid-based boattail design delivers excellent long-range accuracy; in .22 calibers, the ballistic plastic polycarbonate Silvertip bullet initiates rapid fragmentation; in medium to larger calibers, special jacket contours extend range and reduce cross-wind drift; harder lead core ensures proper bullet expansion
Available in: .22-250 Rem., .223 Rem., .223 WSSM, .243 Win., .243 WSSM, .25-06 Rem., .25 WSSM, .270 Win., .270 WSM, .280 Rem., .300 Win. Mag., .30–06 Spfd., .300 WSM, .30–30 Win., .308 Win., 7mm Rem. Mag., 7mm-08 Rem., 7mm WSM, .45-70 Gov't.
Box of 20: . . . .$26.99–$43.99

DEER SEASON XP

Features: Large diameter polymer tip accelerates bullet expansion; built specifically for deer hunting and taking down big bucks; alloyed leather core; contoured jacket
Available in: .223 Rem., .243 Win., 25-06 Win., .270 Win., .270 WSM, .30-06 Spfd., .30-30 Win., .350 Legend, 7.62X39
Box: . . . .$19.99–$27.99

PDX1 DEFENDER

Features: Given the recent popularity of modern sporting rifles (MSR) among shooters and hunters, Winchester has designed a product using Split Core Technology (SCT) for personal defense; SCT technology, using a quick expansion front lead core and a deep driving bonded rear lead core, creates the ultimate .223 Rem. Home Defense load
Available in: .223 Rem., .308 Win., 7.62x39
Box 20: . . . .$31.99–$42.99

EXPEDITION BIG GAME

Features: Polymer tip; bonded alloyed lead core; jacket technology; Lubalox (black oxide) coating; controlled expansion
Available in: .270 Win., .270 WSM, .30-06 Spfd., .300 Win. Mag., .300 WSM, .325 WSM, .338 Win. Mag., .338 Lapua Mag., 7mm Rem. Mag.
Box 20: . . . .$39.99–$89.99

AMMUNITION

WINCHESTER AMMUNITION MATCH

WINCHESTER M-22 SUBSONIC

WINCHESTER AMMUNITION SUPER CLEAN

M-22 SUBSONIC

Features: Specifically designed to reliably function semiautomatic rifles and pistols at subsonic velocities. Subsonic velocities offer low noise in both suppressed and non-supressed firearms. Bullet is a black copper-plated roundnose.
Available in: .22 LR (45 gr.)
Bpx of 100: **$8.99**
Box of 800: **$51.99**

MATCH

Features: Combining proven Winchester technology with proven bullets, the hollow point boat tail design provides the precision match shooters demand; sleek bullet profile, large boattail and small hollow point maximizes long-range accuracy
Available in: .223 Rem., 5.56 NATO, 6.5 Creedmoor, .308 Win., .338 Lapua
Box 20: . . . .**$26.99–$91.99**

SUPER-X HOLLOW POINT

Available in: .204 Ruger, .218 Bee, .22 Hornet, .30-30 Win., .45-70 Gov't.
MSRP . . . .**$22.69–$38.99**

SUPER-X HOLLOW SOFT POINT

Available in: .30 Carbine, .44 Rem. Mag.
Box of 50 .30 Carbine: **$57.99**
Box of 20 .44 Rem. Mag.: **$25.99**

SUPER-X JACKETED SOFT POINT

Available in: .22 Hornet, .22-250 Rem.
Box of 50 .22 Hornet: **$52.49**
Box of 20 .22-250 Rem.: **$30.99**

SUPER-X LEAD

Available in: .32-20 Win.
Box of 50: **$48.99**

SUPER-X POSITIVE EXPANDING POINT

Available in: .25-06 Rem., .25 WSSM
Box of 20 .25-06 Rem: **$36.99**
Box of 20 .25 WSSM: **$37.99**

SUPER-X POWER CORE

Features: Start with a 95/5 copper alloy, integrate a highly engineered contoured cavity—and you have a new benchmark in lead-free big-game cartridges; features a devastating effective bullet with massive initial impact shock plus deep penetration and virtually 100 percent retained weight to assure maximum trauma to bone and vitals
Available in: .223 Rem., .243 Win., .270 Win., .270 WSM, .30-06 Spfd., .300 Win. Mag., .300 WSM, .30-30 Win., .308 Win., 7mm-08 Rem., 7mm Rem. Mag., 7mm WSM
Box 20: . . . .**$26.99–$46.99**

SUPER-X POWER-POINT

Available in: .22-250 Rem., .223 Rem., .223 WSSM, .243 Win., .243 WSSM, .25-35 Win., .257 Roberts +P, .264 Win. Mag., .270 Win., .270 WSM, .284 Win., .300 Savage, .30-06 Spfd., .300 WSM, .30–30 Win., .303 British, .30-40 Krag, .307 Win., .308 Win., .300 Win. Mag., .325 WSM, .32 Win. Spl., .338 Win. Mag., .348 Win. Mag., .356 Win., 35 Rem., .375 Win., .38-40 Win., .38-55 Win., .44-40 Win., 6.5x55 Swede, 6mm Rem., 7.62x39mm, 7x57 Mauser, 7mm Rem. Mag., 7mm-08 Rem., 8x57 Mauser, .350 Legend
Box 20: . . . .**$16.99–$73.99**

VARMINT X

Features: Polymer tip, alloy jacket, lead core, and rapid fragmentation
Available in: .17 Hornet, .22 Hornet, .204 Ruger; .22-250 Rem.; .223 Rem.; .243 Win.
Box 20: . . . .**$19.99–$28.99**

Handgun Ammunition

DEFENDER HANDGUN

Features: The Winchester Supreme Elite Bonded PDX1, which was chosen by the FBI as their primary service round, is engineered to maximize terminal ballistics, as defined by the demanding FBI test protocol, which simulates real-world threats
Available in: .357 Mag., .357 SIG, .380 ACP, .38 Spl., +P, .40 S&W, .45 Colt, .45 ACP, 9mm Luger +P, 9mm, 10mm Auto
Box of 20: . . . .**$18.99–$32.99**

DUAL BOND

Features: Dual Bond offers a large hollow point cavity, which provides consistent upsets at a variety of ranges and impact velocities; the heavy outer jacket is mechanically bonded to the inner bullet; inner bullet utilizes a proprietary bonding process for a combination of knockdown power, solid penetration, and significant tissue damage
Available in: .44 Rem. Mag., .454 Cassull, .460 S&W Mag., .500 S&W Mag.
Box 20: . . . .**$39.99–$64.98**

PLATINUM TIP HOLLOW POINT

Features: Patented notched reserve taper bullet jacket, plated heavy wall jacket, and two-part hollow point cavity for uniform bullet expansion, massive energy depot
Available in: .41 Rem. Mag., .44 Rem. Mag., .454 Casull, .500 S&W
Box 20: . . . .**$33.49–$67.99**

SUPER-X BLANK-BLACK POWDER

Available in: .32 S&W
Box 50: **$37.99**

SUPER-X BLANK-SMOKELESS

Available in: .38 Spl.
Box 50: **$40.99**

SUPER-X EXPANDING POINT

Available in: .25 ACP
Box 50: **$41.77**

SUPER-X JACKETED HOLLOW POINT

Available in: .357 Mag., .38 Spl. +P, .454 Casull, .45 Win. Mag., .460 S&W Mag., .500 S&W Mag.
Box 20: . . . .**$32.99–$59.99**
Box of 50 .38/.357: . . .**$26.99–$49.99**

Winchester Ammunition

SUPER-X JACKETED SOFT POINT
Available in: .357 Mag., .38 Spl.
Box 50: . . . . **$26.99–$49.99**

SUPER-X LEAD ROUND NOSE
Available in: .32 Short Colt, .32 S&W Long, .32 S&W, .38 Spl., .38 S&W, .44 S&W Spl., .45 Colt
Box of 50: . . . . **$21.99–$50.99**

SUPER-X LEAD SEMI-WAD CUTTER
Available in: .38 Spl.
Box 50: **$39.99**

SUPER-X LEAD SEMI-WAD CUTTER HP
Available in: .38 Spl. +P
Box 50: **$51.82**

SUPER-X LEAD SEMI-WADCUTTER SUPER MATCH
Available in: .38 Spl.
Box 50: **$36.99**

SUPER-X SILVERTIP HOLLOW POINT
Available in: 10mm Auto, .32 ACP, .357 Mag., .380 ACP, .38 Super Auto +P, .38 Spl. +P, .38 Spl., .40 S&W, .41 Rem. Mag., .44 Rem. Mag., .44 S&W Spl., .45 ACP, .45 Colt, .45 GAP, 9x23 Win., 9mm Luger
Box 20, 50: . . . . **$23.99–$65.84**

USA FULL METAL JACKET (USA WHITE BOX)
Available in: .25 ACP, .32 ACP, .357 SIG, .38 Spec., .38 Super +P, .380 ACP, .40 S&W, .45 ACP, .45 G.A.P., 7.62X39 Tokarev, 9mm, 9mm Makarov, 9mm NATO, 10MM
From: . . . . **$12.99–$31.99**

VARMINT X LEAD FREE
Features: Features zinc core technology used in Winchester's Super Clean pistol ammo
Available in: .22-250 Rem., .223 Rem., .243 Rem.
Box 20: . . . . **$24.99–$32.99**

W TRAIN & DEFEND
Features: A straightforward solution for new shooters interested in training to become more proficient with their personal defense ammunition; ballistically-matched ammunition pairs range-ready TRAIN (T) rounds with threat-stopping, technologically-driven DEFEND (D) rounds, each designed for less felt recoil
Available in: .38 Spl., .380 ACP, .40 S&W, 9mm, .45 ACP
Box of 50: . . . .**$15.99–$25.99**

WIN1911
Features: Provides a choice of personal defense or training ammunition that has been matched for ballistic performance and engineered for the same feel and function; high-accuracy, ballistically matched full metal jacket and jacketed hollow point offerings make this an ideal ammunition choice
Available in: .45 ACP
Box 50: **$42.99**

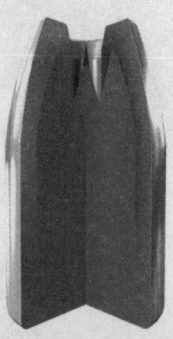

WINCHESTER AMMUNITION SUPER-X PLATINUM TIP HOLLOW POINT

WINCHESTER AMMUNITION DUAL BOND

WINCHESTER AMMUNITION SUPER-X SILVERTIP HOLLOW POINT

WINCHESTER AMMUNITION W TRAIN & DEFEND

WINCHESTER AMMUNITION WIN3GUN PISTOL

WINCHESTER M-22 SUBSONIC

Winchester Ammunition

Rimfire Ammunition

SUPER-X #12 SHOT
Available in: .22 LR
Box 50:. $10.99

SUPER-X FULL METAL JACKET
Available in: .22 Win. Mag.
Box 50:. $11.99

SUPER-X JACKETED HOLLOW POINT
Available in: .17 HMR, .22 Win. Mag.
Box 50, 250: . . . .$9.99–$11.99

SUPER-X LEAD ROUND NOSE
Available in: .22 LR, .22 Long, .22 Short
Box 100:. $7.99

SUPER-X LEAD ROUND NOSE, STANDARD VELOCITY
Available in: .22 LR
Box of 50:. $3.20

SUPER-X POWER-POINT PLATED LEAD HOLLOW POINT
Available in: .22 LR
Box 50:. $8.99

VARMINT HIGH ENERGY
Available in: .22 LR, .22 Win. Mag., .17 WSM
Box of 50:. . . . .$6.99–$16.99

VARMINT HIGH VELOCITY
Available in: .22 Win. Mag., .17 HMR, .17 WSM
Box of 50:. . . . .$13.99–$16.99

VARMINT LEAD FREE
Available in: .22 LR
Box of 50:. $7.88

Shotgun Ammunition

AA STEEL
Features: Steel shot; high-strength hull; AA wads
Available in: 12 (2¾ in.); Shot sizes: 7.5, 8
Box of 25:. $7.99

AA TARGET LOADS
Features: The hunter's choice for a wide variety of game bird applications, available in an exceptionally broad selection of loadings, from 12-gauge to .410 bore, with shot size options ranging from BBs all the way down to 9s—suitable for everything from quail to farm predators
Available in: 12, 20, 28 Ga. (2¾ in.), .410 (2½ in.); Shot sizes: 7.5, 8, 8.5, 9
Box 25:. . . . .$9.99–$11.99

AA TRAACKER
Features: Stay centered in the pattern all the way to the target; Shot-trap core design captures a portion of the shot to stabilize the wad; unique dove-tail petals allows the wad to spin-stabilize and track in the center of the pattern; available in bright orange for low light conditions and in black for bright light conditions
Available in: 12 Ga. (2 ¾ in.), 20 Ga. (2 ¾ in.)
Box 25:. $11.49

WINCHESTER AMMUNITION AA TRAACKER

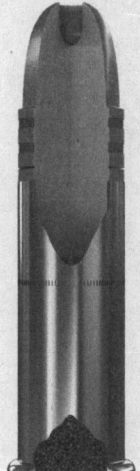

WINCHESTER AMMUNITION VARMINT LEAD FREE

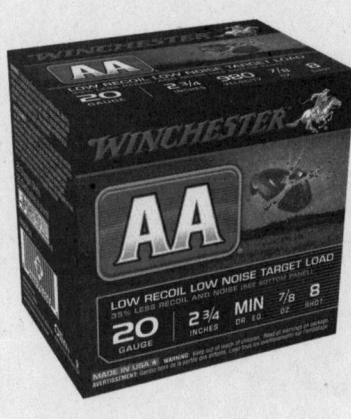

WINCHESTER AMMUNITION AA FEATHERLITE

WINCHESTER AMMUNITION AA STEEL

Winchester Ammunition

BLIND SIDE MAGNUM PHEASANT

Features: High Packing density for increased powder charge with hinged wad results in 1675 fps; high velocity HEX Shot allows reduced leads and increased pellet energy; diamond cut wad design provides choke responsiveness for increased kill zone; Drylok Super Steel System keeps your powder dry
Available in: 12 (2 ¾ in., 3 in.)
Box: $21.39

BLIND SIDE MAGNUM WATERFOWL

Features: High Packing density for increased powder charge with hinged wad results in 1675 fps; high velocity HEX Shot allows reduced leads and increased pellet energy; diamond cut wad design provides choke responsiveness for increased kill zone; Drylok Super Steel System keeps your powder dry
Available in: 12 (2 ¾ in., 3 in., 3 ½ in.), 20 (3 in.)
Box: ....$19.99–$29.99

LONG BEARD XR

Features: Features Shot-Lok technology; offers the tightest patterns and longest shot capability of any traditional turkey load with twice the pellets in a 10-in. circle out to 60 yds
Available in: 12 Ga. (3 in., 3 ½ in.), 20 Ga. (3 in.)
Box 10: ....$19.99–$24.99

ROOSTER LOK'D & LETHAL XR

Features: Protects shot during in-bore acceleration; shot launches from barrel near perfectly round for extremely tight long-range patterns; greater penetration over standard lead loads beyond 50 yards; devastating terminal on-target performances
Available in: 12 (2 ¾ in., 3 in.)
Box: ....$22.99–$29.99

SUPER TARGET

Available in: 12, 20 Ga. (2¾ in.); Shot sizes: 7, 7.5, 8, 9
Box 25: $7.49

SUPER PHEASANT

Available in: 12 Ga. (2¾ in., 3 in.), 20 Ga. (3 in.); Shot sizes: 4, 5, 6
Box 25: ....**N/A**

SUPER PHEASANT STEEL

Available in: 12 Ga. (3 in.); Shot size: 4
Box 25: ....$21.99–$23.99

SUPER-X TRIALS AND BLANKS

Available in: 10 Ga. (2⁷/₈ in.), 12 Ga. (2¾ in.)
Box 25: ....$25.33–$54.95

SUPER-X TURKEY LOADS

Available in: 12 Ga. (2¾ in., 3 in.); Shot sizes: 4, 5, 6
Box 10: ....$9.99–$10.99

WINCHESTER AMMUNITION BLIND SIDE

WINCHESTER AMMUNITION LONG BEARD XR

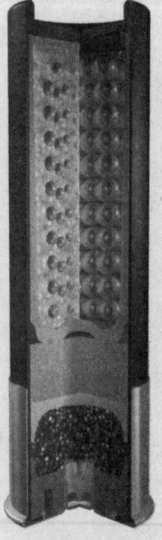

WINCHESTER AMMUNITION ROOSTER LOK'D & LETHAL XR

WINCHESTER AMMUNITION ROOSTER XR

Winchester Ammunition

SUPER-X XPERT HI-VELOCITY STEEL

Available in: 12 Ga. (2¾ in., 3 in.), 20 Ga. (3 in.); Shot sizes: BB, 1, 2, 3, 4
Box 25:. . . . .**$12.99–$14.99**

SUPER-X XPERT STEEL

Available in: 12, 20, 28 Ga., .410 bore (2¾ in.); Shot sizes: 6, 7
Box 25:. . . . . **N/A**

VARMINT-X

Features: Shot-Lok technology; 50 percent more pellets in a 10 in. circle at 40 yds; greater penetration over standard lead loads beyond 40 yds; devastating terminal on-target performance
Available in: 12 Ga. (3 in.); Shot size: BB
Box 10:. **$17.99**

Shotgun Ammunition– Slugs & Buckshot

PDX1 12 SLUG AND BUCK

Features: The 12-gauge PDX1 Defender ammunition features a distinctive black hull, black oxide high-base head and three pellets of Grex buffered 00 plated buckshot nested on top of a 1 oz. rifled slug; an ideal, tight patterning personal defense load; slug/buckshot combination provides optimum performance at short and long ranges while compensating for aim error
Available in: 12 Ga. (2¾ in.)
Box 10:. **$14.99**

PDX1 DEFENDER SEGMENTING SLUG

Features: The uniquely designed slug segments into three pieces when fired into FBI protocol barriers such as bare, light cloth, and heavy cloth covered ballistic gelatin; the round is designed to compensate for aim error over traditional slugs.
Available in: 12 Ga. (2¾ in.), 20 Ga. (2¾ in.)
Box 10: . . . . **N/A**

SUPER-X BUCKSHOT

Available in: 12 Ga. (2¾ in., 3 in., 3½ in.), 20 Ga. (2¾ in.), .410 (2½ in., 3 in.); Shot sizes: 4, 3, 1, 00, 000
Box 5:. . . . .**$4.99–$11.99**

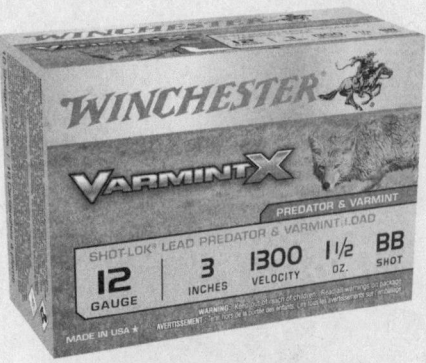

WINCHESTER AMMUNITION VARMINT-X

WINCHESTER AMMUNITION PDX1 DEFENDER SEGMENTING SLUG

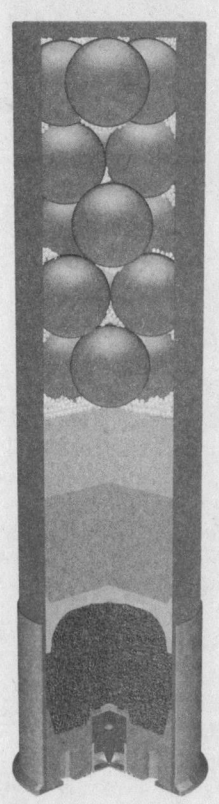

WINCHESTER AMMUNITION SUPER-X BUCKSHOT

AMMUNITION

MUZZLELOADING BULLETS

Barnes Bullets

H15045BR

**HARVESTER MUZZLELOADING
CRUSHED RIB SABOT**

EXPANDER MZ
Features: 100 percent copper with a large, hollow cavity; six copper petals with double-diameter expansion; full weight retention
Available in: .45 (195 gr.), .50 (250, 300 gr.), .54 (275, 325 gr.)
Box of 15:. . . . .$16.9–$24.99
Box of 24:. . . . .$24.79–$28.99

SPIT-FIRE MZ
Features: A streamlined semi-spitzer give, boattail base and tack-driving accuracy; six razor-sharp copper petals create massive shock, deep penetration, and double-diameter expansion; retains virtually 100 percent of its original weight; available in 15 and 24-bullet packs
Available in: .50 (245, 285 gr.)
Box of 15:. $19.49
Box of 24:. $24.99

SPIT-FIRE TMZ
Features: 100 percent copper boattail design with streamlined polymer tip for faster expansion; expands at 1050 fps.; remains intact at extreme velocities; redesigned sabot loads faster while retaining tight gas seal
Available in: .50 (250, 290 gr.)
Box of 15:. . . . .$19.49–$22.99
Box of 24:. . . . .$26.99–$29.99

Harvester Muzzleloading (J-Ron, Inc.)

CRUSHED RIB SABOT
Features: 50 percent less loading friction; consistent ignition and superb accuracy
Available in: .45 (.400); .50 (.400, .429–.430, .451–.452)
Box 50: . . .$9.49–$10.49

SABER TOOTH BELTED
Features: Copper-clad belted bullets in Harvester Crush Rib Sabot
Available in: .50 (250, 270, 300, 350 gr.)
MSRP. $15.99

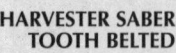

**HARVESTER SABER
TOOTH BELTED**

**BARNES BULLETS
SPIT-FIRE TMZ**

Harvester Muzzleloading (J-Ron, Inc.)

HARVESTER SCORPION FUNNEL POINT MAG

HARVESTER SCORPION PT GOLD

SCORPION FUNNEL POINT MAG

Features: Electroplated copper plating does not separate from lead core; loaded in Harvester Crush Rib Sabots
Available in: .50 (240, 260, 300 gr.); .54 (240, 260, 300 gr.)
MSRP . . . . $9.99–$13.99

SCORPION PT GOLD

Features: Scorpion PT Gold Ballistic Tip Bullets are electroplated with copper plating that does not separate from lead core; offers greater accuracy at longer ranges than a hollow point; 3 percent antimony makes the bullet harder than pure lead
Available in: .45 (240, 260, 300 gr.); .50 ((240, 260, 300 gr.)
MSRP . . . . $14.99–$25.99

Hodgdon Powder Co.

TRIPLE SEVEN FIRESTAR PELLETS

Features: Star-shaped pellet designed for .50-caliber muzzleloaders utilizing 209 primers for ignition; long grooves provide more surface for ignition

compared to traditional pellets
Available in: .50-caliber
Box of: 60
MSRP: $25.99

Hornady Manufacturing

HORNADY GREAT PLAINS - PA CONICAL

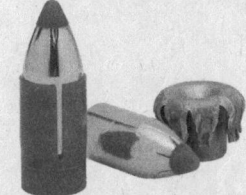

HORNADY MONOFLEX ML

GREAT PLAINS - PA CONICAL

Features: Delivers greater accuracy and more knock-down power; PA bullets are prelubed with special knurled grooves on the bearing sur-

face to hold the lubricant on the bullet—no need for a patch or sabot
Available: in .50-caliber 240-grain
Box of 50: $13.99

MONOFLEX ML

Features: Constructed with the Hornady Flex Tip and retaining 95 percent of its original weight, it's available in both a High Speed/Low Drag sabot and Lock-N-Load Speed Sabot
Available in: .50 cal. sabot with .45 cal. (250 gr.) bullet
Box of 20: $22.99

Knight Rifles

BLOODLINE BULLETS

Features: Individually machined, double knurled bullets for increased visual blood trails
Available in: .45 (185, 200 gr.); .50 (220, 250, 275, 300, 350 gr.); .52 (220, 275, 300, 350 gr.); .54 (325 gr.)
Box 20: . . . . $29.99–$37.99

RED HOT BULLETS

Features: Saboted Barnes solid copper bullet with superior expansion
Available in: .45 (175, 195 gr.); .50 (250, 300, 350 gr.); .52 (275, 350, 375 gr.)
MSRP . . . . $26.99–$37.99

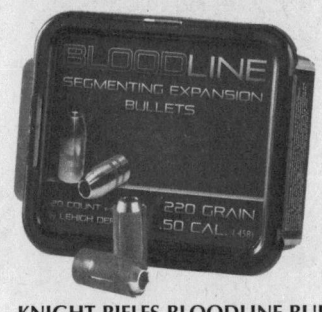

KNIGHT RIFLES BLOODLINE BULLETS

PowerBelt Bullets

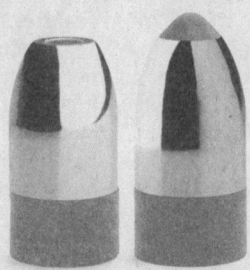
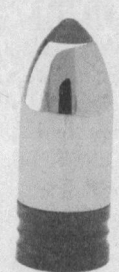
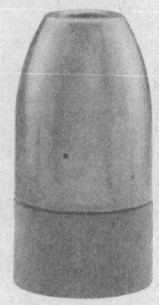

POWERBELT AEROLITE

POWERBELT COPPER

POWERBELT PLATINUM AEROTIP

POWERBELT PURE LEAD HOLLOW POINT

AEROLITE

Features: Designed specifically for use with standard 100-grain loads; AeroLite's shape is noticeably longer and more aerodynamic than other PowerBelts of similar weight; longer length is made possible by the massive hollow point cavity that is filled by an oversized polycarbonate point
Available in: .45 (250 gr.), .50 (250, 300 gr.)
MSRP $22.50

COPPER

Features: Thin copper plating reduces bore friction while allowing for optimal bullet expansion; available in four tip designs: Hollow Point,

AeroTip, Flat Point, and Steel Tip
Available in: .45 (195, 225, 275 gr.); .50 (223, 245, 295, 348, 405, 444 gr.); .54 (295, 348 gr.)
Box of 15: . . . .$18.00–$28.95
Box of 50: . . . .$53.10–$57.60

PLATINUM

Features: Proprietary hard plating and aggressive bullet taper design for improved ballistic coefficient; large-size fluted gas check produces higher and more consistent pressures
Available in: .45 (223, 300 gr.); .50 (270, 300, 338 gr.)
MSRP $22.50

PURE LEAD

Features: Pure lead, available in four different grain weights in Hollow Point and 444 in Flat Point
Available in: .50 (295, 348 gr.); **.54 (345, 405 gr.)**
Box of 15 .50-caliber: $22.05
Box of 15 .54-caliber: . . $23.95–$24.95

Swift Bullet Company

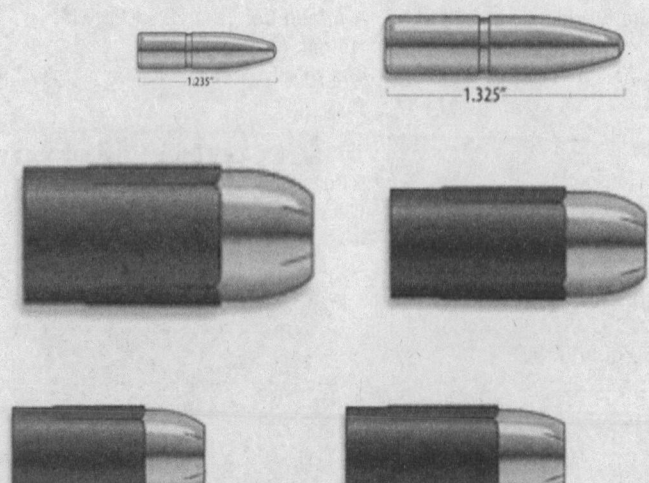

A-FRAME MUZZLELOADING BULLETS

Features: Muzzleloader and heavy revolver A-Frame bullets are one in the same; initiate expansion at 950 feet per second, expand to .65x their original caliber, and maintain 97% of their weight; virtually indestructible at velocities in excess of 3000 feet per second
Available in: .50 (240, 300 gr.); .54 (265, 325 gr.)
Box of 10: . . . . $14.39–$16.99

SWIFT A-FRAME MUZZLELOADING BULLETS

AMMUNITION

Thompson/Center Arms

MAXI-BALL

Features: An exceptionally accurate bullet and the preferred bullet for penetration needed for large game like elk; lubricating grooves (maxi wide grooves)
Available in: .50 (275, 350 gr.)
Box 20: . . . .$20.99–$26.99

SHOCK WAVE SABOTS

Features: Polymer tip spire point bullet with sabot; incorporates harder lead core with walls interlocked with the jacket for maximum weight retention and expansion; available with spire point or bonded bullets
Available in: Bonded Core in Super Glide Sabots .50 (250 gr.); Controlled Expansion in Super Glide Sabot .50 (250, 300 gr.); Bonded Core in Mag Express Sabots .50 (250, 300 gr.); Controlled Expansion in Mag Express Sabots .50 (200, 250, 300 gr.) and .45

(200 gr.)
Bonded Core Super Glide: . . .$20.99
Controlled Expansion Super Glide: $15.99
Bonded Core Mag Express: . . .$20.99
Controlled Expansion Mag Express: . . . .$14.99–$15.99

SUPER 45 XR SABOTS

Features: Centerfire weight performance without the recoil, Super 45 XR sabots have a flatter trajectory, provide deep penetration, and nearly 2 times the expansion of its original diameter.
Available in: .45 (155 gr.)
Box 30: $18.99

THOMPSON/CENTER SHOCK WAVE SABOTS

THOMPSON/CENTER SUPER 45 XR SABOTS

     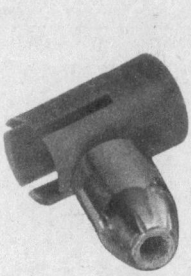 

THOMPSON/CENTER MAXI-BALL

Umarex

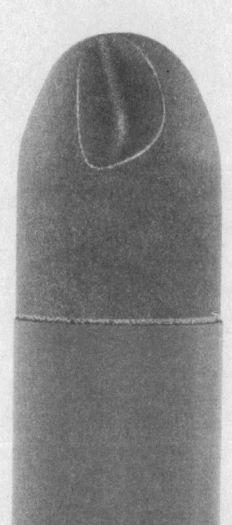

UMAREX RX

ARX

Features: Designed in conjunction with PolyCase Ammunition Development Lab; SpeedBand sabot available calibers include .357, .40, and .45, while a .45-caliber option has Umarex's base-style SpeedBelt; acceptable for use in large-bore airguns, including Umarex's Hammer .50-caliber
Available in: .50
Box of 15: $24.99

Barnes Bullets

Barnes continues to develop leading-edge products with a wide range of workability and functionality using an incredibly broad range of purpose-built components and ammunition. Barnes's most popular hunting bullets, the all-copper TSX line, also comes with a streamlined polymer tip. The Barnes Buster line can be used for both rifles and handguns.

Rifle Bullets

Banded Solids

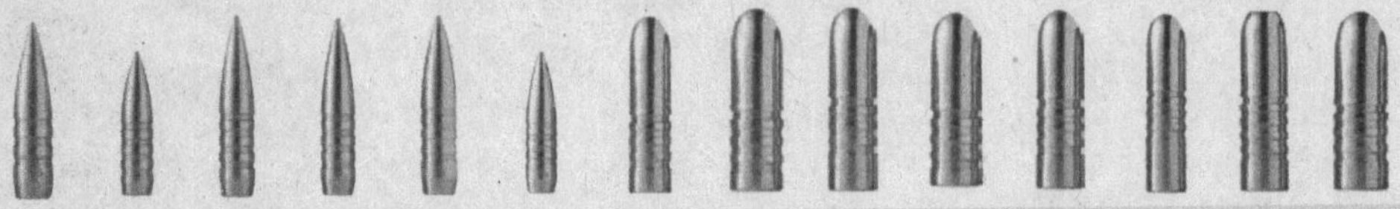

Caliber & Description	6MM S BT	25 S BT	6.5MM S BT	270 S BT	7MM S BT	30 S BT	338 RN	9.3MM RN	9.3MM RN	375 RN	375 RN	375 RN	450/400 FN	416 RN
Diameter, Inches	.243	.257	.264	.277	.284	.308	.338	.366	.366	.375	.375	.375	.410	.416
Weight, Grains	75	90	110	120	140	165	250	250	286	270	300	350	400	350
Density	.181	.195	.225	.223	.248	.248	.313	.267	.305	.274	.305	.356	.340	.289
Ballistic Coefficient	.341	.325	.452	.438	.464	.438	.247	.214	.247	.207	.230	.283	.292	.217
Catalog Number	24375	25793	26422	27763	28464	30816	33825	30466	30467	37512	37525	37527	40935	30520

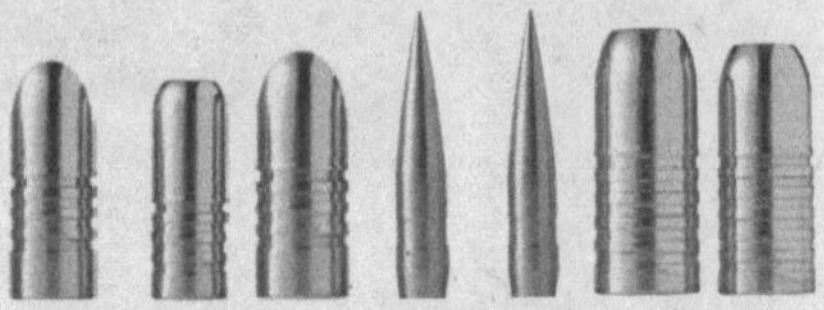

Caliber & Description	505 GIBBS RN	500 NITRO FN	500 JEFF RN	50 BMG BORE RIDER	50 BMG BORE RIDER	577 NITRO FN	600 NITRO FN
Diameter, Inches	.504	.509	.510	.510	.510	.583	.618
Weight, Grains	525	570	535	750	800	750	900
Density	.295	.314	.294	.412	.439	.315	.337
Ballistic Coefficient	.267	.243	-	1.070	1.095	.257	.380
Catalog Number	30685	30690	30694	30703	30707	30713	30714

LEGEND

Type of Bullet

- **BT** – Boattail
- **FB** – Flat Base
- **FN** – Flat Nose
- **RN** – Round Nose
- **S** – Spitzer
- **SP** – Soft Point
- **SS** – Semi-Spitzer

From: $30.00–$59.00

Barnes Buster

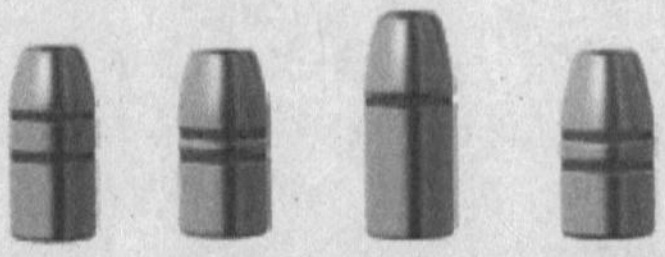

Caliber & Description	44 MAG. FN FB	454 CASULL FN FB	45/70 FN FB	500 S&W FN FB
Diameter, Inches	.429	.451	.458	.500
Weight, Grains	300	325	400	400
Density	.233	.228	.272	.229
Ballistic Coefficient	.241	.206	.242	.220
Catalog Number	30545	30572	30644	30672

Box 50: $50.00–$60.00

Barnes Bullets

BARNES ORIGINAL

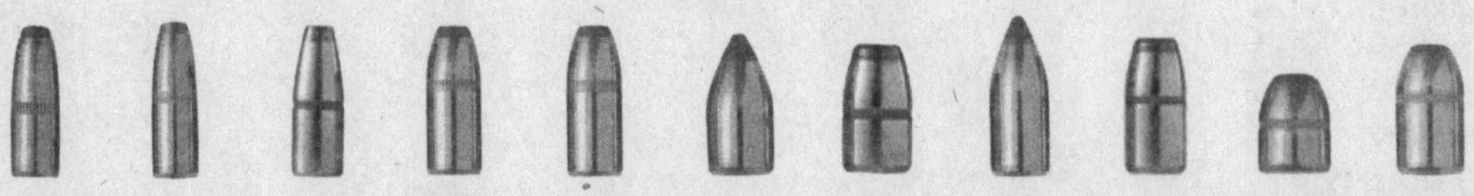

Caliber & Description	348 WIN FN SP	348 WIN FN SP	375 WIN FN SP	38/55 FN SP	38/55 FN SP	"45/70 SSSP"	45/70 FN SP	45/70 SSSP	45/70 FN SP	50/110 WIN FN SP	50/110 WIN FN SP
Diameter, Inches	.348	.348	.375	.375	.377	.458	.458	.458	.458	.510	.510
Weight, Grains	220	250	255	255	255	300	300	400	400	300	450
Jckt.	.032	.032	.032	.032	.032	.032	.032	.032	.032	.032	.032
Density	.260	.295	.259	.259	.256	.204	.204	.272	.272	.165	.247
Ballistic Coefficient	.301	.327	.290	.290	.290	.291	.227	.389	.302	.183	.274
Catalog Number	30437	30438	30496	30498	30611	30612	30612	30613	30614	30682	30683

From: $20.00–$56.00

LRX BULLETS

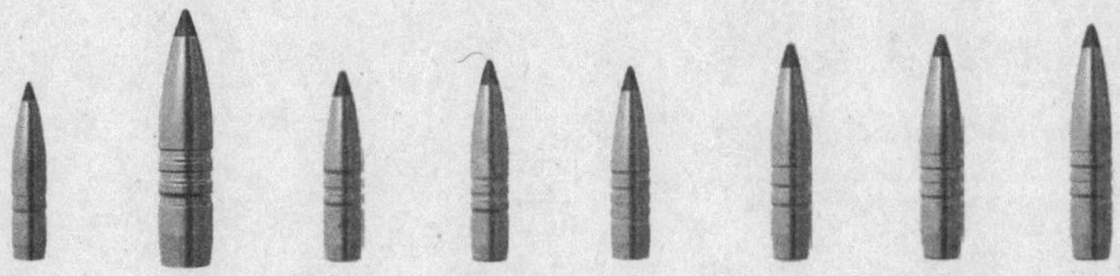

Caliber & Description	6.5MM BT	270 BT	7MM BT	7MM BT	30 BT	30 BT	338 LAPUA BT	338 LAPUA BT
Diameter, Inches	.264	.277	.284	.284	.308	.308	.338	.338
Weight, Grains	127	129	145	168	175	200	265	280
Density	.257	.240	.257	.257	.264	.301	.331	.350
Ballistic Coefficient	.468	.463	.486	.550	.508	.546	.575	.667
Catalog Number	30228	30262	30282	30284	30318	30374	30434	30432

Box 50: $37.00–$49.00

MATCH BURNER BULLETS

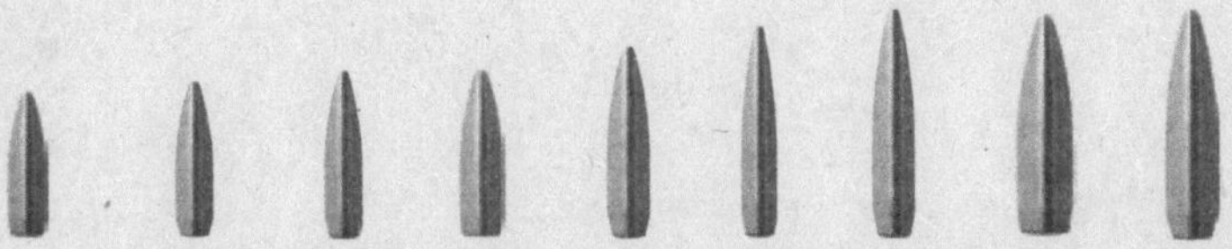

Caliber & Description	22 FB	22 BT	22 BT	6MM FB	6MM BT	6.5MM BT	7MM BT	"30 PALMA FB"	30 BT
Diameter, Inches	.224	.224	.224	.243	.243	.264	.284	.308	.308
Weight, Grains	52	69	85	68	105	140	171	155	175
Density	.148	.196	.242	.165	.254	.287	.303	.233	.264
Ballistic Coefficient	.224	.339	.410	.267	.511	.586	.645	.467	.521
Catalog Number	30160	30162	30164	30205	30206	30230	30285	30381	30385

Box 100: $20.00–$33.00

LEGEND
Type of Bullet
BT – Boattail
FB – Flat Base
FN – Flat Nose
RN – Round Nose
S – Spitzer
SP – Soft Point
SS – Semi-Spitzer

AMMUNITION

Barnes Bullets

M/LE Reduced Ricochet, Limited Penetration (RRLP) Bullets

Caliber & Description	223/5.56 FB	6.8MM FB	30 FB	7.62X39 FB
Diameter, Inches	.224	.277	.308	.310
Weight, Grains	55	85	150	108
Density	.157	.158	.226	.161
Ballistic Coefficient	.225	.229	.357	.243
Catalog Number	80161	30252	30313	30390

From: $19.00–31.00

M/LE TAC-TX Bullets

Caliber & Description	6.5mm BT	6.5mm BT	6.8mm BT	300 BLK	300 BLK	30 FB	30 BT	338 BT	338 BT	458 SOCOM BT
Diameter, Inches	.264	.264	.277	.308	.308	.308	.308	.338	.338	.458
Weight, Grains	100	120	95	110	120	110	168	225	265	300
Density	.205	.246	.177	.166	.181	.166	.253	.281	.331	.204
Ballistic Coefficient	-	.443	.292	.289	.358	.295	.470	.514	.575	.236
Catalog Number	30236	30237	30253	30321	30813	30358	30359	30420	30419	30640

From: $34.00–$52.00

Multi-Purpose Green (MPG) Bullets

Caliber & Description	223 FB	6.8MM FB	30 FB	7.62X39 FB
Diameter, Inches	.224	.277	.308	.310
Weight, Grains	55	85	150	108
Density	.157	.158	.226	.161
Ballistic Coefficient	.225	.229	.357	.243
Catalog Number	30195	30249	30331	30388

From: $19.00–$31.00

LEGEND

Type of Bullet

BT – Boattail
FB – Flat Base
FN – Flat Nose
RN – Round Nose
S – Spitzer
SP – Soft Point
SS – Semi-Spitzer

TSX Bullets

Caliber & Description	22 FB	22 FB	22 FB	22 FB	22 BT	22 BT	6MM BT	25 BT	25 FB	6.5MM BT	6.5MM FB	6.8MM FB	6.8MM BT	270 BT	270 BT
Diameter, Inches	.224	.224	.224	.224	.224	.224	.243	.257	.257	.264	.264	.277	.277	.277	.277
Weight, Grains	45	50	53	55	62	70	85	100	115	120	130	85	110	130	140
Density	.128	.142	.151	.157	.177	.199	.206	.216	.249	.246	.266	.158	.205	.242	.261
Ballistic Coefficient	.188	.197	.204	.209	.287	.314	.333	.336	.335	.381	.365	.246	.323	374	.404
Catalog Number	30176	30174	30180	30182	30190	30193	30212	30222	30224	30244	30246	30254	30260	30264	30266

AMMUNITION

Barnes Bullets

Caliber & Description	270 FB	7MM BT	7MM BT	7MM BT	7MM FB	7MM FB	30 FN FB	30 FB	30 BT	30 BT	30 BT	30 BT	30 BT	30 FB	7.62X39 BT
Diameter, Inches	.277	.284	.284	.284	.284	.284	.308	.308	.308	.308	.308	.308	.308	.308	.310
Weight, Grains	150	120	140	150	160	175	150	110	130	150	165	168	180	200	123
Density	.279	.213	.248	.266	.283	.310	.226	.166	.196	.226	.248	.253	.271	.301	.183
Ballistic Coefficient	.386	.349	.394	.408	.392	.417	.184	.264	.340	.369	.398	.404	.453	.423	.275
Catalog Number	30269	30287	30289	30293	30291	30294	30334	30341	30345	30347	30349	30351	30353	30356	30391

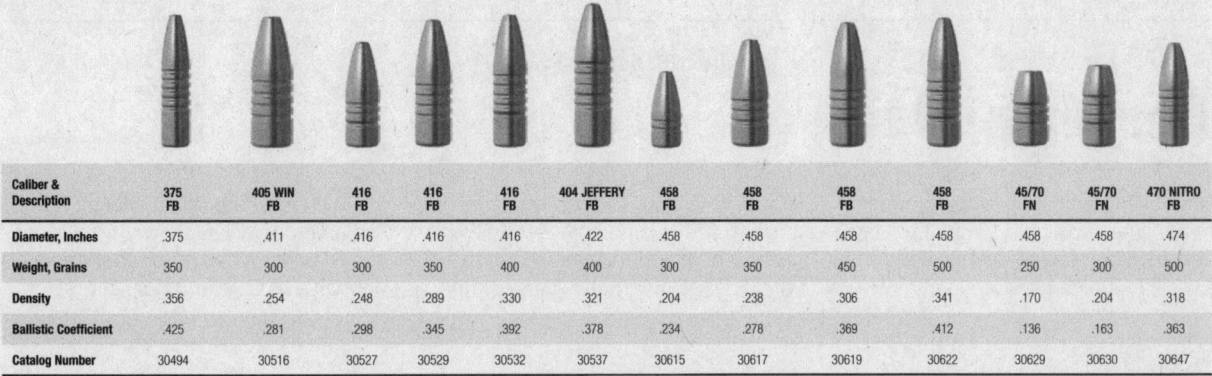

Caliber & Description	303/7.65MM FB	8MM BT	8MM BT	338 BT	338 BT	338 FB	338 FB	338 LAPUA BT	35 FB	35 FB	9.3MM FB	9.3MM FB	375 FB	375 FB	375 FB
Diameter, Inches	.311	.323	.323	.338	.338	.338	.338	.338	.358	.358	.366	.366	.375	.375	.375
Weight, Grains	150	180	200	185	210	225	250	285	200	225	250	286	235	270	300
Density	.222	.246	.274	.231	.263	.281	.313	.356	.223	.251	.267	.305	.239	.274	.305
Ballistic Coefficient	.322	.381	.421	.352	.404	.386	.425	.585	.284	.359	.361	.411	.270	.326	.357
Catalog Number	30393	30396	30398	30408	30410	30412	30415	30417	30455	30457	30469	30473	30486	30489	30491

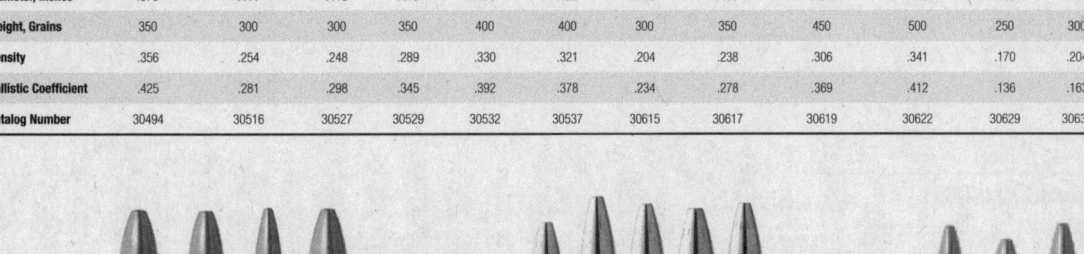

Caliber & Description	375 FB	405 WIN FB	416 FB	416 FB	416 FB	404 JEFFERY FB	458 FB	458 FB	458 FB	458 FB	45/70 FN	45/70 FN	470 NITRO FB
Diameter, Inches	.375	.411	.416	.416	.416	.422	.458	.458	.458	.458	.458	.458	.474
Weight, Grains	350	300	300	350	400	400	300	350	450	500	250	300	500
Density	.356	.254	.248	.289	.330	.321	.204	.238	.306	.341	.170	.204	.318
Ballistic Coefficient	.425	.281	.298	.345	.392	.378	.234	.278	.369	.412	.136	.163	.363
Catalog Number	30494	30516	30527	30529	30532	30537	30615	30617	30619	30622	30629	30630	30647

Caliber & Description	505 GIBBS FB	500 NITRO FB	50 BMG BT	577 NITRO FB
Diameter, Inches	.505	.509	.510	.583
Weight, Grains	525	570	647	750
Density	.294	.314	.355	.315
Ballistic Coefficient	.320	.369	.572	.402
Catalog Number	30688	30692	30700	30712

From: $19.00–$62.00

VARMIN-A-TOR

Caliber & Description	20 FB	22 FB	22 FB	6mm FB	6mm FB
Diameter, Inches	.204	.224	.224	.243	.243
Weight, Grains	32	40	50	58	72
Density	.110	.114	.142	.140	.174
Ballistic Coefficient	.159	.153	.192	.173	.208
Catalog Number	30092	30168	30178	30207	30210

From: $20.00–$23.00

VARMINT GRENADE

Caliber & Description	20 FB	22 HORNET FB	22 FB	223 FB	6MM FB
Diameter, Inches	.204	.224	.224	.224	.243
Weight, Grains	26	30	36	50	62
Density	.089	.085	.102	.142	.150
Ballistic Coefficient	.131	.101	.149	.183	.199
Catalog Number	30090	30170	30171	30198	30214

Box 100: $18.00–$59.00

AMMUNITION

Barnes Bullets

Handgun Bullets

M/LE TAC-XP PISTOL BULLETS

Caliber & Description	380 ACP	9MM	9MM	.357 SIG	38 SPL.	357 MAG.	10MM/40 S&W	10MM/40 S&W	10MM/40 S&W	44 SPL.	45 ACP/45 GAP	45 ACP
Diameter, Inches	.355	.355	.355	.355	.355	.357	.400	.400	.400	.429	.451	.451
Weight, Grains	80	95	115	125	110	125	125.	140	155	200	160	185
Density	.091	.108	.130	.142	.123	.140	.112	.125	.138	.155	.112	.130
Ballistic Coefficient	.107	.120	.167	.159	.156	.160	-	.128	.189	.138	.133	.167
Catalog Number	30440	30444	30442	30446	30449	30451	30500	30502	30504	30539	30550	30552

Box 40: $28.00–$49.00

XPB PISTOL BULLETS

Caliber & Description	357 Mag.	41 Mag.	44 Mag.	44 Mag.	45 Colt	45 Colt	454 Casull	460 S&W	460 S&W	480 Ruger	500 S&W XPB	500 S&W XPB	500 S&W XPB
Diameter, Inches	.357	.410	.429	.429	.451	.451	.451	.451	.451	.475	.500	.500	.500
Weight, Grains	140	180	200	225	200	225	250	200	275	275	275	325	375
Density	.157	.153	.155	.175	.140	.158	.176	.140	.193	.174	.157	.186	.214
Ballistic Coefficient	.150	.126	.138	.166	-	.146	.141	.160	.215	.155	.141	.228	.261
Catalog Number	30453	30512	30541	30543	30556	30558	30562	30554	30548	30659	30663	30665	30667

Box 20: $16.00–$26.00

Berger Bullets

Famous for their superior performance in benchrest matches, Berger bullets also include hunting designs. From .17 to .30, all Bergers feature fourteen jackets with a wall concentricity tolerance of .0003. Lead cores are 99.9 percent pure and swaged in dies to within .0001 of a round. Berger's line includes several profiles: Match, Low Drag, Very Low Drag, Length Tolerant, and Maximum-Expansion, besides standard flat-base and boattail.

HUNTING

Caliber & Description	6mm VLD	6mm VLD	6mm	6mm VLD	6mm VLD	25 VLD"	6.5mm VLD	6.5mm VLD	270 VLD	270 Classic	270 VLD	270 VLD	7mm VLD	270 EOL	7mm VLD	7mm Classic	7mm VLD	7mm EOL	30 VLD	30 VLD	30 Classic	30 VLD	30 VLD	30 Classic	30 VLD	30 VLD	338 Elite	338 Elite
Diameter, Inches	.243	.243	.243	.243	.243	.257	.264	.264	.277	.277	.277	.277	.284	.277	.284	.284	.284	.284	.308	.308	.308	.308	.308	.308	.308	.308	.338	.338
Weight, Grains	87	95	95	105	115	115	130	140	130	130	140	150	140	170	168	168	180	195	155	168	168	175	185	185	190	210	250	300
Density	.210	.230	-	.254	.278	.249	.266	.287	.241	-	.260	.279	.248	-	.298	-	.319	.345	.233	.253	-	.264	.279	-	.286	.316	-	-
Ballistic Coefficient	.412	.480	.427	.532	.545	.466	.552	.612	.452	.497	.487	.531	.510	.662	.617	.604	.659	.754	.439	.473	.496	.498	.549	.547	.570	.631	.682	.818
Catalog Number	24524	24527	24570	24528	24530	25513	26503	26504	27501	27570	27502	27503	28503	27575	28501	28570	28502	28550	30508	30510	30570	30512	30513	30571	30514	30515	33554	33556

Box 100: $40.00–$91.00

Berger Bullets

TARGET

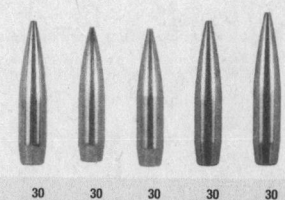

Caliber & Description	22 FBHP	22 FBHP	22 VLD	22 BTHP	22 VLD	22 VLD	22 VLD	22 LRBTHP	22 VLD	6mm FBHP	6mm BR	6mm BTHP	6mm FBHP	6mm FBHP	6mm BTHP	6mm VLD
Diameter, Inches	.224	.224	.224	.224	.224	.224	.224	.224	.224	.243	.243	.243	.243	.243	.243	.243
Weight, Grains	52	55	70	73	75	80	80.5	82	90	62	-	65	65	68	90	95
Density	.148	.157	.199	.208	.214	.228	.229	.233	.256	.150	-	.157	.157	.165	.218	.230
Ballistic Coefficient	.242	.262	.371	.343	.423	.445	.436	.444	.551	.253	.277	.270	.265	.280	.411	.480
Catalog Number	22408	22410	22418	22420	22421	22422	22427	22424	22423	24404	24407	24408	24409	24411	24425	24427

Caliber & Description	6mm BTHP	6mm VLD	6mm Hybrid	6mm BTHP	6mm VLD	6.5mm BTHP	6.5mm VLD	6.5mm VLD	6.5mm LRBTHP	6.5mm Hybrid	7mm VLD	7mm VLD	7mm Hybrid
Diameter, Inches	.243	.243	.243	.243	.243	.264	.264	.264	.264	.264	.284	.284	.284
Weight, Grains	105	105	105	108	115	120	130	140	140	140	168	180	180
Density	.254	.254	.254	.261	.278	.245	.266	.287	.287	.287	.298	.319	.319
Ballistic Coefficient	.493	.495	.547	.551	.545	.453	.552	.612	.592	.618	.617	.659	.674
Catalog Number	24428	24429	24433	24431	24430	26402	26403	26401	26409	26414	28401	28405	28407

Caliber & Description	30 FBHP	30 FBHP	30 VLD	30 Hybrid	30 LRBTHP	30 VLD	30 Hybrid	30 LRBTHP	30 VLD	30 Juggernaut	30 VLD	30 Hybrid
Diameter, Inches	.308	.308	.308	.308	.308	.308	.308	.308	.308	.308	.308	.308
Weight, Grains	115	150	155	155	155.5	168	168	175	175	185	185	185
Density	.183	.226	.233	.233	.234	.253	.253	.264	.264	.279	.279	.279
Ballistic Coefficient	.296	.398	.439	.483	.464	.473	.519	.515	.498	.560	.549	.569
Catalog Number	30421	30407	30408	30426	30416	30410	30425	30420	30412	30418	30413	30424

Caliber & Description	30 Hybrid	30 LRBTHP	30 VLD	30 Hybrid	30 Hybrid
Diameter, Inches	.308	.308	.308	.308	.308
Weight, Grains	200	210	210	215	230
Density	.301	.316	.316	-	-
Ballistic Coefficient	.624	.626	.631	.696	.743
Catalog Number	30427	30419	30415	30429	30430

Box 100: $31.00–$72.00

LEGEND
Type of Bullet
BT – Boattail
FB – Flat Base
HP – Hollow Point
LD – Low Drag
LR – Long Range
VLD – Very Low Drag

AMMUNITION

Berger Bullets

VARMINT

Caliber & Description	17 FBHP	20 FBHP	20 BTHP	20 LRBTHP	22 FBHP	22 FBHP	22 FBHP	22 FBHP	22 FBHP	6mm LDHP	6mm FBHP	6mm LDHP
Diameter, Inches	.172	.204	.204	.204	.224	.224	.224	.224	.224	.243	.243	.243
Weight, Grains	25	35	40	55	40	52	55	60	64	69	80	88
Density	.121	.120	.137	.188	.114	.148	.157	.171	.182	.167	.194	.213
Ballistic Coefficient	.150	.176	.225	.381	.155	.197	.210	.278	.294	.291	.306	.391
Catalog Number	17308	20303	20304	20306	22303	22309	22311	22312	22316	24313	24321	24323

Box 100: $31.00–$64.00

Hornady Bullets

Hornady's product line includes over 300 bullets, ranging from .17 caliber all the way up to the .50 caliber A-MAX bullet for the .50 BMG. Hornady is always working to originate the next technological innovation. From prairie dogs to dangerous game, they have the perfect bullet to meet every hunting and shooting need.

Rifle Bullets

ELD MATCH

Caliber & Description	6.5mm	7mm	30	338
Diameter, Inches	.264	.284	.308	.338
Weight, Grains	140	162	208	285
Density	.287	.287	.313	.356
Ballistic Coefficient	.305	.329	.335	.394
Catalog Number	26331	28403	30731	33381

MSRP $45.00–$53.28

ELD-X

Caliber & Description	30	30	30	30	6.5mm	7mm	7mm
Diameter, Inches	.308	.308	.308	.308	.264	.284	.284
Weight, Grains	178	200	212	220	143	162	175
Density	.268	.301	.319	.331	.293	.287	.310
Ballistic Coefficient	.271	.315	.336	.325	.315	.315	.340
Catalog Number	3074	3076	3077	3078	2635	2840	2841

MSRP N/A

FMJ BULLETS

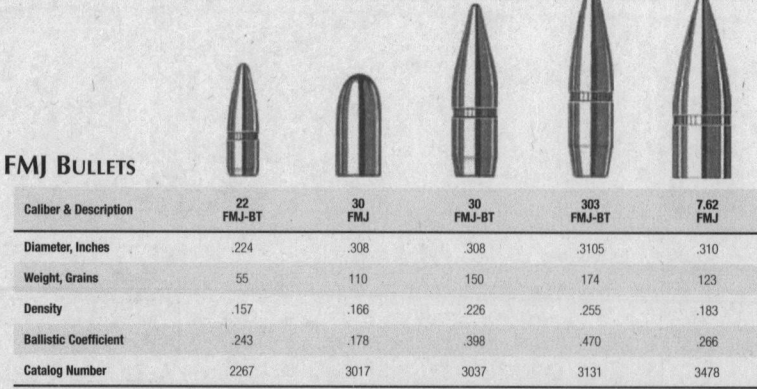

Caliber & Description	22 FMJ-BT	30 FMJ	30 FMJ-BT	303 FMJ-BT	7.62 FMJ
Diameter, Inches	.224	.308	.308	.3105	.310
Weight, Grains	55	110	150	174	123
Density	.157	.166	.226	.255	.183
Ballistic Coefficient	.243	.178	.398	.470	.266
Catalog Number	2267	3017	3037	3131	3478

MSRP $19.00–$42.00

InterBond

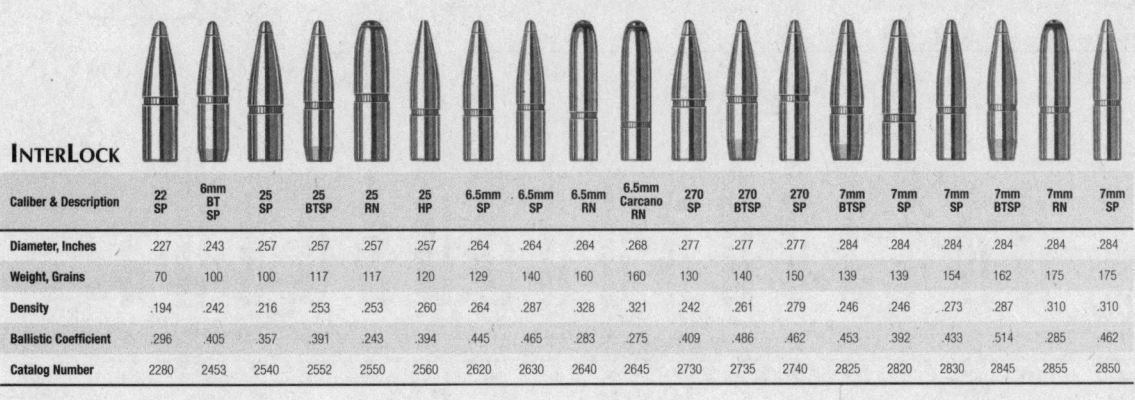

Caliber & Description	6mm BT	25 BT	6.5mm BT	270 BT	270 BT	7mm BT	7mm BT	30 BT	30 BT	30 BT	338 BT	416 RN
Diameter, Inches	.243	.257	.264	.277	.277	.284	.284	.308	.308	.308	.338	.416
Weight, Grains	85	110	129	130	150	139	154	150	165	180	225	400
Density	.206	.238	.264	.242	.279	.246	.525	.226	.248	.271	.281	.330
Ballistic Coefficient	.395	.390	.485	.460	.525	.486	.273	.415	.447	.480	.515	.311
Catalog Number	24539	25419	26209	27309	27409	28209	28309	30309	30459	30709	33209	41659

MSRP $61.00–$89.00

InterLock

Caliber & Description	22 SP	6mm BT SP	25 SP	25 BTSP	25 RN	25 HP	6.5mm SP	6.5mm SP	6.5mm RN	6.5mm Carcano RN	270 SP	270 BTSP	270 SP	7mm BTSP	7mm SP	7mm SP	7mm BTSP	7mm RN	7mm SP
Diameter, Inches	.227	.243	.257	.257	.257	.257	.264	.264	.264	.268	.277	.277	.277	.284	.284	.284	.284	.284	.284
Weight, Grains	70	100	100	117	117	120	129	140	160	160	130	140	150	139	139	154	162	175	175
Density	.194	.242	.216	.253	.253	.260	.264	.287	.328	.321	.242	.261	.279	.246	.246	.273	.287	.310	.310
Ballistic Coefficient	.296	.405	.357	.391	.243	.394	.445	.465	.283	.275	.409	.486	.462	.453	.392	.433	.514	.285	.462
Catalog Number	2280	2453	2540	2552	2550	2560	2620	2630	2640	2645	2730	2735	2740	2825	2820	2830	2845	2855	2850

Caliber & Description	30 BTSP	30 RN	30 SP	30 BTSP	30 SP	30 FP	30 BTSP	30 RN	30 SP	30 BTSP	30 RN	7.62 SP	303 SP	303 RN	32 FP	8mm SP
Diameter, Inches	.308	.308	.308	.308	.308	.308	.308	.308	.308	.308	.308	.310	.312	.312	.321	.323
Weight, Grains	150	150	150	165	165	170	180	180	180	190	220	123	150	174	170	150
Density	.226	.226	.226	.248	.248	.256	.271	.271	.271	.286	.331	.183	.220	.255	.236	.205
Ballistic Coefficient	.349	.186	.338	.435	.387	.189	.452	.241	.425	.491	.300	.252	.361	.262	.249	.290
Catalog Number	3033	3035	3031	3045	3040	3060	3072	3075	3070	3085	3090	3140	3120	3130	3210	3232

Hornady Bullets

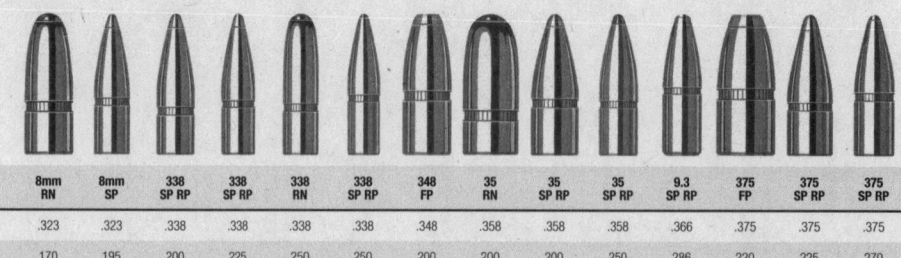

Caliber & Description	8mm RN	8mm SP	338 SP RP	338 SP RP	338 RN	338 SP RP	348 FP	35 RN	35 SP RP	35 SP RP	9.3 SP RP	375 FP	375 SP RP	375 SP RP
Diameter, Inches	.323	.323	.338	.338	.338	.338	.348	.358	.358	.358	.366	.375	.375	.375
Weight, Grains	170	195	200	225	250	250	200	200	200	250	286	220	225	270
Density	.233	.267	.250	.281	.313	.313	.236	.223	.223	.279	.305	.223	.229	.229
Ballistic Coefficient	.217	.410	.361	.397	.291	.431	.246	.195	.282	.375	.410	.217	.320	.380
Catalog Number	3235	3236	3310	3320	3330	3335	3410	3515	3510	3520	3560	3705	3706	3711

Caliber & Description	405 FP	405 SP	416 RN	44 FP	45 HP	45 FP	45 RN	45 RN
Diameter, Inches	.411	.411	.416	.430	.458	.458	.458	.458
Weight, Grains	300	300	400	265	300	350	350	500
Density	.251	.251	.330	.205	.204	.238	.238	.341
Ballistic Coefficient	.215	.250	.311	.186	.197	.195	.189	.287
Catalog Number	41050	41051	4165	4300	4500	4503	4502	4504

MSRP $29.00–$69.00

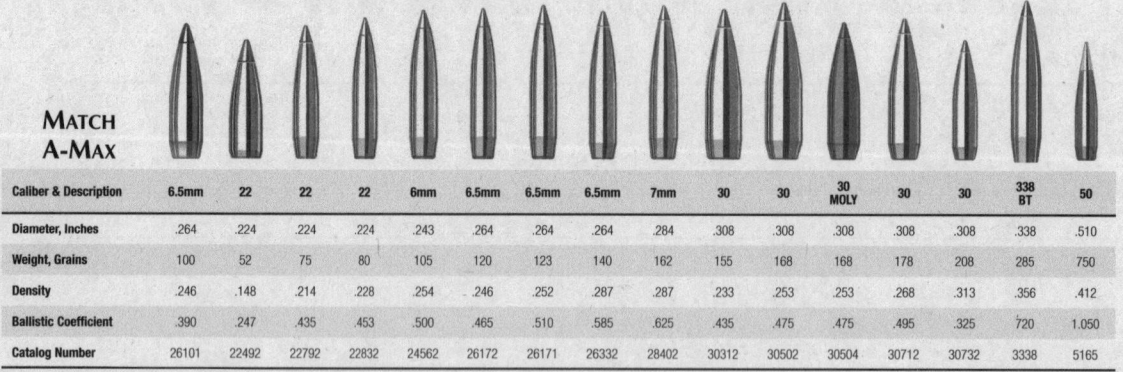

MATCH A-MAX

Caliber & Description	6.5mm	22	22	22	6mm	6.5mm	6.5mm	6.5mm	7mm	30	30	30 MOLY	30	30	338 BT	50
Diameter, Inches	.264	.224	.224	.224	.243	.264	.264	.264	.284	.308	.308	.308	.308	.308	.338	.510
Weight, Grains	100	52	75	80	105	120	123	140	162	155	168	168	178	208	285	750
Density	.246	.148	.214	.228	.254	.246	.252	.287	.287	.233	.253	.253	.268	.313	.356	.412
Ballistic Coefficient	.390	.247	.435	.453	.500	.465	.510	.585	.625	.435	.475	.475	.495	.325	.720	1.050
Catalog Number	26101	22492	22792	22832	24562	26172	26171	26332	28402	30312	30502	30504	30712	30732	3338	5165

MSRP $26.00–$64.00

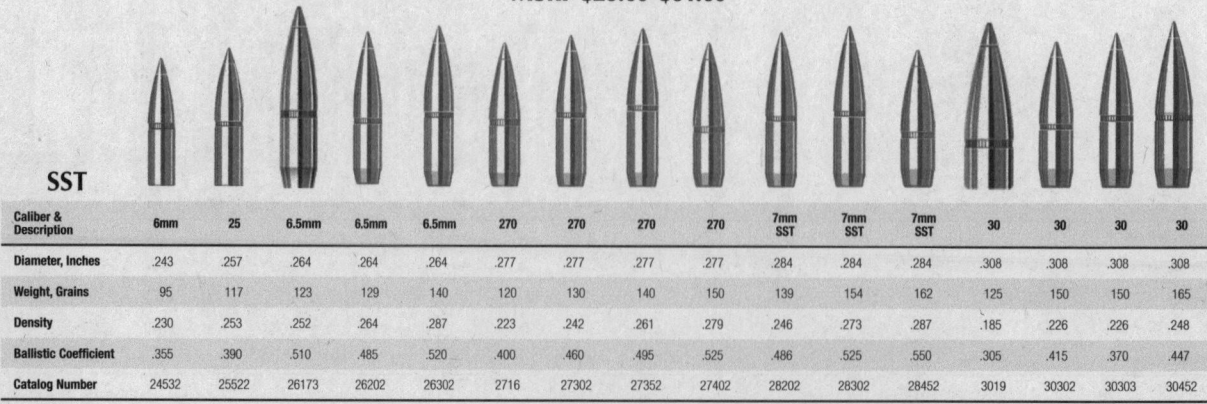

SST

Caliber & Description	6mm	25	6.5mm	6.5mm	6.5mm	270	270	270	270	7mm SST	7mm SST	7mm SST	30	30	30	30
Diameter, Inches	.243	.257	.264	.264	.264	.277	.277	.277	.277	.284	.284	.284	.308	.308	.308	.308
Weight, Grains	95	117	123	129	140	120	130	140	150	139	154	162	125	150	150	165
Density	.230	.253	.252	.264	.287	.223	.242	.261	.279	.246	.273	.287	.185	.226	.226	.248
Ballistic Coefficient	.355	.390	.510	.485	.520	.400	.460	.495	.525	.486	.525	.550	.305	.415	.370	.447
Catalog Number	24532	25522	26173	26202	26302	2716	27302	27352	27402	28202	28302	28452	3019	30302	30303	30452

AMMUNITION

Hornady Bullets

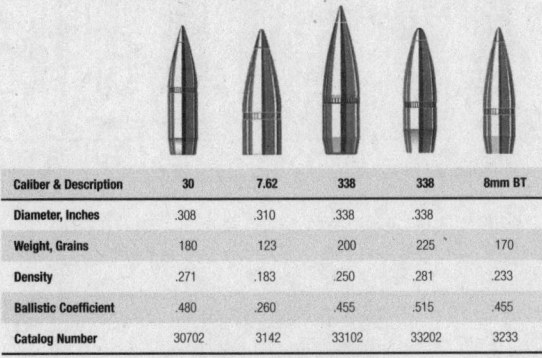

Caliber & Description	30	7.62	338	338	8mm BT
Diameter, Inches	.308	.310	.338	.338	
Weight, Grains	180	123	200	225	170
Density	.271	.183	.250	.281	.233
Ballistic Coefficient	.480	.260	.455	.515	.455
Catalog Number	30702	3142	33102	33202	3233

MSRP $40.00–$54.00

TRADITIONAL VARMINT

Caliber & Description	17 HP	20 SP	22 JET	22 Hornet	22 Hornet	22 HP BEE	22 SP	22 SP SX	22 SP	22 SP	22 SP SX	22 HP	22 SP	6mm HP
Diameter, Inches	.172	.204	.222	.223	.224	.224	.224	.224	.224	.224	.224	.224	.224	.243
Weight, Grains	25	45	40	45	45	45	50	50	55	55	55	60	60	75
Density	.121	.155	.116	.129	.128	.128	.142	.142	.157	.157	.157	.171	.171	.181
Ballistic Coefficient	.187	.245	.104	.202	.202	.108	.214	.214	.235	.235	.235	.271	.264	.294
Catalog Number	1710	22008	2210	2220	2230	2229	2245	2240	2265	2266	2260	2275	2270	2420

Caliber & Description	6mm BTHP	6mm SP	25 FP	25 HP	25 SP	270 SP	270 HP	270 BTHP	7mm HP	30 Short Jacket	30 SP	30 RN	30 SP
Diameter, Inches	.243	.243	.257	.257	.257	.277	.277	.277	.284	.308	.308	.308	.308
Weight, Grains	87	87	60	75	87	100	110	110	120	100	110	110	130
Density	.210	.210	.130	.162	.188	.186	.205	.205	.213	.151	.166	.166	.196
Ballistic Coefficient	.376	.327	.101	.257	.322	.307	.352	.360	.334	.152	.256	.150	.295
Catalog Number	2442	2440	2510	2520	2530	2710	2720	27200	2815	3005	3010	3015	3020

MSRP $18.00–$38.00

Hornady Bullets

V-MAX

Caliber & Description	17	17	20	20	22	22	22	22 MOLY	22	22	22	22 MOLY	22	6mm
Diameter, Inches	.172	.172	.204	.204	.224	.224	.224	.224	.224	.224	.224	.224	.224	.243
Weight, Grains	20	25	32	40	35	40	50	50	53	55	55	55	60	58
Density	.097	.121	.110	.137	.100	.114	.142	.142	.151	.157	.157	.157	.171	.140
Ballistic Coefficient	.185	.230	.210	.275	.109	.200	.242	.242	.290	.255	.255	.255	.265	.250
Catalog Number	21710	17105	22004	22006	22252	22241	22261	22613	22265	22272	22271	22713	22281	22411

Caliber & Description	6mm	6mm	6mm	25	6.5mm	270	7mm	30
Diameter, Inches	.243	.243	.243	.257	.264	.277	.284	.308
Weight, Grains	65	75	87	75	95	110	120	110
Density	.157	.181	.210	.162	.195	.205	.213	.166
Ballistic Coefficient	.280	.330	.400	.290	.365	.370	.365	.290
Catalog Number	22415	22420	22440	22520	22601	22721	22810	23010

MSRP $24.00–$38.00

Handgun Bullets

FMJ BULLETS

Caliber & Description	9mm FMJ-RN	9mm FMJ-RN	10mm FMJ-FP	45 SWC	45 FMJ-RN	9mm FMJ	9mm FMJ-RN	10mm FMJ-FP	45 FMJ-CT
Diameter, Inches	.355	.355	.400	.451	.451	.355	.355	.400	.451
Weight, Grains	115	124	180	185	230	100	147	200	200
Density	.130	.141	N/A	.130	.162	.141	.167	.179	.140
Ballistic Coefficient	.140	.145	N/A	.068	.184	.158	.212	.182	.115
Catalog Number	35557	355771	400471	45137	45177	35527B	35597B	40077B	45157B

MSRP $23.00–$33.00

FRONTIER LEAD BULLETS

Caliber & Description	32 HBWC	32 SWC	38	38 HBWC	38 LRN	38 SWC	38 SWC HP	44 Cowboy	44 Cowboy
Diameter, Inches	.314	.314	.358	.358	.358	.358	.358	.427	.430
Weight, Grains	90	90	140	148	158	158	158	205	180
Density	.130	.130	.157	.165	.176	.176	.176	.161	.139
Ballistic Coefficient	.040	.096	.127	.047	.159	.135	.139	.123	.114
Catalog Number	10028	10008	10078	10208	10508	10408	10428	11208	11058

AMMUNITION

FRONTIER/ LEAD BULLETS (CONT.)

Caliber & Description	44 SWC	44 SWC HP	45 L-C/T	45 SWC	45 LRN	45 FP Cowboy
Diameter, Inches	.430	.430	.452	.452	.452	.454
Weight, Grains	240	240	200	200	230	255
Density	.185	.185	.140	.140	.162	.177
Ballistic Coefficient	.182	.204	.081	.070	.207	.117
Catalog Number	11108	11118	12208	12108	12308	12458

MSRP $32.00–$51.00

HAP BULLETS

Caliber & Description	9mm	9mm	10mm	45	45	10mm	45
Diameter, Inches	.356	.356	.400	.451	.451	.400	.451
Weight, Grains	115	125	180	185	230	200	200
Density	.130	.141	.161	.130	.162	.179	.140
Ballistic Coefficient	.129	.158	.164	.139	.188	.199	151
Catalog Number	355281	355721	400421	451051	451611	40061B	45159B

MSRP $78.00–$139.00

LEGEND
Type of Bullet
BT	–	Boat Tail
CT	–	Combat Target
FMJ	–	Full Metal Jacket
FP	–	Flat Point
HB	–	Hollow Base
L	–	Lead
RN	–	Round Nose
SP	–	Spire Point
SX	–	Super Explosive
SWC	–	Semi-Wadcutter
WC	–	Wadcutter

XTP BULLETS

Caliber & Description	30 RN	30 HP	32 HP	32 HP	32 HP	9mm HP	9mm HP	38 HP	9mm HP	38 FP	9mm HP	38 HP	38 HP	38 FP	38 HP	38 HP	9x18mm HP	10mm HP	10mm HP
Diameter, Inches	.308	.309	.312	.312	.312	.355	.355	.357	.355	.357	.355	.357	.357	.357	.357	.357	.365	.400	.400
Weight, Grains	86	90	60	85	100	90	115	110	124	125	147	125	140	158	158	180	95	155	180
Density	.130	.136	.088	.125	.147	.102	.130	.123	.141	.140	.167	.140	.157	.177	.177	.202	.102	.138	.161
Ballistic Coefficient	.105	.115	.090	.145	.170	.099	.129	.131	.165	.148	.212	.151	.169	.199	.206	.230	.127	.137	.164
Catalog Number	3100	31000	32010	32050	32070	35500	35540	35700	35571	35730	35580	35710	35740	35780	35750	35771	36500	40000	40040

Caliber & Description	10mm HP	41 HP	44 HP	44 HP	44 HP	44 HP	45 HP	45 HP	45 HP	45	45 HP	45 HP	45	475 MAG	50	500 MAG	500 FP
Diameter, Inches	.400	.410	.430	.430	.430	.300	.451	.451	.451	.452	.452	.452	.452	.475	.500	.500	.500
Weight, Grains	200	210	180	200	240	300	185	200	230	240	250	300	300	325	300	350	500
Density	.179	.178	.139	.155	.185	.232	.130	.140	.162	.168	.175	.210	.210	.206	.171	.192	.275
Ballistic Coefficient	.199	.182	.138	.170	.205	.245	.139	.151	.188	.160	.146	.180	.200	.150	.120	.145	.185
Catalog Number	40060	41000	44050	44100	44200	44280	45100	45140	45160	45220	45200	45230	45235	47500	50101	50100	50105

MSRP $22.00–$61.00

AMMUNITION

Lapua

Rifle Bullets

Lapua precision bullets are made from the best raw materials and meet the toughest precision specifications. Each bullet is subject to visual inspection and tested with advanced measurement devices.

D46
Manufactured to the strictest tolerances for concentricity, uniformity of shape, and weight; 7.62mm (.308) available
Box 100: $50.00

D166
Superbly accurate FMJBT bullet for 7.62mm (.311) cartridges
Box 100: $52.00

FMJ
Ten rounds loaded with Lapua's .30 S374 8.0/123gr FMJ bullet from 100m can easily achieve groupings less than; 30mm .224, 6.5mm, 7.62mm (.308, .311) available
Box 100: . . . . $35.00–$44.00

LOCK BASE
A distinctive Full Metal Jacket Boat Tail bullet that has many applications from sport shooting to battlefield; streamlined ballistic shape combined with patented base design; 7.62mm and .338 available
Box 100: . . . . $50.00–$77.00

MEGA
Soft point bullet with a protective copper jacket bullet at its best in the field and typically more than duplicates on impact; mechanical bonding locks the lead alloy in place; 6.5mm, 7.62mm, and 9.3mm available
Box 100: . . . . $52.00–$72.00

LAPUA NATURALIS THIRD GENERATION
Market leaders in terminal ballistic performance, and they can be used in hunting areas where lead-core bullets are prohibited. 5.69 (50 gr.), 6mm (90 gr.), 6.5mm (140 gr.), 7mm (155 gr.), 8mm (180 gr.), 9.3mm (250 gr.), .338 (231 gr.) available.
Box 50: . . . . $66.99–$113.99

SCENAR
Scenar Hollow Point Boat Tail bullets have the IBS World Record in 600 yard Heavy Gun 5-shot group (.404") and hold the official world ISSF record of 600 out of 600 possible; also available in Coated Silver Jacket version; .244, 6mm, 6.5mm, 7.62mm, and .338 available
Box 100: . . . . $37.00–$88.00

SCENAR-L
A refinement in all manufacturing steps that has resulted in closer weight tolerances, tighter jacket wall concentricity standards, and greater uniformity in every dimension, including the gilding metal cup, lead wire and jacket forming, ending up to core-jacket assembly, boat tail pressing, and tipping ; 6mm, 6.5mm, 7mm, and 7.62mm (.308) available
Box 100: . . . . $49.00–$58.00

LAPUA D46

LAPUA D166

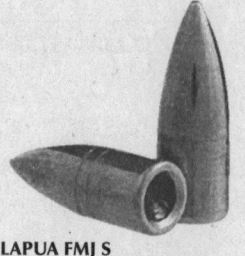

LAPUA FMJ S

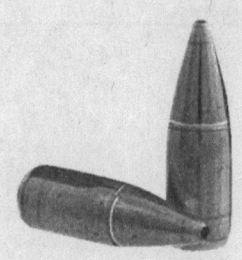

LAPUA HP

LAPUA LOCK BASE

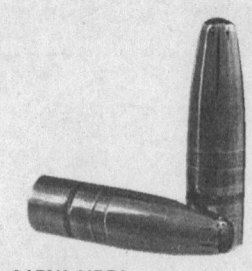

LAPUA MEGA

LAPUA SCENAR

LAPUA NATURALIS THIRD GENERATION

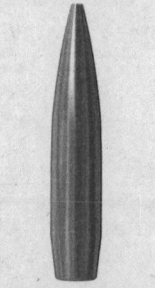

LAPUA SCENAR-L

Rifle Bullets

Accubond

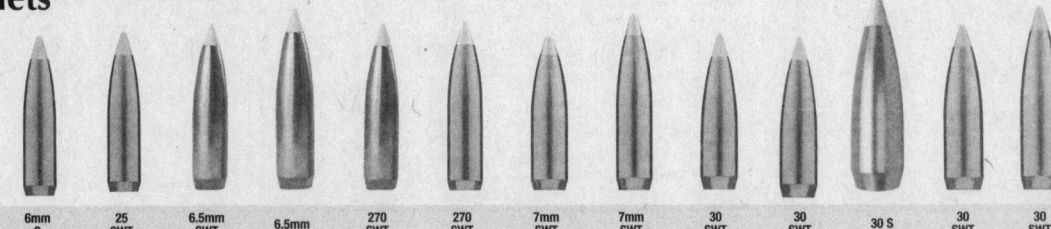

Caliber & Description	6mm S	25 SWT	6.5mm SWT	6.5mm	270 SWT	270 SWT	7mm SWT	7mm SWT	30 SWT	30 SWT	30 S	30 SWT	30 SWT
Diameter, inches	.243	.257	.264	.264	.277	.277	.277	.277	.284	.284	.308	.308	.308
Weight, Grains	90	110	130	140	100	110	130	140	140	160	125	150	165
Density	.218	.238	.266	.287	.186	.205	.242	.261	.248	.283	.188	.226	.248
Ballistic Coefficient	.376	.418	.488	.509	.323	.370	.435	.496	.485	.531	.366	.435	.475
Catalog Number	56357	53742	56902	57873	57845	54382	54987	54765	59992	54932	52165	56719	55602

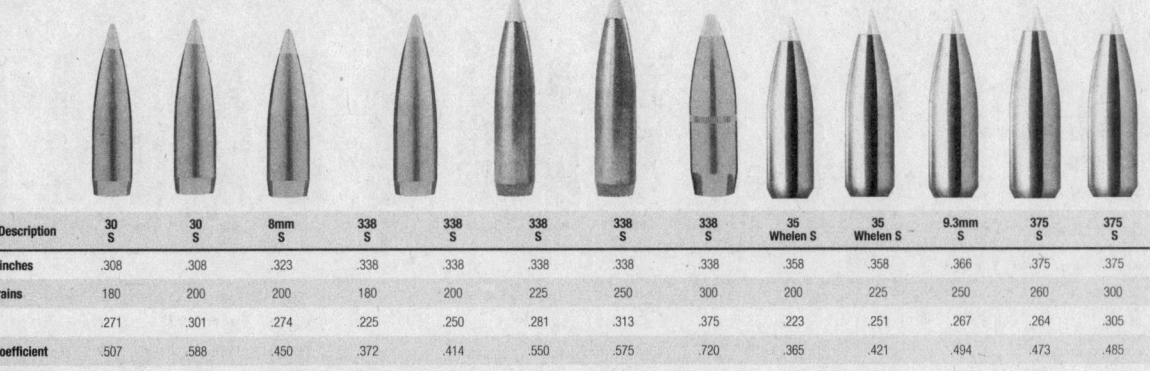

Caliber & Description	30 S	30 S	8mm S	338 S	338 S	338 S	338 S	338 S	35 Whelen S	35 Whelen S	9.3mm S	375 S	375 S
Diameter, inches	.308	.308	.323	.338	.338	.338	.338	.338	.358	.358	.366	.375	.375
Weight, Grains	180	200	200	180	200	225	250	300	200	225	250	260	300
Density	.271	.301	.274	.225	.250	.281	.313	.375	.223	.251	.267	.264	.305
Ballistic Coefficient	.507	.588	.450	.372	.414	.550	.575	.720	.365	.421	.494	.473	.485
Catalog Number	54825	54618	54374	57625	56382	54357	57287	54851	54425	50712	59756	54413	53662

Box 50, 100: $27.00–$63.00

Ballistic Tip Hunting

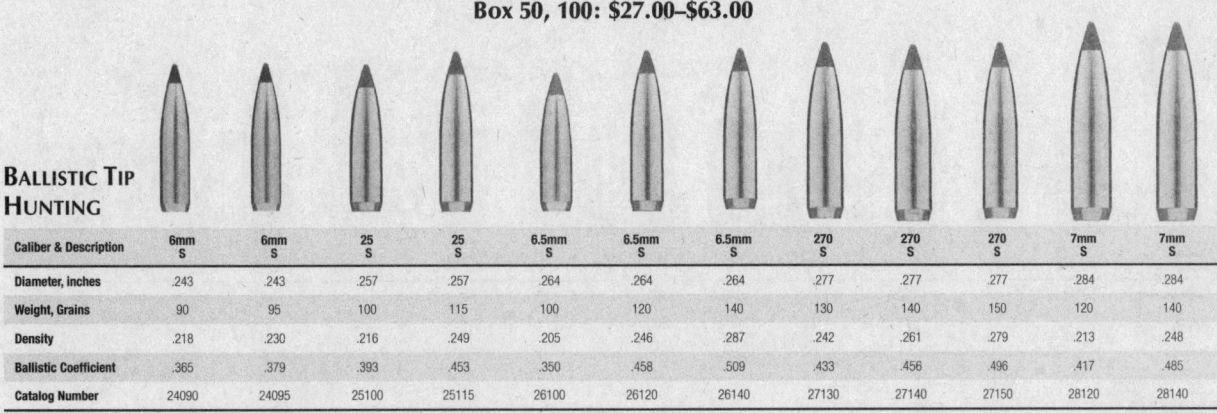

Caliber & Description	6mm S	6mm S	25 S	25 S	6.5mm S	6.5mm S	6.5mm S	270 S	270 S	270 S	7mm S	7mm S
Diameter, inches	.243	.243	.257	.257	.264	.264	.264	.277	.277	.277	.284	.284
Weight, Grains	90	95	100	115	100	120	140	130	140	150	120	140
Density	.218	.230	.216	.249	.205	.246	.287	.242	.261	.279	.213	.248
Ballistic Coefficient	.365	.379	.393	.453	.350	.458	.509	.433	.456	.496	.417	.485
Catalog Number	24090	24095	25100	25115	26100	26120	26140	27130	27140	27150	28120	28140

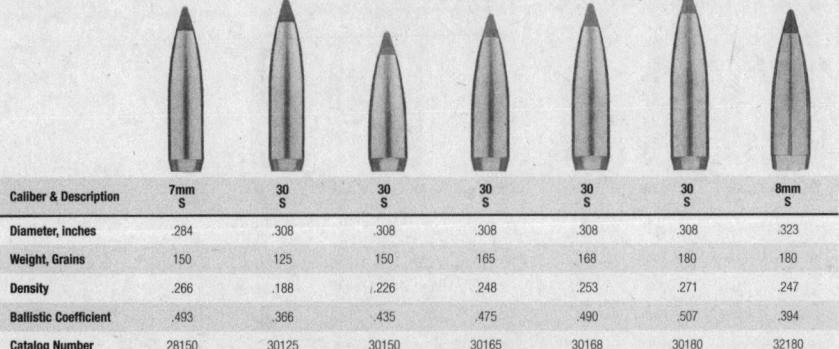

Caliber & Description	7mm S	30 S	30 S	30 S	30 S	30 S	8mm S
Diameter, inches	.284	.308	.308	.308	.308	.308	.323
Weight, Grains	150	125	150	165	168	180	180
Density	.266	.188	.226	.248	.253	.271	.247
Ballistic Coefficient	.493	.366	.435	.475	.490	.507	.394
Catalog Number	28150	30125	30150	30165	30168	30180	32180

LEGEND

Type of Bullet		Type of Tip	
BT	– Boat Tail	PT	– Purple Tip
HP	– Hollow Point	BT	– Blue Tip
J	– Jacketed	BrT	– Brown Tip
PP	– Protected Point	BuT	– Buckskin Tip
RN	– Round Nose	GT	– Green Tip
S	– Spitzer	GuT	– Gunmetal Tip
SS	– Semi Spitzer	MT	– Maroon Tip
W	– Whelen	OT	– Olive Tip
		RT	– Red Tip
		SLT	– Soft Lead Tip
		YT	– Yellow Tip

Box 50: $17.00–$30.00

AMMUNITION

Nosler Bullets

BALLISTIC TIP VARMINT

Caliber & Description	204 S	204 S	22 S	22 S	22 S	22 S	6mm S	6mm S	6mm S	25 S
Diameter, inches	.204	.204	.224	.224	.224	.224	.243	.243	.243	.257
Weight, Grains	32	40	40	50	55	60	55	70	80	85
Density	.110	.137	.114	.142	.157	.171	.133	.169	.194	.184
Ballistic Coefficient	.206	.239	.221	.238	.27	.270	.276	.310	.329	.329
Catalog Number	35216	52111	39510	39522	39526	34992	24055	39532	24080	43004

Box 100: $23.00–$36.00

CT BALLISTIC SILVERTIP HUNTING

Caliber & Description	6mm S	25 S	270 S	270 S	7mm S	7mm S	30 S	30 RN	30 S	30 S	8mm S	45-70 RN	338 S
Diameter, inches	.243	.257	.277	.277	.284	.284	.308	.308	.308	.308	.323	.458	.338
Weight, Grains	95	115	130	150	140	150	150	150	168	180	180	300	200
Density	.230	.249	.242	.279	.248	.266	.226	.226	.253	.271	.247	.204	.250
Ballistic Coefficient	.379	.453	.433	.496	.485	.493	.435	.232	.490	.507	.394	.191	.414
Catalog Number	51040	51050	51075	51100	51105	51110	51150	51165	51160	51170	51693	51834	51200

Box 50: $27.00

CUSTOM COMPETITION

Caliber & Description	22 HPBT	22 HPBT	22 HPBT	22 HPBT	6mm HPBT	6mm HPBT	6.5mm HPBT	6.5mm HPBT	6.8mm HPBT	7mm HPBT	30 HPBT	30 HPBT	30 HPBT	30 HPBT	30 HPBT	45 JHP
Diameter, inches	.224	.224	.224	.224	.243	.243	.264	.264	.277	.284	.308	.308	.308	.308	.308	.451
Weight, Grains	52	69	77	80	105	107	123	140	115	168	140	155	168	175	190	185
Density	.148	.196	.219	.228	.254	.259	.252	.287	.214	.298	.211	.233	.253	.264	.286	.130
Ballistic Coefficient	.220	.305	.340	.415	.517	.525	.510	.529	.375	.520	.396	.450	.462	.505	.530	.142
Catalog Number	53294	17101	22421	25116	53614	49742	53415	26725	45357	53418	53152	53155	53164	53952	53412	44847

Box 100, 250: $19.00–$36.00

E-TIP

Caliber & Description	6mm S	25 S	6.8mm S	270 S	7mm S	7mm S	30 S	30 S	30 S	8mm S	338 S	6.5MM S
Diameter, inches	.243	.257	.277	.277	.284	.284	.308	.308	.308	.323	.338	264
Weight, Grains	90	100	85	130	140	150	150	168	180	180	200	120
Density	.218	.216	.158	.242	.248	.266	.226	.253	.271	.246	.250	.246
Ballistic Coefficient	.403	.409	.273	.459	.489	.498	.469	.503	.523	.427	.425	.497
Catalog Number	59165	59456	59543	59298	59955	59426	59378	59415	59180	59265	59186	59765

Box 50: $29.00–$49.00

AMMUNITION

PARTITION

Caliber & Description	22 S	6mm S	6mm S	6mm S	25 S	25 S	25 S	6.5mm S	6.5mm S	6.5mm S	270 S	270 S	270 S	270 SS
Diameter, Inches	.224	.243	.243	.243	.257	.257	.257	.264	.264	.264	.277	.277	.277	.277
Weight, Grains	60	85	95	100	100	115	120	100	125	140	130	140	150	160
Density	.171	.206	.230	.242	.216	.249	.260	.205	.256	.287	.242	.261	.279	.298
Ballistic Coefficient	.228	.315	.365	.384	.377	.389	.391	.326	.4479	.490	.416	.432	.465	.434
Catalog Number	16316	16314	16315	35642	16317	16318	35643	16319	16320	16321	16322	35200	.16323	16324

Caliber & Description	7mm S	7mm S	7mm S	7mm S	30 S	30 S	30 RN	30 PP	30 S	30 S	30 SS	8mm S	338 S	338 S
Diameter, Inches	.284	.284	.284	.284	.308	.308	.308	.308	.308	.308	.308	.323	.338	.338
Weight, Grains	140	150	160	175	150	165	170	180	180	200	220	200	210	225
Density	.248	.266	.283	.310	.226	.248	.256	.271	.271	.301	.331	.274	.263	.281
Ballistic Coefficient	.434	.456	.475	.519	.387	.410	.252	.361	.474	.481	.351	.426	.400	.454
Catalog Number	16325	16326	16327	35645	16329	16330	16333	25396	16331	35626	16332	35277	16337	16336

Caliber & Description	338 S	35 S	35 S	9.3mm S	375 S	375 S	416 S	458 PP
Diameter, Inches	.338	.358	.358	.366	.375	.375	.416	.458
Weight, Grains	250	225	250	286	260	300	400	500
Density	.313	.251	.279	.307	.264	.305	.330	.389
Ballistic Coefficient	.473	.430	.446	.482	.314	.398	.390	.341
Catalog Number	35644	44800	44801	44750	44850	44845	45200	44745

Box 25, 50: $26.00–$119.00

LEGEND

Type of Bullet
- BT – Boat Tail
- HP – Hollow Point
- J – Jacketed
- PP – Protected Point
- RN – Round Nose
- S – Spitzer
- SS – Semi Spitzer
- W – Whelen

Type of Tip
- PT – Purple Tip
- BT – Blue Tip
- BrT – Brown Tip
- BuT – Buckskin Tip
- GT – Green Tip
- GuT – Gunmetal Tip
- MT – Maroon Tip
- OT – Olive Tip
- RT – Red Tip
- SLT – Soft Lead Tip
- YT – Yellow Tip

SOLID

Caliber & Description	9.3mm Solid	375 Solid	375 Solid	416 Solid	458 Solid	470 NE Solid
Diameter, Inches	.366	.375	.375	.416	.458	.474
Weight, Grains	286	260	300	400	500	500
Density	.305	.264	.305	.330	.341	.318
Ballistic Coefficient	.350	.254	.300	.289	.246	.237
Catalog Number	29825	29755	28451	23654	27452	28455

MSRP $70.00–$89.00

LEGEND

Type of Bullet
- BT – Boattail
- FMJ – Full Metal Jacket
- J – Jacketed
- PP – Protected Point
- RN – Round Nose
- S – Spitzer

AMMUNITION

Nosler Bullets

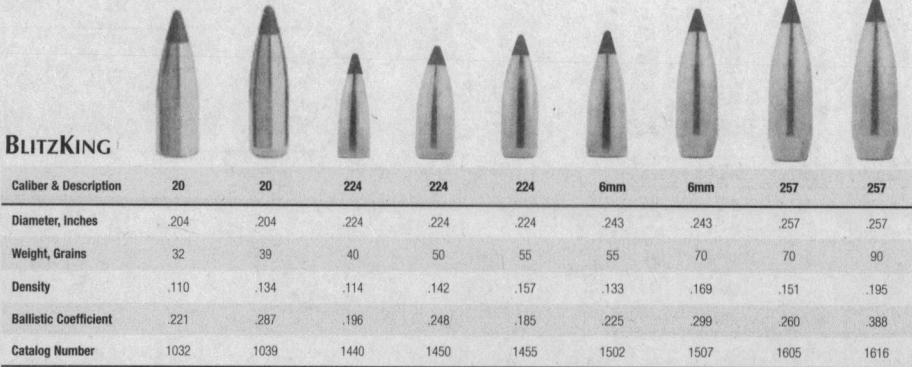

Varmageddon

Caliber & Description	17 FBHP	17 FB Tipped	20 FBHP	20 FB Tipped	22 FB Tipped	22 FBHP	22 FB Tipped	22 FBHP	22 FB Tipped	22 FBHP	6mm FBHP	6mm FB Tipped	6mm FB Tipped	30 FB Tipped
Diameter, Inches	.172	.172	.204	.204	.224	.224	.224	.224	.224	.224	.243	.243	.243	.308
Weight, Grains	20	20	32	32	35	40	40	55	55	62	55	55	70	110
Density	.097	.097	.110	.110	.100	.114	.114	.157	.157	.176	.133	.133	.169	.166
Ballistic Coefficient	.119	.183	.131	.204	.120	.158	.211	.210	.218	.251	.192	.252	.334	.293
Catalog Number	17205	17210	17215	17220	36763	17225	17230	17235	17240	35631	17245	17250	26123	34057

Box 100, 250: $15.00–$25.00

Handgun Bullets

Sporting Pistol

Caliber & Description	9mm JHP	9mm JHP	10mm JHP	10mm JHP	10mm JHP	10mm JHP	45 JHP	45 FMJ
Diameter, Inches	.355	.355	.400	.400	.400	.400	.451	.451
Weight, Grains	115	124	135	150	180	200	230	230
Density	.109	.141	.093	.106	.161	.179	.1625	.162
Ballistic Coefficient	.130	.118	.121	.134	.147	.163	.175	.183
Catalog Number	44848	43123	44852	44860	44885	44952	44922	44964

LEGEND
Type of Bullet
BT – Boattail
FB – Flat Base
FN – Flat Nose
RN – Round Nose
S – Spitzer
SP – Soft Point
SS – Semi-Spitzer

Box 250: $42.00–$60.00

Sporting Revolver

Caliber & Description	38 JHP	41 JHP	44 JHP	44 JHP	44 JHP	44 JHP	45 Colt JHP
Diameter, Inches	.357	.410	.429	.429	.429	.429	.451
Weight, Grains	158	210	200	240	240	300	250
Density	.182	.170	.151	.173	.177	.206	.177
Ballistic Coefficient	.177	.178	155	.186	.186	.233	.176
Catalog Number	44841	43012	44846	44842	44868	42069	43013

Box 100, 250: $28.00–$58.00

Sierra Bullets

Rifle Bullets

BlitzKing

Caliber & Description	20	20	224	224	224	6mm	6mm	257	257
Diameter, Inches	.204	.204	.224	.224	.224	.243	.243	.257	.257
Weight, Grains	32	39	40	50	55	55	70	70	90
Density	.110	.134	.114	.142	.157	.133	.169	.151	.195
Ballistic Coefficient	.221	.287	.196	.248	.185	.225	.299	.260	.388
Catalog Number	1032	1039	1440	1450	1455	1502	1507	1605	1616

From: $28.00–$34.00

AMMUNITION

GameKing

Caliber & Description	22 FMJBT	22 SBT	22 HPBT	22 SBT	6mm HPBT	6mm FMJBT	6mm SBT	25 HPBT	25 SBT	25 SBT	25 HPBT	6.5mm HPBT
Diameter, Inches	.224	.224	.224	.224	.243	.243	.243	.257	.257	.257	.257	.264
Weight, Grains	55	55	55	65	85	90	100	90	100	117	120	130
Density	.157	.257	.157	.185	.206	.218	.242	.195	.216	.253	.260	.266
Ballistic Coefficient	.272	.250	.185	.303	.282	.387	.430	.250	.355	.410	.350	.355
Catalog Number	1355	1365	1390	1395	1530	1535	1560	1615	1625	1630	1650	1728

Caliber & Description	6.5mm SBT	270 SBT	270 HPBT	270 SBT	270 SBT	7mm HPBT	7mm SBT	7mm SBT	7mm SBT	7mm HPBT	7mm SBT	30 FMJBT
Diameter, Inches	.264	.277	.277	.277	.277	.284	.274	.284	.284	.284	.284	.308
Weight, Grains	140	130	140	140	150	140	140	150	160	160	175	150
Density	.287	.242	.261	.261	.279	.248	.248	.266	.283	.283	.310	.226
Ballistic Coefficient	.495	.436	.337	.457	.483	.375	.416	.436	.455	.384	.533	.408
Catalog Number	1730	1820	1835	1845	1840	1912	1905	1913	1920	1925	1940	2115

Caliber & Description	30 SBT	30 HPBT	30 SBT	30 SBT	30 SBT	8mm SBT	338 SBT	338 SBT	35 SBT	375 SBT	375 SBT
Diameter, Inches	.308	.308	.308	.308	.308	.323	.338	.338	.358	.375	.375
Weight, Grains	150	165	165	180	200	220	215	250	225	250	300
Density	.226	.248	.248	.271	.301	.301	.269	.313	.251	.254	.305
Ballistic Coefficient	.380	.363	.404	.501	.560	.521	.485	.565	.370	.353	.475
Catalog Number	2125	2140	2145	2160	2165	2420	2610	2600	2850	2950	3000

From: $21.00–$45.00

MatchKing

Caliber & Description	22 HPBT	22 HP	22 HPBT	22 HPBT	22 HPBT	22 HPBT	6mm HPBT	6mm HPBT	6mm HPBT	25 HPBT	6.5mm HPBT	6.5mm HPBT	6.5mm HPBT	6.5mm HPBT
Diameter, Inches	.224	.224	.224	.224	.224	.224	.243	.243	.243	.257	.264	.264	.264	.264
Weight, Grains	52	53	69	77	80	90	70	107	95	100	107	120	123	140
Density	.148	.151	.196	.219	.228	.256	.169	.259	.230	.216	.219	.246	.252	.287
Ballistic Coefficient	.225	.224	.301	.372	.420	.504	.259	.527	.480	.394	.430	.421	.510	.535
Catalog Number	1410	1400	1380	9377T	9390T	9290T	1505	1570	1537	1628	1715	1725	1727	1740

AMMUNITION

Sierra Bullets

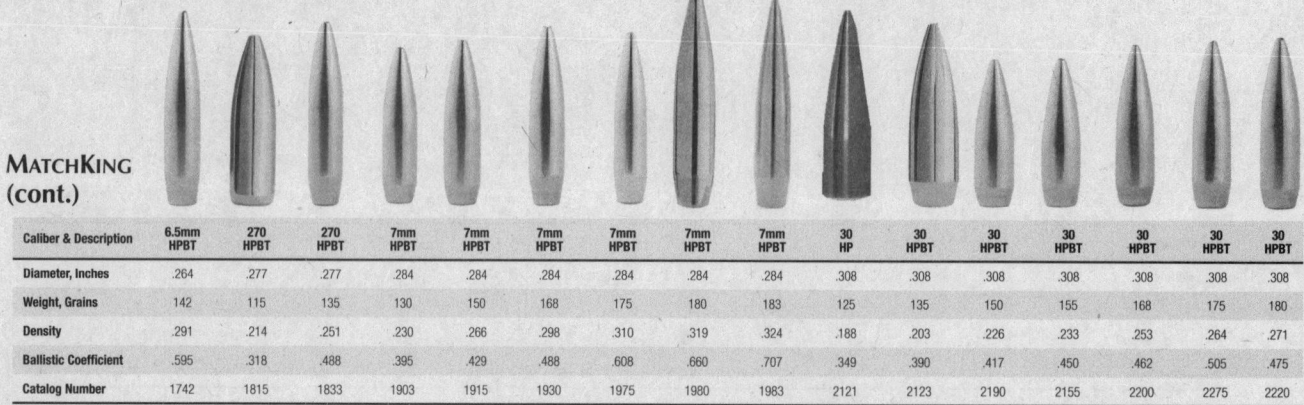

MatchKing (cont.)

Caliber & Description	6.5mm HPBT	270 HPBT	270 HPBT	7mm HPBT	7mm HPBT	7mm HPBT	7mm HPBT	7mm HPBT	7mm HPBT	30 HP	30 HPBT	30 HPBT	30 HPBT	30 HPBT	30 HPBT	30 HPBT
Diameter, Inches	.264	.277	.277	.284	.284	.284	.284	.284	.284	.308	.308	.308	.308	.308	.308	.308
Weight, Grains	142	115	135	130	150	168	175	180	183	125	135	150	155	168	175	180
Density	.291	.214	.251	.230	.266	.298	.310	.319	.324	.188	.203	.226	.233	.253	.264	.271
Ballistic Coefficient	.595	.318	.488	.395	.429	.488	.608	.660	.707	.349	.390	.417	.450	.462	.505	.475
Catalog Number	1742	1815	1833	1903	1915	1930	1975	1980	1983	2121	2123	2190	2155	2200	2275	2220

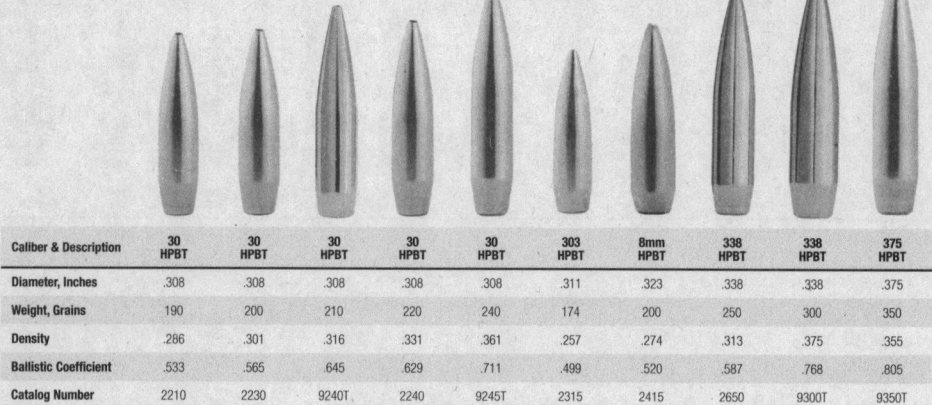

Caliber & Description	30 HPBT	30 HPBT	30 HPBT	30 HPBT	30 HPBT	303 HPBT	8mm HPBT	338 HPBT	338 HPBT	375 HPBT
Diameter, Inches	.308	.308	.308	.308	.308	.311	.323	.338	.338	.375
Weight, Grains	190	200	210	220	240	174	200	250	300	350
Density	.286	.301	.316	.331	.361	.257	.274	.313	.375	.355
Ballistic Coefficient	.533	.565	.645	.629	.711	.499	.520	.587	.768	.805
Catalog Number	2210	2230	9240T	2240	9245T	2315	2415	2650	9300T	9350T

From: $25.00–$54.00

LEGEND
- **BT** – Boattail
- **FMJ** – Full Metal Jacket
- **FN** – Flat Nose
- **HC** – Hollow Cavity
- **HP** – Hollow Point
- **J** – Jacketed
- **RN** – Round Nose
- **S** – Spitzer
- **SMP** – Semi-Pointed
- **SP** – Soft Point

Pro-Hunter

Caliber & Description	6mm S	25 S	25 S	6.5mm S	270 S	270 S	7mm S	7mm S	30 HP/FN	30 FN	30 FN
Diameter, Inches	.243	.257	.257	.264	.277	.277	.284	.284	.308	.308	.308
Weight, Grains	100	100	117	120	110	130	120	140	125	150	170
Density	.242	.216	.253	.246	.205	.242	.213	.248	.188	.226	.256
Ballistic Coefficient	.373	.330	.388	.356	.318	.370	.328	.377	.119	.185	.205
Catalog Number	1540	1620	1640	1720	1810	1830	1900	1910	2020	2000	2010

Caliber & Description	30 RN	30 FMJ	30 S	30 S	30 RN	30 S	30 RN	30 RN
Diameter, Inches	.308	.308	.308	.308	.308	.308	.308	.308
Weight, Grains	110	110	125	150	150	180	180	220
Density	.166	.166	.188	.226	.226	.271	.271	.331
Ballistic Coefficient	.144	.144	.279	.336	.200	.407	.240	.310
Catalog Number	2100	2105	2120	2130	2135	2150	2170	2180

Sierra Bullets

PRO-HUNTER (CONT.)

Caliber & Description	303 S	303 S	303 S	8mm S	8mm S	338 S	35 RN	375 FN	45-70 HP/FN
Diameter, Inches	.311	.311	.311	.323	.323	.338	.358	.375	.458
Weight, Grains	125	150	180	150	175	225	200	200	300
Density	.185	.222	.266	.205	.240	.281	.223	.203	.204
Ballistic Coefficient	.274	.344	.411	.336	.381	.462	.148	.195	.120
Catalog Number	2305	2300	2310	2400	2410	2620	2800	2900	8900

From: $20.00–$37.00

VARMINTER

Caliber & Description	22 Hornet	22 Hornet	22 Hornet	22 Hornet	22 HP
Diameter, Inches	.223	.223	.224	.224	.224
Weight, Grains	40	45	40	45	40
Density	.115	.129	.114	.128	.114
Ballistic Coefficient	.117	.132	.116	.131	.155
Catalog Number	1100	1110	1200	1210	1385

Caliber & Description	22 S	22 S	22 S	22 Blitz	22 Blitz	22 SMP	22 S	22 HP	22 SMP	6mm HP	6mm HP	6mm SBT Blitz	6mm S	25 HP	25 S	6.5mm HP	6.5mm HP	270 HP	7mm HP	30 HP
Diameter, Inches	.224	.224	.224	.224	.224	.224	.224	.224	.224	.243	.243	.243	.243	.257	.257	.264	.264	.277	.284	.308
Weight, Grains	45	50	50	50	55	55	55	60	63	60	75	80	85	75	87	85	100	90	100	110
Density	.128	.142	.142	.142	.157	.157	.157	.171	.179	.145	.181	.194	.206	.162	.188	.174	.205	.168	.177	.166
Ballistic Coefficient	.210	.192	.222	.222	.237	.204	.237	.246	.231	.182	.217	.319	.315	.189	.293	.225	.259	.195	.209	.177
Catalog Number	1310	1320	1330	1340	1345	1350	1360	1375	1370	1500	1510	1515	1520	1600	1610	1700	1710	1800	1895	2110

From: $20.00–$32.00

TIPPED MATCHKING

Caliber & Description	224	224	243	264	284	308	308	308	308
Diameter, Inches	.224	.224	.243	.264	.284	.308	.308	.308	.308
Weight, Grains	69	77	95	130	160	125	155	168	175
Density	.196	.219	.243	.264	.284	.188	.233	.253	.264
Ballistic Coefficient	.375	.420	.500	.518	.600	.343	.519	.535	.545
Catalog Number	7169	7177	7295	7430	7660	7725	7755	7768	7775

From: $30.54–$48.44

Handgun Bullets

SPORTS MASTER

Caliber & Description	30 RN	32 JHC	9mm JHP	9mm JHP	9mm JHP	38 JHP Blitz	38 JHP	38 JSP	38 JHP	38 JHC	38 JSP	10mm JHP	10mm JHP
Diameter, Inches	.308	.312	.355	.355	.355	.357	.357	.357	.357	.357	.357	.400	.400
Weight, Grains	85	90	90	115	125	110	125	125	140	158	158	135	150
Density	.128	.132	.102	.130	.142	.123	.140	.140	.157	.177	.177	.121	.134
Ballistic Coefficient	.102	.125	.095	.107	.124	.120	.133	.133	.0776	.100	.100	.105	.120
Catalog Number	8005	8030	8100	8110	8125	8300	8320	8310	8325	8360	8340	8425	8430

Sierra Bullets

Handgun Bullets

Caliber & Description	10mm JHP	10mm JHP	41 JHC	41 JHC	44 JHC	44 JHC	44 JHC	44 JSP	45 JHP	45 JHP	45 JHC	45 JSP	50 JHP	50 JSP
Diameter, Inches	.400	.400	.410	.410	.4295	.4295	.4295	.4295	.4515	.4515	.4515	.4515	.500	.500
Weight, Grains	165	180	170	210	180	210	240	300	185	230	240	300	350	400
Density	.147	.161	.144	.178	.139	.163	.186	.232	.130	.161	.168	.210	.200	.229
Ballistic Coefficient	.130	.140	.123	.165	.130	.160	.185	.230	.100	.145	.150	.192	.155	.185
Catalog Number	8445	8460	8500	8520	8600	8620	8610	8630	8800	8805	8820	8830	5350	5400

From: $22.00–$37.00

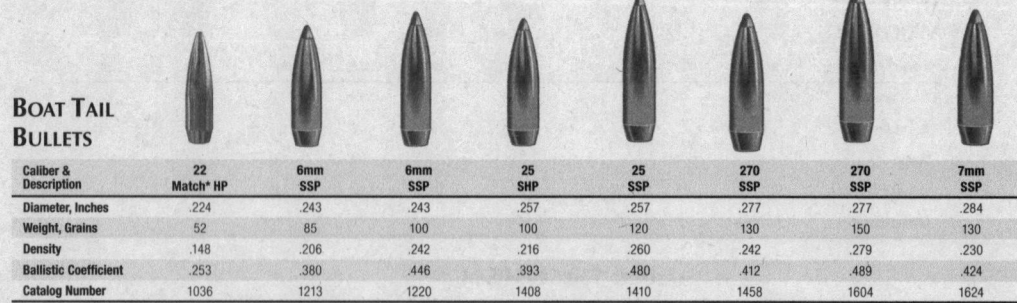

V-Crown

Caliber & Description	9mm JHP	9mm JHP	9mm JHP	10mm JHP	45 JHP
Diameter, Inches	.355	.355	.355	.400	.4515
Weight, Grains	90	124	125	165	200
Density	.109	.160	.168	.147	.143
Ballistic Coefficient	.094	.120	.122	.132	.118
Catalog Number	9990	9924	9925	9465	9820

Box 100: . . . . . . $24.46–$34.80

Speer Bullets

Rifle Bullets

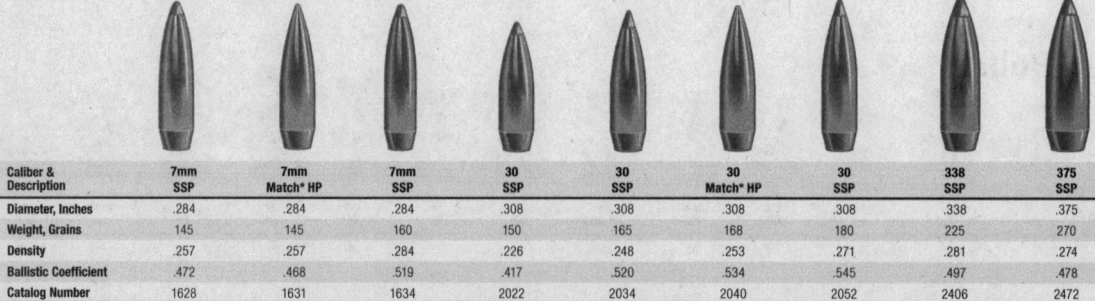

BOAT TAIL BULLETS

Caliber & Description	22 Match* HP	6mm SSP	6mm SSP	25 SHP	25 SSP	270 SSP	270 SSP	7mm SSP
Diameter, Inches	.224	.243	.243	.257	.257	.277	.277	.284
Weight, Grains	52	85	100	100	120	130	150	130
Density	.148	.206	.242	.216	.260	.242	.279	.230
Ballistic Coefficient	.253	.380	.446	.393	.480	.412	.489	.424
Catalog Number	1036	1213	1220	1408	1410	1458	1604	1624

*Match bullets are not recommended for use on game animals.

Caliber & Description	7mm SSP	7mm Match* HP	7mm SSP	30 SSP	30 SSP	30 Match* HP	30 SSP	338 SSP	375 SSP
Diameter, Inches	.284	.284	.284	.308	.308	.308	.308	.338	.375
Weight, Grains	145	145	160	150	165	168	180	225	270
Density	.257	.257	.284	.226	.248	.253	.271	.281	.274
Ballistic Coefficient	.472	.468	.519	.417	.520	.534	.545	.497	.478
Catalog Number	1628	1631	1634	2022	2034	2040	2052	2406	2472

*Match bullets are not recommended for use on game animals.

From: $27.00–$39.00

Speer Bullets

GRAND SLAM

Caliber & Description	6mm SP	25 HCSP	270 HCSP	270 HCSP	7mm HCSP	7mm HCSP	7mm HCSP	30 HCSP	30 HCSP	30 HCSP	338 HCSP	375 HCSP
Diameter, Inches	.243	.257	.277	.277	.284	.284	.284	.308	.308	.308	.338	.375
Weight, Grains	100	120	130	150	145	160	175	150	165	180	250	285
Density	.242	.260	.242	.279	.257	.283	.310	.226	.248	.271	.313	.290
Ballistic Coefficient	.327	.356	.332	.378	.353	.389	.436	.295	.354	.374	.436	.354
Catalog Number	1222	1415	1465	1608	1632	1638	1643	2026	2038	2063	2408	2473

From: $31.00–$66.00

HOT-COR BULLETS*

Caliber & Description	6mm SSP	25 SPFN	25 SSP	25 SSP	25 SSP	6.5mm SSP	6.5mm SSP	270 SSP	270 SSP	7mm SSP	7mm SPFN	7mm SSP
Diameter, Inches	.243	.257	.257	.257	.257	.264	.264	.277	.277	.284	.284	.284
Weight, Grains	90	75	87	100	120	120	140	130	150	130	130	145
Density	.218	.162	.188	.216	.260	.246	.287	.242	.279	.230	.230	.257
Ballistic Coefficient	.365	.135	.300	.334	.405	.392	.498	.383	.455	.394	.257	.416
Catalog Number	1217	1237	1241	1405	1411	1435	1441	1459	1605	1623	1625	1629

* Not recommended for lever-action rifles.

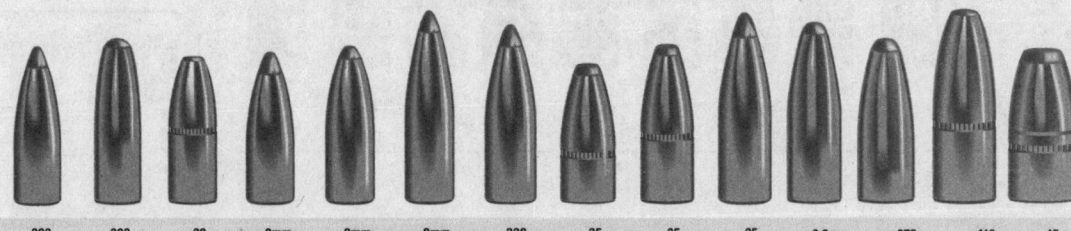

Caliber & Description	7mm SSP	30 Spire SP	30 FNSP	30 SPFN	30 RNSP	30 SSP	30 Mag-Tip	30 SSP	30 SSP	30 SPRN	30 SSP	30 SSP	7.62x39 SSP
Diameter, Inches	.284	.308	.308	.308	.308	.308	.308	.308	.308	.308	.308	.308	.310
Weight, Grains	160	110	130	150	150	150	150	165	170	180	180	200	123
Density	.283	.166	.196	.226	.226	.226	.226	.248	.256	.271	.271	.301	.183
Ballistic Coefficient	.504	.245	.213	.255	.235	.377	.301	.444	.298	.304	.441	.478	.283
Catalog Number	1635	1855	2007	2011	2017	2023	2025	2035	2041	2047	2053	2211	2213

* Not recommended for lever-action rifles.

Caliber & Description	303 SSP	303 RNSP	32 FNSP	8mm SSP	8mm SSSP	8mm SSP	338 SSP	35 FNSP	35 FNSP	35 SSP	9.3mm SSSP	375 SSSP	416 Mag-Tip	45 FNSP
Diameter, Inches	.311	.311	.321	.323	.323	.323	.338	.358	.358	.358	.366	.375	.416	.458
Weight, Grains	150	180	170	150	170	200	200	180	220	250	270	235	350	350
Density	.222	.266	.236	.205	.233	.274	.250	.201	.245	.279	.288	.239	.289	.238
Ballistic Coefficient	.351	.299	.283	.343	.311	.440	.426	.236	.286	.422	.361	.301	.332	.218
Catalog Number	2217	2223	2259	2277	2283	2285	2405	2435	2439	2453	2459	2471	2477	2478

From: $20.00–$44.00

AMMUNITION

Speer Bullets

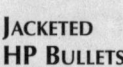

Jacketed HP Bullets

Caliber & Description	22 Hornet	45
Diameter, Inches	.224	.458
Weight, Grains	33	300
Density	.094	.204
Ballistic Coefficient	.080	.206
Catalog Number	1014	2482

From: $21.00–$36.00

Special Purpose Bullets*

Caliber & Description	30 SPRN	30 HP	45 SPFN
Diameter, Inches	.308	.308	.458
Weight, Grains	100	110	400
Density	.151	.166	.272
Ballistic Coefficient	.144	.128	.259
Catalog Number	1805	1835	2479

From: $20.00–$34.00

TNT Bullets

Caliber & Description	204 HP	22 HP	22 HP	6mm HP	25 HP	6.5mm HP	270 HP	7mm HP	30 HP
Diameter, Inches	.204	.224	.224	.243	.247	.264	.277	.284	.308
Weight, Grains	39	50	55	70	87	90	90	110	125
Density	.134	.142	.157	.169	.188	.184	.168	.195	.188
Ballistic Coefficient	.202	.228	.233	.279	.337	.281	.303	.384	.341
Catalog Number	1015	1030	1032	1206	1246	1445	1446	1616	1986

From: $20.00–$33.00

Handgun Bullets

Gold Dot Bullets

Caliber & Description	25 HP	32 Auto HP	327 Fed. Mag. HP	327 Fed. Mag. HP	380 Auto HP	9mm HP	9mm HP	9mm HP	357 SIG HP	38 Spl. HPSB	38 HPSB	357 Mag. HP	40/10mm HP
Diameter, Inches	.251	.312	.312	.312	.355	.355	.355	.355	.355	.357	.357	.357	.400
Weight, Grains	35	60	100	115	90	115	124	147	125	110	135	125	155
Density	.079	.088	.147	.168	.102	.130	.141	.167	.142	.123	.151	.177	.138
Ballistic Coefficient	.091	.118	.137	.180	.101	.125	.134	.164	.141	.117	.141	.140	.123
Catalog Number	3985	3986	3990	3988	3992	3994	3998	4002	4360	4009	4014	4012	4400

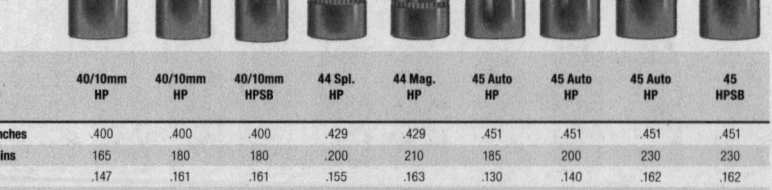

Caliber & Description	40/10mm HP	40/10mm HP	40/10mm HPSB	44 Spl. HP	44 Mag. HP	45 Auto HP	45 Auto HP	45 Auto HP	45 HPSB
Diameter, Inches	.400	.400	.400	.429	.429	.451	.451	.451	.451
Weight, Grains	165	180	180	200	210	185	200	230	230
Density	.147	.161	.161	.155	.163	.130	.140	.162	.162
Ballistic Coefficient	.138	.143	.148	.145	.154	.109	.138	.143	.148
Catalog Number	4397	4406	4401	4427	4428	4470	4478	4483	4482

From: $22.00–$36.00

LEGEND

BT	– Boat Tail	S	– Spitzer
FB	– Fusion Bonded	SS	– Semi-Spitzer
FMJ	– Full Metal Jacket	SB	– For Short-Barrel Firearms
FN	– Flat Nose		
GD	– Gold Dot	SP	– Soft Point
HC	– Hot-Cor	TMJ	– Encased-Core Full Jacket
HP	– Hollow Point		
L	– Lead	RN	– Round Nose
MHP	– Molybdenum Disulfide Impregnated	SWC	– Semi-Wadcutter
		UC	– Uni-Cor
		WC	– Wadcutter

AMMUNITION

Speer Bullets

Jacketed Bullets

Caliber & Description	9mm Luger FN JSP	38 Spl./357 Mag. JHP	38 Spl./357 Mag. JSP	38 Spl./357 Mag. JHP	38 Spl./357 Mag. JHP	38 Spl./357 Mag. JHP	38 Spl./357 Mag. JSP
Diameter, Inches	.355	.357	.357	.357	.357	.357	.357
Weight, Grains	124	110	125	125	140	158	158
Density	.141	.123	.140	.140	.157	.177	.177
Ballistic Coefficient	.115	.113	.129	.129	.145	.163	.164
Catalog Number	3997	4007	4011	4013	4203	4211	4217

Caliber & Description	44 Mag. JSP	44 Mag. JSP	45 Colt/460 S&W JHP	45 Colt/460 S&W JSP	50 Action Express JHP
Diameter, Inches	.429	.429	.451	.451	.186
Weight, Grains	240	300	260	300	325
Density	.186	.233	.183	.211	.186
Ballistic Coefficient	.169	.213	.183	.199	.169
Catalog Number	4454	4463	4481	4485	4495

From: $18–$31

LEGEND

FN	– Flat Nose	S	– Spitzer
HB	– Hollow Base	SP	– Soft Point
HC	– Hot-Cor	SS	– Semi-Spitzer
HP	– Hollow Point	SWC	– Semi-Wadcutter
J	– Jacketed	WC	– Wadcutter
RN	– Round Nose		

Lead Handgun Bullets

Caliber & Description	32 S&W HBWC	9mm Luger RN	38 HBWC	38 SWC	38 SWC HP	38 RN	44 SWC	45 Auto SWC	45 Auto RN	45 Colt SWC
Diameter, Inches	.314	.356	.358	.358	.358	.358	.430	.452	.452	.452
Weight, grains	98	125	148	158	158	158	240	200	230	250
Density	.142	.141	.165	.176	.176	.176	.185	.140	.161	.175
Ballistic Coefficient	.044	.155	.050	.123	.121	.170	.151	.078	.160	.117
Bulk Part No.	4600	4602	4618	4624	4628	4648	4661	4678	4691	4684
Bulk Count	1000	500	500	500	500	500	500	500	500	500

From: $46.00–$84.00

AMMUNITION

Swift Bullet Company

Rifle Bullets

The Scirocco II rifle bullet starts with a tough, pointed polymer tip that reduces air resistance, prevents tip deformation, and blends into the radius of its secant ogive nose section.

The Scirocco II has a bonded core construction with a pure lead core encased in a tapered, progressively thickening jacket of pure copper. The Swift A-Frame bullet with its midsec-tion wall of copper is less aerodynamic than the Scirocco, but it produces a broad mushroom while carrying almost all its weight through muscle and bone.

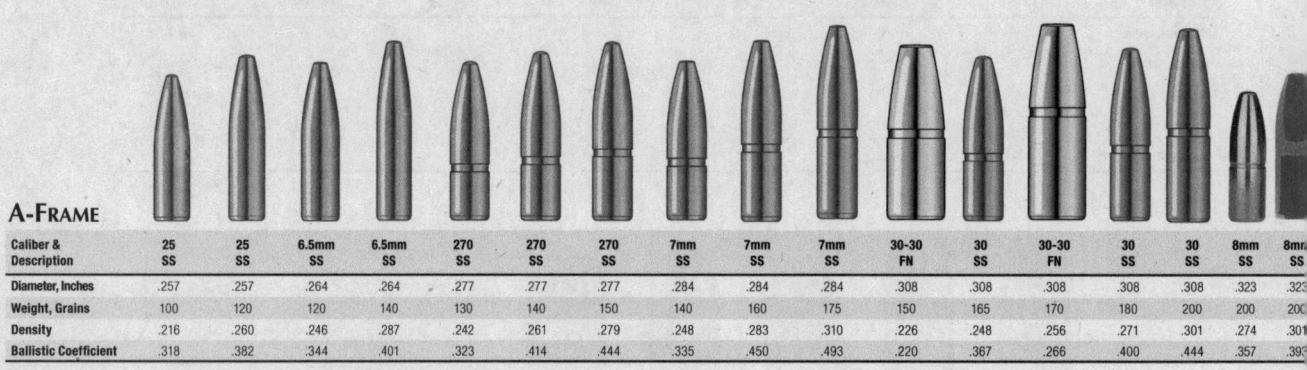

A-FRAME

Caliber & Description	25 SS	25 SS	6.5mm SS	6.5mm SS	270 SS	270 SS	270 SS	7mm SS	7mm SS	7mm SS	30-30 FN	30 SS	30-30 FN	30 SS	30 SS	8mm SS	8mm SS
Diameter, Inches	.257	.257	.264	.264	.277	.277	.277	.284	.284	.284	.308	.308	.308	.308	.308	.323	.323
Weight, Grains	100	120	120	140	130	140	150	140	160	175	150	165	170	180	200	200	200
Density	.216	.260	.246	.287	.242	.261	.279	.248	.283	.310	.226	.248	.256	.271	.301	.274	.301
Ballistic Coefficient	.318	.382	.344	.401	.323	.414	.444	.335	.450	.493	.220	.367	.266	.400	.444	.357	.393

Caliber & Description	338 SS	338 SS	338 SS	348 FN	35 SS	35 SS	35 SS	9.3mm SS	9.3mm SS	9.3mm SS	375 SS	375 SS	375 SS	400 SS	400 SS
Diameter, Inches	.338	.338	.338	.348	.358	.358	.358	.366	.366	.366	.375	.375	.375	.410	.410
Weight, Grains	225	250	275	200	225	250	280	250	286	300	250	270	300	350	400
Density	.281	.313	.344	.236	.251	.279	.312	.267	.305	.320	.254	.274	.305	.297	.339
Ballistic Coefficient	.384	.427	.469	.245	.312	.347	.388	.285	.385	.342	.271	.349	.325	.321	.367

LEGEND

Type of Bullet

BT	–	Boat Tail
CT	–	Combat Target
FMJ	–	Full Metal Jacket
FP	–	Flat Point
HB	–	Hollow Base
L	–	Lead
RN	–	Round Nose
SP	–	Spire Point
SX	–	Super Explosive
SWC	–	Semi-Wadcutter
WC	–	Wadcutter

AMMUNITION

Swift Bullet Company

Caliber & Description	416 SS	416 SS	404 SS	45-70 FN	458 FN	458 FN	458 SS	470 RN	505 RN	505 RN	50 FN	500 RN	500 RN
Diameter, Inches	.416	.416	.423	.457	.458	.458	.458	.475	.505	.505	.509	.509	.509
Weight, Grains	350	400	400	350	400	450	500	500	535	570	450	535	570
Density	.289	.330	.319	.238	.272	.307	.341	.329	.300	.319	.247	.294	.313
Ballistic Coefficient	.321	.367	.375	.172	.258	.325	.361	.364	.285	.306	.180	.285	.306

MSRP $55.00–$115.00

Scirocco

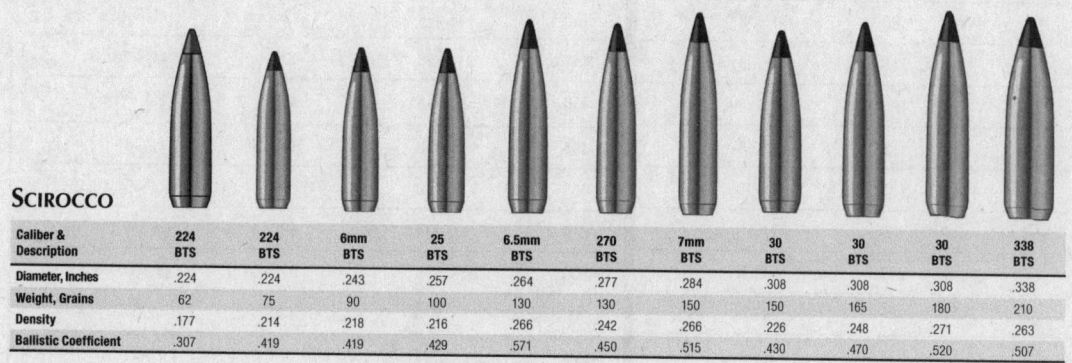

Caliber & Description	224 BTS	224 BTS	6mm BTS	25 BTS	6.5mm BTS	270 BTS	7mm BTS	30 BTS	30 BTS	30 BTS	338 BTS
Diameter, Inches	.224	.224	.243	.257	.264	.277	.284	.308	.308	.308	.338
Weight, Grains	62	75	90	100	130	130	150	150	165	180	210
Density	.177	.214	.218	.216	.266	.242	.266	.226	.248	.271	.263
Ballistic Coefficient	.307	.419	.419	.429	.571	.450	.515	.430	.470	.520	.507

MSRP $52.00–$69.00

LEGEND
BT – Boattail
FN – Flat Nose
HP – Hollow Point
RN – Round Nose
S – Spitzer
SS – Semi-Spitzer

Handgun Bullets

A-Frame Hunting Revolver Bullets

Caliber & Description	357 HP	357 HP	41 HP	44 HP	44 HP	44 HP	45 HP	45 HP	45 HP	50 HP
Diameter, Inches	.357	.357	.410	.430	.430	.430	.452	.452	.452	.499
Weight, Grains	158	180	210	240	280	300	265	300	325	325
Density	.177	.202	.178	.185	.216	.232	.185	.210	.227	.186
Ballistic Coefficient	.183	.189	.159	.119	.139	.147	.129	.153	.171	.135

MSRP $54.00

LEGEND
BT – Boattail
FN – Flat Nose
HP – Hollow Point
RN – Round Nose
S – Spitzer
SS – Semi-Spitzer

Woodleigh Bullets

HYDROSTATICALLY STABILIZED

Hydrostatic stabilization is a method of producing pierced hollow bars to very precise concentricity to produce a bullet that resists deflection and achieves deep straight-line penetration. It's non-toxic and environmentally sensitive. It can be used in most nitro double and magazine rifles.

10–20 per box: $31.00–$80.00

Caliber	Diameter	"Weight, Grains"	Catalog Number
7mm	.284	140	H7mm
308	.308	150	H308A
308	.308	180	H308
303	.312	215	H303
8mm	.323	170	H8mm
338	.338	185	H338A
338	.338	225	H338
358	.358	225	H358
9.3	.366	232	H9.3A
9,3	.366	286	H9.3
375 Win.	.375	235	H375A
375	.375	300	H375
450/400 3"	.410	400	H450/400

Caliber	Diameter	"Weight, Grains"	Catalog Number
416	.416	400	H416
404 Jeffery	.422	400	H404
450	.458	325	H450BPE
45/70	.458	400	H45/70
458	.458	450	H458A
458	.458	480	H458
465	.468	480	H465
470	.474	500	H470
500	.510	570	H500
50 Alaskan	.510	400	H50 Alaskan
505	.505	525	H505
577	.585	750	H577

98% & 95% RETAINED WEIGHT 300 WIN MAG 180GR PP

458 X 500GN SN RECOVERED FROM BUFFALO

270 WIN 150GN PP 86% RETAINED WEIGHT

94% RETAINED WEIGHT 300 WIN MAG 180GR PP

500/465 RECOVERED FROM BUFFALO

Woodleigh Bullets

TRADITIONAL BULLETS

Fashioned from gilding-metal-clad steel 2mm thick, jackets on FMJ bullets are heavy at the nose for extra impact resistance. The jacket then tapers toward the base to assist rifling engraving. Woodleigh Weldcore Soft Nose bullets are made from 90/100 gilding metal (90 percent copper; 10 percent zinc) 1.6 mm thick.

50 per box: $36.00–$86.00

Caliber Diameter	Type	Weight, Grains	SD	BC	Catalog Number
6.5mm .264	PP SN	140	.287	.444	80
	PP SN	160	.328	.509	80A
	RN SN	160	.328	.285	80B
270 Win. .277	PP SN	130	.242	.409	72
	PP SN	150	.279	.463	73
	PP SN	180	.334	.513	73A
7mm .284	PP SN	140	.248	.436	74
	PP SN	160	.283	.486	75
	PP SN	175	.310	.510	76
275 H&H .287	PP SN	160	.277	.474	77
	PP SN	175	.304	.509	78
308 .308	PP SN	130	.189	.302	65I
	PP SN	150	.226	.310	65F
	PP SN	165	.248	.320	65A
	PP SN	180	.271	.376	65B
	RN SN	220	.331	.367	65C
	FMJ	220	.331	.359	65
30-30 .308	FN SN	150	.226	.246	65H
30-06 .308	PP SN	240	.361	.401	65G
300 Win. Mag. .308	PP SN	180	.271	.435	65D
	PP SN	200	.301	.450	65E
303 British .312	PP SN	174	.255	.362	68A
	RN SN	215	.316	.359	68
303/ 7.62x39mm .312	PP SN	130	.180	.295	68B
8mm .323	RN SN	196	.268	.315	64B
	RN SN	220	.301	.355	64C
	RN SN	250	.343	.403	64D
325 Win. (8mm) .323	PP SN	200	.274	.406	64F
	PP SN	220	.301	.448	64G
8x57 .318	RN SN	200	.283	.331	64E
318 WR .330	RN SN	250	.328	.420	63
	FMJ	250	.328	.364	64
333 Jeffery .333	RN SN	250	.322	.335	60
	RN SN	300	.386	.418	61
	FMJ	300	.386	.418	62
338 Fed .338	PP SN	180	.226	.361	56C
	PP SN	200	.251	.401	56D
33 Win. .338	FN SN	200	.246	.234	56E
338 Mag .338	PP SN	225	.281	.425	56A
	RN SN	250	.313	.332	56
	PP SN	250	.313	.431	56B
	FMJ	250	.313	.326	57
	RN SN	300	.375	.416	58
	FMJ	300	.375	.414	59
348 Win. .348	FN SN	250	.295	.281	348

Caliber Diameter	Type	Weight, Grains	SD	BC	Catalog Number
358 .358	RN SN	225	.251	.263	51
	PP SN	225	.251	.372	51A
	FMJ	225	.251	.263	52
	RN SN	250	.279	.300	53
	PP SN	250	.279	.400	53A
	PP SN	275	.307	.450	53B
	RN SN	310	.346	.458	54
	FMJ	310	.346	.458	55
9.3 .366	RN SN	250	.267	.281	47A
	PP SN	250	.267	.381	47C
	RN SN	286	.305	.321	47
	PP SN	286	.305	.396	47B
	FMJ	286	.305	.305	48
	RN SN	320	.341	.359	49
	PP SN	320	.341	.457	49A
	FMJ	320	.341	.341	50
375 Mag. .375	PP SN	235	.239	.310	42A
	RN SN	270	.274	.250	42
	PP SN	270	.274	.370	43A
	RN SN	300	.305	.277	44HD
	RN SN	300	.305	.277	44
	PP SN	300	.305	.380	45A
	FMJ	300	.305	.275	46
	RN SN	350	.356	.321	46B
	RN SN	350	.356	.323	46BHD
	PP SN	350	.356	.400	46C
	FMJ	350	.356	.307	46D
400 Purdey .405	RN SN	230	.200	.181	81
450/400 Nitro .408	RN SN	400	.344	.307	40A
450/400 Nitro .411	RN SN	400	.338	.307	40
450/400 Ruger .410	RN SN	400	.338	.307	40B
450/400 Ruger .408	FMJ	400	.344	.300	41A
.410 Ruger	FMJ	400	.338	.300	41
405 Win. .412	RN SN	300	.252	.194	71
416 Rigby .416	PP SN	340	.281	.330	39
	RN SN	410	.338	.307	37A
	FMJ	410	.338	.300	38
	RN SN	450	.371	.338	37B
	FMJ	450	.371	.330	38B"
416 Rem. .416	RN SN	400	.330	.305	37C
	FMJ	400	.330	.300	38C
	RN SN	450	.371	.338	37N
	FMJ	450	.371	.330	38N
404 Jeffery .422	RN SN	350	.281	.293	35
	RN SN	400	.321	.335	33A
	FMJ	400	.321	.330	34
	RN SN	450	.361	.360	33B
	FMJ	450	.361	.355	34B
10.75x68mm .423	RN SN	347	.277	.290	36
	FMJ	347	.277	.288	36A
444 Marlin .430	FN SN	280	.216	.186	444

Woodleigh Bullets

Caliber Diameter	Type	Weight, Grains	SD	BC	Catalog Number
425 WR .435	RN SN	410	.310	.222	31
	FMJ	410	.310	.221	32
11.2 Schuler .440	RN SN	401	.296	.325	67
458 Mag. .458	PP SN	400	.272	.340	30
	RN SN	480	.327	.328	24A
	FMJ	480	.327	.325	25A
	RN SN	500	.341	.310	26
	PP SN	500	.341	.378	26A
	FMJ	500	.341	.310	28
	RN SN	550	.375	.340	27
	FMJ	550	.375	.326	29
450 BPE .458	RN SN	350	.238	.250	30A
45/70 .458	FN SN	405	.276	.204	30B
	FN SN	300	.205	.196	30C
450 Nitro .458	RN SN	480	.327	.328	24
	FMJ	480	.327	.325	25
465 Nitro .468	RN SN	480	.313	.334	22
	FMJ	480	.313	.330	23
470 Nitro .474	RN SN	500	.318	.374	20
	FMJ	500	.318	.370	21
476 WR .476	RN SN	520	.328	.385	18
	FMJ	520	.328	.380	19
475 No. 2 .483	RN SN	480	.294	.309	15
	FMJ	480	.294	.300	16
475 No. 2 Jeffery .488	RN SN	500	.300	.315	13
	FMJ	500	.300	.300	14

Caliber Diameter	Type	Weight, Grains	SD	BC	Catalog Number
500 S&W MAG .500	FN SN	400	.229	.182	83
505 Gibbs .505	RN SN	525	.294	.345	11
	FMJ	525	.294	.340	12
	PP SN	600	.336	.360	11A
	FMJ	600	.336	.360	12A
500 Jeffery .510	RN SN	535	.294	.350	9
	PP SN	535	.294	.310	9A
	FMJ	535	.294	.340	10
	PP SN	600	.330	.350	10B
	FMJ	600	.330	.355	10A
500 BP .510	RN SN	440	.242	.255	8
50 Alaskan & 50/110 Win. .510	FN SN	500	.275	.219	82
500 Nitro .510	RN SN	450	.247	.257	06A
	RN SN	570	.313	.368	6
	FMJ	570	.313	.350	7
577 BP Express .585	RN SN	650	.271	.292	5
577 Nitro .585	RN SN	650	.271	.292	3A
	RN SN	750	.313	.346	3
577 Nitro .584	FMJ	650	.272	.292	4A
	FMJ	750	.314	.351	4
600 Nitro .620	RN SN	900	.334	.371	1
	FMJ	900	.334	.334	2
700 Nitro .700	RN SN	1000	.292	.340	A
	FMJ	1000	.292	.340	B

AMMUNITION

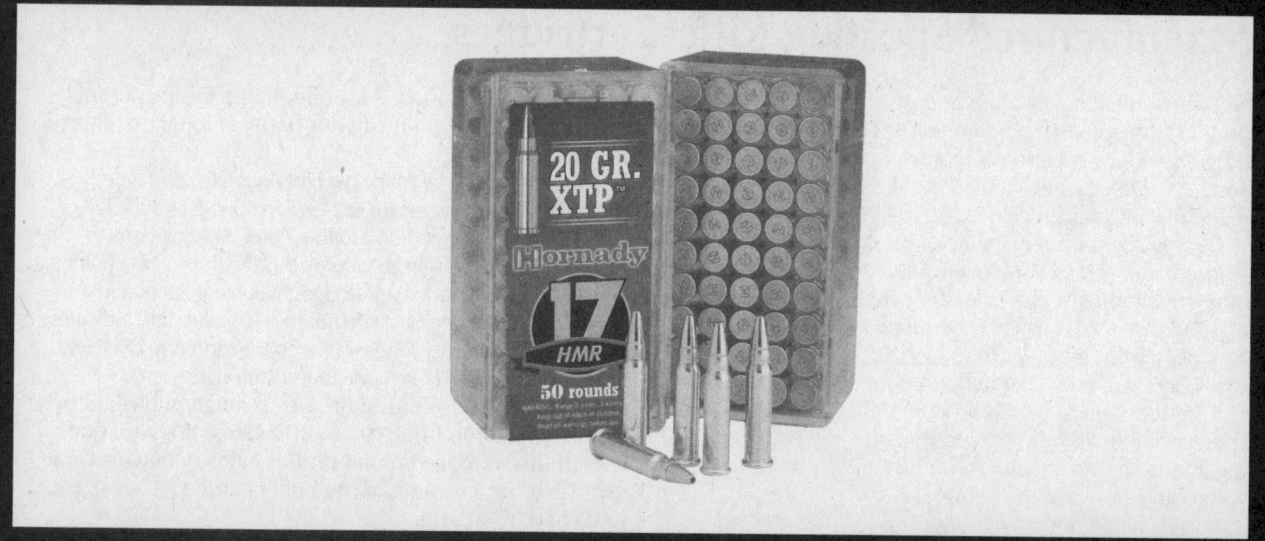

556 CENTERFIRE RIFLE BALLISTICS

590 LONG RANGE RIFLE

591 RIMFIRE BALLISTICS

593 CENTERFIRE HANDGUN BALLISTICS

Centerfire Rifle Ballistics
Comprehensive Ballistics Tables for Currently Manufactured Sporting Rifle Cartridges

No more collecting catalogs and peering at microscopic print to find out what ammunition is offered for a cartridge, and how it performs relative to other factory loads! *Shooter's Bible* has assembled the data for you, in easy-to-read tables, by cartridge.

Data is taken from manufacturers' charts; your chronograph readings may vary. Listings are not intended as recommendations. For example, the data for the .44 Magnum at 400 yards shows its effective range is much shorter. The lack of data for a 285-grain .375 H&H bullet beyond 300 yards does not mean the bullet has no authority farther out. Besides ammunition, the rifle, sights, conditions and shooter ability all must be considered when contemplating a long shot. Accuracy and bullet energy both matter when big game is in the offing.

Barrel length affects velocity, and at various rates depending on the load. As a rule, figure 50 fps per inch of barrel, plus or minus, if your barrel is longer or shorter than 22 inches.

Bullets are given by make, weight (in grains) and type. Most type abbreviations are self-explanatory: BT=Boat-Tail, FMJ=Full Metal Jacket, HP=Hollow Point, SP=Soft Point—except in Hornady listings, where SP is the firm's Spire Point. TNT and TXP are trademarked designations of Speer and Norma. XLC identifies a coated Barnes X bullet. HE indicates a Federal High Energy load, similar to the Hornady LM (Light Magnum) and HM (Heavy Magnum) cartridges.

Arc (trajectory) is based on a zero range published by the manufacturer, from 100 to 300 yards. If a zero does not fall in a yardage column, it lies halfway between—at 150 yards, for example, if the bullet's strike is "+" at 100 yards and "-" at 200.

.17 HORNET TO .222 REMINGTON

CARTRIDGE BULLET	RANGE, YARDS:	0	100	200	300	400
.17 HORNET						
Hornady 15.5 NXT SPF		0	100	200	300	400
	velocity, fps:	3860	2924	2159	1531	1108
	energy, ft-lb:	513	294	160	81	42
	arc, inches:	-1.5	+1.4	0	-9.1	-33.7
Hornady 20 V-MAX		0	100	200	300	400
	velocity, fps:	3650	3077	2574	2122	1721
	energy, ft-lb:	592	420	294	200	132
	arc, inches:	-1.5	+1.1	0	-6.4	-20.7
.17 REMINGTON						
Rem. 20 AccuTip BT	velocity, fps	4250	3594	3028	2529	2081
	energy, ft-lb:	802	574	407	284	192
	arc, inches:		+1.3	+1.3	-2.5	-11.8
Rem. 20 Fireball	velocity, fps	4000	3380	2840	2360	1930
	energy, ft-lb	710	507	358	247	165
	arc, inches		+1.6	+1.5	-2.8	-13.5
Rem. 25 HP Power-Lokt	velocity, fps	4040	3284	2644	2086	1606
	energy, ft-lb:	906	599	388	242	143
	arc, inches:		+1.8	0	-3.3	-16.6
.204 RUGER						
Federal 32 Nosler Ballistic Tip	velocity, fps	4030	3465	2968	2523	2119
	arc, inches		+0.7	0	-4.7	-14.9
Federal 40 Ballistic Tip	velocity, fps:	3650	3200	2790	2420	2080
	energy, ft-lb:	1185	910	695	520	385
	arc, inches:		+1.0	0	-5.4	-16.9
Hornady 32 V-Max	velocity, fps:	4225	3632	3114	2652	2234
	energy, ft-lb:	1268	937	689	500	355
	arc, inches:		+0.6	0	-4.2	-13.4
Hornady 40 V-Max	velocity, fps:	3900	3451	3046	2677	2335
	energy, ft-lb:	1351	1058	824	636	485
	arc, inches:		+0.7	0	-4.5	-13.9
Rem. 32 AccuTip	velocity, fps:	4225	3632	3114	2652	2234
	Energy, ft-lb:	1268	937	689	500	355
	Arc, inches:		+0.6	0	-4.1	-13.1
Rem. 40 AccuTip	velocity, fps:	3900	3451	3046	2677	2336
	energy, ft-lb:	1351	1058	824	636	485
	arc, inches:		+0.7	0	-4.3	-13.2
Win. 32 Ballistic Silver Tip	velocity, fps	4050	3482	2984	2537	2132
	energy, ft-lb	1165	862	632	457	323
	arc, inches		+0.7	0	-4.6	-14.7
Win. 34 HP	velocity, fps:	4025	3339	2751	2232	1775
	energy, ft-lb:	1223	842	571	376	238
	arc, inches:		+0.8	0	-5.5	-18.1

CARTRIDGE BULLET	RANGE, YARDS:	0	100	200	300	400
.218 BEE						
Win. 46 Hollow Point	velocity, fps:	2760	2102	1550	1155	961
	energy, ft-lb:	778	451	245	136	94
	arc, inches:		0	-7.2	-29.4	
.22 HORNET						
Federal 30 Speer TNT	velocity, fps:	3150	2150	1390	990	830
	energy, ft-lb:	660	310	130	65	45
	arc, inches:		+3.3	0	-22.8	-78.7
Federal 45 JSP	velocity, fps:	2690	2100	1590	1210	1000
	energy, ft-lb:	725	440	255	145	100
	arc, inches:		+3.3	0	-17.6	-59.5
Hornady 35 V-Max	velocity, fps:	3100	2278	1601	1135	929
	energy, ft-lb:	747	403	199	100	67
	arc, inches:		+2.8	0	-16.9	-60.4
Rem. 35 AccuTip	velocity, fps:	3100	2271	1591	1127	924
	energy, ft-lb:	747	401	197	99	66
	arc, inches:		+1.5	-3.5	-22.3	-68.4
Rem. 45 Pointed Soft Point	velocity, fps:	2690	2042	1502	1128	948
	energy, ft-lb:	723	417	225	127	90
	arc, inches:		0	-7.1	-30.0	
Rem. 45 Hollow Point	velocity, fps:	2690	2042	1502	1128	948
	energy, ft-lb:	723	417	225	127	90
	arc, inches:		0	-7.1	-30.0	
Win. 34 Jacketed HP	velocity, fps:	3050	2132	1415	1017	852
	energy, ft-lb:	700	343	151	78	55.
	arc, inches:		0	-6.6	-29.9	
Win. 45 Soft Point	velocity, fps:	2690	2042	1502	1128	948.
	energy, ft-lb:	723	417	225	127	90
	arc, inches:		0	-7.7	-31.3	
Win. 46 Hollow Point	velocity, fps:	2690	2042	1502	1128	948.
	energy, ft-lb:	739	426	230	130	92
	arc, inches:		0	-7.7	-31.3	
.221 REMINGTON FIREBALL						
Rem. 50 AccuTip BT	velocity, fps:	2995	2605	2247	1918	1622
	energy, ft-lb:	996	753	560	408	292
	arc, inches:		+1.8	0	-8.8	-27.1
.222 REMINGTON						
Federal 40 Ballistic Tip	velocity, fps:	3450	2990	2570	2190	1840
	energy, ft-lb:	1055	790	585	425	300
	arc, inches:		+1.2	0	-6.5	-20.4

CARTRIDGE BULLET	RANGE, YARDS:	0	100	200	300	400
Federal 43 Speer TNT	velocity, fps:	3400	2750	2180	1680	1290
	energy, ft-lb:	1105	720	450	270	160
	arc, inches:		+1.6	0	-9.2	-31.4
Federal 50 Hi-Shok	velocity, fps:	3140	2600	2120	1700	1350
	energy, ft-lb:	1095	750	500	320	200
	arc, inches:		+1.9	0	-9.7	-31.6
Federal 55 FMJ boat-tail	velocity, fps:	3020	2740	2480	2230	1990
	energy, ft-lb:	1115	915	750	610	484
	arc, inches:		+1.6	0	-7.3	-21.5
Hornady 40 V-Max	velocity, fps:	3600	3117	2673	2269	1911
	energy, ft-lb:	1151	863	634	457	324
	arc, inches:		+1.1	0	-6.1	-18.9
Hornady 50 V-Max	velocity, fps:	3140	2729	2352	2008	1710
	energy, ft-lb:	1094	827	614	448	325
	arc, inches:		+1.7	0	-7.9	-24.4
Norma 50 Soft Point	velocity, fps:	3199	2667	2193	1771	
	energy, ft-lb:	1136	790	534	348	
	arc, inches:		+1.7	0	-9.1	
Norma 50 FMJ	velocity, fps:	2789	2326	1910	1547	
	energy, ft-lb:	864	601	405	266	
	arc, inches:		+2.5	0	-12.2	
Norma 62 Soft Point	velocity, fps:	2887	2457	2067	1716	
	energy, ft-lb:	1148	831	588	405	
	arc, inches:		+2.1	0	-10.4	
PMC 50 Pointed Soft Point	velocity, fps:	3044	2727	2354	2012	1651
	energy, ft-lb:	1131	908	677	494	333
	arc, inches:		+1.6	0	-7.9	-24.5
PMC 55 Pointed Soft Point	velocity, fps:	2950	2594	2266	1966	1693
	energy, ft-lb:	1063	822	627	472	350
	arc, inches:		+1.9	0	-8.7	-26.3
Rem. 50 Pointed Soft Point	velocity, fps:	3140	2602	2123	1700	1350
	energy, ft-lb:	1094	752	500	321	202
	arc, inches:		+1.9	0	-9.7	-31.7
Rem. 50 HP Power-Lokt	velocity, fps:	3140	2635	2182	1777	1432
	energy, ft-lb:	1094	771	529	351	228
	arc, inches:		+1.8	0	-9.2	-29.6
Rem. 50 AccuTip BT	velocity, fps:	3140	2744	2380	2045	1740
	energy, ft-lb:	1094	836	629	464	336
	arc, inches:		+1.6	0	-7.8	-23.9
Win. 40 Ballistic Silvertip	velocity, fps:	3370	2915	2503	2127	1786
	energy, ft-lb:	1009	755	556	402	283
	arc, inches:		+1.3	0	-6.9	-21.5
Win. 50 Pointed Soft Point	velocity, fps:	3140	2602	2123	1700	1350
	energy, ft-lb:	1094	752	500	321	202
	arc, inches:		+2.2	0	-10.0	-32.3

.222 REMINGTON MAGNUM

CARTRIDGE BULLET	RANGE, YARDS:	0	100	200	300	400
Nosler 40 BT	velocity, fps:	3600	3140	2726	2347	2000
	energy, ft-lb:	1150	876	660	489	355
	arc, inches:	-1.5	+1.0	0	-5.7	-17.8
Nosler 50 BT	velocity, fps:	3340	2917	2533	2179	1855
	energy, ft-lb:	1238	945	712	527	382
	arc, inches:	-1.5	+1.3	0	-6.8	-20.9

.223 REMINGTON

CARTRIDGE BULLET	RANGE, YARDS:	0	100	200	300	400
Black Hills 36 Varmint Grenade	velocity, fps:	w3750				
	energy, ft-lb:	1124				
	arc, inches:					
Black Hills 40 Nosler B. Tip	velocity, fps:	3600				
	energy, ft-lb:	1150				
	arc, inches:					
Black Hills 50 V-Max	velocity, fps:	3300				
	energy, ft-lb:	1209				
	arc, inches:					
Black Hills 52 Match HP	velocity, fps:	3300				
	energy, ft-lb:	1237				
	arc, inches:					
Black Hills 55 Softpoint	velocity, fps:	3250				
	energy, ft-lb:	1270				
	arc, inches:					

CARTRIDGE BULLET	RANGE, YARDS:	0	100	200	300	400
Black Hills 55 TSX	velocity, fps:	3200				
	energy, ft-lb:	1250				
	arc, inches:					
Black Hills 60 SP or V-Max	velocity, fps:	3150				
	energy, ft-lb:	1322				
	arc, inches:					
Black Hills 60 Partition	velocity, fps:	3150				
	energy, ft-lb:	1322				
	arc, inches:					
Black Hills 62 TSX	velocity, fps:	3100				
	energy, ft-lb:	1323				
	arc, inches:					
Black Hills 68 Heavy Match	velocity, fps:	2850				
	energy, ft-lb:	1227				
	arc, inches:					
Black Hills 69 OTM	velocity, fps:	2875				
	energy, ft-lb:	1266				
	arc, inches:					
Black Hills 69 Sierra MK	velocity, fps:	2850				
	energy, ft-lb:	1245				
	arc, inches:					
Black Hills 73 Berger BTHP	velocity, fps:	2750				
	energy, ft-lb:	1226				
	arc, inches:					
Black Hills 75 Heavy Match	velocity, fps:	2750				
	energy, ft-lb:	1259				
	arc, inches:					
Black Hills 77 Sierra MKing	velocity, fps:	2750				
	energy, ft-lb:	1293				
	arc, inches:					
Black Hills 77 Tipped MatchKing	velocity, fps:	2750				
	energy, ft-lb:	1293				
	arc, inches:					
Federal 40 Ballistic Tip	velocity, fps:	3700	3210	2770	2370	2010
	energy, ft-lb:	1215	915	680	500	360
	arc, inches:		+0.9	0	-5.5	-17.3
Federal 43 Speer TNT	velocity, fps:	3600	2920	2330	1810	1390
	energy, ft-lb:	1235	810	515	315	185
	arc, inches:		+1.3	0	-7.9	-27.1
Federal 50 Jacketed HP	velocity, fps:	3400	2910	2460	2060	1700
	energy, ft-lb:	1285	940	675	470	320
	arc, inches:		+1.3	0	-7.1	-22.7
Federal 50 Speer TNT HP	velocity, fps:	3300	2860	2450	2080	1750
	energy, ft-lb:	1210	905	670	480	340
	arc, inches:		+1.4	0	-7.3	-22.6
Federal 52 Sierra MatchKing BTHP	velocity, fps:	3300	2860	2460	2090	1760
	energy, ft-lb:	1255	945	700	505	360
	arc, inches:		+1.4	0	-7.2	-22.4
Federal 55 Hi-Shok	velocity, fps:	3240	2750	2300	1910	1550
	energy, ft-lb:	1280	920	650	445	295
	arc, inches:		+1.6	0	-8.2	-26.1
Federal 55 FMJ boat-tail	velocity, fps:	3240	2950	2670	2410	2170
	energy, ft-lb:	1280	1060	875	710	575
	arc, inches:		+1.3	0	-6.1	-18.3
Federal 55 Sierra GameKing BTHP	velocity, fps:	3240	2770	2340	1950	1610
	energy, ft-lb:	1280	935	670	465	315
	arc, inches:		+1.5	0	-8.0	-25.3
Federal 55 Trophy Bonded	velocity, fps:	3100	2630	2210	1830	1500
	energy, ft-lb:	1175	845	595	410	275
	arc, inches:		+1.8	0	-8.9	-28.7
Federal 55 Nosler Bal. Tip	velocity, fps:	3240	2870	2530	2220	1920
	energy, ft-lb:	1280	1005	780	600	450
	arc, inches:		+1.4	0	-6.8	-20.8
Federal 55 Sierra BlitzKing	velocity, fps:	3240	2870	2520	2200	1910
	energy, ft-lb:	1280	1005	775	590	445
	arc, inches:		+-1.4	0	-6.9	-20.9

Centerfire Rifle Ballistics

.223 REMINGTON TO 5.6X52 R

BALLISTICS

CARTRIDGE BULLET	RANGE, YARDS:	0	100	200	300	400
Federal 60 Partition	velocity, fps:	3160	2740	2350	2000	1680
	energy, ft-lb:	1330	1000	735	530	375
	arc, inches:		+1.6	0	-7.9	-24.8
Federal 62 FMJ	velocity, fps:	3020	2650	2310	2000	1710
	energy, ft-lb:	1225	970	735	550	405
	arc, inches:		+1.7	0	-8.4	-25.5
Federal 64 Hi-Shok SP	velocity, fps:	3090	2690	2325	1990	1680
	energy, ft-lb:	1360	1030	770	560	400
	arc, inches:		+1.7	0	-8.2	-25.2
Federal 69 Sierra MatchKing BTHP	velocity, fps:	3000	2720	2460	2210	1980
	energy, ft-lb:	1380	1135	925	750	600
	arc, inches:		+1.6	0	-7.4	-21.9
Hornady 40 V-Max	velocity, fps:	3800	3305	2845	2424	2044
	energy, ft-lb:	1282	970	719	522	371
	arc, inches:		+0.8	0	-5.3	-16.6
Hornady 53 Hollow Point	velocity, fps:	3330	2882	2477	2106	1710
	energy, ft-lb:	1305	978	722	522	369
	arc, inches:		+1.7	0	-7.4	-22.7
Hornady 55 V-Max	velocity, fps:	3240	2859	2507	2181	1891
	energy, ft-lb:	1282	998	767	581	437
	arc, inches:		+1.4	0	-7.1	-21.4
Hornady 75 BTHP Superformance Match	velocity, fps:	2930	2695	2471	2259	2057
	energy, ft-lb:	1430	1209	1017	850	705
	arc, inches:		+1.7	0	-7.4	-21.6
Hornady 55 TAP-FPD	velocity, fps:	3240	2854	2500	2172	1871
	energy, ft-lb:	1282	995	763	576	427
	arc, inches:		+1.4	0	-7.0	-21.4
Hornady 55 Urban Tactical	velocity, fps:	2970	2626	2307	2011	1739
	energy, ft-lb:	1077	842	650	494	369
	arc, inches:		+1.5	0	-8.1	-24.9
Hornady 60 Soft Point	velocity, fps:	3150	2782	2442	2127	1837
	energy, ft-lb:	1322	1031	795	603	450
	arc, inches:		+1.6	0	-7.5	-22.5
Hornady 60 TAP-FPD	velocity, fps:	3115	2754	2420	2110	1824
	energy, ft-lb:	1293	1010	780	593	443
	arc, inches:		+1.6	0	-7.5	-22.9
Hornady 60 Urban Tactical	velocity, fps:	2950	2619	2312	2025	1762
	energy, ft-lb:	1160	914	712	546	413
	arc, inches:		+1.6	0	-8.1	-24.7
Hornady 75 BTHP Match	velocity, fps:	2790	2554	2330	2119	1926
	energy, ft-lb:	1296	1086	904	747	617
	arc, inches:		+2.4	0	-8.8	-25.1
Hornacy 75 TAP-FPD	velocity, fps:	2790	2582	2383	2193	2012
	energy, ft-lb:	1296	1110	946	801	674
	arc, inches:		+1.9	0	-8.0	-23.2
Hornady 75 BTHP Tactical	velocity, fps:	2630	2409	2199	2000	1814
	energy, ft-lb:	1152	966	805	666	548
	arc, inches:		+2.0	0	-9.2	-25.9
PMC 40 non-toxic	velocity, fps:	3500	2606	1871	1315	
	energy, ft-lb:	1088	603	311	154	
	arc, inches:		+2.6	0	-12.8	
PMC 50 Sierra BlitzKing	velocity, fps:	3300	2874	2484	2130	1809
	energy, ft-lb:	1209	917	685	504	363
	arc, inches:		+1.4	0	-7.1	-21.8
PMC 52 Sierra HPBT Match	velocity, fps:	3200	2808	2447	2117	1817
	energy, ft-lb:	1182	910	691	517	381
	arc, inches:		+1.5	0	-7.3	-22.5
PMC 53 Barnes XLC	velocity, fps:	3200	2815	2461	2136	1840
	energy, ft-lb:	1205	933	713	537	398
	arc, inches:		+1.5	0	-7.2	-22.2
PMC 55 HP boat-tail	velocity, fps:	3240	2717	2250	1832	1473
	energy, ft-lb:	1282	901	618	410	265
	arc, inches:		+1.6	0	-8.6	-27.7
PMC 55 FMJ boat-tail	velocity, fps:	3195	2882	2525	2169	1843
	energy, ft-lb:	1246	1014	779	574	415
	arc, inches:		+1.4	0	-6.8	-21.1
PMC 55 Pointed Soft Point	velocity, fps:	3112	2767	2421	2100	1806
	energy, ft-lb:	1182	935	715	539	398
	arc, inches:		+1.5	0	-7.5	-22.9

CARTRIDGE BULLET	RANGE, YARDS:	0	100	200	300	400
PMC 64 Pointed Soft Point	velocity, fps:	2775	2511	2261	2026	1806
	energy, ft-lb:	1094	896	726	583	464
	arc, inches:		+2.0	0	-8.8	-26.1
PMC 69 Sierra BTHP Match	velocity, fps:	2900	2591	2304	2038	1791
	energy, ft-lb:	1288	1029	813	636	492
	arc, inches:		+1.9	0	-8.4	-25.3
Rem. 50 AccuTip BT	velocity, fps:	3300	2889	2514	2168	1851
	energy, ft-lb:	1209	927	701	522	380
	arc, inches:		+1.4	0	-6.9	-21.2
Rem. 55 Pointed Soft Point	velocity, fps:	3240	2747	2304	1905	1554
	energy, ft-lb:	1282	921	648	443	295
	arc, inches:		+1.6	0	-8.2	-26.2
Rem. 55 HP Power-Lokt	velocity, fps:	3240	2773	2352	1969	1627
	energy, ft-lb:	1282	939	675	473	323
	arc, inches:		+1.5	0	-7.9	-24.8
Rem. 55 AccuTip BT	velocity, fps:	3240	2854	2500	2172	1871
	energy, ft-lb:	1282	995	763	576	427
	arc, inches:		+1.5	0	-7.1	-21.7
Rem. 55 Metal Case	velocity, fps:	3240	2759	2326	1933	1587
	energy, ft-lb:	1282	929	660	456	307
	arc, inches:		+1.6	0	-8.1	-25.5
Remington 62 Core-Lokt Ultra Bonded	velocity, fps:	3100	2695	2324	1983	1676
	energy, ft-lb:	1323	1000	743	541	386
	arc, inches:		+1.7			
Rem. 62 HP Match	velocity, fps:	3025	2572	2162	1792	1471
	energy, ft-lb:	1260	911	643	442	298
	arc, inches:		+1.9	0	-9.4	-29.9
Rem. 69 BTHP Match	velocity, fps:	3000	2720	2457	2209	1975
	energy, ft-lb:	1379	1133	925	747	598
	arc, inches:		+1.6	0	-7.4	-21.9
Win. 40 Ballistic Silvertip	velocity, fps:	3700	3166	2693	2265	1879.
	energy, ft-lb:	1216	891	644	456	314
	arc, inches:		+1.0	0	-5.8	-18.4
Win. 45 JHP	velocity, fps:	3600				
	energy, ft-lb:	1295				
	arc, inches:					
Win. 50 Ballistic Silvertip	velocity, fps:	3410	2982	2593	2235	1907.
	energy, ft-lb:	1291	987	746	555	404
	arc, inches:		+1.2	0	-6.4	-19.8
Win. 53 Hollow Point	velocity, fps:	3330	2882	2477	2106	1770
	energy, ft-lb:	1305	978	722	522	369
	arc, inches:		+1.7	0	-7.4	-22.7
Win. 55 Pointed Soft Point	velocity, fps:	3240	2747	2304	1905	1554.
	energy, ft-lb:	1282	921	648	443	295
	arc, inches:		+1.9	0	-8.5	-26.7
Win. 55 Super Clean NT	velocity, fps:	3150	2520	1970	1505	1165
	energy, ft-lb:	1212	776	474	277	166
	arc, inches:		+2.8	0	-11.9	-38.9
Win. 55 FMJ	velocity, fps:	3240	2854			
	energy, ft-lb:	1282	995			
	arc, inches:					
Win. 55 Ballistic Silvertip	velocity, fps:	3240	2871	2531	2215	1923
	energy, ft-lb:	1282	1006	782	599	451
	arc, inches:		+1.4	0	-6.8	-20.8
Win. 64 Power-Point	velocity, fps:	3020	2656	2320	2009	1724
	energy, ft-lb:	1296	1003	765	574	423
	arc, inches:		+1.7	0	-8.2	-25.1
Win. 64 Power-Point Plus	velocity, fps:	3090	2684	2312	1971	1664
	energy, ft-lb:	1357	1024	760	552	393
	arc, inches:		+1.7	0	-8.2	-25.4
Winchester 69 BTHP Match	velocity, fps:	3060	2740	2442	2163	1902
	energy, ft-lb:	1434	1150	913	716	554
	arc, inches:		+1.6	0	-7.4	-22.4

5.6x52 R

CARTRIDGE BULLET	RANGE, YARDS:	0	100	200	300	400
Norma 71 Soft Point	velocity, fps:	2789	2446	2128	1835	
	energy, ft-lb:	1227	944	714	531	
	arc, inches:		+2.1	0	-9.9	

.22 PPC

CARTRIDGE BULLET	RANGE, YARDS:	0	100	200	300	400
A-Square 52 Berger	velocity, fps:	3300	2952	2629	2329	2049
	energy, ft-lb:	1257	1006	798	626	485
	arc, inches:		+1.3	0	-6.3	-19.1

.225 WINCHESTER

CARTRIDGE BULLET	RANGE, YARDS:	0	100	200	300	400
Win. 55 Pointed Soft Point	velocity, fps:	3570	3066	2616	2208	1838.
	energy, ft-lb:	1556	1148	836	595	412
	arc, inches:		+2.4	+2.0	-3.5	-16.3

.224 WEATHERBY MAGNUM

CARTRIDGE BULLET	RANGE, YARDS:	0	100	200	300	400
Wby. 55 Pointed Expanding	velocity, fps:	3650	3192	2780	2403	2056
	energy, ft-lb:	1627	1244	944	705	516
	arc, inches:		+2.8	+3.7	0	-9.8

.22-250 REMINGTON

CARTRIDGE BULLET	RANGE, YARDS:	0	100	200	300	400
Black Hills 50 Nos. Bal. Tip	velocity, fps:	3700				
	energy, ft-lb:	1520				
	arc, inches:					
Black Hills 60 Nos. Partition	velocity, fps:	3550				
	energy, ft-lb:	1679				
	arc, inches:					
Federal 40 Nos. Bal. Tip	velocity, fps:	4150	3610	3130	2700	2300
	energy, ft-lb:	1530	1155	870	645	470
	arc, inches:		+0.6	0	-4.2	-13.2
Federal 40 Sierra Varminter	velocity, fps:	4000	3320	2720	2200	1740
	energy, ft-lb:	1420	980	660	430	265
	arc, inches:		+0.8	0	-5.6	-18.4
Federal 43 Speer TNT	velocity, fps:	4000	3250	2650	2070	1590
	energy, ft-lb:	1530	1010	655	405	240
	arc, inches:		+0.9	0	-6.1	-20.8
Federal 55 Hi-Shok	velocity, fps:	3680	3140	2660	2220	1830
	energy, ft-lb:	1655	1200	860	605	410
	arc, inches:		+1.0	0	-6.0	-19.1
Federal 55 Sierra BlitzKing	velocity, fps:	3680	3270	2890	2540	2220
	energy, ft-lb:	1655	1300	1020	790	605
	arc, inches:		+0.9	0	-5.1	-15.6
Federal 55 Sierra GameKing BTHP	velocity, fps:	3680	3280	2920	2590	2280
	energy, ft-lb:	1655	1315	1040	815	630
	arc, inches:		+0.9	0	-5.0	-15.1
Federal 55 Trophy Bonded	velocity, fps:	3600	3080	2610	2190	1810.
	energy, ft-lb:	1585	1155	835	590	400.
	arc, inches:		+1.1	0	-6.2	-19.8
Hornady 35 NTX Superformance Varmint	velocity, fps:	4450	3736	3128	2598	2125
	energy, ft-lb:	1539	1085	761	524	351
	arc, inches:		+0.5	0	-4.1	-13.4
Hornady 40 V-Max	velocity, fps:	4150	3631	3147	2699	2293
	energy, ft-lb:	1529	1171	879	647	467
	arc, inches:		+0.5	0	-4.2	-13.3
Hornady 50 V-Max	velocity, fps:	3800	3349	2925	2535	2178
	energy, ft-lb:	1603	1245	950	713	527
	arc, inches:		+0.8	0	-5.0	-15.6
Hornady 50 V-Max Superformance Varmint	velocity, fps:	4000	3517	3086	2696	2337
	energy, ft-lb:	1776	1373	1057	807	606
	arc, inches:		+0.7	0	-4.3	-13.5
Hornady 53 Hollow Point	velocity, fps:	3680	3185	2743	2341	1974.
	energy, ft-lb:	1594	1194	886	645	459
	arc, inches:		+1.0	0	-5.7	-17.8
Hornady 55 V-Max	velocity, fps:	3680	3265	2876	2517	2183
	energy, ft-lb:	1654	1302	1010	772	582
	arc, inches:		+0.9	0	-5.3	-16.1
Hornady 60 Soft Point	velocity, fps:	3600	3195	2826	2485	2169
	energy, ft-lb:	1727	1360	1064	823	627
	arc, inches:		+1.0	0	-5.4	-16.3

CARTRIDGE BULLET	RANGE, YARDS:	0	100	200	300	400
Norma 53 Soft Point	velocity, fps:	3707	3234	2809	1716	
	energy, ft-lb:	1618	1231	928	690	
	arc, inches:		+0.9	0	-5.3	
PMC 50 Sierra BlitzKing	velocity, fps:	3725	3264	2641	2455	2103
	energy, ft-lb:	1540	1183	896	669	491
	arc, inches:		+0.9	0	-5.2	-16.2
PMC 50 Barnes XLC	velocity, fps:	3725	3280	2871	2495	2152
	energy, ft-lb:	1540	1195	915	691	514.
	arc, inches:		+0.9	0	-5.1	-15.9.
PMC 55 HP boat-tail	velocity, fps:	3680	3104	2596	2141	1737
	energy, ft-lb:	1654	1176	823	560	368
	arc, inches:		+1.1	0	-6.3	-20.2
PMC 55 Pointed Soft Point	velocity, fps:	3586	3203	2852	2505	2178
	energy, ft-lb:	1570	1253	993	766	579
	arc, inches:		+1.0	0	-5.2	-16.0
Rem. 50 AccuTip BT (also in EtronX)	velocity, fps:	3725	3272	2864	2491	2147
	energy, ft-lb:	1540	1188	910	689	512
	arc, inches:		+1.7	+1.6	-2.8	-12.8
Rem. 55 Pointed Soft Point	velocity, fps:	3680	3137	2656	2222	1832
	energy, ft-lb:	1654	1201	861	603	410
	arc, inches:		+1.9	+1.8	-3.3	-15.5
Rem. 55 HP Power-Lokt	velocity, fps:	3680	3209	2785	2400	2046.
	energy, ft-lb:	1654	1257	947	703	511
	arc, inches:		+1.8	+1.7	-3.0	-13.7
Rem. 60 Nosler Partition (also in EtronX)	velocity, fps:	3500	3045	2634	2258	1914
	energy, ft-lb:	1632	1235	924	679	488
	arc, inches:		+2.1	+1.9	-3.4	-15.5
Win. 40 Ballistic Silvertip	velocity, fps:	4150	3591	3099	2658	2257
	energy, ft-lb:	1530	1146	853	628	453
	arc, inches:		+0.6	0	-4.2	-13.4
Win. 50 Ballistic Silvertip	velocity, fps:	3810	3341	2919	2536	2182
	energy, ft-lb:	1611	1239	946	714	529.
	arc, inches:		+0.8	0	-4.9	-15.2
Win. 55 Pointed Soft Point	velocity, fps:	3680	3137	2656	2222	1832
	energy, ft-lb:	1654	1201	861	603	410
	arc, inches:		+2.3	+1.9	-3.4	-15.9
Win. 55 Ballistic Silvertip	velocity, fps:	3680	3272	2900	2558	2240
	energy, ft-lb:	1654	1307	1027	799	613
	arc, inches:		+0.9	0	-5.0	-15.4
Win. 64 Power-Point	velocity, fps:	3500	3086	2708	2360	2038
	energy, ft-lb:	1741	1353	1042	791	590
	arc, inches:		+1.1	0	-5.9	-18.0

.220 SWIFT

CARTRIDGE BULLET	RANGE, YARDS:	0	100	200	300	400
Federal 52 Sierra MatchKing BTHP	velocity, fps:	3830	3370	2960	2600	2230
	energy, ft-lb:	1690	1310	1010	770	575
	arc, inches:		+0.8	0	-4.8	-14.9
Federal 55 Sierra BlitzKing	velocity, fps:	3800	3370	2990	2630	2310.
	energy, ft-lb:	1765	1390	1090	850	650
	arc, inches:		+0.8	0	-4.7	-14.4
Federal 55 Trophy Bonded	velocity, fps:	3700	3170	2690	2270	1880
	energy, ft-lb:	1670	1225	885	625	430
	arc, inches:		+1.0	0	-5.8	-18.5
Hornady 40 V-Max	velocity, fps:	4200	3678	3190	2739	2329
	energy, ft-lb:	1566	1201	904	666	482
	arc, inches:		+0.5	0	-4.0	-12.9
Hornady 50 V-Max	velocity, fps:	3850	3396	2970	2576	2215.
	energy, ft-lb:	1645	1280	979	736	545
	arc, inches:		+0.7	0	-4.8	-15.1
Hornady 50 SP	velocity, fps:	3850	3327	2862	2442	2060.
	energy, ft-lb:	1645	1228	909	662	471
	arc, inches:		+0.8	0	-5.1	-16.1
Hornady 55 V-Max	velocity, fps:	3680	3265	2876	2517	2183
	energy, ft-lb:	1654	1302	1010	772	582
	arc, inches:		+0.9	0	-5.3	-16.1
Hornady 60 Hollow Point	velocity, fps:	3600	3199	2824	2475	2156
	energy, ft-lb:	1727	1364	1063	816	619
	arc, inches:		+1.0	0	-5.4	-16.3
Norma 50 Soft Point	velocity, fps:	4019	3380	2826	2335	
	energy, ft-lb:	1794	1268	887	605	
	arc, inches:		+0.7	0	-5.1	

Centerfire Rifle Ballistics

.220 SWIFT TO .243 WINCHESTER

CARTRIDGE BULLET	RANGE, YARDS:	0	100	200	300	400
Rem. 50 Pointed Soft Point	velocity, fps:	3780	3158	2617	2135	1710
	energy, ft-lb:	1586	1107	760	506	325
	arc, inches:		+0.3		-1.4	-8.2
Rem. 50 V-Max boat-tail (also in EtronX)	velocity, fps:	3780	3321	2908	2532	2185
	energy, ft-lb:	1586	1224	939	711	530
	arc, inches:		+0.8	0	-5.0	-15.4
Win. 40 Ballistic Silvertip	velocity, fps:	4050	3518	3048	2624	2238
	energy, ft-lb:	1457	1099	825	611	445
	arc, inches:		+0.7	0	-4.4	-13.9
Win. 50 Pointed Soft Point	velocity, fps:	3870	3310	2816	2373	1972
	energy, ft-lb:	1663	1226	881	625	432
	arc, inches:		+0.8	0	-5.2	-16.7

.223 WSSM

CARTRIDGE BULLET	RANGE, YARDS:	0	100	200	300	400
Win. 55 Ballistic Silvertip	velocity, fps:	3850	3438	3064	2721	2402
	energy, ft-lb:	1810	1444	1147	904	704
	arc, inches:		+0.7	0	-4.4	-13.6
Win. 55 Pointed Softpoint	velocity, fps:	3850	3367	2934	2541	2181
	energy, ft-lb:	1810	1384	1051	789	581
	arc, inches:		+0.8	0	-4.9	-15.1
Win. 64 Power-Point	velocity, fps:	3600	3144	2732	2356	2011
	energy, ft-lb:	1841	1404	1061	789	574
	arc, inches:		+1.0	0	-5.7	-17.7

6MM PPC

CARTRIDGE BULLET	RANGE, YARDS:	0	100	200	300	400
A-Square 68 Berger	velocity, fps:	3100	2751	2428	2128	1850
	energy, ft-lb:	1451	1143	890	684	516
	arc, inches:		+1.5	0	-7.5	-22.6

6x70 R

CARTRIDGE BULLET	RANGE, YARDS:	0	100	200	300	400
Norma 95 Nosler Bal. Tip	velocity, fps:	2461	2231	2013	1809	
	energy, ft-lb:	1211	995	810	654	
	arc, inches:		+2.7	0	-11.3	

.243 WINCHESTER

CARTRIDGE BULLET	RANGE, YARDS:	0	100	200	300	400
Black Hills 55 Nosler B. Tip	velocity, fps:	3800				
	energy, ft-lb:	1763				
	arc, inches:					
Black Hills 95 Nosler B. Tip	velocity, fps:	2950				
	energy, ft-lb:	1836				
	arc, inches:					
Federal 70 Nosler Bal. Tip	velocity, fps:	3400	3070	2760	2470	2200
	energy, ft-lb:	1795	1465	1185	950	755.
	arc, inches:		+1.1	0	-5.7	-17.1
Federal 70 Speer TNT HP	velocity, fps:	3400	3040	2700	2390	2100
	energy, ft-lb:	1795	1435	1135	890	685
	arc, inches:		+1.1	0	-5.9	-18.0
Federal 80 Sierra Pro-Hunter	velocity, fps:	3350	2960	2590	2260	1950
	energy, ft-lb:	1995	1550	1195	905	675
	arc, inches:		+1.3	0	-6.4	-19.7
Federal 85 Sierra GameKing BTHP	velocity, fps:	3320	3070	2830	2600	2380
	energy, ft-lb:	2080	1770	1510	1280	1070
	arc, inches:		+1.1	0	-5.5	-16.1
Federal 85 Trophy Copper	velocity, fps:	3200	2950	2710	2480	2270
	energy, ft-lb:	1935	1640	1385	1160	970
	arc, inches:		+1.3	0	-6.0	-17.6
Federal 90 Trophy Bonded	velocity, fps:	3100	2850	2610	2380	2160.
	energy, ft-lb:	1920	1620	1360	1130	935
	arc, inches:		+1.4	0	-6.1	-19.2
Federal 100 Hi-Shok	velocity, fps:	2960	2700	2450	2220	1990
	energy, ft-lb:	1945	1615	1330	1090	880
	arc, inches:		+1.6	0	-7.5	-22.0
Federal 100 Sierra GameKing BTSP	velocity, fps:	2960	2760	2570	2380	2210
	energy, ft-lb:	1950	1690	1460	1260	1080
	arc, inches:		+1.5	0	-6.8	-19.8
Federal 100 Nosler Partition	velocity, fps:	2960	2730	2510	2300	2100
	energy, ft-lb:	1945	1650	1395	1170	975.
	arc, inches:		+1.6	0	-7.1	-20.9
Hornady 58 V-Max Superformance Varmint	velocity, fps:	3925	3465	3052	2676	2330
	energy, ft-lb:	1984	1546	1200	922	699
	arc, inches:		+0.7	0	-4.4	-13.8
Hornady 75 Hollow Point	velocity, fps:	3400	2970	2578	2219	1890
	energy, ft-lb:	1926	1469	1107	820	595
	arc, inches:		+1.2	0	-6.5	-20.3
Hornady 80 GMX Superformance	velocity, fps:	3425	3081	2763	2468	2190
	energy, ft-lb:	2084	1686	1357	1082	852
	arc, inches:		+1.1	0	-5.7	-17.1
Hornady 87 SST Custom Lite	velocity, fps:	2800	2574	2359	2155	1961
	energy, ft-lb:	1514	1280	1075	897	743
	arc, inches:		+1.9	0	-8.1	-23.8
Hornady 95 SST Superformance	velocity, fps:	3185	2908	2649	2404	2172
	energy, ft-lb:	2140	1784	1480	1219	995
	arc, inches:		+1.3	0	-6.3	-18.6
Hornady 100 BTSP	velocity, fps:	2960	2728	2508	2299	2099
	energy, ft-lb:	1945	1653	1397	1174	979
	arc, inches:		+1.6	0	-7.2	-21.0
Hornady 100 BTSP LM	velocity, fps:	3100	2839	2592	2358	2138
	energy, ft-lb:	2133	1790	1491	1235	1014
	arc, inches:		+1.5	0	-6.8	-19.8
Norma 80 FMJ	velocity, fps:	3117	2750	2412	2098	
	energy, ft-lb:	1726	1344	1034	782	
	arc, inches:		+1.5	0	-7.5	
Norma 100 FMJ	velocity, fps:	3018	2747	2493	2252	
	energy, ft-lb:	2023	1677	1380	1126	
	arc, inches:		+1.5	0	-7.1	
Norma 100 Soft Point	velocity, fps:	3018	2748	2493	2252	
	energy, ft-lb:	2023	1677	1380	1126	
	arc, inches:		+1.5	0	-7.1	
Norma 100 Oryx	velocity, fps:	3018	2653	2316	2004	
	energy, ft-lb:	2023	1563	1191	892	
	arc, inches:		+1.7	0	-8.3	
PMC 80 Pointed Soft Point	velocity, fps:	2940	2684	2444	2215	1999
	energy, ft-lb:	1535	1280	1060	871	709
	arc, inches:		+1.7	0	-7.5	-22.1
PMC 85 Barnes XLC	velocity, fps:	3250	3022	2805	2598	2401
	energy, ft-lb:	1993	1724	1485	1274	1088
	arc, inches:		+1.6	0	-5.6	16.3
PMC 85 HP boat-tail	velocity, fps:	3275	2922	2596	2292	2009
	energy, ft-lb:	2024	1611	1272	991	761
	arc, inches:		+1.3	0	-6.5	-19.7
PMC 100 Pointed Soft Point	velocity, fps:	2743	2507	2283	2070	1869
	energy, ft-lb:	1670	1395	1157	951	776
	arc, inches:		+2.0	0	-8.7	-25.5
PMC 100 SP boat-tail	velocity, fps:	2960	2742	2534	2335	2144
	energy, ft-lb:	1945	1669	1425	1210	1021
	arc, inches:		+1.6	0	-7.0	-20.5
Rem. 75 AccuTip BT	velocity, fps:	3375	3065	2775	2504	2248
	energy, ft-lb:	1897	1564	1282	1044	842
	arc, inches:		+2.0	+1.8	-3.0	-13.3
Remington 80 Copper Solid Tipped	velocity, fps:	3350	3011	2696	2403	2128
	energy, ft-lb:	1993	1610	1291	1025	894
	arc, inches:		+1.2	0	-6.1	-18.1
Rem. 80 Pointed Soft Point	velocity, fps:	3350	2955	2593	2259	1951
	energy, ft-lb:	1993	1551	1194	906	676
	arc, inches:		+2.2	+2.0	-3.5	-15.8
Rem. 80 HP Power-Lokt	velocity, fps:	3350	2955	2593	2259	1951
	energy, ft-lb:	1993	1551	1194	906	676
	arc, inches:		+2.2	+2.0	-3.5	-15.8
Rem. 90 Nosler Bal. Tip (also in EtronX) or Scirocco	velocity, fps:	3120	2871	2635	2411	2199
	energy, ft-lb:	1946	1647	1388	1162	966
	arc, inches:		+1.4	0	-6.4	-18.8
Rem. 95 AccuTip	velocity, fps:	3120	2847	2590	2347	2118
	energy, ft-lb:	2053	1710	1415	1162	946
	arc, inches:		+1.5	0	-6.6	-19.5
Rem. 100 PSP Core-Lokt (also in EtronX)	velocity, fps:	2960	2697	2449	2215	1993
	energy, ft-lb:	1945	1615	1332	1089	882
	arc, inches:		+1.6	0	-7.5	-22.1
Rem. 100 PSP boat-tail	velocity, fps:	2960	2720	2492	2275	2069
	energy, ft-lb:	1945	1642	1378	1149	950
	arc, inches:		+2.8	+2.3	-3.8	-16.6
Speer 100 Grand Slam	velocity, fps:	2950	2684	2434	2197	
	energy, ft-lb:	1932	1600	1315	1072	
	arc, inches:		+1.7	0	-7.6	-22.4

BALLISTICS

CARTRIDGE BULLET	RANGE, YARDS:	0	100	200	300	400
Win. 55 Ballistic Silvertip	velocity, fps:	4025	3597	3209	2853	2525
	energy, ft-lb:	1978	1579	1257	994	779
	arc, inches:		+0.6	0	-4.0	-12.2
Win. 80 Pointed Soft Point	velocity, fps:	3350	2955	2593	2259	1951.
	energy, ft-lb:	1993	1551	1194	906	676
	arc, inches:		+2.6	+2.1	-3.6	-16.2
Win. 95 Ballistic Silvertip	velocity, fps:	3100	2854	2626	2410	2203
	energy, ft-lb:	2021	1719	1455	1225	1024
	arc, inches:		+1.4	0	-6.4	-18.9
Win. 95 Supreme Elite XP3	velocity, fps	3100	2864	2641	2428	2225
	energy, ft-lb	2027	1730	1471	1243	1044
	a rc, inches		+1.4	0	-6.4	-18.7
Win. 100 Power-Point	velocity, fps:	2960	2697	2449	2215	1993
	energy, ft-lb:	1945	1615	1332	1089	882
	arc, inches:		+1.9	0	-7.8	-22.6.
Win. 100 Power-Point Plus	velocity, fps:	3090	2818	2562	2321	2092
	energy, ft-lb:	2121	1764	1458	1196	972
	arc, inches:		+1.4	0	-6.7	-20.0

6MM REMINGTON

CARTRIDGE BULLET		0	100	200	300	400
Federal 80 Sierra Pro-Hunter	velocity, fps:	3470	3060	2690	2350	2040
	energy, ft-lb:	2140	1665	1290	980	735
	arc, inches:		+1.1	0	-5.9	-18.2
Federal 100 Hi-Shok	velocity, fps:	3100	2830	2570	2330	2100
	energy, ft-lb:	2135	1775	1470	1205	985
	arc, inches:		+1.4	0	-6.7	-19.8
Federal 100 Nos. Partition	velocity, fps:	3100	2860	2640	2420	2220
	energy, ft-lb:	2135	1820	1545	1300	1090
	arc, inches:		+1.4	0	-6.3	-18.7
Hornady 95 SST Superformance	velocity, fps:	3235	2955	2693	2445	2211
	energy, ft-lb:	2207	1842	1530	1261	1031
	arc, inches:		+1.3	0	-6.1	-18.0
Hornady 100 SP boat-tail	velocity, fps:	3100	2861	2634	2419	2231
	energy, ft-lb:	2134	1818	1541	1300	1088
	arc, inches:		+1.3	0	-6.5	-18.9
Hornady 100 SPBT LM	velocity, fps:	3250	2997	2756	2528	2311
	energy, ft-lb:	2345	1995	1687	1418	1186
	arc, inches:		+1.6	0	-6.3	-18.2
Rem. 75 V-Max boat-tail	velocity, fps:	3400	3088	2797	2524	2267
	energy, ft-lb:	1925	1587	1303	1061	856
	arc, inches:		+1.9	+1.7	-3.0	-13.1
Rem. 100 PSP Core-Lokt	velocity, fps:	3100	2829	2573	2332	2104.
	energy, ft-lb:	2133	1777	1470	1207	983
	arc, inches:		+1.4	0	-6.7	-19.8
Rem. 100 PSP boat-tail	velocity, fps:	3100	2852	2617	2394	2183.
	energy, ft-lb:	2134	1806	1521	1273	1058
	arc, inches:		+1.4	0	-6.5	-19.1
Win. 100 Power-Point	velocity, fps:	3100	2829	2573	2332	2104
	energy, ft-lb:	2133	1777	1470	1207	983
	arc, inches:		+1.7	0	-7.0	-20.4

.243 WSSM

CARTRIDGE BULLET		0	100	200	300	400
Win. 55 Ballistic Silvertip	velocity, fps:	4060	3628	3237	2880	2550
	energy, ft-lb:	2013	1607	1280	1013	794
	arc, inches:		+0.6	0	-3.9	-12.0
Win. 95 Ballistic Silvertip	velocity, fps:	3250	3000	2763	2538	2325
	energy, ft-lb:	2258	1898	1610	1359	1140
	arc, inches:		+1.2	0	5.7	16.9
Win. 95 Supreme Elite XP3	velocity, fps	3150	2912	2686	2471	2266
	energy, ft-lb	2093	1788	1521	1287	1083
	arc, inches		+1.3	0	-6.1	-18.0
Win. 100 Power Point	velocity, fps:	3110	2838	2583	2341	2112
	energy, ft-lb:	2147	1789	1481	1217	991
	arc, inches:		+1.4	0	-6.6	-19.7

.240 WEATHERBY MAGNUM

CARTRIDGE BULLET	RANGE, YARDS:	0	100	200	300	400
Wby. 87 Pointed Expanding	velocity, fps:	3523	3199	2898	2617	2352
	energy, ft-lb:	2397	1977	1622	1323	1069
	arc, inches:		+2.7	+3.4	0	-8.4
Wby. 90 Barnes-X	velocity, fps:	3500	3222	2962	2717	2484
	energy, ft-lb:	2448	2075	1753	1475	1233
	arc, inches:		+2.6	+3.3	0	-8.0
Wby. 95 Nosler Bal. Tip	velocity, fps:	3420	3146	2888	2645	2414
	energy, ft-lb:	2467	2087	1759	1475	1229
	arc, inches:		+2.7	+3.5	0	-8.4
Wby. 100 Pointed Expanding	velocity, fps:	3406	3134	2878	2637	2408
	energy, ft-lb:	2576	2180	1839	1544	1287
	arc, inches:		+2.8	+3.5	0	-8.4
Wby. 100 Partition	velocity, fps:	3406	3136	2882	2642	2415
	energy, ft-lb:	2576	2183	1844	1550	1294
	arc, inches:		+2.8	+3.5	0	-8.4

.25-20 WINCHESTER

CARTRIDGE BULLET		0	100	200	300	400
Rem. 86 Soft Point	velocity, fps:	1460	1194	1030	931	858
	energy, ft-lb:	407	272	203	165	141
	arc, inches:		0	-22.9	-78.9	-173.0
Win. 86 Soft Point	velocity, fps:	1460	1194	1030	931	858.
	energy, ft-lb:	407	272	203	165	141
	arc, inches:		0	-23.5	-79.6	-175.9

.25-35 WINCHESTER

CARTRIDGE BULLET		0	100	200	300	400
Win. 117 Soft Point	velocity, fps:	2230	1866	1545	1282	1097
	energy, ft-lb:	1292	904	620	427	313
	arc, inches:		+2.1	-5.1	-27.0	-70.1

.250 SAVAGE

CARTRIDGE BULLET		0	100	200	300	400
Rem. 100 Pointed SP	velocity, fps:	2820	2504	2210	1936	1684.
	energy, ft-lb:	1765	1392	1084	832	630
	arc, inches:		+2.0	0	-9.2	-27.7
Win. 100 Silvertip	velocity, fps:	2820	2467	2140	1839	1569
	energy, ft-lb:	1765	1351	1017	751	547
	arc, inches:		+2.4	0	-10.1	-30.5

.257 ROBERTS

CARTRIDGE BULLET		0	100	200	300	400
Federal 120 Nosler Partition	velocity, fps:	2780	2560	2360	2160	1970
	energy, ft-lb:	2060	1750	1480	1240	1030
	arc, inches:		+1.9	0	-8.2	-24.0
Hornady 117 SP boat-tail	velocity, fps:	2780	2550	2331	2122	1925
	energy, ft-lb:	2007	1689	1411	1170	963
	arc, inches:		+1.9	0	-8.3	-24.4
Hornady 117 SP boat-tail LM	velocity, fps:	2940	2694	2460	2240	2031
	energy, ft-lb:	2245	1885	1572	1303	1071
	arc, inches:		+1.7	0	-7.6	-21.8
Hornady 117 SST Superformance	velocity, fps:	2946	2707	2480	2265	2060
	energy, ft-lb:	2255	1903	1598	1332	1102
	arc, inches:		+1.6	0	-7.3	-21.4
Rem. 117 SP Core-Lokt	velocity, fps:	2650	2291	1961	1663	1404
	energy, ft-lb:	1824	1363	999	718	512
	arc, inches:		+2.6	0	-11.7	-36.1
Win. 117 Power-Point	velocity, fps:	2780	2411	2071	1761	1488
	energy, ft-lb:	2009	1511	1115	806	576.
	arc, inches:		+2.6	0	-10.8	-33.0

.25-06 REMINGTON

CARTRIDGE BULLET		0	100	200	300	400
Black Hills 100 Nos. Bal. Tip	velocity, fps:	3200				
	energy, ft-lb:	2273				
Black Hills 100 Barnes XLC	velocity, fps:	3200				
	energy, ft-lb:	2273				
	arc, inches:					
Black Hills 115 Barnes X	velocity, fps:	2975				
	energy, ft-lb:	2259				
	arc, inches:					

Centerfire Rifle Ballistics

.25-06 REMINGTON TO 6.5X55 SWEDISH

CARTRIDGE BULLET	RANGE, YARDS:	0	100	200	300	400
Federal 90 Sierra Varminter	velocity, fps:	3440	3040	2680	2340	2030
	energy, ft-lb:	2365	1850	1435	1100	825
	arc, inches:		+1.1	0	-6.0	-18.3
Federal 100 Barnes XLC	velocity, fps:	3210	2970	2750	2540	2330
	energy, ft-lb:	2290	1965	1680	1430	1205
	arc, inches:		+1.2	0	-5.8	-17.0
Federal 100 Nosler Bal. Tip	velocity, fps:	3210	2960	2720	2490	2280
	energy, ft-lb:	2290	1940	1640	1380	1150.
	arc, inches:		+1.2	0	-6.0	-17.5
Federal 100 Trophy Copper	velocity, fps:	3210	2970	2740	2520	2310
	energy, ft-lb:	2290	1955	1665	1410	1185
	arc, inches:		+1.2	0	-5.9	-17.2
Federal 115 Nosler Partition	velocity, fps:	2990	2750	2520	2300	2100
	energy, ft-lb:	2285	1930	1620	1350	1120
	arc, inches:		+1.6	0	-7.0	-20.8
Federal 115 Trophy Bonded	velocity, fps:	2990	2740	2500	2270	2050
	energy, ft-lb:	2285	1910	1590	1310	1075
	arc, inches:		+1.6	0	-7.2	-21.1
Federal 117 Sierra Pro Hunt.	velocity, fps:	2990	2730	2480	2250	2030
	energy, ft-lb:	2320	1985	1645	1350	1100
	arc, inches:		+1.6	0	-7.2	-21.4
Federal 117 Sierra GameKing BTSP	velocity, fps:	2990	2770	2570	2370	2190
	energy, ft-lb:	2320	2000	1715	1465	1240
	arc, inches:		+1.5	0	-6.8	-19.9
Hornady 90 GMX Superformance	velocity, fps:	3350	3001	2679	2378	2098
	energy, ft-lb:	2243	1799	1434	1130	879
	arc, inches:		+1.2	0	-6.0	-18.3
Hornady 117 SP boat-tail	velocity, fps:	2990	2749	2520	2302	2096
	energy, ft-lb:	2322	1962	1649	1377	1141
	arc, inches:		+1.6	0	-7.0	-20.7
Hornady 117 SP boat-tail LM	velocity, fps:	3110	2855	2613	2384	2168
	energy, ft-lb:	2512	2117	1774	1476	1220
	arc, inches:		+1.8	0	-7.1	-20.3
Hornady 117 SST Superformance	velocity, fps:	3110	2862	2627	2405	2193
	energy, ft-lb:	2513	2127	1793	1502	1249
	arc, inches:		+1.4	0	-6.4	-18.9
PMC 100 SPBT	velocity, fps:	3200	2925	2650	2395	2145
	energy, ft-lb:	2273	1895	1561	1268	1019
	arc, inches:		+1.3	0	-6.3	-18.6
PMC 117 PSP	velocity, fps:	2950	2706	2472	2253	2047
	energy, ft-lb:	2261	1900	1588	1319	1088
	arc, inches:		+1.6	0	-7.3	-21.5
Rem. 100 PSP Core-Lokt	velocity, fps:	3230	2893	2580	2287	2014
	energy, ft-lb:	2316	1858	1478	1161	901
	arc, inches:		+1.3	0	-6.6	-19.8
Rem. 115 Core-Lokt Ultra	velocity, fps:	3000	2751	2516	2293	2081
	energy, ft-lb:	2298	1933	1616	1342	1106
	arc, inches:		+1.6	0	-7.1	-20.7
Rem. 120 PSP Core-Lokt	velocity, fps:	2990	2730	2484	2252	2032
	energy, ft-lb:	2382	1985	1644	1351	1100
	arc, inches:		+1.6	0	-7.2	-21.4
Speer 120 Grand Slam	velocity, fps:	3130	2835	2558	2298	
	energy, ft-lb:	2610	2141	1743	1407	
	arc, inches:		+1.4	0	-6.8	-20.1
Win. 85 Ballistic Silvertip	velocity, fps	3470	3156	2863	2589	2331
	energy, ft-lb:	2273	1880	1548	1266	1026
	arc, inches:		+1.0	0	-5.2	-15.7
Win. 90 Pos. Exp. Point	velocity, fps:	3440	3043	2680	2344	2034
	energy, ft-lb:	2364	1850	1435	1098	827
	arc, inches:		+2.4	+2.0	-3.4	-15.0
Win. 110 AccuBond CT	velocity, fps:	3100	2870	2651	2442	2243
	energy, ft-lb:	2347	2011	1716	1456	1228
	arc, inches:		+1.4	0	-6.3	-18.5
Win. 115 Ballistic Silvertip	velocity, fps:	3060	2825	2603	2390	2188
	energy, ft-lb:	2391	2038	1729	1459	1223
	arc, inches:		+1.4	0	-6.6	-19.2
Win. 120 Pos. Pt. Exp.	velocity, fps:	2990	2717	2459	2216	1987
	energy, ft-lb:	2382	1967	1612	1309	1053
	arc, inches:		+1.6	0	-7.4	-21.8

CARTRIDGE BULLET	RANGE, YARDS:	0	100	200	300	400
.25 WINCHESTER SUPER SHORT MAGNUM						
Win. 85 Ballistic Silvertip	velocity, fps:	3470	3156	2863	2589	2331
	energy, ft-lb:	2273	1880	1548	1266	1026
	arc, inches:		+1.0	0	-5.2	-15.7
Win. 110 AccuBond CT	velocity, fps:	3100	2870	2651	2442	2243.
	energy, ft-lb:	2347	2011	1716	1456	1228
	arc, inches:		+1.4	0	-6.3	-18.5
Win. 115 Ballistic Silvertip	velocity, fps:	3060	2844	2639	2442	2254
	energy, ft-lb:	2392	2066	1778	1523	1298
	arc, inches:		+1.4	0	-6.4	-18.6
Win. 120 Pos. Pt. Exp.	velocity, fps:	2990	2717	2459	2216	1987
	energy, ft-lb:	2383	1967	1612	1309	1053
	arc, inches:		+1.6	0	-7.4	-21.8
.257 WEATHERBY MAGNUM						
Federal 115 Nosler Partition 2220	velocity, fps:	3150	2900	2660	2440	
	energy, ft-lb:	2535	2145	1810	1515	1260
	arc, inches:		+1.3	0	-6.2	-18.4
Federal 115 Trophy Bonded	velocity, fps:	3150	2890	2640	2400	2180
	energy, ft-lb:	2535	2125	1775	1470	1210
	arc, inches:		+1.4	0	-6.3	-18.8
Wby. 87 Pointed Expanding	velocity, fps:	3825	3472	3147	2845	2563
	energy, ft-lb:	2826	2328	1913	1563	1269
	arc, inches:		+2.1	+2.8	0	-7.1
Wby. 100 Pointed Expanding	velocity, fps:	3602	3298	3016	2750	2500
	energy, ft-lb:	2881	2416	2019	1680	1388
	arc, inches:		+2.4	+3.1	0	-7.7
Wby. 115 Nosler Bal. Tip	velocity, fps:	3400	3170	2952	2745	2547
	energy, ft-lb:	2952	2566	2226	1924	1656.
	arc, inches:		+3.0	+3.5	0	-7.9
Wby. 115 Barnes X	velocity, fps:	3400	3158	2929	2711	2504
	energy, ft-lb:	2952	2546	2190	1877	1601
	arc, inches:		+2.7	+3.4	0	-8.1
Wby. 117 RN Expanding	velocity, fps:	3402	2984	2595	2240	1921
	energy, ft-lb:	3007	2320	1742	1302	956
	arc, inches:		+3.4	+4.31	0	-11.1
Wby. 120 Nosler Partition	velocity, fps:	3305	3046	2801	2570	2350
	energy, ft-lb:	2910	2472	2091	1760	1471
	arc, inches:		+3.0	+3.7	0	-8.9
6.53 (.257) SCRAMJET						
Lazzeroni 85 Nosler Bal. Tip	velocity, fps:	3960	3652	3365	3096	2844
	energy, ft-lb:	2961	2517	2137	1810	1526
	arc, inches:		+1.7	+2.4	0	-6.0
Lazzeroni 100 Nosler Part.	velocity, fps:	3740	3465	3208	2965	2735
	energy, ft-lb:	3106	2667	2285	1953	1661.
	arc, inches:		+2.1	+2.7	0	-6.7
6.5x50 JAPANESE						
Norma 156 Alaska	velocity, fps:	2067	1832	1615	1423	
	energy, ft-lb:	1480	1162	904	701	
	arc, inches:		+4.4	0	-17.8	
6.5x52 CARCANO						
Norma 156 Alaska	velocity, fps:	2428	2169	1926	1702	
	energy, ft-lb:	2043	1630	1286	1004	
	arc, inches:		+2.9	0	-12.3	
6.5x55 SWEDISH						
Federal 140 Hi-Shok	velocity, fps:	2600	2400	2220	2040	1860
	energy, ft-lb:	2100	1795	1525	1285	1080
	arc, inches:		+2.3	0	-9.4	-27.2

CARTRIDGE BULLET	RANGE, YARDS:	0	100	200	300	400
Federal 140 Trophy Bonded	velocity, fps:	2550	2350	2160	1980	1810
	energy, ft-lb:	2020	1720	1450	1220	1015
	arc, inches:		+2.4	0	-9.8	-28.4
Federal 140 Sierra MatchKg. BTHP	velocity, fps:	2630	2460	2300	2140	2000
	energy, ft-lb:	2140	1880	1640	1430	1235
	arc, inches:		+16.4	+28.8	+33.9	+31.8
Hornady 129 SP LM	velocity, fps:	2770	2561	2361	2171	1994
	energy, ft-lb:	2197	1878	1597	1350	1138
	arc, inches:		+2.0	0	-8.2	-23.2
Hornady 140 SP Interlock	velocity, fps	2525	2341	2165	1996	1836
	energy, ft-lb:	1982	1704	1457	1239	1048
	arc, inches:		+2.4	0	-9.9	-28.5
Hornady140 SP LM	velocity, fps:	2740	2541	2351	2169	1999
	energy, ft-lb:	2333	2006	1717	1463	1242
	arc, inches:		+2.4	0	-8.7	-24.0
Norma 120 Nosler Bal. Tip	velocity, fps:	2822	2609	2407	2213	
	energy, ft-lb:	2123	1815	1544	1305	
	arc, inches:		+1.8	0	-7.8	
Norma 139 Vulkan	velocity, fps:	2854	2569	2302	2051	
	energy, ft-lb:	2515	2038	1636	1298	
	arc, inches:		+1.8	0	-8.4	
Norma 140 Nosler Partition	velocity, fps:	2789	2592	2403	2223	
	energy, ft-lb:	2419	2089	1796	1536	
	arc, inches:		+1.8	0	-7.8	
Norma 156 TXP Swift A-Fr.	velocity, fps:	2526	2276	2040	1818	
	energy, ft-lb:	2196	1782	1432	1138	
	arc, inches:		+2.6	0	-10.9	
Norma 156 Alaska	velocity, fps:	2559	2245	1953	1687	
	energy, ft-lb:	2269	1746	1322	986	
	arc, inches:		+2.7	0	-11.9	
Norma 156 Vulkan	velocity, fps:	2644	2395	2159	1937	
	energy, ft-lb:	2422	1987	1616	1301	
	arc, inches:		+2.2	0	-9.7	
Norma 156 Oryx	velocity, fps:	2559	2308	2070	1848	
	energy, ft-lb:	2269	1845	1485	1183	
	arc, inches:		+2.5	0	-10.6	
PMC 139 Pointed Soft Point	velocity, fps:	2850	2560	2290	2030	1790
	energy, ft-lb:	2515	2025	1615	1270	985
	arc, inches:		+2.2	0	-8.9	-26.3
PMC 140 HP boat-tail	velocity, fps:	2560	2398	2243	2093	1949
	energy, ft-lb:	2037	1788	1563	1361	1181
	arc, inches:		+2.3	0	-9.2	-26.4
PMC 140 SP boat-tail	velocity, fps:	2560	2386	2218	2057	1903
	energy, ft-lb:	2037	1769	1529	1315	1126
	arc, inches:		+2.3	0	-9.4	-27.1
PMC 144 FMJ	velocity, fps:	2650	2370	2110	1870	1650
	energy, ft-lb:	2425	1950	1550	1215	945
	arc, inches:		+2.7	0	-10.5	-30.9
Rem. 140 PSP Core-Lokt	velocity, fps:	2550	2353	2164	1984	1814
	energy, ft-lb:	2021	1720	1456	1224	1023
	arc, inches:		+2.4	0	-9.8	-27.0
Speer 140 Grand Slam	velocity, fps:	2550	2318	2099	1892	
	energy, ft-lb:	2021	1670	1369	1112	
	arc, inches:		+2.5	0	-10.4	-30.6
Win. 140 Soft Point	velocity, fps:	2550	2359	2176	2002	1836
	energy, ft-lb:	2022	1731	1473	1246	1048.
	arc, inches:		+2.4	0	-9.7	-28.1

6.5 GRENDEL

CARTRIDGE BULLET	RANGE, YARDS:	0	100	200	300	400
Hornady 123 A-MAX	velocity, fps:	2590	2420	2256	2099	1948
	energy, ft-lb:	1832	1599	1390	1203	1037
	arc, inches:	-2.4	+1.8	0	-8.6	-25.1
Hornady 123 SST	velocity, fps:	2620	2449	2284	2126	1974

CARTRIDGE BULLET	RANGE, YARDS:	0	100	200	300	400
	energy, ft-lb:	1875	1638	1425	1234	1064
	arc, inches:	-2.4	+1.7	0	-8.4	-24.5

6.5 CREEDMOOR

CARTRIDGE BULLET	RANGE, YARDS:	0	100	200	300	400
Hornady 120 GMX	velocity, fps:	3050	2850	2659	2476	2300
	energy, ft-lb:	2479	2164	1884	1634	1410
	arc, inches:	-1.5	+1.4	0	-6.3	-18.3
Hornady 129 SST	velocity, fps:	2950	2756	2571	2394	2223
	energy, ft-lb:	2493	2176	1894	1641	1415
	arc, inches:	-1.5	+1.5	0	-6.8	-19.7
Hornady 140 A-MAX	velocity, fps:	2710	2557	2410	2267	2129
	energy, ft-lb:	2283	2033	1805	1598	1410
	arc, inches:	-1.5	+1.9	0	-7.9	-22.6
Nosler 140 BT	velocity, fps:	2550	2380	2217	2060	1910
	energy, ft-lb:	2021	1761	1527	1319	1134
	arc, inches:	-1.5	+2.3	0	-9.4	-27.0

.260 REMINGTON

CARTRIDGE BULLET	RANGE, YARDS:	0	100	200	300	400
Federal 140 Sierra GameKing BTSP	velocity, fps:	2750	2570	2390	2220	2060
	energy, ft-lb:	2350	2045	1775	1535	1315
	arc, inches:		+1.9	0	-8.0	-23.1
Federal 140 Trophy Bonded	velocity, fps:	2750	2540	2340	2150	1970
	energy, ft-lb:	2350	2010	1705	1440	1210
arc, inches:		+1.9	0	-8.4	-24.1	
Rem. 120 Nosler Bal. Tip	velocity, fps:	2890	2688	2494	2309	2131
	energy, ft-lb:	2226	1924	1657	1420	1210
	arc, inches:		+1.7	0	-7.3	-21.1
Rem. 120 AccuTip	velocity, fps:	2890	2697	2512	2334	2163
	energy, ft-lb:	2392	2083	1807	1560	1340
	arc, inches:		+1.6	0	-7.2	-20.7
Rem. 125 Nosler Partition	velocity, fps:	2875	2669	2473	2285	2105.
	energy, ft-lb:	2294	1977	1697	1449	1230
arc, inches:	+1.71	0	-7.4	-21.4		
Rem. 140 PSP Core-Lokt (and C-L Ultra)	velocity, fps:	2750	2544	2347	2158	1979
	energy, ft-lb:	2351	2011	1712	1448	1217
	arc, inches:		+1.9	0	-8.3	-24.0
Speer 140 Grand Slam	velocity, fps:	2750	2518	2297	2087	
	energy, ft-lb:	2351	1970	1640	1354	
	arc, inches:		+2.3	0	-8.9	-25.8

6.5-284

CARTRIDGE BULLET	RANGE, YARDS:	0	100	200	300	400
Norma 120 Nosler Bal. Tip	velocity, fps:	3117	2890	2674	2469	
	energy, ft-lb:	2589	2226	1906	1624	
	arc, inches:		+1.3	0	-6.2	
Norma 140 Nosler Part.	velocity, fps:	2953	2750	2557	2371	
	energy, ft-lb:	2712	2352	2032	1748	
	arc, inches:		+1.5	0	-6.8	

6.5-284 NORMA

CARTRIDGE BULLET	RANGE, YARDS:	0	100	200	300	400
Nosler 120 Ballistic Tip	velocity, fps:	3000	2792	2594	2404	2223
	energy, ft-lb:	2398	2077	1793	1540	1316
	arc, inches:	-1.5	+1.4	0	-6.6	-17.1
Nosler 125 PT	velocity, fps:	3000	2788	2585	2392	2207
	energy, ft-lb:	2497	2157	1855	1588	1352
	arc, inches:	-1.5	+1.5	0	-6.7	-19.5
Nosler 130 AccuBond	velocity, fps:	2900	2709	2526	2351	2182
	energy, ft-lb:	2427	2118	1842	1595	1374
	arc, inches:	-1.5	+1.5	0	-6.9	-18.4

6.5 REMINGTON MAGNUM

CARTRIDGE BULLET	RANGE, YARDS:	0	100	200	300	400
Nosler 125 PT	velocity, fps:	3025	2811	2608	2414	2228
	energy, ft-lb:	2539	2194	1888	1617	1377
	arc, inches:	-1.5	+1.5	0	-6.6	-19.1

Centerfire Rifle Ballistics

6.5 REMINGTON MAGNUM TO .270 WINCHESTER

CARTRIDGE BULLET	RANGE, YARDS:	0	100	200	300	400
Rem. 120 Core-Lokt PSP	velocity, fps:	3210	2905	2621	2353	2102
	energy, ft-lb:	2745	2248	1830	1475	1177
	arc, inches:		+2.7	+2.1	-3.5	-15.5

.264 WINCHESTER MAGNUM

CARTRIDGE BULLET	RANGE, YARDS:	0	100	200	300	400
Nosler 100 Ballistic Tip	velocity, fps:	3400	3105	2829	2569	2324
	energy, ft-lb:	2567	2141	1777	1465	1199
	arc, inches:	-1.5	+1.0	0	-5.5	-16.1
Nosler 130 AccuBond	velocity, fps:	3100	2900	2709	2527	2351
	energy, ft-lb:	2774	2428	2119	1843	1595
	arc, inches:	-1.5	+1.2	0	-6.0	-17.5
Rem. 140 PSP Core-Lokt	velocity, fps:	3030	2782	2548	2326	2114
	energy, ft-lb:	2854	2406	2018	1682	1389
	arc, inches:		+1.5	0	-6.9	-20.2
Win. 140 Power-Point	velocity, fps:	3030	2782	2548	2326	2114.
	energy, ft-lb:	2854	2406	2018	1682	1389
	arc, inches:		+1.8	0	-7.2	-20.8

6.8MM REMINGTON SPC

CARTRIDGE BULLET	RANGE, YARDS:	0	100	200	300	400
Hornady 110 BTHP	velocity, fps:	2570	2332	2107	1895	1697
(16-in. barrel)	energy, ft-lb:	1613	1328	1084	877	703
	arc, inches:	-2.4	+2.0	0	-9.9	-29.5
Hornady 120 SST	velocity, fps:	2460	2250	2051	1863	1687
(16-in. barrel)	energy, ft-lb:	1612	1349	1121	925	758
	arc, inches:	-2.4	+2.3	0	-10.5	-31.1
Rem. 115 Open Tip Match	velocity, fps:	2800	2535	2285	2049	1828
(and HPBT Match)	energy, ft-lb:	2002	1641	1333	1072	853
	arc, inches:		+2.0	0	-8.8	-26.2
Rem. 115 Metal Case	velocity, fps:	2800	2523	2262	2017	1789
	energy, ft-lb:	2002	1625	1307	1039	817
	arc, inches:		+2.0	0	-8.8	-26.2
Rem. 115 Sierra HPBT	velocity, fps:	2775	2511	2263	2028	1809
(2005; all vel. @ 2775)	energy, ft-lb:	1966	1610	1307	1050	835
	arc, inches:		+2.0	0	-8.8	-26.2.
Rem. 115 CL Ultra	velocity, fps:	2775	2472	2190	1926	1683
	energy, ft-lb:	1966	1561	1224	947	723
	arc, inches:		+2.1	0	-9.4	-28.2

.270 WINCHESTER

CARTRIDGE BULLET	RANGE, YARDS:	0	100	200	300	400
Black Hills 130 Nos. Bal. T.	velocity, fps:	2950				
	energy, ft-lb:	2512				
	arc, inches:					
Black Hills 130 Barnes XLC	velocity, ft-lb:	2950				
	energy, ft-lb:	2512				
	arc, inches:					
Federal 130 Barnes XLC	velocity, fps:	3060	2840	2620	2420	2220
And Triple Shock	energy, ft-lb:	2705	2320	1985	1690	1425
	arc, inches:		+1.4	0	-6.4	-18.9
Federal 130 Hi-Shok	velocity, fps:	3060	2800	2560	2330	2110
	energy, ft-lb:	2700	2265	1890	1565	1285
	arc, inches:		+1.5	0	-6.8	-20.0
Federal 130 Nosler Bal. Tip	velocity, fps:	3060	2840	2630	2430	2230
	energy, ft-lb:	2700	2325	1990	1700	1440
	arc, inches:		+1.4	0	-6.5	-18.8
Federal 130 Nos. Partition	velocity, fps:	3060	2830	2610	2400	2200
And Solid Base	energy, ft-lb:	2705	2310	1965	1665	1400
	arc, inches:		+1.4	0	-6.5	-19.1
Federal 130 Sierra GameKing	velocity, fps:	3060	2830	2620	2410	2220
	energy, ft-lb:	2700	2320	1980	1680	1420
	arc, inches:		+1.4	0	-6.5	-19.0
Federal 130 Sierra Pro-Hunt.	velocity, fps:	3060	2830	2600	2390	2190
	energy, ft-lb:	2705	2305	1960	1655	1390
	arc, inches:	+1.4	0	-6.4	-19.0	
Federal 130 Trophy Bonded	velocity, fps:	3060	2810	2570	2340	2130
	energy, ft-lb:	2705	2275	1905	1585	1310
	arc, inches:		+1.5	0	-6.7	-19.8
Federal 130 Trophy	velocity, fps:	3060	2840	2630	2430	2240
Bonded Tip	energy, ft-lb:	2705	2330	2000	1710	1455
	arc, inches:		+1.4	0	-6.4	-18.7
Federal 140 Trophy Bonded	velocity, fps:	2940	2700	2480	2260	2060
	energy, ft-lb:	2685	2270	1905	1590	1315
	arc, inches:		+1.6	0	-7.3	-21.5

CARTRIDGE BULLET	RANGE, YARDS:	0	100	200	300	400
Federal 140 Trophy	velocity, fps:	2950	2740	2550	2360	2180
Bonded Tip	energy, ft-lb:	2705	2340	2015	1730	1475
	arc, inches:		+1.6	0	-6.9	-20.1
Federal 140 Tr. Bonded HE	velocity, fps:	3100	2860	2620	2400	2200.
	energy, ft-lb:	2990	2535	2140	1795	1500
	arc, inches:		+1.4	0	-6.4	-18.9
Federal 140 Nos. AccuBond	velocity, fps:	2950	2760	2580	2400	2230.
	energy, ft-lb:	2705	2365	2060	1790	1545
	arc, inches:		+1.5	0	-6.7	-19.6
Federal 150 Hi-Shok RN	velocity, fps:	2850	2500	2180	1890	1620
	energy, ft-lb:	2705	2085	1585	1185	870
	arc, inches:		+2.0	0	-9.4	-28.6
Federal 150 Sierra GameKing	velocity, fps:	2850	2660	2480	2300	2130
	energy, ft-lb:	2705	2355	2040	1760	1510
	arc, inches:		+1.7	0	-7.4	-21.4
Federal 150 Sierra GameKing	velocity, fps:	3000	2800	2620	2430	2260
HE	energy, ft-lb:	2995	2615	2275	1975	1700
	arc, inches:		+1.5	0	-6.5	-18.9
Federal 150 Nosler Partition	velocity, fps:	2850	2590	2340	2100	1880.
	energy, ft-lb:	2705	2225	1815	1470	1175
	arc, inches:		+1.9	0	-8.3	-24.4
Hornady 120 SST Custom Lite	velocity, fps:	2675	2288	1935	1619	1351
	energy, ft-lb:	1907	1395	998	699	486
	arc, inches:		+2.6	0	-12.0	-37.4
Hornady 130 GMX	velocity, fps:	3190	2975	2770	2575	2387
Superformance	energy, ft-lb:	2937	2554	2215	1913	1645
	arc, inches:		+1.2	0	-5.7	-16.8
Hornady 130 SST	velocity, fps:	3060	2845	2639	2442	2254
(or Interbond)	energy, ft-lb:	2700	2335	2009	1721	1467
	arc, inches:		+1.4	0	-6.6	-19.1
Hornady 130 SST LM	velocity, fps:	3215	2998	2790	2590	2400
(or Interbond)	energy, ft-lb:	2983	2594	2246	1936	1662
	arc, inches:		+1.2	0	-5.8	-17.0
Hornady 130 SST	velocity, fps:	3200	2984	2779	2583	2396
Superformance	energy, ft-lb:	2956	2570	2229	1926	1656
	arc, inches:		+1.2	0	-5.7	-16.7
Hornady 140 SP boat-tail	velocity, fps:	2940	2747	2562	2385	2214
	energy, ft-lb:	2688	2346	2041	1769	1524
	arc, inches:		+1.6	0	-7.0	-20.2
Hornady 140 SP boat-tail LM	velocity, fps:	3100	2894	2697	2508	2327.
	energy, ft-lb:	2987	2604	2261	1955	1684
	arc, inches:		+1.4	0	6.3	-18.3
Hornady 140 SST	velocity, fps:	3090	2894	2707	2568	2355
Superformance	energy, ft-lb:	2968	2604	2278	1986	1724
	arc, inches:		+1.3	0	-6.1	-17.6
Hornady 150 SP	velocity, fps:	2800	2684	2478	2284	2100
	energy, ft-lb:	2802	2400	2046	1737	1469
	arc, inches:		+1.7	0	-7.4	-21.6
Norma 130 SP	velocity, fps:	3140	2862	2601	2354	
	energy, ft-lb:	2847	2365	1953	1600	
	arc, inches:		+1.3	0	-6.5	
Norma 130 FMJ	velocity, fps:	2887	2634	2395	2169	
	energy, ft-lb:					
	arc, inches:		+1.8	0	-7.8	
Norma 150 SP	velocity, fps:	2799	2555	2323	2104	
	energy, ft-lb:	2610	2175	1798	1475	
	arc, inches:		+1.9	0	-8.3	
Norma 150 Oryx	velocity, fps:	2854	2608	2376	2155	
	energy, ft-lb:	2714	2267	1880	1547	
	arc, inches:		+1.8	0	-8.0	
PMC 130 Barnes X	velocity, fps:	2910	2717	2533	2356	2186
	energy, ft-lb:	2444	2131	1852	1602	1379
	arc, inches:		+1.6	0	-7.1	-20.4
PMC 130 SP boat-tail	velocity, fps:	3050	2830	2620	2421	2229
	energy, ft-lb:	2685	2312	1982	1691	1435
	arc, inches:		+1.5	0	-6.5	-19.0
PMC 130 Pointed Soft Point	velocity, fps:	2950	2691	2447	2217	2001
	energy, ft-lb:	2512	2090	1728	1419	1156
	arc, inches:		+1.6	0	-7.5	-22.1
PMC 150 Barnes X	velocity, fps:	2700	2541	2387	2238	2095
	energy, ft-lb:	2428	2150	1897	1668	1461
	arc, inches:		+2.0	0	-8.1	-23.1

CARTRIDGE BULLET	RANGE, YARDS:	0	100	200	300	400
PMC 150 SP boat-tail	velocity, fps:	2850	2660	2477	2302	2134
	energy, ft-lb:	2705	2355	2043	1765	1516.
	arc, inches:		+1.7	0	-7.4	-21.4
PMC 150 Pointed Soft Point	velocity, fps:	2750	2530	2321	2123	1936
	energy, ft-lb:	2519	2131	1794	1501	1248
	arc, inches:		+2.0	0	-8.4	-24.6
Rem. 100 Pointed Soft Point	velocity, fps:	3320	2924	2561	2225	1916
	energy, ft-lb:	2448	1898	1456	1099	815
	arc, inches:		+2.3	+2.0	-3.6	-16.2
Rem. 115 PSP Core-Lokt mr	velocity, fps:	2710	2412	2133	1873	1636
	energy, ft-lb:	1875	1485	1161	896	683
	arc, inches:		+1.0	-2.7	-14.2	-35.6
Rem. 130 PSP Core-Lokt	velocity, fps:	3060	2776	2510	2259	2022
	energy, ft-lb:	2702	2225	1818	1472	1180
	arc, inches:		+1.5	0	-7.0	-20.9
Rem. 130 Bronze Point	velocity, fps:	3060	2802	2559	2329	2110
	energy, ft-lb:	2702	2267	1890	1565	1285
	arc, inches:		+1.5	0	-6.8	-20.0
Rem. 130 Swift Scirocco	velocity, fps:	3060	2838	2677	2425	2232
	energy, ft-lb:	2702	2325	1991	1697	1438
	arc, inches:		+1.4	0	-6.5	-18.8
Rem. 130 AccuTip BT	velocity, fps:	3060	2845	2639	2442	2254
	energy, ft-lb:	2702	2336	2009	1721	1467
	arc, inches:		+1.4	0	-6.4	-18.6
Rem. 140 Swift A-Frame	velocity, fps:	2925	2652	2394	2152	1923
	energy, ft-lb:	2659	2186	1782	1439	1150
	arc, inches:		+1.7	0	-7.8	-23.2
Rem. 140 PSP boat-tail	velocity, fps:	2960	2749	2548	2355	2171
	energy, ft-lb:	2723	2349	2018	1724	1465
	arc, inches:		+1.6	0	-6.9	-20.1
Rem. 140 Nosler Bal. Tip	velocity, fps:	2960	2754	2557	2366	2187
	energy, ft-lb:	2724	2358	2032	1743	1487
	arc, inches:		+1.6	0	-6.9	-20.0
Rem. 140 PSP C-L Ultra	velocity, fps:	2925	2667	2424	2193	1975
	energy, ft-lb:	2659	2211	1826	1495	1212
	arc, inches:		+1.7	0	-7.6	-22.5
Rem. 150 SP Core-Lokt	velocity, fps:	2850	2504	2183	1886	1618
	energy, ft-lb:	2705	2087	1587	1185	872
	arc, inches:		+2.0	0	-9.4	-28.6
Rem. 150 Nosler Partition	velocity, fps:	2850	2652	2463	2282	2108
	energy, ft-lb:	2705	2343	2021	1734	1480
	arc, inches:		+1.7	0	-7.5	-21.6
Speer 130 Grand Slam	velocity, fps:	3050	2774	2514	2269	
	energy, ft-lb:	2685	2221	1824	1485	
	arc, inches:		+1.5	0	-7.0	-20.9
Speer 150 Grand Slam	velocity, fps:	2830	2594	2369	2156	
	energy, ft-lb:	2667	2240	1869	1548	
	arc, inches:		+1.8	0	-8.1	-23.6
Win. 130 Power-Point	velocity, fps:	3060	2802	2559	2329	2110
	energy, ft-lb:	2702	2267	1890	1565	1285.
	arc, inches:		+1.8	0	-7.1	-20.6
Win. 130 Power-Point Plus	velocity, fps:	3150	2881	2628	2388	2161
	energy, ft-lb:	2865	2396	1993	1646	1348
	arc, inches:		+1.3	0	-6.4	-18.9
Win. 130 Silvertip	velocity, fps:	3060	2776	2510	2259	2022.
	energy, ft-lb:	2702	2225	1818	1472	1180
	arc, inches:		+1.8	0	-7.4	-21.6
Win. 130 Ballistic Silvertip	velocity, fps:	3050	2828	2618	2416	2224
	energy, ft-lb:	2685	2309	1978	1685	1428
	arc, inches:		+1.4	0	-6.5	-18.9
Win. 140 AccuBond	velocity, fps:	2950	2751	2560	2378	2203
	energy, ft-lb:	2705	2352	2038	1757	1508
	arc, inches:		+1.6	0	-6.9	-19.9

CARTRIDGE BULLET	RANGE, YARDS:	0	100	200	300	400
Win. 140 Fail Safe	velocity, fps:	2920	2671	2435	2211	1999
	energy, ft-lb:	2651	2218	1843	1519	1242
	arc, inches:		+1.7	0	-7.6	-22.3
Win. 150 Power-Point	velocity, fps:	2850	2585	2336	2100	1879
	energy, ft-lb:	2705	2226	1817	1468	1175
	arc, inches:		+2.2	0	-8.6	-25.0
Win. 150 Power-Point Plus	velocity, fps:	2950	2679	2425	2184	1957
	energy, ft-lb:	2900	2391	1959	1589	1276
	arc, inches:		+1.7	0	-7.6	-22.6
Win. 150 Partition Gold	velocity, fps:	2930	2693	2468	2254	2051
	energy, ft-lb:	2860	2416	2030	1693	1402
	arc, inches:		+1.7	0	-7.4	-21.6
Win. 150 Supreme Elite XP3	velocity, fps:	2950	2763	2583	2411	2245
	energy, ft-lb:	2898	2542	2223	1936	1679
	arc, inches:		+1.5	0	-6.9	-15.5

.270 WINCHESTER SHORT MAGNUM

CARTRIDGE BULLET	RANGE, YARDS:	0	100	200	300	400
Black Hills 140 AccuBond	velocity, fps:	3100				
	energy, ft-lb:	2987				
	arc, inches:					
Federal 130 Nos. Bal. Tip	velocity, fps:	3300	3070	2840	2630	2430
	energy, ft-lb:	3145	2710	2335	2000	1705
	arc, inches:		+1.1	0	-5.4	-15.8
Federal 130 Nos. Partition And Nos. Solid Base And Barnes TS	velocity, fps:	3280	3040	2810	2590	2380
	energy, ft-lb:	3105	2665	2275	1935	1635
	arc, inches:		+1.1	0	-5.6	-16.3
Federal 130 Trophy Copper	velocity, fps:	3280	3060	2850	2650	2460
	energy, ft-lb:	3105	2700	2345	2025	1745
	arc, inches:		+1.1	0	-5.4	-15.8
Federal 140 Nos. AccuBond	velocity, fps:	3200	3000	2810	2630	2450
	energy, ft-lb:	3185	2795	2455	2145	1865
	arc, inches:		+1.2	0	-5.6	-16.2
Federal 140 Trophy Bonded	velocity, fps:	3130	2870	2640	2410	2200
	energy, ft-lb:	3035	2570	2160	1810	1500
	arc, inches:		+1.4	0	-6.3	18.7
Federal 140 Trophy Bonded Tip	velocity, fps:	3200	2980	2770	2580	2390
	energy, ft-lb:	3185	2765	2390	2060	1770
	arc, inches:		+1.2	0	-5.8	-16.7
Federal 150 Nos. Partition	velocity, fps:	3160	2950	2750	2550	2370
	energy, ft-lb:	3325	2895	2515	2175	1870
	arc, inches:		+1.3	0	-5.9	-17.0
Norma 130 FMJ	velocity, fps:	3150	2882	2630	2391	
	energy, ft-lb:					
	arc, inches:		+1.5	0	-6.4	
Norma 130 Ballistic ST	velocity, fps:	3281	3047	2825	2614	
	energy, ft-lb:	3108	2681	2305	1973	
	arc, inches:		+1.1	0	-5.5	
Norma 140 Barnes X TS	velocity, fps:	3150	2952	2762	2580	
	energy, ft-lb:	3085	2709	2372	2070	
	arc, inches:		+1.3	0	-5.8	
Norma 150 Nosler Bal. Tip	velocity, fps:	3280	3046	2824	2613	
	energy, ft-lb:	3106	2679	2303	1972	
	arc, inches:		+1.1	0	-5.4	
Norma 150 Oryx	velocity, fps:	3117	2856	2611	2378	
	energy, ft-lb:	3237	2718	2271	1884	
	arc, inches:		+1.4	0	-6.5	
Win. 130 Bal. Silvertip	velocity, fps:	3275	3041	2820	2609	2408
	energy, ft-lb:	3096	2669	2295	1964	1673
	arc, inches:		+1.1	0	-5.5	-16.1
Win. 140 AccuBond	velocity, fps:	3200	2989	2789	2597	2413
	energy, ft-lb:	3184	2779	2418	2097	1810
	arc, inches:		+1.2	0	-5.7	-16.5
Win. 140 Fail Safe	velocity, fps:	3125	2865	2619	2386	2165
	energy, ft-lb:	3035	2550	2132	1769	1457
	arc, inches:		+1.4	0	-6.5	-19.0
Win. 150 Ballistic Silvertip	velocity, fps:	3120	2923	2734	2554	2380.
	energy, ft-lb:	3242	2845	2490	2172	1886.
	arc, inches:		+1.3	0	-5.9	-17.2

Centerfire Rifle Ballistics

.270 WINCHESTER SHORT MAGNUM TO 7MM-08 REMINGTON

CARTRIDGE BULLET	RANGE, YARDS:	0	100	200	300	400
Win. 150 Power Point	velocity, fps:	3150	2867	2601	2350	2113
	energy, ft-lb:	3304	2737	2252	1839	1487
	arc, inches:		+1.4	0	-6.5	-19.4
Win. 150 Supreme Elite XP3	velocity, fps:	3120	2926	2740	2561	2389
	energy, ft-lb:	3242	2850	2499	2184	1901
	arc, inches:		+1.3	0	-5.9	-17.1

.270 WEATHERBY MAGNUM

CARTRIDGE BULLET	RANGE, YARDS:	0	100	200	300	400
Federal 130 Nosler Partition	velocity, fps:	3200	2960	2740	2520	2320
	energy, ft-lb:	2955	2530	2160	1835	1550
	arc, inches:		+1.2	0	-5.9	-17.3
Federal 130 Sierra GameKing BTSP	velocity, fps:	3200	2980	2780	2580	2400
	energy, ft-lb:	2955	2570	2230	1925	1655
	arc, inches:		+1.2	0	-5.7	-16.6
Federal 140 Trophy Bonded	velocity, fps:	3100	2840	2600	2370	2150.
	energy, ft-lb:	2990	2510	2100	1745	1440
	arc, inches:		+1.4	0	-6.6	-19.3
Federal 130 Trophy Bonded Tip	velocity, fps:	3200	2970	2760	2560	2360
	energy, ft-lb:	2955	2555	2200	1885	1610
	arc, inches:		+1.2	0	-5.9	-16.9
Wby. 100 Pointed Expanding	velocity, fps:	3760	3396	3061	2751	2462
	energy, ft-lb:	3139	2560	2081	1681	1346
	arc, inches:		+2.3	+3.0	0	-7.6
Wby. 130 Pointed Expanding	velocity, fps:	3375	3123	2885	2659	2444
	energy, ft-lb:	3288	2815	2402	2041	1724
	arc, inches:		+2.8	+3.5	0	-8.4
Wby. 130 Nosler Partition	velocity, fps:	3375	3127	2892	2670	2458.
	energy, ft-lb:	3288	2822	2415	2058	1744
	arc, inches:		+2.8	+3.5	0	-8.3
Wby. 140 Nosler Bal. Tip	velocity, fps:	3300	3077	2865	2663	2470.
	energy, ft-lb:	3385	2943	2551	2204	1896
	arc, inches:		+2.9	+3.6	0	-8.4
Wby. 140 Barnes X	velocity, fps:	3250	3032	2825	2628	2438
	energy, ft-lb:	3283	2858	2481	2146	1848
	arc, inches:		+3.0	+3.7	0	-8.7
Wby. 150 Pointed Expanding	velocity, fps:	3245	3028	2821	2623	2434
	energy, ft-lb:	3507	3053	2650	2292	1973
	arc, inches:		+3.0	+3.7	0	-8.7
Wby. 150 Nosler Partition	velocity, fps:	3245	3029	2823	2627	2439.
	energy, ft-lb:	3507	3055	2655	2298	1981
	arc, inches:		+3.0	+3.7	0	-8.

7-30 WATERS

CARTRIDGE BULLET	RANGE, YARDS:	0	100	200	300	400
Federal 120 Sierra GameKing BTSP	velocity, fps:	2700	2300	1930	1600	1330.
	energy, ft-lb:	1940	1405	990	685	470
	arc, inches:		+2.6	0	-12.0	-37.6

7MM MAUSER (7x57)

CARTRIDGE BULLET	RANGE, YARDS:	0	100	200	300	400
Federal 140 Sierra Pro-Hunt.	velocity, fps:	2660	2450	2260	2070	1890.
	energy, ft-lb:	2200	1865	1585	1330	1110
	arc, inches:		+2.1	0	-9.0	-26.1
Federal 140 Nosler Partition	velocity, fps:	2660	2450	2260	2070	1890.
	energy, ft-lb:	2200	1865	1585	1330	1110
	arc, inches:		+2.1	0	-9.0	-26.1
Federal 175 Hi-Shok RN	velocity, fps:	2440	2140	1860	1600	1380
	energy, ft-lb:	2315	1775	1340	1000	740
	arc, inches:		+3.1	0	-13.3	-40.1
Hornady 139 SP boat-tail	velocity, fps:	2700	2504	2316	2137	1965
	energy, ft-lb:	2251	1936	1656	1410	1192
	arc, inches:		+2.0	0	-8.5	-24.9
Hornady 139 SP Interlock	velocity, fps:	2680	2455	2241	2038	1846
	energy, ft-lb:	2216	1860	1550	1282	1052
	arc, inches:		+2.1	0	-9.1	-26.6
Hornady 139 SP boat-tail LM	velocity, fps:	2830	2620	2450	2250	2070
	energy, ft-lb:	2475	2135	1835	1565	1330
	arc, inches:		+1.8	0	-7.6	-22.1
Hornady 139 SP LM	velocity, fps:	2950	2736	2532	2337	2152.
	energy, ft-lb:	2686	2310	1978	1686	1429
	arc, inches:		+2.0	0	-7.6	-21.5

CARTRIDGE BULLET	RANGE, YARDS:	0	100	200	300	400
Hornady 139 SST Superformance	velocity, fps:	2760	2575	2397	2227	2063
	energy, ft-lb:	2351	2046	1774	1530	1314
	arc, inches:		+1.9	0	-7.9	-22.9
Norma 150 Soft Point	velocity, fps:	2690	2479	2278	2087	
	energy, ft-lb:	2411	2048	1729	1450	
	arc, inches:		+2.0	0	-8.8	
PMC 140 Pointed Soft Point	velocity, fps:	2660	2450	2260	2070	1890
	energy, ft-lb:	2200	1865	1585	1330	1110.
	arc, inches:		+2.4	0	-9.6	-27.3
PMC 175 Soft Point	velocity, fps:	2440	2140	1860	1600	1380
	energy, ft-lb:	2315	1775	1340	1000	740
	arc, inches:		+1.5	-3.6	-18.6	-46.8
Rem. 140 PSP Core-Lokt	velocity, fps:	2660	2435	2221	2018	1827
	energy, ft-lb:	2199	1843	1533	1266	1037
	arc, inches:		+2.2	0	-9.2	-27.4
Win. 145 Power-Point	velocity, fps:	2660	2413	2180	1959	1754
	energy, ft-lb:	2279	1875	1530	1236	990
	arc, inches:		+1.1	-2.8	-14.1	-34.4

7x57 R

CARTRIDGE BULLET	RANGE, YARDS:	0	100	200	300	400
Norma 150 FMJ	velocity, fps:	2690	2489	2296	2112	
	energy, ft-lb:	2411	2063	1756	1486	
	arc, inches:		+2.0	0	-8.6	
Norma 154 Soft Point	velocity, fps:	2625	2417	2219	2030	
	energy, ft-lb:	2357	1999	1684	1410	
	arc, inches:		+2.2	0	-9.3	
Norma 156 Oryx	velocity, fps:	2608	2346	2099	1867	
	energy, ft-lb:	2357	1906	1526	1208	
	arc, inches:		+2.4	0	-10.3	

7MM-08 REMINGTON

CARTRIDGE BULLET	RANGE, YARDS:	0	100	200	300	400
Black Hills 140 AccuBond	velocity, fps:	2700				
	energy, ft-lb:					
	arc, inches:					
Federal 140 Nosler Partition	velocity, fps:	2800	2590	2390	2200	2020
	energy, ft-lb:	2435	2085	1775	1500	1265
	arc, inches:		+1.8	0	-8.0	-23.1
Federal 140 Nosler Bal. Tip And AccuBond	velocity, fps:	2800	2610	2430	2260	2100
	energy, ft-lb:	2440	2135	1840	1590	1360.
	arc, inches:		+1.8	0	-7.7	-22.3
Federal 140 Tr. Bonded HE	velocity, fps:	2950	2660	2390	2140	1900
	energy, ft-lb:	2705	2205	1780	1420	1120
	arc, inches:		+1.7	0	-7.9	-23.2
Federal 140 Trophy Copper	velocity, fps:	2800	2610	2440	2260	2100
	energy, ft-lb:	2435	2125	1845	1595	1370
	arc, inches:		+1.8	0	-7.7	-22.2
Federal 150 Sierra Pro-Hunt.	velocity, fps:	2650	2440	2230	2040	1860
	energy, ft-lb:	2340	1980	1660	1390	1150
	arc, inches:		+2.2	0	-9.2	-26.7
Hornady 120 SST Custom Lite	velocity, fps:	2675	2435	2207	1992	1790
	energy, ft-lb:	1907	1579	1298	1057	854
	arc, inches:		+2.2	0	-9.4	-27.5
Hornady 139 SP boat-tail LM	velocity, fps:	3000	2790	2590	2399	2216
	energy, ft-lb:	2777	2403	2071	1776	1515
	arc, inches:		+1.5	0	-6.7	-19.4
Norma 140 Ballistic ST	velocity, fps:	2822	2633	2452	2278	
	energy, ft-lb:	2476	2156	1870	1614	
	arc, inches:		+1.8	0	-7.6	
PMC 139 PSP	velocity, fps:	2850	2610	2384	2170	1969
	energy, ft-lb:	2507	2103	1754	1454	1197
	arc, inches:		+1.8	0	-7.9	-23.3
Rem. 120 Hollow Point	velocity, fps:	3000	2725	2467	2223	1992
	energy, ft-lb:	2398	1979	1621	1316	1058
	arc, inches:		+1.6	0	-7.3	-21.7
Rem. 140 PSP Core-Lokt	velocity, fps:	2860	2625	2402	2189	1988
	energy, ft-lb:	2542	2142	1793	1490	1228
	arc, inches:		+1.8	0	-7.8	-22.9
Rem. 140 PSP boat-tail	velocity, fps:	2860	2656	2460	2273	2094
	energy, ft-lb:	2542	2192	1881	1606	1363
	arc, inches:		+1.7	0	-7.5	-21.7

CARTRIDGE BULLET	RANGE, YARDS:	0	100	200	300	400
Rem. 140 AccuTip BT	velocity, fps:	2860	2670	2488	2313	2145
	energy, ft-lb:	2543	2217	1925	1663	1431
	arc, inches:		+1.7	0	-7.3	-21.2
Rem. 140 Nosler Partition	velocity, fps:	2860	2648	2446	2253	2068
	energy, ft-lb:	2542	2180	1860	1577	1330
	arc, inches:		+1.7	0	-7.6	-22.0
Speer 145 Grand Slam	velocity, fps:	2845	2567	2305	2059	
	energy, ft-lb:	2606	2121	1711	1365	
	arc, inches:		+1.9	0	-8.4	-25.5
Win. 140 Power-Point	velocity, fps:	2800	2523	2268	2027	1802.
	energy, ft-lb:	2429	1980	1599	1277	1010
	arc, inches:		+2.0	0	-8.8	-26.0
Win. 140 Power-Point Plus	velocity, fps:	2875	2597	2336	2090	1859
	energy, ft-lb:	2570	1997	1697	1358	1075
	arc, inches:		+2.0	0	-8.8	26.0
Win. 140 Fail Safe	velocity, fps:	2760	2506	2271	2048	1839
	energy, ft-lb:	2360	1953	1603	1304	1051
	arc, inches:		+2.0	0	-8.8	-25.9
Win. 140 Ballistic Silvertip	velocity, fps:	2770	2572	2382	2200	2026
	energy, ft-lb:	2386	2056	1764	1504	1276
	arc, inches:		+1.9	0	-8.0	-23.8

7x64 BRENNEKE

CARTRIDGE BULLET	RANGE, YARDS:	0	100	200	300	400
Federal 160 Nosler Partition	velocity, fps:	2650	2480	2310	2150	2000
	energy, ft-lb:	2495	2180	1895	1640	1415
	arc, inches:		+2.1	0	-8.7	-24.9
Norma 140 AccuBond	velocity, fps:	2953	2759	2572	2394	
	energy, ft-lb:	2712	2366	2058	1782	
	arc, inches:		+1.5	0	-6.8	
Norma 154 Soft Point	velocity, fps:	2821	2605	2399	2203	
	energy, ft-lb:	2722	2321	1969	1660	
	arc, inches:		+1.8	0	-7.8	
Norma 156 Oryx	velocity, fps:	2789	2516	2259	2017	
	energy, ft-lb:	2695	2193	1768	1410	
	arc, inches:		+2.0	0	-8.8	
Norma 170 Vulkan	velocity, fps:	2756	2501	2259	2031	
	energy, ft-lb:	2868	2361	1927	1558	
	arc, inches:		+2.0	0	-8.8	
Norma 170 Oryx	velocity, fps:	2756	2481	2222	1979	
	energy, ft-lb:	2868	2324	1864	1478	
	arc, inches:		+2.1	0	-9.2	
Norma 170 Plastic Point	velocity, fps:	2756	2519	2294	2081	
	energy, ft-lb:	2868	2396	1987	1635	
	arc, inches:		+2.0	0	-8.6	
PMC 170 Pointed Soft Point	velocity, fps:	2625	2401	2189	1989	1801
	energy, ft lb:	2601	2175	1808	1493	1224
	arc, inches:		+2.3	0	-9.6	-27.9
Rem. 175 PSP Core-Lokt	velocity, fps:	2650	2445	2248	2061	1883
	energy, ft-lb:	2728	2322	1964	1650	1378
	arc, inches:		+2.2	0	-9.1	-26.4
Speer 160 Grand Slam	velocity, fps:	2600	2376	2164	1962	
	energy, ft-lb:	2401	2006	1663	1368	
	arc, inches:		+2.3	0	-9.8	-28.6
Speer 175 Grand Slam	velocity, fps:	2650	2461	2280	2106	
	energy, ft-lb:	2728	2353	2019	1723	
	arc, inches:		+2.4	0	-9.2	-26.2

7x65 R

CARTRIDGE BULLET	RANGE, YARDS:	0	100	200	300	400
Norma 150 FMJ	velocity, fps:	2756	2552	2357	2170	
	energy, ft-lb:	2530	2169	1850	1569	
	arc, inches:		+1.9	0	-8.2	
Norma 156 Oryx	velocity, fps:	2723	2454	2200	1962	
	energy, ft-lb:	2569	2086	1678	1334	
	arc, inches:		+2.1	0	-9.3	

CARTRIDGE BULLET	RANGE, YARDS:	0	100	200	300	400
Norma 170 Plastic Point	velocity, fps:	2625	2390	2167	1956	
	energy, ft-lb:	2602	2157	1773	1445	
	arc, inches:		+2.3	0	-9.7	
Norma 170 Vulkan	velocity, fps:	2657	2392	2143	1909	
	energy, ft-lb:	2666	2161	1734	1377	
	arc, inches:		+2.3	0	-9.9	
Norma 170 Oryx	velocity, fps:	2657	2378	2115	1871	
	energy, ft-lb:	2666	2135	1690	1321	
	arc, inches:		+2.3	0	-10.1	

.284 WINCHESTER

CARTRIDGE BULLET	RANGE, YARDS:	0	100	200	300	400
Win. 150 Power-Point	velocity, fps:	2860	2595	2344	2108	1886
	energy, ft-lb:	2724	2243	1830	1480	1185
	arc, inches:		+2.1	0	-8.5	-24.8

.280 REMINGTON

CARTRIDGE BULLET	RANGE, YARDS:	0	100	200	300	400
Federal 140 Sierra Pro-Hunt.	velocity, fps:	2990	2740	2500	2270	2060
	energy, ft-lb:	2770	2325	1940	1605	1320
	arc, inches:		+1.6	0	-7.0	-20.8
Federal 140 Trophy Bonded	velocity, fps:	2990	2630	2310	2040	1730
	energy, ft-lb:	2770	2155	1655	1250	925
	arc, inches:		+1.6	0	-8.4	-25.4
Federal 140 Trophy Bonded Tip	velocity, fps:	2950	2730	2520	2330	2140
	energy, ft-lb:	2705	2320	1980	1680	1420
	arc, inches:		+1.6	0	-7.0	-20.6
Federal 140 Tr. Bonded HE	velocity, fps:	3150	2850	2570	2300	2050
	energy, ft-lb:	3085	2520	2050	1650	1310
	arc, inches:		+1.4	0	-6.7	-20.0
Federal 140 Nos. AccuBond And Bal. Tip And Solid Base	velocity, fps:	3000	2800	2620	2440	2260
	energy, ft-lb:	2800	2445	2130	1845	1590
	arc, inches:		+1.5	0	-6.5	-18.9
Federal 150 Hi-Shok	velocity, fps:	2890	2670	2460	2260	2060
	energy, ft-lb:	2780	2370	2015	1695	1420
	arc, inches:		+1.7	0	-7.5	-21.8
Federal 150 Nosler Partition	velocity, fps:	2890	2690	2490	2310	2130
	energy, ft-lb:	2780	2405	2070	1770	1510.
	arc, inches:		+1.7	0	-7.2	-21.1
Federal 150 Nos. AccuBond	velocity, fps	2800	2630	2460	2300	2150
	energy, ft-lb:	2785	2455	2155	1885	1645
	arc, inches:		+1.8	0	-7.5	-21.5
Federal 160 Trophy Bonded	velocity, fps:	2800	2570	2350	2140	1940
	energy, ft-lb:	2785	2345	1960	1625	1340
	arc, inches:		+1.9	0	-8.3	-24.0
Hornady 139 SPBT LMmoly	velocity,·fps:	3110	2888	2675	2473	2280.
	energy, ft-lb:	2985	2573	2209	1887	1604
	arc, inches:		+1.4	0	-6.5	-18.6
Hornady 139 SST Superformance	velocity, fps:	3090	2891	2700	2518	2343
	energy, ft-lb:	2947	2579	2250	1957	1694
	arc, inches:		+1.3	0	-6.1	-17.7
Norma 156 Oryx	velocity, fps:	2789	2516	2259	2017	
	energy, ft-lb:	2695	2193	1768	1410	
	arc, inches:		+2.0	0	-8.8	
Norma 170 Plastic Point	velocity, fps:	2707	2468	2241	2026	
	energy, ft-lb:	2767	2299	1896	1550	
	arc, inches:		+2.1	0	-9.1	
Norma 170 Vulkan	velocity, fps:	2592	2346	2113	1894	
	energy, ft-lb:	2537	2078	1686	1354	
	arc, inches:		+2.4	0	-10.2	
Norma 170 Oryx	velocity, fps:	2690	2416	2159	1918	
	energy, ft-lb:	2732	2204	1760	1389	
	arc, inches:		+2.2	0	-9.7	
Rem. 140 PSP Core-Lokt	velocity, fps:	3000	2758	2528	2309	2102
	energy, ft-lb:	2797	2363	1986	1657	1373
	arc, inches:		+1.5	0	-7.0	-20.5
Rem. 140 PSP boat-tail	velocity, fps:	2860	2656	2460	2273	2094
	energy, ft-lb:	2542	2192	1881	1606	1363
	arc, inches:		+1.7	0	-7.5	-21.7
Rem. 140 Nosler Bal. Tip	velocity, fps:	3000	2804	2616	2436	2263
	energy, ft-lb:	2799	2445	2128	1848	1593
	arc, inches:		+1.5	0	-6.8	-19.0

Centerfire Rifle Ballistics

.280 REMINGTON TO 7MM REMINGTON MAGNUM

CARTRIDGE BULLET	RANGE, YARDS:	0	100	200	300	400
Rem. 140 AccuTip	velocity, fps:	3000	2804	2617	2437	2265
	energy, ft-lb:	2797	2444	2129	1846	1594
	arc, inches:		+1.5	0	-6.8	-19.0
Rem. 150 PSP Core-Lokt	velocity, fps:	2890	2624	2373	2135	1912
	energy, ft-lb:	2781	2293	1875	1518	1217
	arc, inches:		+1.8	0	-8.0	-23.6
Rem. 165 SP Core-Lokt	velocity, fps:	2820	2510	2220	1950	1701
	energy, ft-lb:	2913	2308	1805	1393	1060.
	arc, inches:		+2.0	0	-9.1	-27.4
Speer 145 Grand Slam	velocity, fps:	2900	2619	2354	2105	
	energy, ft-lb:	2707	2207	1784	1426	
	arc, inches:		+2.1	0	-8.4	-24.7
Speer 160 Grand Slam	velocity, fps:	2890	2652	2425	2210	
	energy, ft-lb:	2967	2497	2089	1735	
	arc, inches:		+1.7	0	-7.7	-22.4
Win. 140 Fail Safe	velocity, fps:	3050	2756	2480	2221	1977
	energy, ft-lb:	2893	2362	1913	1533	1216
	arc, inches:		+1.5	0	-7.2	-21.5
Win. 140 Ballistic Silvertip	velocity, fps:	3040	2842	2653	2471	2297
	energy, ft-lb:	2872	2511	2187	1898	1640
	arc, inches:		+1.4	0	-6.3	-18.4

.280 ACKLEY IMPROVED

CARTRIDGE BULLET	RANGE, YARDS:	0	100	200	300	400
Nosler 140 AccuBond	velocity, fps:	3150	2947	2753	2567	2389
	energy, ft-lb:	3084	2700	2355	2048	1774
	arc, inches:	-1.5	+1.1	0	-5.0	-16.8
Nosler 150 ABLR	velocity, fps:	2930	2775	2626	2482	2342
	energy, ft-lb:	2858	2565	2297	2052	1827
	arc, inches:	-1.5	+1.5	0	-6.6	-18.7
Nosler 160 Partition	velocity, fps:	2950	2752	2562	2380	2206
	energy, ft-lb:	3091	2690	2332	2013	1729
	arc, inches:	-1.5	+1.5	0	-6.7	-19.4

7MM REMINGTON MAGNUM

CARTRIDGE BULLET	RANGE, YARDS:	0	100	200	300	400
A-Square 175 Monolithic Solid	velocity, fps:	2860	2557	2273	2008	1771
	energy, ft-lb:	3178	2540	2008	1567	1219
	arc, inches:		+1.92	0	-8.7	-25.9
Black Hills 140 Nos. Bal. Tip	velocity, fps:	3150				
	energy, ft-lb:	3084				
	arc, inches:					
Black Hills 140 Barnes XLC	velocity, fps:	3150				
	energy, ft-lb:	3084				
	arc, inches:					
Black Hills 140 Nos. Partition	velocity, fps:	3150				
	energy, ft-lb:	3084				
	arc, inches:					
Federal 140 Nosler Bal. Tip And AccuBond	velocity, fps:	3110	2910	2720	2530	2360.
	energy, ft-lb:	3005	2630	2295	1995	1725
	arc, inches:		+1.3	0	-6.0	-17.4
Federal 140 Nosler Partition	velocity, fps:	3150	2930	2710	2510	2320
	energy, ft-lb:	3085	2660	2290	1960	1670
	arc, inches:		+1.3	0	-6.0	-17.5
Federal 140 Trophy Bonded	velocity, fps:	3150	2910	2680	2460	2250.
	energy, ft-lb:	3085	2630	2230	1880	1575
	arc, inches:		+1.3	0	-6.1	-18.1
Federal 140 Trophy Copper	velocity, fps:	3150	2950	2760	2570	2400
	energy, ft-lb:	3085	2705	2360	2055	1785
	arc, inches:		+1.3	0	-5.9	-16.9
Federal 150 Hi-Shok	velocity, fps:	3110	2830	2570	2320	2090
	energy, ft-lb:	3220	2670	2200	1790	1450
	arc, inches:		+1.4	0	-6.7	-19.9
Federal 150 Nosler Bal. Tip	velocity, fps:	3110	2910	2720	2540	2370
	energy, ft-lb:	3220	2825	2470	2150	1865
	arc, inches:		+1.3	0	-6.0	-17.4
Federal 150 Nos. Solid Base	velocity, fps:	3100	2890	2690	2500	2310
	energy, ft-lb:	3200	2780	2405	2075	1775
	arc, inches:		+1.3	0	-6.2	-17.8
Federal 150 Sierra GameKing BTSP	velocity, fps:	3110	2920	2750	2580	2410
	energy, ft-lb:	3220	2850	2510	2210	1930
	arc, inches:		+1.3 0	-5.9	-17.0	

CARTRIDGE BULLET	RANGE, YARDS:	0	100	200	300	400
Federal 150 Trophy Copper	velocity, fps:	3025	2830	2650	2470	2300
	energy, ft-lb:	3045	2675	2335	2035	1765
	arc, inches:		+1.4	0	-6.4	-18.4
Federal 160 Barnes XLC	velocity, fps:	2940	2760	2580	2410	2240
	energy, ft-lb:	3070	2695	2360	2060	1785
	arc, inches:		+1.5	0	-6.8	-19.6
Federal 160 Sierra Pro-Hunt.	velocity, fps:	2940	2730	2520	2320	2140
	energy, ft-lb:	3070	2640	2260	1920	1620
	arc, inches:		+1.6	0	-7.1	-20.6
Federal 160 Nosler Partition	velocity, fps:	2950	2770	2590	2420	2250.
	energy, ft-lb:	3090	2715	2375	2075	1800
	arc, inches:		+1.5	0	-6.7	-19.4
Federal 160 Nos. AccuBond	velocity, fps:	2950	2770	2600	2440	2280.
	energy, ft-lb:	3090	2730	2405	2110	1845
	arc, inches:		+1.5	0	-6.6	-19.1
Federal 160 Trophy Bonded	velocity, fps:	2940	2660	2390	2140	1900
	energy, ft-lb:	3070	2505	2025	1620	1280.
	arc, inches:		+1.7	0	-7.9	-23.3
Federal 165 Sierra GameKing BTSP	velocity, fps:	2950	2800	2650	2510	2370.
	energy, ft-lb:	3190	2865	2570	2300	2050
	arc, inches:		+1.5	0	-6.4	-18.4
Federal 175 Hi-Shok	velocity, fps:	2860	2650	2440	2240	2060
	energy, ft-lb:	3180	2720	2310	1960	1640
	arc, inches:		+1.7	0	-7.6	-22.1
Federal 175 Trophy Bonded	velocity, fps:	2860	2600	2350	2120	1900
	energy, ft-lb:	3180	2625	2150	1745	1400
	arc, inches:		+1.8	0	-8.2	-24.0
Hornady 139 SPBT	velocity, fps:	3150	2933	2727	2530	2341
	energy, ft-lb:	3063	2656	2296	1976	1692
	arc, inches:		+1.2	0	-6.1	-17.7
Hornady 139 SPBT HMmoly	velocity, fps:	3250	3041	2822	2613	2413
	energy, ft-lb:	3300	2854	2458	2106	1797
	arc, inches:		+1.1 0	-5.7	-16.6	
Hornady 139 SST (or Interbond)	velocity, fps:	3150	2948	2754	2569	2391
	energy, ft-lb:	3062	2681	2341	2037	1764
	arc, inches:		+1.1	0	-5.7	-16.7
Hornady 139 SST Custom Lite	velocity, fps:	2800	2613	2434	2262	2097
	energy, ft-lb:	2420	2108	1829	1579	1357
	arc, inches:		+1.8	0	-7.7	-22.2
Hornady 139 SST LM (or Interbond)	velocity, fps:	3250	3044	2847	2657	2475
	energy, ft-lb:	3259	2860	2501	2178	1890
	arc, inches:		+1.1	0	-5.5	-16.2
Hornady 139 SPBT HMmoly	velocity, fps:	3250	3041	2822	2613	2413
	energy, ft-lb:	3300	2854	2458	2106	1797.
	arc, inches:		+1.1	0	-5.7	-16.6
Hornady 154 Soft Point	velocity, fps:	3035	2814	2604	2404	2212
	energy, ft-lb:	3151	2708	2319	1977	1674
	arc, inches:		+1.3	0	-6.7	-19.3
Hornady 154 SST (or Interbond)	velocity, fps:	3035	2850	2672	2501	2337
	energy, ft-lb:	3149	2777	2441	2139	1867
	arc, inches:		+1.4	0	-6.5	-18.7
Hornady 162 SP boat-tail	velocity, fps:	2940	2757	2582	2413	2251
	energy, ft-lb:	3110	2735	2399	2095	1823
	arc, inches:		+1.6	0	-6.7	-19.7
Hornady 162 SST Superformance	velocity, fps:	3030	2856	2689	2527	2372
	energy, ft-lb:	3302	2933	2600	2298	2023
	arc, inches:		+1.4	0	-6.2	-17.8
Hornady 175 SP	velocity, fps:	2860	2650	2440	2240	2060.
	energy, ft-lb:	3180	2720	2310	1960	1640
	arc, inches:		+2.0	0	-7.9	-22.7
Norma 140 Nosler Bal. Tip	velocity, fps:	3150	2936	2732	2537	
	energy, ft-lb:	3085	2680	2320	2001	
	arc, inches:		+1.2	0	-5.9	
Norma 140 Barnes X TS	velocity, fps:	3117	2912	2716	2529	
	energy, ft-lb:	3021	2637	2294	1988	
	arch, inches:		+1.3	0	-6.0	
Norma 150 Scirocco	velocity, fps:	3117	2934	2758	2589	
	energy, ft-lb:	3237	2869	2535	2234	
	arc, inches:		+1.2	0	-5.8	
Norma 156 Oryx	velocity, fps:	2953	2670	2404	2153	
	energy, ft-lb:	3021	2470	2002	1607	
	arc, inches:		+1.7	0	-7.7	

7MM REMINGTON MAGNUM TO 7MM WINCHESTER SHORT MAGNUM

CARTRIDGE BULLET	RANGE, YARDS:	0	100	200	300	400
Norma 170 Vulkan	velocity, fps:	3018	2747	2493	2252	
	energy, ft-lb:	3439	2850	2346	1914	
	arc, inches:		+1.5	0	-2.8	
Norma 170 Oryx	velocity, fps:	2887	2601	2333	2080	
	energy, ft-lb:	3147	2555	2055	1634	
	arc, inches:		+1.8	0	-8.2	
Norma 170 Plastic Point	velocity, fps:	3018	2762	2519	2290	
	energy, ft-lb:	3439	2880	2394	1980	
	arc, inches:		+1.5	0	-7.0	
PMC 140 Barnes X	velocity, fps:	3000	2808	2624	2448	2279
	energy, ft-lb:	2797	2451	2141	1863	1614
	arc, inches:		+1.5	0	-6.6	18.9
PMC 140 Pointed Soft Point	velocity, fps:	3099	2878	2668	2469	2279
	energy, ft-lb:	2984	2574	2212	1895	1614
	arc, inches:		+1.4	0	-6.2	-18.1
PMC 140 SP boat-tail	velocity, fps:	3125	2891	2669	2457	2255
	energy, ft-lb:	3035	2597	2213	1877	1580
	arc, inches:		+1.4	0	-6.3	-18.4
PMC 160 Barnes X	velocity, fps:	2800	2639	2484	2334	2189
	energy, ft-lb:	2785	2474	2192	1935	1703
	arc, inches:		+1.8	0	-7.4	-21.2
PMC 160 Pointed Soft Point	velocity, fps:	2914	2748	2586	2428	2276
	energy, ft-lb:	3016	2682	2375	2095	1840
	arc, inches:		+1.6	0	-6.7	-19.4
PMC 160 SP boat-tail	velocity, fps:	2900	2696	2501	2314	2135
	energy, ft-lb:	2987	2582	2222	1903	1620
	arc, inches:		+1.7	0	-7.2	-21.0
PMC 175 Pointed Soft Point	velocity, fps:	2860	2645	2442	2244	2957
	energy, ft-lb:	3178	2718	2313	1956	1644
	arc, inches:		+2.0	0	-7.9	-22.7
Remington 140 Copper Solid Tipped	velocity, fps:	3175	2964	2762	2570	2385
	energy, ft-lb:	3133	2730	2372	2053	1768
	arc, inches:		+1.4	0	-6.0	-17.6
Rem. 140 PSP Core-Lokt mr	velocity, fps:	2710	2482	2265	2059	1865
	energy, ft-lb:	2283	1915	1595	1318	1081
	arc, inches:		+1.0	-2.5	-12.8	-31.3
Rem. 140 PSP Core-Lokt	velocity, fps:	3175	2923	2684	2458	2243
	energy, ft-lb:	3133	2655	2240	1878	1564
	arc, inches:		+2.2	+1.9	-3.2	-14.2
Rem. 140 PSP boat-tail	velocity, fps:	3175	2956	2747	2547	2356
	energy, ft-lb:	3133	2715	2345	2017	1726
	arc, inches:		+2.2	+1.6	-3.1	-13.4
Rem. 150 AccuTip	velocity, fps:	3110	2926	2749	2579	2415
	energy, ft-lb:	3221	2850	2516	2215	1943
	arc, inches:		+1.3	0	-5.9	-17.0
Rem. 150 PSP Core-Lokt	velocity, fps:	3110	2830	2568	2320	2085
	energy, ft-lb:	3221	2667	2196	1792	1448
	arc, inches:		+1.3	0	-6.6	-20.2
Rem. 150 Nosler Bal. Tip	velocity, fps:	3110	2912	2723	2542	2367
	energy, ft-lb:	3222	2825	2470	2152	1867
	arc, inches:		+1.2	0	-5.9	-17.3
Rem. 150 Swift Scirocco	velocity, fps:	3110	2927	2751	2582	2419
	energy, ft-lb:	3221	2852	2520	2220	1948
	arc, inches:		+1.3	0	-5.9	-17.0
Rem. 160 Swift A-Frame	velocity, fps:	2900	2659	2430	2212	2006
	energy, ft-lb:	2987	2511	2097	1739	1430
	arc, inches:		+1.7	0	-7.6	-22.4
Rem. 160 Nosler Partition	velocity, fps:	2950	2752	2563	2381	2207
	energy, ft-lb:	3091	2690	2333	2014	1730
	arc, inches:		+0.6	-1.9	-9.6	-23.6
Rem. 175 PSP Core-Lokt	velocity, fps:	2860	2645	2440	2244	2057
	energy, ft-lb:	3178	2718	2313	1956	1644
	arc, inches:		+1.7	0	-7.6	-22.1
Speer 145 Grand Slam	velocity, fps:	3140	2843	2565	2304	
	energy, ft-lb:	3174	2602	2118	1708	
	arc, inches:		+1.4	0	-6.7	

CARTRIDGE BULLET	RANGE, YARDS:	0	100	200	300	400
Speer 175 Grand Slam	velocity, fps:	2850	2653	2463	2282	
	energy, ft-lb:	3156	2734	2358	2023	
	arc, inches:		+1.7	0	-7.5	-21.7
Win. 140 Fail Safe	velocity, fps:	3150	2861	2589	2333	2092
	energy, ft-lb:	3085	2544	2085	1693	1361
	arc, inches:		+1.4	0	-6.6	-19.5
Win. 140 Ballistic Silvertip	velocity, fps:	3100	2889	2687	2494	2310
	energy, ft-lb:	2988	2595	2245	1934	1659.
	arc, inches:		+1.3	0	-6.2	-17.9
Win. 140 AccuBond CT	velocity, fps:	3180	2965	2760	2565	2377
	energy, ft-lb:	3143	2733	2368	2044	1756
	arc, inches:		+1.2	0	-5.8	-16.9
Win. 150 Power-Point	velocity, fps:	3090	2812	2551	2304	2071
	energy, ft-lb:	3181	2634	2167	1768	1429
	arc, inches:		+1.5	0	-6.8	-20.2
Win. 150 Power-Point Plus	velocity, fps:	3130	2849	2586	2337	2102
	energy, ft-lb:	3264	2705	2227	1819	1472
	arc, inches:		+1.4	0	-6.6	-19.6
Win. 150 Ballistic Silvertip	velocity, fps:	3100	2903	2714	2533	2359
	energy, ft-lb:	3200	2806	2453	2136	1853
	arc, inches:		+1.3	0	-6.0	-17.5
Win. 160 AccuBond	velocity, fps:	2950	2766	2590	2420	2257
	energy, ft-lb:	3091	2718	2382	2080	1809
	arc, inches:		+1.5	0	-6.7	-19.4
Win. 160 Partition Gold	velocity, fps:	2950	2743	2546	2357	2176
	energy, ft-lb:	3093	2674	2303	1974	1682
	arc, inches:		+1.6	0	-6.9	-20.1
Win. 160 Fail Safe	velocity, fps:	2920	2678	2449	2331	2025
	energy, ft-lb:	3030	2549	2131	1769	1457
	arc, inches:		+1.7	0	-7.5	-22.0
Win. 175 Power-Point	velocity, fps:	2860	2645	2440	2244	2057
	energy, ft-lb:	3178	2718	2313	1956	1644
	arc, inches:		+2.0	0	-7.9	-22.7

7MM REMINGTON SHORT ULTRA MAGNUM

CARTRIDGE BULLET	RANGE, YARDS:	0	100	200	300	400
Rem. 140 PSP C-L Ultra	velocity, fps:	3175	2934	2707	2490	2283
	energy, ft-lb:	3133	2676	2277	1927	1620.
	arc, inches:		+1.3	0	-6.0	-17.7
Rem. 150 PSP Core-Lokt	velocity, fps:	3110	2828	2563	2313	2077
	energy, ft-lb:	3221	2663	2188	1782	1437
	arc, inches:		+2.5	+2.1	-3.6	-15.8
Rem. 160 Partition	velocity, fps:	2960	2762	2572	2390	2215
	energy, ft-lb:	3112	2709	2350	2029	1744
	arc, inches:		+2.6	+2.2	-3.6	-15.4
Rem. 160 PSP C-L Ultra	velocity, fps:	2960	2733	2518	2313	2117
	energy, ft-lb:	3112	2654	2252	1900	1592
	arc, inches:		+2.7	+2.2	-3.7	-16.2

7MM WINCHESTER SHORT MAGNUM

CARTRIDGE BULLET	RANGE, YARDS:	0	100	200	300	400
Federal 140 Nos. AccuBond	velocity, fps:	3250	3040	2840	2660	2470
	energy, ft-lb:	3285	2875	2515	2190	1900
	arc, inches:		+1.1	0	-5.5	-15.8
Federal 140 Nos. Bal. Tip	velocity, fps:	3310	3100	2900	2700	2520
	energy, ft-lb:	3405	2985	2610	2270	1975
	arc, inches:		+1.1	0	-5.2	15.2
Federal 150 Nos. Solid Base	velocity, fps:	3230	3010	2800	2600	2410
	energy, ft-lb:	3475	3015	2615	2255	1935
	arc, inches:		+1.3	0	-5.6	-16.3
Federal 150 Trophy Copper	velocity, fps:	3140	2940	2750	2570	2400
	energy, ft-lb:	3285	2885	2525	2205	1915
	arc, inches:		+1.3	0	-5.9	-16.9
Federal 160 Nos. AccuBond	velocity, fps:	3120	2940	2760	2590	2430
	energy, ft-lb:	3460	3065	2710	2390	2095
	arc, inches:		+1.3	0	-5.9	-16.8
Federal 160 Nos. Partition	velocity, fps:	3160	2950	2750	2560	2380.
	energy, ft-lb:	3545	3095	2690	2335	2015.
	arc, inches:		+1.2	0	-5.9	-16.9

Centerfire Rifle Ballistics

7MM WINCHESTER SHORT MAGNUM TO 7MM REMINGTON ULTRA MAGNUM

BALLISTICS

CARTRIDGE BULLET	RANGE, YARDS:	0	100	200	300	400
Federal 160 Barnes TS	velocity, fps:	2990	2780	2590	2400	2220
	energy, ft-lb:	3175	2755	2380	2045	1750
	arc, inches:		+1.5	0	-6.6	-19.4
Federal 160 Trophy Bonded	velocity, fps:	3120	2880	2650	2440	2230
	energy, ft-lb:	3460	2945	2500	2105	1765
	arc, inches:		+1.4	0	-6.3	-18.5
Federal 160 Trophy Bonded Tip	velocity, fps:	3000	2820	2640	2470	2310
	energy, ft-lb:	3195	2820	2480	2170	1895
	arc, inches:		+1.5	0	-6.4	-18.5
Win. 140 Bal. Silvertip	velocity, fps:	3225	3008	2801	2603	2414
	energy, ft-lb:	3233	2812	2438	2106	1812
	arc, inches:		+1.2	0	-5.6	-16.4
Win. 140 AccuBond CT	velocity, fps:	3225	3008	2801	2604	2415
	energy, ft-lb:	3233	2812	2439	2107	1812
	arc, inches:		+1.2	0	-5.6	-16.4
Win. 150 Power Point	velocity, fps:	3200	2915	2648	2396	2157
	energy, ft-lb:	3410	2830	2335	1911	1550
	arc, inches:		+1.3	0	-6.3	-18.6
Win. 160 AccuBond	velocity, fps:	3050	2862	2682	2509	2342
	energy, ft-lb:	3306	2911	2556	2237	1950
	arc, inches:		1.4	0	-6.2	-17.9
Win. 160 Fail Safe	velocity, fps:	2990	2744	2512	2291	2081
	energy, ft-lb:	3176	2675	2241	1864	1538
	arc, inches:		+1.6	0	-7.1	-20.8

7MM WEATHERBY MAGNUM

CARTRIDGE BULLET	RANGE, YARDS:	0	100	200	300	400
Federal 160 Nosler Partition	velocity, fps:	3050	2850	2650	2470	2290
	energy, ft-lb:	3305	2880	2505	2165	1865
	arc, inches:		+1.4	0	-6.3	-18.4
Federal 160 Sierra GameKing BTSP	velocity, fps:	3050	2880	2710	2560	2400
	energy, ft-lb:	3305	2945	2615	2320	2050
	arc, inches:		+1.4	0	-6.1	-17.4
Federal 160 Trophy Bonded	velocity, fps:	3050	2730	2420	2140	1880.
	energy, ft-lb:	3305	2640	2085	1630	1255
	arc, inches:		+1.6	0	-7.6	-22.7
Federal 160 Trophy Bonded Tip	velocity, fps:	3100	2910	2730	2560	2390
	energy, ft-lb:	3415	3015	2655	2330	2035
	arc, inches:		+1.3	0	-6.0	-17.2
Hornady 139 GMX Superformance	velocity, fps:	3300	3091	2891	2701	2519
	energy, ft-lb:	3361	2948	2580	2252	1958
	arc, inches:		+1.1	0	-5.2	-15.2
Hornady 154 Soft Point	velocity, fps:	3200	2971	2753	2546	2348.
	energy, ft-lb:	3501	3017	2592	2216	1885
	arc, inches:		+1.2	0	-5.8	-17.0
Hornady 154 SST (or Interbond)	velocity, fps:	3200	3009	2825	2648	2478
	energy, ft-lb:	3501	3096	2729	2398	2100
	arc, inches:		+1.2	0	-5.7	-16.5
Hornady 175 Soft Point	velocity, fps:	2910	2709	2516	2331	2154
	energy, ft-lb:	3290	2850	2459	2111	1803
	arc, inches:		+1.6	0	-7.1	-20.6
Wby. 139 Pointed Expanding	velocity, fps:	3340	3079	2834	2601	2380.
	energy, ft-lb:	3443	2926	2478	2088	1748
	arc, inches:		+2.9	+3.6	0	-8.7
Wby. 140 Nosler Partition	velocity, fps:	3303	3069	2847	2636	2434
	energy, ft-lb:	3391	2927	2519	2159	1841
	arc, inches:		+2.9	+3.6	0	-8.5
Wby. 150 Nosler Bal. Tip	velocity, fps:	3300	3093	2896	2708	2527
	energy, ft-lb:	3627	3187	2793	2442	2127
	arc, inches:		+2.8	+3.5	0	-8.2
Wby. 150 Barnes X	velociy, fps:	3100	2901	2710	2527	2352
	energy, ft-lb:	3200	2802	2446	2127	1842
	arc, inches:		+3.3	+4.0	0	-9.4
Wby. 154 Pointed Expanding	velocity, fps:	3260	3028	2807	2597	2397
	energy, ft-lb:	3634	3134	2694	2307	1964
	arc, inches:		+3.0	+3.7	0	-8.8
Wby. 160 Nosler Partition	velocity, fps:	3200	2991	2791	2600	2417
	energy, ft-lb:	3638	3177	2767	2401	2075.
	arc, inches:		+3.1	+3.8	0	-8.9
Wby. 175 Pointed Expanding	velocity, fps:	3070	2861	2662	2471	2288
	energy, ft-lb:	3662	3181	2753	2373	2034
	arc, inches:		+3.5	+4.2	0	-9.9

CARTRIDGE BULLET	RANGE, YARDS:	0	100	200	300	400
7MM DAKOTA						
Dakota 140 Barnes X	velocity, fps:	3500	3253	3019	2798	2587
	energy, ft-lb:	3807	3288	2833	2433	2081
	arc, inches:		+2.0	+2.1	-1.5	-9.6
Dakota 160 Barnes X	velocity, fps:	3200	3001	2811	2630	2455
	energy, ft-lb:	3637	3200	2808	2456	2140
	arc, inches:		+2.1	+1.9	-2.8	-12.5
7MM STW						
A-Square 140 Nos. Bal. Tip	velocity, fps:	3450	3254	3067	2888	2715
	energy, ft-lb:	3700	3291	2924	2592	2292
	arc, inches:		+2.2	+3.0	0	-7.3
A-Square 160 Nosler Part.	velocity, fps:	3250	3071	2900	2735	2576.
	energy, ft-lb:	3752	3351	2987	2657	2357
	arc, inches:		+2.8	+3.5	0	-8.2
A-Square 160 SP boat-tail	velocity, fps:	3250	3087	2930	2778	2631
	energy, ft-lb:	3752	3385	3049	2741	2460
	arc, inches:		+2.8	+3.4	0	-8.0
Federal 140 Trophy Bonded	velocity, fps:	3330	3080	2850	2630	2420
	energy, ft-lb:	3435	2950	2520	2145	1815
	arc, inches:		+1.1	0	-5.4	-15.8
Federal 150 Trophy Bonded	velocity, fps:	3250	3010	2770	2560	2350.
	energy, ft-lb:	3520	3010	2565	2175	1830
	arc, inches:		+1.2	0	-5.7	-16.7
Federal 160 Sierra GameKing BTSP	velocity, fps:	3200	3020	2850	2670	2530.
	energy, ft-lb:	3640	3245	2890	2570	2275
	arc, inches:		+1.1	0	-5.5	-15.7
Federal 160 Trophy Bonded Tip	velocity, fps:	3100	2910	2730	2560	2390
	energy, ft-lb:	3415	3015	2655	2330	2035
	arc, inches:		+1.3	0	-6.0	-17.2
Nosler 175 ABLR	velocity, fps:	2900	2760	2625	2493	2366
	energy, ft-lb:	3267	2960	2677	2416	2175
	arc, inches:	-1.5	+1.5	0	-6.6	-18.8
Rem. 140 PSP Core-Lokt	velocity, fps:	3325	3064	2818	2585	2364
	energy, ft-lb:	3436	2918	2468	2077	1737
	arc, inches:		+2.0	+1.7	-2.9	-12.8
Rem. 140 Swift A-Frame	velocity, fps:	3325	3020	2735	2467	2215
	energy, ft-lb:	3436	2834	2324	1892	1525
	arc, inches:		+2.1	+1.8	-3.1	-13.8
Speer 145 Grand Slam	velocity, fps:	3300	2992	2075	2435	
	energy, ft-lb:	3506	2882	2355	1909	
	arc, inches:		+1.2	0	-6.0	-17.8
Win. 140 Ballistic Silvertip	velocity, fps:	3320	3100	2890	2690	2499
	energy, ft-lb:	3427	2982	2597	2250	1941
	arc, inches:		+1.1	0	-5.2	-15.2
Win. 150 Power-Point	velocity, fps:	3250	2957	2683	2424	2181
	energy, ft-lb:	3519	2913	2398	1958	1584
	arc, inches:		+1.2	0	-6.1	-18.1
Win. 160 Fail Safe	velocity, fps:	3150	2894	2652	2422	2204
	energy, ft-lb:	3526	2976	2499	2085	1727
	arc, inches:		+1.3	0	-6.3	-18.5
7MM REMINGTON ULTRA MAGNUM						
Nosler 175 ABLR	velocity, fps:	3040	2896	2756	2621	2490
	energy, ft-lb:	3590	3258	2952	2669	2409
	arc, inches:	-1.5	+1.3	0	-5.9	-16.9
Rem. 140 PSP Core-Lokt	velocity, fps:	3425	3158	2907	2669	2444
	energy, ft-lb:	3646	3099	2626	2214	1856
	arc, inches:		+1.8	+1.6	-2.7	-11.9
Rem. 140 Nosler Partition	velocity, fps:	3425	3184	2956	2740	2534
	energy, ft-lb:	3646	3151	2715	2333	1995
	arc, inches:		+1.7	+1.6	-2.6	-11.4
Rem. 160 Nosler Partition	velocity, fps:	3200	2991	2791	2600	2417
	energy, ft-lb:	3637	3177	2767	2401	2075
	arc, inches:		+2.1	+1.8	-3.0	-12.9

7.21 (.284) FIREHAWK

CARTRIDGE BULLET	RANGE, YARDS:	0	100	200	300	400
Lazzeroni 140 Nosler Part.	velocity, fps:	3580	3349	3130	2923	2724
	energy, ft-lb:	3985	3488	3048	2656	2308
	arc, inches:		+2.2	+2.9	0	-7.0
Lazzeroni 160 Swift A-Fr.	velocity, fps:	3385	3167	2961	2763	2574
	energy, ft-lb:	4072	3565	3115	2713	2354
	arc, inches:		+2.6	+3.3	0	-7.8

7.5x55 SWISS

CARTRIDGE BULLET	RANGE, YARDS:	0	100	200	300	400
Norma 180 Soft Point	velocity, fps:	2651	2432	2223	2025	
	energy, ft-lb:	2810	2364	1976	1639	
	arc, inches:		+2.2	0	-9.3	
Norma 180 Oryx	velocity, fps:	2493	2222	1968	1734	
	energy, ft-lb:	2485	1974	1549	1201	
	arc, inches:		+2.7	0	-11.8	

7.62x39 RUSSIAN

CARTRIDGE BULLET	RANGE, YARDS:	0	100	200	300	400
Federal 123 Hi-Shok	velocity, fps:	2300	2030	1780	1550	1350
	energy, ft-lb:	1445	1125	860	655	500.
	arc, inches:		0	-7.0	-25.1	
Federal 124 FMJ	velocity, fps:	2300	2030	1780	1560	1360
	energy, ft-lb:	1455	1135	875	670	510
	arc, inches:		+3.5	0	-14.6	-43.5
PMC 123 FMJ	velocity, fps:	2350	2072	1817	1583	1368
	energy, ft-lb:	1495	1162	894	678	507
	arc, inches:		0	-5.0	-26.4	-67.8
PMC 125 Pointed Soft Point	velocity, fps:	2320	2046	1794	1563	1350
	energy, ft-lb:	1493	1161	893	678	505.
	arc, inches:		0	-5.2	-27.5	-70.6
Rem. 125 Pointed Soft Point	velocity, fps:	2365	2062	1783	1533	1320
	energy, ft-lb:	1552	1180	882	652	483
	arc, inches:		0	-6.7	-24.5	
Win. 123 Soft Point	velocity, fps:	2365	2033	1731	1465	1248
	energy, ft-lb:	1527	1129	818	586	425
	arc, inches:		+3.8	0	-15.4	-46.3

.30 CARBINE

CARTRIDGE BULLET	RANGE, YARDS:	0	100	200	300	400
Federal 110 Hi-Shok RN	velocity, fps:	1990	1570	1240	1040	920
	energy, ft-lb:	965	600	375	260	210
	arc, inches:		0	-12.8	-46.9	
Federal 110 FMJ	velocity, fps:	1990	1570	1240	1040	920
	energy, ft-lb:	965	600	375	260	210
	arc, inches:		0	-12.8	-46.9	
Hornady 110 FTX (20-inch barrel)	velocity, fps:	2000	1601	1279	1067	
	energy, ft-lb:	977	626	399	278	
	arc, inches:		0	-12.9	-47.2	
Magtech 110 FMC	velocity, fps:	1990	1654			
	energy, ft-lb:	965	668			
	arc, inches:		0			
PMC 110 FMJ	(and RNSP)velocity, fps:	1927	1548	1248		
	energy, ft-lb:	906	585	380		
	arc, inches:		0	-14.2		
Rem. 110 Soft Point	velocity, fps:	1990	1567	1236	1035	923
	energy, ft-lb:	967	600	373	262	208
	arc, inches:		0	-12.9	-48.6	
Win. 110 Hollow Soft Point	velocity, fps:	1990	1567	1236	1035	923
	energy, ft-lb:	967	600	373	262	208
	arc, inches:		0	-13.5	-49.9	

.30 T/C HORNADAY

CARTRIDGE BULLET	RANGE, YARDS:	0	100	200	300	400
Hornady 150	velocity, fps	3000	2772	2555	2348	
	energy, ft-lb	2997	2558	2176	1836	
	arc, inches	-1.5	+1.5	0	-6.9	

CARTRIDGE BULLET	RANGE, YARDS:	0	100	200	300	400
Hornady 165	velocity, fps	2850	2644	2447	2258	
	energy, ft-lb	2975	2560	2193	1868	
	arc, inches	-1.5	+1.7	0	-7.6	

.30-30 WINCHESTER

CARTRIDGE BULLET	RANGE, YARDS:	0	100	200	300	400
Federal 125 Hi-Shok HP	velocity, fps:	2570	2090	1660	1320	1080
	energy, ft-lb:	1830	1210	770	480	320
	arc, inches:		+3.3	0	-16.0	-50.9
Federal 150 Hi-Shok FN	velocity, fps:	2390	2020	1680	1400	1180
	energy, ft-lb:	1900	1355	945	650	460
	arc, inches:		+3.6	0	-15.9	-49.1
Federal 170 Hi-Shok RN	velocity, fps:	2200	1900	1620	1380	1190
	energy, ft-lb:	1830	1355	990	720	535
	arc, inches:		+4.1	0	-17.4	-52.4
Federal 170 Sierra Pro-Hunt.	velocity, fps:	2200	1820	1500	1240	1060
	energy, ft-lb:	1830	1255	845	575	425
	arc, inches:		+4.5	0	-20.0	-63.5
Federal 170 Nosler Partition	velocity, fps:	2200	1900	1620	1380	1190
	energy, ft-lb:	1830	1355	990	720	535
	arc, inches:		+4.1	0	-17.4	-52.4
Hornady 150 Round Nose	velocity, fps:	2390	1973	1605	1303	1095
	energy, ft-lb:	1902	1296	858	565	399
	arc, inches:		0	-8.2	-30.0	
Hornady 160 Evolution	velocity, fps:	2400	2150	1916	1699	
	energy, ft-lb:	2046	1643	1304	1025	
	arc, inches:		+3.0	0.2	-12.1	
Hornady 170 Flat Point	velocity, fps:	2200	1895	1619	1381	1191
	energy, ft-lb:	1827	1355	989	720	535
	arc, inches:		0	-8.9	-31.1	
Norma 150 Soft Point	velocity, fps:	2329	2008	1716	1459	
	energy, ft-lb:	1807	1344	981	709	
	arc, inches:		+3.6	0	-15.5	
PMC 150 Starfire HP	velocity, fps:	2100	1769	1478		
	energy, ft-lb:	1469	1042	728		
	arc, inches:		0	-10.8		
PMC 150 Flat Nose	velocity, fps:	2300	1943	1627		
	energy, ft-lb:	1762	1257	881		
	arc, inches:		0	-7.8		
PMC 170 Flat Nose	velocity, fps:	2150	1840	1566		
	energy, ft-lb:	1745	1277	926		
	arc, inches:		0	-8.9		
Rem. 55 PSP (sabot) "Accelerator"	velocity, fps:	3400	2693	2085	1570	1187
	energy, ft-lb:	1412	886	521	301	172
	arc, inches:		+1.7	0	-9.9	-34.3
Rem. 150 SP Core-Lokt	velocity, fps:	2390	1973	1605	1303	1095
	energy, ft-lb:	1902	1296	858	565	399
	arc, inches:		0	-7.6	-28.8	
Rem. 170 SP Core-Lokt	velocity, fps:	2200	1895	1619	1381	1191
	energy, ft-lb:	1827	1355	989	720	535
	arc, inches:		0	-8.3	-29.9	
Rem. 170 HP Core-Lokt	velocity, fps:	2200	1895	1619	1381	1191.
	energy, ft-lb:	1827	1355	989	720	535
	arc, inches:		0	-8.3	-29.9	
Speer 150 Flat Nose	velocity, fps:	2370	2067	1788	1538	
	energy, ft-lb:	1870	1423	1065	788	
	arc, inches:		+3.3	0	-14.4	-43.7
Win. 150 Hollow Point	velocity, fps:	2390	2018	1684	1398	1177
	energy, ft-lb:	1902	1356	944	651	461
	arc, inches:		0	-7.7	-27.9	
Win. 150 Power-Point	velocity, fps:	2390	2018	1684	1398	1177
	energy, ft-lb:	1902	1356	944	651	461
	arc, inches:		0	-7.7	-27.9	
Win. 150 Silvertip	velocity,fps:	2390	2018	1684	1398	1177
	energy, ft-lb:	1902	1356	944	651	461
	arc, inches:		0	-7.7	-27.9	

Centerfire Rifle Ballistics

.30-30 WINCHESTER TO .308 WINCHESTER

CARTRIDGE BULLET	RANGE, YARDS:	0	100	200	300	400
Win. 150 Power-Point Plus	velocity, fps:	2480	2095	1747	1446	1209
	energy, ft-lb:	2049	1462	1017	697	487
	arc, inches:		0	-6.5	-24.5	
Win. 170 Power-Point	velocity, fps:	2200	1895	1619	1381	1191
	energy, ft-lb:	1827	1355	989	720	535.
	arc, inches:		0	-8.9	-31.1	
Win. 170 Silvertip	velocity, fps:	2200	1895	1619	1381	1191
	energy, ft-lb:	1827	1355	989	720	535
	arc, inches:		0	-8.9	-31.1	

.300 SAVAGE

CARTRIDGE BULLET	RANGE, YARDS:	0	100	200	300	400
Federal 150 Hi-Shok	velocity, fps:	2630	2350	2100	1850	1630
	energy, ft-lb:	2305	1845	1460	1145	885
	arc, inches:		+2.4	0	-10.4	-30.9
Federal 180 Hi-Shok	velocity, fps:	2350	2140	1940	1750	1570
	energy, ft-lb:	2205	1825	1495	1215	985
	arc, inches:		+3.1	0	-12.4	-36.1
Hornady 150 SST	velocity, fps:	2740	2499	2272	2056	1852
	energy, ft-lb:	2500	2081	1718	1407	1143
	arc, inches:		+2.1	0	-8.8	-25.8
Rem. 150 PSP Core-Lokt	velocity, fps:	2630	2354	2095	1853	1631
	energy, ft-lb:	2303	1845	1462	1143	806.
	arc, inches:		+2.4	0	-10.4	-30.9
Rem. 180 SP Core-Lokt	velocity, fps:	2350	2025	1728	1467	1252
	energy, ft-lb:	2207	1639	1193	860	626
	arc, inches:		0	-7.1	-25.9	
Win. 150 Power-Point	velocity, fps:	2630	2311	2015	1743	1500
	energy, ft-lb:	2303	1779	1352	1012	749
	arc, inches:		+2.8	0	-11.5	-34.4

.307 WINCHESTER

CARTRIDGE BULLET	RANGE, YARDS:	0	100	200	300	400
Win. 180 Power-Point	velocity, fps:	2510	2179	1874	1599	1362
	energy, ft-lb:	2519	1898	1404	1022	742
	arc, inches:		+1.5	-3.6	-18.6	-47.1

.30-40 KRAG

CARTRIDGE BULLET	RANGE, YARDS:	0	100	200	300	400
Rem. 180 PSP Core-Lokt	velocity, fps:	2430	2213	2007	1813	1632.
	energy, ft-lb:	2360	1957	1610	1314	1064
	arc, inches, s:		0	-5.6	-18.6	
Win. 180 Power-Point	velocity, fps:	2430	2099	1795	1525	1298
	energy, ft-lb:	2360	1761	1288	929	673
	arc, inches, s:		0	-7.1	-25.0	

7.62x54R RUSSIAN

CARTRIDGE BULLET	RANGE, YARDS:	0	100	200	300	400
Norma 150 Soft Point	velocity, fps:	2953	2622	2314	2028	
	energy, ft-lb:	2905	2291	1784	1370	
	arc, inches:		+1.8	0	-8.3	
Norma 180 Alaska	velocity, fps:	2575	2362	2159	1967	
	energy, ft-lb:	2651	2231	1864	1546	
	arc, inches:		+2.9	0	-12.9	
Winchester 180 FMJ	velocity, fps:	2580	2401	2230	2066	1909
	energy, ft-lb:	2658	2304	1987	1706	1457
	arc, inches:	-1.5	+2.6	0	-9.6	-27.3
Winchester 180 SP	velocity, fps:	2625	2302	2003	1729	1485
	energy, ft-lb:	2751	2117	1603	1195	882
	arc, inches:	-1.5	+2.9	0	-11.6	-34.9

.308 MARLIN EXPRESS

CARTRIDGE BULLET	RANGE, YARDS:	0	100	200	300	400
Hornady 160	velocity, fps	2660	2438	2226	2026	1836
	energy, ft-lb	2513	2111	1761	1457	1197
	arc, inches	-1.5	+3.0	+1.7	-6.7	-23.5
Hornady 140 MonoFlex	velocity, fps	2800	2532	2279	2040	1818

CARTRIDGE BULLET	RANGE, YARDS:	0	100	200	300	400
	energy, ft-lb:	2437	1992	1614	1294	1027
	arc, inches:	-1.5	+2.0	0	-8.7	-25.8

.308 WINCHESTER

CARTRIDGE BULLET	RANGE, YARDS:	0	100	200	300	400
Black Hills 150 Nosler B. Tip	velocity, fps:	2800				
	energy, ft-lb:	2611				
	arc, inches:					
Black Hills 165 Nosler B. Tip (and SP)	velocity, fps:	2650				
	energy, ft-lb:	2573				
	arc, inches:					
Black Hills 168 Barnes X (and Match)	velocity, fps:	2650				
	energy, ft-lb:	2620				
	arc, inches:					
Black Hills 175 Match	velocity, fps:	2600				
	energy, ft-lb:	2657				
	arc, inches:					
Black Hills 180 AccuBond	velocity, fps:	2600				
	energy, ft-lb:	2701				
	arc, inches:					
Federal 150 Barnes XLC	velocity, fps:	2820	2610	2400	2210	2030
	energy, ft-lb:	2650	2265	1925	1630	1370
	arc, inches:		+1.80	-7.8	-22.9	
Federal 150 FMJ Boat-Tail	velocity, fps:	2820	2620	2430	2250	2070
	energy, ft-lb:	2650	2285	1965	1680	1430
	arc, inches:		+1.80	-7.7	-22.4	
Federal 150 Hi-Shok	velocity, fps:	2820	2530	2260	2010	1770
	energy, ft-lb:	2650	2140	1705	1345	1050
	arc, inches:		+2.0	0	-8.8	-26.3
Federal 150 Nosler Bal. Tip.	velocity, fps:	2820	2610	2410	2220	2040
	energy, ft-lb:	2650	2270	1935	1640	1380
	arc, inches:		+1.8	0	-7.8	-22.7
Federal 150 Trophy Copper	velocity, fps:	2820	2630	2440	2260	2090
	energy, ft-lb:	2650	2295	1980	1700	1455
	arc, inches:		+1.8	0	-7.6	-22.2
Federal 155 Sierra MatchKg. BTHP	velocity, fps:	2950	2740	2540	2350	2170
	energy, ft-lb:	2995	2585	2225	1905	1620
	arc, inches:		+1.9	0	-8.9	-22.6
Federal 165 Sierra GameKing BTSP	velocity, fps:	2700	2520	2330	2160	1990
	energy, ft-lb:	2670	2310	1990	1700	1450
	arc, inches:		+2.0	0	-8.4	-24.3
Federal 165 Trophy Bonded	velocity, fps:	2700	2440	2200	1970	1760
	energy, ft-lb:	2670	2185	1775	1425	1135
	arc, inches:		+2.2	0	-9.4	-27.7
Federal 165 Tr. Bonded HE	velocity, fps:	2870	2600	2350	2120	1890
	energy, ft-lb:	3020	2485	2030	1640	1310
	arc, inches:		+1.8	0	-8.2	-24.0
Federal 168 Sierra MatchKg. BTHP	velocity, fps:	2600	2410	2230	2060	1890
	energy, ft-lb:	2520	2170	1855	1580	1340.
	arc, inches:		+2.1	0	+8.9	+25.9
Federal 180 Hi-Shok	velocity, fps:	2620	2390	2180	1970	1780
	energy, ft-lb:	2745	2290	1895	1555	1270
	arc, inches:		+2.3	0	-9.7	-28.3
Federal 180 Nosler Partition	velocity, fps:	2620	2430	2240	2060	1890
	energy, ft-lb:	2745	2355	2005	1700	1430.
	arc, inches:		+2.2	0	-9.2	-26.5
Federal 180 Nosler Part. HE	velocity, fps:	2740	2550	2370	2200	2030
	energy, ft-lb:	3000	2600	2245	1925	1645
	arc, inches:		+1.9	0	-8.2	-23.5
Federal 180 Sierra Pro-Hunt.	velocity, fps:	2620	2410	2200	2010	1820
	energy, ft-lb:	2745	2315	1940	1610	1330
	arc, inches:		+2.3	0	-9.3	-27.1
Federal 180 Trophy Bonded Tip	velocity, fps:	2620	2450	2280	2120	1960
	energy, ft-lb:	2745	2390	2070	1790	1535
	arc, inches:		+2.2	0	-8.9	-25.5
Hornady 110 TAP-FPD	velocity, fps:	3165	2830	2519	2228	1957
	energy, ft-lb:	2446	1956	1649	1212	935
	arc, inches:		+1.4	0	-6.9	-20.9
Hornady 110 Urban Tactical	velocity, fps:	3170	2825	2504	2206	1937
	energy, ft-lb:	2454	1950	1532	1189	916
	arc, inches:		+1.5	0	-7.2	-21.2

Centerfire Rifle Ballistics

BALLISTICS

CARTRIDGE BULLET	RANGE, YARDS:	0	100	200	300	400
Hornady 125 SST Custom Lite	velocity, fps:	2675	2389	2121	1871	1642
	energy, ft-lb:	1986	1584	1248	971	748
	arc, inches:		+2.3	0	-10.1	-30.1
Hornady 150 SP boat-tail	velocity, fps:	2820	2560	2315	2084	1866
	energy, ft-lb:	2648	2183	1785	1447	1160
	arc, inches:		+2.0	0	-8.5	-25.2
Hornady 150 SP LM	velocity, fps:	2980	2703	2442	2195	1964
	energy, ft-lb:	2959	2433	1986	1606	1285
	arc, inches:	+1.6 0	-7.5	-22.2		
Hornady 150 SST (or Interbond)	velocity, fps:	2820	2593	2378	2174	1984
	energy, ft-lb:	2648	2240	1884	1574	1311
	arc, inches:		+1.9	0	-8.1	-22.9
Hornady 150 SST LM (or Interbond)	velocity, fps:	3000	2765	2541	2328	2127
	energy, ft-lb:	2997	2545	2150	1805	1506
	arc, inches:		+1.5	0	-7.1	-20.6
Hornady 155 A-Max	velocity, fps:	2815	2610	2415	2229	2051
	energy, ft-lb:	2727	2345	2007	1709	1448
	arc, inches:		+1.9	0	-7.9	-22.6
Hornady 155 TAP-FPD	velocity, fps:	2785	2577	2379	2189	2008
	energy, ft-lb:	2669	2285	1947	1649	1387
	arc, inches:		+1.9	0	-8.0	-23.3
Hornady 165 GMX Superformance	velocity, fps:	2750	2550	2358	2174	1999
	energy, ft-lb:	2771	2381	2037	1732	1464
	arc, inches:		+1.9	0	-8.2	-23.8
Hornady 165 SP boat-tail	velocity, fps:	2700	2496	2301	2115	1937
	energy, ft-lb:	2670	2283	1940	1639	1375
	arc, inches:		+2.0	0	-8.7	-25.2
Hornady 165 SPBT LM	velocity, fps:	2870	2658	2456	2283	2078
	energy, ft-lb:	3019	2589	2211	1877	1583
	arc, inches:		+1.7	0	-7.5	-21.8
Hornady 165 SST LM (or Interbond)	velocity, fps:	2880	2672	2474	2284	2103
	energy, ft-lb:	3038	2616	2242	1911	1620
	arc, inches:		+1.6	0	-7.3	-21.2
Hornady 168 BTHP Match	velocity, fps:	2700	2524	2354	2191	2035.
	energy, ft-lb:	2720	2377	2068	1791	1545
	arc, inches:		+2.0	0	-8.4	-23.9
Hornady 168 BTHP Match LM	velocity, fps:	2640	2630	2429	2238	2056
	energy, ft-lb:	3008	2579	2201	1868	1577
	arc, inches:		+1.8	0	-7.8	-22.4
Hornady 168 A-Max Match	velocity, fps:	2620	2446	2280	2120	1972
	energy, ft-lb:	2560	2232	1939	1677	1450
	arc, inches:		+2.6	0	-9.2	-25.6
Hornady 168 A-Max	velocity, fps:	2700	2491	2292	2102	1921
	energy, ft-lb:	2719	2315	1959	1648	1377
	arc, inches:		+2.4	0	-9.0	-25.9
Hornady 168 TAP-FPD	velocity, fps:	2700	2513	2333	2161	1996
	energy, ft-lb:	2719	2355	2030	1742	1486
	arc, inches:		+2.0	0	-8.4	-24.3
Hornady 178 BTHP Match	velocity, fps:	2600	2436	2278	2125	1979
	energy, ft-lb:	2672	2345	2050	1785	1548
	arc, inches:		+2.2	0	-8.9	-25.5
Hornady 180 A-Max Match	velocity, fps:	2550	2397	2249	2106	1974
	energy, ft-lb:	2598	2295	2021	1773	1557
	arc, inches:		+2.7	0	-9.5	-26.2
Norma 150 Nosler Bal. Tip	velocity, fps:	2822	2588	2365	2154	
	energy, ft-lb:	2653	2231	1864	1545	
	arc, inches:		+1.6	0	-7.1	
Norma 150 Soft Point	velocity, fps:	2861	2537	2235	1954	
	energy, ft-lb:	2727	2144	1664	1272	
	arc, inches:		+2.0	0	-9.0	
Norma 165 TXP Swift A-Fr.	velocity, fps:	2700	2459	2231	2015	
	energy, ft-lb:	2672	2216	1824	1488	
	arc, inches:		+2.1	0	-9.1	
Norma 180 Plastic Point	velocity, fps:	2612	2365	2131	1911	
	energy, ft-lb:	2728	2235	1815	1460	
	arc, inches:		+2.4	0	-10.1	
Norma 180 Nosler Partition	velocity, fps:	2612	2414	2225	2044	
	energy, ft-lb:	2728	2330	1979	1670	
	arc, inches:		+2.2	0	-9.3	
Norma 180 Alaska	velocity, fps:	2612	2269	1953	1667	
	energy, ft-lb:	2728	2059	1526	1111	
	arc, inches:		+2.7	0	-11.9	
Norma 180 Vulkan	velocity, fps:	2612	2325	2056	1806	
	energy, ft-lb:	2728	2161	1690	1304	
	arc, inches:		+2.5	0	-10.8	
Norma 180 Oryx	velocity, fps:	2612	2305	2019	1755	
	energy, ft-lb:	2728	2124	1629	1232	
	arc, inches:		+2.5	0	-11.1	
Norma 200 Vulkan	velocity, fps:	2461	2215	1983	1767	
	energy, ft-lb:	2690	2179	1747	1387	
	arc, inches:		+2.8	0	-11.7	
PMC 147 FMJ boat-tail	velocity, fps:	2751	2473	2257	2052	1859
	energy, ft-lb:	2428	2037	1697	1403	1150
	arc, inches:		+2.3	0	-9.3	-27.3
PMC 150 Barnes X	velocity, fps:	2700	2504	2316	2135	1964
	energy, ft-lb:	2428	2087	1786	1518	1284
	arc, inches:		+2.0	0	-8.6	-24.7
PMC 150 Pointed Soft Point	velocity, fps:	2750	2478	2224	1987	1766
	energy, ft-lb:	2519	2045	1647	1315	1039
	arc, inches:		+2.1	0	-9.2	-27.1
PMC 150 SP boat-tail	velocity, fps:	2820	2581	2354	2139	1935
	energy, ft-lb:	2648	2218	1846	1523	1247.
	arc, inches:		+1.9	0	-8.2	-24.0
PMC 168 Barnes X	velocity, fps:	2600	2425	2256	2095	1940
	energy, ft-lb:	2476	2154	1865	1608	1379
	arc, inches:		+2.2	0	-9.0	-26.0
PMC 168 HP boat-tail	velocity, fps:	2650	2460	2278	2103	1936
	energy, ft-lb:	2619	2257	1935	1649	1399
	arc, inches:		+2.1	0	-8.8	-25.6
PMC 168 Pointed Soft Point	velocity, fps:	2559	2354	2160	1976	1803
	energy, ft-lb:	2443	2067	1740	1457	1212
	arc, inches:		+2.4	0	-9.9	-28.7
PMC 168 Pointed Soft Point	velocity, fps:	2600	2404	2216	2037	1866
	energy, ft-lb:	2476	2064	1709	1403	1142
	arc, inches:		+2.3	0	-9.8	-28.7
PMC 180 Pointed Soft Point	velocity, fps:	2550	2335	2132	1940	1760
	energy, ft-lb:	2599	2179	1816	1504	1238.
	arc, inches:		+2.5	0	-10.1	-29.5
PMC 180 SP boat-tail	velocity, fps:	2620	2446	2278	2117	1962
	energy, ft-lb:	2743	2391	2074	1790	1538
	arc, inches:		+2.2	0	-8.9	-25.4
Rem. 125 PSP C-L MR	velocity, fps:	2660	2348	2057	1788	1546
	energy, ft-lb:	1964	1529	1174	887	663
	arc, inches:		+1.1	-2.7	-14.3	-35.8
Rem. 150 PSP Core-Lokt	velocity, fps:	2820	2533	2263	2009	1774
	energy, ft-lb:	2648	2137	1705	1344	1048
	arc, inches:		+2.0	0	-8.8	-26.2
Rem. 150 PSP C-L Ultra	velocity, fps:	2620	2404	2198	2002	1818
	energy, ft-lb:	2743	2309	1930	1601	1320
	arc, inches:		+2.3	0	-9.5	-26.4
Rem. 150 Swift Scirocco	velocity, fps:	2820	2611	2410	2219	2037
	energy, ft-lb:	2648	2269	1935	1640	1381
	arc, inches:		+1.8	0	-7.8	-22.7
Rem. 165 AccuTip	velocity, fps:	2700	2501	2311	2129	1958.
	energy, ft-lb:	2670	2292	1957	1861	1401.
	arc, inches:		+2.0	0	-8.6	-24.8
Rem. 165 PSP boat-tail	velocity, fps:	2700	2497	2303	2117	1941.
	energy, ft-lb:	2670	2284	1942	1642	1379
	arc, inches:		+2.0	0	-8.6	-25.0
Rem. 165 Nosler Bal. Tip	velocity, fps:	2700	2613	2333	2161	1996
	energy, ft-lb:	2672	2314	1995	1711	1460
	arc, inches:		+2.0	0	-8.4	-24.3

Centerfire Rifle Ballistics

.308 WINCHESTER TO .30-06 SPRINGFIELD

CARTRIDGE BULLET	RANGE, YARDS:	0	100	200	300	400
Rem. 165 Swift Scirocco	velocity, fps:	2700	2513	2233	2161	1996
	energy, fps:	2670	2313	1994	1711	1459
	arc, inches:		+2.0	0	-8.4	-24.3
Rem. 168 HPBT Match	velocity, fps:	2680	2493	2314	2143	1979
	energy, ft-lb:	2678	2318	1998	1713	1460
	arc, inches:		+2.1	0	-8.6	-24.7
Rem. 180 SP Core-Lokt	velocity, fps:	2620	2274	1955	1666	1414
	energy, ft-lb:	2743	2066	1527	1109	799
	arc, inches:		+2.6	0	-11.8	-36.3
Rem. 180 PSP Core-Lokt	velocity, fps:	2620	2393	2178	1974	1782
	energy, ft-lb:	2743	2288	1896	1557	1269
	arc, inches:		+2.3	0	-9.7	-28.3
Rem. 180 Nosler Partition	velocity, fps:	2620	2436	2259	2089	1927.
	energy, ft-lb:	2743	2371	2039	1774	1485
	arc, inches:		+2.2	0	-9.0	-26.0
Speer 150 Grand Slam	velocity, fps:	2900	2599	2317	2053	
	energy, ft-lb:	2800	2249	1788	1404	
	arc, inches:		+2.1	0	-8.6	-24.8
Speer 165 Grand Slam	velocity, fps:	2700	2475	2261	2057	
	energy, ft-lb:	2670	2243	1872	1550	
	arc, inches:		+2.1	0	-8.9	-25.9
Speer 180 Grand Slam	velocity, fps:	2620	2420	2229	2046	
	energy, ft-lb:	2743	2340	1985	1674	
	arc, inches:		+2.2	0	-9.2	-26.6
Win. 150 Power-Point	velocity, fps:	2820	2488	2179	1893	1633
	energy, ft-lb:	2648	2061	1581	1193	888
	arc, inches:		+2.4	0	-9.8	-29.3
Win. 150 Power-Point Plus	velocity, fps:	2900	2558	2241	1946	1678
	energy, ft-lb:	2802	2180	1672	1262	938
	arc, inches:		+1.9	0	-8.9	-27.0
Win. 150 Partition Gold	velocity, fps:	2900	2645	2405	2177	1962
	energy, ft-lb:	2802	2332	1927	1579	1282.
	arc, inches:		+1.7	0	-7.8	-22.9
Win. 150 Ballistic Silvertip	velocity, fps:	2810	2601	2401	2211	2028
	energy, ft-lb:	2629	2253	1920	1627	1370.
	arc, inches:		+1.8	0	-7.8	-22.8
Win. 150 Fail Safe	velocity, fps:	2820	2533	2263	2010	1775
	energy, ft-lb:	2649	2137	1706	1346	1049
	arc, inches:		+2.0	0	-8.8	-26.2
Win. 150 Supreme Elite XP3	velocity, fps:	2825	2616	2417	2226	2044
	energy, ft-lb:	2658	2279	1945	1650	1392
	arc, inches:		+1.8	0	-7.8	-22.6
Win. 168 Ballistic Silvertip	velocity, fps:	2670	2484	2306	2134	1971
	energy, ft-lb:	2659	2301	1983	1699	1449
	arc, inches:		+2.1	0	-8.6	-24.8
Win. 168 HP boat-tail Match	velocity, fps:	2680	2485	2297	2118	1948
	energy, ft-lb:	2680	2303	1970	1674	1415
	arc, inches:		+2.1	0	-8.7	-25.1
Win. 180 Power-Point	velocity, fps:	2620	2274	1955	1666	1414
	energy, ft-lb:	2743	2066	1527	1109	799
	arc, inches:		+2.9	0	-12.1	-36.9
Win. 180 Silvertip	velocity, fps:	2620	2393	2178	1974	1782
	energy, ft-lb:	2743	2288	1896	1557	1269
	arc, inches:		+2.6	0	-9.9	-28.9

.30-06 SPRINGFIELD

CARTRIDGE BULLET	RANGE, YARDS:	0	100	200	300	400
A-Square 180 M & D-T	velocity, fps:	2700	2365	2054	1769	1524
	energy, ft-lb:	2913	2235	1687	1251	928
	arc, inches:		+2.4	0	-10.6	-32.4
A-Square 220 Monolythic Solid	velocity, fps:	2380	2108	1854	1623	1424
	energy, ft-lb:	2767	2171	1679	1287	990
	arc, inches:		+3.1	0	-13.6	-39.9
Black Hills 150 Nosler B. Tip	velocity, fps:	2900				
	energy, ft-lb:	2770				
	arc, inches:					
Black Hills 165 Nosler B. Tip	velocity, fps:	2750				
	energy, ft-lb:	2770				
	arc, inches:					
Black Hills 168 Hor. Match	velocity, fps:	2700				
	energy, ft-lb:	2718				
	arc, inches:					
Black Hills 180 Barnes X	velocity, fps:	2650				
	energy, ft-lb:	2806				
	arc, inches:					
Black Hills 180 AccuBond	velocity, fps:	2700				
	energy, ft-lb:					
	arc, inches:					
Federal 125 Sierra Pro-Hunt.	velocity, fps:	3140	2780	2450	2140	1850
	energy, ft-lb:	2735	2145	1660	1270	955
	arc, inches:		+1.5	0	-7.3	-22.3
Federal 150 Hi-Shok	velocity, fps:	2910	2620	2340	2080	1840
	energy, ft-lb:	2820	2280	1825	1445	1130
	arc, inches:		+1.8	0	-8.2	-24.4
Federal 150 Sierra Pro-Hunt.	velocity, fps:	2910	2640	2380	2130	1900
	energy, ft-lb:	2820	2315	1880	1515	1205
	arc, inches:		+1.7	0	-7.9	-23.3
Federal 150 Sierra GameKing BTSP	velocity, fps:	2910	2690	2480	2270	2070
	energy, ft-lb:	2820	2420	2040	1710	1430
	arc, inches:		+1.7	0	-7.4	-21.5
Federal 150 Nosler Bal. Tip	velocity, fps:	2910	2700	2490	2300	2110
	energy, ft-lb:	2820	2420	2070	1760	1485
	arc, inches:		+1.6	0	-7.3	-21.1
Federal 150 FMJ boat-tail	velocity, fps:	2910	2710	2510	2320	2150
	energy, ft-lb:	2820	2440	2100	1800	1535
	arc, inches:		+1.6	0	-7.1	-20.8
Federal 165 Sierra Pro-Hunt.	velocity, fps:	2800	2560	2340	2130	1920
	energy, ft-lb:	2875	2410	2005	1655	1360
	arc, inches:		+1.9	0	-8.3	-24.3
Federal 165 Sierra GameKing BTSP	velocity, fps:	2800	2610	2420	2240	2070.
	energy, ft-lb:	2870	2490	2150	1840	1580
	arc, inches:		+1.8	0	-7.8	-22.4
Federal 165 Sierra GameKing HE	velocity, fps:	3140	2900	2670	2450	2240.
	energy, ft-lb:	3610	3075	2610	2200	1845
	arc, inches:		+1.5	0	-6.9	-20.4
Federal 165 Nosler Bal. Tip	velocity, fps:	2800	2610	2430	2250	2080
	energy, ft-lb:	2870	2495	2155	1855	1585
	arc, inches:		+1.8	0	-7.7	-22.3
Federal 165 Trophy Bonded	velocity, fps:	2800	2540	2290	2050	1830.
	energy, ft-lb:	2870	2360	1915	1545	1230
	arc, inches:		+2.0	0	-8.7	-25.4
Federal 165 Tr. Bonded HE	velocity, fps:	3140	2860	2590	2340	2100
	energy, ft-lb:	3610	2990	2460	2010	1625.
	arc, inches:		+1.6	0	-7.4	-21.9
Federal 165 Trophy Copper	velocity, fps:	2800	2620	2450	2280	2120
	energy, ft-lb:	2870	2515	2190	1900	1645
	arc, inches:		+1.8	0	-7.6	-22.0
Federal 168 Sierra MatchKg. BTHP	velocity, fps:	2700	2510	2320	2150	1980
	energy, ft-lb:	2720	2350	2010	1720	1460
	arc, inches:		+16.2	+28.4	+34.1	+32.3
Federal 180 Barnes XLC	velocity, fps:	2700	2530	2360	2200	2040
	energy, ft-lb:	2915	2550	2220	1930	1670
	arc, inches:	+2.0	0	-8.3	-23.8	
Federal 180 Hi-Shok	velocity, fps:	2700	2470	2250	2040	1850
	energy, ft-lb:	2915	2435	2025	1665	1360
	arc, inches:		+2.1	0	-9.0	-26.4
Federal 180 Sierra Pro-Hunt. RN	velocity, fps:	2700	2350	2020	1730	1470
	energy, ft-lb:	2915	2200	1630	1190	860
	arc, inches:		+2.4	0	-11.0	-33.6
Federal 180 Nosler Partition	velocity, fps:	2700	2500	2320	2140	1970
	energy, ft-lb:	2915	2510	2150	1830	1550
	arc, inches:		+2.0	0	-8.6	-24.6

Centerfire Rifle Ballistics

BALLISTICS

CARTRIDGE BULLET	RANGE, YARDS:	0	100	200	300	400
Federal 180 Nosler Part. HE	velocity, fps:	2880	2690	2500	2320	2150
	energy, ft-lb:	3315	2880	2495	2150	1845
	arc, inches:		+1.7	0	-7.2	-21.0
Federal 180 Sierra GameKing BTSP	velocity, fps:	2700	2540	2380	2220	2080
	energy, ft-lb:	2915	2570	2260	1975	1720
	arc, inches:		+1.9	0	-8.1	-23.1
Federal 180 Barnes XLC	velocity, fps:	2700	2530	2360	2200	2040.
	energy, ft-lb:	2915	2550	2220	1930	1670
	arc, inches:		+2.0	0	-8.3	-23.8
Federal 180 Sierra Pro-Hunt. RN	velocity, fps:	2700	2350	2020	1730	1470
	energy, ft-lb:	2915	2200	1630	1190	860
	arc, inches:		+2.4	0	-11.0	-33.6
Federal 180 Trophy Bonded	velocity, fps:	2700	2460	2220	2000	1800
	energy, ft-lb:	2915	2410	1975	1605	1290
	arc, inches:		+2.2	0	-9.2	-27.0
Federal 180 Tr. Bonded HE	velocity, fps:	2880	2630	2380	2160	1940
	energy, ft-lb:	3315	2755	2270	1855	1505
	arc, inches:		+1.8	0	-8.0	-23.3
Federal 180 Trophy Bonded Tip	velocity, fps:	2700	2520	2350	2190	2030
	energy, ft-lb:	2915	2540	2219	1910	1645
	arc, inches:		+2.0	0	-8.4	-23.9
Federal 200 Trophy Bonded	velocity, fps:	2540	2320	2120	1920	1740
	energy, ft-lb:	2865	2395	1990	1640	1345
	arc, inches:		+2.5	0	-10.1	-29.9
Federal 220 Sierra Pro-Hunt. RN	velocity, fps:	2410	2130	1870	1630	1420
	energy, ft-lb:	2835	2215	1705	1300	985
	arc, inches:		+3.1	0	-13.1	-39.3
Hornady 125 SST Custom Lite	velocity, fps:	2700	2412	2143	1891	1660
	energy, ft-lb:	2023	1615	1274	993	765
	arc, inches:		+2.3	0	-9.9	-29.5
Hornady 150 GMX Superformance	velocity, fps:	3080	2848	2628	2418	2218
	energy, ft-lb:	3159	2701	2300	1948	1639
	arc, inches:		+1.4	0	-6.4	-18.8
Hornady 150 SP	velocity, fps:	2910	2617	2342	2083	1843
	energy, ft-lb:	2820	2281	1827	1445	1131
	arc, inches:		+2.1	0	-8.5	-25.0
Hornady 150 SP LM	velocity, fps:	3100	2815	2548	2295	2058
	energy, ft-lb:	3200	2639	2161	1755	1410
	arc, inches:		+1.4	0	-6.8	-20.3
Hornady 150 SP boat-tail	velocity, fps:	2910	2683	2467	2262	2066.
	energy, ft-lb:	2820	2397	2027	1706	1421
	arc, inches:		+2.0	0	-7.7	-22.2
Hornady 150 SST (or Interbond)	velocity, fps:	2910	2802	2599	2405	2219
	energy, ft-lb:	3330	2876	2474	2118	1803
	arc, inches:		+1.5	0	-6.6	-19.3
Hornady 150 SST LM	velocity, fps:	3100	2860	2631	2414	2208
	energy, ft-lb:	3200	2724	2306	1941	1624
	arc, inches:		+1.4	0	-6.6	-19.2
Hornady 165 GMX Superformance	velocity, fps:	2940	2731	2532	2341	2158
	energy, ft-lb:	3167	2732	3248	2007	1706
	arc, inches:		+1.5	0	-7.0	-20.4
Hornady 165 SP boat-tail	velocity, fps:	2800	2591	2392	2202	2020
	energy, ft-lb:	2873	2460	2097	1777	1495
	arc, inches:		+1.8	0	-8.0	-23.3
Hornady 165 SPBT LM	velocity, fps:	3015	2790	2575	2370	2176
	energy, ft-lb:	3330	2850	2428	2058	1734
	arc, inches:		+1.6	0	-7.0	-20.1
Hornady 165 SST (or Interbond)	velocity, fps:	2800	2598	2405	2221	2046
	energy, ft-lb:	2872	2473	2119	1808	1534
	arc, inches:		+1.9	0	-8.0	-22.8
Hornady 165 SST LM	velocity, fps:	3015	2802	2599	2405	2219
	energy, ft-lb:	3330	2878	2474	2118	1803.
	arc, inches:		+1.5	0	-6.5	-19.3
Hornady 168 A-Max Garand Match	velocity, fps:	2710	2523	2343	2171	2006
	energy, ft-lb:	2739	2374	2048	1758	1501
	arc, inches:		+2.3	0	-8.6	-24.6
Hornady 168 HPBT Match	velocity, fps:	2790	2620	2447	2280	2120.
	energy, ft-lb:	2925	2561	2234	1940	1677.
	arc, inches:		+1.7	0	-7.7	-22.2
Hornady 180 SP	velocity, fps:	2700	2469	2258	2042	1846
	energy, ft-lb:	2913	2436	2023	1666	1362
	arc, inches:		+2.4	0	-9.3	-27.0
Hornady 180 SPBT LM	velocity, fps:	2880	2676	2480	2293	2114
	energy, ft-lb:	3316	2862	2459	2102	1786
	arc, inches:		+1.7	0	-7.3	-21.3

CARTRIDGE BULLET	RANGE, YARDS:	0	100	200	300	400
Norma 150 Nosler Bal. Tip	velocity, fps:	2936	2713	2502	2300	
	energy, ft-lb:	2872	2453	2085	1762	
	arc, inches:		+1.6	0	-7.1	
Norma 150 Soft Point	velocity, fps:	2972	2640	2331	2043	
	energy, ft-lb:	2943	2321	1810	1390	
	arc, inches:		+1.8	0	-8.2	
Norma 180 Alaska	velocity, fps:	2700	2351	2028	1734	
	energy, ft-lb:	2914	2209	1645	1202	
	arc, inches:		+2.4	0	-11.0	
Norma 180 Nosler Partition	velocity, fps:	2700	2494	2297	2108	
	energy, ft-lb:	2914	2486	2108	1777	
	arc, inches:		+2.1	0	-8.7	
Norma 180 Plastic Point	velocity, fps:	2700	2455	2222	2003	
	energy, ft-lb:	2914	2409	1974	1603	
	arc, inches:		+2.1	0	-9.2	
Norma 180 Vulkan	velocity, fps:	2700	2416	2150	1901	
	energy, ft-lb:	2914	2334	1848	1445	
	arc, inches:		+2.2	0	-9.8	
Norma 180 Oryx	velocity, fps:	2700	2387	2095	1825	
	energy, ft-lb:	2914	2278	1755	1332	
	arc, inches:		+2.3	0	-10.2	
Norma 180 TXP Swift A-Fr.	velocity, fps:	2700	2479	2268	2067	
	energy, ft-lb:	2914	2456	2056	1708	
	arc, inches:		+2.0	0	-8.8	
Norma 180 AccuBond	velocity, fps:	2674	2499	2331	2169	
	energy, ft-lb:	2859	2497	2172	1881	
	arc, inches:		+2.0	0	-8.5	
Norma 200 Vulkan	velocity, fps:	2641	2385	2143	1916	
	energy, ft-lb:	3098	2527	2040	1631	
	arc, inches:		+2.3	0	-9.9	
Norma 200 Oryx	velocity, fps:	2625	2362	2115	1883	
	energy, ft-lb:	3061	2479	1987	1575	
	arc, inches:		+2.3	0	-10.1	
PMC 150 X-Bullet	velocity, fps:	2750	2552	2361	2179	2005
	energy, ft-lb:	2518	2168	1857	1582	1339
	arc, inches:		+2.0	0	-8.2	-23.7
PMC 150 Pointed Soft Point	velocity, fps:	2773	2542	2322	2113	1916
	energy, ft-lb:	2560	2152	1796	1487	1222.
	arc, inches:		+1.9	0	-8.4	-24.6
PMC 150 SP boat-tail	velocity, fps:	2900	2657	2427	2208	2000
	energy, ft-lb:	2801	2351	1961	1623	1332
	arc, inches:		+1.7	0	-7.7	-22.5
PMC 150 FMJ	velocity, fps:	2773	2542	2322	2113	1916
	energy, ft-lb:	2560	2152	1796	1487	1222
	arc, inches:		+1.9	0	-8.4	-24.6
PMC 168 Barnes X	velocity, fps:	2750	2569	2395	2228	2067
	energy, ft-lb:	2770	2418	2101	1818	1565
	arc, inches:		+1.9	0	-8.0	-23.0
PMC 180 Barnes X	velocity, fps:	2650	2487	2331	2179	2034
	energy, ft-lb:	2806	2472	2171	1898	1652
	arc, inches:		+2.1	0	-8.5	-24.3
PMC 180 Pointed Soft Point	velocity, fps:	2650	2430	2221	2024	1839
	energy, ft-lb:	2807	2359	1972	1638	1351
	arc, inches:		+2.2	0	-9.3	-27.0
PMC 180 SP boat-tail	velocity, fps:	2700	2523	2352	2188	2030
	energy, ft-lb:	2913	2543	2210	1913	1646
	arc, inches:		+2.0	0	-8.3	-23.9
PMC 180 HPBT Match	velocity, fps:	2800	2622	2456	2302	2158
	energy, ft-lb:	3133	2747	2411	2118	1861
	arc, inches:		+1.8	0	-7.6	-21.7
Rem. 55 PSP (sabot) "Accelerator"	velocity, fps:	4080	3484	2964	2499	2080
	energy, ft-lb:	2033	1482	1073	763	528.
	arc, inches:		+1.4	+1.4	-2.6	-12.2
Rem. 125 PSP C-L MR	velocity, fps:	2660	2335	2034	1757	1509
	energy, ft-lb:	1964	1513	1148	856	632
	arc, inches:		+1.1	-3.0	-15.5	-37.4
Rem. 125 Pointed Soft Point	velocity, fps:	3140	2780	2447	2138	1853
	energy, ft-lb:	2736	2145	1662	1269	953.
	arc, inches:		+1.5	0	-7.4	-22.4
Rem. 150 AccuTip	velocity, fps:	2910	2686	2473	2270	2077
	energy, ft-lb:	2820	2403	2037	1716	1436
	arc, inches:		+1.8	0	-7.4	-21.5

Centerfire Rifle Ballistics

.30-06 SPRINGFIELD TO .300 BLK

CARTRIDGE BULLET	RANGE, YARDS:	0	100	200	300	400
Rem. 150 PSP Core-Lokt	velocity, fps:	2910	2617	2342	2083	1843
	energy, ft-lb:	2820	2281	1827	1445	1131
	arc, inches:		+1.8	0	-8.2	-24.4
Rem. 150 Bronze Point	velocity, fps:	2910	2656	2416	2189	1974
	energy, ft-lb:	2820	2349	1944	1596	1298
	arc, inches:		+1.7	0	-7.7	-22.7
Rem. 150 Nosler Bal. Tip	velocity, fps:	2910	2696	2492	2298	2112.
	energy, ft-lb:	2821	2422	2070	1769	1485
	arc, inches:		+1.6	0	-7.3	-21.1
Rem. 150 Swift Scirocco	velocity, fps:	2910	2696	2492	2298	2111
	energy, ft-lb:	2820	2421	2069	1758	1485
	arc, inches:		+1.6	0	-7.3	-21.1
Rem. 165 AccuTip	velocity, fps:	2800	2597	2403	2217	2039
	energy, ft-lb:	2872	2470	2115	1800	1523
	arc, inches:		+1.8	0	-7.9	-22.8
Rem. 165 PSP Core-Lokt	velocity, fps:	2800	2534	2283	2047	1825.
	energy, ft-lb:	2872	2352	1909	1534	1220
	arc, inches:		+2.0	0	-8.7	-25.9
Rem. 165 PSP boat-tail	velocity, fps:	2800	2592	2394	2204	2023
	energy, ft-lb:	2872	2462	2100	1780	1500
	arc, inches:		+1.8	0	-7.9	-23.0
Rem. 165 Nosler Bal. Tip	velocity, fps:	2800	2609	2426	2249	2080.
	energy, ft-lb:	2873	2494	2155	1854	1588
	arc, inches:		+1.8	0	-7.7	-22.3
Rem. 168 PSP C-L Ultra	velocity, fps:	2800	2546	2306	2079	1866
	energy, ft-lb:	2924	2418	1984	1613	1299
	arc, inches:		+1.9	0	-8.5	-25.1
Rem. 180 SP Core-Lokt	velocity, fps:	2700	2348	2023	1727	1466
	energy, ft-lb:	2913	2203	1635	1192	859
	arc, inches:		+2.4	0	-11.0	-33.8
Rem. 180 PSP Core-Lokt	velocity, fps:	2700	2469	2250	2042	1846
	energy, ft-lb:	2913	2436	2023	1666	1362
	arc, inches:		+2.1	0	-9.0	-26.3
Rem. 180 PSP C-L Ultra	velocity, fps:	2700	2480	2270	2070	1882
	energy, ft-lb:	2913	2457	2059	1713	1415
	arc, inches:		+2.1	0	-8.9	-25.8
Rem. 180 Bronze Point	velocity, fps:	2700	2485	2280	2084	1899.
	energy, ft-lb:	2913	2468	2077	1736	1441
	arc, inches:		+2.1	0	-8.8	-25.5
Rem. 180 Swift A-Frame	velocity, fps:	2700	2465	2243	2032	1833
	energy, ft-lb:	2913	2429	2010	1650	1343
	arc, inches:		+2.1	0	-9.1	-26.6
Rem. 180 Nosler Partition	velocity, fps:	2700	2512	2332	2160	1995
	energy, ft-lb:	2913	2522	2174	1864	1590
	arc, inches:		+2.0	0	-8.4	-24.3
Rem. 220 SP Core-Lokt	velocity, fps:	2410	2130	1870	1632	1422
	energy, ft-lb:	2837	2216	1708	1301	988
	arc, inches, s:		0	-6.2	-22.4	
Speer 150 Grand Slam	velocity, fps:	2975	2669	2383	2114	
	energy, ft-lb:	2947	2372	1891	1489	
	arc, inches:		+2.0	0	-8.1	-24.1
Speer 165 Grand Slam	velocity, fps:	2790	2560	2342	2134	
	energy, ft-lb:	2851	2401	2009	1669	
	arc, inches:		+1.9	0	-8.3	-24.1
Speer 180 Grand Slam	velocity, fps:	2690	2487	2293	2108	
	energy, ft-lb:	2892	2472	2101	1775	
	arc, inches:		+2.1	0	-8.8	-25.1
Win. 125 Pointed Soft Point	velocity, fps:	3140	2780	2447	2138	1853
	energy, ft-lb:	2736	2145	1662	1269	953
	arc, inches:		+1.8	0	-7.7	-23.0
Win. 150 Power-Point	velocity, fps:	2920	2580	2265	1972	1704
	energy, ft-lb:	2839	2217	1708	1295	967
	arc, inches:		+2.2	0	-9.0	-27.0
Win. 150 Power-Point Plus	velocity, fps:	3050	2685	2352	2043	1760
	energy, ft-lb:	3089	2402	1843	1391	1032
	arc, inches:		+1.7	0	-8.0	-24.3
Win. 150 Silvertip	velocity, fps:	2910	2617	2342	2083	1843
	energy, ft-lb:	2820	2281	1827	1445	1131
	arc, inches:		+2.1	0	-8.5	-25.0

CARTRIDGE BULLET	RANGE, YARDS:	0	100	200	300	400
Win. 150 Partition Gold	velocity, fps:	2960	2705	2464	2235	2019
	energy, ft-lb:	2919	2437	2022	1664	1358.
	arc, inches:		+1.6	0	-7.4	-21.7
Win. 150 Ballistic Silvertip	velocity, fps:	2900	2687	2483	2289	2103
	energy, ft-lb:	2801	2404	2054	1745	1473
	arc, inches:		+1.7	0	-7.3	-21.2
Win. 150 Fail Safe	velocity, fps:	2920	2625	2349	2089	1848
	energy, ft-lb:	2841	2296	1838	1455	1137
	arc, inches:		+1.8	0	-8.1	-24.3
Win. 165 Pointed Soft Point	velocity, fps:	2800	2573	2357	2151	1956
	energy, ft-lb:	2873	2426	2036	1696	1402
	arc, inches:		+2.2	0	-8.4	-24.4
Win. 165 Fail Safe	velocity, fps:	2800	2540	2295	2063	1846
	energy, ft-lb:	2873	2365	1930	1560	1249
	arc, inches:		+2.0	0	-8.6	-25.3
Win. 168 Ballistic Silvertip	velocity, fps:	2790	2599	2416	2240	2072
	energy, ft-lb:	2903	2520	2177	1872	1601
	arc, inches:		+1.8	0	-7.8	-22.5
Win. 180 Ballistic Silvertip	velocity, fps:	2750	2572	2402	2237	2080
	energy, ft-lb:	3022	2644	2305	2001	1728
	arc, inches:		+1.9	0	-7.9	-22.8
Win. 180 Power-Point	velocity, fps:	2700	2348	2023	1727	1466
	energy, ft-lb:	2913	2203	1635	1192	859
	arc, inches:		+2.7	0	-11.3	-34.4
Win. 180 Power-Point Plus	velocity, fps:	2770	2563	2366	2177	1997
	energy, ft-lb:	3068	2627	2237	1894	1594
	arc, inches:		+1.9	0	-8.1	-23.6
Win. 180 Silvertip	velocity, fps:	2700	2469	2250	2042	1846
	energy, ft-lb:	2913	2436	2023	1666	1362
	arc, inches:		+2.4	0	-9.3	-27.0
Win. 180 AccuBond	velocity, fps:	2750	2573	2403	2239	2082
	energy, ft-lb:	3022	2646	2308	2004	1732
	arc, inches:		+1.9	0	-7.9	-22.8
Win. 180 Partition Gold	velocity, fps:	2790	2581	2382	2192	2010
	energy, ft-lb:	3112	2664	2269	1920	1615
	arc, inches:		+1.9	0	-8.0	-23.2
Win. 180 Fail Safe	velocity, fps:	2700	2486	2283	2089	1904
	energy, ft-lb:	2914	2472	2083	1744	1450
	arc, inches:		+2.1	0	-8.7	-25.5
Win. 150 Supreme Elite XP3	velocity, fps:	2925	2712	2508	2313	2127
	energy, ft-lb:	2849	2448	2095	1782	1507
	arc, inches:		+1.6	0	-7.2	-20.8
Win. 180 Supreme Elite XP3	velocity, fps:	2750	2579	2414	2256	2103
	energy, ft-lb:	3022	2658	2330	2034	1768
	arc, inches:		+1.9	0	-7.8	-22.5

.300 BLK (.300 Whisper)

CARTRIDGE BULLET	RANGE, YARDS:	0	100	200	300	400
Barnes 110 Tac/TX	velocity, fps:	2350	1810	1369		
	energy, ft-lb:	1349	800	458		
	arc, inches:	-1.5	-6.7	-55.5		
Black Hills 125 OTM	velocity, fps:	2200				
	energy, ft-lb:	1343				
	arc, inches					
Black Hills 220 OTM	velocity, fps:	1000				
	energy, ft-lb:	488				
	arc, inches					
Hornady 110 V-Max (16-inch barrel)	velocity, fps:	2375	2094	1834	1597	1389
	energy, ft-lb:	1378	1071	821	623	471
	arc, inches:		+3.20	0	-13.7	-41.0
Hornady 110 V-MAX	velocity, fps:	2375	2094	1834	1597	
	energy, ft-lb:	1378	1071	821	623	
	arc, inches:	-1.5	+3.2	0	-13.7	
Hornady 208 A-MAX	velocity, fps:	1020	987	959		
	energy, ft-lb:	480	450	424		
	arc, inches:	-1.5	0	-34.1		

BALLISTICS

.300 H&H MAGNUM

CARTRIDGE BULLET	RANGE, YARDS:	0	100	200	300	400
Federal 180 Barnes TSX	velocity, fps:	2880	2680	2480	2290	2120
	energy, ft-lb:	3315	2860	2460	2105	1790
	arc, inches:	-1.5	+1.7	0	-7.3	-21.3
Federal 180 Nosler Partition	velocity, fps:	2880	2620	2380	2150	1930
	energy, ft-lb:	3315	2750	2260	1840	1480
	arc, inches:		+1.8 0	-8.0	-23.4	
Federal 180 Trophy Bonded Tip	velocity, fps:	2880	2700	2520	2350	2180
	energy, ft-lb:	3315	2900	2530	2200	1900
	arc, inches:		+1.6	0	-7.1	-20.6
Handload, 165 Sierra HP	velocity, fps:	3000	2784	2579	2382	2195
	energy, ft-lb:	3297	2840	2436	2079	1764
	arc, inches:	-1.5	+1.5	0	-6.7	-19.5
Handload, 190 Hornady	velocity, fps:	2800	2615	2437	2266	2102
	energy, ft-lb:	3307	2884	2505	2166	1864
	arc, inches:	-1.5	+1.8	0	-7.7	-22.1
Hornady 180 InterBond	velocity, fps:	2870	2678	2493	2316	2146
	energy, ft-lb:	3292	2865	2484	2144	1841
	arc, inches:	-1.5	+1.	0	-7.3	-21.0
Win. 180 Fail Safe	velocity, fps:	2880	2628	2390	2165	1952
	energy, ft-lb:	3316	2762	2284	1873	1523
	arc, inches:		+1.8 0	-7.9	-23.2	

.308 NORMA MAGNUM

CARTRIDGE BULLET	RANGE, YARDS:	0	100	200	300	400
Norma 180 TXP Swift A-Fr.	velocity, fps:	2953	2704	2469	2245	
	energy, ft-lb:	3486	2924	2437	2016	
	arc, inches:		+1.6	0	-7.3	
Norma 180 Oryx	velocity, fps:	2953	2630	2330	2049	
	energy, ft-lb:	3486	2766	2170	1679	
	arc, inches:		+1.8	0	-8.2	
Norma 200 Vulkan	velocity, fps:	2903	2624	2361	2114	
	energy, ft-lb:	3744	3058	2476	1985	
	arc, inches:	0	+1.8	0	-8.0	
Nosler 180 AB	velocity, fps:	2975	2787	2608	2435	2269
	energy, ft-lb:	3536	3105	2718	2371	2058
	arc, inches:	-1.5	+1.5	0	-6.6	-19.1

.300 WINCHESTER MAGNUM

CARTRIDGE BULLET	RANGE, YARDS:	0	100	200	300	400
A-Square 180 Dead Tough	velocity, fps:	3120	2756	2420	2108	1820
	energy, ft-lb:	3890	3035	2340	1776	1324
	arc, inches:		+1.6	0	-7.6	-22.9
Black Hills 180 Nos. Bal. Tip	velocity, fps:	3100				
	energy, ft-lb:	3498				
	arc, inches:					
Black Hills 180 Barnes X	velocity, fps:	2950				
	energy, ft-lb:	3498				
Black Hills 180 AccuBond	velocity, fps:	3000				
	energy, ft-lb:	3597				
	arc, inches:					
Black Hills 190 Match	velocity, fps:	2950				
	energy, ft-lb:	3672				
	arc, inches:					
Federal 150 Sierra Pro Hunt.	velocity, fps:	3280	3030	2800	2570	2360.
	energy, ft-lb:	3570	3055	2600	2205	1860
	arc, inches:		+1.1	0	-5.6	-16.4
Federal 150 Trophy Bonded	velocity, fps:	3280	2980	2700	2430	2190
	energy, ft-lb:	3570	2450	2420	1970	1590
	arc, inches:		+1.2	0	-6.0	-17.9
Federal 165 Trophy Copper	velocity, fps:	3050	2860	2680	2500	2330
	energy, ft-lb:	3410	2995	2620	2290	1990
	arc, inches:		+1.4	0	-6.3	-18.0
Federal 180 Sierra Pro Hunt.	velocity, fps:	2960	2750	2540	2340	2160
	energy, ft-lb:	3500	3010	2580	2195	1860
	arc, inches:		+1.6	0	-7.0	-20.3

CARTRIDGE BULLET	RANGE, YARDS:	0	100	200	300	400
Federal 180 Barnes XLC	velocity, fps:	2960	2780	2600	2430	2260
	energy, ft-lb:	3500	3080	2700	2355	2050
	arc, inches:		+1.5	0	-6.6	-19.2
Federal 180 Trophy Bonded	velocity, fps:	2960	2700	2460	2220	2000
	energy, ft-lb:	3500	2915	2410	1975	1605
	arc, inches:		+1.6	0	-7.4	-21.9
Federal 180 Tr. Bonded HE	velocity, fps:	3100	2830	2580	2340	2110
	energy, ft-lb:	3840	3205	2660	2190	1790
	arc, inches:		+1.4	0	-6.6	-19.7
Federal 180 Nosler Partition	velocity, fps:	2960	2700	2450	2210	1990
	energy, ft-lb:	3500	2905	2395	1955	1585
	arc, inches:		+1.6	0	-7.5	-22.1
Federal 190 Sierra MatchKg. BTHP	velocity, fps:	2900	2730	2560	2400	2240
	energy, ft-lb:	3550	3135	2760	2420	2115
	arc, inches:		+12.9	+22.5	+26.9	+25.1
Federal 200 Sierra GameKing BTSP	velocity, fps:	2830	2680	2530	2380	2240
	energy, ft-lb:	3560	3180	2830	2520	2230
	arc, inches:		+1.7	0	-7.1	-20.4
Federal 200 Nosler Part. HE	velocity, fps:	2930	2740	2550	2370	2200
	energy, ft-lb:	3810	3325	2885	2495	2145
	arc, inches:		+1.6	0	-6.9	-20.1
Federal 200 Trophy Bonded	velocity, fps:	2800	2570	2350	2150	1950
	energy, ft-lb:	3480	2935	2460	2050	1690
	arc, inches:		+1.9	0	-8.2	-23.9
Hornady 150 SP boat-tail	velocity, fps:	3275	2988	2718	2464	2224
	energy, ft-lb:	3573	2974	2461	2023	1648
	arc, inches:		+1.2	0	-6.0	-17.8
Hornady 150 SST (and Interbond)	velocity, fps:	3275	3027	2791	2565	2352
	energy, ft-lb:	3572	3052	2593	2192	1842
	arc, inches:		+1.2	0	-5.8	-17.0
Hornady 150 SST Custom Lite	velocity, fps:	2800	2582	2375	2177	1988
	energy, ft-lb:	2611	2220	1878	1578	1316
	arc, inches:		+1.9	0	-8.0	-23.5
Hornady 165 SP boat-tail	velocity, fps:	3100	2877	2665	2462	2269.
	energy, ft-lb:	3522	3033	2603	2221	1887
	arc, inches:		+1.3	0	-6.5	-18.5
Hornady 165 SST	velocity, fps:	3100	2885	2680	2483	2296
	energy, ft-lb:	3520	3049	2630	2259	1930
	arc, inches:		+1.4	0	-6.4	-18.6
Hornady 180 SP boat-tail	velocity, fps:	2960	2745	2540	2344	2157
	energy, ft-lb:	3501	3011	2578	2196	1859
	arc, inches:		+1.6	0	-7.3	-20.9
Hornady 180 SST	velocity, fps:	2960	2764	2575	2395	2222
	energy, ft-lb:	3501	3052	2650	2292	1974
	arc, inches:		+1.6	0	-7.0	-20.1.
Hornady 180 SPBT HM	velocity, fps:	3100	2879	2668	2467	2275
	energy, ft-lb:	3840	3313	2845	2431	2068
	arc, inches:		+1.4	0	-6.4	-18.7
Hornady 190 BTHP Match	velocity, fps:	2930	2760	2596	2438	2286
	energy, ft-lb:	3717	3297	2918	2574	2262
	arc, inches:		+1.5	0	-6.7	-19.3
Hornady 190 SP boat-tail	velocity, fps:	2900	2711	2529	2355	2187
	energy, ft-lb:	3549	3101	2699	2340	2018
	arc, inches:		+1.6	0	-7.1	-20.4
Norma 150 Nosler Bal. Tip	velocity, fps:	3250	3014	2791	2578	
	energy, ft-lb:	3519	3027	2595	2215	
	arc, inches:		+1.1	0	-5.6	
Norma 150 Barnes TS	velocity, fps:	3215	2982	2761	2550	
	energy, ft-lb:	3444	2962	2539	2167	
	arc, inches:		+1.2	0	-5.8	
Norma 165 Scirocco	velocity, fps:	3117	2921	2734	2554	
	energy, ft-lb:	3561	3127	2738	2390	
	arc, inches:		+1.2	0	-5.9	
Norma 180 Soft Point	velocity, fps:	3018	2780	2555	2341	
	energy, ft-lb:	3641	3091	2610	2190	
	arc, inches:		+1.5	0	-7.0	
Norma 180 Plastic Point	velocity, fps:	3018	2755	2506	2271	
	energy, ft-lb:	3641	3034	2512	2062	
	arc, inches:		+1.6	0	-7.1	
Norma 180 TXP Swift A-Fr.	velocity, fps:	2920	2688	2467	2256	
	energy, ft-lb:	3409	2888	2432	2035	
	arc, inches:		+1.7	0	-7.4	

Centerfire Rifle Ballistics

.300 WINCHESTER MAGNUM TO .300 REMINGTON SHORT ULTRA MAGNUM

CARTRIDGE BULLET	RANGE, YARDS:	0	100	200	300	400
Norma 180 AccuBond	velocity, fps:	2953	2767	2588	2417	
	energy, ft-lb:	3486	3061	2678	2335	
	arc, inches:		+1.5	0	-6.7	
Norma 180 Oryx	velocity, fps:	2920	2600	2301	2023	
	energy, ft-lb:	3409	2702	2117	1636	
	arc, inches:		+1.8	0	-8.4	
Norma 200 Vulkan	velocity, fps:	2887	2609	2347	2100	
	energy, ft-lb:	3702	3023	2447	1960	
	arc, inches:		+1.8	0	-8.2	
Norma 200 Oryx	velocity, fps:	2789	2510	2248	2002	
	energy, ft-lb:	3455	2799	2245	1780	
	arc, inches:		+2.0	0	-8.9	
PMC 150 Barnes X	velocity, fps:	3135	2918	2712	2515	2327
	energy, ft-lb:	3273	2836	2449	2107	1803
	arc, inches:		+1.3	0	-6.1	-17.7
PMC 150 Pointed Soft Point	velocity, fps:	3150	2902	2665	2438	2222
	energy, ft-lb:	3304	2804	2364	1979	1644.
	arc, inches:		+1.3	0	-6.2	-18.3
PMC 150 SP boat-tail	velocity, fps:	3250	2987	2739	2504	2281
	energy, ft-lb:	3517	2970	2498	2088	1733
	arc, inches:		+1.2	0	-6.0	-17.4
PMC 180 Barnes X	velocity, fps:	2910	2738	2572	2412	2258
	energy, ft-lb:	3384	2995	2644	2325	2037
	arc, inches:		+1.6	0	-6.9	-19.8
PMC 180 Pointed Soft Point	velocity, fps:	2853	2643	2446	2258	2077
	energy, ft-lb:	3252	2792	2391	2037	1724
	arc, inches:		+1.7	0	-7.5	-21.9
PMC 180 SP boat-tail	velocity, fps:	2900	2714	2536	2365	2200
	energy, ft-lb:	3361	2944	2571	2235	1935
	arc, inches:		+1.6	0	-7.1	-20.3
PMC 180 HPBT Match	velocity, fps:	2950	2755	2568	2390	2219
	energy, ft-lb:	3478	3033	2636	2283	1968
	arc, inches:		+1.5	0	-6.8	-19.7
Rem. 150 PSP Core-Lokt	velocity, fps:	3290	2951	2636	2342	2068
	energy, ft-lb:	3605	2900	2314	1827	1859
	arc, inches:		+1.6	0	-7.0	-20.2
Rem. 150 PSP C-L MR	velocity, fps:	2650	2373	2113	1870	1646
	energy, ft-lb:	2339	1875	1486	1164	902
	arc, inches:		+1.0	-2.7	-14.3	-35.8
Rem. 150 PSP C-L Ultra	velocity, fps:	3290	2967	2666	2384	2120
	energy, ft-lb:	3065	2931	2366	1893	1496
	arc, inches:		+1.2	0	-6.1	-18.4
Rem. 180 AccuTip	velocity, fps:	2960	2764	2577	2397	2224
	energy, ft-lb:	3501	3053	2653	2295	1976
	arc, inches:		+1.5	0	-6.8	-19.6
Rem. 180 PSP Core-Lokt	velocity, fps:	2960	2745	2540	2344	2157
	energy, ft-lb:	3501	3011	2578	2196	1424
	arc, inches:		+2.2	+1.9	-3.4	-15.0
Rem. 180 PSP C-L Ultra	velocity, fps:	2960	2727	2505	2294	2093
	energy, ft-lb:	3501	2971	2508	2103	1751
	arc, inches:		+2.7	+2.2	-3.8	-16.4
Rem. 180 Nosler Partition	velocity, fps:	2960	2725	2503	2291	2089
	energy, ft-lb:	3501	2968	2503	2087	1744
	arc, inches:		+1.6	0	-7.2	-20.9
Rem. 180 Nosler Bal. Tip	velocity, fps:	2960	2774	2595	2424	2259.
	energy, ft-lb:	3501	3075	2692	2348	2039
	arc, inches:		+1.5	0	-6.7	-19.3
Rem. 180 Swift Scirocco	velocity, fps:	2960	2774	2595	2424	2259
	energy, ft-lb:	3501	3075	2692	2348	2039
	arc, inches:		+1.5	0	-6.7	-19.3
Rem. 190 PSP boat-tail	velocity, fps:	2885	2691	2506	2327	2156
	energy, ft-lb:	3511	3055	2648	2285	1961
	arc, inches:		+1.6	0	-7.2	-20.8
Rem. 190 HPBT Match	velocity, fps:	2900	2725	2557	2395	2239
	energy, ft-lb:	3547	3133	2758	2420	2115
	arc, inches:		+1.6	0	-6.9	-19.9
Rem. 200 Swift A-Frame	velocity, fps:	2825	2595	2376	2167	1970
	energy, ft-lb:	3544	2989	2506	2086	1722
	arc, inches:		+1.8	0	-8.0	-23.5
Speer 180 Grand Slam	velocity, fps:	2950	2735	2530	2334	
	energy, ft-lb:	3478	2989	2558	2176	
	arc, inches:		+1.6	0	-7.0	-20.5
Speer 200 Grand Slam	velocity, fps:	2800	2597	2404	2218	
	energy, ft-lb:	3481	2996	2565	2185	
	arc, inches:		+1.8	0	-7.9	-22.9
Win. 150 Power-Point	velocity, fps:	3290	2951	2636	2342	2068.
	energy, ft-lb:	3605	2900	2314	1827	1424
	arc, inches:		+2.6	+2.1	-3.5	-15.4
Win. 150 Fail Safe	velocity, fps:	3260	2943	2647	2370	2110
	energy, ft-lb:	3539	2884	2334	1871	1483
	arc, inches:		+1.3	0	-6.2	-18.7
Win. 165 Fail Safe	velocity, fps:	3120	2807	2515	2242	1985
	energy, ft-lb:	3567	2888	2319	1842	1445
	arc, inches:		+1.5	0	-7.0	-20.0
Win. 180 Power-Point	velocity, fps:	2960	2745	2540	2344	2157
	energy, ft-lb:	3501	3011	2578	2196	1859
	arc, inches:		+1.9	0	-7.3	-20.9
Win. 180 Power-Point Plus	velocity, fps:	3070	2846	2633	2430	2236
	energy, ft-lb:	3768	3239	2772	2361	1999
	arc, inches:		+1.4	0	-6.4	-18.7
Win. 180 Ballistic Silvertip	velocity, fps:	2950	2764	2586	2415	2250
	energy, ft-lb:	3478	3054	2673	2331	2023
	arc, inches:		+1.5	0	-6.7	-19.4
Win. 180 AccuBond	velocity, fps:	2950	2765	2588	2417	2253
	energy, ft-lb:	3478	3055	2676	2334	2028
	arc, inches:		+1.5	0	-6.7	-19.4
Win. 180 Fail Safe	velocity, fps:	2960	2732	2514	2307	2110
	energy, ft-lb:	3503	2983	2528	2129	1780
	arc, inches:		+1.6	0	-7.1	-20.7
Win. 180 Partition Gold	velocity, fps:	3070	2859	2657	2464	2280
	energy, ft-lb:	3768	3267	2823	2428	2078
	arc, inches:		+1.4	0	-6.3	-18.3
Win. 150 Supreme Elite XP3	velocity, fps:	3260	3030	2811	2603	2404
	energy, ft-lb:	3539	3057	2632	2256	1925
	arc, inches:		+1.1	0	-5.6	-16.2
Win. 180 Supreme Elite XP3	velocity, fps:	3000	2819	2646	2479	2318
	energy, ft-lb:	3597	3176	2797	2455	2147
	arc, inches:		+1.4	0	-6.4	-18.5

.300 REMINGTON SHORT ULTRA MAGNUM

CARTRIDGE BULLET	RANGE, YARDS:	0	100	200	300	400
Rem. 150 PSP C-L Ultra	velocity, fps:	3200	2901	2672	2359	2112
	energy, ft-lb:	3410	2803	2290	1854	1485
	arc, inches:		+1.3	0	-6.4	-19.l
Rem. 165 PSP Core-Lokt	velocity, fps:	3075	2792	2527	2276	2040
	energy, ft-lb:	3464	2856	2339	1828	1525
	arc, inches:		+1.5	0	-7.0	-20.7
Rem. 180 Partition	velocity, fps:	2960	2761	2571	2389	2214
	energy, ft-lb:	3501	3047	2642	2280	1959
	arc, inches:		+1.5	0	-6.8	-19.7
Rem. 180 PSP C-L Ultra	velocity, fps:	2960	2727	2506	2295	2094
	energy, ft-lb:	3501	2972	2509	2105	1753
	arc, inches:		+1.6	0	-7.1	-20.9
Rem. 190 HPBT Match	velocity, fps:	2900	2725	2557	2395	2239
	energy, ft-lb:	3547	3133	2758	2420	2115
	arc, inches:		+1.6	0	-6.9	-19.9

BALLISTICS

.300 WINCHESTER SHORT MAGNUM

CARTRIDGE BULLET	RANGE, YARDS:	0	100	200	300	400
Black Hills 175 Sierra MKing	velocity, fps:	2950				
	energy, ft-lb:	3381				
	arc, inches:					
Black Hills 180 AccuBond	velocity, fps:	2950				
	energy, ft-lb:	3478				
	arc, inches:					
Federal 150 Nosler Bal. Tip	velocity, fps:	3200	2970	2755	2545	2345
	energy, ft-lb:	3410	2940	2520	2155	1830.
	arc, inches:		+1.2	0	-5.8	-17.0
Federal 160 Trophy Bonded Tip	velocity, fps:	3130	2910	2710	2510	2320
	energy, ft-lb:	3590	3110	2680	2305	1970
	arc, inches:		+1.3	0	-6.0	-17.6
Federal 165 Nos. Partition	velocity, fps:	3130	2890	2670	2450	2250
	energy, ft-lb:	3590	3065	2605	2205	1855.
	arc, inches:		+1.3	0	-6.2	-18.2
Federal 165 Nos. Solid Base	velocity, fps:	3130	2900	2690	2490	2290
	energy, ft-lb:	3590	3090	2650	2265	1920
	arc, inches:		+1.3	0	-6.1	-17.8
Federal 180 Barnes TS And Nos. Solid Base	velocity, fps:	2980	2780	2580	2400	2220
	energy, ft-lbs:	3550	3085	2670	2300	1970
	arc, inches:		+1.5	0	-6.7	-19.5
Federal 180 Grand Slam	velocity, fps:	2970	2740	2530	2320	2130
	energy, ft-lb:	3525	3010	2555	2155	1810
	arc, inches:		+1.5	0	-7.0	-20.5
Federal 180 Trophy Bonded	velocity, fps:	2970	2730	2500	2280	2080
	energy, ft-lb:	3525	2975	2500	2085	1725
	arc, inches:		+1.5	0	-7.2	-21.0
Federal 180 Nosler Partition	velocity, fps:	2975	2750	2535	2290	2126
	energy, ft-lb:	3540	3025	2570	2175	1825
	arc, inches:		+1.5	0	-7.0	-20.3
Federal 180 Nos. AccuBond	velocity, fps:	2960	2780	2610	2440	2280
	energy, ft-lb:	3500	3090	2715	2380	2075
	arc, inches:		+1.5	0	-6.6	-19.0
Federal 180 Hi-Shok SP	velocity, fps:	2970	2520	2115	1750	1430
	energy, ft-lb:	3525	2540	1785	1220	820
	arc, inches:		+2.2	0	-9.9	-31.4
Norma 150 FMJ	velocity, fps:	2953	2731	2519	2318	
	energy, ft-lb:					
	arc, inches:		+1.6	0	-7.1	
Norma 150 Barnes X TS	velocity, fps:	3215	2982	2761	2550	
	energy, ft-lb:	3444	2962	2539	2167	
	arc, inches:		+1.2	0	-5.7	
Norma 180 Nosler Bal. Tip	velocity, fps:	3215	2985	2767	2560	
	energy, ft-lb:	3437	2963	2547	2179	
	arc, inches:		+1.2	0	-5.7	
Norma 180 Oryx	velocity, fps:	2936	2542	2180	1849	
	energy, ft-lb:	3446	2583	1900	1368	
	arc, inches:		+1.9	0	-8.9	
Win. 150 Power-Point	velocity, fps:	3270	2903	2565	2250	1958
	energy, ft-lb:	3561	2807	2190	1686	1277
	arc, inches:		+1.3	0	-6.6	-20.2
Win. 150 Ballistic Silvertip	velocity, fps:	3300	3061	2834	2619	2414
	energy, ft-lb:	3628	3121	2676	2285	1941
	arc, inches:		+1.1	0	-5.4	-15.9
Win. 165 Fail Safe	velocity, fps:	3125	2846	2584	2336	2102
	energy, ft-lb:	3577	2967	2446	1999	1619
	arc, inches:		+1.4	0	-6.6	-19.6
Win. 180 Ballistic Silvertip	velocity, fps:	3010	2822	2641	2468	2301.
	energy, ft-lb:	3621	3182	2788	2434	2116
	arc, inches:		+1.4	0	-6.4	-18.6
Win. 180 AccuBond	velocity, fps:	3010	2822	2643	2470	2304
	energy, ft-lb:	3622	3185	2792	2439	2121
	arc, inches:		+1.4	0	-6.4	-18.5

CARTRIDGE BULLET	RANGE, YARDS:	0	100	200	300	400
Win. 180 Fail Safe	velocity, fps:	2970	2741	2524	2317	2120
	energy, ft-lb:	3526	3005	2547	2147	1797
	arc, inches:		+1.6	0	-7.0	-20.5
Win. 180 Power Point	velocity, fps:	2970	2755	2549	2353	2166
	energy, ft-lb:	3526	3034	2598	2214	1875
	arc, inches:		+1.5	0	-6.9	-20.1
Win. 150 Supreme Elite XP3	velocity, fps:	3300	3068	2847	2637	2437
	energy, ft-lb:	3626	3134	2699	2316	1978
	arc, inches:		+1.1	0	-5.4	-15.8
Win. 180 Supreme Elite XP3	velocity, fps:	3010	2829	2655	2488	2326
	energy, ft-lb:	3621	3198	2817	2473	2162
	arc, inches:		+1.4	0	-6.4	-18.3

.300 RUGER COMPACT MAGNUM

CARTRIDGE BULLET	RANGE, YARDS:	0	100	200	300	400
Hornady 150 SST	velocity, fps:	3310	3065	2833	2613	2404
	energy, ft-lb:	3648	3128	2673	2274	1924
	arc, inches:	-1.5	+1.1	0	-5.4	-16.0
Hornady 165 GMX	velocity, fps:	3130	2911	2703	2504	2314
	energy, ft-lb:	3589	3105	2677	2297	1963
	arc, inches:	-1.5	+1.3	0	-6.1	-17.7
Hornady 180 SST	velocity, fps:	3040	2840	2649	2466	2290
	energy, ft-lb:	3693	3223	2804	2430	2096
	arc, inches:	-1.5	+1.4	0	-6.4	-18.5

.300 WEATHERBY MAGNUM

CARTRIDGE BULLET	RANGE, YARDS:	0	100	200	300	400
A-Square 180 Dead Tough	velocity, fps:	3180	2811	2471	2155	1863.
	energy, ft-lb:	4041	3158	2440	1856	1387
	arc, inches:		+1.5	0	-7.2	-21.8
A-Square 220 Monolithic Solid	velocity, fps:	2700	2407	2133	1877	1653
	energy, ft-lb:	3561	2830	2223	1721	1334
	arc, inches:		+2.3	0	-9.8	-29.7
Federal 180 Nosler Partition	velocity, fps:	3190	2980	2780	2590	2400
	energy, ft-lb:	4055	3540	3080	2670	2305
	arc, inches:		+1.2	0	-5.7	-16.7
Federal 180 Nosler Part. HE	velocity, fps:	3330	3110	2810	2710	2520
	energy, ft-lb:	4430	3875	3375	2935	2540
	arc, inches:		+1.0	0	-5.2	-15.1
Federal 180 Sierra GameKing BTSP	velocity, fps:	3190	3010	2830	2660	2490
	energy, ft-lb:	4065	3610	3195	2820	2480
	arc, inches:		+1.2	0	-5.6	-16.0
Federal 180 Trophy Bonded	velocity, fps:	3190	2950	2720	2500	2290
	energy, ft-lb:	4065	3475	2955	2500	2105
	arc, inches:		+1.3	0	-5.9	-17.5
Federal 180 Tr. Bonded HE	velocity, fps:	3330	3080	2850	2750	2410
	energy, ft-lb:	4430	3795	3235	2750	2320
	arc, inches:		+1.1	0	-5.4	-15.8
Federal 180 Trophy Copper	velocity, fps:	3100	2910	2740	2560	2400
	energy, ft-lb:	3840	3395	2990	2625	2300
	arc, inches:		+1.3	0	-6.0	-17.1
Federal 200 Trophy Bonded	velocity, fps:	2900	2670	2440	2230	2030
	energy, ft-lb:	3735	3150	2645	2200	1820
	arc, inches:		+1.7	0	-7.6	-22.2
Hornady 150 SST (or Interbond)	velocity, fps:	3375	3123	2882	2652	2434
	energy, ft-lb:	3793	3248	2766	2343	1973
	arc, inches:		+1.0	0	-5.4	-15.8
Hornady 165 GMX Superformance	velocity, fps:	3140	2921	2713	2515	2325
	energy, ft-lb:	3612	3126	2697	2317	1980
	arc, inches:		+1.3	0	-6.0	-17.5
Hornady 180 SP	velocity, fps:	3120	2891	2673	2466	2268.
	energy, ft-lb:	3890	3340	2856	2430	2055
	arc, inches:		+1.3	0	-6.2	-18.1
Hornady 180 SST	velocity, fps:	3120	2911	2711	2519	2335
	energy, ft-lb:	3890	3386	2936	2535	2180
	arc, inches:		+1.3	0	-6.2	-18.1
Rem. 180 PSP Core-Lokt	velocity, fps:	3120	2866	2627	2400	2184
	energy, ft-lb:	3890	3284	2758	2301	1905
	arc, inches:		+2.4	+2.0	-3.4	-14.9

Centerfire Rifle Ballistics

.300 WEATHERBY MAGNUM TO .303 BRITISH

CARTRIDGE BULLET	RANGE, YARDS:	0	100	200	300	400
Rem. 190 PSP boat-tail	velocity, fps:	3030	2830	2638	2455	2279
	energy, ft-lb:	3873	3378	2936	2542	2190.
	arc, inches:		+1.4	0	-6.4	-18.6
Rem. 200 Swift A-Frame	velocity, fps:	2925	2690	2467	2254	2052
	energy, ft-lb:	3799	3213	2701	2256	1870
	arc, inches:	/	+2.8	+2.3	-3.9	-17.0
Speer 180 Grand Slam	velocity, fps:	3185	2948	2722	2508	
	energy, ft-lb:	4054	3472	2962	2514	
	arc, inches:		+1.3	0	-5.9	-17.4
Wby. 150 Pointed Expanding	velocity, fps:	3540	3225	2932	2657	2399
	energy, ft-lb:	4173	3462	2862	2351	1916
	arc, inches:		+2.6	+3.3	0	-8.2
Wby. 150 Nosler Partition	velocity, fps:	3540	3263	3004	2759	2528
	energy, ft-lb:	4173	3547	3005	2536	2128
	arc, inches:		+2.5	+3.2	0	-7.7
Wby. 165 Pointed Expanding	velocity, fps:	3390	3123	2872	2634	2409
	energy, ft-lb:	4210	3573	3021	2542	2126
	arc, inches:		+2.8	+3.5	0	-8.5
Wby. 165 Nosler Bal. Tip	velocity, fps:	3350	3133	2927	2730	2542
	energy, ft-lb:	4111	3596	3138	2730	2367
	arc, inches:		+2.7	+3.4	0	-8.1
Wby. 180 Pointed Expanding	velocity, fps:	3240	3004	2781	2569	2366
	energy, ft-lb:	4195	3607	3091	2637	2237
	arc, inches:		+3.1	+3.8	0	-9.0
Wby. 180 Barnes X	velocity, fps:	3190	2995	2809	2631	2459
	energy, ft-lb:	4067	3586	3154	2766	2417
	arc, inches:		+3.1	+3.8	0	-8.7
Wby. 180 Bal. Tip	velocity, fps:	3250	3051	2806	2676	2503
	energy, ft-lb:	4223	3721	3271	2867	2504
	arc, inches:		+2.8	+3.6	0	-8.4
Wby. 180 Nosler Partition	velocity, fps:	3240	3028	2826	2634	2449
	energy, ft-lb:	4195	3665	3193	2772	2396
	arc, inches:		+3.0	+3.7	0	-8.6
Wby. 200 Nosler Partition	velocity, fps:	3060	2860	2668	2485	2308
	energy, ft-lb:	4158	3631	3161	2741	2366
	arc, inches:		+3.5	+4.2	0	-9.8
Wby. 220 RN Expanding	velocity, fps:	2845	2543	2260	1996	1751.
	energy, ft-lb:	3954	3158	2495	1946	1497
	arc, inches:		+4.9	+5.9	0	-14.6

.300 DAKOTA

CARTRIDGE BULLET	RANGE, YARDS:	0	100	200	300	400
Dakota 165 Barnes X	velocity, fps:	3200	2979	2769	2569	2377
	energy, ft-lb:	3751	3251	2809	2417	2070
	arc, inches:		+2.1	+1.8	-3.0	-13.2
Dakota 200 Barnes X	velocity, fps:	3000	2824	2656	2493	2336
	energy, ft-lb:	3996	3542	3131	2760	2423
	arc, inches:		+2.2	+1.5	-4.0	-15.2

.300 PEGASUS

CARTRIDGE BULLET	RANGE, YARDS:	0	100	200	300	400
A-Square 180 SP boat-tail	velocity, fps:	3500	3319	3145	2978	2817
	energy, ft-lb:	4896	4401	3953	3544	3172
	arc, inches:		+2.3	+2.9	0	-6.8
A-Square 180 Nosler Part.	velocity, fps:	3500	3295	3100	2913	2734
	energy, ft-lb:	4896	4339	3840	3392	2988
	arc, inches:		+2.3	+3.0	0	-7.1
A-Square 180 Dead Tough	velocity, fps:	3500	3103	2740	2405	2095
	energy, ft-lb:	4896	3848	3001	2312	1753
	arc, inches:		+1.1	0	-5.7	-17.5

.300 REMINGTON ULTRA MAGNUM

CARTRIDGE BULLET	RANGE, YARDS:	0	100	200	300	400
Federal 180 Trophy Bonded	velocity, fps:	3250	3000	2770	2550	2340
	energy, ft-lb:	4220	3605	3065	2590	2180
	arc, inches:		+1.2	0	-5.7	-16.8
Federal 180 Trophy Copper	velocity, fps:	3150	2960	2780	2610	2440
	energy, ft-lb:	3965	3505	3090	2715	2380
	arc, inches:		+1.2	0	-5.8	-16.6

CARTRIDGE BULLET	RANGE, YARDS:	0	100	200	300	400
Federal 200 Partition	velocity, fps:	3070	2870	2680	2490	2320
	energy, ft-lb:	4185	3655	3180	2760	2380
	arc, inches:		+1.4	0	-6.2	-18.0
Rem. 150 Swift Scirocco	velocity, fps:	3450	3208	2980	2762	2556
	energy, ft-lb:	3964	3427	2956	2541	2175
	arc, inches:		+1.7	+1.5	-2.6	-11.2
Remington 165 Copper Solid	velocity, fps:	3250	3035	2821	2617	2422
	energy, ft-lb:	3893	3373	2916	2602	2390
	arc, inches:		+1.4	0	-5.8	-16.7
Rem. 180 Nosler Partition	velocity, fps:	3250	3037	2834	2640	2454
	energy, ft-lb:	4221	3686	3201	2786	2407
	arc, inches:		+2.4	+1.8	-3.0	-12.7
Rem. 180 Swift Scirocco	velocity, fps:	3250	3048	2856	2672	2495
	energy, ft-lb:	4221	3714	3260	2853	2487
	arc, inches:		+2.0	+1.7	-2.8	-12.3
Rem. 180 PSP Core-Lokt	velocity, fps:	3250	2988	2742	2508	2287
	energy, ft-lb:	3517	2974	2503	2095	1741
	arc, inches:		+2.1	+1.8	-3.1	-13.6
Rem. 200 Nosler Partition	velocity, fps:	3025	2826	2636	2454	2279
	energy, ft-lb:	4063	3547	3086	2673	2308
	arc, inches:		+2.4	+2.0	-3.4	-14.6

.30-378 WEATHERBY MAGNUM

CARTRIDGE BULLET	RANGE, YARDS:	0	100	200	300	400
Nosler 210 ABLR	velocity, fps:	3040	2907	2778	2653	2531
	energy, ft-lb:	4308	3940	3599	3282	2987
	arc, inches:	-1.5	+1.3	0	-5.8	-16.6
Wby. 165 Nosler Bal. Tip	velocity, fps:	3500	3275	3062	2859	2665
	energy, ft-lb:	4488	3930	3435	2995	2603
	arc, inches:		+2.4	+3.0	0	-7.4
Wby. 180 Nosler Bal. Tip	velocity, fps:	3420	3213	3015	2826	2645
	energy, ft-lb:	4676	4126	3634	3193	2797
	arc, inches:		+2.5	+3.1	0	-7.5
Wby. 180 Barnes X	velocity, fps:	3450	3243	3046	2858	2678.
	energy, ft-lb:	4757	4204	3709	3264	2865
	arc, inches:		+2.4	+3.1	0	-7.4
Wby. 200 Nosler Partition	velocity, fps:	3160	2955	2759	2572	2392.
	energy, ft-lb:	4434	3877	3381	2938	2541
	arc, inches:		+3.2	+3.9	0	-9.1

7.82 (.308) WARBIRD

CARTRIDGE BULLET	RANGE, YARDS:	0	100	200	300	400
Lazzeroni 150 Nosler Part.	velocity, fps:	3680	3432	3197	2975	2764
	energy, ft-lb:	4512	3923	3406	2949	2546.
	arc, inches:		+2.1	+2.7	0	-6.6
Lazzeroni 180 Nosler Part.	velocity, fps:	3425	3220	3026	2839	2661
	energy, ft-lb:	4689	4147	3661	3224	2831
	arc, inches:		+2.5	+3.2	0	-7.5
Lazzeroni 200 Swift A-Fr.	velocity, fps:	3290	3105	2928	2758	2594.
	energy, ft-lb:	4808	4283	3808	3378	2988
	arc, inches:		+2.7	+3.4	0	-7.9

7.65x53 ARGENTINE

CARTRIDGE BULLET	RANGE, YARDS:	0	100	200	300	400
Norma 174 Soft Point	velocity, fps:	2493	2173	1878	1611	
	energy, ft-lb:	2402	1825	1363	1003	
	arc, inches:		+2.0	0	-9.5	
Norma 180 Soft Point	velocity, fps:	2592	2386	2189	2002	
	energy, ft-lb:	2686	2276	1916	1602	
	arc, inches:		+2.3	0	-9.6	

.303 BRITISH

CARTRIDGE BULLET	RANGE, YARDS:	0	100	200	300	400
Federal 150 Hi-Shok	velocity, fps:	2690	2440	2210	1980	1780
	energy, ft-lb:	2400	1980	1620	1310	1055
	arc, inches:		+2.2	0	-9.4	-27.6
Federal 180 Sierra Pro-Hunt.	velocity, fps:	2460	2230	2020	1820	1630
	energy, ft-lb:	2420	1995	1625	1315	1060
	arc, inches:		+2.8	0	-11.3	-33.2
Federal 180 Tr. Bonded HE	velocity, fps:	2590	2350	2120	1900	1700
	energy, ft-lb:	2680	2205	1795	1445	1160
	arc, inches:		+2.4	0	-10.0	-30.0
Hornady 150 Soft Point	velocity, fps:	2685	2441	2210	1992	1787
	energy, ft-lb:	2401	1984	1627	1321	1064
	arc, inches:		+2.2	0	-9.3	-27.4

CARTRIDGE BULLET	RANGE, YARDS:	0	100	200	300	400
Hornady 150 SP LM	velocity, fps:	2830	2570	2325	2094	1884.
	energy, ft-lb:	2667	2199	1800	1461	1185
	arc, inches:		+2.0	0	-8.4	-24.6
Hornady 174 BTHP	velocity, fps:	2430	2252	2082	1919	1765
	energy, ft-lb:	2281	1959	1674	1423	1204
	arc, inches:		+2.7	0	-10.7	-30.9
Norma 150 Soft Point	velocity, fps:	2723	2438	2170	1920	
	energy, ft-lb:	2470	1980	1569	1228	
	arc, inches:		+2.2	0	-9.6	
PMC 174 FMJ (and HPBT)	velocity, fps:	2400	2216	2042	1876	1720
	energy, ft-lb:	2225	1898	1611	1360	1143
	arc, inches:		+2.8	0	-11.2	-32.2
PMC 180 SP boat-tail	velocity, fps:	2450	2276	2110	1951	1799
	energy, ft-lb:	2399	2071	1779	1521	1294
	arc, inches:		+2.6	0	-10.4	-30.1
Rem. 180 SP Core-Lokt	velocity, fps:	2460	2124	1817	1542	1311
	energy, ft-lb:	2418	1803	1319	950	687
	arc, inches, s:		0	-5.8	-23.3	
Win. 180 Power-Point	velocity, fps:	2460	2233	2018	1816	1629
	energy, ft-lb:	2418	1993	1627	1318	1060
	arc, inches, s:		0	-6.1	-20.8	

7.7X58 JAPANESE ARISAKA

CARTRIDGE BULLET	RANGE, YARDS:	0	100	200	300	400
Norma 174 Soft Point	velocity, fps:	2493	2173	1878	1611	
	energy, ft-lb:	2402	1825	1363	1003	
	arc, inches:		+2.0	0	-9.5	
Norma 180 Soft Point	velocity, fps:	2493	2291	2099	1916	
	energy, ft-lb:	2485	2099	1761	1468	
	arc, inches:		+2.6	0	-10.5	

.32-20 WINCHESTER

CARTRIDGE BULLET	RANGE, YARDS:	0	100	200	300	400
Rem. 100 Lead	velocity, fps:	1210	1021	913	834	769
	energy, ft-lb:	325	231	185	154	131
	arc, inches:		0	-31.6	-104.7	
Win. 100 Lead	velocity, fps:	1210	1021	913	834	769
	energy, ft-lb:	325	231	185	154	131
	arc, inches:		0	-32.3	-106.3	

.32 WINCHESTER SPECIAL

CARTRIDGE BULLET	RANGE, YARDS:	0	100	200	300	400
Federal 170 Hi-Shok	velocity, fps:	2250	1920	1630	1370	1180
	energy, ft-lb:	1910	1395	1000	710	520
	arc, inches:		0	-8.0	-29.2	
Hornady 165 FTX	velocity, fps:	2410	2145	1897	1669	
	energy, ft-lb:	2128	1685	1318	1020	
	arc, inches:	-1.5	+3.0	0	-12.8	
Rem. 170 SP Core-Lokt	velocity, fps:	2250	1921	1626	1372	1175
	energy, ft-lb:	1911	1393	998	710	521
	arc, inches:		0	-8.0	-29.3	
Win. 170 Power-Point	velocity, fps:	2250	1870	1537	1267	1082
	energy, ft-lb:	1911	1320	892	606	442
	arc, inches:		0	-9.2	-33.2	

8MM MAUSER (8X57)

CARTRIDGE BULLET	RANGE, YARDS:	0	100	200	300	400
Federal 170 Hi-Shok	velocity, fps:	2360	1970	1620	1330	1120
	energy, ft-lb:	2100	1465	995	670	475
	arc, inches:		0	-7.6	-28.5	
Hornady 195 SP	velocity, fps:	2550	2343	2146	1959	1782
	energy, ft-lb:	2815	2377	1994	1861	1375
	arc, inches:		+2.3	0	-9.9	-28.8.
Hornady 195 SP (2005)	velocity, fps:	2475	2269	2074	1888	1714
	energy, ft-lb:	2652	2230	1861	1543	1271
	arc, inches:		+2.6	0	-10.7	-31.3
Norma 123 FMJ	velocity, fps:	2559	2121	1729	1398	
	energy, ft-lb:	1789	1228	817	534	
	arc, inches:		+3.2	0	-15.0	

CARTRIDGE BULLET	RANGE, YARDS:	0	100	200	300	400
Norma 196 Oryx	velocity, fps:	2395	2146	1912	1695	
	energy, ft-lb:	2497	2004	1591	1251	
	arc, inches:		+3	0	-12.6	
Norma 196 Vulkan	velocity, fps:	2395	2156	1930	1720	
	energy, ft-lb:	2497	2023	1622	1289	
	arc, inches:		3.0	0	-12.3	
Norma 196 Alaska	velocity, fps:	2395	2112	1850	1611	
	energy, ft-lb:	2714	2190	1754	1399	
	arc, inches:		0	-6.3	-22.9	
Norma 196 Soft Point (JS)	velocity, fps:	2526	2244	1981	1737	
	energy, ft-lb:	2778	2192	1708	1314	
	arc, inches:		+2.7	0	-11.6	
Norma 196 Alaska (JS)	velocity, fps:	2526	2248	1988	1747	
	energy, ft-lb:	2778	2200	1720	1328	
	arc, inches:		+2.7	0	-11.5	
Norma 196 Vulkan (JS)	velocity, fps:	2526	2276	2041	1821	
	energy, ft-lb:	2778	2256	1813	1443	
	arc, inches:		+2.6	0	-11.0	
Norma 196 Oryx (JS)	velocity, fps:	2526	2269	2027	1802	
	energy, ft-lb:	2778	2241	1789	1413	
	arc, inches:		+2.6	0	-11.1	
PMC 170 Pointed Soft Point	velocity, fps:	2360	1969	1622	1333	1123
	energy, ft-lb:	2102	1463	993	671	476
	arc, inches:		+1.8	-4.5	-24.3	-63.8
Rem. 170 SP Core-Lokt	velocity, fps:	2360	1969	1622	1333	1123
	energy, ft-lb:	2102	1463	993	671	476
	arc, inches:		+1.8	-4.5	-24.3	-63.8.
Win. 170 Power-Point	velocity, fps:	2360	1969	1622	1333	1123
	energy, ft-lb:	2102	1463	993	671	476
	arc, inches:		+1.8	-4.5	-24.3	-63.8

.325 WSM

CARTRIDGE BULLET	RANGE, YARDS:	0	100	200	300	400
Win. 180 Ballistic ST	velocity, fps:	3060	2841	2632	2432	2242
	energy, ft-lb:	3743	3226	2769	2365	2009
	arc, inches:		+1.4	0	-6.4	-18.7
Win. 200 AccuBond CT	velocity, fps:	2950	2753	2565	2384	2210
	energy, ft-lb:	3866	3367	2922	2524	2170
	arc, inches:		+1.5	0	-6.8	-19.8
Win. 220 Power-Point	velocity, fps:	2840	2605	2382	2169	1968
	energy, ft-lb:	3941	3316	2772	2300	1893
	arc, inches:		+1.8	0	-8.0	-23.3

8MM REMINGTON MAGNUM

CARTRIDGE BULLET	RANGE, YARDS:	0	100	200	300	400
A-Square 220 Monolythic Solid	velocity, fps:	2800	2501	2221	1959	1718
	energy, ft-lb:	3829	3055	2409	1875	1442
	arc, inches:		+2.1	0	-9.1	-27.6
Nosler 180 BT	velocity, fps:	3200	2923	2662	2416	2183
	energy, ft-lb:	4092	3414	2832	2333	1905
	arc, inches:	-1.5	+1.3	0	-6.2	-18.4
Rem. 200 Swift A-Frame	velocity, fps:	2900	2623	2361	2115	1885
	energy, ft-lb:	3734	3054	2476	1987	1577
	arc, inches:		+1.8	0	-8.0	-23.9

.338 FEDERAL

CARTRIDGE BULLET	RANGE, YARDS:	0	100	200	300	400
Federal 180 AccuBond	velocity, fps:	2830	2590	2350	2130	1930
	energy, ft-lb:	3200	2670	2215	1820	1480
	arc, inches:	-1.5	+1.8	0	-8.2	-23.9
Federal 185 Barnes TSX	velocity, fps:	2750	2500	2260	2030	1820
	energy, ft-lb:	3105	2560	2090	1695	1355
	arc, inches:	-1.5	+2.0	0	-8.9	-26.2
Federal 200 Tr. Bonded T	velocity, fps:	2630	2430	2240	2060	1890
	energy, ft-lb:	3070	2625	2230	1885	1580
	arc, inches:	-1.5	+2.2	0	-9.2	-26.3
Federal 210 Partition	velocity, fps:	2630	2410	2200	2010	1820
	energy, ft-lb:	3225	2710	2265	1880	1545
	arc, inches:	-1.5	+2.3	0	-9.4	-27.3

Centerfire Rifle Ballistics

.338 MARLIN EXPRESS TO .340 WEATHERBY MAGNUM

BALLISTICS

CARTRIDGE BULLET	RANGE, YARDS:	0	100	200	300	400
.338 MARLIN EXPRESS						
Hornady 200 FTX	velocity, fps:	2565	2365	2174	1992	`1820
	energy, ft-lb:	2922	2484	2099	1762	1471
	arc, inches:	-1.5	+3.0	+1.2	-7.9	-25.9
.338-06						
A-Square 200 Nos. Bal. Tip	velocity, fps:	2750	2553	2364	2184	2011
	energy, ft-lb:	3358	2894	2482	2118	1796
	arc, inches:		+1.9	0	-8.2	-23.6
A-Square 250 SP boat-tail	velocity, fps:	2500	2374	2252	2134	2019
	energy, ft-lb:	3496	3129	2816	2528	2263
	arc, inches:		+2.4	0	-9.3	-26.0
A-Square 250 Dead Tough	velocity, fps:	2500	2222	1963	1724	1507
	energy, ft-lb:	3496	2742	2139	1649	1261
	arc, inches:		+2.8	0	-11.9	-35.5
Nosler 180 AB	velocity, fps:	2950	2698	2460	2234	2020
	energy, ft-lb:	3477	2909	2418	1994	1631
	arc, inches:	-1.5	+1.6	0	-7.4	-21.8
Nosler 225 AB	velocity, fps:	2600	2441	2287	2139	1997
	energy, ft-lb:	3376	2976	2614	2286	1992
	arc, inches:	-1.5	+2.2	0	-8.8	-25.3
Wby. 210 Nosler Part.	velocity, fps:	2750	2526	2312	2109	1916
	energy, ft-lb:	3527	2975	2403	2074	1712
	arc, inches:		+4.8	+5.7	0	-13.5
.338 RUGER COMPACT MAGNUM						
Hornady 185 GMX	velocity, fps:	2980	2755	2542	2338	2143
	energy, ft-lb:	3647	3118	2653	2242	1887
	arc, inches:	-1.5	+1.5	0	-6.9	-20.3
Hornady 200 SST	velocity, fps:	2950	2744	2547	2358	2177
	energy, ft-lb:	3846	3342	2879	2468	2104
	arc, inches:	-1.5	+1.6	0	-6.9	-20.1
Hornady 225 SST	velocity, fps:	2750	2575	2407	2245	2089
	energy, ft-lb:	3778	3313	2894	2518	2180
	arc, inches:	-1.5	+1.9	0	-7.9	-22.7
.338 WINCHESTER MAGNUM						
A-Square 250 SP boat-tail	velocity, fps:	2700	2568	2439	2314	2193
	energy, ft-lb:	4046	3659	3302	2972	2669
	arc, inches:		+4.4	+5.2	0	-11.7
A-Square 250 Triad	velocity, fps:	2700	2407	2133	1877	1653
	energy, ft-lb:	4046	3216	2526	1956	1516
	arc, inches:		+2.3	0	-9.8	-29.8
Federal 200 Trophy Bonded Tip	velocity, fps:	2930	2720	2520	2320	2140
	energy, ft-lb:	3810	3280	2810	2395	2025
	arc, inches:		+1.6	0	-7.1	-20.7
Federal 210 Nosler Partition	velocity, fps:	2830	2600	2390	2180	1980
	energy, ft-lb:	3735	3160	2655	2215	1835
	arc, inches:		+1.8	0	-8.0	-23.3
Federal 225 Sierra Pro-Hunt.	velocity, fps:	2780	2570	2360	2170	1980
	energy, ft-lb:	3860	3290	2780	2340	1960
	arc, inches:		+1.9	0	-8.2	-23.7
Federal 225 Trophy Bonded	velocity, fps:	2800	2560	2330	2110	1900
	energy, ft-lb:	3915	3265	2700	2220	1800
	arc, inches:		+1.9	0	-8.4	-24.5
Federal 225 Tr. Bonded HE	velocity, fps:	2940	2690	2450	2230	2010
	energy, ft-lb:	4320	3610	3000	2475	2025
	arc, inches:		+1.7	0	-7.5	-22.0
Federal 225 Barnes XLC	velocity, fps:	2800	2610	2430	2260	2090
	energy, ft-lb:	3915	3405	2950	2545	2190
	arc, inches:		+1.8	0	-7.7	-22.2
Federal 250 Nosler Partition	velocity, fps:	2660	2470	2300	2120	1960
	energy, ft-lb:	3925	3395	2925	2505	2130.
	arc, inches:		+2.1	0	-8.8	-25.1
Federal 250 Nosler Part HE	velocity, fps:	2800	2610	2420	2250	2080
	energy, ft-lb:	4350	3775	3260	2805	2395
	arc, inches:		+1.8	0	-7.8	-22.5
Hornady 185 GMX Superformance	velocity, fps:	3080	2851	2633	2426	2228
	energy, ft-lb:	3897	3338	2848	2417	2038
	arc, inches:		+1.4	0	-6.4	-18.8
Hornady 200 SST Superformance	velocity, fps:	3030	2820	2620	2429	2246
	energy, ft-lb:	4077	3532	3049	2621	2240
	arc, inches:		+1.4	0	-6.5	-18.9
Hornady 225 Soft Point HM	velocity, fps:	2920	2678	2449	2232	2027
	energy, ft-lb:	4259	3583	2996	2489	2053
	arc, inches:		+1.8	0	-7.6	-22.0
Norma 225 TXP Swift A-Fr.	velocity, fps:	2740	2507	2286	2075	
	energy, ft-lb:	3752	3141	2611	2153	
	arc, inches:		+2.0	0	-8.7	
Norma 230 Oryx	velocity, fps:	2756	2514	2284	2066	
	energy, ft-lb:	3880	3228	2665	2181	
	arc, inches:		+2.0	0	-8.7	
Norma 250 Nosler Partition	velocity, fps:	2657	2470	2290	2118	
	energy, ft-lb:	3920	3387	2912	2490	
	arc, inches:		+2.1	0	-8.7	
PMC 225 Barnes X	velocity, fps:	2780	2619	2464	2313	2168
	energy, ft-lb:	3860	3426	3032	2673	2348.
	arc, inches:		+1.8	0	-7.6	-21.6
Rem. 200 Nosler Bal. Tip	velocity, fps:	2950	2724	2509	2303	2108
	energy, ft-lb:	3866	3295	2795	2357	1973
	arc, inches:		+1.6	0	-7.1	-20.8
Rem. 210 Nosler Partition	velocity, fps:	2830	2602	2385	2179	1983
	energy, ft-lb:	3734	3157	2653	2214	1834
	arc, inches:		+1.8	0	-7.9	-23.2
Rem. 225 PSP Core-Lokt	velocity, fps:	2780	2572	2374	2184	2003
	energy, ft-lb:	3860	3305	2815	2383	2004
	arc, inches:		+1.9	0	-8.1	-23.4
Rem. 225 PSP C-L Ultra	velocity, fps:	2780	2582	2392	2210	2036
	energy, ft-lb:	3860	3329	2858	2440	2071
	arc, inches:		+1.9	0	-7.9	-23.0
Rem. 225 Swift A-Frame	velocity, fps:	2785	2517	2266	2029	1808
	energy, ft-lb:	3871	3165	2565	2057	1633
	arc, inches:		+2.0	0	-8.8	-25.2
Rem. 250 PSP Core-Lokt	velocity, fps:	2660	2456	2261	2075	1898
	energy, ft-lb:	3927	3348	2837	2389	1999
	arc, inches:		+2.1	0	-8.9	-26.0
Speer 250 Grand Slam	velocity, fps:	2645	2442	2247	2062	
	energy, ft-lb:	3883	3309	2803	2360	
	arc, inches:		+2.2	0	-9.1	-26.2
Win. 200 Power-Point	velocity, fps:	2960	2658	2375	2110	1862
	energy, ft-lb:	3890	3137	2505	1977	1539
	arc, inches:		+2.0	0	-8.2	-24.3
Win. 200 Ballistic Silvertip	velocity, fps:	2950	2724	2509	2303	2108
	energy, ft-lb:	3864	3294	2794	2355	1972
	arc, inches:		+1.6	0	-7.1	-20.8
Win. 225 AccuBond	velocity, fps:	2800	2634	2474	2319	2170
	energy, ft-lb:	3918	3467	3058	2688	2353
	arc, inches:		+1.8	0	-7.4	-21.3
Win. 230 Fail Safe	velocity, fps:	2780	2573	2375	2186	2005
	energy, ft-lb:	3948	3382	2881	2441	2054
	arc, inches:		+1.9	0	-8.1	-23.4
Win. 250 Partition Gold	velocity, fps:	2650	2467	2291	2122	1960
	energy, ft-lb:	3899	3378	2914	2520	2134
	arc, inches:		+2.1	0	-8.7	-25.2
.340 WEATHERBY MAGNUM						
A-Square 250 SP boat-tail	velocity, fps:	2820	2684	2552	2424	2299
	energy, ft-lb:	4414	3999	3615	3261	2935
	arc, inches:		+4.0	+4.6	0	-10.6
A-Square 250 Triad	velocity, fps:	2820	2520	2238	1976	1741
	energy, ft-lb:	4414	3524	2781	2166	1683
	arc, inches:		+2.0	0	-9.0	-26.8
Federal 225 Trophy Bonded	velocity, fps:	3100	2840	2600	2370	2150
	energy, ft-lb:	4800	4035	3375	2800	2310
	arc, inches:		+1.4	0	-6.5	-19.4

582 • Shooter's Bible 111th Edition

www.skyhorsepublishing.com

.340 WEATHERBY MAGNUM TO .35 REMINGTON

CARTRIDGE BULLET	RANGE, YARDS:	0	100	200	300	400
Wby. 200 Pointed Expanding	velocity, fps:	3221	2946	2688	2444	2213
	energy, ft-lb:	4607	3854	3208	2652	2174
	arc, inches:		+3.3	+4.0	0	-9.9
Wby. 200 Nosler Bal. Tip	velocity, fps:	3221	2980	2753	2536	2329
	energy, ft-lb:	4607	3944	3364	2856	2409
	arc, inches:		+3.1	+3.9	0	-9.2
Wby. 210 Nosler Partition	velocity, fps:	3211	2963	2728	2505	2293
	energy, ft-lb:	4807	4093	3470	2927	2452
	arc, inches:		+3.2	+3.9	0	-9.5
Wby. 225 Pointed Expanding	velocity, fps:	3066	2824	2595	2377	2170
	energy, ft-lb:	4696	3984	3364	2822	2352
	arc, inches:		+3.6	+4.4	0	-10.7
Wby. 225 Barnes X	velocity, fps:	3001	2804	2615	2434	2260
	energy, ft-lb:	4499	3927	3416	2959	2551
	arc, inches:		+3.6	+4.3	0	-10.3
Wby. 250 Pointed Expanding	velocity, fps:	2963	2745	2537	2338	2149
	energy, ft-lb:	4873	4182	3572	3035	2563
	arc, inches:		+3.9	+4.6	0	-11.1
Wby. 250 Nosler Partition	velocity, fps:	2941	2743	2553	2371	2197
	energy, ft-lb:	4801	4176	3618	3120	2678
	arc, inches:		+3.9	+4.6	0	-10.9

.330 DAKOTA

CARTRIDGE BULLET	RANGE, YARDS:	0	100	200	300	400
Dakota 200 Barnes X	velocity, fps:	3200	2971	2754	2548	2350
	energy, ft-lb:	4547	3920	3369	2882	2452
	arc, inches:		+2.1	+1.8	-3.1	-13.4
Dakota 250 Barnes X	velocity, fps:	2900	2719	2545	2378	2217
	energy, ft-lb:	4668	4103	3595	3138	2727
	arc, inches:		+2.3	+1.3	-5.0	-17.5

.338 REMINGTON ULTRA MAGNUM

CARTRIDGE BULLET	RANGE, YARDS:	0	100	200	300	400
Federal 210 Nosler Partition	velocity, fps:	3025	2800	2585	2385	2190
	energy, ft-lb:	4270	3655	3120	2645	2230
	arc, inches:		+1.5	0	-6.7	-19.5
Federal 250 Trophy Bonded	velocity, fps:	2860	2630	2420	2210	2020
	energy, ft-lb:	4540	3850	3245	2715	2260.
	arc, inches:		+0.8	0	-7.7	-22.6
Rem. 250 Swift A-Frame	velocity, fps:	2860	2645	2440	2244	2057
	energy, ft-lb:	4540	3882	3303	2794	2347
	arc, inches:		+1.7	0	-7.6	-22.1
Rem. 250 PSP Core-Lokt	velocity, fps:	2860	2647	2443	2249	2064
	energy, ft-lb:	4540	3888	3314	2807	2363
	arc, inches:		+1.7	0	-7.6	-22.0

.338 NORMA MAGNUM

CARTRIDGE BULLET	RANGE, YARDS:	0	100	200	300	400
Black Hills 300 MatchKing	velocity, fps:	2725				
	energy, ft-lb:	4946				
	arc, inches					

.338 LAPUA

CARTRIDGE BULLET	RANGE, YARDS:	0	100	200	300	400
Black Hills 250 Sierra MKing	velocity, fps:	2950				
	energy, ft-lb:	4831				
	arc, inches:					
Black Hills 300 Sierra MKing	velocity, fps:	2800				
	energy, ft-lb:	5223				
	arc, inches:					
Hornady 250 BTHP Match	velocity, fps:	2900	2761	2626	2495	2368
	energy, ft-lb:	4668	4230	3827	3455	3112
	arc, inches:		+1.5	0	-6.6	-18.8
Hornady 285 BTHP	velocity, fps:	2745	2616	2491	2369	2251
	energy, ft-lb:	4768	4331	3926	3552	3206
	arc, inches:	-1.5	+1.8	0	-7.4	-21.0

CARTRIDGE BULLET	RANGE, YARDS:	0	100	200	300	600
Lapua 250 Scenar	velocity, fps:	2970	2823	2680	2539	2141
	energy, ft-lb:	4896	4424	3985	3579	2545
	arc, inches:	-1.5	+3.0	+4.0	0	-47.0
Lapua 300 Scenar	velocity, fps:	2723	2600	2482	2367	2042
	energy, ft-lb:	4938	4504	4102	3731	2778
	arc, inches:	-1.5	+4.0	+5.0	0	-54.0

CARTRIDGE BULLET	RANGE, YARDS:	0	100	200	300	400
Nosler 225 AB	velocity, fps:	3000	2826	2659	2498	2342
	energy, ft-lb:	4495	3990	3532	3117	2741
	arc, inches:	-1.5	+1.4	0	-6.3	-18.3

.338-378 WEATHERBY MAGNUM

CARTRIDGE BULLET	RANGE, YARDS:	0	100	200	300	400
Wby. 200 Nosler Bal. Tip	velocity, fps:	3350	3102	2868	2646	2434
	energy, ft-lb:	4983	4273	3652	3109	2631
	arc, inches:	0	+2.8	+3.5	0	-8.4
Wby. 225 Barnes X	velocity, fps:	3180	2974	2778	2591	2410.
	energy, ft-lb:	5052	4420	3856	3353	2902
	arc, inches:	0	+3.1	+3.8	0	-8.9
Wby. 250 Nosler Partition	velocity, fps:	3060	2856	2662	2475	2297
	energy, ft-lb:	5197	4528	3933	3401	2927
	arc, inches:	0	+3.5	+4.2	0	-9.8

8.59 (.338) TITAN

CARTRIDGE BULLET	RANGE, YARDS:	0	100	200	300	400
Lazzeroni 200 Nos. Bal. Tip	velocity, fps:	3430	3211	3002	2803	2613
	energy, ft-lb:	5226	4579	4004	3491	3033
	arc, inches:		+2.5	+3.2	0	-7.6
Lazzeroni 225 Nos. Partition	velocity, fps:	3235	3031	2836	2650	2471
	energy, ft-lb:	5229	4591	4021	3510	3052
	arc, inches:		+3.0	+3.6	0	-8.6
Lazzeroni 250 Swift A-Fr.	velocity, fps:	3100	2908	2725	2549	2379
	energy, ft-lb:	5336	4697	4123	3607	3143
	arc, inches:		+3.3	+4.0	0	-9.3

.338 A-SQUARE

CARTRIDGE BULLET	RANGE, YARDS:	0	100	200	300	400
A-Square 200 Nos. Bal. Tip	velocity, fps:	3500	3266	3045	2835	2634
	energy, ft-lb:	5440	4737	4117	3568	3081
	arc, inches:		+2.4	+3.1	0	-7.5
A-Square 250 SP boat-tail	velocity, fps:	3120	2974	2834	2697	2565.
	energy, ft-lb:	5403	4911	4457	4038	3652
	arc, inches:		+3.1	+3.7	0	-8.5
A-Square 250 Triad	velocity, fps:	3120	2799	2500	2220	1958
	energy, ft-lb:	5403	4348	3469	2736	2128
	arc, inches:		+1.5	0	-7.1	-20.4.

.338 EXCALIBER

CARTRIDGE BULLET	RANGE, YARDS:	0	100	200	300	400
A-Square 200 Nos. Bal. Tip	velocity, fps:	3600	3361	3134	2920	2715
	energy, ft-lb:	5755	5015	4363	3785	3274
	arc, inches:		+2.2	+2.9	0	-6.7
A-Square 250 SP boat-tail	velocity, fps:	3250	3101	2958	2684	2553
	energy, ft-lb:	5863	5339	4855	4410	3998
	arc, inches:		+2.7	+3.4	0	-7.8
A-Square 250 Triad	velocity, fps:	3250	2922	2618	2333	2066
	energy, ft-lb:	5863	4740	3804	3021	2370
	arc, inches:		+1.3	0	-6.4	-19.2

.348 WINCHESTER

CARTRIDGE BULLET	RANGE, YARDS:	0	100	200	300	400
Win. 200 Silvertip	velocity, fps:	2520	2215	1931	1672	1443.
	energy, ft-lb:	2820	2178	1656	1241	925
	arc, inches:		0	-6.2	-21.9	

.357 MAGNUM

CARTRIDGE BULLET	RANGE, YARDS:	0	100	200	300	400
Federal 180 Hi-Shok HP Hollow Point	velocity, fps:	1550	1160	980	860	770
	energy, ft-lb:	960	535	385	295	235
	arc, inches:		0	-22.8	-77.9	-173.8
Win. 158 Jacketed SP	velocity, fps:	1830	1427	1138	980	883
	energy, ft-lb:	1175	715	454	337	274
	arc, inches:		0	-16.2	-57.0	-128.3

.35 REMINGTON

CARTRIDGE BULLET	RANGE, YARDS:	0	100	200	300	400
Federal 200 Hi-Shok	velocity, fps:	2080	1700	1380	1140	1000
	energy, ft-lb:	1920	1280	840	575	445
	arc, inches:		0	-10.7	-39.3	

Centerfire Rifle Ballistics

.35 REMINGTON TO 9.3X74 R

CARTRIDGE BULLET	RANGE, YARDS:	0	100	200	300	400
Hornady 200 Evolution	velocity, fps:	2225	1963	1721	1503	
	energy, ft-lb:	2198	1711	1315	1003	
	arc, inches:		+3.0	-1.3	-17.5	
Rem. 150 PSP Core-Lokt	velocity, fps:	2300	1874	1506	1218	1039
	energy, ft-lb:	1762	1169	755	494	359
	arc, inches:		0	-8.6	-32.6	
Rem. 200 SP Core-Lokt	velocity, fps:	2080	1698	1376	1140	1001
	energy, ft-lb:	1921	1280	841	577	445
	arc, inches:		0	-10.7	-40.1	
Win. 200 Power-Point	velocity, fps:	2020	1646	1335	1114	985
	energy, ft-lb:	1812	1203	791	551	431
	arc, inches:		0	-12.1	-43.9	

.356 WINCHESTER

CARTRIDGE BULLET	RANGE, YARDS:	0	100	200	300	400
Win. 200 Power-Point	velocity, fps:	2460	2114	1797	1517	1284
	energy, ft-lb:	2688	1985	1434	1022	732
	arc, inches:		+1.6	-3.8	-20.1	-51.2

.358 WINCHESTER

CARTRIDGE BULLET	RANGE, YARDS:	0	100	200	300	400
Hornady 200 SP	velocity, fps:	2475	2180	1906	1655	1434
	energy, ft-lb:	2720	2110	1612	1217	913
	arc, inches:	-1.5	+2.9	0	-12.6	-37.9
Win. 200 Silvertip	velocity, fps:	2490	2171	1876	1610	1379
	energy, ft-lb:	2753	2093	1563	1151	844
	arc, inches:		+1.5	-3.6	-18.6	-47.2

.35 WHELEN

CARTRIDGE BULLET	RANGE, YARDS:	0	100	200	300	400
Federal 225 Trophy Bonded	velocity, fps:	2600	2400	2200	2020	1840
	energy, ft-lb:	3375	2865	2520	2030	1690.
	arc, inches:		+2.3	0	-9.4	-27.3
Hornady 200 SP	velocity, fps:	2910	2585	2283	2001	1742
	energy, ft-lb:	3760	2968	2314	1778	1347
	arc, inches:	-1.5	+1.9	0	-8.6	-25.9
Rem. 200 Pointed Soft Point	velocity, fps:	2675	2378	2100	1842	1606
	energy, ft-lb:	3177	2510	1958	1506	1145
	arc, inches:		+2.3	0	-10.3	-30.8
Rem. 250 Pointed Soft Point	velocity, fps:	2400	2197	2005	1823	1652
	energy, ft-lb:	3197	2680	2230	1844	1515
	arc, inches:		+1.3	-3.2	-16.6	-40.0

.350 REMINGTON MAGNUM

CARTRIDGE BULLET	RANGE, YARDS:	0	100	200	300	400
Nosler 225 PT	velocity, fps:	2550	2349	2158	1976	1804
	energy, ft-lb:	3248	2758	2327	1951	1626
	arc, inches:	-1.5	+2.4	0	-9.9	-28.7

.358 NORMA MAGNUM

CARTRIDGE BULLET	RANGE, YARDS:	0	100	200	300	400
A-Square 275 Triad	velocity, fps:	2700	2394	2108	1842	1653
	energy, ft-lb:	4451	3498	2713	2072	1668
	arc, inches:		+2.3	0	-10.1	-29.8
Norma 250 TXP Swift A-Fr.	velocity, fps:	2723	2467	2225	1996	
	energy, ft-lb:	4117	3379	2748	2213	
	arc, inches:		+2.1	0	-9.1	
Norma 250 Woodleigh	velocity, fps:	2799	2442	2112	1810	
	energy, ft-lb:	4350	3312	2478	1819	
	arc, inches:		+2.2	0	-10.0	
Norma 250 Oryx	velocity, fps:	2756	2493	2245	2011	
	energy, ft-lb:	4217	3451	2798	2245	
	arc, inches:		+2.1	0	-9.0	

.358 STA

CARTRIDGE BULLET	RANGE, YARDS:	0	100	200	300	400
A-Square 275 Triad	velocity, fps:	2850	2562	2292	2039	1764
	energy, ft-lb:	4959	4009	3208	2539	1899.
	arc, inches:		+1.9	0	-8.6	-26.1

9.3x57

CARTRIDGE BULLET	RANGE, YARDS:	0	100	200	300	400
Norma 232 Vulkan	velocity, fps:	2329	2031	1757	1512	
	energy, ft-lb:	2795	2126	1591	1178	
	arc, inches:		+3.5	0	-14.9	
Norma 232 Oryx	velocity, fps:	2362	2058	1778	1528	
	energy, ft-lb:	2875	2182	1630	1203	
	arc, inches:		+3.4	0	-14.5	
Norma 285 Oryx	velocity, fps:	2067	1859	1666	1490	
	energy, ft-lb:	2704	2188	1756	1404	
	arc, inches:		+4.3	0	-16.8	
Norma 286 Alaska	velocity, fps:	2067	1857	1662	1484	
	energy, ft-lb:	2714	2190	1754	1399	
	arc, inches:		+4.3	0	-17.0	

9.3x62

CARTRIDGE BULLET	RANGE, YARDS:	0	100	200	300	400
Federal 286 Swift A-Frame	velocity, fps:	2360	2150	1950	1760	1580
	energy, ft-lb:	3535	2930	2405	1960	1590
	arc, inches:		+2.9	0	-11.6	-31.0
Federal 286 TSX	velocity, fps:	2360	2160	1970	1790	
	energy, ft-lb:	3535	2965	2465	2035	
	arc, inches:	-1.5	+3.0	0	-12.0	
Federal 286 Woodleigh Hydro	velocity, fps:	2360	2050	1760	1510	
	energy, ft-lb:	3535	2665	1975	1445	
	arc, inches::	-1.5	+3.4	0	-14.7	
Hornady 286 SP-HP	velocity, fps:	2350	2155	1961	1778	
	energy, ft-lb:	3537	2949	2442	2008	
	arc, inches:	-1.5	+3.0	0	-12.1	
Norma 232 Oryx	velocity, fps:	2625	2294	1988	1708	
	energy, ft-lb:	3535	2700	2028	1497	
	arc, inches:	-1.5	+2.5	0	-11.4	
Norma 250 A-Frame	velocity, fps:	2625	2322	2039	1778	
	energy, ft-lb:	3826	2993	2309	1755	
	arc, inches:	-1.5	+2.5	0	-10.9	
Norma 286 Plastic Point	velocity, fps:	2362	2141	1931	1736	
	energy, ft-lb:	3544	2911	2370	1914	
	arc, inches:	-1.5	+3.1	0	-12.4	
Nosler 250 AccuBond	velocity, fps:	2550	2376	2208	2048	1894
	energy, ft-lb:	3609	3133	2707	2328	1992
	arc, inches:	-1.5	+2.3	0	-9.5	-27.2
Nosler 286 Partition	velocity, fps:	2350	2179	2015	1859	1711
	energy, ft-lb:	3506	3014	2578	2194	1859
	arc, inches:	-1.5	+2.9	0	-11.5	-33.1

9.3x64

CARTRIDGE BULLET	RANGE, YARDS:	0	100	200	300	400
A-Square 286 Triad	velocity, fps:	2700	2391	2103	1835	1602
	energy, ft-lb:	4629	3630	2808	2139	1631
	arc, inches:		+2.3	0	-10.1	-30.8

.370 SAKO

CARTRIDGE BULLET	RANGE, YARDS:	0	100	200	300	400
Federal 286 TSX	velocity, fps:	2550	2370	2190	2020	1860
	energy, ft-lb:	4130	3555	3045	2595	2195
	arc, inches:	-1.5	+2.4	0	-9.6	-27.5

370 SAKO MAGNUM

CARTRIDGE BULLET	RANGE, YARDS:	0	100	200	300	400
Federal 286 Swift A-Frame	velocity, fps:	2550	2330	2120	1920	1730
	energy, ft-lb:	4130	3440	2845	2330	1900
	arc, inches:		+2.5	0	-10.1	-30.0
Federal 286 TSX	velocity, fps:	2550	2370	2190	2020	1860
	energy, ft-lb:	4130	3555	3045	2595	2195
	arc, inches:		+2.4	0	-9.5	-27.5
Federal 286 Woodleigh Hydro Solid	velocity, fps:	2550	2230	1920	1650	1410
	energy, ft-lb:	4130	3145	2350	1730	1265
	arc, inches:		+2.8	0	-12.4	-37.5

9.3x74 R

CARTRIDGE BULLET	RANGE, YARDS:	0	100	200	300	400
A-Square 286 Triad	velocity, fps:	2360	2089	1844	1623	
	energy, ft-lb:	3538	2771	2157	1670	
	arc, inches:		+3.6	0	-14.0	
Federal 286 Swift A-Frame	velocity, fps:	2360	2150	1950	1760	1580
	energy, ft-lb:	3535	2930	2405	1960	1590
	arc, inches:		+2.9	0	-11.6	-31.0
Federal 286 TSX	velocity, fps:	2360	2160	1970	1790	1630
	energy, ft-lb:	3535	2965	2465	2035	1675
	arc, inches:		+2.9	0	-11.1	-29.9
Federal 286 Woodleigh Hydro Solid	velocity, fps:	2360	2050	1760	1510	1300
	energy, ft-lb:	3535	2665	1975	1445	1065
	arc, inches:		+3.4	0	-14.7	-45.0
Hornady 286	velocity, fps	2360	2136	1924	1727	1545
	energy, ft-lb	3536	2896	2351	1893	1516
	arc, inches	-1.5	0	-6.1	-21.7	-49.0
Norma 232 Vulkan	velocity, fps:	2625	2327	2049	1792	
	energy, ft-lb:	3551	2791	2164	1655	
	arc, inches:		+2.5	0	-10.8	
Norma 232 Oryx	velocity, fps:	2526	2191	1883	1605	
	energy, ft-lb:	3274	2463	1819	1322	
	arc, inches:		+2.9	0	-12.8	

Centerfire Rifle Ballistics

9.3X74 R TO .375 WEATHERBY MAGNUM

CARTRIDGE BULLET	RANGE, YARDS:	0	100	200	300	400
Norma 285 Oryx	velocity, fps:	2362	2114	1881	1667	
	energy, ft-lb:	3532	2829	2241	1758	
	arc, inches:		+3.1	0	-13.0	
Norma 286 Alaska	velocity, fps:	2362	2135	1920	1720	
	energy, ft-lb:	3544	2894	2342	1879	
	arc, inches:		+3.1	0	-12.5	
Norma 286 Plastic Point	velocity, fps:	2362	2135	1920	1720	
	energy, ft-lb:	3544	2894	2342	1879	
	arc, inches:		+3.1	0	-12.5	

.375 WINCHESTER

CARTRIDGE BULLET	RANGE, YARDS:	0	100	200	300	400
Win. 200 Power-Point	velocity, fps:	2200	1841	1526	1268	1089
	energy, ft-lb:	2150	1506	1034	714	
	arc, inches:		0	-9.5	-33.8	

.375 FLANGED

CARTRIDGE BULLET	RANGE, YARDS:	0	100	200	300	400
Nosler 300 PT	velocity, fps:	2400	2191	1993	1806	1632
	energy, ft-lb:	3836	3198	2646	2173	1775
	arc, inches:	-1.5	+2.9	0	-11.7	-34.0

.375 H&H MAGNUM

CARTRIDGE BULLET	RANGE, YARDS:	0	100	200	300	400
A-Square 300 SP boat-tail	velocity, fps:	2550	2415	2284	2157	2034
	energy, ft-lb:	4331	3884	3474	3098	2755
	arc, inches:		+5.2	+6.0	0	-13.3
A-Square 300 Triad	velocity, fps:	2550	2251	1973	1717	1496
	energy, ft-lb:	4331	3375	2592	1964	1491
	arc, inches:		+2.7	0	-11.7	-35.1
Federal 250 Trophy Bonded	velocity, fps:	2670	2360	2080	1820	1580
	energy, ft-lb:	3955	3100	2400	1830	1380
	arc, inches:		+2.4	0	-10.4	-31.7
Federal 270 Hi-Shok	velocity, fps:	2690	2420	2170	1920	1700
	energy, ft-lb:	4340	3510	2810	2220	1740
	arc, inches:		+2.4	0	-10.9	-33.3
Federal 300 Hi-Shok	velocity, fps:	2530	2270	2020	1790	1580
	energy, ft-lb:	4265	3425	2720	2135	1665
	arc, inches:		+2.6	0	-11.2	-33.3
Federal 300 Nosler Partition	velocity, fps:	2530	2320	2120	1930	1750
	energy, ft-lb:	4265	3585	2995	2475	2040
	arc, inches:		+2.5	0	-10.3	-29.9
Federal 300 Trophy Bonded	velocity, fps:	2530	2280	2040	1810	1610
	energy, ft-lb:	4265	3450	2765	2190	1725
	arc, inches:		+2.6	0	-10.9	-32.8
Federal 300 Tr. Bonded HE	velocity, fps:	2700	2440	2190	1960	1740
	energy, ft-lb:	4855	3960	3195	2550	2020
	arc, inches:		+2.2	0	-9.4	-28.0
Federal 300 Trophy Bonded Sledgehammer Solid	velocity, fps:	2530	2160	1820	1520	1280.
	energy, ft-lb:	4265	3105	2210	1550	1090
	arc, inches, s:		0	-6.0	-22.7	-54.6
Federal 300 TSX	velocity, fps:	2470	2240	2010	1800	1610
	energy, ft-lb:	4065	3325	2700	2170	1735
	arc, inches:		+2.7	0	-11.3	-33.6
Federal 300 Woodleigh Hydro Solid	velocity, fps:	2500	2180	1880	1610	1380
	energy, ft-lb:	4165	3160	2355	1735	1270
	arc, inches:		+2.9	0	-20.1	-46.3
Hornady 250 GMX Superformance	velocity, fps:	2890	2675	2471	2275	2088
	energy, ft-lb:	4636	3973	3388	2873	2421
	arc, inches:		+1.7	0	-7.4	-21.5
Hornady 270 SP HM	velocity, fps:	2870	2620	2385	2162	1957
	energy, ft-lb:	4937	4116	3408	2802	2296
	arc, inches:		+2.2	0	-8.4	-23.9
Hornady 300 FMJ RN HM	velocity, fps:	2705	2376	2072	1804	1560
	energy, ft-lb:	4873	3760	2861	2167	1621
	arc, inches:		+2.7	0	-10.8	-32.1
Norma 300 Soft Point	velocity, fps:	2549	2211	1900	1619	
	energy, ft-lb:	4329	3258	2406	1747	
	arc, inches:		+2.8	0	-12.6	
Norma 300 TXP Swift A-Fr.	velocity, fps:	2559	2296	2049	1818	
	energy, ft-lb:	4363	3513	2798	2203	
	arc, inches:		+2.6	0	-10.9	

CARTRIDGE BULLET	RANGE, YARDS:	0	100	200	300	400
Norma 300 Oryx	velocity, fps:	2559	2292	2041	1807	
	energy, ft-lb:	4363	3500	2775	2176	
	arc, inches:		+2.6	0	-11.0	
Norma 300 Barnes Solid	velocity, fps:	2493	2061	1677	1356	
	energy, ft-lb:	4141	2829	1873	1234	
	arc, inches:		+3.4	0	-16.0	
PMC 270 PSP	velocity, fps:					
	energy, ft-lb:					
	arc, inches:					
PMC 270 Barnes X	velocity, fps:	2690	2528	2372	2221	2076
	energy, ft-lb:	4337	3831	3371	2957	2582
	arc, inches:		+2.0	0	-8.2	-23.4
PMC 300 Barnes X	velocity, fps:	2530	2389	2252	2120	1993
	energy, ft-lb:	4263	3801	3378	2994	2644
	arc, inches:		+2.3	0	-9.2	-26.1
Rem. 270 Soft Point	velocity, fps:	2690	2420	2166	1928	1707
	energy, ft-lb:	4337	3510	2812	2228	1747
	arc, inches:		+2.2	0	-9.7	-28.7
Rem. 300 Swift A-Frame	velocity, fps:	2530	2245	1979	1733	1512
	energy, ft-lb:	4262	3357	2608	2001	1523
	arc, inches:		+2.7	0	-11.7	-35.0
Speer 285 Grand Slam	velocity, fps:	2610	2365	2134	1916	
	energy, ft-lb:	4310	3540	2883	2323	
	arc, inches:		+2.4	0	-9.9	
Speer 300 African GS Tungsten Solid	velocity, fps:	2609	2277	1970	1690	
	energy, ft-lb:	4534	3453	2585	1903	
	arc, inches:		+2.6	0	-11.7	-35.6
Win. 270 Fail Safe	velocity, fps:	2670	2447	2234	2033	1842
	energy, ft-lb:	4275	3590	2994	2478	2035
	arc, inches:		+2.2	0	-9.1	-28.7
Win. 300 Fail Safe	velocity, fps:	2530	2336	2151	1974	1806
	energy, ft-lb:	4265	3636	3082	2596	2173
	arc, inches:		+2.4	0	-10.0	-26.9

.375 DAKOTA

CARTRIDGE BULLET	RANGE, YARDS:	0	100	200	300	400
Dakota 270 Barnes X	velocity, fps:	2800	2617	2441	2272	2109
	energy, ft-lb:	4699	4104	3571	3093	2666
	arc, inches:		+2.3	+1.0	-6.1	-19.9
Dakota 300 Barnes X	velocity, fps:	2600	2316	2051	1804	1579
	energy, ft-lb:	4502	3573	2800	2167	1661
	arc, inches:		+2.4	-0.1	-11.0	-32.7

.375 RUGER

CARTRIDGE BULLET	RANGE, YARDS:	0	100	200	300	400
Hornady 250 GMX Superformance	velocity, fps:	2890	2675	2471	2275	2088
	energy, ft-lb:	4636	3973	3388	2873	2421
	arc, inches:		+1.7	0	-7.4	-21.5
Hornady 270 SP	velocity, fps:	2840	2600	2372	2156	1951
	energy, ft-lb:	4835	4052	3373	2786	2283
	arc, inches:	-1.5	+1.8	0	-8.0	-23.6
Hornady 300 Solid	velocity, fps	2660	2344	2050	1780	1536
	energy, ft-lb	4713	3660	2800	2110	1572
	arc, inches	-1.5	+2.4	0	-10.8	-32.6
Nosler 260 AB	velocity, fps:	2900	2703	2514	2333	2160
	energy, ft-lb:	4854	4217	3649	3143	2693
	arc, inches:	-1.5	+1.6	0	-7.1	-20.7

.375 WEATHERBY MAGNUM

CARTRIDGE BULLET	RANGE, YARDS:	0	100	200	300	400
A-Square 300 SP boat-tail	velocity, fps:	2700	2560	2425	2293	2166
	energy, ft-lb:	4856	4366	3916	3503	3125
	arc, inches:		+4.5	+5.2	0	-11.9
A-Square 300 Triad	velocity, fps:	2700	2391	2103	1835	1602
	energy, ft-lb:	4856	3808	2946	2243	1710
	arc, inches:		+2.3	0	-10.1	-30.8
Wby. 300 Nosler Part.	velocity, fps:	2800	2572	2366	2140	1963
	energy, ft-lb:	5224	4408	3696	3076	2541
	arc, inches:		+1.9	0	-8.2	-23.9

BALLISTICS

Centerfire Rifle Ballistics

.375 JRS TO .416 REMINGTON MAGNUM

CARTRIDGE BULLET	RANGE, YARDS:	0	100	200	300	400
.375 JRS						
A-Square 300 SP boat-tail	velocity, fps:	2700	2560	2425	2293	2166.
	energy, ft-lb:	4856	4366	3916	3503	3125
	arc, inches:		+4.5	+5.2	0	-11.9
A-Square 300 Triad	velocity, fps:	2700	2391	2103	1835	1602
	energy, ft-lb:	4856	3808	2946	2243	1710
	arc, inches:		+2.3	0	-10.1	-30.8
.375 REMINGTON ULTRA MAGNUM						
Nosler 260 AB	velocity, fps:	2950	2750	2560	2377	2202
	energy, ft-lb:	5023	4367	3783	3262	2799
	arc, inches:	-1.5	+1.6	0	-6.9	-19.9
Nosler 300 PT	velocity, fps:	2750	2524	2309	2105	1912
	energy, ft-lb:	5036	4244	3553	2953	2435
	arc, inches:	-1.5	+2.0	0	-8.5	-24.9
Rem. 270 Soft Point	velocity, fps:	2900	2558	2241	1947	1678
	energy, fps:	5041	3922	3010	2272	1689
	arc, inches:		+1.9	0	-9.2	-27.8
Rem. 300 Swift A-Frame	velocity, fps:	2760	2505	2263	2035	1822
	energy, fps:	5073	4178	3412	2759	2210
	arc, inches:		+2.0	0	-8.8	-26.1
.375 A-SQUARE						
A-Square 300 SP boat-tail	velocity, fps:	2920	2773	2631	2494	2360
	energy, ft-lb:	5679	5123	4611	4142	3710
	arc, inches:		+3.7	+4.4	0	-9.8
A-Square 300 Triad	velocity, fps:	2920	2596	2294	2012	1762
	energy, ft-lb:	5679	4488	3505	2698	2068
	arc, inches:		+1.8	0	-8.5	-25.5
.376 STEYR						
Hornady 225 SP	velocity, fps:	2600	2331	2078	1842	1625
	energy, ft-lb:	3377	2714	2157	1694	1319
	arc, inches:		+2.5	0	-10.6	-31.4
Hornady 270 SP	velocity, fps:	2600	2372	2156	1951	1759
	energy, ft-lb:	4052	3373	2787	2283	1855
	arc, inches:		+2.3	0	-9.9	-28.9
.378 WEATHERBY MAGNUM						
A-Square 300 SP boat-tail	velocity, fps:	2900	2754	2612	2475	2342
	energy, ft-lb:	5602	5051	4546	4081	3655
	arc, inches:		+3.8	+4.4	0	-10.0
A-Square 300 Triad	velocity, fps:	2900	2577	2276	1997	1747
	energy, ft-lb:	5602	4424	3452	2656	2034
	arc, inches:		+1.9	0	-8.7	-25.9
Wby. 270 Pointed Expanding	velocity, fps:	3180	2921	2677	2445	2225
	energy, ft-lb:	6062	5115	4295	3583	2968
	arc, inches:		+1.3	0	-6.1	-18.1
Wby. 270 Barnes X	velocity, fps:	3150	2954	2767	2587	2415
	energy, ft-lb:	5948	5232	4589	4013	3495
	arc, inches:		+1.2	0	-5.8	-16.7
Wby. 300 RN Expanding	velocity, fps:	2925	2558	2220	1908	1627.
	energy, ft-lb:	5699	4360	3283	2424	1764
	arc, inches:		+1.9	0	-9.0	-27.8
Wby. 300 FMJ	velocity, fps:	2925	2591	2280	1991	1725
	energy, ft-lb:	5699	4470	3461	2640	1983
	arc, inches:		+1.8	0	-8.6	-26.1
.38-40 WINCHESTER						
Win. 180 Soft Point	velocity, fps:	1160	999	901	827	
	energy, ft-lb:	538	399	324	273	
	arc, inches:		0	-23.4	-75.2	

CARTRIDGE BULLET	RANGE, YARDS:	0	100	200	300	400
.38-55 WINCHESTER						
Black Hills 255 FN Lead	velocity, fps:	1250				
	energy, ft-lb:	925				
	arc, inches:					
Win. 255 Soft Point	velocity, fps:	1320	1190	1091	1018	
	energy, ft-lb:	987	802	674	587	
	arc, inches:			0	-33.9	-110.6
.41 MAGNUM						
Win. 240 Platinum Tip	velocity, fps:	1830	1488	1220	1048	
	energy, ft-lb:	1784	1180	792	585	
	arc inches:			0	-15.0	-53.4
.450/.400 NITRO EXPRESS						
A-Square 400 Triad	velocity, fps:	2150	1910	1690	1490	
	energy, ft-lb:	4105	3241	2537	1972	
	arc, inches:		+4.4	0	-16.5	
Hornady 400 DGS, DGX	velocity, fps:	2050	1820	1609	1420	
	energy, ft-lb:	3732	2940	2298	1791	
	arc, inches:	-0.9	0	-9.7	-32.8	
.404 JEFFERY						
A-Square 400 Triad	velocity, fps:	2150	1901	1674	1468	1299
	energy, ft-lb:	4105	3211	2489	1915	1499
	arc, inches:		+4.1	0	-16.4	-49.1
Hornady 400 DGS, DGX	velocity, fps:	2300	2046	1809	1592	
	energy, ft-lb:	4698	3717	2906	2251	
	arc, inches:	-1.5	0	-6.9	-24.4	
Norma 450 Woodleigh SP	velocity, fps:	2150	2048	1949	1853	1760
	energy, ft-lb:	4620	4191	3795	3430	3096
	arc, inches:	-1.5	+.2	0	-2.5	-7.6
.405 WINCHESTER						
Hornady 300 Flatpoint	velocity, fps:	2200	1851	1545	1296	
	energy, ft-lb:	3224	2282	1589	1119	
	arc, inches:		0	-8.7	-31.9	
Hornady 300 SP Interlock	velocity, fps:	2200	1890	1610	1370	
	energy, ft-lb:	3224	2379	1727	1250	
	arc, inches:		0	-8.3	-30.2	
.416 TAYLOR						
A-Square 400 Triad	velocity, fps:	2350	2093	1853	1634	1443
	energy, ft-lb:	4905	3892	3049	2371	1849
	arc, inches:		+3.2	0	-13.6	-39.8
.416 HOFFMAN						
A-Square 400 Triad	velocity, fps:	2380	2122	1879	1658	1464
	energy, ft-lb:	5031	3998	3136	2440	1903
	arc, inches:		+3.1	0	-13.1	-38.7
.416 REMINGTON MAGNUM						
A-Square 400 Triad	velocity, fps:	2380	2122	1879	1658	1464
	energy, ft-lb:	5031	3998	3136	2440	1903
	arc, inches:		+3.1	0	-13.2	-38.7
Federal 400 Trophy Bonded Sledgehammer Solid	velocity, fps:	2400	2150	1920	1700	1500
	energy, ft-lb:	5115	4110	3260	2565	2005
	arc, inches:		0	-6.0	-21.6	-49.2
Federal 400 Trophy Bonded	velocity, fps:	2400	2180	1970	1770	1590
	energy, ft-lb:	5115	4215	3440	2785	2245
	arc, inches:		0	-5.8	-20.6	-46.9
Rem. 400 Swift A-Frame	velocity, fps:	2400	2175	1962	1763	1579
	energy, ft-lb:	5115	4201	3419	2760	2214
	arc, inches:		0	-5.9	-20.8	

.416 RIGBY

CARTRIDGE BULLET	RANGE, YARDS:	0	100	200	300	400
A-Square 400 Triad	velocity, fps:	2400	2140	1897	1673	1478
	energy, ft-lb:	5115	4069	3194	2487	1940
	arc, inches:		+3.0	0	-12.9	-38.0
Federal 400 Trophy Bonded	velocity, fps:	2370	2150	1940	1750	1570
	energy, ft-lb:	4990	4110	3350	2715	2190
	arc, inches:		0	-6.0	-21.3	-48.1
Federal 400 Trophy Bonded Sledgehammer Solid	velocity, fps:	2370	2120	1890	1660	1460
	energy, ft-lb:	4990	3975	3130	2440	1895
	arc, inches:		0	-6.3	-22.5	-51.5
Federal 410 Woodleigh Weldcore	velocity, fps:	2370	2110	1870	1640	1440
	energy, ft-lb:	5115	4050	3165	2455	1895
	arc, inches:		0	-7.4	-24.8	-55.0
Federal 410 Solid	velocity, fps:	2370	2110	2870	1640	1440
	energy, ft-lb:	5115	4050	3165	2455	1895
	arc, inches:		0	-7.4	-24.8	-55.0
Hornady 400 DGX, DGS	velocity, fps:	2415	2156	1915	1691	
	energy, ft-lb:	5180	4130	3256	2540	
	arc, inches:	-1.5	0	-6.0	-21.6	
Norma 400 TXP Swift A-Fr.	velocity, fps:	2350	2127	1917	1721	
	energy, ft-lb:	4906	4021	3266	2632	
	arc, inches:		+3.1	0	-12.5	
Norma 400 Barnes Solid	velocity, fps:	2297	1930	1604	1330	
	energy, ft-lb:	4687	3310	2284	1571	
	arc, inches:		+3.9	0	-17.7	

.416 RUGER

CARTRIDGE BULLET	RANGE, YARDS:	0	100	200	300	400
Hornady 400 DGS, DGX	velocity, fps:	2400	2151	1917	1700	
	energy, ft-lb:	5116	4109	3264	2568	
	arc, inches:	-1.5	0	-6.0	-21.6	

.500/416 NITRO EXPRESS

CARTRIDGE BULLET	RANGE, YARDS:	0	50	100	150	200
Norma 450 Woodleigh SP	velocity, fps:	2100	1991	1886	1785	1688
	energy, ft-lb:	4408	3963	3556	3185	2849
	arc, inches:	-1.5	+.3	0	-2.7	-8.2

.416 DAKOTA

CARTRIDGE BULLET	RANGE, YARDS:	0	100	200	300	400
Dakota 400 Barnes X	velocity, fps:	2450	2294	2143	1998	1859
	energy, ft-lb:	5330	4671	4077	3544	3068
	arc, inches:		+2.5	-0.2	-10.5	-29.4

.416 WEATHERBY

CARTRIDGE BULLET	RANGE, YARDS:	0	100	200	300	400
A-Square 400 Triad	velocity, fps:	2600	2328	2073	1834	1624
	energy, ft-lb:	6004	4813	3816	2986	2343
	arc, inches:		+2.5	0	-10.5	-31.6
Wby. 350 Barnes X	velocity, fps:	2850	2673	2503	2340	2182
	energy, ft-lb:	6312	5553	4870	4253	3700
	arc, inches:		+1.7	0	-7.2	-20.9
Wby. 400 Swift A-Fr.	velocity, fps:	2650	2426	2213	2011	1820
	energy, ft-lb:	6237	5227	4350	3592	2941
	arc, inches:		+2.2	0	-9.3	-27.1
Wby. 400 RN Expanding	velocity, fps:	2700	2417	2152	1903	1676
	energy, ft-lb:	6474	5189	4113	3216	2493
	arc, inches:		+2.3	0	-9.7	-29.3
Wby. 400 Monolithic Solid	velocity, fps:	2700	2411	2140	1887	1656
	energy, ft-lb:	6474	5162	4068	3161	2435
	arc, inches:		+2.3	0	-9.8	-29.7

10.57 (.416) METEOR

CARTRIDGE BULLET	RANGE, YARDS:	0	100	200	300	400
Lazzeroni 400 Swift A-Fr.	velocity, fps:	2730	2532	2342	2161	1987
	energy, ft-lb:	6621	5695	4874	4147	3508
	arc, inches:		+1.9	0	-8.3	-24.0

.425 EXPRESS

CARTRIDGE BULLET	RANGE, YARDS:	0	100	200	300	400
A-Square 400 Triad	velocity, fps:	2400	2136	1888	1662	1465
	energy, ft-lb:	5115	4052	3167	2454	1906
	arc, inches:		+3.0	0	-13.1	-38.3

.44-40 WINCHESTER

CARTRIDGE BULLET	RANGE, YARDS:	0	100	200	300	400
Rem. 200 Soft Point	velocity, fps:	1190	1006	900	822	756
	energy, ft-lb:	629	449	360	300	254
	arc, inches:		0	-33.1	-108.7	-235.2
Win. 200 Soft Point	velocity, fps:	1190	1006	900	822	756
	energy, ft-lb:	629	449	360	300	254
	arc, inches:		0	-33.3	-109.5	-237.4

.44 REMINGTON MAGNUM

CARTRIDGE BULLET	RANGE, YARDS:	0	100	200	300	400
Federal 240 Hi-Shok HP	velocity, fps:	1760	1380	1090	950	860
	energy, ft-lb:	1650	1015	640	485	395
	arc, inches:		0	-17.4	-60.7	-136.0
Rem. 210 Semi-Jacketed HP	velocity, fps:	1920	1477	1155	982	880
	energy, ft-lb:	1719	1017	622	450	361
	arc, inches:		0	-14.7	-55.5	-131.3
Rem. 240 Soft Point	velocity, fps:	1760	1380	1114	970	878
	energy, ft-lb:	1650	1015	661	501	411
	arc, inches:		0	-17.0	-61.4	-143.0
Rem. 240 Semi-Jacketed Hollow Point	velocity, fps:	1760	1380	1114	970	878
	energy, ft-lb:	1650	1015	661	501	411
	arc, inches:		0	-17.0	-61.4	-143.0
Rem. 275 JHP Core-Lokt	velocity, fps:	1580	1293	1093	976	896
	energy, ft-lb:	1524	1020	730	582	490
	arc, inches:		0	-19.4	-67.5	-210.8
Win. 210 Silvertip HP	velocity, fps:	1580	1198	993	879	795
	energy, ft-lb:	1164	670	460	361	295
	arc, inches:		0	-22.4	-76.1	-168.0
Win. 240 Hollow Soft Point	velocity, fps:	1760	1362	1094	953	861
	energy, ft-lb:	1650	988	638	484	395
	arc, inches:		0	-18.1	-65.1	-150.3
Win. 250 Platinum Tip	velocity, fps:	1830	1475	1201	1032	931
	energy, ft-lb:	1859	1208	801	591	481
	arc, inches:		0	-15.3	-54.7	-126.6.

.444 MARLIN

CARTRIDGE BULLET	RANGE, YARDS:	0	100	200	300	400
Rem. 240 Soft Point	velocity, fps:	2350	1815	1377	1087	941
	energy, ft-lb:	2942	1755	1010	630	472
	arc, inches:		+2.2	-5.4	-31.4	-86.7
Hornady 265 Evolution	velocity, fps:	2325	1971	1652	1380	
	energy, ft-lb:	3180	2285	1606	1120	
	arc, inches:		+3.0	-1.4	-18.6	
Hornady 265 FP LM	velocity, fps:	2335	1913	1551	1266	
	energy, ft-lb:	3208	2153	1415	943	
	arc, inches:		+2.0	-4.9	-26.5	
Hornady 265 InterLock FP	velocity, fps:	2400	1974	1601	1295	
	energy, ft-lb:	3389	2294	1508	987	
	arc, inches:		+3.8	0	-17.5	
Rem. 240 Soft Point	velocity, fps:	2350	1815	1377	1087	941
	energy, ft-lb:	2942	1755	1010	630	472
	arc, inches:		+2.2	-5.4	-31.4	-86.7

.45-70 GOVERNMENT

CARTRIDGE BULLET	RANGE, YARDS:	0	100	200	300	400
Black Hills 405 FPL	velocity, fps:	1250				
	energy, ft-lb:					
Federal 300 Sierra Pro-Hunt. HP FN	velocity, fps:	1880	1650	1430	1240	1110
	energy, ft-lb:	2355	1815	1355	1015	810
	arc, inches:		0	-11.5	-39.7	-89.1
PMC 350 FNSP	velocity, fps:					
	energy, ft-lb:					
	arc, inches:					
Rem. 300 Jacketed HP	velocity, fps:	1810	1497	1244	1073	969
	energy, ft-lb:	2182	1492	1031	767	625
	arc, inches:		0	-13.8	-50.1	-115.7

Centerfire Rifle Ballistics

.45-70 GOVERNMENT TO .460 WEATHERBY MAGNUM

CARTRIDGE BULLET	RANGE, YARDS:	0	100	200	300	400
Rem. 405 Soft Point	velocity, fps	1330	1168	1055	977	918
	energy, ft-lb:	1590	1227	1001	858	758
	arc, inches:		0	-24.0	-78.6	-169.4
Win. 300 Jacketed HP	velocity, fps	1880	1650	1425	1235	1105
	energy, ft-lb:	2355	1815	1355	1015	810
	arc, inches:		0	-12.8	-44.3	-95.5
Win. 300 Partition Gold	velocity, fps	1880	1558	1292	1103	988
	energy, ft-lb:	2355	1616	1112	811	651
	arc, inches:		0	-12.9	-46.0	-104.9

.450 BUSHMASTER

	RANGE, YARDS:	0	100	200	300	400
Hornady 250 SST-ML	velocity, fps	2200	1840	1524	1268	
	energy, ft-lb	2686	1879	1289	893	
	arc, inches	-2.0	+2.5	-3.5	-24.5	

.450 MARLIN

	RANGE, YARDS:	0	100	200	300	400
Hornady 325 FTX	velocity, fps	2225	1887	1585	1331	
	energy, ft-lb:	3572	2569	1813	1278	
	arc, inches:	-1.5	+3.0	-2.2	-21.3	
Hornady 350 FP	velocity, fps	2100	1720	1397	1156	
	energy, ft-lb:	3427	2298	1516	1039	
	arc, inches:		0	-10.4	-38.9	

.450 NITRO EXPRESS (3¼")

	RANGE, YARDS:	0	100	200	300	400
A-Square 465 Triad	velocity, fps	2190	1970	1765	1577	
	energy, ft-lb:	4952	4009	3216	2567	
	arc, inches:		+4.3	0	-15.4	
Hornady 480 DGS, DGX	velocity, fps	2150	1881	1635	1418	
	energy, ft-lb:	4927	3769	2850	2144	
	arc, inches:	-1.5	0	-8.4	-29.9	

.450 #2

	RANGE, YARDS:	0	100	200	300	400
A-Square 465 Triad	velocity, fps	2190	1970	1765	1577	
	energy, ft-lb:	4952	4009	3216	2567	
	arc, inches:		+4.3	0	-15.4	

.458 WINCHESTER MAGNUM

	RANGE, YARDS:	0	100	200	300	400
A-Square 465 Triad	velocity, fps	2220	1999	1791	1601	1433
	energy, ft-lb:	5088	4127	3312	2646	2121
	arc, inches:		+3.6	0	-14.7	-42.5
Federal 350 Soft Point	velocity, fps	2470	1990	1570	1250	1060
	energy, ft-lb:	4740	3065	1915	1205	870
	arc, inches:		0	-7.5	-29.1	-71.1
Federal 400 Trophy Bonded	velocity, fps	2380	2170	1960	1770	1590
	energy, ft-lb:	5030	4165	3415	2785	2255
	arc, inches:		0	-5.9	-20.9	-47.1
Federal 500 Solid	velocity, fps	2090	1870	1670	1480	1320
	energy, ft-lb:	4850	3880	3085	2440	1945
	arc, inches:		0	-8.5	-29.5	-66.2
Federal 500 Trophy Bonded	velocity, fps	2090	1870	1660	1480	1310
	energy, ft-lb:	4850	3870	3065	2420	1915
	arc, inches:		0	-8.5	-29.7	-66.8
Federal 500 Trophy Bonded Sledgehammer Solid	velocity, fps	2090	1860	1650	1460	1300
	energy, ft-lb:	4850	3845	3025	2365	1865
	arc, inches:		0	-8.6	-30.0	-67.8
Federal 510 Soft Point	velocity, fps	2090	1820	1570	1360	1190
	energy, ft-lb:	4945	3730	2790	2080	1605
	arc, inches:		0	-9.1	-32.3	-73.9
Hornady 500 FMJ-RN HM	velocity, fps	2260	1984	1735	1512	
	energy, ft-lb:	5670	4368	3341	2538	
	arc, inches:		0	-7.4	-26.4	
Norma 500 TXP Swift A-Fr.	velocity, fps	2116	1903	1705	1524	
	energy, ft-lb:	4972	4023	3228	2578	
	arc, inches:		+4.1	0	-16.1	

CARTRIDGE BULLET	RANGE, YARDS:	0	100	200	300	400
Norma 500 Barnes Solid	velocity, fps	2067	1750	1472	1245	
	energy, ft-lb:	4745	3401	2405	1721	
	arc, inches:		+4.9	0	-21.2	
Rem. 450 Swift A-Frame PSP	velocity, fps	2150	1901	1671	1465	1289
	energy, ft-lb:	4618	3609	2789	2144	1659
	arc, inches:		0	-8.2	-28.9	
Speer 500 African GS Tungsten Solid	velocity, fps	2120	1845	1596	1379	
	energy, ft-lb:	4989	3780	2828	2111	
	arc, inches:		0	-8.8	-31.3	
Speer African Grand Slam	velocity, fps	2120	1853	1609	1396	
	energy, ft-lb:	4989	3810	2875	2163	
	arc, inches:		0	-8.7	-30.8	
Win. 510 Soft Point	velocity, fps	2040	1770	1527	1319	1157
	energy, ft-lb:	4712	3547	2640	1970	1516
	arc, inches:		0	-10.3	-35.6	

.458 LOTT

	RANGE, YARDS:	0	100	200	300	400
A-Square 465 Triad	velocity, fps	2380	2150	1932	1730	1551
	energy, ft-lb:	5848	4773	3855	3091	2485
	arc, inches:		+3.0	0	-12.5	-36.4
Federal 500 TSX	velocity, fps	2280	2090	1900	1730	1560
	energy, ft-lb:	5770	4825	4000	3305	2715
	arc, inches:		0	-6.4	-22.7	-50.7
Hornady 500 RNSP or solid	velocity, fps	2300	2022	1776	1551	
	energy, ft-lb:	5872	4537	3502	2671	
	arc, inches:		+3.4	0	-14.3	
Hornady 500 InterBond	velocity, fps	2300	2028	1777	1549	
	energy, ft-lb:	5872	4535	3453	2604	
	arc, inches:		0	-7.0	-25.1	

CARTRIDGE BULLET	RANGE, YARDS:	0	50	100	150	200
Norma 500 Woodleigh SP	velocity, fps	2100	1982	1868	1758	1654
	energy, ft-lb:	4897	4361	3874	3434	3039
	arc, inches:	-1.5	+.3	0	-2.8	-8.4

.450 ACKLEY

CARTRIDGE BULLET	RANGE, YARDS:	0	100	200	300	400
A-Square 465 Triad	velocity, fps	2400	2169	1950	1747	1567
	energy, ft-lb:	5947	4857	3927	3150	2534
	arc, inches:		+2.9	0	-12.2	-35.8

.450 RIGBY

CARTRIDGE BULLET	RANGE, YARDS:	0	50	100	150	200
Norma 550 Woodleigh SP	velocity, fps	2100	1992	1887	1787	1690
	energy, ft-lb:	5387	4847	4352	3900	3491
	arc, inches:	-1.5	+.3	0	-2.7	-8.2

.460 SHORT A-SQUARE

CARTRIDGE BULLET	RANGE, YARDS:	0	100	200	300	400
A-Square 500 Triad	velocity, fps	2420	2198	1987	1789	1613
	energy, ft-lb:	6501	5362	4385	3553	2890
	arc, inches:		+2.9	0	-11.6	-34.2

.450 DAKOTA

	RANGE, YARDS:	0	100	200	300	400
Dakota 500 Barnes Solid	velocity, fps	2450	2235	2030	1838	1658
	energy, ft-lb:	6663	5544	4576	3748	3051
	arc, inches:		+2.5	-0.6	-12.0	-33.8

.460 WEATHERBY MAGNUM

	RANGE, YARDS:	0	100	200	300	400
A-Square 500 Triad	velocity, fps	2580	2349	2131	1923	1737
	energy, ft-lb:	7389	6126	5040	4107	3351
	arc, inches:		+2.4	0	-10.0	-29.4
Wby. 450 Barnes X	velocity, fps	2700	2518	2343	2175	2013
	energy, ft-lb:	7284	6333	5482	4725	4050
	arc, inches:		+2.0	0	-8.4	-24.1

.460 WEATHERBY MAGNUM TO .700 NITRO EXPRESS

CARTRIDGE BULLET	RANGE, YARDS:	0	100	200	300	400
Wby. 500 RN Expanding	velocity, fps:	2600	2301	2022	1764	1533.
	energy, ft-lb:	7504	5877	4539	3456	2608
	arc, inches:		+2.6	0	-11.1	-33.5
Wby. 500 FMJ	velocity, fps:	2600	2309	2037	1784	1557
	energy, ft-lb:	7504	5917	4605	3534	2690
	arc, inches:		+2.5	0	-10.9	-33.0

.500/.465

		0	100	200	300	400
A-Square 480 Triad	velocity, fps:	2150	1928	1722	1533	
	energy, ft-lb:	4926	3960	3160	2505	
	arc, inches:		+4.3	0	-16.0	

.470 NITRO EXPRESS

		0	100	200	300	400
A-Square 500 Triad	velocity, fps:	2150	1912	1693	1494	
	energy, ft-lb:	5132	4058	3182	2478	
	arc, inches:		+4.4	0	-16.5	
Federal 500 Trophy Bond (and Sledgehammer solid)	velocity, fps:	2150	1890	1660	1450	
	energy, ft-lb:	5130	3975	3045	2320	
	arc, inches:	-1.5	0	-9.4	-29.3	
Hornady 500 DGX, DGS	velocity, fps:	2150	1885	1643	1429	
	energy, ft-lb:	5132	3946	2998	2267	
	arc, inches:	-1.5	0	-8.9	-30.9	

CARTRIDGE BULLET	RANGE, YARDS:	0	50	100	150	200
Norma 500 Woodleigh (soft and solid)	velocity, fps:	2100	2002	1906	1814	1725
	energy, ft-lb:	4897	4449	4035	3654	3304
	arc, inches:	-1.5	+.3	0	-2.7	-8.0

.470 CAPSTICK

CARTRIDGE BULLET	RANGE, YARDS:	0	100	200	300	400
A-Square 500 Triad	velocity, fps:	2400	2172	1958	1761	1553
	energy, ft-lb:	6394	5236	4255	3445	2678
	arc, inches:		+2.9	0	-11.9	-36.1

.475 #2

		0	100	200	300	400
A-Square 480 Triad	velocity, fps:	2200	1964	1744	1544	
	energy, ft-lb:	5158	4109	3240	2539	
	arc, inches:		+4.1	0	-15.6	

.475 #2 JEFFERY

		0	100	200	300	400
A-Square 500 Triad	velocity, fps:	2200	1966	1748	1550	
	energy, ft-lb:	5373	4291	3392	2666	
	arc, inches:		+4.1	0	-15.6	

.495 A-SQUARE

		0	100	200	300	400
A-Square 570 Triad	velocity, fps:	2350	2117	1896	1693	1513
	energy, ft-lb:	6989	5671	4552	3629	2899
	arc, inches:		+3.1	0	-13.0	-37.8

.50 BMG

		0	100	200	300	400
Hornady 750 A-Max	velocity, fps:	2815	2727	2641	2557	2474
	energy, ft-lb:	13,196	12,386	11,619	10,889	10,196
	arc, inches:		+1.4	0	-6.4	-18.2

.500 NITRO EXPRESS (3")

		0	100	200	300	400
A-Square 570 Triad	velocity, fps:	2150	1928	1722	1533	
	energy, ft-lb:	5850	4703	3752	2975	
	arc, inches:		+4.3	0	-16.1	

CARTRIDGE BULLET	RANGE, YARDS:	0	100	200	300	400
Federal 570 TSX	velocity, fps:	2100	1890	1700	1520	1370
	energy, ft-lb:	5580	4530	3655	2935	2355
	arc, inches:	0	-8.4	-28.7	-64.2	
Hornady 570 DGX, DGS	velocity, fps:	2150	1881	1635	1419	
	energy, ft-lb:	5850	4477	3384	2547	
	arc, inches:	-.9	0	-9.0	-31.1	

CARTRIDGE BULLET	RANGE, YARDS:	0	50	100	150	200
Norma 570 Woodleigh SP	velocity, fps:	2100	2000	1903	1809	1719
	energy, ft-lb:	5583	5064	4585	4145	3742
	arc, inches:	-1.5	+.3	0	-2.7	-8.0
50 BMG Hornady 750 A-MAX	velocity, fps:	2815	2727	2641	2557	2474
	energy, ft-lb:	13196	12386	11619	10889	10196
	arc, inches:	-1.8	+1.4	0	-6.4	-18.2

.500 JEFFERY

CARTRIDGE BULLET	RANGE, YARDS:	0	50	100	150	200
Norma 570 Woodleigh SP	velocity, fps:	2200	2097	1997	1901	1807
	energy, ft-lb:	6127	5568	5050	4573	4134
	arc, inches:	-1.5	+.2	0	-2.4	-7.1

.500 A-SQUARE

CARTRIDGE BULLET	RANGE, YARDS:	0	100	200	300	400
A-Square 600 Triad	velocity, fps:	2470	2235	2013	1804	1620
	energy, ft-lb:	8127	6654	5397	4336	3495
	arc, inches:		+2.7	0	-11.3	-33.5

.505 GIBBS

		0	100	200	300	400
A-Square 525 Triad	velocity, fps:	2300	2063	1840	1637	
	energy, ft-lb:	6166	4962	3948	3122	
	arc, inches:		+3.6	0	-14.2	

CARTRIDGE BULLET	RANGE, YARDS:	0	50	100	150	200
Norma 600 Woodleigh SP	velocity, fps:	2100	1998	1899	1803	1711
	energy, ft-lb:	5877	5319	4805	4334	3904
	arc, inches:	-1.5	+.3	0	-2.7	-8.1

.577 NITRO EXPRESS

CARTRIDGE BULLET	RANGE, YARDS:	0	100	200	300	400
A-Square 750 Triad	velocity, fps:	2050	1811	1595	1401	
	energy, ft-lb:	6998	5463	4234	3267	
	arc, inches:		+4.9	0	-18.5	

.577 TYRANNOSAUR

		0	100	200	300	400
A-Square 750 Triad	velocity, fps:	2460	2197	1950	1723	1516
	energy, ft-lb:	10077	8039	6335	4941	3825
	arc, inches:		+2.8	0	-12.1	-36.0

.600 NITRO EXPRESS

		0	100	200	300	400
A-Square 900 Triad	velocity, fps:	1950	1680	1452	1336	
	energy, ft-lb:	7596	5634	4212	3564	
	arc, inches:		+5.6	0	-20.7	

.700 NITRO EXPRESS

		0	100	200	300	400
A-Square 1000 Monolithic Solid	velocity, fps:	1900	1669	1461	1288	
	energy, ft-lb:	8015	6188	4740	3685	
	arc, inches:		+5.8	0	-22.2	

Long Range Rifle

6.6 CREEDMOOR TO .338 LAPUA

BALLISTICS

6.6 CREEDMOOR

CARTRIDGE BULLET	RANGE, YARDS:	0	400	600	800	1000
Nosler 140 HPBT	velocity, fps:	2550	2229	1932	1662	1426
	energy, ft-lb:	2021	1544	1160	859	632
	arc, inches:	-1.5	0	-26.7	-90.9	-205.9

.264 WINCHESTER MAGNUM

		0	400	600	800	1000
Nosler 130 AccuBond	velocity, fps:	3100	2709	2350	2019	1718
	energy, ft-lb:	2773	2118	1594	1176	852
	arc, inches:	-1.5	0	-17.6	-60.6	-137.9

6.5-284 NORMA

		0	400	600	800	1000
Nosler 129 AccuBond	velocity, fps:	2965	2633	2324	2036	1771
Long Range	energy, ft-lb:	2517	1985	1547	1188	899
	arc, inches:	-1.5	0	-18.7	-63.2	-141.6

.270 WSM

		0	400	600	800	1000
Nosler 150 AccuBond	velocity, fps:	2960	2661	2381	2118	1873
Long Range	energy, ft-lb:	2917	2358	1888	1495	1169
	arc, inches:	-1.5	0	-18.2	-61.1	-135.1

7MM REMINGTON MAGNUM

		0	400	600	800	1000
Nosler 168 AccuBond	velocity, fps:	2880	2598	2333	2084	1851
Long Range	energy, ft-lb:	3093	2518	2030	1620	1278
	arc, inches:	-1.5	0	-19.2	-64.0	-141.0

7MM STW

		0	400	600	800	1000
Nosler 175 AccuBond	velocity, fps:	2900	2625	2366	2122	1893
Long Range	energy, ft-lb:	3267	2677	2175	1750	1393
	arc, inches:	-1.5	0	-18.8	-62.4	-137.1

7MM REMINGTON ULTRA MAG

		0	400	600	800	1000
Nosler 175 AccuBond	velocity, fps:	3040	2756	2490	2239	2002
Long Range	energy, ft-lb:	3590	2952	2409	1948	1558
	arc, inches:	-1.5	0	-16.9	-56.2	-123.5

.308 WINCHESTER

		0	400	600	800	1000
Barnes 175 OTM	velocity, fps:	2650	2318	2011	1730	1480	1272
	energy, ft-lb:	2730	2089	1571	1163	852	629
	arc, inches:	-1.5	0	-24.6	-83.8	-189.9	-360.0

.300 WSM

		0	400	600	800	1000
Nosler 190 AccuBond	velocity, fps:	2875	2588	2319	2066	1830
Long Range	energy, ft-lb:	3486	2826	2269	1801	1413
	arc, inches:	-1.5	0	-19.3	-64.7	-142.7

.300 WINCHESTER MAGNUM

CARTRIDGE BULLET	RANGE, YARDS:	0	400	600	800	1000
Barnes 220 OTM	velocity, fps:	2700	2420	2158	1912	1685	1481
	energy, ft-lb:	3562	2862	2275	1786	1387	1072
	arc, inches:	-1.5	0	-22.4	-74.7	-165.4	-305.3
Nosler 190 AccuBond	velocity, fps:	2870	2583	2314	2062	1826
Long Range	energy, ft-lb:	3474	2816	2260	1794	1407
	arc, inches:	-1.5	0	-19.4	-64.9	-143.3

.300 WEATHERBY MAGNUM

		0	400	600	800	1000
Nosler 210 AccuBond	velocity, fps:	2825	2575	2339	2115	1905
Long Range	energy, ft-lb:	3720	3092	2551	2087	1691
	arc, inches:	-1.5	0	-19.5	-64.6	-140.8

.300 REMINGTON ULTRA MAG

		0	400	600	800	1000
Nosler 210 AccuBond	velocity, fps:	2920	2665	2424	2196	1980
Long Range	energy, ft-lb:	3975	3311	2740	2248	1828
	arc, inches:	-1.5	0	-18.1	-60.0	-130.8

.30-378 WEATHERBY MAGNUM

		0	400	600	800	1000
Nosler 210 AccuBond	velocity, fps:	3040	2778	2531	2297	2076
Long Range	energy, ft-lb:	4308	3599	2987	2461	2009
	arc, inches:	-1.5	0	-16.6	-54.9	-119.7

.338 REMINGTON ULTRA MAG

		0	400	600	800	1000
Nosler 300 AccuBond	velocity, fps:	2600	2359	2131	1916	1716
	energy, ft-lb:	4502	3707	3026	2447	1963
	arc, inches:	-1.5	0	-23.6	-77.9	-170.2

.338 LAPUA

		0	400	600	800	1000
Barnes 300 OTM	velocity, fps:	2600	2375	2161	1958	1767	1591
	energy, ft-lb:	4504	3757	3110	2554	2081	1687
	arc, inches:	-1.5	0	-23.2	-76.4	-165.9	-300.1
Nosler 300 AccuBond	velocity, fps:	2650	2406	2176	1959	1755
	energy, ft-lb:	4677	3857	3154	2555	2053
	arc, inches:	-1.5	0	-22.6	-74.7	-163.1

Rimfire Ballistics

Rimfire cartridges have had a longer run than any centerfire you can name. Horace Smith and Daniel Wesson came up with the first successful .22 rimfires in the United States in 1857. Thirty years later the .22 Long Rifle arrived, courtesy of the J. Stevens Arms & Tool Company. It used 5 grains of black powder to drive a 40-grain bullet, shortly making the transition to smokeless in a case crimped on a heeled bullet. Remington produced the first modern high-speed load in 1930. Current .22 ammo includes myriad Long Rifle listings. The Long (essentially a Short bullet in a Long Rifle case), like the CB and WRF cartridges, is going the way of the dodo. The shot load of #12 "dust" has faded too, though it has dispatched many snakes, and was once hailed as just the ticket for barn mice and rats when you didn't want to perforate the boards. New rimfires have joined the versatile Long Rifle. The .22 WMR (Winchester Magnum Rimfire) came in 1959. More than four decades passed before Hornady necked down the WMR case to form the .17 HMR. A sibling on the CCI Stinger variation of the .22 LR appeared in 2004. Hornady dubbed it the .17 Mach 2. The newest .17, Winchester's Super Mag, arrived in 2013. The .17s and the .22 WMR feature jacketed hollowpoint and polymer-tipped bullets, just like centerfires.

This list is incomplete. For convenience (and given space constraints), it omits duplicate loads—those by the same manufacturer but under different labels). Units: velocity in feet per second, energy in foot-pounds, drop in inches.

.22 TO .17 HORNADY MAGNUM RIMFIRE

CARTRIDGE BULLET	LOAD	MUZZLE VEL./ENERGY	100-YD. VEL./ENERGY	CARTRIDGE BULLET	LOAD	MUZZLE VEL./ENERGY	100-YD. VEL./ENERGY
.22				Remington .22 LR	36-gr. Viper Truncated Cone	1410/159	1056/89
CCI .22 CB Short	29-gr. RN	710/32	607/24	Remington .22 LR	36-gr. Cyclone HP	1280/131	1010/82
CCI .22 CB Long	29-gr. RN	710/32	607/24	Remington .22 LR	38-gr. Sub-sonic HP	1050/93	901/69
CCI .22 Short	27-gr. HP	1105/73	868/45	Remington .22 LR	40-gr. Target	1150/117	976/85
CCI .22 Short	29-gr. RN	1080/75	857/47	Remington .22 LR	40-gr. Thunderbolt	1255/140	1017/92
CCI .22 Short	29-gr. Target RN	830/44	704/32	Remington .22 LR	40-gr. Competition RN	1085/105	941/79
CCI .22 Long	29-gr. RN	1215/95	908/53				
CCI .22 LR	21-gr. Short Range Green HP	1650/127	912/38	Winchester .22 Short	29-gr. RN	1095/77	903/52
CCI .22 LR	31 gr. #12 birdshot	1000		Winchester .22 Long	29-gr. RN	770/38	681/30
CCI .22 LR	32-gr. Stinger HP	1640/191	1066/81	Winchester .22 LR	31-gr. #12 birdshot	1000	
CCI .22 LR	36-gr. HP	1260/127	1003/80	Winchester .22 LR	26-gr. Varmint LF HP	1650/157	1023/60
CCI .22 LR	40-gr. Tactical RN	1200/128	964/82	Winchester .22 LR	32-gr. Xpediter HP	1640/191	1078/83
CCI .22 LR	40-gr. Mini-Mag RN	1235/135	998/88	Winchester .22 LR	29-gr. Super-X sub-sonic	770/38	681/30
CCI .22 LR	40-gr. Sub-sonic HP	1050/98	897/72	Winchester .22 LR	36-gr. HP	1280/131	975/76
CCI .22 LR	40-gr. Velocitor HP	1435/183	1084/104	Winchester .22 LR	37-gr. Super-X HP	1280/135	1015/85
CCI .22 LR	40-gr. Small Game Bullet LFN	1235/135	992/87	Winchester .22 LR	37-gr. Super Speed HP	1330/154	1038/88
CCI .22 LR	40-gr. Quiet-22 HP	710/45	640/36	Winchester .22 LR	37-gr. Varmint HE HP	1435/169	1080/96
CCI .22 LR	40-gr. Select RN	1200/128	964/82	Winchester .22 LR	40-gr. Super-X low-report	1065/101	922/76
CCI .22 LR	40-gr. Green Tag RN	1070/102	908/73	Winchester .22 LR	40-gr. DynaPoint	1150/117	976/85
CCI .22 LR	45-gr. HP Suppressor	970/95	892/75	Winchester .22 LR	40-gr. M22 LRN Black	1255/140	1017/92
				Winchester .22 LR	40-gr. Power-Point HP	1280/145	1001/89
Federal .22 LR	25 gr. #12 birdshot			Winchester .22 LR	40-gr. Super-X	1300/150	1038/96
Federal .22 LR	31-gr. Game-Shok HP	1430/140	1050/75	Winchester .22 LR	40-gr. Hyper Speed HP	1435/183	1070/102
Federal .22 LR	36-gr. Champion HP	1260/125	1000/80	**.17 HORNADY MAGNUM RIMFIRE**			
Federal .22 LR	38-gr. Game-Shok HP	1260/135	1010/85	CCI .17 HMR	16-gr. TNT Green HP	2500/222	1642/96
Federal .22 LR	38-gr. Amer. Eagle HP	1260/135	1010/85	CCI .17 HMR	17-gr. TNT JHP	2550/245	1757116
Federal .22 LR	40-gr. Prem. Gold Medal	1200/130	990/85	CCI .17 HMR	17-gr. Poly-Tip V-Max	2550/245	1915/138
Federal .22 LR	40-gr. Game-Shok HP	1240/135	1010/90	CCI .17 HMR	20-gr. FMJ	2375/250	1776/140
Federal .22 LR	40-gr. Champion	1240/135	1010/90	CCI .17 HMR	20-gr. JSP	2375/250	1754/137
Federal .22 LR	45-gr. Amer. Eagle Suppressed	1050/105	910/75	Federal .17 HMR	17-gr. Prem. V-Shok TNT JHP	2530/240	1800/125
Lapua .22 LR	40-gr. Polar Biathlon	1106/109	914/74	Federal .17 HMR	17-gr. Prem. Hornady V-Max	2530/240	1880/135
Remington .22 Short	29-gr. RN	1095/77	903/52				
Remington .22 LR	33-gr. CBee Low Noise HP	740/40	638/30	Hornady .17 Mach 2	15.5-gr. NTX Lead-Free	2050/149	1450/75
Remington .22 LR	33-gr. Yellow Jacket T. C.	1500/165	1075/85	Hornady .17 Mach 2	17-gr. V-Max	2100/166	1530/88

Rimfire Ballistics

.17 HORNADY MAGNUM RIMFIRE TO .22 WINCHESTER RIMFIRE

BALLISTICS

CARTRIDGE BULLET	LOAD	MUZZLE VEL./ENERGY	100-YD. VEL./ENERGY
Hornady .17 HMR	15.5-gr. NTX Lead-Free	2525/236	1829/119
Hornady .17 HMR	17-gr. V-Max	2550/245	1901/136
Hornady .17 HMR	20-gr. XTP	2375/250	1776/140
Remington.17 HMR	17-gr. AccuTip-V	2550/245	1901/136
Winchester .17 HMR	15.5-gr. Varmint LF NTX	2550/224	1901/124
Winchester .17 HMR	17-gr. Poly Tip V-Max	2550/245	1915/138
Winchester .17 HMR	20-gr. Super-X JHP	2375/250	1776/140

.22 WINCHESTER MAGNUM RIMFIRE

CARTRIDGE BULLET	LOAD	MUZZLE VEL./ENERGY	100-YD. VEL./ENERGY
CCI .22 WMR	30 Maxi Mag HP + V	2200/322	1375/126
CCI .22 WMR	30 Poly-Tip V-Max	2200/322	1571/164
CCI .22 WMR	30 TNT JHP	2200/322	1405/131
CCI .22 WMR	30 TNT Green HP	2050/280	1317/116
CCI .22 WMR	40 Maxi Mag HP	1875/312	1319/155
CCI .22 WMR	40 Maxi Mag TMJ	1875/312	1366/166
CCI .22 WMR	40 GamePoint JSP	1875/312	1385/170
CCI .22 WMR	52 #12 birdshot	1000	
Federal .22 WMR	30-gr. Speer TNT HP	2200/320	1420/135
Federal .22 WMR	40-gr. FMJ	1880/315	1310/155
Hornady .22 WMR	30-gr. V-Max	2200/322	1421/134
Remington .22 WMR	33-gr. AccuTip-V	2000/293	1495/164

CARTRIDGE BULLET	LOAD	MUZZLE VEL./ENERGY	100-YD. VEL./ENERGY
Remington .22 WMR	40-gr. JHP	1910/324	1350/162
Remington .22 WMR	40-gr. PSP	1910/324	1340/159
Winchester .22 WMR	28-gr. Varmint LF JHP	2200/301	1394/121
Winchester .22 WMR	30-gr. Varmint HV V-Max	2250/337	1490/148
Winchester .22 WMR	30-gr. Varmint HV JHP	2250/337	1450/140
Winchester .22 WMR	34-gr. Varmint HE JHP	2120/339	1437/156
Winchester .22 WMR	40-gr. Super-X JHP (and FMJ)	1910/324	1326/156
Winchester .22 WMR	45-gr. USA DynaPoint	1550/240	1147/131

.17 WINCHESTER SUPER MAG.

CARTRIDGE BULLET	LOAD	MUZZLE VEL./ENERGY	100-YD. VEL./ENERGY
Winchester .17 Super Mag	20-gr. Varmint HV	3000/400	2504/278
Winchester .17 Super Mag	25-gr. Polymer Tip	2600/375	2230/276

.22 WINCHESTER RIMFIRE

CARTRIDGE BULLET	LOAD	MUZZLE VEL./ENERGY	100-YD. VEL./ENERGY
CCI .22 WRF	45 JHP	1300/169	1013/103
Winchester .22 WRF	45 FN	1300/169	1023/105

Centerfire Handgun Ballistics

Data shown here is taken from manufacturers' charts; your chronograph readings may vary. Barrel lengths for pistol data vary, and depend in part on which pistols are typically chambered in a given cartridge. Velocity variations due to barrel length depend on the baseline bullet speed and the load. Velocity for the .30 Carbine, normally a rifle cartridge, was determined in a pistol barrel.

Listings are current as of February the year *Shooter's Bible* appears (not the cover year). Listings are not intended as recommendations. For example, the data for the .25 Auto gives velocity and energy readings to 100 yards. Few handgunners would call the little .25 a 100-yard cartridge.

Abbreviations: Bullets are designated by loading company, weight (in grains) and type, with these abbreviations for shape and construction: BJHP= brass-jacketed hollowpoint; FN=Flat Nose; FMC=Full Metal Case; FMJ=Full Metal Jacket; HP=Hollowpoint; L=Lead; LF=Lead-Free; +P=a more powerful load than traditionally manufactured for that round; RN=Round Nose; SFHP=Starfire (PMC) Hollowpoint; SP=Softpoint; SWC=Semi Wadcutter; TMJ=Total Metal Jacket; WC=Wadcutter; CEPP, SXT and XTP are trademarked designations of Lapua, Winchester and Hornady, respectively.

.25 AUTO TO .32 S&W LONG

CARTRIDGE BULLET	RANGE, YARDS:	0	25	50	75	100
.25 AUTO						
Federal 50 FMJ	velocity, fps:	760	750	730	720	700
	energy, ft-lb:	65	60	60	55	55
Hornady 35 JHP/XTP	velocity, fps:	900		813		742
	energy, ft-lb:	63		51		43
Magtech 50 FMC	velocity, fps:	760		707		659
	energy, ft-lb:	64		56		48
PMC 50 FMJ	velocity, fps:	754	730	707	685	663
	energy, ft-lb:	62				
Rem. 50 Metal Case	velocity, fps:	760		707		659
	energy, ft-lb:	64		56		48
Speer 35 Gold Dot	velocity, fps:	900		816		747
	energy, ft-lb:	63		52		43
Speer 50 TMJ (and Blazer)	velocity, fps:	760		717		677
	energy, ft-lb:	64		57		51
Win. 45 Expanding Point	velocity, fps:	815		729		655
	energy, ft-lb	66		53		42
Win. 50 FMJ	velocity, fps:	760		707		
	energy, ft-lb	64		56		
.30 LUGER						
Win. 93 FMJ	velocity, fps:	1220		1110		1040
	energy, ft-lb	305		255		225
7.62x25 TOKAREV						
PMC 93 FMJ	velocity and energy figures not available					
.30 CARBINE						
Win. 110 Hollow SP	velocity, fps:	1790		1601		1430
	energy, ft-lb	783		626		500
.32 AUTO						
Federal 65 Hydra-Shok JHP	velocity, fps:	950	920	890	860	830
	energy, ft-lb:	130	120	115	105	100
Federal 71 FMJ	velocity, fps:	910	880	860	830	810
	energy, ft-lb:	130	120	115	110	105
Hornady 60 JHP/XTP	velocity, fps:	1000		917		849
	energy, ft-lb:	133		112		96
Hornady 71 FMJ-RN	velocity, fps:	900		845		797
	energy, ft-lb:	128		112		100
Magtech 71 FMC	velocity, fps:	905		855		810
	energy, ft-lb:	129		115		103
Magtech 71 JHP	velocity, fps:	905		855		810
	energy, ft-lb:	129		115		103

CARTRIDGE BULLET	RANGE, YARDS:	0	25	50	75	100
PMC 60 JHP	velocity, fps:	980	849	820	791	763
	energy, ft-lb:	117				
PMC 70 SFHP	velocity, fps:	velocity and energy figures not available				
PMC 71 FMJ	velocity, fps:	870	841	814	791	763
	energy, ft-lb:	119				
Rem. 71 Metal Case	velocity, fps:	905		855		810
	energy, ft-lb:	129		115		97
Speer 60 Gold Dot	velocity, fps:	960		868		796
	energy, ft-lb:	123		100		84
Speer 71 TMJ (and Blazer)	velocity, fps:	900		855		810
	energy, ft-lb:	129		115		97
Win. 60 Silvertip HP	velocity, fps:	970		895		835
	energy, ft-lb	125		107		93
Win. 71 FMJ	velocity, fps:	905		855		
	energy, ft-lb	129		115		
.32 S&W						
Rem. 88 LRN	velocity, fps:	680		645		610
	energy, ft-lb:	90		81		73
Win. 85 LRN	velocity, fps:	680		645		610
	energy, ft-lb	90		81		73
.32 S&W LONG						
Federal 98 LWC	velocity, fps:	780	700	630	560	500
	energy, ft-lb:	130	105	85	70	55
Federal 98 LRN	velocity, fps:	710	690	670	650	640
	energy, ft-lb:	115	105	100	95	90
Lapua 83 LWC	velocity, fps:	240		189*		149*
	energy, ft-lb:	154		95*		59*
Lapua 98 LWC	velocity, fps:	240		202*		171*
	energy, ft-lb:	183		130*		93*
Magtech 98 LRN	velocity, fps:	705		670		635
	energy, ft-lb:	108		98		88
Magtech 98 LWC	velocity, fps:	682		579		491
	energy, ft-lb:	102		73		52
Norma 98 LWC	velocity, fps:	787	759	732		683
	energy, ft-lb:	136	126	118		102
PMC 98 LRN	velocity, fps:	789	770	751	733	716
	energy, ft-lb:	135				
PMC 100 LWC	velocity, fps:	683	652	623	595	569
	energy, ft-lb:	102				
Rem. 98 LRN	velocity, fps:	705		670		635
	energy, ft-lb:	115		98		88

.32 S&W LONG TO 9MM LUGER

CARTRIDGE BULLET	RANGE, YARDS:	0	25	50	75	100
Win. 98 LRN	velocity, fps:	705		670		635
	energy, ft-lb:	115		98		88

.32 Short Colt

CARTRIDGE BULLET	RANGE, YARDS:	0	25	50	75	100
Win. 80 LRN	velocity, fps:	745		665		590
	energy, ft-lb	100		79		62

.32-20

CARTRIDGE BULLET	RANGE, YARDS:	0	25	50	75	100
Black Hills 115 FPL	velocity, fps:	800				
	energy, ft-lb:					

.32 H&R Mag

CARTRIDGE BULLET	RANGE, YARDS:	0	25	50	75	100
Black Hills 85 JHP	velocity, fps	1100				
	energy, ft-lb	228				
Black Hills 90 FPL	velocity, fps	750				
	energy, ft-lb					
Black Hills 115 FPL	velocity, fps	800				
	energy, ft-lb					
Federal 85 Hi-Shok JHP	velocity, fps:	1100	1050	1020	970	930
	energy, ft-lb:	230	210	195	175	165
Federal 95 LSWC	velocity, fps:	1030	1000	940	930	900
	energy, ft-lb:	225	210	195	185	170

Hornady 80 FTX		0		50 yds.		100.
	velocity, fps:	1150		1039		963
	energy, ft-lb:	235		192		165

.38 Special Lite, 4"BBL

CARTRIDGE BULLET	RANGE, YARDS:	0	25	50	75	100
Hornady 90 FTX	velocity, fps:	1200		1037		938
	energy, ft-lb:	288		215		176

9mm Makarov

CARTRIDGE BULLET	RANGE, YARDS:	0	25	50	75	100
Federal 90 Hi-Shok JHP	velocity, fps:	990	950	910	880	850
	energy, ft-lb:	195	180	165	155	145
Federal 90 FMJ	velocity, fps:	990	960	920	900	870
	energy, ft-lb:	205	190	180	170	160
Hornady 95 JHP/XTP	velocity, fps:	1000		930		874
	energy, ft-lb:	211		182		161
PMC 100 FMJ-TC	velocity, fps:	velocity and energy figures not available				
Speer 95 TMJ Blazer	velocity, fps:	1000		928		872
	energy, ft-lb:	211		182		161

9x21 IMI

CARTRIDGE BULLET	RANGE, YARDS:	0	25	50	75	100
PMC 123 FMJ	velocity, fps:	1150	1093	1046	1007	973
	energy, ft-lb:	364				

9mm Luger

CARTRIDGE BULLET	RANGE, YARDS:	0	25	50	75	100
Black Hills 115 JHP	velocity, fps:	1150				
	energy, ft-lb:	336				
Black Hills 115 FMJ	velocity, fps:	1150				
	energy, ft-lb:	336				
Black Hills 115 JHP +P	velocity, fps:	1300				
	energy, ft-lb:	431				
Black Hills 115 EXP JHP	velocity, fps:	1250				
	energy, ft-lb:	400				
Black Hills 124 JHP +P	velocity, fps:	1250				
	energy, ft-lb:	430				
Black Hills 124 JHP	velocity, fps:	1150				
	energy, ft-lb:	363				
Black Hills 124 FMJ	velocity, fps:	1150				
	energy, ft-lb:	363				
Black Hills 147 JHP subsonic	velocity, fps:	975				
	energy, ft-lb:	309				
Black Hills 147 FMJ subsonic	velocity, fps:	975				
	energy, ft-lb:	309				
Federal 105 EFMJ	velocity, fps:	1225	1160	1105	1060	1025
	energy, ft-lb:	350	315	285	265	245

CARTRIDGE BULLET	RANGE, YARDS:	0	25	50	75	100
Federal 115 Hi-Shok JHP	velocity, fps:	1160	1100	1060	1020	990
	energy, ft-lb:	345	310	285	270	250
Federal 115 FMJ	velocity, fps:	1160	1100	1060	1020	990
	energy, ft-lb:	345	310	285	270	250
Federal 124 FMJ	velocity, fps:	1120	1070	1030	990	960
	energy, ft-lb:	345	315	290	270	255
Federal 124 Hydra-Shok JHP	velocity, fps:	1120	1070	1030	990	960
	energy, ft-lb:	345	315	290	270	255
Federal 124 TMJ TMF Primer	velocity, fps:	1120	1070	1030	990	960
	energy, ft-lb:	345	315	290	270	255
Federal 124 Truncated FMJ Match	velocity, fps:	1120	1070	1030	990	960
	energy, ft-lb:	345	315	290	270	255
Federal 124 Nyclad HP	velocity, fps:	1120	1070	1030	990	960
	energy, ft-lb:	345	315	290	270	255
Federal 124 FMJ +P	velocity, fps:	1120	1070	1030	990	960
	energy, ft-lb:	345	315	290	270	255
Federal 135 Hydra-Shok JHP	velocity, fps:	1050	1030	1010	980	970
	energy, ft-lb:	330	315	300	290	280
Federal 147 Hydra-Shok JHP	velocity, fps:	1000	960	920	890	860
	energy, ft-lb:	325	300	275	260	240
Federal 147 Hi-Shok JHP	velocity, fps:	980	950	930	900	880
	energy, ft-lb:	310	295	285	265	255
Federal 147 FMJ FN	velocity, fps:	960	930	910	890	870
	energy, ft-lb:	295	280	270	260	250
Federal 147 TMJ TMF Primer	velocity, fps:	960	940	910	890	870
	energy, ft-lb:	300	285	270	260	245
Hornady 115 JHP/XTP	velocity, fps:	1155		1047		971
	energy, ft-lb:	341		280		241
Hornady 124 JHP/XTP	velocity, fps:	1110		1030		971
	energy, ft-lb:	339		292		259
Hornady 124 TAP-FPD	velocity, fps:	1100		1028		967
	energy, ft-lb:	339		291		257
Hornady 147 JHP/XTP	velocity, fps:	975		935		899
	energy, ft-lb:	310		285		264
Hornady 147 TAP-FPD	velocity, fps:	975		935		899
	energy, ft-lb:	310		285		264
Lapua 116 FMJ	velocity, fps:	365		319*		290*
	energy, ft-lb:	500		381*		315*
Lapua 120 FMJ CEPP Super	velocity, fps:	360		316*		288*
	energy, ft-lb:	505		390*		324*
Lapua 120 FMJ CEPP Extra	velocity, fps:	360		316*		288*
	energy, ft-lb:	505		390*		324*
Lapua 123 HP Megashock	velocity, fps:	355		311*		284*
	energy, ft-lb:	504		388*		322*
Lapua 123 FMJ	velocity, fps:	320		292*		272*
	energy, ft-lb:	410		342*		295*
Lapua 123 FMJ Combat	velocity, fps:	355		315*		289*
	energy, ft-lb:	504		397*		333*
Magtech 115 JHP +P	velocity, fps:	1246		1137		1056
	energy, ft-lb:	397		330		285
Magtech 115 FMC	velocity, fps:	1135		1027		961
	energy, ft-lb:	330		270		235
Magtech 115 JHP	velocity, fps:	1155		1047		971
	energy, ft-lb:	340		280		240
Magtech 124 FMC	velocity, fps:	1109		1030		971
	energy, ft-lb:	339		292		259
Norma 84 Lead Free Frangible (Geco brand)	velocity, fps:	1411				
	energy, ft-lb:	371				
Norma 124 FMJ (Geco brand)	velocity, fps:	1120				
	energy, fps:	341				
Norma 123 FMJ	velocity, fps:	1099	1032	980		899
	energy, ft-lb:	331	292	263		221
Norma 123 FMJ	velocity, fps:	1280	1170	1086		972
	energy, ft-lb:	449	375	323		259

Centerfire Handgun Ballistics

9MM LUGER TO .380 AUTO

BALLISTICS

9MM Luger (continued)

CARTRIDGE BULLET	RANGE, YARDS:	0	25	50	75	100
PMC 75 Non-Toxic Frangible	velocity, fps:	1350	1240	1154	1088	1035
	energy, ft-lb:	303				
PMC 95 SFHP	velocity, fps:	1250	1239	1228	1217	1207
	energy, ft-lb:	330				
PMC 115 FMJ	velocity, fps:	1157	1100	1053	1013	979
	energy, ft-lb:	344				
PMC 115 JHP	velocity, fps:	1167	1098	1044	999	961
	energy, ft-lb:	350				
PMC 124 SFHP	velocity, fps:	1090	1043	1003	969	939
	energy, ft-lb:	327				
PMC 124 FMJ	velocity, fps:	1110	1059	1017	980	949
	energy, ft-lb:	339				
PMC 124 LRN	velocity, fps:	1050	1006	969	937	908
	energy, ft-lb:	304				
PMC 147 FMJ	velocity, fps:	980	965	941	919	900
	enerby, ft-lb:	310				
PMC 147 SFHP	velocity, fps:	velocity and energy figures not available				
Rem. 101 Lead Free Frangible	velocity, fps:	1220		1092		1004
	energy, ft-lb:	334		267		226
Rem. 115 FN Enclosed Base	velocity, fps:	1135		1041		973
	energy, ft-lb:	329		277		242
Rem. 115 Metal Case	velocity, fps:	1135		1041		973
	energy, ft-lb:	329		277		242
Rem. 115 JHP	velocity, fps:	1155		1047		971
	energy, ft-lb:	341		280		241
Rem. 115 JHP +P	velocity, fps:	1250		1113		1019
	energy, ft-lb:	399		316		265
Rem. 124 JHP	velocity, fps:	1120		1028		960
	energy, ft-lb:	346		291		254
Rem. 124 FNEB	velocity, fps:	1100		1030		971
	energy, ft-lb:	339		292		252
Rem. 124 BJHP	velocity, fps:	1125		1031		963
	energy, ft-lb:	349		293		255
Rem. 124 BJHP +P	velocity, fps:	1180		1089		1021
	energy, ft-lb:	384		327		287
Rem. 124 Metal Case	velocity, fps:	1110		1030		971
	energy, ft-lb:	339		292		259
Rem. 147 JHP subsonic	velocity, fps:	990		941		900
	energy, ft-lb:	320		289		264
Rem. 147 BJHP	velocity, fps:	990		941		900
	energy, ft-lb:	320		289		264
Speer 90 Frangible	velocity, fps:	1350		1132		1001
	energy, ft-lb:	364		256		200
Speer 115 JHP Blazer	velocity, fps:	1145		1024		943
	energy, ft-lb:	335		268		227
Speer 115 FMJ Blazer	velocity, fps:	1145		1047		971
	energy, ft-lb:	341		280		241
Speer 115 FMJ	velocity, fps:	1200		1060		970
	energy, ft-lb:	368		287		240
Speer 115 Gold Dot HP	velocity, fps:	1200		1047		971
	energy, ft-lb:	341		280		241
Speer 124 FMJ Blazer	velocity, fps:	1090		989		917
	energy, ft-lb:	327		269		231
Speer 124 FMJ	velocity, fps:	1090		987		913
	energy, ft-lb:	327		268		230
Speer 124 TMJ-CF (and Blazer)	velocity, fps:	1090		989		917
	energy, ft-lb:	327		269		231
Speer 124 Gold Dot HP	velocity, fps:	1150		1030		948
	energy, ft-lb:	367		292		247
Speer 124 Gold Dot HP+P	velocity, ft-lb:	1220		1085		996
	energy, ft-lb:	410		324		273
Speer 147 TMJ Blazer	velocity, fps:	950		912		879
	energy, ft-lb:	295		272		252

CARTRIDGE BULLET	RANGE, YARDS:	0	25	50	75	100
Speer 147 TMJ	velocity, fps:	985		943		906
	energy, ft-lb:	317		290		268
Speer 147 TMJ-CF (and Blazer)	velocity, fps:	985		960		924
	energy, ft-lb:	326		300		279
Speer 147 Gold Dot	velocity, fps:	985		960		924
	energy, ft-lb:	326		300		279
Win. 105 Jacketed FP	velocity, fps:	1200		1074		989
	energy, ft-lb:	336		269		228
Win. 115 Silvertip HP	velocity, fps:	1225		1095		1007
	energy, ft-lb:	383		306		259
Win. 115 Jacketed HP	velocity, fps:	1225		1095		
	energy, ft-lb:	383		306		
Win. 115 FMJ	velocity, fps:	1190		1071		
	energy, ft-lb:	362		293		
Win. 115 EB WinClean	velocity, fps:	1190		1088		
	energy, ft-lb:	362		302		
Win. 124 FMJ	velocity, fps:	1140		1050		
	energy, ft-lb:	358		303		
Win. 124 EB WinClean	velocity, fps:	1130		1049		
	energy, ft-lb:	352		303		
Win. 147 FMJ FN	velocity, fps:	990		945		
	energy, ft-lb:	320		292		
Win. 147 SXT	velocity, fps:	990		947		909
	energy, ft-lb:	320		293		270
Win. 147 Silvertip HP	velocity, fps:	1010		962		921
	energy, ft-lb:	333		302		277
Win. 147 JHP	velocity, fps:	990		945		
	energy, ft-lb:	320		291		
Win. 147 EB WinClean	velocity, fps:	990		945		
	energy, ft-lb:	320		291		

9 x 23 WINCHESTER

CARTRIDGE BULLET	RANGE, YARDS:	0	25	50	75	100
Win. 124 Jacketed FP	velocity, fps:	1460		1308		
	energy, ft-lb:	587		471		
Win. 125 Silvertip HP	velocity, fps:	1450		1249		1103
	energy, ft-lb:	583		433		338

.38 S&W

CARTRIDGE BULLET	RANGE, YARDS:	0	25	50	75	100
Rem. 146 LRN	velocity, fps:	685		650		620
	energy, ft-lb:	150		135		125
Win. 145 LRN	velocity, fps:	685		650		620
	energy, ft-lb:	150		135		125

.38 SHORT COLT

CARTRIDGE BULLET	RANGE, YARDS:	0	25	50	75	100
Rem. 125 LRN	velocity, fps:	730		685		645
	energy, ft-lb:	150		130		115

.38 LONG COLT

CARTRIDGE BULLET	RANGE, YARDS:	0	25	50	75	100
Black Hills 158 RNL	velocity, fps:	650				
	energy, ft-lb:					

.380 AUTO

CARTRIDGE BULLET	RANGE, YARDS:	0	25	50	75	100
Black Hills 90 JHP	velocity, fps:	1000				
	energy, ft-lb:	200				
Black Hills 95 FMJ	velocity, fps:	950				
	energy, ft-lb:	190				
Federal 90 Hi-Shok JHP	velocity, fps:	1000	940	890	840	800
	energy, ft-lb:	200	175	160	140	130
Federal 90 Hydra-Shok JHP	velocity, fps:	1000	940	890	840	800
	energy, ft-lb:	200	175	160	140	130
Federal 95 FMJ	velocity, fps:	960	910	870	830	790
	energy, ft-lb:	190	175	160	145	130
Hornady 90 JHP/XTP	velocity, fps:	1000		902		823
	energy, ft-lb:	200		163		135

.380 AUTO TO .38 SPECIAL

CARTRIDGE BULLET	RANGE, YARDS:	0	25	50	75	100
Magtech 85 jHP + P	velocity, fps:	1082		999		936
	energy, ft-lb:	221		188		166
Magtech 95 FMC	velocity, fps:	951		861		781
	energy, ft-lb:	190		156		128
Magtech 95 JHP	velocity, fps:	951		861		781
	energy, ft-lb:	190		156		128
PMC 77 NT/FR	velocity, fps:	1200	1095	1012	932	874
	energy, ft-lb:	223				
PMC 90 FMJ	velocity, fps:	910	872	838	807	778
	energy, ft-lb:	165				
PMC 90 JHP	velocity, fps:	917	878	844	812	782
	energy, ft-lb:	168				
PMC 95 SFHP	velocity, fps:	925	884	847	813	783
	energy, ft-lb:	180				
Rem. 88 JHP	velocity, fps:	990		920		868
	energy, ft-lb:	191		165		146
Rem. 95 FNEB	velocity, fps:	955		865		785
	energy, ft-lb:	190		160		130
Rem. 95 Metal Case	velocity, fps:	955		865		785
	energy, ft-lb:	190		160		130
Rem. 102 BJHP	velocity, fps:	940		901		866
	energy, ft-lb:	200		184		170
Speer 88 JHP Blazer	velocity, fps:	950		920		870
	energy, ft-lb:	195		164		148
Speer 90 Gold Dot	velocity, fps:	990		907		842
	energy, ft-lb:	196		164		142
Speer 95 TMJ Blazer	velocity, fps:	945		865		785
	energy, ft-lb:	190		160		130
Speer 95 TMJ	velocity, fps:	950		877		817
	energy, ft-lb:	180		154		133
Win. 85 Silvertip HP	velocity, fps:	1000		921		860
	energy, ft-lb:	189		160		140
Win. 95 SXT	velocity, fps:	955		889		835
	energy, ft-lb:	192		167		147
Win. 95 FMJ	velocity, fps:	955		865		
	energy, ft-lb:	190		160		
Win. 95 EB WinClean	velocity, fps:	955		881		
	energy, ft-lb:	192		164		

.38 SPECIAL

CARTRIDGE BULLET	RANGE, YARDS:	0	25	50	75	100
Black Hills 125 JHP +P	velocity, fps:	1050				
	energy, ft-lb:	306				
Black Hills 148 HBWC	velocity, fps:	700				
	energy, ft-lb:					
Black Hills 158 SWC	velocity, fps:	850				
	energy, ft-lb:					
Black Hills 158 CNL	velocity, fps:	800				
	energy, ft-lb:					
Federal 110 Hydra-Shok JHP	velocity, fps:	1000	970	930	910	880
	energy, ft-lb:	245	225	215	200	190
Federal 110 Hi-Shok JHP +P	velocity, fps:	1000	960	930	900	870
	energy, ft-lb:	240	225	210	195	185
Federal 125 Nyclad HP	velocity, fps:	830	780	730	690	650
	energy, ft-lb:	190	170	150	130	115
Federal 125 Hi-Shok JSP +P	velocity, fps:	950	920	900	880	860
	energy, ft-lb:	250	235	225	215	205
Federal 125 Hi-Shok JHP +P	velocity, fps:	950	920	900	880	860
	energy, ft-lb:	250	235	225	215	205
Federal 125 Nyclad HP +P	velocity, fps:	950	920	900	880	860
	energy, ft-lb:	250	235	225	215	205
Federal 129 Hydra-Shok JHP+P	velocity, fps:	950	930	910	890	870
	energy, ft-lb:	255	245	235	225	215
Federal 130 FMJ	velocity, fps:	950	920	890	870	840
	energy, ft-lb:	260	245	230	215	205

CARTRIDGE BULLET	RANGE, YARDS:	0	25	50	75	100
Federal 148 LWC Match	velocity, fps:	710	670	630	600	560
	energy, ft-lb:	165	150	130	115	105
Federal 158 LRN	velocity, fps:	760	740	720	710	690
	energy, ft-lb:	200	190	185	175	170
Federal 158 LSWC	velocity, fps:	760	740	720	710	690
	energy, ft-lb:	200	190	185	175	170
Federal 158 Nyclad RN	velocity, fps:	760	740	720	710	690
	energy, ft-lb:	200	190	185	175	170
Federal 158 SWC HP +P	velocity, fps:	890	870	860	840	820
	energy, ft-lb:	280	265	260	245	235
Federal 158 LSWC +P	velocity, fps:	890	870	860	840	820
	energy, ft-lb:	270	265	260	245	235
Federal 158 Nyclad SWC-HP+P	velocity, fps:	890	870	860	840	820
	energy, ft-lb:	270	265	260	245	235
Hornady 125 JHP/XTP	velocity, fps:	900		856		817
	energy, ft-lb:	225		203		185
Hornady 140 JHP/XTP	velocity, fps:	825		790		757
	energy, ft-lb:	212		194		178
Hornady 140 Cowboy	velocity, fps:	800		767		735
	energy, ft-lb:	199		183		168
Hornady 148 HBWC	velocity, fps:	800		697		610
	energy, ft-lb:	210		160		122
Hornady 158 JHP/XPT	velocity, fps:	800		765		731
	energy, ft-lb:	225		205		188
Lapua 123 HP Megashock	velocity, fps:	355		311*		284*
	energy, ft-lb:	504		388*		322*
Lapua 148 LWC	velocity, fps:	230		203*		181*
	energy, ft-lb:	254		199*		157*
Lapua 150 SJFN	velocity, fps:	325		301*		283*
	energy, ft-lb:	512		439*		388*
Lapua 158 FMJLF	velocity, fps:	255		243*		232*
	energy, ft-lb:	332		301*		275*
Lapua 158 LRN	velocity, fps:	255		243*		232*
	energy, ft-lb:	332		301*		275*
Magtech 125 JHP +P	velocity, fps:	1017		971		931
	energy, ft-lb:	287		262		241
Magtech 148 LWC	velocity, fps:	710		634		566
	energy, ft-lb:	166		132		105
Magtech 158 LRN	velocity, fps:	755		728		693
	energy, ft-lb:	200		183		168
Magtech 158 LFN	velocity, fps:	800		776		753
	energy, ft-lb:	225		211		199
Magtech 158 SJHP	velocity, fps:	807		779		753
	energy, ft-lb:	230		213		199
Magtech 158 LSWC	velocity, fps:	755		721		689
	energy, ft-lb:	200		182		167
Magtech 158 FMC-Flat	velocity, fps:	807		779		753
	energy, ft-lb:	230		213		199
PMC 85 Non-Toxic Frangible	velocity, fps:	1275	1181	1109	1052	1006
	energy, ft-lb:	307				
PMC 110 SFHP +P	velocity, fps:	velocity and energy figures not available				
PMC 125 SFHP +P	velocity, fps:	950	918	889	863	838
	energy, ft-lb:	251				
PMC 125 JHP +P	velocity, fps:	974	938	906	878	851
	energy, ft-lb:	266				
PMC 132 FMJ	velocity, fps:	841	820	799	780	761
	energy, ft-lb:	206				
PMC 148 LWC	velocity, fps:	728	694	662	631	602
	energy, ft-lb:	175				
PMC 158 LRN	velocity, fps:	820	801	783	765	749
	energy, ft-lb:	235				
PMC 158 JSP	velocity, fps:	835	816	797	779	762
	energy, ft-lb:	245				

Centerfire Handgun Ballistics

.38 SPECIAL TO .357 MAGNUM

.38 Special

CARTRIDGE BULLET	RANGE, YARDS:	0	25	50	75	100
PMC 158 LFP	velocity, fps:	800		761		725
	energy, ft-lb:	225		203		185
Rem. 101 Lead Free Frangible	velocity, fps:	950		896		850
	energy, ft-lb:	202		180		162
Rem. 110 SJHP	velocity, fps:	950		890		840
	energy, ft-lb:	220		194		172
Rem. 110 SJHP +P	velocity, fps:	995		926		871
	energy, ft-lb:	242		210		185
Rem. 125 SJHP +P	velocity, ft-lb:	945		898		858
	energy, ft-lb:	248		224		204
Rem. 125 BJHP	velocity, fps:	975		929		885
	energy, ft-lb:	264		238		218
Rem. 125 FNEB	velocity, fps:	850		822		796
	energy, ft-lb:	201		188		176
Rem. 125 FNEB +P	velocity, fps:	975		935		899
	energy, ft-lb:	264		242		224
Rem. 130 Metal Case	velocity, fps:	950		913		879
	energy, ft-lb:	261		240		223
Rem. 148 LWC Match	velocity, fps:	710		634		566
	energy, ft-lb:	166		132		105
Rem. 158 LRN	velocity, fps:	755		723		692
	energy, ft-lb:	200		183		168
Rem. 158 SWC +P	velocity, fps:	890		855		823
	energy, ft-lb:	278		257		238
Rem. 158 SWC	velocity, fps:	755		723		692
	energy, ft-lb:	200		183		168
Rem. 158 LHP +P	velocity, fps:	890		855		823
	energy, ft-lb:	278		257		238
Speer 125 JHP +P Blazer	velocity, fps:	945		898		858
	energy, ft-lb:	248		224		204
Speer 125 Gold Dot +P	velocity, fps:	945		898		858
	energy, ft-lb:	248		224		204
Speer 158 TMJ +P (and Blazer)	velocity, fps:	900		852		818
	energy, ft-lb:	278		255		235
Speer 158 LRN Blazer	velocity, fps:	755		723		692
	energy, ft-lb:	200		183		168
Speer 158 Trail Blazer LFN	velocity, fps:	800		761		725
	energy, ft-lb:	225		203		184
Speer 158 TMJ-CF +P (and Blazer)	velocity, fps:	900		852		818
	energy, ft-lb:	278		255		235
Win. 110 Silvertip HP	velocity, fps:	945		894		850
	energy, ft-lb:	218		195		176
Win. 110 Jacketed FP	velocity, fps:	975		906		849
	energy, ft-lb:	232		201		176
Win. 125 Jacketed HP	velocity, fps:	945		898		
	energy, ft-lb:	248		224		
Win. 125 Jacketed HP +P	velocity, fps:	945		898		858
	energy, ft-lb:	248		224		204
Win. 125 Jacketed FP	velocity, fps:	850		804		
	energy, ft-lb:	201		179		
Win. 125 Silvertip HP + P	velocity, fps:	945		898		858
	energy, ft-lb:	248		224		204
Win. 125 JFP WinClean	velocity, fps:	775		742		
	energy, ft-lb:	167		153		
Win. 130 FMJ	velocity, fps:	800		765		
	energy, ft-lb:	185		169		
Win. 130 SXT +P	velocity, fps:	925		887		852
	energy, ft-lb:	247		227		210
Win. 148 LWC Super Match	velocity, fps:	710		634		566
	energy, ft-lb:	166		132		105
Win. 150 Lead	velocity, fps:	845		812		
	energy, ft-lb:	238		219		
Win. 158 Lead	velocity, fps:	800		761		725
	energy, ft-lb:	225		203		185
Win. 158 LRN	velocity, fps:	755		723		693
	energy, ft-lb:	200		183		168
Win. 158 LSWC	velocity, fps:	755		721		689
	energy, ft-lb:	200		182		167
Win. 158 LSWC HP +P	velocity, fps:	890		855		823
	energy, ft-lb:	278		257		238

.38-40

CARTRIDGE BULLET	RANGE, YARDS:	0	25	50	75	100
Black Hills 180 FPL	velocity, fps:	800				
	energy, ft-lb:					

.38 SUPER

CARTRIDGE BULLET	RANGE, YARDS:	0	25	50	75	100
Federal 130 FMJ +P	velocity, fps:	1200	1140	1100	1050	1020
	energy, ft-lb:	415	380	350	320	300
PMC 115 JHP	velocity, fps:	1116	1052	1001	959	923
	energy, ft-lb:	318				
PMC 130 FMJ	velocity, fps:	1092	1038	994	957	924
	energy, ft-lb:	348				
Rem. 130 Metal Case	velocity, fps:	1215		1099		1017
	energy, ft-lb:	426		348		298
Win. 125 Silvertip HP +P	velocity, fps:	1240		1130		1050
	energy, ft-lb:	427		354		306
Win. 130 FMJ +P	velocity, fps:	1215		1099		
	energy, ft-lb:	426		348		

.357 SIG

CARTRIDGE BULLET	RANGE, YARDS:	0	25	50	75	100
Federal 125 FMJ	velocity, fps:	1350	1270	1190	1130	1080
	energy, ft-lb:	510	445	395	355	325
Federal 125 JHP	velocity, fps:	1350	1270	1190	1130	1080
	energy, ft-lb:	510	445	395	355	325
Federal 150 JHP	velocity, fps:	1130	1080	1030	1000	970
	energy, ft-lb:	420	385	355	330	310
Hornady 124 JHP/XTP	velocity, fps:	1350		1208		1108
	energy, ft-lb:	502		405		338
Hornady 147 JHP/XTP	velocity, fps:	1225		1138		1072
	energy, ft-lb:	490		422		375
PMC 85 Non-Toxic Frangible	velocity, fps:	1480	1356	1245	1158	1092
	energy, ft-lb:	413				
PMC 124 SFHP	velocity, fps:	1350	1263	1190	1132	1083
	energy, ft-lb:	502				
PMC 124 FMJ/FP	velocity, fps:	1350	1242	1158	1093	1040
	energy, ft-lb:	512				
Rem. 104 Lead Free Frangible	velocity, fps:	1400		1223		1094
	energy, ft-lb:	453		345		276
Rem. 125 Metal Case	velocity, fps:	1350		1146		1018
	energy, ft-lb:	506		422		359
Rem. 125 JHP	velocity, fps:	1350		1157		1032
	energy, ft-lb:	506		372		296
Speer 125 TMJ (and Blazer)	velocity, fps:	1350		1177		1057
	energy, ft-lb:	502		381		307
Speer 125 TMJ-CF	velocity, fps:	1350		1177		1057
	energy, ft-lb:	502		381		307
Speer 125 Gold Dot	velocity, fps:	1375		1203		1079
	energy, ft-lb:	525		402		323
Win. 105 JFP	velocity, fps:	1370		1179		1050
	energy, ft-lb	438		324		257
Win. 125 FMJ FN	velocity, fps:	1350		1185		
	energy, ft-lb	506		390		

.357 MAGNUM

CARTRIDGE BULLET	RANGE, YARDS:	0	25	50	75	100
Black Hills 125 JHP	velocity, fps:	1500				
	energy, ft-lb:	625				
Black Hills 158 CNL	velocity, fps:	800				
	energy, ft-lb:					
Black Hills 158 SWC	velocity, fps:	1050				
	energy, ft-lb:					

Centerfire Handgun Ballistics

.357 MAGNUM TO .40 S&W

CARTRIDGE BULLET	RANGE, YARDS:	0	25	50	75	100
Black Hills 158 JHP	velocity, fps:	1250				
	energy, ft-lb:					
Federal 110 Hi-Shok JHP	velocity, fps:	1300	1180	1090	1040	990
	energy, ft-lb:	410	340	290	260	235
Federal 125 Hi-Shok JHP	velocity, fps:	1450	1350	1240	1160	1100
	energy, ft-lb:	580	495	430	370	335
Federal 130 Hydra-Shok JHP	velocity, fps:	1300	1210	1130	1070	1020
	energy, ft-lb:	490	420	370	330	300
Federal 158 Hi-Shok JSP	velocity, fps:	1240	1160	1100	1060	1020
	energy, ft-lb:	535	475	430	395	365
Federal 158 JSP	velocity, fps:	1240	1160	1100	1060	1020
	energy, ft-lb:	535	475	430	395	365
Federal 158 LSWC	velocity, fps:	1240	1160	1100	1060	1020
	energy, ft-lb:	535	475	430	395	365
Federal 158 Hi-Shok JHP	velocity, fps:	1240	1160	1100	1060	1020
	energy, ft-lb:	535	475	430	395	365
Federal 158 Hydra-Shok JHP	velocity, fps:	1240	1160	1100	1060	1020
	energy, ft-lb:	535	475	430	395	365
Federal 180 Hi-Shok JHP	velocity, fps:	1090	1030	980	930	890
	energy, ft-lb:	475	425	385	350	320
Federal 180 Castcore	velocity, fps:	1250	1200	1160	1120	1080
	energy, ft-lb:	625	575	535	495	465
Hornady 125 JHP/XTP	velocity, fps:	1500		1314		1166
	energy, ft-lb:	624		479		377
Hornady 125 JFP/XTP	velocity, fps:	1500		1311		1161
	energy, ft-lb:	624		477		374
Hornady 140 Cowboy	velocity, fps:	800		767		735
	energy, ft-lb:	199		183		168
Hornady 140 JHP/XTP	velocity, fps:	1400		1249		1130
	energy, ft-lb:	609		485		397
Hornady 158 JHP/XTP	velocity, fps:	1250		1150		1073
	energy, ft-lb:	548		464		404
Hornady 158 JFP/XTP	velocity, fps:	1250		1147		1068
	energy, ft-lb:	548		461		400
Lapua 150 FMJ CEPP Super	velocity, fps:	370		527*		303*
	energy, ft-lb:	664		527*		445*
Lapua 150 SJFN	velocity, fps:	385		342*		313*
	energy, ft-lb:	719		569*		476*
Lapua 158 SJHP	velocity, fps:	470		408*		359*
	energy, ft-lb:	1127		850*		657*
Magtech 158 SJSP	velocity, fps:	1235		1104		1015
	energy, ft-lb:	535		428		361
Magtech 158 SJHP	velocity, fps:	1235		1104		1015
	energy, ft-lb:	535		428		361
PMC 85 Non-Toxic Frangible	velocity, fps:	1325	1219	1139	1076	1025
	energy, ft-lb:	331				
PMC 125 JHP	velocity, fps:	1194	1117	1057	1008	967
	energy, ft-lb:	399				
PMC 150 JHP	velocity, fps:	1234	1156	1093	1042	1000
	energy, ft-lb:	512				
PMC 150 SFHP	velocity, fps:	1205	1129	1069	1020	980
	energy, ft-lb:	484				
PMC 158 JSP	velocity, fps:	1194	1122	1063	1016	977
	energy, ft-lb:	504				
PMC 158 LFP	velocity, fps:	800		761		725
	energy, ft-lb:	225		203		185
Rem. 110 SJHP	velocity, fps:	1295		1094		975
	energy, ft-lb:	410		292		232
Rem. 125 SJHP	velocity, fps:	1450		1240		1090
	energy, ft-lb:	583		427		330
Rem. 125 BJHP	velocity, fps:	1220		1095		1009
	energy, ft-lb:	413		333		283
Rem. 125 FNEB	velocity, fps:	1450		1240		1090
	energy, ft-lb:	583		427		330

CARTRIDGE BULLET	RANGE, YARDS:	0	25	50	75	100
Rem. 158 SJHP	velocity, fps:	1235		1104		1015
	energy, ft-lb:	535		428		361
Rem. 158 SP	velocity, fps:	1235		1104		1015
	energy, ft-lb:	535		428		361
Rem. 158 SWC	velocity, fps:	1235		1104		1015
	energy, ft-lb:	535		428		361
Rem. 165 JHP Core-Lokt	velocity, fps:	1290		1189		1108
	energy, ft-lb:	610		518		450
Rem. 180 SJHP	velocity, fps:	1145		1053		985
	energy, ft-lb:	542		443		388
Speer 125 Gold Dot	velocity, fps:	1450		1240		1090
	energy, ft-lb:	583		427		330
Speer 158 JHP Blazer	velocity, fps:	1150		1104		1015
	energy, ft-lb:	535		428		361
Speer 158 Gold Dot	velocity, fps:	1235		1104		1015
	energy, ft-lb:	535		428		361
Speer 170 Gold Dot SP	velocity, fps:	1180		1089		1019
	energy, ft-lb:	525		447		392
Win. 110 JFP	velocity, fps:	1275		1105		998
	energy, ft-lb:	397		298		243
Win. 110 JHP	velocity, fps:	1295		1095		
	energy, ft-lb:	410		292		
Win. 125 JFP WinClean	velocity, fps:	1370		1183		
	energy, ft-lb:	521		389		
Win. 145 Silvertip HP	velocity, fps:	1290		1155		1060
	energy, ft-lb:	535		428		361
Win. 158 JHP	velocity, fps:	1235		1104		1015
	energy, ft-lb:	535		428		361
Win. 158 JSP	velocity, fps:	1235		1104		1015
	energy, ft-lb:	535		428		361
Win. 180 Partition Gold	velocity, fps:	1180		1088		1020
	energy, ft-lb:	557		473		416

.40 S&W

CARTRIDGE BULLET	RANGE, YARDS:	0	25	50	75	100
Black Hills 155 JHP	velocity, fps:	1150				
	energy, ft-lb:	450				
Black Hills 165 EXP JHP	velocity, fps:	1150 (2005: 1100)				
	energy, ft-lb:	483				
Black Hills 180 JHP	velocity, fps:	1000				
	energy, ft-lb:	400				
Black Hills 180 JHP	velocity, fps:	1000				
	energy, ft-lb:	400				
Federal 135 Hydra-Shok JHP	velocity, fps:	1190	1050	970	900	850
	energy, ft-lb:	420	330	280	245	215
Federal 155 FMJ Ball	velocity, fps:	1140	1080	1030	990	960
	energy, ft-lb:	445	400	365	335	315
Federal 155 Hi-Shok JHP	velocity, fps:	1140	1080	1030	990	950
	energy, ft-lb:	445	400	365	335	315
Federal 155 Hydra-Shok JHP	velocity, fps:	1140	1080	1030	990	950
	energy, ft-lb:	445	400	365	335	315
Federal 165 EFMJ	velocity, fps:	1190	1060	970	905	850
	energy, ft-lb:	520	410	345	300	265
Federal 165 FMJ	velocity, fps:	1050	1020	990	960	935
	energy, ft-lb:	405	380	355	335	320
Federal 165 FMJ Ball	velocity, fps:	980	950	920	900	880
	energy, ft-lb:	350	330	310	295	280
Federal 165 Hydra-Shok JHP	velocity, fps:	980	950	930	910	890
	energy, ft-lb:	350	330	315	300	290
Federal 180 High Antim. Lead	velocity, fps:	990	960	930	910	890
	energy, ft-lb:	390	365	345	330	315
Federal 180 TMJ TMF Primer	velocity, fps:	990	960	940	910	890
	energy, ft-lb:	390	370	350	330	315
Federal 180 FMJ Ball	velocity, fps:	990	960	940	910	890
	energy, ft-lb:	390	370	350	330	315

Centerfire Handgun Ballistics

BALLISTICS

CARTRIDGE BULLET	RANGE, YARDS:	0	25	50	75	100
Federal 180 Hi-Shok JHP	velocity, fps:	990	960	930	910	890
	energy, ft-lb:	390	365	345	330	315
Federal 180 Hydra-Shok JHP	velocity, fps:	990	960	930	910	890
	energy, ft-lb:	390	365	345	330	315
Hornady 155 JHP/XTP	velocity, fps:	1180		1061		980
	energy, ft-lb:	479		387		331
Hornady 155 TAP-FPD	velocity, fps:	1180		1061		980
	energy, ft-lb:	470		387		331
Hornady 180 JHP/XTP	velocity, fps:	950		903		862
	energy, ft-lb:	361		326		297
Hornady 180 TAP-FPD	velocity, fps:	950		903		862
	energy, ft-lb:	361		326		297
Magtech 155 JHP	velocity, fps:	1025		1118		1052
	energy, ft-lb:	500		430		381
Magtech 180 JHP	velocity, fps:	990		933		886
	energy, ft-lb:	390		348		314
Magtech 180 FMC	velocity, fps:	990		933		886
	energy, ft-lb:	390		348		314
PMC 115 Non-Toxic Frangible	velocity, fps:	1350	1240	1154	1088	1035
	energy, ft-lb:	465				
PMC 155 SFHP	velocity, fps:	1160	1092	1039	994	957
	energy, ft-lb:	463				
PMC 165 JHP	velocity, fps:	1040	1002	970	941	915
	energy, ft-lb:	396				
PMC 165 FMJ	velocity, fps:	1010	977	948	922	899
	energy, ft-lb:	374				
PMC 180 FMJ/FP	velocity, fps:	985	957	931	908	885
	energy, ft-lb:	388				
PMC 180 SFHP	velocity, fps:	985	958	933	910	889
	energy, ft-lb:	388				
Rem. 141 Lead Free Frangible	velocity, fps:	1135		1056		996
	energy, ft-lb:	403		349		311
Rem. 155 JHP	velocity, fps:	1205		1095		1017
	energy, ft-lb:	499		413		356
Rem. 165 BJHP	velocity, fps:	1150		1040		964
	energy, ft-lb:	485		396		340
Rem. 180 JHP	velocity, fps:	1015		960		914
	energy, ft-lb:	412		368		334
Rem. 180 FN Enclosed Base	velocity, fps:	985		936		893
	energy, ft-lb:	388		350		319
Rem. 180 Metal Case	velocity, fps:	985		936		893
	energy, ft-lb:	388		350		319
Rem. 180 BJHP	velocity, fps:	1015		960		914
	energy, ft-lb:	412		368		334
Speer 105 Frangible	velocity, fps:	1380		1128		985
	energy, ft-lb:	444		297		226
Speer 155 TMJ Blazer	velocity, fps:	1175		1047		963
	energy, ft-lb:	475		377		319
Speer 155 TMJ	velocity, fps:	1200		1065		976
	energy, ft-lb:	496		390		328
Speer 155 Gold Dot	velocity, fps:	1200		1063		974
	energy, ft-lb:	496		389		326
Speer 165 TMJ Blazer	velocity, fps:	1100		1006		938
	energy, ft-lb:	443		371		321
Speer 165 TMJ	velocity, fps:	1150		1040		964
	energy, ft-lb:	484		396		340
Speer 165 Gold Dot	velocity, fps:	1150		1043		966
	energy, ft-lb:	485		399		342
Speer 180 HP Blazer	velocity, fps:	985		951		909
	energy, ft-lb:	400		361		330
Speer 180 FMJ Blazer	velocity, fps:	1000		937		886
	energy, ft-lb:	400		351		313
Speer 180 FMJ	velocity, fps:	1000		951		909
	energy, ft-lb:	400		361		330

CARTRIDGE BULLET	RANGE, YARDS:	0	25	50	75	100
Speer 180 TMJ-CF (and Blazer)	velocity, fps:	1000		951		909
	energy, ft-lb:	400		361		330
Speer 180 Gold Dot	velocity, fps:	1025		957		902
	energy, ft-lb:	420		366		325
Win. 140 JFP	velocity, fps:	1155		1039		960
	energy, ft-lb:	415		336		286
Win. 155 Silvertip HP	velocity, fps:	1205		1096		1018
	energy, ft-lb:	500		414		357
Win. 165 SXT	velocity, fps:	1130		1041		977
	energy, ft-lb:	468		397		349
Win. 165 FMJ FN	velocity, fps:	1060		1001		
	energy, ft-lb:	412		367		
Win. 165 EB WinClean	velocity, fps:	1130		1054		
	energy, ft-lb:	468		407		
Win. 180 JHP	velocity, fps:	1010		954		
	energy, ft-lb:	408		364		
Win. 180 FMJ	velocity, fps:	990		936		
	energy, ft-lb:	390		350		
Win. 180 SXT	velocity, fps:	1010		954		909
	energy, ft-lb:	408		364		330
Win. 180 EB WinClean	velocity, fps:	990		943		
	energy, ft-lb:	392		356		

10 MM AUTO

CARTRIDGE BULLET	RANGE, YARDS:	0	25	50	75	100
Federal 155 Hi-Shok JHP	velocity, fps:	1330	1230	1140	1080	1030
	energy, ft-lb:	605	515	450	400	360
Federal 180 Hi-Shok JHP	velocity, fps:	1030	1000	970	950	920
	energy, ft-lb:	425	400	375	355	340
Federal 180 Hydra-Shok JHP	velocity, fps:	1030	1000	970	950	920
	energy, ft-lb:	425	400	375	355	340
Federal 180 High Antim. Lead	velocity, fps:	1030	1000	970	950	920
	energy, ft-lb:	425	400	375	355	340
Federal 180 FMJ	velocity, fps:	1060	1025	990	965	940
	energy, ft-lb:	400	370	350	330	310
Hornady 155 JHP/XTP	velocity, fps:	1265		1119		1020
	energy, ft-lb:	551		431		358
Hornady 180 JHP/XTP	velocity, fps:	1180		1077		1004
	energy, ft-lb:	556		464		403
Hornady 200 JHP/XTP	velocity, fps:	1050		994		948
	energy, ft-lb:	490		439		399
PMC 115 Non-Toxic Frangible	velocity, fps:	1350	1240	1154	1088	1035
	energy, ft-lb:	465				
PMC 170 JHP	velocity, fps:	1200	1117	1052	1000	958
	energy, ft-lb:	543				
PMC 180 SFHP	velocity, fps:	950	926	903	882	862
	energy, ft-lb:	361				
PMC 200 TC-FMJ	velocity, fps:	1050	1008	972	941	912
	energy, ft-lb:	490				
Rem. 180 Metal Case	velocity, fps:	1150		1063		998
	energy, ft-lb:	529		452		398
Speer 200 TMJ Blazer	velocity, fps:	1050		966		952
	energy, ft-lb:	490		440		402
Win. 175 Silvertip HP	velocity, fps:	1290		1141		1037
	energy, ft-lb:	649		506		418

.41 REMINGTON MAGNUM

CARTRIDGE BULLET	RANGE, YARDS:	0	25	50	75	100
Federal 210 Hi-Shok JHP	velocity, fps:	1300	1210	1130	1070	1030
	energy, ft-lb:	790	680	595	540	495
PMC 210 TCSP	velocity, fps:	1290	1201	1128	1069	1021
	energy, ft-lb:	774				
PMC 210 JHP	velocity, fps:	1289	1200	1127	1068	1020
	energy, ft-lb:	774				
Rem. 210 SP	velocity, fps:	1300		1162		1062
	energy, ft-lb:	788		630		526

Centerfire Handgun Ballistics

.41 REMINGTON MAGNUM TO .45 AUTOMATIC (ACP)

CARTRIDGE BULLET	RANGE, YARDS:	0	25	50	75	100
Win. 175 Silvertip HP	velocity, fps:	1250		1120		1029
	energy, ft-lb:	607		488		412
Win. 240 Platinum Tip	velocity, ft-lb:	1250		1151		1075
	energy, ft-lb:	833		706		616

.44 COLT

CARTRIDGE BULLET	RANGE, YARDS:	0	25	50	75	100
Black Hills 230 FPL	velocity, fps:	730				
	energy, ft-lb:					

.44 RUSSIAN

CARTRIDGE BULLET	RANGE, YARDS:	0	25	50	75	100
Black Hills 210 FPL	velocity, fps:	650				
	energy, ft-lb:					

.44 SPECIAL

CARTRIDGE BULLET	RANGE, YARDS:	0	25	50	75	100
Black Hills 210 FPL	velocity, fps:	700				
	energy, ft-lb:					
Federal 200 SWC HP	velocity, fps:	900	860	830	800	770
	energy, ft-lb:	360	330	305	285	260
Federal 250 CastCore	velocity, fps:	1250	1200	1150	1110	1080
	energy, ft-lb:	865	795	735	685	645
Hornady 180 JHP/XTP	velocity, fps:	1000		935		882
	energy, ft-lb:	400		350		311
Magtech 240 LFN	velocity, fps:	750		722		696
	energy, ft-lb:	300		278		258
PMC 180 JHP	velocity, fps:	980	938	902	869	839
	energy, ft-lb:	383				
PMC 240 SWC-CP	velocity, fps:	764	744	724	706	687
	energy, ft-lb:	311				
PMC 240 LFP	velocity, fps:	750		719		690
	energy, ft-lb:	300		275		253
Rem. 246 LRN	velocity, fps:	755		725		695
	energy, ft-lb:	310		285		265
Speer 200 HP Blazer	velocity, fps:	875		825		780
	energy, ft-lb:	340		302		270
Speer 200 Trail Blazer LFN	velocity, fps:	750		714		680
	energy, ft-lb:	250		226		205
Speer 200 Gold Dot	velocity, fps:	875		825		780
	energy, ft-lb:	340		302		270
Win. 200 Silvertip HP	velocity, fps:	900		860		822
	energy, ft-lb:	360		328		300
Win. 240 Lead	velocity, fps:	750		719		690
	energy, ft-lb	300		275		253
Win. 246 LRN	velocity, fps:	755		725		695
	energy, ft-lb:	310		285		265

.44 REMINGTON MAGNUM

CARTRIDGE BULLET	RANGE, YARDS:	0	25	50	75	100
Black Hills 240 JHP	velocity, fps:	1260				
	energy, ft-lb:	848				
Black Hills 300 JHP	velocity, fps:	1150				
	energy, ft-lb:	879				
Federal 180 Hi-Shok JHP	velocity, fps:	1610	1480	1370	1270	1180
	energy, ft-lb:	1035	875	750	640	555
Federal 240 Hi-Shok JHP	velocity, fps:	1180	1130	1080	1050	1010
	energy, ft-lb:	740	675	625	580	550
Federal 240 Hydra-Shok JHP	velocity, fps:	1180	1130	1080	1050	1010
	energy, ft-lb:	740	675	625	580	550
Federal 240 JHP	velocity, fps:	1180	1130	1080	1050	1010
	energy, ft-lb:	740	675	625	580	550
Federal 300 CastCore	velocity, fps:	1250	1200	1160	1120	1080
	energy, ft-lb:	1040	960	885	825	775
Hornady 180 JHP/XTP	velocity, fps:	1550		1340		1173
	energy, ft-lb:	960		717		550
Hornady 200 JHP/XTP	velocity, fps:	1500		1284		1128
	energy, ft-lb:	999		732		565

CARTRIDGE BULLET	RANGE, YARDS:	0	25	50	75	100
Hornady 240 JHP/XTP	velocity, fps:	1350		1188		1078
	energy, ft-lb:	971		753		619
Hornady 300 JHP/XTP	velocity, fps:	1150		1084		1031
	energy, ft-lb:	881		782		708
Magtech 240 SJSP	velocity, fps:	1180		1081		1010
	energy, ft-lb:	741		632		623
PMC 180 JHP	velocity, fps:	1392	1263	1157	1076	1015
	energy, ft-lb:	772				
PMC 240 JHP	velocity, fps:	1301	1218	1147	1088	1041
	energy, ft-lb:	900				
PMC 240 TC-SP	velocity, fps:	1300	1216	1144	1086	1038
	energy, ft-lb:	900				
PMC 240 SFHP	velocity, fps:	1300	1212	1138	1079	1030
	energy, ft-lb:	900				
PMC 240 LSWC-GCK	velocity, fps:	1225	1143	1077	1025	982
	energy, ft-lb:	806				
Rem. 180 JSP	velocity, fps:	1610		1365		1175
	energy, ft-lb:	1036		745		551
Rem. 210 Gold Dot HP	velocity, fps:	1450		1276		1140
	energy, ft-lb:	980		759		606
Rem. 240 SP	velocity, fps:	1180		1081		1010
	energy, ft-lb:	721		623		543
Rem. 240 SJHP	velocity, fps:	1180		1081		1010
	energy, ft-lb:	721		623		543
Rem. 275 JHP Core-Lokt	velocity, fps:	1235		1142		1070
	energy, ft-lb:	931		797		699
Speer 240 JHP Blazer	velocity, fps:	1200		1092		1015
	energy, ft-lb:	767		636		549
Speer 240 Gold Dot HP	velocity, fps:	1400		1255		1139
	energy, ft-lb:	1044		839		691
Speer 270 Gold Dot SP	velocity, fps:	1250		1142		1060
	energy, ft-lb:	937		781		674
Win. 210 Silvertip HP	velocity, fps:	1250		1106		1010
	energy, ft-lb:	729		570		475
Win. 240 Hollow SP	velocity, fps:	1180		1081		1010
	energy, ft-lb:	741		623		543
Win. 240 JSP	velocity, fps:	1180		1081		
	energy, ft-lb:	741		623		
Win. 250 Partition Gold	velocity, fps:	1230		1132		1057
	energy, ft-lb:	840		711		620
Win. 250 Platinum Tip	velocity, fps:	1250		1148		1070
	energy, ft-lb:	867		732		635

.44-40

CARTRIDGE BULLET	RANGE, YARDS:	0	25	50	75	100
Black Hills 200 RNFP	velocity, fps:	800				
	energy, ft-lb:					
Hornady 205 Cowboy	velocity, fps:	725		697		670
	energy, ft-lb:	239		221		204
Magtech 225 LFN	velocity, fps:	725		703		681
	energy, ft-lb:	281		247		232
PMC 225 LFP	velocity, fps:	725		723		695
	energy, ft-lb:	281		261		242
Win. 225 Lead	velocity, fps:	750		723		695
	energy, ft-lb:	281		261		242

.45 AUTOMATIC (ACP)

CARTRIDGE BULLET	RANGE, YARDS:	0	25	50	75	100
Black Hills 185 JHP	velocity, fps:	1000				
	energy, ft-lb:	411				
Black Hills 200 Match SWC	velocity, fps:	875				
	energy, ft-lb:	340				
Black Hills 230 FMJ	velocity, fps:	850				
	energy, ft-lb:	368				

CARTRIDGE BULLET	RANGE, YARDS:	0	25	50	75	100
Black Hills 230 JHP	velocity, fps:	850				
	energy, ft-lb:	368				
Black Hills 230 JHP +P	velocity, fps:	950				
	energy, ft-lb:	460				
Federal 165 Hydra-Shok JHP	velocity, fps:	1060	1020	980	950	920
	energy, ft-lb:	410	375	350	330	310
Federal 165 EFMJ	velocity, fps:	1090	1045	1005	975	942
	energy, ft-lb:	435	400	370	345	325
Federal 185 Hi-Shok JHP	velocity, fps:	950	920	900	880	860
	energy, ft-lb:	370	350	335	315	300
Federal 185 FMJ-SWC Match	velocity, fps:	780	730	700	660	620
	energy, ft-lb:	245	220	200	175	160
Federal 200 Exp. FMJ	velocity, fps:	1030	1000	970	940	920
	energy, ft-lb:	470	440	415	395	375
Federal 230 FMJ	velocity, fps:	850	830	810	790	770
	energy, ft-lb:	370	350	335	320	305
Federal 230 FMJ Match	velocity, fps:	855	835	815	795	775
	energy, ft-lb:	375	355	340	325	305
Federal 230 Hi-Shok JHP	velocity, fps:	850	830	810	790	770
	energy, ft-lb:	370	350	335	320	300
Federal 230 Hydra-Shok JHP	velocity, fps:	850	830	810	790	770
	energy, ft-lb:	370	350	335	320	305
Federal 230 FMJ	velocity, fps:	850	830	810	790	770
	energy, ft-lb:	370	350	335	320	305
Federal 230 TMJ TMF Primer	velocity, fps:	850	830	810	790	770
	energy, ft-lb:	370	350	335	315	305
Hornady 185 JHP/XTP	velocity, fps:	950		880		819
	energy, ft-lb:	371		318		276
Hornady 200 JHP/XTP	velocity, fps:	900		855		815
	energy, ft-lb:	358		325		295
Hornady 200 HP/XTP +P	velocity, fps:	1055		982		925
	energy, ft-lb:	494		428		380
Hornady 200 TAP-FPD	velocity, fps:	1055		982		926
	energy, ft-lbs:	494		428		380
Hornady 230 FMJ/RN	velocity, fps:	850		809		771
	energy, ft-lb:	369		334		304
Hornady 230 FMJ/FP	velocity, fps:	850		809		771
	energy, ft-lb:	369		334		304
Hornady 230 HP/XTP +P	velocity, fps:	950		904		865
	energy, ft-lb:	462		418		382
Hornady 230 TAP-FPD	velocity, fps:	950		908		872
	energy, ft-lb:	461		421		388
Magtech 185 JHP +P	velocity, fps:	1148		1066		1055
	energy, ft-lb:	540		467		415
Magtech 200 LSWC	velocity, fps:	950		910		874
	energy, ft-lb:	401		368		339
Magtech 230 FMC	veloctiy, fps:	837		800		767
	energy, ft-lb:	356		326		300
Magtech 230 FMC-SWC	velocity, fps:	780		720		660
	energy, ft-lb:	310		265		222
PMC 145 Non-Toxic Frangible	velocity, fps:	1100	1045	999	961	928
	energy, ft-lb:	390				
PMC 185 JHP	velocity, fps:	903	870	839	811	785
	energy, ft-lb:	339				
PMC 200 FMJ-SWC	velocity, fps:	850	818	788	761	734
	energy, ft-lb:	321				
PMC 230 SFHP	velocity, fps:	850	830	811	792	775
	energy, ft-lb:	369				
PMC 230 FMJ	velocity, fps:	830	809	789	769	749
	energy, ft-lb:	352				
Rem. 175 Lead Free Frangible	velocity, fps:	1020		923		851
	energy, ft-lb:	404		331		281

CARTRIDGE BULLET	RANGE, YARDS:	0	25	50	75	100
Rem. 185 JHP	velocity, fps:	1000		939		889
	energy, ft-lb:	411		362		324
Rem. 185 BJHP	velocity, fps:	1015		951		899
	energy, ft-lb:	423		372		332
Rem. 185 BJHP +P	velocity, fps:	1140		1042		971
	energy, ft-lb:	534		446		388
Rem. 185 MC	velocity, fps:	1015		955		907
	energy, ft-lb:	423		375		338
Rem. 230 FN Enclosed Base	velocity, fps:	835		800		767
	energy, ft-lb:	356		326		300
Rem. 230 Metal Case	velocity, fps:	835		800		767
	energy, ft-lb:	356		326		300
Rem. 230 JHP	velocity, fps:	835		800		767
	energy, ft-lb:	356		326		300
Rem. 230 BJHP	velocity, fps:	875		833		795
	energy, ft-lb:	391		355		323
Speer 140 Frangible	velocity, fps:	1200		1029		928
	energy, ft-lb:	448		329		268
Speer 185 Gold Dot	velocity, fps:	1050		956		886
	energy, ft-lb:	453		375		322
Speer 185 TMJ/FN	velocity, fps:	1000		909		839
	energy, ft-lb:	411		339		289
Speer 200 JHP Blazer	velocity, fps:	975		917		860
	energy, ft-lb:	421		372		328
Speer 200 Gold Dot +P	velocity, fps:	1080		994		930
	energy, ft-lb:	518		439		384
Speer 200 TMJ/FN	velocity, fps:	975		897		834
	energy, ft-lb:	422		357		309
Speer 230 FMJ (and Blazer)	velocity, fps:	845		804		775
	energy, ft-lb:	363		329		304
Speer 230 TMJ-CF (and Blazer)	velocity, fps:	845		804		775
	energy, ft-lb:	363		329		304
Speer 230 Gold Dot	velocity, fps:	890		845		805
	energy, ft-lb:	405		365		331
Win. 170 JFP	velocity, fps:	1050		982		928
	energy, ft-lb:	416		364		325
Win. 185 Silvertip HP	velocity, fps:	1000		938		888
	energy, ft-lb:	411		362		324
Win. 185 FMJ FN	velocity, fps:	910		861		
	energy, ft-lb:	340		304		
Win. 185 EB WinClean	velocity, fps:	910		835		
	energy, ft-lb:	340		286		
Win. 230 JHP	velocity, fps:	880		842		
	energy, ft-lb:	396		363		
Win. 230 FMJ	velocity, fps:	835		800		
	energy, ft-lb:	356		326		
Win. 230 SXT	velocity, fps:	880		846		816
	energy, ft-lb:	396		366		340
Win. 230 JHP subsonic	velocity, fps:	880		842		808
	energy, ft-lb:	396		363		334
Win. 230 EB WinClean	velocity, fps:	835		802		
	energy, ft-lb:	356		329		

.45 GAP

CARTRIDGE BULLET	RANGE, YARDS:	0	25	50	75	100
Federal 185 Hydra-Shok JHP And Federal TMJ	velocity, fps:	1090	1020	970	920	890
	energy, ft-lb:	490	430	385	350	320
Federal 230 Hydra-Shok And Federal FMJ	velocity, fps:	880	870	850	840	820
	energy, ft-lb:	395	380	3760	355	345
Win. 185 STHP	velocity, fps:	1000		938		887
	energy, ft-lb:	411		361		323
Win. 230 JHP	velocity, fps:	880		842		
	energy, ft-lb:	396		363		

.45 GAP TO .500 SMITH & WESSON

CARTRIDGE BULLET	RANGE, YARDS:	0	25	50	75	100
Win. 230 EB WinClean	velocity, fps:	875		840		
	energy, ft-lb:	391		360		
Win. 230 FMJ	velocity, fps:	850		814		
	energy, ft-lb:	369		338		

.45 WINCHESTER MAGNUM

CARTRIDGE BULLET	RANGE, YARDS:	0	25	50	75	100
Win. 260 Partition Gold	velocity, fps:	1200		1105		1033
	energy, ft-lb:	832		705		616
Win. 260 JHP	velocity, fps:	1200		1099		1026
	energy, ft-lb:	831		698		607

.45 SCHOFIELD

CARTRIDGE BULLET	RANGE, YARDS:	0	25	50	75	100
Black Hills 180 FNL	velocity, fps:	730				
	energy, ft-lb:					
Black Hills 230 RNFP	velocity, fps:	730				
	energy, ft-lb:					

.45 COLT

CARTRIDGE BULLET	RANGE, YARDS:	0	25	50	75	100
Black Hills 250 RNFP	velocity, fps:	725				
	energy, ft-lb:					
Federal 225 SWC HP	velocity, fps:	900	880	860	840	820
	energy, ft-lb:	405	385	370	355	340
Hornady 255 Cowboy	velocity, fps:	725		692		660
	energy, ft-lb:	298		271		247
Magtech 250 LFN	velocity, fps:	750		726		702
	energy, ft-lb:	312		293		274
PMC 250 LFP	velocity, fps:	800		767		736
	energy, ft-lb:	355		331		309
PMC 300 +P+	velocity, fps:	1250	1192	1144	1102	1066
	energy, ft-lb:	1041				
Rem. 225 SWC	velocity, fps:	960		890		832
	energy, ft-lb:	460		395		346
Rem. 250 RLN	velocity, fps:	860		820		780
	energy, ft-lb:	410		375		340
Speer 200 FMJ Blazer	velocity, fps:	1000		938		889
	energy, ft-lb:	444		391		351
Speer 230 Trail Blazer LFN	velocity, fps:	750		716		684
	energy, ft-lb:	287		262		239
Speer 250 Gold Dot	velocity, fps:	900		860		823
	energy, ft-lb:	450		410		376
Win. 225 Silvertip HP	velocity, fps:	920		877		839
	energy, ft-lb:	423		384		352
Win. 255 LRN	velocity, fps:	860		820		780
	energy, ft-lb:	420		380		345
Win. 250 Lead	velocity, fps:	750		720		692
	energy, ft-lb:	312		288		266

.454 CASULL

CARTRIDGE BULLET	RANGE, YARDS:	0	25	50	75	100
Federal 300 Trophy Bonded	velocity, fps:	1630	1540	1450	1380	1300
	energy, ft-lb:	1760	1570	1405	1260	1130
Federal 360 CastCore	velocity, fps:	1500	1435	1370	1310	1255
	energy, ft-lb:	1800	1640	1500	1310	1260
Hornady 240 XTP-MAG	velocity, fps:	1900		1679		1483
	energy, ft-lb:	1923		1502		1172
Hornady 300 XTP-MAG	velocity, fps:	1650		1478		1328
	energy, ft-lb:	1813		1455		1175
Magtech 260 SJSP	velocity, fps:	1800		1577		1383
	energy, ft-lb:	1871		1437		1104
Rem. 300 Core-Lokt Ultra	velocity, fps:	1625		1472		1335
	energy, ft-lb:	1759		1442		1187

CARTRIDGE BULLET	RANGE, YARDS:	0	25	50	75	100
Speer 300 Gold Dot HP	velocity, fps:	1625		1477		1343
	energy, ft-lb:	1758		1452		1201
Win. 250 JHP	velocity, fps:	1300		1151		1047
	energy, ft-lb:	938		735		608
Win. 260 Partition Gold	velocity, fps:	1800		1605		1427
	energy, ft-lb:	1871		1485		1176
Win. 260 Platinum Tip	velocity, fps:	1800		1596		1414
	eneryg, ft-lb:	1870		1470		1154
Win. 300 JFP	velocity, fps:	1625		1451		1308
	energy, ft-lb:	1759		1413		1141

.460 SMITH & WESSON

CARTRIDGE BULLET	RANGE, YARDS:	0	25	50	75	100
Federal 275 Expander	velocity, fps:	1800		1640		1500
	energy, ft-lb:	1980		1650		1370
Federal 300 A-Frame	velocity, fps:	1750		1510		1300
	energy, ft-lb:	2040		1510		1125
Hornady 200 SST	velocity, fps:	2250		2003		1772
	energy, ft-lb:	2248		1395		1081
Win. 260 Supreme Part. Gold	velocity, fps	2000		1788		1592
	energy, ft-lb	2309		1845		2012

.475 LINEBAUGH

CARTRIDGE BULLET	RANGE, YARDS:	0	25	50	75	100
Hornady 400 XTP-MAG	velocity, fps:	1300		1179		1093
	energy, ft-lb:	1501		1235		1060

.480 RUGER

CARTRIDGE BULLET	RANGE, YARDS:	0	25	50	75	100
Federal 275 Expander	velocity, fps:	1350		1190		1080
	energy, ft-lb:	1115		870		710
Hornady 325 XTP-MAG	velocity, fps:	1350		1191		1076
	energy, ft-lb:	1315		1023		835
Hornady 400 XTP-MAG	velocity, fps:	1100		1027		971
	energy, ft-lb:	1075		937		838
Speer 275 Gold Dot HP	velocity, fps:	1450		1284		1152
	energy, ft-lb:	1284		1007		810
Speer 325 SP	velocity, fps:	1350		1224		1124
	energy, ft-lb:	1315		1082		912

.50 ACTION EXPRESS

CARTRIDGE BULLET	RANGE, YARDS:	0	25	50	75	100
Hornady 300 XTP/HP	velocity, fps:	1475		1251		1092
	energy, ft-lb:	1449		1043		795
Speer 300 Gold Dot HP	velocity, fps:	1550		1361		1207
	energy, ft-lb:	1600		1234		970
Speer 325 UCHP	velocity, fps:	1400		1232		1106
	energy, ft-lb:	1414		1095		883

.500 SMITH & WESSON

CARTRIDGE BULLET	RANGE, YARDS:	0	25	50	75	100
Federal 275 Expander	velocity, fps:	1660		1440		1250
	energy, ft-lb:	1680		1255		950
Federal 325 A-Frame	velocity, fps:	1800		1560		1350
	energy, ft-lb:	2340		1755		1315
Hornady 350 XTP Mag	velocity, fps:	1900		1656		1439
	energy, ft-lb:	2805		2131		1610
Hornady 500 FP-XTP	velocity, fps:	1425		1281		1164
	energy, ft-lb:	2254		1823		1505
Win. 350 Super-X	velocity, fps	1400		1231		1106
	energy, ft-lb	1523		1178		951
Win. 400 Platinum Tip	velocity, fps:	1800		1647		1505
	energy, ft-lb:	2877		2409		2012

BALLISTICS

Gunfinder Index

GUNFINDER INDEX

Gunfinder Index